June 16–19, 2014
Bretton Woods, NH, USA

I0047652

Association for Computing Machinery

Advancing Computing as a Science & Profession

MobiSys'14
Proceedings of the 12th Annual International Conference on Mobile Systems, Applications, and Services

Sponsored by:
ACM SIGMOBILE

Supported by:
National Science Foundation, Facebook, Google, HTC, Intel, Microsoft, Nokia, Telefonica, Brocade, Hewlett-Packard, IBM Research, & Dartmouth College

Association for Computing Machinery

Advancing Computing as a Science & Profession

The Association for Computing Machinery
2 Penn Plaza, Suite 701
New York, New York 10121-0701

ISBN: 978-1-4503-2793-0 (Digital)

ISBN: 978-1-4503-3087-9 (Print)

Additional copies may be ordered prepaid from:

ACM Order Department
PO Box 30777
New York, NY 10087-0777, USA

Phone: 1-800-342-6626 (USA and Canada)
+1-212-626-0500 (Global)
Fax: +1-212-944-1318
E-mail: acmhelp@acm.org
Hours of Operation: 8:30 am – 4:30 pm ET

Printed in the USA

General Chairs' Welcome

As general chairs it is our great pleasure to welcome you to the 12th *International Conference on Mobile Systems, Applications, and Services – MobiSys'14 –* and to the beautiful Mount Washington Hotel and Resort, located in Bretton Woods, New Hampshire. Since its inception in 2003, MobiSys has been the leading forum for mobile-systems research. The conference has a tradition of being highly interactive, including workshops on hot new topics, demos, posters and videos presenting early work or new technologies, a single-track paper program presenting the best research ideas in mobile computing, and a thought-provoking keynote.

We are excited to host this year's conference at the stunningly beautiful Mount Washington Hotel and Resort nestled in the White Mountains of New Hampshire. We have been honored to work with a superb team, working behind the scenes on behalf of the conference and our community. Key to the success of any technical conference is the quality, dedication, and leadership of the technical program chairs. We are very fortunate to have Landon Cox and Morley Mao at the helm of the committee this year. Landon and Morley are a pleasure to work with and we thank them and their technical program committee for putting together a stellar program of high-quality papers.

We are especially excited about our keynote speaker, James Landay, whose talk kicks off the technical program. He has held leadership positions at University of California Berkeley, University of Washington, and Intel Research Lab; he recently joined Cornell Tech in New York City. James is widely recognized as one of the key figures driving ubiquitous computing forward. His current research interests include automated usability evaluation, demonstrational interfaces, and user-interface design tools. We are very happy that James could join us at MobiSys this year.

Anyone who has chaired a conference knows that the key to success is having a great organizing committee. Perhaps the key person in the organization committee – a third general chair – is the Local Arrangements Chair. We offer our deep thanks to Guanling Chen for taking care of all the details that slipped through our fingers.

Speaking of details, we thank Andrés Molina-Markham, publication chair, for dealing with the many details in assembling the proceedings. His tireless work in dealing with all the paper, poster, video, and demo authors/chairs, and the publisher's pressing deadlines, has led to a great product.

Part of the MobiSys culture is the demonstration of new technologies and the informal presentation of work-in-progress. This year we have a large number of demos and posters. We would like to thank our demo and poster chairs Hong Lu and Souvik Sen for doing a terrific job and for keeping the spirit of MobiSys alive with these cutting-edge presentations.

Our workshop chairs Tristan Henderson and Xia Zhou have put together an outstanding set of four workshops: the *Ph.D. Forum* led by Andrius Aucinas, Aaron Yi Ding, Aarathi Prasad and Ardalan Amiri Sani; the *Workshop on Mobile Augmented Reality and Robotic Technology-based Systems* led by Mooi Choô Chuah and Pan Hui; the *Workshop on Physical Analytics* led by Deborah Estrin and Venkat Padmanabhan; and the *Workshop on Mobile Cloud Computing and Services* led by Lin Zhong and Yuvraj Agarwal. These four workshops, some new and some returning, should spark discussion on new challenges in mobile computing. Thank you Tristan, Xia and all the workshop organizers. MobiSys started an experimental new video program last year and we thank Deepak Ganesan and Ben Greenstein for organizing our video program.

Another critical task of running a top conference is making sure we come in on, or very near, budget. We enjoyed working with Jacob Sorber as our treasurer and finance chair; Jacob developed and managed the budget and kept us in check. Thank you Jacob!

Our publicity chair Minkyong Kim did a splendid job at getting the various calls out for the different parts of the meeting and being proactive in pushing us to get the word out early. If you like our website then you should thank our web chair Jing Xu who was super responsive at keeping the site current and looking great. Eduardo Cuervo did an outstanding job handling registration this year, with great attention to detail. Mount Washington Hotel is located over two hours from major airports, so we sought Tim Pierson's help providing attendees alternatives to renting a car. He organized a bus between two airports and the Mount Washington Hotel and partnered with ZimRide to create opportunities for attendees to share rides. Thank you Minkyong, Jing, Eduardo, and Tim!

MobiSys has a long tradition of fostering student participation. As chairs we have tried to keep the cost of student registrations as low as possible and continue to help provide student travel grants with the help of industrial supporters and National Science Foundation (NSF). Furthermore, we see the students participating in the conference and our Ph.D. Forum as tomorrow's leaders. We thank Ehsan Hoque for doing a tremendous job coordinating student travel grants. We thank Thyagarajan Nandagopal, who serves in the Division of Computer and Network Systems at NSF, for his assistance in obtaining NSF support for travel grants and for leading a discussion on large-scale infrastructure needs for research in mobile computing during the conference.

ACM and ACM SIGMOBILE are our proud sponsors, but a conference like MobiSys cannot be accomplished without help from many partners. We are deeply grateful for the financial support from Brocade, Facebook, Google, HP Labs, HTC, IBM Research, Intel, ISTS at Dartmouth, Microsoft, Nokia Research, NSF, and Telefonica. As a result of their generous support we can bring many students to MobiSys this year who would most likely not have been able to attend without this generous support for travel and registration.

Many people volunteer their time and energy to pull everything together, including our supportive steering committee members led by Victor Bahl. But the success of MobiSys is mainly due to the hard work of all those people who submit papers, demos, video and posters. We thank you all. On behalf of the whole team, welcome to Bretton Woods – enjoy the conference!

Andrew Campbell and David Kotz
MobiSys'14 General Chairs
Dartmouth College, USA

Program Chairs' Welcome

Welcome to MobiSys 2014, the 12th Conference on Mobile Systems, Applications, and Services.

This year's technical program covers a wide range of topics in mobile systems. The program both deepens our understanding of several long-standing problems and explores an expanding set of emerging mobile applications and technologies. Topics include automated user-interface exploration, efficient resource usage, gesture recognition, localization, privacy and security, wearable computing, wireless networks, and more.

We are thrilled to begin the technical program with a keynote talk by Professor James Landay of Cornell NYC Tech. Dr. Landay has been a leading researcher on human-computer interaction and ubiquitous computing for over twenty years. After the keynote, we have an exciting technical program that includes 25 full-length technical papers chosen by the technical program committee (TPC) from 185 submissions.

As interest in the conference has grown over the last several years, so too has the review load for MobiSys TPCs. To reduce the number of reviews each TPC member had to write, we augmented the TPC with an external review committee (ERC) of experts. Most ERC members reviewed six papers during the initial round of the review process.

Our review process consisted of three rounds of decisions. During the first round, all submissions received three or four reviews, each written by a member of the TPC or ERC. If a reviewer recommended that a paper be accepted, the paper advanced to the second round. During the second round, papers received three or four additional reviews, almost entirely from the TPC. At the end of the second round, reviewers discussed each remaining paper online to determine whether it should advance to the third round of decisions. The third round of decisions occurred during an all-day face-to-face meeting of the TPC. By the conclusion of this meeting, the TPC had identified the 25 papers in the program. Finally, all accepted papers were shepherded by a TPC member to ensure that the final manuscripts met the standards of the committee.

We took strict precautions throughout the review process to avoid conflicts of interest. Furthermore, as the TPC chairs, we did not submit papers to avoid conflicts of interest.

Creating the technical program for MobiSys 2014 was a team effort, and we would like to thank the TPC members, ERC members, and shepherds who worked extremely hard reading papers and providing feedback to paper authors. We would also like to thank the authors for sending us a pool of very high-quality submissions.

We are also grateful to our colleagues who helped organize the conference, including the steering committee, the poster and demo chairs (Hong Lu and Souvik Sen), the treasurer (Jacob Sorber), the publicity chair (Minkyong Kim), the publication chair (Andrés Molina-Markham), the workshop co-chairs (Tristan Henderson and Xia Zhou), the video-program co-chairs (Deepak Ganesan and Ben Greenstein), the transportation chair (Tim Pierson), the student-travel grants chair (M. Ehsan Hoque), the registration chair (Eduardo Cuervo), and the web chair (Jing Xu).

We would especially like to thank the general chairs, Andrew Campbell and David Kotz, and the local arrangements chair, Guanling Chen. Their handling of the conference logistics was invaluable. Finally, we thank our sponsors, ACM SIGMOBILE, and our supporters, Facebook, Google, HTC, Intel, Microsoft Research, Nokia, Telefonica, the National Science Foundation, Brocade, Dartmouth College, and Hewlett Packard. We hope that you will find the technical program exciting and thought provoking, and that the conference will provide you with a valuable opportunity to share experiences and ideas with others from around the world.

Landon P. Cox
MobiSys '14 Program Co-Chair
Duke University, USA

Z. Morley Mao
MobiSys '14 Program Co-Chair
University of Michigan, USA

Table of Contents

Session: Gestures

Session: UI Automation

Session: Resource Usage

Session: Performance

Session: Localization

Session: Demonstrations

Poster Session

Video Presentation Abstracts

Author Index

MobiSys 2014 – The Twelfth International Conference on Mobile Systems, Applications, and Services

General Co-Chairs: Andrew Campbell *(Dartmouth College, USA)*
David Kotz *(Dartmouth College, USA)*

Technical Program Co-Chairs: Landon Cox *(Duke University, USA)*
Z. Morley Mao *(University of Michigan, USA)*

Local Arrangements Chair: Guanling Chen *(University of Massachusetts Lowell, USA)*

Treasurer: Jacob Sorber *(Clemson University, USA)*

Workshop Co-Chairs: Tristan Henderson *(University of St Andrews, UK)*
Xia Zhou *(Dartmouth College, USA)*

Posters/Demos Co-Chairs: Hong Lu *(Intel, USA)*
Souvik Sen *(HP labs, USA)*

Video Program Co-Chairs: Deepak Ganesan *(University of Massachusetts Amherst, USA)*
Ben Greenstein *(Google)*

Publication Chair: Andrés Molina-Markham *(Dartmouth College, USA)*

Publicity Chair: Minkyong Kim *(IBM Research, USA)*

Steering Committee Chair: Victor Bahl *(Microsoft Research, USA)*

Transportation Chair: Tim Pierson *(Dartmouth College, USA)*

Web Chair: Jing Xu *(University of Massachusetts Lowell, USA)*

Student Travel Grants Chair: M. Ehsan Hoque *(University of Rochester, USA)*

Registration Chair: Eduardo Cuervo *(Microsoft, USA)*

Technical Program Committee: Sharad Agarwal *(Microsoft Research, Redmond, USA)*
Mary Baker *(HP Labs, USA)*
Rajesh Balan *(Singapore Management University, Singapore)*
Aruna Balasubramanian *(University of Washington, USA)*
Gaetano Borriello *(University of Washington, USA)*
David Choffnes *(Northeastern University, USA)*
Romit Roy Choudhury *(University of Illinois, USA)*
David Chu *(Microsoft Research, Redmond, USA)*

Technical Program Committee
(Continued): Sunny Consolvo *(Google, USA)*
Prabal Dutta *(University of Michigan, USA)*
William Enck *(NC State University, USA)*
Marco Grutesser *(Rutgers University, USA)*
Wen Hu *(CSIRO, Australia)*
Polly Huang *(National Taiwan University, Taiwan)*
Xiaofan (Fred) Jiang *(Intel Labs, China)*
Kyu-Han Kim *(HP Labs, USA)*
Ulas Kozat *(DOCOMO Innovations, Palo Alto, CA)*
Robin Kravets *(University of Illinois, USA)*
Anthony LaMarca *(Intel Labs, USA)*
Cecilia Mascolo *(University of Cambridge, USA)*
Jeff Pang *(AT&T Labs-Research, USA)*
Chunyi Peng *(Ohio State University, USA)*
Feng Qian *(AT&T Labs-Research, USA)*
Zhiyun Qian *(NEC Labs, USA)*
Mahadev Satyanarayanan *(Carnegie Mellon University, USA)*
Junehwa Song *(KAIST, Republic of Korea)*
Matt Welsh *(Google, USA)*
Guoliang Xing *(Michigan State University, USA)*
Koji Yatani *(Microsoft Research, Asia)*
Lin Zhong *(Rice University, USA)*

External Review Committee:

Yuvraj Agarwal	Li Erran Li
Suman Banerjee	Dimitrios Lymberopoulos
Ramon Caceres	Justin Manweiler
Geoffrey Challen	Emiliano Miluzzo
Eduardo Cuervo Laffaye	Iqbal Mohomed
Maria Ebling	Suman Nath
Deepak Ganesan	Rama Ramasubramanian
Peter Gilbert	Bodhi Priyantha
Shyam Gollakota	Thomas Schmid
Ben Greenstein	Souvik Sen
Urs Hengartner	Subhabrata Sen
Jason Hong	Kaushik Veeraraghavan
Y. Charlie Hu	Alec Wolman
Ethan Katz-Bassett	Pei Zhang
Youngki Lee	Ying Zhang

MobiSys 2014 Sponsor & Supporters

Sponsor:

Gold Supporters:  National Science Foundation
(student travel grants)

Silver Supporters: facebook Google

hTC (intel)

Microsoft NOKIA

Telefónica

Bronze Supporters: BROCADE  hp

IBM Research Dartmouth College
INSTITUTE for SECURITY,
TECHNOLOGY, and SOCIETY

Locally organized by:  Dartmouth

Balancing Design and Technology to Tackle Global Grand Challenges

James A. Landay
Cornell Tech
New York, NY, USA

Abstract

There are many urgent problems facing the planet: a degrading environment, a healthcare system in crisis, and educational systems that are failing to produce creative, innovative thinkers to solve tomorrow's problems. Technology influences behavior, and I believe when we balance it with revolutionary design, we can reduce a family's energy and water use by 50%, double most people's daily physical activity, and educate any child anywhere in the world to a level of proficiency on par with the planet's best students. My research program tackles these grand challenges by using a new model of interdisciplinary research that takes a long view and encourages risk-taking and creativity. I will illustrate how we are addressing these grand challenges in our research by building systems that balance innovative user interfaces with novel activity inference technology. These systems have helped individuals stay fit, led families to be more sustainable in their everyday lives, and supported learners in acquiring second languages. I will also introduce the World Lab, a cross-cultural institute that embodies my balanced approach to attack the world's biggest problems today, while preparing the technology and design leaders of tomorrow.

Categories and Subject Descriptors

H.5.m. Information interfaces and presentation (e.g., HCI): Miscellaneous.

Keywords

Activity inference; ubiquitous computing; HCI; design; innovation; sustainability; health; fitness; language learning

Short Bio

James Landay is a Professor of Information Science at Cornell Tech, specializing in human-computer interaction. He will become a Professor of Computer Science at Stanford in August, 2014. Previously, James was a Professor of Computer Science & Engineering at the University of Washington. His current research interests include Technology to Support Behavior Change, Demonstrational Interfaces, Mobile & Ubiquitous Computing, and User Interface Design Tools. He is the founder and co-director of the World Lab, a joint research and educational effort with Tsinghua University in Beijing.

Landay received his BS in EECS from UC Berkeley in 1990 and MS and PhD in Computer Science from Carnegie Mellon University in 1993 and 1996, respectively. His PhD dissertation was the first to demonstrate the use of sketching in user interface design tools. He was previously the Laboratory Director of Intel Labs Seattle, a university affiliated research lab that explored the new usage models, applications, and technology for ubiquitous computing. He was also the chief scientist and co-founder of NetRaker, which was acquired by KeyNote Systems in 2004. From 1997 through 2003 he was a professor in EECS at UC Berkeley. He was named to the ACM SIGCHI Academy in 2011. He currently serves on the NSF CISE Advisory Committee.

MobiSys14, June 16–19, 2014, Bretton Woods, New Hampshire, USA.
ACM 978-1-4503-2793-0/14/06.
http://dx.doi.org/10.1145/2594368.2620048

BodyBeat: A Mobile System for Sensing Non-Speech Body Sounds

Tauhidur Rahman[1], Alexander T Adams[2], Mi Zhang[1], Erin Cherry[3], Bobby Zhou[1],
Huaishu Peng[1], Tanzeem Choudhury[1]

[1]Cornell University, [2]University of North Carolina at Charlotte, [3]University of Rochester

tr266@cornell.edu, aadams85@uncc.edu, mizhang@cornell.edu,
erinc@cs.rochester.edu, bz88@cornell.edu, hp356@cornell.edu, tkc28@cornell.edu

ABSTRACT

In this paper, we propose BodyBeat, a novel mobile sensing system for capturing and recognizing a diverse range of non-speech body sounds in real-life scenarios. Non-speech body sounds, such as sounds of food intake, breath, laughter, and cough contain invaluable information about our dietary behavior, respiratory physiology, and affect. The BodyBeat mobile sensing system consists of a custom-built piezoelectric microphone and a distributed computational framework that utilizes an ARM microcontroller and an Android smartphone. The custom-built microphone is designed to capture subtle body vibrations directly from the body surface without being perturbed by external sounds. The microphone is attached to a 3D printed neckpiece with a suspension mechanism. The ARM embedded system and the Android smartphone process the acoustic signal from the microphone and identify non-speech body sounds. We have extensively evaluated the BodyBeat mobile sensing system. Our results show that BodyBeat outperforms other existing solutions in capturing and recognizing different types of important non-speech body sounds.

Keywords

Mobile Sensing, Non-Speech Body Sound, Acoustic Signal Processing, Embedded Systems

Categories and Subject Descriptors

C.3 [**Special-Purpose and Application-Based Systems**]: Signal Processing Systems

General Terms

Algorithm, Design, Experimentation, Measurement

1. INTRODUCTION

Human speech processing has been studied extensively over the last few decades. The emergence of Apple Siri, the speech recognition software on iPhones, in many ways, is a mark of success for speech recognition technology. However, there is very little research on using sensing and computing technologies for recognizing and interpreting non-speech body sounds. Non-Speech body sounds contain invaluable information about human physiological and psychological conditions. With regard to food and beverage consumption, body sounds enable us to discriminate characteristics of food and drinks [12]. Longer term tracking of eating sounds could be very useful in dietary monitoring applications. Breathing sounds, generated by the friction caused by the air flow from our lungs through the vocal organs (e.g. trachea, larynx, etc.) to the mouth or nasal cavity [26], are highly indicative of the conditions of our lungs. Body sounds such as laughter and yawn are good indicators of affect. Therefore, automatic tracking these non-speech body sounds can help in early detection of negative health indicators by performing regular dietary monitoring, pulmonary function testing, and affect sensing.

During the past few years, a number of mobile and wearable sensing systems have been developed to detect non-speech body sounds. For example, Larson et al. [17] used the smartphone's microphone to detect cough. Hao et al. [14] also used the smartphone's microphone to capture both snoring and coughing sounds for assessing the quality of sleep. In [30], Yatani and Khai developed a wearable system that used a condenser microphone with a stethoscope head to capture a variety of non-speech sounds. Nirjon et al. [23] integrated a standalone microphone into an earphone to extract heartbeat information. All these existing work used condenser microphones that capture sounds via air pressure variations. However, we argue that the condenser microphone is not the most appropriate microphone to capture non-speech body sounds. One reason is that some non-speech body sounds such as eating and drinking sounds are very subtle and thus generate very weak air pressure variations. This makes them very difficult to be captured by condenser microphones. Second, the condenser microphone is very susceptible to external sounds and ambient noises. As a result, the quality of body sounds captured by condenser microphones decreases significantly in real-world settings.

In this paper, we present the design, implementation, and evaluation of BodyBeat: a mobile sensing system that is capable of capturing a diverse set of non-speech body sounds and recognizing physiological reactions that generate these sounds. BodyBeat is built on top of a novel piezoelectric sensor-based microphone that captures body sounds conducted through the body surface. This custom-made microphone is designed to be highly sensitive to subtle body sounds and less sensitive to external ambient sounds or external noise. To recognize these non-speech body sounds, we carefully selected a set of discriminative acoustic features and developed a body sound classification algorithm. Given the computational complexity of this algorithm and the resource limitation of the smartphone, we partitioned the whole computational framework and implemented a distributed computing system that consists of an ARM micro-controller and an Android smartphone. To evaluate the effectiveness of BodyBeat, we tested the custom-made microphone, the classification algorithm, and the distributed computing system using non-speech body sounds collected from 14 participants. Specifically, the main contributions of this paper are: (1) we design and implement a custom-made piezoelectric sensor-based microphone that is able to capture a diverse set of body sounds whiling dampening external sounds and ambient noises; (2) we develop a body sound classification algorithm based on a set of discriminative acoustic features; (3) we implement the signal processing and machine learning algorithm on an ARM micro-controller and an Android smartphone; and finally (4) we benchmark the performance of our custom-made microphone against other state-of-the-art microphones, evaluate the performance of the body sound classification algorithm, and profile the system performance in terms of CPU and memory usage and power consumption.

The paper is organized as follows. Section 2 outlines the challenges and design considerations of the development of the body sound sensing system. Section 3 presents the design and test results of our custom-made piezoelectric sensor-based microphone. In Section 4, we describe our feature selection and classification algorithms for recognizing a diverse set of body sounds. In Section 5, we explain in details the implementation of the computational framework on the ARM micro-controller and the Android smartphone. We discuss the potential applications of BodyBeat in Section 6. Finally, we give a brief review on some of the existing work in Section 7 and conclude this paper in Section 8.

2. DESIGN CONSIDERATIONS

In this section, we discuss the challenges of capturing and recognizing non-speech body sounds. We also describe how we tackled these challenges in the design of BodyBeat. The detailed design is described in Section 3 and 4.

2.1 Capturing Non-Speech Body Sounds

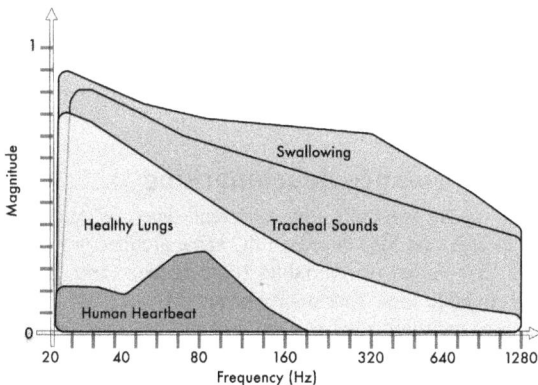

Figure 1: Illustrates approximate frequency range and relative loudness of selected body sounds

In the context of mobile sensing, the built-in microphone is the most widely used sensor for detecting acoustic events [22, 20, 21]. However, the mobile phone microphone (typically an electret or condenser microphone) is specifically designed for the purpose of voice communication and thus the frequency band is optimized for speech. Non-speech body sounds are generated by complex physiological processes inside the human body. After body sounds is

produced inside our body, the energy of the body sounds decreases significantly by the time they reach the body surface. Therefore, non-speech body sounds are in general barely audible. Based on the frequency differences between voice and body sounds, the mobile phone microphone is not the best acoustic sensor for capturing non-speech body sounds. In building the BodyBeat microphone, we considered the following design requirements:

1. The microphone should capture a wide array of subtle body sounds lying in different portion of the frequency spectra.

2. The microphone should be robust against any external sound or ambient noise.

3. The microphone should have mechanisms compensating friction noise due to user's body movement.

The first two requirements are essential for continuous capture of different body sounds with a high signal-to-noise ratio. In the third requirement, the mechanical movement of the body may generate noise due to the friction between body surface and the microphone, which may render captured body sounds uninterpretable. Therefore, we should have mechanism with the microphone to avoid the generation of the friction noise due to users' body movement.

We propose a new microphone, BodyBeat, that captures a wide range of non-speech body sounds. Specifically, BodyBeat adopts a custom-built piezo-electric sensor to capture these sounds. Since its worn around the user's throat, the bone conduction sensor is very sensitive to the vibration caused by non-speech body sounds in the frequency spectrum of 20Hz to 1300Hz. In addition, BodyBeat is also customized to dampen any external sound or noise from the ambient environment. In this manner, most of the features of non-speech body sounds are preserved and captured without being skewed by external sounds. In Section 3, we describe our custom-built microphone and demonstrate its superior performance in capturing non-speech body sounds, compared to a range of other state-of-the art microphones.

2.2 Recognizing Non-Speech Body Sounds

Compared to speech sounds, non-speech body sounds have distinct frequency spectrum. Specifically, the frequencies of speech sounds range from 300Hz to 3500Hz. In comparison, non-speech body sounds are located within the lower region of the frequency spectrum, ranging from 20Hz to 1300Hz. As an example, Figure 1 illustrates the frequency spectrum of four non-speech body sounds. As shown, the human heartbeat is one of the more subtle body sounds with a low magnitude from 20Hz to 200Hz. Breathing sounds (ranging from 20Hz to 1300Hz) are much louder in the 20Hz to 200Hz range but have a large loss in magnitude as the frequency range increases [29]. The unique nature of the body sound's power spectra suggests that spectral features such as power in different filter banks or spectral centroid, spectral variance, spectral entropy might contain valuable information to discriminate among body sounds. Moreover, the concentration of the body sound in the low frequencies warrants higher attention to the minute changes in the low frequencies, in other words higher frequency resolution in the low frequencies. In a previous exploration, Yatani and Khai [30] also used logarithmic filter banks (having center frequencies and bandwidth increase logarithmically).

We begin our exploration by designing and extracting a variety of acoustic and statistical features with the objective of comprehensively describing the characteristics of body sounds. We critically examine the performance of the feature pool and selected a subset of them, which are the best in modeling body sounds. Lastly, we train our inference algorithm and optimize for different parameters.

Sensor ID	Origin	Type of Mic Sensor	Diaphragm Material	Using Stethoscope Head	Reference
M1	Custom-made	brass piezo	latex	no	-
M2	Custom-made	brass piezo	silicon	no	-
M3	Custom-made	film piezo	latex	no	-
M4	Custom-made	brass piezo	latex	yes	-
M5	Custom-made	condenser	plastic	yes	BodyScope [30]
M6	Off-the-shelf	unknown	unknown	no	Invisio [3]
M7	Off-the-shelf	unknown	unknown	no	Temcom [7]

Table 1: Introducing all the microphones considered for recording subtle body sounds

2.3 Resource Limitations and Privacy Issues

While designing BodyBeat, we considered the resource requirements of various computational frameworks and opted for techniques that were capable of running analog to digital conversion of the audio signal; acoustic feature extraction; and classification of body sounds in real-time. Implementing the algorithm entirely in the Android smartphone would be very computationally expensive, and it would cause an unnecessary battery drain. In contrast, another extreme implementation approach would be transferring all the data to a web-based service that classifies the raw (or semi-processed audio signal) to different body sounds. This approach requires good internet connectivity to transfer large amounts of data. Therefore, we optimized our approach by implementing our algorithm in two different platforms: an ARM micro-controller and an Android smartphone.

The audio codec and portions of the feature extraction were implemented on the ARM micro-controller. The ARM unit also employed a frame admission control using some acoustic features, which filtered unnecessary frames that contained no body sounds of interest. If the ARM unit finds a frame containing a specified body sound, it sends the frequency spectrum of the current frame to the Android phone via Bluetooth. We employed a fast and computationally efficient fix-point signal processing algorithm in the ARM unit. Unlike a web-based implementation, this distributed implementation infers body sounds in real-time, which will allow for real-time intervention applications in the future.

We also take the privacy issues into consideration in the design of BodyBeat. To safeguard privacy, BodyBeat filters out the user's raw speech data via an admission control mechanism. In addition, the BodyBeat microphone is specifically designed to be robust against external sounds and thus any speech from other conversation partners is not captured.

3. MICROPHONE DESIGN AND EVALUATION

In this section, we present the design of our BodyBeat microphone for capturing non-speech body sounds. We compare the performance of a set of seven microphones based on the design requirements presented in Section 2.1.

3.1 Microphone Design

Figure 2 illustrates the architecture of our custom-built piezoelectric sensor-based microphone. The microphone was built around a piezoelectric sensor and a 3D printed capsule. This capsule is made with a 3D printer using Polyactic Acid (PLA) filament. The capsule was then filled with a soft silicone (shore hardness of 10) as internal acoustic isolation material. The piezoelectric sensor was then placed in the capsule with the back of the sensor lying on top of the soft silicone filling to capture the subtle body sound vibrations. After the silicone filling cured, the exposed

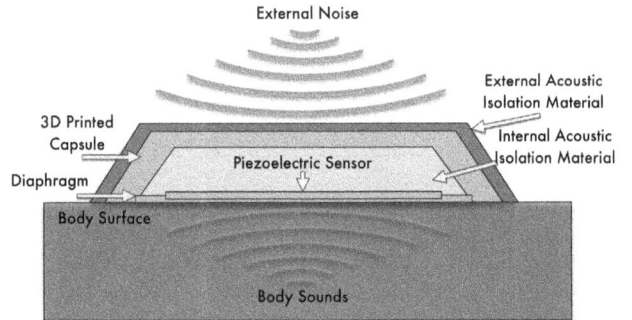

Figure 2: Diagram of piezoelectric sensor-based microphone

front of the piezoelectric sensor was covered with a thin diaphragm (~.001mm), made of either silicone or a piece of latex. Lastly, the exterior of the capsule was covered using external acoustic isolation material, which is a hard, dense, brushable silicone (shore hardness of 50). The internal and external acoustic isolation material (respectively the soft silicone layers inside the capsule and hard silicone layer outside the capsule) act as acoustic isolators, which helps to reduce external noise. In addition, the soft silicone inside the capsule helps the piezoelectric sensor to absorb the surface vibrations without damping the piezoelectric transduction too much. For this design, selecting the right diaphragm material is crucial. A material that has very similar acoustic properties of muscle and skin will maximize the signal transfer to the microphone. Moreover, as the diaphragm is placed on users' skin, we considered inert materials so as to not irritate users' skin.

3.2 Performance Benchmarking

In this work, we built four different types of microphones (M1, M2, M3, and M4) based on the same architecture shown in Figure 2. We varied two variables (type of piezo and diaphragm material) to build these four microphones (M1, M2, M3, and M4). In addition, we duplicated the microphone proposed in [30]. It (M5) is made with a small condenser microphone attached to a stethoscope head. We also considered two additional state of the art commercial bone conduction microphones: M6 [3] and M7 [7]. Instead of capturing sound directly from the air, both M6 and M7 are designed to pick up sound conducted through bone from direct body contact. They also have been extensively used for speech communication under highly noisy environment for army, law enforcement agencies, fire rescuers etc. We ran two tests using the seven microphones listed in table 1. Firstly, a frequency response test is ran to compare the sensitivity of different microphones. Then we run an external noise test to compare the susceptibility of different microphones. Based on these two test, we select a microphone that is highly sensitive to the body sound and less susceptible to external sound. Lastly, we run a microphone position test to select the optimal head location to attach the BodyBeat microphone to capture a wide range of body sounds.

3.2.1 Frequency Response Test

We ran a series of frequency response tests from 20Hz to 16,000Hz with all microphones (M1 to M7). The frequency response test allowed us to measure the inherent characteristics of each microphone. This is a common test to help engineering build microphones according to certain specifications and to classify them based on what they are best at recording. For our requirements, a higher and relatively flat and unaltered response in the low frequency range allows us to detect subtle sounds and indicates that no anomalies were introduced during the recording.

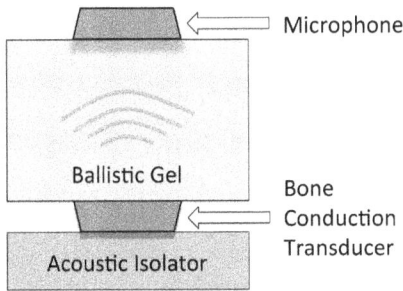

Figure 3: Frequency Response test setup, used to establish the sensitivity of each microphone from 20Hz to 16kHz

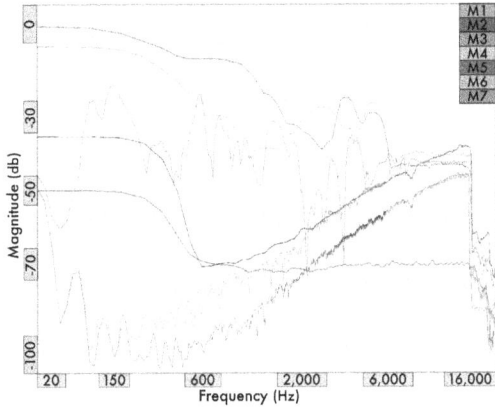

Figure 4: Frequency Response comparison of different microphones from 20Hz to 16kHz

We used a bone conducting transducer as our output device and created a sweeping tone that changed its frequency from 20 Hz to 16,000 Hz. An 8 x 8 x 5.5 centimeter block of ballistic gel was placed on top of the bone conducting transducer. The ballistic gel block is a standard proxy of human flesh or muscle because of its similarity in acoustic properties (e.g. speech of sound, density, etc.). We firmly attached different microphones to the other side of the ballistic gel block. Figure 3 shows the setup of the frequency response test. We ran this experiment for all the seven different microphones listed in table 1.

Figure 4 shows the frequency responses of different microphones. Our results indicate that with a constant gain, M1, M2, and M3 are the most sensitive below 700Hz. M3 maintained the flattest response, but lower than that of M1's and M2's. The most inconsistent response pattern was found in M4, which showed

significant peaks and drop-offs at seemingly random intervals along the frequency axis. M6 and M7 have similar response patterns. M5's response was mostly flat under 600Hz, but it showed similar trends to M6 and M7 above 600Hz. Above 700Hz, M1-M5 had similar response patterns though the magnitude of M5's response was significantly lower. Unlike other microphones, we found a very irregular oscillating frequency response for M6 and M7, which is also considerably lower in the lower part of the frequency range (below 7000 Hz). One explanation of this phenomenon is that most of the off-the-shelf microphones (M6 and M7) are designed for recording speech; thus, they are not optimized for body sounds that lie in relatively lower part of the frequency spectrum. As most of our targeted non-speech body sounds are in a lower part of the frequency range, the frequency response of M2 suggests that it is the most appropriate microphone for capturing subtle body sounds.

3.2.2 External Noise Test

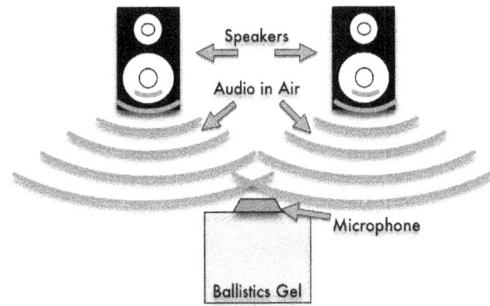

Figure 5: External noise test setup

The external noise test was performed to compare the microphone's robustness against any external or ambient noise. Four prerecorded external noises were played through two speakers to recreate the scenarios in this experiment. These sounds included: white noise, social noise (recorded in a restaurant), traffic noise (recorded in an intersection of a highway), and conversational noise (recorded while another person was talking). For this test, each microphone was positioned over the ballistic gel so that the element was facing the gel and the speakers were facing the back of the microphone. The different recordings were played through the speakers (i.e., audio in air), approximately one meter above the microphone. Figure 5 illustrates the setup of the external noise test.

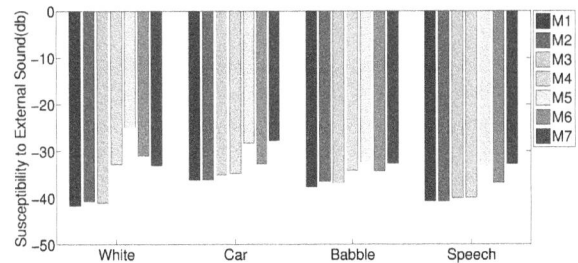

Figure 6: Comparison of different microphone's susceptibility to different type of external sounds or ambient noises

We measure susceptibility (in db) using equation 1, where $Power_{mic}$ is the power of the signal recorded by the microphone and $Power_{speaker}$ is the power emitted from the speaker. We used the standard Root Mean Square (RMS) metric to measure the power. Figure 6 illustrates the susceptibility of different microphones under different types of external sounds. The smaller value of the susceptibility metric of the custom-built M1, M2 and M3 shows that they are more sound proof against external sounds. M5 turned out to be the least robust against external noise. The two off-the-shelf microphones (M6 and M7) were less robust against external sound than M1-M3.

$$Susceptibility = 10 * \log(\frac{Power_{mic}}{Power_{speaker}}) \qquad (1)$$

Based on the frequency response test and the external noise test, we found our custom-built microphone, M2, to be the optimal microphone. While the external noise test was better for M1 than M2, the overall frequency response of M2 was consistently higher in magnitude, up to approximately 2000Hz. The difference in external noise was much less significant than the difference in frequency response between M1 and M2. The construction of these two microphones was identical except for one feature: the diaphragm of M1 was covered with a thin piece of latex, while the diaphragm of M2 was covered with a thin piece of silicone. This leads us to the conclusion that latex is mildly better at preventing external noise than silicone, but silicone is much better at transferring vibration below 2000Hz than latex. Therefore, we selected M2 for the BodyBeat microphone, as it is very insensitive to external sounds and highly sensitive to any sound generated inside the body (including speech).

3.3 Microphone Position Test

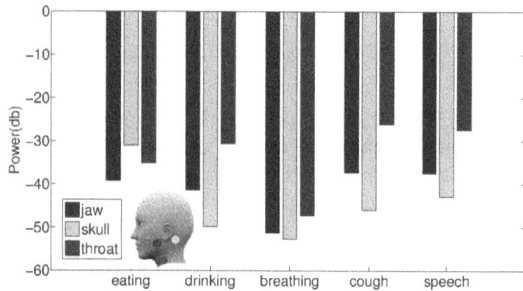

Figure 7: Comparing different body positions (jaw, skull, and throat) for capturing different types of body sounds

We conducted a microphone position test to find the optimal position to place the custom microphone (M2) in order to enable it to capture a wide range of body sounds. This test consisted of two parameters: the first being body position (jaw, skull, & throat) and the second being body sounds (eating, drinking, breathing, coughing, & speech). We recorded the five types of body sounds with M2 in each of the three body positions, and we then compared the power of the captured signals across different body positions. Figure 7 illustrates the power ($10log(P)$ in decibel unit) of the signals captured at different body positions.

Among the three locations, the throat gives us the maximum power (db) for all types of non-vocal body sounds, except eating. The power of the captured eating sounds was similar in all three locations. However, the eating sound captured in the skull contained slightly higher power than that captured in other positions. This is likely because the eating sound can very easily propagate through the teeth and then through the jaw to the skull. Considering our goal of capturing the wide range of body sound classes, the throat is the right location for the BodyBeat microphone.

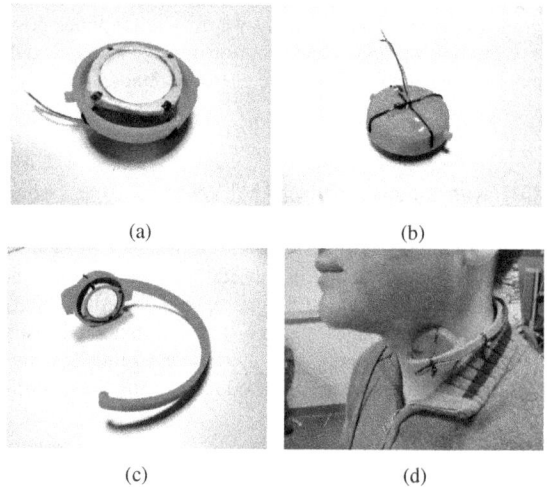

Figure 8: (a) Microphone attached to suspension mechanism (front view), (b) Microphone attached to suspension (back view), (c) 3D printed neck band, (d) Neck band, suspension capsule, and microphone fully assembled, (e) User wearing the fully assembled system

3.4 Neckpiece Design

To capture a wide range of non-speech body sounds from the throat area, we designed a neckpiece to securely attach the custom-made microphone to the throat area. In order to handle users' daily interactions and maintain performance, we also considered friction noise when designing the neckpiece. Human body movements generate noise due to the friction between the silicone diaphragm and the skin. We maintained usability by adopting a suspension mechanism, which allows the microphone's position to be partially independent of the neckpiece. In other words, the microphone remains in place and firmly attached to the neckpiece even when moving, thus minimizing friction noise. Figures 8a and 8b illustrate the top and bottom view of the microphone attached to the suspension capsule.

The microphone is attached to the suspension capsule with four elastic strings (approximately 1mm in diameter). The suspension allows for approximately four millimeters of movement on all sides and four millimeters of vertical movement (for a total of eight millimeters of movement on all three axes). Figure 8c shows the 3D printed neck band. The suspension capsule is attached to the neck band by placing the two cylindrical knobs into the corresponding holes on the two small, inward pointing extensions on the neck band. The band is flexible, which allows for the capsule to be easily placed in (or taken out) and still be tightly attached to the neck band (Figure 9). This design also allows the suspension capsule and microphone to pivot on the horizontal axis, allowing users to adjust for comfort. In figure 8, the current BodyBeat wearable system is still relatively big in size, which may cause some wearability issues. we will iteratively improve the design of *BodyBeat*. We will also look for opportunities to integrate *BodyBeat* into promising wearable systems (such as Google Glass) to enhance wearability.

4. CLASSIFICATION ALGORITHM

4.1 Data Collection

We recruited 14 participants (5 females) with different heights and weights to collect a wide range of body sounds. The partici-

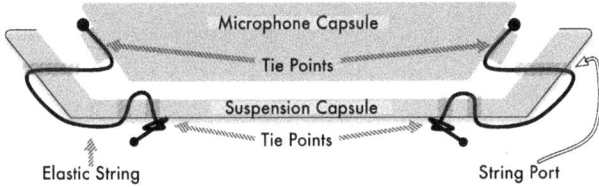

Figure 9: Microphone and Suspension Capsules

Index	Non-Speech Body Sound	Description
1	Eating	Eat a crunchy cookie
2	Eating	Eat an apple
3	Eating	Eat a piece of bread
4	Eating	Eat a banana
5	Drinking	Drink water
6	Deep Breathing	Deeply breath
7	Clearing Throat	Clear your throat
8	Coughing	Cough
9	Sniffling	Sniffle
10	Laugh	Laugh aloud
Index	**Other Sounds**	**Description**
11	Silence	Take a moment to relax
12	Speech	Tell us about yourself

Table 2: The list of non-speech body sounds and other sounds collected in this work

pants are asked to wear the BodyBeat neckpiece and to adjust the position of the microphone so that it is placed beside the vocal chord. The types of body sounds and a short description of each task are listed in table 2. We also collected silence and human speech sounds. Since our primary focus is detecting non-speech body sounds, we treat silence and human speech sounds as sounds that our classification algorithm should be able to recognize them and filter them out. During data collection, all body sounds were recorded with a sampling rate of 8kHz and a resolution of 16-bit. In total, each of our participants contributed approximately 15 minutes of recordings.

To examine the acoustic characteristics of the collected body sounds, we plot their corresponding spectrograms in Figure 10. Spectrogram illustrates a visual representation of the frequency spectrum in a sound as it varies with time. As a comparison, the spectrograms of both silence and speech are also incorporated. As expected, silence spectrogram contains almost no energy throughout the duration of the recording. On the other hand, the spectrogram of speech contains significantly more energy due to the vibration of vocal fold during speech utterances. Among non-speech body sounds, the swallowing sound during drinking generates a distinct frequency pattern. Coughing sound generates two harmonic frequencies following a particular time varying pattern in the spectrogram. When eating crispy hard foods (like chips), chewing is much more pronounced and visible in the spectrogram than that of soft food like bread. The frequency response of deep breathing is much more powerful than that of normal breathing, although both of the breathing variants follow similar trend (in terms of changes of frequency distributino over time). Lastly, the two spectrograms of eating soft food (bread) and normal breathing (in Figure 10) follow a very similar trend.

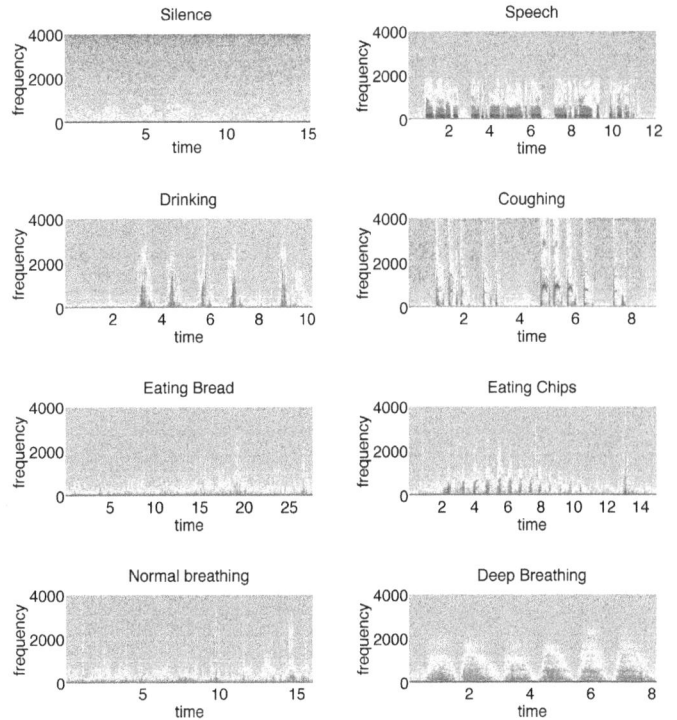

Figure 10: The spectrograms of silence, speech, and non-speech body sounds

4.2 Feature Extraction

The raw audio data sampled from the microphone was first segmented into frames with uniform length and 50% overlap. The length of the segmented frame is critical for the classification procedure that follows. In this work, we considered the frame length in the range from 16ms to 256ms. The optimal frame length is determined empirically based on the classification performance.

To characterize body sounds, we employed a two-step feature extraction procedure. In the first step, we extract a number of acoustic features from each frame to construct frame-level features. Acoustic features for analyzing human speech have been studied extensively in the past decades. However, limited research has been done to interpret non-speech body sounds. Therefore, in this work, we include a standard set of acoustic features used in human speech analysis and a number of other features that have been demonstrated to perform well in capturing paralinguistic features of vocal sounds. Table 3 lists all the frame-level features and their corresponding acronyms. Specifically, the frame-level features include 8 sub-band power features, RMS energy, zero crossing rate (ZCR), 9 spectral features, 12 Mel Frequency Cepstral Coefficients (MFCCs). Let us consider that the sampling frequency is f_s (8000 hz). Now for extracting the 8 log subband power features, we divide the spectrum into 8 subbands respectively having the following frequency ranges $(0, f_s/256)$, $(f_s/256, f_s/128)$, $(f_s/128, f_s/64)$, $(f_s/64, f_s/32)$, $(f_s/32, f_s/16)$, $(f_s/16, f_s/8)$, $(f_s/8, f_s/4)$, $(f_s/4, f_s/2)$. The first sub-band power represents the total power in a very small frequency region from 0 to 31.25 Hz. From the second sub-band, the bandwidth of each sub-band is twice as much as that of the former sub-band. The logarithm (base 10) is applied to represent the power of each sub-band in a bel scale. The spectral features are used to characterize different

7

Group	Frame level descriptors	Acronym
Energy	log power of 8 subbands	LogSubband[i]
	Total RMS Energy	RMSenergy
Spectral	Spectral Centroid	SpectCent
	Spectral Flux	SpectFlux
	Spectral Variance	SpectVar
	Spectral Skewness	SpectSkew
	Spectral Kurtosis	SpectKurt
	Spectral Slope	SpectSlope
	Spectral Rolloff 25%	SpectROff25
	Spectral Rolloff 50%	SpectROff50
	Spectral Rolloff 75%	SpectROff75
	Spectral Rolloff 90%	SpectROff90
Crossing Rate	Zero Crossing Rate	ZCR
MFCC	12 Mel Frequency Cepstral Coefficients	mfcc[i]

Table 3: The list of frame-level features

Type	Statistical Functions	Acronym
Extremes	Minimum	min
	Maximum	max
Average	Mean	mean
	Root Mean Square	RMS
	Median	median
Quartiles	1st and 3rd Quartile	qrtl1, qrtl3
	Interquartile Range	iqrl
Moments	Standard Deviation	std
	Skewness	skew
	Kurtosis	kurt
Peaks	Number of peaks	numOfPeaks
	Mean Distance of Peaks	meanDistPeaks
	Mean Amplitude of Peaks	meanAmpPeaks
Rate of Change	Mean Crossing Rate	mcr
Shape	Linear Regression Slope	slope

Table 4: The list of statistical functions applied to the frame-level features for extracting window-level features

aspects of spectra including the 'center of mass' (spectral centroid), 'change of spectra' (spectral flux), 'variance of the frequency' (spectral variance), 'skewness of the spectral distribution' (spectral skewness), 'the shape of spectra' (spectral slope, spectral rolloffs) etc. Lastly, MFCC coefficients capture the Cepstral coefficients using the source vocal tract model in speech signal processing.

Based on those extracted frame-level features, we grouped frames into windows with much longer duration and extract features at the window-level. We considered the window length in the range of 1s–5s, also determined empirically based on the classification performance. To extract window-level features, we applied a set of statistical functions across all the frame-level features within each window. Table 4 lists all the statistical functions applied to the frame-level features within the window to capture different aspect of the frame-level features. Specifically, the window-level features capture the averages, extremes, rate of change, and shape of the frame-level features within each window. For example, one window-level feature is the mean value of the zero crossing rates (ZCR) in frames, which is measured by at first estimating the ZCR of individual frames and then calculating the arithmetic mean value across all the ZCRs in a particular window. In total, we extracted 512 window-level features.

4.3 Feature Selection

The two-step feature extraction in the last section generates a total of 512 features. Since we are going to implement the overall feature extraction and classification framework on resource limited smartphone and wearable platform, it is not computationally efficient to include all these features. Therefore, the goal is to select a minimum number of features that achieve reasonably good

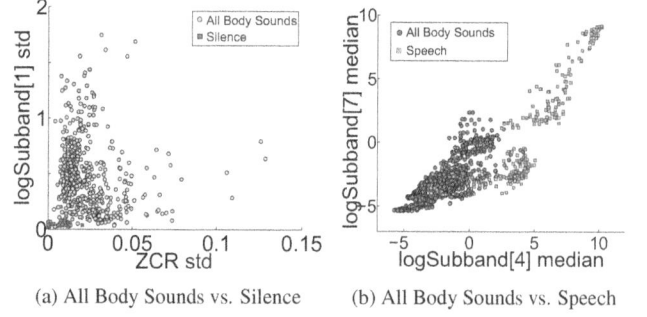

(a) All Body Sounds vs. Silence   (b) All Body Sounds vs. Speech

Figure 11: Scatter plots in 2D feature spaces

classification performance. In our work, we use the *correlation feature selection* (CFS) algorithm to select the subset of features [13]. In general, the CFS algorithm evaluates the goodness of features based on two criteria. First, the feature is highly indicative of the target class. Second, the new feature select must be highly uncorrelated with the features already selected. We used CFS algorithm to select a set of 30 features.

From these 30 features we further select the most optimized feature set for the target classifier. To do this, we run a sequential forward feature selection algorithm with the classifier's performance as criteria to select the top N best features. As a classifier we used Linear Discriminative Classifier which will be explained in further detail in Section 4.4. The best features selected includes logSubband[1] std, logSubband[4] median, specQrtl25 min, logSubband[4] std, logSubband[5] qrtl75, logSubband[5] numOfPeaks, ZCR std, logSubband[6] std, logSubband[6] mean, specRoff50 meanCrossingRate, and logSubband[7] median.

To show the performance of these selected features, a series of scatter plots in 2D feature space are shown in Figure 11 and 12. First, Figure 11a shows the scatter plot of silence and all the body sound classes with respect to the two features: the standard deviation of zero crossing rate and the log of first sub-band power (logSubband[1] std). Silence typically consisted of low energy random signal. The signal's zero crossing rate and the logSubband[1] does not vary much across frames. Thus, using these two features, we can discriminate all body sounds from silence. Figure 11b shows speech and all the body sounds in the feature space of logSubband[4] median and logSubband[7] median. As illustrated, speech signals contain much higher power in both of the sub-bands. Thus, using these two features, we can discriminate speech from all the body sounds considered for this study.

Figure 12 shows the difference among different body sounds in different pairs of selected features. Figure 12a indicates that eating sounds are fairly different from cough, laughter, and clearing the throat in the 2 dimensional feature space of logSubband[4] std and logSubband[5] qrtl75. Both of the features have the low values for eating sounds. The 5th sub-band laughter contains slightly higher energy than others. Figure 12b shows that the most discriminative feature for separating eating from drinking is logSubband[6] std. It means that the 6th sub-band's log energy varies more for the drinking sound than that of eating sounds. Figure 12c shows that deep breathing sounds contain lower energy in 6th sub-band. The standard deviation of the 4th sub-band's log energy also varies much less for deep breathing sounds compared to cough and clearing throat.

(a) Eating vs. Clearing Throat vs. Cough vs. Laugh

(b) Eating vs. Drinking

(c) Clearing Throat vs. Cough vs. Deep Breath

Figure 12: Scatter plots in 2D feature spaces

4.4 Classification

We use Linear Discriminant Classifier (LDC) as the classification algorithm. We chose LDC over other classification algorithms such as Support Vector Machine (SVM), Gaussian Mixture Model (GMM) and Adaboost because LDC is also computationally efficient and lightweight enough to be implemented in resource-limited smartphone. Table 5 shows the results of different classifiers with different feature sets. We used two different cross-validation experiments: a Leave-One-Person-Out (LOPO) and a Leave-One-Sample-Out (LOSO) cross-validation experiment. The LOPO cross-validation results are the most unbiased estimate of our classifier's performance, when the classifier is asked to detect the body sounds of a new person that the classifier has not seen before. In contrast, the LOSO cross-validation assumes that the classifier is trained on the data collected from the target user. The performance results from the LOSO cross-validation can be thought as the ceiling performance of the system. The best performance is achieved using LDC and energy, spectral features, and MFCC is used to extract the initial set of window-level features for selecting the top window-level features. The performance reaches to 72.5 (average recall) and 63.4 (precision). Table 5 also shows that with only energy and spectral features as frame-level features, the LDC classifier can get a nice performance, which is 71.2 (recall), 61.5 (precision), and 66.5 (accuracy) from the LOPO experiment. Moreover, if a user contributes some training data towards making the classifier, the performance measure reaches to 88.1% recall (from LOSO experiment). Notice that losing MFCC from our frame-level feature set does not affect the classifier's performance much (absolute reduction in terms of recall is 1.3 %), but if we don't have to extract MFCC features, that indicates that we could save a lot of system's resource in terms of power [22], speed, and memory. Considering this factor, we decided to use just energy and spectral features as frame-level features with LDC as classifier for the rest of our analysis and system implementation. Lastly, we also build the classification algorithm used by a recent study [30] to compare with our proposed BodyBeat classification algorithm. We find that our system outperforms BodyScope [30]. Lastly, table 6 shows the class level recall and precision from the LOPO experiment this classifier.

The choice of both the frame and window size length used to extract features significantly impacts classification performance. A coarse frame or window size may not capture the local dynamic (time variant) properties of the body sounds. On the other hand a very fine frame or window may be prone to noise and thus may decrease the discriminative properties of the features. We run

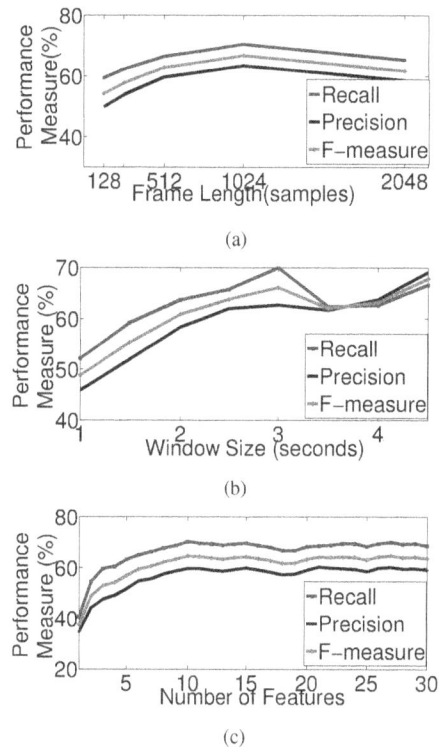

Figure 13: shows the impact of (a) frame size (b) window size (c) total number of features on the performance of classifier

this analysis to find the optimal frame and window size. Figure 13a and 13b shows the impact of the frame and window size on the classifier's performance. The frame size of 1024 samples (125 milliseconds) and the window size of 3 seconds maximize the classifier's performance. The number of features selected using the feature selection also plays a very important role on the performance measure of the classifier. Figure 13c shows that the performance measures in terms of recall, precision and F-measure saturates when we use 10 window-level features.

5. SYSTEM IMPLEMENTATION

The BodyBeat non-speech body sound sensing mobile system is implemented using an embedded system unit and an Android application unit. The custom-made microphone of BodyBeat system is

Frame-level Features	LOPO			LOSO		
	R	P	F	R	P	F
Energy & Spectral	71.2	61.5	66.5	88.1	81.9	86.5
MFCC	66.3	52.8	57.8	75.0	71.5	73.2
Energy & Spectral & MFCC	72.5	63.4	67.6	90.3	82.3	86.6
BodyScope[30]	57.6	55.5	56.5	76.6	71.5	73.8

Table 5: Classification performance in terms of Recall (R), Precision (P) and F-measure (F) based on both Leave-One-Person-Out (LOPO) and a Leave-One-Sample-Out (LOSO) cross-validation

	Eating	Drinking	Deep Breathing	Clearing Throat	Coughing	Sniffling	Laugh	Silence	Speech
Recall	70.35	72.09	64.09	68.75	80.00	75.00	61.90	74.38	81.06
Precision	73.29	57.21	60.95	61.11	62.07	58.00	61.90	61.66	84.69

Table 6: The Recall and Precision for each class from the LOPO experiment using LDC as classifier and energy and spectral features as frame-level features

directly attached to the embedded system. The embedded system unit utilizes an ARM microcontroller unit, an audio codec and a Bluetooth module to implement capture, preprocessing and frame admission control of the raw acoustic data from the microphone. The Android application unit on the other hand implements the two stage feature extraction, and inference algorithm. These two units communicate with each other through Bluetooth. Figure 14 illustrates the system architecture of the overall system. In what follows, we present the system implementation details of both the embedded system unit and the Android application unit.

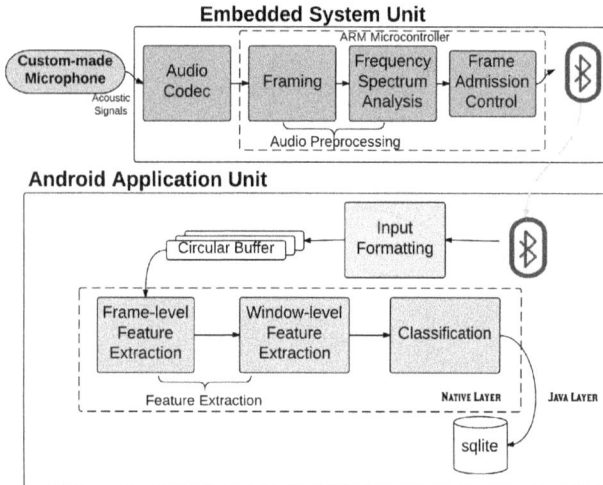

Figure 14: The Block Diagram of BodyBeat System Architecture

5.1 Embedded System Unit

At the center of the embedded system unit, we used a commercially available Maple ARM microcontroller [4]. The board consists of a 72MHz ARM cortex M3 chip with most of the standard peripherals including digital and analog input/output pins, 1 USB, and 3 Universal Asynchronous Receiver/Transmitters (UARTs), and Serial Peripheral Interface (SPI). The clock speed, advanced peripherals, and interrupt capabilities enables us to do some rudimentary real-time audio signal processing and at the same time to drive a Bluetooth codec to communicate with the Android application unit.

As seen in Figure 14, the ARM microcontroller connects to an audio codec via SPI [6]. The audio codec ([6]) contains a Wolfson WM8731 chip. The audio codec receives the analog audio signal using a 1/8 inch input jack and samples the audio with an array sampling frequency up to 88000 Hz and with a resolution up to 24 bit/sample. The ARM unit is also connected with a class 2 Bluetooth ratio modem (commercially called BlueSMiRF Silver [5]). The Bluetooth modem contains the RN-42 chip that receives data from the ARM unit via UART and sends data to the Android application with an SPP profile with a data rate of 115000bps. The Bluetooth modem ensures reliable wireless connectivity with the Android device up to a distance of 18 meters. A rechargeable LiPo battery is used to power the ARM microcontroller, including the audio codec and Bluetooth modem. Figure 15 shows the prototype of embedded unit.

Figure 15: The ARM Micro-Controller Unit

5.1.1 Audio Preprocessing

Audio preprocessing is the first step that happens in the ARM microcontroller, which receives the digital samples of the Body-Beat microphone's analog audio stream by the Audio Codec. The sampling frequency and bit resolution are chosen to be 8000Hz and 16 bit, respectively, as it provides us with a detailed picture of the audio and lowers the computational load of the system at the same time. As the Audio Codec samples the analog audio signal and sends a digital signal to the ARM microcontroller unit via SPI, the interrupt in the ARM microcontroller unit collects the data in a circular buffer. The audio data stored in the circular buffer is then segmented with a frame length of 1024 samples (125 milliseconds). While the interrupt fills the circular buffer, the main thread essentially checks continuously if another 1024 samples has filled the circular buffer. Upon detecting the arrival of a new frame, the ARM unit stars a RADIX-4 Complex Fast

Fourier Transformation (FFT) implementation, which is written in C language [2]. The FFT implementation uses fixed-point arithmetic with a sine table for optimizing speed by sacrificing some memory. To prevent an arithmetic overflow, fixed scaling is employed.

5.1.2 Frame Admission Control

The ARM microcontroller also does a frame admission control to filter out audio frames that do not contain any body sounds. After getting the FFT of the Hanning windowed audio frame of 1024 samples, we extracted a few important sub-band power and zero crossing rate features to detect the presence of speech and silence. In Figure 11, we already demonstrated how with a few features we can filter out frames containing silence and speech. We took a few measures to optimize our implementation in this regard. For example, one of the features that we implemented in our ARM microcontroller is logSubband[4] median. Floating point logarithm calculation is heavy in terms of both CPU. We used a log table to lower the CPU requirements by sacrificing some memory. When a certain frame is detected not to contain any silence or speech, the ARM microcontroller transfers the power spectrum of the current frame to the Android unit. To asynchronously transfer different frames, we send a preamble to mark the start of a frame.

5.2 Android Application Unit

The Android application unit, which is approximately 2200 lines of Java, C, and C++ code, includes the input formatting of the data, which is followed by feature extraction and classification. The android unit implements a feature extraction and classification algorithm in the native layer using C and C++ for faster execution. The complete binary package including resource files is approximately 1280 KB.

5.2.1 Input formatting

The Android unit receives data via Bluetooth from the embedded system unit as shown in Figure 14. This module used the Android Bluetooth APIs to scan for other Bluetooth devices around the phone, to fetch the information of the paired (or already authenticated) remote Bluetooth modem in the embedded system unit, and to establish wireless communication channel. The Android application receives each frame asynchronously from the embedded unit. The Android Bluetooth adapter continuously looks for a four byte long preamble, which indicates the start of a new frame is being sent by the embedded system unit. Upon receiving the preamble, the input processing module continuously stores all the received data in a temporary buffer. As soon as the temporary buffer is full (received 513 samples, each 16 bit), the input processing module takes all the data of the current frame from the temporary buffer and updates a two dimensional circular buffer. At the same time, the input processing unit starts to look for another preamble indicating the start of another frame. This preamble helps the Android application unit to receive each frame of data separately. The two dimensional circular buffer is shared by both the producer thread and the consumer thread as data storage and data source. The two dimensional circular buffer stores each frame's data (513 samples) in a row. Thus, consecutive frame data is stored in different rows in the two-dimensional circular buffer. All the work in input processing happens in producer thread. To facilitate the two dimensional circular buffer sharing by the two threads, it includes two separate pointers for the two threads (producer and consumer) at different rows of the two dimensional circular buffer.

5.2.2 Feature Extraction and Classification

Once the two dimensional circular buffer contains 24 frames of data (window length 3 seconds) for the feature extraction and inference, the consumer thread passes the data to the native layer. To ensure 50% overlap between two consecutive windows, the consumer thread's pointer moves to 16 rows to point to the new frame. The entire feature extraction and classification algorithm is implemented in the native layer considering the speed requirements for real-time passive body sound sensing. Section 4 gives the detailed description of the discriminative features for body sound classification. The frame-level features are first extracted from frame-level data. We used various statistical functions to extract window-level features at this stage. The window-level features are then used to infer the body sound. While implementing the feature extraction and classification, we took several measures to optimize power, CPU, and memory usage. We used additional memory for lowering CPU load. All the memory blocks are pre-allocated during the initialization of the Android application unit and are shared across multiple native layer calls.

5.3 System Evaluation

In this section, we present the system evaluation of the BodyBeat system. We first discuss CPU and memory benchmarks, which is then followed by the detailed time and power benchmarks, including both the embedded system unit and the Android application unit. All the measurement of the Android application unit is done with Google Nexus 4.

5.3.1 CPU and Memory Benchmarks

Status	CPU Usage	Memory Usage
Silence or speech	8-12%	45MB
Body Sound	15-22%	47MB

Table 7: CPU and Memory Benchmarks of the Android Application Unit

Table 7 shows the CPU and memory benchmarks of our system. When the BodyBeat microphone captures either silence or speech, the Android application unit consumes less than 12% of the CPU and 45 MB of memory, because of embedded system's frame admission control. During the presence of body sounds, the CPU and memory usage increases and reaches up to 22% and 47 MB.

5.3.2 Time and Power Benchmarks

Figure 8 shows the average running time of different routines in both the embedded system unit and Android application unit for processing 3 seconds of audio from the BodyBeat microphone that contains some body sound. In the embedded unit, the first routine forms a frame of 1024 samples and multiplies it with the Hanning windowing function to compensate Gibbs phenomena. The framing only takes 5 milliseconds where the next process Fast Fourier Transformation (FFT) takes 80 milliseconds. The frame admission control takes up to 20 milliseconds.

The input processing in the Android application unit takes the most of the time, as it includes the delay due to Bluetooth communication. The feature extraction passes each frame (power spectra received via Bluetooth, length 513 data) in the window to the native layer to extract frame-level features. The frame-level feature extraction takes a moderate amount of time, as this is one of the most heavy routine in Android application unit. Lastly, the window-level feature and classification takes only 5 and 1.5 milliseconds to run.

11

Unit	Routine	Time (ms)
Embedded	Framing	5
	FFT	80
	Frame admission control	20
Android	Input Processing	2448
	Frame-level feature extraction	84
	Window-level feature extraction	5
	Classification	1.5

Table 8: Average running time of different routines in the ARM microcontroller unit and the Android application unit to process 3 seconds (one window) of audio data containing some body sound

Routine	Average Power (milliWatt)
Input Processing (IP)	343.74
IP & Feature Extraction (FE)	362.84
IP & FE & Classification	374.49

Table 9: The Power benchmarking of Android app unit

The embedded system unit consumes 256.64 milliwatt(mW) when the system is waiting to be paired and connected with an Android system. The embedded system unit consumes about 333.3 mW power while the raw audio data contains valuable body sounds and the frame admission control allows the data to be transferred to the Android system unit. On the other hand, when frame admission control detects either silence or speech in the signal and stops transmission of the data to Android unit, the embedded system unit's power consumption decreases to 289.971mW. Table 9 illustrates the average power (in milliwatt unit) consumed by different routines of the Android application unit. The average power consumption by the Android application unit is about 374.49 mW, when the application unit runs all the routines (input processing, frame- and window-level feature extraction and classification).

6. POTENTIAL APPLICATIONS

An increasing number of mobile systems are bringing health sensing to the masses. In this regard, we were inspired to build a mobile system for sensing a wide range of non-speech body sounds. By listening to the internal sounds that our bodies naturally produce, we can continuously sense many medical and behavioral problems in a wearable form factor. Here, we highlight some future applications that can be developed with our BodyBeat sensor:

6.1 Food Journaling

Since BodyBeat can recognize eating and drinking sounds, it has the potential to be used in food journaling applications. Despite technological advancements, developing automatic (or semi-automatic) systems for food journaling is very challenging. For example, the PlateMate [24] system demonstrated the feasibility of using Amazon Mechanical Turk to label photographs of users' meals with caloric information. However, this system required that users actually remember to take a photo of what they eat. With the invention of BodyBeat, you can imagine a future system that detects when a user is eating. The system then either automatically takes a picture of their food with a life-logging camera (e.g. Microsoft SenseCam, Google Glass), or simply reminds the user to take a photo of their food. Lastly, it uploads the image to Mechanical Turk for caloric labeling.

6.2 Illness Detection

The BodyBeat system allows us to detect coughing, deep or heavy breathing, which can be indicative of many pulmonary diseases. While a few previous studies have illustrated success detecting these body sounds indicative of illness (e.g. [17, 30]), BodyBeat mobile system can be used in an application which will detect the onset, frequency, and the location of coughing, heavy breathing or any other kind of pulmonary sounds. As sensing devices become more ubiquitous, cough detection could allow us to track the spread of illnesses, with similar motivation to TwitterHealth research [27]. In future work, we plan to work with medical doctors to expand the BodyBeat system to detect other body sounds of interest, such as sneezing and specific types of coughing (e.g., wheezing, dry cough, productive cough).

7. RELATED WORK

The microphone is a rich sensor stream that contains information about our surroundings and us. Many studies proposed mobile systems that leverage the smartphone's built-in microphone to infer the surroundings of a person [21], physiological state (sleep [14], cough [17]), and psychological state (stress [20]). A recent study proposed Aditeur, a mobile system that detects audio events in real-time using the phone's built-in microphone, backed by a cloud service[22]. Such mobile systems are becoming very popular in the mobile health domain, especially among clinicians and patients for detection of disease, monitoring of health variables, etc. [16]. However, the smartphone's built-in microphone (typically a condenser) is actually optimized for capturing speech. It is difficult to capture subtle non-speech body sounds because of the placement of the smartphone and external noise levels. A few recent studies proposed contact microphone designs. Hirahara et al. proposed a customized microphone with Eurathane elastomer designed to capture non-audible murmur, which is a very weak whispered voice [15]. Various contact microphones are also used in music industry that are designed to directly capture vibrations from musical instruments [1]. None of these contact microphones are not designed and optimized to capture subtle body sounds.

Yatani and Khai [30] proposed BodyScope, a wearable neck-piece with a standard condenser microphone augmented with a stethoscope head, in order to capture an array of body sounds to predict activity. In our study, we designed and implemented a customized microphone based on piezo-electric sensor that are optimized for subtle body sounds. We also propose a neckpiece that is designed with a consideration on the microphone's longer-term wearability and users' comfort. The neckpiece also employ a suspension mechanism to compensate friction noise due to user's body movement. Body sounds are a fundamental source of health information and are being used by physicians since almost the beginning of modern medical science [18]. Due to the subtle nature of body sounds, it is difficult to reliably and passively capture body sound signals with a built-in smartphone microphone. As a result, some studied have explored the feasibility of a customized-wearable microphone for recognizing eating behaviors, breathing patterns, etc. Amft and Troster [10] used a combination of sensors to model eating behavior. They modeled hand gestures with inertial sensors in users' hands; chewing with ear attached microphones; and swallowing with rubber elongation sensors in the throat areas. Recent studies also tried to detect different eating sounds collected from a tri-axial accelerometer implanted inside teeth and using textile neckband [19, 11]. The scalability of this approach might be significantly constricted because of the sensor placement, which is close to oral activity. Another study used the built-in microphone of a hearing aid to recognize chewing events [25]. Some studies have used off-the-shelf bone conduction and condenser microphones to capture audio of eating and then classify the type of food consume and mastication counts [9, 8, 28]. Body vibration captured by inertial sensors have also been used to estimate heartbeat [23]. The recent studies in the literature are mostly confined to offline exploration of discriminative acoustic features and machine learning. In addition, most studies did not provide information about the implementation of the signal processing and machine learning algorithms in resource-limited hardware. In our work, we presented the implementation of our signal processing and machine learning algorithms in the context of a distributed system, consisting of an ARM micro-controller and an Android phone. We compared our algorithms to baseline algorithms, and we also presented the results from the CPU, memory, and power benchmarking experiments.

8. CONCLUSION AND FUTURE WORK

In this paper, we presented the design, implementation and evaluation of BodyBeat, a wearable sensing system that captures and recognizes non-speech body sounds. We have described the design of our custom-built piezoelectric sensor-based microphone and showed that our microphone outperforms other existing solutions in capturing non-speech body sounds. In addition, we have developed a classification algorithm based on a set of carefully selected features and achieved an average classification average recall of 71.2%. Finally, we have implemented BodyBeat and benchmarked its performance.

In the future, we plan to reduce the form factor of BodyBeat to improve its wearability and minimize its obtrusiveness to users. We also want to keep exploring the potential of BodyBeat on detecting other non-speech body sounds. We also aim to process non-speech body sounds at a lower sampling rate and run the end-to-end evaluation of the system. Finally, based on the promising results reported in this paper, we plan to bring BodyBeat to life by deploying it in the aforementioned applications.

9. ACKNOWLEDGMENTS

This work was partially supported by NSF IIS#1202141 and Intel Science and Technology Center for Pervasive computing.

10. REFERENCES

[1] http://contactmicrophones.com/index.html.
[2] http://coolarduino.wordpress.com/2012/03/24/radix-4-fft-integer-math/.
[3] http://invisio.com/products/headsets/invisio-m3.aspx.
[4] http://leaflabs.com.
[5] https://www.sparkfun.com/products/10269.
[6] http://www.openmusiclabs.com/projects/codec-shield/.
[7] http://www.temco-j.co.jp.
[8] Amft, O., Kusserow, M., and Troster, G. Bite weight prediction from acoustic recognition of chewing. *IEEE Transactions on Biomedical Engineering 56*, 6 (June 2009), 1663–1672.
[9] Amft, O., StÃd'ger, M., and TrÃűster, G. Analysis of chewing sounds for dietary monitoring. In *UbiComp '05* (2005), 56–72.
[10] Amft, O., and Troster, G. On-body sensing solutions for automatic dietary monitoring. *IEEE Pervasive Computing 8*, 2 (2009), 62–70.
[11] Cheng, J., Zhou, B., Kunze, K., Rheinländer, C., Wille, S., Wehn, N., Weppner, J., and Lukowicz, P. Activity recognition and nutrition monitoring in every day situations with a textile capacitive neckband. UbiComp '13 Adjunct (2013), 155–158.
[12] Dacremont, C. Spectral composition of eating sounds generated by crispy, crunchy and crackly foods. *Journal of Texture Studies 26*, 1 (1995), 27–43.
[13] Hall, M. A. Correlation-based Feature Selection for Machine Learning. *PhD Thesis* (April 1999).
[14] Hao, T., Xing, G., and Zhou, G. isleep: Unobtrusive sleep quality monitoring using smartphones. SenSys '13 (2013), 1–14.
[15] Hirahara, T., Shimizu, S., and Otani, M. Acoustic characteristics of non-audible murmur. *The Japan China Joint Conference of Acoustics 100* (2007), 4000.
[16] Lane, N., Miluzzo, E., Lu, H., Peebles, D., Choudhury, T., and Campbell, A. A survey of mobile phone sensing. *Communications Magazine, IEEE 48*, 9 (2010), 140–150.
[17] Larson, E., Lee, T., Liu, S., Rosenfeld, M., and Patel, S. Accurate and privacy preserving cough sensing using a low-cost microphone. UbiComp '11 (2011), 375–384.
[18] Levine, S., and Harvey, W. *Clinical auscultation of the heart*. W. B. Saunders, 1959.
[19] Li, C.-Y., Chen, Y.-C., Chen, W.-J., Huang, P., and Chu, H.-H. Sensor-embedded teeth for oral activity recognition. ISWC '13 (2013), 41–44.
[20] Lu, H., Frauendorfer, D., Rabbi, M., Mast, M., Chittaranjan, G., Campbell, A., Gatica-Perez, D., and Choudhury, T. Stresssense: Detecting stress in unconstrained acoustic environments using smartphones. UbiComp '12 (2012), 351–360.
[21] Lu, H., Pan, W., Lane, N. D., Choudhury, T., and Campbell, A. T. Soundsense: Scalable sound sensing for people-centric applications on mobile phones. MobiSys '09 (2009), 165–178.
[22] Nirjon, S., Dickerson, R. F., Asare, P., Li, Q., Hong, D., Stankovic, J., Hu, P., Shen, G., and Jiang, X. Auditeur: A mobile-cloud service platform for acoustic event detection on smartphones. MobiSys '13 (2013), 403–416.
[23] Nirjon, S., Dickerson, R. F., Li, Q., Asare, P., Stankovic, J., Hong, D., Zhang, B., Jiang, X., Shen, G., and Zhao, F. Musicalheart: A hearty way of listening to music. SenSys '12, ACM (2012), 43–56.
[24] Noronha, J., Hysen, E., Zhang, H., and Gajos, K. Platemate: crowdsourcing nutritional analysis from food photographs. In *UIST '11* (Oct. 2011).
[25] Passler, S., and Fischer, W.-J. Evaluation of algorithms for chew event detection. BodyNets '12 (2012), 20–26.
[26] Reichert, S., Gass, R., Brandt, C., and Andrès, E. Analysis of respiratory sounds: state of the art. *Clinical medicine. Circulatory, respiratory and pulmonary medicine 2* (2008), 45.
[27] Sadilek, A., and Kautz, H. Modeling the impact of lifestyle on health at scale. In *WSDM '13* (2013), 637–646.
[28] Shuzo, M., Lopez, G., Takashima, T., Komori, S., Delaunay, J.-J., Yamada, I., Tatsuta, S., and Yanagimoto, S. Discrimination of eating habits with a wearable bone conduction sound recorder system. In *IEEE Sensors '09* (2009), 1666–1669.
[29] Whittaker, A., Lucas, M., Carter, R., and Anderson, K. Limitations in the use of median frequency for lung sound analysis. *Journal of Engineering in Medicine 214*, 3 (2000), 265–275.
[30] Yatani, K., and Truong, K. Bodyscope: A wearable acoustic sensor for activity recognition. UbiComp '12 (2012), 341–350.

Ubiquitous Keyboard for Small Mobile Devices: Harnessing Multipath Fading for Fine-Grained Keystroke Localization

Junjue Wang, Kaichen Zhao and Xinyu Zhang
University of Wisconsin-Madison
{jwang283, kzhao25}@wisc.edu, xyzhang@ece.wisc.edu

Chunyi Peng
The Ohio State University
chunyi@cse.ohio-state.edu

ABSTRACT

A well-known bottleneck of contemporary mobile devices is the inefficient and error-prone touchscreen keyboard. In this paper, we propose UbiK, an alternative portable text-entry method that allows user to make keystrokes on conventional surfaces, *e.g.*, wood desktop. UbiK enables text-input experience similar to that on a physical keyboard, but it only requires a keyboard outline printed on the surface or a piece of paper atop. The core idea is to leverage the microphone on a mobile device to accurately localize the keystrokes. To achieve fine-grained, centimeter scale granularity, UbiK extracts and optimizes the location-dependent multipath fading features from the audio signals, and takes advantage of the dual-microphone interface to improve signal diversity. We implement UbiK as an Android application. Our experiments demonstrate that UbiK is able to achieve above 95% of localization accuracy. Field trial involving first-time users shows that UbiK can significantly improve text-entry speed over current on-screen keyboards.

Categories and Subject Descriptors

H.5.2 [**Information Interfaces and Presentation**]: User Interfaces—*Input devices and strategies*

Keywords

UbiK; mobile text-entry; paper keyboard; acoustic localization

1. INTRODUCTION

Despite the increasing sophistication of mobile technology, interacting with today's mobile devices can involve painful contortions. Miniature circuits and displays keep pushing portable devices to a smaller form factor — down to stamp-size for emerging wearable computers — but human fingers and hands do not shrink accordingly. As a result, on-screen keyboard, a daily part of life for many people, remains as

MobiSys'14, June 16 - 19 2014, Bretton Woods, NH, USA
Copyright 2014 ACM 978-1-4503-2793-0/14/06 ...$15.00.
http://dx.doi.org/10.1145/2594368.2594384.

an obstacle that prevents the anticipated role switching for mobile devices from information consumers to providers.

This grand challenge has prompted considerable research in the field of mobile text entry. Existing work in human computer interaction addressed the problem by redesigning keyboard layout [1], adapting key size [2], expanding keyboard area [3,4], *etc.* However, users are highly resistant to learning new methods, particularly new keyboard layouts or key shapes [5]. Projection keyboard [6–8] provides a more palatable solution for heavy typists, but they require bulky new hardware to accompany mobile devices, which compromises their portability.

In this paper, we propose UbiK, a new approach to mobile text input that recognizes keystrokes through fine-grained localization. UbiK enables PC-like text-entry experience, by allowing users to click on solid surfaces, and then localizing the key symbol through the keystroke's acoustic patterns. A keyboard outline can be drawn on the surface, or printed on a piece of paper atop. The keystrokes can be sensed using microphones that are readily available on today's mobile devices. With such simple setup, UbiK can serve as a spontaneous and efficient keyboard in a wide range of scenarios, *e.g.*, on an office desk, conference room table, or an airplane tray table.

The key challenge for UbiK lies in fine granularity. Inter-key distance on typical PC keyboard is only around 2 centimeters. Wireless localization, even those requiring user to carry active radios, can only achieve several feet of granularity [9]. Using microphone arrays, existing sound source localization algorithms [10] can achieve a few meters of accuracy based on time-difference-of-arrival (TDOA) information. Theoretically, sound waves are coherent within their meters-scale wavelength, and audio sources within this range are hardly distinguishable. However, this holds only for point sound source in free-space. Practical clicks on solid surfaces generate entangled audio waves that undergo complex multipath reflection patterns on the surface and the body of the mobile device, as they propagate towards the microphone. Although such patterns worsen the unpredictability and compromise accuracy of audio ranging [11], they can create location-dependent miniature sound signatures, thus improving the granularity of sound source localization.

To verify the above principle, we use commercial off-the-shelf (COTS) smartphones to conduct a comprehensive measurement study of acoustic multipath patterns produced by keystrokes on conventional solid surfaces. We find that finger clicks on the same spot exhibit highly consistent fading patterns, due to soundwave reflections cancelling or strengthening each other. Such patterns depend on the sound frequency or wavelength, and can be characterized by the amplitude spectrum density (ASD) of the click sound. A more important observation is that the ASD of different keystroke locations reveals highly distinguishable profiles and can be conveniently used as location signatures. The signatures exhibit a certain level of correlation within a short distance of several millimeters, but the correlation diminishes monotonically as physical separation increases. Since neighboring key distance on a PC keyboard is roughly 20 millimeters, ASD has potential to enable keystroke-level location granularity.

UbiK synthesizes these experimental observations to realize a fine-grained, fingerprinting-based keystroke identification system comprised of three key components: detection, localization and adaptation. We design an online detection algorithm that adapts noise-floor threshold to single out keystroke signals, and augments motion sensors to isolate the impact of bursty interference such as human voices. We introduce a keystroke localization framework that uses simple nearest neighbor search for signature matching, while optimizing the signatures to maximize the feature separation between keys. In particular, we leverage dual-microphone interface on typical mobile devices to improve the audio signal diversity and hence signature diversity. We formulate an optimization-based solution to cap the frequency range of the ASD profile, so as to prevent the noisy features from polluting localization accuracy. In addition, we take advantage of the unique opportunity offered by users' online feedback to calibrate the training signatures and discriminate their significance.

We build UbiK as a prototype application for Android devices. Our implementation achieves real-time keystroke detection and localization without noticeable latency. Our baseline evaluation demonstrates that UbiK can easily achieve 90+% of localization accuracy, even with 3 training instances per key and without user calibration. Coupled with its online adaptation, its accuracy quickly escalates to around 95%. UbiK works consistently on a variety of solid surfaces and keyboard layouts. An experimental study involving first-time users show that UbiK maintains high performance across different users. UbiK is robust against minor displacement of the keyboard or mobile devices, and can rapidly converge to high accuracy after significant disturbance. Typing is not as rapid as on a mechanical keyboard but easily outperforms thumb-operated keyboards.

The main contribution of this paper is to address mobile text entry problem using a fine-grained keystroke localization system. This contribution breaks down into the following aspects:

- We provide measurement based evidence that verifies the feasibility of fine-grained, centimeter scale click sound localization using acoustic multipath signatures.

- We design UbiK, a practical framework that optimizes the location signatures and enables detection/localization of keystrokes on solid surfaces and in real-world environment.

- We implement UbiK as an efficient application running on COTS Android devices, and further validate UbiK's performance through comprehensive micro-benchmark tests and users' field trials.

Figure 1: A typical use case of UbiK.

The remainder of this paper is structured as follows. Section 2 presents an overview of the operations, architectures and design objectives underlying UbiK. Section 3 elaborates on our feasibility study of UbiK and verifies the premises behind it. Then, Sections 4, 5 and 6 describe UbiK's main modules in detail. Section 7 presents our implementation of UbiK on Android, followed by a comprehensive experimental evaluation in Section 8. We discuss UbiK's limitations in Section 9 and related work in Section 10. Finally, Section 11 concludes the paper.

2. UbiK OVERVIEW

UbiK facilitates small form-factor, touchscreen-based mobile devices with an *external, virtual, paper-printed*[1] keyboard. Although such a keyboard does not provide the same kinesthetic feedback as a mechanical one, it saves the precious touch-screen area and allows ten-finger typing on a larger workspace. Unlike on-screen virtual keyboard, UbiK is insensitive to gentle taps and touches. It allows finger/wrist rest on the touch surface, thus relieving fatigue [2] caused by hovering.

Figure 1 illustrates a typical use case of UbiK. The mobile device is placed near the printed keyboard, so as to capture the keystroke sound using its microphones. Before running UbiK, an initial setup is needed, whereby the user types all the printed keys at least once and generates "training sounds". UbiK runs a set of novel keystroke detection/localization mechanisms in the mobile device, which learn highly distinguishable acoustic features from the keystrokes, and then use such features to detect subsequent keypress events and localize the corresponding keys.

Usage conditions   UbiK is applicable under two basic conditions: *(i)* The surface can generate audible sounds when the user clicks it with fingertip and nail margin. *(ii)* Throughout the usage life-cycle, the positions of the mobile device and the printed keyboard do not change significantly.

The first condition can be easily satisfied in real-life environment. Through experiments, we show that UbiK works on a wide range of surfaces, *e.g.*, on top of a wood table, hard-covered paper, metal cabinet, plastic board, *etc.*. UbiK does not rely on the timbre of the keystroke sounds.

---

[1]Throughout this paper, we print the keyboard on a letter-sized paper. But any tangible and visible keyboard layout (*e.g.*, drawn on a surface) works for UbiK. The keyboard outline is not mandatory. It mainly serves as a visual assistant that helps users to maintain keystroke positions consistent.

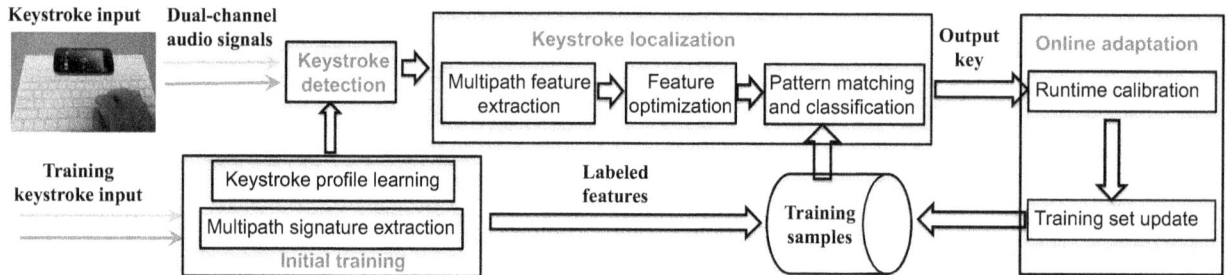

Figure 2: Architecture of UbiK.

Keystrokes can be identified even on a flat, homogeneous surface that makes the same audible sound everywhere.

Regarding the second condition, we note that keyboard input is necessary only when the mobile device acts as a static screen, where user can type and monitor the input text in real-time. Thus, it is reasonable to assume the printed keyboard and mobile devices sit on fixed positions that can be identified using arbitrary anchoring marks on the surface. The user can always move the mobile device away and reposition it back to the anchoring points to continue UbiK's usage life cycle. But whenever the keyboard and mobile device are put to a new location or surface, UbiK requires repeating the initial setup to start a new life cycle.

Design goals and challenges UbiK is designed to meet the following goals, which are geared towards similar user experience as on a desktop keyboard.

(i) Portability. UbiK should not rely on any extra hardware, bulky keyboards or external infrastructure support. It should allow spontaneous setup and usage, using only hardware/software built in existing mobile devices.

(ii) Fine-grained, centimeter-scale keystroke localization. Typical inter-key separation on a PC keyboard is only around 2 cm when printed on letter-sized paper. Thus, UbiK needs a localization mechanism that matches the centimeter-scale granularity and can identify keystrokes with high accuracy. There exists a vast literature of algorithms for audio-source localization leveraging Time-Difference-of-Arrival (TDOA) or energy difference between multiple microphones [10, 12]. Yet such algorithms can only achieve meter-scale accuracy in practical environment with rich reverberation effects.

(iii) Processing efficiency. UbiK's spontaneous keyboard setup requires user to traverse all keys to generate training data for localization. Such training procedure must be brief and should not compromise usability. Ideally, a few repetitions of training should ensure high localization accuracy. In addition, since UbiK runs on the mobile device directly, it must process the keystrokes without any noticeable latency.

(iv) Robustness. UbiK's localization mechanism must be resilient against minor displacement of the keyboard or mobile device, which may be caused by unintended movement or inaccurate repositioning during the usage life cycle. It should not be affected significantly by variations of user's finger/hand posture. In addition, UbiK should accurately detect the presence of keystrokes even in noisy environment.

System architecture UbiK architects the following three major components to build a full-fledged keystroke localization system for mobile devices.

(i) Keystroke detection. UbiK runs a keystroke detection algorithm that takes advantage of the audio signal onset patterns generated by keystrokes. It isolates noise and in-terference by fusing audio and motion sensing data. It is used to trigger the subsequent keystroke localization.

(ii) Keystroke localization. Instead of attempting to combat multipath reflections as in existing localization schemes [13, 14], UbiK's keystroke localization algorithm harnesses the location-dependent audio signal cancellation/enhancement features, and optimize them to achieve high accuracy at a fine granularity. Further, UbiK migrates the principles of multi-antenna spatial diversity in wireless communications [15], and uses dual-microphones on typical mobile devices to enhance localization accuracy.

(iii) Online calibration and adaptation. UbiK takes advantage of run-time user feedback on-screen to correct occasional localization errors. It further employs an online adaptation algorithm to refresh the training data to prevent error propagation.

Figure 2 illustrates the work-flow inside UbiK. During the initial training stage, UbiK learns acoustic parameters and features that later assist run-time keystroke detection and localization. Afterwards, it runs the keystroke detection algorithm to extract audio signals specifically generated by key presses. The keystroke localization algorithm extracts and optimizes acoustic features from those signals and finds the best match in the trained benchmark. It then outputs the resulting key symbol along with alternative candidates on-screen, which can be calibrated by the user. The calibrated result is fed back to the online adaptation algorithm to refresh the training data.

3. FEASIBILITY STUDY OF UbiK

UbiK is built on the hypothesis that audio channel's multipath profile can enable fine-grained keystroke distinction. In particular, the audio channel contains a rich set of characteristics that is consistent over time for each key, but differs across key locations. In this section, we conduct a comprehensive set of experiments to verify this hypothesis through addressing the following three questions: *(i)* Do different keystrokes generate unique audio signatures? *(ii)* Do these signatures exhibit fine-granularity and temporal stability? *(iii)* Can these signatures be enhanced using COTS hardware?

3.1 Preliminaries

We first describe the preliminaries to the feasibility study, covering the basics of sound signals and our experimental setting.

Basics of Sound Signals Sound is a wave phenomenon in air, fluid or solid medium. Mechanical vibrations at a sound source causes compression and decompression of the

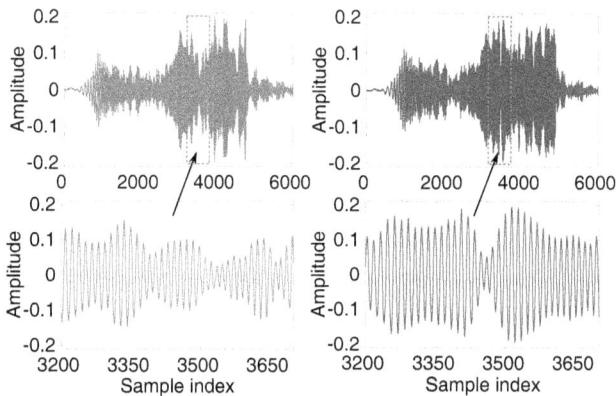

(a) Signals from key location 'A'   (b) Signals from key location 'D'

Figure 3: Received chirp signals sent by a speaker at two different key locations: 'A' and 'D'.

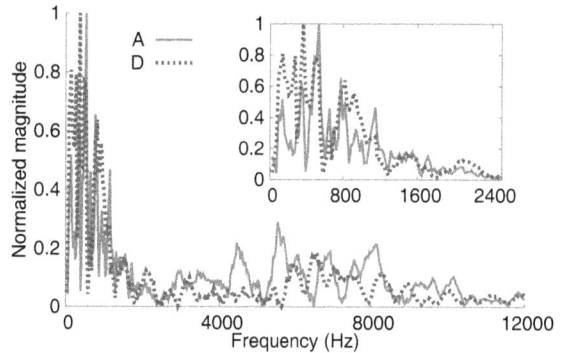

Figure 6: Amplitude spectrum density of two key strokes 'A' and 'D' on a wood table.

medium, which propagates over distance and attenuates following a inverse-square law [16].

Practical audio channel adds more intricacies than attenuation. Solid surface or objects near sound source or microphones can reflect or scatter the original audio source, causing a myriad of "image sources". Phantom waves produced by such image sources can either cancel or strengthen the original wave at different locations. Even for the same location, a sound wave can either be faded or strengthened, depending on its wavelength or frequency. In UbiK, we aim to extract such location and frequency dependent features from keystroke sounds to pinpoint the keystroke location.

Experimental Setup   Our experiment setup complies with UbiK's typical usage scenario. We print the Apple Wireless Keyboard (AWK) layout on a piece of letter paper, and put it on a solid surface – a wood table by default. A Galaxy Nexus (GT-I9250) Android smartphone is placed close to the top-level of the printed keyboard to capture the keystroke sounds, at 48 kHz sampling rate. We redrew the exceptionally big keys on AWK, including Shift, Enter, Space, etc., and limit them to be the same size as others. All experiments run in an office environment, with moderate noise coming from desktop computers and a server room nearby. Our experiments require a dual-microphone setup. Though equipped with two microphones, the Android application framework only allows user access to one microphone. We circumvented this limitation by enabling the Tinyalsa driver in Android OS (Section 7).

We next present our experimental validation of the aforementioned hypothesis.

3.2   Multipath Channel Profile-based Signature

Frequency and location dependent fading effects   We first design experiments to understand the variation of multipath fading effects across different frequencies and locations. We place a smartphone's speaker at two key locations, 'A' and 'D', on the printed AWK. The speaker emits a 100 ms chirp sound, with magnitude being constant but frequencies linearly increasing from 10 Hz to 5 kHz. Fig. 3 plots the audio signals captured by the front-microphone of the listening smartphone.

Despite the constant magnitude sound source, received signals manifest substantial variations across the sampling indices. This verifies the intuition that waves with different frequencies experience different fading levels at the same lo-

cation. Further, even around the same frequency, location 'A' and 'D' exhibit different fading profile — one may be deeply faded while the other experience peak signal strength. Hence, multipath fading effects are also location dependent.

We further investigate the frequency-domain patterns of two actual keystrokes. We characterize such patterns by using the received signals' amplitude spectrum density (ASD). Suppose $R(t)(t = 0 \cdots T)$, are the discrete signal samples captured by the microphone, then the ASD is defined as: $FFT(R(t))$. Since audio signals are real numbers, their ASD is symmetric with respect to the half-frequency (e.g., 24 kHz at 48 kHz sampling rate). We only use the first half to avoid duplication.

Figure 6 plots the ASD corresponding to user-generated click sounds at key locations 'A' and 'D', normalized with respect to the maximum across all frequency bins of each. We see that the majority of frequency components concentrate within 10 Hz and 1 kHz. The ASD of two locations peak at different frequency bins, and exhibit distinct values across frequencies. This provides us with a first hint for using ASD as location signature.

Summary of observation 1:   *Multipath channel profile represents unique audio signatures for different keystrokes and enable signature-based localization.*

3.3   Spatial Granularity and Temporal Stability of Channel Profile

Consistency of ASD on the same key location   Given the potential of ASD as location hint, one would ask: is ASD consistent across clicks of the same key, and will it be fine-grained enough to distinguish adjacent key locations? Figure 4(a) plots the Euclidean distance between the normalized ASD of 9 closely located keys. Each key is clicked by 5 times using finger tip and nail on a wood table, generating a total of 45 signatures.

We observe that short Euclidean distances are concentrated for each 5 keystrokes on the same location. Occasionally, a keystroke may have similar ASD with nearby or distant keys, yet the most similar ones almost always fall in the same location. Note that the diagonal line represent the zero distance between each key press and itself.

One may wonder if the ASD profile is possibly attributed to heterogeneous acoustic profile of the touch surface. To rule out this possibility, we place a speaker at the 9 key locations and repeat the chirp sounds 5 times each. Figure 4(b) plots the resulting Euclidean distances between the bursts of chirp tones. Now the ASD signatures show a more clear

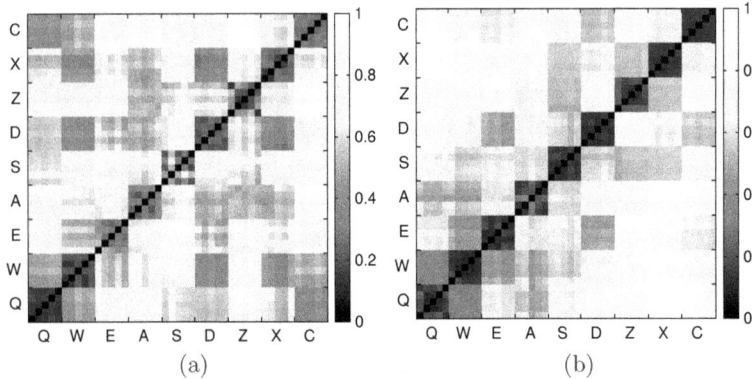

Figure 4: Euclidean distance between ASD of sounds at 9 key locations, each repeated 5 times in two cases: (a) each sound source is created by finger/nail clicking on the key locations; (b) the sound source is a chirp tone emitted from the key locations.

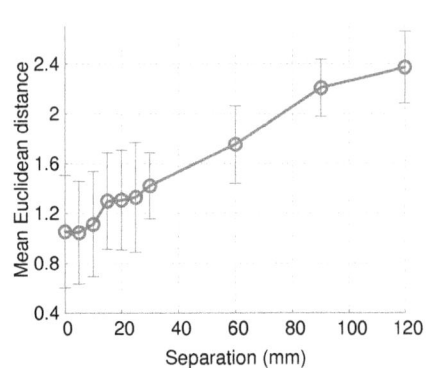

Figure 5: Euclidean distance between a group of keystrokes at a testing position and those at an anchoring position.

location-dependent trend. This confirms that there is no need to use heterogeneous surface materials. On the other hand, the better Euclidean distance profile of chirp tones implies that user's inconsistent click behavior can cause variation of the location signatures.

Spatial correlation of ASD signature   We now examine in more detail how resilient ASD is to minor deviation of click positions, which can naturally happen because users' finger touch positions are not perfectly consistent. We first create an anchoring group of 25 clicks at a fixed position, and then generate testing keystrokes, which deviate from the anchoring position by 5 mm to 120 mm. For each testing position, we calculate the Euclidean distances of all (*testing, anchoring*) pairs, using ASD as the feature vector. Figure 5 plots the mean and standard deviation of the Euclidean distances. We observe that the Euclidean distance increases almost monotonically with the physical separation between keys. For physical separation of 5mm, the change of Euclidean distance is minor, implying that spatial correlation does exist between ASDs of closeby clicks. However, on average, keystrokes with physical separation of more than 1cm (roughly the distance between the center of one key and edge of a neighboring key) have larger ASD separation than those below 1cm. Therefore, clicks on the same key can be separated from those a neighboring key. Note that the Euclidean distances exhibit variance, mainly because the user cannot perfectly control the click positions.

Temporal stability of ASD   To test temporal stability, we repetitively create groups of 10 clicks on the same key location. The experiment spans over one month, while the keyboard and phone are fixed on the same location. Ambient environment changes are minor, including placement/displacement of chairs, laptops, cups *etc.* Figure 7 plots the Euclidean distance between the ASD of a random keystroke in each group with that of all keystrokes in the first group. Over time, the mean Euclidean distance does not show significant change, although variance increases slightly after one month. Thus, compared with radio channels [17], the multipath profile of audio channels is more stable over time. It is also less sensitive to ambient objects movement, likely because reflected waves from those objects may be too weak and below the sensitivity of the microphone. We gauge the multi-path effects mainly come

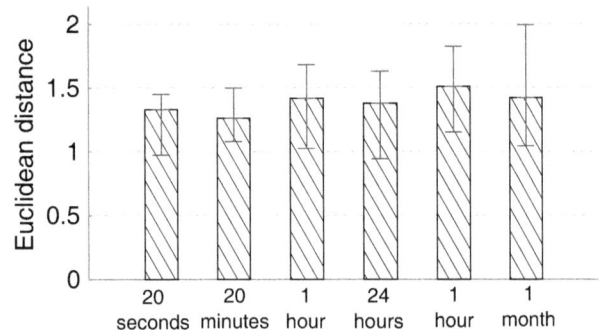

Figure 7: Euclidean distance between keystrokes varies negligibly over time. Error bars show the max-min values.

from keystroke sounds' propagation along the surface and reflections/diffractions around the smartphone body.

Summary of Observation 2:   *The keystrokes' audio signatures follow consistent patterns within a key-size area, so the localization algorithm can be resilient to minor displacement of device and small variation of key-press positions. The signatures are also highly stable over time.*

3.4   Diversity from Multiple Microphones

Channel diversity from dual-microphone   Inspired by the diversity gain in multi-antenna wireless communications, we examine whether dual-microphone, a standard equipment in modern smartphones, can enrich the ASD signature of a key location. Figure 8 plots the ASD of 10 consecutive clicks of the same location, received by two microphones on Galaxy Nexus. The ASD curves of different clicks show a highly consistent pattern on the same microphone. Yet across different microphones, they differ drastically. This implies that audio channel diversity does exist, even though the microphones separate at a much shorter distance (12.5 cm) than the half-wavelength (*e.g.*, 34.3 cm at 500 Hz frequency) of audible keystroke signals.

Coarse-grained localization in conventional dual-mic algorithms   Microphone-array has been extensively used for sound source localization (SSL), *e.g.*, localization a speaker in a lecture room. The principle resembles human perception of sound direction, inferred by time-difference-of arrival

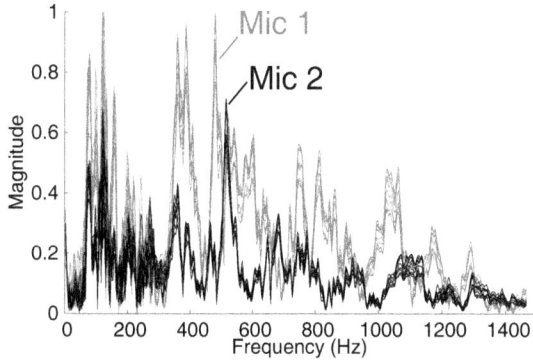

Figure 8: ASD of 10 key presses received by two microphones on the same smartphone. The ASD is normalized by the maximum across all frequency bins and keystrokes.

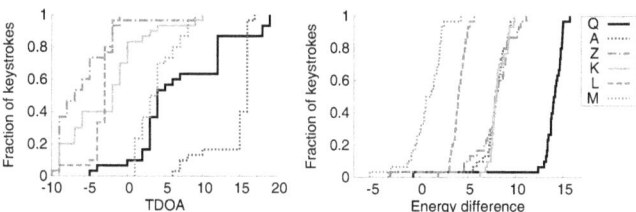

Figure 9: Distribution of the TDOA and EDIF between two microphones.

(TDOA) and energy difference (EDIF) between signals received by two ears [16].

Our earliest attempt to build UbiK followed this principle. Theoretically, on a 2D space, locations of the same TDOA value form two hyperbolas centered around the two microphones, and those of the same EDIF value form a circle centered around one microphone [18]. Intersections between these two form two points, but one can be eliminated as the microphones in UbiK always reside on one side of the keyboard. We compute the TDOA between two microphones using GCC-PHAT (generalized correlation with phase transform), a state-of-the-art algorithm widely used for SSL in practice [19]. The total energy received by each microphone can be derived by summing up the power spectrum density.

Figure 9 shows the distribution of TDOA and EDIF of each key, repetitively clicked by 20 times. Even for the same key, its TDOA values are inconsistent across clicks. TDOA algorithms assume a single non-reverberant path between sound source and microphone, hence it is highly sensitive to multipath reflections and minor deviation in click positions (which is unavoidable). Similarly, the EDIF of the same key spreads over a wide range, and even distant keys (*e.g.*, 'Z' and 'K') can have similar EDIF. Therefore, conventional dual-microphone SSL algorithms cannot achieve fine-grained localization as required by UbiK.

Summary of Observation 3: *Multiple microphones on mobile devices can provide spatial diversity and improve granularity of keystroke localization. The diversity mechanism should embrace, instead of avoid multipath reflections.*

4. KEYSTROKE DETECTION

UbiK's keystroke detection algorithm identifies the signals generated by key-presses. Its core design goal is to ensure

(i) low false-alarm and mis-detection rate and (ii) resilience to noise coming from the user and ambient environment.

4.1 Basic Detection Mechanism

The audio signals produced by a key-press event manifests a common onset pattern, with a few outstanding peaks in the beginning followed by small reverberations, which together form a cluster of energy burst rising above noise. Since the printed keyboard is close to the mobile device, keystroke sounds are much stronger than ambient noises. UbiK leverages such unique profiles to single out the keystroke signals.

In its simplest form, the detection algorithm computes the received signal magnitude or power and declares a keystroke if it exceeds a threshold. Yet no different environment bears different noise levels. A keystroke detection mechanism must adaptively configure the threshold that separates keystrokes from noise. UbiK meets this goal by adapting the Constant False Alarm Rate (CFAR) algorithm [20], a statistical approach historically used in Radar systems to identify signals reflected by intruding objects.

CFAR approximates ambient noise power with a Gaussian distribution $\mathcal{N}(\mu, \sigma^2)$. A significant energy burst is detected if the incoming signal power passes a threshold value of $(\mu + \gamma\sigma)$, or γ standard deviations above the mean noise floor. Given the noise distribution, the detection may also be a false alarm triggered by noise, with probability $1 - erf(\frac{\gamma}{\sqrt{2}})$, which decreases exponentially with γ.

In UbiK's CFAR implementation, we estimate the noise power μ through a moving average window with size W:

$$\mu(t) = \frac{1}{W}A(t) + (1 - \frac{1}{W})\mu(t-1),$$

where $A(t)$ is short-term average noise power right before t. Denote $x(t)$ as the received audio signal at time t, then,

$$A(t) = \frac{1}{W}\sum_{k=t-W+1}^{t}|x(t)|^2.$$

Estimation of variance $\sigma(t)$ follows the same way as $\mu(t)$. We choose the window size W to be much shorter than the duration of environment sounds, so that even if bursty interference occur, the interfering signals within W can still be approximated as Gaussian. An empirical value of 1 ms (48 samples at 48 kHz sampling rate) for W works across a wide range of environment according to our experiments.

UbiK declares a key-press event at t if: *(i)* incoming signal's energy $|x(t)|^2$ passes the CFAR threshold $(\mu + \gamma\sigma)$, and *(ii)* current detection separates from previous one by a safe margin. For devices with dual microphones, either one satisfying these conditions is accepted. We configure γ during the initial training stage, by linearly searching through all integer multiples of 0.5 within the range $[1, 10]$, and pick the highest one that results in zero mis-detections and false alarms for the known keystrokes. The safe margin between keys is configured to a value smaller than the minimum separation between two consecutive keytrokes.

4.2 Combating Bursty Noise

Since UbiK relies on energy based detection, it can be easily disturbed by bursty noise. However, the smartphone's microphones fall within a short-range to keystrokes, typically 10 to 20 centimeters, whereas sound signal power decreases with distance following a inverse-square law [16].

Therefore, far-field noise sources, *e.g.*, a few meters away from the microphone, cause negligible interference to keystroke detection unless they are exceptionally loud.

According to our field test of UbiK, near-field noise mainly comes from two sources: human voices nearby, and user tapping on the smartphone screen which causes non-trivial noise bursts due to close proximity to the microphones.

UbiK utilizes a sensor fusion technique to combat both noises. Gyroscope, which senses rotations in three dimensions, serves as a secondary source for keystroke detection in UbiK. At start-up time, UbiK assumes the phone remains stationary on the surface and collects gyroscope data for a short period for calibration. A threshold ϵ_1 for determining the existence of keystrokes, is then set at two times of the maximum of gyroscope readings during calibration. UbiK declares a keystroke only if both the audio and gyro confirm its presence. In such way, false alarms caused by human voice are eliminated since it does not cause surface vibrations.

Tapping actions on screen (caused by user's runtime feedback) disturb the gyroscope reading to a much larger degree compared to tapping on desk surface. A threshold ϵ_2 for tapping-on-screen is determined when user first taps the on-screen button to start training. ϵ_2 is empirically set to $\frac{1}{2}$ of the maximum gyroscope output during the user tapping. At run-time, only when the gyroscope readings are above ϵ_1 and below ϵ_2, a potential keystroke is confirmed.

Recent work has shown that accelerometers can detect keystrokes tapped on a physical keyboard [21]. In UbiK's usage case, smartphone's motion variations are much smaller. Since tapping bends the area closer to tapping point more than the area further away, a rotation of the smartphone can be captured more easily by gyroscope. Accelerometers, designed to measure larger movements, have more noises at such granular level. From our experiment using Galaxy Nexus and Nexus 7, gyroscope yields cleaner and larger distinctions between a steady phone and a shaking phone caused by key tapping.

5. KEYSTROKE LOCALIZATION

In this section, we describe how UbiK's keystroke localization algorithm leverages the previous experimental observations (Section 3) to distinguish the keystrokes.

5.1 Location Signature Design

Our measurements have established Amplitude Spectrum Density (ASD) as a promising location hints. ASD reflects the frequency domain acoustic channel profile caused by sound waves' multipath fading. Compared with the signal-power based fingerprinting widely used in geo-location systems, ASD incorporates a richer set of features, thus finer granularity. Compared with a time domain approach that uses the sound waves directly as fingerprint, ASD is insensitive to waveform ambiguities and unpredictable stretches. To synthesize such advantages and make ASD a practically useful signature, we still need to address the following problems.

Estimating keystroke duration UbiK uses D samples following the start of a keystroke to compute ASD. D represents an estimation of keystroke duration, which depends on surface type and users' click actions. We obtain D from the initial training setup. For each known keystroke in

the training set, we first obtain the noise floor P_n preceding it (Section 4). A keystroke usually corresponds to a sudden jump in signal power that quickly reaches a peak level $P_{\max}$. Then, D is estimated as the number of samples between the start point and the point when mean signal power first drops to below $P_n + (P_{\max} - P_n) \times 10\%$. Capping the keystroke duration at a power level slightly (10%) above noise floor prevents UbiK from incorporating unnecessary noise following the actual keystroke signals. The estimated keystroke durations of all keystrokes in the training set are averaged to obtain D.

Optimizing frequency range Our previous measurement on a woodtable revealed that the main ASD features concentrate within a small frequency range. Adding higher frequencies into the signature increases the computational load during signature matching, which may worsen processing latency. Moreover, it may invite high-frequency noises that are not generated by the keystroke. The key problem here is how to determine the critical frequency range, which may vary on different solid surfaces. Our solution to this problem is inspired by the optimal separating hyperplane problem in statistical learning [22].

Conventionally, optimal separating hyperplane is used for binary classification, *i.e.*, finding a hyperplane that separates two classes of data and maximizes the distance to the closest point from either class. Denote $\boldsymbol{\beta}$ as the vector normal to the hyperplane, x_{i*} the vector of features in i-th data set, and $\boldsymbol{y}$ the correct prediction (either 1 or -1). Then the classification problem for a given x_{i*} can be cast as:

$$y_i = sgn(\boldsymbol{\beta}\boldsymbol{x} + b) = sgn(\sum_{j=1}^{N} \beta_j x_{ij} + b) \quad (1)$$

where $sgn(\cdot)$ is the sign function. The training process in binary classification solves the following optimization problem to obtain the optimal weights vector $\boldsymbol{\beta}$ and offset b [22]:

$$\arg_{\boldsymbol{\beta},b} \min ||\boldsymbol{\beta}||^2 \quad (2)$$

$$\text{s.t.} \quad y_i \left(\sum_{j=1}^{N} \beta_j x_{ij} + b \right) \geq 1, i = 1, 2, \cdots, S_t \quad (3)$$

where S_t is the number of instances in the training set.

In UbiK, we cast the problem of finding the critical frequency range as a similar problem but with much lower complexity. Denote J as the "sweet spot" frequency below which the ASD features should be included. Since the frequency bins are not weighted, we only need to find:

$$\arg_{J,b} \min ||J||^2 \quad (4)$$

$$\text{s.t.} \quad y_i \left(\sum_{j=1}^{J} x_{ij} + b \right) \geq 1, i = 1, 2, \cdots, S_t \quad (5)$$

This is a mixed-integer program, generally intractable. However, observing that there are only a limited number of possible values for J, we reformulate the optimization problem as a feasibility problem, and solve it by searching for the minimum J that results in a feasible value for b, such that:

$$b \geq \frac{1}{y_i} - \sum_{j=1}^{J} x_{ij}, i = 1, 2, \cdots, S_t \quad (6)$$

In the common cases, the critical frequency J is above 100 Hz. Thus we only need to start searching from the frequency bin: $B \cdot 100/F_s$, where F_s is the audio sampling frequency and B the FFT size (total number of frequency bins). In our actual implementation, by default $B = 4096, F_s =$

48000, $S_t = 3$ and the maximum search range is 5000 Hz. Thus, the maximum number of operations of Eq. (6) is $S_t \cdot B \cdot (5000 - 100)/F_s \approx 1254$, which can easily run in real-time on a modern mobile device.

Determining frequency resolution When computing ASD, a large B results in more frequency bins, thus higher frequency resolution, yet it also increases computational load. In UbiK, we empirically set B to the first 2's power larger than the keystroke duration. A typical keystroke (*e.g.*, on wood table or hard-cover paper) spans around 2000 samples (at 48 kHz sampling rate). Correspondingly, $B = 2048$.

5.2 Initial Training

During initial setup, UbiK displays instructions on the mobile device's screen to guide the user to sequentially click all keys (A–Z, 0–9, and symbolic/functional keys) on the printed keyboard. On a printed Apple Wireless Keyboard (AWK), with 56 keys in total (excluding PC-specific functional keys), this training process takes only around 1 minute, even for first-time users. Users are encouraged to use the same finger to click a key as they would in actual typing.

The audio samples generated by training keystrokes have known labels and are used for three purposes: *(i)* optimizing core parameters in UbiK's keystroke detection algorithm (Section 4); *(ii)* initializing and optimizing the ASD signatures as discussed above; *(iii)* providing benchmark ASD signatures to be used in keystroke localization.

Intuitively, repeating the training procedure multiple times can improve the keystroke localization accuracy. This entails more user workload. However, as shown in our evaluation (Section 8), it only takes 3 training samples each for UbiK to escalate its accuracy from 70% to above 91%. Such overhead is negligible if the keyboard is to be used for hours, *e.g.*, in a coffee shop, on an office desk or tray table of an airplane.

5.3 Localization Algorithm

UbiK's keystroke localization algorithm is a pattern classification scheme that matches the ASD features of user-typed keystrokes with those instances in the training set.

Basic classification After detecting a key-press event, UbiK extracts the ASD features from corresponding audio signals of both microphones, which together form a vector of length $2D$. Depending on the relative location of a keystroke, the two microphones may detect the event with different starting point. UbiK computes the ASD of the two sequences of signals, with the starting point of each separately, but keeping the same keystroke duration parameter D. This ensures the ASD features are best aligned in time and compared in a consistent manner.

Then, UbiK runs a nearest-neighbor based pattern matching (classification) algorithm that compares the extracted features with those in the training set. The training key with minimum distance is declared as the current keystroke and output to the user interface. In the simplest form, we use Euclidean distance as the metric of comparison.

Optimizing ASD features for classification Our controlled experiments (Section 3) have shown that click sounds on the same key location tend to have much shorter Euclidean distance (*w.r.t.* ASD features) than that between different keys. In practice, the Euclidean distance can be disturbed by multiple uncontrollable factors.

Recall that the ASD represents a mix of features from the click sound and the multipath channel distortion. The strength of user's clicks may vary over time, thus causing ASD variation even for the same key. However, the variation tends to simply scale the entire ASD curve. The frequency bin with maximum magnitude remains consistent. We thus normalize each ASD feature with its highest magnitude to improve resilience to variation of click strength.

Further, we observe that the variance of ASD feature within the same frequency bin (but across training instances) can reflect the confidence of pattern matching. For the same key, if the amplitude of a certain frequency bin exhibits a small variance, then that frequency bin should be considered as a highly reliable feature element. Thus, at run-time, for each frequency bin f of the user-typed keystroke, we scale its magnitude by $\frac{1}{V_f}$, where V_f is the magnitude *std.* of the training instances. Note that such scaling should be done before the above feature normalization. The frequency bin with peak magnitude is ignored since it tends to have standard deviation after normalization.

Fail-safe mode adaptation UbiK's keystroke detection algorithm can prevent false triggering by nearby bursty interferences, most commonly, human voice. However, a tougher case comes when human voice and keystroke sounds overlap, which contaminates the keystroke's ASD feature. UbiK tackles such cases by adapting to a fail-safe mode. Rather than outputting a wrong key value, which entails user correction and causes extra burden, UbiK outputs nothing but a "interference" warning on the user interface.

To identify such heavily interfered keystrokes, we observe that human speech tends to show a consistent amplitude for at least tens of milliseconds. In contrast, a keystroke features a cluster of high-amplitude signals, for a few milliseconds, followed by small vibrations. Therefore, whenever an energy bust is detected, UbiK takes the derivative of the signal amplitude envelop, starting from the highest peak and spanning one keystroke duration D. If the derivative's magnitude is below 50% than that of keystrokes in the training set, then UbiK decides the keystroke to be contaminated.

6. ONLINE CALIBRATION AND ADAPTATION

UbiK presumes the keyboard and mobile device are kept at stable positions throughout its usage life-cycle. In practice, the positions may be disturbed by, *e.g.*, surface vibration, screen touches, and user's repositioning of the mobile device. Over time, user's typing posture may also vary due to fatigue, rendering ASD features in the initial training set outdated. UbiK employs a run-time calibration and adaptation framework to tackle such problems.

6.1 Runtime Calibration

UbiK executes run-time calibration by combining user correction with its own localization hints. For each keystroke, besides the output from the localization algorithm, it also displays the top 5 *candidate keys*, *i.e.*, those with shortest feature distance. User can click a candidate if it is the actual intended key. In the rare case when the candidate list does not contain the intended key, the user can reenter the key using the built-in on-screen keyboard. UbiK places the

"Delete" key on the screen instead of the printed keyboard, since it must be reliably recognized for calibration purpose. To minimize disturbance to the ASD features, the mobile device should remain on the surface when user performs on-screen correction.

6.2 Adapting and Optimizing Training Set

UbiK updates the training data set progressively while the user types in more keys. The update opportunistically employs feedback hints about correctness of a localization decision. UbiK deems a localization output as correct if the user does not execute run-time correction. Since the user may not immediately correct a character error, UbiK defers the decision on correctness until then end of the current word input (using space and punctuation as a hint). Besides, user tapping a character on the candidate list implies that an localization error occurred. Notably, user pressing the "Delete" button is not necessarily a hint for localization error because it may be the user's own input error.

If a keystroke is correctly located, the corresponding ASD feature will be put into that key's training set as a new training instance. In addition, UbiK employs a feedback based weighting mechanism to rank the significance of existing training instances.

Weight design for correctly located keys. At time t, UbiK associates a weight $w_{ki}(t)$ to the i-th instance of key k in the training set. t is discrete and simply counts the number of localization runs. $w_{ki}(0)$ equals 1 for all instances. Suppose $d(k, i, S(t))$ denotes the distance metric between each training instance and the incoming key features $S(t)$, then UbiK uses $d(k, i, S(t)) \cdot w_{ki}(t)$ as the distance metric to decide the nearest training instance for $S(t)$.

If a keystroke is correctly located, the corresponding training instances decreases its weight as:

$$w_{ki}(t+1) = V(w_{ki}(t)) \qquad (7)$$

where $V(\cdot)$ is a convex function, such that the decreasing step becomes smaller if $w_{ki}(t)$ is already small. To prevent a small set of instances biasing the classification, $w_{ki}(t)$ is capped between 0.8 and 1.2. Accordingly, we set

$$V(x) = 0.8 + (x - 0.8)^2 \qquad (8)$$

to ensure convexity within this range.

Weight design upon localization error. If a keystroke is located wrongly, the nearest training instance decreases its weight as:

$$w_{ki}(t+1) = X(w_{ki}(t)) \qquad (9)$$

where $X(x)$ is a concave function, designed following similar intuition as $V(x)$, as:

$$X(x) = 1.2 - (x - 1.2)^2 \qquad (10)$$

In addition, after user enters the correct key, the nearest instance to that key will update its weight following Eq. (8). To prevent bias by frequently used keys, we further normalize $w_{ki}(t)$ by t, $i.e.$, the number of times instance i is updated. Here the frequency of usage means the frequency when a training instance is updated, which in turn depends on how frequently the corresponding key is pressed. Without the normalization operation, a frequently used key, say 'A', may have training instances with very small weights, which results in small Euclidean distances between 'A' and all other keys, thereby causing localization errors.

7. IMPLEMENTING UbiK ON ANDROID

We implemented UbiK as a standalone application program running directly on Android devices. Specifically, we implement all the components described in Section 4, 5 and 6. In implementing the online adaptation, we eliminate training instances with largest weights, and keep a constant training set size of 10. We found the user may occasionally miss the localization error and the corresponding instance will be mistakenly put into the training set. However, such instance does not pollute the training set in a significantly way, because it does not contribute to correct localization and thus will be replaced from the training set in a short time with online adaptations.

As for dual-microphone audio acquisition, the Android application framework blocks the stereo recording (the back microphone is only used for noise cancellation by the framework). We overcame this constraint by bypassing the build-in framework and using the low-level tinyalsa driver instead. We modified the tinyalsa driver so that it can stream dual-channel audio samples to applications through standard I/O. UbiK's Java implementation triggers the recording by forking tinyalsa as a child process. The implementation gets recorded samples from tinyalsa every 10 ms. These samples are then put into a 100 ms audio buffer. Our keystroke detection algorithm runs on these 10 ms audio instances. When a keystroke occurs, the application continues to collect audio until enough samples are obtained for extracting ASD signatures.

To benchmark the run-time efficiency of UbiK in our implementation, we use a Galaxy Nexus smartphone to record a keystroke sound, and replay it while running UbiK. Then we measure the latency between the time when the faked keystroke sound is played back and when UbiK outputs the localization result on the screen. We found an average processing latency of 51.4 ms, and standard deviation 2.7 ms. Such latency is well below human response time. In fact, we experience no lagging effects when using UbiK.

8. SYSTEM EVALUATION

In this section, we first evaluate each design component of UbiK, as well as the underlying impact factors in a variety of test scenarios. We then conduct a user study to verify the effectiveness and usability of UbiK in comparison with existing text-entry methods.

8.1 Micro-benchmark Tests

We run experiments using the following default setting unless explicitly specified. We use a Galaxy Nexus phone, which is placed near the edge of a printed keyboard on top of a wood table. We use AWK as the default keyboard and test design components with online-adaptation disabled (except in the adaptation test).

Accuracy of keystroke detection We first evaluate UbiK's keystroke detection in four scenarios, specifically, in an office environment (wood table), a server room (metal cabinet), at food court (wood table) and on a flying airplane (tray table). The former three represent typical, daily environments such as office and cafeteria, and the latter is used to examine UbiK in an extremely noisy environment. These our test scenarios reflect a variety of realistic noise levels, which ranges from 23.2 to 76.5 dB. Noise level is measured by Sound Meter Pro, an Android app calibrated by a

	Office	Server room	Food court	Airplane
Noise level	23.2 dB	45.8 dB	41.0 dB	76.5 dB
P_{mis}	0.33%	1.33%	0.33%	1.67%
P_{fls}	0.0%	0.0%	0.67%	5.0%
P_{mis} (no gyro)	0.0%	2.0%	4.0%	8.67%
P_{fls} (no gyro)	0.67%	0.33%	7.33%	8.67%

Table 1: Keystroke detection accuracy in four environments.

	Office	Server room	Food court	Airplane
Loc. accuracy	97.1%	94.0%	91.9%	92.4%

Table 2: A baseline accuracy test of keystroke localization in four environments.

professional acoustic meter [23]. In each test, a user uses finger tip plus nail margin to make 300 clicks, each on a randomly selected key position. The click strength is empirically maintained to be audible by the user, at a similar level as PC keyboard click sound. Across all the experiments, the detection algorithm uses the default set of parameters described in Section 4.

Table 1 presents the resulting mis-detection (P_{mis}) and false-alarm (P_{fls}) rates. It reveals that the keystroke detection is accurate, robust and reliable. Here are two observations. First, the error rates are kept below a reasonable level ($< 5\%$ in the worst case). In the relatively quiet environment (office and food court), both P_{mis} and P_{fls} are negligible. On an extremely noisy airplane with occasional vibration, they only increase to 1.67% and 5%, respectively. Second, gyroscope improves the accuracy, especially in case of noise. The noise level is lower at food court than in the server room, but P_{fls} can be up to 7.33% without gyroscope. This is mainly attributed to the interference from nearby human voices. Falsely detected keys trigger a chain effect, leading to subsequent miss detections (recall the safe margin between keystrokes). As a result, error rate becomes unacceptably high when gyro is disabled. Note that, in a quiet environment, CFAR based detection maintains an error rate below 2%, even with gyro sensor disabled. Clearly, UbiK is able to effectively eliminate the negative impacts of noise and yield a robust and accurate detection.

Accuracy of baseline localization We perform a baseline test of keystroke localization in the above environments. The keyboard setting remains the same as above, except that all 56 keys on the AWK are pressed sequentially, each repeated 25 times. We carry on a conventional leave-one-out cross-validation. This statistic tends to be generous, since training and testing datasets are collected from the same user and adjacent in time (which will naturally tend to be more similar). Nonetheless, it provides a micro-benchmark to validate the effectiveness of UbiK's location signature design and optimization. Note that add-on features such as online-adaptation and calibration are disabled.

Figure 10 plots the resulting confusion matrix in the office room. Each element (i, j) represents the probability that key i's nearest neighbor is one of the clicks on key j. Clearly, keystrokes localized by UbiK densely overlap with the actual ones. Among those few erroneous localization results, most are mistaken with one or two other keys. Intuitively, such errors can be further reduced or eliminated by online

adaptation (the training set is updated as user inputs more keys).

Table 2 enumerates the average localization accuracy in different environment, where false detection and miss detection are manually eliminated in order to isolate the impact of keystroke detection. The results demonstrate remarkably high accuracy, above 97% in office environment, and around 92% in adverse acoustic environment.

Impact of initial training The initial training set size affects UbiK's usability and accuracy — a tradeoff that deserves a fine-balance. Figure 11 plots the achieved accuracy as the number of initial training instances increases. It shows that localization accuracy is around 70% even with one initial training. As the number of training instances grows up to 3, accuracy escalates to above 91% on average. Further increasing the number beyond 5 provides marginal improvement only. Therefore, the user only needs to input 3 training instances per key to achieve reasonable performance. This is a small burden to pay if the keyboard life cycle spans more than a few minutes but may be undesirable otherwise. Later we will show that the training can be embedded in subsequent typing to reduce user work load at the start.

Effectiveness of frequency range optimization Our initial implementation of UbiK used an empirical frequency range of 0 to 5 kHz — roughly the same as that of human voice — in the ASD feature selection. This worked well if the user carefully stays consistent in terms of finger gesture, click position and strength, when making the keystrokes. However, the performance becomes erratic once she types rapidly. Figure 12 plots the localization accuracy resulting from this empirical approach, in comparison with that after UbiK's frequency-range optimization mechanism (Section 5.1). The experiments run on four different types of solid surfaces, each repeated 8 times (std. shown by error bars). UbiK can maintain above 95% of accuracy across all the experiments, whereas the empirical frequency setting achieves only around 80%.

Resilience to keyboard/phone displacement Recall that the ASD features are coherent within about a key-sized area. Thus minor displacement of the mobile device or printed keyboard should be tolerable. We investigate this intuition by placing the smartphone in various ways and test the effectiveness of the online-adaptation algorithm. The resulting impact on accuracy is shown in Figure 13. Each sample counts the localization accuracy averaged over past 50 keystrokes. Localization accuracy may drop to around 80% if the phone is moved by one key's edge size. With less displacement (1/3 or 1/2 key), the decrease is much smaller. Occasionally, accuracy can be disturbed by other factors, such as user clicking the boarder between keys. However, in all these cases, UbiK's online adaptation scheme can quickly restore the accuracy to above 95% after a few tens of inputs. When user moves the phone away and tries to restore it to the original position ("best realignment"), the accuracy is virtually unaffected. We expect the best realignment to be a common case user may encounter in practical usage of UbiK.

Fail-safe mode under bursty interference Bursty interferences pose a greater challenge than noises with a high but stable power. UbiK's fail-safe adaptation strives to alleviate the impact of bursty noise. Figure 14 verifies the effectiveness of this approach, where we use a speaker to play

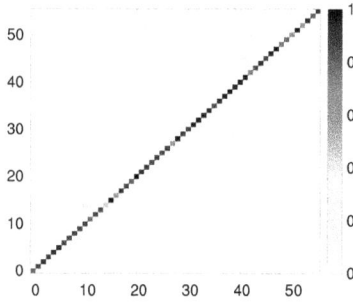

Figure 10: Confusion matrix of 56 keys on AWK.

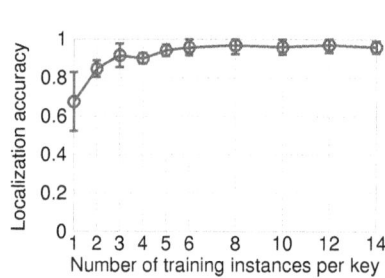

Figure 11: Impact of initial training set size. Error bars show std. across 8 experimental runs.

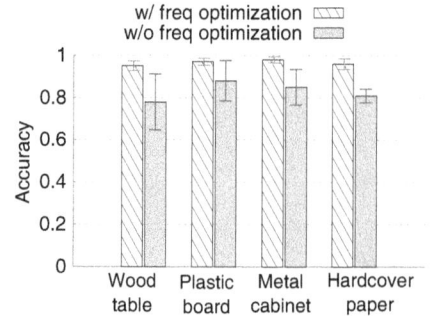

Figure 12: Impact of frequency range optimization when running UbiK on different surfaces.

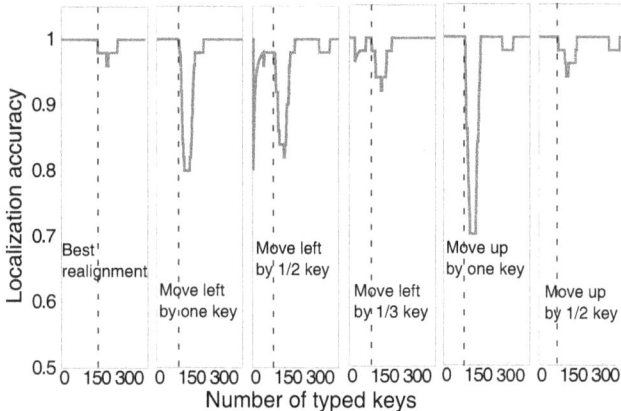

Figure 13: UbiK's online calibration and adaptation helps to quickly restore its high accuracy after a phone displacement. Dotted lines denote the time when displacement occurs.

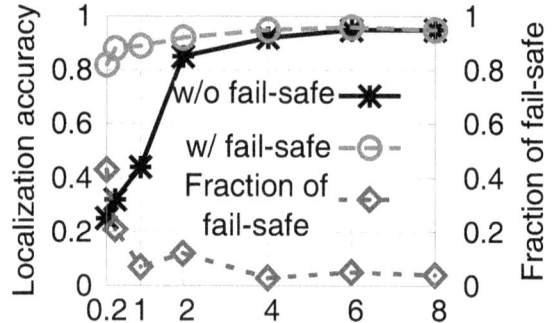

Figure 14: UbiK alleviates the impact of bursty interference by adapting to the fail-safe mode.

	US ANSI	UK ISO	AWK	Split
Accuracy	96.0%	92.5%	94.7%	98.2%

Table 3: Localization accuracy on different keyboard layouts.

human voice and vary its distance to the keyboard to create different levels of interference. Fail-safe mode isolates the keystrokes polluted by bursty interference, thus maintaining above 81% of localization accuracy even if the interferer is 20 cm away from the keyboard. Accuracy increases to above 89% as the interferer moves beyond 1 meter. In contrast, accuracy is degraded to as low as 22% without fail-safe adaptation. Notably, the fraction of keystrokes that are muted by the fail-safe adaptation can be 4% to 11% when the interference source is 1 or 2 meters nearby, which may result in undesirable experience for the typist.

Impact of keyboard layout We test UbiK on four keyboard layouts: US ANSI, UK ISO, AWK and Split keyboard. All keyboards are scaled on letter-size paper while maintaining the length/width aspect ratio. After scaling, the inter-key distance is comparable (1 to 2 mm shorter) to a physical keyboard like AWK. Table 3 shows the average localization accuracy. Keyboard layouts cause at most 5.7% of performance variation. In general, keyboards with slightly smaller key sizes (e.g., US ANSI and AWK) performs better than those with larger ones (e.g., UK ISO). This is mainly because of less variation in click positions. Similarly, keyboards with larger key separation (e.g., the split keyboard) outperform others. Nonetheless, all keyboards experience an accuracy of above 92%, and have space to be improved after augmenting online adaptation.

Power consumption We have used the Monsoon mobile power monitor [24] to profile the power cost of UbiK. Specifically, we put a Galaxy Nexus phone in three states: (1) idle with display on; (2) running UbiK but without key input; (3) running UbiK with fast typing (more than 2 characters per second). Each state is maintained for 1 minute. The resulting average power consumption in each state is 1049.3 mW, 1160.8 mW, 1244.0 mW, respectively. Thus, UbiK incurs an additional 194.7 mW on top of the base power consumption (18.5% of power cost). To put the statistics in perspective, we also conducted measurement when browsing a CNN website through WiFi, which results in 1233.8 mW of power consumption — comparable to that of UbiK in active typing mode.

Impact of mobile device models Besides Galaxy Nexus, we have tested UbiK on alternative hardware platforms: Galaxy Note and Nexus 7. Both block dual microphone recording from firmware level. So we can only test with a single microphone. We find the keystroke localization accuracy on different devices varies slightly, possibly due to varying microphone quality. On Nexus 7, even with a single microphone enabled, the accuracy is comparable to Galaxy Nexus with two microphones. The Galaxy Note's accuracy is only 1–3% lower, under the default test setting. Notably, for Galaxy Nexus, its accuracy can drop by around 5% if a

	U1	U2	U3	U4	U5	U6	U7
PC	1000	2000	3000	1000	500	1000	1000
Onscreen	800	100	1500	100	100	500	500
UbiK	$> 10^4$	> 5000	$> 10^3$	New	New	New	New

Table 4: User reported proficiency with PC, Onscreen (average number of characters per day) and UbiK (total characters tried). All users have little experience with Swype except U3, who inputs > 2000 characters per day using Swype.

single microphone is used. We plan to test UbiK on other device models in future.

8.2 User Study

To evaluate the usability of UbiK in practice, we develop a standard text-entry field trial to compare our approach to others in a user study.

Experiment setup   Seven participants (2 females and 5 males) are recruited from our university. They ran UbiK in several different environment, including home, library and office. Each participant completes four sessions, each involving typing regular text sentences and random characters. The random characters are uniformly selected from A-Z, digits and symbols on the AWK. The text sentences are randomly picked from the standard MacKenzie set [25], which well represents the usage frequency of English characters and words. Each sentence begins with a numerical index and ends with a random punctuation (, or .).

In the user study, we compare UbiK with three other popular input methods: a Dell PC keyboard, Google's Android on-screen keyboard, and Swype [26], which allows the user to enter words by sliding a finger across characters, and then uses a language model to guess the intended word. Before using each input method, the user is given a 10-minute warm-up period to familiarize themselves with the keyboard. Users are given the freedom to choose the solid surface from wood table, hard-covered paper, plastic board, and metal cabinet, as they prefer. The whole study is run in an office environment.

In all trials, participants are instructed to type as they do on a physical keyboard. They are allowed to correct erroneous input as they go. However, if they are unaware of a mistake until several characters later, they then should ignore the mistake and continue. This imitates occasional typos on a physical keyboard [25]. We evaluate the fraction of residual errors as well as the number of characters (including space and enter keys) per second.

Text input   Table 4 lists user proficiency with various keyboard input methods. It is based on the interviews before the study. Figure 15 plots user performance when they enter the benchmark text. Two performance metrics of input speed and error rate are measured.

We make three observations. First, UbiK improves the input speed in real use. For users with less on-screen keyboard experience (*e.g.*, U2, U4 and U5) , their input speed can be more than doubled with UbiK. For U1 who is the most proficient UbiK user, even though she is also a heavy on-screen keyboard user, her input speed is improved by 83% with UbiK, with only slight increase of error rate (around 2%). Notably, two users (U6 and U7) had short nail margins, and struggled to maintain high input accuracy, and thus they do not witness much improvement with UbiK.

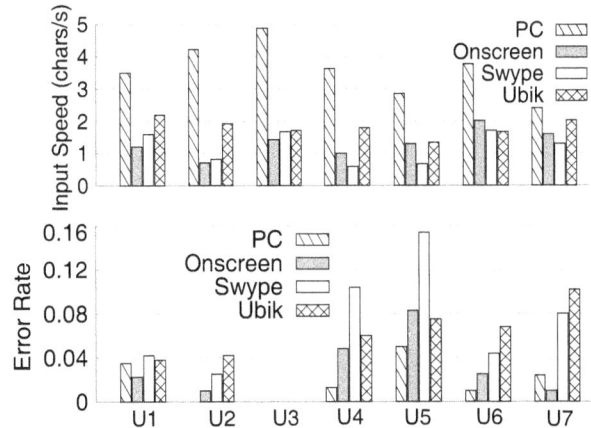

Figure 15: Text entry performance of different users with different keyboards.

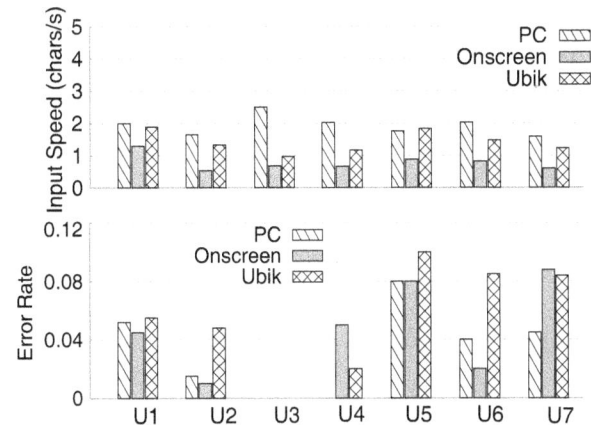

Figure 16: Random text entry performance of different users with different keyboards. Swype performs the same as Onscreen as dictionary is not applicable.

Second, UbiK is easy to use. After a quick warm up, four new users (U4-U7) can type 1.2–2 characters per second, slightly smaller than the proficient users.

Third, accuracy is relevant (sensitive) to user proficiency. The four new users tend to make more mistakes. We gauge they are less familiar with input tricks. Another factor is their personal behaviors; they seldom identify and correct typing errors immediately. We admit UbiK is relatively more erroneous than other methods. Yet as a new technique, its error rate is still comparable and tolerable. Moreover, it is promising to further lower its error rate (as U3 does). The Swype input method does not noticeably improve performance compared with on-screen, primarily because most users are unfamiliar with it and needs to waste time pondering about how to move their fingers.

Random character input   Figure 16 shows the results of random text input. As the text involve a substantial amount of digits and punctuations, the on-screen keyboard suffers from high latency in switching between character/symbol keyboards. Thus, UbiK easily outperforms on-screen keyboard for all users. Note however in both text and random input, UbiK still lags far behind the conventional PC keyboard, partly because of user proficiency, and partly because of the overhead when users attempt to calibrate localization errors from UbiK.

9. DISCUSSION

As a first attempt to realize mobile text entry through fine-grained localization, UbiK still bears several limitations that worth further investigation.

Usability Although the size of the printed keyboard is the same as a physical keyboard, it cannot emulate the kinesthetic and tactile feedback that PC users feel. Existing studies targeting such PC typists pointed out that the removal of feedback significantly reduces the typing performance [27]. Thus, lack of such feedback is another reason why UbiK's input speed is lower than that of a PC keyboard. We also find that inexperienced users pay substantial visual attention on the printed keyboard to navigate their fingers to the correct key position, which further reduces input efficiency.

Tradeoff between accuracy and input speed Localization accuracy has been our primary objective in UbiK. We observe that even for first-time users, accuracy can be above 95% if the user is encouraged to keep consistent keystroke patterns, *e.g.*, always using nail margin plus finger tip to click the keys. However, for inexperienced users, this imposes mental and behavioral burden and hampers input speed. This is the primary reason why the input speed is incomparable to a PC keyboard. An immediate solution is to augment UbiK with a dictionary based error-correction model. This is likely to boost robustness to typing inconsistencies, thus improving input speed.

Robustness in keyboard choices and key clicking It should be noted that UbiK does not rely on the consistency of click strength to distinguish keys. As mentioned in Section 5.3, we normalize each ASD feature vector with its highest-magnitude element so that the keystroke detection can be resilient to the variation of click strength. After the normalization, the frequency-domain ASD features are highly distinguishable (Section 3).

Despite users are encouraged to use the same finger to click a key as they would in actual typing (Section 5.2), it is not mandatory. Such operation improves consistency between the training keystrokes and actually typed keystrokes, thereby improving the typing accuracy. However, UbiK still achieves high accuracy in our experiments even if different fingers are used to press the same key, as long as there is some consistency (*e.g.*, keep using nail tip to press the key).

Security concerns High accuracy in keystroke localization might raise security concerns. An attacker may be able to decipher a user's keystrokes by eavesdropping the keystrokes and stealthily training UbiK on the keyboard. To mitigate it, one possible shield is to use an randomized order for initial training. Without knowing the exact mapping between the ASD features and the keys, it turns much harder (*e.g.*, it requires a large amount of eavesdropping samples) to infer the corresponding keys. Developing counter-measures to such attacks are beyond the scope of our current work.

Other mobile devices Due to lack of hardware, we mainly used smartphones throughout our tests. UbiK is likely to make more difference for small wearable devices like smart watches and glasses, which we will explore in future.

10. RELATED WORK

Fine-grained wireless localization. Fingerprinting based localization, the basic idea behind UbiK, is known to achieve fine-granularity compared with timing-based approaches in wireless location frameworks. Recent measurement study [9] revealed that a combination of WiFi access points and FM broadcast stations' RSS signatures can enable localization accuracy at 1 foot level. Wireless multipath fading profile can be extracted using sophisticated virtual antenna arrays, and used as location signature for objects attached with RFID tags [14]. Frequency-dependent fading characteristics have also been employed [17] for indoor localization with 1 meter accuracy. In contrast to these wireless location solutions, UbiK represents the first work to achieve ultra fine-grained, centimeter scale localization. Further, UbiK cannot take advantage of any well-designed beacon signal patterns. Instead, it faces the unreliability and variation of click patterns even for keystrokes on the same location.

Acoustic ranging and sound source localization. UbiK is reminiscent of the classical sound source localization problem, which has a wide range military, scientific and commercial applications. Due to long propagation time, audio signals' TDOA or directional-of-arrival can be easily measured using a microphone array [10]. However, as verified in Section 3, such non-parametric solutions are extremely vulnerable to indoor reverberation effects and unsuitable for fine-grained localization. Using active audio beacons, it is feasible to achieve localization accuracy on the order of several centimeters [11, 28]. Unfortunately, UbiK's keystrokes cannot be generated using audio beacons.

Keyboard eavesdropping. UbiK is closely related with recent works in keyboard emanation. Asonov *et al.* [29] investigated acoustic emanations of a PC keyboard generated by click sounds. FFT results of keystroke signals are directly used as features to train a neural network. However, even with 100 trainings per key, the approach can only achieve 79% accuracy. The problem is revisited in [30] using an unsupervised learning approach, which heavily rely on dictionary and is unsuitable for real-time keystroke recognition. SpiPhone [21] uses sensing data from accelerometers to decipher keystrokes, base on an artificial neural network. Similar to [29], substantial training (150 instances per key) is needed and best accuracy is only 80%. However, since these approaches mainly target security/privacy, even a low level of accuracy may raise alarming problems.

Customized keyboard for mobile devices. Text-entry method has been an active research area in mobile human-computer interaction. Substantial efforts have been devoted in redesigning the keyboard to improve usability, *i.e.*, by adaptively zooming the keys [2,5], rearranging characters, leveraging context information or additional virtual space on the mobile device [3,4]. A class of projection based mobile keyboards have been studied in the past decade of HCI research [6–8,31]. They use an infrared or visible light projector to cast a keyboard on a surface, and then run sophisticated optical ranging or image recognition algorithms to identify the keystroke. Since additional hardware platforms are needed, such solutions are not yet ready to solve the keyboard bottleneck for mobile devices.

Acoustic touch sensing has been exploited recently in novel human-computer interaction applications. TapSense [32] extracts acoustic features from different part of fingers to create additional dimensions of input information. Touch&Activate [33] enables touch sensing on everyday objects, again through acoustic signals collected from closely attached microphones. The interactive window project and follow-on works [34,35] localize clicks on hard surfaces using surface-mounted high sampling-rate microphones. It is unknown if such approaches work with COTS devices.

11. CONCLUSION

In this paper, we have designed and implemented UbiK, which enables a novel text-input solution for mobile devices via keystrokes on external, solid surfaces. UbiK is grounded on experimental evidences that verify the feasibility of fine-grained, centimeter-scale sound source localization, by using the multipath channel profile as location signatures. These observations are consolidated in a complete system design that realizes accurate detection and localization of keystrokes, and online adaptation of keystroke signatures based on user feedback. Our evaluation of UbiK demonstrates around 95% of localization accuracy across a variety of settings. A field trial involving new and experienced users shows that UbiK can significantly outperform current on-screen keyboards in terms of input efficiency, with slight increase of error rate. Although a physical keyboard is clearly preferable, UbiK provides a viable means for small mobile devices to support text entry.

12. REFERENCES

[1] M. Kölsch and M. Turk, "Keyboards without Keyboards: A Survey of Virtual Keyboards," in *Proceedings of Sensing and Input for Media-centric Systems*, 2002.

[2] K. Al Faraj, M. Mojahid, and N. Vigouroux, "BigKey: A Virtual Keyboard for Mobile Devices," in *Proceedings of International Conference on Human-Computer Interaction*, 2009.

[3] M. Goel, A. Jansen, T. Mandel, S. N. Patel, and J. O. Wobbrock, "ContextType: Using Hand Posture Information to Improve Mobile Touch Screen Text Entry," in *Proc. of ACM CHI*, 2013.

[4] O. Schoenleben and A. Oulasvirta, "Sandwich keyboard: Fast ten-finger typing on a mobile device with adaptive touch sensing on the back side," in *Proc. of ACM MobileHCI*, 2013.

[5] S. Oney, C. Harrison, A. Ogan, and J. Wiese, "ZoomBoard: A Diminutive Qwerty Soft Keyboard Using Iterative Zooming for Ultra-small Devices," in *Proc. of ACM CHI*, 2013.

[6] H. Du, T. Oggier, F. Lustenberger, and E. Charbon, "A Virtual Keyboard Based on True-3D Optical Ranging," in *Proceedings of the British Machine Vision Conference*, 2005.

[7] H. Roeber, J. Bacus, and C. Tomasi, "Typing in Thin Air: The Canesta Projection Keyboard - a New Method of Interaction with Electronic Devices," in *ACM CHI Extended Abstracts*, 2003.

[8] C. Harrison, H. Benko, and A. D. Wilson, "OmniTouch: Wearable Multitouch Interaction Everywhere," in *Proc. of ACM UIST*, 2011.

[9] Y. Chen, D. Lymberopoulos, J. Liu, and B. Priyantha, "FM-based Indoor Localization," in *Proc. of ACM MobiSys*, 2012.

[10] T. Gustafsson, B. Rao, and M. Trivedi, "Source Localization in Reverberant Environments: Modeling and Statistical Analysis," *IEEE Transactions on Speech and Audio Processing*, vol. 11, no. 6, 2003.

[11] C. Peng, G. Shen, Y. Zhang, Y. Li, and K. Tan, "BeepBeep: a High Accuracy Acoustic Ranging System Using COTS Mobile Devices," in *Proc. of ACM SenSys*, 2007.

[12] K. Ho and M. Sun, "Passive Source Localization Using Time Differences of Arrival and Gain Ratios of Arrival," *IEEE Transactions on Signal Processing*, vol. 56, no. 2, 2008.

[13] S. Sen, J. Lee, K.-H. Kim, and P. Congdon, "Avoiding Multipath to Revive Inbuilding WiFi Localization," in *Proc. of ACM MobiSys*, 2013.

[14] J. Wang and D. Katabi, "Dude, Where's My Card?: RFID Positioning That Works with Multipath and Non-Line of Sight," in *Proc. of ACM SIGCOMM*, 2013.

[15] D. Tse and P. Viswanath, *Fundamentals of Wireless Communication*. Cambridge University Press, 2005.

[16] M. Vorlander, *Fundamentals of Acoustics, Modelling, Simulation, Algorithms and Acoustic Virtual Reality*. Springer, 2008.

[17] S. Sen, B. Radunovic, R. R. Choudhury, and T. Minka, "You Are Facing the Mona Lisa: Spot Localization Using PHY Layer Information," in *Proc. of ACM MobiSys*, 2012.

[18] W. Cui, Z. Cao, and J. Wei, "Dual-Microphone Source Location Method in 2-D Space," in *Proc. of IEEE International Conference on Acoustics, Speech and Signal Processing (ICASSP)*, 2006.

[19] J. H. DiBiase, "A High-Accuracy, Low-Latency Technique for Talker Localization in Reverberant Environment," Ph.D. dissertation, Brown University, 2000.

[20] R. Blum, S. Kassam, and H. Poor, "Distributed Detection With Multiple Sensors I. Advanced topics," *Proceedings of the IEEE*, vol. 85, no. 1, 1997.

[21] P. Marquardt, A. Verma, H. Carter, and P. Traynor, "(Sp)iPhone: Decoding Vibrations from Nearby Keyboards Using Mobile Phone Accelerometers," in *Proc. of ACM CCS*, 2011.

[22] T. Hastie, R. Tibshirani, and J. Friedman, *The Elements of Statistical Learning*. Springer, 2013.

[23] Smart Tool Co., "Sound Meter Pro." [Online]. Available: https://play.google.com/store/apps/details?id=kr.aboy.sound

[24] Monsoon Solutions, Inc., "Monsoon Power Monitor," http://www.msoon.com/LabEquipment/PowerMonitor/.

[25] I. S. MacKenzie and R. W. Soukoreff, "Phrase Sets for Evaluating Text Entry Techniques," in *ACM CHI Extended Abstracts*, 2003.

[26] Swype Inc., "The Swype Virtual Keyboard," 2013. [Online]. Available: http://www.swype.com/

[27] S. Kim, J. Son, G. Lee, H. Kim, and W. Lee, "TapBoard: Making a Touch Screen Keyboard More Touchable," in *Proc. of ACM CHI*, 2013.

[28] Z. Zhang, D. Chu, X. Chen, and T. Moscibroda, "SwordFight: Enabling a New Class of Phone-to-phone Action Games on Commodity Phones," in *Proc. of ACM MobiSys*, 2012.

[29] D. Asonov and R. Agrawal, "Keyboard Acoustic Emanations," in *IEEE Symposium on Security and Privacy*, 2004.

[30] L. Zhuang, F. Zhou, and J. D. Tygar, "Keyboard Acoustic Emanations Revisited," *ACM Transactions on Information System Security*, vol. 13, no. 1, 2009.

[31] J. Mantyjarvi, J. Koivumaki, and P. Vuori, "Keystroke Recognition for Virtual Keyboard," in *Proc. of IEEE International Conference on Multimedia and Expo (ICME)*, 2002.

[32] C. Harrison, J. Schwarz, and S. E. Hudson, "TapSense: Enhancing Finger Interaction on Touch Surfaces," in *Proc. of ACM UIST*, 2011.

[33] M. Ono, B. Shizuki, and J. Tanaka, "Touch & Activate: Adding Interactivity to Existing Objects Using Active Acoustic Sensing," in *Proc. of ACM UIST*, 2013.

[34] J. A. Paradiso, C. K. Leo, N. Checka, and K. Hsiao, "Passive Acoustic Knock Tracking for Interactive Windows," in *ACM CHI Extended Abstracts*, 2002.

[35] D. T. Pham, Z. Ji, M. Yang, Z. Wang, and M. Al-Kutubi, "A Novel Human-computer Interface Based on Passive Acoustic Localisation," in *Proc. of International Conference on Human-computer Interaction*, 2007.

Autodirective Audio Capturing Through a Synchronized Smartphone Array

Sanjib Sur[†], Teng Wei[†] and Xinyu Zhang
University of Wisconsin-Madison
{sur2, twei7}@wisc.edu and xyzhang@ece.wisc.edu
[†]Co-primary authors

ABSTRACT

High-quality, speaker-location-aware audio capturing has traditionally been realized using dedicated microphone arrays. But high cost and lack of portability prevents such systems from being widely adopted. Today's smartphones are relatively more convenient for audio recording, but the audio quality is much lower in noisy environment and speaker location cannot be readily obtained. In this paper, we design and implement Dia, which leverages smartphone cooperation to overcome the above limitations. Dia supports spontaneous setup, by allowing a group of users to rapidly assemble an array of smartphones to emulate a dedicated microphone array. It employs a novel framework to accurately synchronize the audio I/O clocks of the smartphones. The synchronized smartphone array further enables autodirective audio capturing, i.e., tracking the speaker's location, and beamforming the audio capturing towards the speaker to improve audio quality. We implement Dia on a testbed consisting of 8 Android phones. Our experiments demonstrate that Dia can synchronize the microphones of different smartphones with sample-level accuracy. It achieves high localization accuracy, and similar beamforming performance compared with a microphone array with perfect synchronization.

Categories and Subject Descriptors

C.3.3 [**Special-Purpose and Application-based Systems**]: Signal processing systems

Keywords

Ad-hoc microphone array; smartphone synchronization; acoustic localization; acoustic beamforming

1. INTRODUCTION

The pervasiveness of smartphones is driving a continuous growth of mobile multimedia applications, which take advantage of the microphone and camera modules for spontaneous audio-visual capturing. Yet such applications are

mostly constrained to short-range individual use, undoubtedly because of the private nature of standalone smartphone devices. Common smartphones are not well suited for demanding multimedia applications. For example, (i) A smartphone's audio-capturing quality can be significantly degraded in noisy environment, with noises coming from ambient electronic devices and interfering voices. (ii) A smartphone does not work well in lecture recording applications, where the lecturer may walk far away from the microphone and her speech may be immersed in noise. (iii) A similar problem occurs in meeting recording or teleconferencing scenarios, where certain speakers can be far from the microphone.

Currently, such challenging audio capturing tasks require dedicated commercial platforms. For example, Polycom CX-5000 [1] and Microsoft RingCam [2] incorporate a microphone array to enhance audio quality and locate speakers. The location information is used to guide a steerable camera to focus its view angle on a main speaker. Ricoh [3] developed an audio-visual recording system with a similar objective, but using video image processing to track conference participants. These high-end systems overcome the narrow view-angle and low audio quality of smartphones, but tend to be expensive and lack portability. Simple solutions using close-talking microphones may be used in lecture-recording cases, but they are intrusive and distracting [4].

In this paper, we propose an alternative system that leverages an ad-hoc group of smartphones (referred to as a *smartphone array*) to enhance audio capturing in the above scenarios. These smartphones may be temporarily collected from participants in a meeting or lecture. Through tight cooperation, their individual microphones can form a virtual microphone array that beamforms to a main speaker, and localizes the speaker in real-time to facilitate video recorders, *e.g.*, a steerable camera [5]. We refer to such a system as auto**D**irective **a**udio (Dia) capturing.

The advantages of Dia are multifold. It inherits all the benefits of a dedicated microphone array. Yet it allows spontaneous setup at almost no extra cost. In addition, Dia has the potential to enable directive, portable audio-visual recording, by aligning multiple smartphones' cameras and triggering each opportunistically according to speaker's location.

Realizing such potential entails several grand challenges, the major one lying in synchronization of the smartphones. Speaker tracking heavily relies on Time-Difference-Of-Arrival (TDOA) statistics among distributed microphones. Therefore, the smartphones must synchronize their microphones with sufficient precision, *i.e.*, the audio sampling clocks must *be triggered simultaneously* and *tick at the same rate*. Similarly, beamforming relies on synchronization to align the audio samples. Sampling offset may cause different microphones to cancel instead of enhancing each other's signals.

Dia meets the above challenges using a distributed two-level synchronization framework. It first synchronizes the CPU clocks of different smartphones, by allowing them to timestamp the WiFi beacons overheard from a nearby access point, and calibrate the CPU time to align with each other. Then, with the help of a PC server, each smartphone's audio I/O clock gets synchronized with its own CPU clock. Consequently, the sampling clocks of distributed microphones are synchronized to a global clock, thus enabling the same functionalities as a dedicated microphone array.

Given this synchronized array of smartphones, Dia incorporates two cooperative audio signal processing modules to achieve autodirective audio capturing. First, it runs a practical beamforming algorithm that assigns weights to the synchronized audio signals captured by different smartphones, the optimal weight vector corresponding to the beam direction that maximizes the speaker's voice quality. Second, Dia estimates the TDOA of audio signals from multiple microphones to track the speaker's angle relative to the smartphone array. It employs a novel *binary mapping* approach to scale the localization scheme to more than two smartphones with unknown separation.

We have implemented Dia based on the Android platform. Our experiments demonstrate that Dia can synchronize distributed smartphones with an accuracy of around 2 samples at 16 kHz sampling rate. With an array of 8 smartphones, Dia is able to boost the voice quality by 11 dB, which is comparable to an oracle scheme with perfect synchronization. More importantly, Dia's performance scales as more smartphones are put together. In addition, our field test shows that Dia is able to track the speaker's direction with an error of around 10 degrees when the smartphones' separation is known, and track the speaker's region with more than 90% of accuracy under unknown smartphone separation.

We make the following contributions in Dia.

(i) We design a novel synchronization mechanism that can synchronize the audio I/O clocks of distributed smartphones at sample-level, which achieves comparable performance as a microphone array. The synchronization algorithm is not only a key component of Dia, but also a standalone contribution. It opens up a wide range of spontaneous audio sensing applications that used to be available only on expensive dedicated hardware platforms.

(ii) We propose a practical audio beamforming system that leverages cooperative signal processing on the synchronized smartphones to boost audio quality. Further, we develop a speaker tracking algorithm on top of Dia that provides location guides to external video capturing devices.

(iii) We implement Dia on a mobile platform and conduct comprehensive experiments to validate its performance, against an oracle scheme and in actual application scenarios.

The remainder of the paper is structured as follows. Sec. 2 presents an overview of Dia and its usage cases. Sec. 3 introduces the design and implementation of the two-level synchronization algorithm, followed by the audio beamforming and speaker localization/tracking algorithms in Sec. 4 and Sec. 5. Sec. 6 elaborates on the experimental evaluation of Dia on top of our Android implementation. Sec. 7 discusses limitations and open problems in Dia. Sec. 8 surveys related work and finally, Sec. 9 concludes the paper.

2. Dia: AN OVERVIEW

2.1 Application Scenarios

Dia enables spontaneous setup of a distributed microphone array using an ad-hoc group of smartphones. It precisely synchronizes the distributed microphones to (i) enhance audio coverage and quality by beamforming speaker's voice to the embedded array of microphones, and (ii) localize and track the speaker's direction relative to the smartphone array. Such functionalities are useful in a wide range of application scenarios. We provide a few examples below.

(i) Smart conferencing. Imagine a conferencing session, where participants intend to start an ad-hoc discussion and spontaneously capture their speech as audio minutes. The conference can occur anywhere and anytime, *e.g.*, in a meeting room, a company cafeteria, a picnic area in a park or a dinning table in a restaurant. Due to lack of portability, dedicated audio recording devices are not readily applicable. Requesting each individual to use their smartphones as close-talking microphones may ensure voice quality, but this is obtrusive and can be distracting [4]. It is also non-trivial to stitch the recordings of individual smartphones to form a coherent piece of meeting record. With Dia, the participants can simply place their smartphones together and record high-quality audio in a similar way to a commercial microphone array [6]. Dia automatically focuses on a main speaker and tracks the speaker in case of movement or role switching. It compiles the audio signals of all smartphones into a single audio track that can also be streamed to a remote site.

(ii) Autonomous lecture recording. In a classroom or lecture hall, Dia can act as a low-cost automatic recording system. It can run on an array of smartphones belonging to the audience. Through synchronous, cooperative audio signal processing, Dia will be able to maintain recording quality even in low signal-to-noise-ratio (SNR) conditions due to, *e.g.*, lecturer walking away from the microphones, and noise from electrical appliances and outside vehicles/machinery.

Dia works under several premises in the above setup. It needs at least two smartphones each equipped with a microphone and WiFi interface. It presumes the smartphone owners trust each other and are willing to allow tight cooperation (exchanging messages) between their phones. In addition, Dia relies on a back-end server to process the audio signals. Thus, the smartphones need to have network connection to the server (*e.g.*, through WiFi or 3G).

The speaker's location information provided by Dia can facilitate a variety of external applications. An immediate one might be a cooperative video capturing system that uses the smartphone array's cameras to capture a meeting, lecture, *etc.* The smartphones may be placed along a line or circle, such that their view angles cover an entire area of interest. At any time, only one camera is triggered that covers the speaker according to Dia's location information. The resulting video frames can be stitched according to their timestamps. Alternatively, Dia can enable a commercial steerable camera system [5] to follow the speaker in real time.

2.2 System Architecture and Basic Operations

Figure 1 illustrates Dia's architecture and basic flow of operations. Dia acts as a software module running on the smartphones and a back-end server. It consists of three ma-

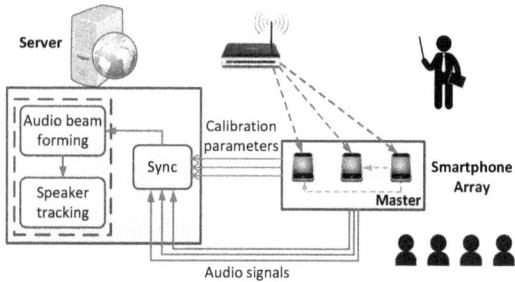

Figure 1: Architecture of Dia.

jor modules: two-level synchronization, audio beamforming, and speaker localization/tracking.

Dia works as follows in a typical use case. First of all, users collect multiple smartphones and place them along a regular geometry shape (*e.g.*, line or circle, to be discussed in Section 5). After such initial setup, *two-level synchronization*, a distributed I/O synchronization protocol, is triggered and operated by both the server and smartphones. Specifically, one smartphone is arbitrarily chosen as the master and it coordinates the other phones to collect relevant timestamp information from ambient WiFi beacons, and from their own audio interface, in order to estimate a set of parameters for timing calibration. The timing calibration is conducted jointly by the server and smartphones, which enables each smartphone to calibrate its CPU clock against a global clock, and its local audio clock against the CPU clock. Afterwards, the smartphones will be able to start audio capturing at the same time, and precisely align their audio samples, even though they are driven by independent CPU clocks and audio I/O clocks rolling at different rates.

The audio streams of all smartphones are delivered to the server through either WiFi or cellular network. The server then runs an *audio beamforming* module that processes the synchronized audio samples to enhance audio quality and suppress noise. The underlying rationale lies in a high level of diversity provided by multiple microphones, similar to multi-antenna spatial diversity in MIMO wireless communications [7]. In addition, the server runs a *speaker localization/tracking* framework that leverages relative timing between the microphones' audio samples to track the speaker's angle relative to the smartphones.

Both of the beamforming and speaker tracking modules benefit from higher performance (in terms of audio SNR and localization granularity) as the number of smartphones increases. Such extensibility is a unique advantage compared with dedicated microphone array hardware.

Note that audio data processed by the server can be either recorded to a file or streamed in real-time to a remote site (we focus on the former case in our implementation). Dia mainly targets the case with one dominating speaker at any time. We will discuss potential approaches to addressing competing speeches in Section 7.

3. AUDIO I/O CLOCK SYNCHRONIZATION AMONG SMARTPHONES

In this section, we first motivate the problem of tight audio clock synchronization by analyzing the application requirement, then we introduce the design and implementation of Dia's two-level synchronization framework in detail.

3.1 Why Synchronization?

Microphone-array based autodirective audio capturing requires tight synchronization between the microphone elements [8]. For audio beamforming, received signals of different microphones need to be coherently combined. Severe timing offset will cause significant phase misalignment between the signals and hence preventing beamforming. Similarly, misalignment induces ambiguities when estimating the signal's TDOA to different microphones, thus causing localization error.

Audio devices' synchronization errors come from two sources: *initial timing offset and sampling-rate difference (clock drift)*. The former is due to the devices' CPU clock difference and timing uncertainties between CPU and audio I/O — even if an application instructs the devices to start simultaneously, the actual time when they are triggered may differ significantly. Human voices commonly fall below 2 kHz, with up to 4 kHz in rare cases [9]. Thus, a constant initial offset of below 1/4000=0.00025 s, or 250 μs, between the different microphones does not noticeably affect the microphone-array's performance. In effect, signals with such offset can be considered as interpolations of the original signal, which can still be coherently combined. For speaker tracking applications, an initial timing offset of 250 μs translates into a distance estimation error of 343 m/s × 0.00025 s=0.086 m, which is easily acceptable in practice.

However, achieving this 250 μs timing alignment is a nontrivial task for COTS smartphones. Due to unpredictable jitter caused by application execution and OS scheduling, existing signaling-based network synchronization protocols can only achieve [10, 11] millisecond-level granularity. GPS can provide μs level synchronization, but it does not work well in indoor environment.

Even after perfect initial synchronization, the second source of errors, *i.e.*, sampling clock drift, remains a serious challenge. Driven by independent oscillators, the smartphones' audio sampling clock rates are bound to differ and, even minor clock skew will accumulate the sampling time offset to quickly diverge beyond the synchronization requirement.

To make the problem more concrete, we measured the audio sampling offset of 5 Galaxy Nexus smartphones (3 I9250 models and 2 I515), by playing a very short 'linear chirp' tone from a sound source at an interval of 15 seconds. We used chirp tones in both human audible frequency range of 10 kHz – 10.5 kHz and inaudible range of 22.05 kHz – 22.3 kHz. To isolate the impact of propagation delay, all the smartphones and the sound source are placed within 6 cm distance. The sampling offsets are obtained by visually checking the onset peak position offset between 'chirp' signals received by the smartphones. Figure 2 plots the relative sampling offset (number of samples drifted) of 4 other phones taking one I9250 as a reference point. Clearly, the audio sample drift between multiple smartphones increases over time and escalates to an intolerable value of up to 22 samples (499 μs) within merely 60 seconds of recording.

Does audio-beacon based synchronization work? At first blush, it might seem sufficient to designate one smartphone as a master node, which periodically broadcasts audio beacon signals as synchronization pilots. All other nodes record the beacons along with desired voice signals. Afterwards, a server can process the signals offline, and synchronize the signals by searching for the optimal beacon-time alignment through cross-correlation. Our earliest attempt to

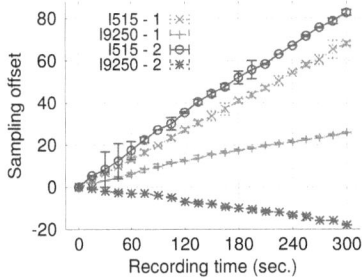

Figure 2: Audio sampling offset between multiple distributed smart phones. Error bars represent maximum and minimum. Sampling rate equals 44.1 kHz.

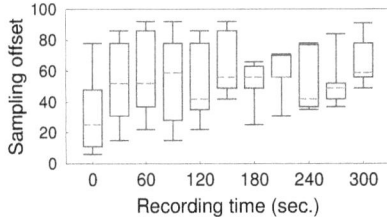

Figure 3: Box plot showing the minimum, first quartile, median, third quartile and maximum sampling offset calculated using audio beacon based synchronization.

build Dia relied on this audio-beacon based synchronization principle. However, two major bottlenecks corrupted the effort.

First of all, we find that audio reverberation and fading effects distort the beacon signals significantly, causing erratic uncertainties in the offline synchronization. We conducted an experiment using a very short 'chirp' tone as beacon and broadcast signal at an interval of 30 seconds. In ideal scenario, the cross-correlation process would have shown the same trend of linear offset increment as in Figure 2. However, we find that cross-correlation process is quite random in nature, as plotted in Figure 3. This is also the reason why, instead of using cross-correlation, we have to visually check the onset peak position offset between the 'chirp' signals as in Figure 2, in order to gauge the sampling offset.

The second bottleneck lies in the conflict between beacons and desired voices. Sampling rate estimation inevitably has some residual errors that accumulate over time. Thus, synchronization beacons need to be broadcast periodically for recalibration purpose. This will interfere the actual recording process, which simply defies the purpose of performing synchronization for high audio quality in first place. Although it is possible to send the audio beacons through inaudible frequency band, the first bottleneck still persists.

3.2 Sample-level Audio I/O Synchronization in Dia

3.2.1 System model and problem formulation

Any hardware clock module $HC(\cdot)$ in the smartphone can be modelled as:

$$HC(t) = \int_{t_0}^{t} r(\tau)d\tau + \theta(t_0) \qquad (1)$$

where $r(\tau)$ is the clock rate at time τ and $\theta(t_0)$ the initial clock offset at time t_0 with respect to an oracle clock.

Ideally, $r(\tau)$ maintains a constant value of 1. In practice, the clock drifts over time. But for bounded time interval, the clock drift is reasonably bounded with a small drift ρ, *i.e.*, $r(\tau) = 1 + \rho$.

In a typical embedded platform, there exists hardware registers that can be probed by software to obtain *logical clock* values $LC(\cdot)$:

$$LC(t) = \int_{t_0}^{t} r(\tau).p(\tau)d\tau + \theta(t_0) \qquad (2)$$

where $p(\tau)$ denotes the software probing interval. For the CPU, $LC(\cdot)$ is simply the system timestamp, whereas for audio I/O, it is the sample index counted from the microphone's triggering time. Henceforth, the clocks we mention are logical clocks by default.

In COTS smartphones, it is infeasible to directly program the audio I/O clock to achieve distributed synchronization. Dia circumvents this barrier via a novel two-level principle: *(i) Inter-device synchronization:* synchronizing the smartphones' CPU clock against a global clock. *(ii) Intra-device synchronization:* synchronizing each smartphone's audio I/O clock against its own CPU clock. We formulate this principle in more detail below.

Suppose the logical CPU clock of smartphone i at time t is $LC_i^{cpu}(t)$. For a bounded time interval, it can be assumed that there exists a linear relationship between $LC_i^{cpu}(t)$ and a global clock $GC(t)$:

$$LC_i^{cpu}(t) = a_i(\delta).GC(t) + b_i(\delta) \qquad (3)$$

where $\delta = (t - t_0)$ is bounded. The timing model parameters $a_i(\delta)$ and $b_i(\delta)$ are constant within δ.

Since both the audio I/O clock and CPU clock advance linearly over time, there is an implicit linear relation between them:

$$LC_i^{audio}(LC_i^{cpu}(t)) = \alpha_i(\delta).LC_i^{cpu}(t) + \beta_i(\delta) \qquad (4)$$

with timing model parameters $\alpha_i(\delta)$ and $\beta_i(\delta)$ being constant within δ. Here, $LC_i^{audio}(LC_i^{cpu}(t))$ is the audio sample index at CPU clock $LC_i^{cpu}(t)$.

Given the above two timing models, the problem of synchronizing the audio samples between multiple smartphones can be formulated as calculating $GC(LC_i^{audio})$, *i.e.*, the global timestamp of audio samples LC_i^{audio}, and compensate for the differences across multiple devices. Said differently, if we know the global clock value corresponding to an audio sample of one smartphone, we can use Eq. (3) and (4) to calculate the audio sample number of a different smartphone at that global clock value, and compensate for the differences. Dia's two-level synchronization algorithm is built atop this principle.

3.2.2 Two-level synchronization algorithm

Illustrative example. Figure 4 showcases an example of how Dia synchronizes two smartphones with 1 sample offset. For simplicity, let us assume the timing model parameters in Eq. (3) and (4), *i.e.*, $a_i(\delta)$, $b_i(\delta)$, $\alpha_i(\delta)$ and $\beta_i(\delta)$, are known for both smartphones. For a given audio sample s_1 in smartphone 1, it knows its local timestamp lt_1 following Eq. (4). It can further infer the corresponding global timestamp gt following Eq. (3). This global time stamp can be passed to smartphone 2, who infers its own local time stamp lt_2 following Eq. (3) (with different timing model parameters). Then, it uses Eq. (4) to calculate the corresponding audio sample number s_2. In this way, both the smartphones know the exact audio sample index corresponding to a particular

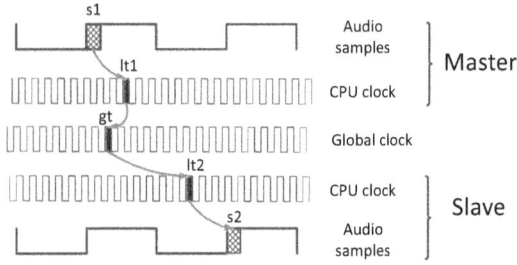

Figure 4: An example timing diagram showing, the audio sample synchronization between two smartphones, having 1 audio sample offset.

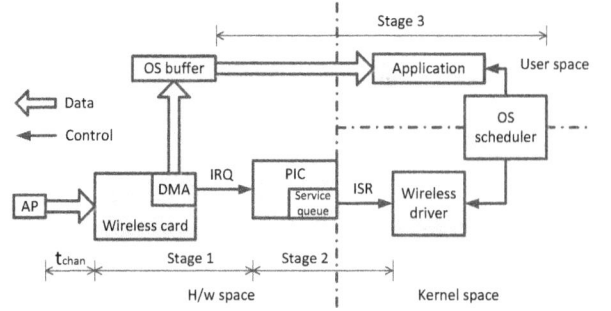

Figure 5: Network I/O control and data flows in smartphone.

global timestamp gt, which in turn synchronizes the audio samples.

The key problem in realizing Dia's principle is to estimate the CPU and audio timing models. In Dia, the smartphones leverage a WiFi AP's beacon messages to estimate parameters for the CPU timing model following Eq. (3) , and then each smartphone locally infers the audio timing model based on CPU/audio timestamps following Eq. (4). This requires each smartphone to obtain highly reliable logical timestamps for the WiFi beacons and audio samples.

Probing logical clock timestamps. Unavailability of hardware timestamps forces us to resort to software probing of timestamps. The software probing interval must be constant across multiple devices (Eq. (2)). This is hard to achieve if we probe the timestamps directly from application-level. We analyze this problem in Figure 5, which shows the processing diagram of the network I/O path in a typical smartphone[1], comprised of 3 stages:

Stage 1. The input data are digitized and partially processed in hardware. The Direct Memory Access (DMA) engine transfers the data to an OS buffer and generates an Interrupt ReQuest (IRQ). In devices with similar hardware, this takes an approximately equal amount of time.

Stage 2. The Programmable Interrupt Controller (PIC) registers the IRQ in an interrupt service queue, and the OS kernel schedules itself to call the Interrupt Service Routine (ISR) of the particular device driver, and then serve the interrupt. Since PIC handles IRQ from multiple hardware modules, a variable amount of delay is introduced here.

Stage 3. Once the interrupt is serviced, the OS delivers the data to the user space. The variable delay in this step is significantly higher than that in *Stage 2*, as it depends on many factors including but not limited to, priority of the application in a multi-processing environment, CPU utilization, *etc.*

Clearly, to fix the software probing interval to a constant value, we should probe in *Stage 1*. Unfortunately, there is no scope of CPU to register the timestamp before the IRQ is serviced by the OS. Thus, in Dia, we aim to achieve a reasonable determinism by probing the hardware clocks only at the ISR (*Stage 2*). However, there could still be jitters, the root cause emerging from the fact that the core OS in today's smartphones is not a real-time. In what follows, we will show how we overcome this jitter in Dia.

Estimating timing parameters under timestamp jitters. Modern 802.11 APs embed a 64-bit timestamp in each broadcast beacon (so called TSF timer), which can be

captured by smartphones as global timestamp. For each Wi-Fi beacon packet j containing timestamp $GC(t^j)$, smartphone i keeps a tuple $\langle GC(t^j), LC_i^{cpu}(t^j)\rangle$ where, $LC_i^{cpu}(t^j)$ denotes the arrival CPU timestamp of the beacon packet j.

Given n sets of observation tuples $\langle GC(t^j), LC_i^{cpu}(t^j)\rangle$ *for* $j = 1, 2, \ldots n$, we want to estimate the parameters $\widehat{a}_i(\delta)$ and $\widehat{b}_i(\delta)$ for bounded δ, following Eq. (3). This is a classical problem of linear curve fitting which can be solved using a linear regression method [12]. However, the jitters in timestamps statistics, obtained by software probing, might reduce the goodness of fitting and hence the reliability of estimation.

We solve this problem by using a least trimmed square (LTS) regression model [13], which removes outlier observations with large residual errors and then computes a least mean square regression model for rest of the observations. This is particularly suitable in reducing the dependency on the OS jitter in serving the ISR.

We apply a similar method to estimating the audio timing model parameters, $\widehat{\alpha}_i(\delta)$ and $\widehat{\beta}_i(\delta)$ following Eq. (4). Corresponding to the audio sample index k, we have the CPU timestamps $LC_i^{cpu}(t^k)$. This gives a set of observation tuple $\langle LC_i^{cpu}(t^k), k\rangle$. Now, given m sets of observation tuple $\langle LC_i^{cpu}(t^k), k\rangle$ *for* $k = 1, 2, \ldots m$, the problem of estimating timing models $\widehat{\alpha}_i(\delta)$ and $\widehat{\beta}_i(\delta)$ is solved again by using LTS regression.

Reliable relationship between logical clocks. A linear relationship between global $\leftrightarrow$ local logical clock and local $\leftrightarrow$ audio I/O logical clock is assumed across the above two-level synchronization algorithm design. We now present an empirical evidence to show this relationship holds in practice for bounded time interval δ.

To this end, we used the same 8 Galaxy Nexus smartphones mentioned in Section 3.1 and register beacon packet arrival times from a single WiFi access point. The timestamps are registered inside the ISR of the Broadcom WiFi driver [14]. We also register the original timestamps that were embedded into the beacon packets which act as the global logical clock of that particular access point.

Table 1 shows the regression results of inter-device synchronization for different smartphones. R^2 is the *Coefficient of Determination*, a widely used measure of how well the result of linear regression method is [12]. We can see that the R^2 values are well above 0.999 for all the smartphones, which indicates very good fitting results. We also performed similar experiment to find the regression results on the relationship between audio sample number to the local CPU

---

[1]The processing diagram of the audio I/O path is similar, except that the data comes from the microphones.

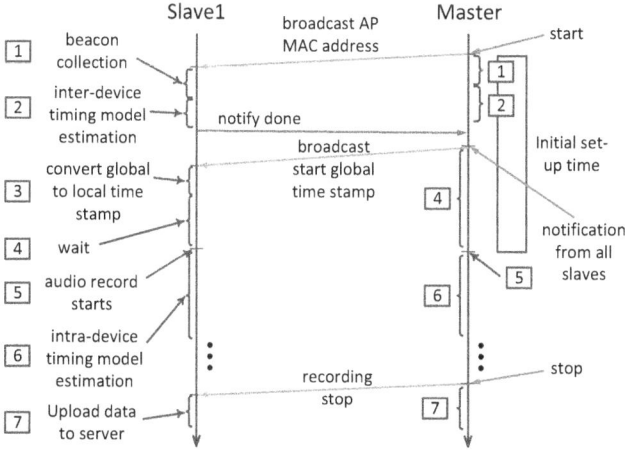

Figure 6: Space-time diagram of the signaling protocol between smartphones.

clock and achieve similar fitting result. We omit this in the interest of space.

Smart Phone	Slope a	Intercept b	R^2
1	0.99998	-34111970	0.99968
2	1.00020	-12020470	0.99962
3	0.99967	18574170	0.99982
4	1.00005	-23536980	0.99977
5	1.00006	-33825370	0.99977
6	1.00008	-46648270	0.99979
7	1.00010	56972960	0.99970
8	1.00010	-55440930	0.99976

Table 1: LTS regression results between the global logical clock and CPU logical clock of 8 smartphones, in the form of $LC_i^{cpu}(t) = a_i(\delta).GC(t) + b_i(\delta)$, where i is the smartphone index. R^2 is the metric indicating the goodness of fitting.

3.3 Implementing Two-Level Synchronization

Dia's implementation of two-level synchronization involves a PC server and multiple smartphones. It extends the prior example of two-smartphone synchronization to multiple smartphones, by designating one of them as master, to whom others (slaves) need to synchronize their audio samples. The master communicate with the slaves through WiFi network.

Signaling protocol. Figure 6 shows the signaling protocol between the master and each of the slave smartphones. When Dia is launched, the master broadcasts a wireless AP MAC address, whose beacons will be monitored by all smartphones. During the beacon capturing process, the smartphones store the timestamps tuple $\langle GC(t^j), LC_i^{cpu}(t^j)\rangle$. After receiving a sufficient amount of beacons, each smartphone runs the inter-device CPU timing model estimation as in Eq. (3). Upon completing this procedure, each slave smartphone sends a notification message to the master.

Once the master has received notifications from all the slaves, it broadcasts a future global triggering timestamp at which all the smartphones should start audio capturing. Note that, by this time a slave already knows the inter-device timing model parameters and thus can convert the global triggering timestamp to its local timestamp following

Eq. (3). Each smartphone, including the master and slaves, waits till its clock hits the local triggering timestamp before it turns on the microphone and starts audio capturing.

During audio capturing, the smartphones keep track of the tuple $\langle LC_i^{cpu}(t^k), k\rangle$ to prepare for the intra-device audio-CPU synchronization. On receiving sufficient number of CPU timestamps corresponding to audio samples, each smartphone runs the intra-device timing model estimation (Eq. (4)). The audio recording runs in parallel to this process. Note that, the intra-device timing model estimation could also be done in the server side. However, this induces tedious message exchanges between the server and the smartphones, who need to send all the CPU timestamps corresponding to each audio samples.

When the user terminates Dia, the master smartphone broadcasts a stop command to all slaves. Each smartphone i then uploads the recorded audio samples A_i along with the inter- and intra-device timing model parameters to the PC server. The server runs Algorithm 1 to synchronize the audio samples of all the slaves with respect to the master smartphone. Specifically, the server first finds out all the global timestamps corresponding to the audio samples of the master smartphone using the timing model parameters. Then, it uses each slave's own timing model parameters to convert the previous global timestamps to the audio sample index. In this way, the audio samples from each slave smartphone get aligned with the master.

Algorithm 1 Audio I/O synchronization: Server

1: **foreach** smartphone i
2:     Receive $\langle A_i, \hat{a}_i(\delta), \hat{b}_i(\delta), \hat{\alpha}_i(\delta), \hat{\beta}_i(\delta)\rangle$
3: **end foreach**
4: **foreach** audio sample j in A_{master}
5:     Calculate $LC_{master}^{cpu}(j)$ such that,
    $j = \hat{\alpha}_{master}(\delta).LC_{master}^{cpu}(j) + \hat{\beta}_{master}(\delta)$
6:     Calculate $GC(j)$ such that,
    $LC_{master}^{cpu}(j) = \hat{a}_{master}(\delta).GC(j) + \hat{b}_{master}(\delta)$
7: **end foreach**
8: **foreach** smartphone $i \setminus master$
9:     Calculate all $LC_i^{cpu}(\cdot)$ such that,
    $LC_i^{cpu}(\cdot) = \hat{a}_i(\delta).GC(\cdot) + \hat{b}_i(\delta)$
10:     Calculate all sample indices $S_i(\cdot)$ such that,
    $S_i(\cdot) = \hat{\alpha}_i(\delta).LC_i^{cpu}(\cdot) + \hat{\beta}_i(\delta)$
11:     Extract samples from A_i using indices from $S_i(\cdot)$
12: **end foreach**

Practical issues. There are a number of additional issues we have addressed in implementing the two-level synchronization algorithm.

(i) Obtaining WiFi beacon timestamps. We register the beacon arrival times from a single Wi-Fi AP on smartphones, by adding flags inside the smartphone's Wi-Fi driver. In particular, for Galaxy Nexus, we register the timestamps inside ISR of the Broadcom Wi-Fi driver [14] to reduce the extraneous jitters introduce in further OS processing. However, registering CPU timestamps inside ISR triggers a severe software bug inside the driver, which was eventually fixed by applying software patches and driver modifications. We also register the original timestamps that was embedded into the beacon packet which acts as the global logical clock of the AP.

(ii) Obtaining fine-grained audio sample timestamps. Audio hardware does not give interrupt until a sufficient amount of audio samples are received. For example, we found out that in Galaxy Nexus, which uses audio hardware of OMAP-4460 [15], the audio driver gets interrupt after every 1056 audio samples, irrespective of the sampling frequency used. Hence, we only receive local CPU timestamps per 1056 audio samples. However, the samples between two CPU timestamps are equally spaced and therefore, to obtain more fine-grained audio sample timestamps, we perform a linear interpolation of the timestamps within the 1056 samples.

(iii) Scanning a fixed wireless channel for beacons. The WiFi driver of the smartphones are pre-programmed to scan all available channels (14 in 2.4 GHz range) for AP discovery. We found that this causes excessive latency for Dia to collect beacons from the target AP. We further modified the wireless driver inside the smartphone's Linux kernel, to scan only on a fixed channel over which the AP transmits beacons.

(iv) Unavailability of beacon timestamps. Some wireless drivers in smartphones hide the WiFi beacon timestamps from user level programs. Few wireless devices for smartphones are implemented as FullMAC [2], and therefore does not even forward the beacon timestamps received from the wireless access point to the kernel driver. In this extreme situations, the master smartphone itself can act as a source of global timestamps and broadcast periodic packets containing global timestamps.

4. ENHANCING AUDIO QUALITY WITH BEAMFORMING

In this section, we introduce how Dia leverages the synchronized smartphone array to develop a beamforming framework for audio enhancement.

4.1 MVDR Beamforming Algorithm

We adopt the state-of-the-art Minimum Variance Distortionless Response (MVDR) [16] algorithm to realize audio beamforming. In theory, MVDR can achieve a high spatial resolution and large SNR improvement with a few number of microphones.

To understand how MVDR works, consider an array of M smartphones. Without loss of generality, we assume each smartphone has one microphone, denoted by $P_1, P_2, \cdots P_M$. Due to spatial separation, the signals from the desired sound source arrive at the microphones with different delays. We can construct a delay vector $\mathbf{T} = [t_{1,2}, \ldots, t_{1,i}, \ldots, t_{1,M}]^T$ representing the relative TDOA between P_1 and all other microphones, *e.g.* P_i. Then the *spatial signature*, $\mathbf{C} = [1, e^{-j\omega t_{1,2}}, \ldots, e^{-j\omega t_{1,M}}]^T$ can represent the phase difference between one smartphone and others at frequency ω. Such signature can be straightforwardly translated from TDOA.

The MVDR algorithm applies complex weight w_i^* to smartphone P_i's audio signals in each frequency bin. The weight will change the phase and amplitude of the signals. If a *weight vector* $\mathbf{W} = [w_1, w_2, \ldots, w_M]^T$ for the M smartphones is properly selected, the desired sound signals can be maintained in the output of summed signals from different smartphones, whereas the noise can be mutually canceled.

---

[2] A wireless device is called FullMAC, when the MAC layer management functionalities, *e.g.*, beaconing, association *etc.* are implemented in h/w to reduce processing latency.

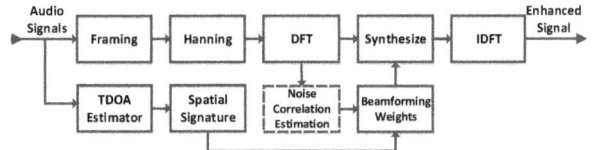

Figure 7: Audio beamforming module in Dia.

To attain such a goal, the weight vector $\mathbf{W}$ has to satisfy two conditions:

(i) It must steer the audio capturing "beam" to the desired direction, *i.e.*, keeping the gain of the signal strength from that direction to be a constant value 1. This gain constraint can be expressed mathematically as $\mathbf{W}^H\mathbf{C} = 1$. In this way, the desired signals can be mutually constructive without loss. This is where the term "distortionless" comes from – to preserve the quality of the desired signals (in both amplitude and phase).

(ii) Meanwhile, it should minimize the output energy of noise signals. Intuitively, the weights in $\mathbf{W}$ can be tuned such that the majority of noise can cancel each other. To this end, $\mathbf{W}$ must capture some statistical information — delay spread and energy distribution in frequency domain — from the noise. The statistical information can be characterized by noise correlation matrix $\mathbf{R_n}$, which describes the phase and amplitude relation among noise signals from different smartphones. Detailed steps to obtain the noise correlation matrix will be introduced in Section 4.2.

The above two conditions in MVDR can be jointly formulated as an optimization problem. The optimal weight vector $\mathbf{W}$ has been proven in closed-form [16] as:

$$\mathbf{W} = \mathbf{R}_n^{-1}\mathbf{C}(\mathbf{C}^H\mathbf{R}_n^{-1}\mathbf{C})^{-1} \tag{5}$$

Below we describe how we incorporate the MVDR theory into Dia's practical beamforming module.

4.2 Audio Beamforming System Design

After synchronizing the audio samples from all smartphones, Dia's server coherently combines the samples to realize MVDR, in order to suppress noise and interference. This is realized in Dia's beamforming module, as shown in figure 7, which comprises the following steps.

(i) Framing the audio signals. Dia processes audio signals on a per-frame basis. A larger frame improves the precision of statistical parameters (*e.g.*, noise correlation) in MVDR, but will incur greater computational complexity and higher latency. In Dia, we choose an empirical frame length of 40 ms, which is found to strike a good balance. To smooth their transition, the frames are partially overlapped by 20 ms and regulated by a Hanning Window. Then, Discrete Fourier Transform (DFT) is applied to the framed signals to split them into frequency bins.

(ii) Estimating noise correlation matrix. The estimation of noise correlation matrix $\mathbf{R_n}$ requires a period that only contains the ambient noise and interference sound. This can often be done prior to the actual audio recording. Let vector $\mathbf{X}_{ik}$ denote the noise signal of frame k from smartphone P_i for one frequency bin (index omitted). The noise correlation matrix can be calculated as:

$$\mathbf{R_n} = \begin{pmatrix} \mathbf{R}_{11} & \cdots & \mathbf{R}_{1M} \\ \vdots & \ddots & \vdots \\ \mathbf{R}_{M1} & \cdots & \mathbf{R}_{MM} \end{pmatrix}$$

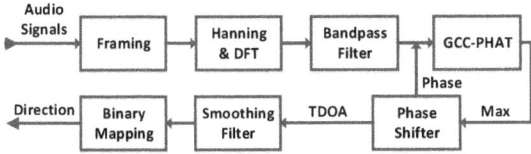

Figure 8: Speaker tracking module in Dia.

where $\mathbf{R}_{ij} = \frac{1}{L}\sum_{k=1}^{L}\mathbf{X}_{ik}\mathbf{X}_{jk}^{H}$. L is the number of frames for noise estimation, default to 60 (or 2.4 s) in Dia.

In our current implementation, Dia only tackles relatively stationary noises, *e.g.*, those from electrical appliances, outdoor machinery and vehicles. Suppressing bursty interference requires adaptive estimation of $\mathbf{R_n}$, which we leave for future work.

(iii) Calculating beamforming weights. Given the estimated TDOA vector $\mathbf{T}$ (to be discussed in Section 5), Dia's server calculates the spatial signature $\mathbf{C}$. Then, using Eq. (5), it computes the beamforming weights. These weights $\mathbf{W}$ are applied into each of the original frames. The weighted frames are converted back to time domain, thus obtaining signals with enhanced quality.

5. SPEAKER TRACKING AND LOCALIZATION

Dia's localization module tracks the speaker's angle relative to the smartphones, based on the TDOA between all the microphones. It can deal with both continuous locations (*e.g.*, a walking lecturer) and discontinuous locations (*e.g.*, role switching in a round-table discussion). Below we detail the components in this module, as shown in Figure 8.

Framing audio signals. Dia's voice tracking scheme frames and windows the audio signals in a similar way to beamforming. The key difference is that TDOA estimation is extremely sensitive to multipath reflections. A larger frame size can amortize the impact but it incurs longer latency for voice tracking. In Dia, we use an empirical frame size of 200 ms — 5 times that of the beamforming frame size — to balance this tradeoff.

Estimating the TDOA. To estimate the TDOA of each slave relative to the master, we adopt the generalized cross correlation with phase transform (GCC-PHAT) algorithm [17], which has been shown to be effective in practical environment. GCC-PHAT computes the cross-correlation between the audio frames of two microphones in frequency domain, and shifts the relative phase between the two frames. The phase that maximizes the cross-correlation corresponds to the time offset between the frames and hence the TDOA. Before running GCC-PHAT, we apply a bandpass filter to attenuate the signals outside the voice frequency range.

Enhancing robustness of TDOA estimation. In implementing GCC-PHAT, we found the discontinuity of human speech induces significant error. Figure 9 shows the GCC-PHAT based TDOA estimation over 20 seconds. Two speakers speak consecutively, each for 10 seconds. Short pauses are intentionally added between speech. The first speaker sits in between two microphones, and thus the TDOA should always equal 0. However, the actual GCC-PHAT estimation varies significantly during the speech gap. We found that speaker movement, ambient noise and the destructive effects of multipath reflections also causes small variations.

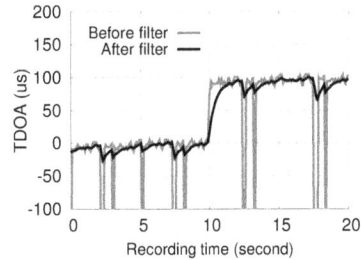

Figure 9: TDOA over time with speaker switching.

To resolve these challenges, we introduce a time-domain linear filter, inspired by the Kalman filter, which removes TDOA outliers via smoothing:

$$T_{i+1} = \alpha D_{i+1} + (1 - \alpha)T_i \qquad (6)$$

where D_i is the GCC-PHAT based TDOA estimation for frame i and T_i the filtered TDOA estimation.

A smaller smoothing factor α can better eliminate outliers, but will cause larger latency during speaker role switching. To balance stability and latency, we adapt α according to the type of TDOA outliers. For minor variation, we choose a larger α_H to reduce latency, because such variations are mostly generated by speaker's movement. Those large variations are incorrect estimations caused by speech gaps. Thus, a smaller value α_L is used for better stability. Formally,

$$\alpha = \begin{cases} \alpha_H & \frac{D_{i+1}}{T_i} < Tres_v \\ \alpha_L & \frac{D_{i+1}}{T_i} >= Tres_v \end{cases}$$

where $Tres_v$ is the threshold determining the type of variation. In Dia, we choose α_H, and α_L to be 0.2 and 0.02 respectively. For the lecture room scenario, $Tres_v$ is chosen to be 0.3 as there is only one target speaker. For conference room case, $Tres_v$ is set to be 0.8 because the audio-beam has to switch among multiple speakers.

Binary mapping: Mapping TDOA to speaker direction. Given TDOA between microphones, a simple and widely used approach for speaker angle estimation is based on the following relation: $TDOA = \frac{d\sin\theta}{c}$, where d is the distance between two microphones and θ the speaker's direction relative to the line segment between them. Dia leverages this approach as a basic speaker tracking mechanism.

However, this approach cannot readily take advantage of the availability of more than two smartphones to improve tracking performance. Also, it assumes known distance between the microphones, which is not always feasible to obtain, considering the fact that Dia's smartphones are placed manually and spontaneously. We have experimented with existing audio-based ranging methods like BeepBeep [18] to estimate the distance, but found the blockage between smartphone bodies caused large estimation errors.

In Dia, we design a novel method called *binary mapping* that leverages multiple smartphones to find the speaker direction without knowing the distance between smartphones. Dia's speaker location information is intended for steerable cameras, which has a view angle of tens of degrees [4]. Thus, it is sufficient to divide the area of interest into fan-shaped regions, and estimate the speaker location on a region basis.

Consider a round-table conference scenario, as shown in Figure 20, where M smartphones are placed in the middle to form a circular array, facing M fan-shaped regions. For each region R_i, there exists a unique TDOA signature vector

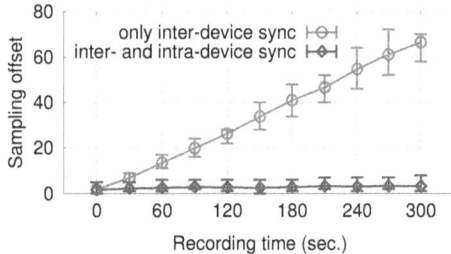

Figure 10: Audio sampling offset between two smartphones. Error bars denote maximum and minimum.

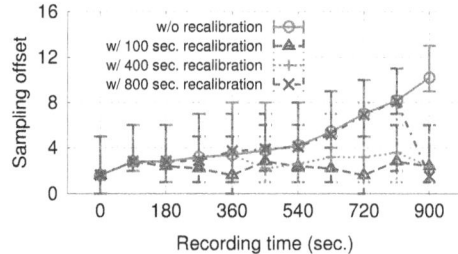

Figure 11: Audio sampling offset with and without periodic recalibration.

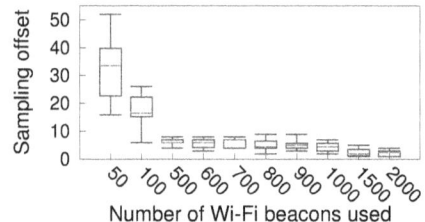

Figure 12: Synchronization accuracy between two distributed smartphones *w.r.t.* number of initial Wi-Fi beacons collected.

$\mathbf{S}_1 = [s_{1,2}^i, s_{1,3}^i, \ldots, s_{1,M}^i]$, where $s_{1,j}^i = sign(t_{1,j}^i)$, and $t_{1,j}^i$ is the TDOA between microphone P_1 and P_j when they receive signals from region R_i. This TDOA signature is unique regardless of the distance between smartphones or between speaker and smartphones. It can be directly computed without any offline training. The TDOA signature for all regions can be presented in a matrix $\mathbf{S} = [\mathbf{S}_1; \mathbf{S}_2; \ldots; \mathbf{S}_M]$.

At run-time, Dia computes the speaker's signature, and matches it to that of different regions. Specifically, taking microphone P_1 as reference, we can obtain a TDOA vector $\mathbf{T}_1 = [t_{1,2}, \ldots, t_{1,M}]$. Then, we map the signed vector $\mathbf{T}_1^{sign} = sign(\mathbf{T}_1)$ to a region by finding the minumum Euclidean distance between $\mathbf{T}_1^{sign}$ and $\mathbf{S}_i$.

$$R_i = \arg\min_i (\mathbf{T}_1^{sign} - \mathbf{S}_i)^2 \qquad (7)$$

The Hamming distance of the TDOA signatures is 2 when $M = 8$. Thus, it can tolerate up to two bits of errors in $\mathbf{T}_1^{sign}$. Occasionally, imperfect TDOA estimation and synchronization may induce more than 2 bits of errors. We adopt two approaches to improve the robustness of our tracking algorithm under such cases.

(i) In order to mitigate the impact of flipped bit from synchronization offset, we normalize the TDOA vector by its maximum absolute value $\mathbf{T}_i = \frac{\mathbf{T}_i}{\max(abs(\mathbf{T}_i))}$, and set $t_{i,i+1}$ to zero if it is smaller than an empirical value of 0.15. This neutralizes the impact of those small TDOA values.

(ii) Instead of only taking one smartphone as reference, we choose multiple smartphones as references, and estimate the region under each reference. Then we run a majority vote to finalize the estimation result.

The above binary mapping algorithm can be applied similarly when the smartphone array is placed in a linear topology. We omit the details due to space constraint.

6. SYSTEM EVALUATION

In this section, we first evaluate the individual modules of Dia, including synchronization, beamforming and localization. Then, we conduct a field trial of Dia in conference round-table and lecture room scenarios.

6.1 Synchronization Performance

To evaluate the accuracy of our two-level synchronization algorithm, we use a smartphone speaker to repetitively play a short 'chirp' tone. Two other smartphones (Galaxy Nexus I9250 & I515) run the synchronization algorithm and record the chirp signals. To isolate the impact of propagation delay, all the phones are placed within 6 cm distance. Unless noted otherwise, both the testing smartphones run at 16 kHz sampling rate and record the chirp tone for 300 seconds.

The separation of onset peaks of their received chirps represents the residual sampling offset after synchronization (same as our measurement in Section 3.1).

Synchronization accuracy. Figure 10 plots the sampling offset between two smartphones over time while performing inter-device and two-level synchronization, respectively. With inter-device (CPU clock) synchronization alone, the synchronization offset is around 2 samples in the beginning, but quickly grows to 20 samples after only 60 seconds of recording. With two-level synchronization, the offset is bounded to 2~3 samples even after 300 seconds.

However, our synchronization algorithm is not perfect. Figure 11 shows that it may slowly accumulate the residual sampling offset over time. Fortunately, smartphones running Dia can always collect fresh CPU/audio timestamps and periodically request the server to recalibrate the sampling offset without disrupting ongoing recording. With a recalibration period of 100 seconds (default value in Dia), the sync error can be kept at 2 to 3 samples. This translates to a timing error of 187.5 μs, easily satisfying the 250 μs requirement mentioned in Section 3.1.

Impact of initialization time on synchronization. Recall that Dia needs to collect WiFi beacons for inter-device synchronization. An immediate question is: how many beacon packets are needed to achieve the desired synchronization accuracy? Figure 12 evaluates the relationship between number of initial Wi-Fi beacons against the sampling offset after running the two-level synchronization algorithm. A larger number of initial beacons allow us to estimate the timing model parameters with better accuracy, thereby increasing the synchronization accuracy. However, beyond 500 beacons, the improvement is marginal. With the default beacon period of 100 ms, this translates to a short initial setup time of 50 s. After the initialization, the two-level synchronization and recalibration runs in background, along with the audio recording, thus eliminating waiting time.

Impact of audio sampling frequency. Ideally, the sampling offset should decrease when decreasing the sam-

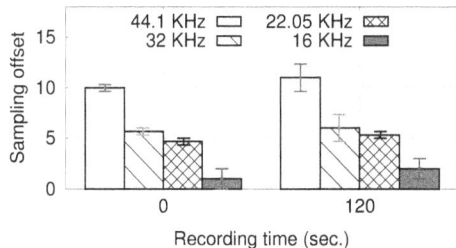

Figure 13: Sampling offset over time between two distributed smartphones *w.r.t.* audio sampling frequency.

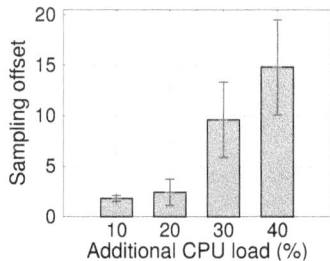

Figure 14: Sampling offset when one smartphone is subject to additional CPU loads. Error bars represent *std.*

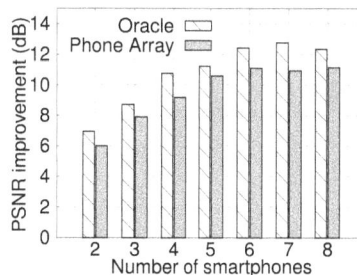

Figure 15: Beamforming gain from Dia's smartphone array, compared with a perfectly synchronized microphone array. Average PSNR of each individual smartphone is 15.73 dB.

pling frequency, to keep the time delay between the samples constant. Figure 13 verifies this property by showing the sampling offset variation across different sampling frequencies. We see that as sampling frequency decreases, the sampling offset decreases proportionally, and the absolute synchronization time error is almost a constant.

Impact of background CPU load. As mentioned in Section 3.3, the jitters in timestamps collected by smartphones depends on the CPU load. We quantify this effect by adding artificial CPU load on top of running Dia, using an open source program, called *cpuloadgen* [19]. This program generates a precise background load on the ARM processor inside the smartphones based on the well-known *dhrystone* [20] benchmark program. Figure 14 shows the resulting sampling offset when one smartphone's CPU load varies. Within 20% of additional CPU load, our synchronization algorithm is virtually unaffected. Beyond that point the sampling offset increases by 4× for only 10% increase in CPU load. The variance also increases significantly. However, we found that background CPU load when running Dia remains at approximately 2~3%, which is far below the critical load of 20%. In addition, when Dia is running and recording (*e.g.*, during a lecture or meeting), it is highly unlikely that the user will be doing any significant background tasks on the smartphones.

6.2 Audio Beamforming Performance

We evaluate Dia's audio beamforming module when running on a synchronized smartphone array. The experiments are conducted in an office environment with ambient noise coming from desktop PCs, servers, and air conditioner. A smartphone playing human voice audio track is used to act as the desired sound source. An additional smartphone generates noise sound with variable power. By default, the smartphones record at 44.1 kHz sampling frequency. We use the conventional peak signal to noise ratio (PSNR) [21] as performance metric. Noise power is measured when the

noise source presents alone. Peak signal power is computed by the maximum total power (measured over consecutive frames containing desired signal and noise) minus noise. PSNR is known to eliminates artifacts caused by speech gap and power variation [21].

Beamforming gain from a smartphone array. We compare Dia's beamforming performance with an oracle microphone array with perfect synchronization. The oracle case is created via a trace-driven approach, which represents the best beamforming performance that can be achieved by smartphones. Specifically, we use one smartphone to emulate multiple smartphones by putting it in different but close-by locations and collect the audio data it captures from the same sound source. We play a short chirp at the beginning of each trace, and manually synchronize the trace data offline. Besides, as we use the same smartphone, there is no sampling rate offset in the audio signals.

Figure 15 shows the resulting beamforming gain, *i.e.*, PSNR improvement *w.r.t.* a single microphone case. We observe that the beamforming gain of both Dia and oracle scales with the growing number of microphones. Dia's beamforming gain is 6.01 dB with 2 smartphones, and escalates to 11.14 dB with 8. More importantly, Dia's performance closely approximates the oracle, with a maximum difference of 1.83 dB and below 1 dB in most cases. This is mainly attributed to the small residual synchronization error, which remains almost constant within each calibration period, and thus does not affect Dia's performance in a noticeable way.

Impact of separation between speaker and microphones. We examine the impact of distance between speaker and microphone on the beamforming gain. We consider a simple topology of two smartphones separated by 16 cm. The desired sound source is located in the middle of two phones moving 20 cm to 260 cm away from the smartphones, representing decreasing PSNR. Figure 16 shows the resulting beamforming gain. We can see that as speaker walks away, even though both original PSNR and beamforming PSNR decrease, the beamforming gain can still sustain at a high level – around $6dB$. In fact, it increases slightly, from $6.31dB$ at 20 cm to $7.79dB$ at 260 cm. Note that, even when the original PSNR is high, Dia can still boost the audio quality by 6+ dB.

Impact of sampling offset on beamforming gain. To verify the necessity of Dia's audio I/O synchronization algorithm, we study the impact of sampling rate offset on beamforming gain. We choose a pair of unsynchronized smartphones which has a sampling rate offset of 0.317 sample/second. We manually align the starting time of their

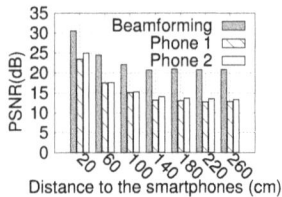

Figure 16: PSNR variation as speaker walks away.

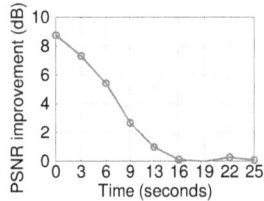

Figure 17: Impact of sampling rate offset on beamforming gain.

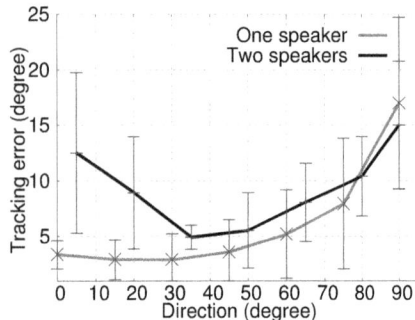

Figure 19: Experimental setup in a typical round-table conference scenario.

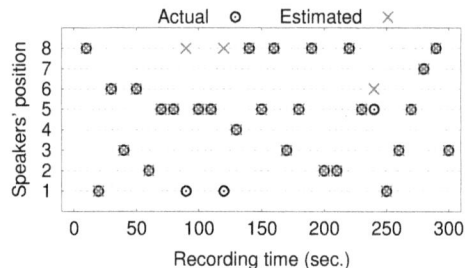

Figure 18: Voice tracking accuracy when the speaker is located in different directions.

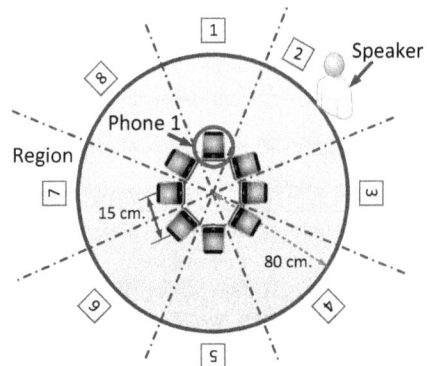

Figure 20: Speakers' position estimation within 8 regions in a typical round-table conference scenario.

recorded audio signals to isolate the impact of CPU time offset. From Figure 17, we can see that sampling rate offset degrades beamforming gain significantly over time. After 16 seconds of recording, the beamforming gain drops below 0.12 dB. This experiment stresses the importance of the intra-device synchronization scheme in Dia. It also implies the infeasibility of the audio beacon alignment approach due to the existence of residual sampling rate errors (Section 3.1).

6.3 Accuracy of Voice Tracking

In this section, we present voice tracking accuracy when running Dia with two smartphones. We use the basic approach introduced in Section 5 that translates TDOA into the angle of the speaker. The two smartphones are placed 16 cm apart and their middle line is the 0 angle reference. We test the system under two scenarios: *(i)* One speaker who moves from 0 to 90 degrees. *(ii)* Two speakers — one as interferer located at 0 angle, the desired one moving from 5 to 90 degrees.

Figure 18 shows the voice tracking accuracy when the desired speaker is located at different angles. For single-speaker case, the tracking error increases as the speaker's angle increases from 0 to 90 degrees. This is mainly due to multipath reflections: At 0 degree, the speaker is facing both microphones, whereas for 90-degree case, one smartphone is partially blocked by the other, which weakens the line-of-sight path, causing the increased uncertainty of TDOA estimation. Besides, when translating TDOA to speaker angle, the angle estimation θ becomes more sensitive to T_i when θ is near 90 degrees (Section 5).

For the case with an interfering speaker, voice tracking can achieve the best accuracy when the two speakers are separated by an intermediate value of around 35 degrees. This is because when two speakers are close to each other, *e.g.*, 5-degree separation, voice tracking cannot reliably differentiate the TDOAs for two speakers. On the other hand, when the speaker is close to 90 degrees, similar tracking error occurs as in the one-speaker case.

In all the cases shown in Figure 18, the basic voice tracking module in Dia can differentiate two simultaneous speakers with granularity of smaller than 10 degrees in most cases. However, this module assumes the smartphones' separation is known. In what follows, we evaluate Dia's tracking performance in two field trials, where the smartphone separation may be unknown.

6.4 System-Level Testing of Dia

In this section we evaluate the performance of Dia in two application scenarios as proposed in Section 2.

6.4.1 Round-table conference meeting

We first evaluate Dia in a typical round-table conference scenario. Here, the whole conference room is divided into 8 regions as shown in Figure 19. We place 8 smartphones in the middle of the table in a circular fashion. The distance between the smartphones' microphones is approximately 15 cm (note that Dia is unaware of this distance value). The speaker is 80 cm away from the smartphone array. A region is randomly selected from those 8 regions and the smartphone plays a speech for 10 seconds therein. Since Dia's beamforming performance has been investigated comprehensively, we only focus on its speaker tracking module, particularly the binary mapping algorithm.

Speaker tracking. Figure 20 shows the true and estimated positions. We test our binary mapping algorithm for 50 times and observe an average accuracy of 90%. Also, we find that the regions for which the mis-detection occurs is always the adjacent region of the true region (*e.g.*, region 1 *w.r.t.* 8). When four smartphones are used to cover four regions (each 90 degrees), we observed zero region estimation error.

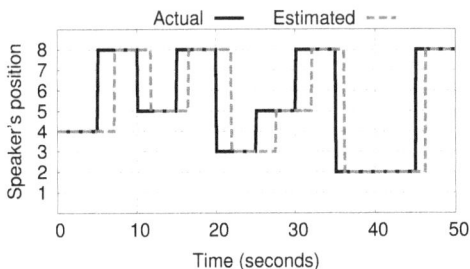

Figure 21: Switching latency in tracking one speaker to another.

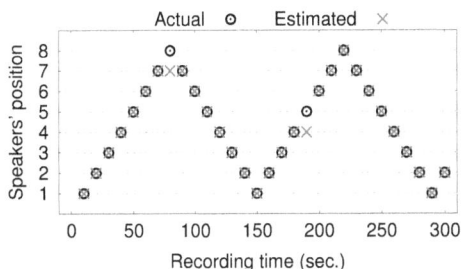

Figure 22: Speaker's position estimation within 8 linear regions in a typical lecture room scenario.

Switching latency. We now consider a scenario where multiple people around the table speaks consecutively. There voices are created by placing 8 smartphone as speakers in the different regions and randomly triggering one at different times. Under this challenging scenario, Figure 21 shows that Dia's binary mapping algorithm tends to lag behind sudden speaker switching by 1 to 2.5 seconds, with mean of 1.7 seconds. This latency may be acceptable if the external video capturing system (*e.g.*, a steerable camera) does not have stringent real-time requirement, but still leaves room for improvement.

6.4.2 Lecture room

Similar to 6.4.1, we measured the performance of Dia in typical lecture room environment. We place 8 smartphones in a linear array, with adjacent separation of 7 cm. The speaker is 70 cm away from the array. We divide the whole lecture stage into 8 partially overlapped regions. The speaker moves from one region to another linearly. Each speech lasts for about 10 s and we measured accuracy of the estimated region from the smartphone array. Figure 22 shows the true and estimated speaker position in one experimental run, lasting 300 seconds. We repeat the experiment 8 times and obtained an average accuracy of 93% in speaker region estimation. In addition, we observed similar tracking latency as in the round-table case. However, note that tracking latency occurs only when the speaker crosses the boundary of two regions, which happens less frequently than the previous case.

7. DISCUSSION

As an early prototype, Dia leaves a number of problems that deserve further investigation.

I/O synchronization in heterogeneous platforms. We have evaluated our I/O synchronization scheme in Galaxy Nexus phones. Even with similar hardware, individual phones exhibit non-trivial CPU timing and audio sampling clock offset. Since Dia's synchronization framework does not rely on

any hardware dependent model, we speculate Dia can be easily migrated to other smartphone platforms. A detailed verification will be left as our future work.

Latency when switching between speakers. As mentioned in Section 6.4.1, Dia's speaker tracking algorithm tends to lag behind sudden speaker switching in a conference room scenario by 1 to 2.5 seconds. As future work, we will improve Dia's tracking algorithm to strike a better balance between accuracy and responsiveness.

Dealing with competing speeches. As shown in Section 5, Dia is able to accurately identify speaker's relative position even when there are two simultaneous speakers. Dealing with more than two speakers is a more challenging scenario. In fact, determining who is the main speaker alone requires human intervention. One possible approach is to degrade Dia to omni-directional recording in this case. This is a matter of our future investigation.

Real-time audio streaming. Currently, the synchronized audio samples recorded by Dia's smartphone array are processed by a server offline. An immediate extension is to enable real-time processing, which will be amenable for teleconferencing scenarios.

Impact of imperfect alignment. As mentioned in Section 2.1, the application scenarios require the smartphones to be grouped together in regular geometry shapes (*i.e.*, line or circle) to run the beamforming and localization algorithms. However, a small misalignment will not reduce the performance of beamforming, because the MVDR can calculate the TDOA and hence beamforming weights irrespective of the smartphone alignment. Also, Dia localizes the sound source in a coarse-grained, region-basis. The accuracy of the region estimation algorithm is unaffected by small changes in alignment or orientation.

Multiple microphones on the smartphone. Certain smartphones like Galaxy Nexus have two microphones, one of which is usually used for noise cancellation. Dia does not leverage the dual microphone capability in its audio capturing. However, we can potentially collect the audio signals from both the microphones (which are synchronized at hardware level) for MVDR beamforming. Dual microphones would not help in Dia's localization algorithm, because they are usually fixed at bottom/back of the smartphones, whereas Dia requires flexible placement of microphones to cover a given region.

Energy overhead. The main step of the synchronization algorithm is to collect the beacon timestamps from an AP at periodic intervals and report it to the application. The beacon packets are by default received by the smartphones for AP discovery and thus require no overhead. Only the interdevice synchronization runs locally in the smartphones and the run time is extremely small compared to the actual audio recording process and thus will consume negligible amount of energy. On the other hand, the beamforming and localization algorithms run only on server side and thus will not consume any extra energy in the smartphones. The main energy cost of Dia thus comes from the continuous operation of microphones and transmission of audio samples to the server through WiFi. Such cost is the same as in typical mobile VoIP applications.

8. RELATED WORK

Autodirective audio-visual capturing. Autodirective audio-visual recording systems have been extensively explored for group meeting, collaborative teleconferencing, and lecture room scenarios [22]. Smart Room technology [23] adopt vision-based algorithms for participant tracking and identification. High-end video-based telepresence systems [4] are able to sense activities through cameras. In many product-oriented systems, panoramic or steerable cameras are combined with microphones for spatial-aware audio-video capturing [3, 24]. Such systems are becoming increasingly important in this era when spontaneous multimedia capturing and distribution becomes prevalent. However, high-cost and lack of portability limits their usage cases. Our Dia system is designed to cover similar application objectives by simply assembling multiple smartphones.

Audio beamforming using microphone arrays. Microphone arrays are often used to emulate the effects of close-up microphones or highly directional microphones to achieve high-quality voice recording. Their unique advantages include hands-free operation and scalable performance with array size. In fact, many contemporary smartphones (*e.g.*, Galaxy Nexus) are equipped with a dual-microphone array for noise cancellation in adverse acoustical environment, *e.g.*, in a cafeteria, on a busy street or in a running vehicle. More powerful microphone array with a large number of elements have been developed. In [25], a 16-microphone array is placed in an office environment for speech enhancement. The LOUD project [21] developed a 1020-microphone array to achieve substantial noise/interference suppression. Adaptive noise suppression and audio beamforming algorithms are studied in [25, 26] and [27] provides an informative survey. Such audio-enhancement algorithms have been applied to in acoustic sensor networks [28] that form a microphone array. Compared with existing work along this line, the main contribution in Dia's beamforming module is the design and implementation of an ad-hoc smartphone array that can serve as a substrate for any acoustic beamforming applications.

Sound source localization. Sound source localization has diverse applications including, *e.g.*, animal population measurement, vehicle speaker tracking, and commercial systems in support of smart spaces. These applications heavily rely on microphone arrays for estimating TDOA. Various microphone array platforms have been developed for such acoustic sensing applications [29, 30]. Chen *et al.* [31] used a distributed microphone array [30] to localize speakers. The algorithm works well when each speaker is close to one microphone element. Since the microphones are separated by a large distance, localization error caused by synchronization offset becomes negligible. However, sampling-rate offset can still become overwhelming and destroy the accuracy. In [32], multiple microphone arrays are used to estimate the direction of animal sounds. Similar architectural concept has been adopted in [33], where an FPGA based 4-channel microphone array is used to localize shooters. We believe Dia can significantly ease the development and deployment of such sound source localization applications.

Network synchronization algorithms. Synchronization is a classical problem for distributed systems and networks. Existing solutions mostly focused on synchronizing the nodes' CPU clocks. In particular, extensive research has been devoted to synchronization in sensor networks (see [34] for a comprehensive survey). The intuition lies in calibrating the CPU clocks through lightweight wireless packet exchanges, in order to achieve network-wide time consis-

tency. Standard synchronization solutions with application-level message exchange (*e.g.*, NTP) can only achieve a granularity of several milliseconds [10]. In Dia, we need to synchronize not only CPU, but also the I/O clocks of different nodes. Distributed synchronization algorithms for microphones on desktop PCs have been proposed in [35, 36], yet a practical, quantitative evaluation of the algorithms are still lacking. To our knowledge, Dia represents the first realization of sample-level I/O synchronization between modern smartphones.

Cooperation between mobile devices. Current smartphones are designed as standalone personal devices. Emerging device-to-device communications technologies, such as WiFi-direct, create new opportunities for cooperative mobile wireless systems. For example, MicroCast [37] allows closely located smartphones to aggregate the cellular bandwidth, and share downloaded data through WiFi-direct to improve video streaming quality. Recent work, like CWC [38], proposed to harness the computational power of many smartphones to establish a distributed computing platform that offload tasks from costly infrastructures. MobiUS [39] split one video frame between two nearby smartphones to enable better-together viewing experience. Many participatory sensing applications [40] have been developed to collect data and reveal interesting context patterns from a large number of distributed smartphones. Compared with the above research, a key distinguishing challenge in Dia is the granularity of cooperation — it requires tight I/O synchronization between close-by smartphones. To our knowledge, Dia represents the first system to tackle this challenge.

9. CONCLUSION

In this paper, we have designed Dia, a novel system that leverages ad-hoc smartphone cooperation to achieve autodirective audio capturing. Dia employs a two-level synchronization framework that can synchronize the audio I/O of distributed smartphones with sample-level accuracy. With this framework, we develop a practical speaker tracking and audio beamforming module that achieves similar performance as a perfectly-synchronized microphone array. Since Dia runs on COTS smartphones and supports spontaneous setup, it has potential to enable a wide range of distributed acoustic sensing and microphone-array based signal processing systems. Our immediate next step to explore Dia's potential is to expand it into a cooperative audio and visual recording system as proposed in Section 2.

10. ACKNOWLEDGMENT

We sincerely thank Dr. Wen Hu for shepherding our paper, as well as the anonymous reviewers for their valuable comments and feedback. This work was partly supported by NSF grant CNS-1318292 and CNS-1350039.

11. REFERENCES

[1] Polycom Inc., "CX5000," 2013. [Online]. Available: http://www.polycom.com/products-services/ products-for-microsoft/lync-optimized/ cx5000-unified-conference-station.html

[2] Microsoft Corporation, "Microsoft RingCam / Roundtable," 2006. [Online]. Available: http://microsoft.blognewschannel.com/2006/05/18/ microsoft-ringcam-microsoft-roundtable/

[3] D.-S. Lee, B. Erol, J. Graham, J. J. Hull, and N. Murata, "Portable Meeting Recorder," in *Proc. of ACM Multimedia*, 2002.

[4] Z. Yu and Y. Nakamura, "Smart Meeting Systems: A Survey of State-of-the-Art and Open Issues," *ACM Computing Survey*, vol. 42, no. 2, 2010.

[5] Ingeniero Marketing Tecnologia, "Fully Steerable Wireless Micro-Camera," 2013. [Online]. Available: http://www.imtsrl.it/wireless.html

[6] Polycom Inc., "Eagle Eye Director Datasheet," 2013. [Online]. Available: http://www.polycom.com/content/dam/polycom/common/documents/data-sheets/eagleeye-director-ds-enus.pdf

[7] D. Tse and P. Viswanath, *Fundamentals of Wireless Communication.* Cambridge University Press, 2005.

[8] J. Benesty, J. Chen, and Y. Huang, *Microphone Array Signal Processing.* Springer, 2008.

[9] M. Vorlander, *Auralization: Fundamentals of Acoustics, Modelling, Simulation, Algorithms and Acoustic Virtual Reality.* Springer, 2008.

[10] M. Laner, S. Caban, P. Svoboda, and M. Rupp, "Time Synchronization Performance of Desktop Computers," in *IEEE International Symposium on Precision Clock Synchronization for Measurement Control and Communication (ISPCS)*, 2011.

[11] The NTP newsgroup, "Network Time Protocol," 2013. [Online]. Available: http://www.ntp.org/

[12] R. Myers, *Classical and modern regression with applications.* Duxbury Press Belmont, CA, 1990, vol. 2.

[13] P. J. Rousseeuw, "Least median-of-squares regression," *American Statistical Association*, vol. 79, 1984.

[14] Broadcom Corporation, "brcmfmac (sdio) drivers," 2013. [Online]. Available: http://wireless.kernel.org/en/users/Drivers/brcm80211

[15] Texas Instrument Inc., "OMAP4460 Multimedia Device - Technical Reference Manual," 2013.

[16] J. J. M. V. de Sande, "Real-time Beamforming and Sound Classification Parameter Generation in Public Environments," Master's thesis, Delft University of Technology, 2012.

[17] "A High-Accuracy, Low-Latency Technique for Talker Localization in Reverberant Environment," Ph.D. dissertation, Brown University, 2000.

[18] C. Peng, G. Shen, Y. Zhang, Y. Li, and K. Tan, "BeepBeep: a High Accuracy Acoustic Ranging System Using COTS Mobile Devices," in *Proc. of ACM SenSys*, 2007.

[19] Texas Instruments Inc., "cpuloadgen," 2013. [Online]. Available: http://github.com/ptitiano/cpuloadgen

[20] "Dhrystone Benchmarking for ARM Cortex Processors," 2011. [Online]. Available: http://infocenter.arm.com/help/index.jsp?topic=/com.arm.doc.dai0273a/index.html

[21] E. Weinstein, K. Steele, A. Agarwal, and J. Glass, "A 1020-Node Modular Microphone Array and Beamformer for Intelligent Computing Spaces," 2004.

[22] Y. Rui, A. Gupta, J. Grudin, and L. He, "Automating Lecture Capture and Broadcast: Technology and Videography," *ACM Multimedia Systems Journal*, vol. 10, 2004.

[23] C. Busso, S. Hernanz, C.-W. Chu, S. il Kwon, S. Lee, P. Georgiou, I. Cohen, and S. Narayanan, "Smart Room: Participant and Speaker Localization and Identification," in *IEEE International Conference on Acoustics, Speech and Signal Processing (ICASSP)*, 2005.

[24] R. Cutler, Y. Rui, A. Gupta, J. Cadiz, I. Tashev, L.-w. He, A. Colburn, Z. Zhang, Z. Liu, and S. Silverberg, "Distributed Meetings: a Meeting Capture and Broadcasting System," in *Proc. of ACM Multimedia*, 2002.

[25] T. Takagi, H. Noguchi, K. Kugata, M. Yoshimoto, and H. Kawaguchi, "Microphone Array Network for Ubiquitous Sound Acquisition," in *Proc. of IEEE ICASSP*, 2010.

[26] M. Jeub, C. Herglotz, C. Nelke, C. Beaugeant, and P. Vary, "Noise Reduction for Dual-Microphone Mobile Phones Exploiting Power Level Differences," in *Proc. of IEEE ICASSP*, 2012.

[27] Y. Huang, J. Benesty, and J. Chen, *Acoustic MIMO Signal Processing.* Springer, 2006.

[28] H. Luo, J. Wang, Y. Sun, H. Ma, and X.-Y. Li, "Adaptive Sampling and Diversity Reception in Multi-hop Wireless Audio Sensor Networks," in *IEEE International Conference on Distributed Computing Systems (ICDCS)*, 2010.

[29] D. Sun and J. Canny, "A High Accuracy, Low-latency, Scalable Microphone-array System for Conversation Analysis," in *Proc. of ACM UbiComp*, 2012.

[30] L. Girod, M. Lukac, V. Trifa, and D. Estrin, "The Design and Implementation of a Self-calibrating Distributed Acoustic Sensing Platform," in *Proc. of ACM SenSys*, 2006.

[31] M. Chen, Z. Liu, L.-W. He, P. Chou, and Z. Zhang, "Energy-Based Position Estimation of Microphones and Speakers for Ad Hoc Microphone Arrays," in *IEEE Workshop on Applications of Signal Processing to Audio and Acoustics*, 2007.

[32] A. M. Ali, K. Yao, T. C. Collier, C. E. Taylor, D. T. Blumstein, and L. Girod, "An Empirical Study of Collaborative Acoustic Source Localization," in *Proc. of ACM/IEEE IPSN*, 2007.

[33] J. Sallai, P. Völgyesi, A. Lédeczi, K. Pence, T. Bapty, S. Neema, and J. R. Davis, "Acoustic Shockwave-Based Bearing Estimation," in *Proc. of ACM/IEEE IPSN*, 2013.

[34] F. Sivrikaya and B. Yener, "Time Synchronization in Sensor Networks: a Survey," *IEEE Network*, vol. 18, no. 4, 2004.

[35] D. Budnikov, I. Chikalov, I. Kozintsev, and R. Lienhart, "Distributed Array of Synchronized Sensors and Actuators," in *Proc. of European Signal Processing Conference (EUSIPCO)*, 2004.

[36] Y. Jia, Y. Luo, Y. Lin, and I. Kozintsev, "Distributed Microphone Arrays for Digital Home and Office," in *Proc. of IEEE ICASSP*, 2006.

[37] L. Keller, A. Le, B. Cici, H. Seferoglu, C. Fragouli, and A. Markopoulou, "MicroCast: Cooperative Video Streaming on Smartphones," in *Proc. of ACM MobiSys*, 2012.

[38] M. Y. Arslan, I. Singh, S. Singh, H. V. Madhyastha, K. Sundaresan, and S. V. Krishnamurthy, "Computing While Charging: Building a Distributed Computing Infrastructure Using Smartphones," in *Proc. of ACM CoNext*, 2012.

[39] G. Shen, Y. Li, and Y. Zhang, "MobiUS: Enable Together-viewing Video Experience Across Two Mobile Devices," in *Proc. of ACM MobiSys*, 2007.

[40] D. Estrin, "Participatory Sensing: Applications and Architecture," *IEEE Internet Computing*, vol. 14, no. 1, 2010.

Tracking Human Queues
Using Single-Point Signal Monitoring

Yan Wang[†], Jie Yang[‡], Yingying Chen[†]
Hongbo Liu[♯], Marco Gruteser[*], Richard P. Martin[*]
[†]Stevens Institute of Technology, Hoboken, NJ 07030, USA
[†]{ywang48,yingying.chen}@stevens.edu
[‡]Oakland University, Rochester, MI 48309, USA
[‡]yang@oakland.edu
[♯]Indiana University-Purdue University Indianapolis, Indianapolis, IN 46202, USA
[♯]hl45@iupui.edu
[*]Rutgers University, North Brunswick, NJ 08902, USA
[*]gruteser@winlab.rutgers.edu, rmartin@cs.rutgers.edu

ABSTRACT

We investigate using smartphone WiFi signals to track human queues, which are common in many business areas such as retail stores, airports, and theme parks. Real-time monitoring of such queues would enable a wealth of new applications, such as bottleneck analysis, shift assignments, and dynamic workflow scheduling. We take a minimum infrastructure approach and thus utilize a single monitor placed close to the service area along with transmitting phones. Our strategy extracts unique features embedded in signal traces to infer the critical time points when a person reaches the head of the queue and finishes service, and from these inferences we derive a person's waiting and service times. We develop two approaches in our system, one is directly feature-driven and the second uses a simple Bayesian network. Extensive experiments conducted both in the laboratory as well as in two public facilities demonstrate that our system is robust to real-world environments. We show that in spite of noisy signal readings, our methods can measure service and waiting times to within a 10 second resolution.

Categories and Subject Descriptors

H.4 [**Information Systems Applications**]: Miscellaneous

Keywords

Human Queue Monitoring; WiFi; Smartphones; Received Signal Strength

1. INTRODUCTION

The popular, almost addictive, usage of smartphones and their data-intensive apps creates novel opportunities to exploit their network traffic for monitoring and optimizing real-world processes. Research has shown, for example, how cellular call data records can be used to infer large scale transportation patterns (e.g., [13]) or how cellular signal traces allow inferring the level of congestion on roadways [4]. In this work, we ask whether signal power readings from cell phone traffic are also sufficient to monitor a much finer-scale, yet common, process: human queues.

Such queues are a familiar and often frustrating occurrence, for example in retail stores, banks, theme parks, hospitals and transportation stations. Figure 1 shows the abstraction we map onto these environments. As people arrive, the *waiting period* is the time spent waiting for service. During the *service period* people receive service, such as paying for items or checking-in travel bags. A person exits the service area during the *leaving period*. Note that we interpret the concept of a queue loosely, people do not need to stand in line but could sit in a waiting room and do not always need to be served in a strict first in, first out order. Real-time quantification of the waiting and service times in such queues allows optimizing service processes, ranging from retail, to heath care, to transportation and entertainment. For example, many hospital emergency departments surveys have average waiting times of several hours [21]. More complete waiting and service time statistics allow customers, travelers, managers and service providers make changes to their behavior and processes. For example, an airport checkpoint might be experiencing abnormal delays and require interventions by diverting screeners from queues with shorter waiting times. Customers also can benefit, for example, knowing at what times retail store checkout lines can be expected to be shorter, and a customer can decide whether to stay in the queue or go to do more urgent tasks. Managers can use such information to make staffing decisions based on the service length. For example, during particular hours in a day, service times may grow at a coffee shop due to increased demands for espresso drinks compared to other items. In such a case, it might be more effective to change the staffing to use experienced baristas as opposed to simply adding staff. A hospital emergency department may shift nursing staff to assist with triage when waiting times become too long. In the transportation field, bus and train schedules or boarding and payment processes could be adjusted.

Existing solutions to the queue monitoring problem rely on cameras [1, 16] or special sensors (e.g., infrared [24] or floor mats [2]) and usually require sensors at multiple locations. The approaches using cameras face occlusion and increased privacy issues. Bluetooth signals emanating from phones have also been used to measure travel times between two sensing points, both at airports [3] and for vehicle traffic [23]. These prior techniques using wireless networks were too coarse-grained to differentiate between the waiting and service time. Moreover, all these solutions require multiple sensors to fully monitor a single longer queue, which increases installation and system cost.

Our approach uses only a single sensor, a WiFi monitor near the head of the queue that measures the received signal strength of packets emitted from phones. Intuitively, the received signal power should follow a known pattern. As the person moves towards the service point, the phone moves closer to the monitor and the received signal power should increase. When the person is receiving service, the signal power should be very strong and relatively constant. Finally, when the person exits the service point, there should be a rapid decline in signal strength. Our approach seeks to exploit this pattern to track service and waiting times of persons in a queue. This does require, of course, that at least some people in the queue carry phones that generate traffic. In our existing system and experiments, we have used a special app to generate periodical beacons. In the future, we expect, however, that it is possible to reuse existing traffic, since it is increasingly the case as people tend to fiddle with their phones while waiting in queues and many venues now offer loyalty apps that customers may use while paying, for example, the Starbucks mobile app has more than 10 million active users [11]. While this approach may also be applicable to other wireless technologies, we have chosen WiFi in our realization because (i) its range is sufficiently large to cover the entire queue in most cases, especially for large-size queues, which usually requires the installation of multiple cameras or sensors in order to obtain the complete view of the queue; (ii) it is particularly easy to monitor WiFi traffic (compared to the complexities tracking Bluetooth frequency hopping sequences, for example); (iii) WiFi traffic is poised to increase due to the WiFi offloading trend [7].

Accurately discerning the points where the person begins and ends service is challenging, however, in this single-point monitoring system, because the multi-path, shadowing, and fading components of a signal are quite dynamic due to the movement of many people. We therefore investigate two approaches for extracting the waiting and service times from a signal trace: a direct feature-driven one and a Bayesian Network one. For both approaches, we use similar filtering techniques to reduce the impact of the dynamic environment. We experimentally evaluate both approaches in three settings: a laboratory, a coffee shop and an airport. We find a simple Bayesian classifier gives the best results, and is able to measure the waiting time to with average errors less than $10s$ and maximum errors below $20s$. Our contributions are:

- Proposing a single-point WiFi monitoring approach for human queue measurement systems that requires less infrastructure and can provide real-time service information for both business and customers.

- Designing queue measurement techniques that can distinguish between important time periods in human queues including waiting, service, and leaving times using unique WiFi signal patterns based on feature extraction and Bayesian networks.

- Leveraging the availability of multiple antennas and multiple smartphone users in the queue to accurately perform queue parameter estimation.

- Demonstrating through extensive experiments with participants randomly placed in a variety of queue patterns in real environments (e.g., a coffee shop and an airport) that it is

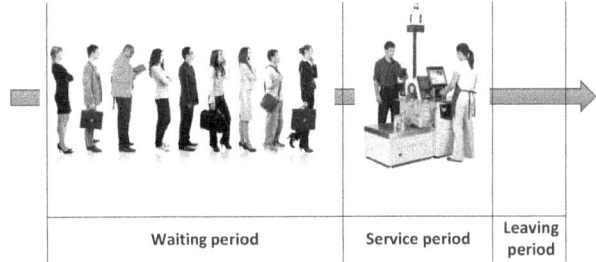

Figure 1: Important time periods and corresponding positions in a human queue.

feasible to track human queues using single-point WiFi monitoring with high accuracy.

The rest of the paper is organized as follows. In Section 2, we investigate whether a sufficient amount of WiFi users are present in human queues to facilitate queue measurements. We describe the challenges, system overview, and two core schemes to measure parameters of human queues in Section 3. We present our system implementation by leveraging multiple antennas and smartphone user traces in Section 4. In Section 5, we perform extensive evaluation of our system in real environments, i.e., a coffee shop and an airport. We discuss limitations in Section 6 and put our work into the context of related research in Section 7. Finally, we conclude in Section 8.

2. PREVALENCE OF WIFI TRAFFIC IN QUEUES

In this section, we investigate whether a sufficient number of WiFi users are present in human queues to facilitate queue measurements.

2.1 WiFi Traffic in Human Queues

An increasing number of facilities, such as retail stores, shopping malls, or airports, offer Internet access through WiFi networks to provide convenience to customers. People visiting these places tend to use the Internet through the WiFi connection because it provides faster speeds than the 3G network [10, 17] and does not count against their data cap. In addition, the increasing trend of the WiFi offloading enables smartphones to automatically switch to WiFi in popular locations where the cellular carriers operate WiFi hotspots [7]. This can be expected to lead to increasing WiFi usage in these locations.

We start by investigating the WiFi device density in a coffee shop over a one month time period. Our objective is to find the percentage of people generating WiFi traffic with their smartphones while standing in the line waiting for service. We utilize a WiFi monitor, placed close to the service desk, to passively monitor WiFi packets sent by mobile devices. To eliminate WiFi devices not in the queue, we use the heuristic that devices with a higher received signal strength (RSS) amplitude, i.e. greater than $-45dBm$, are likely to be in the queue. We have empirically determined this threshold by observing the RSS of a known smartphone placed in the queue close to the service desk. We use the MAC address extracted from captured packets to identify different devices. Meanwhile, we manually count the arrival time of each new customer and the length of the queue as the ground-truth for comparison.

Date	1/21 (noon)	1/28 (noon)	2/3 (noon)	2/7 (noon)	2/12 (noon)	2/14 (morn.)	2/16 (noon)
Time length (hrs)	2	2	2	1.5	1	1	2.5
Discoverable WiFi devices in the queue (w. Max. RSS$> -45dBm$)	24	36	88	26	37	45	84
Discoverable Bluetooth devices in the queue	7	7	6	7	6	6	8
People in the queue (manually counted)	153	82	205	78	88	87	128
Average length of the queue	2.55	1.83	5.19	4.03	3.55	5.47	5.38
Discoverable WiFi devices in the store	307	280	410	278	364	384	608

Table 1: Data collected in a coffee shop from seven days time period.

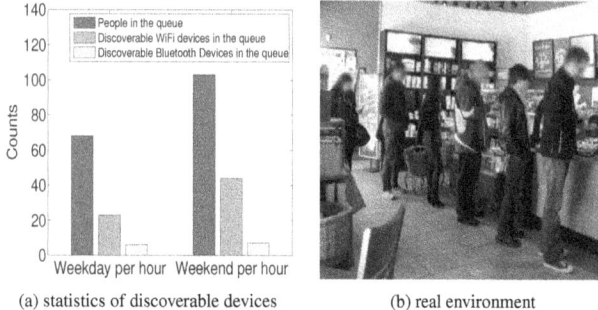

(a) statistics of discoverable devices   (b) real environment

Figure 2: Comparison of the manually counted number of people, discoverable WiFi and Bluetooth devices in queues within a coffee shop, and the illustration of customers using smartphones while waiting for service.

We show detailed data collected for seven days in Table 1. An interesting observation is that the number of discoverable WiFi devices in queues is higher when the average queue length is longer. For example, on both Feb. 3rd and Feb. 16th of 2013, the discoverable WiFi devices in queues are almost doubled compared to other days. This observation implies that a longer waiting time triggers people in the queue to use smartphones more, thus generating more WiFi traffic. We present the comparison of discoverable WiFi devices with a manual count of people in the queue over the one-month study in Figure 2. It shows that statistically there are about 34% customers using WiFi (most likely using smartphones) while waiting in queues in the coffee shop during weekdays and increases to 43% during weekends. While this analysis is based on heuristics, the result is encouraging as it indicates that the number of WiFi signal emitting devices in the queue may already be large and can be exploited for real-time human queue measurements.

2.2 Bluetooth Signals in Human Queues

Since Bluetooth is another wireless technology that has been widely used in mobile applications, we also examine the Bluetooth signals presented in a human queue of the same coffee shop for comparison. We place a Bluetooth dongle close to the service desk running a self-developed software program under Ubuntu 10.04, which can detect Bluetooth devices that are in *discoverable mode*. Because most Bluetooth modules used in mobile devices have a communication range of about 10 meters [17], all devices captured by the Bluetooth dongle are considered valid devices close enough to be within the queue. We find many few Bluetooth devices than WiFi devices in the same store on the same days. Figure 2 shows that there are about 74% and 84% less discoverable Bluetooth devices than WiFi devices during weekdays and weekends respectively in the queue. In principle, our technique should also work with Bluetooth signals, particularly with the expanded range of newer Bluetooth versions. These results support, however,

that WiFi may already be an attractive alternative since monitoring Bluetooth communications requires more effort.

3. SYSTEM DESIGN

In this section, we discuss the challenges and goals of our approach and provide an overview of our system.

3.1 Challenges and Goals

We explore the approach of using low infrastructure and low cost sensing technology that can infer important queueing times from smartphone WiFi signals. Our goal is to employ a single monitor and utilize the smartphones carried by the people waiting in the queue to perform real-time tracking of human queues. To implement such a system, we need to address a number of challenges.

Tracking Queues Using a Single Monitor. If multiple monitors (e.g., WiFi hotspots) were employed, the phone could be localized and hence the queue parameters could be derived from the localization results. However, installing additional monitors are quite costly due to installation costs. The low infrastructure approach by using only a single WiFi monitor cannot uniquely determine the phone's position. To address this challenge, our solution should be able to identify the unique characteristics presented in the smartphone's Received Signal Strength (RSS) traces, which may be utilized to perform queue parameter estimation without the need of explicitly localizing the phone.

Robustness to Real Environments. Although the distance between the smartphone and the service desk dominates the RSS, the RSS is affected by a number of factors including user movements, changing environments, and signal interference. Furthermore, different holding styles and vibrations of smartphones also cause noisy RSS readings. Thus, the system should be designed in such a way that can cope with noisy signal readings.

Identifying Queue Related RSS Traces. The RSS traces extracted from smartphones cannot be directly used to estimate queue parameters, since there could be trends of the received signal happening after the queue process that are similar to the RSS trend within the queue. An effective data calibration mechanism is required to identify the right segment of the RSS trace that includes only the important periods of queue process, i.e., the waiting period, service period, and leaving period.

3.2 System Overview

By placing a WiFi monitor close to the service area, our system can monitor human queues in real-time through examining the unique patterns exhibited in the WiFi signals, which are extracted from smartphones carried by people waiting in the queue. It can also utilize a WiFi hotspot if it is located close to the service area. Our system exploits the change of RSS trends from smartphones carried by people going through a queue process. We find that with the monitor located at the service area, each phase of the queue creates unique signal patterns that can be used to identify different

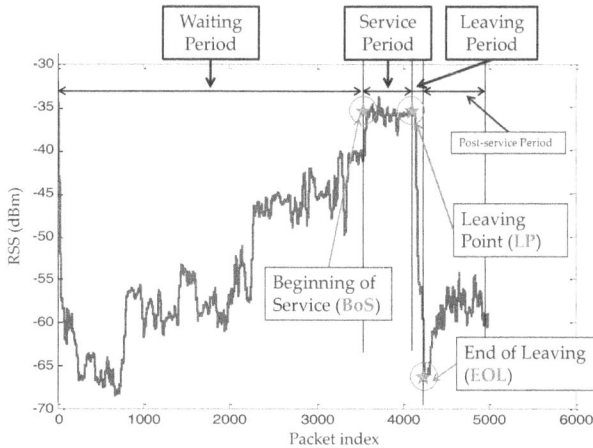

Figure 3: Illustration of special queue-related patterns embedded in the RSS trace collected from a smartphone in a human queue.

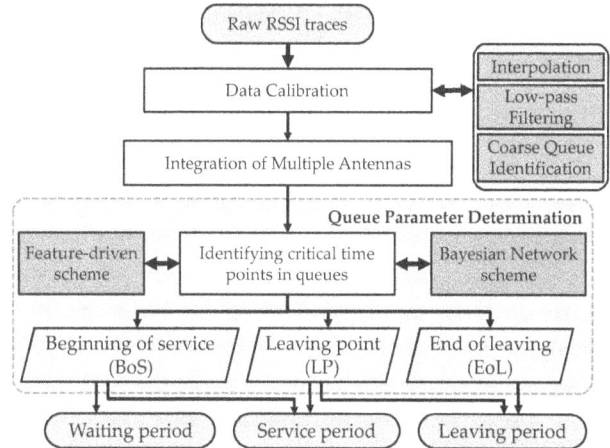

Figure 4: Overview of system flow.

periods of the queue for statistical queue measurement. For example, Figure 3 presents the RSS trace of a smartphone in a queue collected from a single WiFi monitor at the service desk in a coffee shop. We observe that the captured RSS trace reflects the pattern of the distance between the person carrying the phone to the service desk. In particular, the RSS exhibits the following unique patterns: (1) the RSS has a slowly increasing trend during the *waiting period*; (2) it then becomes stable at high RSS values when the person carrying the phone is in the *service period*; and (3) it finally drops quickly when the person leaves the service desk after having received service in his *leaving period*.

The major advantage of this solution is that it can work under real-world queue scenarios in variant environments without requiring a specialized infrastructure and incurring manpower overheads. In addition, our solution is based on the detection of the important time points associated with the service period, which involves the strongest and the most stable signal strength of the smartphone when it is at the closest position to the service desk (WiFi monitor), thus it can work in typical indoor environments with multi-path effects. Furthermore, our solution does not require all the people in the queue to carry phones. Instead, it only requires a sample of phones generating WiFi traffic to track human queues. This is increasingly the case: since people tend to use their phones in WiFi Hotspots when waiting in a queue, and many venues provide customer loyalty apps for people to use in the stores, and these could also be customized. Our feasibility analysis in Section 2 confirms this observation.

We realize our approach with three main sub-tasks: *Data Calibration*, *Integration of Multiple Antennas*, and *Queue Parameter Determination*. Figure 4 shows the flow of our system. We assume the user gets in the queue right after he enters the facility (e.g., a customer enters a coffee shop to buy coffee or a passenger gets on a platform waiting for a train). When the smartphone carried by the user is discovered by the WiFi monitor as the user goes in the queue, the WiFi monitor extracts RSS readings of this device. Based on the RSS trace, our system first performs *Data Calibration*, which aims to preserve the unique trend presented in the raw RSS trace while removing high frequency noise, and to identify segments of the RSS trace that contains related time periods for measuring queue parameters. The *Data Calibration* sub-task contains three steps: *Interpolation*, *Low-pass Filtering* and *Coarse Queue Identification*.

To filter out outliers and obtain a reliable RSS trace, the system further conducts *Integration of Multiple Antennas* by exploiting the availability of multiple antennas, which exists in many WiFi access points already. This subtask combines the selected RSS traces from two antennas in the WiFi monitor to generate an integrated RSS trace that fortifies the unique pattern of RSS associated with important time periods of the queue. Finally, *Queue Parameter Determination* implements two schemes, called: feature-driven and Bayesian Network, to infer the critical time points in the queue. The important time points: the beginning of service (BoS), leaving point (LP) and end of leaving point (EoL) are further utilized to estimate the queue parameters including waiting period, service period, and leaving period. We next present the two schemes developed in the core component *Queue Parameter Determination*. We leave the detailed presentation of *Data Calibration* and *Integration of Multiple Antennas* to the next section (Section 4).

3.3 Queue Parameter Determination

We find that the important periods of a human queue are separated by three critical time points, namely BoS, LP, and EoL, as shown in Figure 3. BoS is the first critical time point, which separates the waiting period and the service period, while LP tells when the service is done and the customer is about to leave the service desk. The third critical time point, EoL, indicates the time that the customer has left the service area, such as goes to a seat or exits the facility. By deducing these three time points, our system is able to track the important queue time periods including waiting, service, and leaving periods. Specifically, the *waiting period* is the time interval between BoS and the starting time of the trace, whereas the *service period* is the time interval between BoS and LP. And the *leaving period* is the time interval between LP and EoL.

Toward this end, we develop two schemes, called *feature-driven* and *Bayesian Network*, in our system to identify the critical time points in a human queue. The feature-driven approach utilizes the unique features extracted from RSS traces to identify these time points. Whereas the Bayesian Network scheme models the detection of BoS and LP as a probabilistic graph based on the statistics of features presented in RSS traces. Comparing these two approaches, the feature-driven scheme requires less prior knowledge on the queue while the Bayesian Network scheme produces more accurate results bounded by the probabilistic graph. We next describe the details of these two approaches.

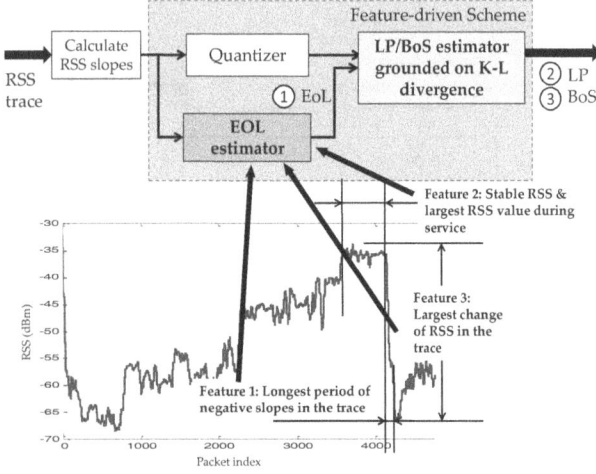

Figure 5: Flow of feature-driven scheme to find EoL, LP, and BoS in a time-reversed way.

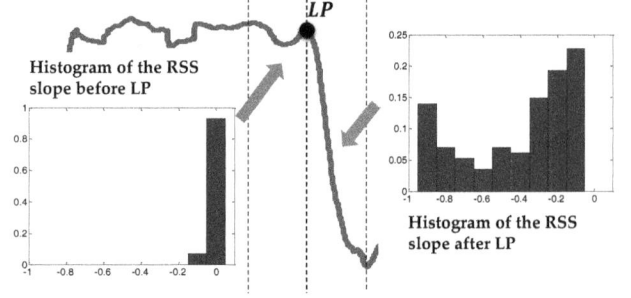

Figure 6: Histogram of the RSS slope before and after the leaving point (LP) from the RSS trace collected from a smartphone in queue.

3.3.1 Feature-Driven Scheme

When designing the feature-driven scheme, we directly apply features associated with the leaving period in the RSS trace to determine the EoL, LP, and BoS in a time-reversed manner. Because the RSS value changes dramatically when people leave the queue after service, the features associated with the leaving period are easier to extract in a reverse order. In particular, we identify three features extracted from the RSS trace associated with the leaving period:

1. The leaving period has the *longest* consecutive negative-slope segments of the selected RSS trace.

2. The RSS values before the leaving period are stable with the *highest* amplitude of the selected RSS trace.

3. The leaving period experiences the *largest* decrease of RSS in the selected RSS trace.

The feature-driven scheme consists of three components: *EoL Estimator*, *Quantizer*, and *LP/BoS Estimator*. We illustrate the flow of the feature-driven scheme in Figure 5.

EoL Estimator. Assume there is a group of M segments with consecutive negative slopes in the RSS trace $\mathbb{G} = \{G_1, \ldots, G_M\}$, and each segment G_i lasts for a period of $T_i = t_1^i - t_0^i$, where t_1^i and t_0^i denote the starting time and the ending time of that segment, respectively. The EoL estimator determines the time t_0^i to be EoL when a segment G_i is most likely to be a leaving period. To determine the likelihood of being a leaving period, we first define the significance of the three features described above as: 1) $\frac{T_i}{\max(\mathbb{T})}$, where $\mathbb{T}$ denotes time length of all the segments in $\mathbb{G}$; 2) $\frac{S_i}{\max(\mathbb{S})}$, where S_i is the average RSS over a time window L before t_1^i, and $\mathbb{S}$ denotes all such average RSS; 3) $\frac{R_i}{\max(\mathbb{R})}$, where R_i is the ratio of the RSS at t_0^i and t_1^i, and $\mathbb{R}$ denotes all such RSS ratio, respectively. We further define an utility function which is a weighted sum of the significance of the three features:

$$u_i = \alpha \cdot \frac{T_i}{\max(\mathbb{T})} + \beta \cdot \frac{S_i}{\max(\mathbb{S})} + \gamma \cdot \frac{R_i}{\max(\mathbb{R})}, \qquad (1)$$

where α, β, and γ are the weights. The leaving period thus can be determined as the segment G_i that maximizes the utility function u_i. And the time t_0^i of such a segment G_i is then declared as the

EoL. To determine the weights in Equation (1), we use a heuristic approach by counting the occurrence of each feature in a small portion of the collected traces (e.g., 20 traces) and respectively using the ratio of each feature's occurrence to the number of traces as their weights. For example, if feature 1 has been found true for 10 times in 20 traces, the weight for feature 1 is then 0.5. Based on our experiments in different scenarios (e.g., the laboratory, the Starbucks coffee shop, and the airport), we empirically find that when $\alpha = 0.4$, $\beta = 0.8$ and $\gamma = 0.8$, the unique features can be extracted from the RSS trace accurately.

Meanwhile, we compute the slopes of each RSS sample in the selected RSS trace. The *Quantizer* performs normalization and quantization on the computed RSS slopes. The detailed implementation of the Quantizer is presented in Section 4.1.3.

LP/BoS Estimator. Our feature-driven scheme then takes the input from the EoL Estimator together with the quantized RSS slopes to identify the leaving point (LP) and beginning of service point (BoS) in the queue following the temporal-reversed order. The LP/BoS Estimator takes the view point that the leaving point separates the service period and the leaving period, and thus the WiFi signals before LP is relatively stable whereas they drop dramatically after the leaving point. This useful observation indicates that the distributions of WiFi signal changes (i.e., slopes of RSS) before and after the leaving point are significantly different. Figure 6 illustrates this significant difference by showing the histogram of the two RSS slope distributions before and after LP. This inspires us to identify LP by using the K-L divergence technique to examine the distribution difference of WiFi signal changes. And LP is determined as the time point (prior to EoL) separating the RSS slopes into two parts that present the most different distributions from each other.

In particular, we calculate the distributions of quantized RSS slopes before and after each time point t_j occurring before EoL, respectively denoted as $P(K_{j-1})$ and $Q(K_j)$, $j = [1, \ldots, J]$, where J is number of time points occurring before EoL. The K-L divergence between these two distributions are derived as:

$$D_{KL}(P(K_{j-1})|Q(K_j)) = \sum_{q \in Q} P(K_{j-1} = q) \ln \frac{P(K_{j-1} = q)}{Q(K_j = q)}, \qquad (2)$$

where Q is the set of all possible values for quantized RSS slopes. LP is then determined as the time point t_j, which maximizes the K-L divergence value:

$$t_j = \arg \max_{t_j} (D_{KL}(P(K_{j-1})|Q(K_j))). \qquad (3)$$

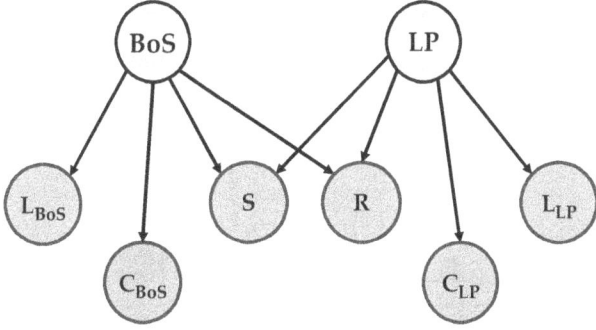

Figure 7: **Bayesian Network model in our system where the random variables** R, S, L_{LP}, C_{LP}, L_{BoS}, **and** C_{BoS} **are computed from unique features embedded in the signal traces.**

Similarly, our scheme can also employ the K-L divergence technique to identify BoS, since WiFi signals are relatively stable during the service period while they exhibit an obvious increasing trend in the waiting period.

3.3.2 Bayesian Network (BN) Scheme

The feature-driven scheme is straightforward and can effectively capture the unique patterns embedded in the WiFi signals when a smartphone is in a human queue. However, it does not consider the dependency among the features, which may place additional constraints to help identifying critical time points in tracking queues. In designing the Bayesian Network scheme, we use a Directed Acyclic Graph (DAG) to represent conditional independencies among the features extracted from the RSS trace. In DAG, a node represents a random variable, while an arrow that connects two nodes represents a direct probabilistic relation. Such a graph is then utilized to construct a *naive Bayesian* classifier [19] for LP and BoS determination. The Bayesian Network scheme first identifies all the RSS segments containing continuous positive RSS slopes and continuous negative RSS slopes respectively in the RSS trace and use them as inputs to run BoS and LP estimation using the constructed Bayesian classifier. The flow of the Bayesian Network approach is depicted in Figure 8.

In particular, we model BoS and LP as two parent nodes in the Bayesian Network and define six attributes (Boolean random variables) based on the features embedded in the RSS trace when a smartphone is in a human queue. The six random variables, R, S, L_{LP}, C_{LP}, L_{BoS}, and C_{BoS}, are represented as the child variables of BoS and LP in the Bayesian graphical model.

Based on the same unique features that we have shown in Section 3.3.1, we define the corresponding random variables as below:

- R: The average RSS within the service period is usually the highest. $R = 1$ when the mean RSS before a specific segment of continuous negative slopes is the highest of all, otherwise $R = 0$.

- S: The RSS within the service period is stable. $S = 1$ when the variation of RSS within a window W before a segment of continuous negative slopes is smaller than a threshold τ, otherwise $S = 0$.

- L_{LP}: The leaving period happens after the service period, which has the strongest RSS. $L_{LP} = 1$ when the starting time of a specific segment of continuous negative slopes is later than the time with the highest RSS value, otherwise $L_{LP} = 0$.

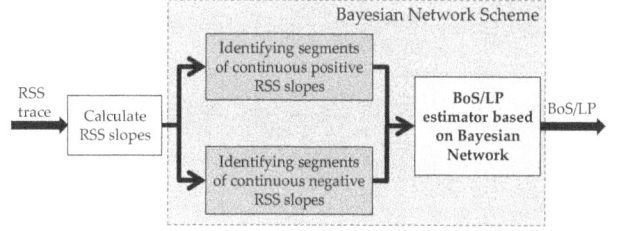

Figure 8: **Flow of the Bayesian Network scheme to find BoS and LP.**

- C_{LP}: The change of RSS after the leaving period usually exhibits the most significant decreasing trend. $C_{LP} = 1$ when the average slope of a specific segment of continuous negative slopes is the smallest of all, otherwise $C_{LP} = 0$.

- L_{BoS}: The waiting period happens before the service period, which has the strongest RSS. $L_{BoS} = 1$ when the end time of a specific segment of continuous positive slopes is earlier than the time with the highest RSS, otherwise $L_{BoS} = 0$.

- C_{BoS}: The change of RSS before the service period usually exhibits the most significant increasing trend. $C_{BoS} = 1$ when the average slope of a specific segment of continuous positive slopes is the largest of all, otherwise $C_{BoS} = 0$.

Assume the scheme identifies a set $\mathbb{U}$ of N segments with continuous positive slopes, and a set $\mathbb{G}$ of M segments with continuous negative slopes in the RSS trace. The naive Bayesian classifier considers the ending time of the segment $U_i \in \mathbb{U}$ with continuous positive slopes as BoS when the segment U_i maximizes the posterior probability:

$$\widehat{U} = \arg\max_{U_i}(P(BoS)\prod_{I \in \mathbb{I}} P(I = 1|Bos)), \qquad (4)$$

where $\mathbb{I} = \{R, S, L_{BoS}, C_{BoS}\}$, and $P(Bos) = \frac{1}{N}$. Similarly, the starting time of the segment $G_i \in \mathbb{G}$ with continuous negative slopes is considered as LP when the segment G_i maximizes the posterior probability:

$$\widehat{G} = \arg\max_{G_i}(P(LP)\prod_{F \in \mathbb{F}} P(F = 1|LP)), \qquad (5)$$

where $\mathbb{F} = \{R, S, L_{LP}, C_{LP}\}$, and $P(LP) = \frac{1}{M}$.

We adopt the traditional two-fold cross-validation approach [12] when applying the Bayesian Network scheme. We randomly separate the collected RSS traces from multiple smartphones in a queue into two folds and use one fold as the training data to learn the probability of each random variable conditioning on its parent variable. The other fold is used as the testing data to obtain the estimation error. Then we switch these two folds and calculate the estimation error again. The final estimation error of the system is the average of the estimation errors observed from previous two tests.

4. IMPLEMENTATION AND LAB EXPERIMENTS

In this section, we present *Data Calibration* and *Signal Integration* sub-tasks in our system. We then describe two approaches to track the important time periods of human queues: *single/multiple antenna* and *single/multiple user*. Furthermore, we provide an evaluation on different queue patterns and energy consumption analysis of our approach.

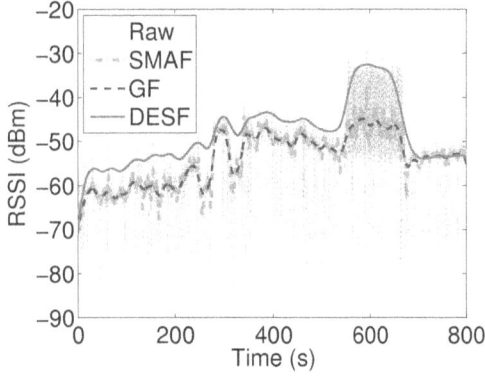

(a) Different filters

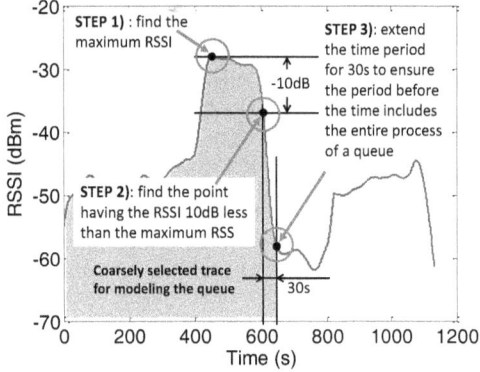

(b) Coarse queue identification

Figure 9: Data calibration: (a) comparison of results from the simple moving average filter (SMAF), the dynamic exponential smoothing filter (DESF) and the gaussian filter (GF); (b) illustration of Coarse Queue Identification: identifying the RSS segment containing the entire process of a human queue.

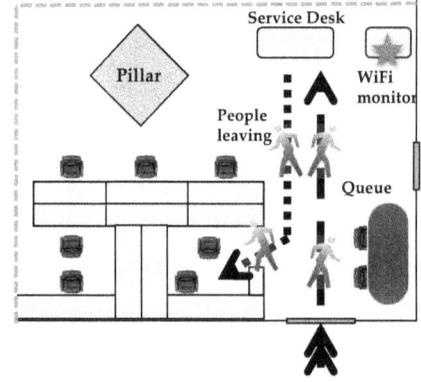

(a) Experimental setup in the lab

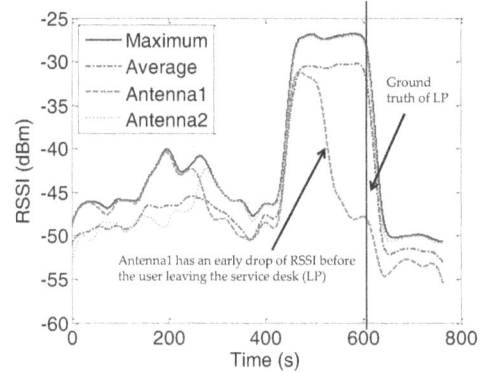

(b) Compare single/multiple antennas

Figure 10: Queue measurement in the laboratory: (a) illustration of Experimental setup; (b) comparison of RSSI traces from two individual antennas and the integrated RSSI trace using both antennas.

4.1 Data Calibration to Maintain Signal Reliability

Although the RSS value is governed by the distance between the smartphone and the monitor, the RSS readings are quite noisy due to the multi-path, shadowing, and fading components of a signal as people move. They are also affected by the way people hold the phones. Further, the collected RSS traces may contain irrelevant time periods, for example, the period after people leave the queue. The *Data calibration* sub-task aims to clean the noisy data, identify the relevant signal segment containing the queue process, and preserve the unique patterns in the signal trace.

4.1.1 Data Interpolation

This step is used to interpolate the RSS samples in evenly spaced time series as we observe that even with an app broadcasting beacon packets periodically, the interval between two adjacent RSS samples has a small variation due to packet delay. Given a sampled RSS trace starting at t_0, we interpolate the RSS trace at the time points $[t_0, t_0 + \Delta, t_0 + 2\Delta, \ldots]$, where Δ is the interpolation step. In our experiments, we find an interpolation step of $0.1s$ is small enough to produce sufficient samples for queue parameter determination.

4.1.2 Low-pass Filtering

Low-pass filtering aims to remove high frequency noise (due to environment dynamics) and yet capture the statistical features pre-

sented in the trace. We experiment with three low-pass filters: simple moving average filter (SMAF), dynamic exponential smoothing filter (DESF) and Gaussian filter (GF). Figure 9 (a) shows the raw RSS trace and the resulted trace after applying these three filters. We observe that both SMAF and GF preserve the rough trend of the trace but fail to capture the exact time points when people arriving at the service desk and moving away after got service due to they has slow roll-off and poor stopband attenuation. We find that DESF not only returns the nicely fitted curve but also preserves those critical points in the RSS trace. This is because DESF is an exponential smoother that changes its smoothing factor dynamically according to previous samples. We thus choose the DESF in our system to remove high frequency noise while preserving the features in the RSS trace. Specifically, we implement DESF based on following equitation:

$$s_i = \begin{cases} \alpha \cdot s_{i-1} + (1 - \alpha) \cdot x_i, \text{if } x_i < s_{i-1} \\ (1 - \alpha) \cdot s_{i-1} + \alpha \cdot x_i, \text{if } x_i \geq s_{i-1}, \end{cases} \quad (6)$$

where s_i is the output sample and x_i is the input sample, s_{i-1} is the previous smoothed sample, α is the smoothing factor that we can choose from $(0.5, 1)$ to favor the samples with larger values.

4.1.3 Coarse Queue Identification

This step is to identify the signal segment that belongs to the human process queue as the collected trace may include the periods that people have left the queue already but still within the monitoring range of the WiFi monitor. The irrelevant time periods con-

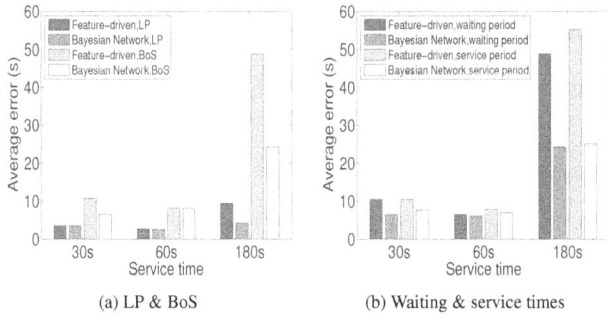

(a) LP & BoS   (b) Waiting & service times

Figure 11: Single-user and single-antenna approach: performance comparison of the feature-driven and Bayesian Network schemes under different service times in laboratory.

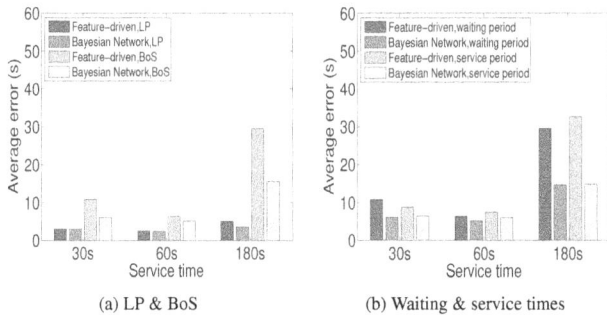

(a) LP & BoS   (b) Waiting & service times

Figure 12: Single-user and two-antenna approach: performance comparison of the feature-driven and Bayesian Network schemes under different service times in Laboratory.

tain useless information and may even affect the accuracy of queue parameter determination due to unpredictable behaviors of people after leaving the queue.

We perform three steps to remove irrelevant time periods: 1) find the time point having the maximum RSS of the entire trace; 2) examine the RSS after that time point to locate the time when the difference between the RSS value and the maximum RSS is larger than a threshold, for example $-10dB$, which is large enough to fall into the leaving period, and 3) remove the time periods after a time interval (e.g., the leaving period is usually within $30s$) on top of the time point we identified in step 2 to ensure that the leaving time period is not excluded. We illustrate these three steps in Figure 9 (b).

Quantizer. After coarse queue identification, we apply a first order linear regression to generate the slope for the RSS segment centered at each RSS sample. The resulting RSS slopes are then normalized and linearly quantized before input into the queue parameter determination algorithms (i.e., feature-driven or Bayesian Network schemes). For normalization and quantization, we use 11 negative levels between $[-1, -0.9, \ldots, -0.1, 0]$ when estimating LP and 11 positive levels between $[0, 0.1, \ldots, 0.9, 1]$ when estimating BoS.

4.2 Inference Using Single and Multiple Antennas

We next show our system implementation with a single antenna as well as two antennas at the WiFi monitor, and evaluate their impacts.

We first conduct experiments with human queues in a laboratory setup as shown in Figure 10 (a). We present the extensive evaluation of our system in two public facilities in Section 5. We place

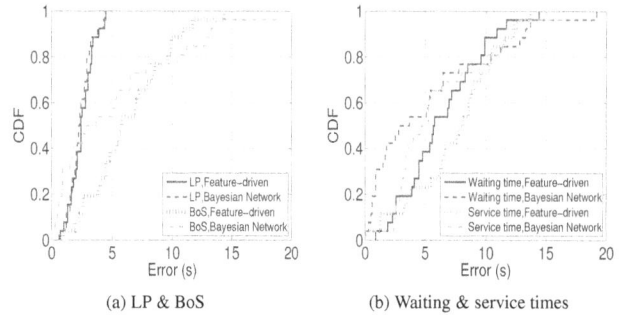

(a) LP & BoS   (b) Waiting & service times

Figure 13: Single-user and two-antenna approach: error CDF using the feature-driven and Bayesian Network schemes under the short ($60s$) service time in Laboratory.

a WiFi monitor equipped with two antennas at the service desk to capture WiFi signals. An Android app is developed to send beacon packets at the rate of $10pkt/sec$ to simulate the normal WiFi traffic, such as the traffic generated by the Starbucks mobile app. We experiment with three different service times, $30s$, $60s$, and $180s$, representing *short*, *normal* and *long* service times, respectively. In total we collect 90 traces in the laboratory environment and we use two-fold cross-validation for evaluation. We calculate the estimation error of the relevant time points and important time periods with regard to the manually logged ground-truth. In our experiments, we have both line-of-sight and non-line-of-sight scenarios, since the signals from smartphones in most cases are blocked by human bodies in the queue.

4.2.1 Single Antenna Approach

We first study the performance of the feature-driven and Bayesian Network schemes based on the signals received from a single antenna at the WiFi monitor. Because the leaving period is a brief period that facilitates the derivation of the service period, in the rest of this paper, we will focus on presenting the results of estimating waiting and service periods. Figure 11(a) compares the average error of estimating the LP and BoS under different lengths of the service time. We observe that both the feature-driven and BN schemes perform well under short ($30s$) and normal ($60s$) service times with the average error less than $10s$. We find that under the long service time ($180s$), the BN scheme outperforms the feature-driven scheme. Moreover, Figure 11(b) depicts the average error of tracking the waiting and service times derived from the estimated BoS and LP. We observe the average error of both waiting and service times is less than $10s$ under short and normal service times. Under the long service times, the BN scheme also outperforms the feature-driven scheme by about 50%, although both schemes experience performance degradation. This is because the BN scheme considers the conditional relationship among multiple features and thus places a tighter bound on the critical queue points estimation even when large RSS fluctuation is experienced during a long service time period.

4.2.2 Multiple Antenna Approach

When multiple antennas are available, integration of signals from them may help to mitigate the multi-path effects and make the wireless signal reception robust to environment dynamics. It is common for a WiFi monitor (e.g., WiFi access point) to have two antennas. We perform a study of integrating the signals from two antennas of the WiFi monitor in our laboratory using two strategies: 1) *Maximum:* taking the maximum RSS from two antennas, 2) *Average:* averaging RSS from two antennas. Figure 10 (b) compares the RSS

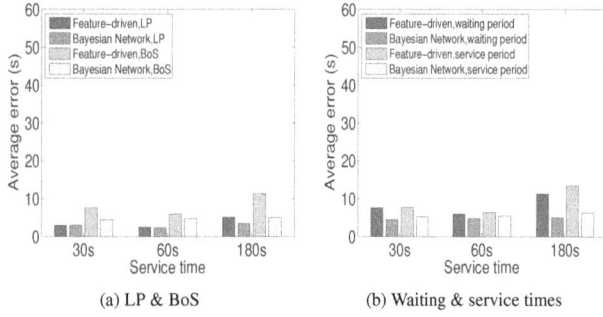

(a) LP & BoS   (b) Waiting & service times

Figure 14: Two-user and two-antenna approach: performance comparison of the feature-driven and Bayesian Network schemes under different service times in Laboratory.

trace from each antenna and the resulted RSS trace after combining from two antennas applying the two strategies. We find that although the RSS from the Antenna 2 drops quickly before reaching LP (affected by multi-path effects and dynamically changed environments), the integrated RSS traces, both *maximum* and *average*, accurately reflect each critical time point in the queue.

Figure 12 shows the average error of BoS and LP estimation and the derived waiting and service times in the laboratory using the *maximum* signal integration strategy (Note that the *average* strategy results in similar performance). Comparing to single antenna results shown in Figure 11, the average error in both Figure 12 (a) and (b) has been reduced over 30% under the long service time, indicating the integration of multiple antennas is highly effective in reducing large errors caused by signal fluctuations. Furthermore, Figure 13 depicts the cumulative distribution function (CDF) of the estimation error of the related time points and time periods in queue under the normal service time. The results confirm that the estimation error of LP is less than $4s$ for 80 percentile and the maximum error for time periods estimation is less than $20s$.

4.3 Inference Using Multiple Users

With the increasing usage of smartphones, it is common to have back-to-back smartphones presenting in the queue. The crucial time points, e.g. BoS and LP, of such back-to-back smartphones have strong correlations. The BoS of the subsequent smartphone happens very soon after the LP of the prior neighbor smartphone. This kind of correlation among neighboring phones can contribute to reducing estimation uncertainties when tracking human queues.

In particular, we observe that the LP estimation error is usually 50% smaller than that of BoS, suggesting that we can leverage the LP estimation of the prior phone as a reference to bound the BoS estimation of the subsequent phone in the queue. Toward this end, we develop a simple yet effective process after estimating BoS of the subsequent smartphone. We compare the estimated BoS of the subsequent smartphone to the estimated LP of its prior neighbor phone: if the difference is larger than a threshold θ, we use the LP of the prior smartphone plus θ as the estimated BoS of the subsequent phone, otherwise we consider the estimation of BoS is accurate and keep it. Theoretically the LP of prior phone should be the same as the BoS of the subsequent phone. However due to the delay of people's movement to the service desk, there could be a time difference between these two. In our approach, we utilize this time delay to determine the θ, which is about $5s$ empirically.

Figure 14 shows the two-antenna results when using the correlation between two smartphone users. Comparing to the BoS estimation errors when using a single user's RSS trace (in Figure 12), we observe a 25% improvement in BoS estimation under the short

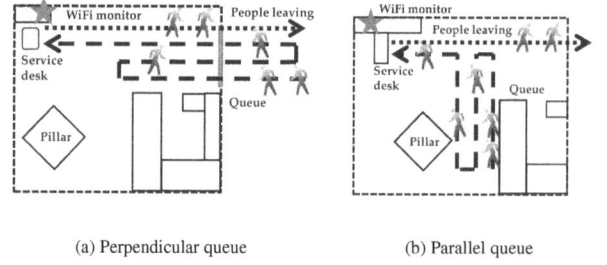

(a) Perpendicular queue   (b) Parallel queue

Figure 15: Two cases of the snaking queue in laboratory.

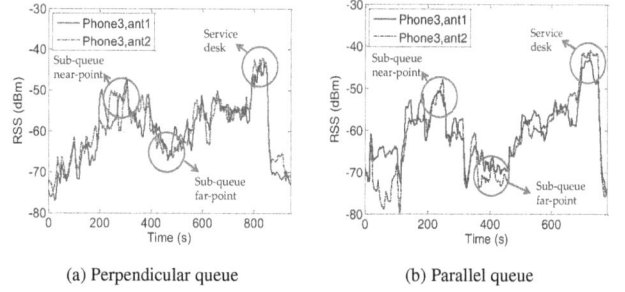

(a) Perpendicular queue   (b) Parallel queue

Figure 16: Example: RSS traces of one smartphone user in two cases of the snaking queue show clearly up-down trends corresponding to the positions of the user in queues.

and normal service times and about 60% improvement under the long service time. In addition, we observe the similar improvement in waiting and service times estimation. This encouraging observation confirms that leveraging the correlation among multiple users in the queue can help reduce large errors when tracking the important time periods in human queues with a single-point signal monitor.

4.4 Evaluation on Snaking Queues

In many scenarios, queues are formed not only in a straight line, but also in folding or zig-zag patterns with multiple subqueues. It is thus important to evaluate the flexibility of our schemes in handling queues with different patterns such as folding or zig-zag queues. We consider a general snaking queue consisting of subqueues with multiple straightlines. We study two representative cases of snaking queues in the laboratory environment: *perpendicular queue* and *parallel queue*. The moving direction of the subqueues in the *perpendicular queue* is perpendicular to the service desk, while they are in parallel to the service desk in the *parallel queue*. The experimental setup of these two queue patterns are illustrated in Figure 15(a) and (b) respectively. The same single monitor is utilized to collect WiFi signals from smartphones. We leave the evaluation in real environments to the next section.

Figure 16 depicts the signal traces collected from these two cases of snaking queues during our experiments. We observe clear and slow up-down trends in the signal trace when the user moves from one subqueue to another in both types of queues. After the user receives the service and leaves the queue finally, a sharp signal drop is observed just as in the single-line queue. Additionally, Figure 17 shows the average estimation error in waiting and service times of snaking queues when the service time is around $60s$ and the waiting time is around $500s$. We utilize the maximum signal integration strategy to combine readings from two antennas before the queue parameter determination. We observe that our feature-driven and Bayesian Network schemes can achieve low estimation errors in

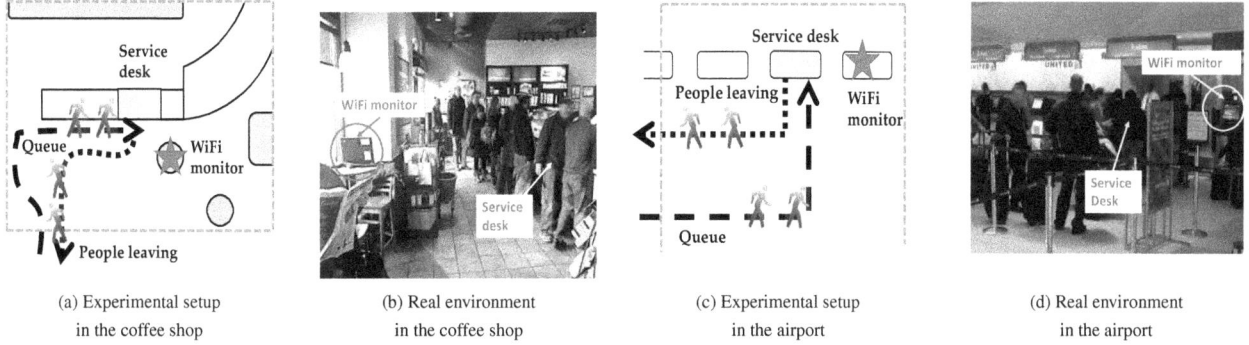

(a) Experimental setup in the coffee shop

(b) Real environment in the coffee shop

(c) Experimental setup in the airport

(d) Real environment in the airport

Figure 18: Illustration of experimental setups and real environments in a coffee shop (a and b) and an airport (c and d).

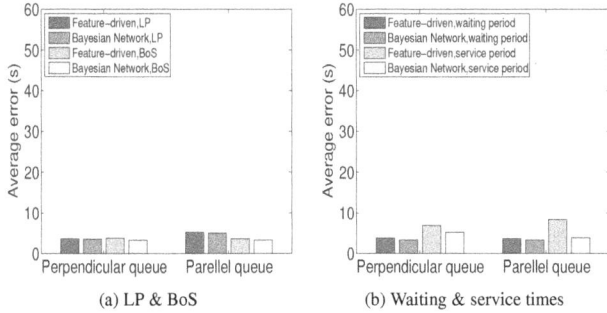

(a) LP & BoS

(b) Waiting & service times

Figure 17: Evaluation of snaking queues in laboratory using single-user and two-antenna approach: feature-driven and Bayesian Network schemes.

both types of snaking queues. Specifically, the average LP and BoS estimation errors are less than $6s$, and the average errors of waiting and service times estimation are about $4s$ and $8s$, respectively. These results are comparable to the ones obtained in single-line queues. This is because our schemes utilize a time-reversed manner to examine the signal traces and the unique features embedded in the signal traces (e.g., the largest signal drop is observed when the user leaves the service desk; the highest and stable signal values are encountered when the user is receiving the service) are still preserved even though the RSS goes up and down when the users go through the snaking queues.

4.5 Energy Consumption Analysis

Our approach require the WiFi interface remains alive during the queue process, we estimate the energy overhead of our approach by utilizing the tool and methodology in [25]. The main power consumption component on the smartphone is an app (e.g., customer loyalty app or a customized app) periodically broadcasting beacons through WiFi. We find that sending these broadcasting beacon packets for $5mins$ (which is the average length of RSS traces that include the entire queue process) with $10pkt/s$ rate takes about 54.3 Joule, which is about $180mW$. Furthermore, with a reduced packet sending rate at $5pkt/s$, our approach can achieve similar estimation accuracy while the power consumption keeps as low as $80mW$. This is much smaller than the average power consumption of a phone (e.g., HTC Evo 4G lasts 12.7 hours with average power of $450mW$). Therefore we conclude that our approach does not pose a burden for the battery life of smartphones.

5. PROTOTYPE EVALUATION IN REAL ENVIRONMENTS

In this section, we evaluate our system of tracking human queues in two real environments with three types of smartphones.[1]

5.1 Experimental Scenarios

To evaluate our system, we conduct experiments in a coffee shop and an airport (a check-in line for domestic flights with both automated machine and a human representative) for over 20 hours and 6 hours, respectively. During the experiments, we place a WiFi monitor close to the service desk in the coffee shop and the check-in desk in the airport. In each round of the experiment, the participants turn on our app to generate WiFi traffic when they get into the queue. Our system tracks the human queues waiting for service in both the coffee shop and the airport as illustrated in Figure 18. The WiFi monitor is made of an Alix system including two $100M$ Ethernet interfaces and two Wistron NeWeb CM9 802.11a/b/g-based WiFi radio modules connecting to two separated antennas. The Alix system runs on a modified Linux OS that allows running customized software to collect and process data. We developed a java program to let the Alix system log RSS traces based on phones' MAC address in the queue. We note that only RSS and the corresponding time stamps are preserved for offline study. The program can fetch the RSS trace per MAC address through the Ethernet connection to further track important time periods of the queue. To validate our system, we do not need to involve many participants inside the same queue. For example, we only place 5 participants in the service queue with the queue length ranging from 7 to 12 people and track the signal changes of their smartphones. These smartphones include HTC 3D, HTC EVO 4G, and Nexus One. In total we collected 72 traces in the coffee shop and 54 traces in the airport. Our scenarios have included both line-of-sight and none-line-of-sight scenarios, and basically the non-line-of-sight scenarios are the majority of the cases. The queue in the coffee shop experiences a normal service time of about $60s$, while the queue in the airport presents a longer average service time around $180s$. We calculate the estimation error with regard to the manually logged ground-truth of the waiting, service, and leaving time.

5.2 Evaluation in a Coffee Shop

We first evaluate the effectiveness of our system in a coffee shop. Figure 19 presents the cumulative distribution function (CDF) of estimation errors in the coffee shop when using the signal integration of two antennas on single user traces. In general, Bayesian Network scheme achieves better accuracy than the feature-driven

---

[1]This project has obtained IRB approval.

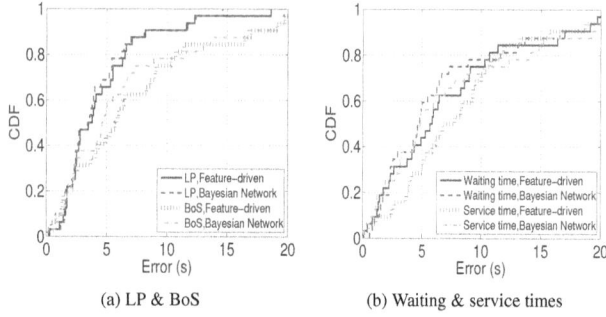

(a) LP & BoS   (b) Waiting & service times

Figure 19: Coffee shop using single-user and two-antenna approach: error CDF using the feature-driven and Bayesian Network schemes with normal service time around $60s$.

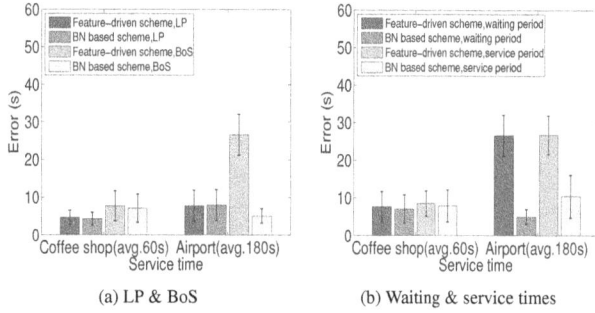

(a) LP & BoS   (b) Waiting & service times

Figure 20: Coffee shop and airport with single-user and two-antenna approach: performance comparison of the feature-driven and Bayesian Network schemes.

scheme. Particularly, Figure 19(a) shows that the median error of LP and BoS estimation is about $4s$ and $5s$ respectively for both schemes. And the median errors of the derived waiting and service time periods are less than $7.5s$ as shown in Figure 19(b). Given the ground-truth of the average service time, the estimation error of the service period is only about 11%. This indicates that our system can track human queues with high accuracy by using only a single-point signal monitor and a sample of phones in the queue.

5.3 Coffee Shop and Airport Performance Comparison

Next, we compare the performance of our system in a coffee shop and an airport with average service time around $60s$ and $180s$ respectively.

Feature-driven scheme. Figure 20(a) shows that the average LP estimation error using feature-driven scheme is low in both environments, around $5s$ and $7s$ for the coffee shop and airport respectively. However, we observe that the average error of BoS estimation in the airport increases, which results in higher average errors on estimating the waiting and service times as shown in Figure 20(b). This error is about 15% of the average service time obtained from the ground-truth, which is a small portion of the total service time and is still under the acceptable range. In addition, this observation is also compatible to the experimental results obtained in the laboratory environment with the long service time. We also observe that the standard deviation of the estimation errors is lower in the coffee shop (around $4s$) and about $8s$ in the airport.

Bayesian Network scheme. Comparing to the feature-driven scheme, the Bayesian Network scheme provides consistent low estimation errors in both environments: The LP and BoS estimation errors are less than $8s$ for both coffee shop and airport. Whereas

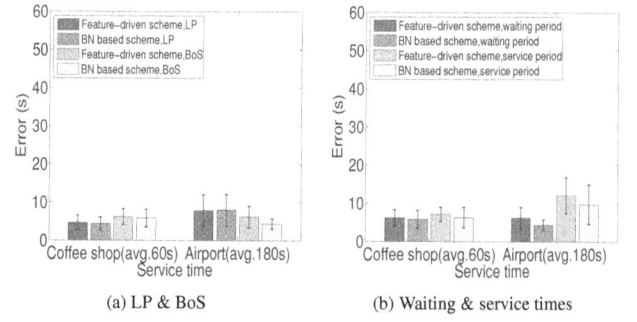

(a) LP & BoS   (b) Waiting & service times

Figure 21: Coffee shop and airport, two-user and two-antenna approach: performance comparison of the feature-driven and Bayesian Network schemes with different service times.

the waiting and service times estimation achieves low average errors less than $8s$ in coffee shop and about $5s$ and $10s$ in the airport, respectively. The standard deviation of estimation errors in both environments is around $3s$ to $7s$. Because passengers in the airport have to pause at a stop line that is about 7 feet from the service desk before they are allowed to proceed to the service desk, this behavior contributes to a more obvious increasing RSS trend when the passenger goes up for service and helps the Bayesian Network scheme maintains its performance to identify the service periods accurately under long service times. We conclude that the Bayesian Network scheme is more robust to real environments but with higher computational cost than the feature-driven scheme.

5.4 Leveraging Multiple Users

Furthermore, we leverage the presence of multiple users in a queue to improve the BoS estimation in both real environments. We follow the same procedure as described in Section 4.3. To make a fair comparison, we apply the same threshold as that in laboratory experiments to both real environments, i.e., $\theta = 5s$. Figure 21 (a) shows that by utilizing the LP estimated from the RSS trace of the prior smartphone, the BoS estimation error of the subsequent smartphone is significantly reduced when using the feature-driven scheme. Comparing to Figure 20, the average BoS estimation error in the airport has about 50% improvement, which is compatible to the results when the Bayesian Network scheme is applied. Additionally, Figure 21 (b) shows that the estimation error of waiting and service times in the airport also have about 50% improvement. Both feature-driven and Bayesian Network schemes reduce the error to $5s$ and $10s$ for waiting and service periods, respectively. The standard deviation of the estimation error is also reduced to about $2s$ in the coffee shop and $6s$ in the airport. This result suggests that employing two consecutive smartphone users (when available) in the queue is helpful to make our system more robust under real-world scenarios.

5.5 Evaluation with Snaking Queues

Finally, to evaluate the performance of our system under snaking queues in real environments, we find a second coffee shop with the presence of a snaking queue as illustrated in Figure 22. We place the WiFi monitor on the service desk, which is about $5m$ away from the nearest point in the sub-queue, and the average service time and waiting time in the coffee shop is about $60s$ and $290s$, respectively. There are about 40 people in the store. Figure 23(a) shows that the average estimation error of the waiting and service times are both less than $10s$ for both the feature-driven and Bayesian Network schemes. In addition, Figure 23(b) presents the CDF of the errors of waiting and service time estimation. It is encouraging that the

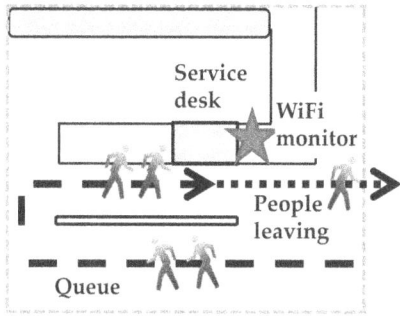

Figure 22: Illustration of experimental setup in a second coffee shop with the presence of a snaking queue.

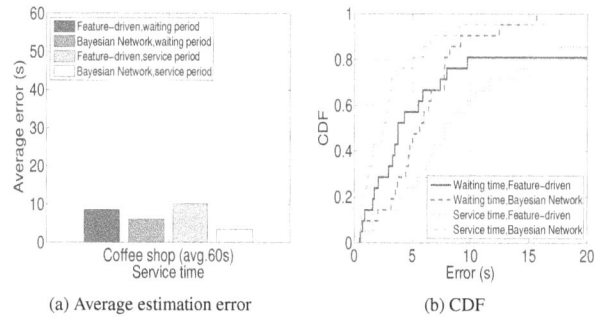

(a) Average estimation error

(b) CDF

Figure 23: Performance under a snaking queue in a second coffee shop using single-user and two-antenna approach: statistics of estimation errors of waiting and service times.

results are comparable to those with single-line queues, indicating that our queue parameter estimation system is flexible and scalable to queues with different patterns.

6. DISCUSSION

The results show that our WiFi-based solution can measure different kinds of queues, especially longer queues, with only a single monitoring station. Earlier camera solutions are prone to occlusion and may require multiple cameras (networked together) to provide a complete measurement. Multi-camera setups are more costly in hardware and installation and may encounter privacy concerns because customers' facial identities are captured by the cameras. There are still, however, some remaining challenges and opportunities for future work that we discuss below.

Opportunistic WiFi Traffic. Additional work may be needed to generalize the system to other WiFi traffic patterns, especially when regular beacons are not available. Our current experiments relied on an app that generates periodic WiFi packet transmissions. While it should be possible to add such functionality to apps that are frequently used in certain queues (e.g., frequent customer apps or airline checkin apps), it would also be desirable for this system to opportunistically use existing WiFi traffic from persons in a queue such as traffic from watching videos, streaming music, checking email, or reading news. Some of these traffic sources are likely to be more sporadic and it is possible that the traffic from a phone stops while the person is still waiting in the queue which poses additional challenges for estimating queue parameters accurately. There are a couple of possible solutions to address these problems: (1) the system can filter out traces that do not possess the sharp drop signal pattern associated with leaving the queue, because this trace is likely incomplete; (2) the system could aggregate multiple signal traces from different users in the queue to reduce the uncertainty of the queue parameter estimation. Although a single phone user in the queue may not be sufficient, the system may still be able to estimate the queue parameters accurately with the help from multiple smartphone users in the queue.

Existing WiFi Access Points. An alternative to deploying a dedicated monitoring device is to utilize existing access points (APs) to capture the WiFi traffic and perform queue measurements. While attractive because the use of multiple APs could improve accuracy, this requires appropriate interfaces to obtain station RSS traces and the placement of existing APs may not be ideal to detect the features we have used in this system. In particular, existing APs are likely placed to maximize coverage in higher locations and may not be close to the service desk of the queue. This means that the signal drop after service can be less pronounced. Still, when appropriate

RSS interfaces are available, this queue monitoring system could potentially make use of existing WiFi infrastructures.

Queue Patterns. Although we show that our queue parameter estimation system can cover a broad range of scenarios, there still exists queues that can present challenges. One are disorganized queues such as those at bus stops or train-station platforms, where the service time is short (e.g., people getting on the bus) and there are no clear first-in and first-out (FIFO) service patterns. Other challenging queues are those in relatively small spaces without pronounced leaving patterns after the service. In such cases, additional or different features need to be identified for integration into our feature-driven and Bayesian Network schemes. For example, when dealing with disorganized queues, new unique features could include a constant observation of multiple mobile devices with stable or small-varying signals for a long period producing a temporal cluster (e.g., people waiting at the bus stop) followed by near-simultaneous departures (e.g., people getting on the bus and departing). These new features will help to estimate critical queue parameters.

7. RELATED WORK

The prevalence of wireless technology and smartphone sensors has enabled great convenience on measuring people's group behavior in daily life. The habitual nature of human mobility in wireless networks have been well investigated [14, 15, 20]. For example, Kim and Kotz analyze users' mobility characteristics including pause time, speed, and direction of movements based on the WiFi traces [14]. And many works [18, 22] recognize human activities (for example walking, sitting, talking, running) by exploiting the readily available sensing capabilities on smartphones such as audio and accelerometer sensors. These works indicate it is feasible to study human group behaviors using existing wireless technology and smartphones.

Turning to examining people staying time in retail stores and business areas, Manweiler et al. [17] designs a coarse-grained dwell-time prediction framework in retail store environments by leveraging the accelerometer and gyroscope sensor readings and WiFi signals from smartphones. Ghosh et al. [8] determines arrival counts and temporal variations, which can be utilized to model the connection time of a user, by modeling the characteristics of traffic observed at a large number of public WiFi hotspots. An anonymous Bluetooth tracking system is deployed at the Indianapolis International Airport to measure the time of passengers staying at security checkpoints [3]. However, none of above works provide detail information to track human queues.

As a particular form of group behavior, queueing has also been studied for many years. The broad utility of queueing in real environments could benefit both service providers as well as customers to adjust their behavior and process accordingly. However, the assumptions of classical queueing theory may not be applicable to model real-world situations exactly [9]. Existing solutions to the queue monitoring problem often rely on additional infrastructures with multiple sensors with high costs and maintenance overheads. For example, the Swedish pavilion at the 2010 World Expo in Shanghai uses multiple video cameras to count people in queues [1] and sensors including light barriers, switching mats, and Bluetooth are exploited to measure the travel and service times in airports [2, 3]. Infrared sensor technique also provides a solution to model vehicle queues on highways [24]. Furthermore, there are several works utilizing virtual queue system to monitor and provide queue information in theme parks [5] and hospitals [6]. But the virtual queue system cannot track human queues in real time. The novelty of our work is that we explore to use a singl-point signal monitor to track human queues leveraging existing WiFi traffic from smartphones in queue. To the best of our knowledge, this work is the first to provide a low infrastructure solution that can accurately estimate queue parameters.

8. CONCLUSION

In this paper, we present a low-infrastructure approach for tracking human queues by extracting unique WiFi signal patterns from smartphones in queues. The approach only requires a small fraction of people in the queue using WiFi on their smartphones and in contrast to earlier solutions needs only a single signal monitor. The insight that the signals from smartphones in a queue follow a predictable pattern as they move through the queue not only allows us to monitor the total time spent inside the queue but also distinguish different phases such as, waiting, service and leaving periods, and estimate the parameters in a queueing model. We propose two core schemes to recognize critical time points that separate these phases: one directly uses special signal features, and the other is based on a Bayesian Network model that considers not only the special features, but also the relation between them.

We demonstrate the generality of our approach applied to a variety of queue patterns through extensive experiments including laboratory, coffee shop, and airport. We observe that our system yields only about $5s$ estimation error when service time is short and normal (about $30s$ and $60s$). Even with service time as long as $180s$, our approaches can achieve the estimation error less than $10s$, which is accurate comparing to the length of service time. Although we only experimented with a first-in first-out queueing process, most other processes still fit into our simplified model, because we leave the service order undefined.

9. ACKNOWLEDGEMENT

This work is supported in part by the National Science Foundation Grants CNS1217387, CCF1018270, CNS1040735, and CNS 0845896.

10. REFERENCES

[1] MultiQ at Shanghai World Expo 2010. http://www.multiq.com/wpcontent/uploads/2013/05/case_study_shanghai_world_expo_2010.pdf.

[2] D. Bauer, M. Ray, and S. Seer. Simple sensors used for measuring service times and counting pedestrians. *Transportation Research Record: Journal of the Transportation Research Board*, 2214(1):77–84, 2011.

[3] D. M. Bullock and et.al. Automated measurement of wait times at airport security. *Transportation Research Record*, 2010.

[4] G. Chandrasekaran and et.al. Vehicular speed estimation using received signal strength from mobile phones. In *ACM Ubicomp*, 2010.

[5] R. F. Cope III, R. F. Cope, and H. E. Davis. Disney's virtual queues: A strategic opportunity to co-brand services? *Journal of Business & Economics Research*, 2011.

[6] D. Dickson, R. C. Ford, and B. Laval. Managing real and virtual waits in hospitality and service organizations. *Cornell Hotel and Restaurant Administration Quarterly*, 2005.

[7] S. Dimatteo, P. Hui, B. Han, and V. Li. Cellular traffic offloading through wifi networks. In *IEEE MASS*, 2011.

[8] A. Ghosh, R. Jana, V. Ramaswami, J. Rowland, and N. Shankaranarayanan. Modeling and characterization of large-scale wi-fi traffic in public hot-spots. In *IEEE INFOCOM*, 2011.

[9] D. Gross, J. F. Shortle, J. M. Thompson, and C. M. Harris. *Fundamentals of Queueing Theory*. Wiley-Interscience, 2008.

[10] D. Hanchard. FCC chairman forecasts wireless spectrum crunch. http://www.zdnet.com, 2010.

[11] R. Handford. Starbucks hits more than 10m active app users. http://www.mobileworldlive.com/starbucks-hits-more-than-10m-active-app-users, 2013.

[12] T. Hastie, R. Tibshirani, and J. H. Friedman. *The elements of statistical learning: data mining, inference, and prediction*. New York: Springer-Verlag, 2001.

[13] S. Isaacman and et.al. Human mobility modeling at metropolitan scales. In *ACM MobiSys*, 2012.

[14] M. Kim and D. Kotz. Extracting a mobility model from real user traces. In *IEEE INFOCOM*, 2006.

[15] B. Liang and Z. J. Haas. Predictive distance-based mobility management for multidimensional PCS networks. *IEEE/ACM Transaction on Networking*, 2003.

[16] I. I. S. Ltd.". Queue management. http://www.irisys.co.uk/queue-management/, 2013.

[17] J. Manweiler, N. Santhapuri, R. R. Choudhury, and S. Nelakuditi. Predicting length of stay at wifi hotspots. In *IEEE INFOCOM*, 2013.

[18] E. Miluzzo and et.al. Sensing meets mobile social networks: the design, implementation and evaluation of the cenceme application. In *ACM SenSys*, 2008.

[19] A. Mittal and A. Kassim. *Bayesian network technologies: applications and graphical models*. IGI publishing, 2007.

[20] A. J. Nicholson and B. D. Noble. Breadcrumbs: forecasting mobile connectivity. In *ACM MobiCom*, 2008.

[21] I. of Medicine (US). *Hospital-Based Emergency Care: At the Breaking Point*. National Academy Press, 2007.

[22] M. Rabbi, S. Ali, T. Choudhury, and E. Berke. Passive and in-situ assessment of mental and physical well-being using mobile sensors. In *ACM UbiComp*, 2011.

[23] I. Siemens Industry. Measure travel time and speed between multiple controller locations. http://www.mobility.siemens.com, 2011.

[24] U. Stilla, E. Michaelsen, U. Soergel, S. Hinz, and H. Ender. Airborne monitoring of vehicle activity in urban areas. *ISPRS*, 2004.

[25] L. Zhang and et.al. Accurate online power estimation and automatic battery behavior based power model generation for smartphones. In *ACM CODES/ISSS*, 2010.

A Wearable System That Knows Who Wears It

Cory Cornelius
Security and Privacy
Research
Intel Labs
Hillsboro, OR

Ronald Peterson
Institute for Security,
Technology, and Society &
Dept. of Computer Science
Dartmouth College
Hanover, NH

Joseph Skinner
Thayer School of Engineering
Dartmouth College
Hanover, NH

Ryan Halter
Thayer School of Engineering
& Geisel School of Medicine
Dartmouth College
Hanover, NH

David Kotz
Institute for Security,
Technology, and Society &
Dept. of Computer Science
Dartmouth College
Hanover, NH

ABSTRACT

Body-area networks of pervasive wearable devices are increasingly used for health monitoring, personal assistance, entertainment, and home automation. In an ideal world, a user would simply wear their desired set of devices with no configuration necessary: the devices would discover each other, recognize that they are on the same person, construct a secure communications channel, and recognize the user to which they are attached. In this paper we address a portion of this vision by offering a wearable system that unobtrusively recognizes the person wearing it. Because it can recognize the user, our system can properly label sensor data or personalize interactions.

Our recognition method uses *bioimpedance*, a measurement of how tissue responds when exposed to an electrical current. By collecting bioimpedance samples using a small wearable device we designed, our system can determine that (a) the wearer is indeed the expected person and (b) the device is physically *on* the wearer's body. Our recognition method works with 98% balanced-accuracy under a cross-validation of a day's worth of bioimpedance samples from a cohort of 8 volunteer subjects. We also demonstrate that our system continues to recognize a subset of these subjects even several months later. Finally, we measure the energy requirements of our system as implemented on a Nexus S smart phone and custom-designed module for the Shimmer sensing platform.

1. MOTIVATION

We are entering a period of rapid expansion of wearable and pervasive computing due to the continuing advances in low-power electronics, including sensors and actuators, Today, it is not uncommon for people to carry multiple computing devices, such as smart phones, music players, and cameras. Increasingly, we carry, hold, or wear devices to measure our physical activity (e.g., Fitbit), to interact with our entertainment devices (e.g., the Xbox One), or to monitor our physiology (e.g., a cardiac patient concerned about

heart arrhythmia or a diabetic managing her blood glucose). These unobtrusive, wearable devices make it possible to continuously or periodically track many health- and lifestyle-related conditions at an unprecedented level of detail. Their use of wireless connectivity enables interaction with other devices nearby (e.g., entertainment systems, climate-control systems, or medical devices), and allows sensor data they collect to be automatically shared with a social-networking service, or (in the case of health applications) uploaded to an Electronic Medical Record system for review by a healthcare provider.

In this paper, we focus on a fundamental problem involving wearable devices: who is wearing the device? The ability to recognize who is interacting with a device is essential for many applications. For an entertainment device, it can recognize the user and load the correct profile. For a home climate control, it can adjust the environment to the wearer's preference. Most compellingly, for a health-monitoring device, it can label the sensor data with the correct identity so that it can be stored in the correct health record. (A mix-up of sensor data could lead to incorrect treatment or diagnosis, with serious harm to the patient.)

In our vision, a person should be able to simply attach the desired set of devices to their body – whether clipped on, strapped on, stuck on, slipped into a pocket, or even implanted or ingested, and have the devices *just work*. That is, without any other action on the part of the user, the devices would discover each other's presence, recognize that they are on the same body (as opposed to devices in radio range but attached to a different body nearby), develop shared secrets from which to derive encryption keys, and establish reliable and secure communications. Furthermore, for many of the interesting applications described above, the devices must also recognize *who* is wearing them.

We have previously developed a method for a networked set of devices to recognize that they are located on the same body; our approach uses correlations in acceleration signals for this purpose [9]. If even one device can recognize *which* body, then transitively the set of devices know who is wearing them. Indeed, it is unlikely that every device will have the technology, or suitable placement, to recognize the user; in our model, only one such device needs that capability.

One easy solution, common in many devices today, is for the device to be statically associated with a given user. This smart phone is *my* phone, whereas that fitness sensor is *your* fitness sensor. The device is assumed to be used by only that user and any data generated

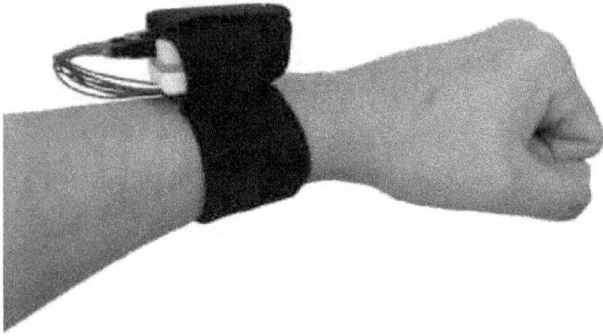

Figure 1: A subject wearing one of our bioimpedance sensors. The exposed wires connect the electrodes to our custom sensor module (which is connected to the Shimmer via the internal expansion port).

by a sensor is associated with that user. There are, however, many situations where this static association fails. In some households, a given device might be shared by many users (e.g., a blood-pressure cuff). In other settings, two people might accidentally wear the wrong sensor (e.g., a couple who go out for a run and accidentally wear the other's fitness sensor). For some applications, a person may actively try to fool the system (e.g., a smoker who places his "smoking" sensor on a non-smoking friend in order to receive incentives for smoking cessation).

What we require is an unobtrusive, wearable device that leverages biometrics to recognize the wearer. It would then share that identity with the body-area network of other devices (earlier confirmed to be on the same body [9]). This device would be trained once for each user that might wear it, but thenceforth be completely automatic and unobtrusive.

Our approach is to use *bioimpedance*, which measures how a living tissue responds when exposed to an electrical current. Our wearable device, shown in Figure 1, places eight electrodes in contact with the wearer's wrist. Using two of these electrodes, the device applies a small, harmless current to the wrist and measures bioimpedance. By comparing these bioimpedance samples with a model of a subject that was built earlier in a training phase, the device can both determine that some person is wearing it and verify the particular subject who is wearing it. If we train the device for a set of users, e.g., the members of a household, then the device can recognize which of those household members is wearing the device, or that none of them are wearing the device. We previously demonstrated the feasibility of this approach [10] on a set of nearly 50 subjects; although that study validated our method's ability to distinguish subjects, all of our data was captured in the lab in a controlled setting using an *unwearable* device.

In this paper we demonstrate the feasibility of our approach by deploying a custom-designed wearable device outside of the lab to collect data over the course of a day for each subject. As in our prior work, we target a household-size cohort of subjects because we believe these kinds of wearable devices will typically be used by a few subjects over their useful lifetime. We also provide evidence that bioimpedance samples remain recognizable even several months later.

Our solution has many advantages. Not all wearable devices require the ability to recognize the user; only one device need do so, assuming it can communicate the identity to other devices proven to be on the same body. The devices may be smaller and simpler than a device like a smart phone since they need no interface for user recognition (or PIN or password for authentication). Use of a biometric

provides important security and privacy properties, preventing unauthorized users from either accessing sensitive data (e.g., in which an adversary Alice tricks Bob's sensor into divulging his activity data to her smart phone), and preventing the mis-labeling of sensor data that might later be used for medically important decisions. Privacy is particularly important in health-related pervasive applications [5]. Furthermore, these methods can support personalization techniques so often envisioned in pervasive computing.

Contributions. First, we devised a wearable sensor system capable of sensing bioimpedance at the wrist. Second, we extend our previous method to include a different set of features that substantially increases recognition performance. Third, we deployed our system outside of the lab to 8 individuals who wore our system for a day. Finally, we demonstrate the feasibility of our device in its ability to recognize the wearer over time and to distinguish among several wearers in identification and verification settings under a naive imposter attack model.

2. WEARABLE SENSOR SYSTEM

We designed our wearable device to be a watch-like bracelet that contains small electrodes to measure bioimpedance. The form factor of a watch has several technical advantages. First, it is worn the same way each time, more or less: issues with placement of the electrodes are diminished because it can sense data from nearly the same location each time and in the same orientation. Second, a watch can be instrumented to detect when it has been placed on and taken off a person. Attachment can be detected, for example, by the ends of the watchband being clasped together or by detecting properties of the skin such as temperature or moisture. Because we require the electrodes to be in contact with the body and not all form factors will afford continuous contact, a mechanism to detect when the device is in contact with a body is necessary. Such simple detection mechanisms also allow us to conserve energy by only performing recognition when the device is actually in contact with a person. We describe such a method in Section 2.4.

2.1 Bioimpedance

Bioimpedance is a physiological property related to a tissue's resistance to electrical current flow and its ability to store electrical charge. In *in vivo* human applications, it is typically measured through metallic electrodes placed on the skin and around an anatomic location of interest (e.g., the wrist). These electrical properties are predominantly a function of the underlying tissue, including the specific tissue types present (e.g., blood, adipose, muscle, bone), the anatomic configuration (i.e., bone or muscle orientation and quantity), and the state of the tissue (normal or osteoporotic bone, edematous versus normally hydrated tissue, and so forth). Significant impedance differences exist between the varying tissue types, anatomic configurations, and tissue states, each of which may provide a unique mechanism for distinguishing among people. Figure 2 shows the anatomy of a human wrist with several electrodes and example paths of where current can travel. For more details about bioimpedance, see Cornelius [8, Section 3.3].

2.2 Hardware

To capture a bioimpedance sample, we designed and manufactured a sensor designed to be worn on a person's wrist. The wearable sensor was built on top of the Shimmer Platform [26] - an open-source, low-power wireless sensing platform - and uses a bioimpedance sensor module we designed. The Shimmer provides processing (via a MSP430 microcontroller), wireless communication (via Bluetooth or 802.15.4), storage capabilities (via SD card), and measurement of movement (via an accelerometer). It also pro-

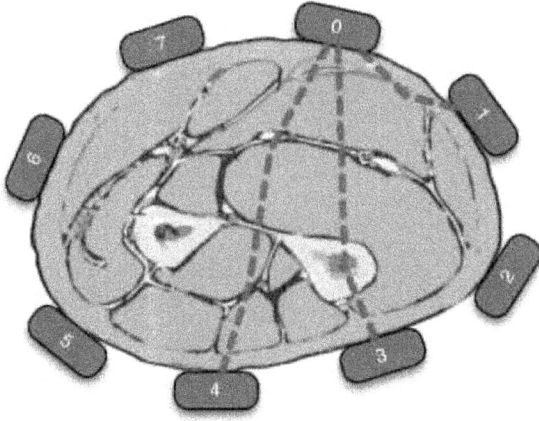

Figure 2: The anatomy of a human wrist [13]. The bones (ulna and radius) are shown in gray, muscle in red, skin in brown. The gray boxes on the outside of the anatomy represent the placement of electrodes with corresponding labels. If electrode 0 were chosen as the current-applying electrode, the blue dashed line represent possible paths from it to electrode 1, 3, or 4. Notice how, depending upon the selected electrodes, the path may pass through a variety of tissues.

Figure 3: Our custom designed sensor module with the major components labeled. It was approximately 45mm long by 19mm wide and fitted comfortably on top of a Shimmer with a custom-designed enclosure.

vides internal and external expansion connectors that allow it to interact with custom sensor modules (e.g., a gyroscope, magnetometer, ECG, EMG, or GSR). Our custom bioimpedance sensor module (Figure 3) used the internal expansion connector, and was enclosed by a custom-designed case. The bioimpedance sensor module included a receptacle that enables a series of electrodes to be connected to it. We designed and manufactured an elastic sleeve with 8 evenly spaced electrodes. The sleeve connected to the bioimpedance sensor module and included a pocket that holds the Shimmer. Both the sleeve and sensor module went through several iterations of design to ensure it would be comfortable for subjects to wear and hold up to daily use. Figures 1 and 4 show the final form factor.

We designed the bioimpedance sensor module (Figure 3) around the Analog Devices AD5933 Impedance Analyzer [3]. The AD5933 includes a frequency generator that allows excitation at a specified frequency between 1 kHz and 100 kHz with a resolution of 0.1 Hz and can measure impedances between 1 kΩ and 100 MΩ to within 0.5% total system accuracy. The Shimmer controlled the AD5933 via the I^2C bus. Because we wanted to allow multiple electrode locations, the sensor module included two Analog Devices ADG1608 8-Channel Multiplexors [4]. Thus, the sensor module was capable of selecting 2 of 8 possible electrodes, called an *electrode pair*, for bi-polar sensing. These multiplexors were controlled by setting specific GPIO pins. The electrodes were connected to the sensor module via an 8-pin Hirose 3260-8S3(55) Connector [16] such that custom electrode configurations could be independently built and interfaced with the sensor module. The Shimmer provided regulated power to the sensor module, which was fed to an Analog Devices ADR433 ultra-low noise voltage reference. This ADR433 [2] provided a stable 3V supply voltage needed for the impedance analyzer while a Microchip MCP1252 charge pump [20] fed a 5V supply voltage to the multiplexors.

Internally, the AD5933 computes the Discrete Fourier Transform of 1024 analog-to-digital samples at each frequency. This computation yields the power of the signal in the form of real r and imaginary

i components. We computed the magnitude of the impedance sample at frequency ω as $|Z(\omega)| = \sqrt{r_\omega^2 + i_\omega^2}$. We computed the phase of the impedance sample as $Z\emptyset(\omega) = \tan^{-1}\left(\frac{i_\omega}{r_\omega}\right)$, taking care to ensure $\frac{i_\omega}{r_\omega}$ was a positive quantity by rotating this angle until it fell into the appropriate quadrant in the complex plane. Given the magnitude and phase, we computed the resistive and reactive components of impedance, represented by $R(\omega)$ and $X(\omega)$ respectively, by projecting onto the Cartesian plane:

$$
\begin{aligned}
Z(\omega) &= R(\omega) + jX(\omega) \\
&= |Z|\cos(Z\emptyset(\omega)) + |Z|\sin(Z\emptyset(\omega))
\end{aligned}
$$

where j is the imaginary number. We calibrated of these values to a known reference impedance as described in Appendix A.

2.3 Software

The Shimmer ran the TinyOS operating system [28]. We wrote custom software to communicate with the impedance analyzer and multiplexors. The software was divided into three major parts: a low-level driver, a high-level driver, and a logging application.

The low-level and high-level drivers allowed applications to communicate with our sensor module. The low-level driver was a barebones interface to the AD5933 that wrapped the I^2C communications. The high-level driver implemented a state machine that allows more natural interaction with the sensor module. It also allowed applications to adjust the settling time (i.e., the amount of time between the stimulus and sampling) and handled failures gracefully. In total, the low-level driver compromised 381 lines of nesC code while the high-level driver compromised 363 lines of nesC code.

The logging application used the high-level driver to interact with the sensor module. Before taking bioimpedance samples, the application collected acceleration for 5 seconds at 50 Hz to classify the type of motion (i.e., low energy, medium energy, high energy) the subject's wrist was experiencing. Next, two electrodes on the wrist strap were selected using the multiplexors. The impedance analyzer was then commanded to measure at 50 logarithmically spaced frequencies from 1 kHz to 100 kHz. Because of the logarithmic spacing of the frequencies, the impedance analyzer's internal mechanism to step through frequencies linearly could not be used, so we

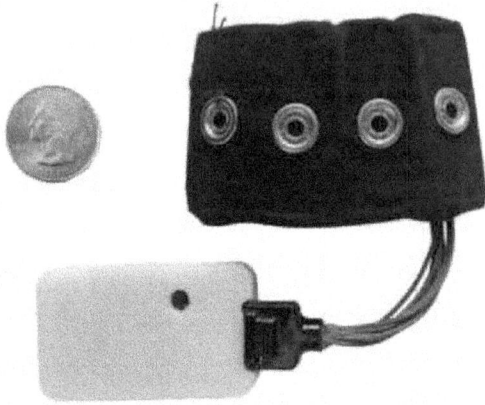

Figure 4: Our wearable bioimpedance sensor. The sleeve (top) is shown inside out to display the electrodes. The Shimmer (bottom) and wires were typically housed within the sleeve, but are shown exposed here. For reference, the Shimmer was approximately 53 mm long by 32 mm wide.

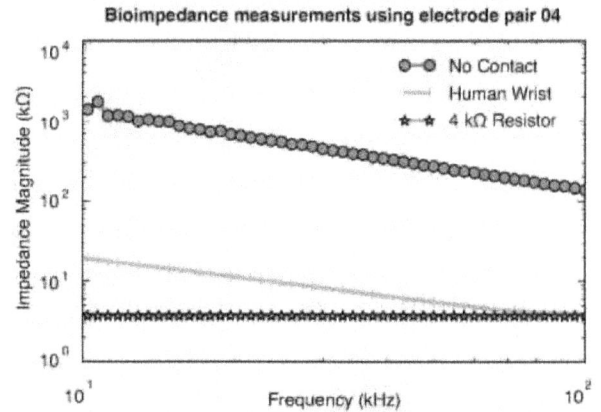

Figure 5: Example impedance samples from electrode pair 0 4 for 1) no contact, 2) bracelet in contact with a human wrist, and 3) bracelet attached to 4 kΩ resistor. In the case of no contact, impedance is effectively infinite. Note: impedance and frequency are plotted on logarithmic scales.

commanded each measurement individually. After one frequency sweep, we selected another set of stimulus and measurement electrodes and another frequency sweep was started. After a complete sample, we commanded the impedance analyzer to conserve power by sleeping. A timer was used to wake the impedance analyzer after a preset interval and start another sample. Sample data could either be stored to a microSD card or sent via the Bluetooth or 802.15.4 radio depending upon the application. In total, the logging application compromised 1570 lines of nesC code.

We also developed a smart phone application that allowed collection of bioimpedance samples via Bluetooth. A Nexus S smart phone [12] communicated with the Shimmer via Bluetooth using the Serial Port Profile. To ensure the confidentiality and integrity of the communications, we relied upon the underlying authentication and confidentiality mechanisms present in Bluetooth. The smart phone application was a 932 line Java Android 4.1 application. We used the OpenUAT toolkit [19] for some of the signal processing and the WEKA toolkit [14] for the machine-learning aspects of the application. We used these toolkits to implement the algorithms described in Section 3 below. We trained each user's model offline using WEKA.

2.4 Detecting presence

Because our device required contact with a person's wrist, we needed to detect when the device was in contact with a person. Fortunately, skin contact was easy to detect. Figure 5 shows some example bioimpedance samples, one of which shows the impedance sample when there was no contact with a human wrist. When there was no contact, the magnitude of the impedance for that sample was high across all frequencies. Thus, we used a simple threshold to detect presence.

This presence-detection scheme, however, required a lot of energy to execute. High security applications, for example, might require near-instant detection of wristband removal. Given that a full impedance sample took 98 mW to measure, this presence-detection method is not suitable for continuous use. It might be feasible to look at an individual electrode pair and a single frequency, but we

leave such optimizations for future work; alternate approaches for presence detection are described in Section 5.

3. RECOGNIZING WEARERS

Recall that the goal of our system is to recognize who is wearing it under a naive imposter attack model. The intuition is quite simple: gather bioimpedance samples from a subject and build a model that represents that subject's bioimpedance samples; later, use that same model to see if a new and unknown bioimpedance sample matches the model. This implies there are two distinct phases: enrollment and recognition. Before we discuss the details of the enrollment and recognition phases, we first discuss the details of the bioimpedance samples and features we use in those phases.

3.1 Bioimpedance samples

It would be infeasible to measure bioimpedance from all pairs of the eight electrodes, so we carefully chose specific electrode pairs. We captured samples from two types of electrode pairs: those electrodes directly across from one another (e.g., electrodes 0 and 4 as shown in Figure 2), since they were the maximal distance away from each other and therefore provide more tissue for the current to travel through; and those electrodes that were exactly one electrode apart (e.g., 0 and 2), since the current would travel through the outer regions of the wrist. We did not measure bioimpedance at electrodes directly next to each other since the skin would be the primary tissue affecting the reading. The skin is subject to variability due to sweat and externally applied fluids (e.g., lotions, hand sanitizers, or topical medicines). Likewise, we did not measure bioimpedance for those electrodes spaced exactly two electrodes apart, because those samples exhibited characteristics similar to those collected from electrodes maximally apart. Figure 6 shows example bioimpedance samples from a single subject for the 12 different electrode pairs we used.

3.2 Feature extraction

Given a set of frequencies and their corresponding bioimpedance measurements, we extracted four features from each bioimpedance sample: two from the bioimpedance magnitude and two from the bioimpedance phase. The features were simple: we fitted one line to

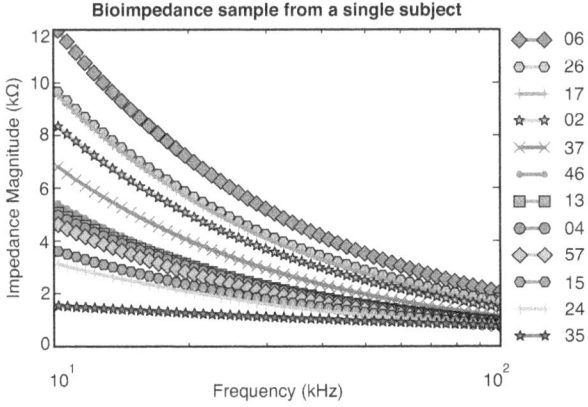

Figure 6: Example bioimpedance samples collected from a single subject for the 12 different electrode pairs after fitting to a line in log-log space. Note: frequency is plotted on a logarithmic scale.

the bioimpedance magnitude and another line to the bioimpedance phase, both in log-log space. The inspiration for this feature can be seen in Figure 5, which shows that a bioimpedance sample of a human wrist is mostly linear in log-log space. Because samples were inherently noisy, fitting a line to a bioimpedance sample smoothed it while preserving its general shape. Fitting a line yields four features because a line is succinctly described by a slope and intercept (a slope and intercept for each of the magnitude and phase components). We thereby reduced the dimensionality of the data from 100 to 4, which in turn lowered the computational and energy requirements. Although we explored other features, including using the raw data itself, we found these features yielded the best recognition performance.

Our final *feature vector* consisted of the concatenation of these features for each electrode pair. Since we took samples from 12 electrode pairs, this resulted in a feature vector of dimension $12 \times 4 = 48$, which was much smaller than the raw data (which is of dimension $12 \times 50 \times 2 = 1200$). This concatenation assumed all electrode pairs would provide some information about the identity of the wearer. (In Section 4 we explore different concatenations of electrode pairs.)

Because many of our studies took place outside of the lab, we had to discard some bioimpedance samples. We discarded those samples where the system failed to measure a complete bioimpedance sample. (In a production system, this could be detected in the moment and the sample could be retaken.) We also discarded all samples where the wrist was deemed to not be in contact with the device. We decided that a sample was not in contact when the maximum bioimpedance magnitude was greater than 10^3 kΩ, a value determined by the maximum non-contact bioimpedance magnitude shown in Figure 5. Finally, we discarded all samples where the sum of squared errors of the fitted line in log-log space was above an empirically determined threshold of 0.5. We discarded these samples because such a poor fit indicated a noisy sample, probably due to motion or other interference with the reading.

3.3 Enrollment

Before a subject could use the system, we trained the system to recognize his/her bioimpedance by putting the system into *enrollment mode*. In this mode the system captured bioimpedance samples for a designated time (12 bioimpedance samples took about 15 seconds). The system then used these training samples as inputs

to an *enrollment algorithm* that learns a model of the enrollee's bioimpedance. (It was necessary to compute this model off the wearable device because of resource constraints.) The model was then loaded into the system for use.

Given a set of *training feature vectors* from a subject, we learned the model of their bioimpedance samples using the enrollment algorithm. There were two modes of operation for these algorithms: *identification* and *verification*. Identification is a many-to-one matching, while verification is a one-to-one matching. Identification is used to determine which person from a population is wearing the device. Verification, on the other hand, is used to confirm that a chosen person is wearing the device. In our experiments, our target population is the size of a household since we believe that over the lifetime of a typical wearable device it will only encounter a few people.

3.3.1 Identification

In identification mode, we used a discriminative algorithm to learn a model of each subjects' bioimpedance. Our method learns a classifier for each subject by using that subject's feature vectors as positive examples (i.e., they are labeled positively) and all other subjects' feature vectors as negative examples (i.e., they are labeled negatively). This is the one-versus-all strategy used for multi-class classification [24]. In this mode, each new subject requires retraining the models; however, we only need to collect samples from the new subject because we can reuse the already enrolled subjects' training data.

We examined two algorithms for use during identification-mode enrollment. The first classifier, Naive Bayes (NB), independently models the mean and variance of each feature. A NB classifier is a relatively simple classifier to train because all it requires is computing the mean and variance of each feature for each label. The second classifier, a Support Vector Machine (SVM), finds the hyperplane that best separates the positive examples from the negative samples (i.e., the maximum-margin hyperplane). The intuition is that only those training examples near the hyperplane (i.e., the "support vectors") are necessary to describe it and thus constitute the model. Even if the data is not linearly separable, one can use the so-called "kernel trick" to map the examples into a higher dimensional space where they might become linearly separable [6].

The SVM classifiers require us to choose some parameters. (The NB classifier has no such parameters.) To choose parameters, we ran a 10-fold cross-validation of a small subset of our dataset over the parameter space of the SVM classifier. In the SVM case, we looked at different kernels (linear, polynomial, and radial-basis function), soft-margin costs, and, in the case of polynomial and radial-basis function kernels, their respective kernel coefficient gamma [6]. Using a grid search, we found that a 3rd degree polynomial kernel with a cost of 32 and gamma of 0.03125 was optimal.

3.3.2 Verification

In verification mode, we used a generative algorithm to learn a model of each subject's bioimpedance. This mode naturally supports multiple subjects because each subject's model can be learned independently of any other subject. Thus, a new subject could simply be loaded into the system without regard to the other subjects already in the system.

We examined one algorithm for use during verification-mode enrollment. A *Gaussian Mixture Model* (GMM) modeled the bioimpedance samples using a weighted linear combination of Gaussian densities, where each Gaussian density was parameterized by a mean vector and covariance matrix. We chose initial Gaussian densities by clustering the set of feature vectors using k-means clustering [17], where k was set to the desired number of Gaussian densities. We then iteratively refined these initial Gaussian densities using the expectation-maximization algorithm [11] until the maximum likelihood remained stable (i.e., the difference between successive iterations was less than 0.01) or after a maximum number of iterations (100). We modeled the full covariance since the dimensionality of a bioimpedance sample was relatively low. Because some values of the covariance matrix could become very small, as in the case of outliers, we enforced a variance floor of 0.001 on the covariance matrix. For our experiments, we found that 4 Gaussian densities best modeled a subject's bioimpedance samples.

3.4 Recognition

Once a subject was enrolled, the system entered *recognition mode*. In recognition mode, the system periodically determined whether it was on a human body (Section 2.4), then collected bioimpedance samples. The system used a *recognition algorithm* to determine whether a bioimpedance sample matches the enrollee's model. Like the enrollment algorithm, this recognition algorithm operated in one of two modes: identification or verification.

3.4.1 Identification

In identification mode, we used the enrolled models to choose which subject best matched a test feature vector from an unknown subject. A feature vector that was classified as positive for a given subject's model was said to match that subject's bioimpedance; otherwise, the test feature vector was classified as negative because it did not match that subject's bioimpedance. Choosing the best match is left to each classifier.

Each classifier has a different mechanism for classifying test feature vectors. The NB classifier chooses the label (i.e., is subject or not) of the test feature vector with the maximum likelihood as the classification. The best match is chosen as the sample with the highest likelihood. That is, it computes the Gaussian probability density function for the test feature vector given each label, and the label with the maximum value is the classification. Since an SVM is a linear classifier, it simply computes the linear transformation of the test feature vector and returns the sign of that value as the predicted label. The best match is chosen by the classifier with the largest margin between the support vectors and the sample.

3.4.2 Verification

In verification mode, we used the enrolled models to decide whether a test feature vector came from a known subject. We did so by asking the generative model to tell us how likely the test feature vector matched the model. Thus, we queried the subject's GMM for the likelihood of the new test feature vector given the model. Given some threshold τ, we accepted those bioimpedance samples came from that subject if the likelihood was greater than τ, and rejected otherwise. Because there is no good way of choosing the threshold *a priori*, we varied this threshold τ to determine how well our method performed.

3.5 Metrics

Consider a set of test feature vectors from a given subject and a set of test feature vectors from other subjects. We labeled the test vectors measured from the given subject as *positive* and all other test vectors as *negative*. We then used the model trained for that subject to classify all the test feature vectors, resulting in a positive or negative classification for each. Thus for each subject, every other subject acted as a naive imposter against that subject's model. Ideally, the model would classify only those test feature vectors from that subject as positive and all other test feature vectors from

other subjects as negative. Given such classification results, we present our results using the following metrics. The *false accept rate* (FAR) is the fraction of negatively labeled feature vectors that were misclassified (i.e., they were classified as positive). A perfect classifier would perform at 0% FAR. The *false reject rate* (FRR) is the fraction of positively labeled feature vectors that were misclassified (i.e., they were classified as negative). A perfect classifier would perform at 0% FRR. The *balanced accuracy* (BAC) is the sum of half of the true accept rate (i.e., the fraction of positively labeled feature vectors that were correctly classified, or $1-$FRR) and half of the true reject rate (the fraction of negatively labeled feature vectors that were correctly classified, or $1-$FAR). This metric weighs the negative and positive examples equally, which is necessary because there were more negatively labeled feature vectors than positively labeled feature vectors (because each subject's model is tested against everyone else's). A perfect classifier would perform at 100% BAC. Finally, the *equal error rate* (EER) is the rate at which the FAR equals the FRR. A perfect classifier would perform at 0% EER.

Although we computed these metrics for every subject in our data sets, we present summary statistics of these metrics over all subjects. In what follows, then, any mentions of BAC, FAR, and FRR should be interpreted as the average BAC, average FAR, and average FRR over all subjects. Where possible, we also include the standard deviation of each metric. Note that because the number of positive samples for any given subject was smaller than the number of negative examples by a factor of $N-1$, where N is the number of subjects, a classifier that always predicts the negative case will perform at a FAR of 0%, BAC of 50%, but FRR of 100%. For comparison's sake, we also computed these metrics under a classifier that predicted randomly based on the frequency of labels present in the training set (i.e., it wholly ignored any feature vectors associated with the labels). This classifier served as a baseline performance measure to compare with our method.

4. EXPERIMENTAL RESULTS

Using the above recognition method, we conducted a series of experiments to evaluate the feasibility of our system. In our first experiment, we replicated our prior work to ensure our device was working properly. Our second and third experiments validate the feasibility of our system when worn in an out-of-lab setting for both identification and verification. Finally, we measured the energy requirements of an implementation of our system.

Recall that our goal is to recognize the wearer in a small cohort of subjects using a custom-designed wearable bioimpedance sensor. Our prior work showed promise that bioimpedance is sufficiently unique among individuals [10]. In this study we sought to validate the use of a wearable bioimpedance sensor by deploying our device to subjects in an out-of-lab study. Such an evaluation will necessarily have some variance in bioimpedance samples and provides some measure of our system's performance in the real world. Furthermore, in this study we evaluate recognition in verification mode as well as identification mode.

4.1 Dataset

We collected bioimpedance samples from 8 people over a period of one day each. We informed participants of the risks involved in wearing the device (e.g., localized skin irritation at electrode site). If they agreed to enroll, we asked each subject to self-report their age and gender, and we measured the circumference of their wrist using a Health-O-Meter Digital Tape Measure at the location shown in Figure 7. We asked each subject to wear the sensor on their non-dominant wrist for as long as possible during the day and to return the device at the end of the day. We informed subjects that

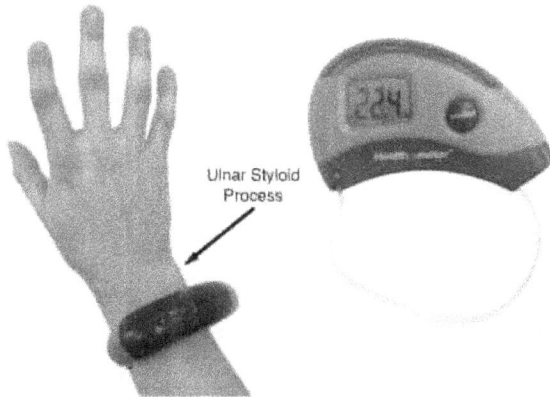

Figure 7: The Health-O-Meter Digital Tape measure we used to measure each subject's wrist circumference. It was placed just above the ulnar styloid process of the subject's non-dominant wrist where the device was worn.

Table 1: The total number of samples taken, the number of samples that were deemed not to be in contact with the subject's wrist, the total time in hours the device was in contact with the subject's wrist, and the subject's wrist circumference in centimeters. We measured each subject's wrist circumference because we believe it can be a useful feature in distinguishing subjects (although we did not use it in these studies). See Cornelius [8, Section 3.6.3 & 3.7.3] for how wrist circumference could be integrated as a feature.

Sub.	Samples	No Cont.	Cont. (h)	Wrist (cm)
1	111	6	8.8	18.2
2	96	8	7.3	16.2
3	107	22	7.1	18.4
4	262	27	19.6	17.0
5	134	12	10.2	19.4
6	123	38	7.1	18.4
7	134	59	6.2	17.6
8	111	13	8.2	19.0
Avg	135 ± 50	23 ± 17	9.3 ± 4.0	18.0 ± 1.0

they could remove the device at their leisure and should certainly remove it if they believed the device would come in contact with water (e.g., before showering or swimming). Should they remove the device, we instructed subjects to put the device back on in the same orientation as it was previously worn. Subjects were paid $8 for their participation and both our device and data-collection protocols were approved by our Institutional Review Board.

The enrolled participants (Table 1), 3 female and 5 male, had an average of 27 ± 8 years. The average wrist circumference was 18.0 ± 1.0 cm, meaning that the group of subjects selected for this study each had a similar wrist circumference. One could use the wrist circumference as a distinguishing factor, but such a device would need to accurately and precisely measure the wearer's wrist circumference. Even with a moderate measurement error of 5 mm, distinguishing the individuals in our dataset would be difficult. On average, the device was in contact with a subject's wrist for 9.3 hours resulting in 112 bioimpedance samples. Note that this group of 8 subjects was larger than the groups we examined in our prior work; we previously examined cohorts of 5 subjects representing a household or similar group that may share devices.

4.2 Replication

We first validated how well our methods performed under conditions similar to our prior work [10]. We ran a 10-fold cross-validation for each subject using only the electrode pairs that were maximally distant (i.e., 04, 15, 26, and 37) as in our prior work. Figure 8 shows the results of this validation for the best-performing combinations of the specified electrode pairs using the NB classifier and SVM classifier. This validation extended our prior work by also examining the use of an SVM classifier. The best performing single-electrode pair in this study (04) confirmed our prior finding that the best performing single-electrode pair was the pair with electrodes on the top and bottom of the wrist. In the SVM case, the best double-electrode pair combination was 04, 37. Due to the the design of our new device, pair 04 did not sit exactly at the top of the wrist (as in our prior experiments), but rather it shared the top of the wrist with electrode pair 37. Overall, the SVM classifier achieved the best performance when all four electrode pairs were combined. It achieved a BAC of $95.0\% \pm 3.00\%$, a FAR of $1.40\% \pm 0.61\%$, and a FRR of $8.62\% \pm 5.74\%$. In contrast, the NB classifier (which was used in our prior study) achieved a BAC of $86.4\% \pm 3.82\%$,

a FAR of $15.4\% \pm 6.35\%$, and a FRR of $11.7\% \pm 3.45\%$, similar findings to our prior experiments. A random classifier achieved $50.2\% \pm 0.87\%$, a FAR of $13.0\% \pm 5.83$, and a FRR of $86.7\% \pm 7.12$. The SVM classifier outperformed our prior work while the NB classifier performed similarly.

4.3 Identification

To examine how well our system performed in the identification setting, we ran a cross-validation over the entire dataset. Recall that identification requires our algorithms to choose which subject is present in a cohort of candidate subjects. This validation assumes that we have nearly an entire day's worth of training samples available, since we train on 90% of the data, leaving 10% for testing. This assumption means the training samples will necessarily capture the variability in a subject's bioimpedance across different environments, motions, and orientations. For each subject we ran a 10-fold cross-validation over the set of feature vectors for each classifier defined in Section 3. That is, we trained our model using 90% of the samples, leaving 10% of the samples to be classified. We computed the FAR, FRR, and BAC for each subject, and we report the average and standard deviation of these measures over all subjects.

Figure 9 shows these results for the top-performing electrode-pair combinations using the NB and SVM classifiers respectively. The top-performing electrode-pair combination (02 04 06 13 15 17 26 37) achieved a BAC of $98.1\% \pm 0.98\%$, FAR of $0.96\% \pm 0.51\%$, and FRR of $2.83\% \pm 1.17\%$ for the SVM classifier. The best the electrode-pair combination (04 06 35 37 46 57) for the NB classifier achieved was a BAC of $87.9\% \pm 3.83\%$, FAR of $14.6\% \pm 8.14\%$, and FRR of $9.62\% \pm 3.44\%$. The SVM classifier benefited from more electrode pairs, while the performance of the NB classifier did not significantly increase except for reductions in FAR and FRR.

Figure 10 shows a visualization of these top-performing electrode-pair combinations for each classifier. In most of the top combinations for the SVM classifier, electrode pairs 04, 37, 02 were present. The electrode locations (see Figure 2) of the top-performing electrode-pair combination correspond to the ulnar side of wrist (or medial side of the forearm) for the SVM classifier, while the top-performing electrode-pair combinations for the NB classifier tend to encompass the whole wrist. In general, as the number of elec-

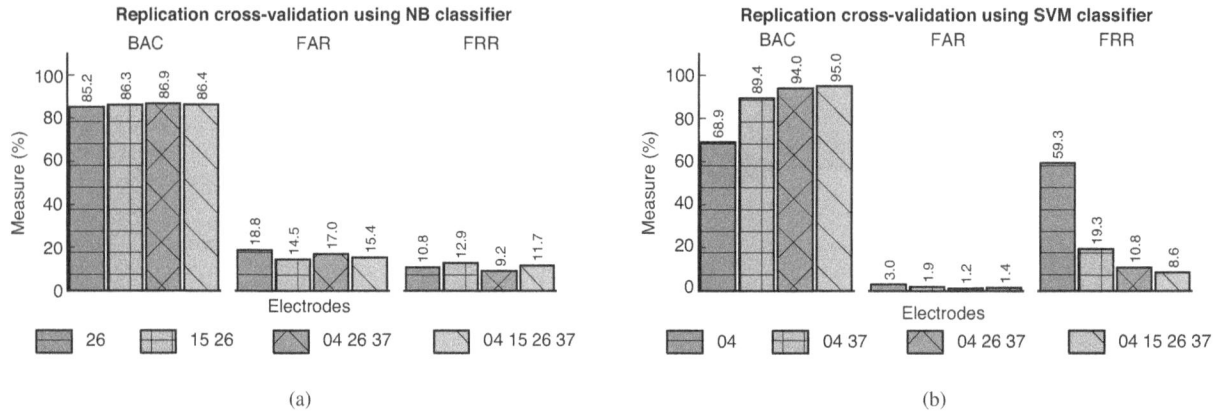

Figure 8: A replication of our prior work using a NB classifier over our dataset restricted to only those electrode pairs maximally distant. For a single electrode pair, 04 performed best, while the full set of electrode pairs does not perform significantly better. The SVM classifier, on the other hand, performed significantly better than the NB classifier when all four electrode pairs were included.

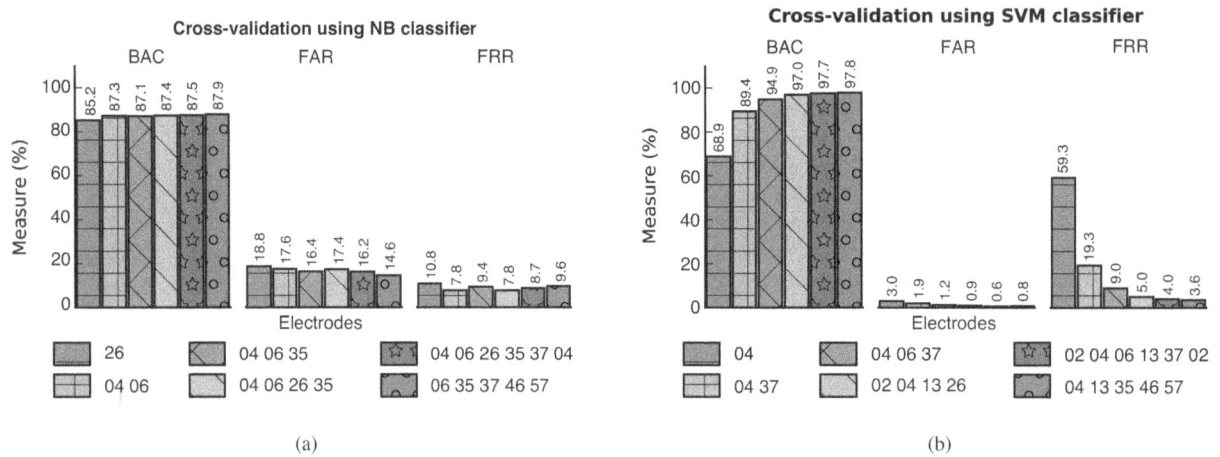

Figure 9: The top-performing electrode-pair combinations of a 10-fold cross-validation as classified by a NB classifier. The performance of the NB classifier was flat while the SVM classifier benefits from more electrode-pair combinations.

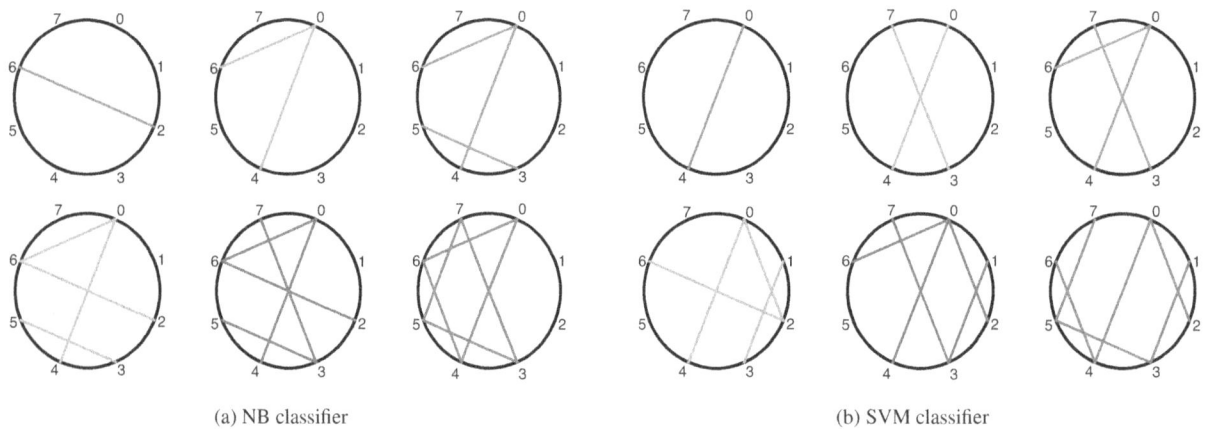

(a) NB classifier

(b) SVM classifier

Figure 10: Visualization of best performing combinations of electrode-pairs in cross validation for the NB classifier and SVM classifier. Notice how the top-performing electrode-pair combination for the NB classifier encompassed much of the wrist, while the top-performing electrode-pair combination for the SVM classifier encompassed the medial side of the wrist.

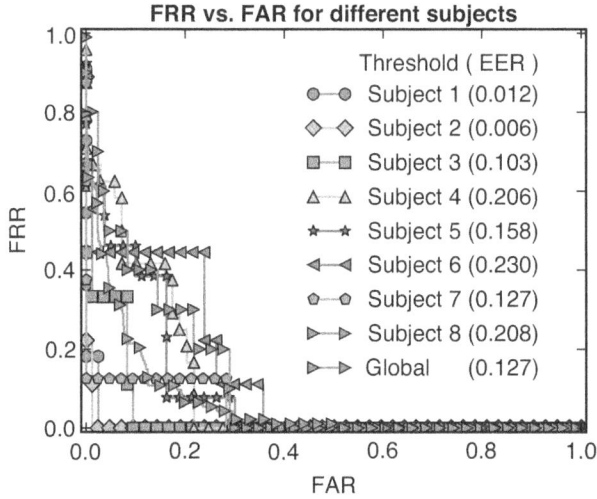

FRR vs. FAR for different subjects

Threshold (EER)
- Subject 1 (0.012)
- Subject 2 (0.006)
- Subject 3 (0.103)
- Subject 4 (0.206)
- Subject 5 (0.158)
- Subject 6 (0.230)
- Subject 7 (0.127)
- Subject 8 (0.208)
- Global (0.127)

Figure 11: The recognition rates for each subject in a verification setting. The average per-subject EER was 13.10 % ± 8.67 %. A global threshold achieved an EER of 12.7 %. The threshold, however, can be changed to suit the needs of the application (i.e., more false-negatives or more false-positives).

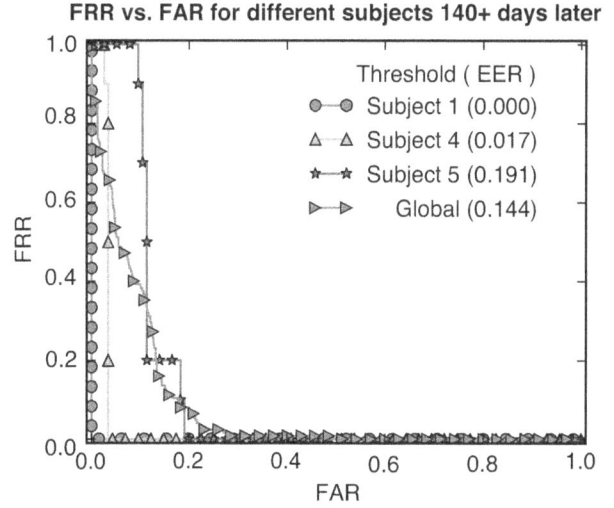

FRR vs. FAR for different subjects 140+ days later

Threshold (EER)
- Subject 1 (0.000)
- Subject 4 (0.017)
- Subject 5 (0.191)
- Global (0.144)

Figure 12: The longitudinal recognition rates of bioimpedance. We collected data from 3 subjects 140 days after their initial enrollment in our wearable study. The per-subject threshold EER was 6.93 % ± 10.60 % while the global threshold EER was 14.4 %, indicating results similar to our wearable verification evaluation.

trode pairs increased, our device sensed more of the geometry of the wrist. This result shows that using electrode pairs that are not just maximally distant (as was done in our prior work) will benefit recognition performance.

4.4 Verification

In this experiment, we sought to understand how well our wearable device performs in a verification setting. Recall that verification is the process of verifying whether the wristband's wearer is its owner, that is, the individual this wristband was trained to recognize. To validate the performance of our system, we used a hold-out validation where we held out the first 90% of a subject's data and left the remaining 10% for testing. We computed the FAR, FRR, and EER for each subject, and we report the average and standard deviation of these measures over all subjects.

Figure 11 shows how well our method performs for a 90 % hold-out validation. Recall that we can vary the threshold τ for each subject and compute the corresponding FAR and FRR for each threshold. At some threshold τ the FAR will equal the FRR, which the legend in Figure 11 also shows as the EER. The EER varied across subjects, but the average per-subject EER was 13.10 % ± 8.67 %. Rather than varying the threshold τ for each subject, we can also vary a global threshold τ over all subjects. That is, rather than computing subject-specific thresholds, we can also compute a threshold that works for any subject. The EER for such a global threshold was 12.7 %. In verification mode, one can easily change the threshold to suit the needs of the application to account for fewer false-positives or false-negatives, as Figure 11 shows. Verification mode, however, tends perform worse than identification mode because identification mode incorporates information about other subjects.

4.5 Longitudinal verification

To understand the longitudinal recognition rates of bioimpedance, we collected 10 additional bioimpedance samples from three subjects (1, 4, and 5) 140 days after their initial enrollment in our wearable study. We ran a hold-out validation where the testing dataset was equal to these new bioimpedance samples for Subjects

1, 4, 5. We used the last 10% of the other subjects' data as negative test data for these three subjects.

Figure 12 shows the results of this longitudinal verification. The average EER for a per-subject threshold was 6.93 % ± 10.60 % while the average EER for a global threshold was 14.4 %. The recognition rates of Subjects 1 and 5 were similar to their recognition rates in the initial verification evaluation, while Subject 4 performed better than its initial rate. Recall that these longitudinal samples were taken immediately after each other and thus would be similar enough that if one should match a subject's model, then the majority of them would. Likewise, the per-subject threshold EER and global threshold EER did not significantly differ from the initial verification evaluation. These results suggest that a subject's bioimpedance remains stable enough to be verified at least 4.5 months later.

4.6 Energy measurements

Wearable devices require careful design for energy conservation. Although our prototype was not optimized for low power, we report here on its power consumption as a worst-case analysis. To capture energy measurements, we used the Monsoon Power Monitor [21] connected to a Windows laptop. The Power Monitor acts like a battery and samples the current drawn every 200 μs. We downsampled the current measurements to 100 ms intervals via averaging.

Figure 13 shows the energy measurement of a Shimmer sampling bioimpedance and sending these values to the smart phone. There are five distinct phases in the energy measurement. In the first phase, the Shimmer was idle. This consumed 6.42 mA on average. Next, the Shimmer turned on its Bluetooth radio (at the 3.0 s dashed line) and attempted to pair with the smart phone. On average, this phase consumed 9.33 mA. Again, the spikes in this phase correspond to the times when the Bluetooth radio was searching for the smart phone. Beginning at the 13.8 s dashed line, the Shimmer and smart phone established a connection. This phase consumed 27.0 mA on average. Next, the smart phone instructed the Shimmer (at the 16.3 s dashed line) to collect 12 bioimpedance samples and send them via Bluetooth. This phase consumed 52.5 mA on average. About 30 %

of this current was due to the actual bioimpedance sensor board, while about 60 % was a result of the Bluetooth radio (the remaining 10 % was the overhead of just running the device). Next, the smart phone told the Shimmer to stop sampling and disconnected at the 35.0 s and 36.5 s dashed lines, respectively. The phase between stopping sampling and disconnecting consumed 26.8 mA on average. Once again, the dominating factor was the Bluetooth radio, although the bioimpedance sensor board required more energy than the accelerometer. A Shimmer with a 450 mAh battery could last more than a day with the Bluetooth radio on continuously and with hourly bioimpedance recognition. In a production system, the wearable device would also compute the classification results (training would probably still have to be done on another device), sending only these results via Bluetooth, thus eliminating the dominant energy cost. The wearable device could easily last for a week. Furthermore, our prototype system was built on top of a commercial off-the-shelf system and so was constrained by the underlying system itself. One could also minimize the energy profile and size by using a system-on-chip that combines the radio and micro-controller into a single chip [22].

Figure 14 shows the energy measurement of a smart phone engaged in bioimpedance recognition. (This figure is not aligned in time with Figure 13 because we could only measure energy from one device at a time.) Like the measurement in Figure 13, we assume the smart phone has already verified that the Shimmer is on the same body. There are four phases in the energy measurement. The first phase was a steady-state energy measurement of the smart phone. This phase consumed 54.5 mA on average. In the next phase, the smart phone turned on its Bluetooth radio at the 5.0 s dashed line and began connecting to the Shimmer. On average, this phase consumed 87.8 mA. At the 13.8 s dashed line, the smart phone was connected to the Shimmer. In this phase, the smart phone collected bioimpedance samples from the Shimmer. The dashed lines at 10.5 s, 12.2 s, 13.9 s, 15.4 s, 17.0 s, 18.8 s, 20.2 s, 21.8 s, 23.5 s, 24.9 s, 26.3 s and 28.1 s correspond to the times when the Shimmer started sensing a new electrode configuration. This phase consumed 67.9 mA on average. At the 29.6 s dashed line, the smart phone ran the recognition algorithm, told the Shimmer to stop sensing, and began disconnecting from the Shimmer. On average, this phase consumed 91.8 mA. Compared to the overhead of the Bluetooth radio and Android operating system, our bioimpedance recognition method did not significantly impact the current drawn; thus, the bioimpedance calculations causes negligible impact on the smart phone.

5. DISCUSSION AND FUTURE WORK

The usefulness of a biometric relates to its ability to recognize a person within some population. The target population is especially important in the forensic sciences. For a long time the Federal Bureau of Investigation believed fingerprints were unique until an innocent man was linked to the 2004 Madrid train bombings using fingerprint matching [30]. In this paper we emphasize that our target population size is that of a household; that is, we ought to be able to distinguish individuals in a household. While bioimpedance may be able to distinguish individuals in larger populations, such explorations remain future work. We believe that tetra-polar sensing combined with different electrode pair combinations will yield recognition rates on par with biometrics like ECG. One could also combine identification and verification to improve robustness. For example, we could use the identification algorithm to identify who is using the device (like a username) and then use the verification algorithm to decide if it is that person with sufficient probability (like a password).

One advantage of the wrist location is that the wristband is placed in about the same location and at about the same orientation every time it is worn. We experimented with changes in wristband orientation, and determined that it does have an effect on the bioimpedance samples, depending upon the amount of rotation about the wrist. A better physical design might reduce this problem by ensuring the proper band orientation on the wrist. If not, it may be possible to use kinematic sensors to determine the orientation of the band and compensate for different orientations. It might also be possible to compute rotation- and reflection-invariant features. The details of such computations are left for future work.

We did not explicitly consider variations in the bioimpedance due to changes in skin temperature (e.g., for a person with a fever, or who steps outside on a cold winter day), or due to changes in diet (e.g., level of hydration or blood sugar). These and other body conditions may have a measurable impact on bioimpedance that could make it more difficult to develop a robust model for each subject. It might be the case, for example, that a change in blood glucose alters bioimpedance samples measured at the wrist. To be truly confident in this method we need to explore the stability of bioimpedance over weeks or even months, to sample a larger number of subjects, and to explicitly and implicitly explore a broader range of environmental conditions than we captured in our day-long field experiment. We plan to perform such validations in the future.

Although we designed the bracelet for ourselves, a few subjects complained about the tightness of the bracelet. Future bracelets would be designed with different wrist sizes in mind and with better electrodes. Some subjects complained that the electrodes pulled the hair on their wrist. Other subjects mentioned that the device was too bulky to fit under a coat. Our reliance on the Shimmer platform is the source of much of the bulk. Future bracelets could incorporate their own storage, processing, communication, and power without relying on external sources. Custom silicon would also allow model training to be done on the wearable itself.

Our method will suffice for the purpose of identifying the bracelet's wearer, in many interesting applications. In some applications, however, there may be individuals with the motivation to fool the sensor into believing that the wearer is a different person – for example, if the bracelet is used as part of a biometric authentication system, or if the person wishes to have body-area sensor data collected under someone else's identity. We believe, however, that it would be exceptionally difficult to 'forge' another person's bioimpedance. In principle, an adversary could capture the desired person's bioimpedance (by hacking our bracelet to extract the data) and then construct a bracelet liner that 'replays' the impedance using fixed resistors, but this attack would be difficult to accomplish given the frequency-dependent nature of bioimpedance. More so, the threshold for verification algorithms can be chosen to produce more false accepts (i.e., affects security) versus false rejects (i.e., affects usability), and so is a policy decision.

Finally, there are several ways the current design could be optimized for lower cost or reduced energy consumption. The current wristband includes 8 electrodes yet we use only two at a time for measuring bioimpedance. It would be worthwhile exploring whether effective models can be built using only a single pair, or perhaps two pairs, of electrodes. Furthermore, we measured bioimpedance across a wide sweep of 50 frequencies; it may be possible to focus on a smaller number of frequencies, decreasing the energy and time needed for each measurement.

Rather than using bioimpedance itself as a presence detection mechanism (Section 2.4), we could integrate capacitive sensing technologies into our device. In particular, the SemTech SX9300 is an ultra low power, Specific Absorption Rate (SAR) controller

Average current drawn for bioimpedance recognition on the Shimmer

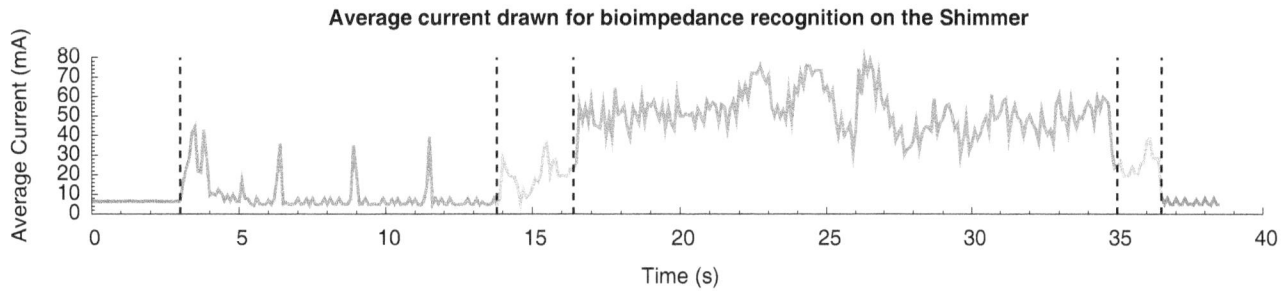

Figure 13: An energy measurement of a Shimmer when collecting bioimpedance data for recognition. The dashed line at 3.0 s is when the Shimmer turned on its Bluetooth radio. The dashed line at 13.8 s is when the smart phone connected to the Shimmer. The dashed line at 16.3 s is when the smart phone told the Shimmer to start sensing bioimpedance. The dashed line at 35.0 s is when the smart phone told the Shimmer to stop sensing bioimpedance. The dashed line at 36.5 s is when the smart phone disconnected from the Shimmer.

Average current drawn for bioimpedance recognition on the Nexus S

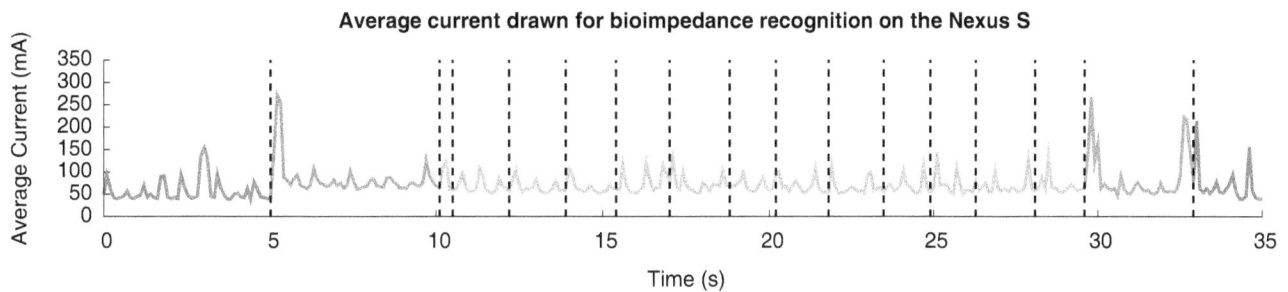

Figure 14: Energy measurement of a Nexus S smart phone when running bioimpedance recognition. The dashed line at 5 s is when the smart phone turned on its Bluetooth radio. The dashed line at 10.1 s is when the smart phone and Shimmer established a connection. The dashed lines at 10.5 s, 12.2 s, 13.9 s, 15.4 s, 17.0 s, 18.8 s, 20.2 s, 21.8 s, 23.5 s, 24.9 s, 26.3 s and 28.1 s are when the Shimmer started sensing a new electrode configuration. The dashed line at 29.6 s is when the smart phone classified the bioimpedance samples and disconnected. The dashed line at 32.9 s is when the smart phone turned off its Bluetooth radio.

that can discriminate between the human body and inanimate objects [25]. It distinguishes a human body from inanimate objects by measuring the permittivity (a measure of how freely charged particles can rotate and become polarized when subject to an electric field) of the space near small capacitive sensors (essentially small land areas on a PCB). The integrated circuit comes in a 3 mm x 3 mm x 0.6 mm QFN-20 package and consumes only 459 µW in active mode. It can generate an interrupt to wake a host microcontroller upon a "body close" or a "body far" event, allowing the controller to sleep until human presence is detected or to react to wristband removal. To reduce power costs further it has a doze mode that can scan for capacitive events at a programmable rate of 30 ms to 400 ms per scan while consuming just 48.6 µW.

Alternatively, we could integrate electric-field sensing technologies into our device. Cohn et al. describe such a low-power wake-up method using electric-field sensing technology [7]. Their sensor, like ours, requires contact with the skin, and using their low-power wake-up method only requires 9.3 µW total, which is three orders of magnitude lower power than required to operate our bioimpedance sensor. It would be easy to adopt this approach for use in our device.

Readers interested in more details about our device or its evaluation may wish to review Cornelius [8, Chapter 3].

6. RELATED WORK

There have been many biometrics proposed in the literature, however not all of them are suitable for a system such as we describe.

Most biometrics are unsuitable for our system because they cannot be captured continuously or they need to interrupt the user. Fingerprint recognition for example, requires the users to swipe or hold their fingers on a sensor. Electrocardiogram (ECG) recognition, while continuous, requires an electrical connection across the heart. Electrodes could be integrated into a shirt, however current form factors require the user to touch two electrodes using both hands.

Bioimpedance is often used to measure a person's body-fat percentage, since they are proportional to each other; several bathroom scales measure both weight and body-fat percentage. There has only been limited use of bioimpedance in support of biometrics, however. Ailisto et al. used body fat (as measured by bioimpedance) and weight to reduce error rates of fingerprint biometrics from 3.9% to 1.5% [1]. Others have used bioimpedance to detect liveness in fingerprint biometrics – see, for example, Martinsen et al. [18] – since a fingerprint reader can be easily fooled; such techniques could be incorporated into our system as well.

We are the first to suggest bioimpedance itself as a biometric. Our prior experiments provided promising evidence that bioimpedance could be a viable method for distinguishing among individuals in a small cohort, such as the members of a household. Those experiments, however, were based on a few samples of each user, under controlled laboratory conditions, using a large bench-top prototype [10]. In this paper we report our success in building such a sensor in the form of a wearable wristband, and demonstrate its potential outside of the lab, with each subject wearing the wristband for the full day. Rasmussen et al. [23] report similar results to ours but for measurements across the whole body (hand-to-hand) using a non-wearable device intended to be integrated to devices like a laptop or automated teller machine.

Others have used capacitive sensing to differentiate subjects using a capacitive touchscreen. Vu et al. [29] require the subject to wear a special ring that would inject a signal through the subject's finger and into the tablet screen while they are touching the screen. They could encode the ring wearer's identity into this signal, but the ring has no ability to biometrically identify its wearer. Indeed, this signal could be used to communicate anything to the tablet while the user touches the screen, although the data rate (4 bit/s to 5 bit/s) limits the amount of information that can be communicated. Harrison et al. [15] show how to differentiate between subjects using a capacitive touchscreen. Rather then identifying each subject, they focus on determining and tracking the number of users touching the screen. They accomplish this by modifying the touchscreen to measure the impedance between the user and ground across many frequencies. By doing this, they differentiate between subjects interacting with the touchscreen.

Finally, Srinivasan et al. [27] used height sensors to distinguish the subjects of a household. Although height might not be a distinguishing factor for large populations, they showed it is sufficiently distinct for a population the size of a household. Our cohort size was inspired by their household population approach. Our method, however, is suitable for wearable sensors that can be used anywhere, even outside of the home.

7. SUMMARY

In this paper we present a wearable system that can continuously recognize the person wearing our system. Our system is intended for applications that need to confirm that the wearer is indeed the device owner, or that need to distinguish among a small cohort such as the members of a household. To recognize people, our system uses a custom-designed bioimpedance sensor that is used for biometric identification. In contrast to our prior work, we show the effectiveness of our system by prototyping it in the form of a wearable, wrist-worn device with electrodes embedded on the inside of the wristband. This wristband was connected to a custom designed impedance-measuring module we built for the Shimmer research platform. We evaluated the ability of our system to correctly identify its wearer within a cohort of eight subjects (modeling a household of eight people). We found that the device was successful in recognizing its wearer almost 98% of the time using data collected outside of the lab. Furthermore, we show that our recognition method does not adversely affect the battery-life of a smart phone and that our wearable bioimpedance sensor could easily last for a day or longer. Finally, showing that a wearable bioimpedance system works provides the foundation for future studies of bioimpedance as a biometric.

Acknowledgments

We thank Rianna Starheim for her invaluable help with data collection. We also thank the anonymous reviewers for their comments, our fellow colleagues in the Dartmouth TISH group for their feedback, and Mary Baker for her feedback and guidance as our paper shepherd. This research results from a research program at the Institute for Security, Technology, and Society at Dartmouth College, supported by the National Science Foundation under Grant Award Number 0910842 and by the Department of Health and Human Services (SHARP program) under award number 90TR0003-01. The views and conclusions contained in this document are those of the authors and should not be interpreted as necessarily representing the official policies, either expressed or implied, of the sponsors.

8. REFERENCES

[1] H. Ailisto, E. Vildjiounaite, M. Lindholm, S.-M. Mäkelä, and J. Peltola. Soft biometrics—combining body weight and fat measurements with fingerprint biometrics. *Pattern Recognition Letters*, 27(5):325–334, Apr. 2006. DOI 10.1016/j.patrec.2005.08.018.

[2] Analog Devices. Analog Devices ADR433 Ultra-low Noise Voltage Reference. Online at http://www.analog.com/en/special-linear-functions/voltage-references/adr433/products/product.html, visited Feb. 2013.

[3] Analog Devices AD5933 Impedance Analyzer. Online at http://www.analog.com/en/rfif-components/direct-digital-synthesis-dds/ad5933/products/product.html, visited Apr. 2013.

[4] Analog Devices ADG1608 8-Channel Multiplexor. Online at http://www.analog.com/en/switchesmultiplexers/multiplexers-muxes/adg1608/products/product.html, visited Apr. 2013.

[5] S. Avancha, A. Baxi, and D. Kotz. Privacy in mobile technology for personal healthcare. *ACM Computing Surveys*, 45(1), Nov. 2012. DOI 10.1145/2379776.2379779.

[6] B. E. Boser, I. M. Guyon, and V. N. Vapnik. A training algorithm for optimal margin classifiers. In *Proceedings of the Fifth Annual Workshop on Computational Learning Theory (COLT)*, pages 144–152, 1992. DOI 10.1145/130385.130401.

[7] G. Cohn, S. Gupta, T. J. Lee, D. Morris, J. R. Smith, M. S. Reynolds, D. S. Tan, and S. N. Patel. An ultra-low-power human body motion sensor using static electric field sensing. In *Proceedings of the 2012 ACM Conference on Ubiquitous Computing (UbiComp)*, pages 99–102, 2012. DOI 10.1145/2370216.2370233.

[8] C. Cornelius. *Usable Security for Wireless Body-Area Networks*. PhD thesis, Dartmouth College Computer Science, Hanover, NH, Sept. 2013. Available as Dartmouth Computer Science Technical Report TR2011-741, Online at http://www.cs.dartmouth.edu/reports/TR2011-741.pdf.

[9] C. Cornelius and D. Kotz. Recognizing whether sensors are on the same body. *Journal of Pervasive and Mobile Computing*, 8(6):822–836, Dec. 2012. DOI 10.1016/j.pmcj.2012.06.005.

[10] C. Cornelius, J. Sorber, R. Peterson, J. Skinner, R. Halter, and D. Kotz. Who wears me? Bioimpedance as a passive biometric. In *Proceedings of the USENIX Workshop on Health Security and Privacy (HealthSec)*, Aug. 2012. Online at http://www.cs.dartmouth.edu/~dfk/papers/cornelius-impedance.pdf.

[11] A. P. Dempster, N. M. Laird, and D. B. Rubin. Maximum likelihood from incomplete data via the EM algorithm. *Journal of the Royal Statistical Society, Series B (Methodological)*, 39(1):1–38, 1977. DOI 10.2307/2984875.

[12] Google. Nexus S – Android Device Gallery. Online at http://www.android.com/devices/detail/nexus-s, visited Dec. 2013.

[13] H. Gray and W. H. Lewis. *Anatomy of the human body*. Lea & Febiger, 20th edition, 1918. Online at http://en.wikipedia.org/wiki/File:Gray417_color.PNG.

[14] M. Hall, E. Frank, G. Holmes, B. Pfahringer, P. Reutemann, and I. H. Witten. The WEKA data mining software: an update. *SIGKDD Explorations Newsletter*, 11(1):10–18, Nov. 2009. DOI 10.1145/1656274.1656278.

[15] C. Harrison, M. Sato, and I. Poupyrev. Capacitive fingerprinting: exploring user differentiation by sensing

electrical properties of the human body. In *Proceedings of the ACM Symposium on User Interface Software and Technology (UIST)*, pages 537–544. ACM, Oct. 2012. DOI 10.1145/2380116.2380183.

[16] Hirose Electric Co., Ltd. Hirose 3260-8S3(55) Connector. Online at http://www.hirose.co.jp/cataloge_hp/e23200014.pdf, visited Mar. 2013.

[17] T. Kanungo, D. M. Mount, N. S. Netanyahu, C. D. Piatko, R. Silverman, and A. Y. Wu. An efficient k-means clustering algorithm: analysis and implementation. *IEEE Transactions on Pattern Analysis and Machine Intelligence*, 24(7):881–892, July 2002. DOI 10.1109/tpami.2002.1017616.

[18] Ø. G. Martinsen, S. Clausen, J. B. Nysæther, and S. Grimnes. Utilizing Characteristic Electrical Properties of the Epidermal Skin Layers to Detect Fake Fingers in Biometric Fingerprint Systems—A Pilot Study. *IEEE Transactions on Biomedical Engineering*, 54(5):891–894, May 2007. DOI 10.1109/tbme.2007.893472.

[19] R. Mayrhofer. OpenUAT: The Open Source Ubiquitous Authentication Toolkit. Online at http://www.openuat.org/, visited Aug. 2013.

[20] Microchip Technology Inc. Microchip MCP1252 Charge Pump. Online at http://ww1.microchip.com/downloads/en/DeviceDoc/21752B.pdf, visited Feb. 2013.

[21] Monsoon Power Monitor. Online at http://www.msoon.com/LabEquipment/PowerMonitor/, visited Nov. 2013.

[22] Nordic Semiconductor. nRF51822. Online at http://www.nordicsemi.com/eng/Products/Bluetooth-R-low-energy/nRF51822, visited Nov. 2013.

[23] K. B. Rasmussen, M. Roeschlin, I. Martinovic, and G. Tsudik. Authentication using pulse-response biometrics. In *Proceedings of the Annual Network and Distributed System Security Symposium (NDSS)*, Feb. 2014.

[24] R. Rifkin and A. Klautau. In defense of one-vs-all classification. *Journal of Machine Learning Research*, 5:101–141, Dec. 2004. Online at http://jmlr.org/papers/v5/rifkin04a.html.

[25] Semtech. SX9300 Ultra Low Power, Dual Channel, Smart Proximity SAR Compliant Solution. Online at http://www.semtech.com/touch-interface/capacitive-touch-controllers/sx9300/, visited Apr. 2013.

[26] Shimmer-Research. Online at http://www.shimmer-research.com/, visited Apr. 2013.

[27] V. Srinivasan, J. Stankovic, and K. Whitehouse. Using Height Sensors for Biometric Identification in Multi-resident Homes. In *Proceedings of the 8th International Conference on Pervasive Computing (PERVASIVE)*, volume 6030 of *LNCS*, pages 337–354. Springer, May 2010. DOI 10.1007/978-3-642-12654-3_20.

[28] TinyOS. Online at http://www.tinyos.net/, visited Apr. 2013.

[29] T. Vu, A. Baid, S. Gao, M. Gruteser, R. Howard, J. Lindqvist, P. Spasojevic, and J. Walling. Distinguishing users with capacitive touch communication. In *Proceedings of the Annual International Conference on Mobile Computing and Networking (Mobicom)*, pages 197–208. ACM, 2012. DOI 10.1145/2348543.2348569.

[30] Wikipedia. Brandon Mayfield — Wikipedia, The Free Encyclopedia. Online at http://en.wikipedia.org/wiki/Brandon_Mayfield, visited Aug. 2013.

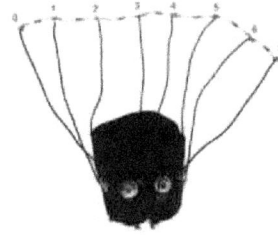

Figure 15: The resistor array used to calibrate our system. The 1 kΩ ± 5% resistors are connected in series. The reference resistance between a pair of electrodes will vary depending on the number of resistors between them. For example, the resistance between electrodes 0–4 is 4 kΩ.

APPENDIX

A. CALIBRATION

To compute impedance from the raw data, we calibrated the system using a reference impedance. Calibration is important because different sensor modules will exhibit different impedances due to different parasitic elements and/or artifacts from the amplifiers present in the hardware. We built three of these sensor modules, so we calibrated each device to be sure that our studies are not affected by the particular choice of hardware. In addition, our particular device senses from different electrode pairs via a pair of multiplexors which can themselves introduce additional parasitic elements. Thus, we also must calibrate for every electrode pair.

To calibrate our devices for an electrode pair, we used a known reference impedance value $|Z|_{ref}$ in the form of an array of 1 kΩ ± 5% resistors (we used a digital multimeter to record the exact values between electrodes) as shown in Figure 15. To calibrate impedance magnitude, we first compute the uncalibrated impedance magnitude $|Z(\omega)|_{uncal}$ of the impedance as described in Section 2.2. Because we know the expected magnitude of the reference impedance $|Z|_{ref}$ (the impedance magnitude of a resistor is equal to its resistance), we computed the *gain factor* as:

$$\text{Gain Factor}(\omega) = \frac{1}{|Z|_{ref} \times |Z(\omega)|_{uncal}}$$

For some new uncalibrated impedance magnitude, we compute the calibrated impedance magnitude as:

$$|Z(\omega)| = \frac{1}{\text{Gain Factor}(\omega) \times |Z(\omega)|_{uncal}}$$

We followed a similar calibration procedure for the impedance phase. Since resistors exhibit no impedance phase shift (aside from some parasitic capacitance, which we ignore because these effects fall outside of the bandwidth of our system), we first compute the uncalibrated impedance phase $Z\emptyset(\omega)_{uncal}$ as above. This value is the *phase difference* that accounts for all phase shift attributed to the hardware itself. For some uncalibrated impedance phase, we computed the calibrated impedance phase as:

$$Z\emptyset(\omega) = Z\emptyset(\omega)_{uncal} - \text{Phase Difference}(\omega)$$

This calibration procedure yields a gain factor and phase difference for each frequency and electrode pair that are specific to that sensor module.

During calibration we noticed the lower frequencies exhibited random noise in the signal, of unknown source, so we discard frequencies below 10 kHz. This left 50 frequencies. The AD5933 evaluation boards exhibited similar noise, so we do not believe it is something inherent in the design of our own sensor module.

Towards Wearable Cognitive Assistance

Kiryong Ha, Zhuo Chen, Wenlu Hu, Wolfgang Richter,
Padmanabhan Pillai[†], and Mahadev Satyanarayanan

Carnegie Mellon University and [†]Intel Labs

ABSTRACT

We describe the architecture and prototype implementation
of an assistive system based on Google Glass devices for
users in cognitive decline. It combines the first-person image capture and sensing capabilities of Glass with remote
processing to perform real-time scene interpretation. The
system architecture is multi-tiered. It offers tight end-to-end
latency bounds on compute-intensive operations, while addressing concerns such as limited battery capacity and limited processing capability of wearable devices. The system
gracefully degrades services in the face of network failures
and unavailability of distant architectural tiers.

Categories and Subject Descriptors

D.4.7 [**Software**]: Operating System – Organization and
Design

General Terms

Design, Experimentation, Measurement

Keywords

wearable computing; mobile computing; cloud computing;
cloudlet; cloud offload; cyber foraging; virtual machine;
Google Glass

1. INTRODUCTION

Today, over 20 million Americans are affected by some
form of cognitive decline that significantly affects their ability to function as independent members of society. This
includes people with conditions such as Alzheimer's disease
and mild cognitive impairment, survivors of stroke, and people with traumatic brain injury. Cognitive decline can manifest itself in many ways, including the inability to recognize
people, locations and objects, loss of short- and long-term
memory, and changes in behavior and appearance. The potential cost savings from even modest steps towards addressing this challenge are enormous. It is estimated that just
a one-month delay in nursing home admissions in the US
could save over \$1 billion annually. The potential win is
even greater when extrapolated to global scale.

Wearable devices such as Google Glass offer a glimmer of
hope to users in cognitive decline. These devices integrate
first-person image capture, sensing, processing and communication capabilities in an aesthetically elegant form factor.
Through context-aware real-time scene interpretation (including recognition of objects, faces, activities, signage text,
and sounds), we can create software that offers helpful guidance for everyday life much as a GPS navigation system
helps a driver. Figure 1 presents a hypothetical scenario
that is suggestive of the future we hope to create.

An ideal cognitive assistive system should function "in the
wild" with sufficient functionality, performance and usability
to be valuable at any time and place. It should also be sufficiently flexible to allow easy customization for the unique
disabilities of an individual. Striving towards this ideal, we
describe the architecture and prototype implementation of a
cognitive assistance system based on Google Glass devices.
This paper makes the following contributions:

- It presents a multi-tiered mobile system architecture
  that offers tight end-to-end latency bounds on compute-
  intensive cognitive assistance operations, while addressing concerns such as limited battery capacity and limited processing capability of wearable devices.

- It shows how the processing-intensive back-end tier of
  this architecture can support VM-based extensibility
  for easy customization, without imposing unacceptable latency and processing overheads on high data-
  rate sensor streams from a wearable device.

- It explores how cognitive assistance services can be
  gracefully degraded in the face of network failures and
  unavailability of distant architectural tiers.

As an initial step towards wearable cognitive assistance,
we focus on the architectural requirements and implementation details needed by such systems in the rest of the paper.
We leave other aspects of this research such as user interface
design and context-sensitive user guidance for future work.

2. BACKGROUND AND RELATED WORK

2.1 Assistive Smart Spaces

One of the earliest practical applications of pervasive com-
puting was in the creation of *smart spaces* to assist people.
These are located in custom-designed buildings such as the
Aware Home at Georgia Institute of Technology [16], the
Gator Tech Smart House at the University of Florida [14],
and Elite Care's Oatfield Estates in Milwaukie, Oregon [36].
These sensor-rich environments detect and interpret the ac-

Ron is a young veteran who was wounded in Afghanistan and is slowly recovering from traumatic brain injury. He has suffered a sharp decline in his mental acuity and is often unable to remember the names of friends and relatives. He also frequently forgets to do simple daily tasks. Even modest improvements in his cognitive ability would greatly improve his quality of life, while also reducing the attention demanded from caregivers. Fortunately, a new Glass-based system offers hope. When Ron looks at a person for a few seconds, that person's name is whispered in his ear along with additional cues to guide Ron's greeting and interactions; when he looks at his thirsty houseplant, "water me" is whispered; when he looks at his long-suffering dog, "take me out" is whispered. Ron's magic glasses travel with him, transforming his surroundings into a helpful smart environment.

Figure 1: Hypothetical Scenario: Cognitive Assistance for Traumatic Brain Injury

tions of their occupants and offer helpful guidance when appropriate. They can thus be viewed as first-generation cognitive assistance systems.

Inspired by these early examples, we aim to free cognitive assistance systems from the confines of a purpose-built smart space. Simultaneously, we aim to enrich user experience and assistive value. These goals are unlikely to be achieved by an evolutionary path from first-generation systems. Scaling up a smart space from a building or suite of buildings to an entire neighborhood or an entire city is extremely expensive and time-consuming. Physical infrastructure in public spaces tends to evolve very slowly, over a time scale of decades. Mobile computing technology, on the other hand, advances much faster.

Instead of relying on sensors embedded in smart spaces, we dynamically inject sensing into the environment through computer vision on a wearable computer. The scenario in Figure 1 is a good example of this approach. Aided by such a system, commonplace activities such as going to a shopping mall, attending a baseball game, or transacting business downtown should become attainable goals for people in need of modest cognitive assistance.

Using computer vision for sensing has two great advantages. First, it works on totally unmodified environments — smart spaces are not needed. Second, the sensing can be performed from a significant physical distance. The video stream can be augmented with additional sensor streams such as accelerometer readings and GPS readings to infer user context. This enables a user-centric approach to cognitive assistance that travels with the user and is therefore available at all times and places.

2.2 Wearable Cognitive Assistance

The possibility of using wearable devices for deep cognitive assistance (e.g., offering hints for social interaction via real-time scene analysis) was first suggested nearly a decade ago [33, 34]. However, this goal has remained unattainable until now for three reasons. First, the state of the art in many foundational technologies (such as computer vision, sensor-based activity inference, speech recognition, and language translation) is only now approaching the required speed and accuracy. Second, the computing infrastructure for offloading compute-intensive operations from mobile devices was absent. Only now, with the convergence of mobile computing and cloud computing, is this being corrected. Third, suitable wearable hardware was not available. Although head-up displays have been used in military and industrial applications, their unappealing style, bulkiness and poor level of comfort have limited widespread adoption. Only now has aesthetically elegant, product-quality hardware technology of this genre become available. Google Glass is the most well-known example, but others are also

being developed. It is the convergence of all three factors at this point in time that brings our goal within reach.

There have been other wearable devices developed for specific types of cognitive decline. For example, SenseCam [15] is a wearable digital camera that takes images of the wearer's day. For those with memory decline, it can be used to review the recorded images in order to boost memory recall. Though valuable, this is a form of offline assistance, and not readily available while performing day-to-day activities. In contrast, our work seeks to augment daily life in an interactive, timely manner and to cover a broader range of cognitive impairments. This leads to different research challenges in the system design and the requirements.

This paper focuses on interactive cognitive assistance using Google Glass, which is the most widely available wearable device today. A Glass device is equipped with a first-person video camera and sensors such as an accelerometer, GPS[1], and compass. Although our experimental results apply specifically to the Explorer version of Glass, our system architecture and design principles are applicable to any similar wearable device. Figure 2 illustrates the main components of a Glass device [20].

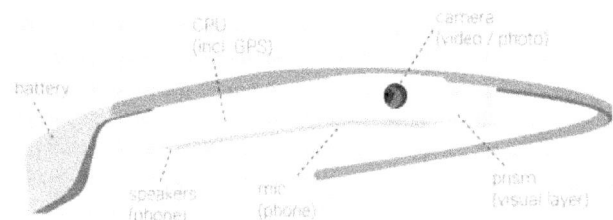

Figure 2: Components of a Google Glass Device (Source: adapted from Missfeldt [20])

2.3 Cyber Foraging

Offloading compute-intensive operations from mobile devices to powerful infrastructure in order to improve performance and extend battery life is a strategy that dates back to the late 1990s. Flinn [8] gives a comprehensive survey of the large body of work in this space. The emergence of cloud computing has renewed interest in this approach, leading to commercial products such as Google Goggles, Amazon Silk, and Apple Siri. Among recent research efforts, MAUI [5] dynamically selects an optimal partitioning of a C# program to reduce the energy consumption of a mobile application. COMET [12] uses distributed shared memory to enable transparent offloading of Android applications. Odessa [29] makes dynamic offloading and parallelism decisions to achieve low latency for interactive perception ap-

---

[1] Google Glass has hardware for GPS but it is not activated. Location is currently estimated with Wi-Fi localization.

| Year | Typical Server | | Typical Handheld or Wearable | |
	Processor	Speed	Device	Speed
1997	Pentium® II	266 MHz	Palm Pilot	16 MHz
2002	Itanium®	1 GHz	Blackberry 5810	133 MHz
2007	Intel® Core™ 2	9.6 GHz (4 cores)	Apple iPhone	412 MHz
2011	Intel® Xeon® X5	32 GHz (2x6 cores)	Samsung Galaxy S2	2.4 GHz (2 cores)
2013	Intel® Xeon® E5	64 GHz (2x12 cores)	Samsung Galaxy S4	6.4 GHz (4 cores)
			Google Glass OMAP 4430	2.4 GHz (2 cores)

Figure 3: Evolution of Hardware Performance (Source: adapted from Flinn [8])

plications. All of these research efforts constrain software to specific languages, frameworks or platforms. In contrast, as discussed in Section 3.5, we aim to support the widest possible range of applications without restrictions on their programming languages or operating systems.

3. DESIGN CONSTRAINTS

The unique demands of cognitive assistance applications place important constraints on system design. We discuss these constraints below, and then present the resulting system architecture in Section 4.

3.1 Crisp Interactive Response

Humans are acutely sensitive to delays in the critical path of interaction. This is apparent to anyone who has used a geosynchronous satellite link for a telephone call. The nearly 500 ms round-trip delay is distracting to most users, and leads to frequent conversational errors.

Normal human performance on cognitive tasks is remarkably fast and accurate. Lewis et al. [17] report that even under hostile conditions such as low lighting and deliberately distorted optics, human subjects take less than 700 milliseconds to determine the absence of faces in a scene. For face recognition under normal lighting conditions, experimental results on human subjects by Ramon et al. [30] show that recognition times range from 370 milliseconds for the fastest responses on familiar faces to 620 milliseconds for the slowest response on an unfamiliar face. For speech recognition, Agus et al. [2] report that human subjects recognize short target phrases within 300 to 450 ms, and are able to detect a human voice within a mere 4 ms.

Ellis et al. [6] report that virtual reality applications that use head-tracked systems require latencies less than 16 ms to achieve perceptual stability. More generally, assistive technology that is introduced into the critical paths of perception and cognition should add negligible delay relative to the task-specific human performance figures cited above. Larger processing delays of more than tens of milliseconds will distract and annoy a mobile user who is already attention challenged and in cognitive decline.

Metric	Standalone	With Offload
Per-image speed (s)	10.49 (0.23)	1.28 (0.12)
Per-image energy (J)	12.84 (0.36)	1.14 (0.11)

Each result is the mean over five runs of an experiment. Standard deviations are shown in parentheses.

Figure 4: OCR Performance on Glass Device

3.2 Need for Offloading

Wearable devices are always resource-poor relative to server hardware of comparable vintage [32]. Figure 3, adapted from Flinn [8], illustrates the consistent large gap in the processing power of typical server and mobile device hardware over a 16-year period. This stubborn gap reflects a fundamental reality of user preferences: Moore's Law works differently on wearable hardware. The most sought-after features of a wearable device are light weight, small size, long battery life, comfort and aesthetics, and tolerable heat dissipation. System capabilities such as processor speed, memory size, and storage capacity are only secondary concerns.

The large gap in the processing capabilities of wearable and server hardware directly impacts the user. Figure 4 shows the speed and energy usage of a Glass device for a representative cognitive assistance application (optical character recognition (OCR), described in detail in Section 5.5). In the configuration labeled "Standalone," the entire application runs on the Glass device and involves no network communication. In the configuration labeled "With Offload," the image is transmitted from the Glass device over Wi-Fi 802.11n to a compute server of modest capability: a Dell Optiplex 9010 desktop with an Intel® Core™ i7 4-core processor and 32GB of memory; the result is transmitted back to the Glass device. As Figure 4 shows, offloading gives almost an order of magnitude improvement in both speed of recognition and energy used on the Glass device. The benefit of offloading is not specific to OCR but applies across the board to a wide range of cognitive assistance applications.

3.3 Graceful Degradation of Offload Services

What does a user do if a network failure, server failure, power failure, or other disruption makes offload impossible? While such failures will hopefully be rare, they cannot be ignored in an assistive system. It is likely that a user will find himself in situations where offloading to Internet-based infrastructure is temporarily not possible. Falling back on standalone execution on his wearable device will hurt user experience. As the results in Figure 4 suggest, it will negatively impact crispness of interaction and battery life. Under these difficult circumstances, the user may be willing to sacrifice some other attribute of his cognitive assistance service in order to obtain crisp interaction and longer battery life. For example, an assistive system for face recognition may switch to a mode in which it can recognize only a few faces, preselected by the user; when offloading becomes possible again, the system can revert to recognizing its full range of faces. Of course, the user will need to be alerted to these transitions so that his expectations are set appropriately.

This general theme of trading off *application-specific fidelity of execution* for response time and battery life was explored by Noble [24], Flinn [9], Narayanan [22], and others in the context of the Odyssey system. Their approach of creating an interface for applications to query system resource state and to leave behind notification triggers is applicable here. However, assistive applications have very different characteristics from applications such as streaming video and web browsing that were explored by Odyssey.

3.4 Context-sensitive Sensor Control

Significant improvements in battery life and usability are possible if high-level knowledge of user context is used to control sensors on a wearable device [4]. For example, consider a user who falls asleep in his chair at home while watching TV. While he is asleep, his Glass device does not have to capture video and stream it for cognitive assistance. In fact, offering whispered hints during his nap might wake him up and annoy him. When he wakes up of his own accord, processing for cognitive assistance should resume promptly. The challenge is, of course, to reliably distinguish between the user's sleeping and waking states. This is the classic problem of activity recognition from body-worn sensor data, on which significant progress has been made in the recent past. These results can be extended to infer context and then use it for adaptive control of sensor streams.

This problem has many subtle aspects. In the above example, if the user falls asleep in a bus or metro rather than in his living room, the cognitive assistance system should give him timely warning of his approaching exit even if it wakes him up from his pleasant nap. In this case, location sensing will need to remain turned on during his nap even though other sensors (such as video) may be turned off. More generally, tight coupling of sensing and context inference in a feedback loop is valuable in a cognitive assistance system.

3.5 Coarse-grain Parallelism

Human cognition involves the synthesis of outputs from real-time analytics on multiple sensor stream inputs. A human conversation, for example, involves many diverse inputs: the language content and deep semantics of the words, the tone in which they are spoken, the facial expressions and eye movements with which they are spoken, and the body language and gestures that accompany them. All of these distinct channels of information have to be processed and combined in real time for full situational awareness. There is substantial evidence [28] that human brains achieve this impressive feat of real-time processing by employing completely different neural circuits in parallel and then combining their outputs. Each neural circuit is effectively a processing engine that operates in isolation of others. Coarse-grain parallelism is thus at the heart of human cognition.

A wide range of software building blocks that correspond to these distinct processing engines exist today: face recognition [38], activity recognition [41] in video, natural language translation [3], OCR [10], question-answering technology such as that used in Watson [7], and so on. These *cognitive engines* are written in a variety of programming languages and use diverse runtime systems. Some of them are proprietary, some are written for closed source operating systems, and some use proprietary optimizing compilers. Each is a natural unit of coarse-grain parallelism. In their entirety, these cognitive engines represent many hundreds to thousands of person years of effort by experts in each domain. To the extent possible we would like to reuse this large body of existing code.

4. ARCHITECTURE

The high-level design of *Gabriel*, our system for wearable cognitive assistance, is strongly influenced by the constraints presented in Section 3. We present an overview of Gabriel here to explain how these constraints are met, and follow with details of our prototype in Section 5.

4.1 Low-latency Offloading

Gabriel faces the difficult problem of simultaneously satisfying the need for crisp, low-latency interaction (Section 3.1) and the need for offloading processing from a wearable device (Section 3.2). The obvious solution of using commercial cloud services over a WAN is unsatisfactory because the RTT is too long. Li et al. [18] report that average RTT from 260 global vantage points to their optimal Amazon EC2 instances is nearly 74 ms, and a wireless first hop would add to this amount. This makes it virtually impossible to meet tight latency goals of a few tens of milliseconds, even if cloud processing takes zero time. There is little evidence that WAN RTTs will improve significantly in the future, since most networking deployments today are working towards improving other aspects of the network such as bandwidth, security, and manageability rather than latency. Mechanisms such as firewalls, overlay networks, traffic engineering, and software defined networking tend to increase the software path length and number of layers traversed by packets, thus potentially hurting latency. Recent work on active control of end-to-end latency shrinks cloud processing time per operation to meet deadlines, and achieves error bounds on the order of 50 ms in an end-to-end latency budget of 1200 ms [31]. Unfortunately, this error bound is comparable to our entire end-to-end latency budget in Gabriel. Further, we strongly believe that degrading cloud processing quality to meet latency bounds should only be a last resort rather than standard operating procedure in cognitive assistance.

Gabriel achieves low-latency offload by using *cloudlets* [34]. A cloudlet is a new architectural element that represents the middle tier of a 3-tier hierarchy: mobile device — cloudlet — cloud. It can be viewed as a "data center in a box" whose goal is to "bring the cloud closer." As a powerful, well-connected and trustworthy cloud proxy that is just one Wi-Fi hop away, a cloudlet is the ideal offload site for cognitive assistance. Although widespread deployment of cloudlets is not yet a reality, commercial interest in cloudlet-like infrastructure is starting. In early 2013, for example, IBM and Nokia-Siemens Networks announced the availability of a "mobile edge computing platform" [1]. Wearable cognitive assistance can be viewed as a "killer app" that has the potential to stimulate investment in cloudlets.

Figure 5(a) illustrates how offload works normally in Gabriel. The user's Glass device discovers and associates with a nearby cloudlet, and then uses it for offload. Optionally, the cloudlet may reach out to the cloud for various services such as centralized error reporting and usage logging. All such cloudlet-cloud interactions are outside the critical latency-sensitive path of device-cloudlet interactions. When the mobile user is about to depart from the proximity of this cloudlet, a mechanism analogous to Wi-Fi handoff is invoked. This seamlessly associates the user with another cloudlet for the next phase of his travels.

4.2 Offload Fallback Strategy

When no suitable cloudlet is available, the obvious fallback is to offload directly to the cloud as shown in Figure 5(b). This incurs the WAN latency and bandwidth issues that were avoided with cloudlets. Since RTT and

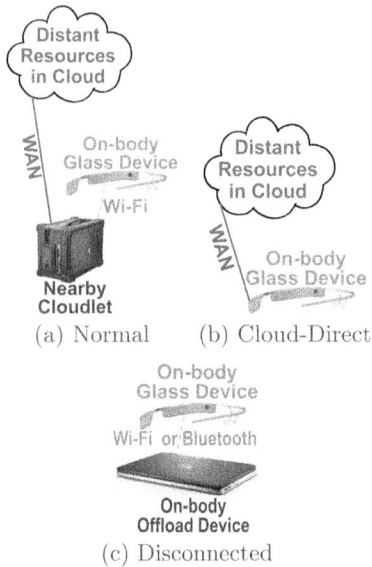

Figure 5: Offload Approaches

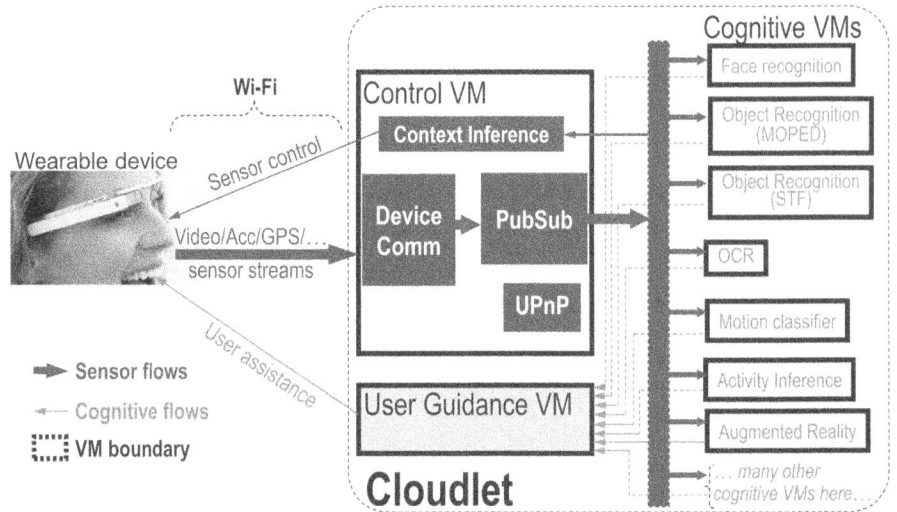

Figure 6: Back-end Processing on Cloudlet

bandwidth are the issues rather than processing capacity, application-specific reduction of fidelity must aim for less frequent synchronous use of the cloud. For example, a vision-based indoor navigation application can increase its use of dead reckoning and reduce how often it uses cloud-based scene recognition. This may hurt accuracy, but the timeliness of guidance can be preserved. When a suitable cloudlet becomes available, normal offloading can be resumed. To correctly set user expectations, the system can use audible or visual signals to indicate fidelity transitions. Some hysteresis will be needed to ensure that the transitions do not occur too frequently.

An even more aggressive fallback approach is needed when the Internet is inaccessible (Section 3.3). Relying solely on the wearable device is not a viable option, as shown by the results of Figure 4. To handle these extreme situations, we assume that the user is willing to carry a device such as a laptop or a netbook that can serve as an offload device. As smartphones evolve and become more powerful, they too may become viable offload devices. The preferred network connectivity is Wi-Fi with the fallback device operating in AP mode, since it offers good bandwidth without requiring any infrastructure. For fallback devices that do not support AP mode Wi-Fi, a lower-bandwidth alternative is Bluetooth. Figure 5(c) illustrates offloading while disconnected.

How large and heavy a device to carry as fallback is a matter of user preference. A larger and heavier fallback device can support applications at higher fidelity and thus provide a better user experience. With a higher-capacity battery, it is also likely to be able to support a longer period of disconnected operation than a smaller and lighter device. However, running applications at higher fidelity shortens battery life. One can view the inconvenience of carrying an offload device as an insurance premium. A user who is confident that Internet access will always be available, or who is willing to tolerate temporary loss of cognitive assistance services, can choose not to carry a fallback offload device.

4.3 VM Ensemble and PubSub Backbone

For reasons explained earlier in Section 3.5, a cloudlet must exploit coarse-grain parallelism across many off-the-shelf cognitive engines of diverse types and constructions. To meet this requirement, Gabriel encapsulates each cognitive engine (complete with its operating system, dynamically linked libraries, supporting tool chains and applications, configuration files and data sets) in its own virtual machine (VM). Since there is no shared state across VMs, coarse-grain parallelism across cognitive engines is trivial to exploit. A cloudlet can be scaled out by simply adding more independent processing units, leading eventually to an internally-networked cluster structure. If supported by a cognitive engine, process-level and thread-level parallelism within a VM can be exploited through multiple cores on a processor — enhancing parallelism at this level will require scaling up the number of cores. A VM-based approach is less restrictive and more general than language-based virtualization approaches that require applications to be written in a specific language such as Java or C#. The specific cognitive engines used in our prototype (discussed in Section 5) span both Windows and Linux environments.

Figure 6 illustrates Gabriel's back-end processing structure on a cloudlet. An ensemble of *cognitive VMs*, each encapsulating a different cognitive engine, independently processes the incoming flow of sensor data from a Glass device. A single *control VM* is responsible for all interactions with the Glass device. The sensor streams sent by the device are received and preprocessed by this VM. For example, the decoding of compressed images to raw frames is performed by a process in the control VM. This avoids duplicate decoding within each cognitive VM. A PubSub mechanism distributes sensor streams to cognitive VMs. At startup, each VM discovers the sensor streams of interest through a UPnP discovery mechanism in the control VM.

The outputs of the cognitive VMs are sent to a single *User Guidance VM* that integrates these outputs and performs higher-level cognitive processing. In this initial implementation of Gabriel, we use very simple rule-based software. As Gabriel evolves, we envision significant improvement in user experience to come from more sophisticated, higher-level cognitive processing in the User Guidance VM. From time to time, the processing in the User Guidance VM triggers output for user assistance. For example, a synthesized voice may say the name of a person whose face appears in the Glass device's camera. It may also convey additional guidance for how the user should respond, such as "John Smith is trying to say hello to you. Shake his hand."

Section 3.4 discussed the importance of context-sensitive control of sensors on the Glass device. This is achieved in Gabriel through a context inference module in the Control VM. In practice, this module determines context from the external cognitive engines and uses this to control sensors. Referring to the example in Section 3.4, it is this module that detects that a user has fallen asleep and sends a control message to the Glass device to turn off the camera.

5. PROTOTYPE IMPLEMENTATION

We have built a prototype of Gabriel that closely follows the architecture described in the previous section. This prototype uses the Explorer edition of Google Glass, which is based on Android 4.0.4. Our cloudlet is composed of 4 desktop machines, each with an Intel® Core® i7-3770 and 32 GB memory, running Ubuntu 12.04.3 LTS server. The control VM runs a UPnP server to allow the Glass device to discover it, and to allow the various VMs to discover the control VM and PubSub system. The cloudlet uses OpenStack Grizzly [27] on QEMU/KVM version 1.0.

5.1 Glass Front-end

A front-end Android application that runs on the Glass device discovers a cloudlet and connects to its Gabriel backend. Our implementation uses the Glass Development Kit (GDK) [11], which enables Glass-specific features such as application control via voice. Thus, users can launch the Gabriel front-end application using voice. After connecting to the Gabriel back-end, the front-end streams video, GPS coordinates, and accelerometer readings over Wi-Fi to the cognitive engines. To achieve low network latency, we have tested both TCP and UDP. Our experiments showed negligible difference in response times between TCP and UDP over Wi-Fi. Since use of UDP adds complexity for maintaining reliable data transmission, we use TCP for each sensor stream. The User Guidance VM digests the outputs of the cognitive engines and presents assistance to the user via text or images on the Glass display or as synthesized speech using the Android text-to-speech API. A single Wi-Fi TCP connection is used for this guidance. In the prototype implementation, the output passes through the DeviceComm module of the Control VM since it represents the single point of contact for all interactions with the Glass device.

5.2 Discovery and Initialization

The architecture of Gabriel is based on many software components in multiple VMs working together. Key to making this composition work is a mechanism for the different components to discover and connect with each other.

In our prototype, the control VM is launched first and provides the servers to which Google Glass and the cognitive engine VMs connect. The User Guidance VM starts next, followed by the cognitive VMs, which are connected together on a private virtual network using OpenStack Nova-networking's VLAN. This private network can span machine boundaries, allowing sizable cloudlets to be used. The control VM is connected to both this private network and the regular LAN, with a public IP address. The latter is used to communicate with the Google Glass device.

A UPnP server, which provides a standard, broadcast-based method of discovering local services in a LAN, runs in the control VM. This allows the other VMs to find the control VM when they start. More specifically, at launch, each VM performs a UPnP query on the private network. The UPnP server, which is tied to our simplified PubSub system, replies with a list of published data streams that are available and the PubSub control channel. The cognitive VMs subscribe to the desired sensor streams and register their own processed data streams through the PubSub system. At a lower level, this establishes TCP connections between the cognitive VMs and the sensor stream servers in the control VM, and to the User Guidance VM that subscribes to all of the processed data streams.

The UPnP server also provides a simple mechanism to let the Glass device discover the Gabriel infrastructure on a LAN. On the public interface of the control VM, the UPnP server replies to queries with the public IP address and port of the Device Comm server. The Glass front end makes multiple TCP connections to this to push its sensors streams and receive cognitive assistance output (passed through from the User Guidance VM) as well as sensor control information.

When the Glass device is not within the broadcast domain of a cloudlet running Gabriel, it falls back to using a cloud-hosted directory of nearby cloudlets. If no cloudlet is found, the client offloads to an instance of Gabriel in the cloud. When all else fails, offload to bigger user-carried devices can be performed, as described in Section 4.2.

5.3 Handling Cognitive Engine Diversity

Our architecture allows cognitive engines to use a variety of programming frameworks and operating systems. For all of these components to work together, we do need them to follow a common communication paradigm. To this end, our system requires a small amount of glue logic to be written for each cognitive engine. This code can be thought of as a wrapper around the cognitive engine, transforming the inputs and outputs to work with our system. It pulls sensor data from the streams and presents it in a manner needed by the cognitive engine (e.g., in the right image format, or as a file). It also extracts results from the engine-specific form and transmits it as a processed data stream. This wrapper is also responsible for discovering and connecting to the PubSub system, subscribing to the required sensor streams, and publishing the outputs. Finally, the wrapper ensures that the cognitive engine processes each data item (e.g., by signaling a continuously running engine that new data is available, or relaunching the engine for each item). All of these functions are simple to implement, and tend to follow straightforward patterns. However, as they are tailored to specific cognitive engines, we expect the wrappers to be packaged with the engines in the cognitive VMs.

5.4 Limiting Queuing Latency

In our flexible and pluggable architecture, a set of components communicate using network connections. Each com-

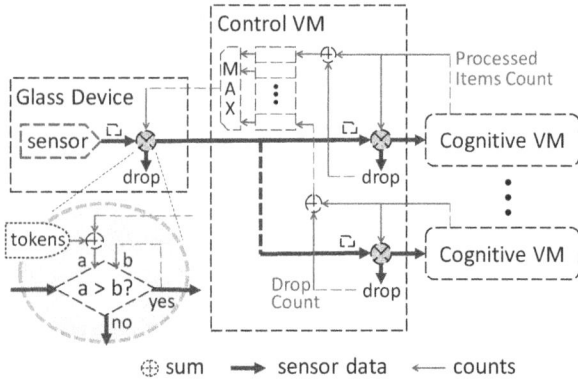

Figure 7: Two Level Token-based Filtering Scheme

munication hop involves a traversal of the networking stacks, and can involve several queues in the applications and guest OSs, over which we have little control. The application and network buffers can be large, and cause many items to be queued up, increasing latency. To minimize queuing, we need to ensure that the data ingress rate never exceeds the bottleneck throughput, whose location and value can vary dramatically over time. The variation arises from fluctuations in the available network bandwidth between the Glass device and cloudlet, and from the dependence of processing times of cognitive engines on data content.

We have devised an application-level, end-to-end flow control system to limit the total number of data items in flight at a given time. We use a token-bucket filter to limit ingress of items for each data stream at the Glass device, using returned counts of completed items exiting the system to replenish tokens. This provides a strong guarantee on the number of data items in the processing pipeline, limits any queuing, and automatically adjusts ingress data rate (frame rates) as network bandwidth or processing times change.

To handle multiple cognitive engines with different processing throughputs, we add a second level of filtering at each cognitive VM (Figure 7). This achieves per-engine rate adaptation while minimizing queuing latency. Counts of the items completed or dropped at each engine are reported to and stored in the control VM. The maximum of these values are fed back to the source filter, so it can allow in items as fast as the fastest cognitive engine, while limiting queued items at the slower ones. The number of tokens corresponds to the number of items in flight. A small token count minimizes latency at the expense of throughput and resource utilization, while larger counts sacrifice latency for throughput. A future implementation may adapt the number of tokens as a function of measured throughput and latency, ensuring optimal performance as conditions change.

5.5 Supported Cognitive Engines

Our prototype incorporates several cognitive engines based on available research and commercial software. These are summarized in Figure 8 and detailed below.

Face Recognition: A most basic cognitive task is the recognition of human faces. Our face recognition engine runs on Windows. It uses a Haar Cascade of classifiers to perform detection, and then uses the Eigenfaces method [38] based on principal component analysis (PCA) to make an identification from a database of known faces. The imple-

mentation is based on OpenCV [26] image processing and computer vision routines.

Object Recognition (MOPED): Our prototype supports two different object recognition engines. They are based on different computer vision algorithms, with different performance and accuracy characteristics. The open source MOPED engine runs on Linux, and makes use of multiple cores. It extracts key visual elements (SIFT features [19]) from an image, matches them against a database, and finally performs geometric computations to determine the pose of the identified object. The database in our prototype is populated with thousands of features extracted from more than 500 images of 13 different objects.

Object Recognition (STF): The other object recognition engine in our prototype is based on machine learning, using the semantic texton forest (STF) algorithm described by Shotton et al [35]. For our prototype, the MSRC21 image dataset mentioned in that work (with 21 classes of common objects) was used as the training dataset. Our Python-based implementation runs on Linux and is single-threaded.

OCR (Open Source): A critical assistance need for users with visual impairments is a way to determine what is written on signs in the environment. Optical character recognition (OCR) on video frames captured by the Glass camera is one way to accomplish this. Our prototype supports two different OCR engines. One of them is the open source Tesseract-OCR package [10], running on Linux.

OCR (Commercial): The second OCR engine supported by our prototype is a Windows-based commercial product: VeryPDF PDF to Text OCR Converter [39]. It provides a command-line interface that allows it to be scripted and readily connected to the rest of our system.

Neither OCR engine is ideal for our purposes. Since they were both intended to operate on scans of printed documents, they do not handle well the wide range of perspective, orientation, and lighting variations found in camera images. They are also not optimized for interactive performance. However, they are still useful as proofs of concept in our prototype.

Motion Classifier: To interpret motion in the surroundings (such as someone is waving to a user or running towards him), we have implemented a cognitive engine based on the MoSIFT algorithm [41]. From pairs of consecutive frames of video, it extracts features that incorporate aspects of appearance and movement. These are clustered to produce histograms that characterize the scene. Classifying the results across a small window of frames, the engine detects if the video fragment contains one of a small number of previously-trained motions, including waving, clapping, squatting, and turning around.

Activity Inference: As discussed in Section 3.4, determining user context is important. Our activity inference engine is based on an algorithm described by Nirjon et al [23] for head-mounted accelerometers. The code first determines a coarse level of activity based on the standard deviation of accelerometer values over a short window. It then uses clues such as inclination to refine this into 5 classes: sit/stand, two variants of lay down, walk, and run/jump.

Engine	Source	OS	VCPU*	Sensors
Face Recognition	open source research code based on OpenCV [38]	Windows	2	images
Object Detection (MOPED)	based on published MOPED [21] code	Linux (32-bit)	4	images
Object Detection (STF)	reimplementation of STF [35] algorithm	Linux	4	images
OCR (Open Source)	open source tesseract-ocr [10] package	Linux	2	images
OCR (Commercial)	closed-source VeryPDF OCR product [39]	Windows	2	images
Motion Classifier	action detection based on research MoSIFT [41] code	Linux	12	video
Activity Inference	reimplementation of algorithm from [23]	Linux	1	accelerometer
Augmented Reality	research code from [37]	Windows	2	images

* Number of virtual CPUs allocated to the cognitive engine at experiment

Figure 8: Summary of Implemented Cognitive Engines in Our Prototype

	CPU	RAM
Cloudlet	Intel® Core™ i7-3770 3.4GHz, 4 cores, 8 threads	32GB
Amazon EC2 Oregon	Intel® Xeon® E5-2680v2 2.8GHz, 8 VCPUs	15GB
Laptop - Dell Vostro 1520	Intel® Core™ 2 Duo P8600 2.4GHz, 2 cores	4GB
Netbook - Dell Latitude 2120	Intel® Atom™ N550 1.5GHz 2 cores, 4 threads	2GB
Google Glass	OMAP4430 ARMv7 Processor rev 3 (v7l)	773MB

Figure 9: Experiment Hardware Specifications

Augmented Reality: Our prototype supports a Windows-based augmented reality engine that identifies buildings and landmarks in images [37]. It extracts a set of feature descriptors from the image, and matches them to a database that is populated from 1005 labeled images of 200 buildings. The implementation is multi-threaded, and makes significant use of OpenCV libraries and Intel Performance Primitives (IPP) libraries. Labeled images can be displayed on the Glass device, or their labels can be read to the user.

5.6 User Guidance VM

The Gabriel architecture envisions sophisticated user guidance that interprets results from multiple cognitive engines, and uses context to intelligently present informative assistance to the user. As the focus of this work is on the architecture and system performance of Gabriel, not cognitive assistance algorithms, our prototype only incorporates a rudimentary place holder for a full-fledged User Guidance service. Our implementation integrates the outputs of the cognitive engines into a single stream of text, which is then converted to speech output on the Glass device. It filters the text stream to remove annoying duplicate messages over short intervals, but is not context-sensitive. The implementation of a complete User Guidance service will entail significant future research, and is beyond the scope of this paper.

6. EVALUATION

Gabriel is an extensible architecture that provides a plug-in interface for the easy addition of new cognitive engines. These cognitive engines are written by third parties, and are of varying quality. In some cases, these engines are closed source and we have no control except through a few external parameters. Our evaluation in this paper focuses on the intrinsic merits of the Gabriel architecture, rather than the speed, accuracy or other attributes of the cognitive engines

or their synthesis into user assistance. Wherever possible, we use real cognitive engines in our evaluation so that the workloads they impose are realistic. In a few cases, we supplement real cognitive engines with synthetic ones to study a particular tradeoff in depth.

We quantify the merits of the Gabriel architecture by asking the following questions:

- How much overhead does the use of VMs impose? Is the complexity of a full-fledged OpenStack cloud computing infrastructure tolerable in the latency-sensitive domain of cognitive assistance? (Section 6.2)
- Are cloudlets really necessary for cognitive assistance? How much benefit do they provide over conventional cloud infrastructure such as Amazon EC2? (Section 6.3)
- Is the implementation complexity of token-based flow control (Section 5.4) necessary? (Section 6.4)
- How easy is it to scale out cognitive engines? Assuming that they are written to exploit parallelism, how well is Gabriel able to provide that parallelism through the use of multiple VMs? (Section 6.5)
- Is Gabriel able to meet latency bounds even when loaded with many cognitive engines processing at full data rate? (Section 6.6)
- Does fallback through fidelity reduction really help in preserving crisp user interaction? What is the tradeoff between loss of fidelity and improvement in response time and battery life? (Section 6.7)

We examine these questions below, in Sections 6.2 to 6.7, after describing the aspects of our setup that are common to all the experiments.

6.1 Experimental Setup

Hardware specifications for our experiments are shown in Figure 9. Experiments using a cloudlet deploy Gabriel inside VMs managed by OpenStack on Linux hosts. For any experiment involving the cloud, we used Amazon EC2 c3.2xlarge VM instances located in Oregon, US. For any experiments involving fallback devices, we run the cognitive engines natively with no virtualization on either a laptop or a netbook. The netbook is comparable in power to a modern smartphone, but it has an x86 processor which means all of our cognitive engines execute unmodified and results are directly comparable with other experiments. The Google Glass device always connects to the cloudlet and cloud via a private Wi-Fi Access Point (AP) which routes over the public university network. For the fallback experiments, we create Wi-Fi hotspots on the offload devices and let the Google Glass directly connect to them.

For reproducibility we use a pre-recorded 360p video to process with the cognitive engines. During experiments, we capture frames from the Glass device, but replace them with

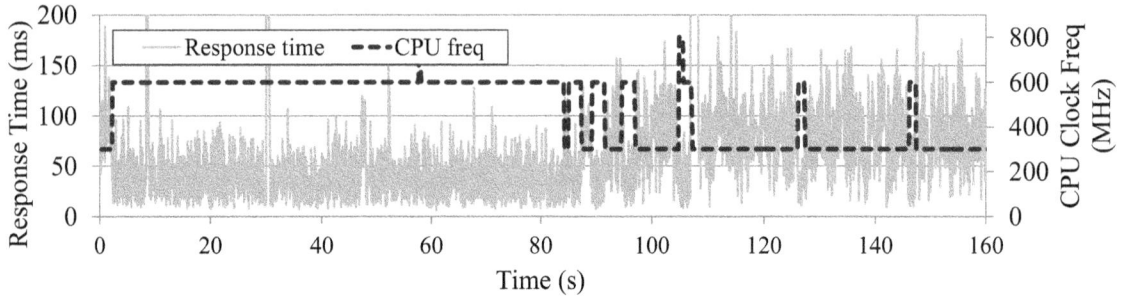

Figure 10: Trace of CPU Frequency, Response Time Changes on Google Glass

percentile	1%	10%	50%	90%	99%
delay (ms)	1.8	2.3	3.4	5.1	6.4

The delay between receiving a sensor data and sending a result using *NULL* engine.

Figure 11: Intrinsic Delay Introduced by Gabriel

frames from the pre-recorded video. This ensures that our energy measurements are consistent and reproducible. We measure the energy consumption of Google Glass using the battery voltage and current reported by the OS[2]. We have verified that this measurement is consistent with the battery capacity specifications. For laptops and netbooks, we use a WattsUp Pro .NET power meter [40] to measure the AC power consumption with batteries removed.

While measuring latency, we noticed anomalous variance during experiments. We found that to reduce discomfort as a wearable device, Glass attempts to minimize heat generation by scaling CPU frequency. Unfortunately, this causes latency to vary wildly as seen in Figure 10. The CPU operates at 300, 600, 800, or 1008 MHz, but uses the higher frequencies only for short bursts of time. Empirically, with ambient room temperature around 70 degrees Fahrenheit, Glass sustains 600 MHz for a few minutes at a time after, which it drops to its lowest setting of 300 MHz. In Figure 10, we let Glass capture images from its camera, send them over Wi-Fi to a server, and report the time from capture to the time of server acknowledgment back to the Glass. Whenever the CPU frequency drops we observe a significant increase in latency. To reduce thermal variability as a source of latency variability in our experiments, we externally cool the Glass device by wrapping it with an ice pack in every experiment, allowing it to sustain 600 MHz indefinitely.

6.2 Gabriel Overhead

Gabriel uses VMs extensively so that there are few constraints on the operating systems and cognitive engines used. To quantify the overhead of Gabriel, we measure the time delay on a cloudlet between receiving sensor data from a Glass device and sending back a result. To isolate performance of the infrastructure, we use a *NULL* cognitive engine, that simply sends a dummy result upon receiving any data. The cognitive VM is run on a separate physical machine from the Control and User Guidance VMs. Figure 11 summarizes the time spent in Gabriel for 3000 request-response pairs as measured on the physical machine hosting the Control VM. This represents the intrinsic overhead of Gabriel. At 2–5 ms, it is surprisingly small, considering that it includes the overheads of the Control, Cognitive, and User

---

[2]In `/sys/class/power_supply/bq27520-0/current_now` and `/sys/class/power_supply/bq27520-0/voltage_now`

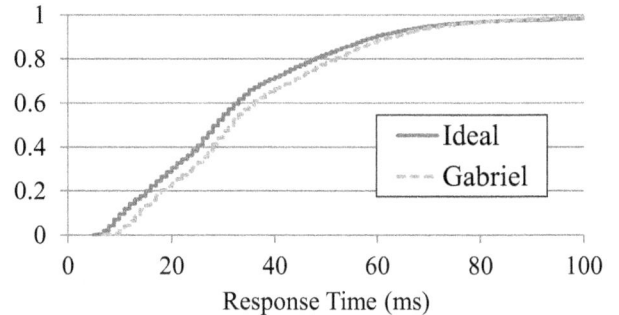

Figure 12: CDF of End-to-end Response Time at Glass Device for the *NULL* Cognitive Engine

Guidance VM stacks, as well as the overhead of traversing the cloudlet's internal Ethernet network.

The end-to-end latency measures at the Glass device are shown in Figure 12. These include processing time to capture images on Glass, time to send 6–67 KB images over the Wi-Fi network, the Gabriel response times with the NULL engine, and transmission of dummy results back over Wi-Fi. We also compare against an ideal server – essentially the NULL server running natively on the offload machine (no VM or Gabriel). Here, Gabriel and the ideal achieve 33 and 29 ms median response times respectively, confirming an approximately 4 ms overhead for the flexible Gabriel architecture. These end-to-end latencies represent the minimum achievable for offload of a trivial task. Real cognitive computations will add to these values.

6.3 Need for Cloudlets

We compare offload on our cloudlet implementation to the same services running in the cloud (Amazon EC2 Oregon datacenter). Figure 13 shows the distribution of end-to-end latencies as measured at the Glass device for face recognition, augmented reality, and both OCR engines. The results show that we do indeed see a significant decrease in latencies using cloudlets over clouds. The median improvement is between 80 ms and 200 ms depending on the cognitive engine. Much of this difference can be attributed to the higher latencies and transfer times to communicate with the distant data center.

In addition, except for augmented reality, the CDFs are quite heavy tailed. This indicates that the time to process each data item can vary significantly, with a small fraction of inputs requiring many times the median processing time. This will make it difficult to achieve the desired tens of milliseconds responses using these cognitive engines, and indicates more effort on the algorithms and implementations of the cognitive engines is warranted. Although this variation exists for both the cloud and cloudlet, the slopes of the curves indicate that our cloudlet instances are actually faster, despite the fact that we employ desktop-class machines for the cloudlet and use Amazon instances with the highest clock rate and network speed available for the cloud.

Finally, the extra latency for cloud offload will also adversely affect the energy consumed on the Glass device. As reported by the MAUI work [5] and others, longer response times for offload requests typically leads to longer total time spent in the tail energy states of hardware components on the mobile device. This leads to more total energy consumed by the mobile device. Our results are consistent with these observations. Figure 14 shows that the energy consumed on the Glass device for four representative cognitive operations is 30–40% lower with cloudlet offload than with cloud offload. Clearly, offload to cloudlets can produce significant latency and energy improvements over offloading to the cloud.

6.4 Queuing Delay Mitigation

In order to evaluate the need for our application-level, end-to-end flow-control mechanism for mitigating queuing, we first consider a baseline case where no explicit flow control is done. Instead, we push data in an open-loop manner, and rely on average processing throughput to be faster than the ingress data rate to keep queuing in check. Unfortunately, the processing times of cognitive engines are highly variable and content-dependent. Measurements summarized in Figure 15 show that computation times for face recognition and OCR (Open Source) can vary by 1 and 2 orders of magnitude, respectively. An image that takes much longer than average to process will cause queuing and an increase in latency for subsequent ones. However, with our two-level token bucket mechanism, explicit feedback controls the input rate to avoid building up queues.

We compare the differences in queuing behavior with and without our flow control mechanism using a synthetic cognitive engine. To reflect high variability, the synthetic application has a bimodal processing time distribution: 90% of images take 20 ms, 10% take 200 ms each. Images are assigned deterministically to the slow or fast category using a content-based hash function. With this distribution, the average processing time is 38 ms, and with an ingress interval of 50 ms (20 fps), the system is underloaded on average. However, as shown in Figure 16-(a), without application-level flow control (labeled TCP), many frames exhibit much higher latencies than expected due to queuing. In contrast, the traces using our token-based flow control mechanism with either 1 or 2 tokens reduce queuing and control latency. There are still spikes due to the arrival of slow frames, but these do not result in increased latency for subsequent frames. We repeat the experiment with a real cognitive engine, OCR (Open Source). Here, the mean processing time is just under 1 second, so we use an offered load of 1 FPS. The traces in Figure 16-(b) show similar results: latency can increase significantly when explicit flow control is not used (TCP), but latency remains under control with our token-based flow control mechanism.

The tight control on latency comes at the cost of throughput – the token based mechanism drops frames at the source to limit the number of data items in flight though the system. Figure 17 shows the number of frames that are dropped, processed on time, and processed but late for the OCR ex-

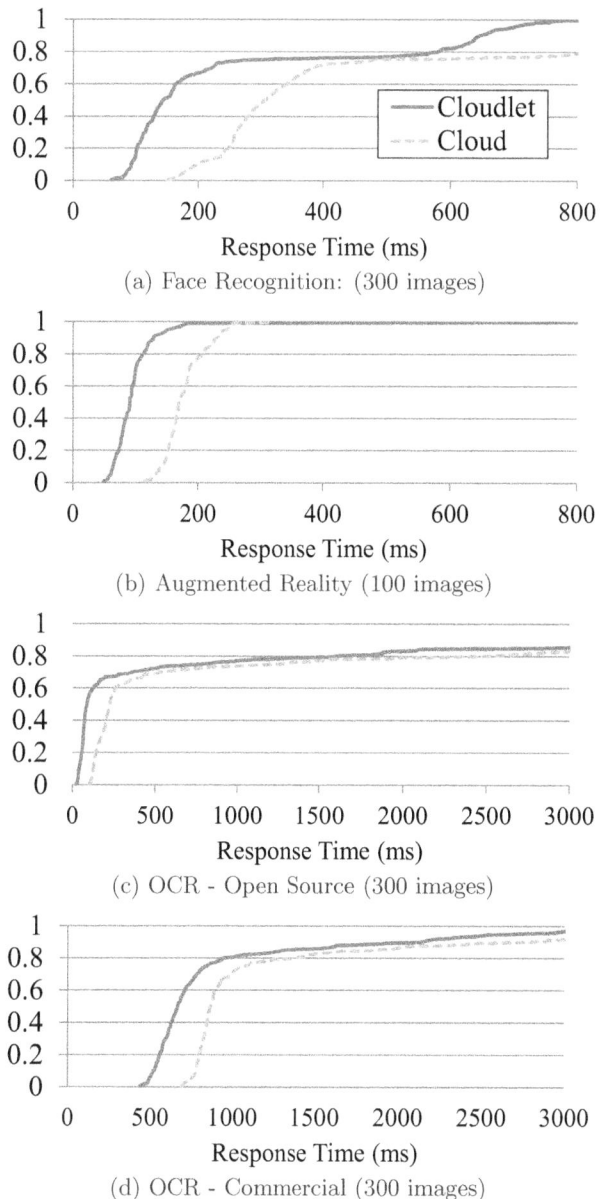

(a) Face Recognition: (300 images)

(b) Augmented Reality (100 images)

(c) OCR - Open Source (300 images)

(d) OCR - Commercial (300 images)

Figure 13: Cumulative distribution function (CDF) of response times in ms

Application	Cloudlet (Joule/query)	Cloud (Joule/query)
Face	0.48	0.82
AR	0.19	0.32
OCR(open)	2.01	3.09
OCR(comm)	1.77	2.41

Figure 14: Energy Consumption on Google Glass

Application	1%	10%	50%	90%	99%
OCR(open)	11ms	13ms	29ms	3760ms	7761ms
Face	21ms	33ms	49ms	499ms	555ms

Figure 15: High Variability in Response Time

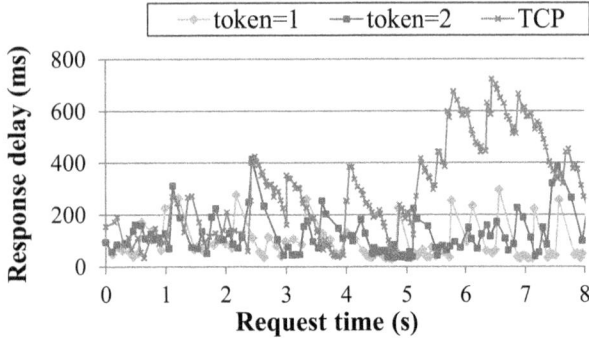

(a) Synthetic Cognitive Engine (20 FPS ingress)

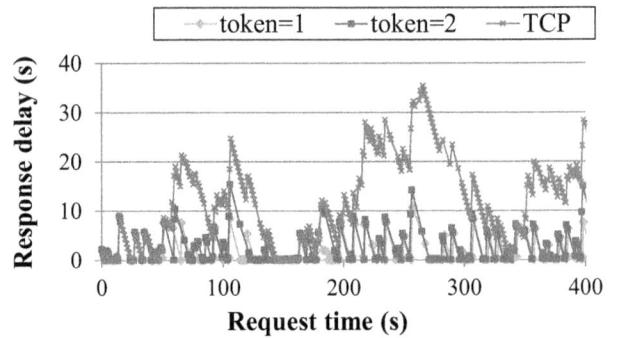

(b) OCR (1 FPS ingress)

Figure 16: Response Delay of Request

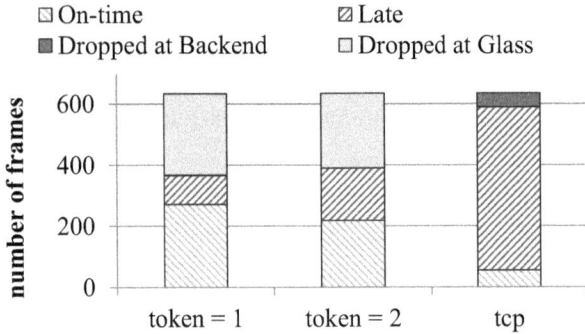

Figure 17: Breakdown of Processed and Dropped Frame for OCR (500ms for on-time response)

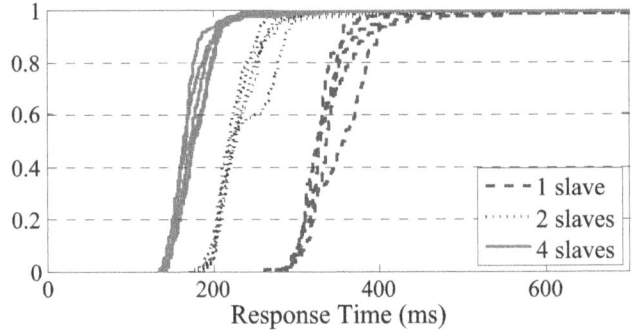

Each family of CDFs shows five experimental runs with the same number of slaves. The tight clustering within each family shows that the observed improvement in latency across families is significant: i.e., increasing the number of slave VMs does indeed reduce latency.

Figure 18: Latency Reduction by VM Scale-Out

periment. Here, we use a threshold of 0.5 s as the "on-time" latency limit. The token-based mechanism (with tokens set to 1) drops a substantial number of frames at the source, but the majority of processed frames exhibit reasonable latency. Increasing tokens (and number of frames in flight) to 2 reduces the dropped frames slightly, but results in more late responses. Finally, the baseline case without our flow-control mechanism attempts to process all frames, but the vast majority are processed late. The only dropped frames are due to the output queues filling and blocking the application, after the costs of transmitting the frames from the Glass front-end have been incurred. In contrast, the token scheme drops frames in the Glass device before they are transmitted over Wi-Fi. These results show that our token-based flow control mechanism is effective and necessary for low latency as well as saving energy.

6.5 Scale-Out of Cognitive Engines

We use the Motion Classifier cognitive engine (Section 5.5) to explore how well Gabriel supports parallelization across multiple VMs. We modified this application to use a master-slave scale-out structure. Feature extraction and classification are both done in parallel on slaves, and pipelined for higher throughput. Feature extraction is parallelized by splitting every image into tiles, and having each slave extract features from a different tile. Classification is parallelized by having each slave receive the full feature vector, but only doing an SVM classification for a subset of classes. The master and each slave are mapped to different VMs. The master receives sensor data from the control VM, distributes it to the

slaves, gathers and merges their results, and returns the final result back to the control VM.

Since the final classification is done based on a window of frames, we define the latency of this offload engine as the time between when the last frame in the window is captured, and when the classification result is returned. Figure 18 shows how latency drops as we use more slave VMs. The 90th percentile latency decreases from about 390 ms with one slave, to about 190 ms with four slaves. Throughput also improves. Using one, two, and four slave VMs, we get frame rates of 9.8 fps, 15.9 fps, and 19.0 fps.

6.6 Full System Performance

Thus far we have presented experimental results examining an individual tradeoff or technique employed by Gabriel to bound latency. In this section we investigate the performance of the entire system with the cognitive engines executing together. We use a different pre-recorded video for this experiment which includes footage recognizable by the cognitive engines such as signs with text for OCR, a Coke can for object recognition, human faces for face recognition, and waving for motion recognition.

Figure 19 shows the performance of each offloading engine during this full system benchmark. Frame rate per second (FPS) and response time is measured at the Glass. Because each cognitive engine's compute time varies drastically

Engine	FPS	Response time (ms) 10%	50%	90%	CPU load(%)
Face	4.4	389	659	929	93.4
MOPED	1.6	962	1207	1647	50.9
STF	0.4	4371	4609	5055	24.9
OCR(Open)	14.4	41	87	147	24.1
OCR(Comm)	2.3	435	522	653	95.8
Motion	14	152	199	260	20.1
AR	14.1	72	126	192	83.8

Figure 19: FPS and Latency of Cognitive Engines

based on content, this experiment is not comparable to the previous microbenchmarks. But, the results reflect that the cognitive engines operate independently within their VMs. Most importantly, the overall system is not limited to the slowest cognitive engine. The cognitive engines that can process frames quickly operate at higher frame rates than the slower cognitive engines, which is precisely what Gabriel promises. In addition, the quickest cognitive engines maintain end-to-end latency of tens of milliseconds.

While we evaluated our system with a single Glass user in this experiment, we provide a mechanism to support multiple users. Since the first-person images are highly personal data, the system isolates each user from others using VLANs. We create a VLAN per user. Thus, a group of cognitive VMs are dedicated to a single user without being shared. This approach cleanly isolates each user, but the number of VMs is proportional to the number of users. Therefore, it is important to assign appropriate amounts of hardware resources to each cognitive engine. In our experiments, the CPU usage of each cognitive engine ranges from 20.1% to 95.8% as in Figure 19. Many of the low CPU utilizations are due to limited parallel sections in the cognitive engine implementations, thus under-utilizing some of the cores. For example, MOPED uses four cores in some sections, but only one or two for the remainder, for an average of 50% utilization. This implies one may be able to statistically multiplex multiple cognitive engines on the same physical cores, but this will have some impact on latency.

We also consider the overhead of provisioning a cloudlet for the first time. Unlike the cloud, where all necessary VM images can be assumed to be present, a new cloudlet may need to be provisioned dynamically. We can use VM synthesis [13] to rapidly provision a cloudlet from the cloud. Our measurements show that it takes around 10 seconds to provision and launch the Control and User Guidance VMs from Amazon EC2 Oregon to our cloudlet on the CMU campus. The provisioning time for a cognitive VM ranges from 10 seconds to 33 seconds depending on VM size. In other words, just 10 seconds after associating with a new cloudlet, a Glass user can start transmitting sensor data to Gabriel. The cloudlet's cognitive engines will start providing answers one by one as they are provisioned and instantiated. It is important to note that provisioning is a one-time operation. Persistent caching of VM images on a cloudlet ensures that re-provisioning is rarely needed.

6.7 Impact of Reducing Fidelity

To study the effect of reducing fidelity, we focus on the most heavyweight cognitive engine in our suite. The response times in Figure 19 indicate that STF object recognition (described in Section 5.5) is very slow even on a cloudlet. On a fallback device, the performance would be even worse.

	Response Time	Glass energy per frame	Glass power	Fallback device power
Cloudlet				
1080p	12.9 (1.2) s	23 J	1.8 W	NA
Laptop				
1080p	27.3 (1.7) s	55 J	2.0 W	31.6 W
720p	12.2 (0.4) s	25 J	2.0 W	31.7 W
480p	6.3 (0.6) s	13 J	2.0 W	31.4 W
360p	4.3 (0.8) s	9 J	2.1 W	31.3 W
Netbook				
480p	32.9 (1.0) s	59 J	1.8 W	14.3 W
360p	20.5 (0.4) s	41 J	2.0 W	14.4 W

Each experiment was run for about 20 minutes to get at least 36 frames processed by STF. Numbers in parentheses are standard deviations of response times across frames. These measurements used token setting 1 to get the best response time possible. The monitor on the fallback device was turned off to save energy.

Figure 20: Energy & Response Time vs. Fidelity

For object recognition, the resolution of individual video frames is a natural parameter of fidelity. The highest resolution supported by a Glass device is 1080p. Lower resolutions are 720p, 480p and 360p. When resolution is lowered, the volume of data transmitted over Wi-Fi is reduced. This lowers transmission time, as well as the energy used for transmission. Lower resolution also reduces the processing time per frame on a fallback offload device.

Figure 20 shows the measured response time and energy usage on the Glass device and on the offload device, as fidelity is reduced. The response time (12.9 s) and Glass energy per frame (23 J) at 1080p with cloudlet offload are baseline values. At 1080p with laptop offload, these values increase to roughly twice their baselines. At 720p with laptop offload, these values are comparable to their baselines. At lower fidelities with laptop offload, these values are below their baselines. The netbook is much too slow at 1080p and 720p, so Figure 20 only shows values for 480p and 360p. Even at these fidelities, response time and Glass energy per frame are both much higher than baseline.

The fourth and fifth columns of Figure 20 show that power consumption on the Glass device and the fallback device are quite stable, regardless of fidelity. This is because the higher frame rate at lower fidelity compensates for the lower energy per frame. At these power draws, a rough estimate of battery life using data sheets gives the following values: 1 hour for Glass device, 1.5 hours for laptop, and 2 hours for netbook. These are long enough to cover Internet coverage gaps in the daily life of a typical user.

Although reducing fidelity hurts the accuracy of object recognition, the relationship is not linear. In other words, relative to the improvement in response time and energy usage, the loss of accuracy due to fidelity reduction is modest. This is illustrated by Figure 21, which shows results based on the processing of 3583 video frames from 12 different video segments. The STF object classifier is trained on the 21 classes of objects in the MSRC21 data set described by Shotton et al. [35]. For brevity, we only show results for 5 representative object classes ("body," "building," "car," "chair," and "dog"). The results for the other 16 classes follows this general pattern. We treat the classifier output at

	body	building	car	chair	dog
1080p	2408	875	122	22	1004
720p					
False neg.	56	5	4	0	39
False pos.	19	137	52	1	14
480p					
False neg.	124	19	11	2	83
False pos.	24	219	136	2	25
360p					
False neg.	223	39	14	3	122
False pos.	23	273	176	5	35

These numbers indicate the quantity of objects in each class detected at different resolutions of the test data set. For each class, the number detected at 1080p is ground truth.

Figure 21: Fidelity versus Accuracy

1080p to be ground truth. At this resolution, there are 2408 instances of "body," 875 instances of "building" and so on.

As fidelity is reduced, classifier performance suffers both through false negatives (i.e., objects that are missed) and through false positives (i.e., detected objects that don't really exist). Figure 21 shows that there are relatively few false negatives. Even in the worst case (for "chair" at 360p), only 3 out of 22 objects (i.e., 13.6%) are missed. The picture is murkier with respect to false positives. The "building" and "car" classes show a high incidence of false positives as fidelity is reduced. However, the "body," "chair," and "dog" classes only show a modest incidence of false positives as fidelity is reduced. For use cases where false negatives are more harmful than false positives, Figure 21 suggests that the wins in Figure 20 come at an acceptable cost.

7. FUTURE WORK AND CONCLUSION

Sustained progress in foundational technologies has brought the decade-long dream of mobile, real-time cognitive assistance via "magic glasses" much closer to reality. The convergence of mobile and cloud computing, the increasing sophistication and variety of cognitive engines, and the widespread availability of wearable hardware are all coming together at a fortuitous moment in time. The work presented here is an initial effort towards understanding this domain in depth and identifying areas where improvements are most critical.

Most urgently, our results show that significant speed improvements are needed in virtually all cognitive engines. The measurements reported in Section 6 indicate typical speeds of a few hundred milliseconds per operation, rather than the desired target of a few tens of milliseconds. In a few cases such as STF object recognition, the speed improvement has to be even larger. Exploiting cloudlet parallelism can help, as shown by the results of Section 6.5. Restructuring the internals of cognitive engines to exploit parallelism and to make them more efficient is a crucial area of future effort.

Our results also show that significant improvements are needed in wearable hardware. The Google Glass devices used in this paper have many of the right attributes in terms of weight, size, and functionality. Their computing power is adequate when combined with cloudlet offloading, although their thermal sensitivity (discussed in Section 6.1) limits their usefulness. However, their battery life of less than two hours on Gabriel workloads is unacceptably short for real-world deployment as assistive devices. A factor of four improvement in battery life on cognitive workloads, without

compromising other attributes, would be highly desirable. Even longer battery life would, of course, be welcome.

Our results reinforce the need for cloudlet infrastructure to attain the low end-to-end latencies that are essential for real-time cognitive assistance. Although cloudlet infrastructure is not yet commercially available, there have been early efforts in this direction [1, 25]. Identifying business models for cloudlet deployments and then catalyzing such deployments will be important for success in this domain. Our measurements suggest that cloudlets have to be substantial computational engines, involving many multi-core processors with large amounts of memory each. They essentially have to be server-class hardware, stationed at the edges of the Internet.

Ultimately, real progress will come from experimental deployments involving users who are genuinely in need of cognitive assistance. Only live use will reveal HCI, usability, robustness and scalability issues that will need to be addressed for a full solution. The Gabriel prototype represents a humble first step, providing an open-source foundation for exploring this exciting new domain.

Acknowledgements

We thank our shepherd Junehwa Song and the anonymous reviewers for their valuable comments and suggestions. We thank Gene Cahill and Soumya Simanta for implementing the SPEECH and FACE applications and Alvaro Collet for implementing the OBJECT application. We also thank Benjamin Gilbert and Jan Harkes for their valuable discussions throughout this work.

This research was supported by the National Science Foundation (NSF) under grant number IIS-1065336, by an Intel Science and Technology Center grant, by DARPA Contract No. FA8650-11-C-7190, and by the Department of Defense (DoD) under Contract No. FA8721-05-C-0003 for the operation of the Software Engineering Institute (SEI), a federally funded research and development center. This material has been approved for public release and unlimited distribution (DM-0000276). Additional support for cloudlet-related research was provided by IBM, Google, Bosch, and Vodafone. Any opinions, findings, conclusions or recommendations expressed in this material are those of the authors and should not be attributed to their employers or funding sources.

References

[1] IBM and Nokia Siemens Networks Announce World's First Mobile Edge Computing Platform. http://www.ibm.com/press/us/en/pressrelease/40490.wss, 2013.

[2] T. Agus, C. Suied, S. Thorpe, and D. Pressnitzer. Characteristics of human voice processing. In *Proceedings of 2010 IEEE International Symposium on Circuits and Systems (ISCAS)*, Paris, France, June 2010.

[3] A. L. Berger, V. J. D. Pietra, and S. A. D. Pietra. A maximum entropy approach to natural language processing. *Comput. Linguist.*, 22(1):39–71, Mar. 1996.

[4] G. Chen and D. Kotz. A survey of context-aware mobile computing research. Technical report, Hanover, NH, USA, 2000.

[5] E. Cuervo, A. Balasubramanian, D. Chok, A. Wolman, S. Saroiu, R. Chandra, and P. Bahl. MAUI: Making Smartphones Last Longer with Code Offload. In *Proceedings of the 8th International Conference on Mobile Systems, Applications, and Services (MobiSys)*, San Francisco, CA, June 2010.

[6] S. R. Ellis, K. Mania, B. D. Adelstein, and M. I. Hill. Generalizeability of Latency Detection in a Variety of Virtual Environments. In *Proceedings of the Human Factors and Ergonomics Society Annual Meeting*, volume 48, 2004.

[7] D. Ferrucci, A. Levas, S. Bagchi, D. Gondek, and E. T. Mueller. Watson: Beyond jeopardy! *Artificial Intelligence*, 199:93–105, 2013.

[8] J. Flinn. *Cyber Foraging: Bridging Mobile and Cloud Computing via Opportunistic Offload*. Morgan & Claypool Publishers, 2012.

[9] J. Flinn and M. Satyanarayanan. Energy-aware Adaptation for Mobile Applications. In *Proceedings of the Seventeenth ACM Symposium on Operating systems Principles*, 1999.

[10] Google. tesseract-ocr. http://code.google.com/p/tesseract-ocr/.

[11] Google. Glass Development Kit. https://developers.google.com/glass/gdk, 2013.

[12] M. S. Gordon, D. A. Jamshidi, S. Mahlke, Z. M. Mao, and X. Chen. COMET: Code Offload by Migrating Execution Transparently. In *Proceedings of the 10th USENIX Symposium on Operating System Design and Implementation*, Hollywood, CA, October 2012.

[13] K. Ha, P. Pillai, W. Richter, Y. Abe, and M. Satyanarayanan. Just-in-time provisioning for cyber foraging. In *Proceeding of the 11th Annual International Conference on Mobile Systems, Applications, and Services*, MobiSys '13, pages 153–166. ACM, 2013.

[14] S. Helal, W. Mann, H. El-Zabadani, J. King, Y. Kaddoura, and E. Jansen. The Gator Tech Smart House: A Programmable Pervasive Space. *IEEE Computer*, 38(3):50–60, 2005.

[15] S. Hodges, E. Berry, and K. Wood. SenseCam: A wearable camera that stimulates and rehabilitates autobiographical memory. *Memory*, 19(7):685–696, 2011.

[16] C. D. Kidd, R. Orr, G. D. Abowd, C. G. Atkeson, I. A. Essa, B. MacIntyre, E. D. Mynatt, T. Starner, and W. Newstetter. The Aware Home: A Living Laboratory for Ubiquitous Computing Research. In *CoBuild '99: Proceedings of the Second International Workshop on Cooperative Buildings, Integrating Information, Organization, and Architecture*, pages 191–198, 1999.

[17] M. B. Lewis and A. J. Edmonds. Face detection: Mapping human performance. *Perception*, 32:903–920, 2003.

[18] A. Li, X. Yang, S. Kandula, and M. Zhang. CloudCmp: comparing public cloud providers. In *Proceedings of the 10th annual conference on Internet measurement*, 2010.

[19] D. G. Lowe. Distinctive image features from scale-invariant keypoints. *International Journal of Computer Vision*, 60(2):91–110, 2004.

[20] M. Missfeldt. How Google Glass Works. http://www.brillen-sehhilfen.de/en/googleglass/, 2013.

[21] MOPED. MOPED: Object Recognition and Pose Estimation for Manipulation. http://personalrobotics.ri.cmu.edu/projects/moped.php.

[22] D. Narayanan and M. Satyanarayanan. Predictive Resource Management for Wearable Computing. In *Proceedings of the 1st international conference on Mobile systems, applications and services*, San Francisco, CA, 2003.

[23] S. Nirjon, R. F. Dickerson, Q. Li, P. Asare, J. A. Stankovic, D. Hong, B. Zhang, X. Jiang, G. Shen, and F. Zhao. Musicalheart: A hearty way of listening to music. In *Proceedings of the 10th ACM Conference on Embedded Network Sensor Systems*, 2012.

[24] B. D. Noble, M. Satyanarayanan, D. Narayanan, J. E. Tilton, J. Flinn, and K. R. Walker. Agile Application-Aware Adaptation for Mobility. In *Proceedings of the 16th ACM Symposium on Operating Systems Principles*, Saint-Malo, France, October 1997.

[25] Nokia Solutions and Networks (NSN). http://nsn.com/portfolio/liquid-net/intelligent-broadband-management/liquid-applications, February 2013.

[26] OpenCV. OpenCV Wiki. http://opencv.willowgarage.com/wiki/.

[27] OpenStack. http://www.openstack.org/software/grizzly/, April 2013.

[28] M. Posner and S. Peterson. The Attention System of the Human Brain. *Annual Review of Neuroscience*, 13:25–42, 1990.

[29] M.-R. Ra, A. Sheth, L. Mummert, P. Pillai, D. Wetherall, and R. Govindan. Odessa: enabling interactive perception applications on mobile devices. In *Proceedings of the 9th International Conference on Mobile systems, Applications, and Services*, Bethesda, Maryland, USA, 2011. ACM.

[30] M. Ramon, S. Caharel, and B. Rossion. The speed of recognition of personally familiar faces. *Perception*, 40(4):437–449, 2011.

[31] L. Ravindranath, J. Padhye, R. Mahajan, and H. Balakrishnan. Timecard: Controlling User-perceived Delays in Server-based Mobile Applications. In *Proceedings of the Twenty-Fourth ACM Symposium on Operating Systems Principles*, Farminton, PA, 2013.

[32] M. Satyanarayanan. Fundamental Challenges in Mobile Computing. In *Proceedings of the ACM Symposium on Principles of Distributed Computing*, Ottawa, Canada, 1996.

[33] M. Satyanarayanan. Augmenting Cognition. *IEEE Pervasive Computing*, 3(2):4–5, April-June 2004.

[34] M. Satyanarayanan, P. Bahl, R. Caceres, and N. Davies. The Case for VM-Based Cloudlets in Mobile Computing. *IEEE Pervasive Computing*, 8(4), October-December 2009.

[35] J. Shotton, M. Johnson, and R. Cipolla. Semantic texton forests for image categorization and segmentation. In *Proc. of IEEE Conf. on Computer Vision and Pattern Recognition*, June 2008.

[36] V. Stanford. Using Pervasive Computing to Deliver Elder Care Applications. *IEEE Pervasive Computing*, 1(1), January-March 2002.

[37] G. Takacs, M. E. Choubassi, Y. Wu, and I. Kozintsev. 3D mobile augmented reality in urban scenes. In *Proceedings of IEEE International Conference on Multimedia and Expo*, Barcelona, Spain, July 2011.

[38] M. Turk and A. Pentland. Eigenfaces for recognition. *Journal of Cognitive Neuroscience*, 3(1):71–86, 1991.

[39] VeryPDF. PDF to Text OCR Converter Command Line. http://www.verypdf.com/app/pdf-to-text-ocr-converter/index.html.

[40] WattsUp. .NET Power Meter. http://wattsupmeters.com/.

[41] M. yu Chen and A. Hauptmann. MoSIFT: Recognizing Human Actions in Surveillance Videos. Technical Report CMU-CS-09-161, CMU School of Computer Science, 2009.

iShadow: Design of a Wearable, Real-Time Mobile Gaze Tracker

Addison Mayberry
University of Massachusetts
Amherst
140 Governor's Drive
Amherst, MA 01003
amayberr@cs.umass.edu

Pan Hu
University of Massachusetts
Amherst
140 Governor's Drive
Amherst, MA 01003
panhu@cs.umass.edu

Benjamin Marlin
University of Massachusetts
Amherst
140 Governor's Drive
Amherst, MA 01003
marlin@cs.umass.edu

Christopher Salthouse
University of Massachusetts
Amherst
100 Natural Resources Rd.
Amherst, MA 01003
salthouse@ecs.umass.edu

Deepak Ganesan
University of Massachusetts
Amherst
140 Governor's Drive
Amherst, MA 01003
dganesan@cs.umass.edu

ABSTRACT

Continuous, real-time tracking of eye gaze is valuable in a variety of scenarios including hands-free interaction with the physical world, detection of unsafe behaviors, leveraging visual context for advertising, life logging, and others. While eye tracking is commonly used in clinical trials and user studies, it has not bridged the gap to everyday consumer use. The challenge is that a real-time eye tracker is a power-hungry and computation-intensive device which requires continuous sensing of the eye using an imager running at many tens of frames per second, and continuous processing of the image stream using sophisticated gaze estimation algorithms. Our key contribution is the design of an eye tracker that dramatically reduces the sensing and computation needs for eye tracking, thereby achieving orders of magnitude reductions in power consumption and form-factor. The key idea is that eye images are extremely redundant, therefore we can estimate gaze by using a small subset of carefully chosen pixels per frame. We instantiate this idea in a prototype hardware platform equipped with a low-power image sensor that provides random access to pixel values, a low-power ARM Cortex M3 microcontroller, and a bluetooth radio to communicate with a mobile phone. The sparse pixel-based gaze estimation algorithm is a multi-layer neural network learned using a state-of-the-art sparsity-inducing regularization function that minimizes the gaze prediction error while simultaneously minimizing the number of pixels used. Our results show that we can operate at roughly 70mW of power, while continuously estimating eye gaze at the rate of 30 Hz with errors of roughly 3 degrees.

Keywords

eye tracking; neural network; lifelog

MobiSys'14, June 16–19, 2014, Bretton Woods, New Hampshire, USA.
Copyright 2014 ACM 978-1-4503-2793-0/14/06 ...$15.00.
http://dx.doi.org/10.1145/2594368.2594388 .

Categories and Subject Descriptors

H.3 [**Special-Purpose and Application-Based Systems**]: Real-time and embedded systems

1. INTRODUCTION

An important aspect of on-body sensing is tracking the eye and visual field of an individual. Continuous real-time tracking of the state of the eye (e.g. gaze direction, eye movements) in conjunction with the field of view of a user is profoundly important to understanding how humans perceive and interact with the physical world. Real-time tracking of the eye is valuable in a variety of scenarios where rapid actuation or intervention is essential, including enabling new "hands-free" ways of interacting with computers or displays (e.g. gaming), detection of unsafe behaviors such as lack of attention on the road while driving, and leveraging visual context as a signal of user intent for context-aware advertising. Continuous eye tracking is also useful in non real-time applications including market research to determine how customers interact with product and advertising placement in stores, and personal health, where the state of the eye provides a continuous window into Parkinson's disease progression, psychiatric disorders, head injuries and concussions, and others.

While our understanding of the human eye and gaze has grown through decades of research on the topic [6, 9], eye tracking remains limited to controlled user studies and clinical trials, and has not bridged the gap to daily consumer use. The central challenge is that the sensing and processing pipeline is extremely complex: the eye-facing imager alone requires continuous operation of a camera at tens of frames per second, and compute-intensive image processing for each frame [2, 13, 24]. Unfortunately, these computational demands are very far from what can be accomplished on low-power microcontrollers and resource-limited embedded platforms. In addition, there are complex camera placement considerations and form-factor demands, making the eyeglass design much more intricate. In all, addressing the myriad technical and design challenges of wearable gaze tracking is a daunting task.

To understand the design challenges, consider an eye tracker equipped with two cameras, one facing the eye and one facing the external world. A VGA-resolution eye facing imager sampled at 30Hz generates a data rate of roughly 4 Mbps. Continuous real-time processing of such an image stream would require computational capability and memory comparable to a high-end smartphone, making the eye tracker both bulky and power hungry. An alternative design might be to wirelessly stream data from the eye tracker to a smartphone for leveraging the phone or cloud-based computational resources. However, the bandwidth requirements for such streaming is substantial — most low-power radios cannot support the demanding data rates of eye trackers, and streaming via WiFi is power-hungry and would greatly limit the lifetime of such a device. Perhaps as a result, many state-of-art eye trackers, such as the Tobii glass [24], operate as data recorders and continuously writes data to a disk that the subject carries in their pocket. (Google Glass, while not equipped with an eye tracker, has similar challenges - in continuous video capture mode, the device lasts for only a few hours.)

We argue that the current approach is fundamentally flawed — existing systems separate image acquisition from the eye state processing, and as a consequence are unable to leverage a variety of optimizations that are possible by a more holistic approach that uses application-driven sampling and processing. Consider, for example, recently available smartphones such as the Samsung Galaxy S IV, which track gaze for eye scrolling; here, the entire image is acquired from the camera, after which it is processed through computer vision techniques to estimate gaze direction. The thesis of our work is that by joint optimization of pixel acquisition and gaze estimation, we can enable real-time, continuous eye tracking while consuming only milliwatts of power, thereby enabling real-time continuous gaze based applications.

At the heart of iShadow is a simple idea: individual eye-facing images are extremely redundant, and thus it should be possible to estimate gaze location using only a small subset of pixel values in each frame. In other words — we can leverage knowledge that the imager is looking at the eye, and that the most useful information for gaze tracking is where the iris is located within the eye. Thus, we can estimate gaze coordinates accurately as long as we can extract the location of the iris and sclera of the eye at low power.

Sparse sampling of pixels has a ripple effect on almost all design choices in our system. From a resource perspective, fewer pixels per frame imply less memory needs, and fewer image processing instructions per frame thereby enabling the entire gaze estimation pipeline to execute on a simple microcontroller. From a latency perspective, fewer pixels implies lower latency for image acquisition and gaze estimation, making it possible to achieve real-time high rate gaze computation despite limited processing capability. From a power perspective, we subsample pixels directly at the imager, and not after acquiring the image, thereby reducing power consumption for image acquisition as well as processing. Fewer pixel acquisitions and less processing translates to less energy consumed per frame capture and gaze computation, which enables longer term operation.

The design of a sparse acquisition-based gaze tracking system presents substantial challenges that we address in this work. First, imagers that operate at the milliwatt power levels need to sacrifice pixel quality for power, hence an important question is whether we can achieve high accuracy despite operating with low quality imagers. Second, we ask whether we can design a gaze estimation algorithm that provides a graceful resource-accuracy tradeoff, where the accuracy of gaze estimation gracefully degrades as the energy budget reduces. Third, the computational demands of gaze tracking are often substantial — for example, several gaze estimation algorithms require processing of the eye image to detect the iris and identify its boundary, which requires processing that is considerably higher than what can be accomplished with a microcontroller.

Thus, we need to understand how to reduce the processing needs to enable real-time gaze estimation while operating on platforms with tens of kilobytes of memory and no floating point units.

The main contributions of our work are the following.

- First, we design a multi-layer neural network-based point-of-gaze predictor that uses offline model training to learn a sparse pixel-based gaze estimation algorithm. A key novelty of this work is the use of a state-of-the-art sparsity-inducing regularization function for identifying pixel subsets[26]. We show such an approach can reduce pixel acquisition by $10\times$ with minimal impact on gaze prediction accuracy.

- Second, we design a real-time gaze estimation algorithm that implements the model learned by the neural network on a prototype computational eyeglass platform equipped with a low-power microcontroller and low-power greyscale cameras with random access capability. We show that our system can operate at frame rates of up to 30Hz with gaze errors of roughly 3 degrees, while executing in real time and at a power consumption of 72 mW.

- Third, we show that our methods can be easily calibrated to a new individual with a calibration dataset that is only one minute long, and without requiring changes to imager placement or adjustment of our hardware prototype. Our user study with ten users shows that, once calibrated, our system works robustly across individuals.

2. BACKGROUND AND RELATED WORK

The gaze tracking problem has a long history and multiple sensing modalities have been developed to address it [25]. In this work, we are specifically interested in gaze tracking using a video stream of eye images, an approach referred to as *video oculography*. We highlight the distinctions between video-based gaze tracking systems that are most relevant to our work in this section and refer readers to the surveys by Young et al. [25], Morimoto et al. [14] and Hansen et al. [7] for further details and references. We organize our review around three important distinctions between gaze tracking systems: (1) whether the hardware system is remote or wearable (typically head mounted), (2) whether the point-of-gaze estimation problem is solved offline or in real time, and (3) the category of algorithm used to solve the gaze inference problem.

Remote vs Wearable Eye Trackers.

Gaze tracking has traditionally been studied and applied in the remote tracking setting [25]. The subject sits facing one or more cameras that record video of the subjects eyes. The subject typically performs a task like reading or viewing images or video. The captured eye images are then used to infer the subject's point of gaze, giving information about what they were attending to while performing the different steps of a task. In early remote systems, chin-rests or other restraints were used to ensure the subject's head was completely motionless relative to the camera system. The gaze inference problem was also solved completely offline.

Subsequent advances have led to gaze tracking systems that can reliably infer gaze direction in real time while allowing subjects a much more comfortable range of motion while seated [5, 1, 18]. Modern instantiations of these techniques use either built-in cameras on laptops and smartphones to estimate gaze direction, or use additional add-on hardware [13] that provides more accuracy for gaze tracking. These approaches are particularly useful for measuring user engagement for online ads, and gaze-based gaming or computer interaction. While very useful, the gaze tracking hardware remains static, and doesn't provide continuous gaze information in natural environments when the user is not interacting with a computing device.

In recent years, more eye trackers are being used in a mobile context. The OpenEyes project is a closely related effort to ours at the hardware layer. It involved the development of an open wearable hardware system for recording eye movements as well as associated algorithms for gaze prediction [13]. While the camera system was also an eyeglass form factor device, it was tethered to a laptop computer worn in a backpack. Rantanen et al. also presented an eyeglass-form-factor tracking device, intended for HCI purposes with disabled users [16]. Their system similarly requires the presence of a computer, though it uses a wireless connection as opposed to a tether. The Aided Eyes project is functionally the most similar system to ours [12]. Their tracking device does some local processing, including gaze prediction, but is a bulky system and there is no emphasis on reducing power consumption. Their tracker uses photodiodes for tracking the limbus, yielding an error of $5°$.

Current commercially available wearable systems remain prohibitively expensive and in most cases are simply video recording devices with no real-time processing capabilities on-board. For example, the ASL MobileEye XG [2] includes an eye glass frame with eye and outward facing cameras, but is tethered to a recording device that can store or transmit data wirelessly. The system records video at 30Hz. While the eyeglass frame and camera system weigh only 0.17lbs, the recording device weighs 1.7lbs and is 7.56 x 4.65 x 2.0 inches in size. The battery life in recording mode is limited to 3 hours and no data processing is done on-board the device. The recently released Tobii Glasses [24] also include an eyeglass form factor camera system tethered to a recording device. The Tobii Glasses also record video at 30Hz with a combined 0.17lbs eyeglass and camera weight. The recording device weighs 0.44lbs and is 4.84 x 3.27 x 1.3 inches in size. However, the battery life in recording mode is limited to only 70 minutes, and no data processing is done on-board the device.

Near-Infrared vs Visible Light.

Commercial eye trackers largely use Near-Infrared (NIR) illumination of the eye to make the pupil appear darker or lighter [14]. The advantage of NIR illumination is that it creates specific reflection patterns on the cornea and pupil of the eye, and these reflections can be captured by one or two imagers. The resulting images can be processed through advanced image processing techniques to robustly extract various aspects of the state of the eye. The disadvantage of this approach is that the device is considerably more complex, and requires an illuminator and reflector to direct the NIR light into the eye, in addition to one or more imagers. This makes the eyeglass design a much more complex engineering problem, with a variety of active and passive elements mounted at different points on the frame. While visible light based eye trackers have been proposed in the past (e.g. OpenEyes), these are far less advanced than the NIR-based counterparts, perhaps because they are perceived as being much less precise and robust to lighting conditions.

While the use of NIR illumination certainly improves image quality and robustness, we argue for an approach that sacrifices some precision for broader utility and applicability. In comparison to NIR-based eyeglasses, a simple visible-light camera integrated with a passive reflector or polarized glasses to reflect the image of the eye is far easier to mount on a regular pair of spectacles. We also argue that the loss of precision may be mitigated through leveraging advances in machine learning techniques to deal with a variety of noise sources in a more robust manner.

Shape-based vs Appearance-based Gaze Estimation.

In terms of gaze tracking algorithms, three primary approaches have been explored in the literature. They are commonly referred to as shape-based, appearance-based and hybrid algorithms [7]. The shape-based approach uses features of the eye image to fit an ellipse to the boundary between the pupil and the iris [7]. The downside of this approach is that it works best with Near-Infrared (NIR) illumination sources, which, through their positioning relative to the camera, can make the pupil appear brighter or darker, thereby making it easier to detect the boundary [14]. When using visible light, shape-based techniques are harder to use since the boundary of the pupil is harder to detect.

Appearance-based gaze tracking algorithms attempt to predict the gaze location directly from the pixels of the eye image without an intermediate geometric representation of the pupil. This approach essentially treats the gaze inference problem as a regression problem where the inputs are the pixels of the eye image and the outputs are the vertical and horizontal components of the point of gaze in the outward facing image plane. Due to the generality of the gaze inference problem when formulated in this way, predictions can be based on essentially any multivariate regression approach. Two prominent approaches used in the gaze tracking literature are multi-layer neural networks [3] and manifold-based regression [21]. This approach is preferable in our scenario, since it is more robust to artifacts observed in a visible-light based image stream of the eye. While we leverage an appearance-based technique, our primary contribution at the algorithmic level is the development of sparse appearance-based models for gaze prediction that optimize gaze estimation accuracy while minimizing the pixel sampling costs.

3. iShadow OVERVIEW

In this section, we provide a brief overview of the iShadow system. The first step in using iShadow is calibration, where a user looks at a few points on a monitor while keeping their head relatively steady, in a manner similar to commercial eye trackers. During this calibration phase, iShadow captures a full image stream from the eye-facing and outward-facing imager, and downloads this data to a computer either via USB or Bluetooth.

The second step is the neural network based sparse pixel selection algorithm. In this stage, the learner divides the calibration dataset into training and testing sets, and sweeps through the regularization parameters to learn a set of models that correspond to different gaze prediction accuracies. Each model specifies both the set of pixels that need to be acquired and the weights on the pixels to use for the activation function that predicts gaze coordinates. Depending on the power constraints of the platform and the accuracy needs of the application, the appropriate model can be downloaded to the iShadow platform for real-time operation.

The third step is the run-time execution of the model that is downloaded onto the iShadow platform. The run-time system acquires the appropriate pixel set and executes the non-linear weighted sum to predict gaze coordinates in real time.

Once gaze coordinates are obtained from the eye-facing imager, they can be used in different ways depending on application needs. For example, it could be used to detect rapid saccades (i.e. rapid eye movements) which correspond to an event in the external field of view of the user. When a saccade is detected, the outward facing imager can be triggered to capture an image or video of the event that could have caused the saccade. Alternately, gaze coordinates

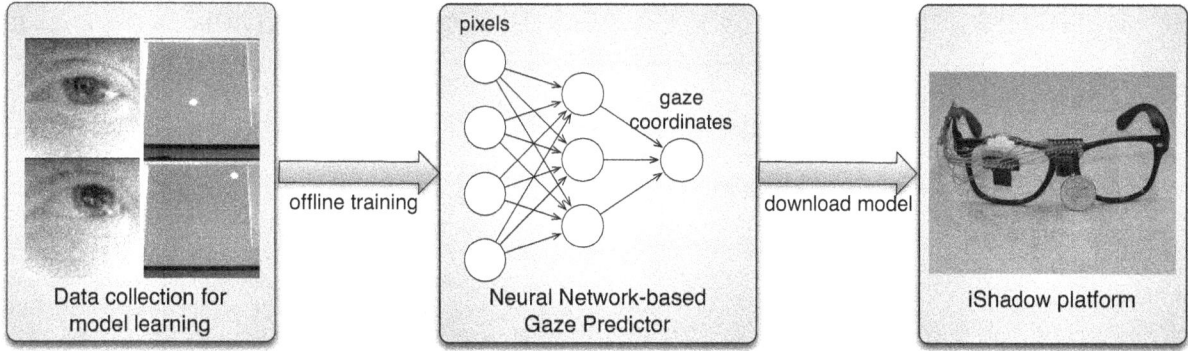

Figure 1: iShadow overview: A user wears the eyeglass and collects a few minutes of calibration data by looking at dots on a computer screen. The calibration data is downloaded from local storage on the eyeglass, and the neural network model is learnt offline. An appropriate model can then be uploaded to the eyeglass for real-time gaze tracking.

could be used to detect fixation and use this information to decide when to trigger the outward facing camera.

4. GAZE TRACKING ALGORITHM

In this section we describe our framework for energy aware gaze tracking. At a high level, the idea involves setting up the prediction problem as a neural network where the inputs are the pixel values obtained from the imager, and the output is the predicted gaze coordinates. A unique aspect of our work is that in addition to determining the parameters of the neural network, we also determine a smaller subset of pixels to sample to reduce power consumption, while minimizing the loss in gaze prediction accuracy.

To enable subset pixel selection, the neural network learning algorithm uses a regularizer that penalizes models that select more pixels; thus, the optimization involves two terms: a) an error term that captures how well the algorithm predicts gaze coordinates, and b) a penalty term that increases with the number of pixels selected. This optimization is done offline using numerical optimization methods, and the parameters are hard-coded into the microcontroller for real-time execution. Thus, the eyeglass is not making any real-time decision about which pixels to sample, or how to map from pixel values to gaze output — it is simply computing a function of the subsampled pixels based on hard-coded parameters from the learnt neural network model. The online operation is therefore lightweight and easy to optimize in hardware. We describe this process in more detail in the rest of this section.

Model Specification.

Our base gaze prediction model is a feed-forward neural network as shown in Figure 2 [1]. The input layer is a $D \times D$ array of values I representing the eye-facing image. The pixel at row i and column j is given by I_{ij}. The desired output of the system is the gaze coordinates in the outward facing image plane (X, Y). The hidden layer of the model consists of K hidden units H_k. The model includes input-to-hidden parameters W_{ijk}^{IH} for each pixel location (i, j) in the eye-facing image and each hidden unit H_k; a hidden unit bias parameter B_k^H for each hidden unit H_k; hidden-to-output parameters W_{kx}^{HO} and W_{ky}^{HO} mapping between hidden unit H_k and the horizontal and vertical gaze coordinates (X, Y); and output bias parameters B_x^O and B_y^O for the horizontal and vertical gaze coordinates (X, Y). The hidden units use a standard hyperbolic tangent (tanh) activation function. The output units use

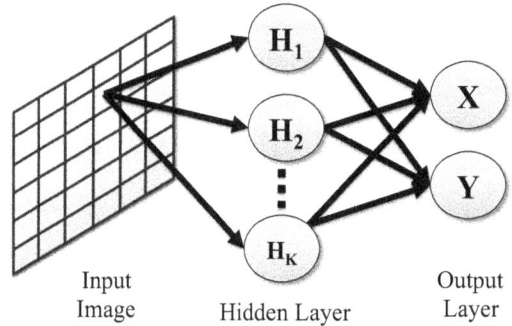

Figure 2: Illustration of the the neural network gaze prediction model.

linear activations. The mathematical formulation of the model is given below.

$$\hat{X} = B_x^O + \sum_{k=1}^{K} W_{kx}^{HO} H_k \qquad (1)$$

$$\hat{Y} = B_y^O + \sum_{k=1}^{K} W_{ky}^{HO} H_k \qquad (2)$$

$$H_k = \tanh\left(B_k^H + \sum_{i=1}^{D} \sum_{j=1}^{D} W_{ijk}^{IH} I_{ij} \right) \qquad (3)$$

Model Learning.

Given a data set $\mathcal{D} = \{I^n, X^n, Y^n\}_{n=1:N}$ consisting of N eye images I^n with corresponding gaze coordinates (X^n, Y^n), our goal is to learn the complete set of neural network model parameters $\theta = \{W^{IH}, W^{HO}, B^H, B^O\}$. We learn the model parameters by minimizing a regularized empirical loss function between the neural network's predicted outputs $(\hat{X}^n, \hat{Y}^n)$ and the true outputs (X^n, Y^n) [1]. In this work, we use squared error as the loss function. The objective function $\mathcal{F}(\theta|\mathcal{D})$ is shown below for an arbitrary regularization function $\mathcal{R}(\theta)$ with regularization parameter λ.

$$\mathcal{F}(\theta|\mathcal{D}) = \sum_{n=1}^{N} (\hat{X}^n - X^n)^2 + (\hat{Y}^n - Y^n)^2 + \lambda \mathcal{R}(\theta) \quad (4)$$

The objective function $\mathcal{F}(\theta|\mathcal{D})$ cannot be analytically minimized with respect to the model parameters θ, so numerical methods are required. The gradients of the model parameters with respect to the loss can be efficiently computed using the standard backpropagation algorithm [17]. For standard, smooth regularization functions like the two norm squared $||\theta||_2^2$, the gradients of the regularization function $\mathcal{R}(\theta)$ are also easy to obtain. The base model can be learned using any numerical optimizer such as the limited memory BFGS algorithm [15].

Pixel Subset Selection.

Given that the eye-facing images are extremely redundant, the central hypothesis of this work is that we can drastically sub-sample the eye facing images while preserving much of the accuracy.

The problem of choosing an optimal set of pixel locations is a subset selection or feature selection problem [8]. We refer to the pixels actually selected as *active pixels*. We can represent the set of active pixel locations using a binary mask A where $A_{ij} = 1$ if the pixel is active and $A_{ij} = 0$ if the pixel is not active. Given such an active pixel mask A, we can modify our neural network to base its prediction on the active pixel locations only. In Figure 2, this would correspond to simply removing all of the edges between the inactive pixels and the hidden units. The computation and communication complexity of image acquisition and gaze estimation are both linear in the number of active pixels in our framework. This means that we should expect a linear decrease in the energy cost of both image acquisition and prediction as the number of active pixels decreases.

To select a smaller active pixel set, we use a state-of-the-art sparsity-inducing group-ℓ_1 regularization function [26]. It is well known that the standard squared-error regularizer commonly used in machine learning and statistics shrinks parameter estimates toward zero, but it typically does not result in actual sparsity in the model coefficients. Tibshirani solved this problem for linear regression through the introduction of a method called the *lasso* for optimizing the least squares loss with a regularizer that penalizes the absolute values of the model parameters [22]. For linear models, setting a coefficient to zero is equivalent removing the underlying variable from the model and, as a result, such ℓ_1 regularization methods have been proven to be very effective at optimally solving subset selection problems.

In the present case, our model is a neural network with one parameter for each pixel in the image and each hidden unit. To solve the subset selection problem we need to simultaneously set all of the outgoing connections from a group of pixels to zero. This is likely not to happen when applying the standard ℓ_1 regularization function in a randomly initialized neural network model. However, the group-ℓ_1 regularizer developed by Yuan and Lin is designed specifically to drive groups of parameters to zero simultaneously. There are several different versions of the group-ℓ_1 regularizer. We make use of the group-ℓ_1/ℓ_2 regularization function as shown below. Note that in our case, we only regularize the input-to-hidden layer weights. The groups consist of all of the parameters from a given pixel to each of the K hidden units.

$$\mathcal{R}(\theta) = \sum_{i=1}^{D} \sum_{j=1}^{d} \left(\sum_{k=1}^{K} (W_{ijk}^{IH})^2 \right)^{1/2} \quad (5)$$

The neural network model parameters can then be learned by optimizing $\mathcal{F}(\theta|\mathcal{D})$ with the choice of regularizer given above.

Real-time Inference: Resource Usage vs Accuracy.

It is important to keep in mind that all model learning described above happens in an offline setting. The real-time component of the gaze estimation system consists only of acquiring an eye facing image and performing a forward pass through the neural network. As shown in Equations (1)-(3), this forward pass requires only floating point addition and multiplication along with the computation of the tanh non-linearity. These are simple enough that they can be performed efficiently even on microcontrollers that do not have a floating point unit, and are limited in RAM.

One of the key benefits of our approach is that the sparse acquisition-based neural network model naturally lends itself to trading off energy consumption or resource usage for the accuracy of gaze prediction. Setting the regularization parameter to larger values will drive the parameters associated with an increasing number of pixel locations to zero while maintaining as much accuracy as possible. Fewer pixels implies a) less energy for using the imager, b) less computational needs for predicting gaze from the pixels, and c) less memory resources needed for storing the weights. All of these have advantages depending on the energy constraints on the eyeglass or the resource constraints on the microcontroller.

5. iShadow CALIBRATION

One important practical aspect of using a gaze tracking system is calibration of the device to each user. We faced three challenges in designing the calibration procedure for the system. (1) There were many idiosyncrasies with the low-power Stonyman imager since it was an early version of a research prototype, and we had to perform extensive experiments across numerous parameters to understand its characteristics. (2) The image stream from the eye-facing imager changes depending on each individual's eye shape and eyeglass position, hence it was important to calibrate for each individual. (3) We needed to find ways to minimize burden on the participant and any manual overhead including adjustment of the imager position, manual labeling of images for learning, etc. all of which would make iShadow difficult to use for a new user. We detail the process by which we addressed these issues and calibrated the iShadow system for a new user.

FPN calibration: One drawback of the Stonyman camera is the noise issues inherent to the logarithmic pixels used by the camera. Such Fixed Pattern Noise (FPN) is typical in digital imagers, and results from small manufacturing imperfections including pixel size, material, interference with circuitry, etc which is unique to each individual imager. However, logarithmic pixels are particularly sensitive to these imperfections, meaning that most pairs of pixels have a noticeably different response to equal incident illumination. This effect yields an extremely noisy image if it is not dealt with.

FPN noise can be easily accounted for under the assumption that the noise remains stationary. In this case, it is simple to correct for the FPN by determining each pixel's response to uniform incident illumination and using this to generate an offset mask over the whole pixel array. The values in this mask are then subtracted from every image captured by the camera, which removes the effects of FPN completely. While FPN will remain constant under consistent lighting conditions and camera configuration settings, the FPN for the Stonyman camera is very sensitive to changes in outdoor lighting conditions. In addition, the dynamic range of imager is relatively low, resulting in saturation effects in bright sunlight.

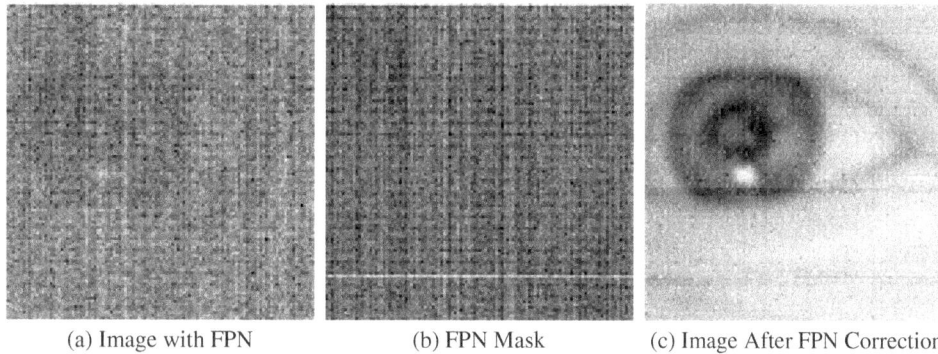

(a) Image with FPN   (b) FPN Mask   (c) Image After FPN Correction

Figure 3: Stages of the fixed-pattern-noise (FPN) correction process. The raw image is collected with FPN present (a), from which the the static FPN mask (b) is subtracted. The resulting image (c) is mostly free of FPN.

Fortunately, we found that the imager's behavior under indoor lighting illumination tends to be relatively uniform, and the we could learn a mask that was reusable over a moderate range of lighting conditions. Under all indoor conditions, we have been able to use a single FPN mask per camera and generate consistently viable images. While this means that our system is not currently useful in outdoor settings, this is an artifact of the camera that will hopefully be resolved with further improvements to the hardware.

The process to learn a new mask for an imager is straightforward, and needs to be only done once prior to mounting the imager on the eyeglass. The imager must be exposed to uniform illumination so as to determine the relative offsets for each pixel in the mask. This should be done using a light-colored diffuser placed over the camera lens. A diffuser can be anything from a nylon mesh, as is often used in professional photography for illumination diffusion, to a thin sheet of paper. Once the lens is covered, the iShadow driver will capture and download an image to process as the new FPN mask for that camera. This process must be performed once for each of the two mounted cameras, and then FPN calibration is complete. See Figure 3 for an example of an image with and without FPN noise.

Collecting training data: Variations between subjects in the shape, position of the eye, and placement of the eyeglass mean that a new neural network model must be trained for each user, and therefore some amount of labeled training data must be generated per user.

The data collection process itself is quite simple. The subject sits in front of a display of some kind for a short period of time. We use a simple script that shows a black field on the display, and a white circle of some small radius on that field. Subjects are fitted with the iShadow glasses and seated in front of the display. To maximize the effectiveness of the training data, the user should be positioned so that the display extends to the edges or just beyond the edges of the scene-facing camera's field of view. This will ensure that there can be training data samples generated over the entire field of view. Checking that the system is in proper position can be done quickly by pulling a few images from the outward-facing camera, and displaying this to the user in real-time so that the user can adjust the position of the eyeglass.

When data collection is triggered to begin, the circle begins moving in a random pattern over the space of the display. Subjects are directed to focus their gaze on the circle as it moves across the screen, and iShadow begins collecting full-frame images from both the eye-facing and world-facing cameras. The exact training time needed depends on how accurate of a model is needed, however,

as we show in our evaluation, after accumulating one minute of labeled training data, adding more does not yield a significant increase in the accuracy of the predictor. Thus, the training session can be very brief without compromising on the accuracy of the generated neural network model.

After training data collection is complete, the collected images need to be transferred to a computer to train the neural network model. This can be done by storing the images on an SD card during the session or live streaming via USB.

Labeling training data: One potentially time-consuming aspect about learning a model for each user is generating labels from the collected data. Since the user's head position depends on height and how he/she is seated, we cannot just use the pixel positions where the target circle is drawn on the computer screen. Instead, we process the image stream from the outward-facing imager, and use a simple computer vision algorithm to detect a light-colored patch on a dark field (rest of the screen). In cases where this process fails (often because the dot is on the edge of the field of view of the imager), the calibration algorithm asks for assistance from the human, but this is largely unnecessary for the training process. Depending on the amount of training data, the process generally takes only a few minutes.

Robustness to blinks and head movements: One question with calibration is whether there is a negative effect of the users blinking or possibly drifting from the target for brief periods. This is not a significant issue since we are able to generate a high volume of data over a short period of time through automatic labeling. As a result, even if there are periods where the user was blinking or the user's gaze moved off-target for a brief of period of time, these are treated as noise by the neural network learner as long as the majority of the samples in the training set involve the user being correctly focused on the target. Our experiments show that training under this assumption yields models that have a high degree of prediction accuracy.

Learning the model: In addition to images from the eye-facing camera, and a corresponding set of gaze coordinates from the labeling session, the model learner also requires a set of regularization parameters λ, each of which will yield a different model with differing sparsity values. The process for choosing the λ values depends upon the application. For our study we swept the training across a series of values ranging from very high to very low sparsity to generate curves for the effect of λ on gaze prediction accuracy as well as power consumption.

The suitable regularization parameter can be chosen in a few different ways. The default option is to find a good tradeoff between prediction accuracy and power. We generally find that there is a sweet spot for each individual i.e. there is a small range of sparsity that yields good prediction accuracy at a very low power cost, and this may be a good standard target for the model generator. Another option is dynamic generation based on the desired value of a certain system parameter, such as prediction accuracy or frame-rate. In this scenario, the model generator would sweep over a standard set of lambda values, generating a prediction model for each one. The model trainer estimates system error based on cross-validation during training, this value can be used to find an acceptable λ value and a corresponding model to meet a prediction accuracy criterion. If the goal is a certain prediction rate, then the same process can be performed using sparsity as the metric.

Once the λs have been decided (or if they are decided dynamically), the calibration program trains a neural network model for each and saves the corresponding model parameters. Once a final model has been chosen to be used for online prediction, it is automatically loaded onto the glasses. At this point, the system is prepared to do gaze prediction for the new subject.

6. iShadow SYSTEM

Figure 4 shows a system diagram and photos a prototype version of iShadow; our current hardware implements all the design elements described in previous sections. We now briefly describe the key hardware sub-components used in the prototype and describe our optimized real-time gaze tracking implementation.

6.1 iShadow Platform

The iShadow platform features a standard glasses frame with two low-power cameras, an inertial sensor, microcontroller, and bluetooth, as seen in Figure 4. One camera is mounted in front of the user's right eye for acquiring eye-facing images. The other is mounted in the center of the frame facing outward to capture the center of the user's field of view. We use the standard optics on the image sensors, which give a $36°$ field of view.

Our hardware is designed with the constraint that needs to be thin and lightweight enough to be mounted on the side frame of a pair of eyeglasses, and roughly the same form-factor as a Google Glass. This required several hardware revisions and optimizations to make all components fit in the appropriate size. Our latest prototype is shown in Figure 4 and the components are described in Table 1. Of the components listed, the focus in this paper is primarily on the eye-facing imager, and computation of gaze on the MCU. Since the imager is central to our algorithm and implementation, we now turn to a more detailed description of its innards.

Eye-facing imager	Stonyman 112x112 greyscale [20]
World-facing imager	Stonyman 112x112 greyscale
Inertial Motion Unit	Invensense 9-axis IMU [10]
Processor	STM32 Arm Cortex M3 microcontroller [19]. 32 MHz processor; 48KB memory; 384KB flash storage
Storage	microSD card, 64GB max
Radio	Bluetooth

Table 1: iShadow platform components

Image Sensors: Our hardware framework is built around the Stonyman Vision Chip produced by Centeye, Inc.[1] This device fits our research purposes for several reasons. First, it is a low-power embedded camera, consuming approximately 3 mW when operating at full power. (see Table 2 for details). Second, the design of the pixel array allows for random access to individual pixel values. The combination of low-power operation and random access capability makes the Stonyman unique among commercially available image sensor chips.

The Stonyman features a 112x112 square grid of pixels. These pixels are characterized by their logarithmic voltage response to lighting conditions. This allows for a greater dynamic range compared to a pixel that operates linearly with respect to lighting conditions. The use of logarithmic pixels allows a random-access interface, which the Stonyman provides via a register-based control scheme. It is this feature specifically that enables the energy-accuracy trade-offs that we explore in this work.

Like many contemporary mobile image sensors, the Stonyman sensor provides a sleep mode. We exploit this feature in iShadow to use power more efficiently. The majority of the power drawn by the camera while it is active comes from the pixel acquisition circuitry, and this can be powered down using a control register. In this low-power state there is only a small power draw - less than a half a microwatt - for the digital control circuitry that maintains the values in the control registers and allows the camera to be switched back to full-power mode. There is a small delay time, on the order of a few microseconds, for the camera to power up and back down. These delay times, as well as the power consumption of the camera in wake and sleep modes, are given in Table 2.

Finally, while we made the choice to use the Stonyman imager as the outward-facing camera in addition to the inward facing one, the outward facing imager can be replaced with a higher-end device if better quality images are needed for vision processing. The insight in this paper is that gaze coordinates can be obtained with a very low-power and low-resolution eye-facing imager such as the Stonyman camera.

Active to Sleep Delay	$4\ \mu s$
Sleep to Active Delay	$10\ \mu s$
Active Power Consumption	3.13 mW
Sleep Power Consumption	$0.041\ \mu W$

Table 2: Stonyman Power Consumption and Transition Times in and out of Sleep Mode

6.2 Basic Operation Modes

At the lowest level, iShadow supports three basic modes of system operation — full image capture, real-time gaze tracking, and life logging. However, the system's functionality is not limited to the modes outlined here, as one of the primary benefits of iShadow over existing commercial eye trackers is its programmability. Users who have a specific application in mind that might benefit from a more complex operating scheme can implement and run it on the system themselves, allowing for a much broader set of usage scenarios than those outlined here.

Full image capture: In this mode, iShadow is continuously capturing full-frame images from the inward and outward-facing imagers and storing it into on-board flash. This mode is intended primarily for offline data analysis, and adjustment of parameters

---

[1] http://centeye.com/products/stonyman-vision-chip-breakout-board

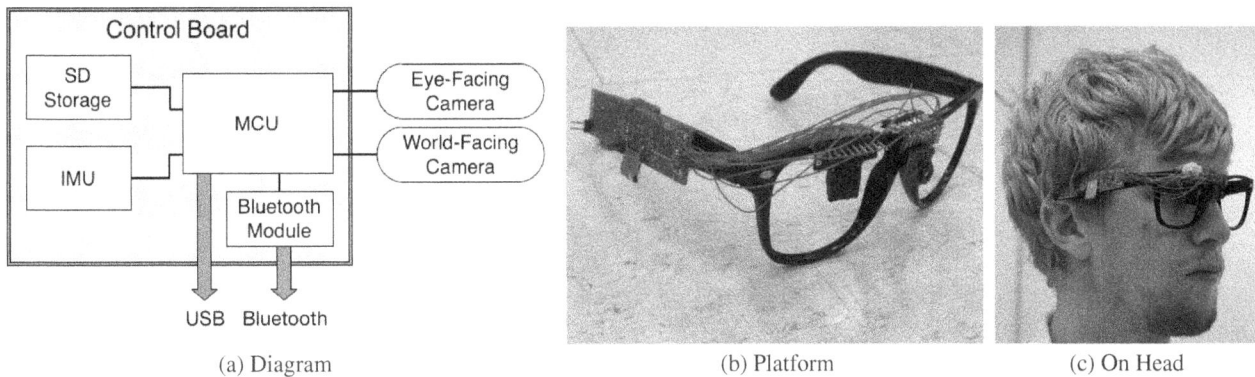

| (a) Diagram | (b) Platform | (c) On Head |

Figure 4: Figures show an architecture diagram and different views of the third-generation iShadow prototype. The prototype has two cameras, one at the center front and one facing the eye, with the electronics mounted on the control board on the side. Batteries, while not shown, are mounted behind the ear.

during the calibration phase (described above). By tightly optimizing the image capture method and interleaving control signals with ADC delays, we are able to drive both cameras at the same capture rate as if we were only driving one. The full-image capture rate for both cameras is 10 Hz.

These images can be stored to an onboard SD card or transmitted to another device via USB or bluetooth. For storage, we have designed our system to use a double-buffered scheme that allows the SD communication peripheral to read and transmit already-collected pixel data while more data is written to the second buffer. There is still some delay introduced by the SD card writes, as there are a small number of operations needed to trigger the SD card write process. However, this improvement hides the majority of the SD write latency. Since our available RAM is too small to hold an entire frame, let alone two double-buffered frames, we write data at regular intervals during image collect to prevent overflow.

Real-time gaze tracking mode: The most useful operating mode of iShadow is real-time gaze prediction, where it is continuously processing the pixels from the eye-facing imager to output gaze coordinates. In this mode, iShadow is solely processing image streams from the eye-facing imager. Once a gaze prediction has been completed and a gaze estimate generated, it can be used in several ways. One option is to store values for some form of post processing later - this is especially useful when run the eye-facing imager runs in conjunction with the world-facing imager, as in the final operating mode below. The gaze data can also be used for triggering more complicated on-board processes or for making higher-level inferences about the state of the eye or the wearer, as discussed in the following section.

Lifelogging mode: iShadow's third operating mode is a simple extension of real-time gaze-tracking. Simply put, it is capturing what in the outside world the user is looking at. By running the real-time gaze inference algorithm using the eye-facing imager and taking full images from the world-facing imager, the system records where the user is looking and what they are looking at. This type of "lifelogging" is becoming more prevalent as wearable computing grows cheaper and more accessible.

In this mode, the bottleneck is the outward-facing image capture. By doing interleaving of prediction operations with ADC reads the predict time can be completely hidden, however, there is no way to significantly reduce the time needed to collect a full-frame image from the outward-facing camera. This operating mode is a simple but straightforward example of the types of applications that

iShadow facilitates, and does not require any additional logic on top of the existing firmware.

6.3 Gaze-triggered applications

While the focus of this paper is not on designing gaze-driven applications, we briefly describe a few example applications that can be designed over the above operating modes. Several higher-level inferences are possible from a continuous stream of gaze coordinates: a) Eye fixations can be detected by looking for windows when the gaze coordinates are relatively steady with small changes due to head movements, b) Smooth Pursuit can be detected by looking for slowly changing gaze coordinates, and c) Sudden events can be detected by looking for a large saccade or change in gaze. These higher-level inferences could suggest different things about the visual state of the outward-facing imager — for example, eye fixations could be during conversation with an individual, smooth pursuit could be while reading from a book or screen, and sudden events could be an unexpected change in the surroundings. In the case of disease progression, abnormal gaze patterns may be detected, for example, abnormally frequent saccades. Once such a high-level inference detects an event of interest, it quickly triggers the outward-facing imager to capture the state of the world, and stores this data into the local SD card or streams the data over bluetooth to a mobile phone.

7. EVALUATION

To test the effectiveness of iShadow at accurately and efficiently predicting the wearer's gaze location, we collected sample data from ten different subjects - eight men and two women from the ages of 22 to 31. We ran each subject through the calibration process outlined in section 5, excluding the FPN mask generation as it does not affect the per-individual results. We generated at least five minutes of labeled data for each subject in full-image-capture mode. To generate the ground-truth labels, we use the approach described in section 5. Running at the maximum framerate of 10 Hz, the resulting dataset includes at least 3000 images per user. We used this data to perform a variety of experiments to determine whether we had reached our design goals.

We present our evaluation in three sections. Section 7.1 details our experiments to determine whether the neural network model and the ℓ_1-subsampling method are capable of accurately estimating the wearer's gaze coordinates. In section 7.2, we evaluate the

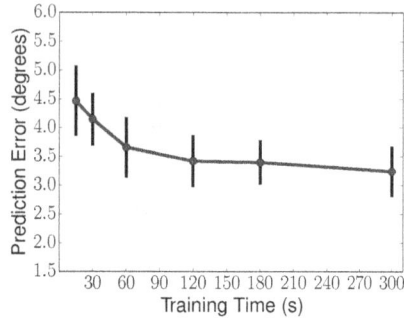

Figure 5: Amount of training time for the system versus the resulting gaze prediction accuracy.

tradeoffs between the model parameters and the resulting performance of the hardware, especially the image capture pipeline.

7.1 Evaluation of Neural-Network-Based Pixel Selection

We first evaluate the benefits of our neural network-based method to select a sparse set of pixels. Using the data collected, we performed a number of experiments to investigate the accuracy of the neural network gaze prediction model as a function of the number of active pixels. We generated a set of 10 values of the regularization parameter λ, and trained each user's data over this same set of λs. Our per-user, per-λ experimental framework is based on a standard five-fold random re-sampling protocol. For each fold, we divided the available data into a training set and a test set completely at random using an 80/20 split.

We use the training set to estimate the parameters of the model and use the learned model parameters to predict gaze locations for each test image. We compute the gaze prediction error for a given test fold in terms of the average squared distance (ℓ_2 distance) between each true gaze location in the test set and the predicted gaze location given each eye image in the test set. We average the prediction error over the five test folds to generate an error value for that user and λ. In addition, the size of the pixel selection mask varies with each fold as the optimizer finds slightly different solutions when using different training data sets. To account for this, we also average the size of the pixel mask generated over the five folds.

After generating per-user data, we average the prediction error and pixel mask sizes across all ten users to generate our results below. While there is moderate variation in the results between users due to differences in eye position and shape, the general trends across users are consistent and can be seen in the results we present here. For all of our results, we present the mean value and the 90% confidence interval unless otherwise indicated.

Accuracy – Model Size tradeoffs.

One of the benefits of our algorithmic framework is that it is able to provide a variety of models that offer different tradeoffs between the overall complexity of the model (i.e. number of pixels sampled, and number of weights for computation) and the accuracy of the model (i.e. the precision in degrees). This tradeoff is enabled by using different choices of the regularization parameter, which varies the penalty for model complexity compared to the accuracy.

First, we look at whether the regularization parameter is a useful knob for tuning model size and accuracy. Figures 6a and 6b show that varying the regularization parameter enables us to select

a spectrum of models with different prediction accuracies and different fractions of selected pixels, respectively.

Figure 6c shows just the prediction accuracy vs model size — interestingly, we see that varying the percentage of activated pixels from 100% down to about 10% only has a minor effect on the prediction accuracy. This shows that there is substantial redundancy in the eye image, and the neural network is able to predict gaze just as well with 10% of the pixels activated as 100% of the pixels. On our imager, this means that sampling 10K pixels per image vs sampling 1K pixels per image has roughly the same prediction error, which in turn can translate to substantial reduction in power consumption.

We also see that the accuracy of the neural network model does not drop below about 2° even when the entire image is sampled. In contrast, high-end mobile eye trackers advertise accuracies of as low as 0.5°. The primary reason for this gap is that the eye-facing imager lens is mounted at a fixed position on our eyeglass in our current iShadow prototype, and has a limited field of view of 36°. As a result, for some individuals, the pupil was rarely completely within the field of view of the imager.

This can be seen in Figure 7, which compares sample eye images between users for whom the predictor performed well, average, and poorly compared to the rest of the set. In general, having the entire range of the pupil's motion visible to the camera, as well as a strong contrast between the iris and the white of the eye (sclera) seem to be the most significant indicators of good predictive performance.

Despite the gap, we argue that a 3° accuracy error is acceptable for a variety of real-world applications, particularly when the object being viewed is in relatively close proximity, for example, detecting the individual with whom a user is engaged in face-to-face conversation. Figure 8 provides a better understanding of the error in the outward image plane. Given that the imager already has a small field of view, gaze coordinates with roughly 3° error is reasonable enough to get a good idea of where the user is looking.

To get a better idea of how the neural network selects weights, we look at some example weights learnt by the hidden units. Figure 9 shows the weights for each hidden unit. Each example has approximately 10% of pixels active We can also see that the group-$\ell 1$ method learns to focus on the region of the eye image where the pupil and the white of the eye are most likely to appear, as one would expect.

Calibration time.

To evaluate how much training data is needed to generate an effective model, we look at how quickly the gaze prediction converges as the amount of data that we use for training increases. Figure 5 shows the results for a particular choice of the regularization parameter ($\lambda = 0.01$). We see that the convergence is very fast — even if there is only 60 seconds of data used for training, that is sufficient for the algorithm to determine the appropriate parameters with little to no improvement as the amount of training data increases. Similar results were seen for other values of λ. Thus, the time for calibration is not a bottleneck in system operation.

7.2 iShadow System Evaluation

We now turn to an evaluation of the iShadow platform predicting gaze in real-time with models trained using the neural network-based sparse sampling algorithm and appropriate regularization parameters, λ, as described earlier.

We wish to evaluate three key performance metrics — gaze tracking rate, prediction accuracy, and energy consumption. While gaze prediction accuracy and energy consumption are self-explanatory, gaze tracking rate requires a bit more explanation. Unlike a traditional eye tracker with an active pixel imager that involves ex-

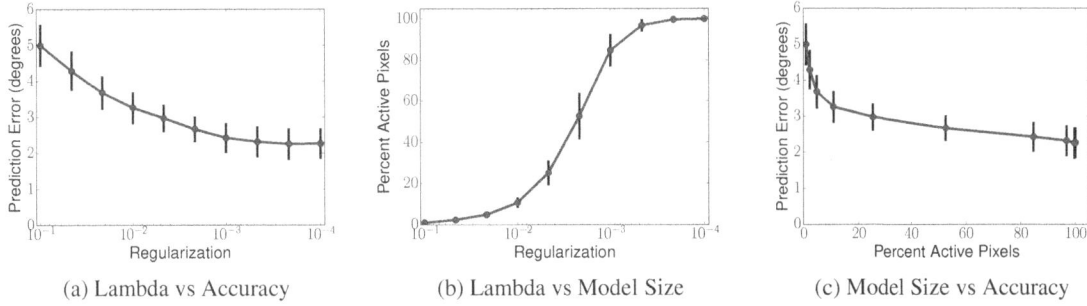

| (a) Lambda vs Accuracy | (b) Lambda vs Model Size | (c) Model Size vs Accuracy |

Figure 6: Plots (a) and (b) show the effect of regularization parameter on gaze prediction accuracy and model size respectively. Plot (c) shows the net result, which is how the number of pixels acquired can be reduced dramatically (up to 10×) with minor effect on gaze prediction accuracy.

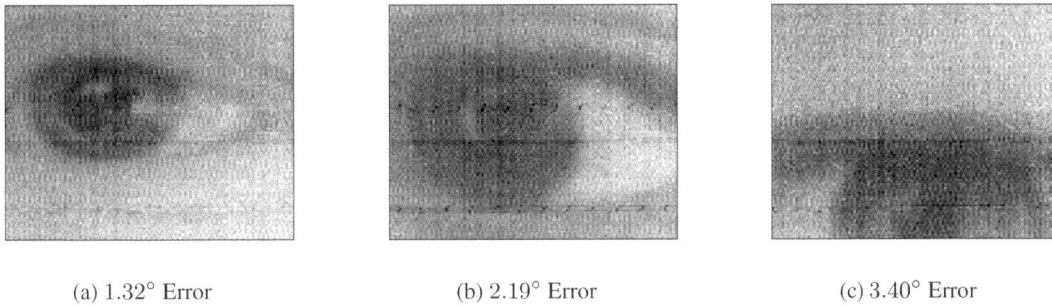

| (a) 1.32° Error | (b) 2.19° Error | (c) 3.40° Error |

Figure 7: Comparison of eye images from multiple users, giving the average prediction error for that user. Notice that the position of the eye in the image and iris / sclera contrast have a prominent effect on prediction accuracy.

posure followed by frame capture and image processing, we use a logarithmic pixel imager where the pixels can be continuously read out at any time. Thus, we refer to gaze tracking time as the amount of time after sampling the first pixel of the pre-selected sparse set until we obtain the results of the gaze. Gaze tracking rate is the number of such gaze predictions we obtain per second.

Tracking rate vs prediction accuracy: By tuning the regularization parameter, λ, we can tradeoff between the three performance metrics. Let us first consider gaze tracking rate vs accuracy while fixing the power budget. Lets start with the case when all pixels are sampled — here, accuracy is high since all pixels are available, but gaze tracking rate is poor since fewer images are sampled per second. By increasing the level of regularization, we can progressively decrease the time needed to make a single prediction since: a) fewer pixels need to be read from the camera and there are fewer calculations to perform, and b) the number of feature weights is proportional to the number of pixels, hence the memory footprint of the model also decreases. Thus, we can increase gaze tracking rate to capture rapid gaze changes, but we suffer in the accuracy of tracking due to a coarser model with fewer pixels.

Figure 11 provides an empirical evaluation of the rate vs accuracy tradeoff on iShadow. We run iShadow in always-on mode and progressively reduce the model size from large (low error, low rate) to small (high error, high rate). The results are as expected — for large models, we get prediction errors of roughly 3° but low gaze tracking rates around 10 Hz. As the models reduce in size, gaze prediction errors increase to roughly 4°, but gaze tracking rates increase to 30+ Hz as well. For reference, commercial eye trackers

operate at 30 Hz or higher, therefore, these results show that with a small reduction in accuracy, iShadow can achieve sampling rates comparable to commercial eye trackers.

Tracking accuracy vs Energy consumption: We now turn to gaze tracking accuracy vs power consumption. When evaluating energy consumption, we need to consider two hardware components, the micro controller (MCU) and the imager, and two software subsystems on the MCU, pixel acquisition from the camera, and the cost of running the gaze prediction algorithm. Thus, we do a three-way breakdown of energy: a) energy consumed for pixel capture by the imager, b) energy consumed for pixel acquisition by MCU, and c) energy consumed for executing the gaze prediction algorithm on the MCU.

Figure 10a shows the results for a fixed gaze tracking rate of 4 Hz. The system is duty-cycled whenever it is not actively performing gaze acquisition or prediction. We measured power between our on-board voltage regulator and the relevant circuit at a rate of 30 KHz, and report the energy breakdown for each gaze prediction across the different components. (Power consumption is just 4× the reported energy number since gaze tracking rate is 4 Hz.)

The general trend in the graph is as expected — a smaller model means less energy consumption but higher error. More interesting is the breakdown across the hardware and software components. The results show that the energy consumed for prediction is roughly the same as the energy consumed by the camera. But the main cost of acquisition is at the MCU, which needs to set appropriate control lines to select pixels, and read-out the pixels over a serial bus. The cost of gaze prediction is about a third or less of acquisition cost.

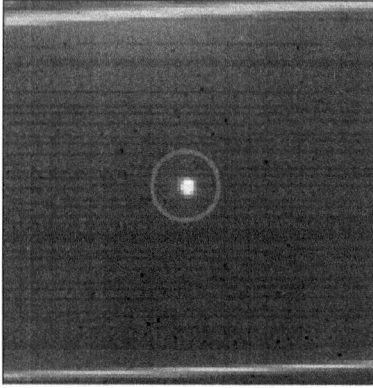

Figure 8: The circle gives an example of 3° of error in the outward imager plane around the white dot. The error is less if the eye is fully within the field of view of the imager, and higher when not fully in the field of view.

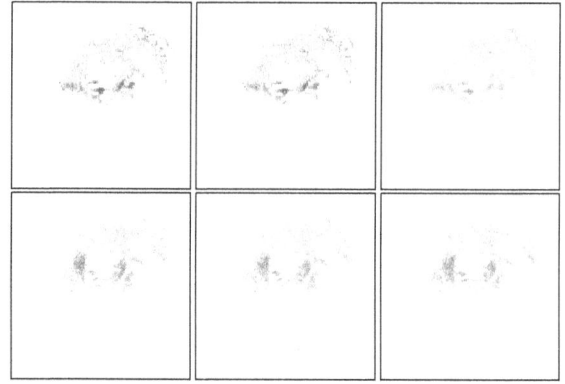

Figure 9: This figure shows the weights learned by each hidden unit in the neural network model for subsets of approximately 10% of pixel locations.

Figure 10b shows the time spent in each subsystem per gaze prediction — since a gaze tracking output is obtained every 250 ms, this shows what portion of this time period is spent per subsystem. Since the camera ON time is the same as acquisition time, we show only the plot for acquisition in the figure. The result shows that the least amount of time is spent in the gaze prediction operation, and more time is spent in pixel capture and acquisition by the MCU.

Overall, these results demonstrate that sub-sampling pixels is extremely important to reduce power consumption of the iShadow platform — gaze prediction consumes less time and energy compared to pixel capture and acquisition, clearly justifying the benefits of sparse acquisition. This is facilitated in hardware by the Stonyman's random-access pixel capability, without which the time and energy for the MCU to acquire all of the pixel data would dwarf the benefits of decreased gaze prediction time and camera sleep.

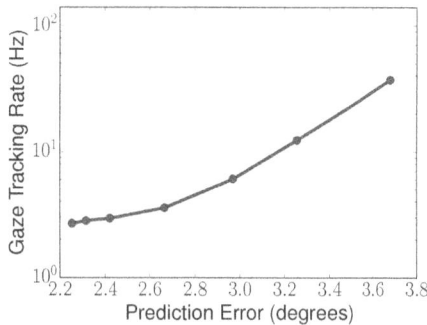

Figure 10: Smooth tradeoff between gaze tracking rate and prediction error as λ is varied. The MCU is always active in this experiment.

8. DISCUSSION

The design of a computational eyeglass platform is extremely complex due to the complexity of the sensors, the positioning and mounting on the eyeglass frame, and the demanding computational needs for processing image streams. While our results are promising, there are several steps to take before such platforms are ready for more widespread use. We discuss some of these steps in this

section, as well as the types of applications that our platform is suitable for.

Imager + IMU fusion: While the techniques that we use in this paper can be used to identify gaze direction, we need additional information about head movement to precisely determine whether the individual is fixated at the same location in the external world. For example, the head might move about during conversation but the eye might continue to track the individuals face. Our platform incorporates an IMU in addition to imagers to enable such fusion, but our algorithms have not yet taken advantage of this capability.

Image field of view: As described in §7, one of the reasons why our gaze tracking performance varies across individuals is because of the field of view of the eye-facing imager. We currently use a lens that has a field of view of 36°, as a result of which the entire eye is not in the visual field of the imager for some subjects. We believe that this issue can be fixed using a lens with a wider field of view, such as a fisheye lens. One important advantage of the neural network-based gaze tracking algorithm used in iShadow is that it is more robust to distortions caused by different lens than canonical vision-based techniques. Even though a fisheye lens may be expected to distort the image, the neural network technique is not sensitive to such distortions compared to an algorithm that does shape fitting, hence our approach can be expected to retain or improve performance.

Inward-facing imager placement: An obvious consideration from an aesthetic perspective is how to place the inward facing imager such that it does not obstruct the field of view of the user. Several possibilities present themselves — for example, the pixels of an imager may be mounted all along the rims of the eyeglass, or the imager may be mounted on the side frame and observe a reflection of the eye on the spectacles lenses. While such design aspects are beyond the scope of this work, we note that a key benefit of the techniques presented in this paper is that it can be easily adapted to new eyeglass designs.

For example, consider the case where pixel imagers are mounted throughout the eyeglass rim. Depending on the shape of a user's eye, different sets of pixels may carry information that is relevant to gaze. These minimal set of pixels can be selected by applying techniques described in this paper. The same is true for the second example, using a reflected eye image. Thus, our methods generalize to a variety of other designs where subsampling of pixels may be useful.

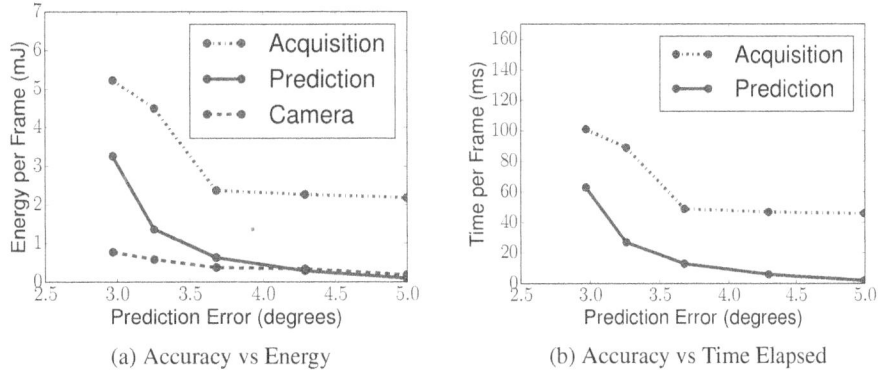

(a) Accuracy vs Energy	(b) Accuracy vs Time Elapsed

Figure 11: Breakdown of energy and time for different subsystems during the capture and predict process. (a) is the amount of energy consumed for pixel acquisition by the MCU, the gaze prediction computation, and cameras, and (b) is the amount of time spent by the MCU in acquisition and prediction.

Robustness across users: We have described the variability of per-user performance and the improvements we plan to implement to make performance better and more consistent across subjects that it has been trained on. However, our end goal is to provide a system that works with little or no per-user training required. This is critically important for accessibility and ease of use. The first step towards this goal is addressing the issue of eye localization in the image, either by altering the hardware to allow repositioning of the camera or by automatically adjusting for the position of the eye in the image. Once that issue has been addressed, we plan to collect data from a much larger number of subjects and begin building and testing "universal" models that will work at least moderately well on a new subject without requiring prior training.

Comparison to other eye tracking devices: The development of specialized eye tracking hardware has accelerated rapidly over the past decade, to the point where remote (non-mobile) devices are expected to have only a few tenths of a degree of predictive error [7]. Even mobile trackers report errors of 1° or less [2]. The fact that the error rates we report are moderately higher than this immediately begs the question of why we chose to introduce this system. Part of the discrepancy is the immaturity of the system - iShadow is still in early development, and accuracy can be expected to improve noticeably as we refine the system and tracking algorithm. It would be overly optimistic, however, to assume that such progression will bring us to the same order of magnitude of accuracy as industrial tracking devices.

However, current mobile trackers remain too bulky to be deployed comfortably in real-life scenarios and have too short of a battery life for even moderate-length studies of 4+ hours. Because of iShadow's low-power design, it offers a significantly longer run time and smaller form factor than existing mobile devices. Once the design of the system has been refined, we envision it being used for long-running experiments in the wild. For these types of applications it is unlikely that extremely fine-grained accuracy will be needed. iShadow's current accuracy is easily enough to identify, for example, what object the user is looking at in a scene. It is not enough to distinguish gaze between lines of text, but tasks of that nature are generally better suited to static test environments.

In short, all eye tracking hardware represents a tradeoff between accuracy and mobility. The current generation of mobile eye trackers give moderate mobility at the cost of some accuracy. We present iShadow as a further step in that same direction, giving excellent mobility at a slight accuracy cost over and above that of current industrial mobile devices. For tasks that require such mobility, we believe that iShadow is the best option currently in existence.

9. CONCLUSIONS

We present a first-of-its-kind low power gaze tracker that is designed to predict gaze in real-time while operating with a power budget of a few tens of milliwatts. This paper presents a soup-to-nuts implementation of such a system, including a full hardware prototype, a new neural-network based algorithm for sparse pixel acquisition, a full implementation of a real-time gaze predictor on a microcontroller, and evaluation on several subjects. Our approach exploits the unique properties of random access pixel cameras to achieve a flexible energy-accuracy trade-off in the wearable/real-time setting. Our results show that we can dramatically reduce power consumption and resource needs by sampling only 10% of pixel values, without compromising accuracy of gaze prediction. These results are highly significant in that they offer a clear path toward ubiquitous gaze tracking for a variety of applications in computer vision, behavioral sensing, mobile health, and mobile advertising. For videos on the working of iShadow, see [11].

Acknowledgements

This paper has benefited from extensive discussions with several people. In particular, we would like to thank Russ Belawski and Prabal Dutta, who have been instrumental in getting earlier prototypes of our platform up and running, and enabling several iterations of initial data collection that helped us bootstrap this work. We would also like to thank Jeremy Gummeson for much needed help with the hardware prototype. We are also very grateful to our shepherd, Prof. Lin Zhong, for extensive interactions and insightful suggestions that helped us improve presentation of results in the paper. This research was partially supported by NSF grants #1239341, #1217606, and #1218586.

10. REFERENCES

[1] A neural-based remote eye gaze tracker under natural head motion. *Computer Methods and Programs in Biomedicine*, 92(1):66 – 78, 2008.
[2] Applied Science Laboratories. NeXtGeneration Mobile Eye: Mobile Eye XG. http://www.asleyetracking.com/Site/Portals/0/MobileEyeXGwireless.pdf, 2013. Online; accessed April 7, 2013.

[3] S. Baluja and D. Pomerleau. Non-intrusive gaze tracking using artificial neural networks. Technical report, Pittsburgh, PA, USA, 1994.

[4] C. M. Bishop. *Neural networks for pattern recognition*. Oxford university press, 1995.

[5] D. Cheng and R. Vertegaal. An eye for an eye: a performance evaluation comparison of the lc technologies and tobii eye trackers. In *Eye Tracking Research & Application: Proceedings of the 2004 symposium on Eye tracking research & applications*, volume 22, pages 61–61, 2004.

[6] A. T. Duchowski. *Eye Tracking Methodology: Theory and Practice*. Springer-Verlag New York, Inc., Secaucus, NJ, USA, 2007.

[7] D. W. Hansen and Q. Ji. In the eye of the beholder: A survey of models for eyes and gaze. *Pattern Analysis and Machine Intelligence, IEEE Transactions on*, 32(3):478–500, 2010.

[8] T. Hastie, R. Tibshirani, J. Friedman, and J. Franklin. The elements of statistical learning: data mining, inference and prediction. *The Mathematical Intelligencer*, 27(2):83–85, 2005.

[9] K. Holmqvist, M. Nyström, R. Andersson, R. Dewhurst, H. Jarodzka, and J. Van de Weijer. *Eye tracking: A comprehensive guide to methods and measures*. OUP Oxford, 2011.

[10] Invensense-9150. MPU-9150 Nine-Axis (Gyro + Accelerometer + Compass) MEMS MotionTracking Device. http://www.invensense.com/mems/gyro/mpu9150.html, 2013.

[11] iShadow. iShadow Videos. http://sensors.cs.umass.edu/projects/eyeglass/, 2013.

[12] Y. Ishiguro, A. Mujibiya, T. Miyaki, and J. Rekimoto. Aided eyes: eye activity sensing for daily life. In *Proceedings of the 1st Augmented Human International Conference*, page 25. ACM, 2010.

[13] D. Li, J. Babcock, and D. J. Parkhurst. openeyes: a low-cost head-mounted eye-tracking solution. In *Proceedings of the 2006 symposium on Eye tracking research & applications*, pages 95–100. ACM, 2006.

[14] C. Morimoto and M. Mimica. Eye gaze tracking techniques for interactive applications. *Computer Vision and Image Understanding*, 98(1):4–24, 2005.

[15] J. Nocedal and S. J. Wright. *Numerical optimization*. Springer Science+ Business Media, 2006.

[16] V. Rantanen, T. Vanhala, O. Tuisku, P. Niemenlehto, J. Verho, V. Surakka, M. Juhola, and J. Lekkala. A wearable, wireless gaze tracker with integrated selection command source for human-computer interaction. *Information Technology in Biomedicine, IEEE Transactions on*, 15(5):795–801, 2011.

[17] D. E. Rumelhart, G. E. Hinton, and R. J. Williams. Learning representations by back-propagating errors. *Nature*, 323(Oct):533–536+, 1986.

[18] W. Sewell and O. Komogortsev. Real-time eye gaze tracking with an unmodified commodity webcam employing a neural network. In *CHI'10 Extended Abstracts on Human Factors in Computing Systems*, pages 3739–3744. ACM, 2010.

[19] STM32. STM32 32-bit ARM Cortex MCUs. http://www.st.com/web/en/catalog/mmc/FM141/SC1169, 2013.

[20] Stonyman. Stonyman Vision Chip. http://centeye.com/products/stonyman-vision-chip-breakout-board/, 2013.

[21] K.-H. Tan, D. Kriegman, and N. Ahuja. Appearance-based eye gaze estimation. In *Proceedings of the Sixth IEEE Workshop on Applications of Computer Vision, 2002.*, pages 191–195, 2002.

[22] R. Tibshirani. Regression shrinkage and selection via the lasso. *Journal of the Royal Statistical Society. Series B (Methodological)*, pages 267–288, 1996.

[23] Tobii. Tobii EyeX Controller. http://www.tobii.com/eye-experience/, 2013.

[24] Tobii Technology. Tobii Glasses Eye Tracker. Online, 2013. Online; accessed April 7, 2013.

[25] L. Young and D. Sheena. Survey of eye movement recording methods. *Behavior Research Methods*, 7(5):397–429, 1975.

[26] M. Yuan and Y. Lin. Model selection and estimation in regression with grouped variables. *Journal of the Royal Statistical Society: Series B (Statistical Methodology)*, 68(1):49–67, 2006.

nShield: A Noninvasive NFC Security System for Mobile Devices

Ruogu Zhou
Michigan State University
3115 Engineering Bld.
East Lansing, MI 48824
zhouruog@msu.edu

Guoliang Xing
Michigan State University
3115 Engineering Bld.
East Lansing, MI 48824
glxing@msu.edu

ABSTRACT

The Near Field Communication (NFC) technology is gaining increasing popularity among mobile users. However, as a relatively new and developing technology, NFC may also introduce security threats that make mobile devices vulnerable to various malicious attacks. This work presents the first system study on the feasibility of and defense again passive NFC eavesdropping. Our experiments show that commodity NFC-enabled mobile devices can be eavesdropped from up to 240 cm away, which is at least an order of magnitude of the intended NFC communication distance. This finding challenges the general perception that NFC is largely immune to eavesdropping because of its short working range. We then present the design of a hardware security system called *nShield*. With a small form factor, nShield can be attached to the back of mobile devices to attenuate the signal strength against passive eavesdropping. At the same time, the absorbed RF energy is scavenged by nShield for its perpetual operation. nShield intelligently determines the right attenuation level that is just enough to sustain reliable data communication. We implement a prototype of nShield, and evaluate its performance via extensive experiments. Our results show that nShield has low power consumption (23 uW), can harvest significant amount of power (55 mW), and adaptively attenuates the signal strength of NFC in a variety of realistic settings, while only introducing insignificant delay (up to 2.2 s).

Categories and Subject Descriptors

C.2.0 [**Computer-communication Networks**]: General—*Security and protection*; B.0 [**Hardware**]: General

Keywords

NFC; Eavesdropping; Smartphone; Energy Harvesting

MobiSys'14, June 16–19, 2014, Bretton Woods, New Hampshire, USA.
Copyright 2014 ACM 978-1-4503-2793-0/14/06 ...$15.00.
http://dx.doi.org/10.1145/2594368.2594376 .

1. INTRODUCTION

In recent years, the Near Field Communication (NFC) technology is increasingly available on the new generation of smartphones, tablets, and smart accessories. It is estimated that more than 200 million NFC-enabled smartphones will be shipped in 2013 [7]. And over 50% of the smart devices to be shipped in 2015 will have NFC support [4]. The growing popularity of NFC has enabled a range of applications, from contactless payment [6] and ticketing [16] to device pairing [15] for ad hoc data exchange.

A major trait of NFC is its short communication range (usually within 10 cm), which is the result of the fast decaying magnetic induction between the antennas of NFC transmitter and receiver. The short communication range is favored by many security-sensitive applications, such as contactless payment, since it provides a natural, physical protection against various attacks, particularly malicious eavesdropping. Unfortunately, as NFC is still a relatively new and developing technology, its implementation on mobile devices often have design flaws, which may be exploited to compromise application security [29]. In particular, our experimental study described in this work shows that, current NFC radios emit significantly more RF energy than intended. With a specially designed portable NFC sniffer, we are able to eavesdrop NFC transmissions from up to 240 cm away, which is at least an order of magnitude further than the intended NFC communication distance. These findings raise major concerns on the physical security of NFC. Moreover, this issue is aggravated by the fact that current NFC chipsets adopt fixed transmission power, which cannot be adjusted to mitigate the potential risks of eavesdropping.

Existing efforts on NFC security can be classified into two basic categories. Several solutions improve the security of NFC by adding more security elements, such as additional secret keys, to the native OS of mobile devices [23]. However, the mobile device would become vulnerable if the integrity of the OS is compromised (e.g., after being rooted). The second category employs additional hardware devices to secure NFC [30][12]. However, these hardware systems are bulky and power-hungry, which are ill-suited for mobile devices. In a recent work [21], a hardware security device is developed to harvest energy from NFC transmissions and jam malicious interactions. However, due to the low energy harvesting efficiency, the system may not provide uninterrupted protection. The above approaches are designed to prevent content-based malicious attacks, and none of them can protect NFC from eavesdropping attacks.

In this paper, we propose a novel, noninvasive NFC security system called *nShield* to protect NFC against passive eavesdropping. nShield is a credit card-sized thin pad that can be easily stuck on the back of mobile devices (see Fig. 6). nShield implements a novel adaptive RF attenuation scheme, in which the extra RF energy of NFC transmissions is determined and absorbed by nShield. At the same time, nShield scavenges the extra RF energy to sustain the perpetual operation. A key contribution of this work is the analysis of the factors affecting the energy harvesting efficiency, and the design of a highly effective energy harvesting system. nSheild is capable of harvesting significant amount of power (55 mW) from commodity mobile devices, which is at least a 1.8X improvement over the state-of-the-art NFC-based energy harvesting systems. Together with the extremely lo-power design, it enables nShield to provide the host uninterrupted protection against malicious eavesdropping. Lastly, the small form factor, self-sustainability, and transparency to OS, makes nShield an attractive solution to retrofit existing mobile devices with protection against passive eavesdropping.

In summary, we make the following key contributions in this paper.

1. We conduct an experimental study on the feasibility of passive NFC eavesdropping, with a specially designed inexpensive NFC sniffer. We show that commodity NFC-enabled devices can be eavesdropped from up to 240 cm away, which is at least an order of magnitude further than the intended NFC communication distance. Moreover, although external signal attenuation is effective in reducing NFC transmission power, the desired attenuation level that can still sustain data communication is highly dependent on the NFC hardware, tags sensitivity, and the physical distance. To our best knowledge, this is the first empirical study on passive NFC eavesdropping in practical settings.

2. We design an NFC security system called nShield to protect NFC from passive eavesdropping attacks. As a key novelty, nShield absorbs the excessive RF energy of NFC to attenuate the signal strength against passive eavesdropping, while the absorbed RF energy is scavenged for its perpetual operation. By exploiting the NFC target discovery process, nShield intelligently determines the right attenuation level that is just enough to sustain reliable data communication. As a result, it can promptly and precisely control the signal strength of NFC transmissions, mitigating the risk of passive eavesdropping.

3. We carefully analyze the factors that affect the NFC energy harvesting efficiency, and apply several design techniques to the antenna and hardware of nShield to maximize the amount of harvested energy, which include quality factor optimization, voltage matching, and tag emulation. As a result, nShield can harvest significantly more power (1.8X and 3.1X) than the two state-of-the-art NFC energy harvesting systems. This capability enables nShield to provide the host uninterrupted protections against passive eavesdropping attacks.

4. We implement a prototype of nShield, and evaluate its performance via extensive experiments. Our results show that nShield has extremely low power consumption, high energy harvesting efficiency, and can adaptively attenuate the signal strength of NFC transmissions in a variety of realistic settings, while only introducing insignificant delay.

2. BACKGROUND

NFC employs the fast decaying magnetic induction between the antennas of transmitter and receiver for communication in close distance. The typical working distance of NFC using compact antenna coils (with the size of a credit card) is a few centimeters. An NFC communication process involves an initiator and a target. Initiator devices are usually smartphones, tablets, and POS terminals, which initiate the NFC communication with the target. The target devices can either be those devices or proximity cards. NFC has two working modes, i.e., passive mode and active mode. The passive mode employs the same communication techniques as those used by the proximity card, in which the target device is powered by the RF field emitted by the initiator, and transmits by modulating the RF field. In the active mode, both initiator and target are powered by their own energy sources. The ASK and PSK modulation schemes are employed by NFC to support a number of data rates (106 kpbs, 212 kbps and 424 kbps).

An NFC communication process always begins with *target discovery*, in which the NFC initiator discovers the nearby NFC targets and learns the capability of the discovered targets. The initial phase of discovery process is probing, in which the initiator broadcasts discovery messages periodically to find nearby target devices. An NFC target device responds after it hears the probe. The initiator and the target then exchange a few parameters back and forth to learn the capabilities of each other before the start of the real data communication. On an NFC-enabled Android phone, when the screen of the phone is unlocked, the NFC radio is activated and the discovery process starts automatically and continues until a target device is discovered. During this process, the discovery probes are broadcast at a frequency of about 1.4 Hz. Using NFC antennas, a device can harvest energy from the RF field generated by NFC initiators within close proximity (a few centimeters). However, the amount of energy that can be harvested during the probing is usually very limited, as NFC radios have a low duty-cycle (10%) during the probing phase.

Passive eavesdropping attacks are harmful to wireless communications in several ways. They could not only compromise the privacy/security of the system, but also serve as the early steps of other more damaging attacks [31], e.g., the man-in-the-middle attacks [31]. Another reason that makes passive eavesdropping attacks especially harmful is that they are hard to detect, as they do not actively transmit any signal and are usually launched from distance. NFC is generally considered to be a secure wireless technology against eavesdropping, due to its short communication range. However, current NFC implementations often emit significantly more RF power than intended. Our study shows that, with specially designed NFC sniffers, NFC signals can be eavesdropped from as far as 2.4 m away, which is much further than the intended NFC working distance. This poses a serious concern for security/privacy-sensitive NFC applications such as contactless payment.

3. A MEASUREMENT STUDY

In this section we experimentally study the passive eavesdropping distance of NFC transmissions. Specifically, we measure the physical distance at which the signals from initiators and targets can be successfully decoded, i.e., eavesdropped. Moreover, we study the impact of transmission power attenuation on the passive eavesdropping distance of different NFC devices. The results provide important motivation for the design of nShield.

We note that the actual eavesdropping distance depends on many factors, such as initiator implementation, initiator position, NFC working mode (active or passive), and environmental factors (e.g., background noise). Our measurements are conducted in typical settings, and an exhaustive evaluation of all these factors is beyond the scope of this paper. Nevertheless, our results raise serious concerns about the physical security of NFC due to the significant discrepancies between the actual and intended working distances, and shed lights on possible defense mechanisms.

3.1 Experimental Setup

Our experiment is conducted using NFC initiators, tags, and a sniffer. Commercial off-the-shelf NFC transceivers do not make good sniffers for two reasons. First, they typically have a small antenna size due to the form factor constraints of mobile devices, which greatly limits the receiving sensitivity. Second, the commercial NFC transceivers are specially optimized for working in close distance with the target. We have designed an NFC sniffer for our experiments. Fig. 4 shows the block diagram of the sniffer, which consists of a 30 cm by 23 cm antenna, a pre-amplifier, and an ADC that is connected to a PC via USB to upload the collected samples. The NFC signal overheard by the antenna is amplified and demodulated by the pre-amplifier and the AM demodulator, respectively. The signal is then digitalized by ADC and transmitted to PC for decoding. Our sniffer has a size of a tablet and average power consumption of 120 mW. Therefore, it can be easily connected to a mobile device via the micro USB interface to form a mobile sniffer. The NFC initiator devices used in this study include a Google Nexus 7 tablet, two smartphones (Google Galaxy Nexus and Samsung Galaxy Note 2), and an Adafruit PN532 NFC breakboard [1]. The NXP PN532 NFC chipset is adopted by the NFC breakboard, while all the other devices employ the NXP PN544 NFC chipset. These two chipsets are currently the most popular NFC chipsets used on commercial off-the-shelf mobile devices. Both chipsets use fixed transmission power which cannot be configured by software [11]. We use an NXP Mifare Classic tag as target.

3.2 Results

In the first experiment, we measure the passive eavesdropping distances of both initiator and tag, without attenuating the RF field radiated by the initiator. We place the initiators on a desk, with the antennas of the devices facing forward. We activate one initiator at a time. The Mifare tag is placed in parallel and 1 cm from the antenna of the activated initiator. We place the sniffer near the initiator, and gradually move it away from the initiator.

Fig. 1 shows the signal strength of the initiators that is measured by the sniffer at different distances. As expected, the received signal strength decreases over distance. We can see that the signal is capped when the initiator-sniffer

distance is short, as the output voltage of the sniffer cannot exceed the voltage of its battery. We implemented a Miller decoder in Matlab to decode these samples. We find that the signal can be decoded if its strength is above 100 mV. When the strength is lower, the signal to noise ratio (SNR) is too low for successful decoding. As shown in Fig. 1, the 100 mV signal strength corresponds to physical distances of 152 cm, 131 cm, 116 cm, and 244 cm, respectively, when Nexus 7, Note 2, Galaxy Nexus, and Adafruit NFC breakboard are used as initiators. We are also able to decode the signal transmitted by the tag at maximum distances of 91 cm with Nexus 7, 85 cm with Note 2, 67 cm with Galaxy Nexus, and 121 cm with Adafruit NFC breakboard. Compared to the initiator transmissions, the eavesdropping distance of tag transmissions is significantly shorter, due to the much weaker signal strength of the tag response. We acknowledge that better hardware design and more advanced signal processing techniques could achieve even longer eavesdropping distances. Nevertheless, our results are already sufficient to demonstrate that the current NFC implementations on smartphone and tablet platforms are subject to passive eavesdropping from a distance at least an order of magnitude longer than the intended NFC communication range.

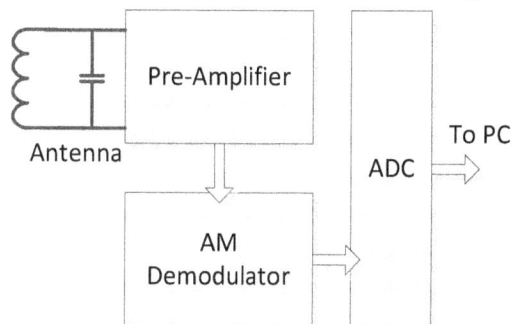

Figure 4: Block diagram of the NFC sniffer used in the measurement study.

A promising approach to defending against passive eavesdropping is to reduce the transmission power of the initiator. However, the current NFC chipsets adopt fixed transmission power, which leaves attenuating the signal externally the only choice. We need to answer the following two questions in order to design an external signal attenuator: 1) what is the maximum attenuation level that could be applied without sacrificing the reliability of data communication, and 2) what is the resulted passive eavesdropping distance. We investigate these questions in the second experiment. We adopt the same experimental setting as in the first experiment, except that we cover the initiators with thin aluminum foils to attenuate the emitted RF field. The thickness and the area of the aluminum foil are adjusted to create different RF field strength, while the maximum passive eavesdropping distances are measured with our sniffer. We use a loop antenna connecting with an Agilent oscilloscope to measure the RF field strength after attenuation.

Fig. 2 shows that, as expected, for all the 4 tested initiators, the passive eavesdropping distances decrease when the attenuation level increases. When the strength of the NFC RF field is just enough to support reliable communication, our sniffer can achieve a maximum passive eavesdropping distance of around 80 cm, which is 67% (NFC Breakboard), 48% (Neuxs 7), 39% (Note 2), and 31% (Galaxy Nexus) shorter than those without attenuation. With such a short

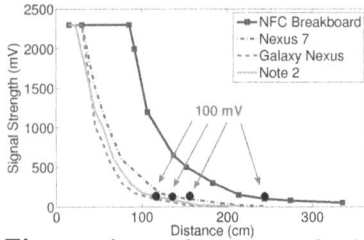

Figure 1: The received signal strength of the unattenuated signal over distance.

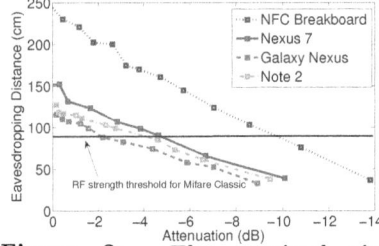

Figure 2: The received signal strength of the attenuated signal over distance.

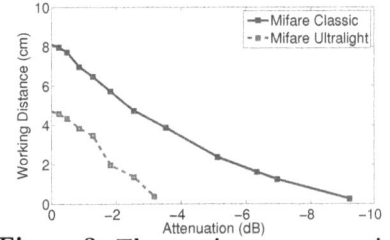

Figure 3: The maximum communication distances of two tags with different attenuation levels.

sniffing distance, the eavesdropping attack becomes significantly more difficult. However, the optimal attenuation level varies significantly for different initiators. Specifically, Fig. 2 shows that, to reduce the signal power to an undecodable level for sniffers, the NFC signal needs to be attenuated by 9.8 dB (NFC Breakboard), 5.9 dB (Neuxs 7), 4.2 dB (Note 2), and 2.2 dB (Galaxy Nexus), respectively. Such significant diversity is caused by the differences in initiator implementations, such as the size of antenna.

We now show that, for a given initiator, the maximum allowed attenuation level also varies significantly across targets. We measure the maximum communication distances between the NFC breakboard and two passive tags, Mifare Classic and Mifare Ultralight, with different attenuation levels applied to the RF field. Fig. 3 shows that the communication distances decrease when the attenuation level increases. However, the Mifare Classic can tolerate a maximum attenuation level of about 9 dB, while Mifare Ultralight can only tolerate about 3 dB. This huge difference is the result of the diverse receiving sensitivities of tags.

3.3 Discussion

We now summarize the results of our experimental study. First, current NFC implementations emit significantly more RF power than intended. As a result, the passive eavesdropping distance is at least an order of magnitude of the intended NFC communication range. This issue greatly increases NFC users' risk of being eavesdropped. Second, the NFC RF field strength can be effectively attenuated externally to enhance the security of NFC without sacrificing the communication reliability. However, the desired attenuation level varies significantly with the specific working conditions, including initiator transmission power, target reception sensitivity, initiator-target distance, and etc. Therefore, simple solutions such as an external signal attenuator with fixed amount of power reduction would not work for all scenarios.

These results have several important implications for the security of NFC systems. Properly implemented cryptosystems can offer strong security assurance even when the communication could be eavesdropped. However, as NFC is usually considered "physically secure", many upper-layer protocols of NFC applications do not implement encryption or only adopt short keys in encryption algorithms (such as DES [3]). With an passive eavesdropping distance up to 244 cm as shown in our study, these systems hence are exposed to malicious attacks. For instance, the leakage of pairing code during NFC-based Bluetooth paring could lead to possible passive eavesdropping or even man-in-the-middle attack on the following data communications. This issue is aggravated in active NFC communication scenarios, where both NFC devices actively transmits using high transmission pow-

er, and eavesdropping attacks on both of the devices could be launched over distance. Moreover, the feasibility of NFC eavesdropping attack renders encryption the last line of defense against attacks. Unfortunately, with the rapid advance of decryption techniques, many once considered "safe" encryption protocols, including WEP [18], DES [3], and RSA [13], have been demonstrated vulnerable when sufficient encrypted data is observed through eavesdropping.

4. OVERVIEW OF nShield

4.1 Design Objectives and Challenges

It is shown in Section 3 that current NFC initiator implementations emit significantly more RF power than intended, which greatly increases the user's risk of being eavesdropped. This result motivates us to develop an NFC security protection device called nShield that dynamically regulates the strength of the RF field radiated by NFC initiators. nShield regulates the RF strength by absorbing the excessive RF power with its own antenna. nShield can be easily stuck on the back of mobile devices, and is solely powered by the absorbed RF energy, thus eliminating offline charging. Specifically, we have the following design objectives.

Adaptive RF field strength regulation. Today's NFC devices exhibit significant diversity in terms of initiator transmission power and the receiver sensitivity. nShield must be able to dynamically adjust the amount of absorbed power to ensure that the remaining RF power is just enough to sustain successful NFC communications. As nShield has no prior knowledge about the receiving sensitivity of the target, a "trial and error" approach is needed to determine whether NFC communications can be sustained at a particular power level. However, trying all possible attenuation levels incurs high delay due to the wide attenuation range and the low frequency of NFC transmissions.

Noninvasive operation. The operation of nShield should not rely on either initiator nor target. In other words, it should work in a standalone manner with no physical connections to neither initiator nor target. This requires nShield to be a self-sustained, self-powered device which has its own CPU and power source. Moreover, it should be transparent to the host, without the need to communicate with the host or modify the NFC protocols. The noninvasive and transparent nature of nShield enables it to easily retrofit the existing NFC devices with security protection. However, a key challenge presented by this design is that, as nShield cannot interact with either initiator or target, it has to determine the right transmission power solely based on the overheard transmissions.

Unintermittent protection. nShield should provide the host devices unintermittent protection against passive eavesdropping. In particular, the down time of protection caused by battery depletion should be minimized. As discussed in Section 2, nShield scavenges energy from the NFC RF field, which is available only when the host device is active (e.g., when the screen of a smartphone is unlocked). When energy harvesting is not possible, nShield has to survive using the energy scavenged previously. Moreover, to keep the small form factor, nShield cannot adopt bulky high capacity batteries. Due to these challenges, nShield must minimize its power consumption as well as maximize the amount of power harvested from the host device. However, wireless charging is inherently inefficient [27], especially for peripherals like nShield that has tight cost budget and form factor constraints.

4.2 System Overview

nShield is composed of two major components, a software-defined passive NFC radio platform and an adaptive RF field attenuation algorithm. The software-defined platform is capable of receiving data from and transmitting data to NFC initiators, attenuating the NFC RF field using its antenna, and harvesting energy from the RF field. The adaptive attenuation algorithm dynamically determines the highest attenuation level that can still ensure communication reliability, according to the overheard NFC traffic. Fig. 5 shows the system architecture of nShield. An on-board MCU runs signal processing tasks such as encoding/decoding. nShield has two tuned loop antennas. The larger antenna is used for harvesting energy from the NFC initiator, as well as transmitting data to the initiator. The smaller antenna is responsible for overhearing data from the initiator. We show in Section 5 that, this dual antenna configuration is essential for maximizing the energy harvesting efficiency without sacrificing the receiving performance, as the receiving antenna and the harvesting antenna require fundamentally different design methods.

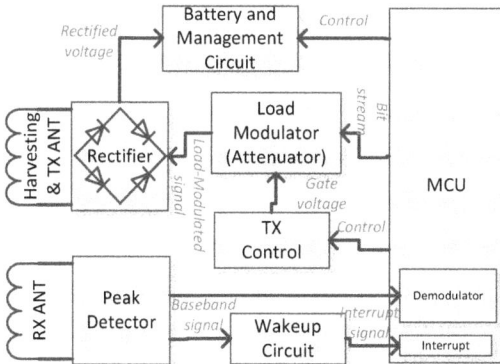

Figure 5: Block Diagram of nShield.

The harvesting antenna is connected with an RF bridge rectifier, which rectifies the RF signal to a DC voltage. The DC voltage is then regulated to provide power to the system and charge a 20 mAh on-board battery. In Section 5 we show that the voltage matching between the harvesting antenna and the battery plays a critical role in maximizing the amount of power harvested by the system. The load modulator is connected with the rectifier, which alters the load of the harvesting antenna to transmit data to the NFC initiator. Since the load modulation-based communication

scheme adopted by NFC standard requires strict timing, nShield employs a hardware TX control circuit to accurately generate the clock used by the load modulation and precisely synchronize the data to be transmitted. The TX control circuit can generate different clock frequencies according to the data rates of the modulation schemes. nShield reduces the risk of eavesdropping by absorbing the excessive RF power radiated by the initiator with an adjustable attenuator, which is multiplexed with the load modulator.

The receiving antenna is connected to a peak detector, which removes the AM carrier from the RF signal. The hardware-based demodulator on the MCU demodulates the baseband signal, from which the raw data is retrieved. A key novelty in the design of nShield is to exploit the hand-shake mechanism in the target discovery process to determine the optimal transmission power of the initiator. Specifically, nShield infers whether the previous messages are successfully received by examining the logical relationship between consecutive initiator messages. To reduce the delay of determining the optimal attenuation level, nShield adopts a binary search algorithm to accelerate the search. nShield falls asleep to conserve energy when no NFC signal is present. A low-power wakeup circuit connected with the peak detector generates an interrupt signal to wake up the system once NFC RF field is present.

Fig. 6 shows a prototype system of nShield. The size of the circuit board and the antenna is 5.5 cm by 5.3 cm and 9.6 cm by 9.6 cm, respectively. We note that this antenna is specially designed for Nexus 7 tablet. The size of antenna can be reduced for smartphones, without sacrificing the energy harvesting efficiency and attenuation performance. The size of the prototype circuit board can be shrunk significantly by removing unnecessary components like debug port, buttons and LEDs. As a result, nShield can be easily fit on diminutive thin-film circuit boards, which could be stuck to the back of small-size mobile devices. The total component cost of our prototype implementation is under $20, and could be further reduced when nShield is mass-manufactured.

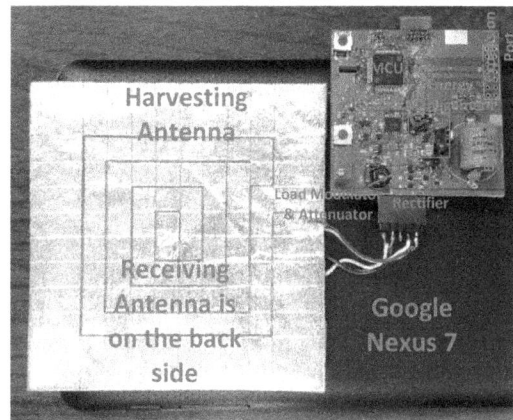

Figure 6: Antenna and circuit of nShield mounted on the back of a Google Nexus 7 tablet.

5. MAXIMIZING HARVESTED ENERGY

nShield is powered solely by the energy harvested from NFC transmissions. The capability of harvesting a large amount of power not only enables the uninterrupted protection of nShield, but also helps increase the attenuation range of the host's NFC transmission power. Fig. 7 shows the block diagram of the energy harvesting subsystem of nShield, which comprises a harvesting antenna and an energy management circuit. These two components work together to determine the amount of power that could be harvested. We show that they must be carefully designed to maximize the harvested power. We define the following two terms to characterize the performance of energy harvesting. *Energy (power) transfer efficiency* is defined as the ratio of the amount of energy (power) transferred to the harvesting antenna, to the amount of energy (power) transmitted by the NFC initiator. *Energy (power) harvesting efficiency* is defined as the ratio of the amount of energy (power) transferred to the receiving system after rectifying and regulation, to the amount of energy (power) transmitted by the NFC initiator. Obviously, for any wireless power transfer system, energy (power) harvesting efficiency is always lower than energy (power) transfer efficiency.

Energy Management Circuit

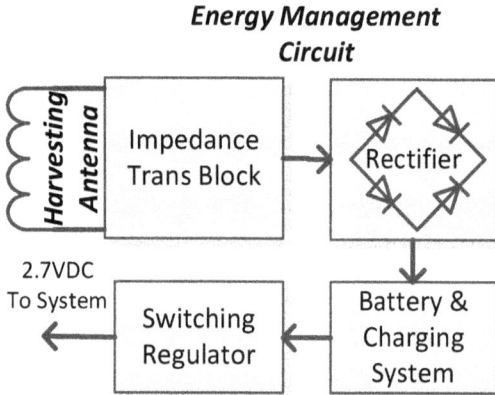

Figure 7: **Block Diagram of energy management circuit on nShield.**

5.1 Harvesting Antenna

When the communication between an NFC initiator and a target device commences, energy transfers from the transmitting antenna to the harvesting antenna via resonant inductive coupling [25] through air. The NFC antennas are essentially inductors, which have inductance as well as series resistance. The radiation efficiency of NFC antennas can be quantified using *quality factor* (or Q-factor), which is the ratio of the inductive reactance to the series resistance of the antenna at 13.56 MHz:

$$Q = \frac{\omega L}{R} = \frac{27.12\pi L}{R} 10^6 \qquad (1)$$

where ω is the working frequency of the antenna, and L and R are the inductance and the series resistance of the antenna, respectively. The Q-factors of the transmitter antenna and the harvesting antenna largely determine the power harvesting efficiency between antennas. Given the Q-factors of transmitter antenna, Q_t, and the harvesting antenna, Q_h, the maximum power transfer efficiency of the NFC antenna pairs can be expressed as [25]:

$$\Pi_{max} = \frac{U^2}{(1 + \sqrt{1 + U^2})^2} \qquad (2)$$

$$U = k\sqrt{Q_t Q_h} \qquad (3)$$

where k is the coupling coefficient, with 0 being completely uncoupled and 1 being perfectly coupled. k depends on many factors such as the distance between the two antennas, antenna alignment, and etc. For NFC, since the communication pairs are always placed in proximity, k is usually

above 0.1 [8]. For each nShield installation, k is largely a constant value, as nShield is fixed on the back of the mobile device. Due to the NFC communication bandwidth requirement (about 1.8 MHz [8]), the Q-factor of the transmitting antennas, Q_t, is about 15 for most NFC devices [17]. As a result, the maximum power transfer efficiency of nShield is largely determined by the Q-factor of the harvesting antenna, Q_h. A high power transfer efficiency can thus be achieved by using harvesting antennas with high Q-factors (above 50). For example, if k, Q_t, and Q_h of an NFC energy harvesting system are 0.2, 15, and 100 respectively, a maximum power transfer efficiency of 77% could be achieved. A key insight of this analysis is that, the harvesting antenna cannot be reused by the NFC transceiver, due to the conflicting requirements of the Q-factors. Therefore, to support efficient energy harvesting and reliable NFC communication at the same time, a dual antenna configuration (one high Q-factor antenna and one low Q-factor antenna) must be adopted.

According to (1), to improve Q-factor of an NFC antenna, we can either increase its inductance or decrease its series resistance. In our harvesting antenna design shown in Fig. 6, we use wide antenna tracks to decrease the series resistance, and closely couple the antenna tracks to increase the inductance. The parasitic capacitance also contributes to the series resistance of the antenna. We adopt a single layer antenna to decease the parasitic capacitance. The resulted high Q-factor ensures that, when the transmitter antenna and the harvesting antenna are closely coupled, the harvesting antenna can receive most of the radiated energy. The implementation details of the harvesting antenna are given in Section 7.

5.2 Energy Management Circuit

Another major factor that affects the amount of power harvested to the system is the design of the energy management circuit. The energy received by the harvesting antenna has to be transferred to the energy storage components in the system, e.g., batteries or super capacitors. A common practice for maximizing power transfer is to match the output impedance of the antenna with the input impedance of the load [24]. The maximum power that can be transferred, P_{load}, can be expressed as:

$$P_{load} = \left(\frac{U_{ant-open}}{R_{ant} + R_{load}}\right)^2 R_{load} = \frac{U_{ant}^2}{4R_{ant}} = 0.25 P_{max} \quad (4)$$

where $U_{ant-open}$ is the open-circuit root-mean-square voltage inducted on the harvesting antenna, R_{ant} and R_{load} are the impedances of the antenna and the load, respectively, and P_{max} is the maximum power that the harvesting antenna can receive. We can see that P_{load} equals a quarter of P_{max}, when and only when $R_{load} = R_{ant}$.

However, the perfect impedance matching is impossible for energy harvesting systems, since the input impedance of the energy management circuit, R_{load}, varies significantly with the system load. To solve this problem, instead of matching impedance, nShield employs *voltage matching*. Since R_{ant} and R_{load} are in series, when $R_{ant} = R_{load}$, the voltage across R_{ant} and R_{load}, denoted as U_{ant} and U_{load}, respectively, are also identical, i.e., $U_{ant} = U_{load} = 0.5U_{ant-open}$. Therefore, an alternative way to achieve the maximum power transfer is to match U_{load} to $0.5U_{ant-open}$. Since $U_{ant-open}$ is a constant value when the harvesting antenna is attached to the initiator, the maximum power transfer can be achieved by letting $U_{load} = 0.5U_{ant-open}$. A key question is how to stabilize U_{load} when system load varies. nShield connects the battery directly to the output of the rectifier, which makes U_{load} stay equal to the voltage of the battery, U_{bat}. Since most batteries have stable output voltage regardless the discharging level and the output current (system load), the optimal energy transfer rate can be always maintained.

However, $0.5U_{ant-open}$ could be difficult to match with U_{bat} in practice, as the harvesting antenna and the energy management circuit are usually separately designed to meet different requirements (e.g., Q-factor, system power consumption, system voltage, etc.). An impedance transformation block, such as L-section circuit or RF transformer [5], can be employed to shift $U_{ant-open}$ to a given voltage. Although an impedance transformation block is not required by our current implementation of nShield, it would be required if nShield employs a Lithium battery (3.6 V). It is also worth noting that, super capacitors are ill-suited for nShield, as their output voltages vary significantly with the discharging levels. To protect the batteries, we use a linear regulator and MOSFET switches to manage the charging. We do not use a switching regulator since it tends to alter the voltage matching point thus reduces the energy harvesting efficiency. Fig. 7 shows the design of energy management circuit of nShield. Our experiment in Section 8.1 shows that nShield can harvest 55 mW power constantly from the NFC initiators on typical smartphones.

5.3 Tag Emulation

As discussed in Section 2, the initiator adopts a low probing rate [21] when no target device is nearby, which only allows limited amount of energy to be harvested. Nevertheless, we show in Section 8.2 that, as long as the host device is active for more than 429 seconds/day, the energy harvested during the probing phase is sufficient for keeping the battery charged. In the rare case when the mobile device is only infrequently unlocked for a long period, nShield may deplete its battery. To address this issue, we adopt a technique called tag emulation to have the initiator significantly increase its duty-cycle. Specifically, nShield emulates itself as a passive ISO14443A tag and responds to the probing messages sent by the initiator. As a result, it triggers the initiator to stay active. This leads to a 10X increase of the initiator output energy, allowing nShield to be rapidly charged. However, this process may interfere with NFC transactions, as the initiator cannot communicate with other target devices when the tag emulation is active. We adopt the following adaptive mechanism to address this issue. First, nShield pauses the tag emulation for 1 second every 2 seconds, allowing the initiator to discover other target devices during the pause. Second, nShield only activates tag emulation when the discharging level of the onboard battery is lower than 30%.

6. ADAPTIVE RF FIELD ATTENUATION

6.1 Attenuator

nShield reduces the risk of being eavesdropped by attenuating the NFC RF field strength using the harvesting antenna. The level of attenuation to the RF field is adjusted by the load of the harvesting antenna. nShield adopts a MOSFET as the variable load, i.e., attenuator to the antenna. The resistance of the MOSFET is controlled by its gate terminal voltage, which is dynamically set by the adaptive RF field attenuation algorithm described in Section 6.2, using an onboard DAC. A novel design of nShield is that the attenuator is multiplexed with the load modulator of the NFC transmitter. This design reduces the cost and size of nShield. Our experiment in Section 8.4 shows that nShield can achieve an attenuation range of 10.86 dB, which is sufficient for the purpose of regulating NFC RF field strength.

6.2 Adaptive RF Field Attenuation Algorithm

nShield adapts the signal attenuation level dynamically to ensure reliable communication between the initiator and the target device. nShield equally divides the whole attenuation range into N discrete levels. The goal of adaptive RF field attenuation is to find the optimal attenuation level in the N levels, with which the attenuated field strength is just enough to support reliable bi-directional communications between the initiator and the target. Fig. 8 illustrates the relationship between Packet Reception Ratio (PRR) and the attenuation levels (AL). nShield tries to use an attenuation level as high as possible, while ensuring the resulted PRR to be close to 1, i.e., high communication reliability. A_{opt} shown on Fig. 8 is the optimal attenuation level.

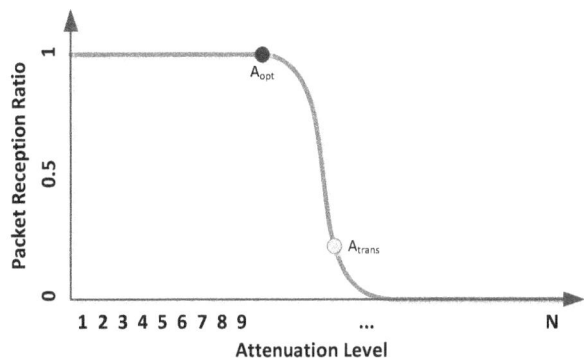

Figure 8: An illustration of the attenuation level vs Packet Reception Ratio relationship.

However, a key challenge in the design of nShield is that, without prior knowledge about the target device, such as reception sensitivity and initiator-target distance, nShield cannot know what RF field strength would support reliable communications. NFC work in a poll-response fashion, in which the target only transmits after it was polled by a message from initiator. We refer to the process of a polling and its subsequent response as a *polling round*. To find out wether an attenuated field strength can support bi-directional communication, the initiator has to attempt a polling round with the attenuation level in question. nShield learns if a polling round is successfully complete, by examining the logic of the polling messages of consecutive polling rounds. In particular, some polling messages, such as the Single Device Detection Request and the Select Request defined in the NFC-A standard, can only be transmitted if the previous polling round succeeds. When overhearing such polling messages, nShield infers that the previous polling round ends successfully.

As shown in Section 8.3, for the passive communication mode, the field strength required for completing the first polling round is lower than that for completing later polling rounds. This phenomenon is caused by insufficient energy left on the tag after the first polling round. Passive tags rely on the energy from the NFC RF field to operate. After activating the RF field, the initiator pauses for certain time to charge the tag before starting the first polling round. The length of this charging period is usually much longer than the interval between consecutive polling rounds. Even if the RF field strength was not sufficient to sustain the successive polling, the first polling round may still succeed due to the energy harvested from the initial charging period. As a result, for passive communication mode, the success of the first polling round after the activation of the RF field is not a good indicator if the field strength is strong enough for sustaining bi-directional communication. In our design, we deem a field strength sufficient only if it can support the first three consecutive polling rounds.

Algorithm 6.1 *Adaptive RF Field Attenuation*

Input: N: number of attenuation levels.
Output: n_{opt}: optimal attenuation level.
Used sub-function: $Comm(n_i)$: attempt communication with attenuation level n_i. This sub-function returns "success" only if the first three polling rounds are completed successfully with the attenuation level n_i

1: $N_{upper} = N$
2: $N_{lower} = 1$
3: $n_{opt} = N/2$
4: **while** $N_{upper} - N_{lower} > 2$ **do**
5:    **if** $Comm(n_{opt}) = success$ **then**
6:       $N_{upper} = round((N_{upper} + n_{opt})/2)$
7:    **else**
8:       $N_{lower} = n_{opt}$
9:    **end if**
10:   $n_{opt} = round((N_{upper} + N_{lower})/2)$
11: **end while**
12: **return** n_{opt}

An interesting question is that, with N different attenuation levels, in what order should nShield attempt communications. A naive solution is to attempt with all N levels from a high-to-low or low-to-high order, until an attenuation level for supporting reliable bidirectional communication is found. However, this approach incurs high delay (at least several seconds). We adopt the Binary Search Algorithm (B-SA) to accelerate the search process. With BSA, the search starts from the middle of all attenuation levels. Depending on whether the following polling rounds are successful or not, BSA discards the lower or higher half of the levels that unlikely contain the optimal level. For example, if any of the three following polling round fails, BSA discards all the levels that are higher than the currently attempted level. BSA repeats this process with the remaining levels until there is only one level left. However, due to the transition region on the PRR-AL curves (see Section 8.3), BSA may fail to locate the optimal attenuation level. This is because whether an attenuation level in the transition region, such as A_{trans} on Fig. 8, can support a successful polling round is probabilistic. When the polling rounds attempted with A_{trans} succeed, all the attenuation levels higher than A_{trans}, including the optimal level A_{opt}, would be discarded. To address this issue, we adopt a modified BSA in nShield. It works in the same way as the original BSA, except that it only discards half of the higher levels after three successful polling rounds. As the transition region of the PRR-AL curve is very narrow (see Section 8.3), this ensures that the optimal level would not be accidentally discarded. Algo-

rithm. 6.1 shows the pseudo-code of the adaptive RF field attenuation algorithm.

nShield exploits the target discovery process, which is always performed by the initiator in the initial phase of the communication, to perform adaptive RF field attenuation. The NFC initiator periodically performs this process by broadcasting NFC discovering probes (at a rate about 3Hz on Android smartphones). If a target NFC device (which can be a tag or another NFC initiator working in active mode) hears this probe, it will send an acknowledgement message back to the initiator. The initiator will then confirm the discovery of the target device by broadcasting a response. The two devices will then exchange a few messages back and forth to learn a few parameters (such as IDs and capabilities). There are several advantages of exploiting this process for adaptive RF field attenuation. First, the NFC target discovery process is mandatory in all NFC communication modes and NFC standards (NFC-A, NFC-B, and NFC-F) [9]. Second, this process does not involve the data payload. The communication conducted during adaptive RF field attenuation might be eavesdropped, due to the possibly high initiator transmission power. However this does not lead to security breach since there is no data payload exchange. Once adaptive RF field attenuation is done, the following data communication is protected from passive eavesdropping. If the adaptive RF field attenuation is not finished yet in the last phase of the target discovery process, nShield will jam the communication to force the initiator to restart the process.

7. IMPLEMENTATION

We implemented a prototype nShield, which is shown in Fig. 6. We use a TI MSP430F2618 as the MCU on nShield. It integrates many low-power components used by nShield, such as comparator, ADC, DAC, and DMA controller. A 4.8 V 20 mAH NiMh battery is adopted to store the harvested energy.

We implement the harvesting antenna using layered tapes and aluminum foil. To maximize the attenuation range, the size of the harvesting antenna should be slightly larger than the antenna on the NFC initiator, so that all magnetic flux generated by the initiator would undergo the attenuation before reaching the target. For example, our prototype antenna attached to Nexus 7 has a dimension of 9.6 cm by 9.6 cm, slightly larger than the NFC antenna in Nexus 7. We build the base of the antenna using 2mm thick layered tapes. We apply the aluminum foil to one side of the base, and cut the foils into 7 mm wide tracks to reduce the series resistance. The tightly coupled tracks increase the inductance of the antenna. The combination of high inductance and low series resistance leads to a high Q-factor (> 100), which is essential for achieving high energy transfer efficiency. The NFC signal reception antenna is prototyped using the same materials and techniques, except that it has much thinner tracks. We use an impedance analyzer to tune the Q-factor of the antenna to the optimal value of 15 [17]. The harvesting and receiving antennas are then glued together. The two prototype antennas can be easily mass-manufactured using flexible thin film circuits.

We implement an NFC transceiver on nShield. The reception path is composed of a peak detector, a comparator, and a software decoder. The RF signal from the antenna is first converted to baseband signal by the peak detector, and then converted to clean logic levels by the comparator. The decoder is implemented in software on the MCU. To decrease the computational overhead, hardware components on the MCU are adopted to assist the decoding. Specifically, a hardware timer is adopted to timestamp the transitions of the logic levels, and a DMA controller is employed to automatically transfer the timestamps to the RAM. This design automatically collects samples without software intervention, enabling low power asynchronous decoding. The data is then verified using CRC and reported to upper layer protocols. For transmission, nShield adopts the load modulation communication techniques [9], in which the load of the antenna is modulated according to the data to be transmitted. We adopt a high speed MOSFET (Fairchild FDV301N) as the load modulator (multiplexed with attenuator), which can be easily driven by the onboard DAC due to its very low gate driving voltage (less than 1 V). The bridge rectifier is implemented by four NXP PMEG600 low forward drop Schottky diodes to minimize the energy loss on rectifying. To generate accurate baud rates and subcarrier frequencies, a 13.56 MHz crystal oscillator and a hardware clock divider are employed. We implemented the ISO14443A (NFC-A) protocol on nShield, which supports a data rate of 106 kbps. Since the modulation/demodulation tasks are mainly handled by hardware, higher data rates can also be easily supported by nShield. Moreover, since many protocols are implemented in software, nShield can be easily customized to meet the requirements of different applications. As a software-defined radio platform, nShield can also be configured to provide malicious content protection functions [21].

nShield employs several techniques to optimize its power consumption. For example, at runtime, unused components are shut down. The clock rate of the MCU is also dynamically adjusted according to the workload. To further reduce power consumption, nShield enters sleep state when no NFC RF field is detected. During sleep, all onboard components except the low-power time keeping timer are shut down.

8. EXPERIMENTATION

In this section, we study the performance of nShield using a set of experiments. We adopt two initiators (Google Nexus 7 tablet and Adafruit PN532 breakboard) and two tags (Mifare Classic and Mifare Ultralight). We choose these devices not only because they are representative NFC devices on the market, but also due to their diverse characteristics. For example, the Adafruit PN532 breakboard has a large antenna and can transmit a large amount of power (about 450 mW), while Google Nexus 7 has a much smaller antenna and much lower transmission power (about 200 mW). The Mifare Classic tag has an antenna size of a credit card which is very common among passive tags, while Mifare Ultralight only has an antenna size of a coin, which is considered to be a "weak" tag. The testing equipments we use include an Agilent DSOX2024 oscilloscope, an Agilent 34410A benchtop multimeter, an Extech handheld multimeter, and an SDR-Kits VNWA3 Vector Network Analyzer.

8.1 Amount of Harvested Power

We measure the amount of power that can be harvested by nShield, and the power transfer and harvesting efficiency with two experiments in this subsection.

In the first experiment, we employ both of the initiators for testing. The harvesting antenna (shown in Fig. 6) is attached to the back of Google Nexus 7, and to the surface of the PCB antenna on PN532 breakboard. We connect a potentiometer to the antenna as the load. The output voltage and current of the antenna under different loads are measured with an Agilent 34410A benchtop multimeter. A linear regression is applied to the results to compute the internal resistances and the open-circuit output voltages of the harvesting antenna. We then compute the power harvested by the system and the power transferred to harvesting antenna under different loads.

Fig. 9 (a) depicts the harvested power under different antenna output voltages. We can see that the curves are parabolas, with the maximum power of 55 mW at 5 V, and 90 mW at 12 V, respectively, when Google Nexus 7 and P-N532 breakboard are used. The amount of power that can be harvested from PN532 breakboard nearly doubles that from Google Nexus 7. This is because PN532 breakboard has a much higher transmission power than Nexus 7, according to our measurement. However, as the antenna is optimized for working with Nexus 7, nShield cannot harvest the maximum amount of power from PN532 breakboard. In particular, the maximum power is harvested at 12 V output and the battery voltage on nShield is only 4.8 V. This voltage mismatch limits the maximum harvested power to be only 57 mW. An impedance matching block is required to shift the open-circuit voltage to around 10 V for PN532 breakboard, as discussed in Section 5.2. On the other hand, nShield can receive the maximum power when working with Nexus 7, due to the tight voltage matching. These results also confirm that a super capacitor is a poor choice for energy storage on nShield, since the voltage of super capacitors varies significantly with its discharging level, resulting a poor voltage matching.

Fig. 9 (b) shows the power transferred to the harvesting antenna at different output voltages. We can see that the transferred power decreases linearly when the output voltage increases. When the output voltage of the harvesting antenna is zero, the antenna receives the maximum power. However, it also delivers virtually no power to the system, resulting in an extremely low power harvesting efficiency, as observed from both Fig. 9 (a) and (b). When the output voltage is about half of the antenna open-circuit voltage, the maximum power is harvested, although the power transferred to the antenna is significantly lower. These results show that, in order to deliver the maximum power to the system, the battery and the harvesting antenna must achieve a voltage matching.

We next evaluate the power harvesting and transfer efficiencies of nShield. We only use Adafruit PN532 breakboard as initiator in this experiment because the transmission power of Nexus 7 cannot be accurately measured due to its packaging. The transmission power of the PN532 board can be obtained by measuring the current draw on the TVDD pin of PN532 chip, which supplies power to its internal coil exciting circuits. The harvesting antenna is connected with a potentiometer which serves as a variable load.

Fig. 10 (a) shows the amount of power transmitted, transferred, and harvested, under different loads to the harvesting antenna. We can see that the transmission power increases when the load becomes lighter. The change of the transmission power is due to the detuning effect, in which the tuning of the initiator's antenna is varied by the mutual coupling between the harvesting antenna and the initiator antenna.

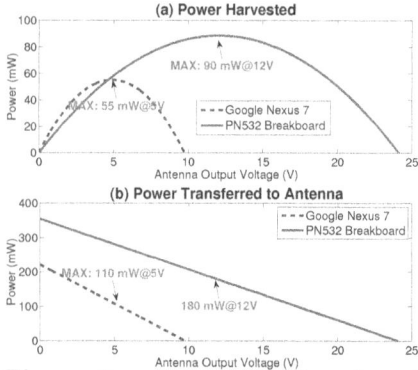

Figure 9: Power transferred and harvested from Nexus 7 and PN532 breakboard.

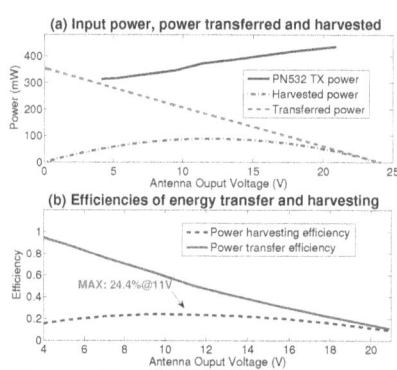

Figure 10: Power harvesting efficiency and power transfer efficiency.

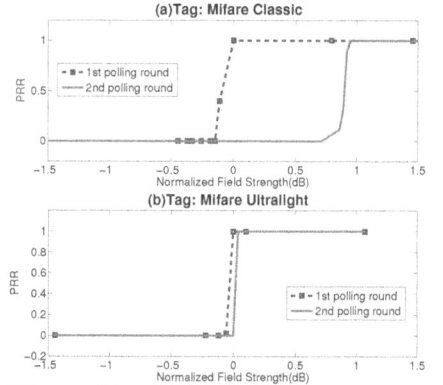

Figure 11: PRR-FS curves of two NFC tags

A heavier (lighter) load to the harvesting antenna creates a slightly stronger (weaker) mutual coupling, which in turn leads to a stronger (weaker) detuning effect. The detuning effect changes the impedance of the antenna, resulting in less power transferred. The highest transmission power is about 440 mW.

Fig. 10 (b) shows the computed energy transfer and harvesting efficiencies. We can observe that the energy transfer efficiency increases linearly with the load to the harvesting antenna, while the energy harvesting efficiency is a parabola curve which peaks at the voltage matching point (11 V). When the output voltage of the harvesting antenna is below 4 V, the energy transfer efficiency is close to 1. At this point, most of the transmitted energy is absorbed by the harvesting antenna, and the strength of the RF field created by the initiator is significantly attenuated. The energy harvesting efficiency peaks at 24.4% when the output voltage of the harvesting antenna is 11 V. We discuss the energy harvesting efficiency in Section 10.

8.2 System Power Consumption and Lifetime

We use an Agilent 34410A benchtop multimeter to measure the power consumption of nShield. The results are summarized in Tab. 1. The most power consuming states are data reception and transmission. This is because the MCU has to work at a higher system clock rate to meet the strict timing requirements of the NFC data reception and transmission, and several system components (e.g., TX control circuit) need to be powered on. Although the idle/RX/TX power consumption are high, their impact on system lifetime is actually insignificant, since nShield spends most of the time in the sleep state with a power consumption of only 23 uW. This is due to the fact that, the NFC initiator is usually inactive most of the time (e.g., when the mobile device is locked), during which nShield is asleep.

Thanks to the large amount of power harvested from NFC transmissions and low power design, nShield can sustain its operation solely on the harvested energy. NFC standard requires initiators to insert long guard time between consecutive polling rounds [9]. As a result, NFC initiators are in idle listening most of the time when activated. This causes nShield to be idle during most of its active period, leading to an average active power consumption of 8.7 mW. As nShield can harvest 55 mW power from an active NFC initiator, it maintains a net power gain of 46.3 mW during its active state. For typical Android devices, the integrated NFC ini-

Sleep	Idle listening	RX	TX	Attenuation
23 uW	8.7 mW	13.1 mW	18.1 mw	9.8 mW

Table 1: System power consumption under different states.

tiators are duty-cycled at 10% [21] during probing. With its low sleep power consumption, the battery on nShield can stay fully charged if the mobile device is unlocked for average 429 seconds per day, which can be met by smartphones and tablets in most circumstances [20][2]. When the discharging level of the onboard battery is low, nShield automatically activates tag emulation, which increases the charging rate by 10X to rapidly charge the battery. Moreover, even when energy harvesting is not possible (e.g., NFC is disabled), the lifetime of a fully charged nShield still exceeds one month, thanks to its low sleep power consumption.

The above results show that nShield's capability of harvesting high amount of power plays a significant role in achieving the perpetual operation. As nShield can be only charged when the screen of the device is unlocked, the minimum harvested power for sustaining nShield depends on how the users interact with mobile devices. A recent survey [28] shows that on average U.S. users spend 58 minutes on smartphones per day, which is more than enough for nShield to stay fully charged. However, for light smartphone users, the harvesting power should be sufficiently high. Compared to EnGarde whose harvested power is only about 30 mW[1], nShield decreases the minimum active time of the phone by more than 50% (7.15 min vs 15.5 min).

8.3 Receiver Characteristics

In this subsection, we study the receiving characteristics of passive NFC tags, by measuring the PRR-FS (Packet Reception Ratio vs Field Strength) curves. The purpose of this experiment is to show two key observations based on which the adaptive RF field attenuation algorithm is designed: 1), the transition regions on the PRR-FS curves are very narrow, and 2), the field strength required for completing the first polling round is higher than the subsequent rounds.

We attach a thin aluminum antenna to the back of each tag to measure the field strength, using an Agilent DSOX2024A

---

[1]The exact amount of harvested power is not given in [21]. However, it is expected to be much lower than 30 mW, due to the load-source mismatch and the loss on rectifying and regulating components.

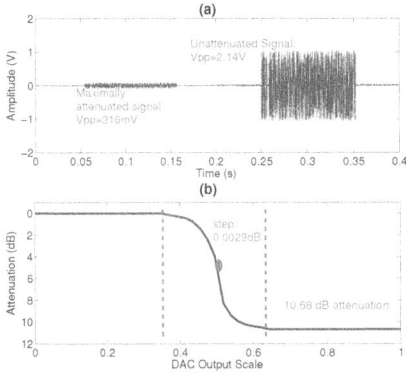

Figure 12: nShield achieves an attenuation range of about 10dB.

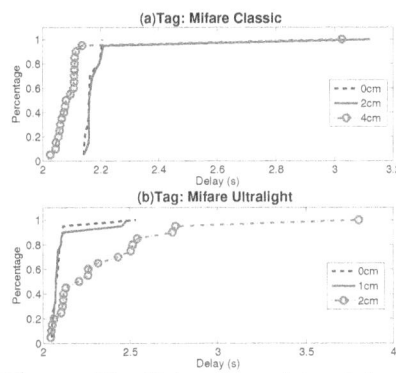

Figure 13: Delay caused by determining attenuation level.

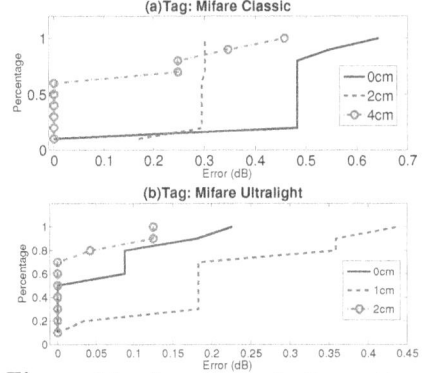

Figure 14: Accuracy of attenuation level determined by nShield.

oscilloscope. A Nexus 7 serves as the NFC initiator in this experiment. We vary the field strength near the tag by changing the distance between the initiator and the tag. The PRR associated with each field strength value is computed from 100 transmissions. The field strength measurements are normalized.

Fig. 11 (a) and (b) show the PRR-FS curves of Mifare Classic tag and Mifare Ultrlight tag, respectively. We can see that, all the curves have narrow transition regions (<0.2 dB) in which the PRR values quickly increase from 0 to 1. We further observe that, Mifare Ultralight tag has a narrower transition region than the Mifare Classic tag (0.05 dB vs 0.2 dB). This is because the Mifare Ultralight tag has a much smaller antenna size, making it more sensitive to the field strength. For each tag, we can see that the field strength required for a successful first polling round is lower than that for the second polling round. As mentioned in Section 6.2, this is due to the fact that the tag has more time to harvest energy before the first round of polling.

8.4 Attenuation Range and Granularity

nShield provides a wide attenuation range and fine attenuation granularity, which allows it to precisely control the strength of the NFC RF field to the optimal level. This subsection evaluates the attenuation range and step that can be achieved by nShield. We manually tune the DAC connected with the attenuator to sweep through its entire voltage output range with a step of 0.05 V. To measure the attenuated signal strength, we use an Agilent probe to form a small loop antenna, and connect the probe to an Agilent DSOX2024A oscilloscope. We record the measured peak-to-peak amplitude (Vpp) of the NFC signal.

Fig. 12 (a) depicts the signals that are maximally attenuated and unattenuated. We can see that nShield can significantly decrease the strength of NFC signals, as the Vpp of the signal decreases from 2.14 V to only 0.216 V after the maximum attenuation level is applied. Fig. 12 (b) shows the computed attenuation levels with different DAC output. We can observe that the effective attenuation region roughly takes about a quarter of the full output scale of the DAC, ranging from 0.8 V to 1.4 V. This is due to the characteristic of the attenuator on nShield, which is a high-speed switching MOSFET. The MOSFET is completely shut down when the gate voltage is below 0.8 V, and is saturated when the gate voltage is above 1.4 V. Therefore, it operates as a variable attenuator only when the gate volt-

age is between 0.8 V and 1.4 V. The maximum attenuation, 10.86 dB, is achieved when the MOSFET is saturated. We can also observe that the attenuation is nonlinear with the DAC output, resulting in a nonconstant attenuation steps. The maximum step occurs when the MOSFET operates near the middle of the effective attenuation region. For a 16 bit DAC with 2.3 V reference, the maximum step is 0.0029 dB. The wide attenuation range and fine attenuation step allows nShield to precisely attenuate the RF field with wide strength range to the optimal level. This ensures nShield to best protect the security of NFC while maintaining reliable communication.

8.5 Delay of Adaptive Attenuation

The delay caused by the adaptive attenuation algorithm is a critical performance metric for nShield, since a long delay would have significant impact on the user's experience. In this section, we measure the delay introduced by the adaptive attenuation algorithm, using a Mifare Classic tag and a Mifare Ultralight tag. We define the delay as the interval from the time instant when the initiator sends the first probe to the tag to the time instant when the optimal attenuation level is determined. We use the hardware timer on nShield to timestamp these events and measure the delay. For each tag, we measure the delay associated with 3 different optimal attenuation levels, by varying the tag-initiator distances. To illustrate the delay in practical settings, we hold the tags with hands, which introduces small tag-initiator distance variations during communications. We repeat the experiment at each distance for 20 times.

Fig. 13 shows that, most of the delays fall below 2.2 s, while the mean delay is 2.1 s. An interesting phenomenon is that the delay of Mifare Classic incurred at a distance of 4 cm is smaller than those incurred at 2 cm and 0 cm. This is because, the delay is largely proportional to the number of steps that the adaptive attenuation algorithm has to take to find the optimal attenuation level, which varies between 6 and 12 in nShield. Thus a longer communication distance could possibly incur a shorter delay. We also notice that the adaptive attenuation algorithm is resilient to minor tag-initiator distance variation, as nShield can almost always find the optimal attenuation level within 2.2 seconds. We did observe some long delays (3s to 4s), although they are rare (< 5%). Our further investigation indicates that they are caused by occasional initiator halts, in which the initiator pauses its transmission for 1 to 2 seconds, while the RF field remaining active. Finding the exact reason of this long initiator halt is left for future work.

8.6 Accuracy and Effectiveness of Adaptive Attenuation

We evaluate the accuracy of adaptive attenuation algorithm in estimating the optimal attenuation level in this subsection. The initiator we use in this experiment is the PN532 breakboard. For each tag under test, we evaluate the optimal attenuation level with different tag-initiator distances. We define the optimal attenuation level as the highest attenuation setting that can support successful initiator-tag communications for 10 seconds. We manually determine the ground-truth optimal attenuation level for each tag-initiator distance, by examining all attenuation levels from a high to low order. We use an Agilent probe to form a small loop antenna, and connect the probe to an Agilent DSOX2024A oscilloscope to measure the attenuated RF field strength. We then run the adaptive attenuation algorithm for ten times, and measure the resulted RF field strength of each run.

Fig. 14 shows that, 90% of the estimation errors of the Mifare Classic tag at distances of 0 cm, 2 cm and 4 cm fall below 0.3 dB, 0.34 dB and 0.52 dB, respectively. For the Mifare Ultralight tag at distances of 0 cm, 1 cm and 2 cm, 90% the errors fall below 0.12 dB, 0.16 dB and 0.35 dB, respectively. The mean errors of the two tags are only 0.29 dB and 0.1 dB, respectively. We can observe that Mifare Ultralight tag generally incurs smaller error than Mifare Classic tag. This may be because the Mifare Ultralight tag has a much smaller antenna size, which makes it more sensitive to the field strength. As a result, it has a narrower transition region, which conforms the finding in Section 8.3. This makes Mifare Ultralight tag more responsive to our adaptive attenuation algorithm, resulting in a smaller estimation error.

Next we evaluate the eavesdropping distances achieved with our sniffer at different initiator-tag distances. We record the eavesdropping distances at which the received signal strength of the initiator falls below 100 mV by following the same procedure of the measurement study in Section 3. The results are summarized in Table 2. It can be seen that, for each tag, the eavesdropping distance decreases with the initiator-tag distance. This is because a longer initiator-tag distance requires a stronger signal strength to ensure reliable communication, which increases the eavesdropping distance. We also notice that the Mifare Ultralight tag always incurs longer eavesdropping distances than Mifare Classic tag. This is because the low-sensitivity receiver of the Mifare Ultralight tag requires higher transmission power to maintain reliable communication. The shortest eavesdropping distances for the two tags are 48 cm and 70 cm, respectively. It is worth noting that, even after significant reduction, the resulted eavesdropping distance may still be further than the expected NFC working distance. This is largely due to the fundamental design trade-off of NFC. nShield could apply higher attenuation to decrease the eavesdropping distance to only a few centimeters, but this would significantly reduce the reliability of the NFC communication.

	Initiator-tag Distance			
	0 cm	1 cm	2 cm	4 cm
Classic	48 cm	75 cm	110 cm	140 cm
Ultralight	70 cm	92 cm	122 cm	151 cm

Table 2: Eavesdropping distances after attenuation.

9. RELATED WORK

Near Field Communication (NFC) is a new short-range wireless communication standard evolved from HF RFID technology. Several studies have been conducted on the distance of eavesdropping RFID proximity cards. In [22], the authors measure the passive eavesdropping distance of the communication between a commercial reader and a Philips Mifare card using a wide band sniffer. The results show that the possible eavesdropping distance is more than 4 m [22]. In [23], the authors analyze the security of NFC and estimate the passive eavesdropping distance of NFC to be about 10m. However, this result is not experimentally validated. In [26], the maximum passive eavesdropping distance of NFC is empirically measured to be 30 cm using Mifare tags and an oscilloscope. However, the antennas of Mifare tags used in their experiments are not optimized for eavesdropping. To our best knowledge, our work is the first empirical study on the practical passive NFC eavesdropping distance under realistic experimental settings. We have designed and implemented a prototype NFC sniffer. Its small form factor and high sensitivity demonstrated the feasibility of launching passive eavesdropping attack from distance. In particular, we are able to achieve a 2.4 m eavesdropping distance with our portable NFC sniffer (see Section 3).

Several approaches have been proposed to protect NFC from malicious attacks. A common solution is to modify the OS of mobile devices [23] to enhance the security of NFC. However, the mobile device would become vulnerable if the integrity of the OS is compromised (e.g., by rooting the device)[21]. To address this issue, several systems adopt additional hardware security devices. RFID guardian [30] provides protection by actively jamming suspicious NFC transactions. However, active jamming consumes considerable power and requires bulky hardware (e.g., RF amplifier and large battery), which significantly limits RFID guardian's applications. Proxmark III [12] is a widely used RFID/NFC software defined radio that is capable of detecting an attack, and generating jam signals. However, it must be plugged in as its FPGA-based design consumes significant power (about several hundred milliwatts). Furthermore, none of these approaches can provide anti-eavesdropping protection.

NFC is ideal for energy harvesting, due to the condensed RF field strength generated by its high transmission power and short communication range. Energy harvesting enables a mobile device to replenish its energy in the presence of NFC RF field. The NFC Discover kit [14] from ST include a sensor board can be wirelessly powered by nearby NFC initiators. NFC-WISP [19][10] is a software defined passive tag platform, which is capable of harvesting energy from NFC transmissions and conducting simple sensing and computational tasks. A key difference between the energy harvesting component of nShield and the above two systems is the amount of power harvested. With extensive optimizations to harvesting antenna and energy management circuit, nShield can harvest a power of about 55 mW, compared to mere 10.2 mW and 17.7 mW of NFC Discover kit and NFC-WISP, respectively. The significant improvement

		nShield	EnGarde
NFC radio	Radio type	Software-define radio	Dedicated ASIC NFC radio
	TX capability	Supports NFC-A (implemented), NFC-B, NFC-F HW accelerated SW encoding	Jamming only No TX support
	RX capability	Supports NFC-A (implemented), NFC-B, NFC-F HW accelerated SW decoding	NFC-A, NFC-B, and NFC-F HW decoding
Energy harvesting	Ant. configuration	Dual antenna	Dual antenna
	Optimization	High Q antenna Voltage matching	N/A
	Harvestable power	55 mW constant	maximum 30 mW transferred to antenna
	Max initiator duty-cycle	100% (tag-emulation)	66% (subcarrier)
System pwr consumption	Active	8.7 mW	32.7 mW
	Sleep	23 uW	38.8 uW

Table 3: Comparison of hardware of nShield and EnGarde.

on the energy harvesting efficiency enables nShield to power additional components and perform sophisticated operations to ensure system security.

To date the most relevant work to ours is EnGarde [21]. EnGarde is a hardware NFC security device that jams on-going malicious NFC transactions. Different from RFID guardian and Proxmark III, EnGarde is optimized for mobile devices and harvests energy from NFC transmissions. However, EnGarde protects NFC by censoring the content of NFC transactions, and hence cannot defend against eavesdropping attacks. We provide a comparison between the hardware of the two systems, which is summarized in Table 3.

nShield is built based on a software-define radio (SDR), which is capable of transmitting to and receiving from NFC initiators. The SDR can be programmed to support standard and custom protocols. However, as SDR relies on software radio stack to decode and encode messages, it tends to incur longer delays. In the case of nShield, hardware components (demodulator, modulator, etc.) are utilized to accelerate the encoding/decoding, which significantly reduces the delay. EnGarde, on the other hand, employs a hardware-based NFC transceiver (TI TRF7970A) that incurs shorter delay than SDR-based transceiver. However, EnGarde only employs the receiving chain of the hardware transceiver, due to its dual antenna configuration. Although EnGarde implements a simple transmitter that can generate jamming signals, it does not support data transmissions. The capability of transmission is critical for tag emulation, which increases the amount of energy harvested from initiator significantly. Another disadvantage of this configuration is the resulted high power consumption, since the hardware transceiver employed by EnGarde is mainly designed for power-hungry NFC initiators. Moreover, the hardware-based transceiver does not support the development of new physical and link-level protocols.

The energy harvesting system of nShield also differs significantly from that of EnGarde. Although a dual antenna configuration is employed by both systems, it is used to meet fundamentally different requirements. Specifically, EnGarde employs the dual antenna configuration for tag proximity detection, while nShield adopts it for improving power harvesting efficiency. The harvesting antenna of nShield is specially designed to achieve high Q-factor. nShield also employs a technique called voltage matching, which carefully matches the output voltage of the antenna to that of the battery to maximize the amount of power harvested. On the another

hand, EnGardes does not perform any load-source matching, which significantly limits the power harvesting efficiency. Moreover, EnGarde does not support tag emulation due to the lack of transmission capability, and can only trigger the initiator to raise its duty-cycle to 66% by using jamming. This further lowers the amount of energy harvested. Lastly, the active power consumption of EnGarde is much higher than nShield (32.7 mW vs 8.7 mW), due to the use of hardware-based transceiver.

10. DISCUSSION

Although NFC does not support single-initiator-multiple-target communication, the presence of multiple target devices may lead to collisions in the discovery process. NFC standards require the initiator to resolve collisions observed in discovery process using anti-collision techniques similar to RFID standards, and interact with resolved targets one by one after the discovery process. nShield currently does not consider the multiple tag case. However, nShield can learn if a collision has occurred by overhearing the traffic from the initiator, and act accordingly. However, this extension is left for future work.

nShield significantly improves the amount of harvested energy over existing NFC-based energy harvesting systems [21][14][19][10]. However, compared to specialized wireless power transfer systems [28] that often achieve power harvesting efficiencies of at least 70%, nShield's efficiency is much lower (24.4%). This is mainly because the current NFC initiator is not optimized for high efficiency wireless power transfer. The antenna on NFC transmitter has low Q-factor, which significantly limits the power transfer efficiency. Moreover, achieving high efficiency also requires that the transmitter and receiver must be precisely tuned to the same resonant frequency, which varies with the transmitter-receiver distance. High efficiency inductive power transfer systems adopt several techniques including resonant frequency auto-tuning and antenna impedance auto-tuning to deal with the detuning effects. Unfortunately, these mechanisms are not implemented on NFC initiators.

We acknowledge that a complete redesign of the NFC initiator would be a more effective way to improve physical security. However, such a "clean-slate" approach may prove challenging in practice due to the need of involving many players (from IC to device manufacturers). Moreover, this would leave the legacy devices already shipped exposed to malicious attacks. The next-generation NFC chipsets may have native transmission control capabilities, which allow mobile devices to configure their NFC transmission power from software. This eliminates the need of accessory security hardware like nShield. In such a case, the adaptive attenuation algorithm of nShield can be integrated by the NFC driver to attenuate the transmission power.

Thanks to the high energy harvesting efficiency, the nShield platform is capable of powering additional hardware components like sensors. Moreover, it can be used as a software-defined radio platform for studying NFC protocols.

11. CONCLUSION

This paper presents a novel, noninvasive security system called nShield to protect NFC against passive eavesdropping. nShield dynamically attenuates the signal strength of NFC transmissions by absorbing the excessive RF energy. nShield intelligently determines the amount of absorbed energy, so that the attenuated signal strength is just enough to sustain successful NFC communications. As a result, in order to launch an attack, the eavesdroppers must be in close proximity of the mobile device, making possible security breach significantly more challenging. We have implemented a prototype of nShield, and evaluated its performance via extensive experiments. We show that nShield can harvest up to 55 mW power, which outperforms two state-of-the-art NFC energy harvesting systems by 1.7X and 3.1X, respectively. Moreover, nShield can accurately attenuate the NFC signal strength in fine granularity, which allows it to provide security protection for a diverse set of NFC platforms. Lastly, nShield only introduces insignificant delay (up to 2.2 s) to NFC data communications.

12. REFERENCES

[1] Adafruit PN532 breakboard. http://www.adafruit.com/products/364.
[2] Americans spend 58 mins a day on smartphones. http://www.experian.com/blogs/marketing-forward/2013/05/28/americans-spend-58-minutes-a-day-on-their-smartphones/.
[3] DES wikipedia site. http://en.wikipedia.org/wiki/Data_Encryption_Standard.
[4] How soon is now: NFC smartphones and physical access control systems. http://blogs.gartner.com/mark-diodati/2011/10/31/how-soon-is-now-nfc-smartphones-and-physical-access-control-systems/.
[5] Impedance matching wikipedia site.
[6] Mobile payments today. http://www.mobilepaymentstoday.com/research/400/Contactless-NFC.
[7] Near field communication (NFC) 2014-2024. http://www.prnewswire.com/news-releases/near-field-communication-nfc-2014-2024-227654461.html.
[8] Near field communication wikipedia. http://en.wikipedia.org/wiki/Near_field_communication.
[9] NFC forum technical specifications. http://www.nfc-forum.org/specs/spec_list/.
[10] NFC-WISP project site. http://www.alansonsample.com/research/NFC-WISP.html.
[11] NXP: PN532 user manual. http://www.nxp.com/documents/user_manual/141520.pdf.
[12] Proxmark 3 project site. http://www.proxmark.org/.
[13] RSA wikipedia site. http://en.wikipedia.org/wiki/RSA_%28cryptosystem%29.
[14] ST discovery kit. http://www.st.com/web/en/catalog/tools/FM116/SC1444/PF253360.
[15] Still not a wallet, NFC has a second life as a safe, simple pairing tool. http://gigaom.com/2013/08/08/still-not-a-wallet-nfc-has-a-second-life-as-a-safe-simple-pairing-tool/.
[16] Strasbourg NFC ticketing moves to commercial launch. http://www.nfcworld.com/2013/07/05/324901/strasbourg-nfc-ticketing-moves-to-commercial-launch/.
[17] Ti:HF antenna design notes. http://www.ti.com/rfid/docs/manuals/appNotes/HFAntennaDesignNotes.pdf.
[18] WEP wikipedia site. http://en.wikipedia.org/wiki/Wired_Equivalent_Privacy.
[19] A. Dementyev, J. Gummeson, D. Thrasher, A. Parks, D. Ganesan, J. R. Smith, and A. P. Sample. Wirelessly powered bistable display tags. In *UbiComp 2013*.
[20] H. Falaki, R. Mahajan, S. Kandula, D. Lymberopoulos, R. Govindan, and D. Estrin. Diversity in smartphone usage. In *Mobisys 2010*.
[21] J. J. Gummeson, B. Priyantha, D. Ganesan, D. Thrasher, and P. Zhang. Engarde: protecting the mobile phone from malicious nfc interactions. In *MobiSys 2013*.
[22] G. Hancke. Practical attacks on proximity identification systems. In *Security and Privacy, 2006 IEEE Symposium on*, pages 6 pp.–333, 2006.
[23] E. Haselsteiner and K. Breitfu? Security in near field communication (nfc). In *Printed handout of Workshop on RFID Security, July 2006*.
[24] J. J. Karakash. *Transmission lines and filter networks*. Macmillan New York, 1950.
[25] M. Kesler. Highly resonant wireless power transfer: Safe, efficient, and over distance. 2013.
[26] H. S. Kortvedt and S. F. Mj?lsnes. Eavesdropping near field communication. In *The Norwegian Information Security Conference (NISK) 2009*.
[27] A. Kurs, A. Karalis, R. Moffatt, J. D. Joannopoulos, P. Fisher, and M. Soljačić. Wireless power transfer via strongly coupled magnetic resonances. *science*, 317(5834):83–86, 2007.
[28] Z. N. Low, R. Chinga, R. Tseng, and J. Lin. Design and test of a high-power high-efficiency loosely coupled planar wireless power transfer system. *Industrial Electronics, IEEE Transactions on*, 56(5):1801–1812, 2009.
[29] C. Miller. Exploring the nfc attack surface. *Proceedings of Blackhat*, 2012.
[30] M. R. Rieback, G. N. Gaydadjiev, B. Crispo, R. F. H. Hofman, and A. S. Tanenbaum. A platform for rfid security and privacy administration. In *LISA 2006*.
[31] D. Welch and S. Lathrop. Wireless security threat taxonomy. In *Information Assurance Workshop, 2003. IEEE Systems, Man and Cybernetics Society*, pages 76–83, 2003.

Sensor-Assisted Facial Recognition: An Enhanced Biometric Authentication System for Smartphones

Shaxun Chen
Department of Computer Science,
University of California Davis, CA,
95616 USA
Phone: 001-530-574-5866
sxch@ucdavis.edu

Amit Pande
Department of Computer Science,
University of California Davis, CA,
95616 USA
Phone: 001-530-752-0870
pande@ucdavis.edu

Prasant Mohapatra
Department of Computer Science,
University of California Davis, CA,
95616 USA
Phone: 001-530-754-8016
prasant@cs.ucdavis.edu

ABSTRACT

Facial recognition is a popular biometric authentication technique, but it is rarely used in practice for device unlock or website / app login in smartphones, although most of them are equipped with a front-facing camera. Security issues (e.g. 2D media attack and virtual camera attack) and ease of use are two important factors that impede the prevalence of facial authentication in mobile devices. In this paper, we propose a new sensor-assisted facial authentication method to overcome these limitations. Our system uses motion and light sensors to defend against 2D media attacks and virtual camera attacks without the penalty of authentication speed. We conduct experiments to validate our method. Results show 95-97% detection rate and 2-3% false alarm rate over 450 trials in real-settings, indicating high security obtained by the scheme ten times faster than existing 3D facial authentications (3 seconds compared to 30 seconds).

Categories and Subject Descriptors

K.6.5 Computing Mileux: Security and Protection - *Authentication*

H.5.2 Information Interfaces and Presentation: *Input devices and strategies*

General Terms

Algorithms, Security, Verification.

Keywords

Biometric; mobile devices; user authentication; smartphone sensors

I. INTRODUCTION

Biometric authentication has many advantages over the traditional credential-based authentication mechanism.

MobiSys'14, June 16 – 19, 2014, Bretton Woods, NH, USA.
Copyright © 2014 ACM 978-1-4503-2793-0/14/06…$15.00
http://dx.doi.org/10.1145/2594368.2594373

It is widely considered to be more secure, because it is based on "who the user is" and biometric information is difficult to forge or spoof. On the contrary, credential-based authentication relies on "what the user knows", which can be lost or stolen and more likely to result in identity theft. If dictionary words are used as password, the risk becomes even higher. In addition, biometric authentication is much easier to use. Users do not need to remember a list of passwords for various websites and apps. Of course, devices or browsers can remember the username and password for users. While eliminating users' memory burden, it introduces additional security threats. For example, when users leave their smartphones or tablets on the desk and leave the office for a while, others can easily get access to their social networks or even bank accounts if the password is memorized. Mobile industry also has paid more and more attention to biometric authentications. For example, Apple launched its latest iPhone with fingerprint readers.

Among various biometric authentication methods, facial recognition is a popular technique that has been continuously improving for the past decade. The recognition accuracy is high for practical use [1] [2]. It is recently reported that facial recognition has already been used for commercial payment systems which requires very high accuracy [16]. On the other hand, most of today's smartphones and tablets are equipped with a front facing camera, and the resolution is now typically higher than one mega pixels, which is very handy and able to capture users' face in high quality. Based on these facts, it seems that facial recognition can be widely used for device unlock and website / app login in smartphones.

However, in practice, facial authentication is rarely used in smartphones even if the device has a front facing camera. Android provides face recognition function (to unlock the device) starting from the version 4.0, but not many users are using it. For the login of social networks, forums, online services and other apps, credential-based authentication is still dominating other methods. Since biometric authentication has great advantages, what is the cause of the current status? Apart from the privacy concerns, the following two factors are very important, which impede the prevalence of facial authentication in mobile devices.

First, there is a trade-off between security and ease of use. The simple 2D face recognition, such as the one used in Android 4.0, can be easily fooled by a photograph of the user (referred to as *photo attack*), which is not difficult to obtain in social networks. An improved version requires the user to blink their eyes during the authentication (e.g. Android 4.1 and [3]), but it still can be circumvented by photo editing [4] or playing a clip of video (referred to as *video attack*) [5]. Apparently, these schemes are not secure enough for serious authentication service. More sophisticated 3D facial authentication techniques have been developed to achieve higher security [6] [7]. A practical example is Toshiba Face Recognition Utility used in recent Toshiba laptops. It requires that users turn their heads towards four directions according to a sequence of arrows shown on the screen. In this way, the authentication program is able to differentiate a real 3D face from a flat photo. However, the whole authentication process takes approximately 30 seconds, which is too long and compromises the ease of use (one of the important advantages of biometric authentication). Since it is more complex than entering a password, why would users choose it? In short, current facial authentication schemes cannot achieve *2D-media-attack*-safety and the ease of use simultaneously (*photo attack* and *video attack* together are referred to *2D-media attack*).

Second, the availability of *virtual cameras*. Virtual camera is a category of software which adds a layer between the real physical camera and the operating system. Virtual Webcam, ManyCam, Magic Camera, etc. are all examples of such software. Currently most of them are developed for PC or tablet platforms, but it is easy to migrate to smartphones. The purpose of these software is to add dynamic effects to the webcam, making the video look more beautiful and live chat more interesting. However, they have now become so powerful that they can not only modify the face, hair and backgrounds, but also stream a pre-recorded video, making the operating system believe it is captured by the physical webcam in real time [8]. Therefore, despite their original purpose, virtual camera software in fact puts a serious threat on the security of facial authentication. While the device unlock lies in the system level and has more control of the hardware (so it is less likely to suffer from *virtual camera attacks*), website and app logins are very susceptible to this type of attack if they choose to use facial authentication.

We want to point out that the security issues we mentioned above are not the weakness of biometric information itself; instead, they stem from the methodology people currently use.

In this paper, our goal is to develop a new facial authentication method which is not only more secure but also easy and quick to use. This method should be safe for

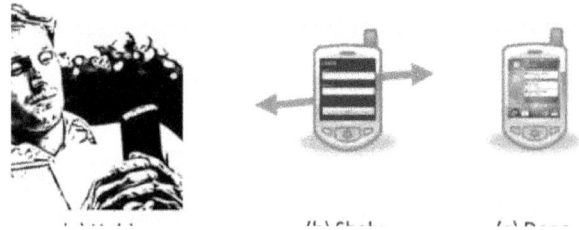

Figure 1. Proposed sensor-assisted user authentication scheme

2D media attacks and *virtual camera attacks*; at the same time, the authentication speed needs to be comparable to or faster than credential-based methods (and much faster than the existing 3D facial authentications). If such a method is achievable, it will make facial authentication more practical and useful in smartphones. It will have the potential to become a practically better solution than credential-based authentication methods, and change the current state of human-device interaction.

To achieve this goal, we propose a sensor-assisted facial authentication system. In our method, motion sensors are employed to infer the position and orientation of the front camera. User head movement is replaced by a small movement of the cellphone, which is able to ensure a real 3D face, and results in a much easier operation and faster authentication. Figure 1 gives an overview of proposed scheme, which is simple and intuitive. In addition, the shake of the video and the shake of the smartphone are extracted separately and then compared to each other, in order to defend against *virtual camera attacks*. To the best of our knowledge, this is the first work to enhance the security and usability of facial authentication by utilizing motion sensors of smartphones. The main contributions of this work are as follows:

1. We propose a sensor-assisted facial authentication system for smartphone users. A Nose Angle Detection algorithm is proposed to counter *2D media attacks*.

2. We propose a Motion-Vector Correlation algorithm to counter *virtual camera attacks*.

3. We implement the proposed algorithms on a Galaxy Nexus smartphone with Android 4.2.2 on top of existing face recognition application. Our system is able to achieve very high detection rate for both *2D media attacks* and *virtual camera attacks*. The average authentication time of our method is approximately 2 seconds, which is about ten times faster than the existing 3D facial authentication methods.

The remainder of this paper is organized as follows. Section II discusses related work. Section III outlines the overall picture and describes the attack model of our work. Section IV introduces our method that defends against *2D media attack* while still conserving the ease of use. Section V presents our technique dealing with the threats of virtual cameras. Section VI evaluates our method and Section VII discusses related issues. Section VIII concludes the paper.

II. RELATED WORK

Face recognition can be divided into two categories: verification and identification [2]. Face verification is a one to one match that compares a face to a template, whose identity is being claimed. Face identification, instead, is a one to N problem that compares a face to all the templates in a face database to determine the identity of the face being queried. Apparently, facial authentication is closely related to the former category.

2D media attack has been a well-known but difficult problem for a long time. The existing efforts can be categorized into three groups. *Liveness detection* tries to capture spontaneous eye blinks or lip movements [3] [9]. While it is useful for photo attacks, it cannot deal with recorded videos. Besides eye-blinks, the authors in [9] also use scene context, which matches background image to a template of background to check for forged video playback. It is effective against imposters but not safe against replay attacks. Moreover, the assumption of fixed camera is not valid for smartphones. *Texture analysis* relies on the different texture patterns of a photo or a real object. It can be further divided into two subcategories. The first focus on the printing failures or overall image blur of the printed photo [10]. However, this method will fail if the photo is of high quality. The second detects micro-textures presented on the printer paper [11], but it requires the input has an extremely high resolution, which is not applicable for front facing cameras on smartphones. *Motion analysis* explores one or multiple images, trying to find clues generated by the planar counterfeits. For example, Tan et al. [12] investigated the Lambertian reflectance information, in order to differentiate 3D faces from 2D images. Bao et al. [13] compared the difference of the optical flow fields under various conditions for the same purpose. These methods require high-quality inputs and the computational complexity is very high. Optical flow computations, for example, are 10000 times slower than regular pixel level operations on a video frame [24]. Besides, their performance largely depends on the complexity of the ambient illumination.

3D face recognition has been widely studied in the recent years [14] [15]. It compares the input to a pre-built 3D head template instead of 2D templates. If the face capturing in each authentication trial is also 3D, this approach is robust to *2D media attacks*. However, 3D face recognition is still in its infancy. Sandbach et al. [21] presented a survey on 3D face expression recognition and concluded that the high frame rate requirements and frame resolution limit its practical usage. More importantly, the 3D capturing process is much more time consuming than 2D methods or entering a password, therefore it is not suitable for device unlock or app login. We will further discuss it in the next section.

There have been some studies on extracting non-intentional motions from videos. For MPEG and MPEG2, motion vectors can be directly used to estimate the motion between frames, but it is not a generally applicable method for arbitrary video formats. Deshaker [17] calculates the shift that can achieve maximum likelihood between frames in a top-down fashion. Vella et al. [18] separated foreground from background before movement estimation. Xu et al. [19] analyzed video motions based on extracted feature points. All these works aimed at improving video quality instead of security purpose, and they were not optimized for facial authentication videos which have their own unique characteristics.

Biggio et al. [23] proposed a multi-modal technique where outputs of fingerprint and face recognition techniques are fused together. [22, 24] presented a magnetic user authentication system to avoid both credentials and images to authenticate a user. It requires users to hold a magnetic pen to draw 3D signature in air which are then authenticated using the magnetic sensor in the smartphone. Unlike those approaches that rely on independent processing of different sensors, our approach relies on integrated processing of accelerometers and camera readings.

III. METHOD OVERVIEW

III.A Sensor Assisted Facial Authentication

Today's smartphones are typically equipped with a plethora of sensors, some of which are not fully utilized. Motion sensors (accelerometers and gyroscopes), proximity sensor, digital compass and ambient light sensor have become de facto equipment. Microphone can be viewed as a sound sensor, and sometimes GPS is referred to as the positioning sensor. Traditional facial authentications only use cameras to capture the user's face image / video and then compare it with pre-known templates. In our proposed sensor-assisted facial authentication, we additionally utilize sensors in smartphones, in order to enhance the security or / and improve the performance of the authentication process.

In this paper, in addition to the video camera and existing face recognition schemes, we use motion sensors and ambient light sensor to defend against *2D media attacks* and *virtual camera attacks*. Motion sensors are used to intelligently choose the necessary frames in the video for further processing, while the ambient light sensor triggers screen brightness adjustment to improve the authentication accuracy.

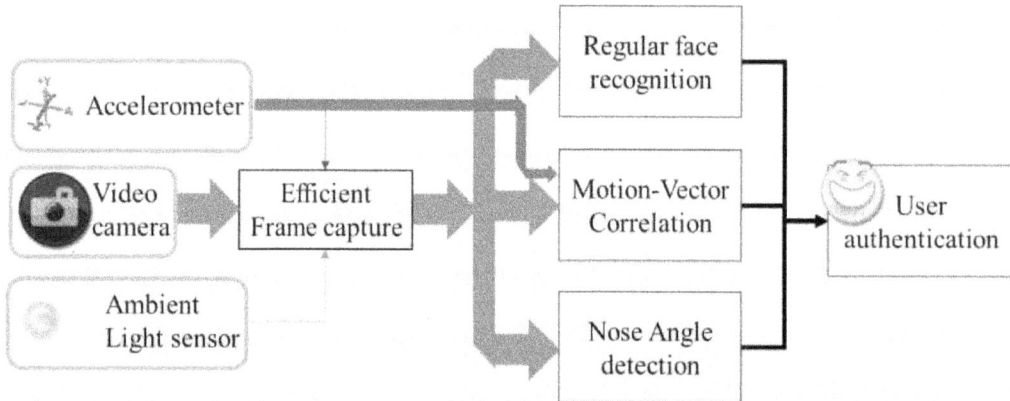

Figure 2. Block diagram of proposed approach. Existing face recognition schemes use 2D frames from smartphone camera to authenticate the user. Our approach builds on top of regular face recognition algorithms to counter 2D media attacks and virtual camera attacks. 2D media attacks are countered by Nose Angle Detection (NAD) algorithm while virtual camera attacks are countered by Motion-Vector Correlation (MVC). The ambient light sensor is used to improve the lightening conditions of face-capture from different angles. The accelerometer sensor is used to select inputs to NAD algorithm and as an input in MVC algorithm

Because these sensors are already built-in for almost all the smartphones, our approach is naturally suitable for smartphone unlock and app login without introducing any extra costs.

III.B Overview of Our Method

As mentioned in Section II, *liveness detection* and *texture analysis* have critical limitations, while *motion analysis* is not reliable under complex illumination. 3D facial authentication is robust to *2D media attacks*. However, they are much more time-consuming and difficult to use. The typical implementation requires that the motion of the user's head is synchronized with system instructions (e.g. the arrows shown on the screen in Toshiba Face Recognition Utility), which puts the burden on the user side. In the experiment (see Section VID), we find that a single trial in Toshiba Face Recognition Utility takes more than 20 seconds, and even for a genuine user, it often needs multiple trials to successfully log in. This fact significantly hurts the usability of 3D facial authentication, for it is more troublesome than simply using a password.

Our proposed approach is simple, intuitive and easy to use. It only requires the user to pick up the phone, move it horizontally for a short distance in front of the face, and it is done. In Section VI, we will show that the average time cost for authentication is less than two seconds, which is significantly faster than the existing 3D recognition methods and comparable to the credential-based method. One of the differences between our method and the existing 3D capturing is that for the former, the synchronization process mentioned above is not needed, which significantly eliminates users' burden. The basic intuition behind our approach is that by utilizing smartphones' motion sensors and object recognition techniques, we are able to infer the

relative position between the camera and the user's face, so that the synchronization can be performed automatically and quickly.

Motion sensor readings are also used to compare the shake of the cellphone with the shake of the video been recorded during the authentication process. In this way, our method can also defend against *virtual camera attacks*, and more importantly, no extra operation is imposed on users. Since our method is of high security and very easy to use, it is a promising technique that can bring the smartphone users with more pleasant authentication experience.

Our work does not touch upon regular face recognition techniques that focus on recognition of facial features to identify and authenticate a person (from adversaries), which are orthogonal to our work (see 4th paragraph of Section VII). The main contribution of our system is nose angle detection algorithm to counter *2D media attacks* and motion-vector correlation algorithm to counter *virtual camera attack*s. Figure 2 gives a block diagram explaining the main working logic of our scheme which will be detailed in the following sections. Section IV discusses nose angle detection scheme, and Section V presents motion vector correlation algorithm, respectively.

III.C Attack Model for 2D Media Attack

In the context of facial authentication, *2D media attack* refers to the attacks that use planar photos or video clips containing user's face to cheat the authentication system, making it believe it is a real user's face. When using photos, such an attack is also referred to as *photo attack* or *print attack* in some literatures.

In our attack model, attackers can use either photographs or videos containing user's face to spoof the authentication system, and we assume the quality of these photos or videos can be sufficiently high. In the authentication process, the users' faces or planar counterfeits are captured by the front-facing camera of smartphones, whose typical resolution is approximately 1 to 2 mega pixels. There is no specific requirement on the illumination conditions when the attack happens.

III.D Attack Model for Virtual Camera Attack

As mentioned in Section I, *virtual camera attack* refers to the attack that virtual camera software streams a clip of pre-recorded video containing a genuine user's face, circumventing the authentication system by making it believe the video is captured in real time.

In the attack model, attackers have the full knowledge of the authentication requirements (e.g. eye-blinks, face expressions, the movement of the head or the movement of the cellphone, etc.). In addition, the attacker may be able to obtain the video in which the genuine user is performing required actions (to log in). In the attack, the pre-recorded video is streamed via virtual camera software to cheat the authentication system. Here we assume the attack's target is websites or smartphone apps, whose authentication system typically locates at the server side.

We also assume the attacker uses the market-available virtual camera tools or lightly modified version of such tools. Their ability is to stream a recorded video, making the operating system believe it is a real-time video captured by a hardware camera in the smartphone. The attacker does not have the power to forge the motion sensor readings of the phone (see last paragraph of Section VII).

IV.   NOSE ANGLE DETECTION

In this section, we explain how our proposed method defends against 2D media attacks without penalizing the authentication speed.

IV.A Differentiate 3D Face from 2D Counterfeits

Assume we have a sequence of images (or video frames) captured by a front-facing camera during the horizontal move in front of the face. In this subsection, we present how to differentiate real 3D faces from 2D counterfeits based on these images. Theoretically two images are good for the detection (one from the left side of the face and the other from right), but more images can improve the accuracy, as well as prevent the attacker from changing the photo in the middle (clever attackers may use different photos to perform the attack). We leave the timing of the image capturing to the next subsection.

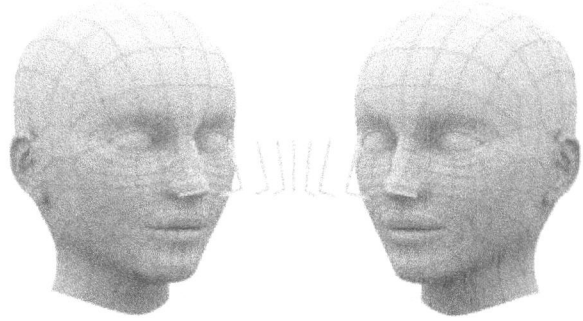

Figure 3. Change of the nose in a sequence of frames

Given an image or video frame P containing user's face, we first transform it to a grayscale image, noted as P'. This operation is trivial; we do it because some libraries only take grayscale inputs. Let the histogram of P' be H', we perform histogram equalization on H' to enhance the contrast. Assume (x, y) is a pixel in P' and its gray level is i, let:

$$p(i) = \frac{n_i}{n} \ (1 \le i \le L)$$

where n is the number of pixels of the image, n_i is the number of occurrences of gray level I, and L is the total number of gray levels. Viewing p as a probability density function, the corresponding cumulative distribution function is:

$$cdf(i) = \sum_{j=0}^{i} p(j) \tag{1}$$

The gray level of the pixel (x, y) in the new image (after histogram equalization) is:

$$cdf(i) \cdot (\max\{i\} - \min\{i\}) + \min\{i\} \tag{2}$$

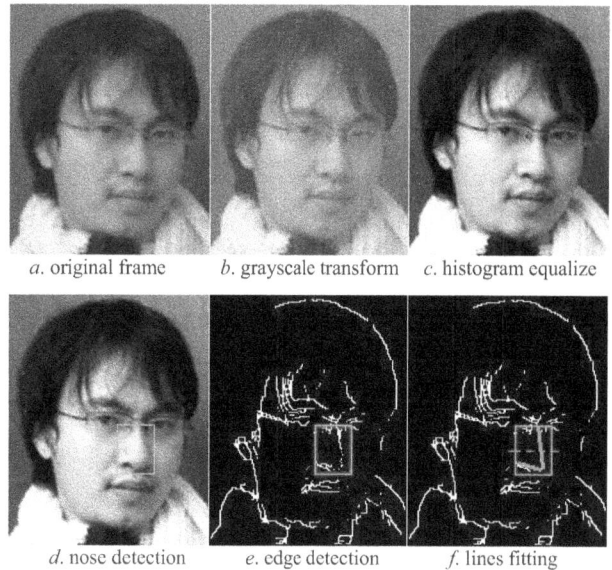

a. original frame   *b.* grayscale transform   *c.* histogram equalize

d. nose detection   *e.* edge detection   *f.* lines fitting

Figure 4. Nose border detection

Here i is the gray level of (x, y) in P'. $\max\{i\}$ $(\min\{i\})$ is the largest (smallest) gray level existed in P'. Note the new image we get as P'', and all of the following processing is performed on P''.

In the next step, we extract the nose region from P''. We put emphasis on the nose because it tends to show significant differences between a real face and a planar photo in our method. Given a series of images (captured by the front-facing camera) of a planar face photo, even if they are taken from different angles, the noses in these images are of the same shape and can match each other after necessary rotation, translation and scale. Instead, given a real 3D face, the noses in multiple images from different angles cannot simply match each other this way. The images taken from left and right will show different sides of the nose. Figure 3 illustrates the change of the nose (of a real 3D face) captured by a front-facing camera when the smartphone moves horizontally from left to right. The solid lines depict the outlines of the nose. We would like to emphasize that in Figure 3, the face on the left and the one on the right are not mirrors, but they present either side of the face respectively.

There are two approaches to detect the nose. The first is using face detection tools to figure out the face region, and then infer the approximate position of the nose based on biology knowledge. The second approach detects the nose directly by utilizing Haar-like features. Haar-like features are useful for real-time detection of face and facial regions such as eyes or nose. They are used in popular Viola-Jones face detection algorithm [20] and implemented in tools such as *Haar Cascades* in OpenCV. We use the second approach for its higher accuracy and faster implementation. Figure 4 illustrates each step starting from the original frame (Figure 4a, 4b, and 4c illustrate P, P' and P'' respectively for a sample image). Figure 4d is the output of nose detection algorithm.

After obtaining the region of the nose in P'', we calculate the nose edges. We test various edge detection operators, such as *prewitt detector, marr detector, canny detector*, etc., and their performances are compared in Section VIB. The detected edges are presented in Figure 4e (in this example, *prewitt operator* is used), and here we only focus on the edges within the nose region which is given by the previous step.

Next, we use two straight lines to perform curve fitting on the nose edge. MMSE (minimum mean square error) is employed for the estimation. Assume a line is expressed as $ax + b$, we have:

$$MSE = \sum_i (ax_i + b - y_i)^2 \quad (3)$$

where (x_i, y_i) are the points in the nose edge (i.e. the edges within the green rectangular in Figure 4e). For a single straight line, we can easily calculate the values of a and b that minimize MSE. However, for the fitting problem with two uncorrelated lines, the computational complexity becomes much higher. We use a heuristic to reduce this complexity. First, we mask the lower half of the

nose area and fit the edge within the upper half with a single line (using Equation 3), noted as l_1. Second, we unmask the lower half, erase all the points that are close to l_1 (within a threshold) or its extension, and then fit the rest of the points by the other line (again, using Equation 3), noted as l_2. The result is illustrated in Figure 4f. Despite a heuristic approach, it shows good accuracy in experiments (see Section VIB) and largely reduces the computational overhead.

Apparently, l_1 and l_2 (or their extensions) will form an angle. If it is a real face, the orientation of this angle will reverse when the camera passes the midline of the face (as the green lines shown in Figure 3). However, if it is a planar photo, this orientation change does not happen. In this way, we are able to differentiate a real face from a 2D counterfeit. The detection accuracy of our method is presented in Section VI.

IV.B Cooperation of Motion Sensor and Camera

In the previous subsection, we talked about how to tell the difference between a genuine user's face and a 2D counterfeit (photos or videos). However, the advantage of our method not only lies in the ability of detecting such attacks, but also it is easy to use and much faster than the existing 3D face authentication methods. To achieve this goal, the key is to utilize smartphones' motion sensors and capture users' face image cleverly. The authentication process of our method is described as follows.

1) As soon as the authentication starts (time noted as T_0), the front-facing camera begins to capture video and perform face detection (detect the existence of human face, OpenCV *haarcascade* is used). Once the face area is greater than or equal to a threshold (in experiment, we set the default value to 40% area of the video frame), the front-facing camera starts recording video (time noted as T_s). The area of the face is approximated by the area of the face detection output (ususally a rectangular). At the same time (T_s), our system starts sampling the readings of accelerometers. If no face is detected, the authentication system will show a prompt and ask the user to move the phone closer to the face.

2) During the video recording, once the face area is smaller than a threshold (by default, 30% of the frame area) or the face can no longer be detected, the video recording stops. If no horizontal move is detected, a prompt will show on the screen asking user to move the phone horizontally in front of the face. If the horizontal move stopped for a time period longer than a threshold, the video recording also stops. The accelerometer sampling always terminates at the same time when video stops recording (time noted as T_e).

3) During the horizontal move, if the light sensor detects that the ambient illumination is very low, the system will change the majority of screen area to brighter colors and turn the screen brightness up, which helps increase the illumination, make the nose outline clearer, and thus improve the accuracy of edge detection.

4) Our system analyzes the accelerometer readings (from T_s to T_e), based on which it calculates the time when the phone is at its left most and right most position during the horizontal move, noted as t_l and t_r , respectively. Then, the video frames captured around time t_l and t_r are used for 2D media attack detection, in which the method introduced in Section IVA is applied. More details are presented as follows.

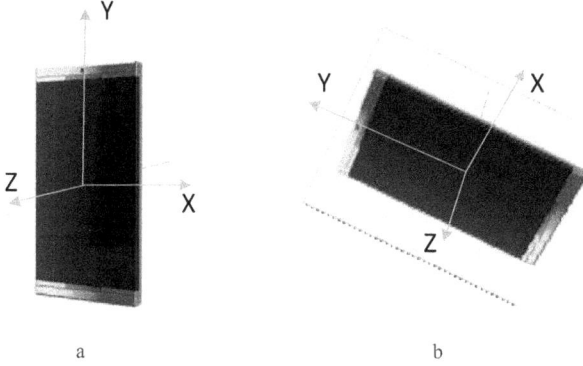

a b

Figure 5. Three axes of the accelerometer and orientation in smartphones

The accelerometer in smartphones typically has three axes, as shown in Figure 5 (z axis is orthogonal to the plane of the phone screen). In order to perform a successful facial authentication, the virtual line linking two eyes should be approximately parallel with the width dimension of the front facing camera. Therefore, the horizontal move required by our method is mostly related with the acceleration along the x axis.

As we know, accelerometers measures the acceleration applied to the devices. An important fact is that when a cellphone is stationary, its accelerometer reads a magnitude of about 9.81 m/s^2, pointing to the direction of gravity; when the phone is in free fall, the accelerometer reads 0. If we use the smartphone when standing or sitting, it is most likely that the gravity only affects y axis (Figure 5a). However, if a user plays with his phone on bed or lying on sofa, gravity can influence x axis readings (Figure 5b). Therefore, we first need to filter out gravity to get the real acceleration of the phone. Let $\vec{G}_{t_i}$ represent the estimate of gravity. Note the accelerometer readings as $\vec{R}$ (this vector has three components: x, y, and z), we calculate:

$$\vec{G}_{t_i} = \alpha \vec{R}_{t_i} + (1 - \alpha)\vec{G}_{t_{i-1}} \quad (4)$$

and note the real acceleration as $\vec{A}$, we have:

$$\vec{A}_{t_i} = \vec{R}_{t_i} - \vec{G}_{t_i} \quad (5)$$

In Equation 4 and 5, t_i ($i \in Z^+$) are the time points that the sensor readings are collected. The basic idea is using exponentially-weighted moving average as a low-pass

filter, which isolates the force of gravity. Then the remaining high frequency part is thereby the real acceleration of the device. α in Equation 4 is a smoothing factor, which defined as:

$$\alpha = \frac{\Delta t}{T + \Delta t} \quad (6)$$

here Δt is the sensor sampling interval (i.e. $t_i - t_{i-1}$), and T is a time constant. By default, we let T = 5Δt.

Having obtained the real acceleration of the device, we can calculate its displacement during the horizontal move. It can be safely assumed that the velocity of the cellphone at T_s is 0 or close to 0, because the horizontal move has not started yet. So we have:

$$s(t) = \iint_{T_s}^{t} A^x(t)\, d^2t \quad (7)$$

where $A^x(t)$ is the x-component of $\vec{A}$, that is, the real acceleration of the phone along the x axis. $s(t)$ is the relative displacement from the original position (position at T_s). Due to the discrete nature of sensor readings, Equation 7 equals:

$$s(i) = (\Delta t)^2 \sum_i \sum_i A^x_{t_i} \quad (8)$$

The smaller Δt is, the more accurate $s(i)$ we get. By default, we use $\Delta t = 0.01$s. Then we calculate the min and max values of $s(i)$ based on Equation 8 such that $T_s \le t_i \le T_s$. They stand for the left-most and right-most position during the horizontal move respectively. Note the values of t_i as t_l and t_r where $s(i)$ reaches its minimum and maximum.

We examine the recorded video around time t_l, and pick up three frames at $t_l - 0.1$s, t_l, and $t_l + 0.1$s (if the video is 30 fps, they are approximately 3 frames away from each other). These three frames are processed using our method discussed in Section IVA, and the frame with minimum *MSE* is retained (refer to Equation 3). The same operation is performed on the frames around time t_r. Finally, two retained frames are compared to each other on the orientation of the angle between l_1 and l_2 (see Section IVA).

So far we have discussed how to quickly differentiate a real 3D face from a 2D photo (or video) with the help of motion sensors. Apart from the frame processing mentioned above, we perform anomaly detection on each frame between t_l and t_r. Face detection is applied on these frames to detect the absence of user's face or duplicated faces, in order to prevent the attacker from changing photos in the middle. Although this operation has to be performed on all the frames between t_l and t_r, the cost is much lower than the 2D counterfeits detection discussed above. Clever attackers will be further discussed in Section VII.

Besides, the frame around time $(t_l + t_r) / 2$ is used as the input for routine face recognition (matching with a template whose identity is being claimed); but for this task, we can employ the existing methods and it is orthogonal to our work.

V. MOTION VECTOR CORRELATION

In Section IV, we present our method that defends against 2D media attacks. Now we move on to the detection of virtual camera attacks, which is another important threat to the facial authentication.

The attack model of the virtual camera attack is described in Section IIID. Since smartphones are hand-held devices, non-intentional shakes are inevitable for facial authentication videos captured by the front-facing camera. The basic idea of our method is to extract these shakes from the video, and compare with the shakes detected by the motion sensors. If it is a match, we can infer that the video is captured in real time; otherwise, it is very likely to be a pre-recorded video streamed via virtual camera software.

An important rule is that only small-scale random shakes (non-intentional hand shaking) are used for the matching, because large-scale motion trajectory can be easily emulated. Our virtual camera detection is performed by reusing the video and sensor readings recorded during T_s and T_e (see Section IVB); no extra operation is required from users.

Now we present our method for video motion extraction. Given two consecutive frames, P_i and P_{i-1}, we first reduce them in scale (resize to $m \times n$). Assuming the frame aspect ratio is 3:4, by default, we let $m = 24$ and $n = 32$. The resized frames are noted as $\overline{P}_i$ and $\overline{P}_{i-1}$ respectively. Then we apply panning (vertical and horizontal), rotation and zooming on $\overline{P}_i$, and the frame after processing is noted as $\widetilde{P}_i$. Our goal is to find the $\widetilde{P}_i$ that best matches $\overline{P}_{i-1}$. In our method, we set a range for the panning, rotation and zoom operations. For example, the panning should be no more than 5 pixels (in each direction) and rotation is less than 10 degrees. The limitation is introduced for two reasons. First, we are only interested in small-scale shakes. The time interval between two consecutive frames is only around 0.03 second. If the difference between them is large, it is very likely that what we detect is large-scale motion instead of a small shake. Second, since we need to try all the combinations of panning, rotation and zoom to find the best match, the search space is considerably large. Putting these physical restrictions on the search space accelerates our method without any negative implications on results.

The degree of match between $\widetilde{P}_i$ and $\overline{P}_{i-1}$ is measured by correlation coefficient. Compared with absolute value matching, it better tolerates the ambient light change and camera ISO / aperture auto adjustments. Correlation coefficient of $\widetilde{P}_i$ and $\overline{P}_{i-1}$ is defined as follows:

Figure 6. Small shake extraction from video

$$r = \frac{\sum_{0 \leq x < m, 0 \leq y < n}(p_{x,y} - \bar{p})(q_{x,y} - \bar{q})}{\sqrt{\sum_{0 \leq x < m, 0 \leq y < n}(p_{x,y} - \bar{p})^2}\sqrt{\sum_{0 \leq x < m, 0 \leq y < n}(q_{x,y} - \bar{q})^2}}$$

where $p_{x,y}$ is the value of pixel (x, y) in $\overline{P}_{i-1}$, and $q_{x,y}$ is the value of pixel (x, y) in $\widetilde{P}_i$. $\bar{p}$ is the mean value for all $p_{x,y}$ while $\bar{q}$ is the average of $q_{x,y}$. For each $\widetilde{P}_i$, we calculate r, and the one with highest r is memorized (noted as $\widehat{P}_i$). The operation performed between $\widetilde{P}_i$ and $\widehat{P}_i$ is noted as OP_i.

If the largest r is smaller than a threshold (0.7 in our settings), it means very likely the motion between P_i and P_{i-1} is so large that any minor shift will not let them match. In this case, the result is discarded and we move on to the next frame pair (P_{i+1} and P_i). Otherwise, the following steps are performed.

We divide P_i into small blocks. For each block, we calculate a shift to make it best match P_{i-1} (in their original resolutions) by using the same approach as for $\widehat{P}_i$. The only difference is that previously we apply panning, rotation and zooming, but now only vertical and horizontal panning is allowed. In other words, now OP_i is fine-tuned in the block level.

The results of the best shift for each block is illustrated on a sample frame in Figure 6 (the arrows stand for the adjustment added to OP_i for each block; OP_i itself is not included). If the majority of these adjustments are the same (or very close), we use this value (or the average) as the shake of P_i, noted as $\vec{K}_i$. Otherwise, we assign a priority to each block. The blocks in the background but with details have the highest priority (such as region A in Figure 6), the blocks in the foreground rank the next (e.g. region C), and the background blocks with few details have the lowest priority (e.g. region B). We choose the average adjustment of the blocks with the highest priority as $\vec{K}_i$. Foreground and background are differentiated by the previous face detection output (blocks within the face region is considered as foreground, otherwise background), and details are judged by the diagonal subband

116

of the wavelet transform of P_i (diagonal subband values are close to zero if few details exist). If the panning component of OP_i is smaller than a threshold, we add this component to $\vec{K}_i$ and note the result as $\vec{\mathcal{K}}_i$. Otherwise, $\vec{\mathcal{K}}_i$ is the same as $\vec{K}_i$. Similarly, we calculate $\vec{\mathcal{K}}$ for each frame during T_s and T_e.

Compared with the standard motion vector extraction method, our method includes a number of modifications in order to improve the performance. Authentication videos have their unique characteristics. For example, the foreground of an authentication video is always a human or human's face; these videos usually do not contain fast moving objects, etc. By utilizing these characteristics, our method presented above can extract motions faster than the standard method without negative implications on results.

In parallel to the motion extraction from video frames, we extract shakes from accelerometer readings, where the method is similar as in Section IVB. The shake of the phone ($\vec{A}$) is calculated by Equation 5 (see Section IVB). In order to remove large-scale motions, we redefine α by letting T = $2\Delta t$ in Equation 6. As T decreases, α increases, and the cutoff frequency of the filter becomes higher. The value of T is determined by the experiments (please refer to Section VIC). Since $\vec{\mathcal{K}}$ is a two dimensional vector that only includes the shifts parallel to the camera sensor plane, we remove the z-component of $\vec{A}$, making it consist of merely the comparable information as in $\vec{\mathcal{K}}$. The trimmed $\vec{A}$ is noted as $\vec{\mathcal{A}}$.

$\vec{\mathcal{K}}$ and $\vec{\mathcal{A}}$ are then aligned according to the time scale. As mentioned previously, some elements of $\vec{\mathcal{K}}$ could be dropped in our method, so we also remove the corresponding elements in $\vec{\mathcal{A}}$ if necessary. Correlation coefficient is employed to measure the similarity between $\vec{\mathcal{K}}$ and $\vec{\mathcal{A}}$:

$$\rho = \frac{E[(\vec{\mathcal{A}} - E(\vec{\mathcal{A}}))(\vec{\mathcal{K}} - E(\vec{\mathcal{K}}))]}{\delta_{\vec{\mathcal{A}}}\delta_{\vec{\mathcal{K}}}} \quad (9)$$

where E is expectation and δ stands for standard deviation. The closer $|\rho|$ is to one, the better $\vec{\mathcal{K}}$ and $\vec{\mathcal{A}}$ matches. Otherwise, if $|\rho|$ is close to zero, a virtual camera attack is assumed. The threshold is determined by experiments (please refer to Section VIC).

VI. EVALUATIONS

We implement our method and conduct real-world experiments to evaluate it. We first talk about the implementation details and experiment settings. Then, we evaluate the accuracy of our 2D media attack detection scheme and virtual camera attack detection approach respectively. After that, the authentication speed of our method, exiting 3D facial authentication and credential-based authentication methods are compared.

VI.A System Implementation and Experiment Preparation

Our system is implemented in a Samsung Galaxy Nexus smartphone. The operating system is Android 4.2.2 and the front-facing camera has 1.3 mega pixels. The video captured in facial authentication is 480×720@24fps, and in the succeeding processing we chop them to 480×640.

We use *Haar Cascades* in OpenCV for face and facial region detection. haarcascade_frontalface_alt2.xml and haarcascade_mcs_nose.xml are employed to detect face and nose region respectively. JavaCV is used as a wrapper to call the native functions.

The main objective of our system is defending against 2D media attacks and virtual camera attacks without introducing high costs. Face identification techniques are orthogonal to our work; any authentication system using 2D face recognition can benefit from our method. But for the completeness, we do include a PCA (principal component analysis) based facial identification module, which is also implemented using OpenCV. The video frames around time $(t_l + t_r) / 2$ are used (see Section IVB) as the input for template matching.

We now compare the face detection accuracy (using the module mentioned above) when the normal operation, hand-picked *best* frame, and automatically extracted frame (by our method) are used, respectively. The purpose of this experiment is to check whether our method is able to pick the appropriate frame for template matching, since face recognition algorithms are usually sensitive to the orientation between the camera and the user.

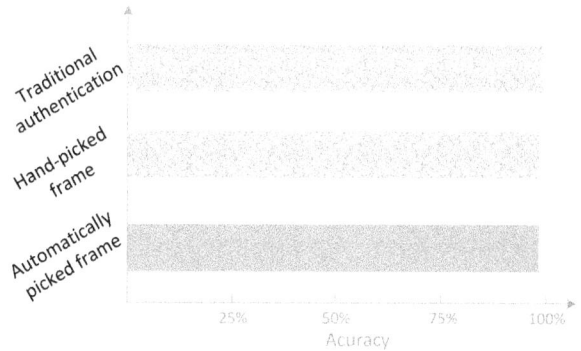

Figure 7. Performance of automatic frame selection

In Figure 7, traditional authentication is the case where a user holds the smartphone, keeps it still, and the smartphone takes a picture of the user's face and performs the recognition. Other two cases use the video collected by our method (horizontally move the phone in front of the user's face); the difference lies in that, "hand-picked frame" refers to the approach in which we manually pick the *best* frame (where the face squarely opposite to the camera) from the video, while "automatically picked frame" fully utilizes our method and the frame is picked by calculating $(t_l + t_r) / 2$. For each case, we plot the accuracy of 180 trials, where data are from 9 volunteers (volunteers will be detailed in Section VIB). The results show that our method is good enough in automatic frame selection (for succeeding template matching).

VI.B Accuracy of 2D Media Attack Detection

In this subsection, we evaluate the 2D media attack detection accuracy of our system.

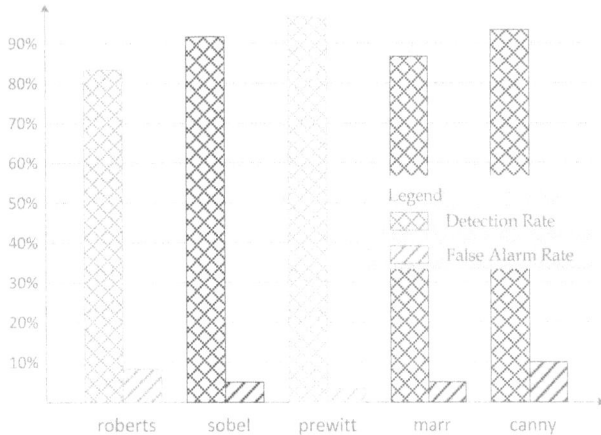

Figure 8. 2D media attack detection accuracy

We have 9 volunteers, each of them performing 20 trials of facial authentication using our system. Besides, we take two pictures and one clip of video for each volunteer, all of which are of high quality and with the head centered. Volunteers include 8 males and 1 female. 6 of them are in their twenties while the other 3 are in their thirties. They are all friends of authors but are not inside or related to our research lab. They participated in experiments voluntarily without compensation and were not aware of the purpose of experiments. For the facial authentication trial using our system, each volunteer was asked to hold the Galaxy Nexus in front of his / her face, click a "start" button on the screen, move the phone horizontally for a short distance, and then click the "complete" button. Besides two buttons mentioned above, the screen shows the real time scene captured by the front facing camera as well as a large green square. We asked the volunteers to locate their face approximately inside this square when moving the phone.

During the attack, pictures are printed on white paper in high quality (in case of the video attack, videos are played in another device), facing the smartphone that is used for authentication. Distance is carefully adjusted, making the size of the face on the planar media the same as the real one. We give each photo (video) ten trials. Therefore, in total we have 180 genuine user trials and 270 attacks (180 photo attacks and 90 video attacks). Half

of them are performed indoor and the other half outdoor. For each test, the smartphone is moved horizontally for a short distance in front of the face (real faces or 2D counterfeits). The experiment result is shown in Figure 8.

Here detection rate refers to the number of detected attacks divided by the total number of attacks, while false alarms stand for genuine users' trials which are reported as attacks by our system. Therefore, a good detection system is expected to have a high detection rate and a low false alarm rate. In Figure 8, x axis exhibits 5 different edge detectors (for nose border extraction, refer to Section IVA). For each detector, we try different thresholds and the best one is used in the final settings. Figure 8 shows that *prewitt* and *canny* detector have the best detection rate (97% and 93%), while *prewitt* and *marr* have the best false alarm rate (3% and 5%). Combining the results, we choose *prewitt* detector for our method. Hereinafter, we use this detector in the rest of experiments unless otherwise specified.

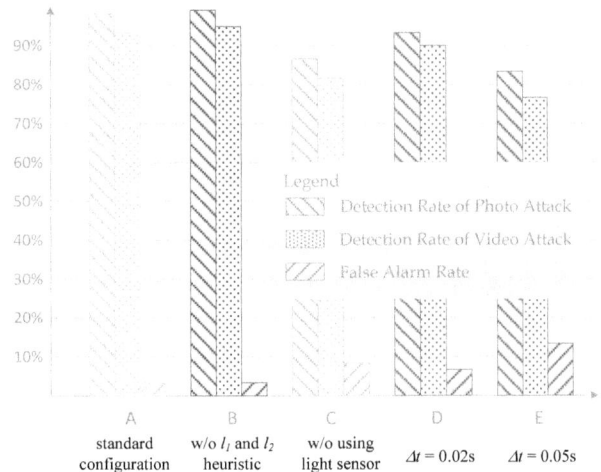

Figure 9. Detection accuracy under different configurations

In Figure 9, we show the detection accuracy of the photo attack and video attack separately. We also twist some configurations of our method to see how they affect the performance. In x axis, A is the standard configuration of our method. B uses brutal force search instead of the heuristic (see Section IVA) to find l_1 and l_2 (two lines used to fit nose edges). The brute force method has negligible performance gain as compared to the increased computational cost (15 times slower). In C, we disable the brightness auto adjustment described in *3)* of Section IVB, and a performance drop is observed. Because only half of our tests are performed indoor, the actual influence might be even stronger than shown in Figure 9. For D and E, we change the motion sensor sampling rate. It can be seen that increased sampling time leads to lower performance. For all the tests, an observation is that video attacks are slightly harder to detect than photo attacks.

Next, we compare the performance of our method to the 3D authentication method as well as the Android face unlock (in version 4.2.2) under 2D media attacks. For the 3D method, we use Toshiba Face Recognition Utility. The results are shown in Figure 10. The result shows that the detection rate of the 3D method is only marginally better than ours for both photo attack and video attack. However, our scheme has a lower false alarm rate than 3D authentication method (up to 10% difference). More important, the detection time of the 3D method is significantly longer than ours, which will be shown later.

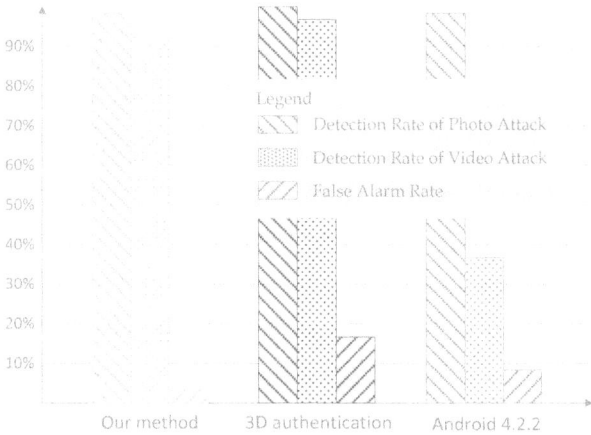

Figure 10. Comparing the detection accuracy with state-of-the-art appraoches

As to the face unlock alternative embedded in the Android system, since it includes an "eye blink" detection mechanism starting from version 4.1, it does a decent job in photo attacks, but it cannot effectively detect video attacks, since many videos naturally contains spontaneous eye blinks. In sum, our method can achieve a detection rate of 97% in 2D media attack detection, and its false alarm rate is as low as 3%. The speed of our method will be evaluated and compared in Section VID.

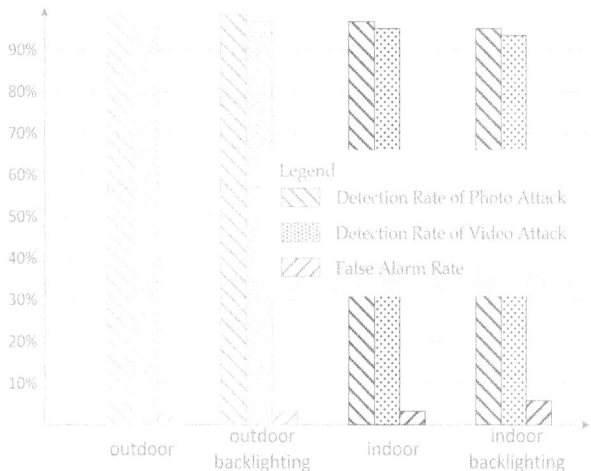

Figure 11. Detection accuracy under different illumi-nance

We now compare the accuracy of our 2D media attack detection algorithm under different illumination conditions. The indoor environment has illuminance of 10 - 50 lux, while the outdoor tests are performed under illuminance that varies from 50 to 200 lux. The averaged results for this set of experiments are shown in Figure 11. We can see from the results that the performance of our method is not greatly affected by the variation of illumination conditions (in contrast, as mentioned in Section II, the performance of motion analysis methods largely depends on the illumination). We also find that if we disable the light sensor and our automatic-screen-brightness-increase (Section IV-B) mechanism, in the indoor backlighting case, the false alarm rate will increase approximately 10 percent.

VI.C Accuracy of Virtual Camera Attack Detection

Now we evaluate our system's detection accuracy of virtual camera attacks. In our implementation, 2D media attacks can be detected either in the smartphone or at the server side (in order to apply to device unlock and website / app login respectively). However, the virtual camera attack detection can only be performed at the server side. A laptop (Toshiba Z930 with Intel i7-3667U CPU) is acting as the server, and the authentication video and sensor readings are streamed to it from the smartphone in real time.

We implement our system this way for two reasons. First, as mentioned in Section I, device unlock lies in the system level and has more control of hardware, so it is less likely to suffer from virtual camera attacks. On the other hand, for website / app login, which are susceptible to this attack, the authentication is always performed at the server side. Second, the computation overhead of virtual camera attack detection is relatively high. Implementation in the server can achieve better performance.

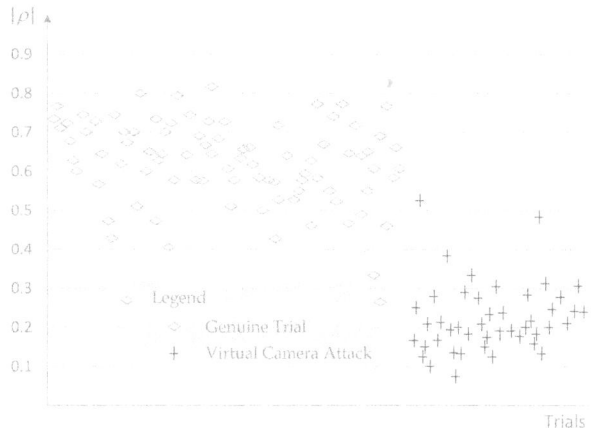

Figure 12. Threshold between attacks and genuine trials

During an attack, a pre-recorded video (with a genuine user's face in it) is streamed to the server instead of the live video captured by the front-facing camera. Meanwhile, the same horizontal move of the smartphone is also performed. The dataset we use is the same as the previous experiments. We have 180 genuine users' trials and 90 pre-recorded videos. They are divided equally into two sets, referred to as D1 and D2 respectively (each contains 90 genuine trials and 45 attacks).

First we use dataset D1 to determine the threshold for $|\rho|$ (see Section V; if $|\rho|$ is smaller than the threshold, an attack is assumed). $|\rho|$ of 90 genuine trials and 45 attacks in D1 are calculated using Equation 9 (T is fixed at $3\Delta t$) and presented in Figure 12. From the result, we can see that the genuine trials and the attacks are separated fairly clearly. $|\rho|$ of most attacks are smaller than 0.4 and genuine trails are the opposite. Based on this observation, we set the threshold of $|\rho|$ at 0.4, which is used as the default value of our method thereinafter.

Next, we vary the value of T (see Sections IVB and V) and see how it affects the detection accuracy. As mentioned before, in our method, large-scale motions are filtered out from both sensor readings and video motion vectors, but the amount that is removed from two sides (sensor readings and video motion vectors) should be approximately the same. Intuitively speaking, adjusting the value of T is the operation that twists the sensitivity of the sensor filter and makes two amounts to be removed approximately the same. The test is performed on dataset D2. The detection rate (solid line) and false alarm rate (dashed line) are plotted in Figure 13.

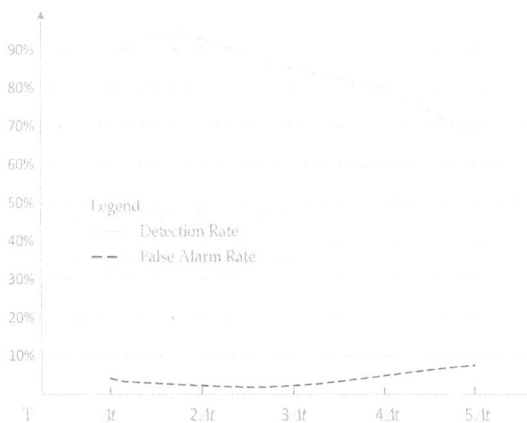

Figure 13. Detection accuracy of virtual camera attacks

The experiment results show that when T is around $2\Delta t$, the best performance can be achieved. So we use T = $2\Delta t$ as the default value in our method for virtual camera attack detection. From the experiment, we can see that our method is able to achieve a detection rate of 95% while the false alarm rate is as low as 2% in virtual camera attack detection.

VI.D Authentication Speed and Usability

In this subsection, we compare the authentication time of our method, 3D facial authentications, and credential based authentications.

In addition to the 180 trials in our system mentioned above, our volunteers perform 90 trials on Toshiba Face Recognition Utility (to log into a Toshiba laptop) using 3D facial authentication, as well as 90 trials to login a website by entering the username and password. For all three schemes, time is counted until the authentication result is sent back. To reduce the influence of network latency, we use local servers in the LAN. The time costs of three schemes are averaged and plotted in Figure 14 (gray bars). We can see that speed-wise, our system is comparable to the credential-based system, and 9 times faster than the 3D facial authentication method.

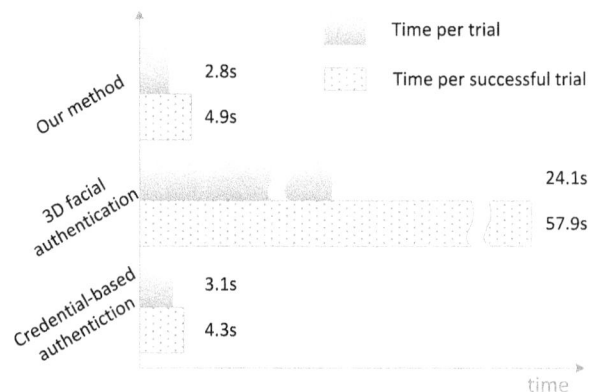

Figure 14. Authentication time comparison

All the trials used for calculation in the last experiment are in fact successful trials. In some cases, a trial can fail even for a genuine user. For example, the user may fail to synchronize the head movement with the instructions given by the 3D scheme; user's face may be too far away from the front camera; the required horizontal move is not detected by our method; or the user enters the wrong password by mistake, etc. In the following test, we include all the trials and calculate the time cost per a successful trial. The result is plotted as dotted bars in Figure 14. Our method is still very close to the credential-based scheme in speed, and its advantage over the 3D facial authentication becomes even larger (13 times faster), which exhibits good usability of our method.

VII. DISCUSSION

We claim that our method can detect 2D media attacks, including photo attacks and video attacks. In Android 4.2, users are required to blink their eyes during the face unlock, which can be easily spoofed by a video containing eye blinks. Our method is safe for such videos. However, clever attackers may think about using more sophisticated videos. Since our system requires a short move of the smartphone from left to right in front of the face, how about using a video in which the genuine user slowly turns his / her head from right to left?

This method sounds good but in fact it can hardly compromise our system. The reason is as follows. First, the feasibility of the video attack against the Android face unlock is based on the fact that videos containing eye blinks are relatively easy to obtain (e.g. through social networks). Blinking is a spontaneous or voluntary action of human eyes. A video with a clear user's face in it has high probability to contain eye blinks as well. On the contrary, finding a video in which the user turns head slowly is much more difficult.

Second, as mentioned above, our method also collects sensor readings during the horizontal move of the smartphone. Keeping the phone still and only relying on the head turn in the video can be easily detected by our system. The attacker must move the phone horizontally and synchronize the smartphone movement with the head turn in the video (making it look like the phone is moving, but the user is not turning head), which is very difficult.

In this work, we have shown a prototype implementation of our system on the top of *haarcascade* face recognition utility available in openCV. On one hand, the recognition accuracy of this default face recognition scheme can limit the overall accuracy of our system. Iris recognition or other advanced facial feature recognition schemes can be used instead of *haarcascade* to achieve higher detection rate and lower false alarm rate for our authentication system. On the other hand, different recognition schemes mentioned above are orthogonal to our research. The method discussed in this paper can still be used to counter against 2D media attacks and virtual camera attacks when the face recognition schemes other than *haarcascade* are used.

As mentioned in Section IIID, the proposed method is based on the assumption that motion sensor readings from the smartphone that performs facial authentication are not compromised. If an attacker is able to forge the sensor readings and manipulate the video (i.e., use a pre-recorded video as if it is captured by the physical front-facing camera of the smartphone) at the same time, our system can be compromised. In this paper, we focus on defending against the virtual camera attacks which take advantage of virtual camera software or lightly modified versions of such software, instead of an omnipotent Trojan which can compromise the OS, manipulate the video and forge the sensor readings simultaneously. The former is the tools that are available on market, while the latter does not exist for now. Of course, an attacker may think of using virtual camera software as well as a Trojan that can modify the sensor readings at the same time. However, it requires that the virtual camera and Trojan cooperate together and synchro-

nize perfectly, which is difficult and significantly raises the bar for breaking into the authentication system.

VIII. CONCLUSION

In this paper, we proposed a novel facial authentication method for smartphones, which can defend against 2D media attacks and virtual camera attacks without penalizing the authentication speed. Motion sensors inside smartphones are employed to achieve this purpose.

We conduct extensive experiments to evaluate our method. The result shows that the attack detection rate of our method is very high, while its speed is comparable to credential-based methods, and over ten times faster than the existing 3D facial authentications. Our work overcomes the most important limitations of current facial authentication techniques, making it more practical and useful for smartphones. It has the potential to change the current state of smartphone authentications.

IX. REFERENCES

[1] R. Jenkins and A. Burton, 100% accuracy in automatic face recognition. *Science*, 319 (5862): 435, January 2008.

[2] A. F. Abate, M. Nappi, D. Riccio, and G. Sabatino. 2D and 3D face recognition: a survey. *Pattern Recognition Letters*, 28(14): 1885-1906, 2007.

[3] G. Pan, L. Sun, Z. Wu, and S. Lao, Eyeblink-based anti-spoofing in face recognition from a generic webcamera. *IEEE 11th International Conference on Computer Vision*, 2007.

[4] www.androidauthority.com/android-jelly-bean-face-unlock-blink-hacking -105556/

[5] www.youtube.com/watch?v=UKIZBbvloO8

[6] C. Queirolo, L. Silva, O. Bellon, and M. Pamplona. 3D face recognition using simulated annealing and the surface interpenetration measure. *IEEE Trans. on Pattern Analysis and Machine Intelligence*, 32(2): 206-219, 2010.

[7] V. Blanz and T. Vetter. Face recognition based on fitting a 3D morphable model. *IEEE Trans. on Pattern Analysis and Machine Intelligence*, 25(9): 1063-1074, 2003.

[8] http://www.manycam.com

[9] G. Pan, L. Sun, Z. Wu, and Y. Wang. Monocular camera-based face liveness detection by combining eye-blink and scene context. *Journal of Telecommunication Systems*, 2009.

[10] J. Li, Y. Wang, T. Tan, and A. K. Jain. Live face detection based on the analysis of fourier spectra. *Biometric Technology for Human Identification*, 2004.

[11] J. Bai, T. Ng, X. Gao, and Y. Shi. Is physics-based liveness detection truly possible with a single image?. *IEEE International Symposium on Circuits and Systems*, 2010.

[12] X. Tan, Y. Li, J. Liu, and L. Jiang. Face liveness detection from a single image with sparse low rank bilinear discriminative model. *Computer Vision ECCV*, vol. 6316, pp. 504-517, 2010.

[13] W. Bao, H. Li, N. Li, and W. Jiang. A liveness detection method for face recognition based on optical field. *IEEE International Conference on Image Analysis and Signal Processing*, 2009.

[14] Y. Wang, J. Liu, and X. Tang. Robust 3D face recognition by local shape difference boosting. *IEEE Trans. on Pattern Analysis and Machine Intelligence*, 32(10): 1858-1870, 2010.

[15] B. Amberg, R. Knothe, and T. Vetter. Expression invariant 3D face recognition with a morphable model. *8th IEEE International Conference on Automatic Face and Gesture Recognition*, 2008.

[16] http://uniqul.com/news/17-launch

[17] http://www.guthspot.se/video/deshaker.htm

[18] F. Vella, A. Castorina, M. Mancuso, and G. Messina. Digital image stabilization by adaptive block motion vectors filtering. *IEEE Trans. on Consumer Electronics*, 48(3): 796-801, 2002.

[19] Y. Xu and S. Qin, A new approach to video stabilization with iterative smoothing. *IEEE International Conference on Signal Processing*, 2010.

[20] P. Viola and M. Jones. Robust real-time face detection. *International Journal of Computer Vision*, (57)2: 137-154, 2004.

[21] G. Sandbach, S. Zaferiou, M. Pantic, and L. Yin. Static and dynamic 3D facial expression recognition: A comprehensive survey. *Image and Vision Computing*, 2012.

[22] S. Shirazi, A. P. Moghadam, H. Ketabdar, and A. Schmidt. Assessing the vulnerability of magnetic gestural authentication to video-based shoulder surfing attacks. In *Proceedings of the 2012 ACM annual conference on Human Factors in Computing Systems*, pages 2045-2048. ACM, 2012.

[23] B. Biggio, Z. Akthar, G. Fumera, G. L. Marcialis, and F. Roli. Security evaluation of biometric authentication systems under realistic spoofing attacks. *IET biometrics*, 1(1): 11-24, 2012.

[24] K. H. Kamer, A. Yüksel, A. Jahnbekam, M. Roshandel, and D. Skirpo. Magisign: User identification/authentication based on 3d around device magnetic signatures. In *Proceedings of 4th International Conference on Mobile Ubiquitous Computing, Systems, Services and Technologies*, pages 31-34. 2010.

MAdFraud: Investigating Ad Fraud in Android Applications

Jonathan Crussell
UC Davis
jcrussell@ucdavis.edu

Ryan Stevens
UC Davis
rcstevens@ucdavis.edu

Hao Chen
UC Davis
chen@ucdavis.edu

ABSTRACT

Many Android applications are distributed for free but are supported by advertisements. Ad libraries embedded in the app fetch content from the *ad provider* and display it on the app's user interface. The ad provider pays the developer for the ads displayed to the user and ads clicked by the user. A major threat to this ecosystem is *ad fraud*, where a miscreant's code fetches ads without displaying them to the user or "clicks" on ads automatically. Ad fraud has been extensively studied in the context of web advertising but has gone largely unstudied in the context of mobile advertising.

We take the first step to study mobile ad fraud perpetrated by Android apps. We identify two fraudulent ad behaviors in apps: 1) requesting ads while the app is in the background, and 2) clicking on ads without user interaction. Based on these observations, we developed an analysis tool, MAdFraud, which automatically runs many apps simultaneously in emulators to trigger and expose ad fraud. Since the formats of ad impressions and clicks vary widely between different ad providers, we develop a novel approach for automatically identifying ad impressions and clicks in three steps: building HTTP request trees, identifying ad request pages using machine learning, and detecting clicks in HTTP request trees using heuristics. We apply our methodology and tool to two datasets: 1) 130,339 apps crawled from 19 Android markets including Play and many third-party markets, and 2) 35,087 apps that likely contain malware provided by a security company. From analyzing these datasets, we find that about 30% of apps with ads make ad requests while in running in the background. In addition, we find 27 apps which generate clicks without user interaction. We find that the click fraud apps attempt to remain stealthy when fabricating ad traffic by only periodically sending clicks and changing which ad provider is being targeted between installations.

Categories and Subject Descriptors

D.4.6 [**Software**]: Security and Protection; K.4.1 [**Computers and Society**]: Public Policy Issues—*Abuse and crime involving computers*

General Terms

Security, Measurement

Keywords

Android; online advertising; click fraud; app testing; data mining; network traffic classification

1. INTRODUCTION

Online advertising is a financial pillar that supports both free Web content and services, and free mobile apps. Both web and mobile advertising use a similar infrastructure: the *ad library* embedded in the web page or mobile app fetches content from *ad providers* and displays it on the web page or the mobile app's user interface. The ad provider pays the developer for the ads displayed (*impressions*) and the ads clicked (*clicks*) by the user. Because web and mobile advertising use a similar infrastructure, they are subject to the same security concerns, such as tracking and privacy infringements [9, 27, 29]. Perhaps the biggest threat to the sustainability of this ecosystem is *ad fraud*, where a miscreant's code fetches ads without displaying them to the user or "clicks" on ads programmatically. Ad fraud has been extensively studied in the context of web advertising but has gone largely unstudied in the context of mobile advertising.

On the web, ad fraud is often perpetrated by botnets, which are collections of compromised user machines called bots. Fraudsters issue fabricated impressions and clicks using bots so that the traffic they generate is varied (i.e., by IP address), making the fraud harder to detect [28]. The two properties of botnets that make them useful for ad fraud are:

- Botnets are comprised bots, which are real user devices.

- Bots can be instructed to make arbitrary network requests silently to the user.

Both of these properties also apply to malicious Android applications. Moreover, while attackers have to compromise desktops to acquire bots, they can simply distribute their malicious applications through Android markets. Based on these observations, we hypothesize that Android (and mobile devices in general) are a lucrative target for those who commit ad fraud professionally.

We take the first step to study fraud and other undesirable behavior in mobile advertising. First, we identify unique characteristics of mobile ad fraud. On Android, at any time at most one app is running in the foreground, where the app has a UI. Our first observation is that when an app fetches ads while it is in the background, this is most likely fraudulent, because the app developer gets credit for this ad impression without displaying it to the user.[1] Our second observation is that when an app *clicks* an ad without user interaction, it is definitely fraudulent.

Based on our observations, we set out to measure the prevalence of ad fraud in the wild. We use two sets of apps: 1) 130,339 apps crawled from 19 Android markets including Play and many third-party markets, and 2) 35,087 apps that likely contain malware provided by a security company. We build a testing infrastructure, where we launch multiple instances of the Android emulator concurrently. In each emulator, we install an app from our datasets, run it for a fixed time, push it to the background, and continue running for a fixed time, while capturing all the network traffic from the emulator. Finally, we extract impressions, clicks, and other ad related activities from the network traffic.

We have to overcome a number of challenges, the biggest of which is how to identify ad impressions and clicks. The formats of impressions and clicks vary widely between different ad providers, so manually compiling a white list is laborious, unreliable, and prone to obsolescence. We propose a novel approach with three steps. First, we build *request trees* to link causally related HTTP requests (Section 4.2). Then, we use machine learning to discover new ad request pages based on known ones. Finally, based on the properties of ad clicks, we create rules to identify clicks from the HTTP request trees. From analyzing our datasets, we find that about 30% of apps with ads make ad requests while in running in the background, which may be malicious or indicate misconfiguration. In addition, 27 apps generate clicks without user interaction, which is definitely malicious. We find that the click fraud apps attempt to remain stealthy when fabricating ad traffic by only periodically sending clicks and changing which ad provider is being targeted between installations.

We call our system MAdFraud, which includes the testing infrastructure we used to run apps as well as the techniques used to identify impressions and clicks. The goal of MAdFraud is to automatically detect fraud behavior through black-box testing of apps alone, without the need to manually reverse engineer apps. In this way, our system can scale to large numbers of apps. Although the definition of ad fraud varies between ad providers as some ad providers only pay developers when ads are clicked, we define fraud as: 1) apps that show ads in the background, and 2) apps that click on ads without user interaction. Thus, MAdFraud exposes potentially fraudulent behaviors in apps but it is up to the ad providers to decide if the behavior is indeed fraudulent. From reviewing the terms and conditions

---

[1]One possibly legitimate exception is when the app tries to cache ad content while it is running in the background, but this is forbidden by the terms of service of many ad providers, as the app may never return to the foreground and therefore cannot guarantee that the cached content will ever be displayed on the UI.

of several ad providers [1, 19, 20], we find that all explicitly disallow (2) while only one explicitly disallows (1). It would be fairly trivial to enforce other definitions of fraud by analyzing the logs of impressions and clicks produced by MAdFraud. For example, the ad providers may restrict which other ad providers an app may contact. MAdFraud can be applied to other deployments, such as identifying ad behavior in network traffic captured from the wild, simply by re-training our machine learner on the new dataset (see Section 7). We make the following contributions:

- We take the first step to study ad fraud in mobile advertising by running a large number of apps and analyzing their network traffic.

- We propose a novel approach for automatically identifying ad impressions and clicks, which is the basis for detecting ad fraud.

- We discovered and analyzed various fraudulent ad behavior in mobile apps on popular markets.

2. BACKGROUND

2.1 Web Advertising

Advertising on the Internet is pervasive, and allows for services such as websites, search, and email to be provided to customers for free by including advertisements (ads) as part of the content displayed to the user. Website owners and other service providers (called *publishers* in advertising jargon) typically include ads through a third party called an *ad provider*, which handles finding and selecting advertisements, as well as paying publishers for ads shown to their users. On the Web, this is typically implemented as an `<iframe>` or `<script>` HTML element embedded in the publisher's webpage, with a `src` attribute that points to the ad provider's ad server. When the web page is loaded by a browser, the ad is populated via an *ad request*, which contains the publisher's ID and information about the user that is used to select a relevant ad (known as targeting information). The ad server returns three pieces of content once an ad is selected: the ad content URL, a click URL, and a pixel URL. The ad content is typically hosted by the ad provider (usually through a CDN) instead of the digital marketer who owns the ad, ensuring the content will be available when the ad is loaded. Marketers who are paying for their ads to be distributed by the ad provider want to guarantee the ad provider is not fraudulently billing them, so they themselves host a *tracking pixel* (or web bug) that is loaded by browsers along with the ad so that the marketers can independently verify that ads are being requested. Finally, the click URL indicates which web page should be opened when a user clicks on an ad. The click URL typically points to the ad provider's ad server, which records the clicks and then redirects the user to the marketer's landing page. A complete ad request, response, and display of the ad and pixel to the user is called an *impression*, and opening the click URL is a *click*. Publishers are paid based on how many impressions and clicks their content generates.

2.2 Web Ad Fraud

Unscrupulous publishers may inflate their ad revenues by having automated bots visit their website and click on ads.

This is referred to as ad fraud (or click fraud), and is a serious security issue as digital marketers who pay to have their ads shown online will not receive any business benefit for ads shown to bots. Although hard numbers on the amount of ad fraud is hard to determine, conservative estimates suggest 10% of Web ad traffic is due to fraud [11]. In order to receive revenue, fraudsters must remain undetected while issuing large numbers of ad requests and clicks. To do so, they employ a number of techniques. First, the ratio of click requests to requested ads is kept low (around 1% [28]) to avoid suspicion, as ads are rarely clicked on by real users. This means fraudsters issue far more ad requests than click requests. Second, fraudsters do not rely on a single publisher account, but rather have many accounts from many ad providers which they rotate through while issuing requests [28]. Not only does this mitigate the impact of any single account being detected, it also decreases the magnitude of fraudulent requests for each publisher ID and ad provider. Finally, fraudsters use botnets as the bots run code that consistently visits the fraudsters' webpages in the background and clicks on the ads located there, so that the fraudsters receive revenue. As mentioned in Section 1, botnets allow fraudsters to remain stealthy as the bots are real user devices which have been compromised.

2.3 Android App Advertising

Many Android applications are distributed for free on app markets, and use ads embedded in the user interface of the app to make money for the developer. The developer must register with an Android ad provider, which provides the developer with a publisher ID and an ad library to include in their app. The library is responsible for fetching and displaying ads when the app is being run. Requesting an ad for an app is analogous to doing so on the web: an ad request is made over HTTP to the ad server which includes the developer's publisher ID and user targeting information. The ad server returns the ad's content URL, click URL, and any tracking pixel URLs which must be fetched to display the ad. In fact, many ad libraries choose to implement making requests and displaying ads simply by loading a traditional HTML ad element in a web view. The primary difference between web and Android app advertising is that ad libraries are implemented in application code, and often contain special application-only logic, for example automatically collecting user targeting information or refreshing the ad.

3. DATASET

3.1 Crawled Apps

We evaluate our assumptions on 713,173 Android apps crawled from 19 markets including Google Play and numerous third-party markets. Since we are only interested in apps that can make network requests, we randomly selected 150,000 apps from the 669,591 apps that have the Internet permission. Due to incompatibilities with our analysis environment (e.g. mismatched API version and missing dependencies), we ran a total of 130,339 apps out of the 150,000 selected apps (see Section 5.1 for details on the failed apps). These apps were crawled between between October 30, 2012 and July 17, 2013. A breakdown of the 130,339 apps by market is shown in Table 1.

Market	Apps
Google Play	83,957
Anzhi	14,273
Gfan	8,423
Brothersoft	7,037
Opera	6,131
SlideME	4,627
m360	3,096
Android Online	2,174
1Mobile	1,650
Eoemarket	1,128
Goapk	628
AndAppStore	283
ProAndroid	278
Freeware Lovers	233
SoftPortal	216
Androidsoft	136
AppChina	74
AndroidDownloadz	39
PocketGear	36

Table 1: Market origins of the apps successfully run by MAdFraud. Since some apps appear on multiple markets, the total apps in the table is slightly more than the total 130,339 apps run.

3.2 Malware Apps

In addition to the dataset described above, we received 38,126 apps from a mobile security company between October 28, 2013 and November 16, 2013. According to the company, the dataset contains apps which are likely malware, but may contain some goodware as well. Regardless, the percentage of apps which are malware in this dataset is expected to be higher than in our crawled apps. We speculate the click fraud will be more pervasive in this dataset as ad fraud on the web is primarily conducted by bots.

3.3 Ad Provider Domains

In order to detect ad behavior, we must know which domains that ad providers use for their ad requests and clicks. We build our list using two domain blacklists [14, 25] which are curated to include only domains related to ad providers and analytics. We then manually removed domains related to the most popular analytics libraries. Unfortunately, even after pulling in two separate blacklists with one being specifically curated to include mobile ad providers, our list was not complete. Therefore, we supplement these lists with ad-related domains that we manually identified using AppBrain's list of popular ad libraries [2]. In total, we identified 3,118 ad-related domains, 3,062 from the blacklists and 56 manually.

4. METHODOLOGY

We wish to measure the prevalence of fraudulent and undesirable ad behavior (abbreviated simply as *ad fraud* henceforth) in Android applications. Based on common guidelines and terms of service in mobile advertising, we identify the following behavior as ad fraud:

- An Android app requesting ads while in the background, as it cannot display ads to the user (see a possible exception to this rule discussed in Section 1).

- An Android app generating clicks without user interaction.

To detect the above behavior, we design a dynamic analysis system to run apps in an emulator, capture their network traffic, and extract ad impressions and clicks from the traffic.

4.1 Running Android Apps

We run apps in our dataset in an Android emulator (API 17) and capture their network traffic. For each app, we create a new emulator image, install the app on the new emulator, run the app in the foreground for 60 seconds, put the app into the background, and run for another 60 seconds. To put the app in the background, we issue an intent to the emulator to open the browser on a static page hosted on our server. The HTTP request to this static page marks the boundary between the app's foreground and background activities in the captured network traffic. As we installed only one third-party app on the emulator, all the captured traffic not from the emulator (evident by a nonstandard TCP port) or browser (evident by our server's IP address in the IP header's source or destination) is attributed to this app. We choose not to interact with the app (i.e., touch events) even when it runs in the foreground to ensure that any ad clicks are generated without user interaction.

To analyze the packets captured by MAdFraud, we use the Bro Network Security Monitor [22]. Using Bro, we can reconstruct TCP flows and extract application protocol entities for HTTP and DNS traffic. For HTTP, these entities include fields from the HTTP request and response. From the HTTP request, we extract header fields as well as the URL and request body. From the HTTP response, we record the status code, response type, and any URLs in the unzipped response body. For DNS, these entities include the hostname in the DNS query and the IP addresses in the DNS response. We store all of these entities in a database for further analysis.

4.2 Request Trees

We can group HTTP requests logically together, as a response from the server may trigger additional HTTP requests. For example, a browser loading a web page may fetch static resources, such as JavaScript or images, to embed in the HTML. In this case, we can group the HTTP requests using the HTTP `referrer` header to form a tree of requests where the request to the HTML page is the root and requests to the static resources are the children. Intelligently constructing this HTTP *Request Tree* is important because it enables a number of techniques for automatically analyzing ad traffic, such as automatically detecting clicks.

We represent each HTTP request in an app's network traffic by a node in a request tree, and connect two nodes if and only if they are related according to three rules. The first two rules are based on the HTTP protocol specifications [3]: 1) the client may set the request `referrer` field to indicate to the server the URL that contained the requested URL, so we consider the former URL as the parent of the latter URL, and 2) the server may set the `location` header along with a redirection status code to redirect the client to a another URL, so we consider the original URL as the parent of the redirected URL. Finally, to account for when the referrer header is missing, we extract all the URLs in the HTTP response body of a node and consider the node as the parent of all the URLs (after URL normalization).

4.3 Ad Request Page Classifier

To identify ad fraud, we must first identify impressions in app network traffic, which begin with an ad request. Since there are many ad providers for Android (over 80 according to [2], and likely many more that are small or operate in other countries), it would be prohibitive to manually reverse engineer each ad provider's ad serving protocol to determine which URLs correspond with ad requests. Instead, we develop an approach for automatically identifying impressions using machine learning. From manually examining mobile ads in our previous work [27], we know ad requests have a common, characteristic format. They typically contain a large number of query parameters, such as the publisher ID and user and device information for selecting relevant ads, will receive at least three URLs in the response body, and are followed by HTTP requests to image content but not HTML or CSS. One naive approach would be to classify whether each HTTP request is an ad request directly; however, since this approach fails to consider any aggregate features, it would severely limit the features available to the classifier. Instead, we classify *request pages*, identified by the host and path names, which is the portion of URL before the '?' character that denotes the beginning of the query parameters. This allows us to extract features over the aggregate of all requests to each request page. We then classify whether each page is for requesting ads.

For each page we extract 33 features from three sources: 10 from query parameters, 16 from request trees, and 7 from HTTP headers. Since our classifier builds decision trees based on the predictiveness of features for the ground truth dataset, we include all the features that may be important based on our observations and then let the classifier determine which of these features are actually predictive. We measure the relative importance of these features in Section 5.2.2.

Features from query parameters.

For each page, we aggregate all the requests to it to measure two properties on each query parameter: whether the parameter is an enumeration and how many bits of entropy it contains. To determine whether a parameter is an enumeration, we compute the ratio of distinct values found for that parameter over the total number of times the parameter appeared in a request. Some parameters will only have a small number of distinct values, and we expect this ratio to be tiny (for example, the IMEI of the emulator will always be the same). On the other hand, if the ratio is near one, it implies that most requests have different values for this parameter, indicating that the parameter may take arbitrary values (for example, a timestamp field). We also compute the ratio of distinct values found for that parameter over the number of distinct apps (to account for fields that remain unchanged between requests for the same app, such as the publisher ID). We then segment these two ratios into several intervals and count the numbers of query parameters whose ratios are in each interval. These counts contribute six features to our classifier. To estimate the entropy of the values of a key, we first attempt to categorize the values into classes (e.g. numeric, alphanumeric) which have different entropy levels per character. We then multiply the determined entropy level by the average length of the values associated with each query parameter to determine the entropy level for the query parameter. We consider an entropy to be high if it has more than 2^{16} bits and low otherwise. We then count the number of query parameters that have high and low entropy, respectively, contributing two features to our classifier. The last two features describe the average and total number of query parameters, respectively.

Features from request trees.

These 16 features describe the structure of the request trees (Section 4.2). These features include the position in the request trees, such as the average height of trees containing the page, the average subtree height below the page, and the average depth of the page in the trees. We also extract features based on the number of children, the MIME types of the children, and the types of edges that connect the children to the parent.

Features from HTTP headers.

These 7 features include the status codes, the length of the requests, and the length of the replies, etc.

4.4 Finding Impressions and Clicks

With the classified ad request pages (Section 4.3) and HTTP request trees (Section 4.2), we can extract impressions and clicks for each app. It is tempting to simply consider each ad request as an impression. However, we found that many ad providers support *reselling* of ad impressions, where an ad request receives a new ad tag (i.e., an ad `<iframe>`) instead of ad content. This new ad tag then initiates another ad request, which may be resold again. Reselling of ad slots is done for business purposes: an ad provider may choose to buy ad slots from another ad provider so that the ad slots can be sold at a higher price to their own marketers, allowing for the provider to reach a larger target audience. For the purpose of measuring ad fraud, however, counting each resold ad request as an impression would be disingenuous, as the developer cannot control ad reselling and is paid only once regardless of how many times the ad is resold. To accurately measure the number of impressions, we consider an ad request as an impression only when none of its ancestors in the request tree are ad requests.

Besides impression fraud, another, perhaps more lucrative, revenue source for misbehaving apps is click fraud, where an app fabricates fraudulent clicks. There are two ways for apps to fabricate clicks without user interaction. First, the app may generate a touch event on the ad to trick the ad library to process it as a user click. Second, the app may parse the response body of the ad request and extract the click URL, and then make an HTTP request to the click URL. To detect either of these cases, we apply rules to the subtrees of ad request nodes in our request trees to determine if there is a path from an ad request node to a click node. We extracted the following rules by manually running apps in an emulator, clicking on their ads, analyzing their network traffic, and examining the properties of paths that led to ad clicks.

- Apps often handle clicks using HTTP redirection to send a request to the ad server before redirecting the user to the marketer's web page. Based on this observation, we look for an HTTP redirection in the subtree of an ad request node that ends on a node that received HTML as its response MIME type.

- Android apps have a variety of unique ways to handle clicks. For example, some clicks redirect to a `loca-tion` URL that has a `market://` schema, indicating the Google Play app should be launched. Similarly, we found an ad provider whose library downloads a `.apk` to the device after the user clicks an ad. To handle these cases as well as marketers that have HTTPS landing pages, we infer that an ad request that has a redirection in its subtree that redirects to a page with a schema other than `http://` contains a click.

Both of these rules require that the landing page be for a non-ad related hostname. We identify clicks in each app by building its request trees, finding all the impression nodes, and applying the above rules to each impression node. Figure 1 shows an example request tree with a click.

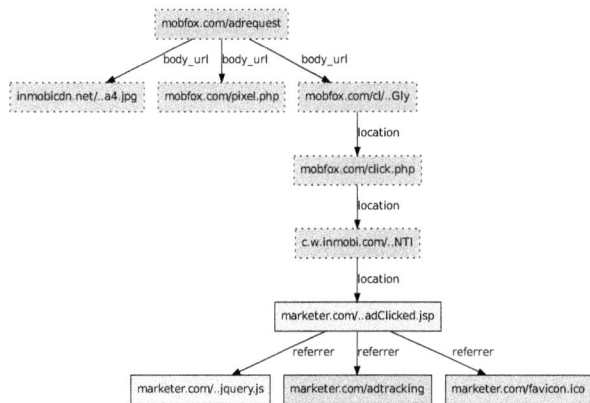

Figure 1: Example ad request tree with click. Nodes in blue are images and nodes in green are static web content. Nodes with a dotted outline are for requests with a known ad provider hostname. The ad request is the root, and its children are the ad image and a tracking pixel. The subtree on the right is the result of a click, with a redirect chain that ends on the marketer's homepage. All nodes have shortened URLs, for simplicity.

5. EVALUATION

We ran 130,339 of our crawled apps through MAdFraud. In total, these apps generated 1,807,379 HTTP requests, 508,005 of which we identify as being ad-related based on the hostname extracted from the request.

5.1 Apps without ad requests

77,461 apps made no HTTP request to a known ad provider hostname during the full duration of their runtime in MAdFraud. The possible reasons are: 1) the app crashes before it makes an ad request, 2) the app includes no ads, 3) the app requires user interaction to reach a UI state where ads are displayed, or 4) the ad library refuses to make ad requests when it detects the emulator environment.[2] To investigate why these apps make no ad requests, we ran a random sample of 7,500 (approx. 10%) apps through a separate tool called PyAndrazzi [12].

---

[2]We know of no ad libraries that do this.

127

Status	Apps
Ran to completion, no ads	3,807
Ran to completion, with ads	957
Missing Native Library	990
Unknown Error	733
App crash	573
API Version Mismatch	440

Table 2: Breakdown of PyAndrazzi's results for the 7,500 apps analyzed that made no ad requests when run through MAdFraud.

		Prediction		
		ARQ	$NARQ$	Recall
Truth	ARQ	28	11	71.8%
	$NARQ$	9	11,475	99.9%
	Precision	75.7%	99.9%	

Table 3: Confusion matrix of our ad request page classifier, computed using 3 fold cross-validation on our ground truth.

PyAndrazzi is a dynamic analysis framework designed to interact with apps and perform UI state exploration. Because it was originally designed to inspect how apps fail when their permissions are revoked, PyAndrazzi monitors apps extensively and can identify when and how the apps crash. This makes PyAndrazzi an ideal tool for determining whether apps are crashing, contain no ad libraries, or require interaction to reach a UI state where ads are displayed.

Table 2 shows that about 37% of the apps that did not generate ad traffic either crashed or failed to install properly on the emulator (due to missing x86 native libraries or an API mismatch). Both MAdFraud and PyAndrazzi use the x86 version of Android to speed up the Android emulator through hardware acceleration. However, some apps include native code for ARM devices but not x86 and thus cannot run correctly. In future work, we could address this limitation by running apps with ARM binaries on an ARM emulator. Among the apps that did run to completion, 957 made requests to a known ad provider. As these apps did not make ad requests during their analysis in MAdFraud, we conclude that these apps likely display ads on UI states that require user interaction.

5.2 Ad Request Page Classifier

5.2.1 Ground Truth

To build the ground truth dataset for identifying ad requests, we started with the most popular ad providers and manually investigated the pages that our apps requested. For each ad provider, if we were able to determine all the ad request pages for this ad provider by manually inspecting the HTTP traffic for each page, we labeled those pages as ARQ (ad requests) and all other pages for the ad provider as $NARQ$ (not ad requests). Otherwise, we excluded this ad provider from our ground truth dataset and instead use our trained classifier to automatically identify the ad request pages for this ad provider. We also identified the top domains used by apps that are not ad providers and labeled all their pages as $NARQ$. In total, we identified 39 pages as ARQ from 25 ad providers and 11,484 pages as $NARQ$.

Since the dataset is heavily skewed towards the $NARQ$ class, we use SMOTE [4] to over-sample the ARQ class. SMOTE is an algorithm for creating synthetic instances of a minority class to improve the classifier's sensitivity to the minority class. Once we have generated the new instances and added them to the ground truth, we then build a classifier using the `RandomForestClassifier` from scikit-learn [23]. The `RandomForestClassifier` creates a forest of decision trees by randomly selecting subsets of the feature space and training a decision tree using each subset. The

most predictive decision trees are weighted appropriately, and in turn indicate which features are the most predictive. Decision trees are an appropriate choice for our feature space as we include categorical (i.e., non-Euclidean) features, which popular algorithms like SVM and K-neighbors do poorly on.

To evaluate the performance of the classifier, we apply cross validation to the ground truth. We split the ground truth into 3 folds, train a classifier on 2 of those folds and then evaluate its performance on the remaining fold. In the evaluation, we include no synthetic data points generated by SMOTE and used for training. Table 3 shows the overall confusion matrix for the classifier during cross validation. It shows that the classifier has a very low false positive rate (00.1%) and that it achieves a reasonable true positive rate (71.8%). Since we will apply the classifier to unknown pages from ad providers to report on the number of ad requests, we prefer the classifier to have erred towards being more precise. Overall, the classifier had a class-weighted accuracy of 85.9%.

5.2.2 Feature Importance

Once we have trained the classifier, we can evaluate the relative importance of its features to investigate which features are the most predictive. We compute feature importance using scikit-learn's built-in method, which measures feature importance by calculating the depth of nodes that use the feature in the decision trees. The higher a feature appears in the trees, the more important it tends to be. Using this methodology, each feature is assigned an importance between 0 and 100% with the sum of all feature importance values equaling 100%.

Figure 2 shows the importance values of features excluding features whose importance values are less than 1%. It shows that nine out of the top ten features are derived from the query parameters, such as the number of enumeration parameters, the number of low and high entropy parameters, and the total number of parameters. Note that many of these features could not be computed from single requests, confirming our assertion that classifying request pages, which are aggregate requests, is more predictive than classifying individual requests (Section 4.3). The most predictive request tree features focus on the height of the tree, as opposed to features measured by analyzing the page's child nodes. This makes sense, as ad requests tend to vary more in their tree heights and their depths in the tree (due to ad reselling) than other types of pages. The fact that features measured from child nodes are not very predictive is likely due to differences between how ad servers respond to ad requests.

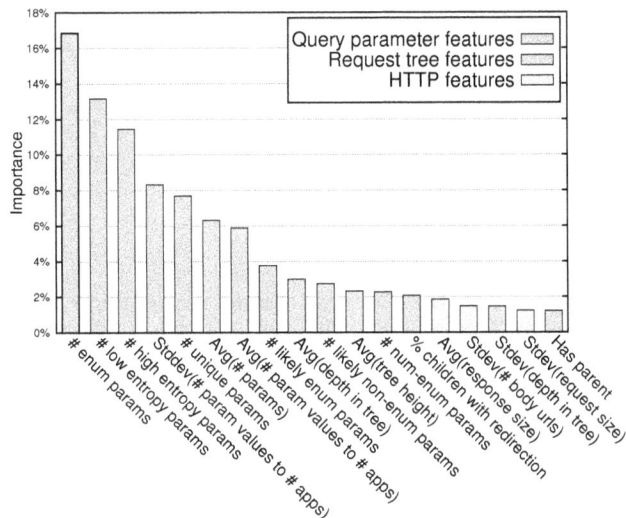

Figure 2: Feature importances ranking the predictability of each feature. Feature importances sum to 100%. Features with less than 1% importance are not shown.

5.2.3 Results

Using the ground truth described in Section 5.2.1, we build a classifier to apply to all the pages requested by apps in our dataset. First, as a prefiltering step, we eliminate all pages whose extension indicate that they are likely a static resource such as an image, JavaScript file, or CSS file, as static resources cannot be used for ad requests. After prefiltering, there are 100,611 pages to classify. When we applied the classifier to these pages, 715 pages were classified as *ARQs*, among them 678 pages were not present in the ground truth and 229 pages were for hostnames that had been known to be ad-related domains. As there are far too many non-ad-related domains to manually investigate, we instead investigated 30 domains whose pages the classifier was most confident were *ARQs* (the classifier computes a probability that the page is in each class). From the 30 domains, we were able to determine that 13 of the domains were ad-related. A common trend we found when analyzing these non-ad-related domains is that the pages used by analytics libraries, which are used to record information about the user's actions, are often misclassified as ad requests. These analytics pages have a very similar format to ad requests as they both rely on many query parameters to pass identifiers for the app, device, and user back to the server. This corroborates our earlier findings in Section 5.2.2 that the classifier primarily uses features based on the query parameters. To avoid over-estimating the number of ad requests performed by apps, we choose to consider only ad requests to pages with known ad-related hostnames. This results in 229 pages for 77 ad providers.

5.3 Request Trees

We build request trees for finding clicks based on impression nodes. Using the rules described in Section 4.4, we automatically found 60 clicks, among which 59 clicks we manually verified. The single false positive was caused by an ad image redirecting to an HTML page. We suspect that this is due to a misconfiguration in either the ad provider or the CDN hosting the ad image.

Apps...	Crawled Apps	Malware Apps
in dataset	150,000	38,126
successfully run	130,339	35,087
with HTTP traffic	88,305	24,957
with ad traffic	52,878	10,960
with impressions	40,409	8,974
with bg impressions	12,421	1,835
with clicks	21	6

Table 4: The number of apps at each stage of our analysis in our two datasets. *in dataset*: the number of apps examined. *successfully run*: the number that actually ran in our dynamic analysis environment. *with HTTP traffic*: the number of apps that had any HTTP traffic (not attributed to the emulator or MAdFraud). *with ad traffic*: the number of apps that have traffic to known ad provider hostnames. *with impressions*: the number of apps with impressions is calculated based on the ARQ pages identified by our classifier. *with bg impressions*: the number of apps making ad requests in the background. *with clicks*: the number of apps issuing clicks.

Occasionally, we cannot link clicks to their impressions due to ad providers that construct click URLs dynamically in application or JavaScript code. To identify clicks for these ad providers, we would have to either reverse engineer this logic to add special cases for them when constructing request trees, or manually determine which pages are associated with clicks and look for requests to these pages in app traffic. This limitation may have caused us to underestimate the number of clicks. In the case that an impression is resold, we find that the subsequent ad requests are always in the response body of their predecessors, as this is intrinsic to the mechanism for reselling ads. One caveat, however, is that it would be impossible to manually determine that two ad requests are part of a reselling chain if there is no referrer, body URL, or redirection to indicate that an impression was resold, without reverse engineering ad library logic. We speculate that this case would occur very rarely, if at all.

6. FINDINGS

We describe the results of our analysis on the network data captured from the crawled app and malware app datasets. We start by focusing on the 130,339 crawled apps, then in Section 6.3 we compare these results with the results of the 35,087 malware apps. Table 4 shows an overview of our results.

6.1 Market Comparison

We investigate the popularity of various ad providers in our crawled app dataset compared with the markets from which we downloaded the apps. We group the providers Admob and Doubleclick together under 'Admob', as they are both owned by Google and often appear together in ad traffic. Overwhelmingly, Admob is the most popular provider among the apps we ran; 47.21% of our apps make a network request to an Admob domain. Figure 3 shows the popularity of Admob across the 9 markets from which we downloaded a majority of our apps. The popularity of the remaining 8 most popular ad providers across these markets is shown in Figure 4. We can see that the Chinese providers WAPS and YouMi have much higher popularity among apps from Chinese markets (Anzhi, Gfan, m360, and Android Online) compared with their popularity on English (language) markets. Similarly, English ad providers are less popular on the Chinese markets, although Admob is still the most popular provider on m360 and Android Online. Finally, the ad provider Adlantis is the only popular ad provider which is neither English or Chinese; Adlantis is a Japanese ad provider. Its popularity in our dataset is surprising, as we do not crawl any Japanese markets.

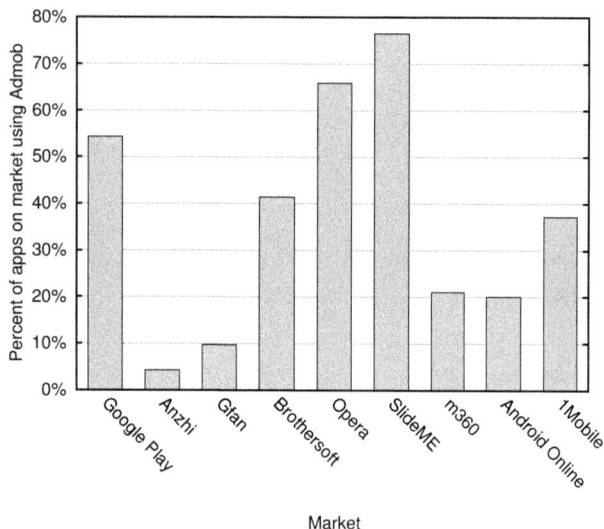

Figure 3: Popularity of Admob for apps from the top 9 Android markets, ordered by number of apps tested from that market. The y-axis is percentage of our crawled app dataset that appear on that market that make a request to an Admob domain.

6.2 Ad Fraud

Here we report on the ad behavior of our crawled app dataset. As previously mentioned, we identify two behaviors that are consistent with ad fraud: 1) apps which make ad requests in the background, and 2) apps that click on ads without user interaction.

6.2.1 Background Requests

We start by investigating which apps made ad requests while in the background. As previously mentioned, we run apps for 60 seconds in the foreground and 60 seconds in the background. We build request trees from the network captures of the apps and find impressions by looking for classified ad request pages in the request trees. Using the list of ARQ pages identified by our classifier, we find that 40,409 of our crawled apps generated a total of 274,128 impressions. Figure 5 shows a distribution of the number of impressions over time, relative to the start time of each app. From this figure, we can see a number of interesting patterns. First, most apps request an ad immediately upon startup without user interaction. 16,755 of the apps only request one ad during their run. Second, there is a clear periodicity to the distribution of impressions. This is because many Android ad libraries are configured to automatically refresh ads at constant intervals, the most common intervals being 30 seconds and 60 seconds. There appears to be a large spike at

60 seconds (the time when we put apps in the background) due to apps which are configured to request ads at these intervals. This is because these apps had initiated their ad request while in the foreground, but did not complete it until being put into the background. We do not wish to consider these impressions as fraudulent, as they do not indicate that the apps would have had the same behavior if they had been put into the background at a different time. Thus, we allow a 5-second grace period after apps are put into the background where we do not consider impressions as fraudulent. Based on this, we found 91,784 background impressions from 12,421 apps.

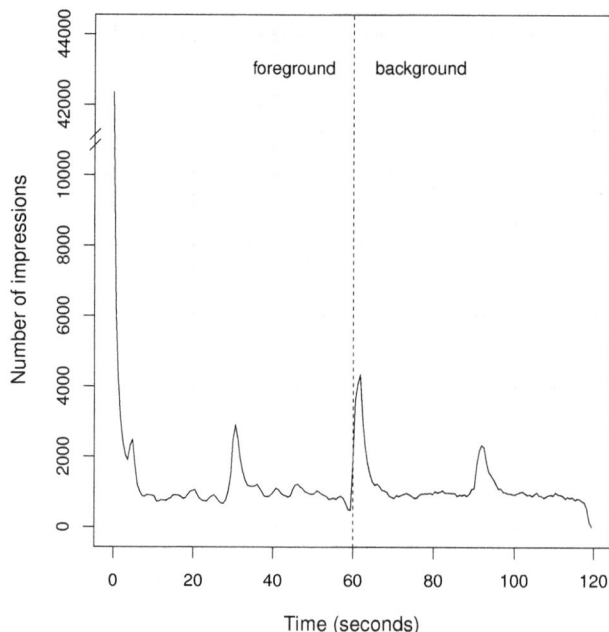

Figure 5: Distribution of the number of impressions over time, relative to the start time of each app.

Finally, the periodicity of ad requests continues after apps have been put into the background, implying some apps continue to run the ad library after losing focus. We expect that some of these cases are due to misconfiguration, however we do not attempt to determine intent. Regardless, requesting ads while the user is not using the app is undesirable behavior, as it is wasteful of device bandwidth and battery life, and may affect the ad provider's bookkeeping.

6.2.2 Click Fraud

We can now use the 274,128 request trees containing impressions that were found in the previous section to find apps that are fabricating clicks. We consider all clicks in our apps as fabricated, regardless of whether they were performed while the app was in the foreground or background, as we do not interact with the UI of our apps while running them. Using the click rules described in Section 4.4, we find that 21 apps fabricate a total of 59 clicks. We find that 24 of the clicks were performed in the foreground and 35 were performed in the background, indicating that the apps fabricating clicks continue doing so regardless of whether they are on the screen. We manually investigate the HTTP traffic for these 21 apps to confirm that they were all indeed

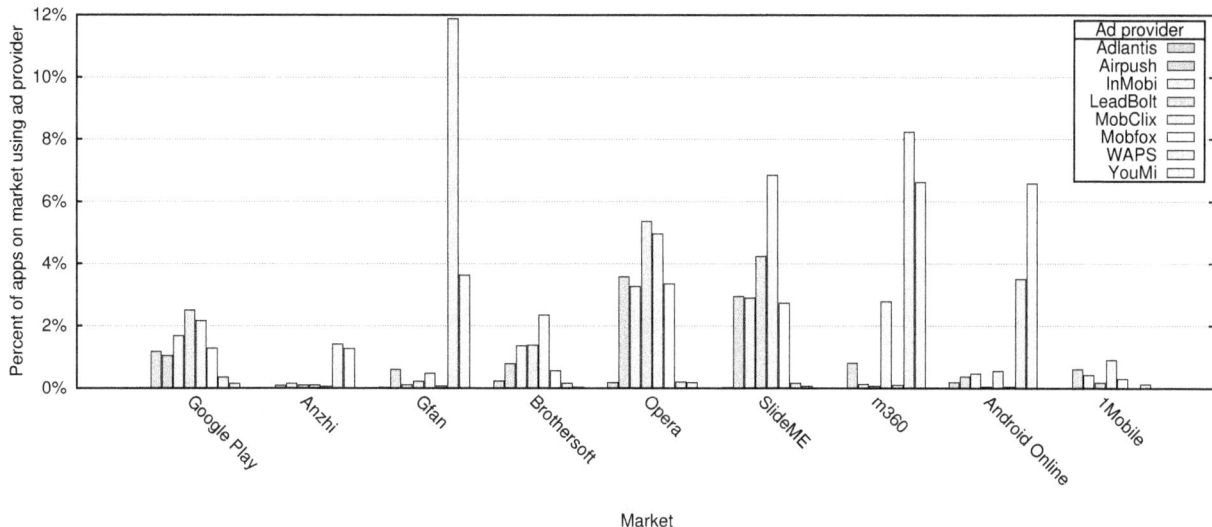

Figure 4: Popularity of the top 8 ad providers on the top 9 Android markets by percentage of apps. We omit Admob from the list of ad providers (but plot it in a separate figure, Figure 3) because of its overwhelming popularity.

click requests. This means that this result is a lower bound for the actual number of clicks across all ad providers. To further investigate the behaviors of these apps, we ran an additional experiment where we left the apps running for a total of twelve hours — six hours in the foreground and six hours in the background. The primary goal of this experiment was to determine whether the apps fabricate clicks for some period of time and then stop, or, if they continue to fabricate clicks on a regular interval indefinitely.

The results from this experiment are shown in Table 5 (along with six apps found to fabricate clicks in the malware dataset). Interestingly, only 16 of the 21 apps fabricated clicks when run a second time, perhaps to stay hidden. For each app, we show its source (either a market, the malware dataset, or '?' if the market information was missing), the number of installs the app had at the time it was crawled along with the number of impressions and clicks during the experiment. Lastly, we report the average interval of time between clicks, calculated as time between the first and last clicks divided by the total number of clicks, and list the ad providers whose impressions were clicked on.

There are a number of surprising results in this table. First, three apps on Google Play, collectively with thousands of installs, fabricated clicks. When we looked up the apps on the market, we found that only one of the three apps were still available. It is unclear whether these apps were removed due to the fraudulent ad behavior or for other reasons. Second, a number of apps have a very similar number of impressions and clicks. We speculate that the same miscreant may have uploaded separate apps with the same click fraud code. Third, only three ad providers appear in the table. This could be for a variety of reasons including, 1) these ad providers are easy to sign-up for, or 2) these ad providers have less sophisticated click fraud detection. Fourth, apps fabricate clicks to at most one ad provider during the experiment. To reduce their risk of being detected, we expect miscreants to rotate between different ad providers but this does not seem to be the case. Interestingly, some apps fabricated clicks to different ad providers during this experiment

than in the previous experiment. We speculate that the apps may select an ad providers on start-up rather than rotating while they are running.

6.3 Dataset Comparison

We analyze the network traffic generated from our malware apps and compare the result with our measurements from the crawled app dataset. Figure 6 shows the popularity of various ad providers in our crawled apps, malware apps, and from App Brain, an organization that presents statistics about Android apps on Google Play. App Brain publishes ad provider statistics [2] based on the *presence* of ad libraries in apps. It provides an interesting comparison to our results, which measure *usage* of ad libraries by apps. There are clear discrepancies between these three datasets. Notably, apps in the malware dataset prefer certain ad providers (WAPS, AdsMogo, AppLovin) while avoiding other (Admob, Mobclix). This could be due to certain providers vetting developers more aggressively, or because malware apps may target non-English markets. The popularity of Airpush in the malware dataset is explained by the numerous security and privacy infringements found in the Airpush ad library [26], meaning some of the apps in the malware dataset may only be there because they include the Airpush library. Finally, we note that App Brain's methodology for measuring ad provider popularity does not indicate which providers are actually used. Unused libraries may be dead code, or used only rarely by apps. In addition, determining which libraries are included in an app using only static analysis is complicated by programs like Proguard [24], which obfuscate package and class names for Android apps.

6.3.1 Ad Fraud Differences between Datasets

We now investigate the prevalence of fraudulent ad behavior in the malware dataset. We find a total of 8,974 apps made 57,619 impressions overall, and that 1,835 apps made 16,565 impressions while in the background. Of the clicks we measured, 27 clicks were generated from 6 apps in the malware dataset. Interestingly, the rates of fraudulent behavior

App	Source	# Installs	# Impressions	# Clicks	Click Interval (s)	Ad providers
79b85a	Opera	236	63	18	1,935.6	MobFox
9e5b41	SlideME	915	63	18	1,925.7	MobFox
f56bda	Google Play	1,000	63	17	2,049.3	MobFox
5a6fc0	Opera	117	54	6	5,795.6	MobFox
63fd85	Opera	255	54	6	5,798.7	MobFox
76a7dc	Opera	125	54	6	5,797.3	MobFox
86cd17	SlideME	915	54	5	6,956.4	MobFox
94bfa8	Google Play*	500	4,366	5	8,353.1	Migital
7bb12f	1Mobile	N/A	4,392	4	6,717.8	Migital
807a0a	BrotherSoft	N/A	98	2	0	AppsGeyser
d9162a	BrotherSoft	N/A	4,385	2	16,919.2	Migital
57b67c	Google Play*	10,000	56	1	N/A	AppsGeyser
a3d816	?	N/A	4,381	3	10,000	Migital
b611ea	?	N/A	4,374	1	N/A	Migital
c7681c	?	N/A	4,416	1	N/A	Migital
d55ece	?	N/A	4,384	1	N/A	Migital
c31310	Malware	N/A	63	15	2,323.1	MobFox
1fcc39	Malware	N/A	54	6	5,796.5	MobFox
247e2e	Malware	N/A	414	6	5,797.6	MobFox
721797	Malware	N/A	414	6	5,796.0	MobFox
35e164	Malware	N/A	54	5	6,956.1	MobFox
9863d9	Malware	N/A	414	5	6,955.2	MobFox
Total		14,063	32,670	139		

Table 5: Results of running apps that fabricate clicks for six hours. During the experiment, only 22 (16 crawled from various markets and 6 from our malware dataset) of the 27 apps tested fabricated clicks after being found doing so in previous experiments. An asterisk next to an app from Google Play indicates that the app is no longer available. Apps whose sources are labeled '?' were downloaded by our crawlers but their markets were not recorded.

in the malware dataset tend to be lower than those in the crawled dataset. For example, 9.5% of crawled apps have an impression in the background, whereas 5.2% of malware apps have an impression in the background. This could be due to a number of factors. First, this could mean that malware apps do not commonly perform ad fraud (remember the malware dataset contains apps that are likely malware, but also includes some goodware). On the other hand, the security company that collected the malware samples may not check for ad fraud. Lastly, malware may be more likely to perform emulator detection and thus would avoid performing malicious activities if the malware apps detect that they are run in an emulator. The relationship between malware and ad fraud on Android is an interesting direction for future work.

7. LIMITATIONS

Here we discuss limitations of our study. We first discuss three limitations that may have led us to underestimate the prevalence of fraud behavior in apps. First, we ran apps in emulators instead of on real devices. It is possible, though we have not observed it, that some ad libraries may refuse to display ads while in an emulator, and some fraud apps may not send fraudulent traffic to avoid being analyzed. Second, we do not interact with the apps and thus we may not reach a UI state where apps would perform fraud. Given that our work was inspired by botnet ad fraud on the web, we would like to find apps which issue fabricated impressions and clicks silently to the user. Fraud apps which only perform fraud on certain UI states risk not being able to perform the fraud when users are not interacting with the app. Regardless, if exploring the UI of apps

is desirable, MAdFraud could be run using a more sophisticated dynamic analysis tool which can explore the UI state of apps without accidentally clicking on ads (in Section 5.1 we ran MAdFraud using the output of the PyAndrazzi dynamic analysis tool, for example). Designing such a system is non-trivial, however, as different ad libraries implement ads differently. Thus, heuristic approaches would be prone to false positives, where ads are clicked accidentally, causing MAdFraud to flag the apps as having click fraud. This may cause us to overestimate our results. Third, we ran all our emulators on a single static IP address. It is possible that some ad providers may have blocked our IP address during our experiments. However, given the prevalence of NAT in our network and that we run no more than 70 apps concurrently, we believe that this is unlikely.

Lastly, we discuss a type of fraud our system cannot detect, *display fraud* where apps obscure or hide ads in the UI of the app. Liu, et al. [13] investigate display fraud on Windows Mobile via a system called DECAF which analyzes the UI structure of apps. Their approach is complementary to our system, as the two systems detect different types of ad fraud. The display fraud detected by DECAF requires the user to run the app (so that ads can be obscured), and to interact with it (so that the user can be coerced into clicking on an ad). On the other hand, MAdFraud detects fraud that is performed silently to the user, either ads requested in the background or ad clicks without user interaction. If we combine the methodologies of MAdFraud and DECAF, we could detect new types of fraud that neither system can detect currently; for example, apps that request ads while running in the foreground but do not put the ad in the UI of the app.

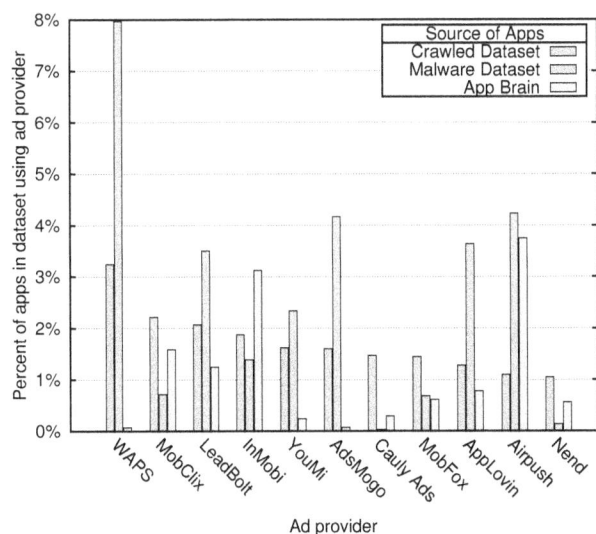

Figure 6: Ad provider popularity by dataset. The list of ad providers differs slightly from those in Figures 4 and 3 because those figures were limited to apps on the top markets. The results from our crawled dataset may overestimate the popularity of ad providers as we only select apps that have the INTERNET permission. Again, we omit Admob from the list of ad providers because of its overwhelming popularity. In comparison, Admob is in 47.21%, 28.3%, and 36.64% of crawled apps, malware apps, and App Brain apps, respectively.

8. RELATED WORK

8.1 Web Advertising

Ad fraud has been studied extensively in the context of online Web advertising. Daswani [6] provides an overview of terms and techniques used for Web ad fraud. Many detection and defense techniques have been proposed to combat web ad fraud. Some detection techniques focus on detecting *duplicate clicks* [30, 17], where a publisher inflates its clicks by clicking the same ad many times. Other techniques detect fabricated impressions and clicks by aggregating ad traffic across client IP addresses and cookie IDs and looking for clients whose ad traffic deviates from expected behavior [16, 18] However, both of these techniques are thwarted by sophisticated botnet ad fraud [28], which uses many compromised machines to vary the IP addresses and cookie ID of fraudulent requests. Fraud performed on many mobile devices would be similarly resistant to these detection techniques. Defenses against ad fraud focus on defeating economic incentives of fraud [21, 15] or using false ads to find malicious publishers [10].

8.2 Mobile Advertising

There is very little security research on ad fraud on mobile devices. Notably, Liu [13] investigates *display fraud* on Windows Mobile, which uses techniques that analyze the UI of apps to determine if developers are hiding, obfuscating, or stacking ads to increase their ad revenue or coercing users to click ads. These techniques would not be able to detect when apps fabricate ad traffic in the background. Symantec [5] and Lookout [7], two security companies, pro-

vide case studies of malware which uses ad fraud to make money. These include a type of click fraud called *search engine poisoning*, where search engine results can be modified by clicking on links in search engine results to increase their page rank. We note that despite similar nomenclature, this type of click fraud is independent of ad click fraud. Finally, plagiarized applications have been found to use advertising to make money by replacing the ad libraries of victim applications with libraries configured to use the plagiarist's account details [8]. Despite the damage that plagiarism causes to developers, this attack is not ad fraud, as plagiarized apps will still show ads to users.

9. CONCLUSION

We have taken the first step to study mobile ad fraud on a large scale. We developed a system and approach, MAdFraud, for running mobile apps, capturing their network traffic, and identifying ad impressions and clicks. To deal with the wide variety of formats of ad impressions and clicks, we proposed a novel approach for automatically identifying ad impressions and clicks in three steps. We discovered and analyzed various fraudulent behavior in mobile ads.

Acknowledgements This paper is based upon work supported by the National Science Foundation under Grant No. 1018964 and by the Intel Science and Technology Center for Secure Computing. Any opinions, findings, and conclusions or recommendations expressed in this material are those of the authors and do not necessarily reflect the views of the National Science Foundation or the Intel Science and Technology Center for Secure Computing.

We would like to thank the anonymous reviewers for their insightful feedback. For his help obtaining Android apps, we would like to thank Clint Gibler. For helping us evaluate our apps that did not make ad requests, we would like to thank Eric Gustafson and Kristen Kennedy. Finally, for helping us manually investigate click URLs, we would like to thank Sam Dawson.

References

[1] *AdSense Terms and Conditions*. URL: https://www.google.com/adsense/localized-terms.

[2] AppBrain. *Android Ad Networks*. 2013. URL: http://www.appbrain.com/stats/libraries/ad.

[3] T. Berners-Lee, R. Fielding, and H. Frystyk. *Hypertext Transfer Protocol – HTTP/1.0*. 1996. URL: http://www.isi.edu/in-notes/rfc1945.txt.

[4] Nitesh V Chawla, Kevin W Bowyer, Lawrence O Hall, and W Philip Kegelmeyer. "SMOTE: Synthetic Minority Over-sampling Technique". In: *Journal of Artificial Intelligence Research* 16 (2002), pp. 321–357.

[5] Eric Chien. *Motivations of Recent Android Malware*. Tech. rep. Technical Report, Symantec Security, 2013.

[6] Neil Daswani et al. "Online advertising fraud". In: *Crimeware: understanding new attacks and defenses* (2008).

[7] John Gamble. *MaClickFraud: Counterfeit Clicks and Search Queries*. 2013. URL: https://blog.lookout.com/blog/2013/11/01/maclickfraud-counterfeit-clicks-and-search-queries/.

[8] Clint Gibler et al. "AdRob: Examining the Landscape and Impact of Android Application Plagiarism". In: *Proceedings of 11th International Conference on Mobile Systems, Applications and Services.* 2013.

[9] Michael C Grace, Wu Zhou, Xuxian Jiang, and Ahmad-Reza Sadeghi. "Unsafe exposure analysis of mobile in-app advertisements". In: *Proceedings of the fifth ACM conference on Security and Privacy in Wireless and Mobile Networks.* ACM. 2012, pp. 101–112.

[10] Hamed Haddadi. "Fighting online click-fraud using bluff ads". In: *ACM SIGCOMM Computer Communication Review* 40.2 (2010), pp. 21–25.

[11] *How Facebook Beats Ad Fraud.* URL: `http : / / www . businessweek . com / articles / 2013 - 11 - 26 / how-facebook-beats-ad-fraud`.

[12] Kristen Kennedy, Eric Gustafson, and Hao Chen. "Quantifying the Effects of Removing Permissions from Android Applications". In: *Workshop on Mobile Security Technologies (MoST).* 2013.

[13] Bin Liu, Suman Nath, Ramesh Govindan, and Jie Liu. "DECAF: Detecting and Characterizing Ad Fraud in Mobile Apps". In: *Presented as part of the 11th USENIX Symposium on Networked Systems Design and Implementation (NSDI 14).* Seattle, WA: USENIX, 2014.

[14] Peter Lowe. *Ad blocking with ad server hostnames and IP addresses.* 2013. URL: `http://pgl.yoyo.org/as/`.

[15] Mohammad Mahdian and Kerem Tomak. "Pay-per-action model for online advertising". In: *Proceedings of the 1st international workshop on Data mining and audience intelligence for advertising.* ACM. 2007, pp. 1–6.

[16] Ahmed Metwally, Divyakant Agrawal, and Amr El Abbadi. "Detectives: detecting coalition hit inflation attacks in advertising networks streams". In: *Proceedings of the 16th international conference on World Wide Web.* ACM. 2007, pp. 241–250.

[17] Ahmed Metwally, Divyakant Agrawal, and Amr El Abbadi. "Duplicate detection in click streams". In: *Proceedings of the 14th international conference on World Wide Web.* ACM. 2005, pp. 12–21.

[18] Ahmed Metwally, Divyakant Agrawal, Amr El Abbadi, and Qi Zheng. "On hit inflation techniques and detection in streams of web advertising networks". In: *Distributed Computing Systems, 2007. ICDCS'07. 27th International Conference on.* IEEE. 2007, pp. 52–52.

[19] *Millennial Media Terms and Conditions.* URL: `https: //tools.mmedia.com/login/termsAndConditions/ index`.

[20] *MobFox Terms of Service.* URL: `http://www.mobfox. com/terms-of-service/`.

[21] Hamid Nazerzadeh, Amin Saberi, and Rakesh Vohra. "Dynamic cost-per-action mechanisms and applications to online advertising". In: *Proceedings of the 17th international conference on World Wide Web.* ACM. 2008, pp. 179–188.

[22] Vern Paxson. "Bro: a system for detecting network intruders in real-time". In: *Computer networks* 31.23 (1999), pp. 2435–2463.

[23] F. Pedregosa et al. "Scikit-learn: Machine Learning in Python". In: *Journal of Machine Learning Research* 12 (2011), pp. 2825–2830.

[24] *ProGuard.* URL: `http://proguard.sourceforge.net/`.

[25] Dominik Schürmann. *Adaway.* 2013. URL: `http:// sufficientlysecure.org/index.php/adaway/`.

[26] T. Spring. *Sneaky Mobile Ads Invade Android Phones.* 2013. URL: `http : / / www . pcworld . com / article / 245305 / sneaky \ _mobile \ _ads \ _invade \ _android \ _phones.html`.

[27] Ryan Stevens, Clint Gibler, Jon Crussell, Jeremy Erickson, and Hao Chen. "Investigating user privacy in android ad libraries". In: *Workshop on Mobile Security Technologies (MoST).* 2012.

[28] Brett Stone-Gross et al. "Understanding fraudulent activities in online ad exchanges". In: *Proceedings of the 2011 ACM SIGCOMM conference on Internet measurement conference.* ACM. 2011, pp. 279–294.

[29] Vincent Toubiana, Arvind Narayanan, Dan Boneh, Helen Nissenbaum, and Solon Barocas. "Adnostic: Privacy Preserving Targeted Advertising." In: *NDSS.* 2010.

[30] Linfeng Zhang and Yong Guan. "Detecting click fraud in pay-per-click streams of online advertising networks". In: *Distributed Computing Systems, 2008. ICDCS'08. The 28th International Conference on.* IEEE. 2008, pp. 77–84.

EnCore: Private, Context-based Communication for Mobile Social Apps

Paarijaat Aditya[†]   Viktor Erdélyi[†]   Matthew Lentz[‡]

Elaine Shi[‡]   Bobby Bhattacharjee[‡]   Peter Druschel[†]

[†]Max Planck Institute for Software Systems   [‡]University of Maryland

ABSTRACT

Mobile social apps provide sharing and networking opportunities based on a user's location, activity, and set of nearby users. A platform for these apps must meet a wide range of communication needs while ensuring users' control over their privacy. In this paper, we introduce EnCore, a mobile platform that builds on *secure encounters* between pairs of devices as a foundation for privacy-preserving communication. An encounter occurs whenever two devices are within Bluetooth radio range of each other, and generates a unique encounter ID and associated shared key. EnCore detects nearby users and resources, bootstraps named communication abstractions called *events* for groups of proximal users, and enables communication and sharing among event participants, while relying on existing network, storage and online social network services. At the same time, EnCore puts users in control of their privacy and the confidentiality of the information they share. Using an Android implementation of EnCore and an app for event-based communication and sharing, we evaluate EnCore's utility using a live testbed deployment with 35 users.

Categories and Subject Descriptors

C.2.0 [**Computer-Communication Networks**]: Security and protection; D.4.4 [**Operating Systems**]: Communications Management—*Network communication*; K.6.5 [**Management of Computing and Information Systems**]: Security and Protection

Keywords

Location-based services, Privacy, Mobile computing, Pervasive computing, Social networking, Proximity-based services

1. INTRODUCTION

Mobile social apps consider users' location, activity, and nearby devices to provide context-aware services; e.g.,

MobiSys'14, June 16–19, 2014, Bretton Woods, New Hampshire, USA.
ACM 978-1-4503-2793-0/14/06.
http://dx.doi.org/10.1145/2594368.2594374.

detecting the presence of friends (Highlight, Foursquare [5, 9]), sharing recommendations about sights, goods and services (Foursquare), sharing content or gossip (FireChat, Whisper, Secret [4, 16, 19]), gaming (Nintendo 3DS, Sony PlayStation Vita [15, 17]), and connecting strangers who met but failed to exchange contact details (SMILE, Smokescreen [29, 49]). Users of these increasingly popular apps are exposed to various privacy risks. Most currently deployed mobile social apps rely on a trusted cloud service [5, 9] to match and relay information, requiring users to reveal their whereabouts, the perils of which have been extensively noted [7, 24, 27, 52, 59].

Some recent apps [1, 4] additionally use device-to-device (D2D) communication via short-range radio (e.g., Bluetooth, Wi-Fi Direct). D2D communication permits new capabilities: first, devices can precisely identify nearby devices, enabling powerful ad hoc communication and sharing. Second, D2D enables devices to create pairwise shared keys, which can be used to bootstrap secure and private communication without a trusted broker.

Recognizing this opportunity, new secure D2D handshake protocols, such as SMILE [49], SmokeScreen [29] and SDDR [47] have been developed. Our own prior work, SDDR, provides a *secure encounter* abstraction: pairs of co-located devices establish a unique encounter ID and associated shared key using D2D communication, which encounter peers can subsequently use for secure communication. While specific apps have been built using encounters [29, 49], no platform exists that relies on encounters to enable a wide range of privacy-preserving mobile social communication and sharing.

In this paper, we leverage the notion of addressable secure encounters introduced in SDDR to build EnCore, a communication platform that provides powerful new capabilities to mobile social apps. Using EnCore, apps can:

- Rely on encounters to conveniently and securely bootstrap *events*, which represent socially meaningful groups of proximal users and are associated with inferred context and user annotations.

- Send, receive, share, organize and search information and contacts by referring to events by their name, time or location, while maintaining confidentiality and full control over participants' anonymity and linkability.

- Use *conduits* to distribute and store information within events, before, during and after the actual social event. Current conduits rely on e-mail, Dropbox and Facebook.

To illustrate the space of apps supported by EnCore, consider a scenario of tourists visiting a site. While there, visitors wish to share live recommendations on nearby sights, shows to attend and eateries to try, but do not wish to reveal any (long-term) linkable information about themselves. If, unbeknownst to them, a friend or person with a shared interest is in the area, they would like to be notified, yet they wish to remain anonymous to all others. At a later time, attendees may like to share content (e.g., photos) and commentary related to the visit, but only with those who were there. Lastly, some might wish to follow up with a special person they met but failed to exchange contact information with. EnCore supports all these capabilities and more.

The primary contributions of this paper are as follows:

- We present the design of EnCore and its implementation on Android devices.

- We demonstrate EnCore's capabilities through *Context*, an Android application that provides communication, sharing, collaboration and organization based on events. The application was shaped by user feedback from a series of testbed deployments.

- We implement a variant of the SDDR protocol over Bluetooth 4.0. SDDR-4 takes full advantage of the new broadcast and low-energy features of Bluetooth 4.0, and is compatible with existing Bluetooth 2.1 accessories without compromising privacy.

- We report on a series of live deployments of *Context* and EnCore, with 35 users at MPI-SWS.

The live deployments described in this paper cover only a subset of the scenarios supported by EnCore, namely those involving colleagues within an organization. Events involving complete strangers, on the other hand, would require physical gatherings of people who do not know each other and who run an app based on EnCore. This requires wide adoption within a local community of sufficient size, or minimally a large event in which participants are incentiviced to run the app. We hope to be able to arrange such deployments as part of future work.

Roadmap.

The rest of this paper is organized as follows: We sketch related work in Section 2, discuss EnCore's capabilities and requirements in Section 3, and present the design of EnCore in Section 4. The *Context* app, which makes the capabilities of EnCore available to mobile users, is described in Section 5. The Android implementation of our prototype is sketched in Section 6. We present the results of our experiments and testbed deployment in Section 7, discuss risks and challenges in Section 8 and conclude in Section 9.

2. RELATED WORK

Mobile social apps Most currently deployed mobile social apps like Foursquare [5], Whisper [19] and Highlight [9] rely on a cloud service to match co-located devices and relay data among them. Users must trust the provider with their whereabouts, activities and social encounters.

More recent systems like LoKast [11], AllJoyn [1], Haggle [8, 57] and Musubi [32], as well as lost-and-found apps like Tile [18], use D2D radio communication, which enables infrastructure-independent and accurate detection of nearby devices (e.g., those within Bluetooth range). In principle, these systems could be designed so that users do not have to trust the cloud provider with their sensitive data. Unfortunately, once Bluetooth discoverability is enabled, devices can be tracked even when they are not actively communicating, introducing a new threat to privacy. Unlike the tracking of cellular phones by mobile operators, such "Bluetooth surveillance" by stores and businesses is not regulated [42].

EnCore relies on D2D radio communication, but incorporates an efficient periodic MAC-address change protocol that ensures users cannot be tracked using their MAC address. The EnCore handshake protocol is provably secure and does not leak users' identity or profile information except to selected users.

The AirDrop [10] service in Apple's iOS 7 enables iPhone users to share content with nearby devices. AirDrop uses Bluetooth for device discovery and token setup, and an ad hoc Wi-Fi network to transfer data. AirDrop is designed for synchronous pairwise sharing among co-located users. Android Beam [2] is similar to AirDrop but relies on NFC [14] to initiate communication by physically placing devices back to back, and uses Bluetooth or Wi-Fi Direct [20] to transfer content. EnCore instead enables communication with all encountered EnCore devices, both during and after co-location. Moreover, EnCore prevents tracking, and supports anonymous and group communication.

Life-logging apps Friday [6] keeps an automated journal of user activities such as calls, SMSes, location history, photos taken and music history for browsing and sharing purposes. Memoto [13] is a life-logging camera that takes a picture every 30 seconds. The Funf framework used in the Social fMRI project [21] is a platform for social and behavioral sensing apps. Since all these services upload the collected data to the cloud, users have to trust the cloud provider with their private information.

Private mobile social communication systems SMILE [49] is a mobile "missed connections" application, which enables users to contact people they previously met, but for whom they do not have contact information. SMILE creates an identifier and an associated shared key for any set of devices that are within Bluetooth range at a given time. Users can subsequently exchange messages (encrypted with the shared key) anonymously through a cloud-based, untrusted mailbox associated with the encounter ID.

In SmokeScreen [29], devices periodically broadcast two types of messages, *clique signals* (CSs) and *opaque identifiers* (OIDs). CSs enable private presence sharing, announcing the device's presence to any nearby member of a mutually trusting clique of devices (e.g., friends). The sender's identity can be determined from the signal only by clique members, who share a secret. OIDs enable communication with strangers. A trusted broker can resolve OIDs to the identity of their sender, assuming that two or more devices agree to mutually reveal their identities. In comparison, EnCore supports anonymous communication with strangers without requiring a trusted broker.

SPATE [48] uses physical encounters among mobile devices to allow users to explicitly establish private communication channels, so that they can communicate and share data securely in the future. SPATE does not address anonymity, does not support communication among strangers who did not explicitly introduce their devices, and does not provide a way to address devices by referring to a shared context.

PIKE [22] is a key exchange protocol designed for secure proximity-based communication among the participants of an event. Keys are exchanged using an existing service like Google Calendar or Facebook, which require knowledge of the contact details for each participant. EnCore, on the other hand, leverages encounters to exchange keys with previously known and unknown participants, and without explicit user action.

SDDR: Secure Device Discovery and Recognition SDDR [47] builds on the encounter-based communication style introduced by SMILE, adding selective and unilaterally revocable linkability. The SDDR handshake protocol is provably secure, non-interactive and energy-efficient. SDDR attempts to form a pairwise encounter with each nearby device, establishing a shared key in the process. SDDR can also recognize specific users or users with specific attributes if both peers in an encounter agree to be recognized by each other, while remaining unlinkable by other devices. This *selective linkability* can be revoked and reinstated efficiently and unilaterally by each peer.

To prevent devices from being linked across encounters by their link-layer addresses, SDDR changes the MAC address every "epoch" (roughly every 15 minutes). However, periodic address changes are not natively supported in Bluetooth 2.1 and cause established connections to reset. As described in Section 6, our SDDR implementation over Bluetooth 4.0 maintains all of the security properties of SDDR over Bluetooth 2.1, and preserves interaction with legacy accessories and devices.

Privacy-preserving MAC protocols SlyFi [36] is a link layer protocol for 802.11 networks that obfuscates packet bits, including MAC address identifiers and management information, in order to prevent adversaries from identifying or tracking users in an application-independent manner. EnCore addresses the complementary concern of enabling anonymous, context-based communication based on encounters. EnCore, however, additionally includes a Bluetooth MAC address change protocol to prevent cross-encounter linking. Bluetooth 4.0 [3] is a new protocol that incorporates low-power, low-latency discovery and security extensions relevant to EnCore. We discuss Bluetooth 4.0 in Section 6.1.

Location privacy Several works investigate location privacy for mobile devices [35, 37, 38, 41, 56]. Roughly speaking, the following two classes of approaches have been proposed. The first class proposes to send fake or perturbed location data, or send location data at coarser granularity [35, 38, 41, 44, 56]. This class of approach essentially trades off utility with privacy. The second class of approaches does not require data obfuscation, but resorts to anonymity [37, 38, 40]. For example, Koi [37] sends unperturbed locations to a cloud server; however, the location is not linkable with a user's identity (assuming two non-colluding servers). In comparison with these approaches, EnCore achieves location privacy without relying on trusted, centralized infrastructure.

Device discovery Energy-efficient device discovery in wireless networks has been studied extensively [25,33,39,45, 60]. EnCore currently uses a simple, static device discovery scheme, but could easily incorporate the more sophisticated protocols in the literature. Other work aims to enable users to prove that they were in a particular location [46, 54]. EnCore addresses the orthogonal problem of allowing users to prove that they were in the vicinity of certain other devices. The Unmanaged Internet Architecture [34] (UIA) provides zero-configuration naming and routing for personal devices. While it shares with EnCore the goal of enabling seamless communication among personal devices, UIA is not concerned with the specific communication model and privacy needs of mobile social applications.

3. ENCORE: CAPABILITIES AND REQUIREMENTS

In this section, we describe EnCore's capabilities in light of the communication requirements of mobile social apps and the privacy needs of users. EnCore provides its capabilities without relying on a third-party provider that is entrusted with users' whereabouts, activities and social encounters.

3.1 Detecting nearby users and resources

A basic requirement of mobile social apps is the detection of nearby resources and users. EnCore's secure encounters enable this capability using D2D communication. Detecting nearby resources has several variants:

Discovering when a known friend is nearby Friends can be members of certain online social network circles (e.g., friends, family, colleagues), or specific users that have previously paired their devices. For privacy reasons, a user should be able to control discoverability by individuals or circles manually, and based on the present time, location, or activity. Moreover, a user's device should be unlinkable by all other devices.

Discovering relevant resources and nearby strangers that match a profile The profile might include interests (e.g., "tango") or relationship status (e.g., "single male age 27 seeking female"). For privacy reasons, a user should be able to control discoverability by individual profile attributes manually, and based on the present time, location, or activity. Moreover, an attribute should be visible only to devices that advertise a matching attribute.

Keeping a record of (strangers') devices encountered This record is useful to communicate and share information related to a shared experience, taking place in the present (e.g., sharing recommendations for menu items while at a restaurant) or in the past (e.g., sharing selected photos from a joint tour bus ride). For privacy reasons, this record must not contain personally identifying or linkable information.

3.2 Event-based communication/sharing

Mobile social apps enable communication among members of a social event like a meeting or gathering. A key abstraction in EnCore is an *event*, a set of encounters relevant to a social event along with inferred context and user annotations. Typically, an event includes a subset of a device's ongoing encounters at a given time, and a device may be part of multiple concurrent events. For instance, while at a restaurant, Alice's device may participate in a dinner event comprising encounters with each of the devices present at her dinner party. Concurrently, her device may be part of a restaurant event comprising encounters with other guests at the restaurant. Both events are socially meaningful, and may be used to share photos and notes about the dinner with her party, and menu suggestions with the other guests, respectively. Note that Alice's device may also encounter devices of people who pass by outside the restaurant, which are not part of any event.

EnCore is able to infer certain types of events automatically, and users can create named events manually by annotating specific encounters. Events occur naturally as users are presented with relevant encounter and context information. For instance, moviegoers at a theatre might wish to share movie recommendations on the spot, while participants of a sightseeing tour may wish to share selected photos and videos days later. Attendees at a conference might wish to virtually carry on a conversation started in the hallway, texting and sharing links long after the conference is over. Supporting events has the following requirements:

Ad hoc event creation The ability to set up an event without the inconvenience of having to pair mobile devices with every attendee or enumerating every attendee by their contact details. This capability lowers the bar for setting up communication and sharing related to an ad hoc event or meeting.

Event-based communication The ability to send, receive, share, organize and search information and contacts by referring to the time/location or name of the appropriate event. This capability makes it easy to communicate with people one has met on a particular occasion, without needing to remember everyone's name or contact details.

Furthermore, the platform must protect user's privacy and data confidentiality, leading to two additional requirements:

Privacy control To protect privacy, users must retain the option to participate in an event with full contact details, a permanent nickname ("Alice"), or under an unlinkable, one-time pseudonym. The former may be appropriate for a meeting with business partners at a conference, while the latter are appropriate for sharing content related to a shared activity with strangers.

Access control The ability to control access to the event is critical for private event-based communication. An event may be restricted to any subset of those physically present during a specific event, and may optionally include additional users who are invited by a member.

4. ENCORE DESIGN

In this section, we describe the services supported by the EnCore platform. Figure 1 depicts the various components of the EnCore architecture. EnCore uses the SDDR protocol to form D2D encounters, and store these in the EnCore database. The Event Generator component groups, under user direction, related encounters into socially relevant named events, and stores these in the database. Users use applications to communicate with event peers. Depending on the event specification and the type of content shared, the Routing module decides how to forward event invitations, content and notifications to the members of an event. The information is sent using Conduits, which

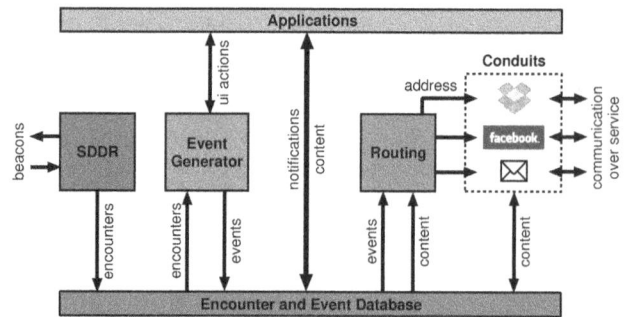

Figure 1: EnCore Architecture

rely on an existing communication, storage or OSN service to effect communication. Applications usually default to specific conduits for particular event and data types, e.g., Dropbox for video sharing. Before describing each of these components, we discuss EnCore's security properties and threat model.

4.1 EnCore security properties

4.1.1 Threat model

We assume that a subset of devices is controlled by attackers who participate in the EnCore protocol as peers and may also collude. Also, attackers can observe network communication and data stored in the Cloud. However, attackers cannot decrypt content without knowledge of the encryption key or invert cryptographic hashes. Furthermore, we assume that user devices are not compromised, i.e., attackers cannot learn honest users' private keys or the shared keys associated with encounters or events in which no attacker was a participant. Finally, honest users do not share event keys with non-members (users not part of an event).

We assume that user devices, including the operating system and any applications the user chooses to run, do not divulge information identifying or linking the device or user through EnCore conduits or other communication channels. (The EnCore protocols themselves do not leak identifiable information, down to the MAC layer.) Finally, we rule out radio fingerprinting attacks, which can identify a device by its unique RF signature [26]. Such attacks require sophisticated, non-standard signal capture hardware, and are outside our threat model.

4.1.2 Security properties

Under the assumptions stated above, EnCore provides the following security properties:

Bluetooth device unlinkability Attackers cannot track a legitimate user's device across Bluetooth radio contacts, unless the user's device remains in Bluetooth contact with some attacker's device for a continuous period that is never interrupted by more than two SDDR epoch changes.[1]

Encounter unlinkability/selective linkability Attackers cannot link different encounters with a user's

---

[1]Device unlinkability for Wi-Fi can be achieved using existing work like SlyFi [36]

device, unless the user has explicitly linked their device with an attacker's device and has not revoked the link.

Communication unlinkability Attackers cannot link communication or posts by a legitimate user in different events, unless the user has explicitly included identifying information, such as a nickname, in the posts.

Anonymity Attackers cannot learn the identity of a legitimate user or user's device with whom they share an event, unless the user explicitly reveals this identity.

Confidentiality Attackers cannot learn the communication content of events in which no attacker participates.

Authenticity Users can verify that the communication or content received in an event originates from a member.

We highlight that EnCore's threat model and security properties are mostly inherited from SDDR [47]. In principle, one could use a different platform, such as SMILE [49] or SmokeScreen [29] to support EnCore's functionality. Minimally, EnCore expects the underlying platform to discover nearby devices, form encounters and provide pairwise shared keys with them. SDDR additionally provides selective linkability and revocation, as well as Bluetooth unlinkability.

4.2 Encounters

EnCore uses a modified version of the SDDR [47] protocol for device discovery and for forming D2D encounters. Below we give a brief overview of how SDDR forms encounters and provides selective linkability. Further details, including SDDR's security guarantees and scalability, are available in [47].

Each device periodically performs a discovery (also known as an inquiry) to identify all nearby devices, collecting their MAC addresses and beacon messages in the process. Every device is also always discoverable, responding to incoming inquiry messages with information on how the discoverer can establish a connection (e.g., MAC address) and an additional payload, referred to as the beacon. This response is sent by the Bluetooth controller autonomously without requiring the attention of the main processor. Therefore, devices must only wake up to perform an inquiry. Otherwise, while simply discoverable, only the Bluetooth controller must be active, allowing the rest of the system to remain in a suspended state (consuming almost no energy).

Once SDDR receives the beacon(s), it forms an encounter with the remote device and computes a shared key. The beacon contains a Diffie-Hellman (DH) [31] public key which is used to compute this shared key.

While processing the beacon, SDDR additionally checks if the device belongs to a known, selectively linkable user. To support this, the beacon also includes a Bloom filter, which represents a set of salted hashes of secrets shared with the devices of linkable users. Two linkable devices advertise the same set member, which guarantees a match in the Bloom filters. The Bloom filters are padded to achieve a uniform load. Moreover, the salt is changed in every successive inquiry, which makes the probability of false positives quickly approach zero with each additional round in which the Bloom filters match. To a third (unlinked) device, on the other hand, the Bloom filters look like randomly changing sets of bits.

SDDR divides time into epochs (typically fifteen minutes long), during which the MAC address and DH public/private key pair remain constant. This allows the devices to track each other during an epoch, but remain unlinkable *across* epochs.

The original SDDR implementation used Bluetooth 2.1 to provide an efficient discovery and encounter formation implementation. Specifically, it encoded the beacons in the additional 240 bytes that the Bluetooth 2.1 Extended Inquiry Response (EIR) feature allows a device to include as part of the inquiry response. However, Bluetooth 2.1 does not support changing MAC addresses, which is *required* by SDDR; otherwise, users could simply be tracked by their MAC addresses regardless of the privacy provided by SDDR. As a result, the original SDDR implementation reset the Bluetooth controller with a new MAC address every epoch, every fifteen minutes or so. While this provided the necessary security guarantees, it also rendered the device unable to maintain long-term connections with other paired accessories such as headsets.

For use in EnCore, we migrated SDDR to Bluetooth 4.0, which provides native support for randomized, ephemeral MAC addresses. This feature enables EnCore to maintain compatibility with legacy accessories. However, the communication model supported by Bluetooth 4.0 is different from Bluetooth 2.1, necessitating an entirely new wire protocol and FEC-based message encoding scheme. Our design and implementation of SDDR over Bluetooth 4.0 is described in Section 6.

4.3 Events

Events are socially meaningful sets of encounters. The *Event Generator* creates events by selecting encounters that are taking (or took) place concurrently and form a social event meaningful to users. There are two methods for generating events: relying on explicit user input from the *Context* application, or using existing user annotations (e.g., the user's calendar entries). Once an event is created, the generator, using suitable conduits (Section 4.4), sends an invitation to all participating encounter peers, containing an event ID and a shared event key, which can be used for communication among event members. For privacy reasons, users are required to explicitly invite others for events inferred from their private calendar entries.

EnCore provides several methods by which users can create events: For small meetings, all participants tend to interact in close proximity with one another, and thus all devices form encounters with each other. Users can manually select appropriate encounters, using cues such as whether an encounter corresponds to a known user, or a received signal strength indicator (RSSI), which helps to distinguish between nearby and distant users.

For larger events and future events, it is inconvenient or impossible for one user to select all participants from the set of encounters they observe at the time of event creation. If the event is managed, and has a list of attendees, it is possible to bootstrap the EnCore event similar to PIKE [22], using Facebook or another existing registration system. However, unlike PIKE, EnCore can also handle ad hoc events. For these events, the event creator can specify a time period and geographic area, such that any devices within the specified space-time region is automatically invited to the event. This can be implemented by having each event member forward invitations over their encounters that meet the spatial and temporal constraints.

Evaluating such policies in a large scale deployment is part of ongoing work.

In designing EnCore, we chose not to use protocol means to disambiguate multiple EnCore events that correspond to the same social event. Thus, users are free to create multiple EnCore events for the same social event, or (somewhat more commonly for large events), a few users may end up creating their own EnCore event corresponding to the same social event. Our experience is that event peers themselves resolve this ambiguity by gravitating to one event, abandoning the others without requiring an arbitration protocol. (This was observed in our deployment as well, see section 7.2). Of course, applications atop EnCore may choose to provide their own arbitration protocol.

4.4 Communication

All application-level communication in EnCore occurs among the members of an event. Two types of components within EnCore are responsible for communication, *Conduits* and the *Router*.

Conduits are adapters to existing communication, storage and online social network services, and are used to convey information between event participants. Conduits accept messages or content and, depending on the type of conduit, either a list of encounter IDs (the communication endpoints for pairwise message transport) or an event ID (the rendezvous point for group communication and sharing). They convert the encounter IDs or event ID into addresses or names used by the underlying communication, storage, or OSN service that the conduit relies on. To provide secure communication among the members of an event, conduits normally encrypt the communication using either the shared encounter key(s) established during the handshake protocols, or the shared event key distributed during the event creation.

The *Router* component decides, based on the event specification and the type of information shared, how information is forwarded among event members. Three types of information are routed: event invitations, content, and notifications. If the conduit used for the event and information type supports multicast or shared storage, then the router delivers the information in one step, using the event ID as an address and the event key to encrypt. If the conduit supports pairwise communication, then the router sends the information to each member with which the local device shares an encounter, using the encounter IDs as addresses and the associated shared keys to encrypt. If not all pairs of event members share an encounter, then the routers on each member device forward the information to all of their local encounter peers that meet the event membership specification and have not already received it.

4.5 Security guarantees

Building EnCore on SDDR guarantees the security properties related to unlinkability. Since SDDR requires periodic MAC address changes, devices are not linkable at the Bluetooth layer unless the tracking device is present whenever the SDDR device changes addresses. Similarly, since SDDR ensures that the advertisements do not carry identifying information (except to linked users), devices remain unlinkable. The confidentiality and authenticity guarantees are provided by ensuring that all communication is encrypted and protected by a message authentication

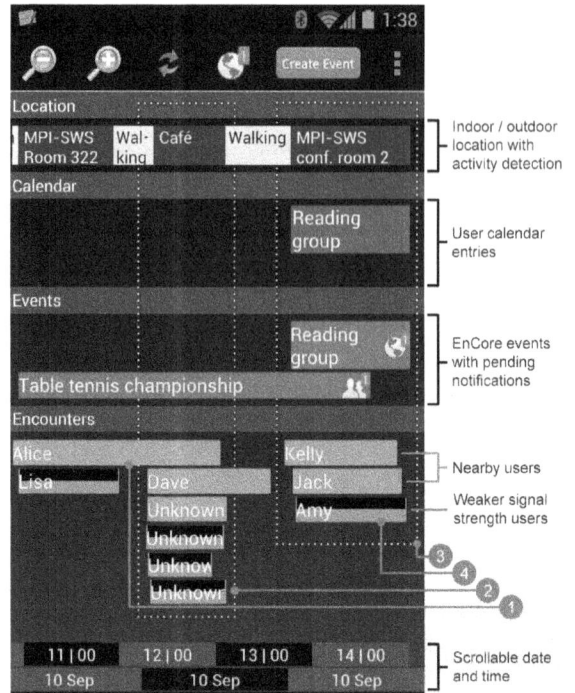

Figure 2: *Context* **Timeline view (User names were changed for privacy)**

code, using either an event key or an encounter key. Since only encounter or event peers possess the same shared keys, this ensures both confidentiality (event peers can decrypt) and authenticity (only encounter or event peers can post).

5. USING EVENTS WITH CONTEXT

We have developed an Android application called *Context* over EnCore. *Context* maintains a private record of the user's activities and social encounters, and allows users to communicate, share, collaborate, organize and search information and contacts using events. The design of *Context* was shaped significantly by user feedback during a series of testbed deployments within our institute community between September, 2012 and September, 2013

Even though *Context* still lacks the feature wealth, sleekness and visual polish of a commercial product, users in our institute-internal deployment have generally found *Context* useful, and have come up with creative uses for its capabilities. We provide quantitative details of *Context*'s usage in our deployment in Section 7.2, as well as qualitative user feedback in Section 8.1. In the rest of this section, we briefly describe the main functions provided by *Context* and their value to the user: browsing the user's timeline and identifying socially relevant encounters, managing events, posting and receiving information, and managing user linkability.

5.1 Browsing the timeline

Figure 2 shows a screenshot of *Context*'s timeline view for a hypothetical user Bob. Bob can navigate this view by scrolling, zooming or searching by keyword or date.

The timeline view shows encounters, events and calendar entries as horizontal bars spanning time intervals. For linked encounters, the peer's name is displayed. Anonymous encounters show "Unknown" as the peer name. The height and color of the encounter bar indicates signal strength and is a rough proxy for proximity. This view scrapes the user's calendar and displays previously scheduled entries. Any EnCore events are displayed in the events area. Events are marked with pending invitations or notifications (if any).

Selecting any UI element reveals more information about, and shows a menu of possible actions on, the element. For example, selecting an event highlights the participating encounters, allows the user to inspect or edit the event's metadata, invite more participants, or launch an application to browse the event's content. Selecting a location switches to a map-based view.

This simple linear view provides remarkable functionality: For instance, as shown by (1) on the Figure, by navigating back to this view, Bob can remind himself that he was with Alice at the table tennis championship before lunch on September 10, and eventually they walked to lunch together. The events pane shows that Bob was invited to the associated event and has a pending notification.

The rectangles (2) and (3) show how social events, both scheduled and impromptu, naturally line up vertically along the timeline. (2) shows that Dave joined Bob and Alice for lunch, and that there was someone else (unknown with high signal strength) nearby. This may be a sufficient hint for Bob to recall that Dave was with his guest at lunch. There were other lower signal strength encounters with unlinked users at lunch. Similarly, (3) shows a scheduled event, the Reading Group, that has a calendar entry and an associated EnCore event. Once again the vertical alignment of the high signal strength encounters with Kelly and Jack serve as reminder that they were at the reading group meeting. The encounter with Amy has low signal strength and likely is an artifact of her being in a nearby room but not at the reading group meeting.

5.2 Creating events

Users create events by touching the "Create Event" button and selecting a set of encounters to be included. If the event was previously scheduled in the calendar, its metadata (name, duration) is automatically imported; otherwise, the user can adjust the default duration inferred from the selected encounters, enter a name for the event, and optionally add the event to the calendar. Once the user confirms, the event is created and invitations are sent to the selected encounters. To support events where some of the users are not physically present (e.g. users attending an event virtually), event members can additionally invite any of their past encounters or known contacts to the event.

For more complex events or future events, the user can specify temporal and spatial (e.g., within the current building) constraints for included encounters. Future and transitive encounters that meet these constraints are invited automatically.

By default, the appropriate conduit to implement an event is chosen automatically. When all participants are linked encounters who provide Facebook account details (as is the case in our deployment at users' request), then a conduit is chosen that maps the event to a private Facebook event. Otherwise, a conduit is chosen that maps the event to a folder in Dropbox. The Dropbox conduit supports anonymous participants and provides the same basic sharing functionality, albeit without the integration and the sophisticated event presentation of Facebook.

These facilities make it easy to set up communication and sharing among a socially meaningful group of users in an ad hoc fashion. The event creator does not require contact details of the participants, and can include anonymous users via unlinked encounters.

5.3 Posting information

Context appears as a choice in Android's Share menu.[2] Therefore, any type of content can be selected (e.g., pictures and videos from the Android gallery, audio from a recording app, pin drops from a map app, text from a notes app) and shared via *Context*. Within *Context*, the user simply touches an event in which the content is to be posted.

As a convenient shortcut, users can post information directly from within *Context* and select encounters with whom the information should be shared, without creating an event. Internally, *Context* creates an event with default metadata to handle the posted information.

These facilities make it very convenient to send messages and share content with nearby or previously encountered users.

5.4 Receiving information

Notifications about incoming messages, posts or pending event invitations are shown as icons with red flags on the corresponding event, or on an encounter in the case of a message sent directly to an encounter. For instance, in Figure 2, there is a new post in the "Reading group" event, and a pending invitation to the "Table tennis championship" event. Notifications are also summarized in the notification center shown as an earth icon at the top of the screen. Touching it will scroll to the nearest event or encounter with a pending notification. Preference settings allow users to suppress notifications by type or source.

To respond to an event invitation, the user touches the event, optionally views the event's metadata, and then accepts, declines or defers the invitation. To read incoming messages or posts, the user selects the relevant event or encounter. Touching an event launches an external application (e.g., Facebook) to show the latest post in the event.

These facilities enable users to prioritize, filter, browse and navigate incoming information according to its context: event, encounter, time and location.

5.5 Controlling linkability

Context allows users to control the information revealed in an encounter in a variety of ways. The user can choose to reveal a linkable nickname or their real identity to selected peer devices. The linkable peers can be selected based on existing relationships in an online social network (e.g., Facebook) or a contact list, or by pairing devices individually. Moreover, linkability can be controlled based on the user's present location or time. For instance, users can choose to be linkable to colleagues only when in the office and not be linkable by anyone at certain times.

Recall that a Facebook private event is used by default for events among linkable encounters who provide Facebook

---

[2]Most Android content apps have a "Share" button, which opens a menu of applications through which the selected content can be shared.

details. User posts are linkable across such events. Users can use a separate Facebook account under a pseudonym for this purpose; in fact, all participants in our deployment use test accounts separate from their main Facebook account. To avoid linkability across events, the creator of an event can choose to use a Dropbox conduit instead, and users can decline invitations to Facebook-backed events if they so choose.

These facilities enable users to effectively control their privacy.

6. IMPLEMENTATION

In this section, we describe the implementation of EnCore and *Context*.

6.1 SDDR over Bluetooth 4.0

We have implemented a modified version of SDDR on the Android platform, using Bluetooth Low-Energy support instead of Bluetooth 2.1. We use Samsung Galaxy Nexus phones running Android 4.1.2 with the android-omap-tuna-3.0-jb-mr0 kernel. We modified this kernel by patching in Bluetooth 4.0 L2CAP communication support present in the Linux 3.7.7 kernel, as well as a power-related bug fix in the Bluetooth controller driver.

As described in [47], in order to provide selective linkability, SDDR devices store an advertised set and a listen set, each containing linkability values (or *link values*); if a value in device A's advertised set exists within device B's listen set, then B can detect A. Upon detection by the underlying radio, the SDDR protocol exchanges a beacon message containing a Diffie-Hellman (DH) [31] public key, and a set digest structure containing salted hashes of the advertised set values. Upon receiving a beacon from a remote device, an SDDR peer computes a shared DH key and checks to see if elements of its listen set are found in the newly advertised set.

The EnCore implementation of SDDR utilizes the broadcast feature of Bluetooth 4.0. Bluetooth 4.0 introduces new roles for devices, two of which are *advertisers* and *scanners*. Advertisers periodically broadcast small messages, containing a 31-byte payload, to nearby scanners who listen for messages. Unlike the exclusively pairwise communication in Bluetooth 2.1, advertisers in Bluetooth 4.0 can broadcast their messages to all nearby devices [3].

SDDR exchanges a beacon, consisting of a 192-bit DH public key and a Bloom filter containing the link values present in the advertised set; however, this beacon cannot fit into the 31-byte limit of Bluetooth 4.0 advertisement messages. Instead, we model the advertisement channel as a packet-erasure channel, i.e., packets are either received correctly or not at all, and send the beacon message, in segments, encoded using Reed-Solomon (RS) coding [53]. RS codes are optimal erasure-correction codes, meaning the receiver can reconstruct the original K data symbols after receiving any K of N total symbols.

Figure 3 illustrates our method for generating advertisements from the beacon information. Each advertisement contains an index to identify the RS and Bloom filter segments. We divide both the public key and the Bloom filter into segments, with each advertisement containing a single RS and Bloom filter segment. In order to produce the RS-coded segments, the coding matrix (in the form of a Vandermonde identity matrix [51]) is

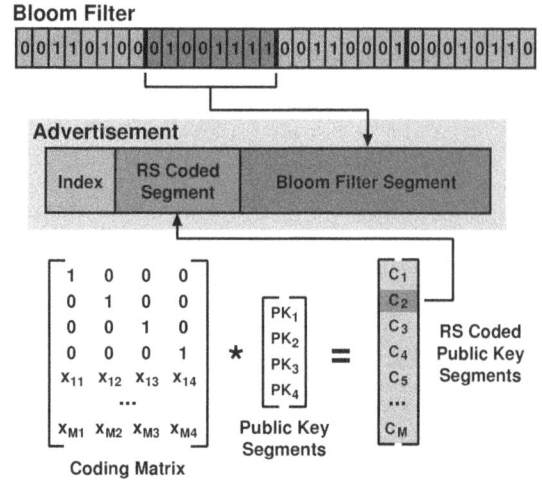

Figure 3: SDDR-4 beacon constructed from RS coded DH public key and Bloom filter segments

multiplied by the vector containing all segments of the public key. Note that the Bloom filter segments do not require forward error correction since if the receiver misses an advertisement, it can simply replace the segment with all 1's in the reconstructed Bloom filter. As more advertisements arrive, the effective false positive rate of the Bloom filter decreases.

The discovery protocol runs periodically (roughly every 15 seconds), acting as both an advertiser and scanner. Using the public key and Bloom filter generated at the start of each epoch, the device computes and starts to broadcast the next advertisement (according to the current index). Devices also scan to capture broadcasts from nearby devices, and report the set of discovered devices to the higher EnCore layers.

Once enough advertisements are received, the handshake protocol attempts to decode the remote device's public key and compute the shared key. Once decoded, the public key is used to query the Bloom filter (which may only be partially received) for all link values in the local listen set; as new Bloom filter fragments are received, the result converges to the true intersection as the number of false positives decreases.

6.2 Conduits and router

EnCore currently supports the following conduits:

SMTP conduit The SMTP conduit allows users to securely exchange e-mails with the participants of an event. The SMTP conduit allows any email client on the device to send a message to the email addresses associated with one or more encounter peers. If an encounter is linkable and has an associated email address, the message is simply sent to that address. If the encounter is unlinkable, then a one-time email address is derived from the encounter ID, and the message is sent to that address. The current implementation uses `mailinator.com` [12] for this purpose, which does not require user registrations and creates mailboxes on-the-fly as mail arrives for an address. The mail is public for all who can guess an email address, but this does not affect confidentiality since all EnCore mail is encrypted using an encounter or event key. The Mailinator conduit is limited by the the fact that Mailinator caches messages only for a few hours, and applications need to periodically resend messages to ensure persistence. Alternatively, one could easily setup a similar one time email system that does not delete messages.[3]

Dropbox conduit The Dropbox conduit converts an event ID into a folder name on Dropbox, and stores all content posted to the event into that folder, encrypted with the shared event key.

Facebook conduit This conduit associates an EnCore event with a private Facebook event. It requires that all participants in the event are linkable and provide details for a Facebook account. The event's participants appear in the Facebook event with the identity of the account they provided. Textual posts, comments, likes and photos are posted in the Facebook event in cleartext, to maintain the flexibility and convenience of the Facebook interface.[4] However, video and audio recording posted to the event are uploaded using the Dropbox conduit (encrypted with the shared event key), and a URL to that content is posted in the Facebook event.

Using Facebook allowed us to leverage the familiarity of users with its app. The Facebook conduit cannot support unlinkable users, which was irrelevant in our deployment. As part of ongoing work, we plan to recreate similar functionality within *Context* with the ability to create events amongst unlinkable users.

Router The current router implementation is limited to forwarding information within events in which all members share pairwise encounters. We are in the process of adding transitive forwarding. There has not been much demand for this feature so far, due to the relatively small size of our deployment and the types of events users have requested.

7. EVALUATION

We have evaluated EnCore using microbenchmarks of CPU usage and power consumption, and also via a series of user studies. All of our experiments used Samsung Galaxy Nexus devices, containing a 1.2 GHz dual-core ARM Cortex-A9 processor. We begin with a description of the microbenchmarks, and conclude with results from our latest user study.

7.1 Microbenchmarks

Protocol computation time We have measured the SDDR-4 handshake protocol computation time while varying the number of link values in the listen and advertised sets. We compare execution time to an implementation [30] of the JL10 scheme [43] for Private Set Intersection (PSI). Results are similar to the original SDDR protocol: For all set sizes, SDDR-4 executes over three orders of magnitude faster than standard PSI.

Energy consumption EnCore runs the SDDR protocol permanently in the background on a mobile device, and therefore power considerations have informed considerable parts of its design. We have collected extensive power

---

^[3] We implemented such a system and used it during one of our initial deployments.
^[4] Note that Facebook has access to cleartext posts; this can be avoided by using the Dropbox conduit or a private OSN platform like Persona [23] to share all information.

Operation	Avg. Power (mW)	Energy (mWs)	When
Idle	1.73	-	-
Suspend/Wakeup	205.94	263.74	-
Bluetooth 2.1			
Inquiry Scan	140.46	1698.36	Every 30s
Name Request	144.97	96.26	-
SDDR-4			
Discovery	236.48	752.67	Every 13.5s
Advertisement	107.22	0.58	Every 700ms

Table 1: Power consumption for Bluetooth 2.1 and SDDR-4 operations. Entries without a value do not have well-defined durations.

traces of different parts of the EnCore protocol using the BattOr [55] power monitor. The BattOr samples the voltage and current across the battery terminals at a rate of 1 kHz, and makes this data available via (its own) USB connection. We collected this data for the SDDR-4 protocol variant, as described in Section 6.1. Detailed energy results for the original SDDR protocol can be found in [47].

Table 1 summarizes the energy consumed and the average power required for each of the different SDDR operations. The idle power consumption while the device is in airplane mode (no radios are enabled) is a negligible 1.73 mW. Since discoveries continually take place in our protocol, we include the power and energy consumption from suspending and waking up the device. As a point of comparison, we have included energy consumed by Bluetooth 2.1 inquiry scans and name requests.

Discoveries are the most expensive operations within SDDR, in part due to the overhead of suspending and waking up the device; for BT 4.0, this overhead makes up ~35% of the energy consumption. BT 4.0 advertisements consume very little energy (< 1mWs), since only the Bluetooth controller (and not the main processor) must run; in addition, the broadcast takes place within a few milliseconds. Overall, the power consumption of SDDR-4 within EnCore is negligible, dominated by the overheads of standard Android services like activity detection and location determination (GPS). Power consumption increases by one order of magnitude once the screen is powered on and the user interacts with *Context*. Even with all features enabled continuously and users performing their normal activities, no user within our deployment had a device run out of battery mid-day during the testing period.

7.2 Live deployment

Our latest EnCore field deployment began on September 9, 2013, with 35 volunteers in the Saarbrücken office of MPI-SWS. The participants were staff members and researchers, and were informed about the purpose of the experiment and what data would be collected. Most of the participants (32 out of 35) were not directly involved in the project.

Deployment setup We provided each participant with a Galaxy Nexus phone running EnCore with *Context* and the Facebook app. All phones were configured with the account details of a different Facebook test account with a pseudonym. At users' request all phones were selectively linked with each other by default. Users were able to change the linkability settings, configure their personal calendars for display in *Context*, and change the pseudonym to their real name if they wished to do so (30 of the 35 users did). None

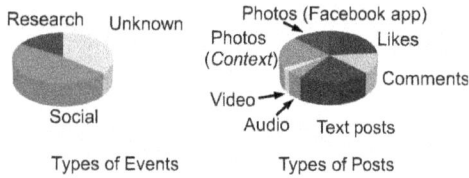

Figure 4: Types of events and posts

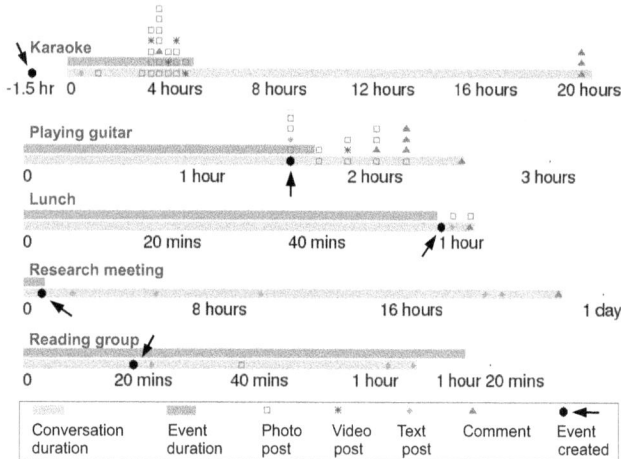

Figure 5: Timelines of five actual events. Each point shows the type of activity performed along with the time elapsed since the specified start time of the event

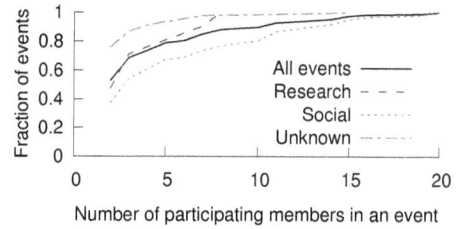

Figure 6: Distribution of event size

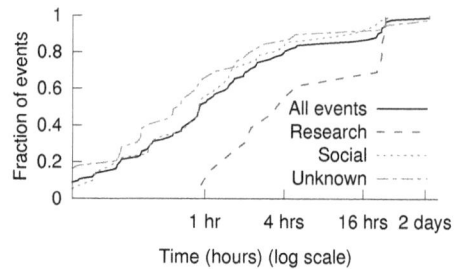

Figure 7: Distribution of conversation durations

of the users modified the default linkability setting (i.e., link with all other users). This is not surprising since the deployment was carried out among mutually trusting users and linkability was limited to experimental devices only.

We requested users to carry the device, and encouraged them to use *Context* to create events, communicate and share content as they saw fit. On September 16, we installed an audio recording and a note taking application on each of the devices because several users requested it, in addition to the default camera, gallery, calendar and map applications already available on each device.

The phones ran EnCore, using the SDDR-4 protocol. The phones executed discoveries every 13.5 seconds and changed MAC addresses every 15 minutes.

Statistics from the deployment After the the first two weeks of the deployment, we collected statistics for all the events created, which we present below. The users' activity level was roughly bimodal. 17 users created fewer than three events and made fewer than five posts, while 18 users exceeded these numbers. Among the users not related to the project, the maximum number of events created by a single user was 12 (median 3) and the maximum number of posts created by a single user were 30 (median 4).

Event usage After removing from consideration a number of events that had been created by project members for demonstration purposes, a total of 128 events remain. We have divided these events into three categories based on their names: research meetings (16%), social events (48%), and unknown (36%). We classified an event as unknown if its purpose was not obvious from its name. Figure 4 shows

the distribution of event types and Figure 5 presents the timelines of a selection of five actual events created during the deployment.

Based on informal feedback from users and our own observations, there was an interesting mix of expected and creative uses of events. Events were created for research gatherings, such as meetings, reading groups, etc., and used to exchange meeting notes, audio recordings, followup comments and links to related papers. The 'research meeting' and the 'reading group' events in Figure 5 show the activity timelines of two events in this category. Also, as seen in Figure 6, these events tend to contain a moderate number of participants, which is what we commonly observe for project/group meetings and reading groups in our institute.

Almost half of the events were created for social or informal gatherings, such as lunches, coffee breaks, sports activities, bus rides, karaoke events, etc., and used to share photos, videos and comments during and after the event. The 'karaoke', 'playing guitar' and 'lunch' events in Figure 5 are typical examples. With the 'karaoke' event we also observed an instance of users resolving multiple EnCore events created for the same social event by gravitating to one event (see Section 4.3). We observed that users stopped posting to one of the two events created for karaoke and continued their interactions on the other. Some creative uses include creating events to invite nearby people for coffee breaks, or to inform nearby people about leftover party food using a picture of the food. The number of members in social events ranges from 2 to 20 users (median 3), which is expected given the size of our deployment (Figure 6).

Figure 5 also highlights that events can be created after the associated event has ended, and that conversations tend to extend beyond the event duration. The former can be observed for the 'Lunch' event by comparing the time when the EnCore event was created (circular dot with an arrow) and the timespan of the actual social event (the first horizontal bar from the top for each event).

144

Figure 7 shows the distribution of conversation durations for different types of events. Even though most of the events did not have conversations longer than five hours, there were cases where users referred back to events they had attended in the past and posted content to them long after the actual event had finished.

Figure 4 shows the distribution of the types of posts within events. Note that the audio recording application was installed one week after the deployment had started; the proportion of audio posts might have been higher had it been installed from the beginning. A large portion of photos were uploaded directly from *Context*, rather than via the Facebook application, which suggests that users found it convenient to refer to an event directly from *Context*'s timeline.

Summary EnCore and *Context* provide a basis for exploring secure ad hoc interactions. Both the analysis of data from the deployment and personal user feedback show that real users find the paradigm useful and found new ways to collaborate and share with colleagues using *Context*.

8. DISCUSSION

In this section, we describe the qualitative feedback we received from our users, and discuss the remaining risks and challenges.

8.1 Qualitative user feedback

Quantitative performance evaluations are often inadequate in capturing the utility of new functionality. User engagement can be an important metric, and here we describe the qualitative feedback we received from our users, both during and after the test deployments. At the end our our latest deployment, many of our users expressed an interest in using the system on a permanent basis once we have a version they can install on their primary devices. We believe this is encouraging since it shows that users (albeit highly technically proficient ones) find the system useful. In the rest of this section, we discuss features that users have requested. We believe feature requests are illuminating. While they obviously point out shortcomings in the existing system, they also point to innovation enabled by, and creative use of, EnCore's capabilities, some of which were not anticipated by the design team.

Support for sharing audio recordings and import/export of events to/from calendar was requested by users and rolled out during the last deployment. Various requests were related to encounter export, to make information about nearby users available to other applications. For instance, exporting a "Nearby" group into the Android address book, which includes the contact details of currently nearby users, if known.

Another feature requested was the ability to create ephemeral pseudonyms as a way to control linkability (in addition to the pairwise linkability offered by EnCore). These pseudonyms allow other users to link their encounters with a device under a pseudonym for a limited period and location (e.g., while attending a conference). Users can change (or remove) their pseudonym and can also choose to stop receiving messages addressed to a pseudonym anytime.

A frequently requested feature is the ability to browse the EnCore timeline, post content and manage events from a desktop computer. Users have also requested the option

to thread recurrent or related events, and view posts and comments within a thread in a linearized manner. Finally, users asked that *Context* suggest events and content to post, based on the users' history, preference, and current context. For instance, if Alice, Bob and Charlie have had frequent meetings recently, then *Context* could automatically suggest another instance of the event when it notices similar circumstances (encounters, location, time). These feature requests suggest that users find it useful to be able to explore an encounter timeline, coupled with the ability to create links, and to relate and recount events.

8.2 Risks and challenges

User privacy and security has informed every step of EnCore's design. Unlike virtually all existing mobile social apps, EnCore does not require the user to reveal their sensitive context data, which often combines location, social contact and communication trace, to a provider. Moreover, EnCore prevents Bluetooth device tracking and provides strong security and privacy guarantees within its threat model. However, privacy risks and usability challenges remain.

EnCore database confidentiality The data logged by EnCore resides on the mobile device, and is susceptible to loss, theft, or subpoena. It is not clear what legal rights regarding privacy and self-incrimination, if any, users can assert with respect to data stored on their personal devices. Encrypting the EnCore database protects the data in the case of loss or theft, though it will not stop a court from compelling the user to provide the decryption keys. The risk can be somewhat reduced by configuring the database to store a limited history. Since the usefulness of encounter information likely diminishes over time, the resultant loss of functionality may be acceptable.

Private profile matching Linking encounters based on shared attributes is supported by EnCore, but currently not fully exported by *Context*. A challenge in this regard is how to prevent attacks where a malicious device advertises attributes in order to learn as many attributes of nearby users as possible. The problem can be partly mitigated by ignoring devices that advertise too many attributes or change their attributes too frequently, but a more general defense is hard, unless attributes can be certified by an external authority.

Reliably identifying socially relevant encounters Identifying relevant encounters (e.g., the participants of a shared event) was not a problem in our deployment. The fact that all participants revealed their name or a pseudonym while in the office, combined with the signal strength indication, proved sufficient.

However, identifying socially relevant encounters in a larger and denser environment with many unlinkable devices is an open challenge. For instance, it is important to reliably identify the attendees of a private, closed-door meeting that takes place in an office building with EnCore devices in adjacent rooms. We are currently experimenting with an audio-based confirmation protocol, where devices have to answer a (fast attenuating) challenge transmitted as an audio chirp, in order to identify devices in the same room. Another option would be to follow a non-interactive approach similar to that of Sound of Silence [58], where each device uploads a signature of their acoustic environment to a cloud service that, by comparing signatures, identifies nearby devices.

In other situations, like a crowded party, distinguishing individual attendees is usually not necessary, because the most likely types of interaction (e.g., sharing photos) are directed to the group as a whole. In situations where users wish to identify individuals within a crowded space (e.g., a dinner party at a busy restaurant), people tend to know each other and have their devices linked already. If not, they can resort to bumping devices via NFC or shake-to-connect [28, 50]. In this case, no contact details would be exchanged (unless desired), but the encounter would be marked as "confirmed" on both devices.

Communication with strangers The limited deployment within our institute has not yet allowed us to experiment with communication among strangers, as it would occur, for instance, in the sightseeing scenario described in the introduction. This case, as well as other challenges described above will require experience with deployments at larger scale. Toward this end, we are developing a version of EnCore that does not require rooting the phone, which is currently a major hurdle for a larger deployment. Nevertheless, we believe we have shown that EnCore provides a robust foundation for building secure, privacy-preserving mobile social applications that exploit the opportunities afforded by D2D communication and secure encounters.

9. CONCLUSION AND FUTURE WORK

We have described the design, implementation, and evaluation of EnCore, a mobile platform for social applications based on secure encounters. EnCore can support a wide range of event-based communication primitives for mobile social apps, with strong security and privacy guarantees, without requiring a trusted provider, and while integrating with existing communication, storage and OSN services. As part of our evaluation, we have conducted small-scale deployments of *Context*, an app for event based communication, sharing and collaboration. User experience was favorable: users were engaged, requested new features, and used the app in interesting ways not envisioned by the designers.

While our small-scale deployments have been invaluable in developing the system, secure encounter-based communication promises more than we have been able to evaluate among a small set of mutually trusting, technically savvy users. Evaluating EnCore's primitives in dense environments and among strangers requires larger scale deployment onto a more heterogeneous population. We are in the process of completing a version of EnCore that can be installed on an unrooted phone, which will be much easier to disseminate at scale. Our experience catalogued in this paper gives us confidence that EnCore and the secure encounter primitive will continue to prove useful, and a larger userbase will yield compelling new ways to communicate using EnCore.

10. REFERENCES

[1] AllJoyn. http://www.alljoyn.org. Last accessed: September 2013.

[2] Android Beam. http://developer.android.com/guide/topics/connectivity/nfc/nfc.html#p2p. Last accessed: June 2013.

[3] Bluetooth Specification Core Version 4.0. https://www.bluetooth.org/docman/handlers/downloaddoc.ashx?doc_id=229737. Last accessed: March 2014.

[4] FireChat. https://itunes.apple.com/us/app/firechat/id719829352?mt=8. Last accessed: March 2014.

[5] Foursquare. https://foursquare.com/. Last accessed: June 2013.

[6] Friday: automated journal. http://www.fridayed.com/. Last accessed: October 2013.

[7] Google fires engineer for violating privacy policies. http://www.physorg.com/news203744839.html. Last accessed: September 2012.

[8] Haggle. http://www.haggleproject.org. Last accessed: September 2013.

[9] Highlight. http://highlig.ht/. Last accessed: December 2013.

[10] iOS 7 AirDrop. http://support.apple.com/kb/HT5887. Last accessed: January 2014.

[11] Lokast. http://www.lokast.com. Last accessed: September 2013.

[12] Mailinator: Free disposable email. http://mailinator.com/. Last accessed: January 2014.

[13] Memoto: automatic lifelogging camera. http://memoto.com/. Last accessed: September 2013.

[14] Near Field Communication – Interface and Protocol (ISO/IEC 18092:2013). http://www.iso.org/iso/home/store/catalogue_ics/catalogue_detail_ics.htm?csnumber=56692. Last accessed: September 2013.

[15] Nintendo 3DS. http://www.nintendo.com/3ds. Last accessed: September 2013.

[16] Secret. https://www.secret.ly/. Last accessed: March 2014.

[17] Sony PlayStation Vita. http://us.playstation.com/psvita/. Last accessed: September 2013.

[18] Tile. http://www.thetileapp.com/. Last accessed: September 2013.

[19] Whisper. http://whisper.sh/. Last accessed: March 2014.

[20] Wi-Fi Direct. http://www.wi-fi.org/discover-and-learn/wi-fi-direct. Last accessed: September 2013.

[21] N. Aharony, W. Pan, C. Ip, I. Khayal, and A. Pentland. Social fMRI: Investigating and shaping social mechanisms in the real world. *Pervasive Mob. Comput.*, 7(6), Dec. 2011.

[22] W. Apolinarski, M. Handte, M. U. Iqbal, and P. J. Marrón. Secure interaction with piggybacked key-exchange. *Pervasive Mob. Comput.*, 10, Feb. 2014.

[23] R. Baden, A. Bender, N. Spring, B. Bhattacharjee, and D. Starin. Persona: an online social network with user-defined privacy. In *Proceedings of the ACM SIGCOMM conference on Data communication*, SIGCOMM '09, 2009.

[24] L. B. Baker and J. Finkle. Sony PlayStation suffers massive data breach. http://www.reuters.com/article/2011/04/26/us-sony-stoldendata-idUSTRE73P6WB20110426. Last accessed: September 2012.

[25] M. Bakht, M. Trower, and R. H. Kravets. Searchlight: won't you be my neighbor? In *Proceedings of the 18th annual international conference on Mobile computing and networking*, MobiCom '12, 2012.

[26] V. Brik, S. Banerjee, M. Gruteser, and S. Oh. Wireless device identification with radiometric signatures. In *Proceedings of the 14th ACM international conference on Mobile computing and networking*, MobiCom '08, 2008.

[27] J. A. Calandrino, A. Kilzer, A. Narayanan, E. W. Felten, and V. Shmatikov. "you might also like: " privacy risks of collaborative filtering. In *Proceedings of the 2011 IEEE Symposium on Security and Privacy*, SP '11, 2011.

[28] C. Castelluccia and P. Mutaf. Shake them up!: a movement-based pairing protocol for CPU-constrained devices. In *Proceedings of the 3rd international conference on Mobile systems, applications, and services*, MobiSys '05, 2005.

[29] L. P. Cox, A. Dalton, and V. Marupadi. Smokescreen: flexible privacy controls for presence-sharing. In *Proceedings of the 5th international conference on Mobile systems, applications and services*, MobiSys '07, 2007.

[30] E. D. Cristofaro, Y. Lu, and G. Tsudik. Efficient techniques for privacy-preserving sharing of sensitive information. Cryptology ePrint Archive, Report 2011/113, 2011. http://eprint.iacr.org/.

[31] W. Diffie and M. Hellman. New Directions in Cryptography. *IEEE Transactions on Information Theory*, 22(6), nov 1976.

[32] B. Dodson, I. Vo, T. Purtell, A. Cannon, and M. Lam. Musubi: disintermediated interactive social feeds for mobile devices. In *Proceedings of the 21st international conference on World Wide Web*, WWW '12, 2012.

[33] P. Dutta and D. Culler. Practical asynchronous neighbor discovery and rendezvous for mobile sensing applications. In *Proceedings of the 6th ACM conference on Embedded network sensor systems*, SenSys '08, 2008.

[34] B. Ford, J. Strauss, C. Lesniewski-Laas, S. Rhea, F. Kaashoek, and R. Morris. Persistent personal names for globally connected mobile devices. In *Proceedings of the 7th symposium on Operating systems design and implementation*, OSDI '06, 2006.

[35] M. Goetz and S. Nath. Privacy-aware personalization for mobile advertising. Technical report.

[36] B. Greenstein, D. McCoy, J. Pang, T. Kohno, S. Seshan, and D. Wetherall. Improving wireless privacy with an identifier-free link layer protocol. In *Proceedings of the 6th international conference on Mobile systems, applications, and services*, MobiSys '08, 2008.

[37] S. Guha, M. Jain, and V. N. Padmanabhan. Koi: a location-privacy platform for smartphone apps. In *Proceedings of the 9th USENIX conference on Networked Systems Design and Implementation*, NSDI'12, 2012.

[38] C. A. Gunter, M. J. May, and S. G. Stubblebine. A formal privacy system and its application to location based services. In *Proceedings of the 4th international conference on Privacy Enhancing Technologies*, PET'04, 2005.

[39] B. Han and A. Srinivasan. ediscovery: Energy efficient device discovery for mobile opportunistic communications. In *Proceedings of the 20th IEEE International Conference on Network Protocols (ICNP)*, ICNP '12, 2012.

[40] B. Hoh, M. Gruteser, R. Herring, J. Ban, D. Work, J.-C. Herrera, A. M. Bayen, M. Annavaram, and Q. Jacobson. Virtual trip lines for distributed privacy-preserving traffic monitoring. In *Proceedings of the 6th international conference on Mobile systems, applications, and services*, MobiSys '08, 2008.

[41] P. Hornyack, S. Han, J. Jung, S. Schechter, and D. Wetherall. These aren't the droids you're looking for: retrofitting android to protect data from imperious applications. In *Proceedings of the 18th ACM conference on Computer and communications security*, CCS '11, 2011.

[42] P. Jappinen, I. Laakkonen, V. Latva, and A. Hamalainen. Bluetooth device surveillance and its implications. *WSEAS Transactions on Information Science and Applications*, 1(4), Oct. 2004.

[43] S. Jarecki and N. Saxena. Authenticated key agreement with key re-use in the short authenticated strings model. In *Proceedings of the 7th international conference on Security and cryptography for networks*, SCN'10, 2010.

[44] P. Kalnis, G. Ghinita, K. Mouratidis, and D. Papadias. Preventing location-based identity inference in anonymous spatial queries. *IEEE Trans. on Knowl. and Data Eng.*, 19(12), Dec. 2007.

[45] A. Kandhalu, K. Lakshmanan, and R. R. Rajkumar. U-connect: a low-latency energy-efficient asynchronous neighbor discovery protocol. In *Proceedings of the 9th ACM/IEEE International Conference on Information Processing in Sensor Networks*, IPSN '10, 2010.

[46] V. Lenders, E. Koukoumidis, P. Zhang, and M. Martonosi. Location-based trust for mobile user-generated content: applications, challenges and implementations. In *Proceedings of the 9th workshop on Mobile computing systems and applications*, HotMobile '08, 2008.

[47] M. Lentz, V. Erdelyi, P. Aditya, E. Shi, P. Druschel, and B. Bhattacharjee. SDDR: Light-Weight Cryptographic Discovery for Mobile Encounters. http://www.cs.umd.edu/projects/encore.

[48] Y.-H. Lin, A. Studer, H.-C. Hsiao, J. M. McCune, K.-H. Wang, M. Krohn, P.-L. Lin, A. Perrig, H.-M. Sun, and B.-Y. Yang. Spate: small-group pki-less authenticated trust establishment. In *Proceedings of the 7th international conference on Mobile systems, applications, and services*, MobiSys '09, 2009.

[49] J. Manweiler, R. Scudellari, and L. P. Cox. Smile: encounter-based trust for mobile social services. In *Proceedings of the 16th ACM conference on Computer and communications security*, CCS '09, 2009.

[50] R. Mayrhofer and H. Gellersen. Shake well before use: authentication based on accelerometer data. In *Proceedings of the 5th international conference on Pervasive computing*, PERVASIVE'07, 2007.

[51] J. S. Plank. A tutorial on reed-solomon coding for fault-tolerance in raid-like systems. *Software-Practice & Experience*, 27(9), Sept. 1997.

[52] F. Y. Rashid. Epsilon data breach highlights cloud-computing security concerns. http://www.eweek.com/c/a/Security/Epsilon-Data-Breach-Highlights-Cloud-Computing-Security-Concerns-637161/. Last accessed: September 2012.

[53] I. S. Reed and G. Solomon. Polynomial codes over certain finite fields. *Journal of the Society for Industrial & Applied Mathematics*, 8(2), jun 1960.

[54] S. Saroiu and A. Wolman. Enabling new mobile applications with location proofs. In *Proceedings of the 10th workshop on Mobile Computing Systems and Applications*, HotMobile '09, 2009.

[55] A. Schulman, T. Schmid, P. Dutta, and N. Spring. Demo: Phone power monitoring with BattOr. In *In the 17th ACM international conference on Mobile computing and networking*, MobiCom '11, 2011.

[56] R. Shokri, G. Theodorakopoulos, J.-Y. Le Boudec, and J.-P. Hubaux. Quantifying location privacy. In *Proceedings of the 2011 IEEE Symposium on Security and Privacy*, SP '11, 2011.

[57] J. Su, J. Scott, P. Hui, J. Crowcroft, E. De Lara, C. Diot, A. Goel, M. H. Lim, and E. Upton. Haggle: seamless networking for mobile applications. In *Proceedings of the 9th international conference on Ubiquitous computing*, UbiComp '07, 2007.

[58] W.-T. Tan, M. Baker, B. Lee, and R. Samadani. The sound of silence. In *Proceedings of the 11th ACM Conference on Embedded Networked Sensor Systems*, SenSys '13, 2013.

[59] K. Thomas. Microsoft cloud data breach heralds things to come. http://www.pcworld.com/article/214775/microsoft_cloud_data_breach_sign_of_future.html. Last accessed: September 2012.

[60] W. Wang, V. Srinivasan, and M. Motani. Adaptive contact probing mechanisms for delay tolerant applications. In *Proceedings of the 13th annual ACM international conference on Mobile computing and networking*, MobiCom '07, 2007.

RisQ: Recognizing Smoking Gestures with Inertial Sensors on a Wristband

Abhinav Parate   Meng-Chieh Chiu   Chaniel Chadowitz   Deepak Ganesan

Evangelos Kalogerakis

University of Massachusetts, Amherst
{aparate,joechiu,cheni,dganesan,kalo}@cs.umass.edu

ABSTRACT

Smoking-induced diseases are known to be the leading cause of death in the United States. In this work, we design *RisQ*, a mobile solution that leverages a wristband containing a 9-axis inertial measurement unit to capture changes in the orientation of a person's arm, and a machine learning pipeline that processes this data to accurately detect smoking gestures and sessions in real-time. Our key innovations are four-fold: a) an arm trajectory-based method that extracts candidate hand-to-mouth gestures, b) a set of trajectory-based features to distinguish smoking gestures from confounding gestures including eating and drinking, c) a probabilistic model that analyzes sequences of hand-to-mouth gestures and infers which gestures are part of individual smoking sessions, and d) a method that leverages multiple IMUs placed on a person's body together with 3D animation of a person's arm to reduce burden of self-reports for labeled data collection. Our experiments show that our gesture recognition algorithm can detect smoking gestures with high accuracy (95.7%), precision (91%) and recall (81%). We also report a user study that demonstrates that we can accurately detect the number of smoking sessions with very few false positives over the period of a day, and that we can reliably extract the beginning and end of smoking session periods.

Keywords

Smoking detection; Inertial measurement unit; Wearables; Mobile computing

Categories and Subject Descriptors

C.5.3 [**Computer System Implementation**]: Microcomputers—*Portable devices*; I.2.10 [**Artificial Intelligence**]: Vision and Scene Understanding—*Motion*

1. INTRODUCTION

Tobacco use remains the single largest preventable cause of death and disease in the United States and worldwide. According to CDC estimates, cigarette smoking kills more than 440,000 Americans each year, either through cancer, heart disease, stroke, or lung diseases. It also increases the chances of other serious illnesses, such as diabetes [2]. In addition, smoking-related illness in the United States costs $96 billion in medical costs and $97 billion in lost productivity each year. The numbers are more alarming worldwide, where tobacco use is increasing rapidly in low- and middle-income countries. In fact, it is estimated that there are about a billion smokers worldwide, with more than 80% in the low and middle-income countries. Of these, about 6 million die through smoking-related causes each year.

At the heart of addressing this scourge is early detection and timely treatment. Several smoking cessation programs have been developed that show that intervening at opportune moments can help a person quit smoking. In theory, continuous sensing using the mobile phone and wearables has the potential to enable such informed and timely interventions both by observing the evolution of a patient's smoking pattern over time, as well as measuring contextual factors that influence smoking (environment, social interactions, stress, etc). However, the first step towards such methods is the ability to detect smoking events in real-world settings, a goal that has proven elusive.

We argue that there is a dire need for a simple and reliable smoking detector that has high sensitivity and specificity, and is easy to wear on a day-to-day basis. Existing methods fall short on one or more of these axes. A sensitive detector for smoking is a tomography meter (e.g. CReSS monitor [1]). However, the user needs to attach the tomography device to the cigarette prior to smoking. This is both burdensome and can change the underlying smoking behavior. A recent alternative is to use the deep respiration cycles associated with inhalation and exhalation of smoke, which can be detected by a respiration chest band (mPuff [4] and Sazonov et al [17]). Unfortunately chest bands are cumbersome to wear for long periods and therefore have limited appeal beyond clinical trials. Other wearables that have been previously proposed include RF-based proximity sensors worn on the collar and wrist to detect when the hand is in the vicinity of the mouth, but this is not robust to confounders [18]. One promising approach is to embed a sensor in a cigarette lighter which detects whenever the lighter is lit [19]. Unfortunately this approach does not provide information about individual puffs and its duration, which is particularly useful for determining the degree of nicotine intake across subjects [11, 12].

Our work relies on a wristband embedded with a single, low-power 9-axis inertial measurement unit (IMU) that fuses information from an accelerometer, gyroscope, and compass to provide 3D orientation of the wrist. IMUs are easy to integrate with wrist-worn wearables, many of which already have accelerometers embedded

MobiSys'14, June 16–19, 2014, Bretton Woods, New Hampshire, USA.
Copyright 2014 ACM 978-1-4503-2793-0/14/06 ...$15.00.
http://dx.doi.org/10.1145/2594368.2594379 .

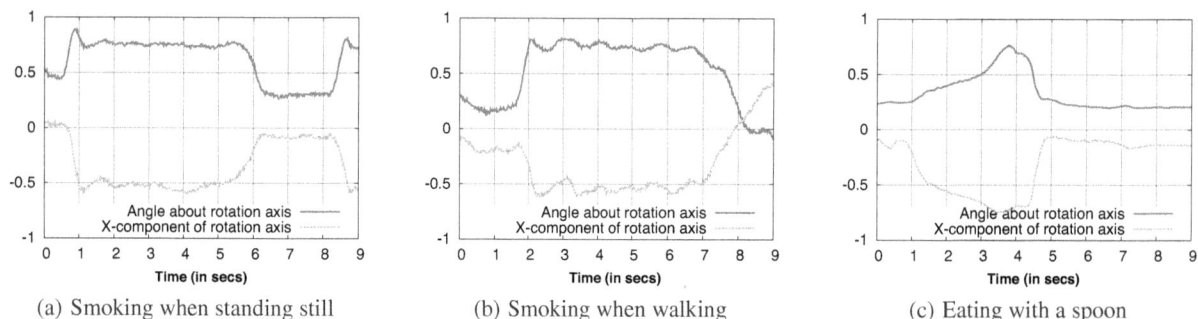

(a) Smoking when standing still   (b) Smoking when walking   (c) Eating with a spoon

Figure 1: Illustration of IMU signals for various hand-to-mouth gestures. (a) & (b) Smoking gestures are characterized by a quick change in orientation when taking a cigarette towards the mouth and a long dwell time while taking a "smoking puff". (c) In contrast, eating gestures are characterized by a slow change when taking a spoonful of food towards the mouth and a very short dwell time.

for calorie or activity tracking. However, there are many challenges in robustly recognizing smoking gestures from orientation data.

1.1 Challenges

The central challenge that we face is that we need to detect and recognize a smoking gesture from a plethora of other gestures that a user performs each day. While recognition of intentional gestures from inertial sensors is commonplace in gaming devices (e.g. Nintendo Wii), there are several challenges in achieving our goal in a natural setting.

Signal variation due to orientation changes: The first challenge is that the signal from the inertial sensor varies significantly depending on the user's body orientation. Thus, if the user changes his/her body orientation while smoking, the orientation output of the sensor will change. An example is shown in Figure 2, where a 180° change in the user's body orientation completely changes the signal. However, we still need to detect the beginning and end of a smoking gesture despite the unknown user's body orientation. Note that this problem is not present in gesture recognition systems designed for user interaction, such as the Nintendo Wii. This is because a user typically faces a fixed direction during the interaction. In addition, the user can consciously adjust the gesture so that it is recognized by the system.

Detecting smoking gestures: A second challenge is that a smoking gesture needs to be detected without any explicit information given by the user regarding the beginning and end of a smoking session. Devices such as the Nintendo Wii address this problem by having the user press a button, thereby explicitly providing information about the beginning and end of the gesture. Other gesture recognition systems such as the Bite-Counter [8] use a similar method: they assume that the user presses a button prior to an eating session. In contrast, we wish to avoid any user interaction altogether, and instead design a passive gesture tracking system. Thus, we aim at designing methods that distinguish a smoking gesture from a huge number of different gestures that a user can perform using his/her hands.

Concurrent activity while smoking: A third challenge is that the user might smoke while performing a concurrent activity. Concurrent activities can modify the characteristic patterns of smoking gestures and further complicate our problem. For example, Figure 1 shows how a smoking gesture looks when the user is stationary (Figure 1a) against when the user is walking (Figure 1b). We can see that smoking gestures have a few bumps when the user walks, in addition to the distortions at the beginning and end of the gesture where the user brings the cigarette down and contin-

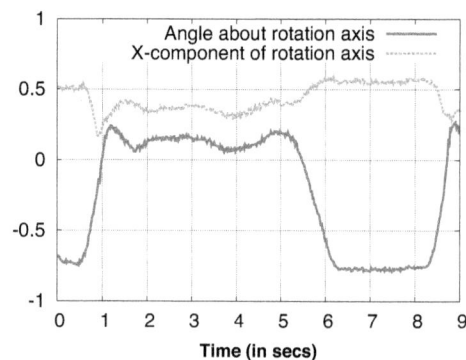

Figure 2: IMU signals for the smoking gesture in Figure 1(a) when the user changes facing direction by 180°. The characteristic patterns observed in IMU signals change with the user's orientation.

ues walking by swinging his/her hand. Similarly, the user might be conversing with a friend while smoking, or might perform other activities while sitting or standing. All such concurrent activities also complicate the smoking gesture recognition problem.

Confounding gestures: A fourth challenge is that many other gestures have arm movement patterns similar to smoking. For example, a user can perform several isolated gestures each day that involve raising the hand towards the mouth and bringing it back down similarly to smoking gestures. In particular, eating and drinking activities not only have similar hand-to-mouth gestures, but also involve repeated sequences of these gestures, as in smoking. Figure 1 shows an example of an eating gesture. Visually, there are differences in the pattern of eating compared to smoking. However, designing an algorithm that robustly distinguishes smoking from other confounding gestures across different users is particularly challenging.

Labeling smoking puffs: In order to recognize smoking gestures robustly, we design a method based on *supervised* classification. However, to train such a classifier, we need training data in the form of fine-grained labels for the beginning and end of each gesture. Many existing approaches for obtaining such labeled data are not feasible or have drawbacks: a) requesting self-reports from the users is impractical, since users cannot possibly label each smoking puff manually while smoking: such an approach would force the users to change their gestures from smoking to interacting with a device to create these self-reports, b) video capture of the smoking session for post-facto annotation is restrictive, since it requires the user to always face the camera, and c) having an observer annotate each smoking puff is cumbersome and not scalable. Thus, one particular challenge is how to enable fine-grained labeled data collection while limiting the burden on participants.

1.2 Contributions

The key innovation of our work is the ability to recognize sequences of hand gestures that correspond to smoking sessions "in the wild". This involves a sensing pipeline with several important aspects: a) we detect candidate hand-to-mouth gestures by continuously tracking and segmenting the 3D trajectory of a user's hand, b) we extract discriminative trajectory-based features that can distinguish a smoking gesture from a variety of other confounding gestures like eating and drinking, c) we design a probabilistic model based on a random forest classifier and a Conditional Random Field that analyze sequences of hand-to-mouth gestures based on their extracted features, and accurately outputs the beginning and end of smoking sessions. Finally, (d) in order to train the classifier and Conditional Random Field, we also propose a simple method to gather training labeled data "in the wild": we ask subjects to wear two IMUs, one on the elbow and one on the wrist, which allows us to build 3D animations of arm movements that can be easily labeled by a third party without compromising the subject's privacy. The only limited burden on the subject is to specify coarse time windows where smoking occurred to verify that we detect gestures within the correct periods of time. Each module in this whole pipeline addresses challenges specific to our problem domain, and we present several new ideas and algorithms.

Our results show that we can detect smoking gestures with 95.7% accuracy and 91% precision. In addition, we can detect smoking session time boundaries reliably: the error in the estimated duration of a smoking session is less than a minute. Finally, we demonstrate with a user study that we can accurately detect the number of users' smoking sessions in the period of a day with only few false positives (less than two in our study). In all, we think that RisQ is a very promising approach for use in smoking cessation and intervention.

2. BACKGROUND

Inertial Measurement Unit: The Inertial Measurement Unit (IMU) is an electronic device consisting of 3-axis accelerometer, 3-axis gyroscope and 3-axis magnetometer. IMU has an on-board processor that fuses the output of these three sensors to compute the orientation of the device in a 3D world (absolute) coordinate system defined by y-axis pointing towards the magnetic north, z-axis pointing perpendicular to the ground in the direction opposite to the earth's gravity and x-axis pointing to the geographical east. We use the Invensense MPU-9150 IMU for our experimental study. This sensor outputs the 3D orientation of a device in the form of a *quaternion*.

Quaternions: Quaternions are convenient mathematical entities for representing orientations and rotations of objects in three dimensions. Quaternions have found a great applicability in robotics, computer graphics, and computer vision communities due to the ease in calculations for performing rotations of objects in 3D space.

Formally, a *quaternion* is defined using a scalar component q_s and a 3D vector (q_x, q_y, q_z). We write a quaternion $\mathbf{q}$ as follows:

$$\mathbf{q} = q_s + q_x\hat{i} + q_y\hat{j} + q_z\hat{k}$$

where $\hat{i}, \hat{j}$ and $\hat{k}$ are imaginary basis elements, each of which squares to -1. A quaternion $\mathbf{q}$ is said to be a *unit quaternion* if its magni-

tude $|\mathbf{q}|$ given by $\sqrt{(q_s^2 + q_x^2 + q_y^2 + q_z^2)}$ is equal to one. 3D rotations can be compactly represented with unit quaternions. Given a 3D rotation defined through a unit vector $\langle x, y, z \rangle$ representing the axis of rotation, and an angle θ representing the amount of rotation about the axis, the corresponding quaternion representing this rotation is defined as:

$$\mathbf{q} = \cos\frac{\theta}{2} + x\sin\frac{\theta}{2}\hat{i} + y\sin\frac{\theta}{2}\hat{j} + z\sin\frac{\theta}{2}\hat{k}$$

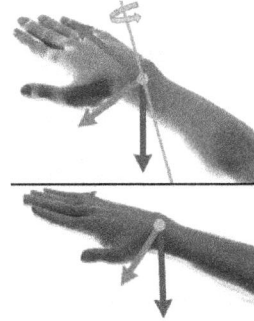

It can be shown that a point $\mathbf{p}$ in 3D space with coordinates $\{p_x, p_y, p_z\}$ can be rotated using a quaternion with the following formula:

$$\mathbf{p}' = \mathbf{q} \cdot \mathbf{p} \cdot \mathbf{q}^{-1}$$

where $\mathbf{p}$ is written as $p_x\hat{i} + p_y\hat{j} + p_z\hat{k}$, and $\mathbf{q}^{-1}$ is the so-called conjugate quaternion of $\mathbf{q}$, which is expressed as:

$$\mathbf{q}^{-1} = \cos\frac{\theta}{2} - x\sin\frac{\theta}{2}\hat{i} - y\sin\frac{\theta}{2}\hat{j} - z\sin\frac{\theta}{2}\hat{k}$$

Figure 3: Top: 3D arm and its initial reference frame. A quaternion rotates the arm about a rotation axis (shown in cyan). Bottom: rotated arm and its updated reference frame.

It is straightforward to see that a quaternion not only represents a 3D rotation, but can also represent the 3D orientation of an object. Given an initial orientation of a 3D object defined by its initial frame of reference, the quaternion q rotates the object yielding a new orientation (see Figure 3).

3. SYSTEM OVERVIEW

In this section, we provide an overview of the RisQ computational pipeline that recognizes smoking gestures and sessions. We also overview the training data collection methodology we used to obtain fine-grained labeled data for the purpose of training our supervised classification method.

Computational pipeline: Figure 4 gives an overview of the computational pipeline that we use for detecting smoking gestures and sessions. At the lowest layer of the pipeline is the extraction of quaternion data from the single wrist-worn 9-axis IMU.

The second layer in the pipeline is the segmentation layer that extracts segments containing candidate gestures from the raw sensor data and filters out extraneous data. The intuition behind the segmentation process is that, while performing a hand gesture, humans start from "a rest position" in which the arm is relaxed, then move their arm, and finally the arm falls back to another, possibly different rest position. Thus, the gestures tend to lie in segments between these resting positions. The segmentation layer accomplishes the segment extraction by computing the spatio-temporal trajectory taken by the wrist using quaternion data and tracking rest positions. Based on the computed trajectory, at each time step it computes the distance of the wrist from rest positions, and identifies segments using a peak-valley detection algorithm. The output of this layer are the extracted segments containing candidate hand gestures.

In the third layer of our pipeline, our method computes a feature vector for each segment, consisting of features that can discriminate hand-to-mouth gestures corresponding to smoking from a large number of other hand-to-mouth gesture candidates. We then

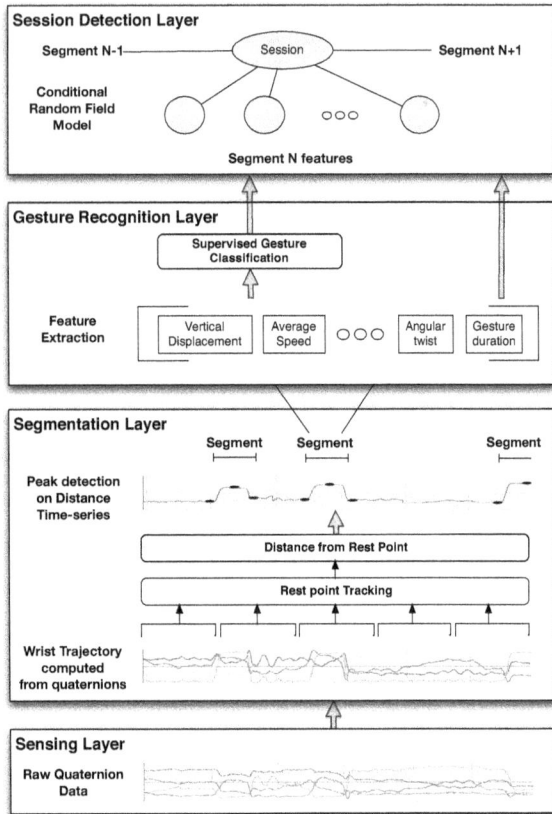

Figure 4: RisQ: Quaternion data processing pipeline

use a supervised classifier, called Random Forests [5, 7], that outputs the probability for the type of gesture ("smoking", "eating" or "other" gesture) based on the extracted features for each segment individually.

The top-most layer in the processing pipeline is a session detection layer that identifies whole sessions ("smoking", "eating", or "other") based on the Random Forest classifier outputs and the segment features. The key intuition behind this layer is that each smoking session involves a continuous sequence of smoking gestures, and is unlikely to contain gestures from other activities. We use a probabilistic model based on a Conditional Random Field (CRF) [14] that captures probabilistic dependencies between the type of gestures contained in consecutive segments. In particular, it has the advantage of filtering out spurious classification outputs of the lower layer and robustly detecting the beginning and end of smoking sessions.

While the focus of this paper is on recognizing smoking gestures and sessions, our approach can be tailored to other instances of repetitive gestures. In §6.3, we use eating sessions to train our method, and we find that it performs considerably better than state-of-art eating detectors that use inertial sensors.

Labeled data collection: We use a novel data collection methodology to obtain fine-grained gesture labeled data from participants for training our method. Our data collection framework consists of two tools: (i) a logging application and (ii) a 3D visualization and labeling tool. The logging application collects data from on-body IMU sensors placed on the user's wrist and upper arm. Since our goal is to reduce the burden of labeling for the user and avoid interfering with his gestures, our logging application provides a sim-

ple user-interface to log events on his mobile phone. This helps us identify time windows that require fine-grained labeling of the smoking or eating gestures. The 3D visualization and labeling tool produces 3D hand animations from the logged sensor data and provides an interface for fine-grained labeling of the gestures, such as "smoking a puff" or "taking a bite of food". The type of gestures can be easily labeled by other users in these animated sequences. Unlike video recording, our visualization tool allows users to see and label gestures from any viewing angle they prefer.

4. GESTURE DETECTION AND RECOGNITION

In this section, we describe how we detect and label hand-to-mouth gestures when the user wears the single IMU on his wristband. The first step in our data processing pipeline is to partition the quaternion time-series obtained from the IMU into segments such that each segment contains a gesture (§4.1). The second step is to extract some features that can be used to discriminate different types of gestures (§4.2). The last step is to recognize the detected gestures and extract smoking sessions (§4.3).

4.1 Gesture detection

In order to detect a gesture, it is essential that we segment the time series of quaternions into segments, such that each segment contains a complete gesture. The problem of correctly segmenting sequences of quaternions presents a number of challenges. First, the segmentation should extract segments representing the entire gesture duration. Otherwise characteristic features that are useful in classifying a gesture will be lost. Moreover, the extracted segments should not be much longer than the gesture, otherwise the computed features related to the gesture will be inaccurate. Another fundamental challenge is that the characteristic patterns observed in a time series of quaternions are dependent on the orientation of the person's body performing the gesture. For example, the pattern observed for a gesture when the person is lying on a bed is very different from the pattern observed when he is standing. The problem gets further complicated due to the large number of variations in the gestures observed for the same activity, within and across users, making the variability of characteristic patterns extremely high. An additional challenge comes from the huge number of all possible gestures and possibly confounding gestures performed by humans throughout their daily life.

The intuition behind our segmentation approach is the observation that the humans tend to perform a gesture starting from an initial rest body pose, and then ending the gesture in another, possibly different, rest pose. This observation holds true for the hand-to-mouth gestures we intend to identify. For example, a person may start a smoking gesture by having his hand lie on an armrest of a chair, then move his hands towards his mouth, then back to the armrest of the chair or the top of a table. Alternatively, the arm might end up being straight, hanging from the body. In general, the beginning and end rest poses are not necessarily stationary and are not necessarily identical. In the following sections, we describe our segmentation approach based on continuous tracking of the rest positions of the fore-arm and computing the spatio-temporal trajectory of the wrist in 3D space.

Relative trajectory computation: Our first step towards identifying hand-to-mouth gestures is computing the spatio-temporal trajectory of the hand from the stream of quaternion data. The main challenge here is that trajectory is affected by body motion and orientation. For example, a smoking gesture when a person is walking takes a much longer path in 3D space compared to the same ges-

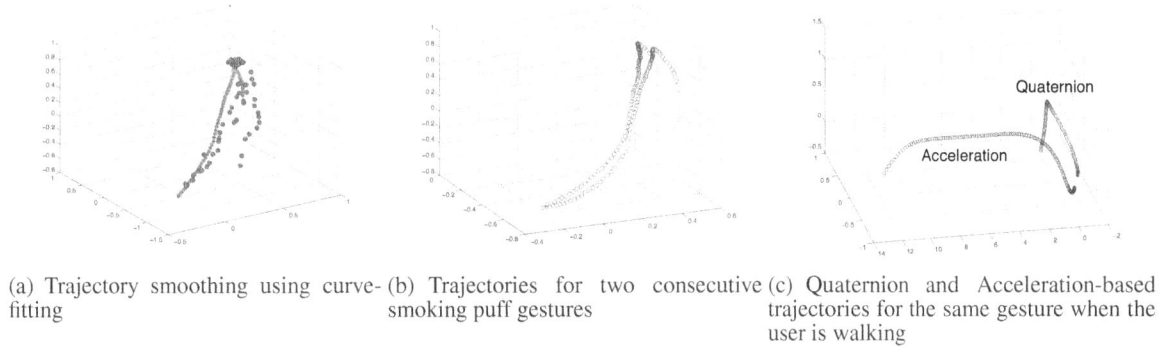

(a) Trajectory smoothing using curve-fitting

(b) Trajectories for two consecutive smoking puff gestures

(c) Quaternion and Acceleration-based trajectories for the same gesture when the user is walking

Figure 5: Figure (a) shows a noisy trajectory for a smoking puff gesture and the smooth trajectory (green curve) obtained after curve-fitting. Figure (b) shows trajectories for two consecutive puffs while standing still. These two trajectories are well-aligned for the isomorphic gestures. Figure (c) shows the trajectory for a smoking puff gesture when the user is walking, computed from acceleration data (blue curve) and quaternion data (brown curve). The acceleration-based trajectory is significantly elongated and distorted when the user is walking, while holding the cigarette in his mouth. The quaternion-based trajectory instead is computed relatively to the elbow and is free of such motion artifacts.

ture performed when the person stands at one place. Similarly, a smoking gesture could be affected by any changes to the pose of the user's body while smoking.

The key insight in our approach is that we care less about the absolute trajectory of the hand in 3D space. We care more about the trajectory of the hand relative to a body joint, such as the shoulder joint. Such a relative trajectory would not depend on the orientation of the person's body, and every smoking gesture should result in roughly isomorphic trajectories with similar shape characteristics.

While such a relative trajectory would be easy to compute if the individual also had an IMU close to the shoulder, the fact that we only have a single wrist-worn IMU complicates the problem. To address this, we make a simplifying assumption that the position of the elbow remains stationary (the shoulder joint does not rotate) while the gesture is being performed. Specifically we compute the trajectory of the wrist relative to a stationary elbow, assuming that the wrist is in a fixed, unit distance away from it. We find that the above assumptions have little influence in our trajectory computation, since hand-to-mouth gestures primarily involve rotating the elbow and not moving the upper arm.

More formally, given a time sequence of quaternions ($\mathbf{q}_1$, $\mathbf{q}_2$, ..., $\mathbf{q}_n$), we can compute the trajectory taken by the wrist by computing the position of the wrist for each time step t ($t = 1...n$). The position of the wrist $\mathbf{w}$ at time t in the elbow's frame of reference $\mathcal{F}$ can be computed as follows:

$$\mathbf{w} = \mathbf{q}_t \cdot \mathbf{w}_0 \cdot \mathbf{q}_t^{-1} \qquad (1)$$

where $\mathbf{w}_0 = 0\hat{i} + 1\hat{j} + 0\hat{k}$ (i.e., has coordinates $\begin{bmatrix} 0 & 1 & 0 \end{bmatrix}$) represents the position of the wrist in the device's local coordinates based on the assumption that the length of the forearm of person has unit length. This assumption also works in our favor as the computed trajectories are independent of the particular variations of the arm length across the population.

Due to this approximating nature of the computed trajectory and the continuous shifts in the elbow position, the wrist trajectory does not always appear smooth. Thus, we smooth the trajectory by fitting a curve using cubic B-splines. Figure 5(a) shows a sample trajectory for a smoking puff gesture before and after the smoothing operation.

IMU vs Accelerometer: One question that is worth asking at this point is whether we really need a 9-axis IMU that provides

quaternion data (by fusing information from the accelerometer, gyroscope, and compass) to compute trajectories, or whether we can do the same with a single accelerometer. Figure 5(b) shows two smoothed sample trajectories taken for two consecutive cigarette puffs while standing still. These trajectories are computed relative to the elbow and align well as the gestures are isomorphic. In Figure 5(c), we show the accelerometer-based and quaternion-based trajectories for the smoking gesture when the user is walking. We see that the accelerometer-based trajectory in this case appears longer. This is because it is relative to the starting point in world coordinates. On the other hand, the trajectory computed using quaternions is relative to the elbow has similar characteristics to trajectories observed when standing still.

Segment Extraction: Our segmentation procedure is based on the observation that humans tend to keep their hands in rest positions and any gesture starts from one rest position and terminates at another rest position. The key challenge is determining these rest positions in a continuous stream of wrist movement. The rest positions need not be the same across gestures (e.g. rest position while sitting and smoking would be different from standing and smoking). Even the beginning rest position for a single smoking puff might be different from the final rest position, since there can be many positions where the human arm is "relaxed".

Our segment extraction method involves four stages:

▶ First, our segment extraction method continuously tracks the rest position from which a current hand gesture started. To detect the rest position, the trajectory is traced according to short sliding time windows (e.g. 10 seconds). Within each window, positions where the wrist velocity is very low are computed. If one or more candidates exist, then we compute the centroid of these low velocity points as the "rest point". Thus, we can now annotate each point in each trajectory trace with the most recent point corresponding to the rest position for which the hand gesture started.

▶ Second, we compute the spatial distance of each point in the trajectory from the most recent rest point. For any hand-to-mouth gesture, we expect that the distance from the rest point should increase rapidly, plateau for a short period, and then return to the next rest point.

▶ Third, we use a peak detector to detect peaks and troughs in the distance time series obtained from the previous stage, and look for a tell-tale trough-peak-trough pattern that is typical of a hand-to-mouth gesture. To filter false positives from either tiny hand movements or very long gestures, we use a relatively loose threshold for distance separation between trough and peak, as well as the expected duration of a typical smoking puff. At this point, the segment extraction pipeline provides the trough-peak-trough segment to the next level of the classification pipeline.

4.2 Segment Feature Extraction

In order to recognize the type of gesture in each segment, we need to compute features that can discriminate different types of gestures. The feature extraction procedure is based on the observation that a hand-to-mouth gesture can be divided into three stages: i) an "ascending" stage that corresponds to the trough to peak movement when the hand goes towards the mouth, ii) a "stationary" stage that corresponds to the period where the hand stays near the peak (close to mouth), and iii) a "descending" stage where the hand goes from peak to trough i.e. back to the rest position. These three sub-segments are useful for extracting features as we describe below.

Table 1 shows the set of features computed for each segment. The following paragraphs describe the features we compute from the smoothed spatio-temporal trajectory and the quaternion information:

▶ **Duration features.** These features measure the time duration of the segment containing the gesture and the durations of the three stages within the segment: ascending, descending and stationary.

▶ **Velocity features.** Second, we use the computed positions of the wrist at each time step to compute the instantaneous velocity of the wrist for the ascending and the descending stages. We compute the average speed, the maximum speed and the variance in speed for both ascending and the descending stages giving us six features.

▶ **Displacement features.** These features measure the displacement of the wrist during the ascending and the descending stages of the wrist motion. We measure the vertical displacement, displacement on the plane parallel to the ground and the net displacement at the end of each stage as features.

▶ **Angle features.** From the orientation information, we can compute the *roll* component of the rotation about the axis of the arm. This is computed by converting the quaternions into Tait-Bryan angles. We call the rate of change in the angle of the rotation along the axis of the arm "roll velocity". We compute the median and the maximum of instantaneous roll velocities and use them as features. Also, we compute the net roll angle as the feature. We extract these 3 features for the ascending and the descending stage. Next, we compute "pitch" that measures the angle between the vector along the arm and the direction of the gravity. We use pitch angle at the peak point of the ascending and the descending stages as features. Next, using the distribution of pitch angles observed at each time step for the ascending stage, we compute 9 values that give the $10^{th}, 20^{th}, ..., 100^{th}$ percentile values as the features. For the descending stage, we use median pitch as a feature.

4.3 Gesture recognition

After extracting segments that contain individual gestures, the next step in our pipeline is to recognize each gesture contained in each segment. The input to this step is a set of segments with their features and the output is a set of labels representing the type of gesture (e.g. "smoking", "eating", or "other" depending on available labels).

Labeling segments poses a number of challenges. First, there is no simple mapping between the duration, velocity, displacement and angular features and the labels. For example, if the duration of the gesture is more than a particular threshold, we cannot infer that the gesture is a "smoking puff" with total certainty. It might be the case that the user instead drinks slowly from a cup. Therefore, we have to also consider other features: for example, smoking is likely to also be strongly correlated with certain ranges of arm twisting angles, wrist velocities, horizontal and vertical displacements and so on. Manually constructing a mathematical formula that detects all smoking gestures based on features is very hard. Noise in the trajectory features make things worse, thus we need to adopt a probabilistic method that outputs the probability of assigning each label to each segment. In the following paragraph, we describe a probabilistic classifier for recognizing each individual gesture. Unfortunately, classifying each gesture independently from all the others in a sequence of segments does not seem to work very well. For example, a sequence of gestures might be labeled as $\{smoking, smoking, eating, smoking, smoking\}$. However, it is very unlikely that the user interrupts and intermixes gestures in a small period of time. Such noisy labelings can easily occur due to feature noise and large deviation of wrist trajectories from the ones in our training data. Thus, we employ a probabilistic model that takes as input the probabilistic output of the classifier for each individual segment, and additionally examines how likely is for successive segments to have the same or different label. Based on this probabilistic model, we estimate the most likely joint labeling of all segments together. We describe this probabilistic model later in this section.

Individual classification of gestures: To build a mapping from segment features to segment labels, we observe that the type of gestures is likely to be correlated with certain value ranges of segment features extracted in the previous section. For this reason, we use a classifier that has a form of a decision tree. A decision tree contains a set of nodes and at each node, the value of an individual feature is compared to a threshold. Then depending on whether the feature of the segment has a smaller or larger value than the threshold, the classifier examines the left or right child node, which in turn examines the value of another feature. When a leaf node is reached, the decision tree outputs a probability based on how many segments in our training data had the same set of splits while traversing the tree.

The thresholds and feature choices at each node of the tree are automatically constructed from the training data during an offline stage. The best choice of features and thresholds are selected to maximize the confidence of predictions [7].

Unfortunately, fitting a single decision tree in the training data results in poor performance. The reason is that a single set of splits yields predictions that are suited only for segments whose features are very similar to the ones of the training segments. A popular alternative is to build an ensemble of decision trees: each decision tree is fitted to small different random subsets of the training data. This leads to decorrelating the individual tree predictions and, in turn, results in improved generalization and robustness [7]. This ensemble of decision trees is called random forest classifier. The output of the random classifier is the probability of assigning a label to each segment, computed as the average of the probabilities outputted by the individual decision trees.

Joint classification of gestures: As we explained in the beginning of the section, classifying each segment independently from all the others in a sequence of segments yields noisy label predictions. Instead, we classify all segments jointly by using the out-

Feature Set		
Duration Features		
Duration	4	Total gesture duration, and duration for the ascending, descending, and the stationary stage.
Velocity Features		
Speed	6	Mean, max and variance of the wrist speed. We compute these for the ascending and the descending stages.
Displacement Features		
distZ	2	Vertical displacement of the wrist during the ascending and descending stage.
distXY	2	Horizontal displacement of the wrist during the ascending and descending stage. This is computed on a plane parallel to the ground.
dist	2	Net displacement between the rest position and the peak position. This is computed for the ascending and the descending stage.
Angle Features		
roll velocity	4	Median and maximum angular velocity about the axis of the arm. We compute 2 features each for the ascending and the descending stage.
roll	2	Net angular change about the axis of the arm during the ascending and the descending stage.
pitch	12	Angle between the arm and the direction of the gravity (pitch angle). We compute the pitch angle at the peak during the ascending and descending stage. Also, we obtain 9 decile features from the pitch pitch distribution for the ascending stage. We compute the median pitch angle for the descending stage.

Table 1: Feature set extracted for a segment containing a gesture. The table describes each feature type and gives the count of features used for each type.

put of the random forest and also considering that consecutive segments in a sequence are more likely to have the same rather than different label.

Given a sequence of $k = 1...K$ segments, we introduce a random variable C_k for each segment representing the type of gesture contained in the segment. We express the joint probability of assigning a sequence of labels to all the random variables $\mathbf{C} = \{C_1, C_2, ..., C_K\}$ of the segments given their features $\mathbf{x} = \{\mathbf{x}_1, \mathbf{x}_2, ..., \mathbf{x}_K\}$ as follows:

$$P(\mathbf{C}|\mathbf{x}) = \frac{1}{Z(\mathbf{x})} \prod_k \phi(C_k, \mathbf{x}_k) \prod_{k,k+1} \psi(C_k, C_{k+1})$$

The unary factors $\phi(C_k, X_k)$ assess the consistency of each individual segment to each label based on the random forest classifier. The pairwise factors $\psi(C_k, C_{k+1})$ assess the consistency of each pair of consecutive segments to their labels. The denominator $Z(\mathbf{x})$ serves as a normalization constant for each input sequence to ensure that the sum of probabilities over all possible label assignments is equal to 1. The type of this model is known as Conditional Random Field [14] in the literature of machine learning.

In our implementation, the unary factors have the following form:

$$\phi(C_k = l, \mathbf{x}_k) = \exp(\theta_l f_l(\mathbf{x}_k) + \theta_{l_0})$$

where $f_l(\mathbf{x}_k)$ are the probabilistic outputs of the random forest classifier for each label $l = \{smoking, eating, other\}$. The parameters $\{\theta_l, \theta_{l,0}\}$ re-scale the probabilities of the random forest classifier, and are learned from the training data. The exp function ensures that the final result will lie in the interval $[0, 1]$ (i.e., will also be a probability) after applying the normalization constant, as typically done in logistic regression and log-linear CRF models [20].

The pairwise factors evaluate how likely is to assign pairs of labels in consecutive segments and are expressed as:

$$\psi(C_k = l, C_{k+1} = l') = \exp(\theta_{l,l'})$$

The parameters $\theta_{l,l'}$ are also learned from the training data. The learned parameters turn out to favor the same label for consecutive segments, as expected.

Parameter learning: It is extremely hard to hand-tune the parameters $\boldsymbol{\theta} = \{\theta_l, \theta_{l,0}, \theta_{l,l'}\}$ in the above probabilistic model. Instead, the model parameters are learned such that they maximize the likelihood of the training sequences. Specifically, the parameters are estimated to maximize the following objective function [13]:

$$L(\{\lambda_k\}) = \sum_{n=1}^{N} \log(P(\mathbf{C}[n] \mid \mathbf{x}[n])) - \mu||\boldsymbol{\theta}||^2$$

where the first term expresses the log likelihood of the training sequences given their features. The second term is a regularization term that penalizes large values in the parameters. Such large values would favor over-fitting of the parameters to the training dataset, and are less likely to generalize to new data. The parameter μ is selected through cross-validation.

The objective function is maximized using the L-BFGS method [15] which is a popular optimization method for solving unconstrained optimization problems. The objective function is convex function, thus, a unique maximum exists [13].

Inference: Given a sequence of segments, we estimate the most likely joint assignment of labels to the segments based on the above model. From the assigned labels, we can simply extract the different gesture sessions by tracking when the label changes in the sequence of segments.

Inference is performed with the technique known as max-product belief propagation [13], which yields the most likely sequence labeling in this type of model. The complexity of the evaluating the unary and pairwise terms, as well as executing belief propagation is linear in the number of segments, thus the labelings can be predicted very efficiently.

5. LABELED DATA COLLECTION

In this section, we describe the framework used to capture ground truth data in uncontrolled environment settings with a low labeling overhead for the user, and the dataset that we obtained through this approach. The main idea is to have the subject wear two inertial sensors, one at the wrist, and one at the elbow, and segment the data post-facto through a 3D visualization tool. We note that the

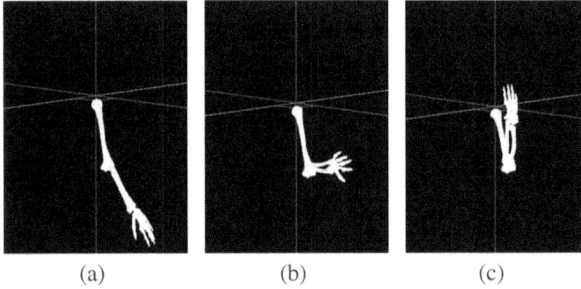

Figure 6: Smoking gesture visualization using sensor data obtained from the two IMUs placed on the upper arm and the wrist.

use of two sensors is used only for gathering training data. During actual usage of RisQ (i.e., during testing), the user always wear a single IMU on a wristband, which is more practical, user-friendly, and less costly.

5.1 Labeling Framework

Sensors: We use Invensense MPU-9150 IMU to obtain orientation data sampled at 50Hz. We fit a user with a wristband and an armband, each containing an IMU device and use a mobile app to log the sensor data on the phone. Our goal is to reconstruct the hand gestures performed by a user using the logged data.

Constructing hand gesture: A human arm consists of an upper arm and a forearm. The upper arm is connected to the shoulder, and is connected with the forearm at the elbow. The forearm extends from the elbow to the wrist. For constructing the hand motion, we assume that the orientation is uniform for the entire forearm and the entire upper arm. This assumption is simplistic as the orientation of the forearm close to the elbow can be different from the orientation of the wrist but this assumption enables us to reconstruct a fairly accurate hand motion with fewer sensors.

In order to reconstruct the hand motion, we use a digital model of a 3D human skeleton in a polygon mesh format (Figure 6). The 3D model consists of skeletal limbs that that can be oriented independently by applying the orientation information in the form of quaternions to the shoulder and elbow joints of the skeleton. The orientations given by the quaternions are applied to the skeleton hierarchically as in skeleton-based animation methods commonly used in computer graphics applications. Given that we log the sensor data at 50Hz, we render the 3D model at 50 frames per seconds where we draw a new pose of the 3D model every frame to enable real-time playback. Rendering is implemented in Processing 2, a popular library used in computer graphics.

Labeling: Using the 3D animation and visualization method described above, we can now mark the start and the end of a gesture like a cigarette puff. However, manually visualizing and marking the gesture for hours of data can be a time-consuming exercise, and in the absence of any additional information, it is difficult to distinguish smoking or eating from any confounding gestures that may look similar. To address this, we ask the participating users in the data collection to mark the beginning and the end of the smoking and eating periods using a mobile app. For fine-grained gesture labeling, we limited our efforts to the marked periods.

5.2 Gesture Dataset

Our dataset consists of IMU data collected for over 32 hours from 15 volunteers for over 20 smoking sessions, 15 eating sessions, 6 drinking sessions, and a variety of other gestures. Users

typically wear sensors for several hours, therefore, our dataset contains many potential confounding gestures. Of this data, we had to discard a few smoking and eating sessions due to interruptions and extreme noise in the data. This left us with 28 hours of data, containing 17 smoking sessions and 10 eating sessions. Overall these sessions include 369 smoking puffs and 252 food bites. The data included users performing several concurrent activities including smoking while standing alone, smoking in a group while having a conversation, smoking using a hand-rolled cigarette and smoking while walking around.

We used our 3D visualization and labeling tool to hand-label the start and end of each smoking puff within the smoking periods reported by the participants. There are a few instances when defining a precise start or a precise end of a gesture is not possible. Since our focus is on detecting a smoking puff, any interval that begins at least 1 second prior to the puff and ends after at least 1 second of the puff is valid for training our algorithm.

6. EVALUATION

Our evaluation has three parts. We start with evaluating how well we detect individual smoking gestures (taking smoking "puffs") and whole smoking sessions. Then, we compare our results against prior work that detects wrist gestures and smoking behavior. Finally, we include a user study for which we implemented the full computational pipeline on a mobile phone, and demonstrate the effectiveness of RisQ for recognizing users' smoking sessions in real-time.

6.1 Recognizing smoking sessions

The ultimate goal of our work is to detect smoking sessions accurately so that we can track: a) how many times a user smoked each day, b) the length of each smoking session, and c) how many puffs they took during each session.

Smoking session detection: First, we look at how many smoking sessions were identified correctly by RisQ. We ran a leave-one-out cross-validation experiment where we leave a single smoking session for testing, and use rest of the data for training. We repeat this procedure for each smoking session in our dataset described in §5. At each time, we evaluate the output of max-product belief propagation in our CRF.

RisQ detected 15 complete sessions out of the 17 sessions in our dataset— it missed 2 smoking sessions for two users who had gestures largely different from other users.

RisQ is also able determine the duration of smoking sessions. Table 2 shows the results of this experiment. The average ground-truth session duration in this set up was 326.2 seconds. We observe an average error of 65.7 seconds in our session duration estimate for the 17 smoking sessions in our leave-one-out cross-validation experiment. We note that when we exclude the two undetected sessions, the average error is reduced to 26.22 seconds. The errors are caused due to the approximate estimates of the beginning and end time-stamps of each session.

Statistic	Avg ± Std. Dev.
Duration of smoking sessions	326.21±19.65 s
Error in estimation	65.7±30.6 s

Table 2: Errors in session duration estimates using our CRF.

6.2 Recognizing smoking gestures

We examine now how well we can recognize individual hand-to-mouth smoking gestures that correspond to each smoking puff in

	Performance Metrics			
	Accuracy	Recall	Precision	False-positive rate
Random Forests	93.00%	0.85	0.72	0.023
CRF	95.74%	0.81	0.91	0.005

Table 3: Performance metrics for smoking puff detection obtained using 10-fold cross-validation evaluation with i) Random Forests classifier (RF), ii) Conditional Random Fields (CRF) with Random Forests. CRF reduces 75.83% of the number of false positives generated by RF, thus improving precision.

a session. Since the total number of smoking gestures is large in our dataset (369 "smoking puffs", 252 "food bites" and 4976 other gestures), we perform a 10-fold cross-validation experiment here: we split the gestures into 10 groups (folds), and of the 10 folds, a single fold is retained for testing, and the remaining 9 are used for training. Then we repeat for each test fold.

First, we evaluate how well individual smoking gestures can be detected by the Random Forest (RF) classifier which examines each segment independently of the others. Then we evaluate the performance of the CRF that infers the type of gesture for each segment by considering the probabilistic dependencies of the segment labels in a sequence.

Gesture detection performance: Table 3 shows the performance metrics for 10-fold cross-validation for smoking puff gesture detection using i) the RF classifier , and ii) CRF. We see that the RF classifier gives 93% accuracy in gesture recognition, and a moderate precision value of 0.72 in detecting smoking gestures. The CRF significantly improves the performance by reducing the number of false positives by 75.83%. This results in a much higher precision value of 0.91 in detecting smoking gestures, and overall 95.74% accuracy in overall gesture recognition. The CRF only causes a slight decrease in recall from 0.85 to 0.81.

Optimizing performance: We now examine how we can optimize the precision and recall for smoking gesture detection by tuning our method. While training the RF classifier, we use a cost function that adds a penalty for missing a training smoking gesture. When this penalty is increased, it increases recall for the smoking gestures, although it also increases the number of false positives. Figure 7 shows the change in precision and recall obtained using RF versus CRF as this penalty increases. We can make two observations here: first, a false positive rate as small as 0.05 results in a significant drop in precision (0.6) of the RF classifier. This is because of the large number of non-smoking hand gestures. Second, the CRF cleans up the mis-classifications of the RF classifier to improve precision. Figure 7 shows that this improvement can be as high as 0.53. However, this improvement comes at a cost of drop in recall, as CRF smooths out some of the true gestures. We can see that the best performance is achieved for a false positive rate of 0.023.

Generalization across subjects: We now examine whether our method can successfully detect gestures for a user by using training data only from other users. In other words, we examine how well our method *generalizes* to new users' data not included during training. For this experiment, we test the smoking gesture detection for each of 14 smokers, given training data from the other 13 in our dataset. Figure 8 shows precision and recall in this "leave-one-user-out" scenario using the Random Forest classifier and the CRF. The precision and recall of our method are high on average which indicates that our method is able to generalize to new users. In particular, the CRF improves precision, but it may occasionally filter out correctly detected puffs. This happens if the user's gestures and their temporal distribution is largely different from what

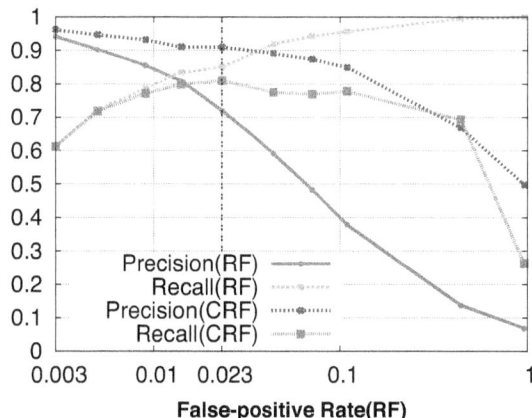

Figure 7: Precision & Recall versus False Positive rate, while adjusting the cost function of the Random Forest (RF) classifier during training. A small increase in false positive rate reduces precision of the RF classifier but the CRF improves the precision dramatically.

	Eating Sessions		All data	
	Recall	Precision	Recall	Precision
Bite-Counter	0.60	0.57	0.65	0.03
RF	0.92	0.78	0.69	0.64
CRF	N/A	N/A	0.64	0.78

Table 4: Eating gesture detection using Bite-counter [8] for cases: i) within eating sessions when it is known that user is having a meal, and ii) when session information is not available.

is observed in the training. This suggests the it is better to acquire training data from a variety of users.

6.3 Comparison #1: Bite Counter

Our first comparison examines a different IMU-based gesture recognition technique, and the benefits of using our computational pipeline.

Bite-Counter [8] is a state-of-art method to detect eating bites while having a meal using angular velocity from a gyroscope worn on the wrist. The intuition is that the angular velocity about the axis along the wrist increases above an empirically observed threshold (T_1) while taking a bite and drops below another threshold (T_2) after taking the bite. Also, there is a minimum time-lapsed (T_3) between these two threshold-crossing events while eating food, and a threshold on the time interval between two consecutive bites (T_4). Thus, this algorithm requires searching for the values of these four parameters: $\{T_1, T_2, T_3, T_4\}$ that have the best score. The score is given by $\frac{4}{7} \times$ precision$+\frac{3}{7} \times$recall. One caveat is that the Bite-Counter algorithm knows when an eating session is in progress

(a) Random Forests

(b) CRF

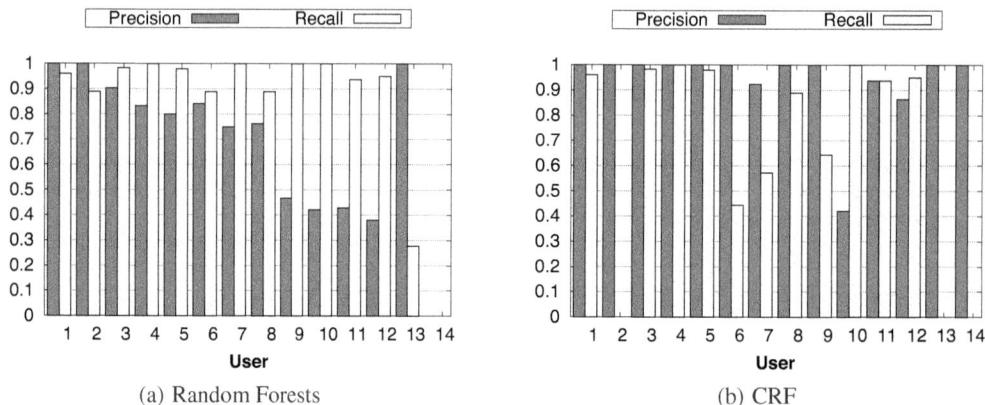

Figure 8: "Leave-one-user-out" evaluation results. The CRF improves precision over the RF classifier. Occasionally the CRF smooths out puffs correctly detected by the RF classifier resulting in a slightly lower recall.

	In-Sessions		All data	
	Recall	Precision	Recall	Precision
Bite-Counter	0.60	0.71	0.73	0.05
RF	0.97	0.95	0.85	0.72
CRF	N/A	N/A	0.81	0.91

Table 5: Smoking gesture detection using Bite-counter [8] for cases: i) within smoking sessions when it is known that user is smoking, and ii) when session information is not available.

since the user presses a button, whereas RisQ requires no such information.

Eating gesture detection: For a fair comparison, we first look exclusively at eating sessions in our dataset, and train RisQ to detect eating gestures using the same feature set and approach that we used for smoking. For this purpose, we labeled the bite gestures in 10 of the eating sessions in our dataset. Table 4 shows the results for two cases — one where we examine eating gesture detection within known eating sessions (case for which Bite-Counter is optimized), and one where we look across the entire data that includes all types of gestures. For evaluation limited to eating sessions, we only use the Random Forest classifier, and excluded CRF as we do not need to detect sessions. Even when only looking within the eating sessions, we see that RisQ has substantially higher precision and recall (21% improvement in precision and 32% improvement in recall). We suspect that our benefits are primarily due to the use of more robust trajectory-based features rather than just the wrist rotation, and the use of the Random Forest classifier as opposed to simple thresholds. As might be expected, when the eating sessions are not known a priori, the performance of Bite-Counter drops substantially. Bite-Counter still has good recall, but the precision is extremely low (0.03) i.e., the algorithm is generating a huge number of mis-classifications since it is picking up a substantial fraction of cases where the wrist is rotated, and detecting them as a bite.

We must note here that RisQ was not designed to detect eating behavior in the first place. Thus, it is possible that with more careful exploration of features, the detection of eating gestures can improve. However, the fact that it performs better even without such tuning demonstrates the broader potential of our approach for gestures other than smoking.

Smoking gesture detection: Just as RisQ can be re-trained to detect eating gestures, Bite-Counter can be re-trained to detect smok-

ing gestures by looking for wrist rotations that are representative of smoking. We use the methodology in [8] to learn appropriate parameters for Bite-Counter if it were used for detection smoking gestures. Table 5 shows the comparative results. The results clearly show that RisQ perform much better than Bite-counter.

6.4 Comparison #2: mPuff

We now turn to an alternate approach for detecting smoking gestures using a respiration chest band: mPuff [4]. Although the results are on different datasets, mPuff reports precision of 91%, true positive rate of 83% and false positive rate of 8%. Our results are similar for precision, and better for other metrics.

To directly compare these methods, we collected several hours of data from the Zephyr Bioharness Chestband for respiration data and the wrist-worn IMUs. Our dataset was captured in the wild, and has several smoking sessions in addition to other activities such as drinking, driving, walking, working on a computer, and so on.

We used the approach suggested in mPuff, which suggests a list of features and the use of an SVM classifier for training the parameters. However, there was substantial noise in the breathing dataset due to other concurrent activities (walking, driving, etc), as a result of which many breathing waveforms had to be discarded prior to training the classifier. The results of training using the clean breathing waveforms were unsuccessful, and we got low precision/recall numbers using mPuff. The results using RisQ instead were similar to those shown earlier.

While further exploration is needed for a quantitative comparison, we highlight that dealing with noise and confounders is a challenge no matter what sensor modality is used for detecting behaviors such as smoking. The fact that RisQ works well despite the confounders is one of its major strengths.

6.5 User Study in the Wild

Our final study looks at the entire computational pipeline learnt using the dataset described in §5, and executed in real time for new users.

Android-based Implementation: Our Android-based implementation for the user study comprises of a wearable wristband with an IMU and bluetooth that continuously streams quaternions at a rate of 50 Hz to an Android phone. The RisQ computational pipeline for real-time smoking session detection is executed on the phone. Our application generates notifications when it detects that a smoking session is in progress and prompts the user to confirm if the detection is correct. Apart from smoking detection, our application

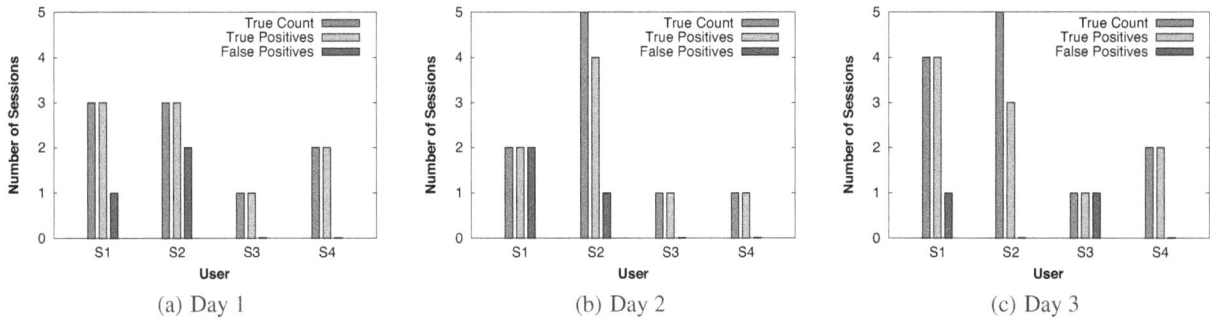

(a) Day 1   (b) Day 2   (c) Day 3

Figure 9: User study results for 4 subjects for 3 days. Figures show the following information for each subject and each day: i) ground-truth count of the smoking sessions, ii) number of sessions detected correctly i.e. true positives, and iii) number of falsely detected sessions i.e. false positives. The results show that we rarely missed a session and had only a few false detections (0-2) per day.

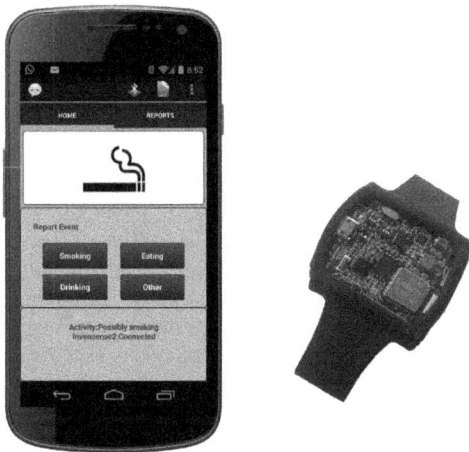

Figure 10: Smoking monitor mobile app and an IMU-equipped wristband.

also acts as a logging app to record data from the IMU worn by a user and to record ground truth events like the beginning and the end of a smoking session.

The complete UI of the mobile application and an IMU equipped wristband are shown in Figure 10. The main interface of the app has a set of UI buttons that can be used by a user to report smoking events as well as confounding events like drinking and eating. A user can use this to report the session boundaries using *before, during* and *after the session* events. In addition, the UI has a tab to view the events previously reported by the user. A user can use this interface to correct the reported event times or to delete a report if there was an error in submitting reports.

The complete gesture recognition pipeline has been implemented in Java. This pipeline detects smoking gestures every 20 seconds in the the buffered sensor data. The classification is done using a Random Forest classification model, learnt using the Weka data mining software [10]. The classification outputs are then buffered for a minute and used in forming a CRF model to detect a smoking session in progress. The inference using CRF is done every minute, thus there is an average latency of 30 seconds in detecting the start of a smoking session.

User study: We recruited 4 users for this study. The users wore the IMU-fitted wristband for four hours per day for three days. We

asked these users to always carry the phone with our mobile application installed. To record the ground truth information, we ask users to report the rough start and the end time for their smoking sessions using our app. Also, our app prompted these users whenever it detected smoking and the users could respond by confirming yes or no. Our goal was to check how well our algorithm would work if it were integrated into a real-world intervention algorithm that a therapist might use, such as a phone call or text message.

How well can RisQ deliver real-time interventions?: Figure 9 shows the actual number of sessions, number of sessions detected by the mobile app correctly and the number of sessions falsely detected for the four users. We see that the number of sessions varied between 1 to 5 in a day for the period that the mobile app was running. Of all the 30 reported smoking sessions, we missed only 3 sessions. The number of false session detections was low and less than or equal to 2 per day. In our informal exit interviews with the users, they reported no discomfort from the small number of false alarms that was raised by RisQ. In summary, the user study provides strong evidence of the effectiveness of our technique in recognizing smoking sessions across users in real-world scenarios.

Statistic	Value
Time for segmentation	92.34±6.85 ms (52-134ms)
Time for feature extraction	79.88±5.30 ms (9-227ms)
Time for CRF Inference	5.89±2.50 ms (1-23ms)
Memory	12-20 MB
Binary Size	1.7 MB

Table 6: System overhead measured on a Galaxy Nexus phone

RisQ Implementation benchmarks: We finalized our evaluation with a brief benchmark of our real-time implementation of RisQ. We first demonstrate that our mobile app has a low system overhead. Table 6 shows the summary of the execution overhead of the smoking detection pipeline measured on Samsung Galaxy Nexus device running Android 4.3 OS. The execution of the three stages in the pipeline: segment extraction, feature vector extraction and session detection using the CRF take an average time of 92.34 ms, 79.88 ms and 6 ms respectively. These overheads are incurred every 20 seconds for segmentation and feature extraction and once in a minute for the CRF inference. The memory requirement to execute our app is modest and varies between 12-20 MB. Users running our application for the user study did not find our app to impact the performance of their phones in their daily usage.

Operating Voltage	2.4-3.6 V
Operating Current (accel,gyro,compass)	4.25 mA
Streaming Data rate	1150 bytes/s

Table 7: Specifications for Invensense MPU-9150 IMU

Power Consumption: Table 7 gives the performance metrics for the operation of Invensense MPU-9150 IMU that we used in our user study. This device comes with a 110mAh battery that provides up to 4 hours of bluetooth streaming of quaternion data sampled at 50Hz. The limited execution time of the device is due to the bluetooth communication overhead that requires an operating current of 50 mA when active. In comparison, the operating currents required for execution of accelerometer, compass (sampled at 8Hz) and gyroscope sensors are 140 μA, 350 μA and 3.6 mA respectively. The execution time can be increased to 12 hours by using a larger battery that fits the form factor of a wristband. This can be increased further by reducing the sampling rate and by switching off the compass. The performance of our approach is not impacted by the lack of compass as the compass is primarily used to correct the drift accumulated around the yaw-axis. Since we extract orientation-independent features for short duration gestures, the impact of the small drift on the features is negligible.

7. RELATED WORK

In this section, we describe the two areas of related work — gesture recognition in computer vision as well as gesture recognition and motion capture using wearable inertial sensors.

Computer Vision: This line of research deal with the problem of gesture detection and recognition using a camera. The camera is used to track a person and the motion of the arm. This gives the coordinates of various points on the body that can be used as features for gesture recognition. Yang et al. [24] used Hidden Markov Models (HMM) for segmenting and identifying the set of gestures for human-robot interaction. Elmezain et al. [9] proposed a method to use Conditional Random Fields to separate gestures from non-gestures without needing to train for non-gestures. Wang et al. [23] combined HMMs with CRFs in a Hidden Conditional Random Field that can be used as a single gesture class detector or a multi-way gesture classifier. All these methods employ similar machine learning formulations, however, recognizing arms accurately in images or video is prone to errors due to occlusions, clothing, illumination changes and other errors in pose tracking from 2D images. These computer vision methods also assume that the user is always expected to turn towards the camera. Yin et al. [25] use HMMs for gesture recognition but it requires a use of special glove to enable the tracking of the arm in a cluttered background.

Wearable sensors: The advances in wearable sensors technology has generated a lot of interest in gesture recognition and other novel uses of these sensors. Vlasic et al. [22] proposed a full body motion capture system using inertial sensors. Such systems are useful to capture a person's full body motion, but require several such sensors, acoustic sensors, careful calibration and initial body pose estimates. Agrawal et al. [3] proposed *PhonePoint Pen* to enable users to use a mobile phone as a pen to write in the air using an accelerometer in the phone. This work identifies six basic strokes in the English characters that are essentially straight lines and two half-circles. These strokes are identified using correlation with the ideal strokes. *u*Wave [16] uses a dynamic time warping (DTW) technique to recognize gestures from the accelerometer present in

Nintendo Wii. DTW is used to match a temporal sequence with a given template, when the number of templates is small. Chen et al. [6] use a 6-axis inertial sensor to track interactive gestures and rely on *push-to-gesture* mechanism to spot the gesture segment. All these approaches detect "control" gestures that have little variations across users. Dong et al. [8] proposed Bite Counter to detect food bites in an eating session using a gyroscope. We compared this with our approach and found it to be less useful for smoking detection. Varkey et al. [21] train two SVMs: first to detect a high-level activity in a window of inertial sensor data and another to detect micro-activities within a window. They evaluated their approach for smoking detection using a synthetic dataset provided by non-smokers who imitated the smoking gestures. Their approach for recognizing puffs relies on detecting two consecutive micro-activites 'arm moving up' and 'arm moving down'. They showed that the cumulative misclassification for micro-activity detection within smoking sessions is around 20%. This approach can lead to a significant error in estimating the number of puffs and the puff duration and may perform worse if the data from confounding gestures is included. This work has not been evaluated for data in the wild and it is unclear if this approach can be used to detect smoking session boundaries reliably.

8. CONCLUSION

Mobile phones can play a major role in detecting and preventing harmful user behavior, such as smoking. In this paper, we tackle the problem of recognizing smoking behavior using a wristband equipped with a single 9-axis inertial sensor and a mobile phone application. Our results demonstrate that we can accurately detect smoking gestures in the wild. While we focus on smoking gesture recognition in this paper, we also have preliminary experiments that indicate that our pipeline can be used for detecting other behaviors such as eating. This could be also useful for preventing harmful eating patterns that can lead to obesity. In the future, we plan to improve our trajectory extraction procedure, enrich our method with more trajectory features, and investigate more complex probabilistic models for recognizing different types of users' gestures and behavioral patterns.

Acknowledgements

This paper has benefitted from extensive discussions with several people. In particular, we would like to thank Annamalai Natarajan who helped us implement an efficient CRF training algorithm. We would also like to thank Rui Wang who has been instrumental in building the prototype of 3D visualization tool. Also, we thank our shepherd, Anthony Lamarca, and the anonymous reviewers for their comments. This research was supported by UMass S&T award, NSF grants CNS-0910900, CNS-0855128, CNS-1239341 and NIH grant M12A11395(A08776).

9. REFERENCES

[1] Cress. http://borgwaldt.hauni.com/en/instruments/smoking-machines/smoking-topography-devices/cress-pocket.html.

[2] Cdc fact sheet on smoking. http://www.cdc.gov/tobacco/data_statistics/fact_sheets/fast_facts/.

[3] S. Agrawal, I. Constandache, S. Gaonkar, R. Roy Choudhury, K. Caves, and F. DeRuyter. Using mobile phones to write in air. In *MobiSys*, 2011.

[4] A. A. Ali, S. M. Hossain, K. Hovsepian, M. M. Rahman, K. Plarre, and S. Kumar. mpuff: Automated detection of cigarette smoking puffs from respiration measurements. In *IPSN*, 2012.

[5] L. Breiman. Random forests. *Machine learning*, 45(1):5–32, 2001.

[6] M. Chen, G. AlRegib, and B.-H. Juang. Feature processing and modeling for 6d motion gesture recognition. *Multimedia, IEEE Trans. on*, 15(3):561–571, 2013.

[7] A. Criminisi, J. Shotton, and E. Konukoglu. Decision forests: A unified framework for classification, regression, density estimation, manifold learning and semi-supervised learning. *Found. Trends. Comput. Graph. Vis.*, 7(2–3):81–227, Feb. 2012.

[8] Y. Dong, A. Hoover, J. Scisco, and E. Muth. A new method for measuring meal intake in humans via automated wrist motion tracking. *Applied psychophysiology and biofeedback*, 37(3):205–215, 2012.

[9] M. Elmezain, A. Al-Hamadi, S. Sadek, and B. Michaelis. Robust methods for hand gesture spotting and recognition using hidden markov models and conditional random fields. In *IEEE ISSPIT*, 2010.

[10] M. Hall, E. Frank, G. Holmes, B. Pfahringer, P. Reutemann, and I. H. Witten. The weka data mining software: An update. In *SIGKDD Explorations*, pages 10–18, 2009.

[11] D. Hammond, G. T. Fong, K. M. Cummings, and A. Hyland. Smoking topography, brand switching, and nicotine delivery: results from an in vivo study. *Cancer Epidemiology Biomarkers & Prevention*, 14(6):1370–1375, 2005.

[12] R. I. Herning, R. T. Jones, J. Bachman, and A. H. Mines. Puff volume increases when low-nicotine cigarettes are smoked. *British medical journal (Clinical research ed.)*, 283(6285):187, 1981.

[13] D. Koller and N. Friedman. *Probabilistic Graphical Models: Principles and Techniques - Adaptive Computation and Machine Learning*. The MIT Press, 2009.

[14] J. D. Lafferty, A. McCallum, and F. C. N. Pereira. Conditional random fields: Probabilistic models for segmenting and labeling sequence data. In *ICML*, 2001.

[15] D. C. Liu and J. Nocedal. On the limited memory bfgs method for large scale optimization. *Math. Program.*, 45(3):503–528, Dec. 1989.

[16] J. Liu, Z. Wang, L. Zhong, J. Wickramasuriya, and V. Vasudevan. uwave: Accelerometer-based personalized gesture recognition and its applications. In *IEEE PerCom 2009*, 2009.

[17] P. Lopez-Meyer, S. Tiffany, and E. Sazonov. Identification of cigarette smoke inhalations from wearable sensor data using a support vector machine classifier. In *IEEE Conf. on EMBC*, 2012.

[18] E. Sazonov, K. Metcalfe, P. Lopez-Meyer, and S. Tiffany. Rf hand gesture sensor for monitoring of cigarette smoking. In *Sensing Technology (ICST), 2011 Fifth International Conference on*, 2011.

[19] P. M. Scholl, N. Kücükyildiz, and K. V. Laerhoven. When do you light a fire?: Capturing tobacco use with situated, wearable sensors. In *UbiComp Adjunct*, 2013.

[20] C. Sutton and A. McCallum. An introduction to conditional random fields. *Foundations and Trends in Machine Learning*, 4(4):267–373, 2012.

[21] J. P. Varkey, D. Pompili, and T. A. Walls. Human motion recognition using a wireless sensor-based wearable system. *Personal Ubiquitous Comput.*, 16(7):897–910, Oct. 2012.

[22] D. Vlasic, R. Adelsberger, G. Vannucci, J. Barnwell, M. Gross, W. Matusik, and J. Popović. Practical motion capture in everyday surroundings. *ACM Trans. Graph.*, 26(3), July 2007.

[23] S. B. Wang, A. Quattoni, L.-P. Morency, and D. Demirdjian. Hidden conditional random fields for gesture recognition. In *Proceedings of the 2006 IEEE Computer Society Conference on Computer Vision and Pattern Recognition - Volume 2*, pages 1521–1527, 2006.

[24] H.-D. Yang, A.-Y. Park, and S.-W. Lee. Gesture spotting and recognition for human-robot interaction. *Robotics, IEEE Transactions on*, 23(2):256–270, 2007.

[25] Y. Yin and R. Davis. Toward natural interaction in the real world: Real-time gesture recognition. In *ICMI-MLMI*, 2010.

An Energy Harvesting Wearable Ring Platform for Gesture Input on Surfaces

Jeremy Gummeson[12], Bodhi Priyantha[2], Jie Liu[2]
[1]University of Massachusetts Amherst, [2]Microsoft Research
gummeson@cs.umass.edu, bodhip@microsoft.com, jie.liu@microsoft.com

ABSTRACT

This paper presents a remote gesture input solution for interacting indirectly with user interfaces on mobile and wearable devices. The proposed solution uses a wearable ring platform worn on a user's index finger. The ring detects and interprets various gestures performed on any available surface, and wirelessly transmits the gestures to the remote device. The ring opportunistically harvests energy from an NFC-enabled phone for perpetual operation without explicit charging. We use a finger-tendon pressure-based solution to detect touch, and a light-weight audio based solution for detecting finger motion on a surface. The two-level energy efficient classification algorithms identify 23 unique gestures that include tapping, swipes, scrolling, and strokes for hand written text entry. The classification algorithms have an average accuracy of 73% with no explicit user training. Our implementation supports 10 hours of interactions on a surface at 2 Hz gesture frequency. The prototype was constructed with off-the-shelf components and has a form factor comparable to a large ring.

Categories and Subject Descriptors

C.3 [**Special-purpose and Application-based Systems**]: [Real-time and Embedded Systems]

Keywords

Near Field Communications; Energy Harvesting; Wearable Computing; Gesture Input; Machine Learning

1. INTRODUCTION

Increasingly, users interact with their mobile devices on the go. Many of us listen to music on mobile devices while traveling, we constantly check our E-mails, shoppers browse through their shopping lists and do price comparisons while shopping, and people constantly access applications such as Facebook, Twitter, and Foursquare.

MobiSys'14, June 16–19, 2014, Bretton Woods, New Hampshire, USA.
Copyright 2014 ACM 978-1-4503-2793-0/14/06 ...$15.00.
http://dx.doi.org/10.1145/2594368.2594389 .

Interacting with mobile devices on-the-go requires the user to enter different gestures to scroll, zoom, flip, and enter text on UI elements. The mobile phone with its relatively large display has provided a unified and convenient platform for such interactions. However, more recent trends in wearable devices such as glasses, wrist bands, and watches have made such interactions limited and awkward due to the lack of touch real estate and the positioning of the device itself [5].

While mobile device interfaces continue to shrink, interfaces of remote display devices such as TVs and game consoles are becoming even more complex, requiring extensive maneuvering via simple remote controllers or requiring remote control with full keyboard-like capability [6]. For example, with a conventional remote control, a simple task such as entering text to search for a movie title becomes a monumental task leading to a poor user experience. The increasing user mobility and availability of ubiquitous computing and entertainment resources will create a strong demand for light-weight solutions that enable rich interaction with remote displays and augmented spaces.

In this paper we present a ring form-factor wearable device for gesture input. The user interacts with an arbitrary surface; such as a desk, chair arm rest, or the users clothing; with the ring-worn finger to enter multiple gestures. Our platform supports a rich set of gestures similar that found on a modern touch based UI. These gestures include "tap" for selection, "flip" gestures that quickly flip through multiple windows or items in a list, "scroll" for scrolling through a web page or a list of items, and writing-based "text-entry". Altogether, our platform can interpret 23 unique gesture primitives made on an arbitrary surface.

Some previous solutions for motion based gesturing support only a limited number of gestures such as a few patterns [13], or only text-entry under constrained conditions such as large character sizes [1] and are implemented on resource rich devices such as cell phones. Other solutions for gesturing on surfaces either required instrumented surfaces [11]; while others use heavy processing such as MFCC computations on audio, and power hungry sensors such as gyroscopes [21] which are impractical on resource limited devices such as a self-contained ring platform. Solutions that instrument the finger tip [20] are inconvenient due to the impact on the user's touch.

Our goal is to develop a wearable platform, which is likely to be adopted by a wide user community, that provides always-available gesture input using gestures typically used in modern touch-based input devices. Developing such a wearable device poses several challenges:

The first challenge is achieving the right balance of usability and performance. A large heavy platform with ample resources would be uncomfortable to wear on a finger continuously, limiting the usability of the device; while a platform with a form factor and weight similar to a typical ring is an ideal platform for achieving the goals of wide adoption and availability.

However, these form factor and weight limitations severely limit the energy and computational resources available on the ring; to make matters worse, the ring needs to use an expensive wireless link to transfer information to a remote device. We use carefully designed sensing techniques, classification algorithms, and compact representation through local processing to achieve an acceptable level of performance without sacrificing usability.

The second challenge is capturing user intent, in the form of accurately detecting the instances of the finger touching surface. For example, when we write on a whiteboard with a marker, we get the immediate visual feedback of what is being written, and the physical feedback of the marker touching the whiteboard. As a consequence of the physical feedback, we know exactly when we are writing on the surface versus when we are moving the marker to a new location.

Similar to writing on a whiteboard, when the user's finger interacts with a surface, we need to capture the instances where the finger is actually touching the surface – indicating actual "writing" – versus the finger gliding in the air. While instrumenting a user's fingertip directly can solve this easily, it will affect the usability significantly since we are obstructing the user's natural touch and providing a platform that is too awkward to wear throughout the day. We use a combination of touch induced pressure and motion induced audio sensing to achieve accurate finger touch and motion detection to capture user intent.

A third challenge is to achieve perpetual operation where users do not have to take off the ring and charge it, giving the user an experience similar to wearing a conventional ring. While this is generally a challenge for an active device with a wireless link, this becomes even more challenging due to the limited battery capacity available on a ring platform.

We implemented a ring prototype that addresses these challenges. The ring uses energy efficient finger-tendon based touch detection and audio-based motion detection to capture user interaction instances. A light-weight multi-classifier solution accurately classifies 23 different gesture primitives. The ring harvests energy from an NFC-enabled phone held in a user's hand to achieve perpetual operation of the ring without the need for explicit charging of the battery. With a 10 mAh battery, the ring can support more than 10 hours of active user interactions.

The remainder of the paper is organized as follows. Section 2, gives an overview of the ring platform. Section 3 describes our solutions for detecting surface interactions. Section 4, describes the design of our gesture classification solutions. Section 5 describes the ring prototype implementation. In section 6, we evaluate the gesture classification solution and quantify the energy consumption and harvesting capabilities of the hardware platform. We present relevant related work in Section 7. Finally, we conclude with discussion and future work in Section 8.

2. PLATFORM DESIGN

Our ring-based gesture input solution consists of 3 components: a finger-worn ring worn by the user, a surface for generating various gestures using the ring-worn finger, and a remote device the user is interacting with that consumes and responds to various gestures.

Figure 1: The ring prototype implementation.

The ring is an active device that detects and parses various gestures that the user performs on the surface, and transmits these gestures to a remote device wirelessly. The energy required for these operations are opportunistically harvested from an NFC-enabled phone held in the user's hand, enabling perpetual operation without explicit recharging. Figure 1 shows our current prototype implementation.

The ring is designed to be worn on the index finger of the user, and the user performs various gestures on an available surface using the index finger. The user can interact with almost any type of surface as long as the surface produces sufficient friction, as explained in Section 3. It can identify 23 different gesture primitives for supporting tap, scroll, swipe, and written text-entry on a remote device UI. The identified gestures are transmitted wirelessly to a remote UI device.

Our current prototype implementation using off-the-shelf components and simple manufacturing has a volume which is $\simeq$ 8 times as large as a typical ring in volume (20 mm $\times$ 20 mm surface area, and 5 mm thickness), which can be easily shrunk to the size of a typical ring using production quality manufacturing techniques.

2.1 Design Overview

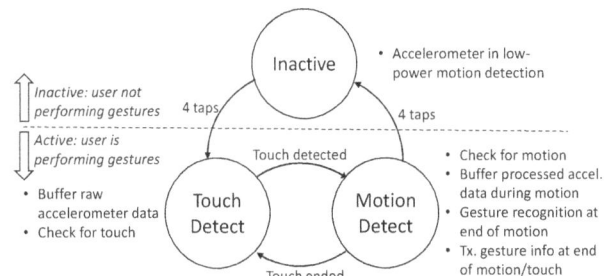

Figure 2: The ring transitions among *active*, *touch-detect*, and *motion-detect* states based on user taps, touch, and motion of the finger on a surface.

The ring has three main sensing elements. An accelerometer is used to capture inertial data during gestures for gesture identification. A force sensitive resistor (FSR), which changes its resistance based on the applied force, is placed next to a tendon of the finger used to detect if the finger is touching a surface. An audio based sensor is used to detect the motion of the finger on the surface, based on the audio generated by the friction between the finger and the surface [21].

During normal operation, the ring is in an *inactive* sleep state to prevent accidental interpretation of day-to-day user activities as gestures. In this state, the ring's accelerometer is in a low-power autonomous motion-detection state.

When the user is ready to enter gestures on an available surface, the ring is brought into active state by tapping the surface 4 times. Once in active state, the ring enters *touch-detect* active state by turning on the touch detection sensor. The 1st tap helps trigger the accelerometer motion-detector, while the rest of the taps are used to reduce accidental triggering of active state. Raw accelerometer readings are collected and buffered during the *touch-detect* state.

When the user touches the surface to enter a gesture, the touch is detected by the touch detector, and the ring enters *motion-detect* state. In the *motion-detect* state, the audio-based motion detector is turned on to detect the motion of the finger along the surface. During this state, processed accelerometer components along plane of the ring are stored. At the end of motion or the touch, these processed accelerometer data is fed to a classifier to identify the gesture.

Once a gesture is identified, this information is transmitted wirelessly to the remote device. Since the user gets immediate feedback on the gesture being received at the remote device, the ring uses a best effort transmission scheme that does not detect or recover from packet loss or collisions.

The gesture classifier on the ring requires the knowledge of the current UI element type when interpreting certain gestures. The ring receives this information from the remote device immediately following the transmission of *tap* gestures which are used for selecting UI elements.

2.2 Gestures

Gesture	Modes	# primitives
Tap	down	1
Swipe	up, down, left, right	4
Scroll	up, down, left, right right-up, left-down	6
Written Text	English characters	12

Table 1: Different gestures, including different modes, and number of classification primitives implemented on the ring.

The ring platform implements the following 4 groups of gestures, which are summarized in Table 1.

Tap. The tap gesture is similar to the typical tap gesture on a touch sensitive surface, or the left mouse click. Similar to touch surfaces and mice, we can use multiple, closely spaced, tap actions to define multiple gestures. We use 2 double-Taps to transition between "active" and "inactive" modes as described above.

Swipe. The swipe gesture is widely popular with touch interfaces for quickly scanning through multiple windows or a collection of items such as photos. The ring platform supports four different swipe actions which include: swipe-up, swipe-down, swipe-left, and swipe-right.

Scroll. The scroll action is also similar to the touch surface or mouse-based scroll. The ring identifies 6 scroll actions: scroll-left, scroll-right, scroll-up, scroll-down, scroll-right-up, and scroll-left-down. The last two diagonal gestures can mimic two-finger based zoom-in and zoom-out on touch displays.

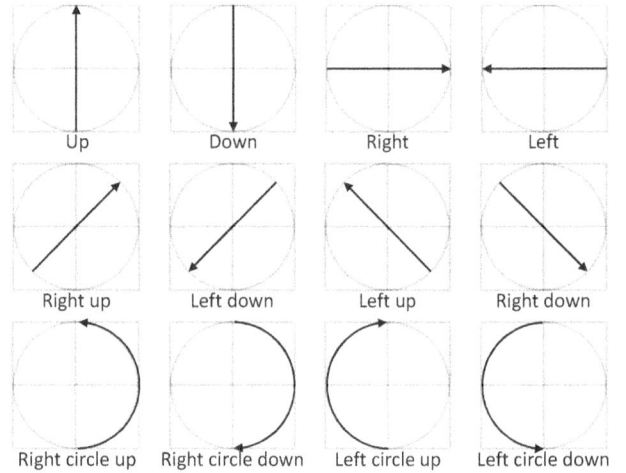

Figure 3: The 12 stroke gesture primitives used for written text entry.

Writing-based text entry We also implement a writing-based English text entry on the ring, where the user simply write the characters on a surface using the index finger.

We use an approach similar to that proposed by Agrawal et al. [1], we treat each character as a combination of multiple primitive shapes called "strokes". Figure 3 shows the 12 strokes used for text entry. The ring identifies these strokes, and also measures inter-stoke latencies which helps identify strikes belonging to a single character. Using techniques similar to those described by Agrawal et al. [1] the stroke identifiers and inter-stroke latencies can be used to identify the individual characters at a remote device.

2.3 Energy Harvesting

The size and weight requirements limit the size of the battery used to power the ring. Based on the size of a typical ring, we selected a 10mAh battery capacity, which can fit in the crown or the band of the ring.

This relatively small 10mAh battery capacity may require the user to recharge the battery several times within a day, which would be a large obstacle to the usability of the platform. To overcome this limitation, we use the *subcarrier based* NFC energy harvesting approach described in [10] to passively recharge the ring battery while the user is holding the phone next to the ring.

To harvest energy from an NFC enabled antenna, the ring has a coil loop wound around the ring band(Figure 1). Winding the coil around the ring band enables us to maximize the size of the loop to achieve better energy harvesting.

3. SURFACE DETECTION

Using an arbitrary, un-instrumented surface for gesture input requires an accurate surface detection mechanism. The benefits of such an approach are twofold: 1) this detection allows the ring to distinguish between gestures made on the surface and spurious motions in the air and 2) provides the user with implicit, natural tactile feedback.

A surface can be detected relatively easily by instrumenting the user's finger tip; however, this is not a practical solution for long-term continuous use due to the impact on the user's touch. Hence, we need to identify and measure indirect physical effects due to touch on a device worn on the user's knuckle. Such indirect measurements require extensive processing to overcome the low signal to noise ratio of the measured signal, making low-power operating challenging.

We use a combination of two techniques to detect the motion of the user's finger on a surface. A pressure sensor embedded in the ring detects the finger touching a surface by sensing the pressure excreted by a *lateral tendon* of the finger, while an energy-efficient audio sensor detects the movement of the finger on the surface by listening to the audio signal generated by the friction between the finger and the surface [21].

3.1 Tendon Pressure-based Touch Detection

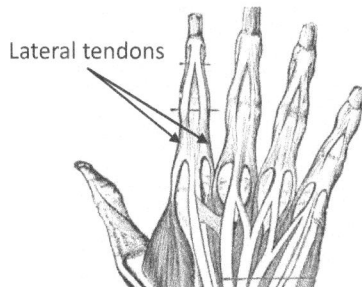

Figure 4: The location of tendons on the back of human hand. The highlighted lateral tendons of the index finger expand outward when the finger touches a surface.

We use the behavior of the lateral tendons of the index finger to detect the finger touching a surface. Figure 4 (copied from *www.wikipedia.org* due the difficulty in accurate reproduction) shows the location of tendons of the human fingers. Of particular interest to us, are the lateral tendons of the fingers.

When a finger touches a surface, these lateral tendons apply a counter force, which causes them to stiffen and move outward laterally. This can be easily observed by gently touching the sides of the index finger between the fist and second knuckle when the finger touches a surface. This lateral motion can be detected using a force sensing resistor (FSR) placed on the inner wall of the ring.

We placed a force sensing resistor between the finger and the inner surface of the ring, and measured the voltage across the sensing resistor.

Figure 5 shows the oscilloscope traces of the measured voltage and the ground truth obtained from a mobile-phone class capacitive touch sensor [4] for both swipe and stroke. We observe that the finger touch can be detected accurately

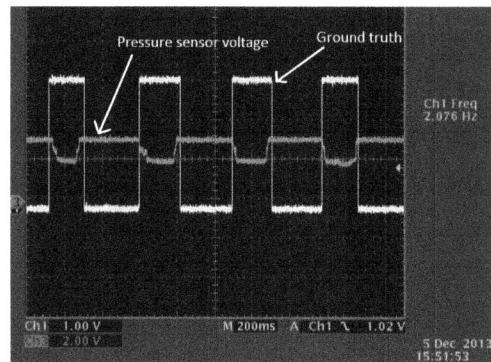

Figure 5: Oscilloscope traces showing the voltage across the force sensing resistor placed between the ring and the finger, and the output from capacitive touch sensor used for ground truth.

by the variation of the measured voltage with a short lag due to the mechanical latency between finger touching the surface and stiffening of the tendon.

We note that a similar stiffening of the tendon happens when the finger is curled. Since a surface interaction session is initiated and terminated by a sequence of taps, the spurious touch detections due to finger curling can be filtered out assuming the user does not curl the finger during the interaction session.

3.2 Audio-based Finger Motion Detection

We use the acoustic signals generated due to the friction when finger moves across the surface to detect finger motion on the surface.

The amount of audio energy emitted from the finger and surface interaction is a function of the speed of finger motion and the physical properties of the surface. The acoustic properties of friction have been well studied in a formal mathematical context [2].

To understand the amount of available acoustic energy on commonly found surfaces, we augmented a glove with a low-power microphone. The microphone is positioned on the index finger's first knuckle, where a ring would typically be worn, with the microphone facing the finger tip. A user performs moderate speed, linear motions across a variety of surfaces in otherwise quiet noise environments. The audio signals picked up by the microphone are recorded by a computer's sound card, while keeping the sound card's gain settings fixed across all experiments. In Figure 6, we show the amount of acoustic energy detected during each experiment normalized by audio length, as well as with respect to each other. As expected, we see rough surfaces, such as wood, cement, or Styrofoam, contain the largest amount of available energy. Smoother surfaces such as paper still emit detectable audio.

Though the acoustic energy of friction is detectable using a low-power microphone, it might be impossible to distinguish the sound of friction from other background noise, it is also important to gain an understanding of the frequency components present in each type of signal. Based on frequency analysis of the audio collected, we find that the frequency components cover a wide band extending from 0 - 15kHz for all the materials tested – this indicates that there are a large

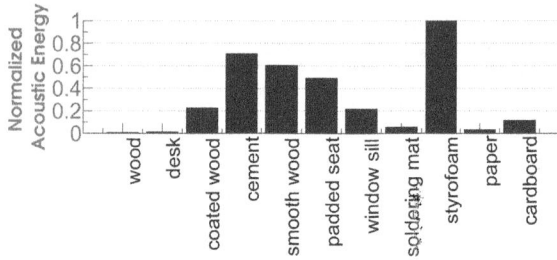

Figure 6: Commonly found materials in office environments produce detectable friction-induced acoustic energy generated by rubbing a finger on their surface.

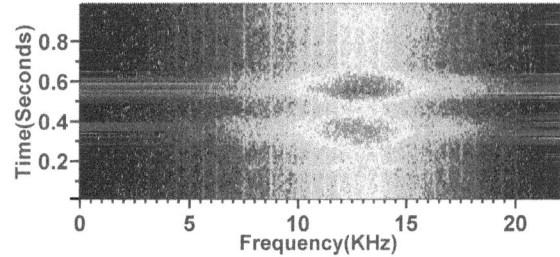

Figure 8: After applying a bandpass filter, the individual strokes of a letter input by a user are easily distinguishable. Here, the pair of red bands denote each line segment of the letter 'L'

number of bands that could be selected that do not overlap with other audio signals present.

To get a better sense of how surface friction sounds interact with extrinsic noise, we perform an experiment where we play an audio track on a set of PC speakers while performing periodic finger movements on a sheet of standard office paper.

The audio track is a recording of children playing on a playground with large amounts of talking, yelling, and mechanical noise from playground equipment. We record the audio (signal+noise) observed during the periodic rubbing and plot the resulting spectrogram in Figure 7. The dark region of the plot that extends from 0 - 6 KHz is the artificially-induced playground noise picked up by the microphone. The time-separate dark bands that extend from 7 - 14 KHz each correspond to one individual stroke of the finger moving across the surface. This result indicates that a high frequency, band-pass filter, could be used to filter many of these noise components.

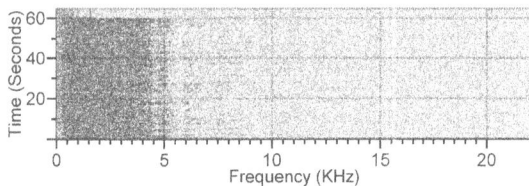

Figure 7: The frequency content of a finger periodically moving across a piece of paper is distinguishable from background noise generated by a PC speaker

To gain a better sense of how bandpass filtering can be used to separate signals from noise, we collect some data from a user entering more realistic gestures and apply a simulated filter to the results – in this experiment, we ask a user to repeatedly input the letter 'L'. After applying a first order bandpass Butterworth filter with corner frequencies at 12 and 14 kHz, we observe the signal plotted in Figure 8. The pair of red bands in the filter frequency range, correspond to individual strokes of the letter 'L'. This indicates that such a filtered audio signal still achieves the necessary time separation required to disambiguate individual strokes of handwriting.

Guided by our results we implemented an audio envelope detector with similar filter characteristics, using low-power operational amplifiers for the filtering, gain, and envelope stages.

Using our hardware filter implementation, we log the analog envelope signal using a microcontroller's ADC; additionally, we log the touch state of our touch sensor for ground truth. Both signals are sampled at a rate of 400 Hz. A user performs periodic rubbing gestures across the surface and a tethered PC logs all of the resulting touch and envelope data. In Figure 9, we plot a segment of both of these signals and observe that the audio envelope positions and widths closely align with the touch state of the capacitive touch sensor.

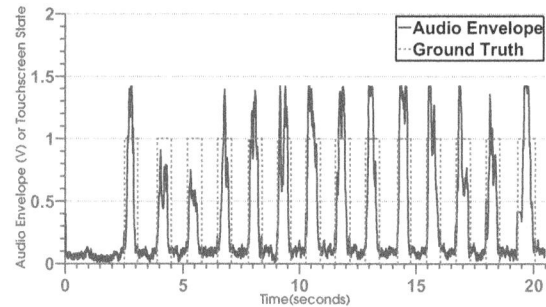

Figure 9: To demonstrate the efficacy of audio envelope-based surface detection, we compare the audio envelope generated by a finger moving along a touchscreen covered with a sheet of office paper. The envelope peaks align closely with the touch state of the capacitive touchscreen.

These results show that audio can be used as a mechanism for surface detection. While audio-based surface detection suffer from intermittent external acoustic noise, the combined pressure and audio based solution can tolerate this noise well.

3.3 Surface detection using Pressure and Audio-based techniques

We use a combination of tendon pressure and audio based techniques for efficient surface detection due to the complementary characteristics of these techniques in terms of power consumption and noise immunity.

The tendon pressure based technique consumes an order of magnitude of power less than the audio-based solution, however, unlike the audio based solution, the pressure-based technique cannot identify finger motion directly. While it might be possible to determine the motion using the accelerometer, the extra processing overhead and segmentation errors introduced can severely affect the system performance.

The audio solution can detect both motion and touch during motion. However, the audio-based solution is affected by ambient audio noise induced errors. While the band-pass filtering removes a significant portion of these errors, we find infrequent short lived errors due to sources such as a high-pitched human voice. The touch detector prevents the accidental triggering of motion sensing due to these errors, while it also prevents cascading failures by touch-based gating of the gesture detection in the presence of noise.

4. GESTURE CLASSIFICATION

As a starting point for designing classifiers for identifying the gesture primitives described in Section 2, we first categorize them based on starting dynamics, real-timeliness, and context dependency of interpretation.

Hard landing gestures start with users finger landing on the surface at a relatively high velocity. Both taps and swipes are hard landing gestures.

Soft landing gestures start with the finger meeting the surface at a low velocity. Both scroll gestures and strokes for text entry are soft landing.

The scroll gestures need **real-time** identification, since the user needs continuous feedback on the current scroll position. Due to short interaction time, both tap and swipe gestures can be identified **non-real-time** after the gesture has completed. The strokes for text entry are also identified **non-real-time**, at the end of each stroke to improve classification accuracy. This is acceptable since the high-level symbols, such as characters, can only be interpreted after collecting all strokes that make up the character, due to lack of absolute position).

Context free gestures are gestures that can be interpreted on the ring without the knowledge of the UI element the user is interacting with. Both tapping and swiping gestures belong to this category.

Context dependent gestures require the knowledge of the current UI element type for correct interpretation by the ring. Some of the stroke and scroll gestures that look identical need to be interpreted differently due to different realtime needs. To enable proper interpretation of these, we assume that the remote device informs the ring when the user starts and stops interacting with a text entry area.

4.1 Resolving Angular Ambiguity of Accelerometer Data

The ring uses the accelerometer data to identify different gestures on a surface. When gestures are performed on a surface, the signature of the gesture is mainly captured in the acceleration components that are parallel to the surface of interaction. Since the ring, when worn on the finger, does not stay parallel to the interaction surface, and since individual users' frame of reference will differ from one another, we need to convert the (X,Y,Z) components of the accelerometer to the (X,Y,Z) components with respect to the interacting plane. In this paper we assume a horizontal plane of interaction, which is true for most of the interaction surfaces available in the environment. We leave the interaction on an arbitrarily inclined plane as future work.

For computing the components along the interacting plane, we use the gravity acceleration vector just prior to movement of the finger to determine the inclination of the finger to the plane, since this angle can vary across users and instances.

To perform this normalization, we need to compute two angles: pitch (θ) and roll (ϕ). To compute these angles, we use well known geometric transformations [7] according to the following equations:

$$\theta_{xyz} = tan^{-1}\left(\frac{-G_{px}}{G_{pz}}\right) \qquad (1)$$

$$\phi_{xyz} = tan^{-1}\left(\frac{G_{py}}{\sqrt{G_{px}^2 + G_{pz}^2}}\right) \qquad (2)$$

After computing these angles while the finger is stationary, they are applied to subsequent accelerometer samples to compensate for finger orientation while the finger is moving:

$$x_{normal} = -x \cdot cos(-\phi) + z \cdot sin(-\phi) \qquad (3)$$

$$y_{normal} = y \cdot cos(\theta) - z \cdot sin(\theta) \qquad (4)$$

There are two limitations to correcting for the finger angle in this way. First, we assume that these angles do not change during a gesture – if this assumption is violated, the gravity vector will pollute the X and Y components, and a fraction of the X and Y accelerations will be falsely attributed to the Z axis. Second, we cannot correct for a third orientation angle, yaw(ψ), since we have no gyro (gravity vector provides no information as to how the finger twists in a plane perpendicular to gravity). Thus, we assume that the users finger motion will be perpendicular to their body and the impact of ψ is negligible. If this assumption is violated, the X and Y acceleration components will not be properly separated. Later, we will show that neither of these limitations has a significant impact on classification accuracy.

4.2 Gesture Classification Overview

We use a two-level classification scheme for gesture classification. When the surface detector indicates a touch event, the top-level classifier, called the landing classifier, is invoked to classify the event as either a soft or hard landing event.

Based on the output of the landing classifier and the UI context reported by the end device, one of the low-level classifiers – swipe-tap, stroke, or scroll – is invoked.

The swipe-tap classifier is invoked to handle a hard landing. This classifier uses the surface touch duration – determined by the length of the audio envelope, and the accelerometer samples to classify the event as either a tap gesture or one of the four swipe gestures.

For a soft landing, if the context reports text input, the stroke classifier is invoked. Since there can be multiple consecutive strokes during a single touch, for example when writing the letter L, accelerometer data collected after the soft landing is segmented based on the audio envelope. This segmented data is fed to the stroke classifier to classify the stroke to one of the 12 possible strokes. This continues until the finger leaves the surface.

For a soft landing with a non-text input context, the scroll classifier is invoked. The scroll classifier first detects a short *nudge* at the start of the scroll based on the audio envelope, and classifies the data collected between the touch event and the end of the nudge to determine the type of scroll event. After this classification stage, the ring periodically transmits *in-scroll* messages to the end device to provide real-time information on the continued scroll event until the finger stops moving and leaves the surface.

Figure 10 shows a state diagram of how different classification stages are invoked. The rest of this section describes these classification stages in more detail.

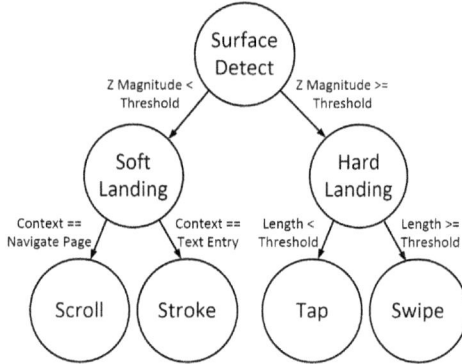

Figure 10: A hard landing has a large magnitude Z-axis component observed at the start of a gesture as compared to the same component of a soft landing.

4.3 Landing classifier

While the finger is moving on a surface, we expect to see negligible activity on an accelerometer's Z-axis. However, when the finger initially lands on the surface, we expect to see the finger abruptly stop, causing large magnitude, short-lived spikes induced by the finger's sudden deceleration. To classify hard landings versus software landings, we exploit this activity on the accelerometer Z-axis at the beginning of a gesture entry. When a surface is initially detected, we look at n samples surrounding the start of motion. These n samples may be used as the input to a heuristic, threshold-based classification or as the input to an SVM classifier. The intuition behind the efficacy of each of these approaches are the existence of large, observable deltas in Z-axis acceleration.

4.4 Swipe-Tap classifier

The swipe-tap classifier is invoked after detecting a hard landing. A tap event is identified by a very short audio envelope length, while a swipe is identified by a longer audio envelope generated as the finger moves across the surface.

A tap gesture requires only the envelope information, while a swipe requires further classification.

4.5 Stroke classifier

To identify strokes, we use an SVM classifier. We use the X, Y, and Z axis accelerometer readings as our feature vector. Since the stroke duration can vary during at different instances as well as across users, we first linearly interpolate 100 points across each x and y axis sample for a given gesture. We then compute a fixed number of averages across these interpolated points for each axis and pass this set of averages to the classifier.

4.6 Scroll classifier

Scroll classification happens after a stroke is detected, based on the context of the remote user interface. A short gesture, called a 'nudge', is detected and classified using an SVM classifier to determine the start of one of the six possible scroll gestures. We mange to accurately classify the scroll action with only a small number of samples since we are using only 6 different scrolls, as opposed to the 12 strokes. After the user performs the nudge, the length of the envelope provides real-time information to the remote device on the progress of the scroll action.

5. NFC ENERGY HARVESTING

A ring platform meant to be worn all the time needs to be of similar size and weight as a typical ring. This requirement limits the size of the battery used to power the ring platform. Based on the size of a typical ring, we assume 10mAh maximum battery capacity.

A small battery may require the user to recharge the battery periodically, which would be a large obstacle to the usability of the platform. To overcome this limitation, we use the `subcarrier based` NFC energy harvesting approach described in [10] to passively recharge the ring battery while the user is holding the phone next to the ring.

To harvest energy from the phone's NFC antenna, the ring has a coil loop wound around the body of the ring as shown in Figure 1. Winding the coil around the ring's body enables us to maximize the size of the loop to achieve better energy harvesting.

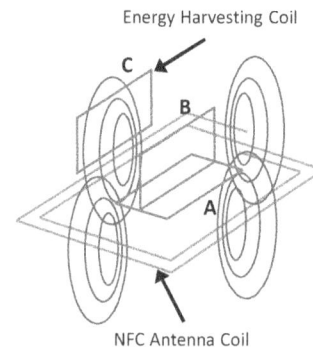

Figure 11: Magnetic field coupling between the energy harvesting coil and the NFC reader coil depends on the relative positioning of coils. Position A has the best magnetic coupling, while B has very little coupling. Position C, representative of the ring, has significant coupling.

Figure 11 illustrates the magnetic field generated by a loop antenna similar to an NFC antenna [19]. We observe that a coil loop placed parallel to the antenna at position **A** has the highest magnetic coupling, hence the best energy scavenging performance. While a loop placed perpendicular to antenna at the center of the antenna (position **B**) has very little flux going through it, a perpendicular loop placed at the edge of the antenna (position **C**) has some flux going through it due to the bending of the flux around the edge of the coil.

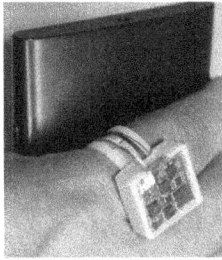

Figure 12: The ring energy harvesting coil is located close to the maximum energy harvesting position when holding a phone.

Figure 12 shows that, when worn on the index finger, the coil of the ring is located close the maximum energy harvesting position (the edge of the NFC coil) of the Nokia Lumia 920 phone, providing significant energy harvesting opportunity.

6. IMPLEMENTATION

6.1 Hardware Platform

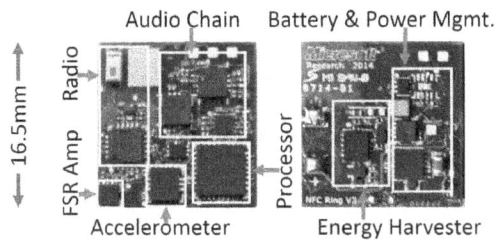

Figure 13: Ring Hardware Modules.

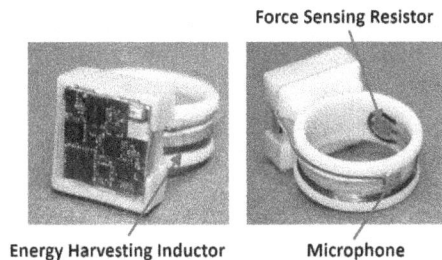

Figure 14: Ring sensing sub modules.

Figure 13 shows various functional sub modules of the Ring circuit board, while figure 14 shows the sensing and energy harvesting peripherals. The circuit board has a MSP430F2274 low-power processor, a CC2500 radio, an ADXL362 accelerometer, audio processing chain, FSR amplifier, a MAX17710 battery manager and power management ICs, and NFC energy harvesting circuitry. The ring has a 10mAh LiPo battery. The energy harvesting coil is wound on the ring band. The FSR and the microphone are also attached to the ring band. The ring PCB and the battery fits within a 16.5mm x 16.5mm x 5mm space.

Figure 15: A bicycle glove, augmented with an accelerometer (left) and MEMS microphone (right) mounted on the first segment of the glove index finger, serves as our data collection platform.

6.2 Surface Detector Implementation

The Surface detector has two pieces: the touch detector and motion detector. The touch detector is implemented using a FSR400 force sensing resistor (FSR) and a LT6003 signal conditioning amplifier. The touch detector can be turned off by power gating.

The audio based motion detector has 4 sub modules: a microphone with a built-in amplifier and high pass filter (SPU0414HR5H-SB), a 4th order high-pass analog filter to filter out typical environmental noise (LT6014), a 40dB amplifier and a low-pass filter (LTC6256), and an envelope detector (LTC6255).

When powered on, the audio stage consumes $670\mu A$, the audio stage can be turned off by power gating.

6.3 SVM Classifier implementation

For gesture classification, we use a multi-class linear-kernel SVM classifier. The classifiers use pair-wise classification, requiring $n(n-1)/$ pair-wise classifers to classify n classes.

Based on our evaluations, we use 4 features for each X and Y axis, resulting in 8 SVM features. Each $(F(i)_X, F(i)_Y)$ feature tuple is calculated by, first breaking all the (x, y) acceleration data in to 4 buckets, and then averaging the data in each bucket. The x and y acceleration component of each data sample is computed immediately after reading the (x, y, z) acceleration data sample from the accelerometer.

Due to limited RAM size, instead of buffering data at 400Hz until the end of a gesture, running averages of each n samples of data is calculated. Value n is selected such that there are at most 60 computed averages for the worst case duration of each gesture class. Once the gesture ends, these precomputed averages are broken into 4 equal-size buckets to compute the 4 feature tuples.

7. EVALUATION

In this section we quantify the ring platform's performance in terms of classification accuracy and rate of energy harvesting and consumption. First, we look at gesture classification accuracy when looking at examples of gesture data (accelerometer and audio) collected from a pool of users. Next, we quantify the energy consumption of the ring and show that we can support the input of many gestures on a single battery charge while being able to quickly replenish the energy buffer using opportunistic NFC-based energy scavenging.

In Section 7.1 all of the data presented is collected using a glove, augmented with acceleration and audio surface detection sensors (depicted in Figure 15). The glove streams 3-axis accelerometer data and and the value of the audio envelope at a rate of 400 Hz. These data samples are stored and collected by a Python script running on a PC; the glove and PC are connected via RS-232. In total, we collected 15 instances of each Swipe and Stroke Gesture from 12 users and 15 instances of each tap and nudge (scroll) gesture from 5 users. Each user's data was collected in a single session, with each type of gesture performed in a group. We also note that the gestures were collected in a relatively quiet noise environment with the gestures performed on a sheet of office paper to mantain a consistent amount of surface friction.

7.1 Gesture Recognition Performance

In this section, we quantify the performance of each classifier component described in Figure 10.

Threshold-based Classifier Evaluation: As described in section 4, the ring needs to be able to distinguish between hard landings and soft landings; after detecting a hard landing, the ring also needs to distinguish between taps and swipes. Since these two types of classification do not rely on time-series accelerometer values, they are likely amenable to a simplistic threshold-based classification algorithm.

To understand how effectively Z-axis magnitude (Hard vs. Soft Landing) or audio envelope width (Tap vs. Swipe) can be used to perform such a classification, we look at the cumulative probability distribution of these features in Figures 16 and 17. The data used to generate these plots was provided by a single user that provided 15 examples of each gesture type. The Z-axis magnitudes were computed as described in Section 4, at the beginning of the audio envelope; the audio envelope width is defined by where the envelope rises and falls above or below 0.2 V. In each of these plots, we observe that most of the probability distribution lies in different halves for each class we attempt to distinguish. For the landing classifier, taps and swipes (hard landings) typically have a much larger Z-axis component than strokes and nudges (soft landings); the CDF indicates that 1.2 G of acceleration might be a good threshold. We make a similar observation for taps versus swipes – taps typically have a much narrower audio envelope than swipes; the CDF indicates that ∼ 0.5 seconds might be a good threshold.

Using the thresholds inferred by the corresponding CDF, we construct simple classifers that indicate a hard landing when larger than the Z-acceleration threshold and a soft landing when smaller; a similar classifier was constructed for swipes versus taps using the audio envelope width. We present the classification results in Table 2. We note that these values can be driven even higher with a form factor implementationt that couples more tightly with the finger and user's that have had more time to pratice entering gestures.

Class	Precision	Recall
Soft Landing	93.81%	96.8%
Hard Landing	89.71%	81.33%
Tap	75%	80%
Swipe	94.92%	93.3%

Table 2: Classification thresholds for Envelope Width or Z-axis magnitude may be selected according to a tradeoff between Precision and Recall.

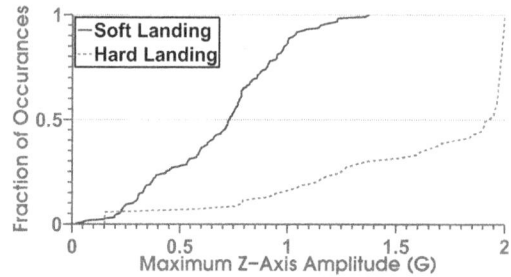

Figure 16: Hard and Soft Landings may be distinguished based on differences in the maximum magnitude of Z-axis acceleration at the beginning of a gesture, as indicated by the audio envelope. This plot shows the cumulative distribution of this magnitude for all 23 gesture classes grouped according to hard versus soft landing types. An acceleration threshold of 1.2 G provides a good tradeoff between precision and recall.

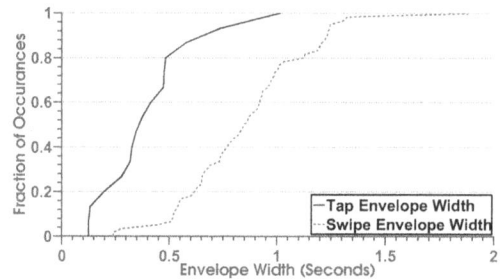

Figure 17: The characterstics of example gestures from one user indicate that most training examples may be correctly classified by using a fixed threshold of 0.51 seconds

After the landing classifer and tap-swipe classifier identify a particular type of gesture, with the exception of the tap gesture, each type is further classified according to time-series accelerometer data segmented by the audio envelope.

Stroke Classifier Evaluation: Unlike the threshold-based classifiers presented previously, strokes require more sophisticated classification techniques. As each gesture is perfomed, the user's finger moves around on a plane defined by the surface – the movements in the X and Y directions can be identified by the X and Y components of acceleration.

There are 3 different types of strokes: orthogonal lines, diagonal lines, and half circles. Orthogonal lines can be identified by looking for acceleration during one half of the gesture, and deceleration during the second half of the gesture – the relative signs of these accelerations indicate the direction, while the dominant axis component defines vertical versus horizontal motions. Diagonal lines are interpreted similarly but with acceleration components in both the X and Y axes. Half circles can be uniquely identified by considering centripetal acceleration, as well as detecting starting and stopping acceleration values with the same sign since the half circle folds back on itself.

One straightforward way to implement a unified classifier for these 3 types of stroke gestures is using a support vector machine. Guided by the previous intuition, we provide averages of the acceleration during different intervals of each gesture example as described in Section 4. A vector of these features is used to train multi-class libsvm [3] using a linear kernel with the C parameter set to 250.

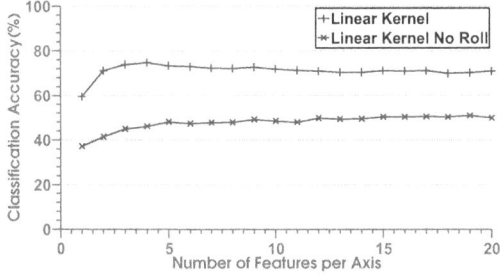

Figure 18: Classification results do not improve significantly beyond 4 features per axis. The metric of evaluation is a per user cross validation across data contributed by 12 users.

Our first evaluation looks at how the trained classifier performs when tested on a new user. The SVM is trained using 11 users' data and tested on the 12th. This process is repeated such that all 12 datasets are cross-validated. In Figure 18 we show the resulting accuracy of this cross-validation. We find that accuracy increases to around 74% as we increase the number of features, saturating with 4 features per axis. To demonstrate the effectiveness of our initial orientation corrections, we plot the classification accuracy when the finger's roll angle is not compensated; we note that the accuracy only reaches around 50%.

Stroke Class	Precision	Recall
Down	61.77%	68.18%
Down Circle Left	82.58%	74.24%
Down Circle Right	80.11%	85.98%
Down Left	58.89%	62.35%
Down Right	60.00%	54.27%
Left	62.36%	63.79%
Right	65.48%	60.44%
Up	67.60%	55.5%
Up Circle Left	86.71%	84.27%
Up Circle Right	86.21%	91.46%
Up Left	68.54%	72.19%
Up Right	53.93%	67.61%

Table 3: Precision and Recall Vary significantly for the 12 Stroke Classes. Circular gestures are easier to classify than diagonals because they are more robust to variations in frame of reference across users.

Next, we look into the confusion matrix for the 12 gesture classes to understand how each class contributes the the aggregate reported accuracy. For each of the 12 swipe classes, we report the precision and recall in Table 3. A key observation here is that the 4 half circle gestures achieve ~20% better performance than the line segments. Since these 4 gestures have a signature different from the line segments, and unique signatures defined by centripetal acceleration, they are more easily disambiguated. The key challenge in

line segments is that untrained users with no feedback from a user interface have difficulty accurately defining the angles required to disambiguate diagonal versus orthogonal lines. More training data and feedback from the user interface could certainly improve this performance, but these improvements are beyond the scope of this work.

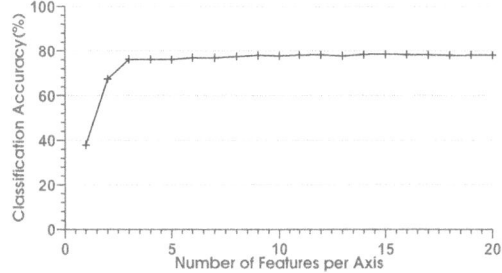

Figure 19: Accuracy results obtained from a ten-fold cross validation applied across all user data indicate that higher accuracy numbers can be achieved given more available training data similar to new users.

To get a better sense of how more training data could potentially help classification, we look at another metric of evaluation. In Figure 19 we look at the accuracy obtained by a 10-fold cross validation that treats all user data uniformly. The user data is randomly partioned into 10 folds; 9 folds are used for training and the remaining fold for testing. These folds are then validated against each other. We note that accuracy improves to around 80%, with accuracy saturating at 10 features per axis.

Swipe Classifier Evaluation: We evaluate the 4 swipe classes using the same approach as strokes. Strokes differ from swipes in two ways: 1) there are fewer swipe classes than stroke classes, and 2) they are typically much shorter in length since they are performed quickly. We peform per user cross-validation and plot the resulting accuracy in Figure 20. We observe around 77% classification accuracy for 4 features per axis. This is because swipes are easier to disambiguate from one another since they are fewer in number and spaced further apart geometrically.

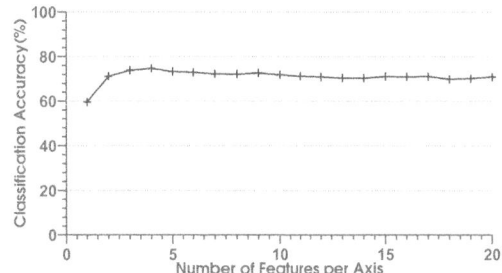

Figure 20: A classifer trained on the swipe classes achieves slightly higher accuracy than the stroke classifier. While swipes typically contain fewer raw samples than strokes, the overall accuracy is higher since there are fewer classes. The test metric is per user cross validation for 12 users.

Nudge Classifier Evaluation: Finally, we present accuracy results for nudge features in Figure 21. The metric of evalution is per user cross-validation and again, note that accuracy saturates at 68% for 4 features per axis. This accuracy is the lowest since each gesture example consists of only a few raw samples. Other sources of error are a result of the diagonal line segments use to implement the "zoom" type gesture. Finally, we note that performance is also diminished as we only currently have training examples of nudges for 5 users as opposed to the 12 used for strokes and swipes.

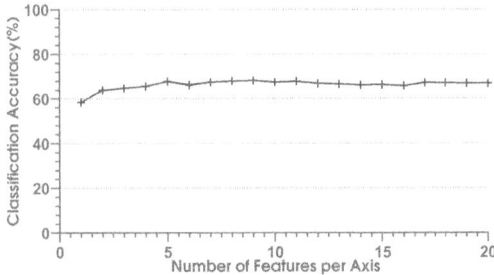

Figure 21: A classifer trained on the nudge classes achieves around 70% accuracy with 4 features of data per X/Y axis. While there are fewer nudge classes and swipes, the small number of samples available makes classification difficult.

Sensitivity to Angular Variations: While we have shown that classification for our collected training and testing data, one question remains: How well does classification perform when there are errors in angular correction for new data with respect to the trained model? Since the classifier is trained with one frame of reference in mind, performance will likely suffer if this frame of reference changes after training (i.e. finger angles are miscalculated). This is a distinct possibility given varying noise environments and differences in surface material properties. To understand how well classification performs in spite of these errors, we train the SVM classifier assuming that angles are computed correctly using our the described techniques, but then perform per user cross-validation using test data with an artificially induced pitch error, applied to all testing examples for all users. We use the a linear kernel with 4 average features per axis and repeatedly run cross validation for different amounts of error. We plot the results in Figure 22. We note that the classification accuracy only diminishes by 2% for angles as large as +/- 3 degrees.

7.2 Power Consumption

To determine the average power consumption and battery life, we assume a workload with 2Hz gesture frequency. We also assume that users spend equal amounts of time touching the the surface and hovering above the surface, resulting in a 50% duty cycle (250ms execution time) for touch detect and motion detect.

Gestures are encoded in 10 byte RF messages. The messages are transmitted using best effort with no collision avoidance or detection. Immediately following the messages with *tap* gestures, the ring expects to receive a 10byte message encoding the current UI element type for context-based gesture classification. We assume that 25% of all the gestures are tap gestures.

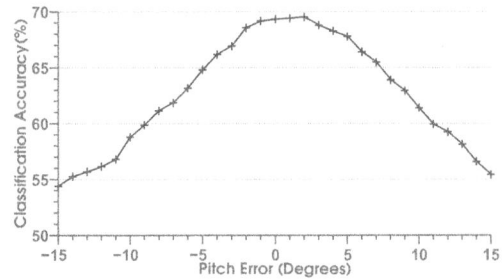

Figure 22: The model learned by the SVM classifer is relatively immune to errors in gesture angle computation. The classifier maintains high accuracy with pitch angle errors consisting of a few degrees in either direction.

The hardware modules on the ring are powered from the battery through low-power linear regulators with negligible leakage current. Hence, the total current drawn from the battery is the sum of currents consumed by individual HW modules.

Since the battery capacity is given in mAh, we use the average current consumption as the measure of power consumption. This enables a direct comparison of how the power consumption of different modules impact the overall battery lifetime. While the active current consumption of hardware modules were measured, the sleep currents were estimated from device data sheets.

The following is a breakdown of current consumption of the different system modules under different operating conditions:

- The MSP430F2274 microcontroller consumes 450 μA at 1MHz clock. It operates at a 30% duty cycle during *touch-detect*, resulting in 135 μA average current.

- During a touch detect, the pressure sensor-based touch detector consumes 11 μA, while the audio-based motion detector is turned off with negligible current consumption. During motion detect, the touch detector and motion detector consume 30 μA and 670 μA respectively.

- After waking up from deep sleep, the CC2500 radio takes 5.52 ms for register configuration and message transmission for a 10 byte message. At -30dBm transmit power, the measured average current consumption within the 5.52 ms interval is 4.32 mA. At 2 Hz gesture frequency, this translates to an average current of 47.7 μA per gesture (neglecting the 0.4 μA sleep current).

- During bi-directional communication, the remote device transmits a 10 byte message immediately following the receipt of a *tap* gesture message. The CC2500 radio takes 8.6 ms for register configuration, message transmission, and reception. The measured average current consumption during this interval is 9.85 mA. This translates to 169 μA average current per gesture.

- Assuming 25% of the gestures are *tap* gestures that require a response from the remote device, the average current consumption of CC2500 per gesture is 78.0 μA.

Module	Touch detect (μA)	Motion detect (μA)	Inactive (μA)
Microcontroller	135	450	0.1
Touch detector	11	30	$\simeq 0$
Motion detector	$\simeq 0$	670	$\simeq 0$
Accelerometer	5	5	0.27
Radio	78		0.4
Total	229	1233	0.77

Table 4: The current consumption of sub-modules of the ring during *touch-detect*, *motion-detect*, and *inactive* states.

Table 4 summarizes the current consumption of modules during touch detect, touch process, and inactive states. Under the given workload, the ring consumes only 731μA when active on average. It consumes only 0.8μA when inactive. With a fully charged 10mAh battery, the ring achieves more than 10 hours of active interaction time.

7.3 Energy Harvesting Performance

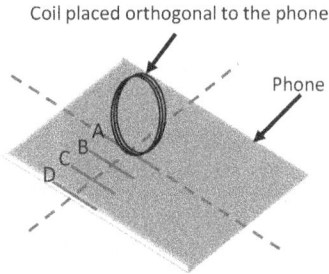

Figure 23: Energy harvested with a tuned coil held perpendicular to the surface of the phone were measured at 4 different locations on the phone.

We first determine the maximum power that can be harvested from the phone using a tuned harvesting coil with a matched resistive load. To measure this, we placed the tuned coil on the back of an Lumia 920 phone, orthogonal to the surface of the phone, at 4 equally spaced locations labeled ($\mathbf{A,B,C,D}$) as shown in Figure 23. We used a 1.5 cm diameter coil with 10 turns.

Figure 24 shows the power that can be harvested at these locations. We observe that the ring can harvest up to 18 mW of power when placed at C, which is right next to where a ring worn on the index finger is typically located.

We next measured the actual power harvested by the ring when charging the built in battery by attaching a resistor between with the battery -ve terminal and the ground. We used a 10 ohm 0.1% resistor for measuring the charging current. We measured a 3.27mA charging current when the battery voltage is lower than the charger cut off voltage. The trickle charge current when the battery voltage is above the charger cut off was negligible.

7.4 Trace-driven Performance Evaluation

To further validate our harvesting claims, we look at a trace driven evaluation of ring harvesting performance

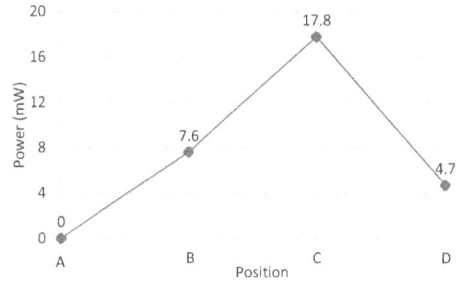

Figure 24: The maximum power harvested by a tuned harvesting coil placed at different locations of a Lumia 920 phone.

across week long intervals of normal phone usage. To understand what normal phone usage looks at, we use a set of traces provided by the LiveLab project at Rice University [18] – these traces give detailed useage logs of 34 iPhone users over the span of one year. Of particular interest to this paper are the intervals during which the phone's screen is unlocked, as these are opportunities to harvest energy from the phone's NFC interface.

Our simulation study assumes that while a user is actively using their phone with the screen unlocked, the ring-worn finger is positioned favorably on the back of the phone, allowing the ring to harvest power according to position B in Figure 24 and assume the harvesting rate measured by the 10 ohm resistor reported in §7.3. While harvesting this power, the ring is able to store energy in its battery equal to the difference of this harvesting rate and the sleep power consumption shown in Table 4. After the battery reaches 96% of its total capacity, the battery is trickle charged – in practice we found the trickle charge current to be negligible, thus our simulation does not consider the final 4% of the battery's capacity. We also assume that the initial 5% of the battery capacity is unavailable, as a protection circuit prevents the battery from going below 2.5 V to prevent damage caused by deep discharge.

The simulation workloads we consider, consist of periodic intervals of gesture inputs that occur once every 2 hours and last for a variable number of minutes. We do not consider intervals that overlap with a screen unlock event, as the user is interacting with their phone rather than a remote device via the ring. During a gesture input session, the ring spends equal amounts of time in power states according to *touch* and *motion detect*, again according to Table 4. This implies that the finger spends the same amount of time in the air and performing gestures on the surface. During each of these gesture input sessions, we consider the amount of energy at the start of each session and consider the ring is "available" if the battery is charged beyond 5% of its total capacity, plus the energy required for the current gesture interval duration. The ring is considered unavailable for gesture input if below this threshold. In Figure 25, we show the fraction of occurances during which the ring is available. Each box plot is computed over all 34 users, for gesture input durations ranging from 1 - 30 minutes. Even under very aggressive workloads where the ring is active for 20 minutes out of every 2 hours, the median of ring availability computed across all 31 users is still around 90%. We also note that these performance numbers are considered a worst-case, since in a real-world scenario, it would be very uncommon for users to perform gesture inputs during the middle of the night.

We further validate the worst case nature of these results by look into the timing characterstics of time periods where the ring was not available. In Figure 26, we plot a CDF showing the amount of time between the last charging opportunity and instance of the ring being unavailable due to energy starvation. We note that even for the 30 minute workload, 75% of failures occur after 4 hours of mobile phone inactivity. These failures are likely induced by the previousy mentioned "night effect" and other longer periods of inactivity. More realistic workloads would likely occur more closely to periods of phone inactivity while people are active and engaged in other activities.

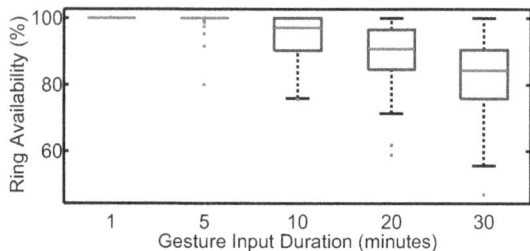

Figure 25: A trace-driven simulation of power harvested opportunistically by the ring platform indicates more than 80% availability for 31 different users over the span of a year. A periodic useage model is considered, where the ring is usd for gesture input for the length specified every 2 hours.

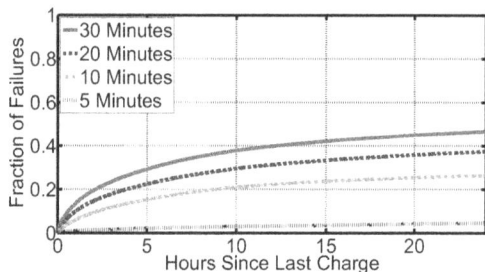

Figure 26: A CDF of the time between last charge interval and gesture failure shows that most failures occur as a a result of energy starvation after long periods of phone activity. In real world use cases, gesture input sessions would likely occur within a couple of hours of phone activity.

8. RELATED WORK

The use of accelerometers for gesture recognition has been studied extensively – we provide a summary of the most relevant related work in Table 5. These systems primarily look at performing gestures in the air using commodity devices such as a mobile phone or the Nintendo Wii Remote – while our work focused on the system power consumption and perpetual availability possible in a wearable ring form factor devices, these systems instead focused on techniques that

maximize classification accuracy. The Nintendo Wiimote was the first widely popular device that used acceleration-based gestures as a primary input mechanism; Schlomer et al. [17] show it was possible to disambiguate a small gesture vocabulary using an HMM-based learning algorithm using the output of the Wii Remote. The uWave system [13] uses a dynamic time warping based technique to align gesture inputs to templates that denote different gestures. Agrawal et al. [1] describe a mobile phone based system for combining indivdual strokes into characters. The PhonePoint system is similar to our work in that it uses stroke primitives to build up more complex characters and words. We view our work as complementary, as we focused primarily on the energy efficient detection of individual strokes.

System Name	Accuracy	Battery Life
Wii Remote [17]	85 - 95%	60 hours
uWave [13]	91 - 99%	60 hours
PhonePoint [1]	46 - 100%	40 hours

Table 5: A number of related gesture-based input solutions have been proposed. None of them simultaneously offer continuous system availability within a self-contained, wearable form factor.

Also similar to our work are other wearable ring-like platforms. Magic Finger [20] is a device worn on the finger tip and uses a low-resolution camera and motion sensor to track movement on a surface. Unlike our work, Magic Finger focuses on UI and does not consider system power consumption. The iRing [16] senses changes in finger position using infrared sensors looking inward at the wearer's skin. Like our platform, the ring platform presented by Zhang et al [21] also uses audio and acceleration sensors to track movements on a surface. This iRing performs audio signal processing on sound conducted through the wearer's bone; in contrast, our ring platform uses the envelope of audio emitted from the surface rather than through the finger and uses an accelerometer to track the direction of motion. We also find that existing commercial ring-based UI controls are currently too bulky to be continuously wearable [8].

Finally, there are other systems that leverage the acoustics of friction [2] to interact with different types of surfaces. Stane [15] consists of a handheld device that used scratching and tapping sounds as gesture inputs to a music player. Several systems [11, 14, 12] instrument the surface itself, rather than the finger and detect the noise produced by user interactions. The SurfaceLink system [9] allows multiple devices to communicate with each other and perform gestures via vibrations and sound travelling along a shared surface. Instead of using a surface directly as a communication channel, our work uses the surface to partition accelerometer data and provide the user with impicit tactile feedback that aids the user in gesture entry tasks.

9. DISCUSSION

This paper focused on the design aspects of an energy-constrained, wearable ring platform. In the future, our system design can be enhanced to tackle other important challenges such as improving classification accuracy, improving noise resilience of audio-based motion detection, and better quantifying the system performance on a larger variety of surfaces.

Classification Accuracy: The gesture classification performance of our system can be improved in several ways. First, in the evaluation presented in this paper, users were not given a frame of reference for gesture entry, likely causing more noise in training data. Another major drawback was the lack of feedback given to a user after performing each gesture input. Adding this feedback would greatly enhance the ability of users to learn how to correctly enter gesture examples. Finally, since machine learning-based classification methods are dependent on the availability of large amounts of training data, our system could greatly benefit from an increase in the number of users and training examples used to build the SVM classifier models. Based on results obtained from self cross-validation, we expect additional training data to increase the overall accuracy by at least 10%.

Noise Resilience: We observed that audio-based surface detection suffers due to high frequency noise, such as noise from ultrasonic room occupancy sensors. This could be mitigated with an audio channel selecting bandpass filter, as well as other time-domain filtering techniques. After adding these techniques, an evaluation would quantify surface detection accuracy in a variety of expected noise envionments.

Performance of Different Surfaces: Our classification results were based on audio data collected from common office paper. We note that in Figure 6, office paper has little acoustic surface friction energy compared to other types of materials we benchmarked making our initial classification results encouraging. However, a more extensive evaluation would look more closely at other commonly available surfaces such as coffee tables and desks; we also note that the type of surface will also have a major impact on its resilience to extrinsic noise.

10. CONCLUSION

This paper presented a low-power wearable ring platform that enables users to enter gestures by interacting on arbitrary surfaces. The ring uses energy efficient finger-tendon based touch detection and audio-based motion detection to capture user interaction instances. A light-weight multi-classifier solution accurately classifies 23 different gesture primitives. Using a 10 mAh battery, charged by energy harvested from an NFC-enabled phone, the ring can support more than 10 hours of active user interactions.

11. ACKNOWLEDGEMENTS

This research was partially funded by NSF grants CNS-1218586, CNS-1217606, and CNS-1239341. We thank our shepherd Prabal Dutta for providing guidance in preparing our final draft and the anonymous reviewers for their insightful comments. We also thank the anonymous volunteers that provided examples of gesture inputs.

12. REFERENCES

[1] S. Agrawal, I. Constandache, S. Gaonkar, R. Roy Choudhury, K. Caves, and F. DeRuyter. Using mobile phones to write in air. In *MobiSys '11*, pages 15–28. ACM.

[2] A. Akay. Acoustics of friction. *The Journal of the Acoustical Society of America*, 111:1525, 2002.

[3] C.-C. Chang and C.-J. Lin. LIBSVM: A library for support vector machines. volume 2, pages 27:1–27:27, 2011. Software available at `http://www.csie.ntu.edu.tw/~cjlin/libsvm`.

[4] Cypress Semiconductor. CY3290-TMA400EVK TrueTouch Gen4 Evaluation Test Kit (`http://www.cypress.com/?rID=58447`), June 2013.

[5] M. Dunlop and S. Brewster. The challenge of mobile devices for human computer interaction. *Personal Ubiquitous Computing*, 6(4):235–236, Jan. 2002.

[6] L. Eronen and P. Vuorimaa. User interfaces for digital television: A navigator case study. In *AVI '00*, pages 276–279. ACM.

[7] Freescale Semiconductor. Tilt Sensing Using a Three-axis Accelerometer (`http://www.freescale.com/files/sensors/doc/app\_note/AN3461.pdf`).

[8] Genius KYE Systems Group. Wireless Thumb Cursor Controller (`http://www.geniusnet.com/wSite/ct?xItem=47711&ctNode=105`), 2011.

[9] M. Goel, B. Lee, M. T. I. Aumi, S. Patel, G. Borriello, S. Hibino, and J. Begole. Surfacelink: Using inertial and acoustic sensing to enable multi-device interaction on a surface. In *CHI '14*.

[10] J. Gummeson, B. Priyantha, D. Ganesan, D. Thrasher, and P. Zhang. EnGarde: protecting the mobile phone from malicious NFC interactions. In *MobiSys '13*, pages 445–458.

[11] C. Harrison and S. E. Hudson. Scratch input: creating large, inexpensive, unpowered and mobile finger input surfaces. In *UIST '08*, pages 205–208. ACM.

[12] C. Harrison, J. Schwarz, and S. E. Hudson. Tapsense: enhancing finger interaction on touch surfaces. In *UIST '11*, pages 627–636. ACM.

[13] J. Liu, L. Zhong, J. Wickramasuriya, and V. Vasudevan. uwave: Accelerometer-based personalized gesture recognition and its applications. *Pervasive and Mobile Computing*, 5(6):657–675, 2009.

[14] P. Lopes, R. Jota, and J. A. Jorge. Augmenting touch interaction through acoustic sensing. In *ITS '11*, pages 53–56. ACM.

[15] R. Murray-Smith, J. Williamson, S. Hughes, and T. Quaade. Stane: synthesized surfaces for tactile input. In *CHI '08*, pages 1299–1302. ACM.

[16] M. Ogata, Y. Sugiura, H. Osawa, and M. Imai. iring: intelligent ring using infrared reflection. In *UIST '12*, pages 131–136. ACM.

[17] T. Schlömer, B. Poppinga, N. Henze, and S. Boll. Gesture recognition with a Wii controller. In *TEI '08*, pages 11–14. ACM.

[18] C. Shepard, A. Rahmati, C. Tossell, L. Zhong, and P. Kortum. Livelab: measuring wireless networks and smartphone users in the field. *ACM SIGMETRICS Performance Evaluation Review*, 38(3):15–20, 2011.

[19] Texas Instruments. HF Antenna Design Notes (http://www.ti.com/lit/an/scba034/scba034.pdf).

[20] X.-D. Yang, T. Grossman, D. Wigdor, and G. Fitzmaurice. Magic finger: Always-available input through finger instrumentation. In *UIST '12*, pages 147–156. ACM.

[21] B. Zhang, Y. Chen, Y. Qian, and X. Wang. A ring-shaped interactive device for large remote display and mobile device control. In *UbiComp '11*, pages 473–474. ACM, 2011.

User-Generated Free-Form Gestures for Authentication: Security and Memorability

Michael Sherman[†], Gradeigh Clark[†], Yulong Yang[†], Shridatt Sugrim[†], Arttu Modig[*],
Janne Lindqvist[†], Antti Oulasvirta[‡*], Teemu Roos[*]
[†]Rutgers University, [‡]Max Planck Institute for Informatics
[*]Saarland University, [*]University of Helsinki

ABSTRACT

This paper studies the security and memorability of free-form multitouch gestures for mobile authentication. Towards this end, we collected a dataset with a generate-test-retest paradigm where participants (N=63) generated free-form gestures, repeated them, and were later retested for memory. Half of the participants decided to generate one-finger gestures, and the other half generated multifinger gestures. Although there has been recent work on template-based gestures, there are yet no metrics to analyze security of either template or free-form gestures. For example, entropy-based metrics used for text-based passwords are not suitable for capturing the security and memorability of free-form gestures. Hence, we modify a recently proposed metric for analyzing information capacity of continuous full-body movements for this purpose. Our metric computed estimated mutual information in repeated sets of gestures. Surprisingly, one-finger gestures had higher average mutual information. Gestures with many hard angles and turns had the highest mutual information. The best-remembered gestures included signatures and simple angular shapes. We also implemented a multitouch recognizer to evaluate the practicality of free-form gestures in a real authentication system and how they perform against shoulder surfing attacks. We discuss strategies for generating secure and memorable free-form gestures. We conclude that free-form gestures present a robust method for mobile authentication.

Categories and Subject Descriptors

H.5.m. [**Information Interfaces and Presentation (e.g. HCI)**]: Miscellaneous

Keywords

gestures; security; mutual information; memorability

1. INTRODUCTION

Smartphones and tablets today are important for secure daily transactions. They are part of multi-factor authentication for enterprises [23], allow us to access our email, make one-click payments on Amazon, allow mobile payments [36] and even access to

MobiSys'14, June 16–19, op2014, Bretton Woods, New Hampshire, USA.
Copyright is held by the owner/author(s). Publication rights licensed to ACM.
ACM 978-1-4503-2793-0/14/06 ...$15.00.
http://dx.doi.org/10.1145/2594368.2594375.

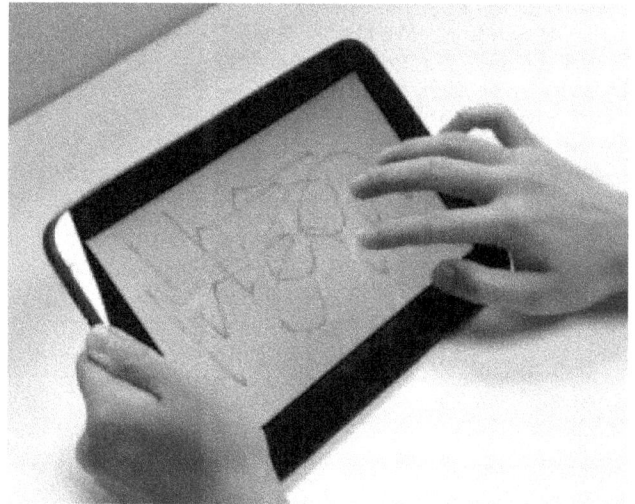

Figure 1: **This paper studies continuous free-form multitouch gestures as means of authentication on touchscreen devices. Authentication on touchscreens is normally done with a grid-based method. Free-form gesture passwords have a larger password space and are possibly less vulnerable to shoulder surfing. We note that there are no visual cues for the gestures, the gesture traces are shown only after creating the gesture. This is for the purposes of testing – a fully trained system does not show the traces.**

our houses [16]. Therefore, it is important to ensure the security of mobile devices.

Recently, mobile devices with touchscreens have made gesture-based authentication common. For example, the Android platform includes a 3x3 grid that is used as a standard authentication method, which allows users to unlock their devices by connecting dots in the grid. Compared with text-based passwords, gestures could be performed faster while requiring less accuracy. Although grid-based gestures better utilize the capabilities of touchscreens as input devices, they are limited as an authentication method. For example, a visual pattern drawn on a grid is prone to attacks such as shoulder surfing [43] and smudge attacks [1].

This paper studies *free-form multitouch gestures* without visual reference, that is, gestures that allow all fingers to draw a trajectory on a blank screen with no grid or other template. An example of the creation process is depicted in Figure 1, where the gesture traces are shown only after the gesture was created. This method bears potential, because it relaxes some of the assumptions that make the grid-based methods vulnerable. In particular, arbitrary shapes can be created. Moreover, as more fingers can be used, in principle more information can be expressed. Technically such gestures can be scale and position invariant, allowing the user to perform gestures on the surface without visually attending the display. Consider, for example, drawing a circle as your password. This may be beneficial for mobile users who need to attend their environment. Nevertheless, although no visual reference is provided, mnemonic cues referring to shapes and patterns can still be utilized for generating the gestures. Finally, when multiple fingers are allowed to move on the surface and no visual reference is provided, observational attacks may be more difficult.

Previous work on gestures as an authentication method has focused on a few directions: one was whether the same gesture can be correctly recognized in general [15, 31] or in a specific environment such as handwriting motion detected by Kinect-cameras [38], predefined whole-body gestures detected from wireless signals [28], and mobile device movement detected by built-in sensors [30]. Studies of the security of gestures look at either the protection of gestures from specific scenarios [43, 33, 38, 11], or an indirect measurement of security [17, 25]. Further, these works have focused on understanding performance of template gestures repeated by participants, not user-generated free-form gestures as the present work.

Our goal is to understand the security of this method by measuring mutual information and studying memorability in a dataset that allowed users to freely choose the kind of multitouch passwords they deemed best. We conducted a controlled experiment with 63 participants in a generate-test-retest design. At first, participants created and repeated a gesture (generate), then tried to recall it after a short break (test) and recalled it again after a period of time at least 10 days (retest). With this paradigm we were able to examine the effect of time on how participants memorize their gestures. To the best of our knowledge, we are the first to present a study on how people actually recall free-form multitouch gestures after a delay.

To analyze the security of the gestures, we use a novel information metric of mutual information in repeated multifinger trajectories. We base our metric on a recent one that was used for a very different purpose, specifically the estimation of throughput (bits/s) in continuous full-body motion [27], and it has not been used previously for authentication. Because multitouch gestures are continuous by nature the standard information metrics cannot be directly applied. What is unique to gesturing over discrete aimed movements (physical and virtual buttons) is that every repetition of a trajectory is inherently somewhat different [20]. However, when this variability grows too large, the password is useless, because it is both not repeatable by the user and not discriminable from other passwords. The information metric should capture this variability. In our metric, a secure gesture should contain a certain amount of "surprise", that is, some turns or changes, while still being able to be reproduced by the user itself. We also include a mutual information calculation to separate the complexity of controlled and intended features of the gesture and that of uncontrolled and unreproducible features.

Our results show that several participants were able to create secure and memorable gestures without guidance and prior practice. However, many participants used multiple fingers in a trivial way, by just repeating the same gesture. Our implementation of a practical multitouch recognizer shows that the free-form gestures can used as a secure authentication mechanism, and are resistant to shoulder-surfing attacks.

Our contributions are as follows:

1. Report on patterns in user-generated free-form multitouch gestures generated from 63 participants with a typical tablet;

2. Adaptation of a recent information theoretic metric for measuring the security and memorability of gestures;

3. A design and implementation of a practical multitouch gesture recognizer to evaluate free-form gestures applicability for authentication;

4. A preliminary study on a shoulder-surfing attack that indicates the potential of free-form gestures against such attacks.

2. RELATED WORK

In this section, we discuss related work on biometric-rich authentication schemes, graphical passwords, and password memorability.

2D gesture authentication schemes. Similar to free-form gestures, biometric-rich authentication schemes are based on the idea that when a user performs a gesture on a touchscreen they will do this in such a way that features can be extracted that will uniquely identify them later on [15, 31, 45, 3]. Similar ideas have been applied to recognizing motions with Kinect [38]. Specifically, Sae-Bae et al. [31] has shown that there is a uniqueness to the way users perform identical set of template 2D gestures based on biometric features (e.g. hand size and finger length). Frank et al. [15] demonstrated that the way a user interacts with a smartphone forms a unique identifier for that user, they showed that the way a user performs simple tasks (e.g. scrolling to read or swiping to the next page) is performed in a unique way such that the coordinates of a stroke, time, finger pressure, and the screen area covered by a finger are measurements that could be used to classify said user. Zheng et al. [45], operating on similar principles, have studied behavioral authentication using the way a user touches the phone – the features extracted included acceleration, pressure, size, and time. Bo et al. [3] performed recognition by mining coordinates, duration, pressure, vibration, and rotation. Cai et al. [8] examined six different features (e.g. sliding) and compared data such as the speed, sliding offset, and variance between finger pressures. De Luca et al. [11] developed a system for authentication by drawing a template 2D gesture on the back of a device using two phones connected back to back. The security of the gesture is analyzed through various methods by an attacker to replicate the original biometric or graphical password – there is no analysis performed as to the security content of the gesture, just its difficulty to be reproduced. Shazad et al. [35] worked on a template-based touchscreen recognition system on smartphones where they used distinguishing features of a gesture other than the shape to recognize users. To that end, they selected (besides the coordinates) features like finger velocity, device acceleration, and stroke time. The motivation here was to create a system where a gesture could not be stolen by sight alone. Their password space, however, is limited to ten gestures and is thus not user-generated or free-form.

3D gesture authentication schemes. 3D gesture recognition can be performed, most recently, using camera-based systems (e.g. Kinect) [38] or using wireless signals [28]. With the camera-based systems, a user would trace a gesture out in space and the image gets compressed into a two dimensional image and processed for recognition [38]. Pu et al. [28] have shown that three-dimensional gestures can be recognized by measuring the Doppler shifts between transmitted and received Wi-Fi signals.

Graphical and text-based passwords security and memorability. Bonneau et al. [5] have studied alternatives to text-based passwords for web authentication and how to comparatively evaluate them. There has been considerable work on cued graphical passwords, a survey is offered by Biddle et al. [2] for the past twelve years. In particular, there has been analysis on how Draw a Secret (DAS) [19] type of graphical passwords measures up to text-based passwords in terms of dictionary attacks [26]. Oorschot et al. [26] go on to describe a set of complexity properties based on DAS passwords and conclude that symmetry and stroke-count are key in how complicated a DAS-password can be. They do not provide a direct measurement of this for DAS-password, the analysis is restricted to constructing a model to perform a dictionary attack and show that there are weak password subspaces based on DAS symmetry. For click-based graphical passwords (e.g. PassPoints [40]), Thorpe et al. [37] found they could seed attacks based on human choices and find hotspots for dictionary attacks. For text-based passwords Florencio et al. [14] studied people's web password habits, and found that people's passwords were generally of poor quality, they are re-used and forgotten a lot. Yan et al. [42] were among the first to study empirically how different password policies affect security and memorability of the text-based passwords. Chiasson et al. [9] conducted laboratory studies on how people recall multiple text-based passwords compared to multiple click-based graphical passwords (PassPoints [40]). They found that the recall rates after two weeks were not statistically significant from each other. Everitt et al. [12] analyzed the memorability of multiple graphical passwords (PassFaces [2]) through a longitudinal study and found that users who authenticate with multiple different graphical passwords per week were more likely to fail authentication than users who dealt with just one password.

Security Analysis of Graphical Passwords and Gestures. Most security analysis focus on preventing shoulder surfing attacks from hijacking a graphical password or gesture [43, 33, 11]. The methods depend on implementing techniques to make the input more difficult to attack (e.g. making the graphical password disappear as it is being drawn [43]). Another team designed an algorithm based on Rubine [29] that told users whether or not their gestures are too similar, although the metric for this is inherently based on the recognizer's scoring capabilities and not on a measure of the gesture by itself [22]. Schaub et al. [33] suggest that the size of the password space for a gesture is based on three spaces: design features (how the user interacts with the device), smartphone capabilities (screen size, etc.), and password characteristics (existing metrics of security, usability, etc). Security in this context refers to a measured resistance to shoulder surfing.

Continuing with security analysis, brute force attacks on gestures have been examined in some studies [38, 44, 2]. Zhao et al. [44] have examined the security of 2D gestures against brute force attacks (assisted or otherwise) when using an authentication system where a user will draw a gesture on a picture. A measure of the password space is developed and an algorithm under which a gesture in that space can be attacked. The attack is capable of guessing the password based on areas of the screen that a user would be drawn towards. This study does not concern itself with the security of the gesture drawn, instead it is focused on where a user would target in a picture-based authentication schema – it does not address free-form gesture authentication. Serwadda et al. [34] showed that authentication schema based on biometric analysis (including one by Frank et al. [15]) can be cracked using a robot to brute force the inputs using an algorithm that is supplied swipe input statistics from the general population.

Finally, on non-security related work, Oulasvirta et al. [27] studied the information capacity of continuous full-body movements. Our metric is motivated by their work. Specifically, they did not study 2D gestures or their security and memorability or use for an authentication system. When asked to create gestures for non-security purposes, previous work [17, 25] indicates that people tend to repeat gestures that are seen on a daily basis and are context-dependent (e.g. that the gestures people perform are dependent on whether they are directing someone to perform a task or receiving directions on a task).

3. SECURITY OF GESTURES

In this section, we present our novel information-theoretic metric for evaluating the security and memorability of gestures. We briefly discuss why existing entropy-based metrics used to evaluate discrete text-based passwords [4] are not suitable for gestures, and move to present our metric for security and memorability of continuous gestures. We have modified a recent metric on analyzing information capacity of full-body movements [27] to estimate the security of a multitouch gesture.

Multitouch gestures on a touchscreen surface produce trajectory data where the positions of one or more end-effectors (finger tips) are tracked over time. The continuous and multi-dimensional nature of multitouch gesture data poses some additional challenges for defining the information content compared to regular text-based passwords that only gauge information in *discrete movements* corresponding to key events (pressing the key down) caused by a single end-effector (e.g. finger, cursor) at a time. *Multitouch gestures* involve multiple end-effectors and continuous movement. To our knowledge, no information theory based security metric has been proposed for multitouch gestures as passwords.

The core idea is to demonstrate that there is an association between the security of a gesture password and the *information content* of the gesture. Intuitively, information content is a property of a message or a signal (such as a recorded gesture): it measures the amount of surprisingness, or unpredictability, of the signal with the important additional constraint that any surprisingness due to random (uncontrolled) component in the signal is excluded. Information-theoretically, the surprisingness of a message, or more precisely, of a source generating messages according to a certain probability distribution, can be measured by the entropy $H(x)$ associated with the random variable, x, whose values are the messages. For instance, the surprisingness of a key stroke chosen uniformly at random among 32 alternatives is $\log_2(32) = 5$ bits; five times that of an answer to a single yes–no question. A similar measure of surprisingness, differential entropy, can also be associated to continuous random variables, but it lacks the same meaning in terms of yes–no questions. For in-depth definitions of the used information-theoretic concepts and their properties, please see e.g. Cover and Thomas [10].

For text-based passwords, in the practically untypical case where a password is chosen uniformly at random, the relationship between entropy and security is straightforward. If the alphabet size is denoted by $|\mathcal{X}|$ and the password is of length n, then the entropy is given by $H(X) = n \log_2 |\mathcal{X}|$ in the uniformly random case. It then holds that the probability that an uninformed guess is successful is $2^{-H(X)} = |\mathcal{X}|^{-n}$ and the expected number of guesses required to guess correctly by an uninformed attacker is $(2^{H(X)} + 1)/2 = |\mathcal{X}|^n/2 + 1/2$, about half the number of possible passwords of length n. However, when the password is not chosen uniformly at random, the entropy has no direct relationship with security and the required number of guesses can vary significantly between different kinds of password generation strategies even if they have exactly the same entropy [4]. Despite this, the entropy $H(X)$ is used as a standard measure of password security even in the non-uniform case [7]. More accurate definitions that take into account the shape of the password distribution have been proposed, see Bonneau [4].

For continuous passwords, one needs to take into account the tolerance for repeatability and recognizability. From an information theoretic point of view, this aspect is captured by the concept of *mutual information*. The mutual information $I(x\,;\,y)$ of two random variables, x and y, gives the reduction in the entropy of one random variable when another one becomes known:

$$I(x\,;\,y) = H(x) - H(x\,|\,y), \qquad (1)$$

where $H(x\,|\,y)$ denotes the conditional entropy. This applies to both discrete as well as continuous variables. The mutual information characterizes the information capacity of noisy channels with the interpretation that x denotes a transmitted signal and y denotes the signal received at the other end of the channel. In the context of the present work, the transmitted signal is the intended gesture and the received signal is the recorded or repeated gesture. The more noisy the channel (less accurately repeated gesture), the lower the mutual information, $I(x\,;\,y)$, and the capacity of the channel, and *vice versa*. Note that a message can have high entropy (complexity) without the mutual information (information content) being high but not the other way around.[1]

The exact operational meaning of mutual information from a communication point of view is that given a channel for which the mutual information between its input and its output equals $I(x\,;\,y)$, it is possible to reliably transmit information at the rate of $I(x\,;\,y)$ bits per use of the channel. In other words, we can communicate a choice among $2^{I(x\,;\,y)}$ different messages so that the receiver can reliably recover the intended message. Getting back to the question of password security, if the mutual information between the intended and the recorded gesture is $I(x\,;\,y)$, and a gesture password is chosen uniformly at random among the $2^{I(x\,;\,y)}$ mutually distinguishable choices, we obtain a result analogous to the case of text-based passwords: the probability of success of an uninformed guess is given by $2^{-I(x\,;\,y)}$ and the attacker will need on the average $2^{I(x;y)-1} + 1/2$ attempts before the guessed gesture is identified as the correct one. Each bit of mutual information will double the effort by the attacker. Thus, the mutual information defines the *effective key-length* [6, 4] of gesture passwords, so that their security becomes directly comparable to the security of text-based passwords.

In practice, it can be questioned whether users will typically choose gesture passwords uniformly at random [37, 44], although the problem is hardly as pronounced as in the case of text-based passwords where a significant portion of passwords are vulnerable to simple dictionary attacks [4]. Another issue that interferes with the above counting argument is the design of the recognizer that is used to accept or reject a gesture. The information-theoretic limit provides an upper bound on the effective key-length. The better the recognizer, the closer to this limit the system will be able to operate.

Based on the above insight, we can now ask what makes a gesture password secure. Recalling Eq. 1, we see that the two factors affecting the mutual information are $i)$ the entropy (uncertainty or surprisingness) of the intended gesture, $H(x)$, and $ii)$ the condi-

tional entropy (remaining uncertainty) of the intended gesture given the observed gesture, $H(x\,|\,y)$. These two factors correspond to the complexity and the accuracy of the gesture, respectively.

The metric we use for the information content in repeated gestures is defined as the mutual information between two realizations of the same gesture. The input to the metric consists of two multitouch movement sequences produced by asking a user to produce a gesture and repeat it.

The first realization will be used to represent the intended gesture, x, and the second realization will be denoted by y. The trajectories record the locations of each of the used fingers over duration of the gesture. In order to estimate the mutual information $I(x\,;\,y)$ between two multitouch trajetories, which describes the security of the gesture in the information-theoretic sense described above, a number of steps are required.

Computation. Computation of the mutual information involves a sequence of steps. First, we need to remove from the sequences their predictable aspects, as far as possible. To do so, we fit a second order autoregressive model for both of the sequences separately. For sequence x, the model is:

$$x_t = \beta_0 + \beta_1 x_{t-1} + \beta_2 x_{t-2} + \varepsilon_t^{(x)}, \qquad (2)$$

where β_0, β_1 and β_2 are parameters that we estimate using the standard least-squares method. The benefit of a second-order model is its interpretability; it captures the physical principle that once the movement vector (direction and velocity) is determined, constant movement contains no information.

After parameter fitting, we obtain residuals $r_t^{(x)}$ for each frame t:

$$r_t^{(x)} = x_t - \hat{x}_t = x_t - (\hat{\beta}_0 + \hat{\beta}_1 x_{t-1} + \hat{\beta}_2 x_{t-2}) \qquad (3)$$

The residuals $r_t^{(x)}$ correspond to deviations from constant movement and are hence the part of the sequence unexplained by the autoregressive model. They can be used to gauge the surprisingness of the trajectory. The same procedure is carried out for sequence y. We could now compute the differential entropy of the residual sequences, but as stated above, it alone has little meaning and we are in fact only interested in the mutual information between the two sequences.

Before we compute the mutual information, *dimension reduction* is performed whereby multitouch gestures are represented using only as many features per measurement as the data requires. The motivation for this step is that one cannot simply add information in the movement features in multitouch gestures together. Instead, any dependencies between the fingers should be removed. Intuitively, a multitouch gesture with all fingers in a fixed constellation contains essentially the same amount of information as the same gesture performed using a single finger. Dimension reduction is performed using principal component analysis (PCA), which removes any linear dependencies. Following common practice, the number of retained dimensions is set by finding the lowest number of dimensions that yields an acceptably low reprojection error (e.g. mean square error [27]).

Once the movement features have been processed by a dimension reduction technique (PCA), we treat them independently which amounts to simply adding up the information content in each feature in the end. Hence, the following discussion only considers the one-dimensional case where both x and y are univariate sequences.

Another issue in gesture data is that the two gestures x and y are often not of equal length due to different speed at which the gestures are performed. This can be corrected by *temporally aligning* the sequences using, for instance, Canonical Time Warping [46]. The result is a pairwise alignment of each of the frames in x and

---

[1]In fact, to be precise, the inequality $I(x;y) \leq H(x)$ which follows directly from Eq. 1, holds only for discrete signals, such as text-based passwords, but not for continuous signals, such as gestures, because continuous signals can have negative (conditional) differential entropy [10]. However, even though there is no theoretical guarantee of it, the intuition that a trivial gesture such as a straight line cannot contain high information content holds true in our experiments; see below.

y achieved by duplicating some of the frames in each sequence. These duplicate frames are skipped when computing mutual information to avoid inflating their effect.

Finally, we form pairs of residual values $(r_t^{(x)}, r_t^{(y)})$ corresponding to each of the frames in the aligned residual sequences and evaluate the mutual information. Since the mutual information is defined for a joint distribution of two random variables, we model the residual pairs $(r_t^{(x)}, r_t^{(y)})$ in each frame $1 \leq t \leq n$ using a bivariate Gaussian model, under which the mutual information is given by the simple formula

$$I(x\,;\,y) = -\frac{n}{2}\log_2(1 - \rho_{x,y}^2), \qquad (4)$$

where $\rho_{x,y}$ is the Pearson correlation coefficient between x and y.

By substituting the sample correlation coefficient, r, estimated from the data in place of $\rho_{x,y}$ and subtracting a term due to the known statistical bias of the estimator (see [27]), we obtain the mutual information estimate

$$\hat{I}(x\,;\,y) = -\frac{n}{2}\log_2(1 - r^2) - \log_2(e)/2, \qquad (5)$$

where $\log_2(e) \approx 1.443$ is the base-2 logarithm of the Euler constant.

The total information content in the gesture, based on two repetitions, is estimated as the sum of the mutual information estimates in each of the movement features after dimension reduction.

Summary. The metric has some appealing properties to serve as an index of security. First, a distinctive feature of our framework that sets it apart from the work on text-based password security is that in dealing with continuous gestures, it is imperative to be able to separate the complexity due to intended aspects of the gesture from that due to its unintended, and hence non-reproducible, aspects. This is the main motivation to use mutual information as a basis for the metric. Second, as mutual information under the bivariate Gaussian model is determined by the correlation between the movement sequences (residuals), it is invariant under linear transformations such as change of scale, translation, or rotation. Hence, the user need not remember the exact scale, position, or orientation of the gesture on the screen. The metric is also independent of the size and the resolution of the used screen unless, of course, the resolution is so low that important details of the gesture are not recorded. Third, the time warping step ensures that variation in the timing within the gesture has only slight effect on the metric. Fourth, the metric enables comparison between gestures of unequal lengths and between single-finger and multi-finger gestures, as well as across different screen sizes and resolutions, on a unified scale (bits).

4. METHOD

Our study design builds on a generate-test-retest paradigm where participants were first asked to create a gesture, recall it, and recall again during the second session, a minimum of 10 days later. Participants were told that they should generate secure gestures as they would do in real situations and that their ability to recall them would be tested later. They were not given any hints about what a secure gesture might be. For understanding the generation and recall process, we used a mixed method approach: after generating a gesture, all participants filled a questionnaire on workload (NASA-TLX [18]) after each task and a short survey at the end of the second session.

We note that a somewhat similar generate-test-retest design has been used before by Chiasson et al. [9] to compare multiple password inference to recall between text-based and graphical pass-

words (PassPoints [40]). However, our work differs for the following reasons: we use TLX forms, focus on free-form multitouch gestures, include more repetitions and recalls, do not require a separate login phase, and postpone questions to the end of a trial.

Next, we describe our volunteer participants, our apparatus, data preprocessing, experiment design and procedure.

Participants. We recruited participants with flyers, email lists, and in-person in cafeterias. We required the participants to be 18 years old or over and familiar with touchscreen devices. We recruited 63 participants in all, from the ages of 18 to 65 (M = 27.2, SD = 9.9); 24 are male and 39 are female. Their educational background varies: 22 have high school diplomas, 23 have a Bachelor's degree, 16 have a graduate degree and two have other degrees.

All 63 participants completed session 1 of our study, and 57 of them returned and participated in session 2. As compensation, participants received $30 for completing the whole study. They also participated in a raffle of three $75 gift cards.

We recruited our participants in two batches: first in May 2013 (33) and second in June 2013 (30). Further, in order to analyze the effect of varying time on recall, the gap between the two sessions of the study varies. The mean time gap for the first participants is 14.53 (SD = 5.81) days and 29.52 (SD = 7.57) days for the second.

Our study was approved by our Institutional Review Board.

Apparatus. The gesture data was recorded on a Google Nexus 10 tablet with Android 4.2.2 as the operating system, at an average of 200 frames per second (FPS).

Preprocessing. The raw data files were preprocessed using MATLAB. In the preprocessing, each gesture file is resampled to 60 FPS, to reduce the effect of the uneven sample rate.

The resampling was done by cubic spline interpolation, via MATLAB's built in function interp1.m. For the x and y coordinates for each finger, it takes the recorded timestamps and resamples to a constant rate. The reduction from 200 to 60 FPS takes into account a large amount of duplicate data created by the touchscreen, and is necessary to prevent artifacts in the resampling.

FFT analysis showed that the frequency reduction combined with the cubic spline method results in low pass filtering of the data, removing high frequency jitter introduced by the touchscreen hardware, but preserving the low frequency content of the gesture data. To deal with the uneven sample rate in the non-interpolated data, the Lomb-Scargle [32] method was used.

At this stage, artifacts in the raw data were detected and corrected as well. The primary such artifact is when a participant fails to place their fingers on the touchscreen in the same order between consecutive trials. As fingers are numbered sequentially upon being detected by the touchscreen, this places them out of order, resulting in artificially low scores in the later analysis. This was corrected by comparing the starting coordinates of each finger, and correcting the order to be consistent.

Experiment Design. The experiment followed a 17 x 2 mixed factor design with a repeated measurement variable of gesture repetition (17 levels) and a between-subject variable of time gap between sessions (2 levels). In the 17 gesture repetitions, 10 were performed during the creation process, followed by another 2 repetitions after a short distraction, and 5 were performed in the second session.

Procedure. We conducted a two-session study. The second session was held after a minimum 10 days after the first session. The details of the procedure were as follows.

First session: First, the participants were introduced to the study, which included reading and signing the consent form, discussion of their rights as participants and how they will be compensated.

Gesture Creation (Generate): Each participant was given the same tablet and was asked to create what they thought would be a secure gesture by drawing on it. The participants were asked to generate a gesture that they think others could not guess, but they could also remember later. The participants could retry until they felt satisfied with their gesture. Then the participant repeated the same gesture for an additional nine times on the same tablet. Participants were presented with a blank screen for drawing their gestures. The application did not limit the number of fingers participants use to create the gesture. However, the number of fingers used could not be changed during the drawing process, that is, the gesture has to be drawn continuously without lifting any fingers from the screen. Once it is completed, the gesture is displayed on the tablet's screen as a colored curve line, as shown in Figure 1. The display was checked visually, to verify that the gesture was recorded properly.

Subjective Workload Assessment: The participants were asked to fill out NASA-TLX form regarding the creation process.

Distraction: The participants were asked to perform a mental rotation task and count down from 20 to 0 silently.

Gesture Recall 1: The participants were asked to recall the gesture by repeating it twice on the same tablet using the same application.

Demographic questions: The participants were asked usual demographics questions that were aggregated and reported above.

Second session:

Gesture Recall 2: The participants were asked to recall their gestures by repeating it for five times on the same tablet using the same application.

Subjective Workload Assessment: The participants were asked to fill out a NASA-TLX form regarding the recall process.

Short Survey: The participants were asked some questions about the recall process and other thoughts about the study.

5. RESULTS

For each participant who completed both sessions, a total of 17 gesture repetitions were recorded. In all, 1038 recordings were generated, as six participants did not attend session 2, and three additional traces were not completed. The groups of repetitions are summarized in Table 1. Because the estimated Mutual Information $(\hat{I})$, is computed in pairs, $\hat{I}$ is reported as the mean for the relevant repetitions.

Session	Trial #	Group
1	1-10	Generate
1	11-12	Recall1
2	13-17	Recall2

Table 1: Repetition Groups by Session # and Trial #. $\hat{I}$ was computed for all pairs of repetitions each group.

5.1 Factors Affecting Security

Figure 2 shows the mean $\hat{I}$ of each repetition across all gestures versus the repetition number. During gesture creation in Generate, $\hat{I}$ trended upwards from repetitions 1-4, and then leveled off from repetitions 5-10. This shows that it takes at least three repetitions for a participant's gesture to become stable.

A second major feature is that by Recall1, repetition 11 and 12, the $\hat{I}$ has dropped suddenly, despite a delay of only a few minutes. Surprisingly, more than 10 days later, $\hat{I}$ did not drop much further in Recall2. The drop between Generate and Recall1 was more severe for single finger gestures, and the drop between Recalls 1 and 2 was more severe for multifinger gestures. In both cases, $\hat{I}$ stabilized, at around 27 bits for single finger and 15 bits for multifinger

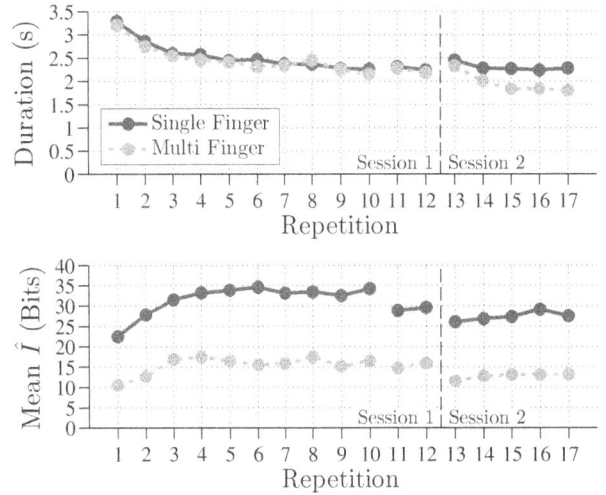

Figure 2: Mean $\hat{I}$ and mean gesture duration vs repetition. Top: Within Generate, mean gesture duration trended downwards as gestures increased in speed. Bottom: Over the same repetitions, $\hat{I}$ trended upwards before leveling out. It then dropped quickly between Generate and the two Recalls.

gestures, having dropped from an initial value of around 35 and 20 bits respectively.

Figure 2 also shows the amount of time taken to record each repetition of each gesture. This duration also changed with repetition. As the number of repetitions increased, the mean duration of each repetition trended downwards from around 3 seconds to around 2. Unlike $\hat{I}$, it remained stable from there through the two recalls. Interestingly, during Recall2 the multifinger gestures sped up from 2.5 seconds to under 2 seconds, whereas the single finger gestures stabilized.

A plot of the mean $\hat{I}$ of each gesture versus mean duration appears in Figure 3. This shows that many gestures with a short duration also had a low $\hat{I}$. The highest $\hat{I}$ gestures had a duration of between 2 and 5 seconds. $\hat{I}$ increased with duration, but had a poor fit, explaining only 5% of the variation, as the highest duration gestures were either very high or very low $\hat{I}$. Long duration could thus indicate either a complex, careful gesture, or a relative lack of practice.

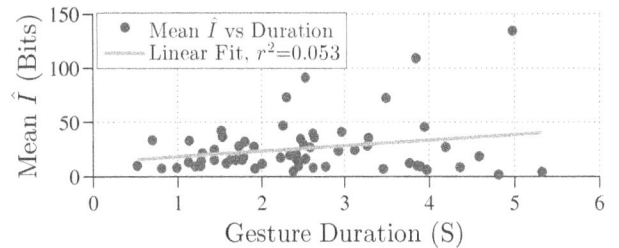

Figure 3: Mean $\hat{I}$ vs. mean gesture duration. The r^2 value indicates a poor linear fit, showing little correlation. However, the highest $\hat{I}$ gestures were all longer than 2 seconds, suggesting that some degree of precision is required.

Figure 4 shows that majority of the user-generated gestures had relatively low $\hat{I}$ with only a small tail of high $\hat{I}$. For Generate, the distribution had a mean of 27.72 bits, and a standard deviation of

26.30 bits. However, taking only the second, stable half of Generate, the mean rose to 33.42 bits, with a standard deviation of 31.13 bits. In both cases, the standard deviation was about the same size as the mean, indicating a large variability. The histogram shifted as well, becoming slightly more uniform. Although many user chosen gestures score poorly, some scored highly as well, suggesting that it is possible to create guidelines to emulate the characteristics of high scoring gestures.

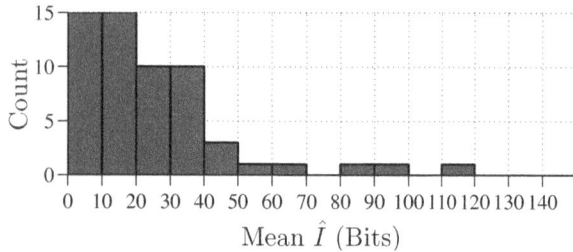

Figure 4: Histogram of mean $\hat{I}$ of Generate, per gesture, showing low scoring, biased distribution.

We compared mean $\hat{I}$ with participant age and gender. There was a mild negative relationship between $\hat{I}$ and age, with a r^2 of 0.08. Seven of the top eight gestures were created by participants under the age of 25, with the remaining one under the age of 30. Mean $\hat{I}$ for male participants (N=23) was 29.82 bits and mean $\hat{I}$ for female participants (N=40) was 25.00 bits.

Finally, we looked for defining visual characteristics of the highest and lowest scoring gestures. We ranked each gesture by its $\hat{I}$ in each of the five categories, and evaluated the top five in each category. There was a high correlation between the categories, and as such, the top five gestures for each category overlapped significantly, having only nine unique gestures. The best gestures fell into two groups, angular paths with many hard turns, and signatures. This matched our expectations, as the algorithm looks for both consistency between trials and for large deviations from a straight line. The defining visual feature of the lowest scoring gestures was having only a few, gentle curves. Many were multifinger, with the additional fingers merely copying the motion of the first. A gallery appears in Figure 5.

5.2 Security of Multitouch Gestures

As seen in Figure 2, the mean $\hat{I}$ of multifinger gestures is lower than that of single finger ones. We compared $\hat{I}$ of these gestures to estimate how much additional information is added by additional fingers. Figure 6 shows the higher mean $\hat{I}$ of single finger gestures, and the rarity of gestures using more than two fingers. Recall2 showed a greater difference in $\hat{I}$ than Generate, as a number of participants failed to use the same number of fingers when they returned in session 2. Of the 63 participants, 32 decided to create multifinger gestures, and 31 chose to create single finger gestures, with only three participants using more than two fingers. Participants were prompted that they could use as many fingers as they liked, but were not instructed on how many to use.

We performed regression analysis on the effect of the number of fingers on $\hat{I}$. The result shows that the effect is significant for the $\hat{I}$ of Generate, $b = 17.948, t(57) = 2.763, p = .0077$, while not for the $\hat{I}$ of Recall2, $b = 11.898, t(57) = 1.841, p = .07$. However, the regression model only explained 11.8% of variance in the $\hat{I}$ for the significant effect. In short, the number of fingers is not the most major factor affecting $\hat{I}$.

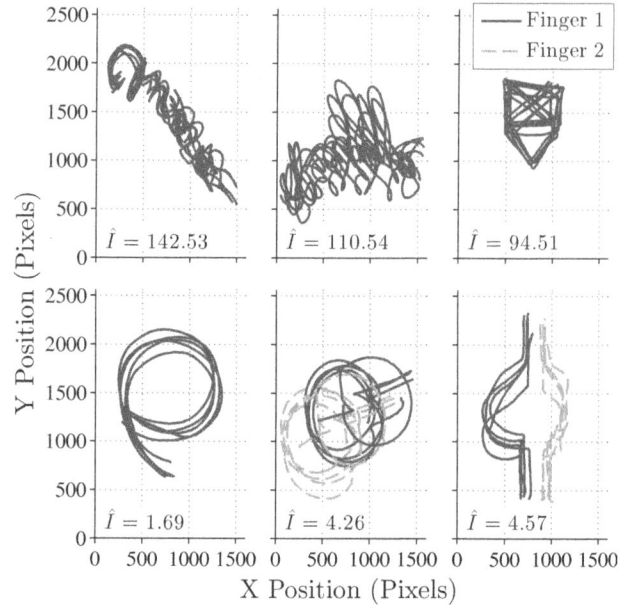

Figure 5: Gestures ranked by $\hat{I}$ for Generate and Recall2. Top: Best three gestures, showing the many tight turns characteristic of high scoring gestures. Bottom: Worst three gestures, Low scoring gestures had few, gentle turns.

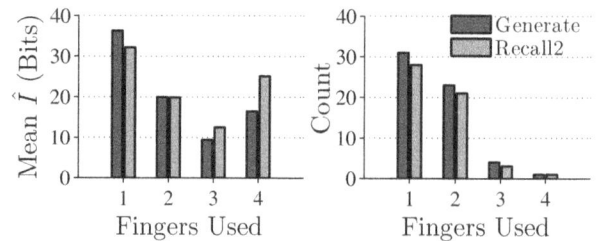

Figure 6: $\hat{I}$ and number of fingers used to perform gesture, and change between sessions 1 and 2. This shows the both the higher performance of single finger gestures, as well as the rarity of using more than two fingers.

5.3 Factors Affecting Memorability

Figure 7 shows the best remembered gestures. To evaluate memorability, we computed the cross-group $\hat{I}$ of Generate and Recall2, with pairs consisting of one from each group, instead of both from within a group. However, the large differences in $\hat{I}$ from gesture complexity obscured the differences from repetition accuracy, as the cross-group $\hat{I}$ has a linear fit with an r^2 of 0.65 with the $\hat{I}$ of Generate. We compensated by dividing the mean cross-group $\hat{I}$ for each gesture by its $\hat{I}$ from Generate.

Gestures that scored highly on the resulting ratio have the best consistency between Generate and Recall2, as compared to the consistency within Generate. The top gestures for memorability are shorter and simpler than the top gestures for security.

Once we had a way of comparing how well gestures are remembered, we investigated what might cause the large difference in $\hat{I}$ between sessions. We compared the memorability ratio to the time interval between Generate and Recall2, as seen in Figure 8. The

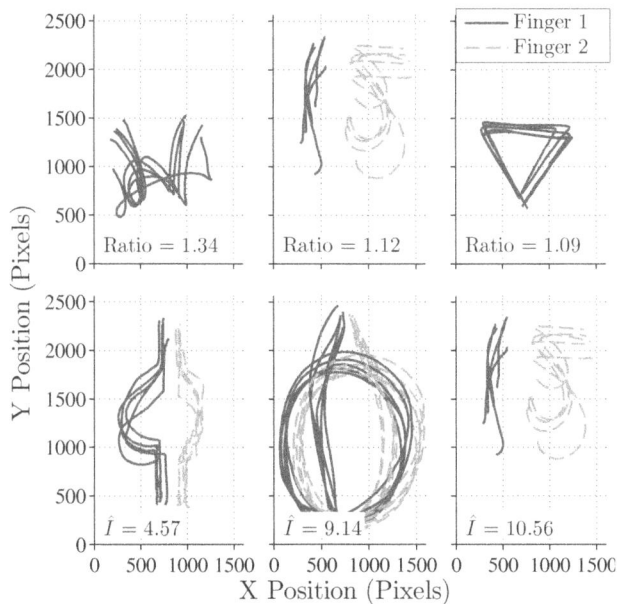

Figure 7: Top: Best 3 Gestures by memorability. These have a shorter length and decreased complexity compared to high $\hat{I}$ gestures. Bottom: These 3 gestures had the greatest difference in path between fingers. Two of the three are a simple mirroring of the path (Left, Middle), while only (Right) adds a large amount of $\hat{I}$.

linear fit however, had a r^2 of less than 0.03, showing minimal dependence on the delay between sessions.

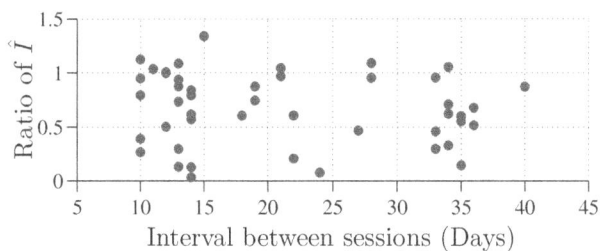

Figure 8: Memorability vs interval between sessions. This plot compares the relative quality of gesture recall versus time between Generate and Recall2. There was no significant correlation with a ($r^2 < 0.03$).

5.4 Individual Differences

Given the surprising deficiency of the multifinger gestures, we looked at specific examples. Only three participants used multitouch gestures with significantly different motions between fingers, and in two of the three cases they were simple mirrorings of the motion. These three gestures appear in Figure 7. All other cases were just translations of the same trace, as if the gesture were made with a rigid hand. Gestures with minimal additional information per finger were in part scored low because all gestures were run through a PCA algorithm to remove redundant information, prior to analysis of $\hat{I}$.

Participants also commonly performed several categories of error. Despite instructions, 19 of the 32 multifinger using participants

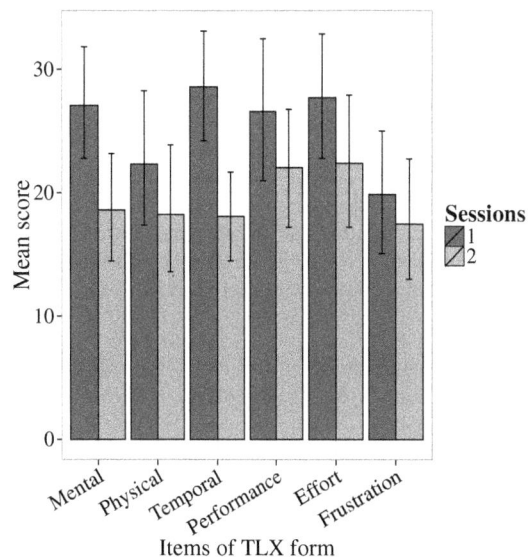

Figure 9: Mean score and corresponding 95% confidence interval for each item on the TLX form, for the two sessions of our study. The mean scores of each item in session two were lower than those of session one.

placed their fingers down in an inconsistent order between sequential trials. This was fixed in preprocessing to ensure that computation of $\hat{I}$ used the same fingers. In addition, some participants rotated the tablet either during or between sessions. This stands out visually when comparing traces, but the metric is negligibly affected by rotations. This was verified by comparing the result with its gesture counterpart from session one or two which did not have a rotation. Some of the lowest scoring gestures featured a rotation between repetitions, and all gestures with rotation between sessions scored poorly on cross-session $\hat{I}$. However, the gestures with cross-session rotation also scored poorly within a session. Only one gesture with rotation between sessions scored significantly higher on its within session $\hat{I}$ than on its cross-session.

Given that error containing gestures scored poorly, even when excluding those repetition pairs containing the errors, we take these errors as an indicator of poor recall. Extra fingers or complex shapes are no guarantees of a high score, without consistent execution. Attention when creating the gesture is thus important, practicing accurate repetition rather than just going through the motions.

5.5 Subjective Task Load

This section contains the analysis of the study's TLX forms. For each session of our study we asked participants to fill out one TLX form, which is used to assess subjective workload of given task. Figure 9 shows the mean score and corresponding 95% confidence interval for each item in the TLX form, for both sessions.

Figure 9 suggests that the mean scores of session two are lower than those of session one. To prove the point we conducted a non-parametric repeated-measure Wilcoxon signed-rank test on the scores of each item from the two sessions, given the fact that the data does not follow a normal distribution. The result is shown in Table 2.

From Table 2 we can see that except for Frustration, all items show significant differences in scores between sessions. It is safe to say that given the data we have, it is very likely that participants felt the recall task was easier than the creation task in terms

Item	Mental	Physical	Temporal
p value	<0.001	0.025	<0.001
effect size	-.038	-0.21	-0.34
Item	Performance	Effort	Frustration
p value	0.029	0.0013	0.072
effect size	-0.20	-0.30	-0.17

Table 2: Subjective task load components compared between the two sessions. Statistical significance calculated using Wilcoxon signed-rank test. The difference was significant at the 0.05 level for all components except Frustration.

of workload. This could be because of increased practice or familiarity, and intuitively agrees with the increase in gesture speed seen in Figure 2.

6. PRACTICAL AUTHENTICATION SYSTEM IMPLEMENTATION

In this section, we describe our extension to a practical single touch gesture recognizer for multitouch gestures, and the results of how the participants' gestures would perform in a real authentication system based on our multitouch recognizer. We also present our trial on shoulder surfing attacks that indicates how free-form gestures are robust against shoulder surfing.

A recognizer works by taking a user's gesture, passing it through a recognition algorithm, and computing whether or not the gesture is a successful match for a stored template. The device will store a series of templates of which the gestures are compared to for authentication. The best score is used and compared to a threshold value. We have the following assumptions for the recognizer: 1) location invariance: No matter where the correct gesture is drawn on the screen, it should be authenticated correctly. 2) scale invariance: No matter what size the correct gesture is drawn to on the screen, it should be authenticated correctly. 3) rotation invariance: No matter what angle the correct gesture is drawn at on the screen, it should be authenticated correctly. Location and scale invariance are important when dealing with cross-platform authentication. The screen dimension inherently limits what size the gesture can be drawn to and the area over which a gesture can be performed would cause wild variations in where it would be drawn depending on the user. Rotation invariance is useful for reducing computational complexity when dealing with individualized free-form gestures as we have in our data set. We note that authentication system designers can opt to restrict or relax these assumptions. Scale invariance, for example, is not inherently necessary. The size of a gesture can be a feature of that gesture depending on how the recognizer is implemented.

We elected to implement and extend the Protractor [21] recognition algorithm, a popular nearest neighbor approach. Given the gesture templates obtained and the two recall sets, we would like to measure how well the gestures perform. Protractor is an improvement upon the $1 Recognizer [41], having both a lower error rate [21] and an effectively constant computational time per training sample as compared to $1's growing cost per training sample. Protractor presents itself further as an attractive algorithm for the data under consideration since it has low computational complexity compared to other techniques, for example, Dynamic Time Warping (DTW) [41] and Hidden Markov Models (HMM) [13, 24]. In general, Protractor's error rate falls with an increasing number of training samples and at 9-10, the error rate is less than 0.5% [21].

Below we describe first the single touch Protractor and we follow with our extension of it to multitouch gestures.

Upon the input of a gesture, the algorithm splits the work into four parts:

1. A gesture is resampled into N equally spaced coordinates.

2. The gesture is translated to the origin of the plane.

3. After translation, the angle between the first point of the gesture and the origin is measured. Then, the entire gesture is rotated until that angle becomes zero degrees.

4. To minimize the distance between the gesture and a template, they need to be aligned such that the angle between them is the smallest. This angle is easily calculated as being the dot product between the gesture and the template. The gesture is subsequently rotated by the dot product angle.

5. The cosine distance is then measured between the template and the gesture. The inverse of this distance defines the recognition score. The smaller the cosine distance, the better the match (and correspondingly, a larger score).

6. The score is compared to a threshold value. If it is greater than the threshold, the gesture and the template are said to match. If it is less than the threshold, they are said not to match.

Again, Protractor is a single touch recognition algorithm. Other projects considering multitouch gestures have used more general techniques for gesture recognition instead of a nearest neighbor approach. For example, Sae-bae et al. [31] applied DTW to deal with their multitouch gesture set. For the authenticator to remain practical, it needs low computational complexity, high speed, and low error rate per template to be implemented on a mobile device – Protractor can meet this demand. As we are dealing with multitouch gestures, it is necessary to modify Protractor. The accounting procedure is as follows:

1. Each finger is split into its own set of points and passed through the algorithm and compared to templates of similar fingers and the score is computed for each individually.

2. They are then averaged together.

3. There are provisions built into place to ensure the authentication failure for the wrong number of fingers. In the case of n fingers versus m, the number of fingers is compared. If n is equal to m, then the recognizer continues to the next step. If n is not equal to m, then the recognizer immediately stops the computation and registers the score as 0: a failure.

4. This score is then compared to the threshold value. If the score is greater than or equal to the threshold then it is considered a positive authentication, otherwise, it is negative.

It is important to note that the threshold should be set high enough such that authentication failure is all but guaranteed for gestures that are being matched to templates other than their own.

As a reminder, when the participants began the study, they were asked to repeat their gestures ten times. Each of these ten trials is used by Protractor as templates for that gesture. There are two authentication data sets under consideration here: the first is where participants were asked to replicate their gesture after a distraction and the second where they were asked to replicate their gesture after at least 10 days.

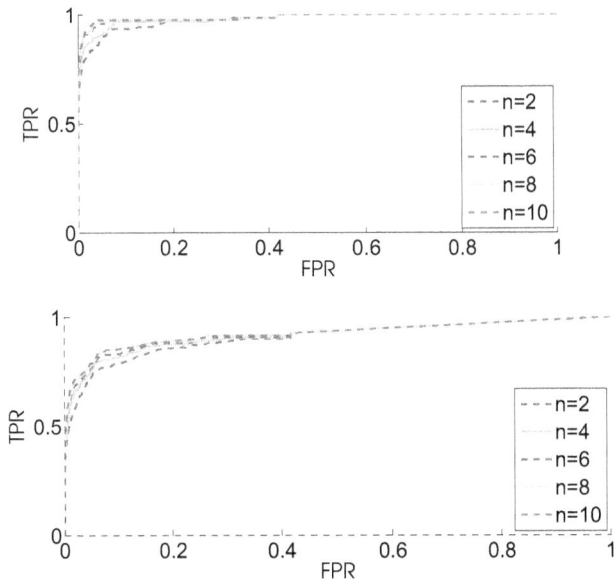

Figure 10: This figure shows the ROC curve for the recognizer across the two data sets with variable template numbers – 'n' corresponds to the number of templates. The top plot is the first data set and the second plot is the second data set. The ROC curve is a measure of the performance of a binary classifier, the closer the top left corner of the plot moves towards the vertical axis, the better the performance. The first data set is closer to that corner than the second, showing that the second data set performed worse and must have a higher equivalent error rate. As the number of templates increases, the closer the curve shifts up and the better the recognizer performs. In general, the recognizer classified the first data set with a lower EER than the second set despite those being the same gesture types, indicating a weakness on the parts of participants to accurately replicate their gestures. The EER values can be read in Table 3.

6.1 Recognizer Performance

We wanted to know how accurately the recognizer is performing across the different gestures in our data sets. To quantify this in terms of a numerical estimate and visualize it, we elected to obtain a Receiver Operating Characteristic (ROC) curve and derive from it an Equivalent Error Rate (EER). The ROC curve gives the visual representation of how our classifier is performing and the EER value gives us the numerical estimate for how it is performing: the lower the EER is, the more accurately the recognizer is performing.

To find the EER value we need to find the rate at which the True Positive Rate (TPR) is equivalent to the False Positive Rate (FPR). These are defined as:

$$TPR = \frac{True\ Positives}{True\ Positives + False\ Negatives} \quad (6)$$

$$FPR = \frac{False\ Positives}{False\ Positives + True\ Negatives} \quad (7)$$

These values are dependent on the threshold parameter that the score computed by the recognizer is compared to. To generate an ROC curve, one must vary the authentication threshold parameter and measure a (TPR,FPR) value for each point and plot them. From there, we can determine the EER visually.

At low threshold values, the classification system would be accepting virtually any gesture as a validation against any template gesture. At high values, all input gestures would be rejected against any other template (even if it is being matched to the correct one). As the EER value climbs higher, the reliability of the gesture or the recognizer can be called into question since false positives are propagating through the system. In the case of our system, the templates are not matched to one another. We have two true cases for a given gesture in the first data set and five true cases for a given gesture in the second data set. All other gesture attempts in all other data sets (exclusively across these two sets, no intersections) are considered false cases.

As such, what this means is that the ROC curves and the EER values are across the entire data set and not per gesture. This is done to avoid generating ROC curves and EER values for every one of the different gestures, which would be an overabundance of data that is not altogether useful. The EER and ROC values given here can be thought of as a measure of performance of the recognizer across the entire set rather than the recognizer and a single gesture.

# of Templates	Set 1 EER	Set 2 EER
2	7.07%	15.97%
4	6.42%	14.45%
6	4.13%	13.94%
8	4.10%	13.09%
10	3.34%	13.16%

Table 3: EER Values, Ranked by Template Number. Listed above are the EER values corresponding to Figure 10. As the number of templates increases, the lower the EER value drops and thus the lower the error in the system and the better the recognizer performs. The lower Set 2 values correlate to the shape of the curves represented in Figure 10: as EER decreases, the better the curve appears. The EER values for the recognizer reduce more slowly with 6 training templates, indicating this to be the ideal starting point when asking a user to train the system.

As for how well the gestures and the recognizer performed in terms of accuracy across the data sets, that information can be gleaned from the ROC plots given in Figure 10 and the EER values shown in Table 3. As a reminder, the further away an ROC curve moves from being a 90-degree box (an EER of 0%), the worse it is performing. Figure 10 shows the ROC curves with a varying number of template sizes. As the number of templates increases, the ROC curves are pushed further towards the corner and the EER values are lowered, telling us that a larger number of training templates leads to improved accuracy. For the first set, the best result (with 10 templates) is 3.34% and the best result for the second set is 13.16%. Note that the higher EER on the second data set does not speak to the weakness of the recognizer but rather those of the participants – some participants who returned to attempt their gestures in the second set forgot the number of fingers they used, registering immediate authentication failure. As such, the increased error in the second set as compared from the first set can be attributed to recall problems rather than weaknesses in the recognizer's ability to classify gestures.

6.2 Threshold Selection

The final stage of the recognition process, the threshold comparision, determines whether or not a gesture is classified as a positive or a negative. So, naturally, the question becomes: How does one select the optimal threshold? Ideally, a perfect threshold would be set at a point where it is possible to accept only the correct gestures and reject all others.

The starting point for considering the optimal threshold would be the ROC curve and the EER. Recall that the EER is the rate at which the true positive rate equals the false positive rate. The EER value occurs at a specific tuning threshold. Meaning, at this specific threshold, the system rejects the same number of true positives as it accepts false positives. An illustrative example is this: if the EER is 2%, then that means 2 out of 100 true attempts are rejected and 2 out of 100 false attempts are accepted. Selecting a threshold above or below the EER threshold can tighten or relax the admission requirements.

At this point, the threshold selection becomes application dependent. For authenticating into a bank, for example, a 2% false acceptance rate is unspeakable. As such, the threshold would be set at a point far above the EER threshold. When this happens, the false acceptance rate drops drastically but the false rejection rate would increase just as drastically; now there is a threshold where is a 0.01% false acceptance rate but a 10% false rejection rate. This is a tradeoff that a bank could accept.

For most gestures in this set, false positives are not an issue. Individual EER ratings on a *per gesture basis* are quite small, as compared to the larger EER of the gesture set. Selection at this threshold for gestures in the data set would be acceptable for authentication.

6.3 Shoulder Surfing Attack Trial

We conducted a preliminary study to understand how free-form gestures would resist shoulder surfing attacks. Towards this end, we recruited seven participants from computer science and engineering schools who had considerable experience with touchscreens. We assume that these volunteers would likely to be more skilled with attacks than the general populace to limit confounding factors. One of the seven volunteers acted as the target who performs gestures and the other six would be attackers who try to replicate target's gestures.

We chose three qualitatively different gestures as shown in Figure 11 as examples. In the experiment, we first had the target of the attacks exercise and get familiar with all three gestures; then we collected gesture data from the target in a way matching the original dataset: for each chosen gesture, the target first repeated ten times; after a short distraction task, which included mental rotation and countdown, the target repeated another two times. Finally, we video recorded one additional repetition the target made for each gesture. Instead of having the target performing gestures in person for every attacker, we played video recordings of that process to the attackers, which ensured attackers would not be affected by any inconsistency or difference within the performance of the target.

During the shoulder surfing process, each attacker was presented with all of the three videos, each of which contained one of the chosen gestures. The attackers were always seated at the same spot, adjacent to the a chair at the table where the display was setup. This was done in order to emulate shoulder surfing. The order of videos played to each attacker was produced in a Latin square to prevent any carry over effect on the attackers' performance. Each video was played only once for each attacker. Then attackers were told to repeat the gesture they observed from the video for five times with the purpose of replicating it as well as possible.

We measured shoulder surfing effectiveness of a gesture using our multitouch recognizer discussed above. The templates we used are the 10 gestures from the Generate phase of the target. Table 4 shows the result. All scores displayed in the table are the maximum score of that category, that is, the best attempt of either the target

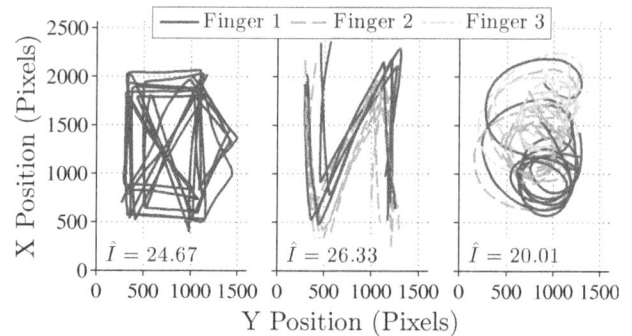

Figure 11: Gallery of Gestures used for shoulder surfing. In order from left to right represents Gesture1, Gesture2, and Gesture3 generated by the Target.

or attackers to replicate the gesture. Scores that are rendered as a 0 are because of the fact that the recognizer immediately rejects template-gesture matching where the finger count is different.

Participant	Gesture1	Gesture2	Gesture3
Target (Recall)	4.36	4.31	6.75
Target (Video)	2.95	4.51	7.27
Attacker 1	0.50	0.00	0.97
Attacker 2	0.43	3.08	0.00
Attacker 3	1.07	0.00	0.00
Attacker 4	0.27	0.00	0.94
Attacker 5	1.10	2.19	3.96
Attacker 6	0.57	0.00	0.53

Table 4: Table of best scores for each attacker for each gesture. The results show that none of the attacks were successful: the passing score for the recognizer can be set so that the Target can authenticate with ease and the attackers are not authenticated.

From the Table 4 we see that there is not any overlapping for scores of target and attackers. This indicates our recognizer correctly differentiates attempts made by the target and that by attackers. In general, the target is always authenticating quite well across the the three gestures in comparison to the poorer scores of the attackers. The only opportunity where an attacker became close enough to steal the gesture (Attacker 2, Gesture 2) still has a one point cushion around it – high enough to prevent authentication by an attacker if the threshold is set appropriately.

7. DISCUSSION AND CONCLUSIONS

We have presented the first study of using free-form multitouch gestures for mobile authentication. Towards the end of analyzing the security and memorability of the gestures, we presented a novel metric based on computing the estimated mutual information of repeated gestures. We designed and implemented a practical multitouch recognizer as an authentication system, and studied the robustness of free-form gestures against shoulder surfing attacks.

Overall, the results are favorable to user-generated free-form gestures as a means of authentication on touchscreen devices.

Security, as estimated by $\hat{I}$, is high enough for most passwords the users generated. We learned that *multi*finger gestures do not show high security in this measure. It should be noted though, most of multifinger gestures in our dataset are gestures of multiple fingers repeating the same simple shape, for example, drawing a circle with three fingers. We believe that the participants may overestimate the increase in security by merely increasing number of fingers. When they decided to use multiple fingers, they tended to choose a simple shape because they might have believed multiple fingers gave them high security despite simple shape. Such inconsistency in participants' perception and the actual security could be advised against in the password generation user interface.

We also learned that, unlike with the length of a text-based password [39], the duration of a gesture does not play an important role in $\hat{I}$. Intuitively speaking, complex gestures with high $\hat{I}$ should take longer time to perform. However, we learned that even brief gestures can have high security. Gestures with duration less than two seconds have an average $\hat{I}$ less than 2% lower than the average $\hat{I}$ for all gestures.

By looking at our dataset, we found out that some simple shapes, even circles, would actually take more time to complete than complex ones like signatures. The possible reasons warrant further studies. At this point, we suspect that complex gestures are also more difficult to reproduce precisely. A good secure gesture should have both: inherent complexity and easiness to perform. It is interesting in this light that signatures are particularly good and resulted in very high $\hat{I}$. This means, although very complex to perform, participants still managed to repeat them quite well.

When it comes to memorability, the data shows that users need a few repetitions to achieve a stable password. Like with text-based passwords, the generation of passwords is experienced as more demanding by users than recall. After generation, $\hat{I}$ drops after an interval of more than 10 days by about 16%. However, they are still recognizable as unique passwords. In addition, for a participant, the value of $\hat{I}$ varies as they repeat the gesture. By continuously repeating, $\hat{I}$ tends to stabilize. Unlike the text-based passwords, which one has to input exactly, free-form gestures involve many sources of variance, which would be very difficult to keep constant across different attempts. Therefore, one alternative way of reporting security of gestures could be a range similar to confidence interval, instead of an exact value. Moreover, studying gesture variability is a good topic for future research, because a good balance must be found between memorability and security. Of course, it is important to note that the memorability could be in our favor as compared to truly random gestures. We asked the participants to generate gestures that would be repeated after at least ten days. As such, there is an incentive on the participants to create something they will be able to recall after some time.

Several participants were able to create highly secure and memorable gestures. Below, we sketch strategies for generating such gestures. We plan to develop and test the guidelines and their effect on creating gestures in further studies. These guidelines are illustrated with the best and worst gestures in Figure 5, especially with the worst gestures being simple multifinger circular motions.

1. General advice to promote consistency and retention: Practice different gestures first in order to get used to the touchscreen. Try out different gestures instead of picking the first one, to find one you prefer. Pick a gesture that will be used frequently to avoid forgetting it. Take more care and pay attention. Do not rush. Practice until faster and still accurate. Try to repeat each trace as closely as possible.

2. Characteristics of High $\hat{I}$ gestures to emulate: Use many sharp turns. Use a familiar gesture, for example, a signature. Use extra fingers to do different motions. Follow the above rules even when adding fingers.

3. Characteristics of Low $\hat{I}$ gestures to avoid: Do not use only few turns. Do not use gentle turns. Do not make turns only to go in the the same direction. For example: avoid doing a circle.

4. Specific errors to avoid: Place fingers down in the same order each time. Use the same number of fingers each time.

Our results from the recognizer show the capability of free-form multitouch gestures to work as passwords in a practical authentication system. The gestures were classified by the recognizer with relatively low error when being compared across all 63 participants, indicating the ability of the participants to generate passwords that a recognizer would not have trouble classifying when comparing against multiple templates. The recognizer generated much higher scores when evaluating a participant's gesture against their template (ranging from three to nine) as compared to when it compared to other templates (ranging from zero to one). Memorability of the free-form gestures are also displayed through the EER values in recognizer results: the lowest EER value for the first set is 3.34% and the lowest for the second set is 13.16%. The disparity in the data sets can be attributed to two factors: 1) the first data set had only two authentication trials compared to the second set's five trials and 2) the second data set was performed after a much longer time span than in the first set, thus, there were memorability effects between the two sessions. The multitouch recognizer we designed and implemented has room for consideration in the future, for example, the effects of rotation, scale, and position invariance as added degrees of freedom with free-form multitouch gestures.

There can be some cause for remark here about whether or not there is a trade-off between memorability and security of a gesture. Heightened EER values between the first and second recall sessions can give rise to the notion that some participants might have trouble remembering certain gestures, in spite of the $\hat{I}$ for those gestures. However, we note that the errors in recognition extend to the number of fingers – the general shape of the free-form gesture is always almost correctly reproduced. So we contend that the trade-off is in the multitouch aspect and not in the free-form aspect. It appears that remembering the number of fingers is difficult for some participants and we contend this is likely due to a lack of adoption of multitouch as an industry standard. Most people are used to using a single finger for interaction with touchscreens and that might have confused participants in the second session after more than ten days.

With our preliminary shoulder surfing attack trial, we also learned that free-form gestures are relatively robust against shoulder surfing. None of the attackers were able to repeat the gestures well enough to be accepted by a practical authentication system. We acknowledge that further more comprehensive studies with several different kinds of gestures and more opportunities for the attackers would be warranted. For example, we could separate attackers into different groups in which half of them are allowed to rewatch the video recordings as many times they want to.

Thinking towards the future, we wondered what would happen if gestural passwords like these become ubiquitous. How would people begin managing multiple passwords across different platforms? Would there be trouble in remembering the correct password for different applications? If that is the case – what is the best way to manage multiple gestural passwords such that someone can recall them? The obvious text-based analogue is a password manager. Although it is outside the scope of this paper, we can consider the concept of a gestural password manager to be important future work.

Going further, we can think about the effect of screen size on gestural password generation. It can be reasonably assumed that both a person's finger size and the screen size will both change what gestures are used for passwords. All of the participants in this study worked off of a Nexus tablet with a fairly large capture area. Future work could focus on seeing what passwords are generated for varying screen sizes or even to see if the gestures in the sets presented in this paper are comfortable to perform on smaller screens.

To conclude, our work shows that free-form gestures present a robust method of authentication for touchscreen devices.

Acknowledgments

This material is based upon work supported by the National Science Foundation under Grant Number 1228777. Any opinions, findings, and conclusions or recommendations expressed in this material are those of the author(s) and do not necessarily reflect the views of the National Science Foundation.

8. REFERENCES

[1] A. J. Aviv, K. Gibson, E. Mossop, M. Blaze, and J. M. Smith. Smudge attacks on smartphone touch screens. In *Proc. of WOOT'10*.

[2] R. Biddle, S. Chiasson, and P. Van Oorschot. Graphical passwords: Learning from the first twelve years. *ACM Comput. Surv.*, Sept. 2012.

[3] C. Bo, L. Zhang, X.-Y. Li, Q. Huang, and Y. Wang. Silentsense: Silent user identification via touch and movement behavioral biometrics. In *Proc. of MobiCom '13*.

[4] J. Bonneau. The science of guessing: Analyzing an anonymized corpus of 70 million passwords. In *Proc. of IEEE SS&P'12*.

[5] J. Bonneau, C. Herley, P. van Oorschot, and F. Stajano. The quest to replace passwords: A framework for comparative evaluation of web authentication schemes. In *Proc. of IEEE SS&P'12*, May 2012.

[6] S. Boztas. Entropies, guessing and cryptography. Technical report, RMIT University Research Report Series, 1999.

[7] W. E. Burr, D. F. Dodson, E. M. Newton, R. A. Perlner, W. T. Polk, S. Gupta, and E. A. Nabbus. NIST SP 800-63-1. Electronic Authentication Guideline, 2011.

[8] Z. Cai, C. Shen, M. Wang, Y. Song, and J. Wang. Mobile authentication through touch-behavior features. In *Proc. of Biometric Recognition*, 2013.

[9] S. Chiasson, A. Forget, E. Stobert, P. C. van Oorschot, and R. Biddle. Multiple password interference in text passwords and click-based graphical passwords. In *Proc. of CCS'09*.

[10] T. M. Cover and J. A. Thomas. *Elements of Information Theory*. Wiley-Interscience, 2006.

[11] A. De Luca, E. von Zezschwitz, N. D. H. Nguyen, M.-E. Maurer, E. Rubegni, M. P. Scipioni, and M. Langheinrich. Back-of-device authentication on smartphones. In *Proc. of CHI '13*.

[12] K. M. Everitt, T. Bragin, J. Fogarty, and T. Kohno. A comprehensive study of frequency, interference, and training of multiple graphical passwords. In *Proc. of CHI'09*.

[13] J. Fierrez, J. Ortega-Garcia, D. Ramos, and J. Gonzalez-Rodriguez. HMM-based on-line signature verification: Feature extraction and signature modeling. *Pattern Recogn. Lett.*, Dec. 2007.

[14] D. Florencio and C. Herley. A large-scale study of web password habits. In *Proc. of WWW'07*.

[15] M. Frank, R. Biedert, E. Ma, I. Martinovic, and D. Song. Touchalytics: On the applicability of touchscreen input as a behavioral biometric for continuous authentication. *IEEE Trans. on Information Forensics and Security*, Jan 2013.

[16] Gogogate. www.gogogate.com. Ref. Dec 3, 2013.

[17] S. A. Grandhi, G. Joue, and I. Mittelberg. Understanding naturalness and intuitiveness in gesture production: insights for touchless gestural interfaces. In *Proc. of CHI '11*.

[18] S. G. Hart and L. E. Staveland. *Development of NASA-TLX (Task Load Index): Results of empirical and theoretical research*. 1988. P. Hancock & N. Meshkati (Eds.), Human mental workload.

[19] I. Jermyn, A. Mayer, F. Monrose, M. K. Reiter, and A. D. Rubin. The design and analysis of graphical passwords. In *Proc. of USENIX Security'99*.

[20] L. A. Jones and S. J. Lederman. *Human hand function*. Oxford University Press, 2006.

[21] Y. Li. Protractor: a fast and accurate gesture recognizer. In *Proc. of CHI '10*.

[22] A. C. Long, J. A. Landay, and L. A. Rowe. "Those look similar!" issues in automating gesture design advice. In *Proc. of PUI'01*.

[23] Microsoft. Windows azure multi-factor authentication. www.windowsazure.com/en-us/documentation/services/multi-factor-authentication. Ref. Dec 3, 2013.

[24] D. Muramatsu and T. Matsumoto. An HMM on-line signature verifier incorporating signature trajectories. In *Proc. of ICDAR '03*.

[25] U. Oh and L. Findlater. The challenges and potential of end-user gesture customization. In *Proc. of CHI '13*.

[26] P. C. v. Oorschot and J. Thorpe. On predictive models and user-drawn graphical passwords. *ACM Trans. Inf. Syst. Secur.*, jan 2008.

[27] A. Oulasvirta, T. Roos, A. Modig, and L. Leppanen. Information capacity of full-body movements. In *Proc. of CHI'13*.

[28] Q. Pu, S. Gupta, S. Gollakota, and S. Patel. Whole-home gesture recognition using wireless signals. In *Proc. of MobiCom '13*.

[29] D. Rubine. Specifying gestures by example. In *Proc. of SIGGRAPH '91*.

[30] J. Ruiz, Y. Li, and E. Lank. User-defined motion gestures for mobile interaction. In *Proc. of CHI '11*.

[31] N. Sae-Bae, K. Ahmed, K. Isbister, and N. Memon. Biometric-rich gestures: a novel approach to authentication on multi-touch devices. In *Proc. of CHI '12*.

[32] D. Savransky. Lomb (lomb-scargle) periodogram, 2008. http://www.mathworks.com/matlabcentral/fileexchange/20004-lomb-lomb-scargle-periodogram. Ref Dec 9, 2013.

[33] F. Schaub, M. Walch, B. Könings, and M. Weber. Exploring the design space of graphical passwords on smartphones. In *Proc. of SOUPS '13*.

[34] A. Serwadda and V. V. Phoha. When kids' toys breach mobile phone security. In *Proc. of CCS '13*.

[35] M. Shahzad, A. X. Liu, and A. Samuel. Secure unlocking of mobile touch screen devices by simple gestures: You can see it but you can not do it. In *Proc. of MobiCom '13*.

[36] Square. www.squareup.com. Ref. Dec 3, 2013.

[37] J. Thorpe and P. C. van Oorschot. Human-seeded attacks and exploiting hot-spots in graphical passwords. In *Proc. of USENIX Security'07*.

[38] J. Tian, C. Qu, W. Xu, and S. Wang. Kinwrite: Handwriting-based authentication using kinect. In *Proc. of NDSS '13*.

[39] B. Ur, P. Kelley, S. Komanduri, J. Lee, M. Maass, M. Mazurek, T. Passaro, R. Shay, T. Vidas, L. Bauer, N. Christin, L. Cranor, S. Egelman, and J. Lopez. Helping users create better passwords. *;login*, Dec. 2012.

[40] S. Wiedenbeck, J. Waters, J.-C. Birget, A. Brodskiy, and N. Memon. Passpoints: design and longitudinal evaluation of a graphical password system. *Int. J. Hum.-Comput. Stud.*, 63(1-2):102–127, July 2005.

[41] J. O. Wobbrock, A. D. Wilson, and Y. Li. Gestures without libraries, toolkits or training: a $1 recognizer for user interface prototypes. In *Proc. of UIST '07*.

[42] J. Yan, A. Blackwell, R. Anderson, and A. Grant. Password memorability and security: Empirical results. *IEEE Security and Privacy*, Sept. 2004.

[43] N. H. Zakaria, D. Griffiths, S. Brostoff, and J. Yan. Shoulder surfing defence for recall-based graphical passwords. In *Proc. of SOUPS'11*.

[44] Z. Zhao and G.-J. Ahn. On the security of picture gesture authentication. In *Proc. of USENIX Security'13*.

[45] N. Zheng, K. Bai, H. Huang, and H. Wang. You are how you touch: User verication on smartphones via tapping behaviors. Technical report, Dec. 2006.

[46] F. Zhou and F. De la Torre. Canonical time warping for alignment of human behavior. In *Proc. of NIPS'09*.

APPENDIX

A. EXAMPLES OF USER-GENERATED GESTURES

The following presents a selection of gesture passwords recorded during this study.

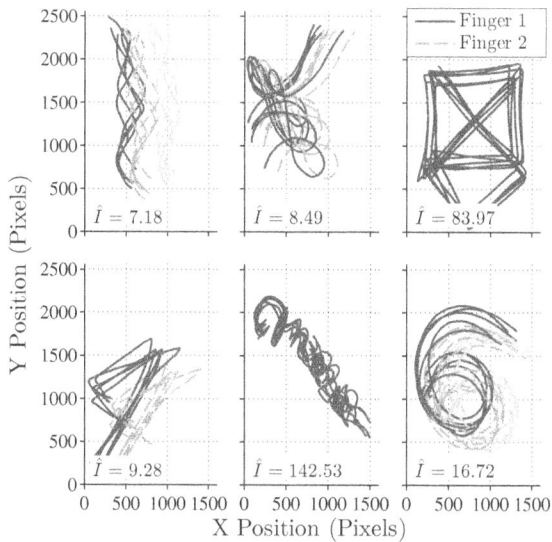

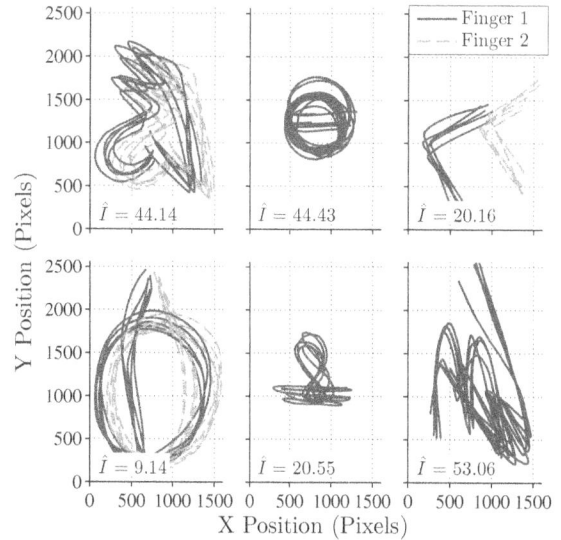

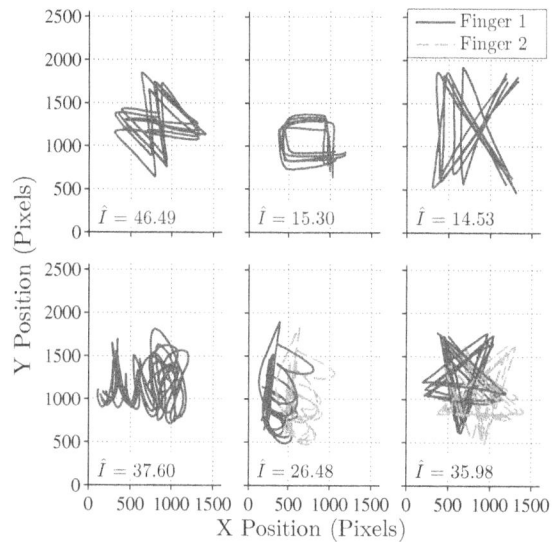

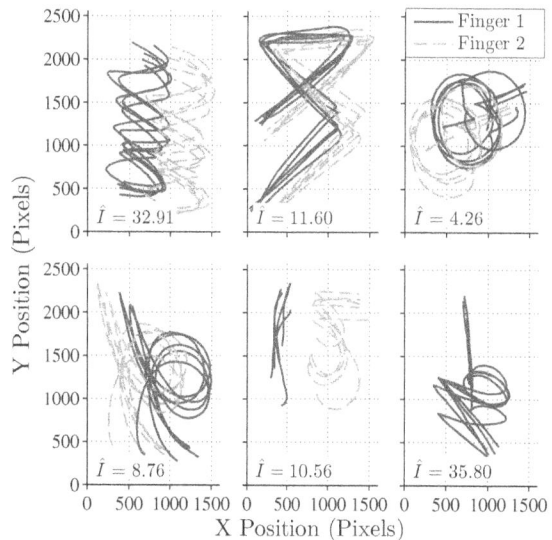

Automatic and Scalable Fault Detection for Mobile Applications

Lenin Ravindranath
lenin@csail.mit.edu
M.I.T. & Microsoft
Research
Cambridge, MA, USA

Suman Nath
sumann@microsoft.com
Microsoft Research
Redmond, WA, USA

Jitendra Padhye
padhye@microsoft.com
Microsoft Research
Redmond, WA, USA

Hari Balakrishnan
hari@csail.mit.edu
M.I.T.
Cambridge, MA, USA

ABSTRACT

This paper describes the design, implementation, and evaluation of VanarSena, an automated fault finder for mobile applications ("apps"). The techniques in VanarSena are driven by a study of 25 million real-world crash reports of Windows Phone apps reported in 2012. Our analysis indicates that a modest number of root causes are responsible for many observed failures, but that they occur in a wide range of places in an app, requiring a wide coverage of possible execution paths. VanarSena adopts a "greybox" testing method, instrumenting the app binary to achieve both coverage and speed. VanarSena runs on cloud servers: the developer uploads the app binary; VanarSena then runs several app "monkeys" in parallel to emulate user, network, and sensor data behavior, returning a detailed report of crashes and failures. We have tested VanarSena with 3000 apps from the Windows Phone store, finding that 1108 of them had failures; VanarSena uncovered 2969 distinct bugs in existing apps, including 1227 that were not previously reported. Because we anticipate VanarSena being used in regular regression tests, testing speed is important. VanarSena uses two techniques to improve speed. First, it uses a "hit testing" method to quickly emulate an app by identifying which user interface controls map to the same execution handlers in the code. Second, it generates a `ProcessingCompleted` event to accurately determine when to start the next interaction. These features are key benefits of VanarSena's greybox philosophy.

1. INTRODUCTION

No one doubts the importance of tools to improve software reliability. For mobile apps, improving reliability is less about making sure that "mission critical" software is bug-free, but more about survival in a brutally competitive marketplace. Because the success of an app hinges on good user reviews, even a handful of poor reviews can doom an app to obscurity. A scan of reviews on mobile app stores shows that an app that crashes is likely to garner poor reviews.

Mobile app testing poses different challenges than traditional "enterprise" software. Mobile apps are typically used in more uncontrolled conditions, in a variety of different locations, over different wireless networks, with a wide range of input data from user interactions and sensors, and on a variety of hardware platforms. Coping with these issues is particularly acute for individual developers or small teams.

There are various approaches for mobile app testing. Static analysis of app binaries [34, 17], although scalable, can fail to uncover app faults due to the runtime issues such as poor network condition and corrupted or unexpected responses from cloud services. Symbolic execution [10] and its hybrid variant, concolic execution, require constructing symbolic model for program execution environment. Although such a model is shown feasible for simple android libraries [37] and UI events [7, 19] of simple apps, applicability of the techniques have been limited for two key reasons. First, it is not easy to model real-world execution environment for mobile apps, consisting of sensors, networks, and cloud services. Second, they do not scale well to real-world apps due to notorious path explosion problem. Recent efforts, therefore, focus on dynamic analysis, where runtime behavior of an app is examined by executing it [41, 16, 8, 31, 35, 32]. We take a similar approach.

Our goal is to develop an easy to use, and scalable system that thoroughly tests mobile apps for common faults. The developer should be able to submit an app binary to the system, and then within a short amount of time obtain a report. This report should provide a correct stack trace and a trace of interactions or inputs for each failure. We anticipate the system being used by developers interactively while debugging, as well as a part of regular nightly and weekly regression tests, so speed is important. An ideal way to deploy the system is as a service in the cloud, so the ability to balance resource consumption and discovering faults is also important.

We describe VanarSena, a system that meets these goals. The starting point in the design is to identify what types of faults have the highest "bang for the buck" in terms of causing real-world failures. To this end, we studied 25 million crash reports from more than 100,000 Windows Phone apps reported in 2012. Three key findings inform our design: first, over 90% of the crashes were attributable to only 10% of all the root causes we observed. Second, although the "90-10" rule holds, the root causes affect a wide variety of execution paths in an app. Third, a significant fraction of these crashes can be mapped to externally induced events, such as unhandled HTTP error codes (see §2).

The first finding indicates that focusing on a small number of root causes will improve reliability significantly. The second suggests that the fault finder needs to cover as many execution paths as possible. The third indicates that software emulation of user inputs, network behavior, and sensor data is likely to be effective, even without deploying on phone hardware.

Using these insights, we have developed VanarSena,[1] a system that finds faults in mobile applications. The developer uploads the app binary to the service, along with any supporting information such as a login and password. VanarSena instruments the app, and launches several *monkeys* to run the instrumented version on phone emulators. As the app is running, VanarSena emulates a variety of user, network and sensor behaviors to uncover and report observed failures.

A noteworthy principle in VanarSena is its "greybox" approach, which instruments the app binary before emulating its execution. Greybox testing combines the benefits of "whitebox" testing, which requires detailed knowledge of an app's semantics to model interactions and inputs, but isn't generalizable, and "blackbox" testing, which is general but not as efficient in covering execution paths.

The use of binary instrumentation enables a form of execution-path exploration we call *hit testing* (§6.1), which identifies how each user interaction maps to an event handler. Hit testing allows VanarSena to cover many more execution paths in a given amount of time. Moreover, app instrumentation makes VanarSena extensible, by inserting our own event handlers that trigger under certain situations, such as network calls and certain user actions. VanarSena can then trap these event handlers to induce specific faults such as emulating slow or faulty networks. We have written several such fault inducers, and more can be easily written. Binary instrumentation also allows VanarSena to determine when to emulate the next user interaction in the app. This task is tricky because emulating a typical user requires knowing when the previous page has been processed and rendered, a task made easier with our instrumentation approach. We call this generation of `ProcessingCompleted` event (§6.2), which leverages our earlier work on AppInsight [37].

We have implemented VanarSena for Windows Phone apps, running it as an experimental service. We evaluated VanarSena empirically by testing 3,000 apps from the Windows Phone store for commonly-occurring faults. VanarSena discovered failures in 1,108 of these apps, which have presumably undergone some testing and real-world use[2]. Overall, VanarSena detected 2,969 crashes, including 1,227 that were not previously reported. The testing took 4500 machine hours on 12 desktop-class machines, at average of 1.5 hours per app. At current Azure prices, the cost of testing is roughly 25 cents per app. These favorable cost and time estimates result from VanarSena's use of *hit testing* and `ProcessingCompleted` event.

While many prior systems [41, 16, 8, 31, 35] have analyzed mobile apps in various ways by exercising them with automated "monkeys" and by inducing various faults, this paper makes three new research contributions, that have general applicability.

Our first contribution is the study of 25 million crash reports from windows phone apps (§2). We believe that this is the first study of its kind. The insights from this study anchor the design of VanarSena. Other mobile app testing systems such as Dynodroid [35] can also benefit from these insights. For example, Dynodroid currently does not inject faults due to external factors such as bad networks or event timing related to unexpected or abnormal user behavior. Our study shows that these are among the most common root causes of real-world crashes.

Our second contribution is the technique of *hit testing* (§6.1). This technique allows VanarSena to speed up testing significantly. Our third contribution is the idea of generation and use of `ProcessingCompleted` event (§6.2). We show that this is nec-

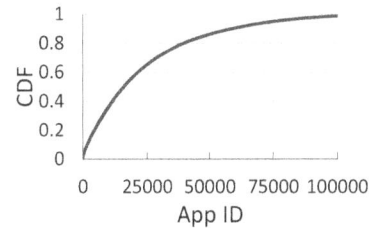

Figure 1: CDF of crash reports per app.

```
0: TransitTracker.BusPredictionManager.ReadCompleted
1: System.Net.WebClient.OnOpenReadCompleted
2: System.Net.WebClient.OpenReadOperationCompleted
...
```

Figure 2: Stack trace fragment for Chicago Transit Tracker crash. The exception was WebException.

essary to both speed up the testing, and to correctly simulate both *patient* and *impatient* users. We are not aware of any other app testing framework that incorporates comparable techniques. Both these techniques leverage our earlier work on AppInsight.

While the implementation details of hit testing and generation of processing completed event are specific to VanarSena, the core ideas behind both of them are quite general, and can be used by other testing frameworks as well.

2. APP CRASHES IN-THE-WILD

To understand why apps crash in the wild, we analyze a large data set of crash reports. We describe our data set, our method for determining the causes of crashes, and the results of the analysis.

2.1 Data Set

Our data set was collected by Windows Phone Error Reporting (WPER) system, a repository of error reports from all deployed Windows Phone apps. When an app crashes due to an unhandled exception, the phone sends a crash report to WPER with a small sampling probability[3]. The crash report includes the app ID, the exception type, the stack trace, and device state information such as the amount of free memory, radio signal strength, etc.

We study over 25 million crash reports from more than 100,000 apps collected in 2012. Figure 1 shows the number of crash reports per app. Observe that the data set is not skewed by crashes from handful of bad apps. A similar analysis shows that the data is not skewed by a small number of device types, ISPs, or countries of origin.

2.2 Root Causes of Observed Crashes

To determine the root cause of a crash, we start with the stack trace and the exception type. An exception type gives a general idea about what went wrong, while the stack trace indicates where things went wrong. An example stack fragment is shown in Figure 2. Here, a WebException was thrown, indicating that something went wrong with a web transfer, causing the `OnOpenReadCompleted` function of the `WebClient` class to throw an exception. The exception surfaced in the `ReadCompleted` event handler of the app, which did not handle it, causing the app to crash.

We partition crash reports that we believe originate due to the same root cause into a collection called a *crash bucket*: each crash bucket has a specific exception type and system function name where the exception was thrown. For example, the crash shown in Figure 2 will be placed in the bucket labeled `WebException`, `System.Net.WebClient.OnOpenReadCompleted`.

---

[1]VanarSena in Hindi means an "army of monkeys".

[2]Thus, VanarSena would be even more effective during earlier stages of development

[3]The developer has no control over the probability.

Given a bucket, we use two techniques to determine the likely root cause of its crashes. First, we use data mining techniques [5] to discover possible patterns of unusual device states (such as low memory or poor signal strength) that hold for all crashes in the bucket. For example, we found that all buckets with label (OutOfMemoryException, *) have the pattern `AvailableMemory = 0`.

Second, given a bucket, we manually search various Windows Phone developer forums such as `social.msdn.microsoft.com` and `stackoverflow.com` for issues related to the exception and the stack traces in the bucket. We limit such analysis to only the 100 largest buckets, as it is not practical to investigate all buckets and developer forums do not contain enough information about less frequent crashes. We learned enough to determine the root causes of 40 of the top 100 buckets. We also manually verified the root causes we determined. The whole process took us around one week.

2.3 Findings

A small number of large buckets cover most of the crashes. Figure 3 shows the cumulative distribution of various bucket sizes. The top 10% buckets cover more than 90% crashes (note the log-scale on the x-axis). This suggests that we can analyze a small number of top buckets and still cover a large fraction of crashes. Table 1 shows several large buckets of crashes.

A significant fraction of crashes can be mapped to well-defined externally-inducible root causes. We use the following taxonomy to classify various root causes. A root cause is *deterministically inducible* if it can be reproduced by deterministically modifying the external factors on which the app depends. For example, crashes of a networked app caused by improperly handling an HTTP Error 404 (Not Found) can be induced by an HTTP proxy that returns Error 404 on a Get request. Some crashes such as those due to memory faults or unstable OS states are not deterministically inducible. We further classify inducible causes into two categories: device and input. Device-related causes can be induced by systematically manipulating device states such as available memory, available storage, network signal, etc. Input-related causes can be induced by manipulating various external inputs to apps such as user inputs, data from network, sensor inputs, etc.

Table 1 shows several top crash buckets, along with their externally-inducible root causes and their categories. For example, the root causes behind the bucket with label (WebException, WebClient.OnDownloadStringCompleted) are various HTTP Get errors such as 401 (Unauthorized), 404 (Not Found), and 405 (Method Not Allowed), and can be induced with a web proxy intercepting all network communication to and from the app.

We were able to determine externally-inducible root causes of 40 of the top 100 buckets; for the remaining buckets, we either could not determine their root causes from information in developer forums or identify any obvious way to induce the root causes. Together, these buckets represent around 48% of crashes in the top 100 buckets (and 35% of all crashes); the number of unique root causes for these buckets is 8.

These results imply that a significant number of crashes can be induced with a relatively small number of root causes.

Although a small number, the dominant root causes affect many different execution paths in an app. For example, the same root cause of HTTP Error 404 can affect an app at many distinct execution points where the app downloads data from a server. To illustrate how often it happens, we consider all crashes from one particular app in Figure 4 and count the number of distinct stack traces in various crash buckets of the app. The higher the number

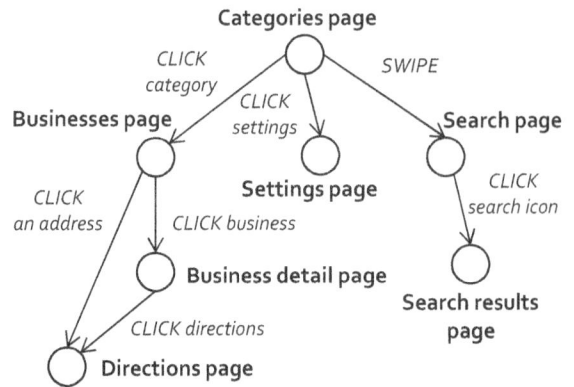

Figure 7: App structure for the example in Figure 6.

of distinct stack traces in a bucket, the more the distinct execution points where the app crashed due to the same root causes responsible for the bucket. As shown in Figure 4, for 25 buckets, the number of distinct stack traces is more than 5. The trend holds in general, as shown in Figure 5, which plots the distribution of distinct stack traces in all (app, bucket) partitions. We find that it is common for the same root cause to affect many tens of execution paths of an app.

3. GOALS AND NON-GOALS

Our goal is to build a scalable, easy to use system that tests mobile apps for common, externally-inducible faults as thoroughly as possible. We want to return the results of testing to the developer as quickly as possible, and for the system to be deployable as a cloud service in a scalable way.

VanarSena does not detect *all* app failures. For example, VanarSena cannot detect crashes that result from hardware idiosyncrasies, or failures caused by specific inputs, or even failures caused by the confluence of multiple simultaneous faults that we do test for. VanarSena also cannot find crashes that result from erroneous state maintenance; for example, an app may crash only after it has been run hundreds of times because some log file has grown too large. VanarSena cannot adequately test apps and games that require complex free-form gestures or specific order of inputs.

Before we describe the architecture of VanarSena, we need to discuss how we measure *thoroughness*, or coverage. Coverage of testing tools is traditionally measured by counting the fraction of basic blocks [9] of code they cover. However, this metric is not appropriate for our purpose. Mobile apps often include third party libraries of UI controls (e.g., fancy UI buttons). Most of the code in these libraries is inaccessible at run time, because the app typically uses only one or two of these controls. Thus, coverage, as measured by basic blocks covered would look unnecessarily poor.

Instead, we focus on the user-centric nature of mobile apps. A mobile app is typically built as a collection of pages. An example app called *AroundMe* is shown in Figure 6. The user navigates between pages by interacting with controls on the page. For example, each category listing on page 1 is a control. By clicking on any of the business categories on page 1, the user would navigate to page 2. Page 1 also has a swipe control. By swiping on the page, the user ends up on the search page (page 4). From a given page, the user can navigate to the parent page by pressing the back button. The navigation graph of the app is shown in Figure 7. The nodes of the graph represent pages, while the edges represent unique *user transactions* [42] that cause the user to move between pages. Thus, we measure coverage in terms of unique pages visited [8], and unique

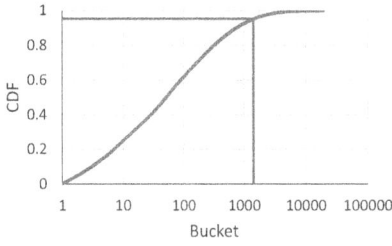

Figure 3: Cumulative distribution of bucket sizes

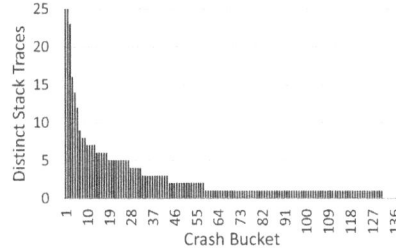

Figure 4: Distinct stack traces in various buckets for one particular app

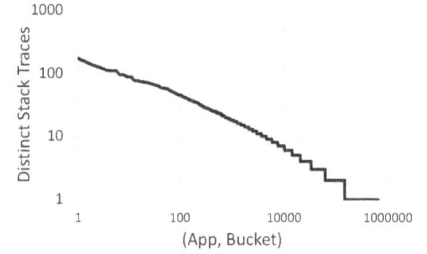

Figure 5: Distinct stack traces in various buckets for all apps

Rank (Fraction)	Bucket		Root Cause	Category	HowToInduce
	Exception	Crash Function			
1 (7.51%)	OutOfMemory Exception	*	WritablePages = 0	Device/Memory	Memory pressure
2 (6.09%)	InvalidOperation Exception	ShellPageManager.CheckHResult	User clicks buttons or links in quick succession, and thus tries to navigate to a new page when navigation is already in progress	Input/User	Impatient user
3 (5.24%)	InvalidOperation Exception	NavigationService.Navigate			
8 (2.66%)	InvalidOperation Exception	NavigationService.GoForwardBackCore			
12 (1.16%)	WebException	Browser.AsyncHelper.BeginOnUI	Unable to connect to remote server	Input/Network	Proxy
15 (0.83%)	WebException	WebClient.OnDownloadStringCompleted	HTTP errors 401, 404, 405		
5 (2.30%)	XmlException	*	XML Parsing Error	Input/Data	Proxy
11 (1.14%)	NotSupportedException	XmlTextReaderImpl.ParseDoctypeDecl			
37 (0.42%)	FormatException	Double.Parse	Input Parsing Error	Input/User, Input/Data	Invalid text entry, Proxy
50 (0.35%)	FormatException	Int32.Parse			

Table 1: Examples of crash buckets and corresponding root causes, categories, and ways to induce the crashes

user transactions mimicked by the tool. In §8.2, we will show that we cover typical apps as thoroughly as a human user.

4. ARCHITECTURE

Figure 8 shows the architecture of VanarSena. VanarSena instruments the submitted app binary. The *Monkey manager* then spawns a number of *monkeys* to test the app. A *monkey* is a UI automation tool built around the Windows Phone Emulator. The monkey can automatically launch the app in the emulator and interact with the UI like a user. When the app is *monkeyed*, we systematically feed different inputs and emulate various faults. If the app crashes, the monkey generates a detailed crash report for the developer. Figure 9 shows the key components of the monkey.

Emulator: We use an off-the-shelf Windows Phone emulator in our implementation. We intentionally do not modify the emulator in any way. The key benefit of using an emulator instead of device hardware is scalability: VanarSena can easily spin up multiple concurrent instances in a cloud infrastructure to accelerate fault-finding.

Instrumentation: The instrumenter runs over the app binary; it adds five modules to the app as shown in Figure 9. At run-time, these modules generate information needed for UI Automator and the Fault Inducer (§5).

UI Automator: The UI Automator (UIA) launches and navigates the instrumented app in the emulator. It emulates user interactions such as clicking buttons, filling textboxes, and swiping. It incorporates techniques to ensure both coverage and speed (§6).

Fault Inducer: During emulated execution, the Fault Inducer (FI) systematically induces different faults at appropriate points during execution (§7).

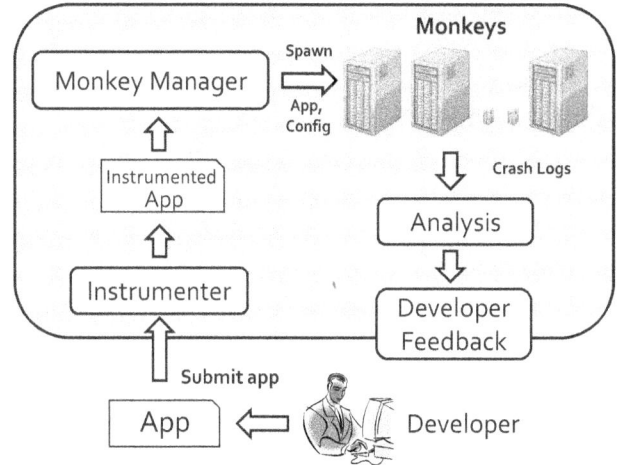

Figure 8: VanarSena Architecture.

5. INSTRUMENTATION

We use the binary instrumentation framework that we developed in AppInsight [42] to rewrite an app binary. The instrumentation is designed for apps written using the Silverlight framework [40]. Silverlight is used by a vast majority of apps in the Windows Phone app store. In Silverlight, the app is written in C# and XAML [46] and compiled to MSIL byte code [33]. We instrument the app at the byte code level.

In VanarSena, the instrumentation injects five modules into the app that provides the information needed for the UI Automator and the Fault Inducer, as shown in Figure 9. The modules communicate with the UI Automator and the Fault Inducer via local sockets.

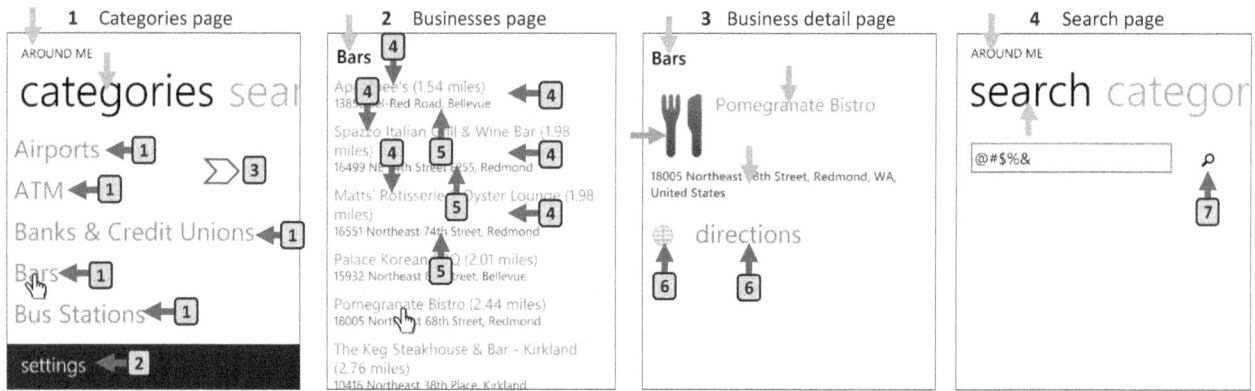

Figure 6: Example app pages. UI elements pointed by red arrows can be interacted with. Arrows and numbers will be explained in Section 6.1.

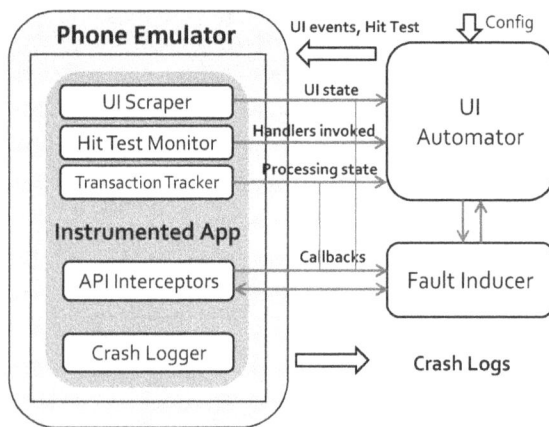

Figure 9: Monkey design.

UI Scraper: In Silverlight, an app page is represented as a DOM tree of UI elements. The UI Scraper, when invoked, serializes the current UI page and sends it to the UIA. For each UI element, it sends the element's type, location and whether it is visible on the current screen. The UI Automator can invoke the UI Scraper on demand to inspect the current UI.

Hit Test Monitor: We instrument every event handler in the app with a Hit Test Monitor. The Hit Test Monitor helps the UIA to decide which controls to interact with. We describe hit testing in detail in §6.1.

Transaction Tracker: The transaction tracker provides the `ProcessingCompleted` event used by the UIA to decide when to interact next. We describe transaction tracking in detail in §6.2.

API Interceptors: The instrumenter rewrites the app to intercept certain API calls to proxy through the Fault Inducer. We describe API interceptors and Fault Inducer in detail in §7.

Crash Logger: To identify that an app has crashed, we rewrite the app to subscribe for the unhandled exception handler [18]. The unhandled exception handler is invoked just before the app crashes with an exception that is not handled by the developer. When the handler is invoked, we log the exception and the stack trace associated with it.

6. UI AUTOMATOR

As the UIA navigates through the app, it needs to make two key decisions: what UI control to interact with next, and how long to

wait before picking the next control. In addition, because of the design of each monkey instance, VanarSena adopts a "many randomized concurrent monkeys" approach, which we discuss below.

To pick the next control to interact with, the UIA asks the *UI Scraper* module (Figure 9) for a list of visible controls on the current page (controls may be overlaid atop each other).

In one design, the UIA can systematically explore the app by picking a control that it has not interacted with so far, and emulating pressing the back button to go back to the previous page if all controls on a page have been interacted with. If the app crashes, VanarSena generates a crash report, and the monkey terminates.

Such a simple but systematic exploration has three problems that make it unattractive. First, multiple controls often lead to the same next page. For example, clicking on any of the business categories on page 1 in Figure 6 leads to the Business page (page 2), a situation represented by the single edge between the pages in Figure 7. We can accelerate testing in this case by invoking only one of these "equivalent" controls, although it is possible that some of these may lead to failures and not others (a situation mitigated by using multiple independent monkeys).

Second, some controls do not have any event handlers attached to them. For example, the title of the page may be a text-box control that has no event handlers attached to it. UIA should not waste time interacting with such controls, because it will run no app code.

Last but not least, a systematic exploration can lead to dead ends. Imagine an app with two buttons on a page. Suppose that the app always crashes when the first button is pressed. If we use systematic exploration, the app would crash after the first button is pressed. To explore the rest of the app, the monkey manager would have to restart the app, and ensure that the UIA does not click the first button again. Maintaining such state across app invocations is complicated and makes the system more complex for many reasons, prominent among which is the reality that the app may not even display the same set of controls on every run.

We address the first two issues using a novel technique we call *hit testing* (§6.1), and the third by running multiple independent random monkeys concurrently (§6.3).

6.1 Hit Testing

Hit testing works as follows. The instrumentation framework instruments all UI event handlers in an app with a *hit test monitor*. It also assigns each event handler a unique ID. Figure 10 shows an example. When hit testing is enabled, interacting with a control will invoke the associated event handler, but the handler will sim-

```
void btnFetch_Click(object sender, EventArgs e) {
  if (HitTestFlag == true) {
    HitTest.MethodInvoked(12, sender, e);
    return;
  }

  // Original Code
}
```

Figure 10: Event Handlers are instrumented to enable Hit Testing. Handler's unique id is 12.

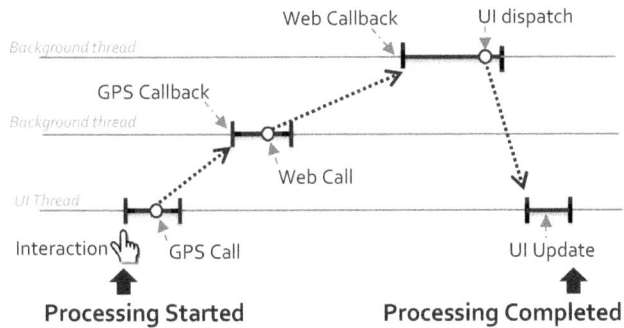

Figure 11: Generating `ProcessingCompleted` **event.**

ply return after informing the UIA about the invocation, without executing the event handler code.

On each new page, UIA sets the HitTestFlag and interacts with all controls on the page, one after the other. At the end of the test, the UIA can determine which controls lead to distinct event handlers. UIA can test a typical page within a few hundred milliseconds.

The arrows and the associated numbers in Figure 6 shows the result of hit tests on pages. For example, clicking any item on the categories page leads to the same event handler, while clicking on the word "categories" on that page does not invoke any event handler (gray arrow). In fact, the controls on the page lead to just three unique event handlers: clicking on one of the categories leads to event handler 1, clicking on settings leads to handler 2 and swiping on the page leads to handler 3. Note also that several controls on page 1 have no event handlers attached them (gray arrows). By using hit testing, the monkey can focus only on controls that have event handlers associated with them. And from different controls associated with the same event handler, it needs to pick only one[4], thereby significantly reducing the testing time. In §8.2, we will evaluate the impact of hit testing.

We stress that the binding of event handlers to controls can be dynamic, (i.e. it can be changed by the app at run time). Thus static analysis is not sufficient to determine which event handler will be triggered by a given control. This issue has also been raised in [34].

6.2 When to interact next?

Emulating an "open loop" or impatient user is straightforward because the monkey simply needs to invoke event handlers independent of whether the current page has properly been processed and rendered, but emulating a real, patient user who looks at the rendered page and then interacts with it is trickier. Both types of interactions are important to test. The problem with emulating a patient user is that it is not obvious when a page has been completely processed and rendered on screen. Mobile applications exhibit significant variability in the time they take to complete rendering: we

show in §8 (Figure 21) that this time could vary between a few hundred milliseconds to several seconds. Waiting for the longest possible timeout using empirical data would slow the monkey down to unacceptable levels.

Fortunately, VanarSena's greybox binary instrumentation provides a natural solution to the problem, unlike blackbox techniques. The instrumentation includes a way to generate a signal that indicates that processing of the user interaction is complete. (Unlike web pages, app pages do not have a well-defined page-loaded event [45] because app execution can be highly asynchronous. So binary instrumentation is particularly effective here.)

We instrument the app to generate a signal that indicates that processing of the user interaction is complete. We use techniques developed in AppInsight [42] to generate the signal, as follows.

The core ideas in AppInsight are the concept of *user transaction*, and techniques to track their progress. For example, Figure 11 shows the user transaction [42] for the interaction with "Bars" in Figure 6. The thick horizontal lines represent thread executions, while the dotted lines link asynchronous calls to their corresponding callbacks [42]. When a category (e.g. "Bars") is clicked on page 1, it calls the associated event handler, which in turn makes an asynchronous call to get GPS location. After obtaining the location, the callback thread makes another asynchronous call to a web server to fetch information about bars near that location. The web callback thread parses the results and initiates a dispatcher call to update the UI with the list of bars. To track this transaction, we instrument the app to add transaction tracker (Figure 9). It monitors the transaction at runtime and generates a `ProcessingCompleted` event when all the processing (synchronous and asynchronous) associated with an interaction is complete. Two key problems in tracking the transaction are (*a*) monitoring thread start and ends with minimal overhead, and (*b*) matching asynchronous calls with their callbacks, across thread boundaries. We address these problems using techniques from AppInsight [42][5]. The key difference between AppInsight and transaction tracker is that our tracker is capable of tracking the transaction in an online manner (i.e. during execution). In contrast, AppInsight generated logs that were analyzed by an offline analyzer.

6.3 Randomized Concurrent Monkeys

VanarSena uses many simple monkeys operating independently and at random, rather than build a single more complicated and stateful monkey.

Each monkey picks a control at random that would activate an event handler that it has not interacted with in past. For example, suppose the monkey is on page 1 of Figure 6, and it has already clicked on settings previously, then it would choose to either swipe (handler 3), or click one of the businesses at random (handler 1).

If no such control is found, the monkey clicks on the back button to travel to the parent page. For example, when on page 3 of Figure 6, the monkey has only one choice (handler 6). If it finds itself back on this page after having interacted with one of the controls, it will click the back button to navigate back to page 2. Pressing the back button in page 1 will quit the app.

Because an app can have loops in its UI structure (e.g. a "Home" button deep inside the app to navigate back to the first page), running the monkey once may not fully explore the app. To mitigate this, we run several monkeys concurrently. These monkeys do not share state, and make independent choices.

Running multiple, randomized monkeys in parallel has two advantages over a single complicated monkey. First, it overcomes the

---

[4]In other words, we assume that two controls that lead to same event handler are equivalent. See §6.3 for a caveat.

[5]We correctly handle thread waits, sleeps, and timers.

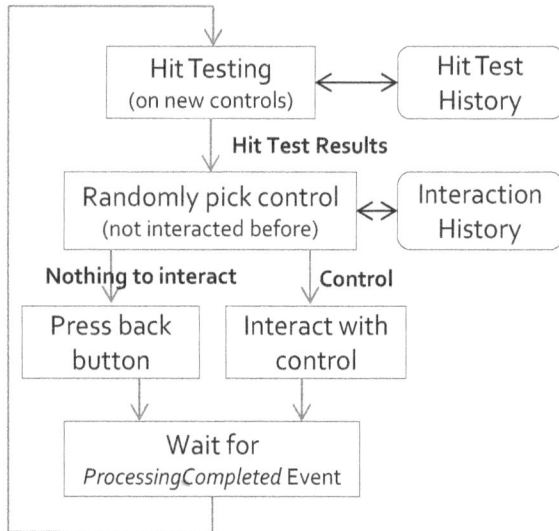

Figure 12: UI automator flow.

```
Original code
void fetch(string url) {
  WebRequest.GetResponse(url, callback);
}
Rewritten code
void fetch(string url) {
  WebRequestIntercept.GetResponse(url, callback);
}
class WebRequestIntercept {
  void GetResponse(string url, delegate callback) {
    if (MonkeyConfig.InducingResponseFaults)
      ResponseFaultInducer.Proxy(url, callback);
    if (MonkeyConfig.InducingNetworkFaults)
      NetworkFaultInducer.RaiseNetworkEvent();
  }
}
```

Figure 13: Intercepting web API to proxy through web response FIM and informing network FIM about the impending network transfer.

problem of deterministic crashes. Second, it can improve coverage. Note that we assumed that when two controls lead to the same event handler, they are equivalent. While this assumption generally holds, it is not a fact. One can design an app where all button clicks are handled by a single event handler, which takes different actions depending on the button's name. Random selection of controls ensures that different monkeys would pick different controls tied to the same event handler, increasing coverage for apps that use this coding pattern.

Putting it all together: Figure 12 shows the overall flow of the UI automator.

7. INDUCING FAULTS

The Fault Inducer (FI) is built as an extensible module in which various fault inducing modules (FIM) can be plugged in. The monkey manager configures each monkey to turn on one or more FIMs.

The FIMs are triggered by the instrumentation added to the app. The binary instrumentation rewrites the app code to intercept calls to specific APIs to proxy them through the appropriate FIM. Figure 13 shows an example. When the call to the HTTP API is made at run-time, it can be proxied through the FIM that mimics web er-

rors. The FIM may return an HTTP failure, garble the response, and so forth.

We built FIMs that help uncover some of the prominent crash buckets in Table 1. The first three intercept API calls and return values that apps may overlook, while the others model unexpected user behavior.

(1) Web errors: When an app makes a HTTP call, the FIM intercepts the calls and returns HTTP error codes such as 404 (Not Found) or 502 (Bad Gateway, or unable to connect). These can trigger WebExceptions. The module can also intercept the reply and garble it to trigger parsing errors. Parsing errors are particularly important for apps that obtain data from third-party sites. We use Fiddler [3] to intercept and manipulate web requests.

(2) Poor Network conditions: Brief disconnections and poor network conditions can trigger a variety of network errors, leading to WebExceptions. To emulate these network conditions, we instrument the app to raise an event to the FI just before an impending network transfer. The FIM can then emulate different network conditions such as brief disconnection, slow network rate, or long latency. We use a DummyNet-like tool [43] to simulate these conditions.

(3) Sensor errors: We introduce sensor faults by returning null values and extreme values for sensors such as GPS and accelerometers.

(4) Invalid text entry: A number of apps do not validate user inputs before parsing them. To induce these faults, the UIA and the FI work together. The UI Scraper generates an event to the FI when it encounters a textbox. The FIM then informs the UIA to either leave the textbox empty, or fill it with text, numbers, or special symbols.

(5) Impatient user: In §6.2, we described how the UIA emulates a patient user by waiting for the ProcessingCompleted event. However, real users are often impatient, and may interact with the app again before processing of the previous interaction is complete. For example, in Figure 6, an impatient user may click on "Bars" on page 1, decide that the processing is taking too long, and click on the back button to try and exit the app. Such behavior may trigger race conditions in the app code. Table 1 shows that it is the root cause of many crashes. To emulate an impatient user, the transaction tracker in the app raises an event to the FI when a transaction starts, i.e., just after the UIA interacted with a control. To emulate an impatient user, the FIM then instructs the UIA to immediately interact with another specific UI control, without waiting for ProcessingCompleted event. We emulate three distinct impatient user behaviors—clicking on the same control again, clicking on another control on the page, and clicking on the back button.

It is important to be careful about when faults are induced. When a FIM is first turned on, it does not induce a fault on every intercept or event, because it can result in poor coverage. For example, consider testing the AroundMe app (Figure 6) for web errors. If the FIM returns 404 for every request, the app will never populate the list of businesses on page 2, and the monkey will never reach page 3 and 4 of the app. Hence, a FIM usually attempts to induce each fault with some small probability. Because VanarSena uses multiple concurrent monkeys, this approach works in practice.

During app testing, VanarSena induces only one fault at a time: each one instance of the monkey runs with just one FIM turned on. This approach helps us pinpoint the fault that is responsible for the crash. The monkey manager runs multiple monkeys concurrently with different FIMs turned on.

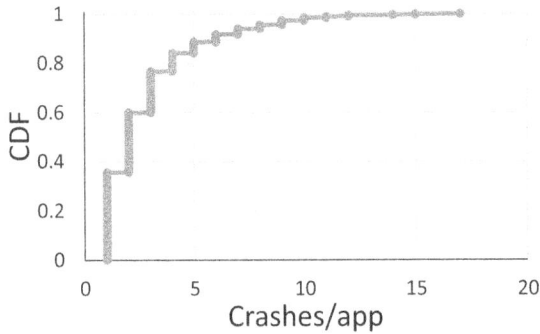

Figure 14: Crashes per app

Rating value	VanarSena	WPER
None	350 (32%)	21%
1	127 (11%)	13%
2	146 (13%)	16%
3	194 (18%)	15%
4	185 (17%)	22%
5	106 (10%)	13%

Table 2: Number of crashed apps for various ratings

8. EVALUATION

We evaluate VanarSena along two broad themes. First, we demonstrate the usefulness of the system by describing the crashes VanarSena found on 3,000 apps from the Windows Phone Store. Then, we evaluate the optimizations and heuristics described in §6.

To test the system, we selected apps as follows. We bucketized all apps that were in the Windows Phone app store in the first week of April 2013 into 6 groups, according to their rating (no rating, rating $\leq 1, \cdots$, rating ≤ 5). We randomly selected 500 apps from each bucket. This process gives us a representative set of 3,000 apps to test VanarSena with.

We found that 15% of these apps had a textbox on the first page. These might have required user login information, but we did not create such accounts for the apps we evaluated. So it is possible (indeed, expected) that for some apps, we didn't test much more than whether there were bugs on the sign-in screen. Despite this restriction, we report many bugs, suggesting that most (but not all) apps were tested reasonably thoroughly. In practice, we expect the developer to supply app-specific inputs such as sign-in information.

8.1 Crashes

We ran 10 concurrent monkeys per run, where each run tests one of the eight fault induction modules from Table 3, as well as one run with no fault induction. Thus, there were 9 different runs for each app, 90 monkeys in all. In these tests, the UIA emulated a patient user, except when the "impatient user" FIM was turned on.

We ran the tests on 12 machines, set up to both emulate Windows Phone 7 and Windows Phone 8 in different tests. Overall, testing 3,000 apps with 270,000 distinct monkey runs took 4,500 machine hours with each app tested for 1.5 hours on average. At current Azure pricing, the cost of testing one app is roughly 25 cents, which is small enough for nightly app tests to be done. The process emulated over 2.5 million interactions, covering over 400,000 pages.

8.1.1 Key Results

Overall, VanarSena flagged 2969 unique crashes[6] in 1108 apps. Figure 14 shows that it found one or two crashes in 60% of the apps. Some apps had many more crashes—one had 17.

Note that these crashes were found in apps that are already in the marketplace; these are not "pre-release" apps. VanarSena found crashes in apps that have already (presumably) undergone some degree of testing by the developer.

Table 2 bucketizes crashed apps according to their ratings rounded to nearest integer values. Note that we have 500 total apps in each rating bucket. We see that VanarSena discovered crashes

---

[6]The uniqueness of the crash is determined by the exception type and stack trace. If the app crashes twice in exactly the same place, we count it only once.

in all rating buckets. For example, 350 of the no-rating 500 apps crashed during our testing. This represents 31% of total (1108) apps that crashed. We see that the crash data in WPER for these 3000 apps has a similar rating distribution except for the 'no-rating' bucket. For this bucket, WPER sees fewer crashes than VanarSena most likely because these apps do not have enough users (hence no ratings).

8.1.2 Comparison Against the WPER Database

It is tempting to directly compare the crashes we found with the crash reports for the same apps in the WPER database discussed in §2. Direct comparison, however, is not possible because both the apps and the phone OS have undergone revisions since the WPER data was collected. But we can compare some broader metrics.

VanarSena found 1,227 crashes not in the WPER database. We speculate that this is due to two key reasons. First, the database covers a period of one year. Apps that were added to the marketplace towards the end of the period may not have been run sufficiently often by users. Also, apps that are unpopular (usually poorly rated), do not get run very often in the wild, and hence do not encounter all conditions that may cause them to crash. To validate this hypothesis, we examined metadata of the apps in Windows Phone Store. The app store provides information such as rating counts and average rating values of apps, but not their actual downloads or usage counts. However, previous works have pointed out that rating count and download count of apps are strongly correlated and hence a high rating count is a strong indication of a high download count [12]. We found that apps for which VanarSena found these 1,227 crashes have, on average, $3\times$ fewer reviews (and hence likely fewer downloads) and 10% worse rating than remaining of the apps we used.

The crashes found by VanarSena cover 16 out of 20 top crash buckets (exception name plus crash method) in WPER, and 19 of the top 20 exceptions. VanarSena does not report any `OutOfMemoryException` because of the following reason. To collect crashes, VanarSena instruments the unhandled exception handler inside the app. Out of memory is a fatal exception that crashes the app without calling the exception handler. WPER collects crash data at the system level instead of the app level where `OutOfMemoryException` is logged.

Figure 15 shows another way to compare VanarSena crash data and WPER. For this graph, we consider the subset of WPER crashes that belong to the crash buckets and the apps for which VanarSena found at least one crash. For each bucket, we take the apps that appear in WPER, and compute what fraction of these apps are also crashed by VanarSena. We call this fraction *bucket coverage*. Figure 15 shows that for 40% of the buckets, VanarSena crashed *all* the apps reported in WPER, which is a significant result suggesting good coverage.

8.1.3 Analysis

Even "no FIM" detects failures. Table 3 shows the breakdown of crashes found by VanarSena. The first row shows that even without turning any FIM on, VanarSena discovered 506 unique crashes

197

FIM	Crashes (Apps)	Example crash buckets	Not in WPER
No FIM	506 (429)	NullReferenceException, InvokeEventHandler	239 (205)
Text Input	215 (191)	FormatException, Int32.Parse	78 (68)
Impatient User	384 (323)	InvalidOperationException, Navigation.GoBack	102 (89)
HTTP 404	637 (516)	WebException, Browser.BeginOnUI	320 (294)
HTTP 502	339 (253)	EndpointNotFoundException, Browser.BeginOnUI	164 (142)
HTTP Bad Data	768 (398)	XmlException, ParseElement	274 (216)
Network Poor	93 (76)	NotSupportedException, WebClient.ClearWebClientState	40 (34)
GPS	21 (19)	ArgumentOutOfRangeException, GeoCoordinate..ctor	9 (9)
Accelerometer	6 (6)	FormatException, Double.Parse	1 (1)

Table 3: Crashes found by VanarSena.

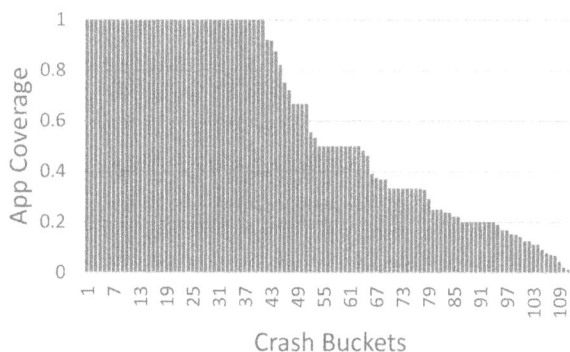

Figure 15: Coverage of crash buckets in WPER data

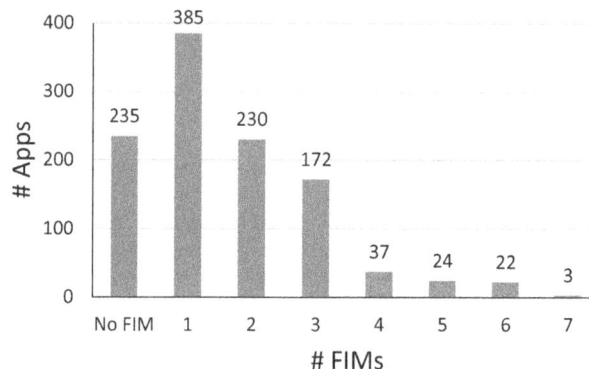

Figure 16: FIMs causing crashes

in 429 apps (some apps crashed multiple times with distinct stack traces; also, the number of apps in this table exceeds 1108 for this reason). The main conclusion from this row is that merely exploring the app thoroughly can uncover faults. A typical exception observed for crashes in this category is the NullReferenceException. The table also shows that 239 of these 506 crashes (205 apps) were not in the WPER database.

We now consider the crashes induced by individual FIMs. To isolate the crashes caused by a FIM, we take a conservative approach. If the signature of the crash (stack trace) is also found in the crashes included in the first row (i.e., no FIM), we do not count the crash. We also manually verified a large sample of crashes to ensure that they were actually being caused by the FIM used.

Most failures are found by one or two FIMs, but some apps benefit from more FIMs. Figure 16 shows the number of apps that crashed as a function of the number of FIMs that induced the crashes. For example, 235 apps required no FIM to crash them at all[7]. Most app crashes are found with less than three FIMs, but complex apps fail for multiple reasons (FIMs). Several apps don't use text boxes, networking, or sensors, making those FIMs irrelevant, but for apps that use these facilities, the diversity of FIMs is useful. The tail of this chart is as noteworthy as the rest of the distribution.

Many apps do not check the validity of the strings entered in textboxes. We found that 191 apps crashed in 215 places due to this error. The most common exception was FormatException. We also found web exceptions that resulted when invalid input was proxied from the cloud service backing the app.

Emulating an impatient user uncovers several interesting crashes. Analysis of stack traces and binaries of these apps showed that the crashes fall in three broad categories. First, a number of apps violate the guidelines imposed by the Windows Phone frame-

work regarding handling of simultaneous page navigation commands. These crashes should be fixed by following suggested programming practices [1]. Second, a number of apps fail to use proper locking in event handlers to avoid multiple simultaneous accesses to resources such as the phone camera and certain storage APIs. Finally, several apps had app-specific race conditions that were triggered by the impatient behavior.

Several apps incorrectly assume a reliable server or network. Some developers evidently assume that cloud servers and networks are reliable, and thus do not handle HTTP errors correctly. VanarSena crashed 516 apps in 637 unique places by intercepting web calls, and returning the common "404" error code. The error code representing Bad Gateway ("502") crashed 253 apps.

Some apps are too trusting of data returned from servers. They do not account for the possibility of receiving corrupted or malformed data. Most of the crashes in this category were due to XML and JSON parsing errors. These issues are worth addressing also because of potential security concerns.

Some apps do not correctly handle poor network connectivity. In many cases, the request times out and generates a web exception which apps do not handle. We also found a few interesting cases of other exceptions, including a NullReferenceException, where an app waited for a fixed amount of time to receive data from a server. When network conditions were poor, the data did not arrive during the specified time. Instead of handling this possibility, the app tried to read the non-existent data.

A handful of apps do not handle sensor failures or errors. When we returned a NaN for the GPS coordinates, which indicates that the GPS is not switched on, some apps crashed with ArgumentOutOfRangeException. We also found a timing-related failure in an app where it expected to get a GPS lock within a certain amount of time, failing when that did not happen.

API compatibility across OS versions caused crashes. For example, in the latest Windows Phone OS (WP8), the behavior of several APIs has changed [2]. WP8 no longer supports the FM radio feature and developers were advised to check the OS version before

---

[7]This number is less than 429 (row 1 of Table 3), because some of those 429 apps crashed with other FIMs as well. Unlike Table 3, apps in Figure 16 add up to 1108.

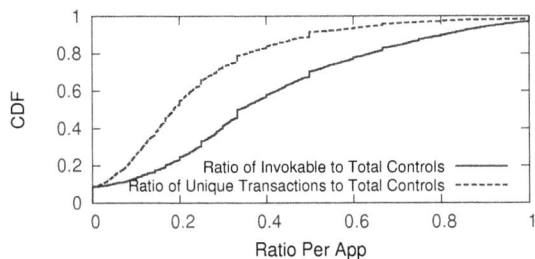

Figure 17: Fraction of invokable to total controls and unique event handlers to total controls in an app.

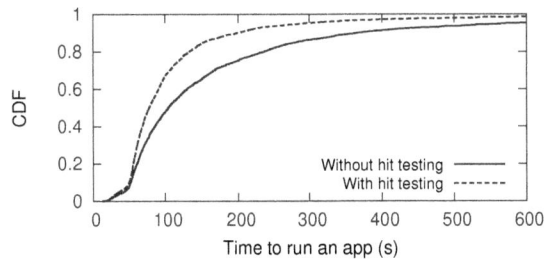

Figure 18: Time to run apps with and without hit testing

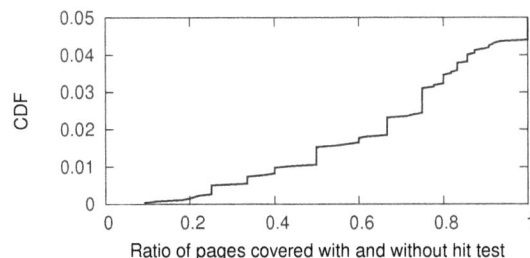

Figure 19: Fraction of pages covered with and without hit testing.

using this feature. Similar changes have been made to camera and GPS APIs. To test whether the apps we selected are susceptible to API changes, we ran them with the emulator emulating WP8. The UIA emulated patient user, and no FIMs were turned on. We found that 8 apps crashed with an `RadioDisabledException`, while the camera APIs crashed two apps. In total, we found about 221 crashes from 212 apps due to API compatibility issues[8].

8.2 Monkey Techniques

We now evaluate the heuristics and optimizations discussed in §6. Unless specified otherwise, the results in this section use the same 3000 apps as before. The apps were run 10 times, with no FIM, and the UIA emulated a patient user.

8.2.1 Coverage

We measure coverage in terms of pages and user transactions. We desire that the monkey should cover as much of the app as possible. However, there is no easy way to determine how many unique pages or user transactions the app contains. Any static analysis may undercount the pages and controls, since some apps generate content dynamically. Static analysis may also overestimate their numbers, since apps often include 3rd party libraries that include a lot of pages and controls, only a few of which are accessible to the user at run-time.

Thus, we rely on human calibration to thoroughly explore a small number of apps and compare it to monkey's coverage. We randomly picked 35 apps and recruited 3 users to manually explore the app. They were specifically asked to click on possible controls and trigger as many unique transactions as possible. We instrumented the apps to log the pages visited and the transactions invoked. Then, we ran the app through our system, with the configuration described earlier.

In 26 out of 35 apps, the monkey covered 100% of pages and more than 90% of all transactions. In five of the remaining nine apps, the monkey covered 75% of the pages. In four apps, the monkey was hampered by the need for app-specific input such as login/passwords and did not progress far. Although this study is small, it gives us confidence that the monkey is able to explore the vast majority of apps thoroughly.

8.2.2 Benefits of Hit Testing

Hit testing accelerates testing by avoiding interacting with non-invokable controls. Among invokable controls, hit testing allows the monkey to interact with only those that lead to unique event handlers.

To evaluate the usefulness of hit testing, we turned off randomization in the UIA, and ran the monkey with and without hit testing once for each app. When running without hit testing, we assume

---

[8]Note that this data is not included in any earlier discussion (e.g. Table 3) since we used Windows 7 emulator for all other data.

that every control leads to a unique event handler, so the monkey interacts with every control on the page.

Figure 17 shows the ratio of invokable controls and unique event handlers to the total controls in each app. We found that in over half the apps, less than 33% of the total controls in the app were invokable, and only 18% lead to unique event handlers.

Figure 18 shows the time to run apps with and without hit testing. The 90th percentile of the time to run the app once with no fault induction was 365 seconds without hit testing, and only 197 seconds with hit testing. The tail was even worse: for one particular app, a single run took 782 seconds without hit testing, while hit testing reduced the time to just 38 seconds, a 95% reduction.

At the same time, we found that hit testing had minimal impact on app coverage (Figure 19 and Figure 20). In 95.7% of the apps, there was no difference in page coverage with and without hit testing, and for 90% of the apps, there was no difference in transaction coverage either. For the apps with less than 100% coverage, the median page and transaction coverage was over 80%. This matches the observation made in [42]: usually, only distinct event handlers lead to distinct user transactions.

8.2.3 Importance of the ProcessingCompleted Event

When emulating a patient user, the UIA waits for the `ProcessingCompleted` event to fire before interacting with the next control. Without such an event, we would need to use a fixed timeout. We now show that using such a fixed timeout is not feasible.

Figure 21 shows distribution of the processing time for transactions in the 3000 apps. Recall (Figure 11) that this includes the time taken to complete all processing associated with a current interaction [42]. For this figure, we separate the transactions that involved network calls and those that did not. We also ran the apps while the FIM emulated typical 3G network speeds. This FIM affects only the duration of transactions that involve networking, and the graph shows this duration as well.

The graph shows that processing times of the transactions vary widely, from a few milliseconds to over 10 seconds. Thus, with a small static timeout, we may end up unwittingly emulating an im-

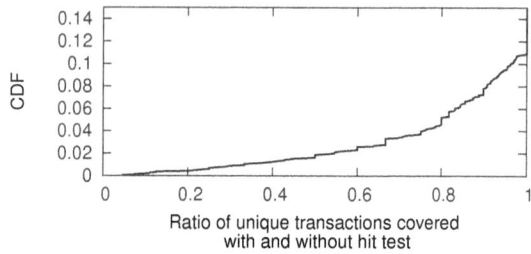

Figure 20: Fraction of transactions covered with and without hit testing.

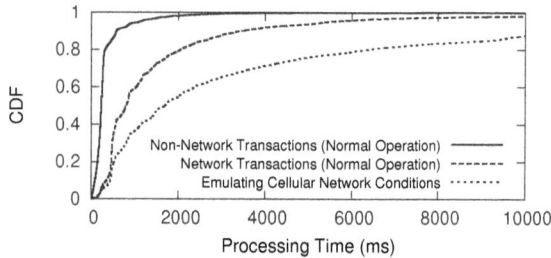

Figure 21: Processing times for transaction.

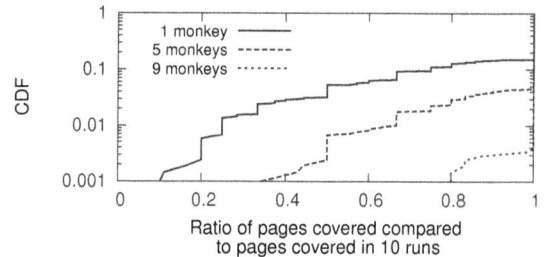

Figure 22: Fraction of pages covered by runs compared to pages covered by 10 runs.

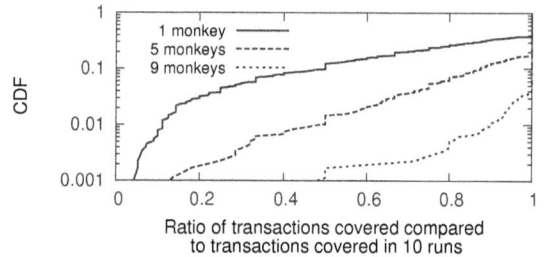

Figure 23: Fraction of transactions covered by runs compared to transactions covered by 10 runs.

patient user for many transactions. Worse yet, we may miss many UI controls that are populated only after the transaction is complete. On the other hand, with a large timeout, for many transactions, the UIA would find itself waiting unnecessarily. For example, a static timeout of 4 seconds covers 90% of the normal networking transactions, but is unnecessarily long for non-networking transactions. On the other hand, this value covers only 60% of the transactions when emulating a 3G network.

This result demonstrates that using the *ProcessingCompleted* event allows VanarSena to maximize coverage while minimizing processing time.

8.2.4 Multiple Concurrent Monkeys are Useful

Figure 22 shows the CDF of the fraction of pages covered with 1, 5, and 9 monkeys compared to the pages covered with 10 monkeys. The y-axis is on a log scale. Although 85% of apps need only one monkey for 100% coverage, the tail is large. For about 1% of the apps, new pages are discovered even by the 9th monkey. Similarly, Figure 23 shows that for 5% of the apps, VanarSena continues to discover new transactions even in the 9th monkey.

We did an additional experiment to demonstrate the value of multiple concurrent runs. Recall that we ran each app through each FIM 10 times. To demonstrate that it is possible to uncover more bugs if we run longer, we selected 12 apps from our set of 3000 apps that had the most crashes in WPER system. We ran these apps 100 times through each FIM. By doing so, we uncovered 86 new unique crashes among these apps (4 to 18 in each) in addition to the 60 crashes that we had discovered with the original 10 runs.

9. DISCUSSION AND LIMITATIONS

Why not instrument the emulator? VanarSena could have been implemented by modifying the emulator to induce faults. As a significant practical matter, however, modifying the large and complex emulator code would have required substantially more development effort than our architecture. Moreover, it would require the fault detection software to be adapted to the emulator evolving.

Why cloud deployment? We envision VanarSena as a cloud service for a couple of reasons. First, the cloud offers elastic resources

– i.e. a large number of emulators can be deployed on demand. Second, a cloud-based deployment also makes for easier updates. We can update the monkey in a variety of ways – e.g. by adding more FIMs based on crash reports from the field, or by using (as yet undiscovered) techniques for improving testing speed or resource consumption. That said, it is easy to envision non-cloud deployment models as well. For example, VanarSena can work by spawning multiple VMs on developer's desktop (resources permitting), or on a network of local machines. These other deployment scenarios have their own advantages and disadvantages. The fact that monkeys run independently of each other allows for many deployment and pricing models.

Target audience: We envision that VanarSena would be primarily used by amateur developers, or small app shops who lack resources to perform thorough testing of their apps. A majority of apps (on any platform) are developed by such entities. However, note that our evaluation did not focus on only such apps, and we were able to crash so-called professionally developed apps as well. Apart from app developers, VanarSena can also be used by app store owners during app ingestion and approval pipeline to test submitted apps for common faults. The extensibility of the fault inducer, and not requiring source code, are both significant assets in realizing this scenario.

Number of monkeys per app: For results reported in this paper, we ran a fixed number of monkeys for every app. However, we also found that running more monkeys often uncovers more crashes (although we expect that the the returns will be diminishing). We also believe that the number of monkeys needed to test an app comprehensively for each fault depends on the complexity of the app. Static analysis of the app should be able to provide some guidance in this matter. We leave this as part of our future work.

Providing inputs in a specific order: Some apps do not make progress until certain inputs are provided in a specific order. For example, log-in button should be clicked only after filling username and password. In VanarSena, we expect developers to provide inputs to textboxes. When the UI Automator discovers textboxes in a page, it fills the textboxes first (with the developer provided input or a random value) before hit testing and clicking controls. This helps the UIA to quickly go past login screens. For all other types of inputs, the UIA picks the controls randomly. If an app requires a specific order of interaction, it might be worthwhile to get hints from the developer to save testing time. We are currently exploring how developers can provide such hints easily.

Testing Games: Many games requires complex, free-form gestures. Thus, trace replay [21] may be a more appropriate testing strategy on game apps, than randomized monkey actions. Our monkey can easily support trace replay, although collection and validation of such traces is a challenging problem that we plan to address in future. We also note that we cannot test certain other kinds of apps with the current version of VanarSena. Some apps launch other apps (e.g. web browser) and terminate. Testing such apps requires keeping careful track of different app contexts – something which we have not yet implemented. This, however, is an engineering challenge only - not a fundamental one.

Overhead: On average, our instrumentation increases the runtime of transactions by 0.02%. This small overhead is unlikely to affect the behavior of the app.

False Positives: The binary instrumentation may itself be buggy, causing "false positive" crashes. We cannot prove that we do not induce such false positives, but careful manual analysis of crash traces shows that none of the crashes occurred in the code VanarSena added.

Combination of fault inducers: We evaluated apps by injecting one fault at a time to focus on individual faults. In reality, multiple faults may happen at the same time. We plan to investigate this in future.

Improving the SDK: Some of the bugs we have uncovered should be fixed in the platform, instead of in the app. For example, crashes due to violation of simultaneous page navigation could be avoided by redesigning the API.

Beyond Windows Phone: VanarSena currently supports Windows Phone applications. However, its techniques are broadly applicable to mobile apps and can be extended to other platforms. In [42], we have described how the instrumentation framework can be extended to other platforms.

Beyond crashes: We currently focus on app crashes only. However, app developers also typically care about performance of their app [42], under a variety of conditions. Extending VanarSena to do performance testing is the primary thrust of our future work.

10. RELATED WORK

At a high level, VanarSena consists of two components: (1) dynamic analysis with a monkey, and (2) fault injection for app testing. Below we discuss how VanarSena compares with prior works in these two aspects.

Static and dynamic analysis of mobile apps. Several prior works have statically analyzed app binaries to uncover energy bugs [39, 44], performance problems [30], app plagiarism [13], security problems [17, 23], and privacy leaks [34, 20]. Static analysis is not suitable for our goal of uncovering runtime faults of apps since it cannot capture runtime issues such as poor network condition and corrupted or unexpected responses from cloud services. Several recent works have proposed using a monkey to automatically execute mobile apps for analysis of app's runtime properties. AppsPlayground [41] runs apps in the Android emulator on top of a modified Android software stack (TaintDroid [15]) in order to track information flow and privacy leaks. Authors evaluate the tool with an impressive 3,968 apps. Recently A^{3}E [8] and Orbit [47] use combinations of static and dynamic analysis to automatically generate test cases to reach various activities of an app. AMC [31] uses a dynamic analysis to check accessibility properties of vehicular apps. It has a UI Automator similar to VanarSena, but unlike our system, it clicks on every control in a given page and waits for a static timeout of 10 seconds before making the next interaction. With hit testing and processing completed event, we believe that VanarSena's UI Automator would be much faster than AMC's. Eprof [38] uses dynamic analysis (without a monkey) for fine-grained energy accounting. ProtectMyPrivacy [4] uses the crowd to analyze app privacy settings and to automatically recommend app-specific privacy recommendations. All these works differ by their end goals and specific optimizations. Similarly, VanarSena differ from them in its end goal of uncovering runtime faults of apps and its novel monkey optimization techniques: hit testing and accurate processing completed event. The optimizations are general and can be used for other systems as well. We cannot directly compare the performance of our monkey with the other systems since all of them are for Android apps.

VanarSena uses AppInsight [42] to instrument Windows Phone app binaries. For Android apps, one could use similar frameworks such as SIF [26] and RetroSkeleton [14].

Mobile app testing with a monkey. As mentioned in Section 1, mobile app testing poses different challenges than traditional "enterprise" software, motivating researchers to develop mobile-specific solutions. Researchers have used Android Monkey [22] for automated fuzz testing [6, 7, 19, 27, 37]. Similar UI automation tools exist for other platforms. VanarSena differs from these tools is two major ways. First, the Android Monkey generates only UI events, and not the richer set of faults that VanarSena induces. Second, it does not optimize for coverage or speed like VanarSena. One can provide an automation script to the Android Monkey to guide its execution paths, but this approach is not scalable when exploring a large number of distinct execution paths.

Closest to our work is DynoDroid [35] that, like VanarSena, addresses the above problems, but with a different approach: it modifies the Android framework and involves humans at run-time to go past certain app pages (e.g., login screen). Another fundamental difference is that it manipulates only UI and system events and does not inject faults due to external factors such as bad network or event timing related to unexpected or abnormal user behavior, which are among the most common root causes in our real-world crash reports. A^{3}E [8] and Orbit [47] use static and dynamic analysis to generate test cases to traverse different app activities, but do not inject external faults. All these systems could benefit from our crash analysis insights to decide what faults to inject.

ConVirt [32] is a related effort on mobile app testing that it explores the concept of contextual fuzzing. Under contextual fuzzing a variety of real world environmental and hardware conditions are systematically explored through both real hardware and emulation; these conditions include: user interaction, geo-locations, network conditions, and device/system configurations. To reduce the time in finding app performance problems, ConVirt implements a set of algorithms that leverage inter-app behavioral similarities. Unlike VanarSena, ConVirt takes a blackbox approach and incorporates actual hardware into the testing process. We envision combining ConVirt and VanarSena into a seamless system [11].

Other software testing techniques. Software testing has a rich history, which cannot be covered in a few paragraphs. We focus only on recent work on mobile app testing, which falls into three broad categories: fuzz testing, which generates random inputs to apps; symbolic testing, which tests an app by symbolically executing it; and model-based testing. Fuzz testing is done with a monkey and is discussed above.

As mentioned in Section 1, symbolic execution [29, 10, 37] and its hybrid variant, concolic execution [7, 28] have found limited success in testing real-world apps due to path explosion problem and difficulty in modeling real-world execution environment with network, sensors, and cloud.

"GUI ripping" [36, 25, 6] systems and GUITAR [24] use model-based testing to mobile apps. Unlike VanarSena, it requires developers to provide a model of the app's GUI and can only check faults due to user inputs. Applicability of these techniques has so far been very limited (e.g., evaluated with a handful of "toy" apps only).

Comparison to AppInsight: VanarSena leverages the instrumentation framework and other techniques developed for AppInsight [42]. However, the goals of VanarSena and AppInsight are very different. Developers use AppInsight to collect analytics, performance and crash data from mobile apps running "in the wild" – i.e. being used by real users. Thus, AppInsight does not include emulator, UI Automator or fault inducer. On the other hand, VanarSena is meant for catching bugs in the app before it is released to end users. Indeed, the development of VanarSena was motivated by our experience with AppInsight and feedback from developers who used it. We found that while AppInsight helped the developers fix bugs in subsequent releases of the app, it was sometimes "too late". Users of mobile apps can be quite unforgiving – once an app gets a poor rating due to crashes, few download subsequent "fixed" versions. The key goal of VanarSena is to detect the common faults in the app before it is released.

11. CONCLUSION

VanarSena is a software fault detection system for mobile apps designed by gleaning insights from an analysis of 25 million crash reports. VanarSena adopts a "greybox" testing method, instrumenting the app binary to achieve both high coverage and speed, using *hit testing* and generation of `ProcessingCompleted` event. We found that VanarSena is effective in practice. We tested it on 3000 apps from the Windows Phone store, finding that 1108 of them had failures. VanarSena uncovered over 2969 distinct bugs in existing apps, including over 1227 that were not previously reported. Each app was tested, on average, in just 1.5 hours. Deployed as a cloud service, VanarSena can provide a automated testing framework to mobile software reliability even for amateur developers who cannot devote extensive resources to testing.

Acknowledgments

We thank the MobiSys reviewers and our shepherd, Zhiyun Qian, for several useful comments and suggestions that improved this paper. We also thank Felix Xiaozhu Lin and Jessica Miller for their support during VanarSena development. LR and HB were supported in part by the National Science Foundation under Grant 0931508 and the MIT Center for Wireless Networks and Mobile Computing (Wireless@MIT).

12. REFERENCES

[1] http://www.magomedov.co.uk/2010/11/navigation-is-already-in-progress.html.

[2] App platform compatibility for Windows Phone. http://msdn.microsoft.com/en-US/library/windowsphone/develop/jj206947(v=vs.105).aspx.

[3] Fiddler. http://fiddler2.com/.

[4] Y. Agarwal and M. Hall. Protectmyprivacy: Detecting and mitigating privacy leaks on ios devices using crowdsourcing. In *Mobisys*, 2013.

[5] R. Agrawal and R. Srikant. Fast algorithms for mining association rules in large databases. In *VLDB*, 1994.

[6] D. Amalfitano, A. R. Fasolino, S. D. Carmine, A. Memon, and P. Tramontana. Using gui ripping for automated testing of android applications. In *ASE*, 2012.

[7] S. Anand, M. Naik, M. J. Harrold, and H. Yang. Automated concolic testing of smartphone apps. In *FSE*, 2012.

[8] T. Azim and I. Neamtiu. Targeted and depth-first exploration for systematic testing of android apps. In *OOPSLA*, 2013.

[9] T. Ball and J. Larus. Efficient Path Profiling. In *PLDI*, 1997.

[10] C. Cadar, D. Dunbar, and D. Engler. Klee: Unassisted and automatic generation of high-coverage tests for complex systems programs. In *OSDI*, 2008.

[11] R. Chandra, B. F. Karlsson, N. Lane, C.-J. M. Liang, S. Nath, J. Padhye, L. Ravindranath, and F. Zhao. Towards Scalable Automated Mobile App Testing. MSR-TR-2014-44.

[12] P. H. Chia, Y. Yamamoto, and N. Asokan. Is this app safe?: A large scale study on application permissions and risk signals. In *Proceedings of the 21st International Conference on World Wide Web*, WWW '12, 2012.

[13] J. Crussell, C. Gibler, and H. Chen. Attack of the clones: Detecting cloned applications on android markets. In *ESORICS*, 2012.

[14] B. Davis and H. Chen. Retroskeleton: Retrofitting android apps. In *Mobisys*, 2013.

[15] W. Enck, P. Gilbert, B.-G. Chun, L. P. Cox, J. Jung, P. McDaniel, and A. Seth. TaintDroid: An Information-Flow Tracking System for Realtime Privacy Monitoring on Smartphones. In *OSDI*, 2010.

[16] W. Enck, P. Gilbert, B.-G. Chun, L. P. Cox, J. Jung, P. McDaniel, and A. N. Sheth. Taintdroid: An information-flow tracking system for realtime privacy monitoring on smartphones. In *OSDI*, 2010.

[17] W. Enck, D. Octeau, P. McDaniel, and S. Chaudhuri. A study of android application security. In *USENIX Security*, 2011.

[18] Unhandled exception handler. http://msdn.microsoft.com/en-us/library/system.appdomain.unhandledexception.aspx.

[19] S. Ganov, C. Killmar, S. Khurshid, and D. Perry. Event listener analysis and symbolic execution for testing gui applications. *Formal Methods and Software Engg.*, 2009.

[20] C. Gibler, J. Crussell, J. Erickson, and H. Chen. Androidleaks: Automatically detecting potential privacy leaks in android applications on a large scale. In *Trust and Trustworthy Computing*, 2012.

[21] L. Gomez, I. Neamtiu, T. Azim, and T. Millstein. Reran: Timing- and touch-sensitive record and replay for android. In *ICSE*, 2013.

[22] Google. UI/Application Exerciser Monkey. http://developer.android.com/tools/help/monkey.html.

[23] M. Grace, Y. Zhou, Q. Zhang, S. Zou, and X. Jiang. Riskranker: Scalable and accurate zero-day android malware detection. In *Mobisys*, 2012.

[24] GUITAR: A model-based system for automated GUI testing. http://guitar.sourceforge.net/.

[25] D. Hackner and A. M. Memon. Test case generator for GUITAR. In *ICSE*, 2008.

[26] S. Hao, D. Li, W. Halfond, and R. Govindan. SIF: A Selective Instrumentation Framework for Mobile Applications. In *MobiSys*, 2013.

[27] C. Hu and I. Neamtiu. Automating gui testing for android applications. In *AST*, 2011.

[28] C. S. Jensen, M. R. Prasad, and A. MÃÿller. Automated testing with targeted event sequence generation. In *Int. Symp. on Software Testing and Analysis*, 2013.

[29] J. C. King. Symbolic execution and program testing. *CACM*, 19(7):385–394, 1976.

[30] Y. Kwon, S. Lee, H. Yi, D. Kwon, S. Yang, B.-G. Chun, L. Huang, P. Maniatis, M. Naik, and Y. Paek. Mantis: Automatic performance prediction for smartphone applications. In *Usenix ATC*, 2013.

[31] K. Lee, J. Flinn, T. Giuli, B. Noble, and C. Peplin. Amc: Verifying user interface properties for vehicular applications. In *ACM Mobisys*, 2013.

[32] C.-J. M. Liang, N. Lane, N. Brouwers, L. Zhang, B. Karlsson, R. Chandra, and F. Zhao. Contextual Fuzzing: Automated Mobile App Testing Under Dynamic Device and Environment Conditions. MSR-TR-2013-100.

[33] S. Lidin. *Inside Microsoft .NET IL Assembler* . Microsoft Press, 2002.

[34] B. Livshits and J. Jung. Automatic mediation of privacy-sensitive resource access in smartphone applications. In *USENIX Security*, 2013.

[35] A. Machiry, R. Tahiliani, and M. Naik. Dynodroid: An input generation system for android apps. In *FSE*, 2013.

[36] A. Memon. Using reverse engineering for automated usability evaluation of gui-based applications. *Human-Centered Software Engineering*, 2009.

[37] N. Mirzaei, S. Malek, C. S. Păsăreanu, N. Esfahani, and R. Mahmood. Testing android apps through symbolic execution. *SIGSOFT Softw. Eng. Notes*, 37(6):1–5, 2012.

[38] A. Pathak, Y. C. Hu, and M. Zhang. Where is the energy spent inside my app? fine grained energy accounting on smartphones with eprof. In *Eurosys*, 2012.

[39] A. Pathak, A. Jindal, Y. C. Hu, , and S. Midkiff. What is keeping my phone awake? characterizing and detecting no-sleep energy bugs in smartphone apps. In *Mobisys*, 2012.

[40] C. Perzold. *Microsoft Silverlight Edition: Programming Windows Phone 7*. Microsoft Press, 2010.

[41] V. Rastogi, Y. Chen, and W. Enck. Appsplayground: Automatic security analysis of smartphone applications. In *CODASPY*, 2013.

[42] L. Ravindranath et al. Appinsight: Mobile app performance monitoring in the wild. In *OSDI*, 2012.

[43] L. Rizzo. Dummynet.

[44] P. Vekris, R. Jhala, S. Lerner, and Y. Agarwal. Towards verifying android apps for the absence of wakelock energy bugs. In *HotPower*, 2012.

[45] X. S. Wang, A. Balasubramanian, A. Krishnamurthy, and D. Wetherall. Demystifying Page Load Performance with WProf. In *NSDI*, 2013.

[46] Xaml. http://msdn.microsoft.com/en-us/library/ms752059(v=vs.110).aspx.

[47] W. Yang, M. R. Prasad, and T. Xie. A Grey-box Approach for Automated GUI-Model Generation of Mobile Applications. In *FASE*, 2013.

PUMA: Programmable UI-Automation for Large-Scale Dynamic Analysis of Mobile Apps*

Shuai Hao*, Bin Liu*, Suman Nath†, William G.J. Halfond*, Ramesh Govindan*
*University of Southern California   †Microsoft Research
{shuaihao, binliu, halfond, ramesh}@usc.edu   sumann@microsoft.com

ABSTRACT

Mobile app ecosystems have experienced tremendous growth in the last six years. This has triggered research on dynamic analysis of performance, security, and correctness properties of the mobile apps in the ecosystem. Exploration of app execution using automated UI actions has emerged as an important tool for this research. However, existing research has largely developed analysis-specific UI automation techniques, wherein the logic for exploring app execution is intertwined with the logic for analyzing app properties. PUMA is a programmable framework that separates these two concerns. It contains a generic UI automation capability (often called a Monkey) that exposes high-level events for which users can define handlers. These handlers can flexibly direct the Monkey's exploration, and also specify app instrumentation for collecting dynamic state information or for triggering changes in the environment during app execution. Targeted towards operators of app marketplaces, PUMA incorporates mechanisms for scaling dynamic analysis to thousands of apps. We demonstrate the capabilities of PUMA by analyzing seven distinct performance, security, and correctness properties for 3,600 apps downloaded from the Google Play store.

Categories and Subject Descriptors

D.3.3 [**Programming Languages**]: Language Constructs and Features—*Frameworks*

General Terms

Design, Experimentation, Languages, Performance

*The first author, Shuai Hao, was supported by Annenberg Graduate Fellowship. This material is based upon work supported by the National Science Foundation under Grant No. CNS-1330118 and CCF-1321141. Any opinions, findings and conclusions or recommendations expressed in this material are those of the author(s) and do not necessarily reflect the views of the National Science Foundation (NSF).

Keywords

Dynamic Analysis; Large Scale; Mobile Apps; Programming Framework; Separation of Concerns; UI-Automation

1. INTRODUCTION

Today's smartphone app stores host large collections of apps. Most of the apps are created by unknown developers who have varying expertise and who may not always operate in the users' best interests. Such concerns have motivated researchers and app store operators to analyze various properties of the apps and to propose and evaluate new techniques to address the concerns. For such analyses to be useful, the analysis technique must be robust and scale well for large collections of apps.

Static analysis of app binaries, as used in prior work to identify privacy [21] and security [10, 12] problems, or app clones [9] *etc.*, can scale to a large number of apps. However, static analysis can fail to capture runtime contexts, such as data dynamically downloaded from the cloud, objects created during runtime, configuration variables, and so on. Moreover, app binaries may be obfuscated to thwart static analysis, either intentionally or unintentionally (such as stripping symbol information to reduce the size of the app binary).

Therefore, recent work has focused on dynamic analyses that execute apps and examine their runtime properties (Section 2). These analyses have been used for analyzing performance [26, 27, 15], bugs [22, 25, 19], privacy and security [11, 24], compliance [20] and correctness [18], of apps, some at a scale of thousands of apps. One popular way to scale dynamic analysis to a large number of apps is to use a software automation tool called a "monkey" that can automatically launch and interact with an app (by tapping on buttons, typing text inputs, *etc.*) in order to navigate to various execution states (or, pages) of the app. The monkey is augmented with code tailored to the target analysis; this code is systematically executed while the monkey visits various pages. For example, in DECAF [20], the analysis code algorithmically examines ads in the current page to check if their placement violates ad network policies.

Dynamic analysis of apps is a daunting task (Section 2). At a high level, it consists of *exploration logic* that guides the monkey to explore various app states and *analysis logic* that analyzes the targeted runtime properties of the current app state. The exploration logic needs to be optimized for *coverage*—it should explore a significant portion of the useful app states, and for *speed*—it should analyze a large collection of apps within a reasonable time. To achieve these goals, existing systems have developed a monkey from scratch and have tuned its exploration logic by leveraging properties of the analysis. For example, AMC [18] and DE-CAF [20] required analyzing one of each type of app page, and hence their monkey is tuned to explore only unique page types. On the other hand, SmartAds [23] crawled data from all pages, so its monkey is tuned to explore *all* unique pages. Similarly, the monkeys of VanarSena [25] and ConVirt [19] inject faults at specific execution points, while those of AMC and DECAF only read specific UI elements from app pages. Some systems even instrument app binaries to optimize the monkey [25] or to access app runtime state [23]. In summary, exploration logic and analysis logic are often intertwined and hence a system designed for one analysis cannot be readily used for another. The end effect is that many of the advances developed to handle large-scale studies are only utilizable in the context of the specific analysis and cannot currently be generalized to other analyses.

Contributions. In this paper we propose PUMA (Section 3), a dynamic analysis framework that can be instantiated for a large number of diverse dynamic analysis tasks that, in prior research, used systems built from scratch. PUMA enables analysis of a wide variety of app properties, allows its users to flexibly specify which app states to explore and how, provides programmatic access to the app's runtime state for analysis, and supports dynamic runtime environment modification. It encapsulates the common components of existing dynamic analysis systems and exposes a number of configurable hooks that can be programmed with a high level event-driven scripting language, called PUMAScript. This language cleanly separates analysis logic from exploration logic, allowing its users to (a) succinctly specify navigation hints for scalable app exploration and (b) separately specify the logic for analyzing the app properties.

This design has two distinct advantages. First, it can simplify the analysis of different app properties, since users do not need to develop the monkey, which is often the most challenging part of dynamic analysis. A related benefit is that the monkey can evolve independently of the analysis logic, so that monkey scaling and coverage improvements can be made available to all users. Second, PUMA can *multiplex* dynamic analyses: it can concurrently run similar analyses, resulting in better scaling of the dynamic analysis.

To validate the design of PUMA, we present the results of seven distinct analyses (many of which are presented in prior work) executed on 3,600 apps from Google Play (Section 4). The PUMAScripts for these analyses are each less than 100 lines of code; by contrast, DECAF [20] required over 4,000 lines of which over 70% was dedicated to app exploration. Our analyses are valuable in their own right, since they present fascinating insights into the app ecosystem: there appear to be a relatively small number (about 40) of common UI design patterns among Android apps; enabling content search for apps in the app store can increase the relevance of results and yield up to 50 additional results per query on average; over half of the apps violate accessibility guidelines; network usage requirements for apps vary by six orders of magnitude; and a quarter of all apps fail basic stress tests.

PUMA can be used in various settings. An app store can use PUMA: the store's app certification team can use it to verify that a newly submitted app does not violate any privacy and security policies, the advertising team can check if the app does not commit any ad fraud, the app store search engine can crawl app data for indexing, etc. Researchers interested in analyzing the app ecosystem can download PUMA and the apps of interest, customize PUMA for their target analysis, and conduct the analysis locally. A third-party can offer PUMA as a service where users can submit their analyses written in PUMAScript for analyzing the app ecosystems.

2. BACKGROUND AND MOTIVATION

In this section, we describe the unique requirements of large-scale studies of mobile apps and motivate the need for a programmable UI-based framework for supporting these studies. We also discuss the challenges associated with satisfying these requirements. In Section 3, we describe how PUMA addresses these challenges and requirements.

2.1 Dynamic Analysis of Mobile Apps

Dynamic analysis of software is performed by executing the software, subjecting it to different inputs, and recording (and subsequently analyzing) its internal states and outputs. Mobile apps have a unique structure that enables a novel form of dynamic analysis. By design, most mobile app actions are triggered by user interactions, such as clicks, swipes etc., through the user interface (UI). Mobile apps are also structured to enable such interactions: when the app is launched, a "home page" is shown that includes one or more *UI elements* (buttons, text boxes, other user interface elements). User interactions with these UI elements lead to other pages, which in turn may contain other UI elements. A user interaction may also result in local computation (*e.g.,* updating game state), network communication (*e.g.,* downloading ads or content), access to local sensors (*e.g.,* GPS), and access to local storage (*e.g.,* saving app state to storage). In the abstract, execution of a mobile app can be modeled as a transition graph where nodes represent various pages and edges represent transitions between pages. The goal of dynamic analysis is to navigate to all pages and to analyze apps' internal states and outputs at each page.

UI-Automation Frameworks. This commonality in the structure of mobile apps can be exploited to automatically analyze their dynamic properties. Recent research has done this using a UI automation framework, sometimes called a *monkey*, that systematically explores the app execution space. A monkey is a piece of software that runs on a mobile device or on an emulator, and extracts the user-interface structure of the current page (*e.g.,* the home page). This UI structure, analogous to the DOM structure of web pages, contains information about UI elements (buttons and other widgets) on the current page. Using this information, the monkey can, in an automated fashion, click a UI element, causing the app to transition to a new page. If the monkey has *not* visited this (or a similar) page, it can interact with the page by clicking its UI elements. Otherwise, it can click the "back" button to return to the previous page, and click another UI element to reach a different page.[1] In the abstract, each page corresponds to a *UI-state* and clicking a clickable UI element results in a state transition; using these, a monkey can effectively explore the UI-state transition graph.

2.2 Related Work on Dynamic Analysis of Mobile Apps

As discussed above, our work is an instance of a class of dynamic analysis frameworks. Such frameworks are widely used in software engineering for unit testing and random (fuzz) testing. The field of software testing is rather large, so we do not attempt to cover it; the interested reader is referred to [6].

Monkeys have been recently used to analyze several dynamic properties of mobile apps (Table 1). AMC [18] evaluates the conformance of vehicular apps to accessibility requirements; for example, apps need to be designed with large buttons and text, to minimize driving distractions. DECAF [20], detects violations of ad placement and content policies in over 50,000 apps. SmartAds [23] crawls contents from an app's pages to enable contextual

---

[1]Some apps do not include back buttons; this is discussed later.

205

System	Exploration Target	Page Transition Inputs	Properties Checked	Actions Taken	Instrumentation
AMC [18]	Distinct types of pages	UI events	Accessibility	None	No
DECAF [20]	Distinct types of pages containing ads	UI events	Ad layouts	None	No
SmartAds [23]	All pages	UI events	Page contents	None	Yes
A^{3}E [8]	Distinct types of pages	UI events	None	None	Yes
AppsPlayGround [24]	Distinct types of pages	UI events, Text inputs	Information flow	None	Yes
VanarSena [25]	Distinct types of pages	UI events, Text inputs	App crashes	Inject faults	Yes
ContextualFuzzing [19]	All pages	UI events	Crashes, performance	Change contexts	No
DynoDroid [22]	Code basic blocks	UI events, System events	App crashes	System inputs	No

Table 1: Recent work that has used a monkey tool for dynamic analysis

advertising for mobile apps. A^{3}E [8] executes and visits app pages to uncover potential bugs. AppsPlayground [24] examines information flow for potential privacy leaks in apps. VanarSena [25], ContextualFuzzing [19], and DynoDroid [22] try to uncover app crashes and performance problems by exposing them to various external exceptional conditions, such as bad network conditions.

At a high-level, these systems share a common feature: they use a monkey to automate dynamic app execution and use custom code to analyze a specific runtime property as the monkey visits various app states. At a lower level, however, they differ in at least the following five dimensions.

Exploration Target. This denotes what pages in an app are to be explored by the monkey. Fewer pages mean the monkey can perform the analysis faster, but that the analysis may be less comprehensive. AMC, A^{3}E, AppsPlayground, VanarSena aim to visit only pages of unique types. Their analysis goals do not require visiting two pages that are of same type but contain different contents (*e.g.,* two pages in a news app that are instantiated from the same page class but displays different news articles), and hence they omit exploring such pages for greater speed. On the other hand, SmartAds requires visiting all pages with unique content. DECAF can be configured to visit only the pages that are of unique types and that are likely to contain ads.

Page Transition Inputs. This denotes the inputs that the monkey provides to the app to cause transitions between pages. Most monkeys generate UI events, such as clicks and swipes, to move from one page to another. Some other systems, such as AppsPlayground and VanarSena, can provide text inputs to achieve a better coverage. DynoDroid can generate system inputs (*e.g.,* the "SMS received" event).

Properties Checked. This defines what runtime properties the analysis code checks. Different systems check different runtime properties depending on what their analysis logic requires. For example, DECAF checks various geometric properties of ads in the current page in order to identify ad fraud.

Actions Taken. This denotes what action the monkey takes at each page (other than transition inputs). While some systems do not take any actions, VanarSena, ContextualFuzzing, and DynoDroid create various contextual faults (*e.g.,* slow networks, bad user inputs) to check if the app crashes on those faults.

Instrumentation. This denotes whether the monkey runs an unmodified app or an instrumented app. VanarSena instruments apps before execution in order to identify a small set of pages to explore. SmartAds instruments apps to retrieve page contents.

Due to these differences, each work listed in Table 1 has developed its own automation components from scratch and tuned the tool to explore a specific property of the researchers' interest. The resulting tools have an intertwining of the app exploration logic and the logic required for analyzing the property of interest. This has meant that many of the advances developed to handle large-scale

studies are only utilizable in the context of the specific analyses and cannot be readily generalized to other analyses.

PUMA. As mentioned in Section 1, our goal is to build a generic framework called PUMA that enables scalable and programmable UI automation, and that can be customized for various types of dynamic analysis (including the ones in Table 1). PUMA separates the analysis logic from the automated navigation of the UI-state transition graph, allowing its users to (a) succinctly specify navigation hints for scalable app exploration and (b) separately specify the logic for analyzing the app properties. This has two distinct advantages. It can simplify the analysis of different app properties, since users do not need to develop UI automation components, and the UI automation framework can evolve independently of the analysis logic. As we discuss later, the design of scalable and robust state exploration can be tricky, and PUMA users can benefit from improvements to the underlying monkey, since their analysis code is decoupled from the monkey itself. Existing monkey tools only generate pseudo-random events and do not permit customization of navigation in ways that PUMA permits. Moreover, PUMA can concurrently run similar analyses, resulting in better scaling of the dynamic analysis. We discuss these advantages below.

2.3 Framework Requirements

Table 1 and the discussion above motivate the following requirements for a programmable UI-automation framework:

- *Support for a wide variety of properties*: The goal of using a UI-automation tool is to help users analyze app properties. But it is hard (if not impossible) for the framework to predefine a set of target properties that are going to be useful for all types of analyses. Instead, the framework should provide a set of necessary abstractions that can enable users to specify properties of interest at a high level.

- *Flexibility in state exploration*: The framework should allow users to customize the UI-state exploration. At a high-level, UI-state exploration decides which UI element to click next, and whether a (similar) state has been visited before. Permitting programmability of these decisions will allow analyses to customize the monkey behavior in flexible ways that can be optimized for the analysis at hand.

- *Programmable access to app state*: Many of the analyses in Table 1 require access to arbitrary app state, not just UI properties, such as the size of buttons or the layout of ads. Examples of app state include dynamic invocations of permissions, network or CPU usage at any given point, or even app-specific internal state.

- *Support for triggered actions*: Some of the analyses in Table 1 examine app robustness to changes in environmental conditions (*e.g.,* drastic changes to network bandwidth) or exceptional inputs. PUMA must support injecting these run-

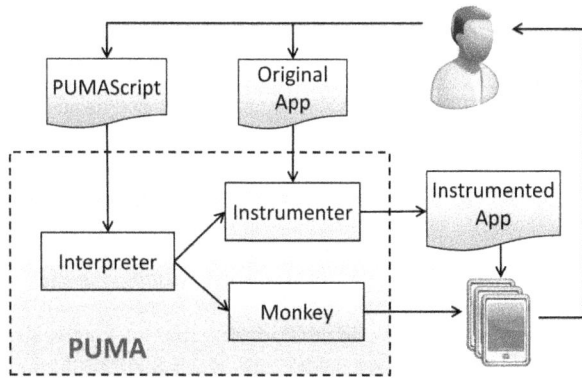

Figure 1: Overview of PUMA

time behaviors based on user-specified conditions (*e.g.,* change network availability just before any call to the network API).

These requirements raise significant research questions and challenges. For example, how can PUMA provide users with flexible and easy-to-use abstractions to specify properties that are unknown beforehand? Recall these properties can range from basic UI attributes to those that aim to diagnose various performance bottlenecks. Also, can it provide flexible control of the state exploration, given that the state space may be huge or even infinite? We now describe how PUMA meets these challenges.

3. PROGRAMMABLE UI-AUTOMATION

In this section, we describe PUMA, a programmable framework for dynamic analysis of mobile apps that satisfies the requirements listed in the previous section. We begin with an overview that describes how a user interacts with PUMA and the workflow within PUMA. We then discuss how users can specify analysis code using a PUMAScript, and then discuss the detailed design of PUMA and its internal algorithms. We conclude the section by describing our implementation of PUMA for Android.

3.1 PUMA Overview and Workflow

Figure 1 describes the overall workflow for PUMA. A user provides two pieces of information as input to PUMA. The first is a set of app binaries that the user wants to analyze. The second is the user-specified code, written in a language called PUMAScript[2]. The script contains all information needed for the dynamic analysis.

In the first step of PUMA's workflow, the *interpreter* component interprets the PUMAScript specification and recognizes two parts in the script: monkey-specific directives and app-specific directives. The former provides necessary inputs or hints on how apps will be executed by the monkey tool, which are then translated as input to our *programmable monkey* component. The latter dictates which parts of app code are relevant for analysis, and specifies what actions are to be taken when those pieces of code are executed. These app-specific directives are fed as input to an *app instrumenter* component.

The *app instrumenter* component statically analyzes the app to determine parts of app code relevant for analysis and instruments the app in a manner described below. The output of this component is the instrumented version of input app that adheres to the app-specific directives in PUMAScript.

---

[2]In the rest of paper, we will use PUMAScript to denote both the language used to write analysis code and the specification program itself; the usage will be clear from the context.

Then, the *programmable monkey* executes the instrumented version of each app, using the monkey-specific directives specified in the PUMAScript. PUMA is designed to execute the instrumented app either on a phone emulator, or on a mobile device. As a side effect of executing the app, PUMA may produce logs which contain outputs specified in the app-specific directives, as well outputs generated by the programmable monkey. Users can analyze these logs using analysis-specific code; such analysis code is not part of PUMA. In the remainder of this section, we describe these components of PUMA.

3.2 The PUMAScript Language

Our first design choice for PUMA was to either design a new domain-specific language for PUMAScript or implement it as an extension of some existing language. A new language is more general and can be compiled to run on multiple mobile platforms, but it may also incur a steeper learning curve. Instead, we chose the latter approach and implemented PUMAScript as a Java extension. This choice has its advantage of familiarity for programmers but also limits PUMA's applicability to some mobile platforms. However, we emphasize that the abstractions in our PUMAScript language are general enough and we should be able to port PUMA to other mobile platforms relatively easily, a task we have left to future work.

The next design challenge for PUMA was to identify abstractions that provide sufficient expressivity and enable a variety of analysis tasks, while still decoupling the mechanics of app exploration from analysis code. Our survey of related work in the area (Table 1) has influenced the abstractions discussed below.

Terminology. Before discussing the abstractions, we first introduce some terminology. The visual elements in a given page of the mobile app consist of one or more *UI element*. A UI element encapsulates a UI widget, and has an associated *geometry* as well as *content*. UI elements may have additional *attributes*, such as whether they are hidden or visible, clickable or not, etc.

The layout of a given page is defined by a *UI hierarchy*. Analogous to a DOM tree for a web page, a UI hierarchy describes parent-child relationships between elements. One can programmatically traverse the UI hierarchy to determine all the UI elements on a given page, together with their attributes and textual content (image or video content associated with a UI element is usually not available as part of the hierarchy).

The *UI state* of a given page is completely defined by its UI hierarchy. In some cases, it might be desirable to define a more general notion of the state of an app page, which includes the internal program state of an app together with the UI hierarchy. To distinguish it from UI state, we use the term *total state* of a given app.

Given this discussion, a monkey can be said to perform a state traversal: when it performs a *UI action* on a UI element (*e.g.,* clicks a button), it initiates a state transition which may, in general, cause a completely different app page (and hence UI state) to be loaded. When this loading completes, the app is said to have reached a new state.

PUMAScript Design. PUMAScript is an event-based programming language. It allows programmers to specify *handlers* for *events*. In general, an event is an abstraction for a specific point in the execution either of the monkey or of a specific app. A handler for an event is an arbitrary piece of code that may perform various actions: it can keep and update internal state variables, modify the environment (by altering system settings), and, in some cases, access UI state or total state. This paradigm is an instance of aspect-oriented programming, where the analysis concerns are cleanly separated from app traversal and execution. The advantage of having a scriptable specification, aside from conciseness, is that it is possible (as shown in Section 3.3) to optimize joint concurrent execution of multiple PUMAScripts, thereby enabling testing of more apps within a given amount of time.

PUMAScript defines two kinds of events: *monkey-specific* events and *app-specific* events.

Monkey-specific Events. A monkey-specific event encapsulates a specific point in the execution of a monkey. A monkey is a conceptually simple tool[3], and Alg. (1) describes the pseudo-code for a generic monkey, as generalized from the uses of the monkey described in prior work (Table 1). The highlighted names in the pseudo-code are PUMA APIs that will be explained later. The monkey starts at an initial state (corresponding to its home page) for an app, and visits other states by deciding which UI action to perform (line 8), and performing the click (line 12). This UI action will, in general, result in a new state (line 13), and the monkey needs to decide whether this state has been visited before (line 15). Once a state has been fully explored, it is no longer considered in the exploration (lines 19-20).

Algorithm 1 Generic monkey tool. PUMA APIs for configurable steps are highlighted.

```
 1:  while not all apps have been explored do
 2:      pick a new app
 3:      S ← empty stack
 4:      push initial page to S
 5:      while S is not empty do
 6:          pop an unfinished page s_i from S
 7:          go to page s_i
 8:          pick next clickable UI element from s_i // Next-Click
 9:          if user input is needed (e.g., login/password) then
10:              provide user input by emulating keyboard clicks // Text Input
11:          effect environmental changes // Modifying Environment
12:          perform the click
13:          wait for next page s_j to load
14:          analyze page s_j // In-line Analysis
15:          flag ← s_j is equivalent to an explored page // State-Equivalence
16:          if not flag then
17:              add s_j to S
18:          update finished clicks for s_i
19:          if all clicks in s_i are explored then
20:              remove s_i from S
21:          flag ← monkey has used too many resources // Terminating App
22:          if flag or S is empty then
23:              terminate this app
```

In this algorithm, most of the steps are mechanistic, but six steps involve *policy* decisions. The first is the decision of whether a state has been visited before (Line 15): prior work in Table 1 has observed that it is possible to reduce app exploration time with analysis-specific definitions of *state-equivalence*. The second is the decision of which UI action to perform next (Line 8): prior work in Table 1 has proposed using out-of-band information to *direct* exploration more efficiently, rather than randomly selecting UI actions. The third is a specification of user-input (Line 10): some apps require some forms of text input (*e.g.,* a Facebook or Google login). The fourth is a decision (Line 11) of whether to modify the environment as the app page loads: for example, one prior work [25] modifies network state to reduce bandwidth, with the aim of analyzing the robustness of apps to sudden resource availability changes. The fifth is analysis (Line 14): some prior work has performed in-line analysis (*e.g.,* ad fraud detection [20]). Finally, the sixth is the decision of whether to terminate an app (Line 21): prior work in Table 1

has used fixed timeouts, but other policies are possible (*e.g.,* after a fixed number of states have been explored). PUMAScript separates policy from mechanism by modeling these six steps as events, described below. When these events occur, user-defined handlers are executed.

(1) State-Equivalence. This abstraction provides a customizable way of specifying whether states are classified as equivalent or not. The inputs to the handler for a state-equivalence event include: the newly visited state s_j, and the set of previously visited states S. The handler should return `true` if this new state is equivalent to some previously visited state in S, and `false` otherwise.

This capability permits an arbitrary definition of state equivalence. At one extreme, two states s_i and s_j are equivalent only if their total states are identical. A handler can code this by traversing the UI hierarchies of both states, and comparing UI elements in the hierarchy pairwise; it can also, in addition, compare program internal state pairwise.

However, several pieces of work have pointed out that this strict notion of equivalence may not be necessary in all cases. Often, there is a trade-off between resource usage and testing coverage. For example, to detect ad violations, it suffices to treat two states as equivalent if their UI hierarchies are "similar" in the sense that they have the same kinds of UI elements. Handlers can take one of two approaches to define such fuzzier notions of equivalence.

They can implement app-specific notions of similarity. For example, if an analysis were only interested in UI properties of specific types of buttons (like [18]), it might be sufficient to declare two states to be equivalent if one had at least one instance of each type of UI element present in the other.

A more generic notion of state equivalence can be obtained by collecting *features* derived from states, then defining similarity based on distance metrics for the feature space. In DECAF [20], we defined a generic feature vector encoding the structure of the UI hierarchy, then used the cosine-similarity metric[4] with a user-specified similarity threshold, to determine state equivalence. This state equivalence function is built into PUMA, so a PUMAScript handler can simply invoke this function with the appropriate threshold.

A handler may also define a different set of features, or different similarity metrics. The exploration of which features might be appropriate, and how similarity thresholds affect state traversal is beyond the scope of this work.

(2) Next-Click. This event permits handlers to customize how to specify which element to click next. The input to a handler is the current UI state, together with the set of UI elements that have already been clicked before. A handler should return a pointer to the next UI element to click.

Handlers can implement a wide variety of policies with this flexibility. A simple policy may decide to explore UI elements sequentially, which may have good coverage, but increase exploration time. Alternatively, a handler may want to maximize the *types* of elements clicked; prioritizing UI elements of different types over instances of a type of UI element that has been clicked before. These two policies are built into PUMA for user convenience.

Handlers can also use out-of-band information to implement *directed exploration*. Analytics from real users can provide insight into how real users prioritize UI actions: for example, an expert user may rarely click a *Help* button. Insights like these, or even actual traces from users, can be used to direct exploration to visit states that are more likely to be visited by real users. Another input to directed exploration is static analysis: the static analysis may reveal that button A can lead to a particular event handler that sends

---

[3]However, as discussed later, the implementation of a monkey can be significantly complex.

[4]http://en.wikipedia.org/wiki/Cosine_similarity

a HTTP request, which is of interest to the specific analysis task at hand. The handler can then prioritize the click of button A in every visited state.

(3) Text Input. The handler of this event provides the text input required for exploration to proceed. Often, apps require login-based authentication to some cloud-service before permitting use of the app. The input to the handler are the UI state and the text box UI element which requires input. The handler's output includes the corresponding text (login, password *etc.*), using which the monkey can emulate keyboard actions to generate the text. If the handler for this event is missing, and exploration encounters a UI element that requires text input, the monkey stops exploring the app.

(4) Modifying the Environment. This event is triggered just before the monkey clicks a UI element. The corresponding handler for this event takes as input the current UI state, and the UI element to be clicked. Based on this information, the handler may enable or disable devices, dynamically change network availability using a network emulator, or change other aspects of the environment in order to stress-test apps. This kind of modification is coarse-grained, in the sense that it occurs before the entire page is loaded. It is also possible to perform more fine-grained modifications (*e.g.,* reducing network bandwidth just before accessing the network) using app-specific events, described below. If a handler for this event is not specified, PUMA skips this step.

(5) In-line Analysis. The in-line analysis event is triggered after a new state has completed loading. The handler for this event takes as input the current total state; the handler can use the total state information to perform analysis-specific computations. For example, an ad fraud detector can analyze the layout of the UI hierarchy to ensure compliance to ad policies [20]. A PUMAScript may choose to forgo this step and perform all analyses off-line; PUMA outputs the explored state transition graph together with the total states for this purpose.

(6) Terminating App Exploration. Depending on the precise definition of state equivalence, the number of states in the UI state transition graph can be practically limitless. A good example of this is an app that shows news items. Each time the app page that lists news items is visited, a new news item may be available which may cause the state to be technically not equivalent to any previously visited state. To counter such cases, most prior research has established practical limits on how long to explore an app. PUMA provides a default *timeout* handler for the termination decision event, which terminates an app after its exploration has used up a certain amount of wall-clock time. A PUMAScript can also define other handlers that make termination decisions based on the number of states visited, or CPU, network, or energy resources used.

App-specific Events. In much the same way that monkey-specific events abstract specific points in the execution of a generic monkey, an *app-specific event* abstracts a specific point in app code. Unlike monkey-specific events, which are predetermined because of the relative simplicity of a generic monkey, app-specific events must be user-defined since it is not known a priori what kinds of instrumentation tasks will be needed. In a PUMAScript, an app-specific event is defined by naming an event and associating the named event with a codepoint set [16]. A codepoint set is a set of instructions (*e.g.,* bytecodes or invocations of arbitrary functions) in the app binary, usually specified as a regular expression on class names, method names, or names of specific bytecodes. Thus, a codepoint set defines a set of points in the app binary where the named event may be said to occur.

Once named events have been described, a PUMAScript can associate arbitrary handlers with these named events. These handlers

```
1  class NetworkProfiler extends PUMAScript {
2    boolean compareState(UIState s1, UIState s2) {
3      return MonkeyInputFactory.stateStructureMatch(s1,
           s2, 0.95);
4    }
5    int getNextClick(UIState s) {
6      return MonkeyInputFactory.nextClickSequential(s);
7    }
8    void specifyInstrumentation() {
9      Set<CodePoint> userEvent;
10     CPFinder.setBytecode("invoke.*", "HTTPClient.
           execute(HttpUriRequest request)");
11     userEvent = CPFinder.apply();
12     for (CodePoint cp : userEvent) {
13       UserCode code = new UserCode("Logger", "
             countRequest", CPARG);
14       Instrumenter.place(code, BEFORE, cp);
15       code = new UserCode("Logger", "countResponse",
             CPARG);
16       Instrumenter.place(code, AFTER, cp);
17     }
18   }
19 }
20 class Logger {
21   void countRequest (HttpUriRequest req) {
22     Log(req.getRequestLine().getUri().getLength());
23   }
24   void countResponse (HttpResponse resp) {
25     Log(resp.getEntity().getContentLength());
26   }
27 }
```

Listing 1: Network usage profiler

have access to app-internal state and can manipulate program state, can output state information to the output logs, and can also perform finer-grained environmental modifications.

A Sample PUMAScript. Listing 1 shows a PUMAScript designed to count the network usage of apps. A PUMAScript is effectively a Java extension, where a specific analysis is described by defining a new class inherited from a `PUMAScript` base class. This class (in our example, `NetworkProfiler`) defines handlers for monkey-specific events (lines 2-7), and also defines events and associated handlers for app-specific events. It uses the inbuilt feature-based similarity detector with a threshold that permits fuzzy state equivalence (line 3), and uses the default next-click function, which traverses each UI element in each state sequentially (line 6). It defines one app-specific event, which is triggered whenever execution invokes the `HTTPClient` library (lines 10-11), and defines two handlers, one (line 21) before the occurrence of the event (*i.e.,* the invocation) and another after (line 24) the occurrence of the event. These handlers respectively log the size of the network request and response. The total network usage of an app can be obtained by post-facto analysis of the log.

3.3 PUMA Design

PUMA incorporates a generic monkey (Alg. (1)), together with support for events and handlers. One or more PUMAScripts are input to PUMA, together with the apps to be analyzed. The PUMAScript interpreter instruments each app in a manner designed to trigger the app-specific events. One way to do this is to instrument apps to transfer control back to PUMA when the specified code point is reached. The advantage of this approach is that app-specific handlers can then have access to the explored UI states, but it would have made it harder for PUMA to expose app-specific internal state. Instead, PUMA chooses to instrument apps so that app-specific handlers are executed directly within the app context; this way, handlers have access to arbitrary program state information. For example, in line 22 of Listing 1, the handler can access the size of the HTTP request made by the app.

After each app has been instrumented, PUMA executes the algorithm described in Alg. (1), but with explicit events and associated handlers. The six monkey-specific event handlers are highlighted in Alg. (1) and are invoked at relevant points. Because app-specific event handlers are instrumented within app binaries, they are implicitly invoked when a specific UI element has been clicked (line 12).

PUMA can also execute multiple PUMAScripts concurrently. This capability provides scaling of the analyses, since each app need only be run once. However, arbitrary concurrent execution is not possible, and concurrently executed scripts must satisfy two sets of conditions.

Consider two PUMAScripts A and B. In most cases, these scripts can be run concurrently only if the handlers for each monkey-specific event for A are identical to or a strict subset of the handlers for B. For example, consider the state equivalence handler: if A's handler visits a superset of the states visited by A and B, then, it is safe to concurrently execute A and B. Analogously, the next-click handler for A must be identical with that of B, and the text input handler for both must be identical (otherwise, the monkey would not know which text input to use). However, the analysis handler for the two scripts can (and will) be different, because this handler does not alter the sequence of the monkey's exploration. By a similar reasoning, for A and B to be run concurrently, their app-specific event handlers must be disjoint (they can also be identical, but that is less interesting since that means the two scripts are performing identical analyses), and they must either modify the environment in the same way or not modify the environment at all.

In our evaluation, we demonstrate this concurrent PUMAScript execution capability. In future work, we plan to derive static analysis methods by which the conditions outlined in the previous paragraph can be tested, so that it may be possible to automate the decision of whether two PUMAScripts can run concurrently. Finally, this static analysis can be simplified by providing, as PUMA does, default handlers for various events.

3.4 Implementation of PUMA for Android

We have designed PUMA to be broadly applicable to different mobile computing platforms. The abstractions PUMA uses are generic and should be extensible to different programming languages. However, we have chosen to instantiate PUMA for the Android platform because of its popularity and the volume of active research that has explored Android app dynamics.

The following paragraphs describe some of the complexity of implementing PUMA in Android. Much of this complexity arises because of the lack of a complete native UI automation support in Android.

Defining a Page State. The UI state of an app, defined as the current topmost foreground UI hierarchy, is central to PUMA. The UI state might represent part of a screen (*e.g.,* a pop-up dialog window), a single screen, or more than one screen (*e.g.,* a webview that needs scrolling to finish viewing). Thus, in general, a UI state may cover sections of an app page that are not currently visible.

In Android, the UI hierarchy for an app's page can be obtained from `hierarchyviewer` [1] or the `uiautomator` [2] tool. We chose the latter because it supports many Android devices and has built-in support for UI event generation and handling, while the former only works on systems with debugging support (*e.g.,* special developer phones from google) and needs an additional UI event generator. However, we had to modify the `uiautomator` to intercept and access the UI hierarchy programmatically (the default tool only allows dumping and storing the UI state to external storage). The `uiautomator` can also report the UI hierarchy for

widgets that are generated dynamically, as long as they support the `AccessibilityService` like default Android UI widgets.

Supporting Page Scrolling. Since smartphones have small screens, it is common for apps to add scrolling support to allow users to view all the contents in a page. However, `uiautomator` only returns the part of the UI hierarchy currently visible. To overcome this limitation, PUMA scrolls down till the end of the screen, extracts the UI hierarchy in each view piecemeal, and merges these together to obtain a composite UI hierarchy that represents the UI state. This turns out to be tricky for pages that can be scrolled vertically and/or horizontally, since `uiautomator` does not report the direction of scrollability for each UI widget. For those that are scrollable, PUMA first checks whether they are horizontally or vertically scrollable (or both). Then, it follows a zig-zag pattern (scrolls horizontally to the right end, vertically down one view, then horizontally to the left end) to cover the non-visible portions of the current page. To merge the scrolled states, PUMA relies on the `AccessibilityEvent` listener to intercept the scrolling response, which contains hints for merging. For example, for `ListView`, this listener reports the start and the end entry indices in the scrolled view; for `ScrollView` and `WebView`, it reports the co-ordinate offsets with respect to the global coordinate.

Detecting Page Loading Completion. Android does not have a way to determine when a page has been completely loaded. State loading can take arbitrary time, especially if its content needs to be fetched over the network. PUMA uses a heuristic that detects page loading completion based on `WINDOW_CONTENT_CHANGED` events signaled by the OS, since this event is fired whenever there is a content change or update in the current view. For example, a page that relies on network data to update its UI widgets will trigger one such event every time it receives new data that causes the widget to be rendered. PUMA considers a page to be completely loaded when there is no content-changed event in a window of time that is conservatively determined from the inter-arrival times of previous content-changed events.

Instrumenting Apps. PUMA uses SIF [16] in the backend to instrument app binaries. However, other tools that are capable of instrumenting Android app binaries can also be used.

Environment Modifications by Apps. We observed that when PUMA runs apps sequentially on one device, it is possible that an app may change the environment (*e.g.,* some apps turn off WiFi during their execution), affecting subsequent apps. To deal with this, PUMA restores the environment (turning on WiFi, enabling GPS, etc.) after completing each app, and before starting the next one.

Implementation Limitations. Currently, our implementation uses Android's `uiautomator` tool that is based on the underlying `AccessibilityService` in the OS. So any UI widgets that do not support such service cannot be supported by our tool. For example, some user-defined widgets do not use any existing Android UI support at all, so are inaccessible to PUMA. However, in our evaluations described later, we find relatively few instances of apps that use user-defined widgets, likely because of Android's extensive support for UI programming.

Finally, PUMA does not support non-deterministic UI events like random swipes, or other customized user gestures, which are fundamental problems for any monkey-based automation tool. In particular, this limitation rules out analysis of games, which is an important category of Android apps. To our knowledge, no existing monkeys have overcome this limitation. It may be possible to overcome this limitation by passively observing real users and "learning" user-interface actions, but we have left this to future work.

4. EVALUATION

The primary motivation for PUMA is rapid development of large-scale dynamic mobile app analyses. In this section, we validate that PUMA enables this capability: *in a space of two weeks, we were able to develop 7 distinct analyses and execute each of them on a corpus of 3,600 apps.* Beyond demonstrating this, our evaluations provide novel insights into the Android app ecosystem. Before discussing these analyses, we discuss our methodology.

4.1 Methodology

Apps. We downloaded 18,962 top free apps[5], in 35 categories, from the Google Play store with an app crawler [4] that implements the Google Play API. Due to the incompleteness of the Dalvik to Java translator tool we use for app instrumentation [16], some apps failed the bytecode translation process, and we removed those apps. Then based on the app name, we removed foreign-language apps, since some of our analyses are focused on English language apps, as we discuss later. We also removed apps in the game, social, or wallpaper categories, since they either require many non-deterministic UI actions or do not have sufficient app logic code (some wallpaper apps have no app code at all). These filtering steps resulted in a pool of 9,644 apps spread over 23 categories, from which we randomly selected 3,600 apps for the experiments below. This choice was dictated by time constraints for our evaluation.

Emulators vs Phones. We initially tried to execute PUMA on emulators running concurrently on a single server. Android emulators were either too slow or unstable, and concurrency was limited by the performance of graphics cards on the server. Accordingly, our experiments use 11 phones, each running an instance of PUMA: 5 Galaxy Nexus, 5 HTC One, and 1 Galaxy S3, all running Android 4.3. The corpus of 3,600 apps is partitioned across these phones, and the PUMA instance on each phone evaluates the apps in its partition sequentially. PUMA is designed to work on emulators as well, so it may be possible to scale the analyses by running multiple cloud instances of the emulator when the robustness of the emulators improves.

4.2 PUMA Scalability and Expressivity

To evaluate PUMA's expressivity and scalability, we used it to implement seven distinct dynamic analyses. Table 2 lists these analyses. In subsequent subsections, we describe these analyses in more detail, but first we make a few observations about these analyses and about PUMA in general.

First, we executed PUMAScripts for three of these analyses concurrently: UI structure classifier, ad fraud detection, and accessibility violation detection. These three analyses use similar notions of state equivalence and do not require any instrumentation. We could also have run the PUMAScripts for network usage profiler and permission usage profiler concurrently, but did not do so for logistical reasons. These apps use similar notions of state equivalence and perform complementary kinds of instrumentation; the permission usage profiler also instruments network calls, but in a way that does not affect the network usage profiler. We have verified this through a small-scale test of 100 apps: the combined analyses give the same results as the individual analyses, but use only the resources required to run one analysis. In future work, we plan to design an optimizer that automatically determines whether two PUMAScripts can be run concurrently and performs inter-script optimizations for concurrent analyses.

Second, we note that for the majority of our analyses, it suffices to have fuzzier notions of state equivalence. Specifically, these analyses declare two states to be equivalent if the cosine similarity between feature vectors derived from each UI structure is above a specified threshold. In practice, this means that two states whose pages have different content, but similar UI structure, will be considered equivalent. This is shown in Table 2, with the value "structural" in the "State-Equivalence" column. For these analyses, *we are able to run the analysis to completion for each of our 3,600 apps: i.e.,* the analysis terminates when all applicable UI elements have been explored. For the single analysis that required an identical match, we had to limit the exploration of an app to 20 minutes. This demonstrates the importance of exposing programmable state equivalence in order to improve the scalability of analyses.

Third, PUMA enables extremely compact descriptions of analyses. Our largest PUMAScript is about 20 lines of code. Some analyses require non-trivial code in user-specified handlers; this is labeled "user code" in Table 2. The largest handler is 60 lines long. So, for most analyses, less than 100 lines is sufficient to explore fairly complex properties. In contrast, the implementation of DECAF [20] was over 4,300 lines of code, almost *50× higher*; almost 70% of this code went towards implementing the monkey functionality. Note that, some analyses require post-processing code; we do not count this in our evaluation of PUMA's expressivity, since that code is presumably comparable for when PUMA is used or when a hand-crafted monkey is used.

Finally, another measure of scalability is the speed of the monkey. PUMA's programmable monkey explored 15 apps per hour per phone, so in about 22 hours we were able to run our structural similarity analysis on the entire corpus of apps. This rate is faster than the rates reported in prior work [18, 20]. The monkey was also able to explore about 65 app *states* per hour per phone for a total of over 100,000 app states across all 7 analyses. As discussed above, PUMA ran to completion for our structural similarity-based analyses for every app. However, we do not evaluate coverage, since our exploration techniques are borrowed from prior work [20] and that work has evaluated the coverage of these techniques.

4.3 Analysis 1: Accessibility Violation Detection

Best practices in app development include guidelines for app design, either for differently-abled people or for use in environments with minimal interaction time requirements (*e.g.,* in-vehicle use). Beyond these guidelines, it is desirable to have automated tests for *accessibility compliance*, as discussed in prior work [18]. From an app store administrator's perspective, it is important to be able to classify apps based on their accessibility support so that users can be more informed in their app choices. For example, elderly persons who have a choice of several email apps may choose the ones that are more accessible (*e.g.,* those that have large buttons with enough space between adjacent buttons.)

In this dynamic analysis, we use PUMA to detect a subset of accessibility violations studied in prior work [18]. Specifically, we flag the following violations: if a state contains more than 100 words; if it contains a button smaller than $80mm^2$; if it contains two buttons whose centers are less than 15mm apart; and if it contains a scrollable UI widget. We also check if an app requires a significant number of user interactions to achieve a task by computing the maximum shortest *round-trip path* between any two UI states based on the transition graph generated during monkey exploration.

This prior work includes other accessibility violations: detecting distracting animations can require a human in the loop, and is not

---

[5]The versions of these apps are those available on Oct 3, 2013.

	Properties Studied	State-Equivalence	App Instrumentation	PUMAScript (LOC)	User Code (LOC)
Accessibility violation detection	UI accessibility violation	structural	no	11	60
Content-based app search	in-app text crawling	exact	no	14	0
UI structure classifier	structural similarity in UI	structural	no	11	0
Ad fraud detection	ad policy violation	structural	no	11	52
Network usage profiler	runtime network usage	structural	yes	19	8
Permission usage profiler	permission usage	structural	yes	20	5
Stress testing	app robustness	structural	yes	16	5

Table 2: List of analyses implemented with PUMA

	user actions per task	words count	button size	button distance	scrolling
#apps	475	552	1276	1147	2003
	1 type	2 types	3 types	4 types	5 types
#apps	752	683	656	421	223

Table 3: Accessibility violation results

suitable for the scale that PUMA targets; and analyzing the text contrast ratio requires OS modifications. Our work scales this analysis to a much larger number of apps (3,600 vs. 12) than the prior work, demonstrating some of the benefits of PUMA.

Our PUMAScript has 11 lines of code (shown in Listing 2), and is similar in structure to ad fraud detection. It uses structural matching for state equivalence, and detects these accessibility violations using an in-line analysis handler AMCChecker.inspect().

Table 3 shows the number of apps falling into different categories of violations, and the number of apps with more than one type of violation. We can see that 475 apps have maximum round-trip paths greater than 10 (the threshold used in [18]), 552 for word count, 1,276 for button size, 1,147 for button distance and 2,003 for scrolling. Thus, almost 55% of our apps violate the guideline that suggests not having a scrollable widget to improve accessibility. About one third of the violating apps have only one type of violation and less than one third have two or three types of violations. Less than one tenth of the apps violate all five properties.

This suggests that most apps in current app stores are not designed with general accessibility or vehicular settings in mind. An important actionable result from our findings is that our analyses can be used to automatically tag apps for "accessibility friendliness" or "vehicle unfriendliness". Such tags can help users find relevant apps more easily, and may incentivize developers to target apps towards segments of users with special needs.

4.4 Analysis 2: Content-based App Search

All app stores allow users to search for apps. To answer user queries, stores index various app metadata: *e.g.,* app name, category, developer-provided description, etc. That index does not use app content—content that an app reveals at runtime to users. Thus, a search query (*e.g.,* for a specific recipe) can fail if the query does not match any metadata, even though the query might match the dynamic runtime content of some of these apps (*e.g.,* culinary apps).

One solution to the above limitation is to crawl app content by dynamic analysis and index this content as well. We program PUMA to achieve this. Our PUMAScript for this analysis contains 14 lines of code (shown in Listing 3) and specifies a strong notion of state equivalence: two states are equivalent only if their UI hierarchies are identical and their contents are identical. Since the content of a given page can change dynamically, even during exploration, the exploration may, in theory, never terminate. So, we limit each app to run for 20 minutes (using PUMA's terminating app exploration

event handler). Finally, the PUMAScript scrapes the textual content from the UI hierarchy in each state and uses the in-line analysis event handler to log this content.

We then post-process this content to build three search indices: one that uses the app name alone, a second that includes the developer's description, and a third that also includes the crawled content. We use Apache Lucene[6], an open-source full-featured text search engine, for this purpose.

We now demonstrate the efficacy of content-based search for apps. For this, we use two search-keyword datasets to evaluate the generated indices: (1) 200 most popular app store queries[7] and (2) a trace of 10 million queries from the Bing search engine. By re-playing those queries on the three indices, we find (Table 4) that the index with crawled content yields at least 4% more non-empty queries than the one which uses app metadata alone. More importantly, on average, each query returns about 50 more apps (from our corpus of 3,600) for the app store queries and about 100 more apps for the Bing queries.

Here are some concrete examples that demonstrate the value of indexing dynamic app content. For the search query "jewelery deals", the metadata-based index returned many "deals" and "jewelery" apps, while the content-based index returned as the top result an app (*Best Deals*) that was presumably advertising a deal for a jewelry store[8]. Some queries (*e.g.,* "xmas" and "bejeweled") returned no answers from the metadata-based index, but the content-based index returned several apps that seemed to be relevant on manual inspection. These examples show that app stores can greatly improve search relevance by crawling and indexing dynamic app content, and PUMA provides a simple way to crawl the data.

4.5 Analysis 3: UI Structure Classifier

In this analysis, we program PUMA to cluster apps based on their UI state transition graphs so that apps within the same cluster have the same "look and feel". The clusters can be used as input to clone detection algorithms [14], reducing the search space for clones: the intuition here is that the UI structure is the easiest part to clone and cloned apps might have very similar UI structures to the original one. Moreover, developers who are interested in improving the UI design of their own apps can selectively examine a few apps within the same cluster as theirs and do not need to exhaustively explore the complete app space.

The PUMAScript for this analysis is only 11 lines (shown in Listing 4) and uses structural page similarity to define state equivalence. It simply logs UI states in the *in-line analysis* event handler. After the analysis, for each app, we represent its UI state transition graph by a binary adjacency matrix, then perform Singular

---

[6] http://lucene.apache.org/core/

[7] http://goo.gl/JGyO5P

[8] In practice, for search to be effective, apps with dynamic content need to be crawled periodically.

Keyword Type	Number	Search Type	Rate of Queries with Valid Search Return (≥ 1)	Statistics of Valid Return			
				Min	Max	Mean	Median
App Store Popular Keywords	200	Name	68%	1	115	17	4
		Name + Desc.	93%	1	1234	156.54	36.50
		Name + Desc. + Crawl	97%	1	1473	200.46	46
Bing Trace Search Keywords	9.5 million	Name	54.09%	1	311	8.31	3
		Name + Desc.	81.68%	1	2201	199.43	66
		Name + Desc. + Crawl	85.51%	1	2347	300.37	131

Table 4: Search results

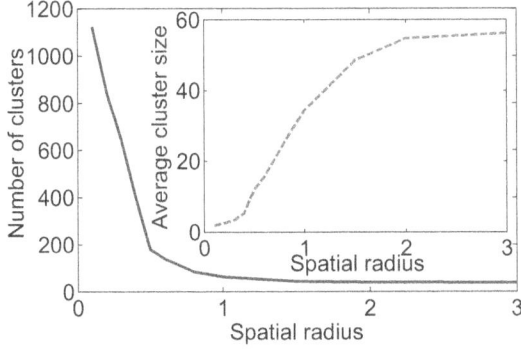

Figure 2: App clustering for UI structure classification

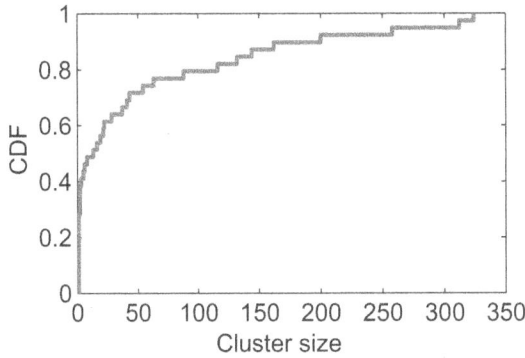

Figure 3: Cluster size for $r_{spatial} = 3$

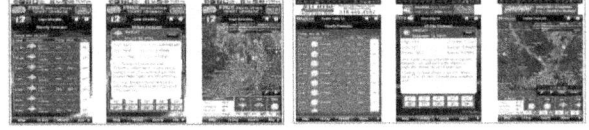

Figure 4: An app clone example (one app per rectangle)

Following the above process, Figure 2 shows the number of clusters and average apps per cluster for different spatial radii. As the radius increases, each cluster becomes larger and the number of clusters decreases, as expected. The number of clusters stabilizes beyond a certain radius and reaches 38 for a radius of 3. The CDF of cluster size for $r_{spatial} = 3$ is shown in Figure 3. By manually checking a small set of apps, we confirm that apps in the same cluster have pages with very similar UI layouts and transition graphs.

Our analysis reveals a few interesting findings. First, there exists a relatively small number of UI design patterns (*i.e.*, clusters). Second, the number of apps in each cluster can be quite different (Figure 3), ranging from one app per cluster to more than 300 apps, indicating that some UI design patterns are more common than the others. Third, preliminary evaluations also suggest that most apps from a developer fall into the same cluster; this is perhaps not surprising given that developers specialize in categories of apps and likely reuse significant portion of their code across apps. Finally, manual verification reveals the existence of app clones For example, Figure 4 shows two apps from one cluster have nearly the same UI design with slightly different color and button styles, but developed by different developers[11].

4.6 Analysis 4: Ad Fraud Detection

Recent work [20] has used dynamic analysis to detect various *ad layout frauds* for Windows Store apps, by analyzing geometry (size, position, etc.) of ads during runtime. Examples of such frauds include (a) hidden ads: ads hidden behind other UI controls so the apps appear to be ad-free; (b) intrusive ads: ads placed very close to or partially behind clickable controls to trigger inadvertent clicks; (c) too many ads: placing too many ads in a single page; (d) small ads: ads too small to see. We program PUMA to detect similar frauds in Android apps.

Our PUMAScript for ad fraud detection catches small, intrusive, and too many ads per page. We have chosen not to implement detection of hidden ads on Android, since, unlike Microsoft's ad network [5], Google's ad network does not pay developers for ad impressions [3], and only pays them by ad clicks, so there is no incentive for Android developers to hide ads.

Our PUMAScript requires 11 lines (shown in Listing 5) and uses structural match for state equivalence. It checks for ad frauds within the in-line analysis handler; this requires about 52 lines of code.

Value Decomposition[9] (SVD) on the matrix, and extract the Singular Value Vector. SVD techniques have been widely used in many areas such as general classification, pattern recognition and signal processing. Since the singular vector has been sorted by the importance of singular values, we only keep those vector elements (called *primary singular values*) which are greater than ten times the first element. Finally, the Spectral Clustering[10] algorithm is employed to cluster those app vectors, with each entry of the similarity matrix being defined as follows:

$$m_{ij} = \begin{cases} 0 & , dim(\mathbf{v}_i) \neq dim(\mathbf{v}_j) \text{ or } d_{ij} > r_{spatial} \\ e^{-d_{ij}} & , \text{otherwise} \end{cases}$$

where $\mathbf{v}_i$ and $\mathbf{v}_j$ are the singular vectors of two different apps i and j, and d_{ij} is the Euclidean distance between them. $dim()$ gives the vector dimension, and we only consider two apps to be in a same cluster if the cardinality of their primary singular values are the same. Finally, the radius $r_{spatial}$ is a tunable parameter for the algorithm: the larger the radius, the further out the algorithm searches for clusters around a given point (singular vector).

---

[9]http://en.wikipedia.org/wiki/Singular_value_decomposition
[10]http://en.wikipedia.org/wiki/Spectral_clustering

---

[11]We emphasize that clone detection requires sophisticated techniques well beyond UI structure matching; designing clone detection algorithms is beyond the scope of this paper.

violation	small	many	intrusive	1 type	2 types	3 types
#apps	13	7	10	3	3	7

Table 5: Ad fraud results

This handler traverses the UI view tree, searches for the WebView generated by ads, and checks its size and relationship with other clickable UI elements. It outputs all the violations found in each UI state.

Table 5 lists the number of apps that have one or more violations. About 13 out of our 3,600 apps violate ad policies. Furthermore, all 13 apps have small ads which can improve user experience by devoting more screen real estate to the app, but can reduce the visibility of the ad and adversely affect the advertiser. Seven apps show more than one ad on at least one of their pages, and 10 apps display ads in a different position than required by ad networks. Finally, if we examine violations by type, 7 apps exhibit all three violations, 3 apps exhibit one and 3 exhibit two violations.

These numbers appear to be surprisingly small, compared to results reported in [20]. To understand this, we explored several explanations. First, we found that the Google AdMob API enforces ad size, number and placement restrictions, so developers cannot violate these policies. Second, we found that 10 of our 13 violators use ad providers other than AdMob, like millennialmedia, medialets and LeadBolt. These providers' API gives developers the freedom to customize ad sizes, conflicting with AdMob's policy of predefined ad size. We also found that, of the apps that did not exhibit ad fraud, only about half used AdMob and the rest used a wide variety of ad network providers. Taken together, these findings suggest that the likely reason the incidence of ad fraud is low in Android is that developers have little incentive to cheat, since AdMob pays for clicks and not impressions (all the frauds we tested for are designed to inflate impressions). In contrast, the occurrence of ad fraud in Windows phones is much higher because (a) 90% of the apps use the Microsoft ad network, (b) that network's API allows developers to customize ads, and (c) the network pays both for impressions and clicks.

4.7 Analysis 5: Network Usage Profiler

About 62% of the apps in our corpus need to access resources from the Internet to function. This provides a rough estimate of the number of cloud-enabled mobile apps in the Android marketplace, and is an interesting number in its own right. But beyond that, it is important to quantify the network usage of these apps, given the prevalence of usage-limited cellular plans, and the energy cost of network communication [15].

PUMA can be used to approximate the network usage of an app by dynamically executing the app and measuring the total number of bytes transferred. Our PUMAScript for this has 19 lines of code (shown in Listing 1), and demonstrates PUMA's ability to specify app instrumentation. This script specifies structural matching for state equivalence; this can undercount the network usage of the app, since PUMA would not visit similar states. Thus, our results present lower bounds for network usage of apps. To count network usage, our PUMAScript specifies a user-defined event that is triggered whenever the HTTPClient library's execute function is invoked (Listing 1). The handler for this event counts the size of the request and response.

Figure 5 shows the CDF of network usage for 2,218 apps; the *x-axis is in logarithmic scale*. The network usage across apps varies by *6 orders of magnitude* from 1K to several hundred MB.

Half the apps use more than 206KB of data, and about 20% use more than 1MB of data. More surprisingly, 5% apps use more than

10MB data; 100 times more than the lowest 40% of the apps. The heaviest network users (the tail) are all video streaming apps that stream news and daily shows. For example, "CNN Student News" app, which delivers podcasts and videos of the top daily news items to middle and high school students has a usage over 700MB. We looked at 508 apps that use more than 1MB data and classified based on their app categories. The top five are "News and Magazines", "Sports", "Library and Demo", "Media and Video", and "Entertainment". This roughly matches our expectation that these heavy hitters would be heavy users of multimedia information.

This diversity in network usage suggests that it might be beneficial for app stores to automatically tag apps with their approximate network usage, perhaps on a logarithmic scale. This kind of information can help novice users determine whether they should use an app when WiFi is unavailable or not, and may incentivize developers to develop bandwidth-friendly apps.

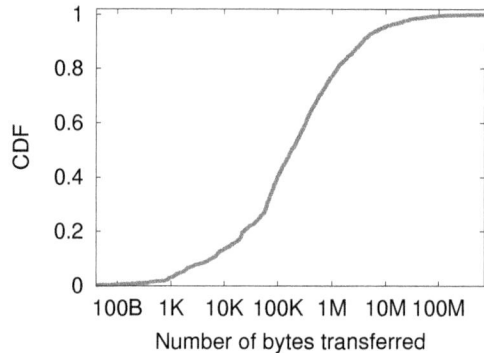

Figure 5: Network traffic usage

4.8 Analysis 6: Permission Usage Profiler

Much research has explored the Android security model, and the use of permissions. In particular, research has tried to understand the implication of permissions [13], designed better user interfaces to help users make more informed decisions [28], and proposed fine-grained permissions [17].

In this analysis, we explore the runtime use of permissions and relate that to the number of permissions requested by an app. This is potentially interesting because app developers may request more permissions than are actually used in the code. Static analysis can reveal an upper bound on the permissions needed, but provides few hints on actual permissions usage.

With PUMA, we can implement a permission usage profiler, which logs every permission usage during app execution. This provides a lower bound on the set of permission required. We use the permission maps provided by [7]. Our PUMAScript has 20 lines of code (shown in Listing 6). It uses a structural-match monkey and specifies a user-level event that is triggered when any API call that requires permissions is invoked (these API calls are obtained from [7]). The corresponding instrumentation code simply logs the permissions used.

Figure 6 shows the CDF of the number of permissions requested and granted to each of the 3,600 apps as well as those used during app exploration. We can see that about 80% are granted less than 15 permissions (with a median of 7) but this number can be as high as 41. Apps at the high end of this distribution include antivirus apps, a battery optimization tool, or utilities like "Anti-Theft" or "AutomateIt". These apps need many permissions because the functionalities they provide require them to access various system resources, sensors and phone private data.

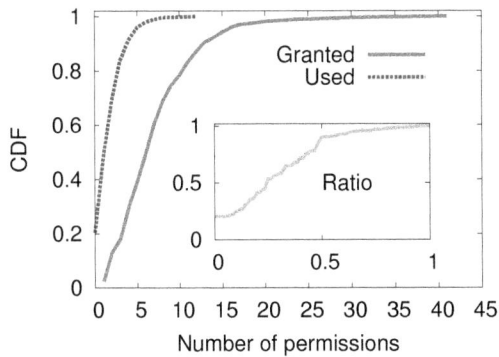

Figure 6: Permission usage: granted vs used

At runtime, apps generally use fewer permissions than granted; about 90% of them used no more than 5 permissions, or no more than half of granted ones. While one expects the number of permissions used in runtime is always less than granted, but the surprisingly low runtime permission usage (about half the apps use less than 30% of their permissions) may suggest that some app developers might request for more permissions than actually needed, increasing the security risks.

4.9   Analysis 7: Stress Testing

Mobile apps are subject to highly dynamic environments, including varying network availability and quality, and dynamic sensor availability. Motivated by this, recent work [25] has explored random testing of mobile apps at scale using a monkey in order to understand app robustness to these dynamics.

In this analysis, we demonstrate PUMA can be used to script similar tests. In particular, we focus on apps that use HTTP and inject null HTTP responses by instrumenting the app code, with the goal of understanding whether app developers are careful to check for such errors. The PUMAScript for this analysis has 16 lines of code (Listing 7) to specify a structural-match monkey and defines the same user-defined event as the network usage profiler (Listing 1). However, the corresponding event handler replaces the `HTTPClient` library invocation with a method that returns a null response. During the experiment, we record the system log (`logcat` in Android) to track exception messages and apps that crash (the Android system logs these events).

In our experiments, apps either crashed during app exploration, or did not crash but logged a null exception, or did not crash and did not log an exception. Out of 2,218 apps, 582 (or 26.2%) crashed, 1,287 (or 58%) continued working without proper exception handling. Only 15.7% apps seemed to be robust to our injected fault.

This is a fairly pessimistic finding, in that a relatively small number of apps seem robust to a fairly innocuous error condition. Beyond that, it appears that developers don't follow Android development guidelines which suggest handling network tasks in a separate thread than the main UI thread. The fact that 26% of the apps crash suggests their network handling was performed as part of the main UI thread, and they did not handle this error condition gracefully. This analysis suggests a different usage scenario for PUMA: as an online service that can perform random testing on an uploaded app.

5.   CONCLUSION

In this paper, we have described the design and implementation of PUMA, a programmable UI automation framework for conducting dynamic analyses of mobile apps at scale. PUMA incorporates a generic monkey and exposes an event driven programming abstraction. Analyses written on top of PUMA can customize app exploration by writing compact event handlers that separate analysis logic from exploration logic. We have evaluated PUMA by programming seven qualitatively different analyses that study performance, security, and correctness properties of mobile apps. These analyses exploit PUMA's ability to flexibly trade-off coverage for speed, extract app state through instrumentation, and dynamically modify the environment. The analysis scripts are highly compact and reveal interesting findings about the Android app ecosystem.

Much work remains, however, including joint optimization for PUMAScripts, conducting a user study with PUMA users, porting PUMA to other mobile platforms, revisiting PUMA abstractions after experimenting with more user tasks, and supporting advanced UI input events for app exploration.

Acknowledgements

We would like to thank our shepherd, Wen Hu, and the anonymous reviewers, for their insightful suggestions that helped improve the technical content and presentation of the paper.

6.   REFERENCES

[1] Android hierarchyviewer. http: //developer.android.com/tools/help/hierarchy-viewer.html.

[2] Android uiautomator. http: //developer.android.com/tools/help/uiautomator/index.html.

[3] Google admob. http://www.google.com/ads/admob/.

[4] Google Play crawler. https://github.com/Akdeniz/google-play-crawler.

[5] Microsoft advertising. http://advertising.microsoft.com/en-us/splitter.

[6] Software Testing Research Survey Bibliography. http: //web.engr.illinois.edu/~taoxie/testingresearchsurvey.htm.

[7] K. W. Y. Au, Y. F. Zhou, Z. Huang, and D. Lie. PScout: Analyzing the Android Permission Specification. In *Proc. of ACM CCS*, 2012.

[8] T. Azim and I. Neamtiu. Targeted and Depth-first Exploration for Systematic Testing of Android Apps. In *Proc. of ACM OOPSLA*, 2013.

[9] J. Crussell, C. Gibler, and H. Chen. Attack of the Clones: Detecting Cloned Applications on Android Markets. In *Proc. of ESORICS*, 2012.

[10] M. Egele, C. Kruegel, E. Kirda, and G. Vigna. PiOS: Detecting Privacy Leaks in iOS Applications. In *Proc. of NDSS*, 2011.

[11] W. Enck, P. Gilbert, B.-G. Chun, L. P. Cox, J. Jung, P. McDaniel, and A. N. Sheth. TaintDroid: An Information-flow Tracking System for Realtime Privacy Monitoring on Smartphones. In *Proc. of ACM OSDI*, 2010.

[12] W. Enck, D. Octeau, P. McDaniel, and S. Chaudhuri. A Study of Android Application Security. In *Proc. of USENIX Security*, 2011.

[13] A. P. Felt, E. Ha, S. Egelman, A. Haney, E. Chin, and D. Wagner. Android Permissions: User Attention, Comprehension, and Behavior. In *Proc. of SOUPS*, 2012.

[14] C. Gibler, R. Stevens, J. Crussell, H. Chen, H. Zang, and H. Choi. AdRob: Examining the Landscape and Impact of Android Application Plagiarism. In *Proc. of ACM MobiSys*, 2013.

[15] S. Hao, D. Li, W. G. J. Halfond, and R. Govindan. Estimating Mobile Application Energy Consumption Using Program Analysis. In *Proc. of ICSE*, 2013.

[16] S. Hao, D. Li, W. G. J. Halfond, and R. Govindan. SIF: A Selective Instrumentation Framework for Mobile Applications. In *Proc. of ACM MobiSys*, 2013.

[17] J. Jeon, K. K. Micinski, J. A. Vaughan, A. Fogel, N. Reddy, J. S. Foster, and T. Millstein. Dr. Android and Mr. Hide: Fine-grained Permissions in Android Applications. In *Proc. of SPSM*, 2012.

[18] K. Lee, J. Flinn, T. Giuli, B. Noble, and C. Peplin. AMC: Verifying User Interface Properties for Vehicular Applications. In *Proc. of ACM MobiSys*, 2013.

[19] C.-J. M. Liang, D. N. Lane, N. Brouwers, L. Zhang, B. Karlsson, R. Chandra, and F. Zhao. Contextual Fuzzing: Automated Mobile App Testing Under Dynamic Device and Environment Conditions. Technical Report MSR-TR-2013-100, Microsoft Research, 2013.

[20] B. Liu, S. Nath, R. Govindan, and J. Liu. DECAF: Detecting and Characterizing Ad Fraud in Mobile Apps. In *Proc. of NSDI*, 2014.

[21] B. Livshits and J. Jung. Automatic Mediation of Privacy-Sensitive Resource Access in Smartphone Applications. In *Proc. of USENIX Security*, 2013.

[22] A. Machiry, R. Tahiliani, and M. Naik. Dynodroid: An Input Generation System for Android Apps. In *Proc. of ESEC/FSE*, 2013.

[23] S. Nath, X. F. Lin, L. Ravindranath, and J. Padhye. SmartAds: Bringing Contextual Ads to Mobile Apps. In *Proc. of ACM MobiSys*, 2013.

[24] V. Rastogi, Y. Chen, and W. Enck. AppsPlayground: Automatic Security Analysis of Smartphone Applications. In *Proc. of ACM CODASPY*, 2013.

[25] L. Ravindranath, S. Nath, J. Padhye, and H. Balakrishnan. Automatic and Scalable Fault Detection for Mobile Applications. In *Proc. of ACM MobiSys*, 2014.

[26] L. Ravindranath, J. Padhye, S. Agarwal, R. Mahajan, I. Obermiller, and S. Shayandeh. AppInsight: Mobile App Performance Monitoring in the Wild. In *Proc. of ACM OSDI*, 2012.

[27] L. Ravindranath, J. Padhye, R. Mahajan, and H. Balakrishnan. Timecard: Controlling User-perceived Delays in Server-based Mobile Applications. In *Proc. of ACM SOSP*, 2013.

[28] S. Rosen, Z. Qian, and Z. M. Mao. AppProfiler: A Flexible Method of Exposing Privacy-related Behavior in Android Applications to End Users. In *Proc. of ACM CODASPY*, 2013.

APPENDIX

A. MORE PUMASCRIPT PROGRAMS

```
1   class AMC extends PUMAScript {
2     boolean compareState(UIState s1, UIState s2) {
3       return MonkeyInputFactory.stateStructureMatch(s1,
            s2, 0.95);
4     }
5     int getNextClick(UIState s) {
6       return MonkeyInputFactory.nextClickSequential(s);
7     }
8     void onUILoadDone(UIState s) {
9       AMCChecker.inspect(s);
10    }
11  }
12  class AMCChecker {
13    Map<String, Integer> BTN_SIZE_DICT = new Hashtable<
          String, Integer>();
14    Map<String, Integer> BTN_DIST_DICT = new Hashtable<
          String, Integer>();
15    static {
16      BTN_SIZE_DICT.put("gn", 12301);
17      BTN_SIZE_DICT.put("s3", 11520);
18      BTN_SIZE_DICT.put("htc", 27085);
19      BTN_DIST_DICT.put("gn", 186);
20      BTN_DIST_DICT.put("s3", 180);
21      BTN_DIST_DICT.put("htc", 276);
22    }
23    static void inspect(UIState s) {
24      String dev = s.getDevice();
25      BasicTreeNode root = s.getUiHierarchy();
26      List<Rectangle> allButtons = new ArrayList<
            Rectangle>();
27      boolean scrolling_vio = false;
28      Queue<BasicTreeNode> Q = new LinkedList<
            BasicTreeNode>();
29      Q.add(root);
30      while (!Q.isEmpty()) {
31        BasicTreeNode btn = Q.poll();
32        if (btn instanceof UiNode) {
33          UiNode uin = (UiNode) btn;
34          String clz = uin.getAttribute("class");
35          boolean enable = uin.getAttribute("enabled");
36          boolean scrolling = uin.getAttribute("
              scrollable");
37          if (clz.contains("Button") && enable) {
38            Rectangle bounds = new Rectangle(uin.x, uin
                .y, uin.width, uin.height);
39            allButtons.add(bounds);
40          }
41          if (scrolling && !scrolling_vio)
42            scrolling_vio = true;
43        }
44        for (BasicTreeNode child : btn.getChildren())
45          Q.add(child);
46      }
47      int btn_size_vio = 0, btn_dist_vio = 0;
48      for (int i = 0; i < allButtons.size(); i++) {
49        Rectangle b1 = allButtons.get(i);
50        double area = b1.getWidth() * b1.getHeight();
51        if (area < BTN_SIZE_DICT.get(dev))
52          btn_size_vio++;
53        for (int j = i + 1; j < allButtons.size(); j++)
              {
54          Rectangle b2 = allButtons.get(j);
55          double d = get_distance(b1, b2);
56          if (d < BTN_DIST_DICT.get(dev))
57            btn_dist_vio++;
58        }
59      }
60      Log(btn_size_vio + "," + btn_dist_vio + "," + (
            scrolling_vio ? 1 : 0));
61    }
62    static double get_distance(Rectangle r1, Rectangle
          r2) {
63      double x1 = r1.getCenterX();
64      double y1 = r1.getCenterY();
65      double x2 = r2.getCenterX();
66      double y2 = r2.getCenterY();
67      double delta_x = Math.abs(x1 - x2);
68      double delta_y = Math.abs(y1 - y2);
69      return Math.sqrt(delta_x * delta_x + delta_y *
            delta_y);
70    }
71  }
```

Listing 2: Accessibility violation detection

```
1   class InAppDataCrawler extends PUMAScript {
2     boolean compareState(UIState s1, UIState s2) {
3       return MonkeyInputFactory.stateExactMatch(s1, s2)
            ;
4     }
5     int getNextClick(UIState s) {
6       return MonkeyInputFactory.nextClickSequential(s);
7     }
8     long getTimeOut() {
9       return 1200000;
10    }
```

```
11    void onUILoadDone(UIState s) {
12      s.dumpText();
13    }
14 }
```

Listing 3: Content-based app search

```
1  class UIStructureClassifier extends PUMAScript {
2    boolean compareState(UIState s1, UIState s2) {
3      return MonkeyInputFactory.stateStructureMatch(s1,
          s2, 0.95);
4    }
5    int getNextClick(UIState s) {
6      return MonkeyInputFactory.nextClickSequential(s);
7    }
8    void onUILoadDone(UIState s) {
9      Log(s.getID());
10   }
11 }
```

Listing 4: UI structure classifier

```
1  class DECAF extends PUMAScript {
2    boolean compareState(UIState s1, UIState s2) {
3      return MonkeyInputFactory.stateStructureMatch(s1,
          s2, 0.95);
4    }
5    int getNextClick(UIState s) {
6      return MonkeyInputFactory.nextClickSequential(s);
7    }
8    void onUILoadDone(UIState s) {
9      DECAFChecker.inspect(s);
10   }
11 }
12 class DECAFChecker {
13   static void inspect(UIState s) {
14     BasicTreeNode root = s.getUiHierarchy();
15     boolean portrait = (root.width < root.height);
16     List<Rectangle> allAds = new ArrayList<Rectangle
         >();
17     List<Rectangle> otherClickables = new ArrayList<
         Rectangle>();
18     Queue<BasicTreeNode> Q = new LinkedList<
         BasicTreeNode>();
19     Q.add(root);
20     while (!Q.isEmpty()) {
21       BasicTreeNode btn = Q.poll();
22       if (btn instanceof UiNode) {
23         UiNode uin = (UiNode) btn;
24         Rectangle bounds = new Rectangle(uin.x, uin.y
             , uin.width, uin.height);
25         String clz = uin.getAttribute("class");
26         boolean enabled = uin.getAttribute("enabled")
             ;
27         boolean clickable = uin.getAttribute("
             clickable");
28         if (clz.contains("WebView") && enabled) {
29           Rectangle tmp = new Rectangle((int) bounds.
               getWidth(), (int) bounds.getHeight());
30           if (portrait) {
31             if (PORTRAIT_AD_SIZE_MAX.contains(tmp))
32               allAds.add(bounds);
33           } else {
34             if (LANDSCAPE_AD_SIZE_MAX.contains(tmp))
35               allAds.add(bounds);
36           }
37         }
38         if (!clz.contains("WebView") && enabled &&
             clickable)
39           otherClickables.add(bounds);
40       }
41       for (BasicTreeNode child : btn.getChildren())
42         Q.add(child);
43     }
44     int num_ads = allAds.size();
45     int small_ad_cnt = 0;
46     for (int i = 0; i < allAds.size(); i++) {
47       Rectangle bounds = allAds.get(i);
48       Rectangle tmp = new Rectangle((int) bounds.
           getWidth(), (int) bounds.getHeight());
```

```
49       if ((portrait && PORTRAIT_AD_SIZE_MIN.contains(
           tmp)) || (!portrait &&
           LANDSCAPE_AD_SIZE_MIN.contains(tmp)))
50         small_ad_cnt++;
51     }
52     int intrusive_ad_cnt = 0;
53     for (int i = 0; i < allAds.size(); i++) {
54       Rectangle ad = allAds.get(i);
55       for (int j = 0; j < otherClickables.size(); j
           ++) {
56         Rectangle clickable = otherClickables.get(j);
57         if (ad.intersects(clickable))
58           intrusive_ad_cnt++;
59       }
60     }
61     Log(num_ads + "," + small_ad_cnt + "," +
         intrusive_ad_cnt);
62   }
63 }
```

Listing 5: Ad fraud detection

```
1  class NetworkProfiler extends PUMAScript {
2    boolean compareState(UIState s1, UIState s2) {
3      return MonkeyInputFactory.stateStructureMatch(s1,
          s2, 0.95);
4    }
5    int getNextClick(UIState s) {
6      return MonkeyInputFactory.nextClickSequential(s);
7    }
8    void specifyInstrumentation() {
9      Set<CodePoint> userEvent;
10     List<String> allPerms = loadPermMap("perm.map");
11     for (String perm : allPerms) {
12       CPFinder.setPerm(perm);
13       userEvent = CPFinder.apply();
14       for (CodePoint cp : userEvent) {
15         UserCode code = new UserCode("Logger", "log",
             CPARG);
16         Instrumenter.place(code, BEFORE, cp);
17       }
18     }
19   }
20 }
21 class Logger {
22   public void log(String perm) {
23     Log(perm);
24   }
25 }
```

Listing 6: Permission usage profiler

```
1  class StressTesting extends PUMAScript {
2    boolean compareState(UIState s1, UIState s2) {
3      return MonkeyInputFactory.stateStructureMatch(s1,
          s2, 0.95);
4    }
5    int getNextClick(UIState s) {
6      return MonkeyInputFactory.nextClickSequential(s);
7    }
8    void specifyInstrumentation() {
9      CPFinder.setBytecode("invoke.*", "HTTPClient.
          execute(HttpUriRequest request)");
10     Set<CodePoint> userEvent = CPFinder.apply();
11     for (CodePoint cp : userEvent) {
12       UserCode code = new UserCode("MyHTTPClient", "
           execute", CPARG);
13       Instrumenter.place(code, AT, cp);
14     }
15   }
16 }
17 class MyHTTPClient {
18   HttpResponse execute(HttpUriRequest request) {
19     return null;
20   }
21 }
```

Listing 7: Stress testing

Characterizing Resource Usage for Mobile Web Browsing

Feng Qian, Subhabrata Sen, and Oliver Spatscheck
AT&T Labs – Research, Bedminster, New Jersey, USA
{fengqian,sen,spatsch}@research.att.com

ABSTRACT

Multiple entities in the smartphone ecosystem employ various methods to provide better web browsing experience. In this paper, we take a first comprehensive examination of the resource usage of mobile web browsing by focusing on two important types of resources: bandwidth and energy. Using a novel traffic collection and analysis tool, we examine a wide spectrum of important factors including protocol overhead, TCP connection management, web page content, traffic timing dynamics, caching efficiency, and compression usage, for the most popular 500 websites. Our findings suggest that that all above factors at different layers can affect resource utilization for web browsing, as they often poorly interact with the underlying cellular networks. Based on our findings, we developed novel recommendations and detailed best practice suggestions for mobile web content, browser, network protocol, and smartphone OS design, to make mobile web browsing more resource efficient.

Categories and Subject Descriptors

C.2.2 [**Computer-Communication Networks**]: Network Protocols – Applications; C.2.1 [**Computer-Communication Networks**]: Network Architecture and Design – Wireless Communication; C.4 [**Performance of Systems**]: Measurement Techniques

Keywords

Mobile Web; HTTP; SSL; SPDY; Energy Consumption; Cellular Networks; Smartphones

1. INTRODUCTION

Web browsing is one of the key applications on mobile devices. Cellular traffic volume of browser-based web browsing surpasses that of any other application except for multimedia streaming [26]. Multiple entities in the smartphone ecosystem employ various methods to provide better web browsing experience. Content providers publish mobile versions of their websites. Based on our examination of the Alexa top 500 websites in February 2013, 327 out of the 500 websites have mobile versions that are specifically designed for smartphone/tablet users (§3). Mobile carriers deploy middleboxes in their networks to specifically optimize web traffic. Mobile browsers also introduce a wide range of techniques to make web browsing on handheld devices easier, safer, and faster (*e.g.*, through the SPDY protocol [9] or a compression proxy).

In this paper, we take a first comprehensive examination of the *resource usage* of mobile web browsing by focusing on two important types of resources: bandwidth and energy. Our study is driven by two facts. *(i)* Bandwidth and energy are the key resource bottlenecks for mobile users. *(ii)* Web developers are often unaware of cellular-specific characteristics. Although mobile websites have tailored their appearances for mobile device screens, it is unclear how well their design fits cellular networks operating under severe resource constraints compared to Wi-Fi and wired networks.

Bandwidth is a vital resource for cellular customers who pay for their traffic. A recent white paper from Mobidia [15] suggests that in UK most smartphone customers (*e.g.*, 70% for Vodafone) use a monthly data plan of no more than 500 MB (less than 16.7 MB per day on average). For all carriers, data roaming is even much more expensive. Therefore under the constraints of delivering necessary contents and providing good user experiences, mobile web browsing should consume as less bandwidth as possible.

Battery Life is another critical bottleneck. We focus on the power consumed by the handset radio interface. When the radio is on, it contributes to 1/3 to 1/2 of the total handset power usage [28]. It is well known that in cellular networks, the radio energy consumption highly depends on network traffic patterns, and it is always more energy-efficient to batch all transfers in one traffic burst than to transfer them intermittently in separate bursts. This is because in 3G/4G networks, there exists a timeout, called *tail time*, for turning off the radio interface after a data transfer. The tail time (T_{tail}) ranges between several seconds to more than 10 seconds depending on the carrier settings [28, 22]. Therefore, if two data bursts are transferred separately, then within the timing gap between the two bursts, the radio interface is still on (and consuming power) for up to T_{tail} seconds, leading to waste of the radio energy.

To understand the resource consumption of mobile web browsing, we collected network traces and browser events for landing pages of the top 500 websites on smartphone, and conducted in-depth analysis on their bandwidth consumption and their energy efficiency. A *landing page* is loaded after a user enters the website URL and hits the "Go" button. The importance of landing pages is well recognized: they are the first and the most frequently viewed pages of websites. A high-quality landing page is one of the key factors of online marketing [11]. Therefore, developers usually put a lot of effort on optimizing this important resource. However, our findings suggest that many of them are far from resource-efficient. Further, web pages are also directly fetched by many smartphone apps that contain programmable browsers (*e.g.,* `WebView` in Android), so making web pages more resource-efficient can benefit many mobile apps as well. We have made the following methodological contributions and new observations.

1. The UbiDump **Tool (§2).** HTTPS and SPDY are becoming increasingly popular (*e.g.,* Google Chrome for Android already supports tunneling all browsing traffic to SPDY proxies [2]). We thus built a measurement tool called UbiDump, which runs on a mobile device and precisely reconstructs all web transfers carried by HTTP, HTTPS, and SPDY [9] from captured `tcpdump` traces. It supports on-device SSL decryption *without* requiring servers' private keys or a man-in-the-middle (MITM) proxy. The decryption is realized by instrumenting the SSL Library and intercepting session keys during SSL handshakes. UbiDump provides a complete view of today's web traffic, and enables cross-layer analysis that cannot be performed by a browser-based data collection approach.

2. Protocol Bandwidth Overhead (§4.2). We performed a first analysis of the bandwidth impact of HTTPS and SPDY protocols based on real smartphone web browsing traffic, and discovered surprisingly high protocol bandwidth overheads. The overall protocol efficiency rate, defined as the size of HTTPS/SPDY payload divided by the total size of data transferred in the network (except for TCP retransmissions), is only 66% to 73% for cold-cache (*i.e.,* empty cache) load. For warm-cache (*i.e.,* non-empty cache) load, the efficiency can be as low as 11%. Such low efficiency is primarily caused by a tendency to open new TCP connections rather than to reuse existing ones. Each new TCP connection incurs high bandwidth overhead due to SSL handshake.

3. New Insights on Mobile Web Contents (§4.4). We examined causes of large websites, objects, and images. We also conduct in-depth analysis on hosts that are accessed by multiple websites, and found that they provide third-party services such as user tracking, and their functionalities are usually not related to the main content of the website (exceptions exist though). Removing them saves at least 39% (20%) of bandwidth for 20% of mobile websites in warm-cache (cold-cache) load.

4. Energy and Root-cause Analysis for Network Idleness (§4.5, §4.6). We perform novel analysis to identify network idle periods during a page load. The idle periods, during which the radio may still be on and be consuming power, can be caused by a few reasons such as delayed transfers triggered by Javascript. Surprisingly, reducing such idle time gaps brings a median radio energy saving of up to 59% across all mobile websites.

5. New Findings of Caching and Compression (§4.7, §4.8). We found that caching is poorly utilized for many mobile sites. 26% of the top mobile sites (*e.g.,* `m.bing.com`) mark their main HTML files as non-storable, leading to potential bandwidth waste. About 23% of objects in mobile sites are cacheable but have freshness lifetime of less than 1 hour. Within them, more than 70% of the objects are images, fonts, CSS, and Javascript whose contents are not likely to change within such a short time period of 1 hour. We investigate compression opportunities for HTTP, SSL, and SPDY, and found SSL stream-level compression outperforms the traditional HTTP object-level compression.

Overall, we found that factors at different layers can affect resource utilization in mobile web browsing, including web contents, HTTP, SSL, and even TCP. In particular, although many mobile websites have tailored their appearances for smartphone screens, many of the adjustments are very superficial, and the resulting sites are often poorly interacting with the cellular network. We observe very little difference between mobile and non-mobile websites in many aspects such as caching aggressiveness and object sizes.

Figure 1: Web protocols supported by UbiDump**.**

And for some metrics such as the number of redirections, mobile websites are even worse. Based on our findings, we developed novel recommendations and detailed best practice suggestions for mobile web content, browser, protocol, and smartphone OS design, to make mobile website access more resource efficient.

The remainder of this paper is organized as follows. §2 and §3 describe the UbiDump tool and our methodology for collecting top 500 landing pages, respectively. §4 details the measurement findings, based on which we provide our recommendations in §5. We present related work in §6 before concluding the paper in §7.

2. THE UbiDump TOOL

The first step towards analyzing mobile web browsing is data collection. This can be obtained directly from a browser (*e.g.,* a browser extension), from a server, from a middlebox (*e.g.,* a proxy server), or from network traces. We adopt the last method by building a measurement tool called UbiDump. It runs on a mobile device, and precisely reconstructs all web transfers from `tcpdump` traces captured on the handset, thus requiring no change to the existing browser, server, or middlebox. Further, since `tcpdump` runs below the application layer, UbiDump allows capturing traffic across all applications (not only browsers). Another advantage of UbiDump is it also captures protocol headers at lower layers such as TCP, IP, and SSL. This enables cross-layer analysis (*e.g.,* §4.2) that cannot be performed by using the browser-based approach.

Handling SSL. SSL is becoming increasingly popular. Previous work handle the decryption of SSL traffic in `tcpdump` traces in three different ways. (*i*) Simply ignore the content of SSL traffic [26, 23, 37]. (*ii*) Some tools such as `Wireshark` [13] and `ssldump` [12] require servers' private keys for decryption. However obtaining private keys of commercial servers is usually impossible. (*iii*) Redirect traffic to a man-in-the-middle (MITM) SSL proxy such as `mitmproxy` [8] and Stanford MITM proxy [10]. HTTPS requests are then terminated by the proxy and resent to the remote web server in a new TCP connection. The certificate of the proxy needs to be installed on the client. To decrypt the SSL traffic, one can provide `Wireshark` or `ssldump` with the private key of the proxy. This MITM approach however has limitations: it requires additional infrastructures and may change traffic pattern and content, as will be shown in §2.2.

A key contribution of UbiDump is it supports *on-device SSL decryption* without requiring servers' private keys or a proxy. Throughout this paper, "SSL" will be used to refer to SSL v2, SSL v3, and TLS v1, all supported by UbiDump. Our key observation is that, unlike a private key that is only known to the server, a *session key* is derived independently by both the client and the server when an SSL session is established. Symmetric encryption is used in subsequent data transfers where data is encrypted and decrypted using this session key. Therefore, UbiDump realizes on-device decryption using an instrumented SSL library, which dumps SSL session keys during SSL handshakes. The session keys are then combined with `tcpdump` traces to derive the decrypted data.

Protocol Analyzers. Today's web traffic is carried by three application-layer protocols: HTTP, HTTPS, and SPDY, with the latter two becoming increasingly popular. UbiDump thus contains analyzers for all three protocols shown in Figure 1, plus DNS. SPDY [9] is developed primarily at Google for transporting web content. It provides an HTTP interface to applications but differs from HTTP mainly in three ways. *(i)* In SPDY, concurrent transfers of multiple web objects belonging to the same domain can be multiplexed in a single TCP connection. *(ii)* SPDY can prioritize some object loads over others. *(iii)* Request and response headers embedded in SPDY headers are always compressed using a customized dictionary.

2.1 System Implementation

UbiDump is a handy traffic capture and analysis tool supporting on-device SSL decryption and web content analysis. We describe the implementation of UbiDump on Android[1]. The system consists of the following three components.

1. A `tcpdump` program running on the handset. It records all network traffic in `pcap` format with negligible runtime overhead incurred.

2. An instrumented Android SSL library (`libssl.so`). During an SSL handshake, it dumps a premaster secret p, and a 48-byte master secret m to the Android debugging log. They will be used for SSL decryption to be explained soon.

3. Protocol analyzers. They parse the `tcpdump` trace from IP to application layers and extract all web transfers over HTTP, HTTPS, and SPDY. The analyses can be performed in an online manner although they are currently offline. We leveraged the existing PCAP/HTTP analyzer implementation in the ARO tool [28], and wrote 4K lines of C++ code for SSL, SPDY, and DNS analyzers. Additionally, we leveraged several cryptographic functions in `openssl` and Linux WPA Supplicant [7] projects.

SSL Decryption is performed as follows. During an SSL handshake, the handset generates a premaster secret p, encrypts p using server's public key into p_e, and then sends p_e to server, which decrypts p_e using its private key. Both sides then independently compute the master secret m:

$$m = \Theta(p, r_c, r_s) \qquad (1)$$

where Θ is a publicly known function, r_c and r_s are random strings generated by client and server, respectively, at the beginning of the handshake. They are exchanged in plain text. Let there be multiple SSL sessions captured by `tcpdump`, which outputs a list of (r_c, r_s, D) triples where D is the traffic data to be decrypted in an SSL session. Meanwhile we obtain from the modified SSL library a list of (p, m) pairs. Equation 1 bridges the two lists so that we can associate each (p, m) pair with its corresponding D. The final session key for decrypting D is derived from m, r_c, and r_s using another publicly known function.

2.2 Discussions

Limitations. We describe cases where UbiDump cannot decrypt SSL traffic from the packet trace. First, if the capture starts in the middle of an SSL session, it is impossible for UbiDump to decrypt that session since the key is not captured. One solution is to instrument all places in the SSL library where decrypted bytes are delivered to upper layers.

Second, the current SSL protocol analyzer only implements the most popular RSA key exchange algorithm. We therefore restrict the set of supported key exchange algorithms in the handshake message sent from the handset by adding one line of code to `libssl.so`. We are working on making our analyzer support

---

[1] An Android device needs to be rooted to run UbiDump.

other key exchange algorithms such as Diffie-Hellman. UbiDump supports all symmetric encryption (AES, 3DES, RC4) and MAC algorithms (SHA, MD5) used by the original Android SSL library.

Third, the entire decryption mechanism can be bypassed if a smartphone app implements its own SSL logic, or if the SSL library is statically linked into the app binary. We examined several popular built-in and third-party apps on Android such as the browser, the Google Map, and banking apps. SSL traffic of the vast majority of those apps can be decrypted by UbiDump. For completeness, UbiDump can also read private keys from files and use them to decrypt SSL. Note none of the above limitations affects the SSL decryption in our measurement study.

Comparing with the MITM-Proxy-based Approach. We perform a case study to show the potential impact of an MITM proxy on the traffic. We collected two traces A and B for the same website (`https://www.chase.com`). The mobile handset (Samsung Galaxy S III running Android 4.0.4), the network (Wi-Fi), the collection time and location are all same for the two traces. Trace A is collected using the MITM-Proxy-based approach (we use `mitmproxy` [8] due to its popularity) and Trace B is collected by UbiDump without a proxy.

By comparing the two traces, we found the following differences. *(i)* In Trace A, the phone issues an `HTTP CONNECT` request to the proxy before establishing the SSL session while in Trace B, the SSL session is established without that additional round trip. *(ii)* Their TCP connections are closed in different ways. This affects handset energy consumption in cellular networks (§4.3). *(iii)* Some objects in Trace B are transferred in SPDY that is never used in Trace A. This is because the proxy does not support SPDY so the handset has to fall back to HTTPS. The above observations indicate that an MITM proxy may change the traffic pattern and content compared to the case where the phone directly connects to the original server.

3. COLLECTING TOP 500 LANDING PAGES

We describe how we use UbiDump to collect landing pages of the top 500 websites to be characterized in §4.

We obtained a list of top 500 U.S. websites from Alexa in February 2013. According to Alexa, the sites are ordered by their one-month traffic ranks, which are calculated "using a combination of average daily visitors and page views over the past month". Although the ranks are derived from the usage of all Internet users, we expect they are also popular among just mobile users.

Automated Testbed. We installed UbiDump on a Samsung Galaxy S III smartphone running Android 4.0.4. We wrote another Android program that loads the website URLs in a `WebView` in an automated manner. A `WebView` is the programmable version of the default Android browser.

Our testbed leverages UbiDump to collect two types of traces: a *cold-cache* load where all caches (DNS/SSL/web content cache caches) are cleared before loading, and a *warm-cache* load right after the cold-cache load without clearing any cache. For each website, we repeat the cold and warm load pair for three times in a row, obtaining six traces. We collected all websites using both a 3G HSPA+ network and a corporate Wi-Fi network, resulting in two datasets which we call DS1 and DS2, respectively. Both DS1 and DS2 were collected at late nights in spring 2013 at good signal strength levels, to minimize the impact of network congestion, as well as to provide a best case for radio energy consumption. All collected SSL sessions were successfully decrypted by UbiDump.

Completion of Page Load (so that we stop the data collection) is determined by a timeout of 30 seconds (*i.e.,* when no request has been made for 30 seconds). To validate that the load is indeed successful, we let the testbed take a picture of the entire rendered page and examine the screenshot manually to check failures such as any unrendered part due to network timeout. For each website, we collect all its six traces again if any of them is found to be problematic. We also impose a limit of 90-second data collection duration for pages that continuously load new data (*e.g.*, due to periodic user tracking).

Landing Pages. Each collected page is a *landing page* that is loaded if a user enters the URL (*e.g.,* `cnn.com`) and hits the "Go" button. The importance of landing pages is well recognized: they are the first and often the most frequently viewed pages of websites. A high-quality landing page is one of the key factors of online marketing as it can keep visitors at the website by capturing their short attention span of 2 to 3 seconds [11]. Therefore, developers usually put a lot of effort on optimizing this important resource. However, we found many of them are far from resource efficient.

Identifying Mobile and Non-mobile Sites. For each website, we manually label it as either mobile version or non-mobile (desktop) version. For most landing pages, this is straightforward to tell from the screenshot. Another obvious clue is that for many mobile websites, their redirected landing page URLs begin with `m.xyz.com` or `xyz.com/mobile`. For a small number of websites, we label them by comparing between the rendering result on the phone and that on a desktop. Among the top 500 websites, 327 (65.4%) are found to be mobile versions designed specifically for mobile handsets. 143 (28.6%) are non-mobile versions *i.e.,* mobile users are served with the same contents as desktop users are. The remaining 30 (6%) websites could not be loaded on either a mobile or a desktop browser, and are therefore excluded from our analysis. Many of such failed websites are "helper" domain names such as `googleusercontent.com` not providing a web interface.

3.1 Discussions

Mobile Apps vs. Websites. About 1/4 of our measured websites provide official apps in Android market (in Feb 2013). Although we do not have the statistics, we do believe many users prefer using the apps to access the content providers, in particular for those popular ones (*e.g.,* top 100). However, lessons and recommendations derived from this study are generally applicable to any mobile web page. Also, web pages are often directly fetched by many smartphone apps containing programmable browsers (*e.g.,* `WebView` in Android), so making web pages more resource efficient can benefit those apps as well. Conducting detailed comparisons between mobile apps and websites is our future work.

Web Page Complexity. It is possible that our analysis underestimates the complexity of today's mobile web pages since landing pages can be simple (*e.g.,* Facebook login page). However, it is difficult to identify "simple" web pages due to a lack of objective criteria. Further, we observe many cases where a visually simple landing page contains complex Javascript and CSS scripts, as well as involves large data transfers when being loaded. We thus include all loadable websites in subsequent analyses. Also, for many sites, their landing pages may not be the pages on which users spends most of their time. But we still believe they are worthy of being studied due to the importance of landing pages described early.

Popularity of HTML5. HTML5 provides new features, such as web sockets, enhanced multimedia, and offline caching, to enhance web browsing experience. We found HTML5 is still not widely used for mobile websites (as of Feb 2013). For example, only eight mobile sites leverage the offline caching feature to enhance the user experience when the device is offline. Studying HTML5 is our future work as it will eventually become popular on mobile devices.

Table 1: Usage of HTTPS and SPDY across landing pages of all websites (the DS1 Dataset).

Protocol	Mobile Sites		Non-mobile Sites	
	Cold	Warm	Cold	Warm
HTTPS	58.7%	48.6%	93.7%	68.5%
SPDY	22.3%	21.4%	42.7%	39.2%

The Connection Split Proxy. Mobile carriers deploy in-network middleboxes or proxies for various purposes. In particular, the carrier from which we collected the DS1 dataset deploys a proxy in the cellular core network for HTTP traffic (server port 80/8080). It transparently splits an end-to-end TCP connection into two, one between a handset and the proxy, and the other between the proxy and the remote server. Although splitting connection can improve TCP performance in certain circumstances [19], it has negligible impact on our measurement results in §4 except for the TCP connection management part, on which the impact is also small. We revisit this in §4.3 and §4.6.

4. MEASUREMENT RESULTS

We next examine various aspects that can affect resource consumption of mobile web browsing: protocol bandwidth overhead (§4.2), TCP connection management (§4.3), page content (§4.4), network idle time during page loading period (§4.5, §4.6), caching semantics (§4.7), and compression usage (§4.8). As will be shown, improving the resource efficiency of mobile web browsing requires *joint efforts* of multiple entities in the smartphone ecosystem.

From this point on, a *website* refers to its landing page unless otherwise noted. An *object* refers to a URL fetched by the handset. The *transfer* of an object includes both sending the request and receiving the response. Each figure or table can present a distribution across websites, TCP connections, or objects, which are clearly stated[2]. Also, the analysis results of DS1 and DS2 are qualitatively similar unless otherwise noted. So we usually only present the results of DS1. We do not find anything distinguishing Wi-Fi and 3G in request headers.

4.1 Protocol Prevalence

Table 1 shows the prevalence of HTTPS and SPDY across websites, for both cold-cache load ("Cold") and warm-cache load ("Warm"). We say a website (*i.e.,* its landing page) uses SSL (SPDY) if we observe at least one TCP flow that carries an SSL (SPDY) session, which is therefore counted by Table 1. Table 1 indicates many top websites use SSL. In DS1, we observed SSL sessions are established to 300 distinct content providers identified by their host names. We also found from the datasets that as of today, SPDY is only employed by a few content providers including Google, YouTube, Facebook, Twitter, and AdMob, *etc.* However, other websites often embed their services (*e.g.,* Facebook feeds, see §4.4). This explains why Table 1 still indicates SPDY is reasonably prevalent among the top websites.

Regarding to traffic volume and object count, HTTP still dominates the web usage in both metrics. For DS1, HTTPS and SPDY together account for around 10% and 6% of the total bytes for mobile sites and non-mobile sites, respectively (similar case for object count). However, SSL and SPDY are becoming increasingly popular. In 2010, Gmail and Twitter made HTTPS the default

---

[2]Each dataset contains 470*3 cold-load traces and 470*3 warm-load traces. All are used in our analysis unless otherwise noted. Therefore, for example, a CDF plot of a certain distribution across all cold-load websites contains 470*3 data points.

Table 2: Protocol byte breakdown for DS1.

Protocol	Category	$tcpip\_ctl$	udp_usr	ssl_ctl	$ssl\_usr\_enc -$ ssl_usr_dec	$http\_ctl$ or $spdy\_ctl$	$http\_usr$ or $spdy\_usr$
HTTP	Cold, Mobile sites	9.0%	0.2%	0	0	6.9%	83.9%
	Cold, Non-mobile	9.2%	0.2%	0	0	8.6%	81.9%
	Warm, Mobile sites	13.2%	0.3%	0	0	21.5%	65.0%
	Warm, Non-mobile	13.6%	0.5%	0	0	25.3%	60.6%
HTTPS	Cold, Mobile sites	8.6%	0.1%	11.6%	0.0%	6.2%	73.4%
	Cold, Non-mobile	9.7%	0.3%	17.0%	0.3%	7.0%	65.8%
	Warm, Mobile sites	12.3%	0.1%	33.9%	0.3%	17.1%	36.2%
	Warm, Non-mobile	13.6%	0.3%	44.5%	-0.4%	16.3%	25.6%
SPDY	Cold, Mobile sites	9.7%	0.4%	10.5%	1.6%	5.2%	72.6%
	Cold, Non-mobile	10.8%	0.4%	12.1%	1.9%	5.2%	69.5%
	Warm, Mobile sites	15.7%	0.3%	24.9%	2.0%	12.0%	45.1%
	Warm, Non-mobile	22.9%	0.5%	44.0%	3.1%	18.3%	11.2%

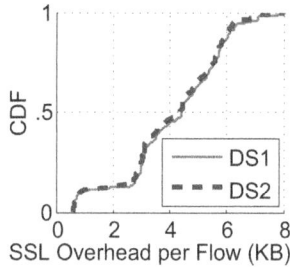

Figure 2: SSL handshake overhead across TCP flows.

for all users [4]. Facebook started to support HTTPS in 2011, and moved all users to HTTPS in 2012 [4]. Google Chrome for Android already supports tunneling all browsing traffic to SPDY proxies [2]. Understanding the resource impact of SPDY and HTTPS is therefore critical.

4.2 Bandwidth Impact of Protocols

The additional protocol layers introduced by HTTPS and SPDY may incur additional overheads. Previous studies mostly focus on their security implications and CPU overhead. Here our emphasis is to understand the *bandwidth* impact of diverse protocols for mobile web browsing.

Our analysis goes from lower layer to higher layer. The raw bytes captured by UbiDump on the wire consist of four components: TCP/UDP/IP headers ($tcpip\_ctl$), UDP payload carrying DNS traffic (udp_usr), TCP payload (tcp_usr), and retransmitted TCP packets (tcp_rt).

$$raw = tcpip\_ctl + udp\_usr + tcp\_usr + tcp\_rt \quad (2)$$

For HTTP, the TCP payload contains HTTP headers ($http\_ctl$) and HTTP payloads ($http\_usr$) in plain text.

$$tcp\_usr = http\_ctl + http\_usr \quad (3)$$

HTTPS and SPDY use SSL. Therefore the TCP payload consists of SSL header and control data (ssl_ctl), as well as the encrypted SSL payload (ssl_usr_enc).

$$tcp\_usr = ssl\_ctl + ssl\_usr\_enc \quad (4)$$

Let the decrypted SSL payload be ssl_usr_dec. For HTTPS, it is comprised of HTTP headers and payloads. SPDY is similar to HTTPS but we use different symbols for SPDY headers/control data ($spdy\_ctl$) and SPDY payloads ($spdy\_usr$). Note $http\_usr$

and $spdy\_usr$ might be encoded by server (*e.g.*, compressed or transferred in HTTP chunked mode).

$$ssl\_usr\_dec = http\_ctl + http\_usr \quad (5)$$

$$ssl\_usr\_dec = spdy\_ctl + spdy\_usr \quad (6)$$

Since UbiDump captures all traffic at the network interface, it can precisely calculate all values in Equations 2 to 6. Table 2 shows the breakdown for DS1. We classify all TCP flows (a TCP flow may include DNS lookup(s) before the flow starts) into 12 categories based on the combinations of (app protocol, cold/warm loads, mobile/non-mobile sites). Also Table 2 excludes all TCP retransmissions which are network-dependent. In other words, we compute the fractions of aforementioned traffic components within ($raw - tcp\_rt$). Numbers in each row add up to 100%.

We describe the findings regarding to Table 2 as follows. *(i)* Byte contributions of TCP/IP headers and HTTP/SPDY headers are non-trivial, especially for warm-cache loads whose website payload sizes (Figure 4), object payload sizes (Figure 5), and packet payload sizes are all statistically smaller than those of cold-cache loads. *(ii)* The $ssl\_usr\_enc - ssl\_usr\_dec$ column quantifies the overhead due to symmetric encryption. Usually it is positive due to the MAC (Message Authentication Code) or paddings (for blocked ciphers) introduced in the encryption process. However, SSL supports stream-level compression that compresses the entire SSL stream before encrypting it. If that option is used, ssl_usr_enc refers to the compressed and encrypted bytes appearing on the wire, and ssl_usr_dec denotes the decrypted and decompressed bytes delivered to the upper layer. In that case, ssl_usr_enc can be smaller than ssl_usr_dec. We found that only a few HTTPS flows use this compression option but none of the SPDY flows uses it (§4.8). This explains why $ssl\_usr\_enc - ssl\_usr\_dec$ for HTTPS is much smaller than that of SPDY. *(iii)* DNS (udp_usr) accounts for negligible traffic.

Why is SSL Overhead so High? Table 2 indicates that SSL header and control traffic (ssl_ctl) is responsible for the highest protocol overhead among all eight non-HTTP categories *e.g.*, as high as 45% for warm-cache load using HTTPS/SPDY. This is explained as follows. *(i)* We found that most such overhead comes from the SSL handshake phase. Figure 2 plots the distribution of the number of bytes incurred by the handshakes across all SSL sessions, for both datasets. The overhead ranging from 0.5 KB to 8 KB (mean: 4.2 KB, median: 4.4 KB) depends on several factors including the certificate size, whether a full or

Table 3: What-if analysis of changing protocols. The numbers shown are the overall protocol efficiency rates (DS1).

What-if Scenario	Mobile Sites		Non-mobile Sites	
	Cold	Warm	Cold	Warm
Original	83.0%	62.3%	81.0%	58.1%
HTTP→ HTTPS	71.1%	42.7%	68.2%	38.6%
Plus GTP	78.2%	57.1%	76.2%	53.1%
HTTP→HTTPS + GTP	66.7%	39.1%	63.9%	35.4%

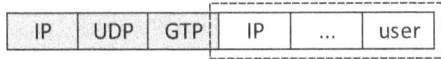

Figure 3: A common configuration of GTP. The user packet is surrounded by dashed line.

an abbreviated handshake is performed, *etc.*[3] (In contrast, the overhead of a TCP handshake is only around 100 bytes). In the SSL data transfer phase, each encrypted data block only has a 5-byte header, and the overhead introduced by symmetric encryption ($ssl\_usr\_enc - ssl\_usr\_dec$) is also small as shown in Table 2 so the SSL overhead in data transfer phase is negligible. *(ii)* TCP connections are not effectively reused. We will detail the connection reuse issue in §4.3. *(iii)* As will be shown in Figure 5 (§4.4), most objects are small in payload size. By putting together the above three observations, we found the high overhead of SSL is caused by inefficient reuse of TCP connections, each incurring high SSL handshake overhead compared to the small payload it carries. Warm-cache loads incur higher SSL overhead than cold-cache loads do because for warm loads, their object payload sizes are smaller (Figure 5) and their connections are more poorly reused.

The Overall Protocol Efficiency Rate is defined to be the fraction of $http\_usr$ or $spdy\_usr$ shown in the rightmost column in Table 2. It quantifies the fraction of data (*i.e.,* the HTTP/SPDY payload) ultimately consumed by the user. HTTP significantly outperforms HTTPS and SPDY, and cold-cache load is more efficient than warm-cache load. Warm-cache load for HTTPS and SPDY always yields efficiency rates less than 50%, and sometime as low as 11%. The reasons have been detailed above.

What if All HTTP is Replaced by HTTPS? We consider a "what-if" scenario where all HTTP flows in the dataset switch to HTTPS. This is possible in the near future given the rapid deployment of HTTPS and SPDY. We construct the what-if scenario by adding to TCP flows carrying HTTP objects dummy SSL handshakes whose sizes conform to the distribution shown in Figure 2. The overhead in the SSL data transfer phase is ignored. Also existing HTTPS and SPDY flows are not changed in the what-if scenario. The "Original" row in Table 3 lists the overall protocol efficiency rates of the original DS1 trace, considering all three protocols. The "HTTP→HTTPS" row corresponds to the what-if scenario. The results indicate that switching to HTTPS will reduce the *overall* protocol efficiency rates by at least 12% to 20%.

What if Transferred in Cellular Core Network? When passing through the 3G/LTE cellular core network, user packets will be tunneled by the GPRS Tunneling Protocol (GTP) [5]. As shown in Figure 3, when tunneled, a user packet (surrounded by dashed line) is encapsulated by an IP header (20 bytes), a UDP header (8 bytes), and a GTP header (at least 8 bytes). In LTE, when a base

Table 4: TCP reuse status across objects.

Data Set	Protocol*	Reused	First	Connection Not Reused		
				Closed	Busy	Other
DS1	HTTP(S)	35.5%	28.6%	4.5%	13.5%	18.0%
	SPDY	47.4%	52.6%	0	0	0
DS2	HTTP(S)	37.2%	28.4%	10.6%	7.3%	16.5%
	SPDY	47.4%	52.6%	0	0	0

* HTTP(S) means HTTP or HTTPS.

station receives a user packet over air interface, it will perform the encapsulation and forward the packet towards the serving gateway (SGW). The GTP header contains the tunnel information, and the outer IP header contains the base station IP as the source address and the SGW IP as the destination address. UMTS uses a conceptually similar scheme for tunneling.

The "Plus GTP" row in Table 3 indicates that under the aforementioned configuration, the overall protocol efficiency rates will decrease by at least 5% due to the additional IP/UDP/GTP headers. If the above two what-if scenarios are combined, the reduction will be up to 23% as shown in the last row of Table 3.

4.3 TCP Connection Management

We study two aspects of TCP connection management policy: connection reuse and connection closure.

Reusing TCP Connection for multiple objects helps reduce the resource utilization in two ways. *(i)* It reduces overheads such as TCP handshake, slow start, and SSL handshake, leading to fewer round trips. In cellular networks with high latency, this means lower radio energy consumption since usually the radio is not turned off during the entire page loading period due to the long tail time explained in §1. *(ii)* Reusing connections also helps lower the bandwidth utilization caused by SSL handshake (§4.2).

To understand whether TCP connections are properly reused, we start by measuring the number of distinct server IPs the handset contacts during loading a website. In DS1, the median values for (mobile sites, cold-cache load), (mobile, warm), (non-mobile, cold), (non-mobile, warm) are 8, 5, 10, and 7, respectively. However, complex sites may involve up to 100 distinct IPs. The number of distinct IP addresses is clearly the *lower bound* of the number of required TCP connections, which we found to be much higher: the median values of the total number of actual established TCP connections of a website are 22, 7, 37, and 12, respectively, for the aforementioned four schemes.

Why are TCP Connections not Reused? To answer this, we classify each object into the following five categories shown in Table 4[4]. *(i)* The object is transferred by reusing an existing TCP connection ("Reused"). *(ii)* Reusing a connection is inherently impossible because it is the first time that the client connects to that server ("First"). *(iii)* No connection is reused because all existing connections are closed or marked as `Connection:close` ("Closed"). *(iv)* All existing connections are busy transferring user data, and (probably because of this) the client opens a new connection ("Busy"). *(v)* There is at least one reusable idle connection, but the client still opens a new connection ("Other").

Table 4 indicates striking differences between HTTP(S) and SPDY in the "Connection Not Reused" categories. *(i)* In HTTP(S), a connection may not be reusable if it closes too soon or if

---

[3]The implementation limitation where only RSA key exchange is used by the modified SSL library of UbiDump has negligible impact on the handshake overhead, based on our local experiments.

[4]Usually a browser does not reuse a single connection for multiple host names, even if they resolve to the same IP address. Our analysis follows this practice although the results are qualitatively similar between IP-based and host-based reuse.

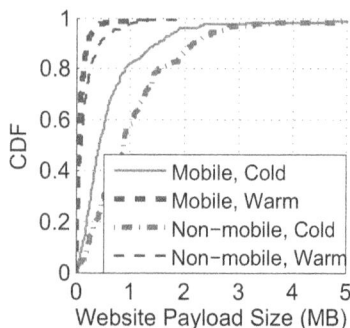

Figure 4: Payload sizes across websites (DS1).

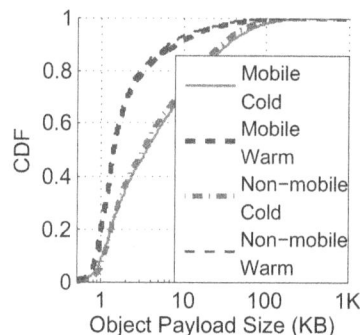

Figure 5: Payload sizes across objects (DS1).

`Connection:close` is used. SPDY addresses this problem by using a much longer timeout (describe soon) and by forbidding to use the `Connection` header field (*i.e.,* SPDY always assumes a persistent connection). *(ii)* In HTTP(S), a busy connection may block a new request to the same server but this does not happen in SPDY, which allows multiplexing transfers of multiple objects of the same domain in a single connection. SPDY's approach can potentially create head-of-line blocking at the transport layer, whose negative effects can somewhat be mitigated by prioritizing object loads [9]. *(iii)* The "Other" category indicates that for HTTP(S), often the client should have reused the connection but it did not, probably due to an implementation issue. Overall, we found SPDY outperforms HTTP(S) in reusing TCP connections, leading to the benefits described at the beginning of this subsection.

Connection Closure: HTTP vs SPDY. When an HTTP(S) data transfer finishes, a client or a server usually waits for a while before sending a FIN, to increase the chance of the TCP connection being reused [27]. Our measurement shows that for HTTP(S), most of their TCP connections are closed by the handset using TCP FIN, and the remaining are usually terminated by FIN initiated by the server, or by the connection split proxy in the studied cellular network for server port 80/8080 (§3.1). Negligible fraction of connections are terminated by TCP RST. The closure delay (*i.e.,* the delay between the last data packet and the FIN/RST) usually ranges between 0 and 10 seconds.

On the other hand, most TCP connections carrying SPDY traffic are not terminated when the data collection terminates. They are kept open for a long time *i.e.,* longer than the 30-second timeout used to determine the completion of a page load (§3). This is because SPDY recommends "clients do not close open connections until the user navigates away from all web pages referencing a connection, or until the server closes the connection". Servers are also encouraged to "leave connections open for as long as possible, but can terminate idle connections if necessary" [9]. This creates more opportunities for reusing TCP connections (Table 4). Note HTTPS/SPDY traffic does not traverse the connection split proxy.

Silent Connection Closure. As mentioned before, it is useful to reuse TCP connections to amortize overheads such as TCP and SSL handshakes. In cellular networks, delayed FIN/RST packets can cause significant radio energy drainage, due to their incurred tail times. To address such a dilemma between connection reuse and delayed connection closure overhead, recent work [27] proposes a TCP extension called Silent TCP connection Closure (STC). The key idea is that both sides close the connection silently without performing FIN handshake based on a negotiated keep-alive timer. It allows both sides to delay connection closure using the negotiated timer (and thus reuse connections). In the meanwhile it eliminates

Table 5: Mobile websites with the largest payload sizes (DS1).

Website (Cold)	Type	# Objs	Avg Size	Height[*]
deadspin.com	Blog	71	6.5 MB	25.3
pinterest.com	OSN	128	5.4 MB	47.2
disney.go.com	Entertain	99	5.3 MB	6.5
salon.com	News	279	5.2 MB	15.2
Website (Warm)	Type	# Objs	Avg Size	Height[*]
disney.go.com	Entertain	26	1.4 MB	6.5
perezhilton.com	Blog	54	1.1 MB	5.9
cbs.com	TV & Video	61	1.0 MB	2.4
yahoo.com	News	62	0.7 MB	14.0

[*] The unit is the screen height in portrait orientation.

the tail time incurred by the FIN/RST packets that usually appear as separate traffic bursts. STC is generally applicable to any mobile application. It is lightweight, incrementally deployable, and backward compatible. All its introduced changes can be confined within cellular networks, which STC is specifically designed for, by upgrading the mobile device and cellular proxy software. In §4.6, we show STC is particularly useful for web browsing.

4.4 Web Page Content

We now shift our focus to the web page content. Figure 4 plots the distribution of the payload sizes of the top websites (*i.e.,* their landing pages). The "payload size" refers to the size of $http\_usr$ or $spdy\_usr$ in Table 2. The payload may be compressed if the server does so. As expected, non-mobile sites are usually larger than mobile sites, and cold-cache loads transfer more bytes than warm-cache loads do.

Large Websites. Figure 4 indicates that for cold-cache load, 20% of mobile sites and more than 40% of non-mobile sites have more than 1 MB of payload. Table 5 lists the largest mobile sites (in terms of the total payload size) for cold and warm load. We found that statistically, large mobile sites tend to be much "taller" in their appearances than small mobile sites do[5]. We measure the height of a website from the captured screenshot in which the width of the page already automatically aligns with the handset screen width in portrait orientation. The "Height" column in Table 5 thus shows the page height in multiples of the handset screen height. The heights are usually far greater than 1 for large mobile sites. In contrast, mobile sites with small sizes are much more likely to have heights of exact one unit. We discuss solutions for reducing sizes of "tall" websites in §5.

---

[5] A few sites may do "infinite scrolling": when the user scrolls to the bottom of a tall page, the browser will load more contents, which are not captured by our automated testbed.

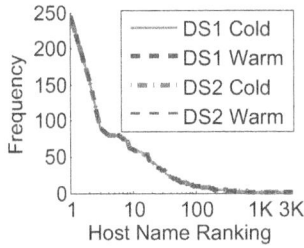

Figure 6: Occurrences of host names in distinct websites.

Table 6: Breakdown of large objects (mobile websites in DS1).

Type	% bytes (objs)	Large images (subset of large objects)	
		Cause	% bytes (objs)
Images	64.5% (60.2%)	High Res. JPG/PNG	78.5% (78.1%)
JS	22.8% (25.5%)	Sprite JPG/PNG	6.7% (7.4%)
Html	4.4% (5.4%)	Animated JPG/PNG	4.1% (2.8%)
Fonts	4.0% (4.7%)	Animated GIF	6.2% (3.7%)
CSS	3.8% (3.9%)	Vector SVG images	4.6% (8.0%)
Json	0.5% (0.3%)		

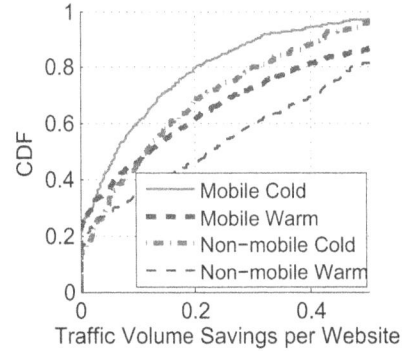

Figure 7: What-if analysis with shared hosts removed (DS1).

Table 7: Top hosts accessed by multiple websites (DS1, cold).

Host name	# Websites	Description
www.google-analytics.com	245	User tracking & stats
b.scorecardresearch.com	156	User tracking & stats
www.facebook.com	91	Facebook
ad.doubleclick.net	81	Advertisements
pixel.quantserve.com	81	User tracking & stats

Large Objects. We now look at individual web objects. As shown in Figure 5, the object payload size (including both request and response, but dominated by response payload) follows a heavy-tail distribution similar to that in Figure 4, except that the difference between mobile and non-mobile object sizes is much smaller. We next study the largest 2,632 objects of mobile websites in DS1 since they are the most bandwidth-consuming. They account of 2.4% of all mobile site objects while their payload size contribution is 50.0%. Their content type breakdown is shown on the left-hand side of Table 6. Images dominate the large objects in terms of both the bytes and the object count.

The right part of Table 6 investigates why the images belonging to the largest 2,632 objects have large sizes based on our visual inspection of more than 1,500 images. 78% of them are single images with (often unnecessarily) high resolutions, while about 10% of the large images consist of multiple sub-images whose resolutions are not high. Those sub-images can be animation frames. Unlike GIF, neither JPEG nor PNG has built-in support for animation so the animation will be "played" by quickly rolling over each sub-image using Javascript. Another usage of such an image slicing technique is called "Sprite Image" i.e., to transfer multiple small images in one large image to save round-trip delays. A potential issue with this approach is the reduced caching efficiency, as the entire sprite image needs to be transferred if any sub-image changes. So sprite image better works with small sub-images.

Hosts Shared by Multiple Websites Providing Third-Party Services. We obtained from both datasets about 3,200 (2,200) unique host names for cold (warm) cache loads. Figure 6 ranks the host names by the number of websites they appear in (i.e., the "frequency" on Y Axis). We found that although most hosts are only associated with one single website, there are a small amount of hosts that are accessed by a large number of websites. The top host name appears in 245 distinct websites. Table 7 describes the top shared hosts for DS1 (cold load for both mobile and non-mobile websites). We also manually verified host names appearing in at least 10 distinct websites in DS1 for both cold and warm load. All those hosts seem to provide third-party "add-on" features such as user tracking, usage measurement, advertisements, and social network feeds for the websites they are embedded in.

What if Shared Hosts are Eliminated? We consider a what-if scenario where the above third-party hosts are eliminated. Specifically, we remove traffic from/to hosts appearing in at least 10 distinct websites since they are verified to be not related to the main content of the website[6]. Doing so reduces both the bandwidth consumption and the radio energy utilization for the mobile handset. We consider the bandwidth saving here and quantify the energy benefits in §4.6. Figure 7 plots the CDF of traffic volume (HTTP/HTTPS/SPDY header and payload) savings across websites in the what-if scenario. For 20% of websites ($y = 0.8$), the bytes reduction achieves at least 20%, 39%, 30%, and 48% for (mobile sites, cold-cache load), (mobile, warm), (non-mobile, cold), and (non-mobile, warm), respectively. The 95-percentiles are even as high as 43%, 75%, 49%, and 73% for the four scenarios, respectively. Note these are the lower bounds of bandwidth savings since hosts shared by less than 10 distinct websites can also provide third-party services. The results indicate that for many websites, compared to their main contents, the embedded third-party services impose high bandwidth overhead, and optimizing them can lead to non-trivial or even significant bandwidth savings.

Redirections. Table 8 lists the distribution of the number of redirections (HTTP 301 or 302) before the main html file is transferred, for cold-cache load of each website[7]. To our surprise, 57.8% of the mobile sites take at least two redirections while 90% non-mobile sites require no more than one redirection. We found that some popular mobile sites have as many as 5 redirections before the phone can fetch the main html file, such as `msn.com`, `wsj.com`, and `bankofamerica.com`. Excessive redirections hurt in particular user experience in cellular networks with high latency by bringing in additional round trips. For example, loading the mobile version of `live.com`, the Microsoft online service gateway, on cellular network takes five redirections, with four having DNS lookup and three being transferred in HTTPS. All redirections take about 6.7

---

[6]We do handle a few exceptions in our analysis e.g., we do not remove the `facebook.com` host from the Facebook website itself.
[7]For most sites, loading `www.xyz.com` instead of `xyz.com` can reduce the number of redirections by one.

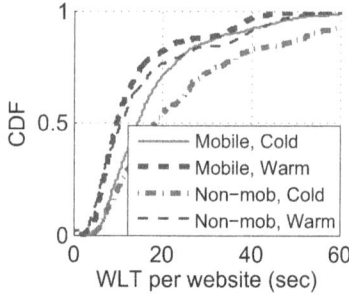

Figure 8: Distributions of WLT across websites (DS1).

Table 8: Number of redirections (DS1, cold load).

# Redirections	Mobile	Non-mobile
0	7.3%	24.7%
1	34.9%	65.3%
2	42.5%	6.3%
3	9.9%	2.3%
4	3.6%	0.7%
5	1.8%	0.7%

seconds (median) in total, leading to significant user experience degradation and radio energy waste.

4.5 Timing Dynamics

In this subsection, we begin by measuring website load time and rendering time. Although performance is not our focus in this study, it is correlated with the radio energy utilization in cellular networks since usually the radio is on during the entire page loading period due to the long tail times. They also lead us to examine a key metric called inter-object idle time, which causes many websites to have very long load time, significantly hurting the resource efficiency.

Website Load Time (WLT) is defined to be the duration from the client sending the first byte of the web/DNS request to the client receiving the last *data* packet from the web server. Note that control data such as TCP FIN can go beyond WLT. Figure 8 plots its distributions for DS1. As expected, mobile sites usually have shorter WLT values than non-mobile sites do, and warm-cache loading outperforms cold-cache loading. Websites in DS2 are loaded faster than DS1 due to lower latency in Wi-Fi networks (figure not shown).

Website Rendering Time (WRT) is defined to be the duration from the client sending the first byte to the moment when the page is fully rendered. It is measured by `WebView.PictureListener.onNewPicture()`, a callback function triggered at each time when the rendering results of the `WebView` changes. One issue of this method is that, for some pages containing animated elements (*e.g.,* an animated ad banner), the callback is being continuously triggered till the end of the data collection. We therefore eliminate from our rendering time analysis such websites (account for about 30% of all websites) whose WRT cannot be accurately determined. We plan to use more accurate metrics (*e.g.,* Speed Index [14]) to quantify WRT in future work.

WRT can be regarded as the *user-perceived* page loading time. Figure 9 plots the distributions of the proportion of rendering time within the total transfer time (*i.e.,* WRT/WLT) across websites for DS1. For 40% of the websites, their page rendering finishes before the data transfer finishes. DS2 exhibits a similar distribution.

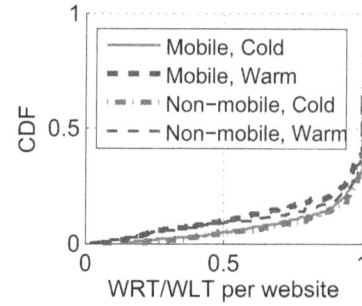

Figure 9: Distributions of WRT/WLT across websites (DS1).

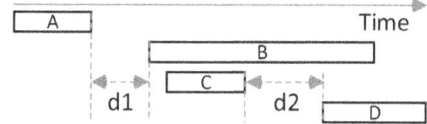

Figure 10: An example illustrating IIT. Each box corresponds to a web object transfer including both request and response.

We are interested in the origins of objects that are transferred after the page is fully rendered. We found that some of them belong to shared hosts providing "add-on" features such as user tracking (Table 7). But many more of them correspond to objects whose transfers are not necessary, such as duplicate contents and not consumed data. For example, a single load of `usmagazine.com` transfers about 650KB of advertisement images that are never displayed on the page, leading to waste of bandwidth utilization.

Figure 8 indicates the WLT can last for more than 60 seconds, because often there are long idle periods among object transfers. Such idle periods can cause energy inefficiencies due to the tail effect. Recall that a tail time (T_{tail}) is the timeout period before the radio is turned off (§1). As an example, in Figure 10, after Transfer A, if $d_1 \geq T_{tail}$, the radio will be on for T_{tail} seconds, then be turned off, and then be switched on by Transfer B. If $d_1 < T_{tail}$, the radio will be always on from A to D (D incurs another tail). The tail can be triggered by any data burst and T_{tail} can last for more than 10 seconds. Our subsequent analysis aims at understanding the root causes of idle periods like d_1 in Figure 10.

Inter-object Idle Time (IIT) depicts the idle time period when no object transfer is in progress. Recall a transfer includes both the request and the response of an object. For a transfer W starting at time t, the IIT *before* W is defined to be $IIT(W) = \max\{0, t-t_L\}$ where t_L is the latest transfer ending time for all other objects whose transfers start before t. Therefore the network is idle from time $t - IIT(W)$ to t waiting for request (but the radio might still be on). For example, in Figure 10 consisting four transfers, $IIT(B) = d_1$ but $IIT(D) = 0$ instead of d_2 since B partially overlaps with D. IIT is a conservative estimation of the part of the website load time (WLT) that can be reduced without violating the dependencies among objects. Eliminating IIT reduces WLT and saves radio energy.

Origins of Long IIT. Figure 11 plots across all websites the distribution of the maximum IIT for each mobile website load. DS1 and DS2 exhibit very similar distributions, because IIT does not consider the idle time *within* a transfer that is usually caused by the network or server latency. Instead, IIT is always caused by the delay introduced by the handset. Figure 11 indicates that for more than 20% of the mobile websites, their maximum IITs are longer than 1 second. Some IITs can be as long as 30 seconds.

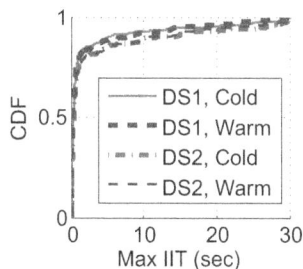

Figure 11: Max IIT across mobile sites.

Table 9: Periodic transfer examples (DS1).

Website	Periodicity
ChartBeat (30+ sites)	≥ 15 sec
`m.espn.go.com`	15 sec
`comcast.net`	10 sec
`m.staple.com`	5 sec
`boston.com`	1,2,4,8,... sec

We are interested in the long IITs that lengthen the WLT and therefore increase the radio energy consumption. By sampling a few long IITs, we classify their root causes as follows. *(i)* Periodic transfers triggered by Javascript. For example, ChartBeat (`http://chartbeat.com`), a popular user tracking service used by more than 30 different websites, sends a beacon to `ping.chartbeat.net` periodically (the periodicity depends on the level of user interaction). *(ii)* Delayed transfers controlled by Javascript. The object is only transferred once instead of periodically. For example, a few mobile sites (*e.g.,* `m.sprint.com`) use the TeaLeaf Customer Experience Management framework (`http://www.tealeaf.com/`), which sends some measurement data 30 seconds after the main page is loaded. *(iii)* Client computation delay such as parsing complex Javascript and CSS files. This usually happens for IITs less than 1 seconds during which the CPU usage is 100% (our testbed logs the CPU usage). *(iv)* Other delays not caused by the CPU bottleneck. For example, some sites use the Google Location Service (`https://www.google.com/loc/m/api`) for mapping a GPS coordinate to a street address. There is usually some network idle period (from hundreds of milliseconds to several seconds) before the request is sent out because the handset is obtaining its location as indicated by the GPS icon displayed on the status bar.

Among the above causes, periodic transfers impose the highest impact on the radio energy utilization. We found that compared with those generated by mobile apps [28], periodic transfers in web pages are more aggressively involving much smaller periodicities (*e.g.,* 5 seconds), which can keep the radio always on as long as the user stays on the page. We show examples of identified periodic transfers in Table 9.

4.6 Energy Impact of Timing Dynamics

We quantify the radio energy impact of three previously described issues: delayed connection closure (§4.3), the shared hosts (§4.4), and the inter-object idle time (IIT, §4.5). All of them can inject network idle time and therefore cause more radio energy consumption due to the tail effect. Our analysis methodology is as follows. For each website, we feed the original trace into a radio energy model and get the energy consumption denoted as E_0. We then construct a what-if scenario (*e.g.,* removing all shared hosts) by modifying the trace. The energy model then computes the radio energy of the modified trace as E_1. The resultant radio energy saving in the what-if scenario is $(E_0 - E_1)/E_0$. We next describe three what-if scenarios S1, S2, and S3.

S1: Silent Connection Closure. As mentioned in §4.3, most FIN/RST packets are delayed, incurring radio energy overhead. In S1, we assume silent TCP connection closure (STC) is used by eliminating FIN handshakes[8]. Similar analysis was performed in the original STC proposal [27] by applying STC to packet traces

collected from a cellular carrier in an application-agnostic manner. Here we investigate whether STC is useful for web browsing.

S2: No Third-Party Services from Shared Hosts. We remove TCP connections containing host names appearing in at least 10 distinct websites. The method and parameters are justified in the what-if analysis of the bandwidth impact of the shared hosts (§4.4).

S3: Reducing Inter-object Idle Time (IIT). We reduce an IIT to δ if it is longer than δ, otherwise we do not modify it. For example, in Figure 10, B, C, and D will be shifted backward by $d_1 - \delta$ if $d_1 > \delta$. The threshold δ specifies the maximum processing delay of each object. We conservatively choose $\delta = 0.5s$ which we believe is achievable if websites are well optimized for smartphones. Changing δ to 0.3s or 0.7s does not affect the results qualitatively.

In fact, to reduce IIT properly without impacting the functionalities, we need IITs' app-level semantics, which however are difficult to infer in an automated manner. We therefore consider the aforementioned upper bound of energy saving by reducing all long IITs to δ. In many cases, objects with long IITs are *delay-tolerant* (*e.g.,* periodic advertisement update and user tracking). Wisely scheduling their transfers using prefetching, batching, or piggyback [16] can eliminate IITs without impacting functionality. Also, even when there are legitimate reasons to use high-energy-overhead features such as periodic transfers, it is a good practice to provide options for users to disable them. We thus believe S3 has practical relevance.

The What-if Analysis Results are shown in Figure 12 and 13 for warm loads of DS1 and DS2, respectively (results for cold loads are similar). We leverage two smartphone radio energy models: the UMTS/HSPA model [28] and the LTE model [22]. Both models[9] take as input a packet trace and compute the radio energy consumption by simulating the Radio Resource Control (RRC) state machine used by the handset to manage the radio interface. We found both models yield very similar results in terms of relative radio energy savings so we present the results using the UMTS model. In each figure, each curve plots the CDF of energy savings across all websites. For example, a point at $(0.2, 0.4)$ means the energy savings are at least 20% for 60% of the websites.

We describe our findings. *(i)* For 60% to 80% of the websites, S2 brings no saving. This is because although shared-hosts are popular (Table 7), their transfers often temporally coexist with other objects. Therefore removing them does not help turn the radio off. The energy savings brought by S3 is also insignificant, because many websites do not have a long IIT of more than 0.5 second (Figure 11). *(ii)* For some websites, S2 or S3 brings considerable energy savings. Fixing their resource-inefficient traffic patterns by removing the third-party objects or reducing the IIT helps save the radio energy by up to 80%. For example, by removing the ChartBeat traffic (Table 9), the overall radio energy saving for `bloomberg.com` (warm-cache load) is 66%. Note the S2 curve

---

[8]We conservatively do not remove any RST packets.

[9]UMTS/HSPA model: Google Nexus One handset, DCH→FACH timer 5s, FACH→IDLE timer 12s; LTE model: HTC Thunderbolt handset, CONNECTED→IDLE timer 11.6s.

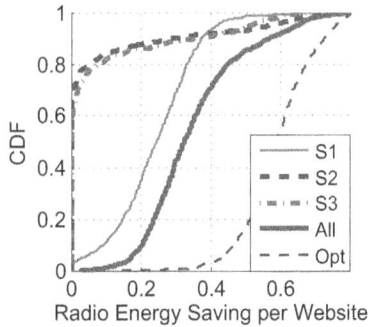

Figure 12: What-if analysis of saving radio energy by changing traffic patterns (mobile sites, warm load, DS1).

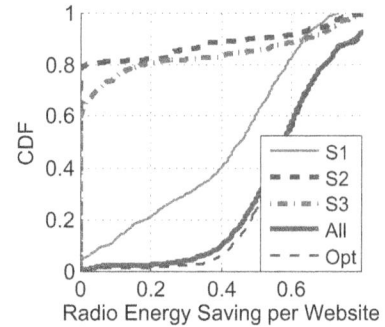

Figure 13: What-if analysis of saving radio energy by changing traffic patterns (mobile sites, warm load, DS2).

Table 10: Cache status across objects (cold load in DS1).

Cacheability Category	Mobile Sites		Non-mobile Sites	
	Objs	Bytes	Objs	Bytes
C1: Cacheable w/ explicit lifetime	51.2%	71.3%	48.3%	67.6%
C2: Cacheable w/o explicit lifetime	23.2%	19.7%	24.6%	22.2%
C3: `no-store` due to server	10.8%	2.4%	11.9%	3.0%
C4: `no-cache` due to server	12.5%	6.2%	13.8%	7.0%
C5: HTTP POST objects	0.6%	0.1%	0.7%	0.1%
C6: Other	1.7%	0.3%	0.7%	0.1%

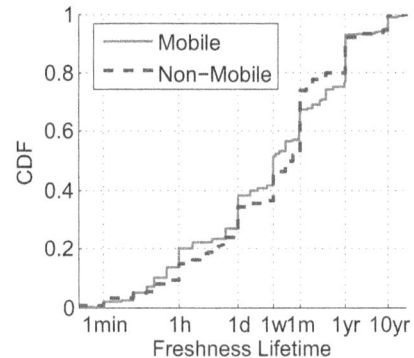

Figure 14: Freshness lifetime across objects (DS1, cold load).

underestimates the savings because hosts shared by less than 10 distinct websites can also provide third-party services but we do not remove them. *(iii)* For S1, it brings the highest radio energy savings, indicating STC is particularly effective for mobile web browsing. The median radio energy saving is 25% for DS1 and 45% for DS2. In contrast, as measured in [27], applying STC to all mobile traffic patterns yields a saving of only 11%, since many long-lived connections (*e.g.,* video streaming) cannot benefit much from STC. Also, the connection split proxy (§3.1) has small impact on the S1 savings for DS1 (Figure 12), because *(i)* the vast majority of connections in both datasets are closed by handsets instead of the proxy or remote servers, and *(ii)* the S1 curves for both datasets exhibit qualitatively similar patterns as shown in Figure 12 and 13.

The "All" curve represents a what-if scenario where S1, S2, and S3 are jointly applied. In that scenario, the median radio energy savings in Figure 12 and 13 are 32.5% and 58.7%, respectively. DS2 achieves higher savings than DS1 does, because for the same website, its overall load time (WLT) in DS2 is shorter than that in DS1, while the absolute durations of eliminated timing gaps are similar for both datasets. Therefore the removed fraction of radio-on time is higher in DS2 than in DS1.

The "Opt" curve refers to a what-if scenario same as that of the "All" curve, plus that all inter-packet time (IPT) longer than δ (0.5s) is reduced to δ. IPT is different from IIT in that IPT further includes timing gaps *within* a transfer. The "Opt" curve depicts the upper bound of the radio energy saving for each website. For DS2, the "All" and "Opt" curves are almost identical, indicating the timing gaps optimized by S1, S2, and S3 contribute to almost all idle time periods except for those caused by the high network latency (*i.e.,* high IPT), which seldom exist in DS2 but often appear in DS1 (so the "All" and "Opt" curves differ a lot in DS1).

4.7 Caching Semantics

Caching effectively reduces network bandwidth consumption and decreases user-perceived latency. In mobile networks, caching on user devices is particularly important because it can poten-

tially eliminate any network-related overhead. Efficient caching relies on two factors: good caching *implementation* and *semantics*. The former requires a browser to strictly conform to the HTTP caching protocol [20], while the latter means proper configuration of caching parameters such as cacheability and expiration time, as the entire caching mechanism will be bypassed if, for example, the server marks all object as `no-store`.

Web caching implementation on mobile devices has been extensively investigated by previous work [26] so here we study the caching semantics. We have verified using the techniques introduced in [26] that our testbed (using `WebView` on Android 4.0.4) does follow the HTTP/1.1 caching protocol except that it does not cache byte-range responses that are not observed in the datasets. The total cache size and the size limit of a single cache entry of the `WebView` are measured to be 20 MB and 2.62 MB, respectively. These are greater than the maximum landing page and object sizes, respectively, in our datasets. Also note HTTP, HTTPS, and SPDY use the same caching protocol.

Object Cacheability is summarized in Table 10, which classifies each object in a cold-cache load into one of the six categories C1 to C6. C1 and C2 are cacheable objects. They differ in that C1 objects have freshness lifetime[10] explicitly set by the server using `Expires` and/or `Cache-Control:max-age` header fields, while C2 objects are without such explicit lifetime. For C2, a client is allowed to use a heuristic lifetime whose value completely depends on the implementation. C3 refers to objects that are not cacheable,

---

[10]The freshness lifetime is used to keep the consistency between a local copy and server's copy. Within the lifetime of an object, a client just uses the local (cached) copy. Otherwise the client needs to contact the server to revalidate the freshness of the object.

Table 11: Caching across main HTML pages (cold load, DS1).

Cacheability Category	Mobile Sites	Non-mobile Sites
C1: Cacheable w/ explicit lifetime	16.5%	15.4%
C2: Cacheable w/o explicit lifetime	33.6%	42.7%
C3: `no-store` due to server	26.0%	18.2%
C4: `no-cache` due to server	23.9%	23.8%

Table 12: Compression what-if analysis (DS1).

What-if	Mobile Sites		Non-mobile Sites	
Scenario	Cold	Warm	Cold	Warm
T1	10.8%	11.9%	11.3%	13.1%
T2	3.1%	10.3%	4.1%	13.0%
T3	13.9%	22.2%	15.4%	26.1%
T4	14.4%	24.5%	16.4%	29.0%

as indicated by the `no-store` cache control directive. C4 corresponds to must-revalidate objects that are tagged by `no-cache` or `must-revalidate` cache control directives. Such objects are cacheable, but a client must always revalidate with the origin server before serving them (*i.e.*, their lifetime is zero). C5 consists of objects requested using HTTP POST (usually not cacheable). Remaining objects are classified as C6.

We describe our findings in Table 10. *(i)* About 23% to 25% of the objects belong to C2, and their lifetimes are determined by heuristic values that vary across diverse HTTP client implementations: a short heuristic lifetime (*e.g.*, 30 minutes used by the `HttpResponseCache` library [26]) can cause unnecessary revalidation requests, while a long lifetime (*e.g.*, 48 hours adopted by the Safari browser) may lead to out-of-date local copies. *(ii)* 11% to 12% of the objects (C3) are tagged by the `no-store` directive so they cannot enjoy any benefit of caching. The situation is improved for those 12% to 14% of the must-revalidate objects (C4), since if the object content does not change, the server only needs to reply a small `304 Not Modified` response header instead of transferring the entire object. However, revalidation requests can still incur additional network round trips and potentially additional resource consumption. In Table 10, 23% of all mobile sites' objects fall into C3 or C4, meaning that every request for any of these objects will involve a request to the remote server and therefore incur at least one round trip. Also recall that in cellular networks, even transferring such small amount of data can turn on the radio and keep it on for T_{tail} seconds when no concurrent transfer is in progress. *(iii)* Both mobile and non-mobile sites share similar distributions in Table 10, implying caching semantics are not specifically optimized for mobile websites that are delivered in a more resource-constrained environment compared to their desktop counterparts.

Cacheability of Main HTML Pages is listed in Table 11. 26% (18%) of mobile (non-mobile) websites mark their main HTML pages as `no-store`, causing bandwidth waste for warm-cache load, as such main HTML pages are frequently accessed and their sizes are often not small. For example, the main HTML pages of `m.bing.com` and `mobile.twitter.com` are non-storable, with sizes (after compression) of 65KB and 85KB, respectively.

Freshness Lifetime. We examine the server-specified lifetime for objects belonging to Category C1 in Table 10. As shown in Figure 14, overall about 75% of the C1 objects have common lifetime values such as one hour, one day, and one month. For objects in mobile websites, their lifetime settings are statistically even shorter than those in non-mobile websites. We found many short lifetime values tend to be aggressive. For example, about 20% of the C1 objects in mobile websites have lifetime shorter than 1 hour. Within such objects, 35.7% are images and fonts, 34.3% are Javascripts, and 7.8% are CSS scripts. It is unlikely that their contents can change within such a short period of 1 hour or less. Given the resource-constrained environments of cellular networks, it is important for web developers to ensure that objects are not assigned too short freshness lifetimes.

4.8 Data Compression

Compression is widely used to reduce bandwidth consumption. Previous work (*e.g.*, [25]) characterized the effectiveness of compression on today's smartphone HTTP traffic. Our analysis goes beyond previous studies by further considering compression at the SSL and SPDY layers.

Compression support provided by HTTP, HTTPS, and SPDY are different. *(i)* For HTTP, the server can choose to compress an individual HTTP response payload (*i.e.*, object-level compression) if the client offers this option in an HTTP request. *(ii)* For SSL, the server can choose to compress the entire SSL stream before encrypting it based on the compression option negotiated during the handshake. *(iii)* In SPDY, web request and response headers are embedded in a particular type of SPDY header, and are mandatorily compressed using a customized dictionary. HTTP, by contrast, never compresses headers.

How Often is Compression Utilized? We summarize our finding for DS1 (DS2 yields similar results). *(i)* For HTTP, compression is always offered by `WebView` while only 31.8% of HTTP `200(OK)` responses are actually compressed by the server. We found that most of the under-utilization is associated with images that are already in compact formats. They account for 82.6% of non-compressed HTTP `200` responses. But as will be shown in Table 12, there still exist non-trivial amount of uncompressed contents compressing which can achieve additional bandwidth savings of up to 11% (13%) for cold (warm) load. *(ii)* In almost all SSL sessions, the client offers the stream-level compression option. But the option is adopted by server in only 8.4% of all SSL sessions. There can be multiple causes for such significant under-utilization *e.g.*, due to unawareness or performance concerns. Note that in fact, the gzip compression scheme used by HTTP, SSL, and SPDY is quite efficient. A single core of a commodity server can achieve throughput of 100+ Mbps [25]. Decompressing data on a commodity smartphone is even faster. So performance concerns should not prevent the use of SSL compression.

What-if Analysis. We study the following what-if scenarios T1 to T4 to understand how compression can be further improved to help reduce the bandwidth consumption. T1 corresponds to the scenario where object-level compression is fully used in HTTP/HTTPS/SPDY response payload. T2 is the hypothetical case where SPDY header compression is also employed in HTTP(S) headers. T3 combines T1 and T2 by compressing both payload and headers separately. In T4, SSL stream-level compression is fully used in HTTPS and SPDY, and it is also ported to HTTP *i.e.*, the entire TCP connection payload carrying HTTP transfers will be compressed as a whole. For each what-if scenario, we first perform the corresponding compression to get a more compact dataset, and then compare it with the original dataset to compute the relative saving of all HTTP/HTTPS/SPDY header and payload bytes.

Table 12 shows the what-if analysis results. *(i)* Full usage of object-level compression for response payload (T1) yields *additional* bandwidth savings of 11% to 13%. Such benefits mainly come from compressing Html/Javascript/CSS/XML objects that

Table 13: A summary of identified resource inefficiencies.

Layer	Description	§
TCP	Inefficient connection reuse	§4.3
SSL	Bandwidth impact of SSL	§4.2
HTTP	Impact of delayed connection closure	§4.6
HTTP	Inefficient caching semantics	§4.7
SSL/HTTP	Inefficient object/stream compression	§4.8
Content	Root causes of large contents	§4.4
Content	Impact of third-party services	§4.4, §4.6
Content	Excessive redirections	§4.4
Content	Unnecessary post-render objects	§4.5
Content	Causes & impact of in-load timing gaps	§4.5, §4.6

are not compressed in the original trace. *(ii)* For T2, surprisingly, just compressing headers brings non-trivial savings (3% to 4%) for cold-cache load. For warm load, the savings are even much higher (10% to 13%), almost as high as those of T1. This is because today's HTTP headers are not as small as one might think. For the entire DS1 dataset, the ratio between total payload size and header size is 12:1 and 3:1 for cold and warm load of mobile sites, respectively. Since HTTP and HTTPS never compress their headers, compressing them reduces the overall header size by more than 40%. *(iii)* The savings achieved by T3 is always the sum of those of T1 and T2. *(iv)* If always used, the stream-level compression (T4) can achieve more savings than T3 does, because it further eliminates redundancies across multiple objects within the same TCP connection. In contrast, T1, T2, and T3 handle each object separately. With SSL compression, HTTP header and payload traffic can be further reduced by 14% and 25% for cold and warm load, respectively, for mobile websites.

5. RECOMMENDATION

We provide detailed recommendations for improving the discovered inefficiencies summarized in Table 13.

1. High SSL Bandwidth Overhead. Mobile OS venders can use the following approaches to mitigate the overhead. *(i)* Perform lightweight SSL handshakes. Specifically, Session Identifier [17] and Session Ticket [29] can be used to resuming previously terminated SSL sessions with low handshake overheads (UbiDump can analyze both of them). Session ticket is preferred because the SSL state is stored at the client side. *(ii)* Reuse TCP connections so that multiple HTTPS/SPDY objects can share the same TCP connection and therefore SSL session.

2. TCP Connection Management. Reuse TCP connections amortizes overheads such as TCP handshake, SSL handshake, and TCP slow start. SPDY outperforms HTTP(S) in connection reuse. Also, delaying closing TCP connections can cause severe radio energy drainage. Such overhead can be eliminated by the silent connection closure scheme, which works particularly well for web browsing.

3. Large Websites and Objects. Under the constraints of delivering necessary contents and providing good user experiences, a mobile website should consume as less bandwidth as possible. The content provider should carefully determine the proper resolution of an image, keeping in mind both the context of the image, and the display capability of the requesting device. Apply "sprite images" only to small sub-images. Double check transfers after the page is fully rendered, as they are often unnecessary (*e.g.,* duplicate or not-consumed objects).

4. Image Lazy-loading Consumes More Energy. One way to mitigate the high bandwidth consumption of the "tall" pages

(Table 5) is to lazily load images *i.e.,* deferring the loading of images until they appear in the client's viewport. This optimization is already implemented by Google modpagespeed [6] using Javascript tricks. In cellular networks, however, doing so can cause intermittent data transfers leading to high radio energy overhead due to the tail effect. In the worst case, the radio can be on as long as the user is scrolling. A better solution might be to split a tall page into several subpages based on content semantics.

5. Excessive Redirections (HTTP 301 and 302) should be minimized as they incur additional round trips especially in cellular networks with high latency.

6. Third-party Services (*e.g.,* ads and user tracking) providers should carefully examine traffic patterns of their data transfers. Javascript-triggered delayed or periodic transfers are particularly energy inefficient in cellular networks. In many cases, transfers incurring long inter-object idle time (IITs) are delay-tolerant or can be prefetched. Wisely scheduling their transfers using prefetching, batching, or piggybacking can minimize IITs without impacting the functionality.

7. Caching Semantics. Content providers should determine carefully if an object should really be marked as **no-store**. For those non-storable large HTML pages (*e.g.,* **mobile.twitter.com**, 85KB), one possible improvement is to separate the html into two parts: a static part and a (usually small) varying part. The static part can have a long lifetime while the varying one can be dynamic content or be marked as **no-cache**. Also, for cacheable objects, good practices are to *(i)* provide explicit freshness lifetimes, and *(ii)* avoid using unnecessarily short lifetimes.

8. Compression. The server should compress large HTML/XML/CSS/Javascript objects. For HTTPS/SPDY, performing compression at the SSL layer saves more bandwidth than using HTTP object-based compression.

6. RELATED WORK

We describe related work in three categories below.

Analyzing SSL Traffic. As described in §2, most previous studies simply ignore the content of SSL traffic [26, 23, 37]. Existing tools such as Wireshark [13] and ssldump [12] require servers' private keys for decryption. The Man-in-the-Middle (MITM) Proxy approach [8, 10] also has limitations as they may change traffic patterns and contents (§2.2). Previous work [30] leverages correlations across protocols and time for classifying HTTPS-based webmail traffic. But the technique does not decrypt the HTTPS traffic. The contribution of the UbiDump tool is it supports on-device SSL decryption without requiring private key or an MITM proxy. Further, previous analysis of SSL usually focuses on its security implications and CPU overhead. We instead study the bandwidth overhead in §4.2.

Mobile Web Measurement and Optimization. Huang *et al.* measured mobile web browsing performance early in 2009 [24]. Gember *et al.* compared web contents consumed by handheld and non-handheld devices [21]. Akamai Mobitest [1] is an online tool measuring performance for web pages loaded on mobile devices. Thiagarajan *et al.* presented a system for measuring the energy consumed by a mobile browser and applied it to diverse websites [32]. The authors provided recommendations such as shrinking Javascript and using energy-efficient image formats. Wang *et al.* studied how client-based caching, prefetching, and speculative loading help improve mobile browser performance [36]. Erman *et al.* examined the interplay between SPDY and the cellular radio layer [18]. Sivakumar *et al.* investigated cloud-based mobile web browsing and revealed that it does not provide clear benefits over the non-cloud-based approach in many cases [31].

Compared with the above work, our study provides new insights on resource efficiency of mobile browsing, considering the content, the browser, the smartphone OS design, and lower-layer protocols. The delayed FIN issue was identified by [28] and was addressed by the recent silent connection closure (STC) proposal [27]. Here we conduct a comprehensive measurement of the benefits of STC on a large number of popular websites. Vallina-Rodriguez *et al.* characterized mobile advertisement traffic [33]. We focus on a broader category of "add-on" services by examining shared hosts and quantifying their energy and bandwidth impact for top websites. Recent work [26] studied implementation issues of HTTP caching on smartphones. Study [25] investigated applying other redundancy elimination (RE) techniques such as object-level compression and delta encoding on smartphone traffic. We complement them by looking at caching semantics and by examining RE techniques used by SSL and SPDY.

General Web Optimization (not mobile-specific) has been a hot area towards which numerous efforts have been made. Recently there are new protocols and optimization frameworks such as Google SPDY [9, 35], QUIC [3], Google modpagespeed [6], and WProf [34] from both industry and academia. We believe our findings will provide them with new insights in the context of mobile devices and cellular networks.

7. CONCLUDING REMARKS

Using the UbiDump tool, we examine a wide spectrum of factors including protocol overhead, TCP connection management, web page content, traffic timing dynamics, caching efficiency, and compression usage, for the landing pages of the most popular 500 websites. As summarized in Table 13, we found that all above factors at different layers can affect resource utilization (*i.e.,* radio energy and/or bandwidth consumption) for mobile web browsing. Our findings and recommendations will assist web developers, browser developers, OS vendors, and protocol designers in making mobile web browsing more resource efficient. In our future work, we plan to thoroughly evaluate the cellular-friendliness of other web optimization approaches (*e.g.,* modpagespeed [6]) and to explore specific optimization techniques for LTE networks.

8. ACKNOWLEDGEMENTS

We would like to thank the anonymous reviewers and especially Sharad Agarwal for shepherding the paper.

9. REFERENCES

[1] Akamai Mobitest. http://mobitest.akamai.com/.
[2] Chrome for Android may get a speedy websurfing boost. http://gigaom.com/2013/03/04/chrome-for-android-may-get-a-speedy-websurfing-boost/.
[3] Experimenting with QUIC. http://blog.chromium.org/2013/06/experimenting-with-quic.html.
[4] Facebook moves all users to HTTPS for added security. http://www.pcworld.com/article/2015185/facebook-moves-all-users-to-https-for-added-security.html.
[5] General Packet Radio Service (GPRS); GPRS Tunnelling Protocol (GTP) across the Gn and Gp interface. 3GPP TS 29.060.
[6] Google modpagespeed. https://code.google.com/p/modpagespeed/.
[7] Linux WPA/WPA2/IEEE 802.1X Supplicant. http://hostap.epitest.fi/wpa_supplicant/.
[8] mitmproxy: an SSL-capable man-in-the-middle proxy. http://mitmproxy.org/.
[9] SPDY Protocol - Draft 3. http://www.chromium.org/spdy/spdy-protocol/spdy-protocol-draft3.
[10] SSL MITM Proxy by Stanford Crypto Group. http://crypto.stanford.edu/ssl-mitm/.
[11] The Importance Of Landing Pages. http://www.connectwisdom.com/the-importance-of-landing-pages/.
[12] The ssldump tool. http://www.rtfm.com/ssldump/.
[13] The Wireshark tool. http://www.wireshark.org/.
[14] Webpage Speed Index. https://sites.google.com/a/webpagetest.org/docs/using-webpagetest/metrics/speed-index.
[15] Understanding Today's Smartphone User (Part 2). Informa White Paper, August 2012.
[16] N. Balasubramanian, A. Balasubramanian, and A. Venkataramani. Energy Consumption in Mobile Phones: A Measurement Study and Implications for Network Applications. In *IMC*, 2009.
[17] T. Dierks and C. Allen. The TLS Protocol Version 1.0. RFC 2246, 1999.
[18] J. Erman, V. Gopalakrishnan, R. Jana, and K. Ramakrishnan. Towards a SPDY'ier Mobile Web. In *CoNEXT*, 2013.
[19] V. Farkas, B. Heder, and S. Novaczki. A Split Connection TCP Proxy in LTE Networks. In *Information and Communication Technologies*, volume 7479, pages 263–274. 2012.
[20] R. Fielding, J. Gettys, J. Mogul, H. F. L. Masinter, P. Leach, and T. Berners-Lee. Hypertext Transfer Protocol - HTTP/1.1 . RFC 2616, 1999.
[21] A. Gember, A. Anand, and A. Akella. A Comparative Study of Handheld and Non-Handheld Traffic in Campus Wi-Fi Networks. In *PAM*, 2011.
[22] J. Huang, F. Qian, A. Gerber, Z. M. Mao, S. Sen, and O. Spatscheck. A Close Examination of Performance and Power Characteristics of 4G LTE Networks. In *Mobisys*, 2012.
[23] J. Huang, F. Qian, Z. M. Mao, S. Sen, and O. Spatscheck. Screen-Off Traffic Characterization and Optimization in 3G/4G Networks. In *IMC*, 2012.
[24] J. Huang, Q. Xu, B. Tiwana, Z. M. Mao, M. Zhang, and P. Bahl. Anatomizing Application Performance Differences on Smartphones. In *Mobisys*, 2010.
[25] F. Qian, J. Huang, J. Erman, Z. M. Mao, S. Sen, and O. Spatscheck. How to Reduce Smartphone Traffic Volume by 30%? In *Proc. of Passive and Active Measurement conference (PAM)*, 2013.
[26] F. Qian, K. S. Quah, J. Huang, J. Erman, A. Gerber, Z. M. Mao, S. Sen, and O. Spatscheck. Web Caching on Smartphones: Ideal vs. Reality. In *Mobisys*, 2012.
[27] F. Qian, S. Sen, and O. Spatscheck. Silent TCP Connection Closure for Cellular Networks. In *CoNEXT*, 2013.
[28] F. Qian, Z. Wang, A. Gerber, Z. M. Mao, S. Sen, and O. Spatscheck. Profiling Resource Usage for Mobile Applications: a Cross-layer Approach. In *Mobisys*, 2011.
[29] J. Salowey, H. Zhou, P. Eronen, and H. Tschofenig. Transport Layer Security (TLS) Session Resumption without Server-Side State. RFC 5077, 2008.
[30] D. Schatzmann, W. Muhlbauer, T. Spyropoulos, and X. Dimitropoulos. Digging into HTTPS: Flow-Based Classification of Webmail Traffic. In *IMC*, 2010.
[31] A. Sivakumar, V. Gopalakrishnan, S. Lee, S. Rao, S. Sen, and O. Spatscheck. Cloud is not a silver bullet: A Case Study of Cloud-based Mobile Browsing. In *Proc. of ACM HotMobile*, 2014.
[32] N. Thiagarajan, G. Aggarwal, A. Nicoara, D. Boneh, and J. Singh. Who Killed My Battery: Analyzing Mobile Browser Energy Consumption. In *WWW*, 2012.
[33] N. Vallina-Rodriguez, J. Shah, A. Finamore, H. Haddadi, Y. Grunenberger, K. Papagiannaki, and J. Crowcroft. Breaking for Commercials: Characterizing Mobile Advertising. In *IMC*, 2012.
[34] X. S. Wang, A. Balasubramanian, A. Krishnamurthy, and D. Wetherall. Demystifying Page Load Performance with WProf. In *NSDI*, 2013.
[35] X. S. Wang, A. Balasubramanian, A. Krishnamurthy, and D. Wetherall. How Speedy is SPDY? In *NSDI*, 2014.
[36] Z. Wang, F. X. Lin, L. Zhong, and M. Chishtie. How Far Can Client-Only Solutions Go for Mobile Browser Speed? In *WWW*, 2012.
[37] Q. Xu, J. Erman, A. Gerber, Z. M. Mao, J. Pang, and S. Venkataraman. Identifying Diverse Usage Behaviors of Smartphone Apps. In *IMC*, 2011.

Procrastinator: Pacing Mobile Apps' Usage of the Network

Lenin Ravindranath
lenin@csail.mit.edu
M.I.T.
Cambridge, MA, USA

Sharad Agarwal
sagarwal@microsoft.com
Microsoft Research
Redmond, WA, USA

Jitendra Padhye
padhye@microsoft.com
Microsoft Research
Redmond, WA, USA

Chris Riederer
cjr2149@columbia.edu
Columbia University
New York, NY, USA

ABSTRACT

Generations of computer programmers are taught to prefetch network objects in computer science classes. In practice, prefetching can be harmful to the user's wallet when she is on a limited or pay-per-byte cellular data plan. Many popular, professionally-written smartphone apps today prefetch large amounts of network data that the typical user may never use. We present Procrastinator, which automatically decides when to fetch each network object that an app requests. This decision is made based on whether the user is on Wi-Fi or cellular, how many bytes are remaining on the user's data plan, and whether the object is needed at the present time. Procrastinator does not require app developer effort, nor app source code, nor OS changes – it modifies the app binary to trap specific system calls and inject custom code. Our system can achieve as little as no savings to 4X reduction in total bytes transferred by an app, depending on the user and the app. These savings for the data-poor user come with a 300ms median latency penalty on LTE.

1. INTRODUCTION

"This app is too slow" is a phrase that app developers dread when reading user reviews for their apps. Over the last 5 years, smartphone users have forced app developers to optimize their apps for performance. App developers now rely heavily on threading and asynchronous programming patterns to keep their app's UI responsive. They rely on prefetching network content at the launch of an app to hide the network latency of cellular communication.

Recently, low-end system-on-chips from companies including MediaTek and Qualcomm have resulted in significantly cheaper smartphones that are flooding phone markets in the Eastern hemisphere. In the US, we can now buy smartphones outright (without a carrier contract) for $59-$99 with a dual-core 1 GHz processor and 8GB storage [3]. This price point, without a requirement to be locked into a large cellular data plan, will attract many users who cannot or do not want to spend money on large cellular data plans. The prefetching nature of apps will hurt these users.

Apps that prefetch network content are downloading content before the user needs it - for example to populate images that are off screen. A typical example is shown in Figure 1. This popular weather app downloads a large amount of data as soon as the app is

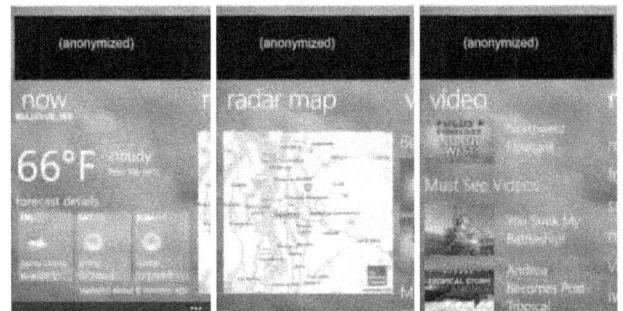

Figure 1: Screenshots of a highly rated and popular weather app. The left screen is visible immediately after app launch. The middle screen is visible after a swipe. The right screen is visible after another swipe.

launched, including many images. While some of the data is necessary to display current weather on the "main" page of the app, many prefetched images are displayed deeper in the app.

Those users that scroll or click through an app to visit that off-screen content will experience a more responsive app. However, for those users that do not visit that off-screen content, the penalty is wasted network consumption. This waste can harm three sets of users – (1) users that are always conscious about data consumption because they are on a pay-per-byte plan; (2) users that start their monthly cellular billing cycle with a large number of bytes (e.g. 2GB), but eventually run low and want the remaining bytes to last them through the end of their cycle; (3) users that have large data plans at home but are temporarily roaming internationally and are paying additional per-byte charges.

This problem cannot be solved by producing two versions of an app – data-light and data-heavy versions – for two different sets of users. A data-rich user can sometimes become data-poor, or vice-versa temporarily when the user connects to Wi-Fi (we assume that Wi-Fi connectivity is free or significantly cheaper) or starts running out of her monthly cellular allotment or is roaming. Alternatively, producing a single adaptive app is difficult for the app developer who has to manage multiple network transfers that affect different parts of the user interface. Worse, the user can be scrolling around in the app while some network transfers are ongoing and connectivity changes between cellular and Wi-Fi.

Our goal is to *automatically* delay prefetching of network content *when appropriate*, to reduce data usage. The system we present in this paper is (aptly) named *Procrastinator*. "Delaying" or "procrastination" of network content is done based on current network connectivity (cellular or Wi-Fi), the status of the user's cellular data plan, where in the app the user is (which parts of the UI are visible), and potential for impact on the functionality of the app beyond the UI (such as playing music or vibrating the phone).

In designing Procrastinator, we strive for *"immediate deployability"* – we do not require changes to the mobile OS, nor runtime. We also attempt to achieve *"zero effort"* for the app developer – we do not want her to write additional code, nor add code annotations. She may need to simply run our system, and can optionally choose to test her app under Procrastinator. We also strive for *"zero functionality impact"* – beyond appearing as though the network is occasionally slower, the user should not experience any other change in the functionality of the app.

We have implemented Procrastinator for the Windows Phone 8 platform. Our system automatically rewrites app binaries without requiring app source code. There are two key challenges in building Procrastinator. First, Procrastinator must automatically identify asynchronous network calls that are candidates for procrastination. This involves careful static analysis of the app code (§3.1). Next, Procrastinator must rewrite the app code, so that at run time (§3.2), it can decide (a) whether to procrastinate each candidate call, and (b) when to execute a previously procrastinated call, if at all.

We make a number of technical contributions in this paper. Our system automatically identifies for each network transfer which part of the app UI it affects. For those parts of the UI that are not visible, it delays network transfers until they become visible. Our system works on arbitrary third party apps without source code nor app developer effort. At run time, it uses dynamic information about network connectivity and data plan information to automatically switch from prefetching behavior to procrastination. Our lab experiments identify the potential network usage savings in 6 popular, professionally-written Windows Phone apps, as well as additional savings that are untapped because of our conservative approach in avoiding any change to the functionality of the app. Our small study of 9 users with those 6 apps demonstrates savings in total network usage by each app ranging from none to 4X. A larger scale evaluation of 140 apps using automated UI behavior demonstrates 2.5X and higher savings in 20-40 apps, or 20% and higher savings in 60-75 apps. These savings come at no noticeable cost to energy consumption, and additional median latency that is under 300ms.

2. PROBLEM

To understand how app developers prefetch network content, we analyzed the binary code of a large number of apps in the Windows Phone app store. While diverse, the programming patterns used tend to fall into three categories. An example of each is shown in Figure 2. Even though we analyzed .NET byte code, for convenience, we show pseudo-code. Before describing these examples, we note two relevant aspects of the Windows Phone programming framework. First, the framework supports only asynchronous network I/O. Second, images and text are displayed on the screen by assigning them to specific UI elements such as a text box.

In Pattern 1, the app developer assigns an image to an image element that is not yet visible on the screen. One app that uses this pattern is a news reader app. Each news story has an associated image. The news stories are displayed as an "infinitely scrolling" list. When the app is launched, only the top three or four stories and images are visible to the user. However, the app continues to fetch images that are "below the fold" in anticipation of user scrolling down. Note that the HTTP fetch call executes asynchronously and the image is populated after the call successfully returns.

Programmers often explicitly handle these asynchronous fetches, especially if additional processing is required before displaying the

```
Pattern 1
void page_load() {
  /* image not visible on the current screen */
  imageElement.Source = http.fetchImage(url1);
}

Pattern 2
void page_load() {
  http.FetchData(url2, callback);
}
void callback(result) {
  var cleanText = clean(result);
  /* text not visible on the current screen */
  textElement.Content = cleanText;
}

Pattern 3
void mainpage_load() {
  http.FetchData(url3, callback);
}
void callback(result) {
  hurricaneWarnings = parseXML(result);
}
/* called when user clicks to navigate to a new page */
void navigate_hurricaneWarningsPage() {
  hurricaneUIElement.Content = hurricaneWarnings;
}
```

Figure 2: Common prefetching patterns in apps.

fetched data. This is illustrated in Pattern 2. The fetched text is "cleaned up" and then displayed by assigning it to a textbox element. The textbox element may not yet be visible on the screen, but once the user scrolls down to it, it will have the text ready for viewing.

Pattern 3 is similar to Pattern 2, but the assignment to the UI element is delayed even further. This pattern is used in a weather app. At launch, the app fetches data about hurricane warnings, which it stores in a global variable. The data is used only if the user navigates to a specific tab (or a "page") within the app that displays hurricane warnings.

These programming patterns are common because app developers typically lay out and pre-populate most or all of the UI of the app at launch. Even though the user may be viewing a specific portion of the UI (for example, what is visible on a 1024x768 resolution screen), there may be additional content virtually off screen below or to the right or left of the physical screen coordinates, or on different pages. When the user scrolls down a list or slides horizontally, the OS's app runtime will change the viewable coordinates relative to the virtual coordinates of the entire UI. This provides a smooth experience to the user. Unfortunately, this further promotes network prefetching behavior.

It is hard for the app developer to restructure their program to dynamically choose between prefetching and procrastinating. One option is for the app developer to detect at launch whether the user is low on cellular data bytes, and then either layout the entire UI or layout only what is visible. In the latter case, each time the user attempts to scroll up or click on something, she needs to trap that call and then re-layout the screen and present that to the user. This has the disadvantage of significantly increasing code complexity, and having to update two different code paths each time the app developer decides to make even a small change to her UI design.

Alternatively, the app developer could lay out the entire UI, but not tie individual network objects to the individual UI elements. At app launch time, the app would check for network cost. If the network is cheap, it can tie all network objects to all UI elements and prefetch. If the network is expensive, the app developer will have to decide which objects are necessary and only tie those. Each

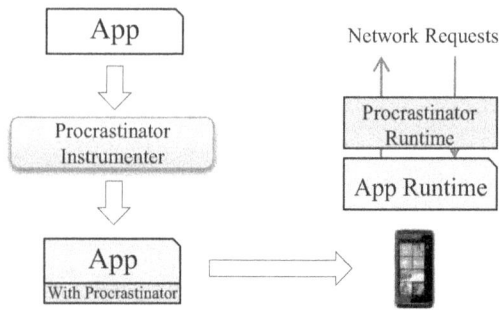

Figure 3: Procrastinator design overview.

Figure 4: Setting image elements using XAML.

time the user makes any move on the UI, such as scroll up a little bit or slide horizontally, the app code will have to re-evaluate which network objects it should fetch, if it has not fetched already. If the network cost changes (such as the user switches to/from Wi-Fi or roaming), then the app code will have to re-evaluate all these decisions again. This adds a significant amount of complexity to the app code.

A third option would be to build a new networking API into the OS. The app developer could specify at the beginning which network objects may be needed, and at different points in the code provide hints to the OS as to whether those objects are definitely needed or no longer needed. We argue that this also adds burden on the app developer – she has to learn a new API and think about every network call and split it into two distinct points in the app code. In the 140 apps that we later evaluate, the number of objects they fetch is 23 on average, and 180 in the highest case. The amount of work that app developers would have to do is not trivial.

We strive for a system that can automatically procrastinate network calls with no app developer effort. We also avoid using app source code. This gives the system the flexibility of being run either by the app marketplace prior to publishing, or by the user, or by the app developer. The trade-offs to explore include data savings versus user responsiveness, delaying network transfers versus energy consumption of cellular radios, and the ability of the app developer to finely control how Procrastinator affects her app.

3. SYSTEM DESIGN & IMPLEMENTATION

We have designed and implemented Procrastinator for Windows Phone apps. As shown in Figure 3, our system consumes an app binary, and outputs a new app binary. It has two main components: the Procrastinator Instrumenter and the Procrastinator Runtime. The Instrumenter takes a Windows Phone app binary and produces a *procrastinated* version. It statically analyzes the app to look for prefetching patterns and finds candidates for procrastination. It then rewrites the associated app code and makes those network calls go through the Procrastinator Runtime.

When producing the new app binary, the Instrumenter will link the Procrastinator Runtime library to the app. When the procrastinated app is run, network calls pass through the Procrastinator Runtime which dynamically checks the state of the network, tracks the UI, and delays those network calls whose results are not immediately needed by the UI. These procrastinated network calls are then fetched on demand if the user navigates to the relevant portions of the UI.

3.1 Procrastinator Instrumenter

The mechanism that we use to instrument apps is similar to what is used in AppInsight [19]. AppInsight was designed to find the critical path in user transactions, to help in performance debugging in real-world usage of mobile apps. Procrastinator is instead designed to alter application logic to optimize network usage. Our Instrumenter exploits the fact that apps are often compiled to an intermediate language. While Android apps are compiled to Java byte code, Windows Phone apps are compiled to MSIL [12]. Our Instrumenter works on apps written using the Microsoft Silverlight framework [13], compiled to MSIL byte code. The MSIL byte code representation of an app preserves the structure of the program, including types and methods.

A key challenge in Procrastinator is to automatically find the relationship between network calls and the UI elements that are updated using the data fetched by the network calls. The Instrumenter statically analyzes the app to find such relationships. When such a relationship is found, the Instrumenter rewrites the network call to explicitly identify the UI elements associated with the network call and makes it go to through the Procrastinator Runtime. This takes care of programming patterns 1 and 2 as described in §2. Pattern 3 uses intermediate global variables to store the fetched data before updating the UI elements. In this case, the Instrumenter automatically identifies the relationship between network calls and global variables being set. When this relationship is found, the Instrumenter rewrites the network call to explicitly identify the global variables associated with the network call and makes it go to through the Procrastinator Runtime. We now describe in detail how the Instrumenter rewrites each of these network patterns.

3.1.1 Pattern 1

In programming pattern 1, the app developer is directly connecting the result of a HTTP fetch to an image element in the UI, even though the network call itself is still asynchronous. In practice, this can manifest itself in a variety of ways. The app developer may provide the URL as a hard-coded string, or may use a variable that contains the string. In Windows Phone apps written using the Silverlight framework, this can alternatively be specified in XAML code. An app developer can construct the entire UI of an app in C# code, or using XAML which is a declarative markup language that looks like XML. XAML allows the app developer to separate the UI definition from the run-time logic by using code-behind files, joined to the markup through partial class definitions. This enables the development environment to provide a GUI editor for the app developer to use in designing the UI of an app. Individual UI elements can refer to corresponding variables in C# code. The top of Figure 4 shows the XAML code where the source of an image

```
Pattern 1:
void page_load() {
  /* image not visible on the current screen */
  CheckProcrastinate(url1, imageElement);
}


Pattern 2:
void page_load() {
  CheckProcrastinate(url2, callback, textElement);
}
void callback(result) {
  var cleanText = clean(result);
  /* text not visible on the current screen */
  textElement.Content = cleanText;
}


Pattern 3:
void mainpage_load() {
  /* 2 is a unique id that identifies the network request */
  Procrastinate(url3, callback, 2);
}
void callback(result) {
  hurricaneWarnings = parseXML(result);
}
/* called when user clicks to navigate to a new page */
void navigate_hurricaneWarningsPage() {
  /* 2 identifies the network request to fetch */
  FetchProcrastinated(2);
  /* wait does not return until network fetch completes */
  wait();
  hurricaneUIElement.Content = hurricaneWarnings;
}
```

Figure 5: Rewriting code to add procrastination.

element is set to a URL. Another common XAML pattern is to bind the source of the UI element to a variable in the C# program – this is the middle example in Figure 4.

Static analysis: To find pattern 1 through static analysis, the Instrumenter looks for any HTTP fetch API calls that are set to a UI element's source. The value passed into the call can be either a static URL string, or a variable that contains the URL. There are several different image element classes in the Windows Phone SDK, as well as several third party image handlers. The Procrastinator Instrumenter handles all of the common image elements that we have encountered. The Instrumenter also statically analyzes XAML code in the app binary package to find both types of image source setting, and rewrites the XAML so that they can be detoured.

Rewriting: The Instrumenter replaces the network call in pattern 1 in Figure 2 with the `CheckProcrastinate` call as shown in Figure 5. The rewritten call explicitly passes the UI element with the url. In the case of XAML, we rewrite the XAML to provide a callback whenever the url is bound to a UI element. We achieve this using the Dependency Property feature of the Windows Presentation Foundation, which can be used to extend the functionality of a common language runtime (CLR) property. Essentially, it gives our code a callback into a user defined function when a property of an element is changed. During the callback, the parameter to the function is the UI element being set and the property value that is bound (URL in this case). We alter the XAML code to trap the image setting and call `CheckProcrastinate` with the two parameters, as shown in the bottom of Figure 4.

3.1.2 Pattern 2

In pattern 2, the developer passes a callback function to the network call. The network call asynchronously fetches data and invokes the callback with the data. The UI elements are then accessed and updated in the callback, as shown in Figure 2. Instrumenting this pattern is more challenging. First, statically identifying the UI

category	num
no side effect	8,869
changes UI	1,053
changes input parameters	275
changes property of instance that the method is called on	2,228
has side effect	756

Table 1: The five categories that we classified each Windows Phone SDK API, system call and popular third party library calls into, and how many are in each category.

elements that are updated is not trivial. In the example shown, the callback method itself updates the UI element. However, the callback method could call other methods (perhaps asynchronously!) and the updated UI elements may lie deep in this call tree. Second, the callback method or any code in its call graph may have *side effects* besides updating the UI. For example, one of the methods may vibrate the phone or write to the file system that another thread reads. If there are any side effects, then those network calls are not candidates for Procrastinator, and we allow them to proceed as normal.

Static analysis: This involves the following steps:

1. find the callback method associated with the call
2. generate a *conservative* call graph (one that includes all possible code paths) that is rooted in the callback method. This call graph contains both synchronous and asynchronous calls.
3. analyze code in the conservative call graph to discover all UI elements being updated
4. analyze code in the call graph to ensure it has no side effects. If any code in the graph has any side effects, the Instrumenter conservatively decides that the call cannot be procrastinated, and the code is not modified.

Call graph: Generating a call graph in the presence of virtual method calls is challenging. At compile time, the type of the instance for which invocation takes place is not known. At run time, when invoking a virtual method, the run-time type of the instance determines the actual method to invoke. To overcome this problem in static analysis, we take a conservative approach. In the call graph, we include *all* the potential calls in the class hierarchy if we are not able to statically resolve the object type reference. Similarly, when a function pointer is used, we include all the potential calls that the function pointer could point to, since we may not decisively know what the contents of that function pointer are during static analysis. When an asynchronous call is made, we identify the potential callback and recursively include the call graph of the callback.

Side effects: Our analysis of all the Windows Phone marketplace apps shows that there are over 13,000 unique system calls, SDK API calls, and third party library calls, that apps use in the call graphs of network callbacks. These range from methods such as Math.Sqrt to VibrateController.Start. Some methods such as Math.Sqrt do not modify any input parameters nor modify the state of the phone, such as the filesystem. Those calls are free of "side effects". Other calls may modify input parameters, which may be global variables that other threads in the app may interact with. We manually sorted these calls into the five categories in Table 1. We conservatively assume that any call that changes an input parameter or class instance that is globally accessible by other threads is not side effect free. If a call graph for a network callback has any system call or SDK call that has a side effect, the Instrumenter ignores that network call for procrastination and leaves it untouched. Each time the API list available to apps changes, which typically happens when there is a major OS update, this categorization will need to be updated.

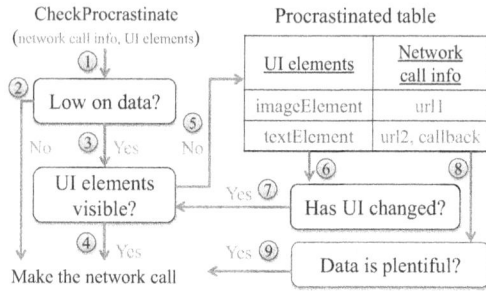

Figure 6: Procrastinator Runtime tracking UI elements.

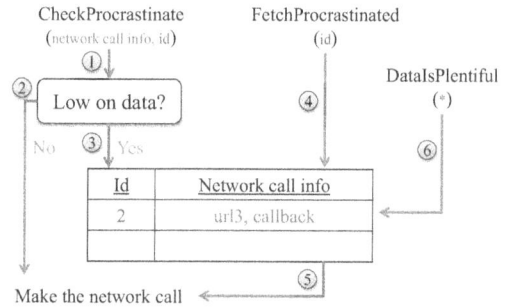

Figure 7: Procrastinator Runtime tracking global variables.

Rewriting: For network callbacks that do not have a side effect, the static analysis outputs a list of UI elements that are updated by a network call. The network call is rewritten as shown in Figure 5. We explicitly pass the UI elements with the network call information into the Procrastinator Runtime, similar to pattern 1.

3.1.3 Pattern 3

In pattern 3, the result of the network request is stored in memory (global variables) and used later. This may be done to prefetch data for UI elements that have not yet been instantiated. Here, the Instrumenter's goal is to find the relationship between network calls and global variables.

Static Analysis: We do two passes of static analysis for this pattern. In the first pass we analyze network callbacks to identify global variables used in *store* operations. In the second pass, we analyze the rest of the app code to identify code where the same global variables are accessed in *load* operations. The first pass analysis is similar to pattern 2. We generate a conservative call graph of the callback and analyze the code in the entire call graph. Instead of looking for UI elements, we look for *store* operations to global variables. Note that we do not consider these store operations to a global variable as a side effect here. We do look for other side effects such as accessing system APIs that affects the phone state, such as the filesystem. If there is a side effect other than updating global variables, we do not consider it for procrastination. In the second pass, we analyze the entire app to find load operations of the same global variables that was identified in the first pass. We instrument both the network call and these load points as follows.

Rewriting: We rewrite the network call to go through the Procrastinator Runtime as shown in Figure 5. Along with the network call information (url and callback), we pass in a unique identifier for the set of global variables stored by the callback. Just before where these global variable are loaded, we instrument the code to inform the Procrastinator Runtime to fetch the network data before it is accessed. The network call to execute is identified by the unique identifier.

3.2 Procrastinator Runtime

The Procrastinator Runtime behavior for patterns 1 and 2 is summarized in Figure 6 and pattern 3 in Figure 7.

Patterns 1 and 2: CheckProcrastinate calls into the Procrastinator Runtime with the network call info (URL and UI elements, and network callback method for pattern 2). The Runtime checks if the user is low on data (1), described below in §3.2.1. If not, the network call is not procrastinated and issued right away (2). Otherwise, the runtime checks the visibility of the UI elements being passed (3), described below in §3.2.2. If at least one UI element is visible, the network call is not procrastinated and continues

to execute (4). If the relevant UI elements are not visible on the current screen, then the network call is procrastinated (5).

Procrastinated network call info and associated UI elements are added to the procrastinated table. This in-memory table maintains requested network calls that have not been issued. Whenever the UI changes (6), described below in §3.2.3, the runtime iterates over this table and checks the visibility of each UI element in it. If any UI element becomes visible, the associated network call is made and the entry is removed from the table (7). The runtime also tracks changes in network connectivity. If data becomes plentiful, *all* outstanding network requests are immediately issued (8).

Pattern 3: CheckProcrastinate calls into the procrastinator runtime with the network call and the unique identifier (1). If the user is not low on data, the network call is made right away (2). Otherwise, the call is procrastinated and added to the procrastinated table indexed by the unique id (3). The call is delayed until one of the global variables is accessed by any thread in the app (4). We intercept all accesses to the identified global variables and pass the same unique identifier to inform the Procrastinator Runtime to fetch the request before the global variable is first accessed. Since all network calls in the Windows Phone SDK are asynchronous, we have to instrument the thread to wait until the transaction is complete before proceeding. When FetchProcrastinated is called, the network call is removed from the table and executed. Again, if data becomes plentiful, *all* outstanding network requests are immediately issued (6).

3.2.1 Checking network connectivity and cost

Procrastinator makes use of a feature called Data Sense that we previously helped build and deploy inside the Windows Phone 8 OS. As shown in Figure 8, it allows the user to enter their cellular data plan information: type (such as monthly or pay-per-byte), limit (such as 200 MB), and reset date (such as 3rd of every month). The OS carefully tracks every byte sent and received over the network and attributes it to the responsible app or OS feature. The user can see the per-app breakdown in the UI, and request that the OS automatically restrict data consumption when nearing the data cap. The OS tracks overall consumption against the data limit and advertises changes in available data to OS services and apps [2]. The app can query (or be alerted) when the network cost type changes ("unrestricted" when on Wi-Fi or unlimited cellular data, "fixed" when on periodic plans, or "variable" when on pay-per-byte plans) and when available data changes ("Approaching-DataLimit", "OverDataLimit", or "Roaming").

Each time a procrastinated app requests a network transfer, the Procrastinator Runtime checks the current network cost type and properties to determine whether procrastination is warranted. If the network cost type is "unrestricted", or "fixed" and not any of "Ap-

Figure 8: Screenshots of Data Sense on Windows Phone 8.

proachingDataLimit", "OverDataLimit", and "Roaming", then the transfer will be allowed. Otherwise, only transfers that affect currently visible UI will go through. Any time network cost changes, the Procrastinator Runtime gets an event up-call from the OS, and will reevaluate all procrastinated network calls. On OSes without Data Sense, we imagine a UI button can be exposed to the user to manually turn procrastination behavior on or off for all apps.

3.2.2 Checking visibility of UI elements

To check if a UI element is visible to the user, the Procrastinator Runtime extracts the current UI tree and traverses it to find the location of this UI element in the tree. We use the size of the UI element, position in the UI tree, the size of the UI page, the resolution of the screen, and current view coordinates to check if it is visible to the user. In most cases, the size or bounding box of the UI element is defined in the app code (such as an image of 500x300 pixels). In these cases, straightforward math can determine if any portion of the UI element is visible to the user. In relatively rare cases, the size of the UI element is not defined by the app code and is instead determined by the downloaded network object. In these cases, if the center of the UI element is not visible, we assume that the UI element is not visible.

3.2.3 Checking if the UI has changed

All procrastinated requests are reevaluated every time the UI changes. To detect UI changes, the Procrastinator Runtime includes event handlers for UI manipulation events and UI update events. Manipulation events are fired whenever the user interacts with the phone (such as click or swipe). Update events are fired whenever a UI element is updated programmatically. When one of the events fires, the runtime iterates over each procrastinated request and checks if any of the UI elements associated with the request is visible. When the procrastinated table is empty, the Runtime will de-register from these event notifications, and re-register if any are later added.

3.3 Implementation

The Procrastinator Runtime is written in 839 lines of C# code, which compiles down to a 46 KB library of MSIL code. This library is included in all procrastinated apps. The Procrastinator Instrumenter, which consumes an app binary and produces a procrastinated app binary, is written in 861 lines of C# code, not including the Microsoft Research Common Compiler Infrastructure libraries [6] that it relies on to parse MSIL code and replace calls.

In practice, many apps and programming constructs rely on virtual method invocations and function pointers at the MSIL level. As a result, when dealing with programming patterns 2 and 3, our Instrumenter tends to construct large call graphs for the network

app	functionality	action
App1	cooking recipes	read top daily recipe
App2	movie times	see details of top movie
App3	movie times	see details of top movie
App4	news aggregator	read top news story
App5	news paper	read top news story
App6	weather reports	see current weather and forecast

Table 2: The six Windows Phone apps we evaluate and the action we perform in each run of the app in lab experiments. Each app is one of the top apps in its category, and is authored by the professional online company that owns both the app and the primary web service that it relies on (e.g. Twitter by Twitter, Inc.).

callbacks. The call graph is large because we conservatively include any possible method that might match the virtual method call or function pointer. The problem with a large call graph is that the chances of encountering a system call or SDK call that has a side effect go up significantly. As a result, in practice, the Procrastinator Instrumenter will procrastinate almost all image transfers because they tend to follow programming pattern 1. Network calls that download non-image content tend to follow programming patterns 2 and 3, and those rarely get procrastinated due to the risk of unintentionally altering app behavior. We expect that images account for the bulk of network bytes and will provide significant savings in our evaluation.

4. EVALUATION METHODOLOGY

To evaluate Procrastinator, we use a three-pronged strategy. We begin by evaluating 6 popular apps in the lab. By manually inspecting every network transfer and the MSIL code for these 6 apps, we can understand the behavior of these apps and of their procrastinated versions. Next, we deploy these 6 apps to 9 users in a small user trial to understand savings that Procrastinator offers in more realistic usage. Finally, we evaluate Procrastinator using a much larger set of 140 apps in Windows Phone emulators using UI automation.

4.1 Lab experiments

To test the effectiveness of Procrastinator, we pick 6 apps from the top 50 in the Windows Phone marketplace, listed anonymously in Table 2. We installed these 6 original apps, as well as their procrastinated versions on a Nokia Lumia 920 smartphone. The procrastinated apps have different app IDs and hence are completely isolated from their original version – they do not share any state, storage, or web caches. The phone had only Wi-Fi connectivity. We configured the phone so that all HTTP and HTTPS traffic was intercepted by a server with the Fiddler [1] proxy.

We ran both versions of each app, performed the action listed in Table 2, and captured traces of network activity. We ensured that there was no background activity from other apps and OS features. Normally, Procrastinator would not procrastinate network calls if the user is connected to Wi-Fi – we turned off this feature here.

We manually inspected the Fiddler traces and compared the content that was fetched to what was displayed on the screen. Apart from verifying what appeared on the screen, we also carefully looked through the app's binary code to determine whether the object was needed to render the page that the user saw. We then classified each web object that was fetched by the original app into one of three buckets. A web object is considered "necessary" if the contents were used to show something to the user on the main screen of the app or any of the subsequent screens when performing the action listed in Table 2. In cases where we cannot deduce whether

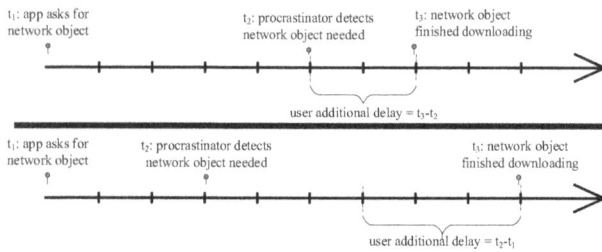

Figure 9: Two examples (top and bottom) of how we calculate the additional delay experienced by a user in a procrastinated app.

the content of web objects is used in the screen, typically when we cannot decipher the web object and the relevant MSIL code, we conservatively assume them to be "necessary". If a web object is not necessary, then it is either "skipped" or "prefetched". If Procrastinator correctly deduces that a network object is not necessary and does not download it, we count this as "skipped". If Procrastinator allows an object to be downloaded that is not necessary, we count this as "prefetched". This happens when Procrastinator cannot determine that not fetching a network object will not cause an unintended side effect in the behavior of the app (such as playing music or vibrating the phone or writing to the filesystem), and hence conservatively allows the network object to be prefetched.

4.2 User trial

Our lab experiments show that Procrastinator can substantially reduce data consumption. However, the savings experienced by real users in the wild will depend on multiple factors including network conditions, specific user interactions, and app caching. These savings can come at the cost of additional delay experienced by the user when a procrastinated network object has to be fetched, such as in App6 in Figure 1, if the user swipes to see the radar image. This additional delay depends on a variety of factors, including the speed of that network, the size of the network object, and how responsive the web server is.

To evaluate these aspects, we deployed the procrastinated versions of these 6 apps to 9 colleagues for 2 months [1]. We asked the users to use any of these 6 apps that they like as normally as they would if they discovered them in the app marketplace. Over this 2 month period, we collected a total of 553 sessions across these users and apps where their phone had network connectivity.

All 9 users have unlimited data on their LTE cellular plans. Since the phones are never in danger of exceeding their data limits, for the purposes of our study, we turned off the Data Sense network check so that Procrastinator would always attempt to procrastinate. We also write a log for every user session. This log records when the user launches the app, what network transfers the app requests, which ones Procrastinator allows through, which ones it procrastinates, when (if at all) a previously procrastinated request becomes necessary to display to the user, and the sizes and end times of all network transfers. To determine the size of any requests that are procrastinated and never fetched by Procrastinator, we download those objects on the side simply to check their size for our evaluation graphs. These logs are periodically uploaded in the background to the Microsoft Azure cloud.

---

[1] This user study was performed in accordance with Microsoft Research privacy guidelines, record #1903.

parameter	value
LTE promotion power	1210.7 mW
LTE promotion duration	260.1 ms
LTE continuous downlink transfer power	1950.1 mW
LTE tail power	1060.0 mW
LTE tail duration	11576.0 ms

Table 3: Parameters of LTE energy model from Tables 3 and 4 of the 4GTest paper in ACM MobiSys 2012. We assume downloads happen in LTE continuous reception mode and we use the power values for median throughput of 12.74 Mbps.

Using these logs, we calculate how much network activity occurred in each user session of each app. We calculate how many bytes were fetched that the app requested that Procrastinator did not interfere with, and label these as "fetched" bytes. We calculate how many bytes Procrastinator did not fetch, and the app did not display to the user – these are "skipped" bytes, and represent our savings. Finally, there are bytes that Procrastinator did not initially fetch, but later detects that they are needed and subsequently fetches, thereby incurring additional delay – these are "delayed" bytes.

For "delayed" bytes, we want to evaluate how much longer the user had to wait as a result of our decision to not initially fetch the network object when the app requested it. Figure 9 shows two example situations that can occur. At time t_1, the app requests a network object that Procrastinator decides not to fetch because the relevant UI is not visible to the user. At a later time t_2, Procrastinator detects that the relevant UI is shown to the user and starts fetching it. This transfer completes at time t_3 and the UI is updated. In the top example, the download time for the object $t_3 - t_2$ is smaller than $t_2 - t_1$ which is the time between the initial request by the app and when Procrastinator starts the fetch. In this case, the *additional* delay that the user experiences is the download time of $t_3 - t_2$. In the bottom example, the download time of $t_3 - t_2$ is longer than $t_2 - t_1$. In this case, the *additional* delay that the user experiences is $t_2 - t_1$, which is the extra delay introduced by Procrastinator.

Finally, we want to evaluate how Procrastinator impacts the phone battery consumption of apps. When Procrastinator does not fetch unnecessary bytes from the network, it should reduce energy consumption by cellular radios since that depends on how much the radio is transferring and how long it is awake for. However, when Procrastinator delays the transfer of network objects, it can potentially increase energy consumption – the radio may have gone to sleep due to network inactivity and may need to spend energy waking up, and now the radio may be up for longer than when network objects were batched under prefetching behavior. Since it is difficult to accurately pinpoint the energy consumption of an LTE radio at fine time granularity and what energy state it is in while an app is running in the hands of a user, we use the empirical energy model constructed by prior work [10]. Table 3 lists the energy model parameters that we use. For each user session of an app, we construct two time series. One time series identifies when the app would normally fetch objects from the network, and the other time series identifies when the app would fetch objects with Procrastinator. By factoring in transfer times, and LTE radio promotion time and tail duration, we calculate the total energy expenditure of the LTE radio in each user app session, assuming the radio is off when the app is launched. We include the LTE tail power consumption both during the session, if the radio would go to sleep, and at the end of the session.

238

monkey	functionality
M1	for up to 15 minutes, random swipes and clicks
M2	for up to 1 minute, random swipes and clicks
M3	launch app, wait for all transactions to finish, quit

Table 4: The 3 automated user profiles (or "monkeys") that we use to evaluate 140 apps in the Windows Phone emulator.

4.3 Automated monkeys

Finally, to understand the data savings and latency penalty of Procrastinator on a broader set of apps, we use UI automation (or "monkeys"). From all the apps in the Windows Phone marketplace (across the entire 5-star rating spectrum) that make at least one network call, we pick a random set of 140 apps. We then apply UI automation to these apps to emulate user behavior. We run these apps in the Windows Phone emulator running on a server. We disable the Data Sense check by Procrastinator, so that it always assumes the phone is on cellular and the user is running out of data plan bytes. We continue to log actions by Procrastinator, and any network objects that are skipped are fetched on the side so that we can calculate their sizes for our graphs.

Table 4 lists the three monkeys that we use. M1 will launch an app and aggressively browse it in a random pattern. It will click on icons and dialog boxes and other UI elements and it will scroll horizontally left and right, but it does not scroll up or down. It will do this for up to 15 minutes, unless the app quits or crashes prematurely. We consider this to represent users that will explore most of an app's UI, but not necessarily the entire UI. M2 is similar to M1, except that it does not run for more than 1 minute. M3 is the least aggressive – it will launch an app, wait for any pending computations to finish, and then exit the app. M3 will explore the least amount of the app's UI, and represents user behavior where the main page of the app displays the information relevant to the user, such as in weather apps. In comparing monkey runs to our user trials, M2 closely matches user behavior with respect to data consumption, and saved and delayed bytes. Details of how our UI automation system works are in [18].

We run each monkey on each app 15 times, though we may get fewer useful logs if the app crashes occasionally on launch. Unlike in our user study where we focused solely on top, professionally-written apps, here we include apps from across the spectrum of user ratings, some of which are buggy. Using logs from these runs, we calculate how many bytes were fetched, skipped, and delayed. The Windows Phone emulator that we run the monkeys on is connected to Ethernet. Hence latency numbers for delayed objects do not make sense, unlike in our user study where users were sometimes on LTE. Instead, we calculate what the latency would be to download delayed objects if the network connection was LTE. We use the median values for LTE throughput and latency from Figure 5 of prior work [10], specifically 12.74 Mbps downlink on LTE and 69.5 ms RTT. We calculate latency while factoring in whether the radio was still connected and awake as a result of prior transfers or asleep, TCP connection setup delay, HTTP request and responses, TCP window ramp up, and whether an existing HTTP connection was open as a result of a prior fetch from the same server. Unlike in the user study, *additional* latency does not make as much sense in this context, so we present the full latency to download delayed objects.

In addition to the LTE model, we also consider a "cloudlet" model. Cloudlets [20] provide an interesting opportunity here. If there is a cloudlet running in the celltower, it can fetch objects that Procrastinator skips on the phone. In case the user does go to that part of the UI, the network object is now sitting at the nearby cloudlet, instead of on a distant webserver. In this way, the la-

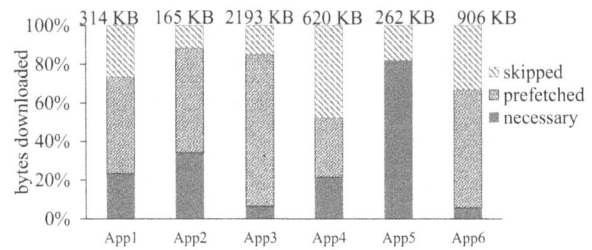

Figure 10: Bytes consumed when running each of the 6 original apps, and their procrastinated versions.

tency of fetching delayed objects is significantly reduced, while still preserving spectrum usage over the air for objects that are not needed at all. In this model, we assume that the phone has a low latency connection to the cloudlet that is still limited on throughput – 12.74 Mbps downlink and 3 ms RTT, while the cloudlet suffers the remainder of the end-to-end RTT latency of 66.5 ms, but is not limited by air spectrum and has 50 Mbps throughput to the Internet. When Procrastinator decides to skip a network object, it sends that URL to the cloudlet, which fetches it. If Procrastinator detects that the object is needed, it fetches it from the cloudlet. We calculate the download latency for the cloudlet, and the download latency between the phone and the cloudlet. In the best case, the initial download to the cloudlet will have finished before the phone needs it, in which case the penalty is the latter download latency. In the worst case, the phone has to wait for the cloudlet to download it and then download it from the cloudlet. While cloudlets do not exist today and hence this depends on a number of assumptions, we nonetheless want to consider how Procrastinator would fare in this future model.

5. EVALUATION RESULTS

We now present results from our evaluation. We begin with our in-lab experiments on 6 popular apps, followed by our small user deployment of the same set of apps with 9 users. Finally, we examine a broader set of 140 apps that we evaluate using UI automation.

5.1 Lab experiments

Our lab results are summarized in Figure 10. For all 6 apps, the unnecessary content dominates the downloaded bytes when performing the actions listed in Table 2.

In Table 5, we list the network objects that the original App6 requests on app launch. It requests 31 web objects, for a total of 906 KB. Refer back to Figure 1. The left picture is the first screen presented to the user. The current weather and the forecast is shown, along with some icons and occasionally ads on the top of the screen. If the user swipes to the right, she is shown the middle picture, which has a large radar map. If user swipes again to the right, a list of four weather videos is presented with images for each of the videos. If the user is only interested in the current weather and forecast, and hence remains on the first screen and does not visit the other screens, then the radar map and the video images are all wasted downloads. Procrastinator correctly identifies those as wasted because the screen coordinates for those images are off screen, and hence does not download those 5 objects listed at the bottom right of Table 5. This corresponds to 301 KB out of 906 KB that are skipped by Procrastinator, leading to roughly 33% of savings for the user.

The app also requests some large XML files that describe photos that people have taken of weather phenomenon across the US and

object	type	bytes
ad	xml	6,226
weather	js	6,096
alerts	xml	54
weather detail	js	6,562
forecast	xml	3,466
weather	js	880
weather	js	640
weather detail	js	5,622
sun rise/set	js	43
storm info	xml	572
weather detail	js	458
ad	text	6,700
ad	js	223
ad	oml	6,546
ad	gif	8,493
ad	gif	1,097
ad	gif	43

object	type	bytes
video list	xml	302,940
photo list	js	107,463
photo status	js	84
regional weather	xml	26,778
photo list	js	11,616
national forecast	xml	4,614
national forecast	xml	12,065
tropical forecast	xml	2,837
weather news	xml	96,810
radar map†	png	280,933
video screenshot†	jpeg	9,965
video screenshot†	jpeg	11,192
video screenshot†	jpeg	2,817
video screenshot†	jpeg	3,681

Table 5: Breakdown of 31 objects fetched by a single run of the unmodified App6. We manually classify the left 17 items as "necessary" objects, and the right 14 items as "prefetched" objects. The objects marked with † are those that Procrastinator did not fetch. The bytes exclude TCP/IP and HTTP headers.

detailed weather news for other parts of the US. These are shown to the user if the user swipes three times over to the right and clicks on a menu item. These objects add up to 552 KB and involve programming patterns 2 and 3 from Figure 2 where static analysis of the app's callback methods could not guarantee that there is no side effect from not downloading these network objects. As a result of our conservative design to avoid any potential for change in app behavior (other than network delays), Procrastinator allows the app to download these objects. These are marked as "prefetched" in Figure 10. Ultimately, this app needs only 52 KB of network objects to show the contents of the first screen to the user.

Other apps are similar. App1 downloads 40 objects. Some are text descriptions of recipes and some are photos of recipes. 10 of these objects are necessary, 6 large objects are skipped by Procrastinator, and another 24 small objects bypass Procrastinator and are still prefetched by the app. App3 downloads several web objects, most of which are small XML blobs describing each movie, review details, news and user comments. App4 downloads news articles and news images, of which Procrastinator skips 303 KB, while the app continues to prefetch 195 KB that it does not need, and 136 KB that it does need, leading to 48% of savings. App5 downloads fewer objects, but does prefetch some large ones, all of which Procrastinator skips.

5.2 User trial

The savings we demonstrate in the lab are highly dependent on what the user does in the app. To understand this in a more realistic setting, we now present results from our deployment of the same apps with 9 users. Figure 11 shows the number of app launches across all users for each app. Our users seem to check the weather more frequently than they cook with a new recipe. We collected data for 553 user sessions in total.

Figure 12 shows the number of bytes spent per user session. Note that the total bytes requested by an app varies across runs, such as when the radar map image for Seattle is of a different size than the radar map image for San Francisco, or when content is cached by the app. We see that in the case of App6, Procrastinator typically reduces the number of bytes by over 4X. In the other extreme, for App2, Procrastinator almost never saves any bytes, perhaps because users scroll through all available movies before leaving the app. In this situation, Procrastinator hurts because any objects that it decides to not prefetch, it will later need to fetch when the user visits that part of the UI, resulting in "delayed" bytes. We also

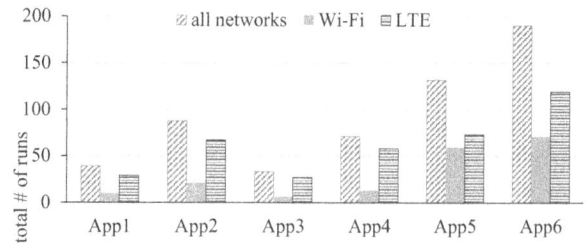

Figure 11: Total number of user sessions per app.

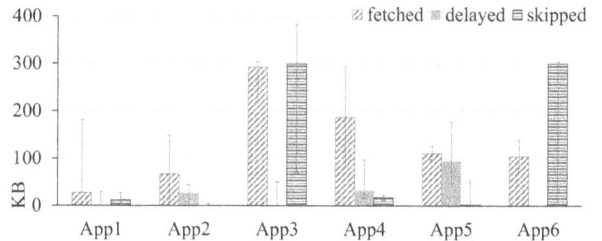

Figure 12: Median KB fetched, delayed and skipped per session, with 25th and 75th percentiles, across all user sessions.

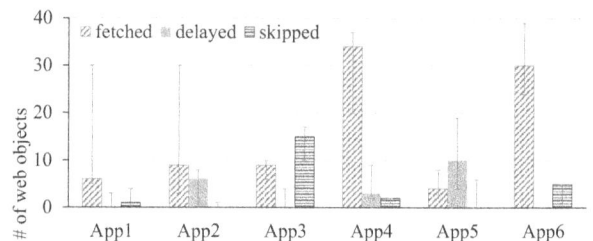

Figure 13: Median number of web objects fetched per session, with 25th and 75th percentiles, across all user sessions.

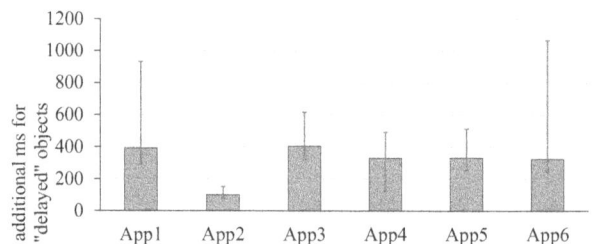

Figure 14: Median additional delay incurred per delayed web object, with 25th and 75th percentiles, across those objects incorrectly procrastinated in user trial, when user was on a cellular connection.

note that for some apps, such as App3 (which shows the user more photos of each movie), there is huge variance in bytes saved.

We contrast this with Figure 13, where for App6, a small number of objects are skipped, but those objects are large and contribute a lot to the savings we achieve. App3 has a lot of small images (stills

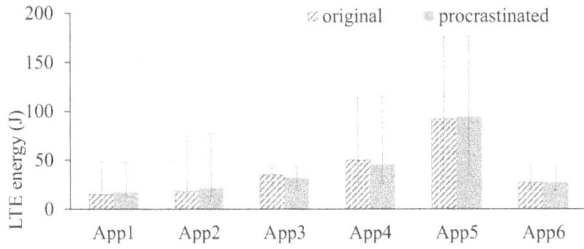

Figure 15: Median energy spent on LTE radio in original and procrastinated behaviors of apps, with 25th and 75th percentiles across all user sessions.

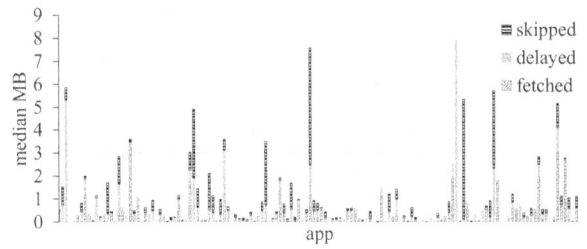

Figure 16: Median MB skipped, delayed and fetched across 140 apps, when using monkey M1.

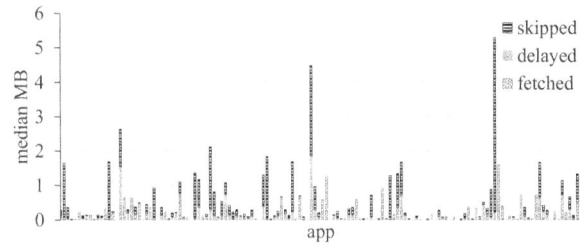

Figure 17: Median MB skipped, delayed and fetched across 140 apps, when using monkey M3.

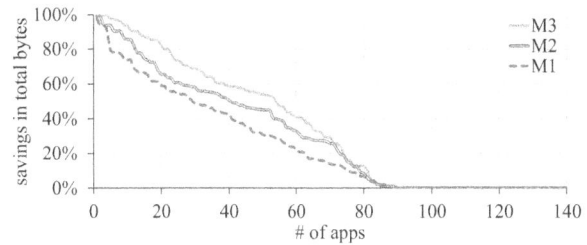

Figure 18: CDF of % of median bytes saved when using Procrastinator on 140 apps. Each line is an independent CDF of a different monkey. Vertical axis is (bytes saved) / (bytes saved + bytes fetched + bytes delayed).

from movies), and procrastinating many of those small objects add up.

In some cases, the user would incur no delay in using a procrastinated app because she does not scroll to a part of the app where a previously skipped image is shown. For other cases where the user is shown a skipped image, we calculate the *additional* delay that she incurs as a result of Procrastinator. This is the smaller value of either the download time for that image, or the difference between when the app originally requests the image and when Procrastinator detects the image is visible. Figure 14 shows this additional delay. We find this is typically under 1 second, and under 300ms in the median across all app sessions. Recall that this is a penalty that a user will experience only when she is on a cellular connection, and running low on her data plan bytes, and visits app content that is not on the first screen of the app. For users in this situation, we believe this is a compelling trade-off.

While we cannot directly measure the energy consumed by the LTE radio on the smartphones that our users used, we apply an empirical model from prior work [10] using the actual timings of network transfers from the user logs. In Figure 15 we show the energy consumed by the app with normal behavior and under Procrastinator. The energy consumption is largely similar. The energy benefit of not transferring unnecessary bytes is balanced by the energy cost of waiting to transfer bytes that later become necessary. We notice that App5 exhibits high variance, partly because users spent variable amounts of time reading articles before clicking on the next article, sometimes as long as 12 seconds which can trigger the LTE radio to sleep.

5.3 Automated monkeys

To understand the performance of Procrastinator in a wider set of apps, we use UI automation to run 140 apps multiple times in the Windows Phone emulator. In Figure 16, we show the number of bytes that were fetched, skipped and delayed when using the most aggressive monkey, M1. In contrast, Figure 17 shows that for the least aggressive M3. Clearly apps consume fewer bytes under M3 (note the different scales on the vertical axes). Even though M3 launches the app and quits soon after without interacting the app's UI, it is possible for there to be delayed network objects. Procrastinator may decide to not download an object, then the app code automatically changes the UI screen despite not having any input from the user, at which point Procrastinator detects the need for previously requested network objects which it will then download.

Figure 18 shows CDFs of the fraction of bytes saved by the three monkeys across the 140 apps. We see that with M3, Procrastinator saves over 60% of bytes in 40 apps. With the most aggressive monkey, it saves over 60% of bytes in 20 apps, and over 40% in 40 apps. There is a tail of over 50 apps where the savings are practi-

cally nothing, but these apps consume relatively less network data. The apps that represent points to the left of 90 on the horizontal axis consume 1.1 MB on average, while the ones to the right consume 475 KB on average.

Figure 19 shows the median latency in downloading delayed objects under an LTE model, and Figure 20 shows that assuming a cloudlet at the LTE celltower. Under M3, almost half of apps experience no delay because there is less opportunity for there to be delayed objects in M3. There are some objects that take more than 500 ms to download – these are all large transfers. In some cases, they are 1 MB files, which is almost a second at 12.74 Mbps, which is sometimes exacerbated if the radio went to sleep due to inactivity or there was no open TCP connection that server. In the case of LTE, we observe that all non-zero latencies start at about 100 ms. This is because the LTE end-to-end RTT is 69.5 ms and if an HTTP connection is already open to a server, it can take a little more than a round-trip to get an entire small object. In contrast, Figure 20 does not show this artifact. In this hypothetical model of a cloudlet at the celltower, the radio latency to the cloudlet is much lower,

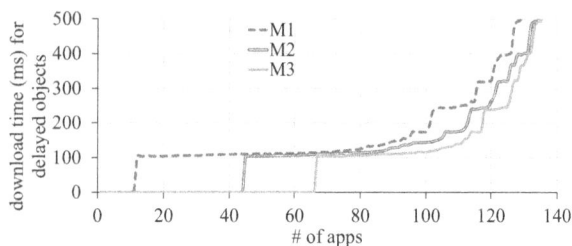

Figure 19: CDF of median download time for delayed objects in 140 apps under Procrastinator when using monkeys. Download times are calculated using LTE parameters from prior work. Each line is an independent CDF representing a different monkey. Vertical axis is chopped at 500ms for readability.

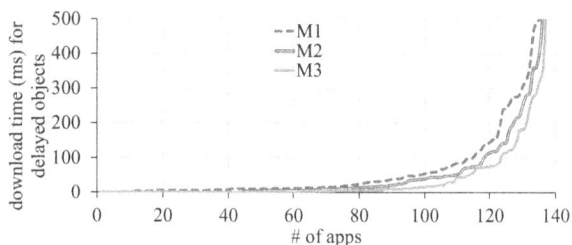

Figure 20: CDF of median download time for delayed objects in 140 apps under Procrastinator when using monkeys. Download times are calculated assuming a Cloudlet at the LTE celltower. Each line is an independent CDF representing a different monkey. Vertical axis is chopped at 500ms for readability.

while the cloudlet continues to experience the bulk of the latency to the Internet. In this way, the cloudlet can hide network delays.

5.4 Overheads

Due to the addition of the Procrastinator Runtime and the code injection in the app's binary, the size of the app package increases. This can impact users in two ways. The bytes spent downloading the app from the marketplace will increase. The bytes consumed by local storage on the phone in storing the app binary will increase. In Figure 21, we present the increase in size of the app package. The compressed line shows the increase in size of the compressed package, which is what the phone will download from the marketplace. The uncompressed line indicates how much storage will be consumed on the phone. The median app size before Procrastinator is 1.6 MB uncompressed and 813 KB compressed. The largest is 29 MB uncompressed and 25 MB compressed. All of the apps with more than 5% increase in uncompressed size were under 1MB in size uncompressed prior to Procrastinator. All of the apps above 10% are under 544 KB in size. While it is unfortunate that using Procrastinator will increase the size of the app that is downloaded by the user and hence consume additional cellular bytes, this minor increase is easily amortized if the user runs the app frequently and thereby saves cellular bytes then.

Another overhead that Procrastinator introduces is the memory consumption in maintaining the two tables that track procrastinated calls as shown in Figures 6 and 7. The number of rows in the tables in any app is bounded by the number of prefetch network calls that the app makes. Each row consists of the URL being procrastinated and any associated callback method reference or UI element refer-

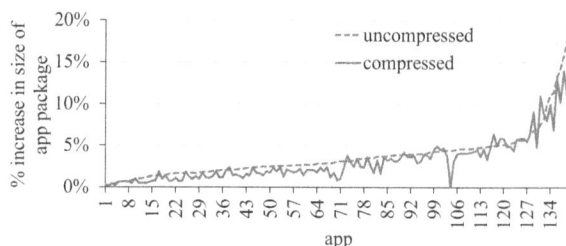

Figure 21: Increase in size of app package as a result of Procrastinator, for 140 apps. Highest point is almost 20%. Apps are sorted on the horizontal by uncompressed increase percentage.

UI tree depth	average delay
3	0.1 ms
13	0.2 ms

Table 6: Delay in checking whether a UI element is visible on the phone's screen. Delay reported is the average of 1000 runs on a Nokia Lumia 920 smartphone. UI depth is the number of levels in the UI tree that the UI element is at.

ence. Similar to Figure 13, we do not see an excessive number of downloads in any run of an app – it is typically well below a hundred. Hence, the memory consumption of these tables is minor in practice.

The Procrastinator Runtime introduces very little delay during program execution. The most common code execution is to check the visibility of UI elements (§ 3.2.2), which may happen each time an app requests a network object, and once per procrastinated network object each time the UI changes. This code traverses the UI tree and does simple math to determine the visibility of each parent node of the UI element in the tree. In Table 6, we evaluate the overhead of this check for two common UI tree depths. In each case, we calculate the time spent in running this code path 1,000 times and then divide that by 1,000. We find that running this code requires 0.1 – 0.2 ms. If an app has 100 UI elements that are procrastinated (far more than we have observed in practice), this overhead will be 10 – 20 ms each time the UI changes.

6. DEPLOYMENT IMPLICATIONS

Here we summarize our thinking on a number of practical issues that one would consider in a public deployment of Procrastinator.

Balancing speed and cost: Our target user for Procrastinator is one who frequently switches between being data cost conscious (when on pay-per-byte data plans or roaming internationally) and data cost oblivious (when on Wi-Fi or at the start of a monthly billing cycle). Procrastinator offers a compelling trade-off of occasional delays in network transfers for data cost savings for these users. There is a middle ground that our system could support. Based on prior usage history, existing machine learning algorithms could learn that a particular user often goes to certain portions of an app's UI. With that knowledge, Procrastinator could choose to fetch additional content, thereby reducing the user experience delay, at the risk of occasionally being wrong and consuming more bytes than needed. In either case, users who prefer to manually turn off Procrastinator can do so using the existing button in Figure 8.

Request prioritization: While our goal is to reduce data consumption, Procrastinator's techniques can be used to improve network performance. Apps tend to intermingle urgent network requests with non-urgent prefetches. Procrastinator automatically identifies which network requests are prefetches. It could hold off on those until the network becomes idle. In this way, prefetch transfers will not compete with more urgent requests for precious available bandwidth.

Impact on server: Procrastinator affects only HTTP(S) GETs. Other traffic, including UDP, ICMP, HTTP POST, and (non-HTTP) TCP remain unaffected by Procrastinator. Semantically, HTTP GET is a mechanism for retrieving content from a server. The same cannot be said of arbitrary TCP or UDP traffic, and certainly not for HTTP POST which is used to commit an action at a server (such as purchase a movie ticket). Hence we do not procrastinate any such traffic. One could design a client-server system where an HTTP GET actually signals an action or commit on the server side. So far, we have not encountered such unusual behavior in the apps we have studied. If that were to happen, and if Procrastinator were to procrastinate such a call, that would affect the broader semantics of the application. It is possible that by not fetching some HTTP objects, Procrastinator may impact analytics done on server-side HTTP logs.

Who runs Procrastinator? We designed Procrastinator to not require mobile OS changes, not require app developer effort, and not require app source code. These design decisions give us significant flexibility in deploying Procrastinator. We can consider three models:

- Developer tool: The app developer can run Procrastinator on their app binary, test the new app binary, and submit that to the app marketplace.
- Marketplace tool: The app marketplace could run Procrastinator on incoming app binaries as part of the app publication process. The marketplace may chose to do this selectively for users, or countries where data costs are a significant concern for the population.
- User tool: The data-conscious user could run Procrastinator on app binaries that she has purchased from the marketplace.

We do not advocate any one model over another. Each group has their own incentives. Some users want to save data costs. An OS vendor may want their phones to be appealing to data conscious users. An app developer may want to support data conscious users without hurting performance demanding users.

Procrastinator versus "Prefetcher": In our experience, most apps prefetch network content, such as images and icons and XML files. Thankfully, apps typically do not prefetch large video files, and will wait for the user to click on a video. Procrastinator works because apps prefetch. Hence our system adaptively procrastinates those prefetches. If apps were to fetch network content solely on demand, we would be faced with the opposite problem of automatically prefetching that on-demand content for non-data-conscious users. That reverse problem is *harder* than the one we tackle. In that problem, the solution will need to hunt the app for URLs to fetch ahead of the app requesting it. These URLs may not be readily available, especially when the app constructs the URLs on the fly (e.g. a weather URL with a zip code embedded in it).

Limited programmer effort: By design, we avoid requiring the app developer to change her code. This ease comes at the penalty of limiting our savings. As shown in Figure 10, our conservative design is leaving additional savings on the table. This is because in some programming patterns, it is difficult for static program analysis to ascertain that there is no side effect in a network callback method. This can happen, for example, in dynamic dispatch where the implementation of a polymorphic operation is chosen at runtime not at compile-time. While Procrastinator's static analysis

is not robust enough and hence is conservative, dynamic analysis could be used in these cases. However, dynamic analysis would add tremendous complexity to our system, and can impose a significant runtime performance penalty on the user of the app. Alternatively, the app developer could give us 1 bit of information for every network call – does the callback have a side effect? That one boolean can help unlock additional data savings. It requires some developer effort in carefully walking through the code affected by every network transfer.

7. PRIOR WORK

Prefetching is a well-studied problem in many areas of computer systems. Here, we focus on prior work in network prefetching in mobile apps.

The most relevant prior work is Informed Mobile Prefetching [9]. IMP is a system where app developers use an API to specify a method that is capable of fetching a network object, a call to consume the network object, or a call to cancel that prefetch. By providing a hint that a network object may be needed, and then later specifying either the immediate need for it or a cancellation, the underlying system can optimize for data, power and performance goals. Procrastinator and IMP represent two different points in the design space. IMP is a system designed to optimize *prefetching*. On the other hand, Procrastinator never prefetches on its own – it only *delays* fetching of network objects. IMP takes energy consumption into account when making prefetching decisions, while Procrastinator does not. IMP requires deliberate rewriting of app by the developer, and thus, the evaluation of IMP was limited to just two apps. On the other hand, Procrastinator works via binary rewriting, without any input from the developer. As a result, we are able to evaluate Procrastinator on many more apps. IMP includes complex mechanisms for self-learning and self-tuning, while the design of Procrastinator is much simpler. However, learning from past history of procrastination may be beneficial for our system as well. We believe that IMP and Procrastinator offer two design choices that are on extreme ends of the developer effort spectrum. As a result, the system design and techniques that we use are completely different.

This paper is an extended version of a short workshop paper [17]. In this paper, we address a number of deficiencies in that workshop paper. We have made our system significantly more robust by handling more prefetch situations and filling gaps in our system design. This is evidenced by the additional detail in § 3, and our ability to run Procrastinator on many more apps. We have added several elements to our evaluation, including energy consumption, UI automated runs of 140 apps, impact on app code size, and runtime delay.

Outside of network consumption, prior work has modified mobile apps to improve performance and reduce battery consumption. RetroSkeleton [7] is a toolbox to rewrite Android apps without using app source code. While they do not use it to improve network efficiency, they do use it to change some network calls, such as changing all HTTP calls to HTTPS.

Researchers have also looked at automatic static and dynamic analysis of call graphs and data flows in mobile apps for other purposes. TaintDroid [8] dynamically monitors the data flow of apps to find privacy leaks. ADEL [21] finds energy leaks in mobile apps by dynamically monitoring the data flow in the app. ADEL identifies network calls that are not useful and reports them as energy leaks. In comparison, Procrastinator not only identifies these calls but also automatically delays them to reduce data consumption.

Improving web caching in apps [15] and redundancy elimination of cellular traffic [14] are two additional techniques for reducing data consumption. Our approach is complementary in nature, in that Procrastinator can further reduce data consumption by eliminating some network transfers. Much of Procrastinator's savings are from not fetching unnecessary images, which are typically already compressed in PNG or JPEG formats and would not see much benefit from additional compression. The open-source PageSpeed module [4] for webservers can speed up web browsing and reduce data consumption by optimizing the layout of web pages. It combines and "minifies" resource files, and resizes and re-encodes images. PageSpeed works on web pages, but not on individual web transfers that apps do. Furthermore, Procrastinator applies techniques that PageSpeed does not.

Prior work has also looked at the related problem of cellular signaling overhead and optimizing network traffic burstiness to reduce such overhead and energy consumption. Huang [11] has studied data transfers when the phone's screen is turned off, and proposes being more aggressive in optimizing traffic then. ARO [16] is a system for optimizing the radio behavior of apps to mitigate the ill effects of bursty network usage.

8. SUMMARY

As more cellular operators transition from unlimited data plans to tiered plans, more users will find themselves needing to curb their cellular data consumption. However, many smartphone apps are designed to prefetch network content. We argue that asking an app developer to modify her app is not a winning proposition because it asks for altruism from the app developer to think hard about each network transfer and rewrite code around it. Conversely, automatically deciding whether to do a requested network transfer is hard because it depends on understanding the intent of the app developer. In Procrastinator, we attempt to automatically understand this intent by tying each network transfer to the portion of the UI that is affected. We run into trouble when a network callback method calls a series of other methods, where programming patterns such as reflection can create type instances at run time. In those situations, we cannot statically determine that there will be no ill effect of not running that code. Even with dynamic analysis we may not know without actually running that code. In those situations, we take the conservative approach of allowing the app to proceed, thereby leaving out some data savings for the user.

Nonetheless, on professionally-written apps, Procrastinator has achieved as much as 4X reduction in bytes transferred by the apps for some users. In lab experiments with UI automation, Procrastinator shows 2.5X and higher savings in 20-40 apps. If the user decides to visit off-screen content that we do not prefetch, the penalty is additional latency, which was under 300ms in the median on LTE in our user study. This is only experienced when the user is on cellular and running low on data bytes – otherwise, normal app behavior occurs. Our measured latency is tolerable, and can be seen in our online video [5] where the smartphone was connected over LTE.

Acknowledgments

We thank our shepherd, Ulas Kozat, and the ACM MobiSys 2014 reviewers for their feedback on our work.

9. REFERENCES

[1] Fiddler. http://fiddler2.com/.
[2] How to adjust data usage using the Data Sense API. http://msdn.microsoft.com/en-us/library/windowsphone/develop/jj207005.aspx.
[3] Nokia Lumia 520 phone, as shown on 4 December 2013. http://www.microsoftstore.com/store/msusa/en_US/pdp/Nokia-Lumia-520-No-Contract-for-ATT/productID.283842800.
[4] PageSpeed Module. https://developers.google.com/speed/pagespeed/module.
[5] Procrastinator demo video. http://research.microsoft.com/apps/video/default.aspx?id=202479.
[6] M. Barnett and M. Fahndrich. Microsoft Research Common Compiler Infrastructure. http://research.microsoft.com/en-us/projects/cci/.
[7] B. Davis and H. Chen. RetroSkeleton: Retrofitting Android Apps. In *ACM MobiSys*, 2013.
[8] W. Enck, P. Gilbert, B. Chun, L. Cox, J. Jung, P. McDaniel, and A. Sheth. TaintDroid: An Information-Flow Tracking System for Realtime Privacy Monitoring on Smartphones. In *USENIX OSDI*, 2010.
[9] B. D. Higgins, J. Flinn, T. Giuli, B. Noble, C. Peplin, and D. Watson. Informed mobile prefetching. In *ACM MobiSys*, 2012.
[10] J. Huang, F. Qian, A. Gerber, Z. M. Mao, S. Sen, and O. Spatscheck. A Close Examination of Performance and Power Characteristics of 4G LTE Networks. In *ACM MobiSys*, 2012.
[11] J. Huang, F. Qian, Z. M. Mao, S. Sen, and O. Spatscheck. Screen-Off Traffic Characterization and Optimization in 3G/4G Networks. In *IMC*, 2012.
[12] S. Lidin. Inside Microsoft .NET IL Assembler. In *Microsoft Press*, 2002.
[13] C. Perzold. Microsoft Silverlight Edition: Programming Windows Phone 7. In *Microsoft Press*, 2010.
[14] F. Qian, J. Huang, J. Erman, Z. M. Mao, S. Sen, and O. Spatscheck. How to Reduce Smartphone Traffic Volume by 30%? In *PAM*, 2013.
[15] F. Qian, K. S. Quah, J. Huang, J. Erman, A. Gerber, Z. M. Mao, S. Sen, and O. Spatscheck. Web Caching on Smartphones: Ideal vs. Reality. In *ACM MobiSys*, 2012.
[16] F. Qian, Z. Wang, A. Gerber, Z. M. Mao, S. Sen, and O. Spatscheck. Profiling Resource Usage for Mobile Applications: a Cross-layer Approach. In *ACM MobiSys*, 2011.
[17] L. Ravindranath, S. Agarwal, J. Padhye, and C. Riederer. Give in to procrastination and stop prefetching. In *HotNets*, 2013.
[18] L. Ravindranath, S. Nath, J. Padhye, and H. Balakrishnan. Automatic and Scalable Fault Detection for Mobile Applications. In *ACM MobiSys*, 2014.
[19] L. Ravindranath, J. Padhye, S. Agarwal, R. Mahajan, I. Obermiller, and S. Shayandeh. Appinsight: Mobile app performance monitoring in the wild. In *USENIX OSDI*, 2012.
[20] M. Satyanarayanan, P. Bahl, R. Caceres, and N. Davies. The Case for VM-based Cloudlets in Mobile Computing. In *IEEE Pervasive*, 2009.
[21] L. Zhang, M. Gordon, R. Dick, Z. M. Mao, P. Dinda, and L. Yang. Adel: An automatic detector of energy leaks for smartphone applications. In *CODES+ISSS*, 2012.

CoAST: Collaborative Application-Aware Scheduling of Last-Mile Cellular Traffic

Cong Shi*, Kaustubh Joshi†, Rajesh K. Panta†, Mostafa H. Ammar*, Ellen W. Zegura*

*School of Computer Science
Georgia Institute of Technology, Atlanta, GA
{cshi7, ammar, ewz}@cc.gatech.edu

†AT&T Labs - Research, Bedminster, NJ
{kaustubh, rpanta}@research.att.com

ABSTRACT

The explosive growth of mobile data traffic poses severe pressure on cellular providers to better manage their finite spectrum. Proposed solutions such as congestion-pricing exist, but they degrade users' ability to use the network when they want. In this paper, we propose a fundamentally different approach - rather than reducing the aggregate busy hour traffic, we seek to smooth the peaks that cause congestion. Our approach is based on two key insights obtained from traffic traces of a large cellular provider. First, mobile traffic demonstrates high short-term variation so that delaying traffic for very short periods of time can significantly reduce peaks. Second, by making collaborative decisions on which traffic gets delayed and by how much across all users of a cell, the delays need not result in any degradation of user experience. We design a system, CoAST, to implement this approach using three key mechanisms: a protocol to allow mobile applications and providers to exchange traffic information, an incentive mechanism to incentivize mobile applications to collaboratively delay traffic at the right time, and mechanisms to delay application traffic. We provide extensive evaluations that show that CoAST reduces traffic peaks by up to 50% even for applications that are not thought to be delay-tolerant, e.g., streaming and web browsing, but which together account for 70% of all cellular traffic.

Categories and Subject Descriptors

C.2.3 [**Computer-Communication Networks**]: Network Operations —*Network Management*

Keywords

Cellular Networks; Peak Throughput; Delay Tolerance; Scheduling

1. INTRODUCTION

The rapid proliferation of smartphones, tablets, and mobile applications has led to a tremendous increase in mobile data traffic in the last few years. For example, the mobile data traffic on major US based mobile carriers has increased by more than 20,000% in

five years [7]. Furthermore, according to forecasts by major equipment manufacturers, this trend is likely to continue in future with 78% compound annual growth rate [1]. In contrast, the capacity of cellular networks, especially the wireless spectrum, has not increased proportionally. The efficient management of mobile traffic is, therefore, critical for cellular network operators.

Various solutions have been proposed to manage the mismatch between the ever-increasing traffic demand and finite wireless spectrum. These solutions can be broadly classified into two categories— adding more network resources to increase the overall capacity (i.e. increasing supply), or managing user demands and behavior to reduce the load on the network (i.e. controlling demand). Examples of the first category include the use of small cells for augmenting the capacity of traditional macro cells, adding WiFi hotspots to offload cellular traffic to WiFi, using portable base stations (e.g. Cells On Wheels or COWs) to meet high traffic demands in event venues where large numbers of users gather for some time periods, etc. Examples of the second category include congestion pricing, off-peak delivery, network-aware throttling, etc. These approaches reduce the aggregate traffic in busy periods by either shifting the parts of traffic that can tolerate some delay to off-peak hours (e.g. backup, synchronization, cloud offload, etc.) [12], or causing the user to use the network less frequently.

These existing approaches have some fundamental limitations. Shifting traffic to off-peak hours can cause degradation of quality of service experienced by the end users. The vast majority of mobile data traffic, including video streaming and mobile web browsing, cannot be shifted to off-peak hours because of latency requirements. Although additional network resources increase the overall capacity, they also incur significant costs. Furthermore, solutions like small cells can be deployed only gradually because of the detail radio engineering trials required for the correct positioning and deployment of such infrastructure.

In this paper, we take a fundamentally different approach to tackle this problem—delaying mobile traffic like video streaming and mobile web browsing that are not traditionally thought to be delay tolerant. This is based on two key insights derived from mobile traffic traces of a large US cellular provider. First, we observe that the mobile data traffic exhibits high burstiness over small time scales (tens of seconds). Thus, to ensure adequate quality of service at all times, it is important to reduce the instantaneous peak traffic, not just the aggregate traffic. Second, even applications like video streaming and mobile web browsing can, in fact, tolerate small delays. For example, a video streaming client can tolerate delays of tens of seconds as long as its playback buffer is not empty. Mobile web browsers can delay downloading the contents that are not currently displayed on the screen. These two insights suggest that if the right user traffic (from the set of all current user traffic in the cell) is delayed at the right time for the right time duration, it is possible to reduce the peak traffic in a cell without affecting the user experience on any mobile device. This requires both device-level information (e.g. tolerable delay values at the given time instant) and cell-level information (e.g. the total traffic demand in the cell at the given time instant). Thus, an efficient interaction mechanism between mobile devices and cellular infrastructure is necessary to enable collaboration between them to make proper decisions about delaying the user traffic.

Using these insights, we present the design, implementation, and extensive evaluation of a novel system called CoAST (**Co**llaborative **A**pplication-Aware **S**cheduling of Last Mile Cellular **T**raffic). CoAST provides an interface to enable an efficient collaboration between mobile devices and the network element to which they are connected (e.g. a base station). The interface is simple and flexible, allowing dynamic policies and protocols to be built on top of it, according to the requirements and capabilities of individual mobile applications. CoAST also provides an incentive mechanism for mobile applications to delay their traffic and the actual mechanisms to delay the application traffic.

In addition to benefits to the mobile network operator, CoAST also improves the application performance for the end user. By delaying traffic of users with enough playback buffer contents, CoAST can aggressively fill the starving buffers of other users, thereby reducing their buffering delays.

In summary, CoAST makes following novel contributions:

1) Rather than reducing the aggregate busy hour traffic, CoAST reduces the instantaneous peak load in a cell, without compromising the quality of service experienced by the end users.

2) CoAST can handle traffic which is not traditionally thought to be delay tolerant.

3) CoAST provides a simple and flexible interface for mobile devices and the cellular network to exchange various information to enable them to make proper decisions about delaying user traffic.

We implement a prototype of CoAST on the Android platform for two sample application categories, streaming (e.g., YouTube) and web browsing, which are the top two generators of cellular network traffic, accounting for nearly 70% of global cellular traffic [25]. We evaluate our implementation on a per-cell basis using emulation based on real YouTube and web browsing traces obtained from a major US cellular provider. Our results show that CoAST reduces traffic peaks by an average of 30-50%, or conversely, increases the capacity of a cell by 20% without compromising the quality of the end user experience. In fact, we show that CoAST achieves a better quality of service in terms of reduced buffering delay compared to the cell that does not use CoAST. Our experiments also show that the control plane overhead introduced by CoAST is negligible.

The rest of the paper is organized as follows. In Section 2, we describe the background of this work and present an overview of CoAST design. We motivate the CoAST design with an analysis on cellular traffic in Section 3. The design details of CoAST is described in Section 4. The deployment and implementation of CoAST system is discussed in Section 5. The system evaluation of CoAST prototype and the trace-driven evaluation of CoAST are presented in Section 6 and 7, respectively. We discuss the related issues in Section 8. Section 9 summarizes the related work. We conclude this paper and discuss future work in Section 10.

2. BACKGROUND AND DESIGN OVERVIEW

In this section, we describe the background of this work and present a high-level overview of CoAST design.

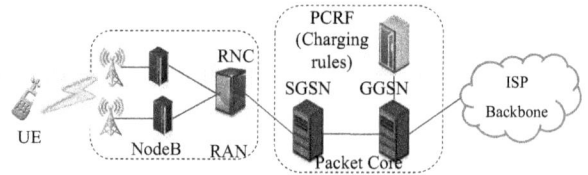

Figure 1: Architecture of UMTS data network.

2.1 Background of Cellular Networks

In this subsection, we first describe the basics of cellular architecture and then provide information about the data set used in our evaluations.

Figure 1 shows the key components of a typical UMTS data network. It consists of 2 major components: the Radio Access Network (RAN) and the Core Network (CN) (or Packet Core). The mobile device, called User Equipment (UE) in UMTS terminology, is connected to one or several cell sectors in RAN. A physical base station (called NodeB in 3G and eNodeB in LTE) can have multiple cell sectors, which provide radio resources to UEs for wireless communications. Cellular data traffic from several NodeBs are then passed to the Radio Network Controller (RNC), which manages handovers, and scheduling of wireless resources among the NodeBs under its control. The RNCs connect to Serving GPRS Support Nodes (SGSNs) at the core network. The SGSNs are connected to the external networks, such as the Internet, via Gateway GPRS Support Nodes (GGSNs). When a UE connects to the network, it establishes a Packet Data Protocol (PDP) context which facilitates tunneling of IP traffic from the UE to the peering GGSN using GPRS Tunneling Protocol (GTP) (see [14] for details of the UMTS network).

We evaluate CoAST using real-world cellular traffic data from a tier-1 cellular network carrier. All device and user identifiers are anonymized for our analysis. The first data set is collected from the link between SGSN and GGSN in the core network. It contains information about IP flows carried in PDP contexts for a 3% random sample of devices collected every minute, e.g. start and end time stamps, per flow traffic volume, application identifier, etc. This data set is used to collect information about the characteristic of video streaming traffic. To gain more fine grained information about the actual traffic volume in a given cell sector, we use another dataset collected every 2 seconds at RNCs in the RAN network.

2.2 Design Overview

CoAST aims to reduce the peak-to-average ratio of the cellular last-hop traffic, and consequently improve application performance for the end user. It is not designed for persistently congested networks whose average traffic is close to the capacity. Such networks need to be upgraded to increase the capacity. We focus primarily on *downstream* as the upstream traffic intensity is not as significant. (Note that CoAST can apply equally to upstream traffic as well. But we do not claim it is the contribution of this paper.) We accomplish this by delaying downstream traffic at times when the link is experiencing heavy load. In order to avoid degrading the quality of service experienced by the end user, the acceptable delays may range from a few to tens of seconds depending on the applications. As will be shown in the next section such relatively short traffic delays are enough to produce the desired effect of reducing traffic peaks.

One key insight of CoAST is that only mobile applications know the delay constraints of their traffic while the eNodeB has the aggregated traffic information. Thus, solutions that rely solely on the eNodeB or on the mobile devices do not have enough information to simultaneously achieve both high utilization and good quality of service. Collaboration between the eNodeB and mobile devices is required to determine if and by how much the downstream data should be delayed. The scheme, described in detail in Section 4, enables the users to optimize their download rates while minimizing the cost of data download and maximizing the quality of service.

It is important to note that the pricing incentive used in our scheme is, strictly speaking, internal to the system and is used to facilitate decision making regarding whether to delay a certain chunk of the download traffic. It is not meant to be exposed directly and as-is to the user, nor is it meant to translate directly into billing. It will be important, however, to incentivize users to deploy this system in their devices. So we expect that there will be some correlation between billing and pricing practices of operators to be influenced by the usage of this system. However, the exact approach here is beyond the scope of our technical discussion.

Although a wide user participation increases the effectiveness of CoAST, it is not necessary that all users in a cell deploy CoAST—only enough number of UEs that can make a difference in traffic peaks is needed. Also note that users who do not deploy the system will not necessarily have any advantage over those who use the system since the user experience is preserved for those using it. So there is no individual incentive to "cheat" the system from this perspective. On the contrary, users will be interested to participate if operator pricing does somehow reflect the usage of the system. CoAST also monitors the behaviors of participating devices to identify potential cheating, which will be discussed in Section 8.

3. FEASIBILITY AND BENEFITS OF DELAYING MOBILE TRAFFIC

In this section we present an analysis of the real-world traffic traces of a large US cellular carrier to provide motivation about the feasibility and potential benefits of delaying mobile traffic for short time durations.

3.1 Short-Term Burstiness of Mobile Traffic

First, we analyze the traffic distribution of a large number of cells (13522 NodeBs) using a large dataset of cellular traffic collected at several RNCs to demonstrate that the mobile data traffic of a typical cell demonstrates high variations over short time scales (e.g. 30 seconds). This dataset provides per cell as well as per UE cellular data records. We focus on the downlink traffic because it is significantly larger than the uplink traffic in cellular networks [9, 18].

Figure 2 plots the downlink throughput along with its 20 second moving average in a typical cell in one day. The traffic is clearly very bursty with large short-term variations. To ensure adequate quality of service at all times, the cellular network provider needs to over-provision the network resources based on the peak traffic demand. Therefore, the burstiness of mobile traffic makes the resources underutilized during most periods of time.

A heuristic idea to better utilize the cellular resources is to delay a portion of mobile traffic for a short period of time to reduce the peak throughput over time. As a simple approximation, we use the moving average in a short period of time to demonstrate the potential benefits of delaying mobile traffic. Figure 2 shows that the peak value of the 20 second moving average is only about 60% of the original peak throughput. This implies that delaying a portion of mobile traffic by 20 seconds or less can result in a significant reduction in the peak throughput demand in the cell. It will lead to two major benefits. First, the reduction in the peak throughput allows the network to support more users and mobile traffic with-

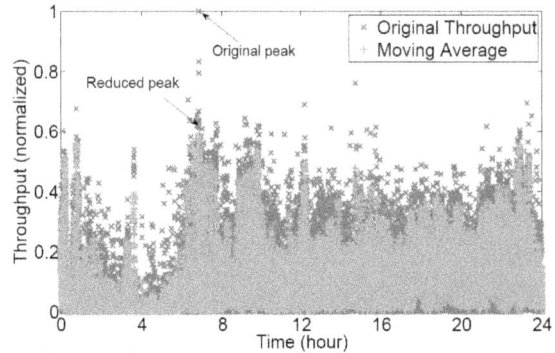

Figure 2: The downlink traffic and its 20 second moving average in a cell in one typical day. The throughput is normalized with the maximal capacity used. The difference between the original traffic and its moving average demonstrates its high short-term variations.

out upgrading the infrastructure. In some cases, it also means that the cellular network may be able to support better quality services. For example, it may be feasible to support a better quality video streaming (say HD video with better resolution) if there is sufficient reduction in the overall load on the cell. Second, this also reduces congestion and helps improve the performance of mobile applications that are sensitive to delays (e.g., VoIP).

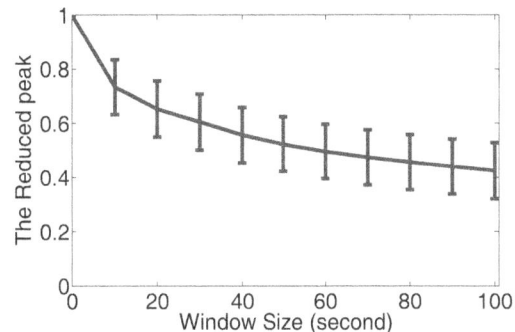

Figure 3: The reduction of the peak downlink throughput for moving averages computed over different time periods. The average and standard deviation are plotted.

To further quantify the relationship between the extra delay and the reduction on the peak throughput, we compare the reduced peak throughput achieved by moving averages computed over different time intervals for the top 200 heavy-loaded cells. The results are plotted in Figure 3. When the window size increases from 1s to 30s, the reduced peak throughput quickly decreases from 100% to 60.5% of the original peak on average. As the window size further increases to 100s, the peak is gradually reduced to 42.5% of the original peak. This figure implies that most benefits in terms of reduction of peak throughput can be obtained by delaying traffic for short time durations (e.g., 30 seconds), with diminishing returns for larger delay intervals.

3.2 Delay Tolerance of Mobile Applications

The real-world cell traffic traces indicate that delaying mobile traffic for a few seconds can reduce the peak load in the cell significantly. The next natural question is: Can real-world mobile applications tolerate such delays without affecting the quality of service experienced by the end-users? To investigate this, we consider following major traffic classes:

3.2.1 Streaming

Streaming applications (e.g., video streaming, audio streaming) account for around 34% of the total mobile traffic [25]. As they usually buffer some data, they can tolerate small delays which are equivalent to the current buffer occupancy of their playback buffer.

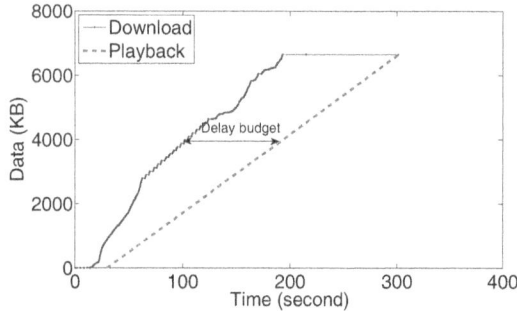

Figure 4: The download and playback progress of a Youtube video on an Android smartphone using a cellular network. The difference between download and playback represents the delay it can tolerate.

To investigate delay tolerance of streaming applications over cellular networks, we play a Youtube video on an Android smartphone and record the cellular traffic using Wireshark. Figure 4 compares the number of downloaded bytes and the actual playback progress during the experiment. Initially, the Youtube client aggressively buffers the video contents. But once the client has sufficient contents to play for some time, it slows the download to avoid downloading unnecessary contents in case the user does not watch the complete video. The difference between the actual download and the playback progress at any given time is the amount of delay the Youtube client can tolerate at that time without affecting the user experience (i.e., pausing the video).

We also see from Figure 4 that depending on the size of the buffered data, the tolerable delay varies from a few seconds to more than one hundred seconds in this example. In addition, user operations like "back" and "forward" will also impact the delay that the video client can tolerate at the specific time.

To accurately predict the future traffic and delay that the video client can tolerate, video size, bitrate, buffered data, and playback progress are required. Specifically, we can predict the amount of data to download based on the video size and buffered data. Meanwhile, the bitrate, buffered data and playback progress can be used to estimate the delay that it can tolerate. Fortunately, all of them are available to the video client. Video size and bitrate can be obtained from the video metadata, while buffered data and playback progress are internal states of the video client. In contrast, delaying the streaming traffic arbitrarily, say from the network side without taking real time input from the application, may affect the user experience.

3.2.2 Web Browsing

Web browsing applications, which are also one of the top generators of cellular mobile traffic [25], are generally not regarded as being delay-tolerant. Due to their small size, mobile devices like smartphones and tablets can display only a small portion of a webpage (e.g., texts, images, and other multimedia contents) at any given time. Thus when a user browses a web page, only contents that are shown on the screen need to be downloaded immediately,

while off-screen contents can be downloaded a little bit later without impacting the user experience. In other words, off-screen contents can be treated as being delay-tolerant. In fact, some websites (e.g., Huffington Post [2]) already support progressive download and display of the web pages. When web pages contain many multimedia contents (e.g., images), the amount of traffic that can be delayed will be significant.

To identify the delay tolerance of web browsing, we analyze the on-screen and off-screen contents of the top 500 Alexa websites [6] in various categories. We only treat off-screen images as off-screen contents and the rest components as on-screen contents. We use PhantomJS [4] to download and render the web pages. For every website, we only download and analyze its home page. We set the user agent of all HTTP requests to that of the Android web browser and let those websites decide whether to return the mobile version or the full version. The screen size is set to 480×800, a typical setting for smartphones. For each web page, we identify all the off-screen images and treat them as off-screen content, while all other contents are treated as on-screen content.

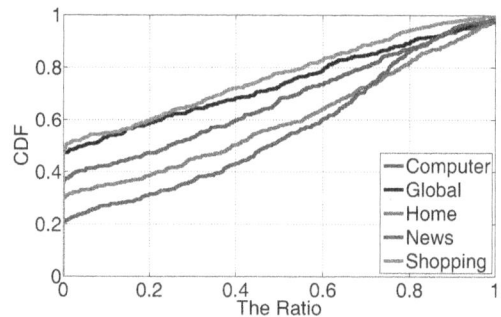

Figure 5: The ratio of off-screen content to the total content on the homepages of the top 500 websites. We also select 4 categories and plot the top 500 websites in these categories.

Figure 5 shows the ratio of the size of the off-screen contents to that of the total contents on the homepage of the top 500 Alexa websites [6]. The category "Global" represents the overall top 500 websites. We also select and plot 4 categories among 16 special categories listed by Alexa. The distributions of other categories are between that of "News" and that of "Shopping". Generally a significant portion of the web content is off-screen and can tolerate short extra delays. For categories like "News", more than 50% of those websites have more than 50% of the contents that can tolerate extra delay. In addition, since the homepages of the websites that we analyzed usually contain less content than other pages, our estimation of the potential benefits as shown in Figure 5 is likely very conservative.

Like streaming applications, we also notice that only the web browser knows which images are off-screen and can tolerate short delay, especially when the user scrolls the web page. Specifically, by parsing the HTML file, the web browser can identify the images that are not shown on the screen. In addition, using the height and width attributes of the corresponding "img" tags, it can estimate their sizes.

4. COAST DESIGN

CoAST enables collaboration among mobile devices for scheduling their mobile traffic, when necessary and feasible, to reduce the peak traffic load on a cell. The basic idea is to use dynamic pricing to motivate the mobile applications to proactively shift their traffic in small time scales (up to 30 seconds) while still satisfying their delay constraints. To realize this idea, CoAST uses three major mechanisms: a protocol to allow mobile applications and their associated cell to exchange traffic information, an incentive mechanism to incentivize mobile applications to collaboratively delay traffic at the right time for the right time duration, and a mechanism to enable applications to delay their traffic. The first two mechanisms are incorporated into the *control plane* of CoAST, while the last one is realized in its *data plane*. However, it should be noted that all CoAST mechanisms are data plane functions from 3GPP protocol perspective, i.e. CoAST does not change the 3GPP protocol itself.

4.1 Design Principles

Minimal modification to mobile applications: For ease of deployment, CoAST requires no modification on the server side, but only small changes on the client side because only mobile applications know the delay constraints of their traffic. CoAST modifies the underlying socket API implementation to allow client applications to specify the tolerable delay information via these socket calls in a transparent manner. The actual value of the tolerable delay at a given time instant depends on the application itself. In this paper, we describe how playback buffer size can be used to figure out the value of tolerable delay for video streaming applications. For other applications, mobile developers may use existing instrumentation systems [13] to determine the tolerable delay, thereby reducing the development efforts.

Privacy preservation: To reduce the peak load on the cell, CoAST relies on collaboration and sharing of traffic information among all mobile devices in that cell. A malicious mobile device may participate CoAST and collect the traffic information of other mobile devices to infer their application usage. To prevent privacy leak under such attack, the control plane is divided into UE proxies on mobile devices and a market proxy on the eNodeB. Each mobile device shares its aggregated traffic demand only with the market proxy and obtains the prices for downloading data only from the market proxy, avoiding the direct sharing of traffic demands among participating devices. With this design, it will be impossible for malicious mobile device to obtain accurate traffic information of mobile applications running on other mobile devices.

Control of demand through pricing: To motivate mobile applications to delay their traffic when necessary, CoAST uses dynamic "prices" to charge mobile traffic at different time instants. The prices used by CoAST can be $ per bit as used in [12]. More generally, it can also be treated as the discount ratio on the accounted traffic. For example, when the price is 0.8, 1 Mb mobile traffic can be accounted as 0.8 Mb. The latter case is compatible with the usage-based pricing model used by most cellular providers nowadays. In this paper, we don't specify the pricing model used by the cellular providers. We treat the price as the ratio of accounted traffic to the transferred traffic.

Tackling system abuse: CoAST requires UEs to report traffic demands to the market proxy, which sets the prices based on demand information from all UEs in the cell. Malicious UEs may attempt to report fake information to abuse the system. To prevent such cheating behavior, CoAST records and compares the reported traffic demands and the real traffic to identify suspicious behavior (please see Section 8 for a detail discussion).

4.2 Overview of CoAST Operation

Figure 6 provides a high-level overview of the CoAST architecture. It consists of two major components: a *market proxy* that resides on a cell-level network element like eNodeB and a *UE proxy* on each mobile device. The market proxy collects the traffic de-

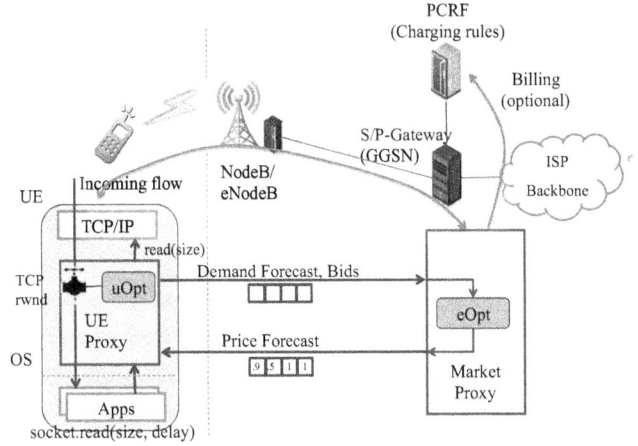

Figure 6: CoAST Architecture.

mands for some future time window from all mobile devices in a cell. These are used by the market proxy as parameters of an optimization problem (eOpt) which determines new future prices for each UE (for the next time window) with the goal of minimizing the traffic peak in the cell. The traffic demands and prices may also be reported to the LTE network for accounting and billing purpose. On the user side, applications determine their traffic demands in a manner that satisfies their delay constraints and sends this information to its UE proxy through the user library. The UE proxy uses these demand information as inputs to an optimization problem (uOpt) that attempts to minimize the cost of satisfying these demands based on prices obtained from the market proxy. CoAST also includes a mechanism by which applications can control their traffic according to the outputs of uOpt.

4.3 Control Plane

CoAST ensures that the traffic demand does not exceed the network capacity at any time without affecting the user experience of mobile applications. Let's denote the capacity of a cell sector by c, the throughput at time t of the ith flow under the control of CoAST by $th_i(t)$, and the total throughput of all other flows by $th_b(t)$. CoAST's goal can be expressed as optimizing an objective function of the difference between the throughput and capacity over time, as follows:

$$\min \ \Phi(\{\sum_{i=1}^{n} th_i(t) + th_b(t) - c\}) \qquad (1)$$

where Φ can be any meaningful utility function. For simplicity of description, we omit the constraints in Eqn 1 and will present them in Eqn 4.

One design challenge is the fact that CoAST has neither control nor accurate information about the background traffic in the cell. By background traffic, we mean all mobile traffic generated by applications that do not use CoAST. Given the burstiness of mobile traffic as shown in Figure 2, it's also hard to accurately predict the background traffic using historical information. To solve this problem, CoAST optimizes the maximal throughput of the flows under its control over time, as follows:

$$\min \ \max_t \sum_{i=1}^{n} th_i(t) \qquad (2)$$

Therefore, no information of the background traffic is required. Let $th_b^* = \max_t th_b(t)$. A pleasant property of this objective function is that it is equivalent to minimizing $\sum_{i=1}^{n} th_i(t) + th_b^*$, which will be proved in Section 4.5. When enough numbers of UEs use CoAST, the peak throughput of total traffic will be minimized.

A centralized solution to Formula 2 would require the market proxy and the UE proxies to share information of all flows, resulting in a lot of control overhead. Moreover, it violates our privacy preservation design goal. Thus, a distributed control protocol that exchanges limited information is required. To solve this problem, we use the dual decomposition method [20] to decompose the original problem into a master problem and multiple independent sub-problems. The master problem (eOpt) is solved by the market proxy, while the independent sub-problems (uOpt) are solved by the UE proxies. We describe this control protocol next.

At a high level, the control plane functions as follows: The market proxy periodically computes the projected prices for mobile traffic for some time window in the future. These prices are calculated based on the traffic demand collected from all connected UEs. The prices are broadcasted to all connected UEs. Each UE proxy uses the price information from the market proxy and the demand information from its mobile applications to schedule the mobile traffic such that the demand of each application is satisfied and the overall cost is minimized. The UE proxy then sends back the traffic demands that it calculates for some future time window to the market proxy, and the process is repeated.

4.3.1 Market Proxy Operations

The market proxy operates in time slots with length τ (e.g., 1 second). The time slot that time t belongs to is denoted as $\lfloor t \rfloor_\tau = \lfloor \frac{t-t_0}{\tau} \rfloor$, where t_0 is the start time. Let $p(\lfloor t \rfloor_\tau)$ represent the price for the downlink traffic through a cell sector during time slot $\lfloor t \rfloor_\tau$. Let $the_e(\lfloor t \rfloor_\tau)$ represent the downlink traffic demand of UE e during time slot $\lfloor t \rfloor_\tau$.

In every δ seconds (e.g., 0.1), the market proxy receives a vector of traffic demand for the next κ (e.g., 30) time slots, i.e., $\overline{the_e} = \{the_e(\lfloor t \rfloor_\tau), the_e(\lfloor t \rfloor_\tau + 1), \dots, the_e(\lfloor t \rfloor_\tau + \kappa)\}$, where t is the current time. Then it updates the price vector, i.e., $\overline{p} = \{p(\lfloor t \rfloor_\tau), \dots, p(\lfloor t \rfloor_\tau + \kappa)\}$, as follows:

$$\overline{p'} = [\overline{p} + \beta(\sum_e \overline{the_e} - \alpha)]_H \qquad (3)$$

where $\alpha = \max_t \sum_e the_e(t)$, $[\overline{p}]_H$ represents the projection of $\overline{p}$ onto the hyperplane $H = \{p(t) | \sum_t p(t) = 1, p(t) \geq 0\}$, and β is the step length. The value of β is set to ensure that $\forall t, |p'(t) - p(t)| < p(t)/10$ in our implementation.

The market proxy then broadcasts the prices to all UEs in the cell.

4.3.2 UE Proxy Operations

The UE proxy collects the information about traffic demand per slot (τ) for κ slots into the future from all mobile applications and periodically receives the future price information from the market proxy. It generates the future traffic demand, $\overline{the_e}$, and sends it to the market proxy.

Each mobile application reports its delay constraints for the next κ time slots to its UE proxy. Let's use $\langle D, t \rangle$, i.e., a tuple of the amount of data D and its deadline t, to express the delay constraint that data D should be downloaded before deadline t. Therefore, for a specific flow i, its delay constraints can be expressed as a set of tuples, i.e., $\{\langle D_{i,0}, t_{i,0} \rangle, \langle D_{i,1}, t_{i,1} \rangle, \dots, \langle D_{i,n}, t_{i,n} \rangle\}$, where $t_{i,0} < t_{i,1} < \dots < t_{i,n}$. Let's define function $d_i(t) = \sum_{j=0}^{T} D_{i,j}$, where $t_{i,T} \leq t \leq t_{i,T+1}$. It represents the amount of data required to be transferred before time t.

When a UE proxy receives the price information from the market proxy, it tries to minimize the cost of transferring data under the constraint that the delay constraints of all flows are satisfied. Specifically, at time t^* the UE proxy solves the following optimization function:

$$\min \quad \sum_i \sum_{t \in T} th_i(t) \times p(t)$$

$$\text{s.t.} \quad \sum_i th_i(t) \leq b_d, \forall t \in T$$

$$\sum_i \sum_{t \leq t'} th_i(t) \times \tau \geq d_i(t), \forall t' \in T \qquad (4)$$

where $th_i(t)$ is the throughput of flow i at time t, b_d is the bandwidth, and $T = \{\lfloor t^* \rfloor_\tau, \dots, \lfloor t^* \rfloor_\tau + \kappa\}$.

By solving the above optimization function we obtain the desired throughput of all downlink flows over time. $th_i(\lfloor t^* \rfloor_\tau)$ corresponds to the bandwidth allocated to flow i in the current time slot. The UE proxy will send this value back to the mobile applications to control their traffic in the data plane accordingly as described in Section 4.4. It should be noted that those constraints may not be satisfied, i.e., the available bandwidth may be smaller than the traffic demand. Under such scenario, CoAST will allow mobile applications to transfer data as fast as possible and let users decide if they want to stop some applications.

The UE proxy will send $\{the_e(t) | the_e(t) = \sum_i th_i(t), t \in T\}$ to the market proxy. The market proxy collects such traffic demands from all UEs in the cell and updates the prices in the next round.

4.4 Data Plane

The primary functionality of the CoAST data plane is to control the downlink traffic based on the throughput cap assigned by the control plane. As most of the mobile applications we are considering use TCP and we don't want to modify the server, we focus on controlling the TCP traffic from the receiver side. It is also important to note that while the control plane operates with a window of projected demands and prices, the data plane only controls the traffic for the current slot.

In TCP the amount of data that the sender can send within an RTT is limited by $\min\{cwnd, rwnd\}$ where $cwnd$ is the congestion window size, and $rwnd$ is the receiver's window size advertised in the acknowledgement packets. When cwnd is larger than rwnd, rwnd will determine the throughput of a TCP flow. To control the downlink traffic from the receiver side, we set an upper-bound on rwnd as:

$$\text{DL\_CAP} = \max\{\text{throughput} \times \text{RTT}, \text{MSS}\} \qquad (5)$$

where $throughput$ is the target throughput assigned by the control plane. When throughput is very small, DL_CAP is set to MSS to avoid totally blocking the flow. In our implementation, we add a new socket option, DL_CAP, to allow applications to dynamically specify the upper-bound on the advertised receiver's window size at runtime.

It's noteworthy that the receiver will obtain the required downlink throughput after one RTT since the sender receives the new advertised rwnd after RTT/2 and then spends RTT/2 to deliver the new packets to the receiver. When RTT is large (e.g., 1 second), the receiver should use the estimated future throughput to set DL_CAP.

4.5 CoAST Performance Guarantee

The primary goal of CoAST is to schedule the last-mile traffic to ensure that the total traffic demand does not exceed the network capacity. For scalability, CoAST is designed as a distributed system that only schedules the traffic under its control. A natural question is whether the CoAST design meets its goal. Here we present a theoretical analysis to answer this question.

CoAST uses an iterative control protocol between a market proxy and a set of UE proxies to schedule the traffic. This control protocol allows CoAST to minimize the maximal throughput of flows under its control over time. Formally, we have the following theorem:

THEOREM 1. *With the interaction interval, δ, approaching 0, CoAST approaches the optimization goal defined in Formula 2.*

Its proof can be found in Proof 1 of the Appendix. As CoAST minimizes the maximal throughput of flows under its control, it also reduces the maximal throughput of all flows including those background traffic. Formally, we have the following theorem:

THEOREM 2. *Assume $\sum_{i=1}^{n} th_i(t)$ and $th_b(t)$ are independent random variables. With $t \to +\infty$, the expected value of the peak throughput obtained by using CoAST approaches $\max_t \sum_{i=1}^{n} th_i(t) + \max_t th_b(t)$.*

The proof can be found in Proof 2 of the Appendix. Thus, when the number of UEs that uses CoAST is large enough, CoAST can significantly reduce the overall peak traffic.

5. DEPLOYMENT AND IMPLEMENTATION

In this section, we discuss various ways in which CoAST can be deployed on a real network and describe our prototype implementation.

5.1 Deployment

CoAST proposes two new functions to be added to the cellular network: a UE proxy for each mobile device and a market proxy for each cell sector. The UE proxy interacts with mobile applications running on the UE to collect their delay constraints and allocates bandwidth to them. The market proxy aggregates demand information from all the UEs in a cell and sets the prices. UE and market proxies communicate with each other to exchange demand and pricing information. The network elements on which these functions are deployed determines both the information available to CoAST and the changes needed to the network. We consider three deployment options and their merits.

Clean Slate: The market proxy for a cell and the UE proxies for all UEs in the cell are hosted in the cell's eNodeB. Mobile applications directly communicate their requirements to their UE proxy through extensions to the 3GPP RAN control plane (via mobile OS APIs to expose these extensions). The UE proxy directly controls bandwidth allocations through the eNodeB scheduler. Because the market proxy also resides on the eNodeB, it has full access to cell utilization information when setting prices and no latency between the UE and market proxy. The market proxy can also compare reported traffic and real traffic to detect price manipulation. While this represents the cleanest and most functional design, it requires changes to the 3GPP protocol to exchange demand and price information, to eNodeBs, and to the mobile OS, and thus may be difficult to deploy.

Incremental: The UE proxy is deployed on the mobile device as a daemon process, while the market proxy is deployed by the network provider as a new network element in the packet core. The UE proxy interacts with mobile applications through user library calls for collecting delay constraints and allocating bandwidth (via a controlled socket abstraction). Interaction between the UE and market proxy for exchanging demand and price information occurs using the normal cellular network data plane, through a well known UDP port and a special destination IP address that points to

the market proxy for the current cell. This configuration imposes higher latency between the UE and market proxies, but because the market proxy is deployed by the network provider, it can be made as low as possible. Also, the market proxy may be given access to real-time traffic information through a private interface to the eNodeB as well as the provider's charging and data metering systems [21]. Thus, it provides most of the benefits of the clean slate design while being easier to deploy - 3GPP protocols or eNodeBs do not have to be extensively modified on the provider side, while the UE proxy can be implemented as a user space library without modifying the mobile OS on the UE side.

Over-the-top: The UE proxy is deployed as a library on the UE just as in the incremental design, but the market proxy is deployed as a third-party service on an external cloud server, possibly even on an application-by-application basis. E.g., a large video streaming provider may have its own market proxy that serves to smooth only its own traffic within a cell and improve the performance for its own users. In this design, when a mobile device connects a cell, its UE proxy uses the cell ID to find the IP address of the corresponding market proxy through standard DNS mechanisms. UE and market proxies exchange information through UDP as in the incremental design, but the third party nature of the market proxy precludes the market proxy from basing its pricing decisions based on real-time traffic information (e.g., it cannot lower prices during periods of low utilization to incentivize more aggressive transfers) or from actually providing real monetary incentives to users. However, the design requires no modification to any cellular network elements, or to the mobile OS, and thus is the easiest to deploy.

Due to its ease of deployment, we chose the over-the-top design for our prototype. However, the goal of this paper is to evaluate the feasibility of CoAST and quantify its benefits and costs instead of advocating a particular deployment choice. Our evaluation will hold irrespective of the design chosen.

5.2 Prototype Implementation

We implemented market proxy on a Linux system with a dual-core 2.53 GHz CPU and 4GB of RAM. The market proxy divides time into 1-second slots and dynamically sets the prices for future 30 time slots. Every 100ms the market proxy collects the traffic demands for the future 30 time slots from all mobile devices that connect to it. Then it updates the prices based on the aggregated traffic demand and sends the new prices to all the mobile devices.

Ideally the market proxy should reside on a cell-level network element like the eNodeB in a 4G LTE network or the RNC in a 3G network where it can also monitor the traffic over the cell. However, because we have no access to such network elements, we have to run the market proxy on a remote server whose RTT to the mobile devices through a 4G LTE network is 57ms on average. Since the RTT between the market proxy and UE proxies is much smaller than their interaction interval (i.e., 100ms), the functionality of the control plane will not be affected.

We implemented the UE proxy on Android 4.1. It is implemented as an Android application collecting delay information from mobile applications and the prices from the market proxy and assigning throughput caps to the mobile traffic. To dynamically control the downlink traffic from the receiver side, we also patched the Android kernel to add a new socket option, DL_CAP, to limit the maximal throughput of the TCP flows at runtime.

5.2.1 Communication and Computation Overhead

The traffic demands and prices are the only data exchanged between the UE proxy and the market proxy. In the current implementation, we use 2 bytes for the traffic demand and 1 byte for the price in each time slot. Therefore, each UE proxy uploads 60 bytes and downloads 30 bytes from the market proxy in every round. Since they exchange information every 100ms, the control overhead in this case is 600 Bytes/s in the upload direction traffic and 300 Bytes/s in the download direction in the worst case. The overhead is much lower in reality because of two reasons. First, the UE proxy will exchange information with the market proxy only if some communication-intensive applications (e.g., video streaming) are running. Second, compared with the high traffic volume of those target applications, the extra communication overhead of CoAST is negligible. As the experiment in Section 6.2 will show, CoAST only leads to 0.07% extra traffic.

The computation overhead is also very low. The market proxy updates the prices by solving a projection problem. Its computational complexity is $O(\kappa)$ where κ is the number of time slots (30 in our implementation). The UE proxy needs to solve an optimization problem that minimizes the cost under the delay constraints. As we discretize time into time slots, the maximal number of delay constraints for a flow is $O(\kappa)$. The optimization problem can be solved by gradually finding the minimal cost for each constraint. Therefore, its computational complexity is $O(f \times \kappa^2 \times log(\kappa))$, where f is the number of concurrent flows. On an old Motorola ATRIX smartphone with Android 2.3, it takes less than 1ms for the UE proxy to solve the problem for 100 concurrent flows.

6. SYSTEM EVALUATION

In this section, we evaluate the CoAST prototype as described in Section 5.2. We will demonstrate how CoAST improves the performance of mobile applications under various LTE network congestion states.

6.1 Experimental Setup

Our testbed is composed of 5 Linux workstations and 4 Android smartphones with 4G LTE capability. The first workstation acts as the market proxy. Its average RTT to these smartphones through the LTE network is 57ms. The other 4 workstations act as the remote mobile application servers, each of which serves one smartphone. The Linux traffic control tool tc is used on application servers to control their available bandwidth. We make sure that all these smartphones connect to the same cell during the experiments by checking the cell id of their connected cell. All experiments are conducted in a residential area around midnight to reduce the impact of other cellular users.

CoAST is designed to improve the performance of mobile applications when the LTE network is congested. We use following mobile streaming strategies to create different levels of network congestion and streaming behavior. The evaluation for other types of mobile applications (e.g. web browsing) will be presented in Section 7. We find that the streaming strategies impact the distribution of mobile traffic and how they interact with each other in CoAST.

- **All-at-once:** strategy aggressively transfers data from the server to the client as fast as possible. This strategy is usually used by some audio streaming [22] and video streaming applications on some specific phones [28].

- **Pacing:** strategy controls the download throughput at the "steady state" after initial buffering. This strategy is widely used in video streaming services such as Youtube, Hulu, and Netflix [10].

- **Bundling:** strategy is proposed to reduce the energy consumption of video streaming applications [28]. It divides

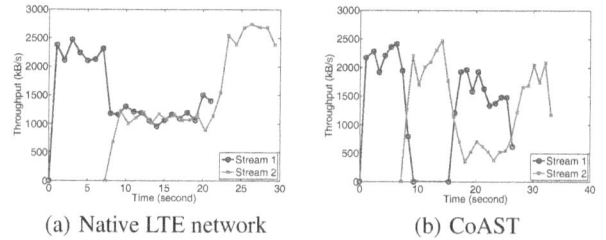

(a) Native LTE network   (b) CoAST

Figure 7: The interaction between two video streams

the entire stream into several large chunks and aggressively transfers each chunk periodically.

We use two metrics to evaluate the impact of CoAST on mobile users:

- **Buffering time:** It is a direct measure of the user experience for streaming applications. We consider both initial buffering period and rebuffering period in the steady state.

- **Energy consumption:** The energy consumption of video streaming is primarily caused by the device screen in the "on" state and the LTE network interface. For fair comparison, we use the LTE energy model that calculates energy consumption based on traffic traces [15].

6.2 The Reduction of Buffering Time in Video Streaming

We first demonstrate the basic mechanism through which CoAST enables collaborative traffic scheduling via a simple two-device video streaming experiment. Let the two devices start streaming two HD videos at time 0s and 7s, respectively. Both of them use the all-at-once strategy. The LTE cell is the only bottleneck of both streams.

Figure 7 plots the throughputs of two streams for the native LTE network and CoAST cases. In the native LTE case, stream1 is unaware of the traffic demand of stream2 and, thus, continues downloading data from its server even after stream2 starts. Therefore, the initial buffering period for stream2 is twice as long as that of stream1. In CoAST, when stream2 starts at 7sec with an empty buffer, it tries to download aggressively, thus causing the market proxy to increase prices due to the increased demand. Because stream1 has a relatively full buffer, it is less willing to pay the increased price than stream2, and thus delays its traffic. After some time, when stream2 has buffered enough data for playback, it reduces its willingness to pay higher prices, and thus begins delaying its data more. In the meantime, stream1 has already played back a portion of data in its buffer and becomes more aggressive to meet its delay constraints. Due to this cooperative inter-play between the UEs — the UE with full buffer deferring its download in favor of the UE with empty buffer— the buffering time of stream2 is reduced by 50% while that of stream1 is not affected.

By exchanging traffic demands and prices between the UE proxies and the market proxy, CoAST incurs a total of 47.5 kB extra traffic in the experiment. Compared with the total download traffic (i.e., 64 MB), CoAST only incurs a 0.07% communication overhead.

6.3 The Impact of Network Congestion

Next we evaluate the impact of traffic demand on CoAST performance by varying the stream bitrate from 400 kb/s (i.e., average Youtube bitrate [11]) to 3200 kb/s while keeping the number of

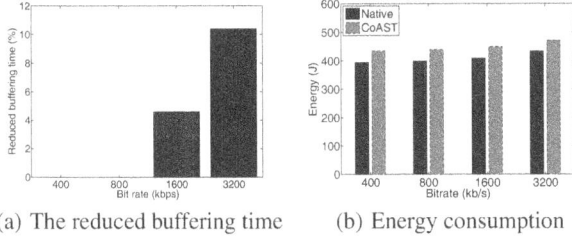

(a) The reduced buffering time   (b) Energy consumption

Figure 8: The impact of taffic demand on CoAST performance

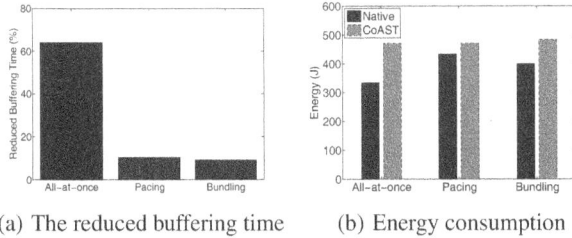

(a) The reduced buffering time   (b) Energy consumption

Figure 9: The impact of streaming strategies on CoAST performance

streams unchanged. We randomly start 4 streams within 30 seconds. The length of each stream is 3.33 minutes, i.e., the median Youtube video length [11]. The upload bandwidth of servers are unlimited, i.e., the LTE cell is the only bottleneck. Each experiment is repeated 3 times with different random seeds. The average values are reported.

Figure 8 plots the reduced buffering time and average energy consumption of the smartphones. It is clear that the benefits of CoAST start increasing with the increase in traffic demand (i.e. bitrate in the experiments). When the bitrate is 3200 kb/s, CoAST is able to reduce buffering time by more than 10% on average. It is exactly the design goal of CoAST, i.e., to reduce the impact of increased mobile traffic on user experience.

Figure 8(b) also shows that CoAST increases the energy consumption by less than 8% in all the experiments. More importantly, with the increase in traffic demand, the extra energy consumption is even smaller (e.g. 7% for 3200 kb/s case). The increase in energy consumption is caused by longer streaming time in CoAST. Note that energy consumption is based on the assumption that there is no background traffic. Otherwise, CoAST will incur even smaller energy consumption overhead.

6.4   The Impact of Streaming Strategies

Finally we evaluate the impact of streaming strategy on the performance of CoAST. The stream bitrate is 3200 kb/s. Other parameters are the same as previous experiments. The experiment results are shown in Figure 9. When the all-at-once strategy is used, CoAST reduces buffering time by 66%. However, it also increases the energy consumption significantly if the entire video is downloaded. Compared to the pacing strategy, CoAST incurs similar buffering time and slightly more energy consumption in the bundling strategy.

7.   TRACE-DRIVEN EVALUATION

In this section, we demonstrate the potential benefits of CoAST by using trace-driven evaluations of real-world cellular traffic traces from a large US mobile network operator.

7.1   Experimental Setup

We implement CoAST on a packet-level simulator, ns-3 [3], which supports the simulation of LTE networks. The network is composed of an eNodeB, a remote server and multiple mobile devices. The market proxy is installed on the eNodeB, while the application servers are installed on the remote server. All mobile devices connect to the same eNodeB during the experiments. We use the default parameters for all the experiments.

Traffic traces: We identify the top 100 heavily-loaded cell sectors in our cellular traffic dataset and evaluate how CoAST reduces their peak throughputs within 1 day. For each cell, we generate the flows for Youtube video streaming and web browsing as follows.

- **YouTube video streaming:** We identify all flows from Youtube servers to the mobile devices in the cellular traffic dataset. But only flows whose size and duration are large enough (i.e., size > 100 kB and duration > 10 s) are treated as streaming flows. Since we don't have video information (e.g., bitrate, video length) in our dataset, we use the empirical models from [11] to generate the video profile for each flow. The pacing strategy is used to control the stream.

- **Web browsing:** We first identify all web traffic using port number 80. If two flows between the same source and destination start within 5 seconds, they are considered as belonging to the same browsing event. Using this method, we obtain a set of browsing events with their start time instants. Since the dataset doesn't contain the identity of the web page, we randomly pick one of the top 500 Alexa websites for each browsing event.

Metrics: We compare CoAST against the native network using the following metrics:

- **Peak reduction:** This is the most important metric because the goal of CoAST is to reduce the peak cell throughput. It is defined as $\frac{Peak_{native} - Peak_{CoAST}}{Peak_{native}}$.

- **Discount:** A key promise of CoAST is that mobile users will also benefit from CoAST and, thus, be willing to use it. We use $\frac{D_t - D_a}{D_t}$ to denote the user benefit, where D_t is the amount of transferred data, D_a is the amount of accounted data.

- **Overhead:** We also analyze if CoAST causes any overhead, including energy consumption and RRC signaling overhead [14].

We acknowledge that our trace-based evaluation has some limitations. First, there is no system feedback. By scheduling the traffic better, CoAST may cause mobile users to use more data and, thus, increase the peak traffic. However, our experiments cannot capture this phenomenon. Second, the user behavior in using applications is not available. For video streaming, the user may skip ahead or pause the video. For web browsing, the user may quickly scroll down in the webpage. These user behaviors impact the delay constraints of the corresponding traffic and, thus, affect the performance of CoAST.

7.2   Experimental Results

7.2.1   Video Streaming Experiments

We first perform simulation-based video streaming experiments using 100 heavy-loaded cells for 1 day. In all experiments we only consider Youtube video streams. As shown in Figure 10, CoAST

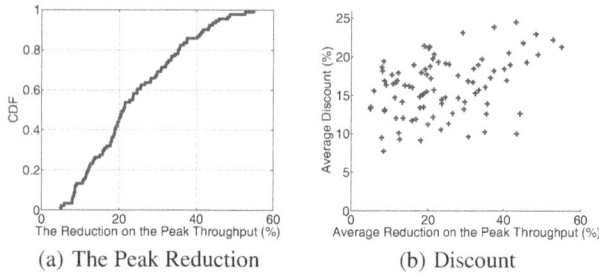

(a) The Peak Reduction   (b) Discount

Figure 10: The performance of video streaming supported by CoAST on various sectors.

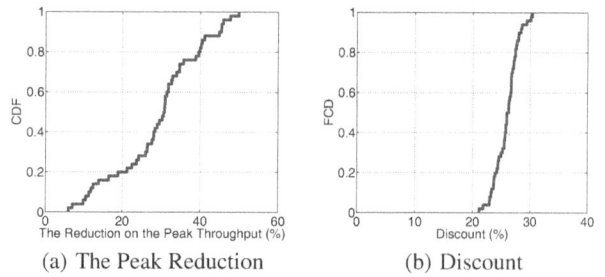

(a) The Peak Reduction   (b) Discount

Figure 12: The performance of web browsing supported by CoAST on various sectors.

successfully reduces the peak throughput for all cells. We also observe the following phenomena. First, the peak reduction ranges from 5% to 55% for different cells, as shown in Figure 10(a). More than 30% cells reduce their peak by 30%. The high variation of the peak reduction among different cells is probably caused by diverse distribution of Youtube video streams among various cells. Cells with more video streams are able to achieve better performance. Second, the average discount obtained by the mobile users correlates with the peak reduction on the cells, as shown in Figure 10(b). Finally, none of the videos is paused during the experiments.

Next we explore how the reduced peaks actually help increase the capacity of cellular networks by examining the impact of increasing user demand on application level performance with and without CoAST. Specifically, we increase the users/spectrum ratio and measure how long the video streams pause waiting for more data. However, rather than increasing the number of users in a cell artificially, we increase the ratio by reducing the effective bandwidth (spectrum) available to a cell by a fraction $\alpha \in [0, 1)$, i.e., Capacity = $(1 - \alpha) \times$ MaxCapacity. The average values of video pause time over 100 cells are reported for different values of α in Figure 11. We see that CoAST results in very little application performance degradation while supporting a capacity increase of up to 20% ($\alpha = 0.2$). Also, for the same value of application performance degradation, CoAST can support more users per unit of available spectrum.

the top 500 Alexa websites in the "news" category. We report the results for the 100 heavy-load cells in Figure 12.

As expected, CoAST-based web browser reduces the peak throughput for all cells. Like in video streaming experiments, the peak reduction varies significantly among cells, ranging from 6% to 50%. However, different from video streaming, CoAST-based web browser helps more than 55% cells achieve more than 30% peak reduction. In addition, as shown in Figure 12(b), the average discount obtained by the mobile users ranges from 22% to 31%, which is more than video streaming case. This is because web browsing flows are usually very small and are able to take advantage of the variation in price.

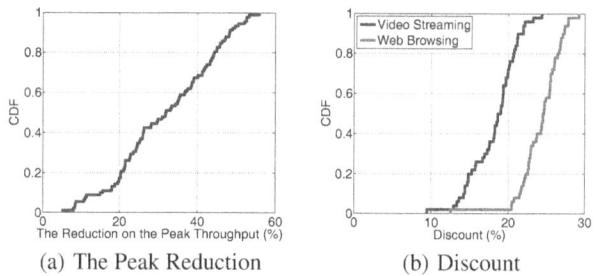

(a) The Peak Reduction   (b) Discount

Figure 13: The performance of both video streaming and web browsing supported by CoAST.

Next, we evaluate the scenario in which both video streaming and web browsing use CoAST to schedule their traffic. Video streaming and web browsing are the most important mobile applications, accounting for more than 70% mobile traffic. The experimental results are plotted in Figure 13. In this more realistic scenario, CoAST helps all cells to reduce their peak throughputs. We also plot the discount obtained by video streaming and web browsing in Figure 13(b). Web browsing is still able to obtain higher discount than video streaming.

In Section 6, we noticed that CoAST slightly increases the energy consumption in some scenarios. This is because by delaying mobile traffic, mobile devices need to keep the network interface active for longer duration, resulting in extra energy consumption. To analyze the overhead of CoAST, we assume that the mobile device is initially in the RRC_IDLE state, and there is no other traffic on the mobile device. We use the RRC state model [15] to analyze the overhead. For both video streaming and web browsing, the mobile devices always stay at the RRC_CONNECTED state when using these applications. Thus, CoAST does not introduce extra RRC state transitions. However, CoAST does keep cellular interface alive for slightly longer duration and, thus, consumes a little more energy. Figure 14 shows that in CoAST, the mobile de-

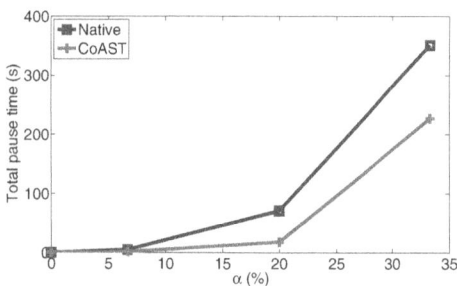

Figure 11: Comparison of video pause time for different number of users with and without CoAST.

7.2.2 Experiments on Web Browsing

Web browsing is another important application that can benefit from CoAST because of its delay tolerance. Unlike video streaming, web browsing flows are relatively small. In this subsection, we analyze the performance of CoAST-based web browser.

First, we consider the simple scenario that all cellular traffic are web traffic. For each browsing event, we randomly choose one of

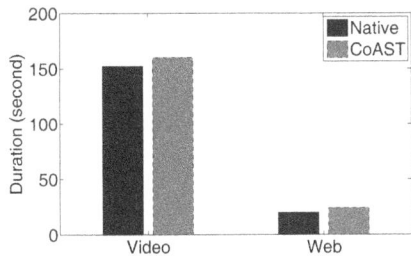

Figure 14: The time duration at RRC_CONNECTED state for video streaming and web browsing.

vices stay slightly longer in the RRC_CONNECTED state than the native case.

7.2.3 The Impact of Partial Deployment

CoAST reduces the peak throughput by rescheduling the traffic of mobile devices under its control. The number of participating mobile devices will impact the CoAST performance. In this subsection, we evaluate the performance of CoAST when only a portion of mobile devices support it.

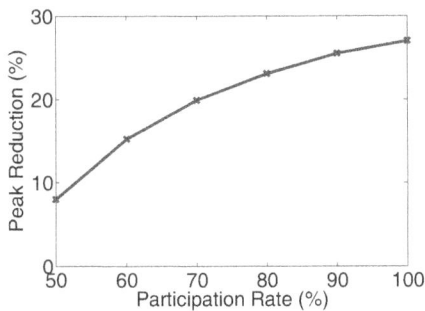

Figure 15: The impact of partial deployment on CoAST performance.

In this set of experiments, we randomly select $r\%$ mobile devices to support CoAST, where r varies from 50 to 100. The video streaming application is used in the evaluation. Each experiment is repeated 10 times with different random seeds. We report the average value of all the 100 cells.

The experimental results are shown in Figure 15. It's clear that the participation rate has significant impact on the CoAST performance. When r reduces from 100 to 50, the average peak reduction decrease from 27% to 8%. We also observe that the slope of the curve decreases with the increase of the r value. This is because the peak value of the background traffic will be higher when the participation rate is low. Thus, according to Theorem 2, the peak reduction achieved by CoAST will be much lower. This set of experiments indicate the importance of increasing the participation rate in CoAST.

To analyze whether partial deployment will impact the user experience of early adopters or non-adopters, we compare the buffering time of streaming applications in the above experiments and that in LTE networks. The buffering time of each stream in both scenarios are the same in all experiments. This is because CoAST tries to satisfy the delay constraints of all adopters. When the network is not very congested, their delay constraints can be easily satisfied. In contrast, when the network is persistently congested which is uncommon in our dataset, adopters behave the same as non-adopters,

i.e., downloading as fast as possible without rescheduling their traffic.

Therefore, the partial deployment will primarily impact the peak reduction with little impact on the user experience of mobile applications.

7.2.4 The Impact of Design Choices

In this subsection, we evaluate the impact of CoAST parameters and network factors on the performance of CoAST.

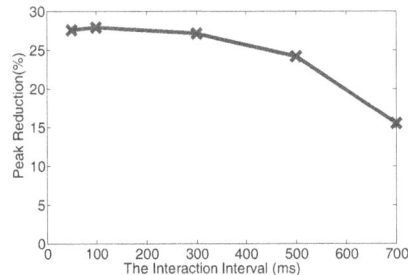

Figure 16: The impact of interaction frequency between UEs and the market proxy.

In the first set of experiments, we analyze the impact of the interaction frequency between the UE and Market proxies. We change the interaction interval (i.e., δ) from 50 ms to 700 ms, while other parameters are kept unchanged. The video streaming application is used in the evaluation. We report the average value of all the cells.

The experimental results are shown in Figure 16. When the interaction interval is less than 100 ms, CoAST achieves similar performance in terms of peak reduction. As the interval increases from 100 ms to 500 ms, the average peak reduction slightly drops from 27% to 24%. When it further increases to 700 ms, the obtained peak reduction is quickly reduced to 15%. This is because the control plane of CoAST utilizes an iterative protocol that gradually optimizes its performance in each iteration. When interaction interval is too large, it is hard for the system to converge to the optimal solution. On the other hand, increase in interaction frequency results in more communication overhead. From our experiments, we find that 100 ms is a good choice as it achieves good tradeoff between performance and overhead.

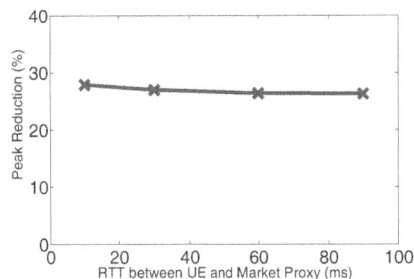

Figure 17: The impact of the delay between UEs and the market proxy. The interaction interval is 100 ms.

In the second set of experiments, we analyze the impact of the distance between the UE and market proxies. We vary the RTT between them from 10 ms to 90 ms. The results are reported in Figure 17. We observe that the RTT between UE proxy and market proxy has very small impact on peak reduction. This indicates that CoAST can still achieve good performance even if it is not possible to deploy the market proxy in cellular network elements close to the end user devices, like eNodeB in LTE or NodeB in 3G networks.

8. DISCUSSION

In this section, we discuss how the mechanisms proposed by CoAST interact with other existing and proposed mechanisms in the RAN.

3GPP quality of service: The LTE specification provides a QoS model based on Quality Class Indicators (QCI) [5]. A UE may create bearers with one of up to 9 QCI classes, each with a different priority (diffserv), packet delay budget, loss rate, and bitrate guarantee. Many cellular providers today reserve QCI only for managed services (e.g., IMS), and do not expose QCI classes to third party applications. Because CoAST is an over-the-top protocol that can operate without any support from 3GPP infrastructure, it is applicable even on networks which do not expose QCI. Furthermore, QCI provides a static and inflexible partitioning of applications into a small number of priorities. It is not sufficient for scenarios presented by both our examples — streaming and web browsing — in which the *same* application requires different QoS and delay tolerance at different times, depending on the context. Furthermore, any non-collaborative mechanism cannot coordinate behavior across multiple UEs the way that CoAST does.

Congestion aware pricing/control: Access to real-time congestion information at the eNodeBs is not exposed through 3GPP standardized interfaces. Therefore, to remain independent of vendors-specific implementations, CoAST does not assume any access to the eNodeB, including information about whether there is cell congestion or not. Instead, it tries to continuously minimize the peaks across the applications whose traffic is managed through its APIs, independently of other background traffic. If real-time congestion information could be made available, it could easily be used to trigger when CoAST optimization mechanisms kick-in and provide improved fidelity and price control to the market proxy's demand estimation step. We leave this extension to future work.

RNC/eNodeB schedulers: The UMTS RNC or LTE eNodeB have a scheduler that allocates scrambling codes (variable sized slices of the spectrum) to UEs every 2ms based on their demands, QCI, channel noise, and overall cell congestion. Beyond differentiation using QCI, this scheduler is *application context agnostic*. CoAST does not interfere with this scheduler because it operates at a much coarser granularity (hundreds of msec). CoAST adds an additional application aware layer of control on the top, and helps the RAN scheduler by reducing demand peaks themselves, thus reducing the need for the RAN scheduler to allocate less than what UEs demand. However, the RAN scheduler can have an impact on applications that use CoAST because it may restrict the bandwidth available to a UE (because of noise or congestion), and thus decrease the amount of time an application's data can be delayed. To solve this problem, CoAST should take the radio link condition into consideration. We leave it for future work since it requires deeper integration with the eNodeB scheduler.

Energy vs. congestion tradeoffs: Several proposals have been made in the literature to help mobile devices save energy by batching mobile traffic into short concentrated bursts and reducing the time UE radios spend in the active state, e.g., [24, 15]. It would seem that CoAST proposes the opposite philosophy—spread out traffic to minimize congestion. However, in reality, these two mechanisms are relatively complementary. CoAST can just as easily work with applications where data transfers occur in bursts—e.g., web browsing. All CoAST advocates is that when there is contention, priority be given to the traffic on which users are waiting as opposed to applications that are just filling up their buffers. While

this can increase the amount of time needed to transfer an application's background data, as Figure 14 shows, the increase is not substantial. An interesting future use of CoAST is for applications to increase their price based on how much available battery they have, thus prioritizing their transfers over everyone else.

Potential for price manipulation: Because CoAST's mechanisms do not force users to transfer any data after they have indicated their demand forecast, it is possible that malicious users may increase the price others have to pay by falsely forecasting high demands. While it is not easy to detect one-off instances of such behavior (a user's demand may legitimately have changed), it is easy to detect systematic abuse over a period of time by statistically comparing forecasts to actual data transfers using cellular providers existing data tracking mechanisms. Abusers may then have their bids ignored in the future, thus effectively removing them from the set of CoAST managed devices. With incremental deployment, it is possible that some legitimate applications don't support CoAST, resulting in the discrepancy between reported traffic and the real traffic. To solve this problem, the UE proxy needs to report the flow information of those adopters, while the CoAST will only monitor those flows.

Impact of handover: Finally, we briefly describe CoAST's interactions with mobility mechanisms, i.e., handover. UEs detect when a handover takes place by querying their baseband chip for the current cell id. They inform the market proxy for every handover, which then simply assigns the UE's projected demand to the new cell and recomputes the demand for both the old and new cells. Because we expect each market proxy to cover a relatively large area (we expect one market proxy per P-GW), the number of inter-proxy handoffs are few and are handled by the UE simply reconnecting to the new market proxy.

9. RELATED WORK

The idea of time shifting traffic to reduce the peak throughput over a link is not brand new. Many ISPs use traffic sharping against bulk flows to reduce the peak of inter-domain traffic [19]. Laoutaris et al. [17, 16] proposed intentionally using diurnal variations in Internet traffic to transfer delay tolerant bulk data over the Internet at off-peak times. With peak pricing, these shifts can also reduce cost. Recently, Ha et al. [12] applied the idea of medium-to-long time scale shifting to cellular networks and proposed a time-dependent pricing mechanism, TUBE, to motivate mobile users to shift some cellular traffic sessions from peak time to off-peak times in exchange for lower prices. CoAST is fundamentally different from TUBE in many aspects. First, TUBE utilizes medium-to-long time-scale variation of the background traffic and thus are only suitable for applications that can tolerate substantial delays. Second, CoAST requires no involvement of mobile users, while TUBE requires user change their behavior. Third, CoAST also has a data plane to schedule traffic, while TUBE only focuses on the control plane. In addition, our approach is compatible with medium and long time scale traffic shifting: our work can reduce the short time scale peaks that will remain after other data is time shifted by hours or 10s of minutes.

In addition to reducing traffic peaks, time shifting mobile traffic can be beneficial in saving device energy. For example, one set of approaches [8, 27] utilize the observation that aggregation of traffic can reduce energy by avoiding the excessive energy-consuming RRC transitions and tail energy that occur in 3G and LTE networks [24, 15] when traffic is transfered in disjoint time periods. Studies show that mobile applications have sufficient periods of sparse traffic transfer to make these approaches useful for energy saving with relatively little traffic delay [23]. Another approach saves device energy by scheduling transfers when signal strength is strong [26], leveraging the observation that energy consumption per bit increases when signal strength degrades.

Our approach is not directly compatible with approaches that use scheduling to reduce energy because both approaches operate on a similar time scale but with different objective functions. To use an energy saving scheduler with a peak reduction scheduler would require an integrated objective function that minimizes a combination of device energy and cost to use the shared link, while meeting deadlines. An adaptive approach may be most appropriate, where reducing cost is favored when device energy is plentiful, and reducing energy is favored when device energy is low. In its most simplistic form, a controller could simply switch from one scheduler to the other based on a device energy threshold. More complex approaches are obviously possible and are left to future work.

10. CONCLUSIONS AND FUTURE WORK

In this paper, we present a new approach to improving the capacity of cellular network cells through application-aware collaborative microscheduling and delaying of traffic. Our implementation, CoAST, supports applications such as streaming and web-browsing that are not normally considered to be delay tolerant, but yet account for over 70% of cellular network traffic today. Our extensive evaluation demonstrates shows the approach's potential by showing that it can reduce traffic peaks by up to 50%, and increase the capacity of cells to serve such workloads by up to 20% without any degradation to user experience. There are a number of future issues to consider. These include implementing a fully functioned web browser that supports CoAST and field test of the system with mobile users, and incorporating additional factors such as energy use and congestion awareness into CoAST's scheduling algorithms.

Acknowledgments

We would like to thank our shepherd, Chunyi Peng, and the anonymous reviewers for their insightful feedback. Cong Shi, Mostafa Ammar, and Ellen Zegura are supported in part by the US National Science Foundation through grant CNS 1161879.

11. REFERENCES

[1] Cisco systems. cisco visual networking index: Forecast and methodology, 2011-2016, may 30 2012. http://tinyurl.com/VNI2012.

[2] Huffington post. http://www.huffingtonpost.com.

[3] ns-3. http://www.nsnam.org/.

[4] PhantomJS: Headless WebKit with JavaScript API. http://phantomjs.org/.

[5] 3GPP TS 25.214: 3rd Generation Partnership Project; Technical Specification Group Radio Access Network; Physical layer procedures (FDD) (Release 8), 2010.

[6] Alexa. Top 500 website. http://www.alexa.com/.

[7] AT&T. 2011 annual report, 2011. http://bit.ly/Lf0goQ.

[8] N. Balasubramanian, A. Balasubramanian, and A. Venkataramani. Energy consumption in mobile phones: a measurement study and implications for network applications. In *ACM IMC*, pages 280–293, 2009.

[9] H. Falaki, D. Lymberopoulos, R. Mahajan, S. Kandula, and D. Estrin. A first look at traffic on smartphones. In *Proceedings of the 10th annual conference on Internet measurement*, pages 281–287. ACM, 2010.

[10] M. Ghobadi, Y. Cheng, A. Jain, and M. Mathis. Trickle: rate limiting youtube video streaming. In *USENIX ATC*, pages 17–17, 2012.

[11] P. Gill, M. Arlitt, Z. Li, and A. Mahanti. Youtube traffic characterization: a view from the edge. In *ACM IMC*, 2007.

[12] S. Ha, S. Sen, C. Joe-Wong, Y. Im, and M. Chiang. Tube: time-dependent pricing for mobile data. In *ACM SIGCOMM*, pages 247–258, 2012.

[13] S. Hao, D. Li, W. G. Halfond, and R. Govindan. Sif: A selective instrumentation framework for mobile applications. In *ACM MobiSys*, 2013.

[14] H. Holma and A. Toskala. *Hsdpa/Hsupa For Umts*. Wiley Online Library, 2006.

[15] J. Huang, F. Qian, A. Gerber, Z. M. Mao, S. Sen, and O. Spatscheck. A close examination of performance and power characteristics of 4g lte networks. In *ACM MobiSys*, pages 225–238, 2012.

[16] N. Laoutaris, M. Sirivianos, X. Yang, and P. Rodriguez. Inter-datacenter bulk transfers with netstitcher. *SIGCOMM Comput. Commun. Rev.*, 41(4):74–85, Aug. 2011.

[17] N. Laoutaris, G. Smaragdakis, P. Rodriguez, and R. Sundaram. Delay tolerant bulk data transfers on the internet. In *ACM SIGMETRICS*, pages 229–238, 2009.

[18] G. Maier, F. Schneider, and A. Feldmann. A first look at mobile hand-held device traffic. In *Passive and Active Measurement*, pages 161–170. Springer, 2010.

[19] M. Marcon, M. Dischinger, K. P. Gummadi, and A. Vahdat. The local and global effects of traffic shaping in the internet. In *IEEE COMSNETS*, pages 1–10, 2011.

[20] D. P. Palomar and M. Chiang. A tutorial on decomposition methods for network utility maximization. *IEEE Journal on Selected Areas in Communications*, 24(8):1439–1451, 2006.

[21] C. Peng, G.-h. Tu, C.-y. Li, and S. Lu. Can we pay for what we get in 3g data access? In *ACM MobiCom*, pages 113–124, 2012.

[22] F. Qian, Z. Wang, A. Gerber, Z. Mao, S. Sen, and O. Spatscheck. Profiling resource usage for mobile applications: A cross-layer approach. In *ACM MobiSys*, 2011.

[23] F. Qian, Z. Wang, A. Gerber, Z. Mao, S. Sen, and O. Spatscheck. Profiling resource usage for mobile applications: a cross-layer approach. In *ACM MobiSys*, pages 321–334, 2011.

[24] F. Qian, Z. Wang, A. Gerber, Z. M. Mao, S. Sen, and O. Spatscheck. Characterizing radio resource allocation for 3g networks. In *ACM IMC*, pages 137–150, 2010.

[25] Sandvine. Global internet phenomena report. http://www.sandvine.com/news/global_broadband_trends.asp, 2012.

[26] A. Schulman, V. Navda, R. Ramjee, N. Spring, P. Deshpande, C. Grunewald, K. Jain, and V. N. Padmanabhan. Bartendr: a practical approach to energy-aware cellular data scheduling. In *ACM MobiCom*, pages 85–96, 2010.

[27] A. Sharma, V. Navda, R. Ramjee, V. N. Padmanabhan, and E. M. Belding. Cool-tether: energy efficient on-the-fly wifi hot-spots using mobile phones. In *ACM CoNEXT*, pages 109–120, 2009.

[28] M. Siekkinen, M. A. Hoque, J. K. Nurminen, and M. Aalto. Streaming over 3g and lte: How to save smartphone energy in radio access network-friendly way. In *Proceedings of the 5th Workshop on Mobile Video*, 2013.

Appendix

PROOF 1. The goal of the market proxy is to minimize the maximal throughput on a cell sector over time, as shown in Formula 2. To decompose this problem and derive a distributed protocol, we rewrite the objective of the market proxy as follows:

$$\min \quad \alpha \tag{6}$$

$$\text{s.t.} \quad \forall t, \sum_i th_i(t) \leq \alpha \tag{7}$$

Introducing a dual variable $p(t) > 0$ (i.e., price for downlink traffic through the cell sector at time slot t) for each constraint of (7), we define the Lagrange dual function

$$L(\{p(t)\}) = \min \alpha + \sum_t p(t)(\sum_i th_i(t) - \alpha) \tag{8}$$

To make $L(\{p(t)\})$ finite, the coefficient of α should be 0:

$$\sum_t p(t) = 1 \tag{9}$$

Then, we simplify $L(\{p(t)\})$ to

$$L(\{p(t)\}) = \min \sum_t p(t) \sum_i th_i(t) \tag{10}$$

$$= \min \sum_i \sum_t p(t) th_i(t) \tag{11}$$

The original problem can be decomposed into independent problems for each mobile applications. If we aggregate the throughput by UEs, we obtain

$$L(\{p(t)\}) = \min \sum_e \sum_{i \in e} \sum_t p(t) th_i(t) \tag{12}$$

$$= \sum_e \min \sum_{i \in e} \sum_t p(t) th_i(t) \tag{13}$$

Therefore, the original problem is decomposed into independent sub-problems for each UE. The objective of each UE is to select $th_e(t)$ among all feasible values so that $\sum_{i \in e} \sum_t p(t) th_i(t)$ is minimized. The derived objective of each UE is exactly the same as (4).

The market proxy, running the master program of the decomposition method, gets feedbacks (i.e., $th_e(t)$) from UE proxies and updates $\{p(t)\}$ using a projected sub-gradient method as described in (3). Therefore, the objective of Formula (2) is equivalent to the control protocol in Section 4.3. □

PROOF 2. Let $x_t = \sum_{i=1}^n th_i(t)$ have a probability density function $f(x_t)$ and a cumulative probability distribution function of $F(x_t)$. Let $y_t = th_b(t_t)$ have a probability density function $g(y_t)$ and a cumulative probability distribution function of $G(y_t)$. Let x_{max} and y_{max} be the lowest value of x_t and y_t such that $F(x_t) = 1$ and $G(y_t) = 1$, respectively. Since the number of flows associated with a cell is limited, x_{max} and y_{max} are finite. Let p be the convolution of f and g, and P be its cumulative probability distribution function. Then the sum $z_t = x_t + y_t$ is a random variable with the density function $p(z_t)$ and the cumulative probability distribution function of $P(z_t)$. Since x_t and y_t are independent, $P(z_t \leq x_{max} + y_{max}) = 1$.

Let $z^* = \max_t z_t$ where $t \in \{1, 2, \ldots, T\}$. The probability density function of z^*, $h(z^*)$ is

$$h(z^*) = T[P(z^*)]^{T-1} p(z^*) \tag{14}$$

The expected value of z^* is

$$E(z^*) = \int_{-\infty}^{+\infty} z^* T[P(z^*)]^{T-1} p(z^*) dz^* \tag{15}$$

$$= \int_0^1 P^{-1}(z^{*\frac{1}{T}}) dz^* \tag{16}$$

Therefore, when $T \to +\infty$, we have

$$\lim_{T \to +\infty} E(z^*) = \int_0^1 P^{-1}(1) dz^* = x_{max} + y_{max} \tag{17}$$

Since CoAST minimizes x_{max} with y_{max} unchanged, it is equivalent to minimizing $\max_t \sum_i th_i(t) + y_{max}$ when $T \to +\infty$. □

Rio: A System Solution for Sharing I/O between Mobile Systems

Ardalan Amiri Sani, Kevin Boos, Min Hong Yun, and Lin Zhong

Rice University, Houston, TX

Abstract

Mobile systems are equipped with a diverse collection of I/O devices, including cameras, microphones, sensors, and modems. There exist many novel use cases for allowing an application on one mobile system to utilize I/O devices from another. This paper presents Rio, an I/O sharing solution that supports unmodified applications and exposes all the functionality of an I/O device for sharing. Rio's design is common to many classes of I/O devices, thus significantly reducing the engineering effort to support new I/O devices. Our implementation of Rio on Android consists of about 7100 total lines of code and supports four I/O classes with fewer than 500 class-specific lines of code. Rio also supports I/O sharing between mobile systems of different form factors, including smartphones and tablets. We show that Rio achieves performance close to that of local I/O for audio devices, sensors, and modem, but suffers noticeable performance degradation for camera due to network throughput limitations between the two systems, which is likely to be alleviated by emerging wireless standards.

Categories and Subject Descriptors

B.4.2 [**Input/Output and Data Communications**]: Input/Output Devices; C.0 [**Computer Systems Organization**]: General—System architectures; C.2.4 [**Computer-Communication Networks**]: Distributed Systems—Client/Server; K.8.0 [**Personal Computing**]: General

Keywords

I/O; Remote I/O; I/O Sharing; Mobile; Rio

1. INTRODUCTION

A user nowadays owns a variety of mobile systems, including smartphones, tablets, smart glasses, and smart watches, each equipped with a plethora of I/O devices, such as cameras, speakers, microphones, sensors, and cellular modems.

MobiSys'14, June 16–19, 2014, Bretton Woods, New Hampshire, USA.
Copyright 2014 ACM 978-1-4503-2793-0/14/06 ...$15.00.
http://dx.doi.org/10.1145/2594368.2594370.

There are many interesting use cases for allowing an application running on one mobile system to access I/O devices on another system, for three fundamental reasons. (*i*) Mobile systems can be in different physical locations or orientations. For example, one can control a smartphone's high-resolution camera from a tablet to more easily capture a self-portrait. (*ii*) Mobile systems can serve different users. For example, one can a play music for another user if one's smartphone can access the other system's speaker. (*iii*) Certain mobile systems have unique I/O devices due to their distinct form factors and targeted use cases. For example, a user can make a phone call from her tablet using the modem and SIM card in her smartphone.

Unsurprisingly, solutions exist for sharing various I/O devices, e.g., camera [3], speaker [4], and modem (for messaging) [11]. However, these solutions have three fundamental limitations. First, they do not support unmodified applications. For example, IP Webcam [3] and MightyText [11] do not allow existing applications to use a camera or modem remotely; they only support their own custom applications. Second, they do not expose all the functionality of an I/O device for sharing. For example, IP Webcam does not support remote configuration of all camera parameters, such as resolution. MightyText supports SMS and MMS from another device, but not phone calls. Finally, existing solutions are I/O class-specific, requiring significant engineering effort to support new I/O devices. For example, IP Webcam [3] can share the camera, but not the modem or sensors.

In this paper, we introduce Rio (*Remote I/O*), an I/O sharing solution for mobile systems that overcomes all three aforementioned limitations. Rio adopts a split-stack I/O sharing model, in which the I/O stack, i.e., all software layers from the application to the I/O device, is split between the two mobile systems at a certain boundary. All communications that cross this boundary are intercepted on the mobile system hosting the application and forwarded to the mobile system with the I/O device, where they are served by the rest of the I/O stack. Rio uses *device files* as its boundary of choice. Device files are used in Unix-like OSes, such as Android and iOS, to abstract many classes of I/O devices, providing an I/O class-agnostic boundary. The device file boundary supports I/O sharing for unmodified applications, as it is transparent to the application layer. It also exposes the full functionality of each I/O device to other mobile systems by allowing processes in one system to directly communicate with the device drivers in another. Rio is not the first system to exploit the device file boundary; our previous work [22] uses device files as the boundary for

I/O virtualization inside a single system. However, sharing I/O devices between two physically separate systems engenders a different set of challenges regarding how to properly exploit this boundary, as elaborated below.

The design and implementation of Rio must address the following fundamental challenges that stem from the I/O stack being split across two systems. (*i*) A process may issue operations on a device file that require the driver to operate on the process memory. With I/O sharing, however, the process and the driver reside in two different mobile systems with separate physical memories. In Rio, we support cross-system memory mapping using a distributed shared memory (DSM) design that supports access to shared pages by the process, the driver, and the I/O device (through DMA). We also support cross-system memory copying with collaboration from both systems. (*ii*) Mobile systems typically communicate through a wireless connection that has a high round-trip latency compared to the latency between a process and driver within the same system. To address this challenge, we reduce the number of round trips between the systems due to file operations, memory operations, or DSM coherence messages. (*iii*) The connection between mobile systems can break at any time due to mobility or reliability issues. This can cause undesirable side-effects in the OSes of all involved systems. We address this problem by properly cleaning up the residuals of a remote I/O connection upon disconnection, switching to a local I/O device of the same class, if present, or otherwise returning appropriate error messages to the applications.

We present a prototype implementation of Rio for Android systems. Our implementation supports four important I/O classes: camera, audio devices such as speaker and microphone, sensors such as accelerometer, and cellular modem (for phone calls and SMS). It consists of about 7100 Lines of Code (LoC), of which less than 500 are specific to I/O classes. It also supports I/O sharing between heterogeneous mobile systems, including tablets and smartphones. See [16] for a video demo of Rio.

We evaluate Rio on Galaxy Nexus smartphones and show that it supports existing applications, allows remote access to all I/O device functionality, requires low engineering effort to support different I/O devices, and achieves performance close to that of local I/O for audio devices, sensors, and modem, but suffers noticeable performance degradation for camera sharing due to Wi-Fi throughput limitation in our setup. With emerging wireless standards supporting much higher throughput, we posit that this degradation is likely to go away in the near future. In addition, we report the throughput and power consumption for using remote I/O devices with Rio and show that throughput highly depends on the I/O device class, and that power consumption is noticeably higher than that of local devices.

2. USE CASES

We envision two categories of use cases for Rio. The first category, already tested with Rio, consists of those that simply combine Rio with existing application (§2.1). This category is the focus of this paper. However, we envision applications developed specifically with I/O sharing in mind. Obviously, such applications do not exist today because I/O sharing is not commonly available. §2.2 presents some of such use cases.

2.1 Use Cases Demonstrated with Rio

Multi-system photography: With Rio, one can use a camera application on one mobile system to take a photo with the camera on another system. This capability can be handy in various scenarios, especially when taking self-portraits, as it decouples the camera hardware from the camera viewfinder, capture button, and settings. Several existing applications try to assist the user in taking self-portraits using voice recognition, audio guidance, or face detection [5]. However, Rio has the advantage in that the user can see the camera viewfinder up close, comfortably configure the camera settings, and press the capture button whenever ready, even if the physical camera is dozens of feet away. Alternatively, one can use the front camera, which typically has lower quality than the rear-facing one.

Multi-system gaming: Many mobile games require the user to physically maneuver the mobile system for control. Tablets provide a large screen for gaming but are bulky to physically maneuver. Moreover, maneuvers like tilting make it hard for the user to concentrate on the content of the display. With Rio, a second mobile system, e.g., a smartphone, can be used for physical maneuvers while the tablet running the game remains stationary.

One SIM card, many systems: Despite many efforts [1], users are still tied to a single SIM card for phone calls or SMS, mainly because the SIM card is associated with a unique number. With Rio, the user can make and receive phone calls and SMS from any of her mobile systems using the modem and SIM card in her smartphone. For example, if a user forgets her smartphone at home, she can still receive phone calls on her tablet at work.

Music sharing: A user might want to allow a friend to listen to some music via a music subscription application on her smartphone. With Rio, the user can simply play the music on her friend's smartphone speaker.

Multi-system video conferencing: When a user is video conferencing on her tablet, she can use the speaker or microphone on her smartphone and move them closer to her mouth for better audio quality in a noisy environment. Or she can use the camera on her smart glasses as an external camera for the tablet to provide a different viewpoint.

2.2 Future Use Cases of Rio

With Rio, new applications can be developed to use the I/O devices available on another system.

Multi-user gaming: The multi-system gaming use case explained in the previous subsection combined with modifications to the application can enable novel forms of multi-user gaming across mobile systems. For example, two players can use their smartphones to wirelessly control a racing game on a single tablet in front of them. The smartphones' displays can even show in-game context menus or game controller keys, similar to those on game consoles, providing a familiar and traditional gaming experience for users.

Music sharing: If supported by the system software (e.g., audio service process in Android (§7)), a user can play the same music on her and her friend's smartphones simultaneously. With proper application support, the user can even play two different sound tracks on these two systems at the same time, much like multi-zone stereo receivers.

Multi-view video conferencing: A video conferencing application can be extended to show side-by-side video streams from the smart glasses and the tablet simultaneously. In this

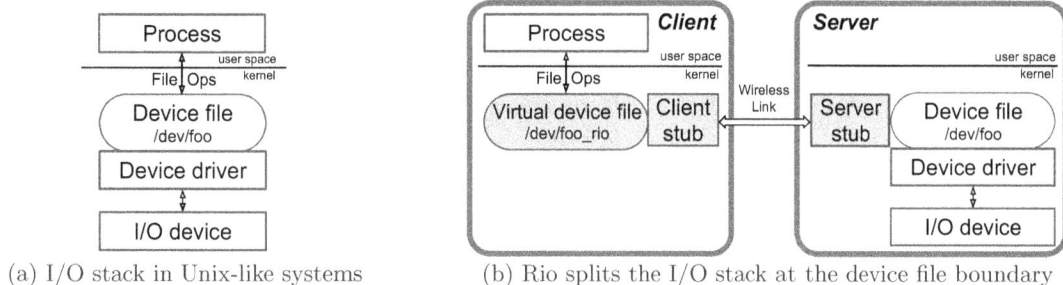

(a) I/O stack in Unix-like systems   (b) Rio splits the I/O stack at the device file boundary

Figure 1: Rio splits the I/O stack at the device file boundary. The process that remotely uses the I/O device resides in the client system and interacts with a virtual device file. The actual device file, device driver, and I/O device all reside in the server system. Rio forwards file operations between the client and server. The wireless link can either be through an AP or a device-to-device connection.

fashion, the user can not only share a video stream of her face with her friend, but she can also share a stream of the scene in front of her at the same time.

Multi-camera photography: Using the cameras on multiple mobile systems, one can realize various computational photography techniques [42]. For example, one can use the cameras of her smartphone and smart glasses simultaneously to capture photos with different exposure times in order to remove motion blur [52], or to increase the temporal/spatial resolution of video by interleaving/merging frames from both cameras [41,50]. One can even use the smartphone as an external flash for the smart glasses camera.

3. DESIGN

We describe the design of Rio, including its architecture and the guarantees it provides to mobile systems using it.

3.1 Split-Stack Architecture

Rio adopts a split-stack model for I/O sharing between mobile systems. It intercepts communications at the device file boundary in the I/O stack on one mobile system and forwards them to the other system to be executed by the rest of the I/O stack.

Unix-like OSes, such as Android and iOS, use device files to abstract many classes of I/O devices. Figure 1(a) shows the typical I/O stack in Unix-like OSes. The device driver runs in the kernel, manages the device, and exports the I/O device functions to user space processes through device files. A process in the user space then issues file operations on the device file in order to interact with the device driver. One advantage of using device files as the I/O sharing boundary is that they are common to many classes of I/O devices, reducing the engineering effort required to support various I/O classes. Moreover, such a boundary is transparent to the application layer and immediately supports existing applications. It also exposes all functionality of an I/O device to other mobile systems by allowing processes to directly communicate with the driver.

Figure 1(b) depicts how Rio splits the I/O stack. It shows two mobile systems: the *server* and the *client*. The server system has an I/O device that the client system wishes to use. Rio creates a *virtual device file* in the client that corresponds to the actual device file in the server. The virtual device file creates the illusion to the client's processes that the I/O device is present locally on the client. To use the

remote I/O device, a process in the client executes file operations on the virtual device file. These file operations are intercepted by the *client stub* module, which packs the arguments of each file operation into a packet and sends it to the *server stub* module. The server stub unpacks the arguments and executes the file operation on the actual device file. It then sends back the return values of the file operation to the client stub, which returns them to the process. Note that Figure 1(b) only shows one client using a single I/O device from a single server. The design of Rio, however, allows a client to use multiple I/O devices from multiple servers. It also allows multiple clients to use an I/O device from a server. Moreover, the design allows a system to act as both a client and a server simultaneously for different devices or for different systems.

In Rio, the client process is always the initiator of communications with the server driver. This is because communications between the process and driver are always initiated by the process via a file operation. When an I/O device needs to notify a process of events, the notification is done using the `poll` file operation. To wait for an event, a process issues a blocking `poll` file operation that blocks in the kernel (and hence, in the server kernel in Rio) until the event occurs. Or, it periodically issues non-blocking `poll`s to check for the occurrence of an event.

Some file operations, such as `read`, `write`, `ioctl`, and `mmap`, require the driver to operate on the process memory. `mmap` requires the driver to map some memory pages into the process address space. For this, Rio uses a DSM design that supports access to shared pages by the client process as well as the server driver and device (through DMA) (§4.1). The other three file operations often ask the driver to copy data to or from the process memory. The server stub intercepts the driver's requests for these copies and services them with collaboration from the client stub (§4.2).

3.2 Guarantees

Using I/O remotely at the device file boundary impacts three expected behaviors of file operations: reliability of connection, latency, and trust model. That is, remote I/O introduces the possibility of disconnection between the process and the driver, adds significant latency to each file operation due to wireless round trips, and allows processes and drivers in different trust domains to communicate. Therefore, Rio provides the following guarantees for the client and server.

First, to avoid undesirable side-effects in the client and

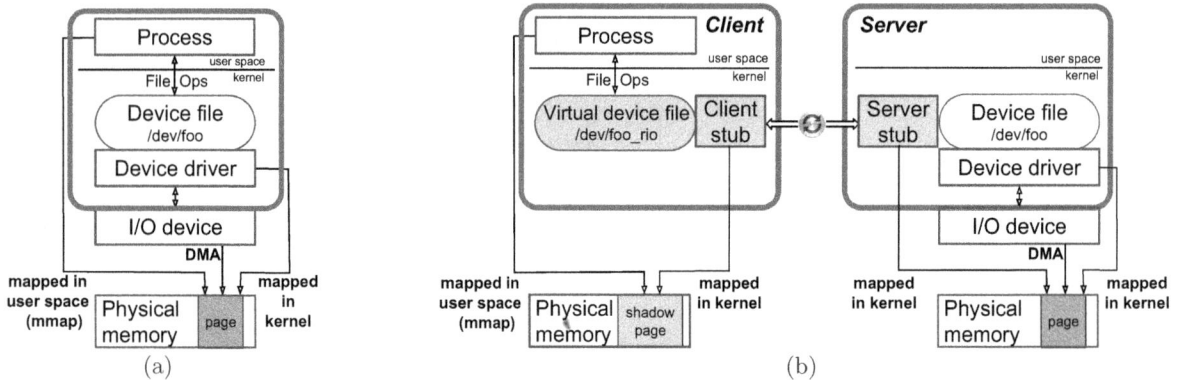

Figure 2: (a) Memory map for a local I/O device. (b) Cross-system memory map in Rio.

server resulting from an unexpected disconnection, Rio triggers a cleanup in both systems upon detecting a disconnection. Rio guarantees the server that a disconnection behaves similar to killing a local process that uses the I/O device. Rio also guarantees the client will transparently switch to a local I/O device of the same class, if possible; otherwise, Rio returns appropriate error messages to the application (§6).

Second, Rio reduces the number of round trips due to file or memory operations and DSM coherence messages (§5) in order to reduce latency and improve performance. Moreover, it guarantees that the additional latency of file operations only impacts the performance, *not the correctness*, of I/O devices. Rio can provide this guarantee because most file operations do not have a time-out threshold, but simply block until the device driver handles them. poll is the only file operations for which a time-out can be set by the process. In §5.4, we explain that poll operations used in Android for I/O devices we currently support do not use the poll time-out mechanism. We also explain how Rio can deal with the poll time-out, if used.

Finally, processes typically trust the device drivers with which they interact through the device file interface, and drivers are vulnerable to attacks by processes [15]. To maintain the same trust and security model in one mobile system, we intend the current design of Rio to be used among trusted mobile systems only. In §10, we discuss how the current design can be enhanced to maintain this guarantee while supporting I/O sharing between untrusted mobile systems.

4. CROSS-SYSTEM MEMORY SUPPORT

In order to handle file operations, the device driver often needs to operate on the process memory by executing memory operations. However, these operations pose a challenge for Rio because the process and the driver reside in different mobile systems with separate physical memories. In this section, we present our solutions.

There are three types of memory operations. The first one is map_page, which the driver uses to map system or device memory pages into the process address space. This memory operation is used for handling the mmap file operation and its supporting page_fault operation. Note that the kernel itself performs the corresponding unmap_page memory operation and not the driver. The other two types of memory operations are copy_to_user and copy_from_user, which the driver uses to copy a buffer from the kernel to the process memory and vice-versa. These two memory operations are typically used for handling read, write, and ioctl file operations.

4.1 Cross-System Memory Map

Cross-system memory map in Rio supports the map_page memory operation across two mobile systems using Distributed Shared Memory (DSM) [27, 31, 37, 47, 53] between them. At the core of Rio's DSM is a simple write-invalidate protocol, similar to [53]. The novelty of the DSM in Rio is that it can support access to the distributed shared memory pages not only by a process, but also by kernel code, such as the driver, and also by the device (through DMA).

Figure 2 illustrates the cross-system memory map in Rio. When intercepting a map_page operation from the server driver, the server stub notifies the client stub, which then allocates a shadow memory page in the client (corresponding to the actual memory page in the server) and maps that shadow page into the client process address space. The DSM modules in these two stubs guarantee that the process, the driver, and the device have consistent views of these pages. That is, updates to both the actual and shadow pages are consistently available to the other mobile system.

We choose a write-invalidate protocol in Rio's DSM for efficiency. Compared to update protocols that proactively propagate the updates to other systems [27], invalidate protocols do so only when the updated data is needed on the other system. This minimizes the amount of data transmitted between the client and server, and therefore minimizes the resource consumption, e.g., energy, in both systems. With the invalidate protocol, each memory page can be in one of three possible states: read-write, read-only, or invalid. Although the invalidate protocol is the default in Rio, we can also use an update protocol if it offers performance benefits.

We use 4 KB pages (small pages) as the coherence unit because it is the unit of the map_page memory operation, meaning the driver can map memory as small as a single small page into the process address space. When many pages are updated together, we batch them altogether to improve performance (§5.3).

To manage a client process's access to the (shadow) page, we use the page table permission bits, similar to some existing DSM solutions [37]. When the shadow page is in the read-write state, the page table grants the process full access permissions to the page, and all of the process's read and write instructions execute natively with no extra overhead. In the read-only state, only write to these pages cause page faults, while both read and write cause page faults in the invalid state. Upon a page fault, the client stub triggers appropriate coherence messages. For a read fault, it fetches the page from the server. For a write fault, it first fetches the page if in invalid state, and then sends an invalidation message to the server.

To manage the server driver's access to the page, we use the page table permission bits for kernel memory since the driver operates in the kernel. However, unlike process memory that uses small 4 KB pages, certain regions of kernel memory, e.g., the identity-mapped region in Linux, use larger pages, e.g., 1 MB pages in ARM [23], for better TLB and memory efficiency. When the driver requests to map a portion of a large kernel page into the process address space, the server stub dynamically breaks the large kernel page into multiple small ones by destroying the old page table entries and creating new ones, similar to the technique used in K2 [38]. With this technique, the server stub can enforce different protection modes against kernel access at the granularity of small pages, rather large pages. To minimize the side-effects of using small pages in the kernel, e.g., higher TLB contention, the server stub immediately stitches the small pages back into a single large page when the pages are unmapped by the process.

To manage the server I/O device's access to the page through DMA, the server stub maintains an explicit state variable for each page, intercepts the driver's DMA request to the device, updates the state variable, and triggers appropriate coherence messages. Note that it is not possible to use page table permission bits for a device's access to the page since devices' DMA operations bypass the page tables.

Rio provides sequential consistency. This is possible for two reasons. First, the DSM module triggers coherence messages immediately upon page faults and DMA completion, and maintains the order of these messages in each system. Second, processes and drivers use file operations to coordinate their own access to mapped pages.

4.2 Cross-System Copy

Cross-system memory copy in Rio supports `copy_from_user` and `copy_to_user` memory operations between two mobile systems. We achieve this through collaboration between the server and client stubs. When intercepting a `copy_from_user` or `copy_to_user` operation from the driver, the server stub sends a request back to the client stub to perform the operation. In the case of `copy_from_user`, the client stub copies the data from the process memory and sends it back to the server stub, which copies it into the kernel buffer determined by the driver. In the case of `copy_to_user`, the server stub copies and sends the data from the kernel buffer to the client stub, which then copies it to the corresponding process memory buffer. Figure 3(b) illustrates the cross-system copy for a typical `ioctl` file operation.

When handling a file operation, the driver may execute several memory copy operations, causing that many round trips between the mobile systems because the server stub has to send a separate request per copy operation. Large numbers of round trips can degrade the I/O performance significantly. In §5.1, we explain how we reduce these round trips to only one per file operation by pre-copying the copy data in the client stub for `copy_from_user` operations, as

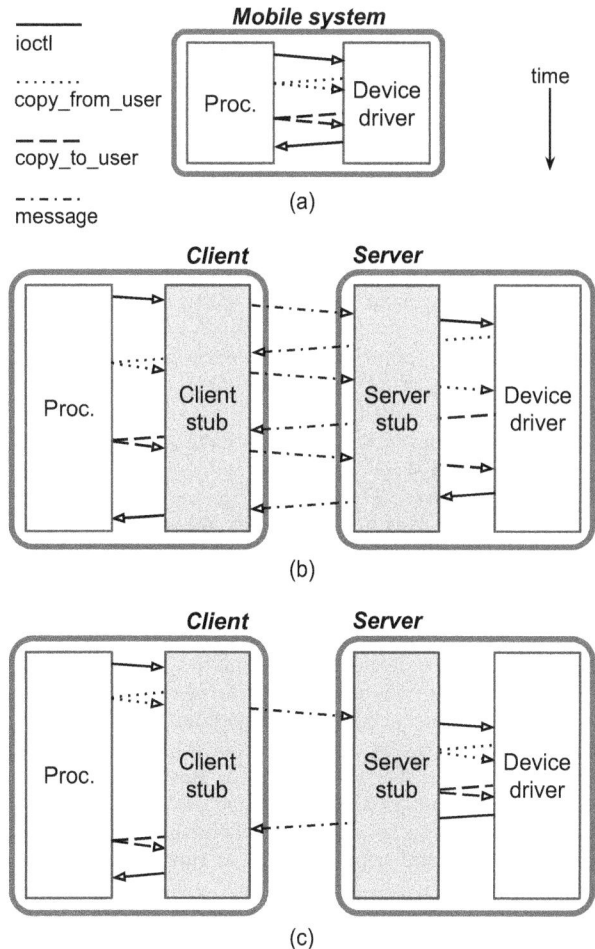

Figure 3: Typical execution of an `ioctl` file operation for (a) a local I/O device, (b) a remote I/O device with unoptimized Rio (§4.2), and (c) a remote I/O device with optimized Rio (§5.1). As the figure shows, optimized Rio reduces the number of round trips from 3 to 1. The reduction can be even more significant if the file operation requires more copy memory operations.

well as batching the data of `copy_to_user` operations in the server stub.

5. MITIGATING HIGH LATENCY

The connection between the client and the server typically has high latency. For example, Wi-Fi and Bluetooth have about 1-2 ms round-trip latency at best [51], which is significantly higher than the few microseconds of latency typical of native communications between a process and device driver (i.e., syscalls). In this section, we discuss the challenges resulting from such high latency and present our solutions to reduce its effect on I/O performance by reducing the number of round trips due to copy memory operations, file operations, and DSM coherence messages.

5.1 Round Trips due to Copies

Round trips due to `copy_from_user` and `copy_to_user` memory operations present a serious challenge to Rio's performance since a single file operation may execute several copy memory operations in succession. For example, a single `ioctl` in Linux's PCM audio driver may execute four `copy_from_user` operations. To solve this problem, we use the following two techniques. (*i*) In the client stub, we determine and pre-copy all the data needed by the server driver and transmit it together with the file operation. With this technique, all `copy_from_user` requests from the driver are serviced locally inside the server. (*ii*) In the server stub, we buffer and batch all data that the driver intends to copy to the process memory and transmit it to the client along with the return values of the file operation. With this technique, all `copy_to_user` operations can be executed locally in the client. Figure 3(c) illustrates these techniques.

Pre-copying the data for driver `copy_from_user` requests requires the client stub module to determine *in advance* the addresses and sizes of the process memory data buffers needed by the driver. This is trivial for the `read` and `write` file operations, as this information is embedded in their input arguments. However, doing so for `ioctl` is non-trivial as the `ioctl` input arguments are not always descriptive enough. Many well-written drivers embed information about some simple driver memory operations in one of the `ioctl` input arguments, i.e., the `ioctl` command number. In such cases, we parse the command number in the client stub to infer the memory operations, similar to [22]. There are cases, however, that the command number does not contain all necessary information. For these cases, we use a static analysis tool from our previous work, [22], that analyses the driver's source code to extract a small part of the driver code, which can then be executed either offline or at runtime in the client stub to infer the parameters of driver memory operations. Finally, to maintain a consistent view of the process memory for the driver, Rio updates the pre-copied data in the server stub upon buffering the `copy_to_user` data if the memory locations overlap.

5.2 Round Trips due to File Operations

File operations are executed synchronously by each process thread, and therefore, each file operation needs one round trip. To optimize performance, the process should issue the minimum number of file operations possible. Changing the number of file operations is not always possible or may require substantial changes to the process source code, e.g., the I/O service code in Android (§7), which is against Rio's goal of reducing engineering effort. However, minimal changes to the process code can occasionally result in noticeable reductions in file operation issuance, justifying the engineering effort. §7.3 explains one example for Android audio devices.

5.3 Round Trips due to DSM Coherence

As mentioned in §4.1, we use 4 KB pages as the DSM coherence unit in Rio. However, when there are updates to several pages at once, such a relatively small coherence unit causes several round trips for all data to be transferred. In such cases, transmitting all updated pages together in a single round trip is much more efficient.

5.4 Dealing with Poll Time-outs

`poll` is the only file operations for which the issuing process can set a time-out. Since Rio adds noticeable latency to each file operation, it can break the semantics of `poll` if a relatively small time-out threshold is used. So far in our Android implementation, all I/O classes we support do not use `poll` time-out (i.e., the process either blocks indefinitely until the event is ready or uses non-blocking `poll`s). If `poll` is used with a time-out, the time-out value should to be adjusted for remote I/O devices. This can be done inside the kernel handler for `poll`-related syscalls, such as `select`, completely transparent to the user space. Using the heartbeat round-trip time (§6), the client stub can provide a best estimate of the additional latency that the syscall handler needs to add to the requested time-out value. Processes typically rely on the kernel to enforce the requested `poll` time-out; therefore, this approach guarantees that the process function will not break in the face of high latency. In the unlikely case that the process uses an external timer to validate its requested time-out, the process must be modified to accommodate additional latency for remote I/O devices.

6. HANDLING DISCONNECTIONS

The connection between the client and the server may be lost at any time due to mobility. If not handled properly, the disconnection can cause the following problems: render the driver unusable, block the client process indefinitely, or leak resources, e.g., memory, in the client and server OSes. When faced with a disconnection, the server and client stubs take the appropriate actions described below.

We use a time-out mechanism to detect a disconnection. At regular intervals, the client stub transmits heartbeat messages to the server stub, which immediately transmits back an acknowledgement. If the client stub does not receive the acknowledgement before a certain threshold, or the server does not hear from the client, they both trigger a disconnection event. We do not use the in-flight file operations as a heartbeat because file operations can take unpredictable amounts of time to complete in the driver. Determining the best heartbeat interval and time-out thresholds to achieve an acceptable trade-off between overhead and detection accuracy is part of future work.

For the server, network disconnection is equivalent to killing a local process that is communicating with the driver. Therefore, just as the OS cleans up the residuals of a killed process, the server stub cleans up the residuals of the disconnected client process. For each `mmap`ed area and each file descriptor, the server stub invokes the driver's `close_map` handler and `release` file operation handler respectively, in order for the driver to release the allocated resources. Finally, it releases its own bookkeeping data structures.

We take two actions in the client upon disconnection. First, we clean up the residuals of the disconnected remote I/O in the client stub, similar to the cleanup process in the server. Next, we try to make the disconnection as transparent to the application as possible. If the client has a local I/O device of the same class, we transparently switch to that local I/O device after the disconnection. If no comparable I/O device is present, we return appropriate error messages supported by the API. These actions require class-specific developments, and §7.3 explains how we achieve this for sensors. Switching to local I/O is possible for three of the I/O classes we currently support, including camera, audio, and sensors such as accelerometer. For the modem, the disconnection means that a phone call will be dropped or not initiated, or that an SMS will not be sent; all behaviors are understandable by existing applications.

Type	Total LoC	Component	LoC
Generic	6618	Server stub	2801
		Client stub	1651
		Shared between stubs	647
		DSM	1192
		Supporting Linux kernel code	327
Class-specific	498	Camera:	
		- HAL	36
		- DMA	134
		Audio device	64
		Sensor	128
		Cellular modem	136

Table 1: Rio code breakdown.

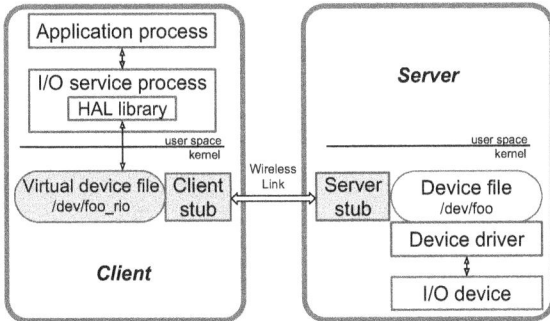

Figure 4: Rio's architecture inside an Android system. Rio forwards to the server the file operations issued by the I/O service process through HAL. Rio supports unmodified applications but requires small changes to the class-specific I/O service process and/or HAL.

7. ANDROID IMPLEMENTATION

We have implemented Rio for Android OS and ARM architecture. The implementation currently supports four classes of I/O devices: sensors (e.g., accelerometer), audio devices (e.g., microphone and speaker), camera, and modem (for phone calls and SMS). It consists of about 7100 LoC, fewer than 500 of which are I/O class-specific as shown in Table 1. We have tested the implementation on Galaxy Nexus smartphones running CyanogenMod 10.1 (Android 4.2.2) atop Linux kernel 3.0, and on a Samsung Galaxy Tab 10.1 tablet running CyanogenMod 10.1 (Android 4.2.2) with Linux kernel 3.1. The implementation can share I/O between systems of different form factors: we have demonstrated this for sharing sensors between a smartphone and a tablet.

Figure 4 shows the architecture of Rio inside an Android system. In Android, the application processes do not directly use the device files to interact with the driver. Instead, they communicate to a class-specific *I/O service process* through class-specific APIs. The I/O service process loads a *Hardware Abstraction Layer (HAL)* library in order to use the device file to interact with the device driver. Rio's device file boundary lies below the I/O service processes, forwarding its file operations to the server. As we will explain in the rest of this section, we need small modifications to the HAL or I/O service process, but no modifications to the applications are needed.

7.1 Client & Server Stubs

The client and server stubs are the two main components of Rio and constitute a large portion of Rio's implementa-

tion. Each stub has three modules. The first module supports interactions with applications and device drivers. In the client stub, this module intercepts the file operations and packs their arguments into a data structure; in the server stub, it unpacks the arguments from the data structure and invokes the file operations of the device driver. This module is about 3000 LoC and is shared with our previous work, Paradice [22]. The second module implements the communication with the other stub by serializing data structures into packets and transmitting them to the other end. Finally, the third module implements Rio's DSM, further explained in §7.2.

We use in-kernel TCP sockets for communication between the client and server stubs [10]. We use TCP to ensure that all the packets are successfully received, otherwise the device, driver, or the application might break.

To handle cross-system memory operations, the server stub intercepts the driver's kernel function calls for memory operations. This includes intercepting 7 kernel functions for `copy_to_user` and `copy_from_user` and 3 kernel functions for `map_page`. Using this technique allows us to support *unmodified drivers*.

7.2 DSM Module

Rio's DSM module is shared between the client and the server. It implements the logic of the DSM protocol, e.g., triggering and handling coherence messages. The DSM module is invoked in two cases: page faults and DMA. We instrument the kernel fault handler to invoke the DSM module when there is a page fault. Additionally, the DSM module must handle device DMA to DSM-protected pages. We monitor the driver's DMA requests to the device and invoke the DSM module upon DMA completion.

To monitor the driver's DMA requests to devices, we instrument the corresponding kernel functions. These functions are typically I/O bus-specific and will apply to all I/O devices using that I/O bus. Specialized instrumentation is needed if the driver uses non-standard interfaces. For example, the camera on the TI OMAP4 SoC inside Galaxy Nexus smartphones uses custom messages between the driver and the Imaging Subsystem (ISS) component, where the camera hardware resides [49]. We instrumented the driver responsible for communications with the ISS to monitor the DMA requests, only with 134 LoC.

When we receive a DMA completion notification for a memory buffer, we may use a DSM update protocol to immediately push the updated buffers to the client, an optional optimization. Moreover, we update the whole buffer in one round trip. These optimizations can improve performance as they minimize the number of round trips between mobile systems (§5.3); as such, we used them for camera frames.

As described in §4.1, certain regions of the kernel's address space, namely the identity-mapped region, use large 1 MB pages known as *Sections* in the ARM architecture. To split these 1 MB Sections into smaller 4 KB pages for use with our DSM module, we first walk the existing page tables to obtain a reference to the Section's first-level descriptor (a PGD entry). We then allocate a single new page that holds 512 second-level page table entries (PTEs), one for each page; altogether, these 512 PTEs reference two 1 MB Sections of virtual memory. We populate each second-level PTE with the correct page frame number and permission bits from the original Section. Finally, we change the first-level descriptor entry to point to our new table of second-level PTEs and flush the corresponding cache and TLB entries.

7.2.1 Support for Buffer Sharing using Android ION

Android uses the ION memory management framework to allocate and share memory buffers for multimedia applications, such as those using the GPU, camera, and audio [2]. The sharing of ION buffers creates unique challenges for Rio, as demonstrated in the following example.

The camera HAL allocates buffers using ION and passes the ION buffer handles to the kernel driver, which translates them to the physical addresses of these buffers and asks the camera to copy new frames to them. Once the frames are written, the HAL is notified and forwards the ION buffer handle to the graphics framework for rendering. Now, imagine using a remote camera in Rio. The same ION buffer handles used by the camera HAL in the client need to be used by both the server kernel driver and the client graphics framework, since the camera frames from the server are rendered on the client display.

To solve this problem, we provide support for global ION buffers that can be used both inside the client and the server. We achieve this by allocating an ION buffer in the server with similar properties (e.g., size) to the one allocated in the client; we use the DSM module to keep the two buffers coherent.

7.3 Class-Specific Developments

Most of Rio's implementation is I/O class-agnostic; our current implementation only requires under 500 class-specific LoC.

Resolving naming conflicts: In case the client has an I/O device of the same class that uses device files with similar names as those used in the server, the virtual device file must assume a different name (e.g., /dev/foo_rio vs. /dev/foo in Figure 1(b)). However, the device file names are typically hard-coded in the HAL, necessitating small modifications to use a renamed virtual device file for remote I/O.

Optimizing performance: As discussed in §5.2, sometimes small changes to the I/O service code and HAL can boost the remote I/O performance significantly by reducing the number of file operations. For example, the audio HAL exchanges buffered audio segments with the driver using ioctls. The HAL determines the size of the audio segment per ioctl. For local devices (with very low latency), these buffered segments can contain as low as 3 ms of audio, less than a single round-trip time in Rio. Therefore, we modify the HAL to use larger buffering segments for remote audio devices. Although this slightly increases the audio latency, it significantly improves the audio rate for remote devices. §8 provides measurements to quantify this trade-off. This modification only required about 30 LoC.

Support for hot-plugging and disconnection: Remote I/O devices can come and go at any time; in this sense, they behave similarly to hot-plugging/removal of local I/O devices. Small changes to the I/O service layer may be required to support hot-plugging and disconnection of remote I/O devices. For example, the Android sensor service layer opens the sensor device files (through the HAL) in the phone initialization process and only uses these file descriptors to read the sensor values. To support hot-plugging remote sensors, we modified the sensor service layer to open the virtual device files and use their file descriptors too when remote sensors are present. Upon disconnection, we switch back to using local sensors to provide application transparency.

Avoiding duplicate I/O initialization: Some HAL libraries, including sensor and cellular modem's, perform initialization of the I/O device upon system boot. However, since the I/O device is already initialized in the server, the client HAL should not attempt to initialize the I/O device. Not only this can break the I/O device, it can also break the HAL because the server device driver rejects initialization-based file operations. Therefore, the HAL must be modified in order to avoid initializing a device twice. Achieving this was trivial for the open-source sensor HAL. However, since the modem's HAL is not open-source, we had to employ a workaround that uses a second SIM card in the client to initialize its modem's HAL. It is possible to develop a small extension to the modem open-source kernel driver in order to fake the presence of the SIM card and allow the client HAL to initialize itself without a second SIM card.

Sharing modem for phone calls: Through the device file interface, Rio can initiate and receive phone calls. However, it requires further development to relay the incoming and outgoing audio for the phone call. A phone call on Android works as follows. The modem HAL uses the modem device file to initiate a call, or to receive one. Once the call is connected, with instructions from the HAL, the modem uses the speaker and microphone for incoming and outgoing audio. The modem directly uses the speaker and microphone; therefore, the audio cannot be automatically supported by Rio's use of the modem device file. To overcome this, we leveraged Rio's ability to share audio devices in order to relay the audio. There are two audio streams to be relayed. The audio from the user (who is using the client device) to the target phone (on the other side of the phone call) and the audio from the target phone to the client. For the former stream, we record the audio on the client using the client's own microphone and play it back on the server's speaker through Rio. The modem on the server then picks up the audio played on the speaker and transmits it to the target phone. For the latter stream, we record the incoming audio data on the server using server's microphone remotely from the client using Rio, and then play it back on the client's own speaker for the user. We used CyanogenMod 10.2 for relaying the audio for phone calls since CyanogenMod 10.1 does not support capturing audio during a phone call.

Currently, we can only support one audio stream at a time. The main reason for this is that supporting both streams will result in the user at the client hearing herself since the audio played on the server's speaker will be picked up by the microphone. While we currently have to manually arbitrate between the two streams, it is possible to support automatic arbitration by measuring the audio intensity on the two streams.

7.4 Sharing between Heterogeneous Systems

Because the device file boundary is common to all Android systems, Rio's design readily supports sharing between heterogeneous systems, e.g., between a smartphone and a tablet. However, the implementation has to properly deal with the HAL library of a shared I/O device because it may be specific to the I/O device or to the SoC used in the server. Our solution is to port the HAL library used in the server to the client. Such a port is easy for two reasons. First, Android's interface to the HAL for each I/O class is the same

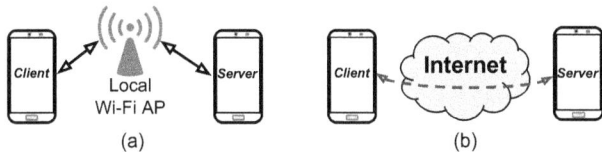

Figure 5: We use two different connections in our evaluation. In (a), the phones are connected to the same AP. This connection represents that used between mobile systems that are close to each other. In (b), the phones are connected over the Internet. This connection represents that used between mobile systems at different geographical locations.

across Android systems of different form factors. Second, all Android systems use the Linux kernel and are mostly shipped with ARM processors. For example, we managed to port the Galaxy Nexus smartphone sensors HAL library to the Samsung Galaxy Tab 10.1 tablet by compiling the smartphone's HAL inside the tablet's source tree.

8. EVALUATION

We evaluate Rio and show that it supports legacy applications, allows access to all I/O device functionality, requires low engineering effort to support different I/O devices, and achieves performance close to that of local I/O for audio devices, sensors, and modem, but exhibits performance drops for the camera due to network throughput limitations. We further discuss that future wireless standards will eliminate this performance issue. In addition, we report the throughput and power consumption for using remote I/O devices with Rio and show that throughput highly depends on the I/O device class, and that power consumption is noticeably higher than that of local devices. Finally, we demonstrate Rio's ability to handle disconnections.

All experiments are performed on two Galaxy Nexus smartphones. We use two connections of differing latencies for the experiments. The first connection (Figure 5(a)) is over a wireless LAN between mobile systems that are close to each other, e.g., both in the same room. We connect both phones to the same Wi-Fi access point. This connection has a latency with median, average, and standard deviation of 4 ms, 8.5 ms, and 16.3 ms, and a throughput of 21.9 Mbps. The second connection (Figure 5(b)) is between mobile systems at different geographical locations, one at home and one 20 miles away at work. We connect these two phones through the Internet using external IPs from commodity Internet Providers. This connection has a latency with median, average, and standard deviation of 55.2 ms 57 ms, and 20.9 ms, and a throughput of 1.2 Mbps. All reported results use the first LAN connection, unless otherwise stated.

8.1 Non-Performance Properties

First, Rio supports existing unmodified applications. We have tested Rio with both stock and third-party applications using different classes of I/O devices.

Second, unlike existing solutions, Rio exposes all functionality of remote I/O devices to the client. For example, the client system can configure every camera parameter, such as resolution, zoom, and white balance. Similarly, an application can configure the speaker with different equalizer effects.

Third, supporting new I/O devices in Rio requires low engineering effort. As shown in Table 1, we only needed 128, 64, 170, and 136 LoC to support sensors, audio devices (both speaker and microphone), camera, and the modem (for phone calls and SMS) respectively.

8.2 Performance Benchmarks

In this subsection, we measure the performance of different I/O classes in Rio and compare them to local performance. Unless otherwise stated, we repeat each experiment three times and report the average and standard deviation of measurements. The phones are rebooted after each experiment.

Audio devices: We evaluate the performance of the speaker and the microphone measuring the audio (sample) rate at different buffering sizes, and hence, different audio latency. Using larger buffering sizes reduces the interactions with the driver but increases the audio latency. Audio latency is the average time it takes a sample to reach the speaker from the process (and vice-versa for microphone), and is directly determined by the buffering size used in the HAL.

Figure 6 shows the achieved rate for different buffering sizes (and hence different latencies) for the speaker and the microphone when accessed locally or remotely through Rio. We use a minimum of 3 ms for the buffering size as it is the smallest size used for local speakers in Android in low latency mode. The figure shows that such a small buffering size degrades the audio rate in Rio. This is mainly because the HAL issues one `ioctl` for each 3 ms audio segment, but the `ioctl` takes longer than 3 ms to finish in Rio due to the network's long round-trip time. However, the figure shows that Rio is able to achieve the desired 48 kHz audio rate at slightly larger buffering sizes of 9 and 10 ms for microphone and speaker, respectively. We believe that Rio achieves acceptably low audio latency because Android uses a buffering size of 308 ms for non-low latency audio mode for speaker, and uses 22 ms for microphone (it uses 3 ms for low latency speaker).

We also measure the performance of audio devices with Rio when mobile systems are connected via the aforementioned high latency connection, e.g., for making a phone call remotely at work using a smartphone at home. Our measurements show that Rio achieves the desired 48 kHz for the microphone using buffering sizes as small as 85 ms. However, for the speaker, Rio can only achieve a maximum sampling rate of 25 kHz using a 300 ms buffer (other buffer sizes performed poorly). We believe this is because the speaker requires a higher link throughput, as demonstrated in §8.3.

Camera: We measure the performance of both a real-time streaming camera preview and that of capturing a photo. In the first case, we measure the frame rate (in frames per second) that the camera application can achieve, averaged over 1000 frames for each experiment. We ignore the first 50 frames to avoid the effects of camera initialization on performance. Figure 7(a) shows that Rio can achieve acceptable performance (i.e., >15 FPS) at low resolutions. The performance at higher resolutions is bottlenecked by network throughput between the client and server. Rio spends most of its time transmitting frames rather than file operations. However, streaming camera frames are uncompressed, requiring, for example, 612 KB of data *per frame* even for VGA (640×480) resolution, necessitating about 72 Mbps of throughput to maintain 15 FPS at this resolution.

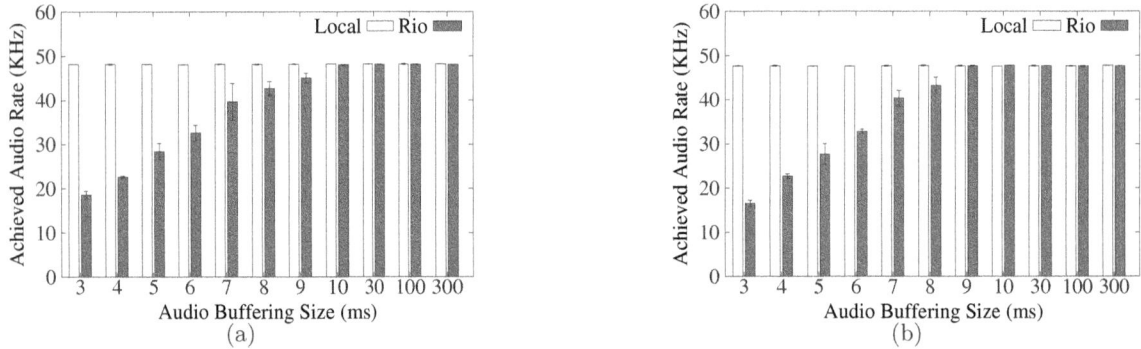

Figure 6: Performance of (a) speaker and (b) microphone. The X axis shows the buffering size in the HAL. The larger the buffer size, the smoother the playback/capture, but the larger the audio latency. The Y axis shows the achieved audio rate.

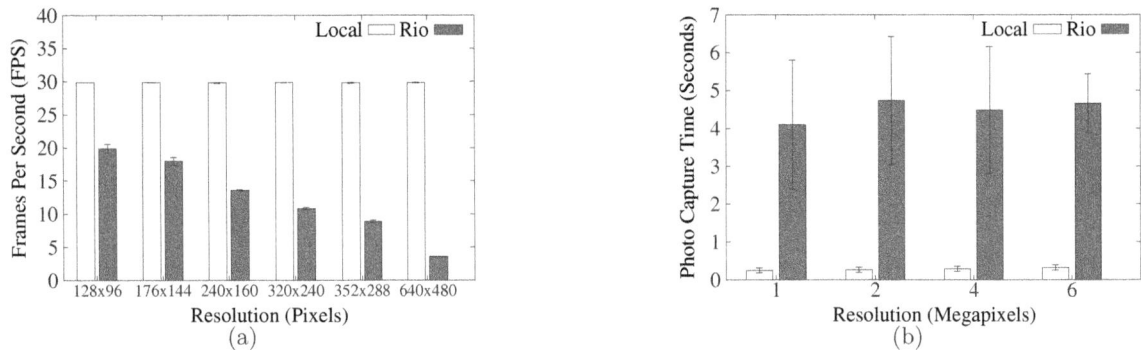

Figure 7: Performance of a real-time streaming camera preview (a) and photo capture (b) with a 21.9 Mbps wireless LAN connection between the client and server. Future wireless standards with higher throughput will improve performance without requiring changes to Rio.

We believe that the lower resolution camera preview supported by Rio is acceptable given that Rio supports capturing photos at maximum resolutions. Rio will support higher real-time camera resolutions using future wireless standards. For example, 802.11n, 802.11ac, and a 802.11ad can achieve around 200 Mpbs, 600 Mbps, and 7 Gbps of throughput respectively [19, 21]. Such throughput capabilities can support real-time camera streaming in Rio at 15 FPS for resolutions of 1280×720 and 1920×1080, which are the highest resolutions supported on Galaxy Nexus. Moreover, Rio can incorporate compression techniques, either in software or using the hardware-accelerated compression modules on mobile SoCs, to reduce the amount of data transferred for real-time camera, although we have not yet explored this optimization.

To evaluate photo capture, we measure the time from when the capture request is delivered to the camera HAL from the application until the HAL notifies the application that the photo is ready. We do not include the focus time since it is mainly dependent on the camera hardware and varies for different scenes. We take three photos in each experiment (totalling 9 photos in three experiments). Figure 7(b) shows the capture time for local and remote cameras using Rio. It shows that Rio adds noticeable latency to the capture time, mostly stemming from the time taken to transfer the raw images from the server to the client. However, the user only needs to point the camera at the targeted scene very briefly (similar to when using a local camera), as

the image will be immediately captured in the server. This means that the *shutter lag is small*. It is important to note that the camera HAL in Galaxy Nexus uses the same buffer size regardless of resolution, hence the capture time is essentially resolution-independent. The buffer size is 8 MB, which takes about 3.1 seconds to transfer over our 21.9 Mbps connection. As with real-time camera streaming, future wireless standards will eliminate this overhead, providing latency on par with local camera capture.

Sensors: To evaluate remote sensor performance, we measure the average time it takes for the sensor HAL to obtain a new accelerometer reading. We measure the average time of 1000 samples for each experiment. Our results of 10 experiments show that the sensor HAL obtains a new local reading in 64.8 ms on average (with a standard deviation of 0.1 ms) and a new remote reading via Rio in 70.5 ms on average (with a standard deviation of 1.9 ms). The sensor HAL obtains a new reading by issuing a blocking `poll` operation that waits in the kernel until the data is ready, at which point the HAL issues a `read` file operation to read the new value. Rio causes overhead in this situation because one and a half round trips are required for the blocking `poll` to return and for the `read` to complete. Fortunately, this overhead is negligible in practice and does not impact the user experience.

Modem: We measure the time it takes the dialer and messaging applications to start a phone call and to send an SMS, respectively. We measure the time from when the

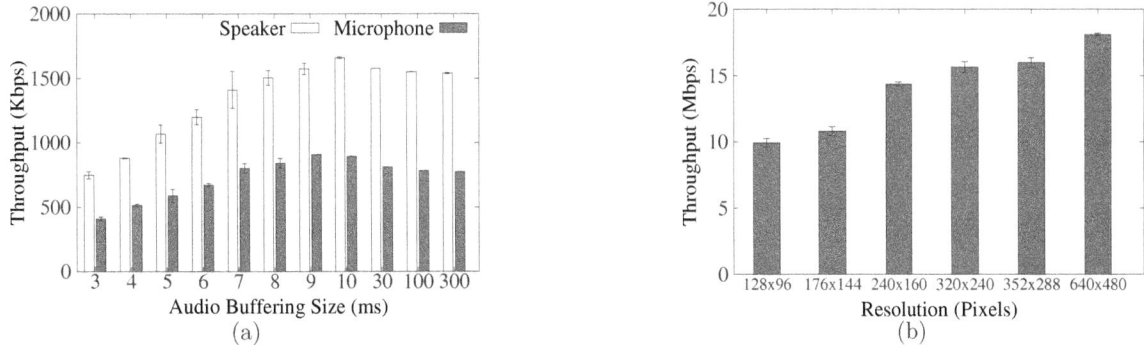

Figure 8: Throughput for using (a) audio devices (speaker and microphone) and (b) the camera (for video streaming) with Rio. Note that the Y axis is in Kbps and Mbps for (a) and (b), respectively.

user presses the "dial" or "send SMS" button until the notification appears on the receiving phone. Our measurements show that local and remote modems achieve similar performance, as the majority of time is spent in carrier networks (from T-Mobile to AT&T). For local and remote modems, the phone call takes an average of 7.8 and 7.9 seconds (with standard deviations of 0.7 and 0.3 seconds) while SMS takes an average of 6.2 and 5.9 seconds (with standard deviations of 0.3 and 0.6 seconds), respectively.

8.3 Throughput

We measure the wireless throughput required for using different classes of I/O devices remotely with Rio. Our results show that using sensors, audio devices, and camera remotely requires small, moderate, and large throughput, respectively.

We quantify the throughput by measuring the amount of data transmitted between the client and the server. We measure the number of bytes transmitted over the TCP socket, therefore, our results does not include the overhead due to the TCP header and headers of lower layers. We run each experiment for one minute and measure the throughput. For microphone, we record a one minute audio segment. For speaker, we play a one minute audio segment. For camera, we stream frames for one minute, and for accelerometer, we receive samples for one minute. We report each experiment three times and report the average and standard deviation. We reboot the phone before each experiment.

Figure 8(a) shows the results for the speaker and microphone. It shows that audio devices require a moderate throughput (hundreds of Kbps) and therefore Rio's performance for these devices is not throughput bounded. The throughput increases as we increase the audio buffering size, caps when the buffering size is 9-10 ms, and then decreases for larger buffering sizes. This trend can be explained as follows: at low buffering sizes, the audio performance on Rio is bounded by the link latency due to the high number of round trips. As a result, fewer audio samples are exchanged, resulting in lower throughput. As the buffering size increases, more audio samples are exchanged, hence requiring higher throughput. The number of audio samples exchanged (i.e., the audio rate) is maximized when the buffering size is 9-10 ms. For larger buffering sizes, the number of audio samples are fixed but the Rio's communication overhead decreases, resulting in a lower overall throughput. Moreover, the results show that speakers uses twice the throughput

used by the microphone. This is because audio samples for the speaker are twice the size of the audio samples used by the microphone in our experiments.

Figure 8(b) shows the throughput results for video streaming from a remote camera using Rio. We show that the camera requires high throughput, which is why the link throughput is a performance bottleneck in our setup. At high resolutions, the link is almost saturated with sending the frame content; Rio's overhead is small (since the number of frames is small). For lower resolutions, more frames are transmitted and therefore the effect of link latency becomes more noticeable. This is why Rio fails to saturate the link throughput at these resolutions.

We also measure the throughput when using the accelerometer remotely with Rio. Our measurements show the average throughput is 52.05 Kbps with a standard deviation of 1.72. This shows that the throughput for sensors is small and therefore we can leverage low throughput, low energy links (such as Bluetooth) for these devices. Also, most of this throughput comes from Rio's overhead since accelerometer data are small.

8.4 Power Consumption

We evaluate the overhead of Rio in terms of both systems' power consumption. For each I/O device, we measure the average power consumption of the client and server in Rio and also the power consumption of the system when the I/O device is used locally. In each experiment, we use the device for one minute, similar to §8.3, and measure the average power consumption using the Monsoon Power Monitor [13]. We repeat each experiment three times and report the average and standard deviation of the experiment. The display consumes a large amount of power; therefore, we try to keep the display powered off whenever possible. More specifically, for the accelerometer and audio devices, we turn off the display on both the client and the server and also on the local system. For camera, we turn off the display only on the server but not on the client or the local system (because the camera frames are being displayed).

Figure 9 shows that Rio consumes noticeably more power than local devices. Considering the sum of the power consumption of client and server for Rio, Rio consume about 4× the power consumed by local accelerometer and audio devices, and 2× the power consumed by the local camera. These are expected results as Rio spans over two systems and uses the Wi-Fi interface. For camera, the source of power

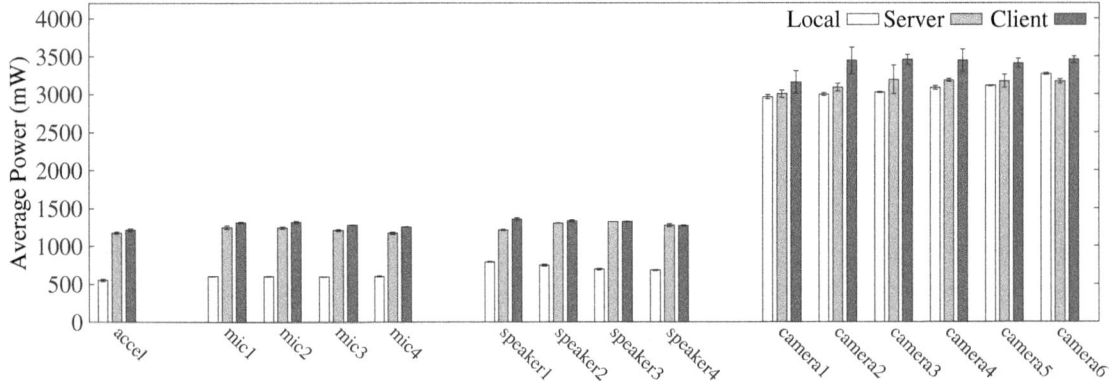

Figure 9: Average system power consumption of when accelerometer, microphone, speaker, and camera (for video streaming) are used locally and remotely with Rio, respectively. For Rio, the power consumption for both the server and the client are shown. Scenarios 1 to 4 for audio devices correspond to audio buffering sizes of 3 ms, 10 ms, 30 ms, and 300 ms, respectively. Scenarios 1 to 6 for camera correspond to resolutions of 128×96, 176×144, 240×160, 320×240, 352×288, and 640×480, respectively.

consumption of the local camera scenario is from the camera itself, the display, the CPU, and even the GPU, which is used for rendering the frames onto the screen. For Rio, the source of power consumption on the client is from the Wi-Fi interface, the display, the CPU, and the GPU, and for the server, from the Wi-Fi interface, the CPU, and the camera. For other devices, the main source of power consumption for the local scenario is the device itself and the CPU. For Rio, the source of power consumption on the client is from the Wi-Fi interface and the CPU, and on the server is from the Wi-Fi interface, the CPU, and the device.

8.5 Handling Disconnections

We evaluate Rio's ability to react to disconnections for the accelerometer. We play a game on the client using the server's accelerometer. Without warning, we disconnect the server and the client, and then trigger a disconnection event after a customizable threshold. Rio then transparently switches to using the local accelerometer so that we can continue to play the game using the client's own accelerometer.

9. RELATED WORK

The value of I/O sharing has been recognized by others for both mobile and non-mobile systems. However, existing solutions have three limitations: They do not support unmodified applications, do not expose all I/O device functions to the client, or are not generic to I/O classes. One possible advantage of these solutions is the incorporation of I/O class-specific optimizations. It is important to note that Rio can adopt I/O class-specific optimizations as well, if needed. For example, we have already incorporated one such optimization for audio devices (§7.3) where we modified the audio buffering size to improve the audio rate. Another possible optimization is the compression of camera frames before transmission.

I/O sharing for mobile systems: Existing I/O sharing solutions for mobile systems all suffer from the fundamental limitations described above. For example, IP Webcam [3] turns a mobile system's camera into an IP camera, which can then be viewed from another mobile system through a

custom viewer application. The client system cannot configure all camera parameters, such as resolution; These parameters must be manually configured on the server. Wi-Fi Speaker [4] allows music to be played on a mobile system's speaker from a PC. It does not, however, support sharing the microphone. MightyText [11] allows the user to send SMS and MMS messages from a PC or a mobile system using the SIM card and modem in another system. It does not support phone calls.

Screen sharing: Applications like Miracast [12] allow one system to display its screen on another system's screen. Thin client solutions also display content received from a server machine on a client. Examples are the X window system [45], THINC [25], Microsoft Remote Desktop [29], VNC [43], Citrix Metaframe [6], and Sun Ray [46]. None of these solutions use the device file boundary; their choice of boundary is usually graphics-specific or even application-specific. For example, X sets the boundary between the application and X server. As a result, these solutions cannot support other classes of I/O devices.

Other I/O sharing solutions: Remote file systems [14,35, 44], network USB devices [7,17,20,34], Wireless Displays [9], remote printers [18], and IP cameras [8] support I/O sharing as well. These solutions are also specific to one I/O class, e.g., storage. Participatory and cooperative sensing systems collect sensor data from registered or nearby mobile systems [30,36]. These systems use custom applications installed on mobile systems and are therefore more limited than Rio, which supports a variety of I/O devices. Indeed, these systems can incorporate Rio to more easily collect sensor data from other systems.

Computation offloading: There is a large body of literature regarding offloading computation from mobile systems [32], e.g., Cyber Foraging [24], MAUI [28], and COMET [33]. I/O sharing, as is concerned in this work, invites a different set of research challenges and has a focus on system support rather than programming support. Nevertheless, both computation offloading and I/O sharing benefit from existing techniques for distributed systems. For example, both Rio and COMET employ DSM, albeit with different designs.

10. CONCLUDING REMARKS

We presented Rio, an I/O sharing solution for mobile systems that adopts a split-stack model at the device file boundary. We demonstrated that Rio overcomes the limitations of existing solutions by supporting unmodified applications, exposing all I/O device functionality to clients, and reducing development effort. We presented an implementation of Rio for Android and showed that it achieves adequate performance for various sharing scenarios and that it supports heterogeneous mobile systems. We next offer some insights into the limitations of the current design and implementation of Rio and possible solutions to overcome some of them.

Supporting more classes of I/O devices: Our current implementation supports four classes of I/O devices. It is possible to extend it to support graphics, touchscreen, and GPS, since they also use the device file interface. There are, however, two classes of I/O that Rio's design cannot support: network and block devices. This is because these I/O devices do not use the device file interface for communications between the process and the driver. Network devices use sockets along with the kernel networking stack and block devices use kernel file systems.

Sharing I/O with untrusted systems: In this paper, we assumed that the systems sharing I/O through Rio trust each other not to be malicious (§3.2). For such scenarios, Rio can simply adopt an authentication mechanism where it asks the client and server's owner(s) to authenticate the I/O sharing, after which Rio assumes that both systems are not malicious. However, supporting I/O sharing between untrusted systems creates new challenges for Rio, which fall into two categories. (*i*) *Protecting the server*. As also discussed in [22], device drivers are buggy, and malicious applications can abuse these bugs through the device file interface to compromise the driver protection domain [15]. In Rio, this means that a malicious process in the client can compromise the server. In order to solve this problem, the device driver and the device need to be sandboxed in a protection domain in the server, using techniques similar to Paradice [22], Nooks [48], and VirtuOS [40]. (*ii*) *Protecting the client*. An untrusted server can issue spurious memory copy operations to the client in order to compromise the client. The client stub can simply protect against this threat by strictly checking the memory copy operations requested by the server, similar to [22]. Note that the server can also snoop the client's data that are shared with the I/O device, e.g., the audio buffers. Since the server is completely untrusted, we cannot provide any isolation for the client's data. This is indeed an inherent problem to any I/O sharing systems, and not only to Rio.

Energy use by Rio: Using an I/O device via a wireless link obviously incurs more energy consumption than using a local one, as demonstrated in §8.4. In this work, we did not address energy optimizations for Rio. Rather, we note that most of the performance optimizations in Rio, e.g., those described in §5, lead to more efficient use of the wireless link and therefore to reduced energy consumption. We also note that Rio's quest to reduce latency rules out the use of the standard 802.11 power-saving mode. On the other hand, many known techniques that trade a little latency for much more efficient use of the wireless link can benefit Rio, e.g., data compression [26] and μPM [39].

Supporting iOS: iOS also uses device files and hence can be supported in Rio. Sharing I/O devices between iOS systems should require similar engineering effort reported in this paper for sharing I/O devices between Android systems. However, sharing I/O devices between iOS and Android systems require potentially non-trivial engineering effort, mainly because these two systems have different I/O stack components and API.

Acknowledgments

The work was supported in part by NSF Awards #1054693, #1065506, and #1218041. The authors would also like to thank Sreekumar Nair, then at Nokia Research, who contributed to an early prototype of I/O sharing for x86/Linux machines that exchanges file operations and memory copy operations over sockets. The authors also thank the anonymous reviewers and their shepherd, Professor Gaetano Borriello, for their useful comments.

11. REFERENCES

[1] http://www.theverge.com/2011/06/09/google-voice-skype-imessage-and-the-death-of-the-phone-number/.

[2] Android ION Memory Allocator. http://lwn.net/Articles/480055/.

[3] Android IP Webcam application. https://play.google.com/store/apps/details?id=com.pas.webcam&hl=en.

[4] Android Wi-Fi Speaker application. https://play.google.com/store/apps/details?id=pixelface.android.audio&hl=en.

[5] Applications for taking self-portraits. http://giveawaytuesdays.wonderhowto.com/inspiration/10-iphone-and-android-apps-for-taking-self-portraits-0129658/.

[6] Citrix Metaframe. http://www.citrix.com.

[7] Digi International: AnywhereUSB. http://www.digi.com/products/usb/anywhereusb.jsp.

[8] Dropcam. https://www.dropcam.com/.

[9] Intel WiDi. http://www.intel.com/content/www/us/en/architecture-and-technology/intel-wireless-display.html.

[10] Linux ksocket. http://ksocket.sourceforge.net/.

[11] MightyText application. http://mightytext.net.

[12] Miracast. http://www.wi-fi.org/wi-fi-certified-miracast%E2%84%A2.

[13] Monsoon Power Monitor. http://www.msoon.com/LabEquipment/PowerMonitor/.

[14] Network File System. http://etherpad.tools.ietf.org/html/rfc3530.

[15] Privilege escalation using NVIDIA GPU driver bug. http://www.securelist.com/en/advisories/50085.

[16] Rio Project Homepage (including a video demo). http://www.ruf.rice.edu/~mobile/rio.html.

[17] USB Over IP. http://usbip.sourceforge.net/.

[18] Web Services on Devices: Devices That Are Controlled on the Network. http://msdn.microsoft.com/en-us/library/windows/desktop/aa826001(v=vs.85).aspx.

[19] Wireless LAN at 60 GHz - IEEE 802.11ad Explained. In *Agilent White Paper*.

[20] Wireless USB. http://www.usb.org/wusb/home/.

[21] 802.11ac: The Fifth Generation of Wi-Fi. In *Cisco White Paper*, 2012.

[22] A. Amiri Sani, K. Boos, S. Qin, and L. Zhong. I/O Paravirtualization at the Device File Boundary. In *Proc. ACM ASPLOS*, 2014.

[23] ARM. Architecture Reference Manual, ARMv7-A and ARMv7-R edition. *ARM DDI*, 0406A, 2007.

[24] R. K. Balan, D. Gergle, M. Satyanarayanan, and J. Herbsleb. Simplifying Cyber Foraging for Mobile Devices. In *Proc. ACM MobiSys*, 2007.

[25] R. A. Baratto, L. Kim, and J. Nieh. THINC: A Remote Display Architecture for Thin-Client Computing. In *Proc. ACM SOSP*, 2004.

[26] K. C. Barr and K. Asanović. Energy-Aware Lossless Data Compression. In *Proc. ACM MobiSys*, 2003.

[27] J. B. Carter, J. K. Bennett, and W. Zwaenepoel. Implementation and Performance of Munin. In *Proc. ACM SOSP*, 1991.

[28] E. Cuervo, A. Balasubramanian, D. Cho, A. Wolman, S. Saroiu, R. Chandra, and P. Bahl. MAUI: Making Smartphones Last Longer with Code Offload. In *Proc. ACM MobiSys*, 2010.

[29] B. C. Cumberland, G. Carius, and A. Muir. *Microsoft Windows NT Server 4.0, Terminal Server Edition: Technical Reference*. Microsoft Press, 1999.

[30] T. Das, P. Mohan, V. Padmanabhan, R. Ramjee, and A. Sharma. PRISM: Platform for Remote Sensing Using Smartphones. In *Proc. ACM MobiSys*, 2010.

[31] G. S. Delp. The Architecture and Implementation of MEMNET: a High-Speed Shared Memory Computer Communication Network. *Doctoral thesis, University of Delaware*, 1988.

[32] J. Flinn. Cyber Foraging: Bridging Mobile and Cloud Computing. *Synthesis Lectures on Mobile and Pervasive Computing*, 2012.

[33] M. S. Gordon, D. A. Jamshidi, S. Mahlke, Z. M. Mao, and X. Chen. COMET: Code Offload by Migrating Execution Transparently. In *Proc. USENIX OSDI*, 2012.

[34] A. Hari, M. Jaitly, Y. J. Chang, and A. Francini. The Switch Army Smartphone: Cloud-based Delivery of USB Services. In *Proc. ACM MobiHeld*, 2011.

[35] P. J. Leach and D. Naik. A Common Internet File System (CIFS/1.0) Protocol. *IETF Network Working Group RFC Draft*, 1997.

[36] Y. Lee, Y. Ju, C. Min, S. Kang, I. Hwang, and J. Song. CoMon: Cooperative Ambience Monitoring Platform with Continuity and Benefit Awareness. In *Proc. ACM MobiSys*, 2012.

[37] K. Li. Ivy: A Shared Virtual Memory System for Parallel Computing. In *Proc. Int. Conf. Parallel Processing*, 1988.

[38] F. X. Lin, Z. Wang, and L. Zhong. K2: A Mobile Operating System for Heterogeneous Coherence Domains. In *Proc. ACM ASPLOS*, 2014.

[39] J. Liu and L. Zhong. Micro Power Management of Active 802.11 Interfaces. In *Proc. ACM MobiSys*, 2008.

[40] R. Nikolaev and G. Back. VirtuOS: An Operating System with Kernel Virtualization. In *Proc. ACM SOSP*, 2013.

[41] S. C. Park, M. K. Park, and M. G. Kang. Super-Resolution Image Reconstruction: a Technical Overview. *IEEE Signal Processing Magazine*, 2003.

[42] R. Raskar, J. Tumblin, A. Mohan, A. Agrawal, and Y. Li. Computational Photography. In *Proc. STAR Eurographics*, 2006.

[43] T. Richardson, Q. Stafford-Fraser, K. R. Wood, and A. Hopper. Virtual Network Computing. *IEEE Internet Computing*, 1998.

[44] A. P. Rifkin, M. P. Forbes, R. L. Hamilton, M. Sabrio, S. Shah, and K. Yueh. RFS Architectural Overview. In *Proc. USENIX Conference*, 1986.

[45] R. W. Scheifler and J. Gettys. The X Window System. *ACM Transactions on Graphics (TOG)*, 1986.

[46] B. K. Schmidt, M. S. Lam, and J. D. Northcutt. The Interactive Performance of SLIM: A Stateless, Thin-Client Architecture. In *Proc. ACM SOSP*, 1999.

[47] I. Schoinas, B. Falsafi, A. R. Lebeck, S. K. Reinhardt, J. R. Larus, and D. A. Wood. Fine-Grain Access Control for Distributed Shared Memory. In *Proc. ACM ASPLOS*, 1994.

[48] M. M. Swift, B. N. Bershad, and H. M. Levy. Improving the Reliability of Commodity Operating Systems. In *Proc. ACM SOSP*, 2003.

[49] Texas Instruments. Architecture Reference Manual, OMAP4430 Multimedia Device Silicon Revision 2.x. SWPU231N, 2010.

[50] B. Wilburn, N. Joshi, V. Vaish, E. Talvala, E. Antunez, A. Barth, A. Adams, M. Horowitz, and M. Levoy. High Performance Imaging Using Large Camera Arrays. *ACM Transactions on Graphics (TOG)*, 2005.

[51] R. Woodings and M. Pandey. WirelessUSB: a Low Power, Low Latency and Interference Immune Wireless Standard. In *Proc. IEEE Wireless Communications and Networking Conference (WCNC)*, 2006.

[52] L. Yuan, J. Sun, L. Quan, and H. Shum. Image Deblurring with Blurred/Noisy Image Pairs. *ACM Transactions on Graphics (TOG)*, 2007.

[53] S. Zhou, M. Stumm, K. Li, and D. Wortman. Heterogeneous Distributed Shared Memory. *IEEE Transactions on Parallel and Distributed Systems*, 1992.

Real-Time Android with RTDroid

Yin Yan, Shaun Cosgrove, Varun Anand, Amit Kulkarni,
Sree Harsha Konduri, Steven Y. Ko, Lukasz Ziarek
Department of Computer Science and Engineering
University at Buffalo, The State University of New York
{yinyan, shaunger, varunana, amitshri, sreehars, stevko, lziarek}@buffalo.edu

ABSTRACT

This paper presents RTDroid, a variant of Android that provides predictability to Android applications. Although there has been much interest in adopting Android in real-time contexts, surprisingly little work has been done to examine the suitability of Android for real-time systems. Existing work only provides solutions to traditional problems, including real-time garbage collection at the virtual machine layer and kernel-level real-time scheduling and resource management. While it is critical to address these issues, it is by no means sufficient. After all, Android is a vast system that is more than a Java virtual machine and a kernel.

Thus, this paper goes beyond existing work and examines the internals of Android. We discuss the implications and challenges of adapting Android constructs and core system services for real-time and present a solution for each. Our system is unique in that it redesigns Android's internal components, replaces Android's Java VM (Dalvik) with a real-time VM, and leverages off-the-shelf real-time OSes. We demonstrate the feasibility and predictability of our solution by evaluating it on three different platforms—an x86 PC, a LEON3 embedded board, and a Nexus S smartphone. The evaluation results show that our design can successfully provide predictability to Android applications, even under heavy load.

Categories and Subject Descriptors

C.3 [**Special-Purpose and Application-Based Systems**]: Real-time and embedded systems

General Terms

Design, Measurement, Experimentation, Performance

Keywords

Real-time Systems, Mobile Systems, Smartphones, Android

1. INTRODUCTION

There is a growing interest in adopting Android in embedded, real-time environments. A DARPA project utilizing Android is currently in development, which creates a plug and play navigation

and sensor network that can scale from personal devices up to aircraft navigators [23, 24]. The UK has recently launched a satellite equipped with an Android smartphone to explore the possibility of using a smartphone as a control system [30]. In health care, much discussion is currently ongoing as to how the medical device industry can adopt Android [1, 4, 6, 7]. In these domains, the benefits are numerous; developers can leverage Android's rich set of APIs to utilize new types of hardware such as sensors and touch screens; Android's well-supported, open-source development environment eases application development; and many applications published in online application stores give an opportunity to incorporate creative functionalities with less effort.

However, surprisingly little work has been done in actually adding real-time capabilities in Android. The current literature only provides a short overview of potential high-level system models [21] and extensions to Android's Java VM (Dalvik) that enable real-time garbage collection [13, 19]. The fundamental question of how to add real-time support to Android *as a whole system* has not been explored.

This paper presents our first step to answering that question. We analyze the real-time capabilities of Android and identify limitations. We then propose and implement redesigns of several internal components of Android to provide real-time support. We recognize, however, that Android is a vast system with many components, and that it is difficult to evaluate every aspect of Android. Thus, our goal for this paper is to identify and redesign core components central to Android, in order to support the execution of a *single* real-time application. As the rest of the paper shows, this goal alone has many hard challenges associated and still has broad applicability in utilizing smartphones in real-time domains such as control, medical, and military devices. It is also a prerequisite to supporting multiple real-time applications (*i.e.*, mixed criticality [15, 17]—the ability to execute multiple components with different criticality levels safely).

More concretely, this paper makes the following four contributions. First, we analyze the real-time capabilities of Android and present the result. In addition to the kernel and JVM layers, we examine Android's application framework, which provides programming constructs and system services to applications. We show that Android, due to its heavy reliance on unpredictable message passing mechanisms, does not provide predictable timing guarantees. We also show that system services (understandably) were not designed to support real-time.

Second, we provide an implementation that addresses the limitations discovered in our analysis. We redesign three of the core components in the application framework—a message-passing mechanism (`Looper-Handler`), the timer service (`AlarmManager`), and the sensor architecture (`SensorManager`)—to provide predictable

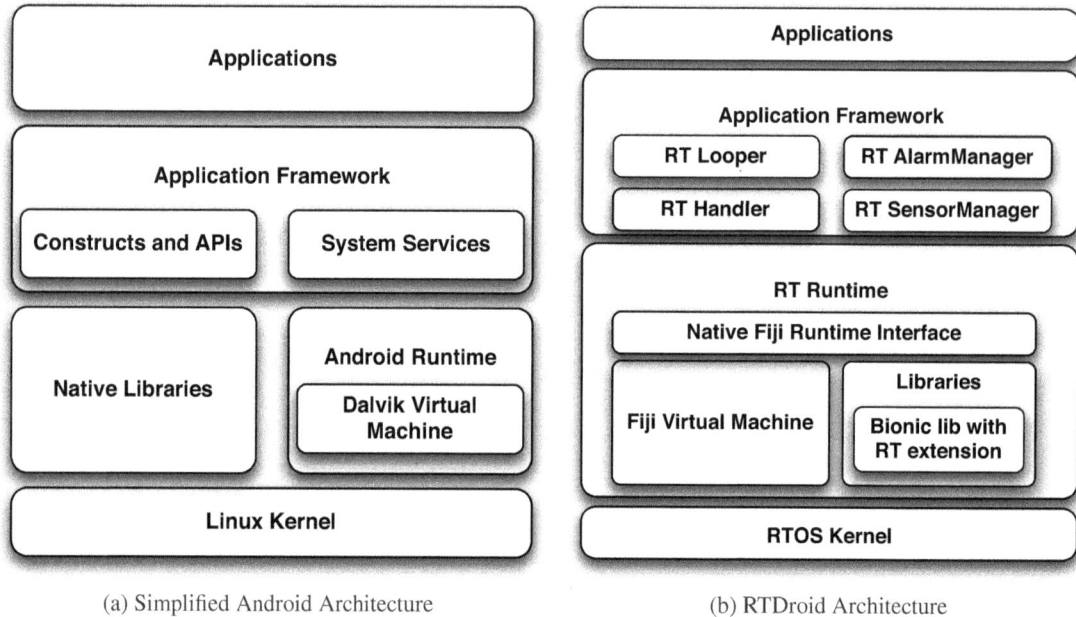

(a) Simplified Android Architecture   (b) RTDroid Architecture

Figure 1: Comparison of Simplified Android and RTDroid Architectures

timing guarantees. We have chosen these components in order to support a class of applications that perform real-time sensing such as fall detection ("man down") applications [18, 29], medical monitors, and control applications.

Third, we report our experience in replacing non-real-time building blocks (Dalvik and Linux) with real-time building blocks. We utilize the Fiji real-time VM [27] as our Java runtime and two real-time OSes (RTLinux [3, 16] and RTEMS [5]) as our kernel options. These building blocks give us a good starting point with sound lower-layer real-time guarantees. In replacing these components, we have encountered practical challenges in modifying both the JVM as well as the kernel layers. We discuss these challenges and our solutions.

Fourth, we demonstrate the real-time capabilities of our redesigns on three different platforms with varying degrees of guarantees: (1) hard real-time on a LEON3 embedded board with the RTEMS RTOS, (2) soft real-time on an x86 PC with RTLinux, and (3) soft real-time on a Nexus S smartphone with the RTLinux patch applied on an Android's version of Linux. In all three platforms, we show that our redesigns provide predictability to applications even under heavily-loaded conditions. As part of this effort, we have implemented, executed, and measured the first real-time Android application: an automatic fall detector deployed on a Nexus S smartphone and on a LEON3 development board. We show that even with hundreds of non-real-time "noise" generating threads, the application shows good timeliness and predictability.

This paper is a continuation of our previous workshop paper [32], which focused on preliminary redesigns of `Looper-Handler` and `AlarmManager`. In this paper, we explore a more comprehensive set of challenges including updated versions of `Looper-Handler` and `AlarmManager`, a redesigned real-time `SensorManager`, and a fall detector that runs on both a smartphone and a LEON3 embedded board. Our prototype presented in this paper enables the execution of a single application while providing real-time guarantees. It serves as a base system on which we will explore multi-application execution in a mixed criticality environment, which is part of our

future work discussed in Section 9. Additional performance measures, experiments, raw data, and plotting scripts are publicly available on our website: `http://rtdroid.cse.buffalo.edu`.

The rest of the paper is organized as follows. Section 2 provides an overview of our system, RTDroid. Sections 3, 4, and 5 show the limitations of three components of Android, presents our redesigns and provide a Worst-Case Execution Time (WCET) formalization for each component to algorithmically quantify an upper bound for each individual component. Section 6 reports our experience in replacing non-real-time components with real-time counterparts. Finally, Section 8 discusses our related work and Section 9 discusses our future work and conclusions.

2. OVERVIEW

In this section, we first examine the architecture of Android and discuss the existing work for real-time Android. We then explore the question of how to add real-time capabilities to Android focusing on time, memory, and resource predictability. Lastly, we present an overview of our system, RTDroid.

2.1 Background

Fig. 1a shows a simplified version of the Android architecture. The purpose of the figure is *not* to give a detailed view of Android; instead, we highlight only those components relevant to our discussion in this section.

As Fig. 1a depicts, we can divide Android into roughly three layers below the application layer: (1) the application framework layer, (2) the runtime and libraries layer, and (3) the kernel layer. Android leverages a modified Linux kernel, which does not provide any real-time features such as priority-based preemption of threads, priority inversion avoidance protocols, and priority based resource management. Previous work [13, 19] has also shown that Android's runtime and libraries provide no real-time guarantees and Dalvik's garbage collector can arbitrarily stall application threads regardless of priority, resulting in non-deterministic behavior. Thus, it is currently well-understood that the bottom layers need real-time support in order to provide a predictable platform.

However, we show in this paper that even with the proper real-time features at the kernel and VM layers, Android cannot provide real-time guarantees. This is due to the fact that the application framework layer does not provide predictability for its core constructs, allowing for arbitrary priority inversion.

Broadly speaking, the application framework layer poses two problems for real-time applications, one rooted in each of its two categories shown in Fig. 1a. The first problem lies in the category shown on the left, *constructs and APIs*, which provides programming constructs [1] and APIs that application developers can use such as `Looper`, `Handler`, and `AsyncTask`. This category poses a problem for real-time applications since the constructs do not provide any time or memory predictability as well as priority awareness. The main issue is that the latency of message delivery in these mechanisms is unpredictable; lower priority threads can unnecessarily prevent higher priority threads from making progress. In Section 3, we discuss this problem in more detail and present our solution. Section 7 demonstrates the problem experimentally.

The second problem occurs in the category shown on the right, *system services*, which provides essential system services. For example, `SensorManager` mediates access to sensors and `AlarmManager` provides system timers. The issue with these system services is that the implementation of the services does not consider real-time guarantees as a requirement. In Sections 4 and 5, we show how two core system services necessary to run a single sensing application, `AlarmManager`, and `SensorManager`, exhibit this general issue and discuss how we redesign these services for real-time support.

2.2 Overview of RTDroid

Our system, RTDroid, aims to add real-time support in Android *as a whole system*, thereby providing the ability to execute a single real-time application that leverages the built-in system services, such as `AlarmManager` and `SensorManager`. This necessitates that our system is predictable in time and memory usage as well as resource management. Our current system design targets a uni-process environment where only a single user-level process (*i.e.*, the application process) executes. However, we believe that the design is extensible to multi-core and mixed-criticality systems. Such extensions are our future work.

2.2.1 RTDroid Architecture

In order to provide real-time support in all three layers depicted in Fig. 1a, we advocate a clean-slate redesign of Android in Fig 1b. Our redesign starts from the ground up, leveraging an established RTOS (*e.g.*, RT Linux or RTEMS) and an RT JVM (*e.g.*, Fiji VM). Upon this foundation we build *Android compatibility*. In other words, our design provides a faithful illusion to an existing Android application running on our platform that it is executing on Android. This entails providing the same set of Android APIs as well as preserving their semantics for both regular Android applications and real-time applications. For real-time applications, Android compatibility means that developers can use standard Android APIs in addition to a small number of additional APIs our platform provides to support real-time features. These additional APIs provide limited Real-Time Specification for Java (RTSJ) [14] support without scoped memory. This goal of providing Android compatibility makes our architecture unique and different from potential architectures discussed previously in the literature [?], where much of the focus is on the kernel and the JVM layers.

2.2.2 Benefits of RTDroid

There are three major benefits of our clean-slate design. First, by using an RTOS and an RT JVM, we can rely on the sound design decisions already made and implemented to support real-time capabilities in these systems. Our RTDroid prototype uses Fiji VM [27], which is designed to support real-time Java programs from the ground up. Fiji VM already provides real-time functionality through static compiler checks, real-time garbage collection [28], synchronization, threading, *etc*. We note, however, that RTDroid's design is VM independent.

The second benefit of our architecture is the flexibility of adjusting the runtime model for different use cases. This is because using an RTOS and an RT JVM provides the freedom to control the runtime model. For example, we can leverage the RTEMS [5] runtime model, where one process is compiled together with the kernel for single application deployment. With this model, an application can fully utilize all the resources of the underlying hardware.Using this runtime model is not currently possible with Android, as Android runs most system services as separate processes. Simply modifying Dalvik or the OS is not enough to augment Android's runtime model; the framework layer itself must be changed.

The third benefit of our architecture is the streamlining of real-time application development. Developers can leverage the rich APIs and libraries that are already implemented and have support for various hardware components. Unlike other mobile OSes, Android excels in supporting a wide variety of hardware with different CPUs, memory capacities, screen sizes, and sensors. Android APIs make it easier to write a single application that can run on different types of hardware. Thus, Android compatibility can reduce the complexity of real-time application development.

2.2.3 Current Scope of Implementation

Our current RTDroid prototype redesigns three core Android components, `Looper` and `Handler`, `AlarmManager` and `SensorManager`. We have chosen these components due to their extensive use in existing Android applications as well as in our target applications. For example, `Handler` and `Looper` are essential to Android applications as they are used implicitly by every application, as we detail in Section 3. `AlarmManager` provides a timer service used by any application that runs periodic tasks; many real-time applications need to run periodic tasks and rely on such a service to trigger their tasks. `SensorManager` provides sensing APIs in Android, which are necessary for our target real-time sensing applications such as fall detectors as well as health monitors.

In addition to redesigning the above three components, we have also ported a subset of other Android programming components necessary to run an application, such as `Service`, `Context`, *etc*. These components do not require a redesign and RTDroid is able to leverage them wholesale. As part of our future work, we plan to increase our coverage to create a more comprehensive system.

2.2.4 Deployment Profiles

RTDroid supports three different types of deployment profiles with varying degrees of guarantees provided by the underlying platform and RTOS kernel. Not all of the deployment profiles currently support hard real-time guarantees due to their use of the RTLinux kernel and closed source drivers as we explain below.

- **Soft Real-time Smartphone:** This profile provides the loosest guarantees due to its reliance on unverified closed source

---

[1] By constructs, we mean abstract Java classes provided by the Android application framework. Application developers can extend these abstract classes to leverage advanced functionalities.

drivers and a partially preemptible RTLinux kernel as opposed to a *fully* preemptible RTLinux kernel. [2] As we detail in Section 6, the Android patch to Linux is incompatible with the RTLinux patch, which prevents us from putting the kernel into a fully-preemptible mode. As such, it is only suited for soft real-time tasks. However, most applications domains, such as medical device monitoring are soft real-time systems. In this profile, task deadlines can be missed due to jitter from the kernel or blocking from the drivers. Nevertheless, we demonstrate in Section 7 that we can still provide tight latency bounds and predictability even on this profile with RTDroid.

- **Soft Real-time Desktop:** This profile provides stricter guarantees than that of the smartphone as it leverages a fully preemptible RTLinux kernel. In this profile, we can leverage verified-and-certified drivers. However, RTLinux, even in the fully preemptible kernel is not typically used in hard real-time systems. Based on current best practices, this deployment should only be used for soft real-time systems. In this profile, deadlines can be missed due to jitter from the kernel.

- **Hard Real-time Embedded:** By moving away from RTLinux and using a certified RTOS such as RTEMS as well as a development board with certified drivers for its hardware sensors, much stricter guarantees can be provided. No deadlines will be missed due to jitter from the kernel or the drivers.

3. RT LOOPER AND RT HANDLER

In this section as well as the next two sections, we discuss how we add real-time support in the application framework layer of Android. As discussed in Section 2, the first issue that the application framework poses lies in its message-passing constructs. These constructs do not provide any predictability or priority-awareness. We detail this issue in this section and discuss how we address it in RTDroid.

3.1 Background and Challenges

Android provides a set of constructs that facilitate communication between different entities, *e.g.*, threads and processes. There are four such constructs—Handler, Looper, Binder, and Messenger. Since any typical Android application uses these constructs, we need to support these constructs properly in a real-time context.

Among these four constructs, Looper and Handler are the most critical constructs for our target scenario of running a single real-time sensing application. This is because Binder and Messenger are inter-process communication constructs, while Looper and Handler are inter-thread communication constructs. Further, Looper and Handler are used not only explicitly by an application, but also *implicitly* by *all* applications. This is due to the fact that Android's application container, ActivityThread, uses Looper and Handler to control the execution of an application. When an application needs to make transitions between its execution states (*e.g.*, start, stop, resume, *etc.*), ActivityThread uses Looper and Handler to signal necessary actions.

Fig. 2 shows how Looper and Handler work. Looper is a per-thread message loop that Android's application framework implements. Its job is to maintain a message queue and dispatch each message to the corresponding Handler that can process the

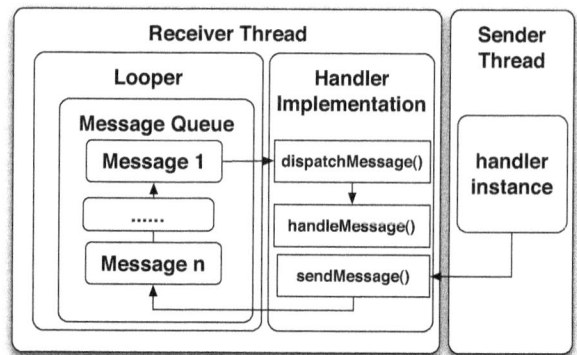

Figure 2: The Use of Looper and Handler

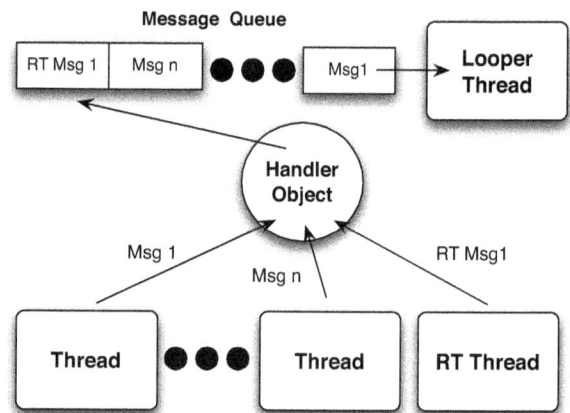

Figure 3: The thread in which the looper executes processes the messages sent through this handler object in the order in which they are received.

message. The developer of the application provides the processing logic for a message by implementing Handler's handleMessage(). A Handler instance is shared between two threads to send and receive messages.

The Looper and Handler mechanism raises a question for real-time applications when there are multiple threads with different priorities sending messages simultaneously. In Android, there are two ways that Looper and Handler process messages. By default, they process messages in the order in which they were received. Additionally, a sending thread can specify a message processing time, in which case Looper and Handler will process the message at the specified time. In both cases, however, the processing of a message is done regardless of the priority of the sending thread or the receiving thread. Consider if multiple user-defined threads send messages to another thread. If a real-time (*i.e.*, high-priority) thread sends a message through a Handler, its message will not be processed until the Looper dispatches every other message prior to its message in the queue regardless of the sender's priority as seen in Fig. 3. The situation is exacerbated by the fact that Android can re-arrange messages in a message queue if there are messages with specific processing times. For example, suppose that there are a number of messages sent by non-real-time (*i.e.*, low-priority) threads in a queue received before a message sent by a real-time thread. While processing those messages, any number of low-priority threads can send messages with specific times. If those times fall within the

---

[2] With a fully preemptible kernel, all parts of the kernel become preemptible by a high priority thread.

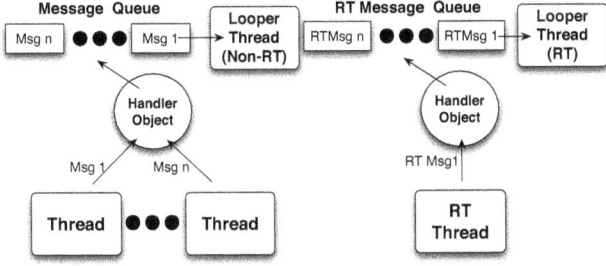

Figure 4: An Example of `Looper` and `Handler` in RTDroid. Each message has a priority and is stored in a priority queue. Processing of messages is also done by priority. The example shows one high-priority thread and multiple non-real-time threads.

processing time window for non-real-time messages, the real-time message will get delayed further by non-real-time messages.

3.2 Redesign

To mitigate the issues mentioned, we redesign `Looper` and `Handler` in two ways. First, we assign a priority to each message sent by a thread. We currently support two policies for priority assignment. These policies are *priority inheritance*, where a message inherits its sender's priority, and *priority inheritance + specified* where a sender can specify the message's priority in relation to other messages it sends.

Second, we create multiple priority queues to store incoming messages according to their priorities. We then associate one `Looper` and `Handler` for each queue to process each message according to its priority. Fig. 4 shows our new implementation for `Looper` and `Handler`. Since we now process each message according to its sender's priority, messages sent by lower priority threads do not delay the messages sent by higher priority threads. For memory predictability, queues can be statically configured in size.

3.3 Worst-Case Execution Time

We now formally show how our new design provides predictability. The worst-case execution time is the best metric for this purpose as it gives the upper bound on execution time. To understand the worst-case execution characteristics of the Real-time `Looper` and `Handler` we must reason about how the constructs process a series of messages and execute each message's callback function. We define T_i^j to be the ith message issued by the application from a thread with priority j. The messages are passed into a real-time `Looper` that has the same priority as the messages and then they are enqueued in a `MessageQueue`. The time cost for handling the ith message in priority level j is shown as S_i^j in Equation (1):

$$S_i^j = \sum_{l=0}^{i} (h_l^j + deq(T_l^j)),\qquad(1)$$

Where h_l^j is the cost of time to handle T_l^j and $deq(T_l^j)$ is the cost of dequeuing from the message queue.

To reason about the worst-case execution time for a message m, we must first calculate the processing time for all messages that have priorities greater than or equal to the priority of message m, shown in Equation (2):

$$phase_0(T_i^j) = \sum_{p>j} S_{last}^p + S_i^j.\qquad(2)$$

Where *last* is the last message in the message queue with priority p that is greater than j. Since the system also handles new incoming

messages, which may have a priority greater than or equal [3] to that of m, we must also define the system in terms of a message arrival rate R for a given priority p.

We divide the amount of time for the system to handle m into a number of phases. During $phase_0$, the system handles all of the messages in the priority queue which are greater than or equal to the priority of m as shown in Equation 2. While handling the message in the current phase, new messages arrive at a given rate per priority level, the system must then handle each of the new messages with priority greater than or equal to m before handling message m.

In order to quantify the number of messages in each priority queue, we define a sending rate for each group of clients with priority p, R_p. When $n \geq 1$, then worst-case handling time is integrating all of the handling times for messages that are greater than or equal to the priority of message m, as shown in Equation (3):

$$phase_n(T_i^j) = \sum_{p\geq j}^{phase_{n-1}(T_i^j)*R_p} \sum_{i=0} \left(h_i^p + deq(T_i^j) + enq(T_i^j)\right).$$
$$(3)$$

Where $enq(T_i^j)$ is the cost of enqueuing in the message queue.

The LHS represents the upper bound of the time cost for message handling for `phase`$_n$, the RHS represents the total time cost for handling all messages that arrive during `phase`$_{n-1}$; The outer summation is the time to handle each priority level and the inner summation is the integration of the time to handle all of the same priority messages that have arrived in the phase$_{n-1}$. phase$_{n-1}(T_i^j)$ represents the time spent in previous phase, and when multiplied by the rate R_p gives the number of messages currently in each priority based queue. The recursion ends when $phase_n$ is smaller than the time unit of R_p. Thus, the summation of all phases is the actual worst-case execution time for handling message, m as shown in Equation (4):

$$WCET(T_i^j) = phase_0(T_i^j) + phase_1(T_i^j)$$
$$+ ... + phase_{n-1}(T_i^j) + phase_n(T_i^j). \quad(4)$$

Notice, the system is only well defined (*i.e.* able to process messages with real-time guarantees) if the worst-case execution time for each message is less than the deadline for processing that message relative to its arrival time and if phase$_n$ is less than phase$_{n-1}$.

4. RT ALARM MANAGER

As mentioned in Section 2, the second issue that Android's application framework layer poses for real-time support is that system services do not provide real-time guarantees. Since Android mediates all access to its core system functionalities through a set of system services, it is critical to provide real-time guarantees in the system services. Just to name a few, these services include `SensorManager` that mediates all sensor access and data acquisition; and `AlarmManager` that provides a timer service.

The presence of these system services raises two questions. First, in our target scenario of running a single real-time application, there is no need to run system services as separate processes; rather it is more favorable to run the application and the system services as a single process to improve the overall efficiency of the system. Then the question is how to redesign the system service architecture in our platform in order to avoid creating separate processes

---

[3]Although our `Looper` and `Handler` uses a FIFO priority queue, we are abstracting the complexities of the data-structure algorithm, such as queuing and dequeuing costs, in the calculation and thus creating a generalized equation applicable to all our RT redesigns.

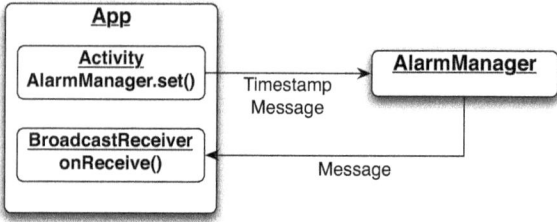

Figure 5: An Example Flow of `AlarmManager`. An application uses `AlarmManager.set()` to register an alarm. When the alarm triggers, the `AlarmManager` sends a message back to the application, and the application's callback (`BroadcastReceiver.onReceive()` in the example) gets executed.

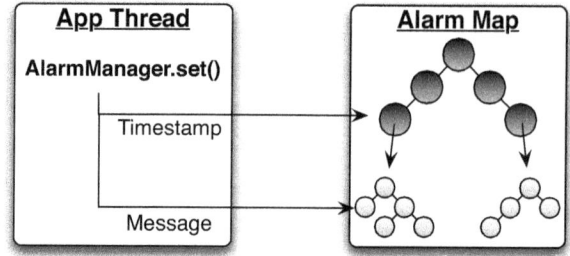

Figure 6: The Implementation of Alarm Execution on RTDroid. The tree colored black at the top maintains timestamps. The trees colored gray are per-timestamp trees maintaining actual alarm messages to be delivered.

while preserving the underlying behavior of Android. Second, as we show in this section and the next section, the internals of these system services do not consider real-time support as a design requirement.

To answer these two questions, we redesign two of the system services—`AlarmManager` and `SensorManager`. In this section we first show how we redesign `AlarmManager` to provide real-time guarantees. In the next section, we discuss our `SensorManager` redesign.

4.1 Background and Challenges

`AlarmManager` receives timer registration requests from applications and sends "timer triggered" messages to these applications when its timer fires. Since real-time applications frequently rely on periodic and sporadic tasks, it is important to provide real-time guarantees in `AlarmManager`.

Fig. 5 shows how `AlarmManager` works, including alarm registration and alarm delivery. An IPC call, with a message [4] and its execution time, is made to the `AlarmManager` every time an application registers an alarm. When the the alarm triggers at the specified time, the `AlarmManager` sends a message back to the application, and the associated callback is executed. The issue with `AlarmManager` is that it provides no guarantee on when or in what order alarm messages are delivered, hence does not provide any timing guarantee or priority-awareness.

4.2 Redesign

We redesign both alarm registration and delivery mechanisms to support predictable alarm delivery. For alarm registration, we use red-black trees to maintain alarms as shown in Fig. 6. This means that we can make the registration process predictable based on the complexity of red-black tree operations, *i.e.*, the longest path of a tree is no longer than twice the shortest path of the tree. We use one red-black tree for storing timestamps and pointers to per-timestamp red-black trees. Per-timestamp trees are leveraged to order alarms with the same timestamp by their sender's priority. Thus, our alarm registration process is essentially one insert operation to the timestamp tree and another insert operation to a per-timestamp tree. By organizing the alarms based on senders' priorities, we guarantee that an alarm message for a low priority thread does not delay an alarm message for a high priority thread. Expired alarms are discarded. Note that this ensures that low priority threads whose alarm

registration rate exceeds the alarm delivery capacity of the system cannot prevent a high priority alarm from being triggered.

For alarm delivery, we create an `AlarmManager` thread and assign the highest priority for timely delivery of alarm messages. This thread replaces the original multi-process message passing architecture of Android. It wakes up whenever an application inserts a new alarm into our red-black trees, then it schedules a new thread at the specified time for the alarm. We associate the application's callback for the alarm message with this new thread. For precise execution timing of this callback thread, we implement Asynchronous Event Handlers (AEH) that Real-Time Specification for Java (RTSJ) [14] specifies the interface for.

We have implemented two versions for AEH. The first is a per-thread AEH implementation used in our workshop paper [32], which creates one thread per handler to process a given event type. This simple mechanism is efficient in handling low numbers of events, but can create memory and processing pressure due to large number of handling threads if a large number of events occur within the same time period. Although most Android applications do not register alarms at a frequency that would cause problems, our system must be resilient to such behavior nonetheless.

The second mechanism leverages a thread pool with a statically configured number of threads, which reduces the number of threads that we need to create. Our implementation is based on Kim *et al.*'s proposed model [20] and is similar to how the jRate [10] implements RTSJ's AEH. The benefit of this implementation is a hard, statically known limit on the number of threads to handle asynchronous events. There is lower memory usage due to less threads being created and the output is deterministic with a well-known, predictable behavior [10].

4.3 Worst-Case Execution Time

The worst-case execution scenario for `AlarmManager` is similar to that discussed for the `Looper` and `Handler` in Section. 3.3. The upper bound of delivery and execution of an alarm a consists of 1) the delivery and execution of all alarms that have been registered with priority greater or equal to that of a, 2) the delivery and execution of all newly registered alarms with priority greater or equal to a based on a per priority rate of alarm delivery and registration. The equation of WCET for `AlarmManager` is the same pattern as shown in Equation (1), (2), (3), (4), but couched in terms of alarm processing instead of message delivery.

- T_i^j represents the ith alarm registered by application with priority j.
- S_i^j represents the time cost for handling the ith alarm in priority level j.

---

[4]This message is associated with a callback for the application which gets executed when the message is delivered.

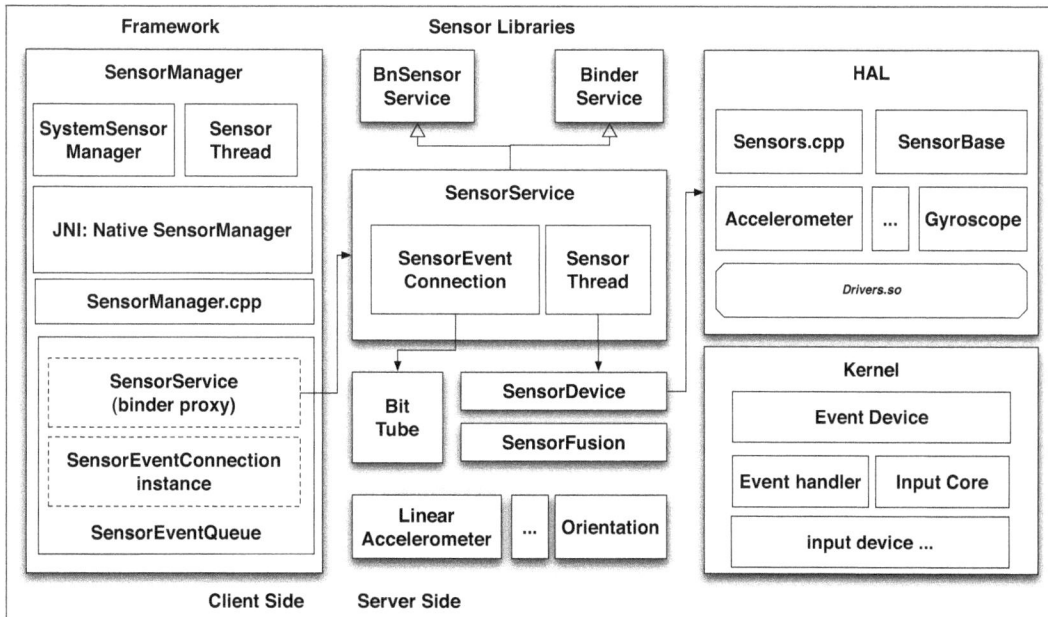

Figure 7: Android Sensor Architecture

- h_i^j is the cost of time to execute the alarm T_i^j.
- *last* is the last alarm in priority p that is greater than j.
- enq(T_i^j) is the cost of alarm registration.
- deq(T_i^j) is the cost of alarm delivery.

5. RT SENSOR ARCHITECTURE

Another system service we redesign in RTDroid is `SensorManager`. Modern mobile devices are equipped with many sensors such as accelerometers, gyroscopes, *etc*. Android, mainly through its `SensorManager`, provides a set of APIs to acquire sensor data. This section examines the current sensor architecture of Android and presents our new design for real-time support.

5.1 Background and Challenges

On Android, sensors are broadly classified into two categories. The first category is *hardware* sensors, which are the sensors that have a corresponding hardware device. For example, accelerometer and gyroscope belong to this category. The second category is *software* sensors, which are "virtual" sensors that exist purely in software. Android fuses different hardware sensor events to provide software sensor events. For example, Android provides an orientation sensor in software. On Nexus S, Android 4.2 has 6 hardware sensors and 7 software sensors.

These sensors are available to applications through `SensorManager` APIs. An application registers sensor event listeners through the provided APIs. These listeners provide the application's callbacks that the Android framework calls whenever there is any requested sensor event available. When registering a listener, an application can also specify its desired delivery rate. The Android framework uses this as a hint when delivering sensor events.

Internally, there are four layers involved in the overall sensor architecture—the kernel, HAL, `SensorService`, and `SensorManager`. Fig. 7 shows a simplified architecture.

1. **Kernel:** The main job of the kernel layer is to pull hardware sensor events and populate the Linux `/dev` file system to make the events accessible from the user space. Each sen-

sor hooks to the circuit board through an I^2C bus and registers itself as an *input device*.

2. **HAL:** The HAL layer provides sensor hardware abstractions by defining a common interface for each hardware sensor type. Hardware vendors provide actual implementations underneath.

3. `SensorService`: `SensorService` converts raw sensor data to more meaningful data using application-friendly data structures. This involves three steps. First, `SensorService` polls the Linux `/dev` file system to read raw sensor input events. Second, it composites both hardware and software sensor events from the raw sensor input events. For hardware sensors, it just reformats the data; for software sensors, it combines different sources to calculate software sensor events via sensor fusion. Finally, it writes each sensor event to the `SensorEventQueue` via `SensorEventConnection`.

4. **Framework Layer:** `SensorManager` delivers the sensor events by reading the data from `SensorEventQueue` and invoking the registered application listeners to deliver sensor events.

There are two issues that the current architecture has in providing predictable sensing. First, there is no priority support in the sensor event delivery mechanism since all sensor events go through the same `SensorEventQueue`. When there are multiple threads with different priorities, the event delivery of lower-priority threads can delay the event delivery of higher-priority threads. Second, the primary event delivery mechanisms poll and buffer at the boundary of different layers (*e.g.*, between the kernel and `SensorService` and between `SensorService` and `SensorManager`) by use of message passing constructs. Android does not provide any guarantee on how long it takes to deliver events through these mechanisms.

5.2 Redesign

We redesign the sensor architecture for RTDroid to address the two issues mentioned above. Our design is inspired by event pro-

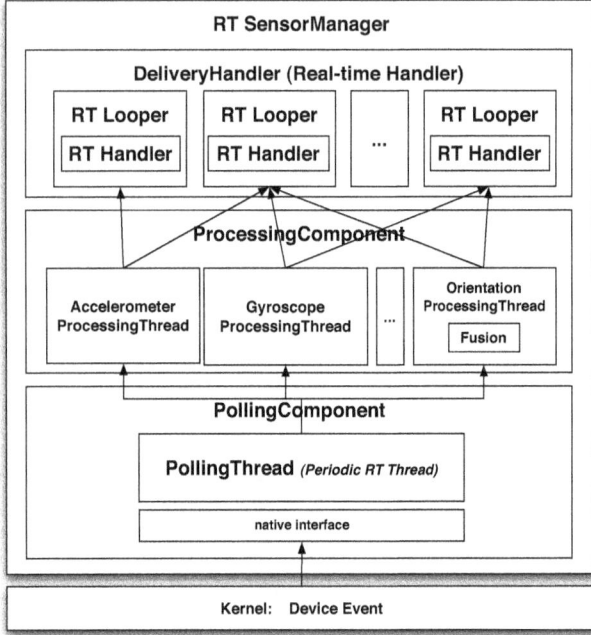

Figure 8: RTDroid Sensor Architecture

cessing architectures used for Web servers [26, 31]. We first describe the architecture and discuss how we address the two problems with our new architecture.

As shown in Fig. 8, there are multiple threads specialized for different tasks. At the bottom, there is a *polling thread* that periodically reads raw sensor data out of the kernel. This polling thread communicates with multiple *processing threads*. We allocate one thread per sensor type as shown in Fig. 8, *e.g.*, one thread for accelerometer, one thread for gyroscope, and one thread for the orientation sensor. The main job of these processing threads is to perform raw sensor data processing for each sensor type. For example, a processing thread for a hardware sensor reformats raw sensor data using an application-friendly format, and a processing thread for a software sensor performs sensor fusion. Once the raw sensor data is properly processed, each processing thread notifies the *delivery thread* whose job is to create a new thread that executes the sensor event listener callback registered by an application thread. To provide predictable delivery, we use notification, not polling, for our event delivery except in the boundary between the kernel and the polling thread. We provide additional predictability through our priority inheritance mechanism described next.

We address the two issues mentioned earlier by priority inheritance. When an application thread of priority p registers a listener for a sensor, say, gyroscope, then the processing thread for gyroscope inherits the same priority p. If there are multiple application threads that register for the same gyroscope, then the gyroscope processing thread inherits the priority of the highest-priority application thread. In addition, when the delivery thread creates a new thread that executes a sensor event listener callback, this new thread also inherits the original priority p of the application thread. We assign the highest priority available in the system to the polling thread to ensure precise timing for data pulling.

This combined use of event-based processing threads and priority inheritance has two implications. First, when an application

thread registers a listener for a sensor, we effectively create a new, isolated event delivery path from the polling thread to the listener. Second, this newly created path inherits the priority of the original application thread. This means that we assign the priority of the application thread to the *whole event delivery path*.

5.3 Worst-Case Execution Time

The worst-case execution scenario for `SensorManager` is slightly different than what we have discussed in Section 3.3 and 4.3. The upper bound for delivery of the sensor event to a sensor listener, l, consists of three parts: (1) the time cost of the system delivery the sensor event to all sensor listeners that registered a listener that are greater or equal to the priority of l, (2) recursively integrate the time cost for register and deliver of the sensor data for the new higher-priority listener arriving at a per priority rate, and (3) the time cost for polling the data from each sensor kernel module. The WCET equation for `SensorManager` is in the same fashion as previously defined in Equation (1), (2), (3), (4), and includes the sensor data polling cost as shown in in Equation. 5, 6:

$$phase_0(T_i^j) = \sum_{p \geq j} P_j(sensor_e) + \sum_{p > j} S_{last}^p + S_i^j \qquad (5)$$

$$phase_n(T_i^j) = \sum_{p \geq j} \sum_{i=0}^{phase_{n-1}(T_i^j)*R_p} \left(h_i^p + deq(T_i^j) + enq(T_i^j) \right). \qquad (6)$$

- T_i^j represents the ith sensor listener in application with priority j.
- S_i^j represent the time cost to execute the ith callback of sensor listener in priority level j.
- h_i^j is the amount of time to execute the callback of sensor listener of T_i^j.
- $deq(T_i^j)$ is the cost of listener registration.
- *last* is the sensor listener in priority p that is greater than j.
- $P_j(sensor_e)$ is the cost of sensor data polling.

6. REAL-TIME BUILDING BLOCKS

In this section, we report our experience in replacing non-real-time building blocks (Dalvik and Linux) with off-the-shelf real-time counterparts (Fiji VM and RTOSes). As mentioned earlier, we support three deployment profiles, an x86 PC environment, an embedded environment with a LEON3 development board, and an ARM-based smartphone environment with a Nexus S smartphone. The x86 and the LEON3 environments do not require any more than replacing the non-real-time kernel with either real-time Linux kernel (by applying an RT-Preempt patch, *i.e.*, RTLinux) or the real-time RTEMS kernel. The same strategy, however, does not work for the smartphone environment because Android has introduced extensive changes in the kernel that are not compatible with RTLinux patches. Thus, we first briefly describe our x86 and LEON3 environments. We then report our experience with the smartphone environment in detail.

6.1 x86 PC and LEON3

For the x86 environment, we apply an RTLinux patch (patch-3.4.45-rt60) to Linux 3.4.45, and use Fiji as the real-time VM. Fiji already runs on RTLinux, thus it did not require any additional effort. This configuration represents our soft real-time deployment. Tighter bounds are provided as RTLinux makes the kernel fully preemptible. Similarly, we can introspect the drivers on the machine to guarantee their timeliness or leverage off-the-shelf drivers that have already been vetted.

To create the LEON3 environment, we use a LEON3 embedded board, GR-XC6S-LX75, manufactured by Gaisler. We then use RTEMS as the real-time kernel and Fiji as the real-time VM. RTEMS has native support for LEON3 and Fiji already supports RTEMS. This configuration represents our hard real-time embedded board deployment, avoiding the issues that plague RTLinux and closed source drivers. The LEON3 manufacturers provide drivers that have previously been certified for automotive, aerospace, and civilian aviation.

In order to test the `SensorManager` on the LEON3 system, we have designed and implemented an accelerometer daughter board as well as the associated RTEMS compliant driver.

6.2 Nexus S Smartphone

Unfortunately, the same approach is not adequate for executing real-time applications on an Android phone. This is mainly due to the incompatibilities between Android and the real-time building blocks in the kernel layer as well as in Android's C library, Bionic. The following are the main challenges to integration.

6.2.1 Bionic

Android does not utilize glibc as the core C library, instead it uses its own library called Bionic [12]. Bionic is a significantly simplified, optimized, light-weight C library specifically design for resource constrained devices with low frequency CPUs and limited main memory. Its architectural targets are only ARM and x86.

Bionic becomes a problem when replacing Dalvik with Fiji; this is because it does not support the real-time extensions for Pthreads and mutexes, which are required by Fiji (or any other real-time Java VM). In addition, it is not POSIX-compliant. Thus, we have modified Bionic to include all necessary POSIX compliant real-time interfaces. This includes all the real-time extensions for Pthreads and mutexes.

6.2.2 Incompatible Kernel Patches

Android has introduced a significant amount of changes specializing the Linux kernel for Android, e.g., low memory killer, wakelock, binder, logger, etc. Due to these changes, automatic patching of an Android kernel with an RTLinux patch is not possible, requiring a manually applied RTLinux patch.

Even after manual patching, however, we have discovered that we are still not able to get a fully-preemptible kernel which can provide tighter latency bounds. The reason is simply that Android's changes are not designed with full preemption in mind. We are currently investigating this issue and it is likely that this is an engineering task. Nevertheless, we are not aware of any report of a fully-preemptible Android kernel.

6.2.3 Non-Real-Time Kernel Features

During our initial testing and experimentation, we have discovered that there are two kernel features that are not real-time friendly. They are the *out of memory killer* (OOM killer) [2] and *CPUFreq governors* [11]. The OOM killer is triggered when there is not enough space for memory allocation. It scans all pages for each process to verify if the system is truly out of memory. It then selects one process and kills it. We have found out that this causes other threads and processes to stop for an arbitrary long time, creating unpredictable spikes in latency. For our target scenario of running a single real-time application, the OOM killer is not only unnecessary, but a source of missed real-time task deadlines. Memory management is provided by Fiji VM's Schism, which is a real-

time, fragmentation tolerant GC [28]. It is therefore, critical to disable OOM killer.

CPUFreq governors offer dynamic CPU frequency scaling by changing the frequency scaling policies. Android uses this to balance between phone performance and battery usage. The problem is that when a CPUFreq governor changes the frequency, it affects the execution time of all running threads, again introducing jitter in the system. Moreover, frequency scaling is not taken into consideration when scheduling threads. The result is missed task deadlines and unpredictable spikes in latency. Although not the focus of our experiments, we note that real-time scheduling that takes voltage scaling into consideration has been vetted for hardware architectures with specialized mechanisms for predictability [9].

In our experiments, we show the behavior of RTDroid with two governors—the "ondemand" governor, which dynamically changes the CPU frequency depending on the current usage, and the "performance" governor, which sets the CPU frequency to the highest frequency possible. We leave it as our future work to handle dynamic frequency scaling. For example, we can apply an existing method for worse case execution time analysis [22] to validate the hardware and leverage this timing analysis to modify the kernel and VM schedulers appropriately.

7. EXPERIMENTAL RESULTS

To measure and validate our prototype of RTDroid, we tested our implementation on three system level configurations, each of which represents one of our target deployments discussed in Section 2.2.4. The first configuration utilizes an Intel Core 2 Duo 1.86 GHz Processor with 2GB of RAM. For precise timing measurements, we disabled one of the cores prior to running the experiments. The second configuration is a Nexus S phone equipped with a 1 GHz Cortex-A8 and 512 MB RAM along with 16GB of internal storage and an accelerometer, gyro, proximity, and compass sensors running Android OS v4.1.2 (Jelly Bean) patched with RT Linux v.3.0.50. For the third configuration we leveraged a GR-XC6S-LX75 LEON3 development board running RTEMS version 4.9.6. The board's Xilinx Spartan 6 Family FPGA was flashed with a modified LEON3 [5] configuration running at 50Mhz. The development board has an 8MB flash PROM and 128MB of PC133 SDRAM. We present observed, end-to-end worst-case execution times as it is difficult to provide the latency breakdown for the whole system without specialized timing hardware. We therefore focus on showing the timeliness of our system on a series of stress tests. We couple the worst observed latency/processing time for each experiment with the algorithmic characterization of each component, individually presented in Sections 3.3, 4.3, and 5.3.

We have designed and developed a daughter board with interface circuitry based on an MMA8452Q triple axis accelerometer. We have developed an RTEMS driver for the accelerometer and integrated it into our RTEMS build.

Due to space constraints, we only show a subset of our experimental results. All of our results are available through our website: `http://rtdroid.cse.buffalo.edu`.

7.1 RT Looper and RT Handler

To measure the effectiveness of our prototype, we have constructed an experiment that leveraged RT Looper and RT Handler. Our microbenchmark creates one real-time task with a 100 ms period that sends a high-priority message. To measure the predictability of the system, we calculate the latency of processing the

---

[5]The LEON3 core was reconfigured to allow access to a specific I^2C bus so that the accelerometer could be connected to the board.

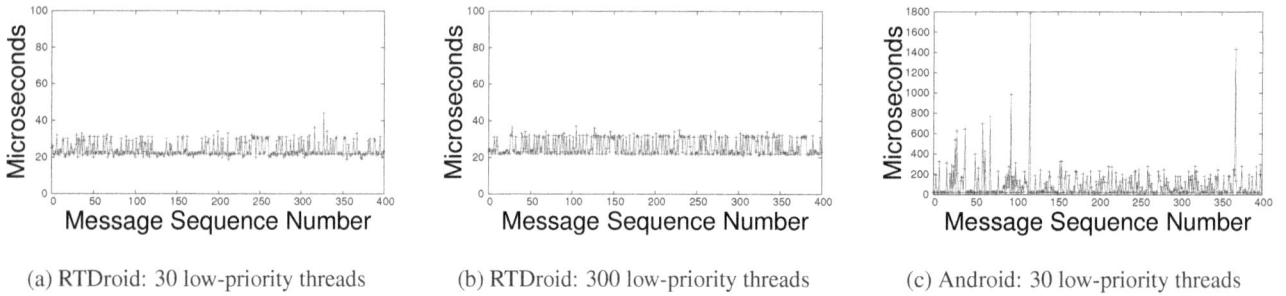

(a) RTDroid: 30 low-priority threads   (b) RTDroid: 300 low-priority threads   (c) Android: 30 low-priority threads

Figure 9: The observed raw latency of `Looper` and `Handler` on x86. Please note graph (c) has a different Y-axis.

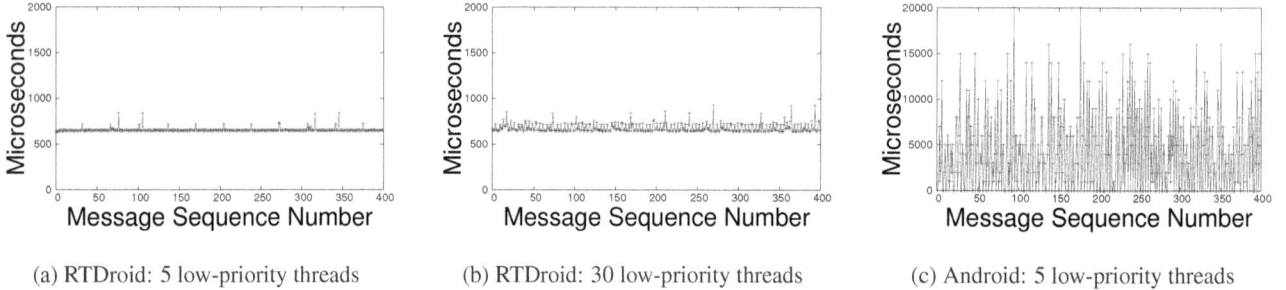

(a) RTDroid: 5 low-priority threads   (b) RTDroid: 30 low-priority threads   (c) Android: 5 low-priority threads

Figure 10: The observed raw latency of `Looper` and `Handler` on LEON3 Please note graph (c) has a different Y-axis.

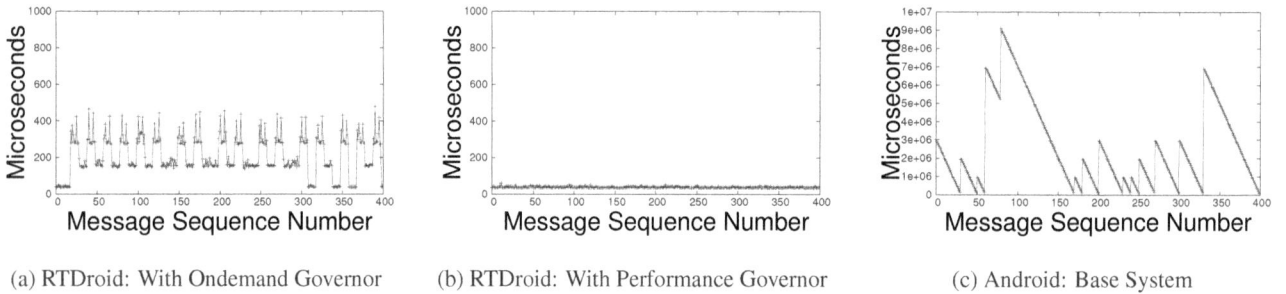

(a) RTDroid: With Ondemand Governor   (b) RTDroid: With Performance Governor   (c) Android: Base System

Figure 11: The observed raw latency of `Looper` and `Handler` on Nexus S. Please note graph (c) has a different Y-axis

message, determined by two timestamps. The first timestamp is taken in the real-time thread prior to sending the message. This timestamp is the data encoded within the message. The second timestamp is taken within the `RT Handler` responsible for processing this message after the message has been received and the appropriate callback invoked. The difference between these two timestamps is the message's latency.

In addition, the experiments include a number of low-priority threads which also leverage `RT Looper` and `RT Handler`. These threads have a period of 10 ms and send 10 messages during each period. To compare the `Looper` and `Handler` designs between RTDroid and Android, we have ported the relevant portion of Android's application framework, including `Looper` and `Handler`, so we can compile and run our benchmark application on x86. Thus, on Android, all threads, regardless of their priorities, use the same `Looper` and `Handler`—this is the default behavior. On RTDroid, each thread uses a different pair of `RT Looper` and `RT Handler` according to its priority—this is opaque to the application developer and handled automatically by the system.

To measure the predictability of our constructs under a loaded system, we increase the number of low-priority threads. We have executed each experiment for 40 seconds, corresponding to 400 releases of the high-priority message, and have a hard stop at 50 seconds. We measure latency only for the high-priority messages and

scale the number of low-priority threads up to the point where the total number of messages sent by the low-priority threads exceeds the ability to process those messages within the 40 second execution window. On both Intel Core 2 Duo and Nexus S, we have varied the number of low-priority threads in increments of 10 from 0-300. Considering memory and other limitations of our resource constrained embedded board, we have run the experiments increasing the low priority threads in increments of 5 from 5-30 when running on the LEON3 board.

Fig. 9 and Fig. 10 demonstrates the consistent latency of our `RT Looper` and `RT Handler` implementation. On the desktop, we observe most of the latency for messaging is between 22 μs and 50 μs with any number of threads, and the variance is around 20 μs from the lowest to the highest latency in any given run. The worst observed latency variance is 26 μs. This degree of variance on the system is attributed to context switch costs and scheduling queue contention. On the LEON3 development board, the result shows a similar pattern. In contrast, the huge variance of Android on both platforms clearly indicate its inability to provide real-time guarantees.

Fig. 11 shows the results on Nexus S. We run two series of experiments, one with the ondemand governor and the other one with the performance governor. It was observed that the latency of the tests with the ondemand governor decreases with an increasing number

282

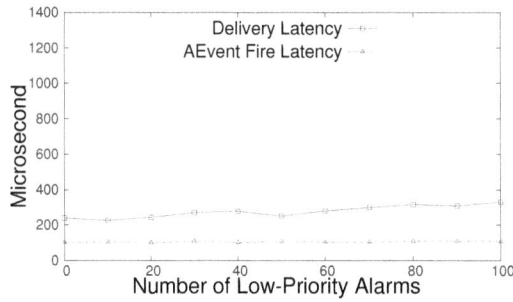

(a) RTDroid: Per Thread AEH

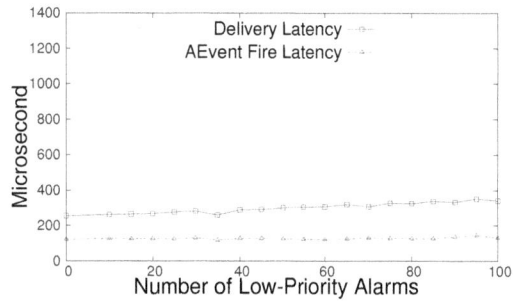

(b) RTDroid: Thread Pool AEH

Figure 12: RTSJ's AEH implementation - Per Thread vs Thread Pool on x86.

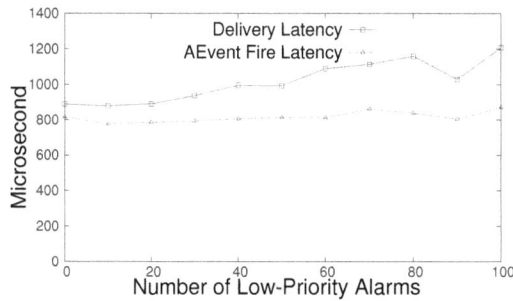

(a) RTDroid: Per Thread AEH

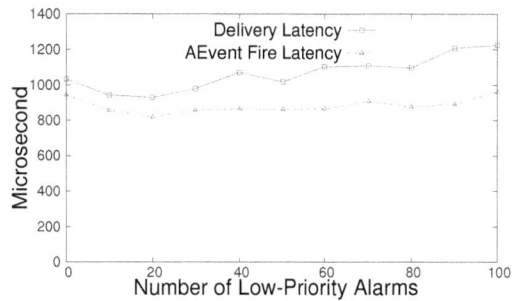

(b) RTDroid: Thread Pool AEH

Figure 13: RTSJ's AEH implementation - Per Thread vs Thread Pool on Nexus S.

of low-priority threads. This is due to the extra load on the system, which results in the CPU's frequency being increased by the ondemand governor. The tests with the performance governor show a consistent latency in any given run, since the CPU frequency does not change. On the other hand, the latency variation from Android is several orders of magnitude greater than that of RTDroid as shown in Fig. 11a.

7.2 RT AlarmManager

Measuring the performance of the `RT AlarmManager` was done with an experiment consisting of scheduling of a single high-priority alarm at the current system time + 40 ms, while increasing the number of low-priority alarms scheduled at the exact same time. We measure two types of latency for the experiment: 1) the entire latency of the alarm delivery (*Delivery latency*), which is the difference between the scheduled time and actual execution time of the high-priority alarm, and 2) the latency of the asynchronous event fire (*AEvent fire latency*), which is the difference between the scheduled time and the actual firing time by the `AlarmManager`. The difference between the two types of latency shows how long it takes for the system to deliver an alarm from the `AlarmManager` to the application. We run the experiment on all three platforms. These results show the timing and latency of the alarm execution process and indicate that the `RT AlarmManager` is efficient at prioritizing high-priority alarms and scheduling them at their specified time.

As mentioned in Section 4, we have implemented two techniques for alarm management in `RT AlarmManager`—one with a per-thread AEH implementation used in our previous workshop paper [32] and another implemented with a thread pool. We show the predictability of RTDroid with each technique by using threads ranging from 5-100 and a thread granularity of 10. To induce queueing in the thread pool implementation, only 3 worker threads are allocated for the thread pool.

7.2.1 x86 Desktop

Fig. 12 shows the results of the per-thread AEH and the thread pool AEH experiments running on RTLinux. The latency of the entire alarm delivery for per-thread AEH on the x86 is bounded from 220 μs to 331 μs with a 32 μs standard deviation. The *Asynchronous event fire* latency is consistently around 105 μs. The thread pool implementation exhibits a slightly slower performance with the alarm delivery bounded from 255 μs to 355 μs with a 29 μs standard deviation. This small performance drop is expected and caused by alarm queuing in the thread pool itself.

7.2.2 Nexus S Smartphone

Fig. 13 demonstrates the results with the same experimental scenario on the Nexus S smartphone. It shows the same pattern as the x86 does, but with a lager value. This is not surprising considering the hardware difference between X86 and smartphone in terms of the type and frequency of their CPU and available memory. On av-

283

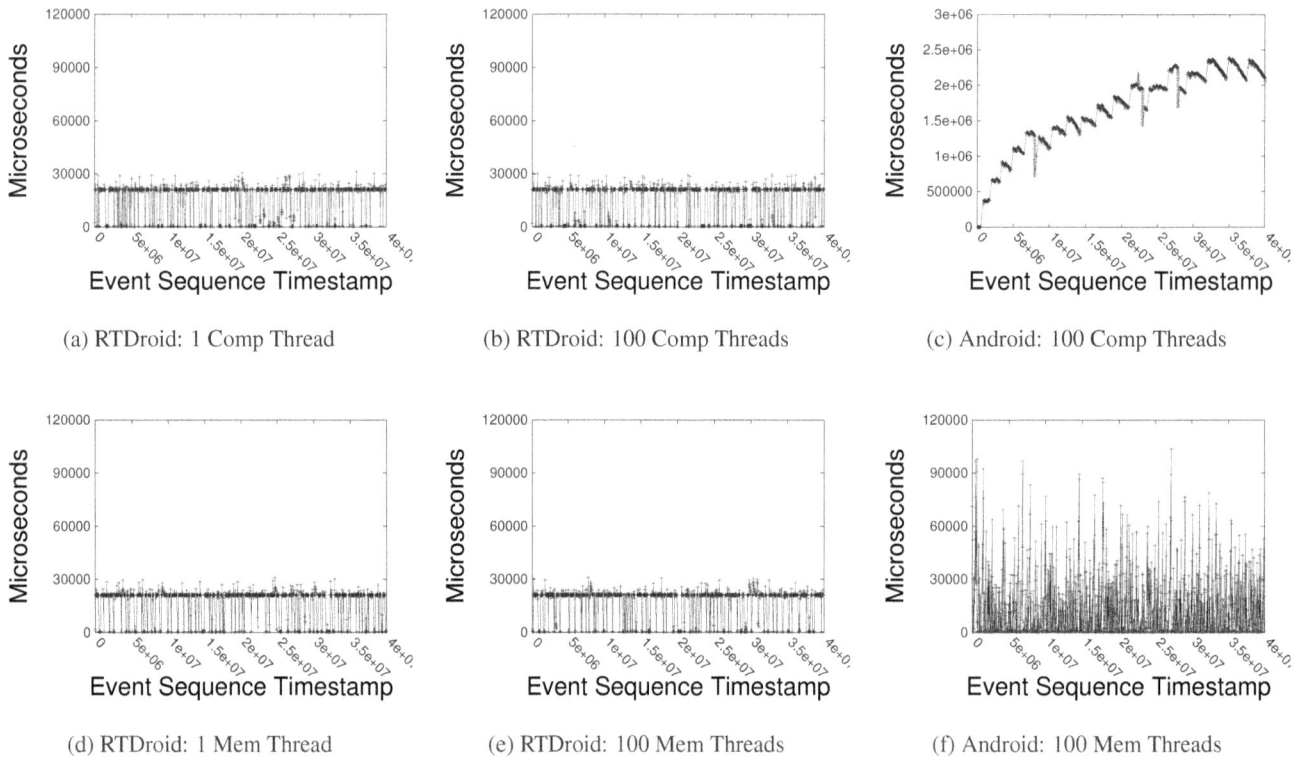

| (a) RTDroid: 1 Comp Thread | (b) RTDroid: 100 Comp Threads | (c) Android: 100 Comp Threads |
| (d) RTDroid: 1 Mem Thread | (e) RTDroid: 100 Mem Threads | (f) Android: 100 Mem Threads |

Figure 14: Memory and Computation stress test for the Fall Detection Application on Nexus S.

erage, the thread pool shows less than 1 ms latency and the worst observed case is 1.2 ms for both of the the per-thread AEH and thread pool implementations, with 108 μs and 92 μs deviation.

7.2.3 LEON3 Embedded Board

We have conducted a similar set of experiments on LEON3. Our results, however, show little difference from our x86 and Nexus S results. Due to this reason and space considerations, we do not include the graphs. Overall, for both AEH implementations across platforms, our experiments show that high-priority threads execute in a deterministic fashion and with tight bounds. This is irrespective of the number of low-priority threads that exist in the system.

7.3 Real-Time Fall Detector

To validate the predictability of our sensor architecture in data delivery, we have created a soft real-time fall detection application that leverages our SensorManager outlined in Section 5. We designed two experiments with two different types of workloads: (1) a memory intensive load and (2) a computation intensive load. The memory intensive experiment creates a varying number of non-real-time priority threads that each allocate a 2.5 MB integer array storing integer objects. The thread then assigns every other entry in the array to null. The effect of this operation is to fragment memory and create memory pressure. The extent of fragmentation is dependent on the VM and underlying GC. RTGCs can minimize and in some cases eliminate fragmentation [28]. The computation intensive experiment creates low-priority, periodic threads with a period of 20 ms. Each thread executes a tight loop performing a floating point multiplication for 1,000 iterations.

The fall detection application is registered as a SensorEventListener with SensorManager and executed with the highest priority in the system. After receiving events from the SensorManager as outlined in Section 5, the application consumes the SensorEvent with the value of x, y, and z coordinates and computes the fall detection algorithm. If a fall is detected the application notifies a server through a direct socket connection using Wi-Fi. Since network does not provide any real-time guarantees, we measure data-passing latency between the time of the sensor raw data detected in the kernel and the time that the sensor event is delivered by SensorManager to the fall detection application.

7.3.1 Nexus S Smartphone

Fig. 14 illustrates the observed latency of the sensor event delivery for the fall detection application. To stress the predictability of our SensorManager implementation, we have injected memory and computationally intensive threads into the application itself that run alongside of the fall detecting thread. We set these additional threads to a low priority. The Fig. 14a, Fig. 14b, Fig. 14d, and Fig. 14e show the latency of sensor event delivery with one low-priority thread and 100 low priority threads. The upper bound of these four runs was always around 30 ms, and there is no perceivable difference between executing the application with or without memory and computationally intensive threads. For comparison we provide Android performance numbers in Fig. 14c and Fig. 14f to show the effect of low-priority threads on sensor event delivery in stock Android.

7.3.2 LEON3

Fig. 15 lists the results of running the system unloaded, with 30 computational threads and with 30 memory intensive threads. The typical latency is 5.5 ms with a very low standard deviation. The memory intensive test shows a greater variability in the sensor event delivery times but they still fall under 6.5 ms and are also typically 5.5 ms also. RTDroid deployed on this platform creates a very stable system, especially when compared to the results of

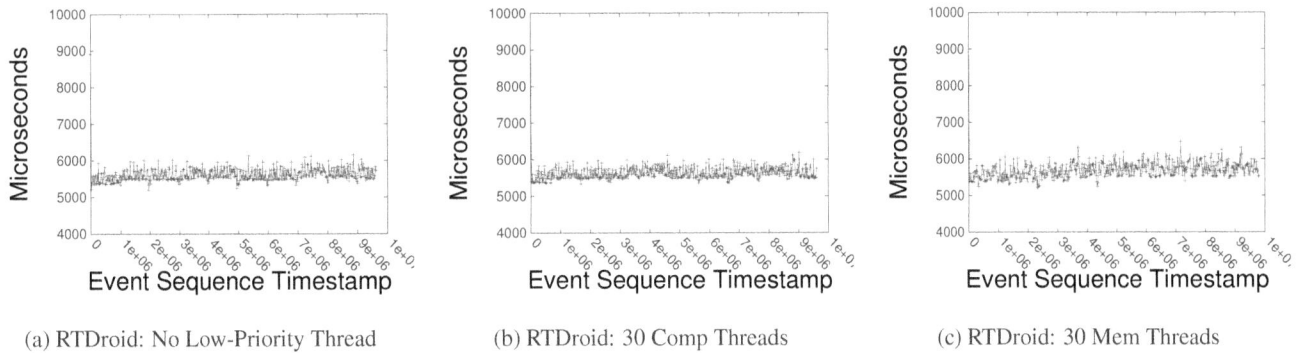

(a) RTDroid: No Low-Priority Thread   (b) RTDroid: 30 Comp Threads   (c) RTDroid: 30 Mem Threads

Figure 15: Memory and Computation stress test for the Fall Detection Application on LEON3.

both Android and RTDroid running on the Nexus S as is shown in Fig. 14.

8. RELATED WORK

Recent work has performed preliminary studies on the real-time capabilities of Android. Maia *et al.* evaluated Android for real-time and proposed the initial models for a high-level architecture [21]. The study did not explore the Android framework, services, IPC, nor core library implementations for their suitability in a real-time context. We believe our work further refines the proposed models.

The overall performance and predictability of DVM in a real-time setting was first characterized by Oh *et al.* [25]. Their findings mirror our general observations on Android. In general, Android performs well in many operational conditions. However, the core system does not provide any guarantees, and the worst-case execution time is parameterized by other applications and components in the system. Thus, to provide real-time guarantees, we need to alter the core system constructs, the libraries, and system services built from them.

Kalkov *et al.* [19] outline how to extend DVM to support real-time; they observed that DVM's garbage collection mechanism suspends all threads until it finishes garbage collection. This design is obviously problematic for applications that need predictability. The suggested solution is to introduce new APIs that allow developers to free objects explicitly. While this design decision does not require a redesign of the whole Dalvik GC, relying on developers to achieve predictability adds a layer of complexity. In addition, their work does not explore how different components within a single application (or across multiple applications) interact through Android's core constructs. We have observed, that the structure of many of Android's core mechanisms, from which many services and libraries are constructed, need to be augmented to provide real-time guarantees. Thus, we believe our implementation is synergistic to such proposals and can be leveraged to provide predictability when applications leverage services, IPC, or the core Android constructs.

9. CONCLUSIONS AND FUTURE WORK

This paper has presented RTDroid, a variation of Android that aims to provide real-time capabilities to Android as a whole system. We have shown that replacing DVM with an RT JVM and Linux with an RTOS is insufficient to run an Android application with real-time guarantees. To address this shortcoming, we have redesigned Android's core constructs and system services to provide tight latency bounds to real-time applications. Our experiments with three platforms—an x86 PC, a LEON3 embedded board, and

a Nexus S smartphone, show that RTDroid has good observed predictability on several microbenchmarks as well as a real-time application across three distinct deployment profiles.

Our future work includes the development of Android specific real-time APIs and the design of new programming constructs that naturally support real-time applications on RTDroid. We also plan to extend the current Android's application manifest in order to enable the static definition of real-time features. In parallel, we are working on supporting multi-application execution using Fiji's mixed-criticality support [8, 33] and just-in-time compilation of real-time applications.

Acknowledgements: We thank our shepherd Feng Qian and the MobiSys 2014 program committee for their constructive feedback. We are also grateful to Ethan Blanton, Karthik Dantu, Kyungho Jeon, Taeyeon Ki, Feng Shen, and Jan Vitek for their insightful comments. This work is supported in part by a National Science Foundation Award, CNS-1205656.

References

[1] Android and RTOS together: The dynamic duo for today's medical devices.
http://embedded-computing.com/articles/android-rtos-duo-todays-medical-devices/.

[2] Linux kernel memory management: Out of memory killer.
http://linux-mm.org/OOM_Killer.

[3] Real-Time Linux Wiki.
https://rt.wiki.kernel.org/index.php/Main_Page.

[4] Roving reporter: Medical Device Manufacturers Improve Their Bedside Manner with Android.
http://goo.gl/d2JF3.

[5] RTEMS. http://www.rtems.org/.

[6] What OS Is Best for a Medical Device?
http://www.summitdata.com/blog/?p=68.

[7] Why Android will be the biggest selling medical devices in the world by the end of 2012. http://goo.gl/G5UXq.

[8] Ethan Blanton and Lukasz Ziarek. Non-blocking inter-partition communication with wait-free pair transactions. In *Proceedings of the 11th International Workshop on Java Technologies for Real-time and Embedded Systems*, JTRES '13, pages 58–67, New York, NY, USA, 2013. ACM.

[9] Jian-Jia Chen and Chin-Fu Kuo. Energy-efficient scheduling for real-time systems on dynamic voltage scaling (dvs) platforms. In *Embedded and Real-Time Computing Systems and Applications, 2007. RTCSA 2007. 13th IEEE International Conference on*, pages 28–38, 2007.

[10] Angelo Corsaro and DouglasC. Schmidt. The design and performance of the jrate real-time java implementation. 2519:900–921, 2002.

[11] Cpu frequency and voltage scaling code in the linux(tm) kernel. https://www.kernel.org/doc/Documentation/cpu-freq/governors.txt.

[12] Android Developers. Bionic c library overview. http://www.kandroid.org/ndk/docs/system/libc/OVERVIEW.html.

[13] Thomas Gerlitz, Igor Kalkov, John Schommer, Dominik Franke, and Stefan Kowalewski. Non-blocking garbage collection for real-time android. In *Proceedings of the 11th International Workshop on Java Technologies for Real-time and Embedded Systems*, JTRES '13, 2013.

[14] James Gosling and Greg Bollella. *The Real-Time Specification for Java*. Addison-Wesley Longman Publishing Co., Inc., Boston, MA, USA, 2000.

[15] Dip Goswami, Martin Lukasiewycz, Reinhard Schneider, and Samarjit Chakraborty. Time-triggered implementations of mixed-criticality automotive software. In *Proceedings of the Conference on Design, Automation and Test in Europe*, DATE '12, pages 1227–1232, San Jose, CA, USA, 2012. EDA Consortium.

[16] D. Hart, J. Stultz, and T. Ts'o. Real-time linux in real time. *IBM Syst. J.*, 47(2):207–220, April 2008.

[17] Mike G. Hill and Thomas W. Lake. Non-interference analysis for mixed criticality code in avionics systems. In *Proceedings of the 15th IEEE International Conference on Automated Software Engineering*, ASE '00, pages 257–, Washington, DC, USA, 2000. IEEE Computer Society.

[18] iOmniscient. Fall and man down detection. http://iomniscient.com/index.php?option=com_content&view=article&id=155&Itemid=53.

[19] Igor Kalkov, Dominik Franke, John F. Schommer, and Stefan Kowalewski. A real-time extension to the Android platform. In *Proceedings of the 10th International Workshop on Java Technologies for Real-time and Embedded Systems*, JTRES '12, pages 105–114, New York, NY, USA, 2012. ACM.

[20] MinSeong Kim and Andy Wellings. An efficient and predictable implementation of asynchronous event handling in the RTSJ. In *Proceedings of the 6th international workshop on Java technologies for real-time and embedded systems*, JTRES '08, pages 48–57, New York, NY, USA, 2008. ACM.

[21] Cláudio Maia, Luís Nogueira, and Luis Miguel Pinho. Evaluating Android OS for embedded real-time systems. In *Proceedings of the 6th International Workshop on Operating Systems Platforms for Embedded Real-Time Applications, Brussels, Belgium*, OSPERT '10, pages 63–70, 2010.

[22] Sibin Mohan, Frank Mueller, Michael Root, William Hawkins, Christopher Healy, David Whalley, and Emilio Vivancos. Parametric timing analysis and its application to dynamic voltage scaling. *ACM Trans. Embed. Comput. Syst.*, 10(2):25:1–25:34, January 2011.

[23] Yolanda Murphy. Northrop grumman news release: DARPA ASPN project article. http://www.irconnect.com/noc/press/pages/news_releases.html?d=10029353.

[24] Northrop to demo darpa navigation system on android. http://goo.gl/bgRggD.

[25] Hyeong-Seok Oh, Beom-Jun Kim, Hyung-Kyu Choi, and Soo-Mook Moon. Evaluation of Android Dalvik virtual machine. In *Proceedings of the 10th International Workshop on Java Technologies for Real-time and Embedded Systems*, JTRES '12, pages 115–124, New York, NY, USA, 2012. ACM.

[26] Vivek S. Pai, Peter Druschel, and Willy Zwaenepoel. Flash: An efficient and portable web server. In *Proceedings of the 1999 USENIX Annual Technical Conference*, USENIX ATC'99, 1999.

[27] Filip Pizlo, Lukasz Ziarek, Ethan Blanton, Petr Maj, and Jan Vitek. High-level programming of embedded hard real-time devices. In *Proceedings of the 5th European conference on Computer systems*, EuroSys '10, pages 69–82, New York, NY, USA, 2010. ACM.

[28] Filip Pizlo, Lukasz Ziarek, Petr Maj, Antony L. Hosking, Ethan Blanton, and Jan Vitek. Schism: fragmentation-tolerant real-time garbage collection. In *Proceedings of the 2010 ACM SIGPLAN conference on Programming language design and implementation*, PLDI '10, pages 146–159, New York, NY, USA, 2010. ACM.

[29] Military Embedded Systems. Rugged handheld computers suit up with android on the battlefield. http://mil-embedded.com/articles/rugged-suit-with-android-the-battlefield/#.

[30] Strand-1 satellite launches Google Nexus One smartphone into orbit. http://www.wired.co.uk/news/archive/2013-02/25/strand-1-phone-satellite.

[31] Matt Welsh, David Culler, and Eric Brewer. Seda: An architecture for well-conditioned, scalable internet services. In *Proceedings of the Eighteenth ACM Symposium on Operating Systems Principles*, SOSP '01, pages 230–243, New York, NY, USA, 2001. ACM.

[32] Yin Yan, Sree Harsha Konduri, Amit Kulkarni, Varun Anand, Steven Y. Ko, and Lukasz Ziarek. Rtdroid: A design for real-time android. In *Proceedings of the 11th International Workshop on Java Technologies for Real-time and Embedded Systems*, JTRES '13, 2013.

[33] Lukasz Ziarek. Prp: Priority rollback protocol – a pip extension for mixed criticality systems: Short paper. In *Proceedings of the 8th International Workshop on Java Technologies for Real-Time and Embedded Systems*, JTRES '10, pages 82–84, New York, NY, USA, 2010. ACM.

Enhancing Vehicular Internet Connectivity using Whitespaces, Heterogeneity, and a Scouting Radio

Tan Zhang
Univ. of Wisconsin-Madison
Madison, WI 53706, USA
tzhang@cs.wisc.edu

Sayandeep Sen[*]
IBM Research India
Bangalore, KA 560045, India
sayandes@in.ibm.com

Suman Banerjee
Univ. of Wisconsin-Madison
Madison, WI 53706, USA
suman@cs.wisc.edu

ABSTRACT

We explore the use of TV whitespace communication systems for providing robust connectivity to vehicles. A key challenge in this setup is the *asymmetry in transmit power limits* – the fixed base station is allowed to communicate at up to 4 W, while the mobile gateways in vehicles are limited to 100 mW. This paper presents a specific solution to deal with this asymmetry in which whitespace transceivers are used in the downlink direction while a more traditional cellular path is used in the uplink one. While heterogeneous communication systems have been considered before (e.g., in some satellite networks), our solution explores some unique opportunities that arise in vehicular systems. In particular, we describe a system called *Scout* that uses a front radio at the head of a vehicle to look ahead and identify the best channel parameters to be used when the rear radio eventually reaches the forward post. We use these channel estimates to adapt a number of transmission mechanisms for improving the performance of flows through this heterogeneous network. We have implemented and deployed this system on moving vehicles in an urban environment, and demonstrated $3 - 8\times$ performance improvement over simpler alternatives that do not use the scouting technique.

Categories and Subject Descriptors

C.2.1 [**Computer-Communication Networks**]: Network Architecture and Design—*Wireless communication*

Keywords

TV Whitespaces; Vehicular Internet Access; Power Asymmetry; Heterogeneous Network; Scouting Radio

1. INTRODUCTION

There is a growing need to provide high bandwidth and robust Internet connectivity to vehicles for supporting diverse applications, e.g., improved traffic intelligence, transportation safety, and infotainment for passengers. Numerous research projects such as

---

[*]The author was a graduate student at University of Wisconsin-Madison during the course of this work.

MobiSys'14, June 16–19, 2014, Bretton Woods, NH, USA.
Copyright 2014 ACM 978-1-4503-2793-0/14/06 ...$15.00.
http://dx.doi.org/10.1145/2594368.2594371.

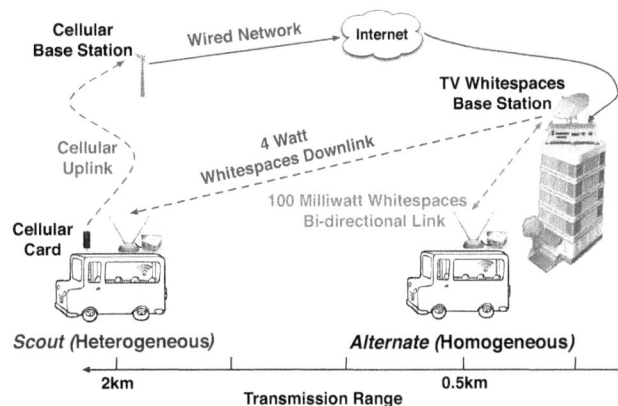

Figure 1: *Scout* uses TV whitespaces path primarily for downlink traffic and cellular path primarily for uplink, unlike a traditional, homogeneous design that uses the same path for both directions.

MAR [19], WiRover [10], ViFi [3], Wiffler [2], CaberNet [7], along with commercial endeavors strive to provide this today primarily using existing cellular technologies, and sometimes enhanced through opportunistic WiFi access. In this paper, we explore the feasibility and design challenges of using the emerging TV whitespaces spectrum for this application.

TV whitespaces ($512 - 698$MHz), recently released for unlicensed usage in some parts of the world (e.g., U.S. [9]), offer a new communication medium to wireless systems. The substantial spectrum resource (up to 180MHz) and good propagation characteristics (up to 30km) make this additional spectrum especially attractive for wide-area communications. In this work, we have explored the use of TV whitespaces spectrum not *merely* because of the low spectrum cost, but for reclaiming additional spectrum resources that is especially suited for long-range communications to match the needs of vehicular connectivity. Our near term goal of this project is to deploy an "on-board" Internet access service over a TV whitespaces network for commuters of a city metro transit operating hundreds of buses at Madison, WI, USA.

To efficiently utilize TV whitespaces, we propose a *heterogeneous* network design called *Scout* that (i) communicates the downlink traffic (usually the dominant fraction of traffic) primarily over TV whitespaces paths while sending the uplink traffic primarily over existing cellular paths, and (ii) uses an additional "scouting" radio in the vehicle to probe the channel condition in advance, thereby compensating for the high feedback latency in making protocol decisions.

Power	Range (km)
100 mW	0.4 – 0.5
4 W	1.9 – 2

Table 1: Transmission range of our whitespace radio at different transmit powers when operating at 1 Mbps PHY rate.

Figure 1 (left side) shows the *Scout* architecture. Gateway nodes (clients) on buses are each equipped with two TV whitespaces radios and one cellular radio. Each of these radios communicates with its corresponding base station — the whitespace radios with our own whitespace base stations and the cellular radio with the usual commercial cellular base stations. The gateway serves as a WiFi hotspot inside the bus, allowing users to connect to the Internet through their WiFi-capable devices. This path diversity, however, is hidden from end applications through an encapsulation tunnel between the gateway and an aggregation proxy situated behind the TV whitespaces and the cellular networks. We contrast this design of *Scout* to a simpler symmetric network where the TV whitespaces path alone is used for both uplink and downlink communications, such as in the WhiteFi system [1] (Figure 1 right side).

Why a heterogeneous network design? Most of communication systems typically use a single network path for transferring both uplink and downlink traffic. Unfortunately, applying this design convention to our vehicular context significantly limits the coverage of the base stations over whitespaces. As per FCC's ruling [9], the transmission power of the mobile whitespace devices (gateway nodes on the bus) is limited to 100 mW, whereas the power of static base stations can be up to 4 W [1]. This $40\times$ difference in the transmit power limit is to prevent mobile devices from causing harmful interference to the primary incumbents during roaming. Since most of the communication protocols need to be bi-directional, a whitespace-only network design as shown in Figure 1 (right side) would limit the operating range of a whitespace path to that of the "weaker" mobile clients.

Experiments with our whitespaces radios show that the operating range of a symmetric, homogeneous system using 100 mW transmit power would be $4\times$ less than our proposed dual network design that uses 4 W power for downlink alone. This is shown in Table 1 [2]. While the operating range can be improved somewhat by choosing a lower rate on the uplink or using more sophisticated signal processing techniques, a significant link asymmetry is expected to remain. To achieve the same coverage, the lower bi-directional range means much more whitespace base stations to be deployed, leading to higher infrastructure and management cost.

Scout circumvents the problem of "weak" whitespaces uplink by adopting a heterogeneous network architecture in which the downlink traffic (from the base station to the vehicle) is mainly communicated over TV whitespaces, while the uplink traffic (from the vehicle to the base station) is sent over a cellular link. This can maximize the downlink coverage of each whitespace base station by leveraging the extensive cellular connectivity in the uplink. Furthermore, since many networking applications are downlink dominated ($10\times$ in WiRover [10]), *Scout* is efficient in utilizing TV whitespaces for relaying traffic.

---

[1] This power limit includes the gain of antennas and regardless of number of channels used for transmission.

[2] The measured transmission ranges are similar to a prior report [6] based on a different hardware platform.

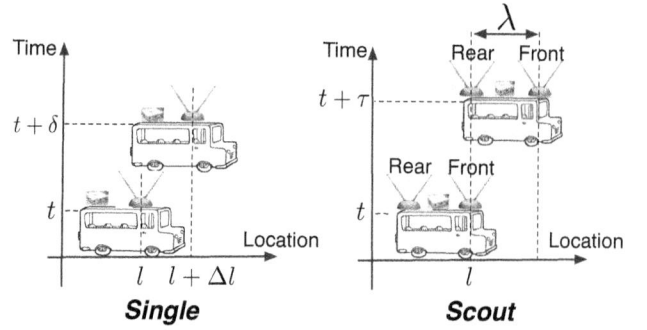

Figure 2: Diagram of *Single* and *Scout*. λ is the antenna separation, τ is the rear radio's travel time to front position, and δ is the cellular path delay ($\delta \leq \tau$).

Why the use of a scouting radio? While effectively extending the coverage, a heterogeneous network based on traditional networking protocols yields poor downlink performance due to the *high feedback latency* in the cellular uplink. First, the stale feedback leads to low accuracy of channel estimation, especially in the mobile environment. Since most of communication systems rely on channel estimation for making *various* protocol decisions, e.g., rate adaptation, FEC, etc., the poor estimation lead to higher packet losses. Second, the feedback delay drastically inflates the bandwidth delay product rendering the performance of TCP based applications extremely susceptible to channel losses. Third, the delayed feedback severely slows down retransmissions that are primarily used in traditional wireless systems for loss recovery. This in turn leads to high bandwidth inefficiency. To tackle these problems caused by the slow feedback, we leverage an extra "scouting" radio to accurately measure channel condition for a location in advance. This information is then used by several aggressive transmission techniques to enhance link performance by minimizing end-to-end loss.

The core intuition of "channel scouting" comes from the simple observation that the reception location of a radio largely determines its experienced channel characteristics [13, 16, 20]. Thus, in a single-radio system as shown in Figure 2 (*Single*), the radio's actual channel experience in a new location would be different from the feedback conveyed at the old location by the time our base station acts on this feedback. This is especially true with a cellular uplink with at least tens of milliseconds delay. In contrast, if we were to place two radios as shown in Figure 2 (*Scout*), the channel condition experienced by the front radio would be somewhat similar to that of the rear radio after it moves forward a short time later. In essence, the front radio can "scout" the likely channel condition for future receptions by the rear radio. Thus, we can send back the observed channel condition by the front radio at its current location l. By the time the rear radio reaches the same location l, the base station can use this feedback made earlier by the front radio to choose better transmission parameters for the rear radio. While the underlying intuition is simple, to successfully realize the benefits of the channel scouting in real settings, we had to address challenges such as identifying relevant feedback to a given location and handling varying vehicle speed and driving patterns, which will be discussed in § 3.1.

Built upon this scouting based channel estimation framework, we design multiple transmission adaptation techniques, i.e., rate adaptation, inter-packet FEC, and intelligent traffic duplication, to enhance the reliability of vehicular connectivity. Since TCP is the dominant transport protocol used by most applications, we demonstrate the efficacy of the combination of our proposed mechanisms by showing how they can improve TCP performance.

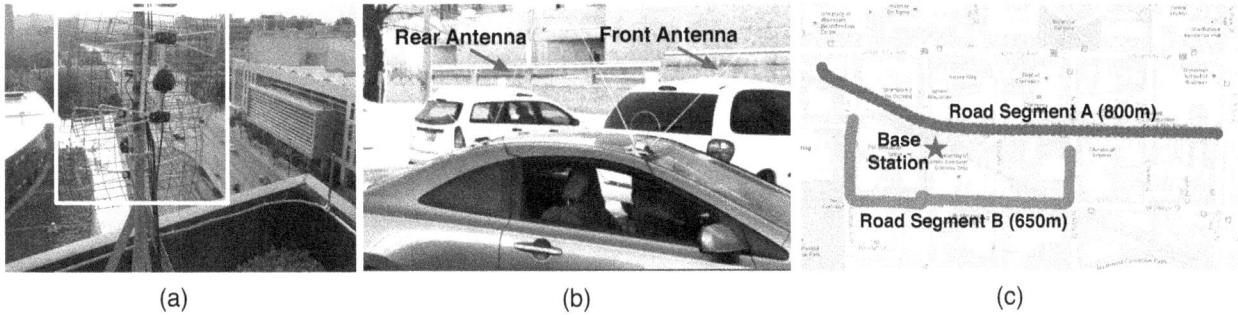

Figure 3: Outdoor deployment at the campus area of Madison, WI: (a) whitespace base station deployed on top of a 8-floor building; (b) vehicular client with two TV antennas mounted atop; (c) two example road segments used in experiments.

We note our dual radio approach is quite successful for a moving vehicle with adequate length (≥ 1.5m). However, this approach as designed, is not relevant to static settings (§ 5.3), or for a platform with limited physical size such as a smart phone. In addition, our use of a scouting radio is *independent* to multi-antenna techniques (MIMO) that combine signals at the physical layer for scaling throughput or enhancing reception robustness. Our scouting radio operates at the MAC and higher layers, and is primarily used to determine channel properties at a reception location where the rear radio visits later. Furthermore, our scouting technique is *complementary* to MIMO, and a significant performance gain can be achieved when a scouting radio is leveraged by MIMO for compensating feedback delay as will be shown in § 5.1.2.

We also note that existing cellular technologies (3G, 4G, etc.) have addressed the problem of power asymmetry in the *licensed* band. The key technique used is *power equalization*, which enables the base station to manage interference among multiple mobile clients by tightly controlling their transmission power [8, 23]. This ensures that the base station receives uplink signals at similar power from different clients, thus being able to decode each one through an amplification process. Unfortunately, imposing centralized power control over the *uncoordinated and opportunistic* TV whitespaces appears to be difficult. Since the whitespaces spectrum is intended for uncoordinated usage, a base station, by design, would be incapable of controlling other unlicensed devices potentially operating with a different communication protocol. The unrestricted interference is likely to overwhelm the weak uplink signal, causing decoding at the base station to fail.

Finally, heterogeneous networks have been widely used in satellite communications in which the downlink connection is established over the satellite link and the uplink is over dial-up lines. While similar in approach, *Scout* is a stylized design to meet the asymmetric power constraints in TV whitespaces. More importantly, *Scout* can *compensate* the disadvantage in the slow cellular uplink through the use of a scouting radio.

Contributions: The key contributions of our work are:

- We present a stylized design of a heterogeneous network structure, which effectively uses TV whitespaces for providing wide-area network connectivity to vehicles. Our system avoids a denser deployment of whitespaces base stations that are otherwise needed in a whitespaces-only network.

- To address the problem of feedback delay over the cellular uplink, we propose a channel estimation technique enabled by an additional scouting radio suited specifically for moving vehicles. We further design and implement a functional system that leverages this channel estimation for three transmis-

sion techniques, i.e., rate adaptation, inter-packet FEC and intelligent traffic duplication over cellular links. Based on our experiments (conducted by driving about 500 miles on different routes around our whitespace base station), *Scout* can enhance TCP performance by $3 - 8\times$ over alternative SISO and MIMO systems.

In the rest of the paper, we first validate the feasibility and advantage of our scouting radio approach in § 2. In § 3, we present the design of *Scout* in detail. We then outline some implementation details in § 4, followed by our evaluation of *Scout* in § 5.

2. ADVANTAGES OF A SCOUTING RADIO

Most wireless communication systems use rate adaptation and link-layer retransmission (or their variants) for adapting to changes in channel conditions. Rate adaptation enables the sender to choose a combination of modulation and channel coding suitable for the channel characteristics experienced by the receiver. Link-layer retransmission allows the sender to retransmit lost frames to avoid their negative impact at higher layers, e.g., TCP. In this section, we will show the limitations of a single radio system under mobility in making these protocol decisions. We then demonstrate the advantage of leveraging a scouting radio in obtaining better channel estimates for improving such decisions. We start by describing our experiment setup.

2.1 Experiment setup

Our testbed is built around the UW campus area with a coverage radius of several kilometers. It currently consists of one base station and several mobile clients. The base station is mounted atop a 8-floor building as shown in Figure 3(a). It is equipped with an Ethernet connection for receiving the uplink traffic and relaying it to the Internet on behalf of the client. It performs downlink transmission using a whitespaces radio, a high-gain power amplifier, and a directional TV antenna. The total transmission power is set to be 3.8 W for extensive downlink coverage. To avoid interfering to primary incumbents, we configure the base station to operate across 4 contiguous, unused TV channels (at a center frequency of 662MHz) as indicated by a spectrum occupancy database [26]. As the mobile client for experiments, we use a personal vehicle carrying two whitespaces radios to receive downlink traffic as shown in Figure 3(b). Each radio is connected to an omni-directional antenna for capturing signal from all directions. A 3G cellular card is used for uplink communications.

Figure 3(c) shows the two of many road segments where our experiments were conducted. These two road segments have very different coverage characteristics — *segment A* is part of one major

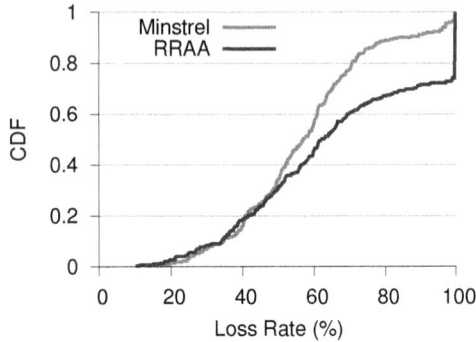

Figure 4: CDF of MAC layer losses of two state-of-the-art rate adaptation algorithms with mobility and under feedback delay in the cellular uplink.

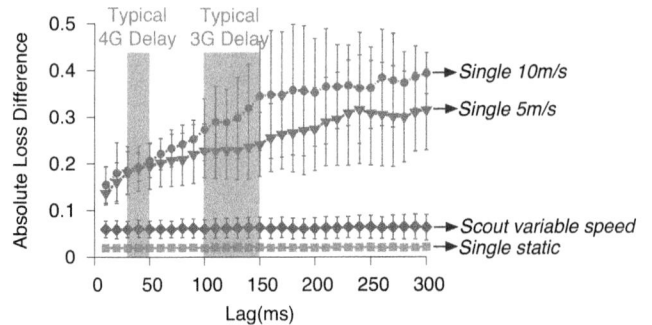

Figure 5: Average of absolute loss differences at various lags for 12Mbps packets. A lag is the elapsed time between two measurements. *Single* denotes one radio and *Scout* is the two radio setup.

bus route we intend to cover. It has good connectivity to the whitespaces base station with more than 70% of the path in line-of-sight to the base station's antenna. In contrast, the *segment B* represents a worse coverage scenario, with more than 60% of the path blocked by several tall buildings. The mobile client drove around this area at speeds between 18 and 35 km/hr (governed by city speed limits).

Our radio platform is similar to the WhiteFi radio [1]. It performs a frequency translation function by converting the signal from commercial WiFi cards to the UHF band. We will describe this platform for more details in § 4.1. Note that most of the techniques in *Scout* are not limited to the 802.11 baseband technology, but applicable to other technologies (WiMax, LTE, etc) as well.

2.2 Limitations of a single-radio system under vehicular mobility

We now discuss how vehicular mobility in a single radio setup impacts the accuracy of rate adaptation and the efficiency of link layer retransmission. In particular, this impact is *exacerbated by the feedback delays* in the cellular uplink.

Rate selection mismatch with mobility: We conducted experiments where we drove a vehicle along road segment A multiple times at speeds of about 35 km/hr. The vehicular gateway sent the feedback over cellular links to the TV whitespace base station for selecting downlink data rates. As the vehicle kept moving, the usable PHY rates relevant to a given location changed quickly. Thus, by the time the base station could act on a received feedback, the location of the receiving radio on the vehicle had changed and the feedback become stale. As a result, any rate selection algorithm that depends on such feedback experienced poor performance. To illustrate this, Figure 4 presents the MAC layer loss rates for two state-of-the-art rate adaptation algorithms (Minstrel [4] and RRAA [29]) calculated over 100 millisecond intervals. We observe a median loss rate of 57% and 62% for each algorithm based on the delayed feedback.

Retransmission overhead: While MAC layer retransmissions can hide some of the packet losses, they introduce bandwidth inefficiency and additional delay that can also limit the performance of a system. Based on our testbed measurements, the current cellular paths (3G and 4G) have a minimum delay of 25 milliseconds and a typical delay between 50 and 150 milliseconds. Each retransmission will therefore inflate the end-to-end path latency by a corresponding amount, significantly cutting down TCP throughput. As will be shown in § 5.1, for a single radio system using a combination of a state-of-the-art rate adaptation algorithm (RRAA), link

layer retransmissions, and a cellular uplink, the achieved downlink TCP throughput can be quite low (about 40 Kbps). In contrast, our alternative design is able to provide a performance more than two orders of magnitude better in many cases. We next validate the intuition of the scouting based channel estimation, which is the *core* technique used in *Scout*.

2.3 Using a scouting radio to improve channel estimation

The advantage of the scouting based channel estimation can be ascertained by comparing the following two schemes as shown in Figure 2. In *Scout*, suppose the front radio measures the loss property at location l, time t. How accurate is this measurement in predicting the channel condition for the rear radio when it reaches the same location l at time $t + \tau$? We contrast this with the alternative design of a single radio (*Single*). In this single radio setup, the only radio will measure the loss property at location l, time t, and use this estimate to predict the channel condition at location $l + \Delta l$, time $t + \delta$.

Metric: We used the packet loss rate as an indicator of channel quality for a given location and at a given time. Each loss rate was calculated for 10 contiguous packets at a fixed PHY rate. We then measured the magnitude of difference in loss rates under different time separations to classify whether channel condition has changed with varying location or time (or both). We denote this time separation as a *lag* in the following discussion.

Evaluation: To understand the stability of channel loss properties as only a function of time, we present the variation of loss rates at same locations with different lags. We measured this by placing a single radio mounted atop a car at 12 equally spaced locations on the road segment A. We then averaged the absolute differences for pairs of loss rates separated by each time lag at all these locations. Figure 5 (*Single static*) shows that the variation of loss rates remains small with a lag below 300 milliseconds for all the measured locations.

We next determine the stability of loss measurements done by the same single radio as a function of both time and location. The speed of the vehicle in these experiments was between 5m/s (18 km/hr) and 10m/s (35 km/hr), which is typical for urban area due to the 40km/hr speed limit. As can be seen from Figure 5 (*Single* 10m/s and 5m/s), the difference in loss rates increased drastically with increasing lags. The degree of variation is expected as the single radio system was measuring the loss rates at different locations and different time. When using the stale channel observation to predict the loss rate, *Single* would make an estimation error of over 30% under the typical delay of a 3G uplink (100 to 150 milliseconds), and over 20% under the delay of a 4G link (25 to 50 milliseconds). Note that these delay values were obtained from our testbed measurement as mentioned before.

We finally benchmark the mismatch in the loss rates under *Scout* setup with two radios (front and rear) aligned *at the same locations* under various lags introduced by different vehicle speeds. The result is again shown in Figure 5 (*Scout variable speed*). For a lag of 300 milliseconds, we note that the difference in loss rates between two radios at the same location remained a fifth of a single radio traveling at 10 m/s speed for a 3G uplink, and within a third for a 4G uplink. This demonstrates that *Scout* can indeed improve the channel estimation for the rear radio.

While our vehicle was driving at a city speed of 18 – 50 km/hr for the experiments reported in this paper, we note much higher speed (up to 120 km/hr) can be supported by *Scout*. In particular, the average length of a car in the US is 5 meter, which sets the maximum limit for the separation of two radios at the client. Assuming this 5 meter separation and a highest vehicular speed of 120 km/hr (33 m/s), it takes at least 150 milliseconds for the rear radio to reach the front radio's location. This delay is typically higher than the observed latency in the cellular links (3G and 4G), thus allowing the base station to receive the front radio's feedback usually before the rear radio reaches the front position.

3. SCOUT: A HETEROGENEOUS DESIGN

Scout adopts a heterogeneous network architecture to take most advantage of power asymmetry between the whitespace base stations and vehicular clients. In this network, the downlink communication is mainly conducted over TV whitespaces with the maximum allowed power, thereby achieving extensive coverage by our whitespace base stations. For uplink communications, we choose to use existing cellular path to circumvent the limited transmission range in TV whitespaces. We further allow downlink traffic to be *intelligently* duplicated over the cellular path when the whitespace link is experiencing an outage [3].

Specifically, we have developed following related mechanisms to enhance whitespace connectivity — an efficient way of estimating channel properties (of the rear radio, using a forward radio) and several transmission techniques based on the obtained channel estimates, i.e., rate adaptation, forward error correction (FEC), and intelligent traffic duplication over cellular links. For uplink communications, we choose to provide best-effort delivery because the loss rates and packet reordering are observed to be very low in the cellular path. Figure 6 shows the overall architecture of *Scout*.

To send downlink traffic, the base station first obtains channel quality estimates based on the feedback generated for both radios by the client (§ 3.1). It then chooses an appropriate link-layer data rate using the obtained channel estimates (§ 3.2.1). Based on the error performance of the chosen data rate, it constructs coded packets for each batch of data packets for forward error correction (§ 3.2.2), then transmitting them over TV whitespaces at the selected rate. Upon detecting connection blackouts in the whitespace link, the base station also sends the data packets in duplicate over the cellular path (§ 3.2.3).

At the client (vehicular gateway), we leverage the dual-radio diversity by combining the coded packets from both radios (§ 3.3).

---

[3]In fact, our system is designed to be opportunistic in both communication directions, e.g., if the vehicle is within the uplink range to a whitespace base station, we also allow uplink traffic to be sent over TV whitespaces.

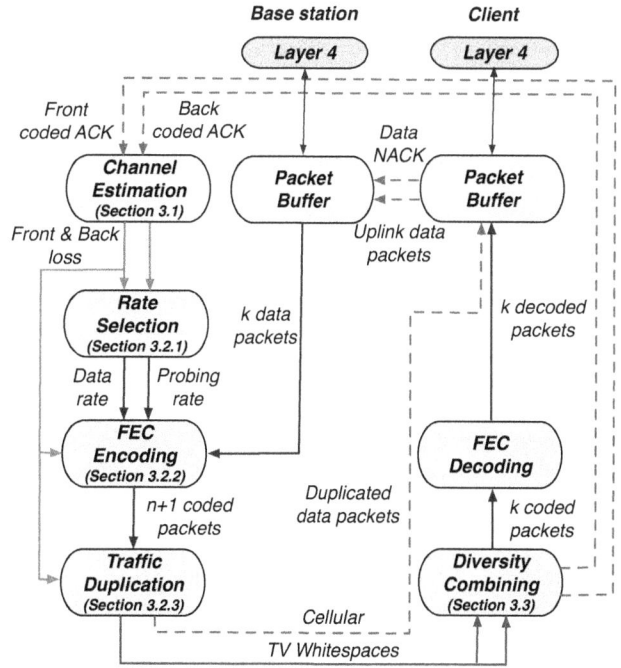

Figure 6: System architecture of Scout.

The client then decodes these packets to obtain data packets. If duplicated packets are received on the cellular path, the client also merges them with the data packets, then passing all the packets received in order to the application. To provide the base station with channel estimates and information about lost packets for retransmission, the client sends feedback for both coded packets and data packets over the cellular link. In addition, the client reports its GPS information periodically to the base station for obtaining relevant feedback to the rear radio's reception location. The pseudocode of *Scout* is shown in Algorithm 1 (appendix). We now explain each of these components in detail.

3.1 Scouting radio based channel estimation

The first and the most important step in the transmission process is for the base station to obtain accurate channel estimates for making various transmission decisions. This is performed by the *ScoutEstimate* procedure in Algorithm 1.

Channel estimation: We use the *loss rates of coded packets* as the estimator of channel quality because such information is readily accessible from the commercial WiFi cards used in our implementation. Note that our proposed technique can be used to collect other types of channel statistics such as channel state information (CSI) and bit error rates in a similar way. To estimate the packet loss rates, the base station first collects feedback generated for the *coded packets* received by both radios at the client. For each PHY rate r, the base station calculates the loss rate $L_f(r)$ for the front radio based on the packets most recently ACKed for the front radio. It also calculates the loss rate $L_r(r)$ for the rear radio based on the packets previously received by the front radio at the current location l of the rear radio. If no coded packets are sent when the front radio was at l, the base station will use the delayed ACKs for the rear radio to calculate $L_r(r)$. To obtain sufficient, yet relevant channel estimates, we choose a time window of 25ms for calculating both loss rates. As a safeguard against random channel fluctuations, we apply exponential averaging with a heavy weight (0.85) on the current estimates to compute the final channel estimates.

291

Feedback alignment: To accurately estimate the channel quality at a given location l, it is critical to identify a relevant set of coded packets that are sent to the front radio at l. As shown in Figure 5, the loss rate estimation can be off by about 40% due to a 3 meter location error (300 milliseconds lag at 10 m/s speed). Unfortunately, our low priced GPS modules used at the clients have a positioning inaccuracy up to 10 meter.

To circumvent this problem, we use the speed reading v instead of the coordinate reading reported by the GPS because it has much lower error (0.1 m/s). Using this speed reading, the base station obtains the radio alignment period τ, which is the time elapsed for the rear radio to reach the location l since the front radio was previously at l (Figure 2). This period is calculated by $\tau = \lambda/v$ where λ is the antenna separation of two radios, which is set to be 1.5 m in our implementation. Note that v remains constant because the GPS reading is updated at short intervals (1 second). The base station then obtains coded packets that are received by the front radio τ time ago for estimating $L_r(r)$ at location l. Since τ is usually below 300 milliseconds (1.5m / 5m/s), the feedback alignment error in *Scout* is less than 0.03 meters (0.1 m/s × 300 milliseconds).

Finally, for the occasional cases when the vehicle stops ($v = 0$), the base station uses the delayed ACKs for the rear radio to calculate $L_r(r)$ because they remain relevant to this radio's reception location. The base station will switch back to use the scouting feedback upon detecting the vehicle to move again. The change of vehicle mobility can be quickly determined by the GPS reading that is updated by the client frequently (every second).

3.2 Utilizing Scout channel estimates

In *Scout*, we utilize the obtained channel quality estimates for improving rate adaptation, forward error correction and intelligent traffic duplication over cellular links. We present the details of these mechanisms next.

3.2.1 PHY rate selection

We start by describing how to use the channel estimates from the scouting radio to choose the first transmission parameter – PHY rates at the base station. Our algorithm – *ScoutRate* proceeds in three steps as shown in Algorithm 1.

The first step is to identify a candidate set of reliable rates C for the rear radio. To this end, we examine the loss rate at both radios – $L_f(r)$ and $L_r(r)$ for each PHY rate r. We only include those PHY rates with both loss rates below a threshold (0.65) into C. This is because our testbed measurements show that higher loss rates usually have large variation, which makes accurately estimating loss properties difficult.

In the second step, we calculate the achievable throughput at the rear radio $T = r \times (1 - L_r(r))$ for each data rate in the candidate set C. We select the rate r_{data} with the highest throughput, and assign it to a batch of coded packets as will be described in § 3.2.2.

Finally, we append an additional *coded* packet at each batch of packets to randomly probe a different rate r_{probe}. The probed rate should be higher than the throughput of the current data rate, but not necessarily in C. Thus, *Scout* can quickly adapt to the improved channel condition through random probing, while promptly adapting to channel degradation via either probing or identifying the change of the candidate rate set.

3.2.2 Inter-packet forward error correction

We now explain the next step of the transmission process that inserts redundant packets into each batch of data packets for forward error correction. All the coded packets are transmitted using the *same* selected rate r_{data} over TV whitespaces. This process is shown by *ScoutFEC* in Algorithm 1.

Inter-packet FEC: To circumvent the high retransmission inefficiency caused by a slow cellular uplink as mentioned in § 2.2, we leverage *inter-packet* forward error correction as the primary mean of error recovery. The base station first groups data packets to be transmitted into batches. It then encodes each batch of k data packets into n coded packets for transmission. Upon receiving *any* k coded packets, the client can decode the original k data packets.

Our motivation of performing encoding *across* packets comes from the empirical analysis of loss characteristics in the vehicular testbed. In particular, we find that most of packet losses ($>80\%$) result from the *failure of detecting packets* at the receiver, rather than *bits corruption*. Two factors might contribute to this fact. First, our vehicular network operates in an urban area with many tall buildings that completely blocks off the whitespaces transmission in certain road segments. Second, the intra-packet FEC used in the 802.11 baseband technology is effective in correcting bit errors within a packet. Thus, we use the inter-packet FEC to complement the intra-packet FEC in the 802.11 technology. We will show in § 5.2.2 that the above choice leads to significant performance gain.

We choose a type of erasure codes based on Vandermode encoding matrices [18] in our implementation, which incurs low computational latency (order of microseconds). The specific erasure codes provide an unique advantage by having data packets as their first k coded packets, denoted as D. Upon successfully receiving all the packets in D, the receiver can directly pass them to the higher layer without incurring any decoding delay. More importantly, when less than k coded packets are received, the receiver can scavenge whatever packets received in D to reduce the penalty of decoding failure.

Redundancy estimation: To determine the number of data packets k and that of coded packets n to be included in a given batch, we calculate the effective loss rates L after the diversity combining at the client. Assuming independent channel losses at both radios, L should be calculated by $L = L_f(r_{data}) \times L_r(r_{data})$, where $L_f(r_{data})$ and $L_r(r_{data})$ are the loss rates of the selected PHY rate r_{data} estimated for both radios. We then determine the *redundancy ratio* rr, which are defined as $rr = (n-k)/n$. rr should be no less than the loss rate L for successful decoding the entire batch. In our implementation, we insert 5% extra redundancy to be conservative, thus $rr = L \times (1 + 0.05)$.

Using the calculated rr, we now determine k and n. n is chosen such that the transmission duration of all the coded packets are within the channel coherence time c (25ms based on our measurements). This is due to our design assumption that all the packets within a batch should experience similar degree of channel losses, thus sharing the same data rate and redundancy. We calculate n by $n = c \times r_{data}/s$, where s is the size of each encoded packet. After determining n, we calculate k by $k = n \times (1 - rr)$. Finally, we append one additional coded packet at the end of each batch for probing a different data rate as mentioned in § 3.2.1.

3.2.3 Intelligent traffic duplication over cellular path

We now present the third transmission technique in *Scout* that intelligently duplicates some downlink packets over the cellular link when necessary to bridge coverage holes. This is shown in the *ScoutDUP* procedure of Algorithm 1.

Our decision of traffic duplication is motivated by non-negligible frequency of connection blackouts (11% for road segment A) observed at the mobile client. Some of the connectivity losses can last for long periods of time (up to 5 seconds), causing a TCP connection to timeout before all the recovery mechanisms over whites-

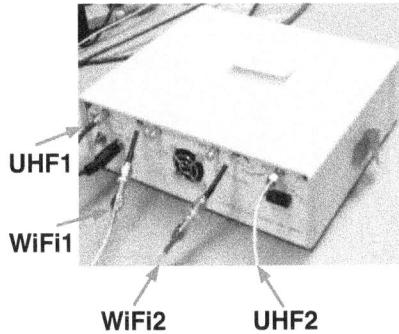

Figure 7: Scout wide band digital radio.

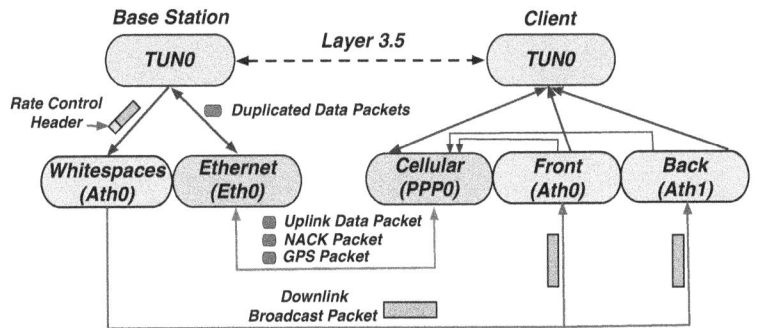

Figure 8: Software architecture of Scout.

paces to take effect. To effectively handle connection blackouts, the base station duplicates traffic on both the whitespace and cellular paths upon detecting intermittent connectivity over TV whitespaces. The reason we duplicate the downlink traffic, instead of sending it solely on the cellular path, is to accurately determine when the connectivity is recovered over whitespace, and stop sending on the cellular path from that point. Furthermore, we only duplicate the *k data packets* in each batch to reduce the cellular usage, since the loss rates in the cellular path are observed to be very low as mentioned before.

The intelligent duplication is triggered when either of the following criterion is met. *Criteria I:* the current data rate r_{data} selected by the base station is the lowest rate (1Mbps) and the corresponding loss reported by the scouting radio is greater than a duplication threshold (0.75). This is to minimize the cellular usage by having the rate adaptation algorithm to decrease the PHY rate first. *Criteria II:* the downlink packet is a retransmission packet. This attempts to minimize further retransmissions, thereby alleviating the effect of head-of-line blocking at the client.

3.3 Additional techniques

We describe two additional techniques used in *Scout*, i.e., dual-radio diversity combining and NACK based retransmissions. These two techniques, albeit simple, are useful in combating end-to-end losses as shown in § 5.2.

Dual-radio diversity combining: Apart from channel estimation, we leverage the additional scouting radio to enhance reception diversity. To this end, we combine the *coded* packets received at both radios, passing those *unique* packets for FEC decoding. Since two radios are likely to capture a different set of packets, a phenomenon widely known as reception diversity [12], combining packets between them can effectively enhance the reception performance.

NACK based retransmission: In *Scout*, the base station and the client follow a sliding-window protocol to provide in-order and optionally reliable delivery in downlink communication. For uplink, *Scout* provides best-effort delivery due to the trivial loss rates observed in the cellular links as discussed. To avoid saturating the cellular path, the client sends a NACK packet for a block of downlink data packets periodically (every 50ms). The base station retransmits each lost packet for a maximum retry count before discarding it. The retry limit is tunable to accommodate various application requirements.

4. IMPLEMENTATION

We describe the hardware platform and the software architecture of *Scout*, along with the rate adaptation algorithms implemented for comparison.

4.1 Hardware platform

Our radio platform, called the *Scout Wide Band Digital Radio* (WDR), is shown in Figure 7. It enables the whitespaces communication by translating the WiFi signals to the UHF band. To support two WiFi radios at the client, we used an enhanced version of WDR equipped with two independent signal processing paths, each of which can translate a stream of the WiFi signal. This allows the use of one WDR for two radios at each client to reduce the hardware cost. Due to some limitations in the RF front-end, the current version of WDR can support 802.11 b/g data rates up to 18Mbps.

4.2 Software architecture

We implement *Scout* with a userspace program running at the 3.5 layer of the networking stack on top of the cellular and whitespaces links. Figure 8 shows our software architecture. We have written this program in about 7000 lines of C++ and added 50 lines of C code to modify the Ath5k and Ath9k driver. The salient characteristics of our implementation are listed below.

Single-link abstraction: To allow traditional applications to run over two heterogeneous links without modifications, we expose the abstraction of a single link using a virtual network device in Linux called *TUN*. All the applications send traffic through this fake device, which is then intercepted by our user-space program, and redirected through UDP tunneling over the underlying physical links (i.e., whitespaces and cellular).

As shown in Figure 8, for downlink communication, the server program at the base station first reads the application traffic from TUN into a packet buffer. It performs all the signal processing as described in § 3, sending the encoded packets through the whitespaces interface (Ath0). It also sends the original data packets via the Ethernet interface (Eth0) upon detecting the outage of the whitespace link. The client program receives the downlink packets from both whitespace interfaces (Ath0, Ath1), and occasionally from the cellular interface (PPP0). It decapsulates these packets and performs various decoding steps as mentioned in § 3. After decoding, the client collates all the unique data packets into the packet buffer, passing those received in-order through TUN to the application layer. The uplink communication is conducted in a similar fashion by having the client program send the uplink traffic over the cellular interface, which will be received at the Ethernet interface of the base station, and passed through the TUN interface by the server program.

Broadcast-based downlink communication: We configure the base station to broadcast downlink traffic to all the clients. The client program is responsible for discarding those packets destined to a different client based on their IP address after decapsulation.

Section	Experiment Setup	Compared Algorithms	Scout Gains
	Overall Performance		
5.1.1	Whitespace + cellular, road A	*Scout* v.s. A1 – A4	23 – 120× over single radio, 3 – 8× over dual radios
5.1.2	WiFi + cellular, road A	*Scout* v.s. MIMO	Scout(2-SISO-Radios): 4×, Scout(2-MIMO-Radios): 7×
5.1.3	Whitespace + cellular, road A (video streaming)	*Scout* v.s. A4	90% reduction in buffering delay
5.1.4	Whitespace + cellular, road B	*Scout* v.s. A3 – A4	9× at 75th quartile
	Microbenchmarks		
5.2.1	Whitespace + cellular, road A	ScoutRate v.s. RRAA and Minstrel	3.6× and 1.3× (with diversity)
5.2.2	Whitespace + cellular, road A	FEC-w-Scouting v.s. No-FEC, FEC-w/o-Scouting	1.5× over No-FEC, 1.3× over FEC-w/o-Scouting
5.2.3	Whitespace + cellular, road A	*Scout* v.s. No-DUP, DUP-w/o-Scouting	1.6× over No-DUP, 1.3× over DUP-w/o-Scouting
5.3	WiFi + cellular, indoor	*Scout* v.s. A3 – A4	0.8× (under-perform)

Table 2: Summary of main evaluation results. Performance gain is reported for TCP throughput unless mentioned otherwise.

There are three reasons for this decision. First, the 802.11 protocol disables the link-layer retransmissions in the broadcast mode. Thus, *Scout* can make its own retransmission decisions based on the NACK packets sent over the cellular link [4]. Second, the broadcast packets can be received by both radios at a client for channel estimation and multi-radio diversity combining. Third, each client can even overhear other clients' downlink traffic for channel estimation. Here we assume that the security is assured by higher layer protocols, e.g., https. We modify the WiFi driver so that the server program can use a specific header field to control the PHY rate of each broadcast packet.

Dual sequence number spaces: *Scout* uses two different spaces of sequence numbers for data packets and coded packets respectively. The *raw sequence numbers* are used to index coded packets for channel estimation. In contrast, the *data sequence numbers* are used to identify data packets for link-layer retransmission. The client program detects packet loss based on the gaps in the sequence numbers of received packets. It generates different types of NACKs, which contain the sequence numbers of the lost data packets and those of missing coded packets respectively.

4.3 Rate adaptation algorithm

We select RRAA [29] and Minstrel [25] as representative rate adaptation algorithms implemented in the alternative systems for comparison with *Scout*. Minstrel is an enhanced version of SampleRate [4], which can respond faster to the channel variation and is the default algorithm used by the Ath5k driver. We further implement a Minstrel variant – Minstrel-HT [24] used by the Ath9k driver for MIMO rate adaptation.

While we experiment with only two rate adaptation algorithms, we expect *any* algorithm that requires accurate channel estimates at the client to be benefited from the scouting feedback in a heterogeneous network. Examples of such algorithms include SNR-triggered protocols [5, 11], which depend on accurate SNR measurements at the receiver to perform well. Similarly, for recently proposed schemes such as SoftRate [28] and AccuRate [21] that require PHY layer feedback from the receiver, and SensorHints [17] that uses mobile sensor inputs to detect the receiver mobility, adoption of the scouting feedback over stale feedback should lead to better performance. Exploring the complexity of adapting all the above algorithms for *Scout*, albeit challenging, is beyond the scope of our current work.

Alternative Systems	Rate Adaptation	Dual-radio Combining
A-1	RRAA	No
A-2	Minstrel	No
A-3	RRAA	Yes
A-4	Minstrel	Yes

Table 3: Alternative systems to be compared against *Scout*.

5. EVALUATION

In this section, we evaluate the performance gains by exploiting the scouting feedback to optimize multiple protocol decisions, which include rate adaptation, inter-packet FEC, and intelligent traffic duplication implemented in our prototype system. For the experiments, we have driven about 500 miles in the neighborhood of our whitespaces base station across various road segments. We primarily use two road segments shown in Figure 3(c) in this evaluation. Table 2 summarizes our main results.

Evaluation metrics: We use a variety of metrics to evaluate the link performance such as TCP throughput, end-to-end packet loss rates, buffering delay of video streaming, etc.

Compared systems: As discussed in § 4.3, we use RRAA and Minstrel as representative algorithms that use packet error rates at the receiver to select PHY rates. Table 3 describes four alternative systems implemented upon these algorithms and using SISO radios for downlink communication. A-1 and A-2 use RRAA and Minstrel respectively. A-3 and A-4 are dual-radio variants of A-1 and A-2, which also instantiate the prior concept of multi-radio diversity (MRD [12]) as done in *Scout*. We further implement a MIMO version of A-2 based on Minstrel-HT to select MIMO PHY rates. All the above systems use link-layer retransmission with a retry limit of 4.

Data collection: We collected measurements from 5 drives for each algorithm along these routes in all the experiments unless mentioned otherwise. The testbed is the same as described in § 2.1.

5.1 Overall performance of Scout

We evaluate the overall performance of *Scout* in supporting TCP downloading and video streaming on the two representative road segments. We quantify the performance gain of *Scout* over the alternative systems using SISO and MIMO radios, respectively.

5.1.1 TCP throughput (road segment A)

Method: We measured the downlink TCP performance of experiments conducted on road segment A, which has a better coverage from our whitespaces base station. The duration of each drive was 60 seconds approximately, and the results were averaged over 1 second bins for each system.

---

[4]If the unicast communication is used otherwise, the WiFi-based radio at the base station would perform unnecessary link-layer retransmission up to the maximum retry limit, since it cannot receive any link-layer ACKs over the weak whitespace uplink.

(a) TCP throughput

(b) End-to-end loss rates

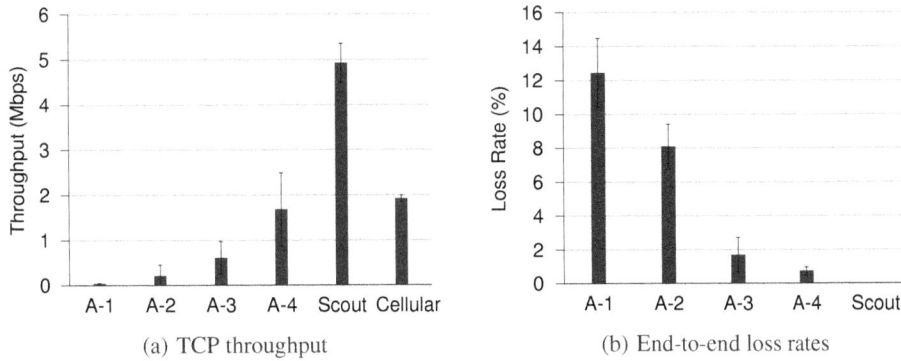

Figure 9: Average downlink TCP performance on road segment A. The error bar shows standard deviation.

Results: Figure 9(a) shows that *Scout* achieved 8× and 3× improvement in TCP throughput over A-3 and A-4, both of which used dual-radio diversity combining in the downlink path. These dual-radio systems outperformed their single-radio counterparts by 15× and 8×, and hence it is sufficient to focus on the dual-radio versions alone. We also provide the TCP throughput of an existing 3G cellular link just for reference. Note that a direct comparison between *Scout* and the cellular link is not useful since the quality of hardware platforms and the load at the base station are different. We envision much higher throughput to be possible in a commercially designed whitespace system with improved antennas, sophisticated placement, and a radio incorporating higher PHY rates and various signal processing optimizations.

To gain some insights behind the throughput performance, we analyzed the end-to-end loss rate and the congestion window size of each TCP connection. Figure 9(b) shows that *Scout* can completely eliminate the end-to-end loss, whereas A-3 and A-4 suffered from 1.69% and 0.72% loss. Thus, we find that the average congestion window in *Scout* was 6× and 3× larger than that in A-3 and A-4.

5.1.2 Scout or MIMO? (road segment A)

One natural question we need to address is how does *Scout* compare to a 2×2 MIMO system, considering both using *two* radio chains at the client. A commercial 2×2 MIMO system based on the 802.11n standard [27] leverages path diversity by simultaneously sending different data streams from the two radios at the transmitter (multiplexing mode) to boost throughput under good channel condition, or by duplicating a single data stream across these radios (diversity mode) to enhance reception under a harsh channel. In order to be effective, a MIMO transmitter needs to select an appropriate operation mode and modulation based on a given channel condition, which is fast varying under vehicular context and can hardly be captured with the delayed feedback. Hence, we find that the use of a scouting radio can be particularly beneficial to a MIMO system in a heterogeneous network.

Method: We compare three multi-radio systems using the cellular uplink to send feedback. (i) Single-MIMO-Radio uses one 2×2 MIMO transceiver at the client for receiving downlink traffic. (ii) Scout (2-SISO-Radios) is the *Scout* design using two SISO radios at the client, thus having a comparable number of radio chains at the client. (iii) Scout (2-MIMO-Radios) is the *Scout* version of MIMO that is enhanced by one extra scouting MIMO radio at the client. We used commercial WiFi radios operating in the 2.4GHz band for downlink communications in all the systems [5], because the dual radio chains in WDR are not sufficiently synchronized for

---

[5]This is the only outdoor experiment not done in TV whitespaces.

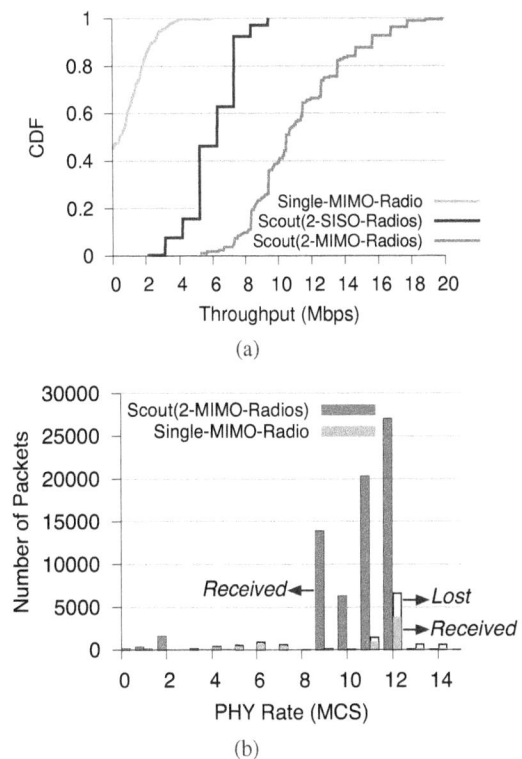

(a)

(b)

Figure 10: TCP performance of *Scout* and MIMO systems on road segment A. (a) CDF of downlink TCP throughput. (b) Distribution of end-to-end packets received and lost at different PHY rates.

MIMO signal processing. The base station was transmitting at a power of 1.4 W. We measured the downlink TCP performance of each system on road segment A, but with shorter drives due to the limited WiFi range. The experiment was conducted at late nights to avoid external interference.

Results: Figure 10(a) shows the CDF of TCP throughputs averaged over 1 second bins of each system. We observe that Single-MIMO-Radio achieved a TCP throughput of less than 2Mbps at 75th quartile due to inappropriate rate decisions caused by delayed feedback. Scout (2-SISO-Radios) had 4× higher throughput compared to Single-MIMO-Radio owing to better channel estimation and aggressive error recovery. Finally, Scout (2-MIMO-Radios) can outperform Scout (2-SISO-Radios) by 1.8× at the 75th quartile by fulfilling the PHY layer diversity gain in MIMO with improved protocol decisions enabled by the scouting radio.

295

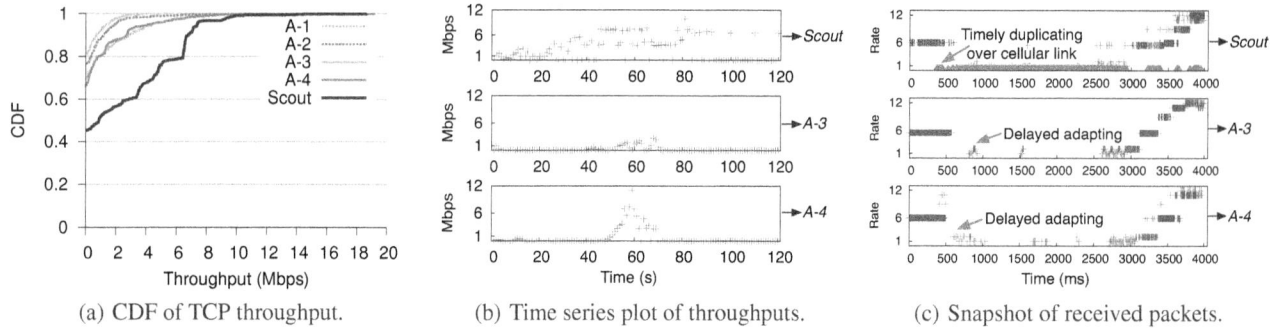

(a) CDF of TCP throughput. (b) Time series plot of throughputs. (c) Snapshot of received packets.

Figure 12: Downlink TCP performance of different systems along road segment B.

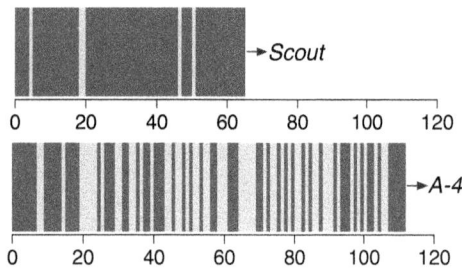

Figure 11: Time series plot of a 60s video played in different systems along road segment A. The dark color shows the playing time and the light color shows the buffering delay.

To understand the reason for the performance difference between the two MIMO systems, Figure 10(b) shows the distribution of end-to-end packets that were received and lost at each modulation and coding index (MCS). A MCS indicates a combination of the operation mode and modulation to be selected by a rate adaptation algorithm; the upper 8 indices select different modulations in the multiplexing mode, whereas the lower 8 choose those in diversity mode. We find that Single-MIMO-Radio based on delayed feedback over-selected MCS, incurring up to 42% loss rates at different MCS. This caused frequent TCP timeout and a small TCP window size (inferred by total packet counts). After enhanced by the scouting MIMO receiver, Scout (2-MIMO-Radios) has reduced loss rates to be less than 0.1%, thus being able to maintain a TCP window $5\times$ larger than that of Single-MIMO-Radio.

5.1.3 Video streaming over TCP (road segment A)

We next evaluate the quality of video streaming in different systems. Video streaming is an application of growing popularity. A lot of emerging streaming services (Netflix, Hulu, YouTube, etc.) are implemented on top of TCP. For these applications, one performance metric is the playing outages due to buffering delays, which have a large impact on the user experience.

Method: We streamed a high definition (1280×720) video clip from YouTube when the client was driving on road segment A. The duration of this video was 60s. We compared the video performance between *Scout* and A-4. Note that A-4 performed the best among all the alternative systems.

Results: Figure 11 shows the time series plot of the video played in both systems based on our captured traces. We observe that the video played in A-4 stopped frequently for buffering, whereas the same video played in *Scout* only stopped for a few times (4), with

each lasting for less than 3 seconds. This leads to an overall buffering delay to be 90% lower than that of A-4, indicating better user experience in *Scout*.

5.1.4 TCP throughput (road segment B)

Method: We measured the downlink TCP throughput along road segment B to study the performance of different systems on a road with poor coverage from the TV whitespaces base station. Each drive lasted about 120 second, corresponding to the time for the vehicle to finish the entire route.

Results: Figure 12(a) presents the CDF of TCP throughputs averaged over 1 second bins from all the drives of each system. We observe that *Scout* achieved $9\times$ gain over A-3 and A-4 at the 75th percentile. Apart from higher throughput, *Scout* reduced the "blackout" period (0 Mbps throughput) in both alternative systems by 25% and 20% due to the intelligent traffic duplication.

Figure 12(b) presents the throughput measurements over time in one of 5 drives for each system. We observe that *Scout* strived to maintain a vehicular connectivity for more than 75% of the time, whereas A-3 and A-4 were able to support connectivity for about 15% of the time. During the first 20 seconds of driving, *Scout* accurately detected the connection outage with the scouting radio, activating the cellular duplication to ensure a minimum connectivity. In contrast, A-3 and A-4 suffered from the link outage with zero throughput. During the period between 20 to 80 seconds, *Scout* detected the recovery of the whitespaces connectivity, thus stopped using the cellular link for traffic duplication. It boosted the throughput performance by selecting aggressive PHY rates while using FEC to guard against channel losses in whitespaces. Finally, all systems failed to provide connectivity at the end of the drive (approximately after 90 second) because both the cellular and whitespace links were severely blocked by the surrounding buildings.

To illustrate how the scouting radio can improve performance, we present a 4 second packet trace for each system along the *same* road segment in Figure 12(c). We observe that all three systems experienced the loss of connectivity over whitespaces during a time period between 500 and 2500 milliseconds. *Scout* immediately detected this channel degradation by observing the packet failures at the front radio. It then enabled the base station to duplicate packets over the cellular link until the connectivity was fully recovered at 3000 milliseconds. In contrast, A-3 and A-4 incurred the delay of 225 milliseconds and 97 milliseconds in adapting to the deteriorating channel. Subsequently, both A-3 and A-4 suffered from a connection "black-out" for about 2 seconds where all packets were lost over the whitespaces. This leads to significant throughput degradation due to TCP timeout, which was avoided by *Scout* with traffic duplication.

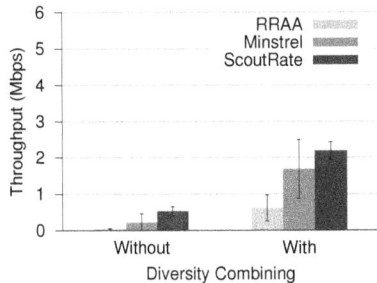

Figure 13: Performance improvement of rate adaptation (microbenchmark).

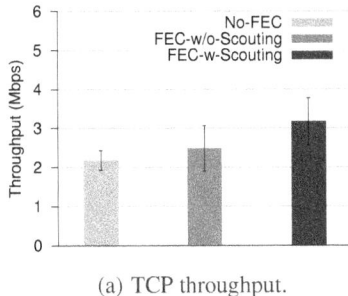

(a) TCP throughput.

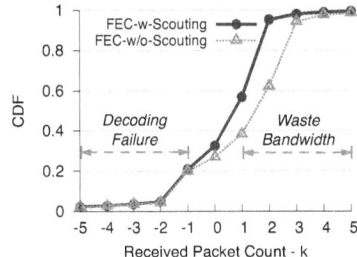

(b) Accuracy of redundancy estimation.

Figure 14: Performance improvement of inter-packet FEC (microbenchmark).

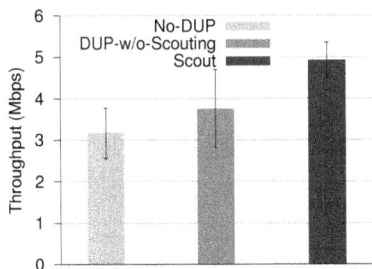

Figure 15: Performance improvement of intelligent traffic duplication over cellular path when needed (microbenchmark). No-DUP is the same as FEC-w-Scouting.

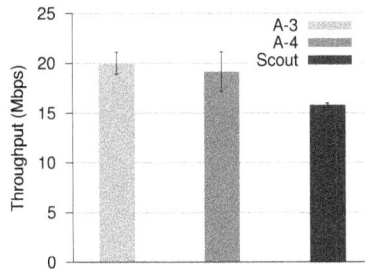

Figure 16: Performance of *Scout* in static scenarios.

5.2 Microbenchmarks of Scout

We benchmark the performance improvement due to individual components in *Scout*, which are rate adaptation, dual-radio diversity, inter-packet FEC, and intelligent traffic duplication. We applied these techniques incrementally to our system while carefully measuring the change in performance before and after adopting each scheme. We further quantified the benefits of the scouting radio in enhancing each transmission decision. The link-layer retransmission was enabled with a retry limit of 4 along with these techniques. All the results were downlink TCP throughputs averaged over 1 second bins from 5 drives on road segment A.

5.2.1 Rate adaptation

Method: To understand the contribution of the scouting radio to rate selection, we evaluated the rate adaptation algorithm used in *Scout* alone, denoted as ScoutRate. We compared ScoutRate against RRAA and Minstrel under the two cases where the dual-radio diversity combining was used or not.

Results: Figure 13 shows that ScoutRate has achieved $13\times$ and $2.5\times$ throughput improvement over RRAA and Minstrel without reception diversity, as well as $3.6\times$ and $1.3\times$ over the two algorithms with reception diversity. We also note that the reception diversity effectively improved the performance of RRAA, Minstrel and ScoutRate by $15\times$, $8\times$ and $4\times$.

5.2.2 Inter-packet Forward Error Correction

Method: To study the efficacy of inter-packet FEC, we compared three systems, which are No-FEC, FEC-w/o-Scouting, and FEC-w-Scouting. No-FEC uses ScoutRate to select PHY rates. FEC-w/o-Scouting uses ScoutRate and FEC, but estimates redundancy based on the delayed feedback for both radios. FEC-w-Scouting uses ScoutRate and FEC based on the channel estimates provided

by the scouting radio. All the systems leverage diversity combining and have taken account its multiplicative effect in loss reduction as described in § 3.2.2.

Results: Figure 14(a) shows that FEC-w-Scouting outperformed No-FEC by 45% due to the use of inter-packet FEC. Our further analysis shows that the inter-packet FEC reduced the number of retransmissions by 62%, thus significantly reducing the bandwidth inefficiency caused by slow retransmission. While both using FEC, FEC-w-Scouting outperformed FEC-w/o-Scouting by 28% due to the improved channel estimates enabled by the scouting radio.

To understand the advantage of the scouting radio based channel estimation, we analyzed the accuracy of redundancy estimation in FEC-w-Scouting and FEC-w/o-Scouting. To this end, we calculated the difference between the number of coded packets received for each batch and the minimum number of packets needed to decode the entire batch. This minimum decodable count is equal to the number of data packets included in the batch – k as described in § 3.2.2. A positive result indicates over-estimation of redundancy, leading to wastage in bandwidth. A negative result means under-estimation of redundancy, resulting in failure of decoding. Figure 14(b) shows the CDF of this metric for all the batches. We observe that the gain of FEC-w-Scouting mainly came from *fewer over-estimations* of redundancy, which allowed better utilization of limited channel capacity.

5.2.3 Intelligent traffic duplication over cellular links

Method: We benchmark the efficacy of the intelligent traffic duplication in *Scout*. We compared the following three systems: (i) No-DUP that is FEC-w-Scouting without the use of duplication, (ii) DUP-w/o-Scouting that additionally performs necessary traffic duplication but based on the delayed feedback, and (iii) *Scout* – the complete version of our system. Again, all the systems use the loss rates at both radios for making transmission decisions.

Results: Figure 15 shows that the intelligent traffic duplication in *Scout* improved the overall TCP throughput by 55% over No-DUP, because whitespace links (like all other links) can experience occasional outages and the ability to divert traffic to alternate paths should always improve performance. *Scout* outperformed DUP-w/o-Scouting by 31% due to the timely duplication based on the scouting radio. Finally, since the duplication in *Scout* was done on demand, i.e., when the whitespace link is considered unresponsive, we find only 7% duplicated data to be unnecessary.

5.3 Scout in static scenarios

As discussed in § 3.1, when a client is static, our base station loses its advantage in channel estimation by reverting to the delayed feedback of the rear radio. Below we evaluate the performance of *Scout* in these static environments.

Method: We measured the downlink TCP throughput in our indoor lab environment where the loss rate was quite low. All the systems used SISO based WiFi radios for downlink communication and a cellular path for uplink. Each experiment was run for 60 seconds.

Results: Figure 16 shows the average TCP throughput of different systems. We observe that *Scout* had 21% and 17% lower throughput compared to A-3 and A-4 since the scouting radio no longer provided any useful feedback to the system. Further, some of the error recovery mechanisms such as FEC were not necessary in this setup, but introducing overheads. Hence, the scouting related functions, while particularly suited for highly mobile scenarios, should be disabled in static situations by the base station, which can quickly detect such cases using the GPS updates from the client.

6. RELATED WORK

We delineate *Scout* from prior work in the following six categories, whitespaces networking, vehicular networking, heterogeneous networking, context-based channel estimation, multi-antenna systems, and rate adaptation.

WhiteFi [1] is a system that operates over TV whitespaces using a WiFi-like protocol. A campus-wide network based on such design for vehicular connectivity has been subsequently reported in [6]. These systems use whitespaces for both uplink and downlink transmissions, thus suffering from the problem of power asymmetry avoided by *Scout*.

A large body of prior work has explored providing Internet connectivity to moving vehicles. Example systems include MAR [19], ViFi [3], CaberNet [7], MobiSteer [13], Wiffler [2], WiRover [10]. These systems use different combinations of cellular and WiFi connectivity, and do not explore the unique challenges related to the use of TV whitespaces for supporting this application.

The heterogeneous architecture has been widely adopted in satellite networks, e.g., direct broadcast satellite. These systems use the satellite link to send the downlink traffic while leveraging the dial-up modem to exchange the uplink traffic. *Scout* is different from them in two major ways. First, *Scout* is a stylized design to mitigate the effect of slow feedback in making transmission decisions over the fast whitespaces downlink. In contrast, the prior designs focus on how to efficiently utilize the slow satellite downlink with a relatively fast feedback path [14, 15]. Second, *Scout* uses link-layer only solutions to establish a robust connection, over which a variety of higher layer protocols can be efficiently supported. On the other hand, some of the solutions [14, 15] proposed in satellite networks are transport-layer centric and focus on TCP enhancements.

To address the feedback delay in a heterogeneous network, *Scout* uses the location specific channel information collected by an extra scouting radio. Predicting network connectivity based on the receiver's location has been explored before (e.g., Bartendr [20],

BreadCrumbs [16], MobiSteer [13]). However, most of these solutions rely on some training information that is updated on a coarse timescale, e.g., order of days [20]. In contrast, *Scout* allows collecting such channel information in real-time, while obviating any training overhead.

In addition to obtaining channel estimates, the extra radio in *Scout* is also used for packet-level diversity combining. Diversity combining techniques have been studied in many multi-radio, multi-antenna systems [12, 22, 27]. These MIMO systems harness the path diversity in wireless channel for robust reception [27], scaling throughput [27], or simultaneous communications with multiple users [22]. However, most of the diversity techniques work at the physical layer of the networking stack whereas *Scout* leverages diversity at the MAC layer. Furthermore, *Scout* is shown to be complementary to these techniques by providing better channel estimates to enhance their transmission decision.

We compare *Scout* with two widely used rate adaptation algorithms, i.e., RRAA [29], Minstrel [25]. RRAA tracks packet loss rates in a short period, and uses some predetermined loss thresholds to adapt data rates. Minstrel is an enhanced version of SampleRate [4], which are used in the Ath5k driver. It periodically probes a random rate, and selects the one with the highest throughput. Recent rate adaptation techniques [17, 21, 28] attempt to collect diversified information such as PHY layer hints and device mobility, to better infer the channel condition experienced at a receiver. To be effective, all these techniques require accurate feedback, and thus can be enhanced by the scouting radio in a heterogeneous network.

Finally, the concept of a scouting radio was first reported in a position paper [30] that explored the feasibility of the idea. In this paper, we build upon this prior concept by evaluating various challenges around building a practical and working system, designing algorithmic techniques to meet such challenges, and performing detailed evaluations on the prototypes developed.

7. CONCLUSIONS

In this work, we explore a heterogeneous network design called *Scout* to provide wide-area Internet connectivity to vehicles. Our system leverages the use of new and additional spectrum available in TV whitespaces and combines it with the already pervasive cellular networks. The proposed architecture significantly enhances the coverage of vehicular whitespace deployments compared to a symmetric whitespace-only architecture.

We also introduce the notion and demonstrate the benefits of a scouting radio in the proposed architecture. In a vehicular setting, since it is natural for a rear radio to follow a front radio along a given path, the scouting radio placed at the head of a vehicle is able to provide accurate channel estimates for the main receiving radio at the rear. This accurate feedback in turn leads to better protocol decisions that ultimately translate to substantial performance improvement $(3 - 8\times)$. A preliminary version of our system has been showcased in a recent conference demo [31] and the video of this demo is at http://www.youtube.com/watch?v=_rnzH7owtBw.

Acknowledgments

We thank Ning Leng for providing various suggestions to improve the techniques developed in this work. We also thank Ren Chao and Lei Kang for their help in some of outdoor experimentation. We are grateful to our shepherd, Romit Roy Choudhury, and the anonymous reviewers whose comments helped bring the paper to its final form. All the authors are supported in part by the following awards of the US National Science Foundation: CNS-1040648, CNS-0916955,CNS-0855201,CNS-0747177, CNS-1064944, CNS-1059306, CNS-1343363, and CNS-1230751.

Algorithm 1 : *Scout*

Input: t: Current time, λ: Antenna separation, v: Vehicle speed,
$\mathcal{D}$: Batch of data packets to be transmitted, $\mathcal{R}$: PHY rates for selection,
$\mathcal{A}_f$: Set of packets ACKed for the front radio,
$\mathcal{A}_r$: Set of packets ACKed for the rear radio.
Output: $\mathcal{P}_{wspace}$: Coded packets sent over TV whitespaces,
$\mathcal{P}_{cell}$: Data packets duplicated over cellular links.

$\qquad \mathcal{L}_f, \mathcal{L}_r = ScoutEstimate(\mathcal{R}, \mathcal{A}_f, \mathcal{A}_r, t, \lambda, v)$
$\qquad R_{data}, R_{probe} = ScoutRate(\mathcal{R}, \mathcal{L}_f, \mathcal{L}_r)$
$\qquad \mathcal{P}_{wspace} = ScoutFEC(\mathcal{D}, \mathcal{L}_f, \mathcal{L}_r, R_{data}, R_{probe})$
$\qquad \mathcal{P}_{cell} = ScoutDUP(\mathcal{P}_{wspace}, \mathcal{L}_r)$
$\qquad$ **return** $(\mathcal{P}_{wspace}, \mathcal{P}_{cell})$

1: **procedure** SCOUTESTIMATE($\mathcal{R}, \mathcal{A}_f, \mathcal{A}_r, t, \lambda, v$)
2: $\quad \tau \leftarrow \lambda / v$
3: $\quad \mathcal{E}_f \leftarrow \{P_i.rate : P_i \in \mathcal{A}_f, t - i \leq W\}$ ▷ W is a time window
4: $\quad \mathcal{E}_r \leftarrow \{P_i.rate : P_i \in \mathcal{A}_f, |(t - \tau) - i| \leq W/2\}$
5: $\quad$ **if** $\mathcal{E}_r = \phi$ **then**
6: $\qquad \mathcal{E}_r \leftarrow \{P_i.rate : P_i \in \mathcal{A}_r, t - i \leq W\}$
7: $\quad$ **end if**
8: $\quad \mathcal{L}_f \leftarrow calculate\_loss\_rates(\mathcal{E}_f, \mathcal{R})$
9: $\quad \mathcal{L}_r \leftarrow calculate\_loss\_rates(\mathcal{E}_r, \mathcal{R})$
10: $\quad$ **return** $(\mathcal{L}_f, \mathcal{L}_r)$
11: **end procedure**

12: **procedure** SCOUTRATE($\mathcal{R}, \mathcal{L}_f, \mathcal{L}_r$)
13: $\quad$ **for** $R_i \in \mathcal{R}$ **do**
14: $\qquad$ **if** $\mathcal{L}_f(R_i) \leq L_{thresh}$ and $\mathcal{L}_r(R_i) \leq L_{thresh}$ **then**
15: $\qquad\quad throughput(R_i) \leftarrow R_i \times (1 - L_r(R_i))$
16: $\qquad$ **end if**
17: $\quad$ **end for**
18: $\quad R_{data} \leftarrow R_i$ with maximum *throughput*
19: $\quad probing\_set \leftarrow \{R_i : R_i \in \mathcal{R}, R_i > throughput(R_{data})\}$
20: $\quad R_{probe} \leftarrow$ a random $R \in probing\_set$
21: $\quad$ **return** (R_{data}, R_{probe})
22: **end procedure**

23: **procedure** SCOUTFEC($\mathcal{D}, \mathcal{L}_f, \mathcal{L}_r, R_{data}, R_{probe}$)
24: $\quad L \leftarrow \mathcal{L}_f(R_{data}) \times \mathcal{L}_r(R_{data})$
25: $\quad rr \leftarrow L \times (1 + extra\_redundancy)$
26: $\quad N \leftarrow coherence\_time \times R_{data} / packet\_size$
27: $\quad K \leftarrow N \times (1 - rr)$
28: $\quad \mathcal{P}_{wspace} \leftarrow encode(\mathcal{D}, K, N + 1)$
29: $\quad$ **for** $P_i \in \mathcal{P}_{wspace}$ **do**
30: $\qquad$ **if** $i = N + 1$ **then**
31: $\qquad\quad P_i.rate \leftarrow R_{probe}$
32: $\qquad$ **else**
33: $\qquad\quad P_i.rate \leftarrow R_{data}$
34: $\qquad$ **end if**
35: $\quad$ **end for**
36: $\quad$ **return** $\mathcal{P}_{wspace}$
37: **end procedure**

38: **procedure** SCOUTDUP($\mathcal{P}_{wspace}, \mathcal{L}_r$)
39: $\quad \mathcal{P}_{cell} \leftarrow \phi$
40: $\quad$ **for** $P_i \in \mathcal{P}_{wspace}$ and $i <= K$ **do**
41: $\qquad$ **if** $P_i.rate = lowest$ and $\mathcal{L}_r(P_i.rate) > L_{dup\_thresh}$ **then**
42: $\qquad\quad \mathcal{P}_{cell} \leftarrow \mathcal{P}_{cell} \cup P_i$
43: $\qquad$ **end if**
44: $\qquad$ **if** $P_i.retransmission = true$ **then**
45: $\qquad\quad \mathcal{P}_{cell} \leftarrow \mathcal{P}_{cell} \cup P_i$
46: $\qquad$ **end if**
47: $\quad$ **end for**
48: $\quad$ **return** $\mathcal{P}_{cell}$
49: **end procedure**

8. REFERENCES

[1] P. Bahl, R. Chandra, T. Moscibroda, R. Murty, and M. Welsh. White space networking with WiFi like connectivity. In *SIGCOMM*, 2009.

[2] A. Balasubramanian, R. Mahajan, and A. Venkataramani. Augmenting mobile 3G using WiFi. In *MobiSys*, 2010.

[3] A. Balasubramanian, R. Mahajan, A. Venkataramani, B. N. Levine, and J. Zahorjan. Interactive WiFi connectivity for moving vehicles. In *SIGCOMM*, 2008.

[4] J. C. Bicket. Bit-rate selection in wireless networks. In *Master's thesis, MIT*, 2005.

[5] J. Camp and E. Knightly. Modulation rate adaptation in urban and vehicular environments: cross-layer implementation and experimental evaluation. In *MobiCom*, 2008.

[6] R. Chandra, T. Moscibroda, P. Bahl, R. Murty, G. Nychis, and X. Wang. A campus-wide testbed over the TV white spaces. *MC2R*, 15, July 2011.

[7] J. Eriksson, H. Balakrishnan, and S. Madden. Cabernet: vehicular content delivery using WiFi. In *MobiCom*, 2008.

[8] Federal Communications Commission. IEEE standard for local and metropolitan area networks, 2009.

[9] Federal Communications Commission. Unlicensed operation in the TV broadcast bands, second memorandum opinion and order, 2010.

[10] J. Hare, L. Hartung, and S. Banerjee. Beyond deployments and testbeds: experiences with public usage on vehicular WiFi hotspots. In *MobiSys*, 2012.

[11] G. Judd, X. Wang, and P. Steenkiste. Efficient channel-aware rate adaptation in dynamic environments. In *MobiSys*, 2008.

[12] A. Miu, H. Balakrishnan, and C. E. Koksal. Improving loss resilience with multi-radio diversity in wireless networks. In *MobiCom*, 2005.

[13] V. Navda, A. P. Subramanian, K. Dhanasekaran, A. Timm-Giel, and S. Das. Mobisteer: using steerable beam directional antenna for vehicular network access. In *MobiSys*, 2007.

[14] Network Working Group. Enhancing TCP over satellite channels using standard mechanisms, 1999.

[15] Network Working Group. Ongoing TCP research related to satellites, 2000.

[16] A. J. Nicholson and B. D. Noble. Breadcrumbs: forecasting mobile connectivity. In *MobiCom*, 2008.

[17] L. Ravindranath, C. Newport, H. Balakrishnan, and S. Madden. Improving wireless network performance using sensor hints. In *NSDI*, 2011.

[18] L. Rizzo. Effective erasure codes for reliable computer communication protocols. *ACM CCR*, 1997.

[19] P. Rodriguez, R. Chakravorty, J. Crowcroft, J. Chesterfield, and S. Banerjee. MAR: A commuter router infrastructure for the mobile Internet. In *Mobisys*, 2004.

[20] A. Schulman, V. Navda, R. Ramjee, N. Spring, P. Deshpande, C. Grunewald, K. Jain, and N. Padmanabhan, Venkata. Bartendr: a practical approach to energy-aware cellular data scheduling. In *MobiCom*, 2010.

[21] S. Sen, N. Santhapuri, R. R. Choudhury, and S. Nelakuditi. Accurate: constellation based rate estimation in wireless networks. In *NSDI*, 2010.

[22] C. Shepard, H. Yu, N. Anand, E. Li, T. Marzetta, R. Yang, and L. Zhong. Argos: practical many-antenna base stations. In *Mobicom*, 2012.

[23] C. Smith and D. Collins. *3G Wireless Networks*. McGraw-Hill, 2001.

[24] D. Smithies and F. Fietkau. Linux wireless minstrel high throughput. http://wireless.kernel.org.

[25] D. Smithies and F. Fietkau. minstrel: Madwifi and linux kernel rate selection algorithm, 2005.

[26] Spectrum Bridge Inc. Spectrum bridge database. http://www.spectrumbridge.com/Home.aspx.

[27] P. Thornycroft. Designed for speed: Network infrastructure in an 802.11n world. In *Aruba Networks white paper*, 2007.

[28] M. Vutukuru, H. Balakrishnan, and K. Jamieson. Cross-layer wireless bit rate adaptation. In *SIGCOMM*, 2009.

[29] S. H. Y. Wong, H. Yang, S. Lu, and V. Bharghavan. Robust rate adaptation for 802.11 wireless networks. In *MobiCom*, 2006.

[30] T. Zhang, S. Sen, and S. Banerjee. Scout: An asymmetric vehicular network design over TV whitespaces. In *ACM HotMobile*, 2013.

[31] T. Zhang, S. Sen, and S. Banerjee. Video streaming using whitespace spectrum for vehicular applications. In *Mobysis video session*, 2013.

COIN-GPS: Indoor Localization from Direct GPS Receiving

Shahriar Nirjon[1], Jie Liu[2], Gerald DeJean[2], Bodhi Priyantha[2], Yuzhe Jin[2], Ted Hart[2]
[1] Department of Computer Science, University of Virginia
[2] Microsoft Research, Redmond, WA
smn8z@virginia.edu, {liuj, dejean, bodhip, yuzjin, tedhar}@microsoft.com

ABSTRACT

Due to poor signal strength, multipath effects, and limited on-device computation power, common GPS receivers do not work indoors. This work addresses these challenges by using a steerable, high-gain directional antenna as the front-end of a GPS receiver along with a robust signal processing step and a novel location estimation technique to achieve direct GPS-based indoor localization. By leveraging the computing power of the cloud, we accommodate longer signals for acquisition, and remove the requirement of decoding timestamps or ephemeris data from GPS signals. We have tested our system in 31 randomly chosen spots inside five single-story, indoor environments such as stores, warehouses and shopping centers. Our experiments show that the system is capable of obtaining location fixes from 20 of these spots with a median error of less than 10 m, where all normal GPS receivers fail.

Categories and Subject Descriptors

C.3 [**Special-Purpose and Application-Based Systems**]: Real-time and embedded systems

Keywords

Indoor GPS, Instant GPS, CO-GPS, COIN-GPS

1. INTRODUCTION

Common wisdom believes that GPS receivers do not work indoors, period. GPS signals are extremely weak when they reach the Earth's surface, and further attenuation and multipath effects caused by the building shell make satellites undetectable. In fact, we have all experienced a frozen 'acquiring satellites' screen or the 'lost satellite reception' message on a GPS receiver when the device is inside a building or when the line-of-sight between the receiver and the satellites is obstructed. This paper presents a method of using GPS-based direct localization in some indoor environments. This is a first step in making GPS feasible indoors. Especially, the theory developed in this paper of combining acquired satellites from multiple directions at different points in time to estimate an indoor location is the first of its kind.

Indoor localization and location-based services have gained great attention recently while people have enjoyed their outdoor counterparts for years. Indoor navigation in shopping malls, indoor location-based advertisements, and tracking friends and family members in indoor public places are a few examples of how indoor location information can make services friendlier and more useful. Because common GPS receivers do not work indoors due to low GPS signal strength and multipath effects, indoor location systems are usually much more complicated than direct GPS receiving. Existing indoor localization approaches are either based on signature matching or continuous tracking.

There are many kinds of signatures that can approximately associate a receiver with an indoor location. Some examples include RF signatures like WiFi [7], FM [10], cellular networks, or Bluetooth beacons; magnetic signatures from either the Earth's magnetic field [12] or deployed beacons [18]; ambient sound signatures [6]; and cameras [23, 31]. The challenges of all these approaches are infrastructure setup and profiling. The accuracy of most signature-based approaches directly relates to the density of signal sources. At the same time, the indoor space must be profiled (in many cases repeatedly to accommodate temporal variations) to map signatures to location coordinates. A second class of localization approaches is based on continuously tracking the movement of the target from a known location [39, 29]. However, motion sensing based on accelerometer, compass, and gyro drifts over time. The methods must rely again on signatures to realign tracking processes. Continuous sensing and processing also challenge the battery lives of mobile devices.

In contrast to the above approaches, GPS receiving, when working effectively, is direct. A device does not need to have prior knowledge of a known location to start with. Each location can be computed independently, and there is no additional infrastructure or profiling necessary. Our goal is to extend GPS receiving to indoor environments, where it can either be used directly by consumer devices, or be used in conjunction with profiling and tracking methods as landmarks.

Building an indoor GPS receiver is challenging for several practical reasons. First, signals from the GPS satellites are inherently weak, and after traveling more than 21000 km to reach the Earth's surface, the signal strength (−125 dBm) is barely enough to decode satellite information outdoors. Note that the thermo-noise floor at GPS frequency is about −111 dBm. Indoors, the signal strength is about 10 to 100 times weaker, and it is almost impossible for a typical GPS receiver to acquire any satellites. Second, even if signals from a satellite are detected indoors, the weaker signal strength combined with increased multipath effects can cause the receiver to compute an inaccurate distance from the satellite and yield an estimated location that is miles away from the true location. Third, location estimation in a typical GPS receiver requires at least 4 visible satellites, which is highly unlikely to be obtained in an indoor environment. In this paper, we address these challenges and propose a high-sensitivity cloud-offloaded instant GPS (COIN-GPS) for indoors.

We take a hardware-software approach in COIN-GPS, in which a high-gain directional antenna is used at the front-end of the receiver, and the locations are computed in the cloud. Due to the size of the antenna and the requirement for it to be controlled by a laptop, COIN-GPS in its current form is not really suitable to be commercialized or sold as a consumer product. However, the system has other applications, such as providing the ground-truth for other indoor profiling techniques, or mapping indoor environments similar to Google's street-view car or Nokia's NAVTEQ system that are used outdoors.

The design of COIN-GPS is motivated by several properties of indoor environments.

- The roof materials of a building are heterogeneous. We perform a simulation study to understand the amount of attenuation a GPS signal undergoes when it penetrates through different building materials. We conclude that a directional antenna obtains a higher SNR in any given direction than an omnidirectional antenna can, and therefore combining multiple readings in different directions from a directional antenna gives a better overall SNR than an omnidirectional antenna is capable of. Directional antennas also help suppress signals of the same frequency from other directions, and thus mitigate the multipath effects introduced by the building structure.

- Indoor GPS signals are too weak to decode any data packets for timestamps and ephemeris. By using a cloud-offloaded approach [22], we eliminate the need to decode any GPS data. We only store the raw signals at the intermediate frequency as necessary and rely upon the cloud for the ephemeris and location calculation.

- Indoor subjects move slowly. The receiver's location does not change much within a short period of time. By exploiting this, we are able to reuse satellites by considering the same satellite, acquired at different points in time, as different satellites. We derive the formula that, for M independent directions, a total of $2M + 3$ satellites are required to get a successful location fix in such cases.

COIN-GPS is inspired by CO-GPS, an energy efficient signal sampling and cloud-offloaded location computation paradigm [22]. However, COIN-GPS is also different in a number of major aspects. For example, the goal of CO-GPS is to save energy, whereas COIN-GPS's aim is to achieve high sensitivity. COIN-GPS uses a custom-designed, high-gain directional antenna, whereas CO-GPS uses a regular omnidirectional antenna. Finally, COIN-GPS incorporates two new signal processing algorithms, one for robust satellite acquisition and another for estimating the location of a stationary receiver when the number of satellites is inadequate. Both of these algorithms are designed specifically for indoors, taking advantage of the relatively low speed of indoor movements. Like CO-GPS, COIN-GPS is suitable for delay-tolerant applications where the data is collected in-situ and processed offline. But compared to a time-to-first-fix of 30 seconds or more in an outdoor GPS with cold start, COIN-GPS's execution-time performance is acceptable for many indoor location-based applications as well. CO-GPS is used as a baseline for comparison in our experiments.

In order to demonstrate the performance of COIN-GPS, we evaluate the system in five randomly chosen public places in the greater Bellevue, WA area: Starbucks, Home Depot, Fred Meyer,

Costco, and Bellevue Square Mall. We perform a series of experiments to show that, by virtue of the directional antenna and the robust acquisition algorithm, COIN-GPS acquires at least 3 satellites more than 60% of the time, and by combining acquired satellites from 3 or more directions, COIN-GPS gets successful location fixes in 65% of the cases, with an average localization error of 17.4 m and a median error of less than 10 m. Compared to this, traditional GPS hardly ever acquires a satellite and never gets a location fix at those locations.

The main contributions of this paper are the following:

- The design and implementation of a high-gain directional antenna and a robust acquisition algorithm that is motivated by the properties of an indoor environment.

- The formulation and implementation of the stationary GPS formula, which says that for M independent directions, a total of $2M + 3$ satellites are required to get a successful location fix.

- The design and implementation of a complete system called COIN-GPS, which is shown to work in several indoor environments with a success rate of 65% and a median localization error of 9.6 m.

The rest of the paper is organized as follows. We briefly introduce necessary GPS concepts in Section 2. In Section 3, we study RF properties of common building materials to motivate our solution. In Section 4, we give an overview of COIN-GPS, and then Sections 5, 6, and 7 drill down to the details of three key technologies in the solution. We evaluate COIN-GPS in Section 8 and provide a discussion in Section 9.

2. GPS TERMINOLOGIES

To make this paper self-contained, we briefly introduce some key GPS concepts. We refer interested readers to [24, 37] for more technical details.

GPS Satellites: There are 32 GNSS satellites in the sky, each orbiting the earth about two cycles a day. The satellites simultaneously and continuously broadcast time and orbit information through CDMA signals at 1.575 GHz towards the Earth. A GPS receiver computes its location by measuring the distance from the receiver to multiple satellites.

Code Phase: Each satellite encodes its signal using a satellite-specific coarse/acquisition (C/A) code of length 1023 chips at 1023 Mbps, i.e. repeating every millisecond. The purpose of the C/A code is to allow a receiver to identify the sending satellite and estimate the propagation delay. Typically, GPS signals take from 64 to 89 ms to travel from a satellite to the earth. To obtain an accurate distance measurement, the receiver must estimate the signal propagation delay to the microsecond level. Since C/A codes repeat every ms, one way to estimate the sub-ms part of the propagation delay is to identify the code phase, i.e. the offset of the C/A code when it was received.

Doppler Shifts: The Doppler frequency shift is caused by the motion of the satellite and by any movement of the receiver. For example, a rising GPS satellite moves at up to 800 m/s towards a receiver, causing a frequency shift of 4.2 kHz. A shift of the same magnitude occurs in the opposite direction for a setting satellite. To reliably compute corrections under this shift, the receiver must generate the C/A code within 500 Hz of the shifted frequency. Therefore, in the frequency dimension, the receiver needs to search up to 18 bins. Most GPS receivers use 25 to 40 frequency bins to provide better receiver sensitivity.

Acquisition, Tracking, and Location Estimation: The task of getting a location fix is divided mainly into two subtasks: satellite acquisition and location estimation. Acquisition usually involves a search process where, for each satellite, the C/A code is correlated with the received signals to check if the satellite is present or not. Once satellites are acquired, tracking is the process of progressively adjusting code phase and Doppler shifts without going through the full acquisition process again. If a satellite is present, its trajectory and a precise timestamp can be decoded from the satellite signal. From that, the distance from the satellite to the receiver, called the pseudo-range, is obtained. Depending on the type of GPS solutions, estimation of location requires pseudo-ranges from 4 to 5 acquired satellites to form a least squares optimization process. More details of these two steps are in Section 5 and Section 6, prior to the description of our own approaches to them.

Acquisition is a computationally intensive process due to the large code phase and Doppler search space: Time-To-First-Fix (TTFF) is the elapsed time between turning on a receiver and obtaining the first location fix. Depending on what prior knowledge the receiver has about the satellites, TTFF varies from 30+ seconds in standalone GPS receivers to 6+ seconds in assisted GPS (AGPS) where the satellite trajectories are provided to the receivers through a separate channel. Typical AGPS receivers still decode timestamps from satellite signals.

CO-GPS: CO-GPS stands for the Cloud Offloaded GPS. CO-GPS is an extremely low power GPS receiver for delay-tolerant applications. The core idea of CO-GPS is to log a minimal amount of signals (1-2 ms) at runtime and process them offline. This allows the device to aggressively duty-cycle in order to increase its lifetime. CO-GPS adopts coarse time navigation (CTN) [37], in which neither ephemeris *nor the time stamp* is decoded from the satellite packet; rather, a coarse time and a reference from a nearby landmark are used to estimate the ms part of the propagation delay, and only the sub-ms part, i.e. the code phase, is computed from the satellite signals. This results in a GPS receiver that uses as little as 1 ms of signal, and hence, the TTFF can be as fast as a few ms. Because of this, a GPS with CTN is often called an Instant GPS. Unlike standard CTN, CO-GPS leverages the computing resources in the cloud to generate a number of candidate landmarks and use other geographical constraints to filter out the wrong solutions. Since CO-GPS does not have to decode the entire data packet, it is less susceptible to errors in environments where signal strength is weak. This is a key advantage that we leverage in COIN-GPS.

3. MOTIVATION OF COIN-GPS DESIGN

The design of COIN-GPS is motivated by observations on indoor signal attenuation and (slow) indoor receiver movements.

3.1 GPS Signal Attenuation Indoors

GPS signals are inherently weak from the source. The total radiated power from a GPS satellite is about 500 W (or 27 dBW). Assuming a 21000 km distance between the satellite and the receiver (the actual distance depends on the elevation angle), the free space path loss is about 182 dB. That results in a received signal strength, in ideal conditions, of -155 dBW (or -125 dBm), which is actually below the ambient RF noise floor (typically around -111 dBm). Traditional GPS receivers use a high-gain front end, precise band pass filters and, most importantly, the SNR gain from C/A code correlation to detect the existence of GPS signals.

Indoor environments bring significant challenges to GPS signal acquisition since building materials further reduce the signal strength by 10 to 100 times, yet the strength of the RF noise floor remains the same. Amplifying the signals at the GPS frequency will not be effective. Using longer, repeated C/A code may appear

to be a promising approach. However, since C/A codes are used to modulate GPS data packets, without knowing the packet content in advance, the correlation operation may go across the boundaries of opposite bits, which cancels out the correlation gain. We will discuss a more robust correlation algorithm in Section 5.

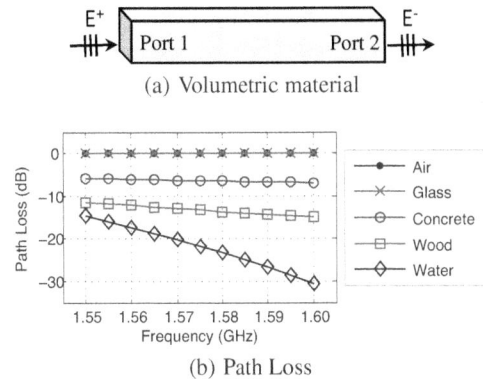

(a) Volumetric material

(b) Path Loss

Figure 1: Path loss of GPS signals through air, glass, concrete, wood, and water. Steel (not drawn) is < -200 dB.

3.1.1 A Simulation Study of GPS Signal Attenuation

To motivate our solution, we first quantify the GPS signal attenuation through different building materials. We use a simulation software called CST Microwave Studio [1], which is one of the most recognized simulators used in the RF and electromagnetic communities. As shown in Figure 1(a), we set up a waveguide of dimensions $6.2 \times 3.1 \times 12$ inches. These dimensions correspond to the fundamental propagating transverse electric mode (TE_{10}) of an air-filled rectangular waveguide. The materials examined in the volume are glass, concrete, wood, water, and steel. In addition, an empty waveguide (simulated as air) is evaluated as a baseline case. The GPS signal is a Gaussian wave propagating in the direction of the volume's length from the Port 1 to the Port 2, and polarized in the direction of the volume's height. We measure the ratio of received voltage signal at Port 2 to the voltage signal transmitted at Port 1, and call it the *path loss*.

Figure 1(b) shows the path loss versus frequency for the 6 cases considered in this study. GPS frequency is 1.575 GHz, which is in the middle of the plot. We see that the signals that propagate through air and glass are unaffected by those materials. The path loss for concrete and wood are in the range of -5 dB to -15 dB, but water and steel present significant obstructions for a GPS signal to be received. Figure 2 illustrates a 2D electric field plot of the GPS signal traveling from transmit Port 1 to receive Port 2, which gives a sense of path loss versus the thickness of the materials.

We have several observations through this simulation study:

- Each foot of concrete or wood attenuates the signal by $5-15$ dB. For multistory buildings, each floor will introduce this amount of path loss, which makes the problem extremely hard. Therefore, in this paper we will focus on single floor structures such as shopping malls, department stores, and business parks.

- The roof of a commercial building is typically made from multiple layers of materials, such as wood, fiberglass, polymer, and asphalt. Its RF path loss property should be close to the combination of wood, glass, and concrete in the simulation, so we expect $10-20$ dB attenuation.

- Many commercial buildings have glass as part of the roof, such as skylights. They allow GPS signals to penetrate the roof with small path loss.

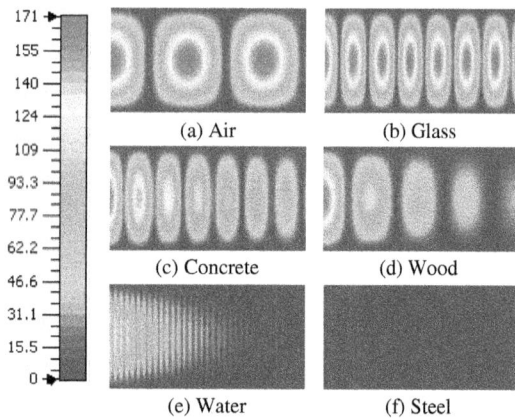

Figure 2: 2D electric field plots of a GPS signal propagating through different materials.

3.2 Motion of an Indoor Receiver

One big difference between an indoor and an outdoor GPS receiver is that the receiver moves slowly indoors. An average person walks about 3 mph, which is $10 - 25$ times slower than a motor vehicle's speed. Compared to the GPS satellites' pseudo-range rate of change of up to 800 m/s, an indoor receiver can be considered stationary. This motivates us to reuse satellites, i.e. to consider the same satellite, acquired at different points in time, as different reference satellites. This is a crucial assumption in COIN-GPS's location estimation algorithm that allows us to overcome the inadequate satellites problem, which is highly likely indoors, and to estimate the location even when the number of unique satellites is less than the required minimum.

4. OVERVIEW OF COIN-GPS

Our high-sensitivity indoor GPS solution incorporates three key technologies: a directional antenna, a robust acquisition algorithm, and a multi-directional location estimation algorithm.

4.1 Directional Antenna

The simulation study and the observations in Section 3.1 motivate us to leverage a directional antenna for GPS receiving. Directional antennas selectively amplify the signals from a chosen direction. As a result, noise (and signals) from other directions are suppressed. For example, in an indoor environment, if we point the antenna towards part of the roof that introduces low signal attenuation, especially skylights, we have a greater opportunity to receive good quality GPS signals while suppressing signals from other directions. GPS satellites scatter in the sky by design. Amplifying towards one satellite may decrease the possibility of acquiring others. That's why we need to point the antenna towards different directions and carefully combine the results.

There are many antenna topologies that can be used to create a directional radiation. Some of the more popular directional antennas are Yagi-Uda arrays [34], slot antennas [14], reflector antennas [30], and patch antenna arrays [27]. Yagi-Uda arrays and reflector antennas are difficult to design in a compact form factor. Although slot antennas over a ground plane have a small form factor, they have a lower gain than desired for highly directional coverage. Patch antenna arrays present a balanced tradeoff between high gain and a compact form factor. They are also highly desirable for their ability to be independent of size and frequency by changing the dielectric material and/or utilizing compact design methods for

miniaturization [20]. We discuss our implementation using a patch antenna array in Section 7.1. For now, it is sufficient to assume a directional antenna that can provide $\approx$ 10 dB gain in the pointed direction.

4.2 Robust Acquisition

The directional antenna is used to sample and store raw GPS signals from multiple directions at the same physical location. Each chunk of samples, obtained from a particular direction, undergoes a robust satellite acquisition process which is described in detail in Section 5. The outcome of the acquisition process is what we call a *directional acquisition*, which consists of a list of satellites with their code phases and Doppler shifts. The directional acquisition processes are run in parallel for a speedup. Once we have results from all N directions at a particular location, those having fewer than 2 acquired satellites are discarded, and the rest are merged to form a combined acquisition result having M ($M \leq N$) directional acquisitions.

The reason a directional acquisition having < 2 satellites is useless is because each time we combine acquired satellites from a certain direction, due to differences in timestamps we introduce 2 new unknown variables into the set of navigational equations. Unless we have 2 or more satellites, adding that direction into consideration will increase the total number of unknowns and thus make the problem worse.

Finally, if the total number of acquired satellites (including repetition) in the combined acquisition is at least $2M + 3$, we proceed to the location estimation phase. In Section 6, we describe how we obtain the $2M + 3$ formula.

4.3 Multi-Directional Location Estimation

The location estimation module takes the combined acquisition result as an input and computes the 3D coordinates of the indoor location. Recall that, to estimate the location, we need a precise timestamp and the ephemeris at that instant. We estimate the ms part of the timestamp from a nearby landmark, which is either generated (as in CO-GPS) or previously known (e.g. a location outside of the building). The sub-ms part of the timestamp is obtained from the code phase, which comes as a byproduct of the acquisition process. The ephemeris is obtained directly from the web. Once we have all this information, we formulate a set of linear equations with $2M + 3$ unknowns and solve them using a least squares solver. The details of how we formulate the set of linear equations are described in Section 6.

5. ACQUISITION FROM WEAK SIGNALS

In this section, we first discuss the standard satellite acquisition process and then describe how to make it robust.

5.1 Standard Acquisition

After receiving GPS packets, a receiver first demodulates the signals and then passes the signals to the acquisition process. Figure 3 shows a simplified diagram of the satellite acquisition process of an Instant GPS. In order to identify the presence of a satellite, the receiver takes any 1 ms chunk of signals and computes the correlation between the signals and the universally known satellite-specific C/A code to find a match. Since the code phase is unknown, the receiver repeatedly shifts the C/A code circularly, and computes the correlation as in Equation 1:

$$\mathcal{R}[m] = \sum_{n=0}^{L-1} x[n].CA[(n+m)_L], 0 \leq m \leq L - 1 \qquad (1)$$

where $x[n]$, $CA[(n+m)_L]$, and $\mathcal{R}[m]$ denote the L-length signals, the C/A code which is shifted m places modulo L, and the mth correlation, respectively. A correlation plot (code phase vs. correlation) is obtained by computing all $\mathcal{R}[m]$s. The unique highest peak in the plot signifies the presence of the satellite, whereas a flat line means the satellite is not acquired. The displacement of the peak in the plot is the code phase which gives us the sub-ms part of the propagation delay.

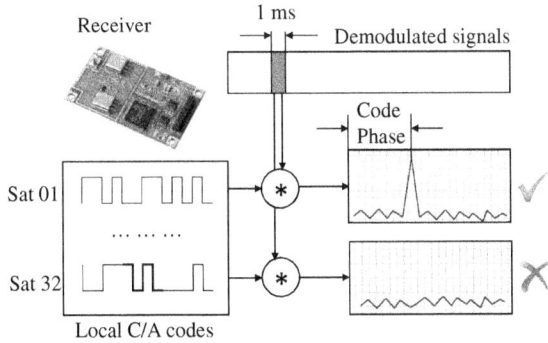

Figure 3: Simplified standard satellite acquisition.

One caveat is that the above algorithm does not deal with Doppler shifts which must be taken into account during acquisition. Taking Doppler effect into account is done simply by replicating the entire process, each time using a different frequency within the range of ±4.2 kHz of the carrier frequency. With this modification, the search space becomes a 2D state space consisting of all possible code phases and Doppler shifts. In our implementation, we use 25 frequency bins and process them in parallel to speed up the search.

5.1.1 Frequency-Domain Search

Most commercial receivers use the above linear search algorithm for its simplicity. However, with computing correlation repeatedly being slow, we use a faster method in COIN-GPS, in which, correlations are computed with the help of FFT as shown in Equation 2. This is possible since Equation 1 resembles a convolution operation which is multiplication in the frequency domain. [38] shows that the FFT search is 2000x faster than the linear search algorithm.

$$\mathcal{R}[m] = x[n] * CA[-n] = \mathcal{F}^{-1}(\mathcal{F}(x[n]) \cdot \mathcal{F}(CA[n])^*) \quad (2)$$

In order to find the unique peak in $\mathcal{R}[m], 0 \leq m \leq L-1$, the ratio of the maximum and the average (or, the second highest peak) of $\mathcal{R}[m]$ is taken, and if it is above a threshold ρ, the satellite is considered acquired. Because of the properties of the C/A codes (which are 1023-length Gold codes), ideally, only a non-delayed exact replica of a C/A code will produce a normalized correlation value of 1 (after dividing by the length 1023). For any other delays or any other satellite's C/A code, the autocorrelation is close to zero, or more precisely one of these three values: $-1/1023$, $63/1023$, or $-65/1023$. Hence, a $\mathcal{R}[m]$ close to 1 and a $\rho > 2$ indicate that we have acquired the satellite.

5.2 Robust Acquisition

5.2.1 Integrating Correlations

In the presence of noise, the idealistic nature of $\mathcal{R}[m]$ does not hold, and detecting the right peak becomes non-trivial. In order to understand the effect of noise on peak $R[m]$, we perform an experiment, where we distort a GPS packet, obtained from a commercial

GPS receiver, by artificially adding Gaussian noise (AWGN) and correlate it with a noise free C/A code. Figure 4 shows that as we vary the SNR from +15 dB to −60 dB, $\mathcal{R}[m]$ deviates from its ideal value of 1, and the peak ratio gets close to 1, which means that the highest peak becomes comparable to noise. Therefore, in indoor environments where SNR is below −30 dB, we won't be able to acquire any satellite with a regular GPS.

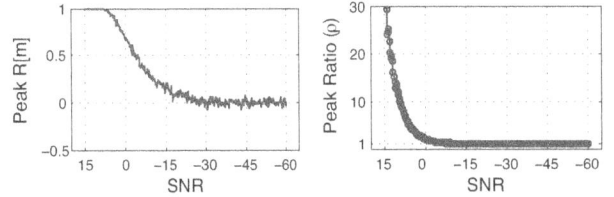

Figure 4: Effect of SNR on correlation peak.

With ≈ 10 dBi directional gain, a directional antenna helps reduce a great deal of noise. However, to complement its capability, we perform additional signal processing during acquisition. To further reduce noise, we use a non-coherent integrator to element-wise add correlations from consecutive 1 ms signal chunks. Assuming $\mathcal{R}^{(i)}[m]$ to be the correlation from the ith chunk of 1 ms signals, the integrated correlations are obtained from Equation 3:

$$\mathcal{R}^2[m] = \sum_{i=1}^{K} |\mathcal{R}^{(i)}[m]|^2 \quad (3)$$

The effect of this integration is illustrated with an example in Figure 5. The first plot having $K = 1$ uses only 1 ms of signals to produce the correlation plot. The seemingly highest peak in this plot is labeled as the wrong peak, which becomes evident when we integrate correlations obtained from 2, 4, and 8 ms of signals in the next three plots. The reason the peak is clearer in the later plots is that the highest peak remains at the same position while the noise varies. The more we integrate, the closer we get to the expected values and the more the variance is reduced.

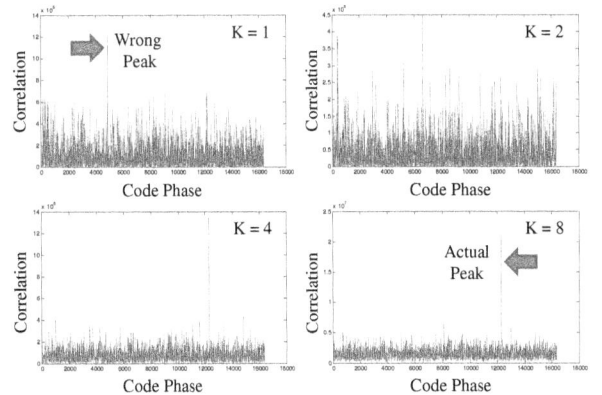

Figure 5: Longer integration produces a better peak.

Analysis: Assuming $E[\mathcal{R}]$ and $E[\mathcal{N}]$ to be the expected values of correlation power and squared noise, respectively, the expected value of peak ratio ρ is:

$$E[\rho] \approx \frac{K \cdot E[\mathcal{N}] + K \cdot E[\mathcal{R}]}{K \cdot E[\mathcal{N}]} = 1 + \frac{E[\mathcal{R}]}{E[\mathcal{N}]} \quad (4)$$

This is consistent with the plot of ρ in Figure 4. For example, when a satellite is not present, $E[\mathcal{R}] = 0$ leads to an $E[\rho]$ of 1; otherwise, the ratio is dictated by the SNR.

5.2.2 Data Bit Flip

The duration of a data bit in a GPS packet is 20 ms. Hence, it is possible that a correlation peak will be lost during a data bit flip. This problem was solved in CO-GPS [22] by taking the maximum of two consecutive correlations. In COIN-GPS, however, due to non-coherent integration of correlator outputs, even if a peak is missed, it is compensated by other $K - 1$ values. Furthermore, as we add absolute values, there is no chance that a positive and a negative correlation will cancel each other in the event of a data bit transition.

5.2.3 Multipath Effect

One effect of multipath is that the combined signals may have multiple correlation peaks which makes the primary peak less detectable. A directional antenna amplifies signals from a certain direction and suppresses the rest. If the pointed direction happens to be the direction towards the satellite, it helps remove the effects of other paths. If the direction is not the straight line of sight towards the satellite, it may pick up a reflected signal. Compared to the distance from the satellite to the earth, indoor reflections only cause a small percentage of error. The least square optimization is capable of eliminating some of those effects. Having said all these, false satellite detections and multipaths are still key causes of location error.

6. INDOOR LOCATION ESTIMATION

Even after using a high-gain directional antenna and a robust acquisition algorithm, it is possible that the number of acquired satellites inside a building is inadequate. This section describes how we exploit the stationarity of an indoor receiver and handle the inadequate satellite problem by combining directional acquisitions.

6.1 Required Number of Satellites

The required number of satellites for location estimation must be greater than or equal to the number of unknown variables. Theoretically, distances from three satellites should be enough to compute the receiver's (X, Y, Z) coordinates. Practically, however, in an Instant GPS, two more satellites are required due to two more unknowns: the *common bias* and the *coarse time error*. Therefore, we need at least 5 acquired satellites to estimate the receiver's position.

6.1.1 Common Bias Error

The pseudo-range error due to the difference between a satellite's clock and a receiver's clock is the common bias. GPS satellites carry high-precision atomic clocks which are always in sync (to a nanosecond level), and even the smallest drift in a satellite clock is included in the message, and hence, it is correctible. Receivers, on the other hand, use cheap, low-power, and small form-factored quartz crystal oscillators which have less precision and larger drifts. A 1 μs offset between the receiver and the satellite clock produces a pseudo-range error of 300 m. This bias term is estimated as an unknown parameter along with the receiver's position in the navigation solution. Figure 6 illustrates the common bias b for three satellites at a particular instant.

6.1.2 Coarse Time Error

In CTN, a coarse time reference from the device's system clock is used, which results in another form of pseudo-range error called the coarse time error. Unlike the common bias which affects the measurements all by the same amount, coarse time error affects the

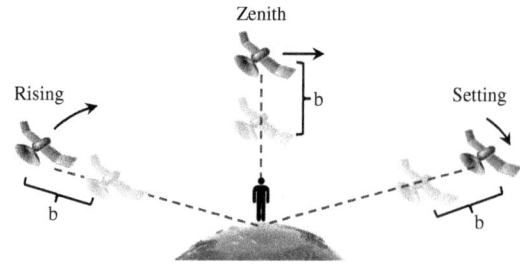

Figure 6: Common clock bias.

pseudo-ranges, each by a different amount, due to erroneous estimates of satellite positions resulting from using an incorrect local time when consulting the ephemeris. These errors are a function of satellite motion relative to the receiver and are thus non-uniform among the satellites.

Figure 7 illustrates this for a coarse time estimate that is later than the actual time. Due to this error, a rising satellite appears to be closer than its actual position, which results in a negative pseudo-range error. For a setting satellite, the error is positive, and a satellite at the zenith, which is neither approaching nor receding from the receiver, is free from this error. Although the coarse time error in terms of pseudo-range is different for each satellite, we know the velocity (pseudo-range rate) of each satellite from the ephemeris, so the error can be expressed as a product of the velocity and the unknown coarse time offset. Like common bias, the coarse time offset is also estimated as an unknown parameter in the navigation solution.

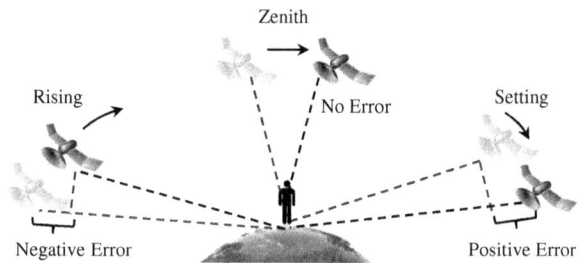

Figure 7: Coarse time error.

6.2 Handling Inadequate Satellites Indoors

A key assumption in COIN-GPS is that the receiver's motion within a short period is so negligible that if we capture multiple time-delayed chunks of GPS signals within that interval, all chunks will result in the same (x, y, z) coordinates. With this assumption that the position of the receiver is essentially fixed during the time interval separating the chunks, we can reuse the physical satellites that are acquired in more than one chunk because their positions will have changed during that time. For example, if only the same 3 satellites are acquired in 3 chunks obtained in an indoor environment, no existing GPS receiver is able to estimate its position. However, COIN-GPS in such a case would acquire those 3 satellites 3 times each for a total of 9 satellite references, and can estimate the location.

Figure 8 depicts an indoor mapping scenario with COIN-GPS. At 10:30 AM, there happens to be 3 satellites in the sky that COIN-GPS acquires from one direction. After about a second, the antenna is pointed towards another direction and from this new direction COIN-GPS acquires 4 satellites. From these two sets of satellites,

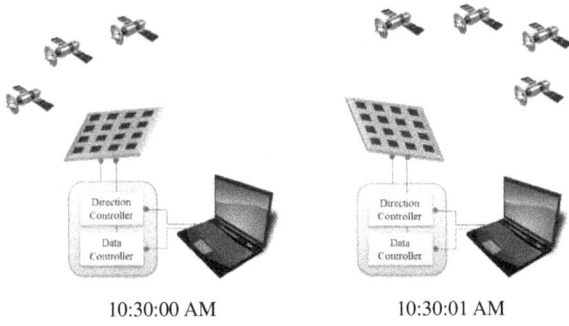

10:30:00 AM　　　10:30:01 AM

Figure 8: Satellites acquired from different directions at different points in time are combined to handle the inadequate satellites problem.

which may or may not have any overlap, we formulate two sets of equations, S_1 and S_2 as shown in Equation 5 and Equation 6. Each element $E^{(k)}_{x_i y_i z_i b_i c_i}$ in S_i is an equation having 5 unknowns: the location coordinates (x_i, y_i, z_i), bias b_i, and the coarse time offset c_i. Since we must have at least 5 equations to solve for these 5 unknowns, none of the two sets individually can be used to estimate the variables. We have placed a question mark '?' explicitly to specify the absence of an equation.

$$S_1 = \left\{ E^{(1)}_{x_1 y_1 z_1 b_1 c_1}, E^{(2)}_{x_1 y_1 z_1 b_1 c_1}, E^{(3)}_{x_1 y_1 z_1 b_1 c_1}, ?, ? \right\} \quad (5)$$

$$S_2 = \left\{ E^{(4)}_{x_2 y_2 z_2 b_2 c_2}, E^{(5)}_{x_2 y_2 z_2 b_2 c_2}, E^{(6)}_{x_2 y_2 z_2 b_2 c_2}, ? \right\} \quad (6)$$

Under the stationary assumption, we set (x_1, y_1, z_1) and (x_2, y_2, z_2) equal, and thus reduce the total number of unknowns from 10 to 7. We now have 7 equations with 7 unknowns, and hence the combined set of equations in Eq. 7 is readily solvable with a least squares solver.

$$S_{12} = \left\{ E^{(1)}_{xyzb_1 c_1}, E^{(2)}_{xyzb_1 c_1}, E^{(3)}_{xyzb_1 c_1}, E^{(4)}_{xyzb_2 c_2}, E^{(5)}_{xyzb_2 c_2}, \right. \quad (7)$$
$$\left. E^{(6)}_{xyzb_2 c_2}, E^{(7)}_{xyzb_2 c_2} \right\}$$

Note that a further reduction in the number of unknowns is possible if we could relate the bias and coarse time offset terms across S_1 and S_2. However, considering unpredictable delays between the start of capturing the signals and logging of timestamps inside the receiver, we decide to keep b_i's and c_i's as independent unknown variables. Generalizing this for M independent acquisitions, we are now ready to state our formula for a stationary receiver:

STATIONARY INSTANT GPS FORMULA 1. *For a stationary receiver, the required total number of visible GPS satellites for an instant GPS is $2M + 3$, where M is the number of independent acquisitions and the same satellite acquired in different readings is considered different.*

PROOF. Each time we consider a new set of acquired satellites, we add two unknowns: the bias and the coarse time offset for that instant. Thus, for M independent acquisitions, we have M bias terms, and M coarse time error terms. Including x, y, and z, which are common, we have a total of $2M + 3$ unknowns. Each acquired satellite contributes one equation involving $2M + 3$ unknowns. Hence, the required number of satellites is $2M + 3$. □

6.3 Navigation Equations

6.3.1 Standard Coarse Time Navigation

Like most navigation problems, CTN [37] uses an iterative approach to estimate the location (x, y, z) and the error terms: bias

(b), and coarse time offset (tc). Let us define the state variable $\mathbf{p}$ having these 5 unknowns as: $\mathbf{p} = [x, y, z, b, tc]^T$. At each iteration, $\mathbf{p}$ is updated by the amount $\delta\mathbf{p} = [\delta_x, \delta_y, \delta_z, \delta_b, \delta_{tc}]$. The following 4 steps are iterated until $|\delta\mathbf{p}| \leq \epsilon$.

Step 1: Start with a priori estimate of $\mathbf{p}$. Initially, $\mathbf{p}_{xyz}$ is the reference location, and $\mathbf{p}_b$ and $\mathbf{p}_{tc}$ are zero.

Step 2: Predict the pseudo-range vector $\hat{\mathbf{z}}$ based on $\mathbf{p}$. The element $\hat{z}^{(k)}$ corresponds to the kth acquired satellite.

Step 3: Measure the pseudo-range vector $\mathbf{z}$. The element $z^{(k)}$ corresponds to the kth acquired satellite.

Step 4: Compute $\delta\mathbf{p}$ as a function of $\delta\mathbf{z} = \mathbf{z} - \hat{\mathbf{z}}$, and update the state variable $\mathbf{p}$.

The fourth step is where we relate the pseudo-range residuals $\delta z^{(k)}$ in terms of the spatial elements of $\delta\mathbf{p}$, i.e. $\delta\mathbf{p}_{xyz}$, the bias δ_b, and the coarse time offset δ_{tc}, all having the units of distance.

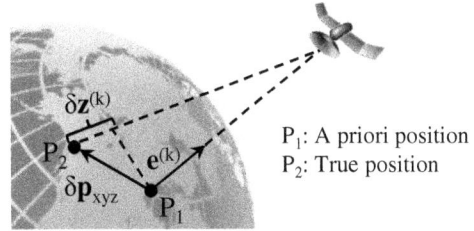

P_1: A priori position
P_2: True position

Figure 9: A priori and true location.

The pseudo-range error due to the spatial elements of $\delta\mathbf{p}$ is illustrated in Figure 9. For each satellite, the error $\delta z^{(k)}$ is expressed by $-\mathbf{e}^{(k)} \cdot \delta\mathbf{p}_{xyz}$, where $\mathbf{e}^{(k)}$ is the unit vector from the priori location estimate P_1 to the kth satellite's position. The bias term δ_b, which is a distance term and is the same for all satellites, is simply added to the error. The coarse time error is expressed by $-v^{(k)} \cdot \delta_{tc}$, where $v^{(k)}$ is the pseudo-range rate which is obtained from the velocity information of each satellite found in the Ephemeris data. Thus, for each satellite, the relationship between $\delta z^{(k)}$ and $\mathbf{p}$ is:

$$\delta z^{(k)} = -\mathbf{e}^{(k)} \cdot \delta\mathbf{p}_{xyz} + \delta_b + v^{(k)} \cdot \delta_{tc} \quad (8)$$

Using matrix notation, the above equation, considering M visible satellites, is expressed by,

$$\delta\mathbf{z} = \mathbf{H} \cdot \delta\mathbf{p} \quad (9)$$

where

$$\mathbf{H} = \begin{bmatrix} -e^{(1)} & 1 & v^{(1)} \\ \vdots & \vdots & \vdots \\ -e^{(M)} & 1 & v^{(M)} \end{bmatrix} \quad (10)$$

Finally, we get $\delta\mathbf{p}$ using the standard least squares solution:

$$\delta\mathbf{p} = (\mathbf{H}^T \mathbf{H})^{-1} \mathbf{H}^T \cdot \delta\mathbf{z} \quad (11)$$

6.3.2 Indoor Navigation Equations

Let us assume that there are M directional acquisitions having $K_1, K_2, \ldots K_M$ acquired satellites respectively. Throughout this section, we use the superscript (i, k) to denote the kth satellite in i^{th} chunk, where $1 \leq i \leq M$ and $1 \leq k \leq K_i$. Before we derive an expression for the pseudo-range error $\delta z^{(i,k)}$, we make the following assumptions:

- The (x, y, z) coordinates are the same in all chunks.
- Each chunk has a bias b_i and a coarse time error tc_i.
- Total number of satellites $\sum_{j=1}^{M} K_j \geq 2M + 3$.

Generalizing Equation 8 we obtain:

$$\delta z^{(i,k)} = -\mathbf{e}^{(i,k)} \cdot \delta \mathbf{p}_{xyz} + \delta_{b_i} + \nu^{(i,k)} \cdot \delta_{tc_i} \qquad (12)$$

Considering all K_i satellites in i^{th} chunk:

$$\delta \mathbf{z}^{(i)} = \mathbf{H}^{(i)} \cdot \delta \mathbf{p}^{(i)} \qquad (13)$$

where

$$\mathbf{H}^{(i)} = \begin{bmatrix} -e^{(i,1)} & 1 & \nu^{(i,1)} \\ \vdots & \vdots & \vdots \\ -e^{(i,K_i)} & 1 & \nu^{(i,K_i)} \end{bmatrix} \qquad (14)$$

Extending the state variable $\mathbf{p}$ by including all $(2M + 3)$ variables, for $\mathbf{p} = [x, y, z, b_1, tc_1, \ldots b_M, tc_M]^T$ we rewrite the above equation as:

$$\mathbf{H}^{(i)} = \begin{bmatrix} -e^{(i,1)} & 0 & 0 & \ldots & 1 & \nu^{(i,1)} & \ldots & 0 & 0 \\ \vdots & \vdots & \vdots & & \vdots & \vdots & & \vdots & \vdots \\ -e^{(i,K_i)} & 0 & 0 & \ldots & 1 & \nu^{(i,K_i)} & \ldots & 0 & 0 \end{bmatrix} \qquad (15)$$

Stacking up all $\mathbf{H}^{(i)}$, $1 \le i \le M$, we get the observation matrix $\mathbf{H}$ for indoor navigation:

$$\mathbf{H} = \begin{bmatrix} -e^{(1,1)} & 1 & \nu^{(1,1)} & \ldots & 0 & 0 \\ \vdots & \vdots & \vdots & & \vdots & \vdots \\ -e^{(1,K_1)} & 1 & \nu^{(1,K_1)} & \ldots & 0 & 0 \\ \vdots & \vdots & \vdots & & \vdots & \vdots \\ -e^{(M,1)} & 0 & 0 & \ldots & 1 & \nu^{(M,1)} \\ \vdots & \vdots & \vdots & & \vdots & \vdots \\ -e^{(M,K_M)} & 0 & 0 & \ldots & 1 & \nu^{(M,K_M)} \end{bmatrix} \qquad (16)$$

Finally, we obtain $\delta \mathbf{p}$ by using the standard least squares solution as done in Equation 11.

7. SYSTEM IMPLEMENTATION

So far we have provided a generic description of how an indoor GPS could be built. This section describes the specific implementation of COIN-GPS.

7.1 Front End Hardware

The front-end of COIN-GPS consists primarily of three components: a high-gain directional antenna, the direction controller, and a GPS signal logger, which are connected to a PC as shown in Figure 10.

7.1.1 Antenna Design

In order to have a reasonable gain and also a reasonable size of the antenna, we built an antenna with a 4×4 array of patches that has the dimensions of 10×10 inches and a thickness of < 0.5 inch. The antenna has a directional gain of 12.3 dBi, a half-power beam width of $35°$, and a broad-side angle of $0.5°$. Figure 11(a) shows the simulated gain of the antenna in 3D. The antenna is directional, which means it receives signals along its Z-axis, and the receiving direction is controllable. Figure 11(b) shows that its receiving frequency is 1.575 GHz, matching the GPS signal frequency.

The antenna is composed of two two-layer boards (boards with two copper layers and one substrate layer) that are physically connected to each other by plastic screws. The substrate used for each two-layer board is RT/Duroid 5880. Its low dielectric constant ($\epsilon_r = 2.2$) and low loss tangent ($\tan \delta = 0.0009$) is the most

Figure 10: The antenna and the signal logger are connected to a PC.

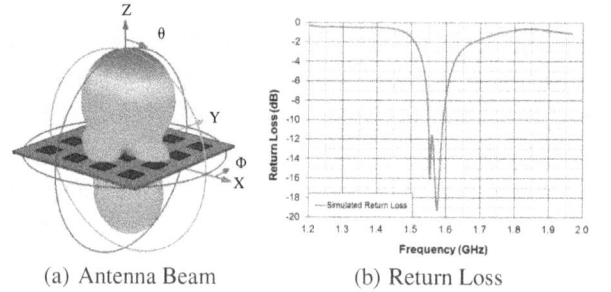

(a) Antenna Beam (b) Return Loss

Figure 11: Antenna Beam and Return Loss.

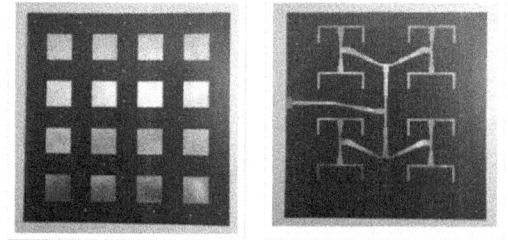

(a) Antenna Front (b) Antenna Back

Figure 12: Front and Back of the Antenna

suitable substrate for producing maximal gain for a given patch antenna topology. One of the boards (Board A) consists of a ground layer that is filled with 16 coupling slots (one for each patch antenna) and a corporate feeding network. The other board (Board B) has an analogous ground layer, filled with 16 coupling slots, and a layer with 16 patches. The size of each patch is 1.25×1.25 inches.

7.1.2 Steering the Antenna

In COIN-GPS, we attempt to receive GPS signals from a total of nine main beam directions with respect to the X-Z and Y-Z elevation planes. These directions are denoted by coordinates (R, S) where R is the main beam tilt angle along the X-axis, and S is the tilt angle along the Y-axis. The directions are $(0, 0)$, $(\pm 15, 0)$, $(\pm 30, 0)$, $(0, \pm 15)$, and $(0, \pm 30)$.

We use a programmable mechanical robot to control the antenna's direction by rotating it physically. The antenna is mounted on top of a mechanical pan-tilt platform, WidowX Robot Turret [3], which provides $360°$ rotation to steer the antenna in any direction. During operation, the antenna is pointed in different directions, and from each direction, we collect raw GPS signals using a GPS signal sampler.

7.1.3 GPS Signal Sampler

We use an off-the-shelf GPS signal sampler, SiGe GN3S Sampler v3 [2]), that connects to the USB port of a laptop. The sampler has an MCX antenna connector port where we connect our high-gain antenna. The sampler directly captures low-level GPS signals at 16368 samples/ms at the intermediate frequency of 4.092 MHz, and sends the samples directly to the laptop. The laptop simultaneously controls the robot, and the GPS signal sampler collects 100 ms of GPS samples from each of the nine directions and stores them into the disk for processing.

7.2 Back End Software

Due to space limitations, we discuss the back-end processing of COIN-GPS in brief. The two main tasks of the back-end are to maintain an up-to-date ephemeris database and to run the algorithms that are described in Section 5 and Section 6. We use the precise ephemeris from the National Geospatial-Intelligence Agency (NGA). All of our web services corresponding to the ephemeris, acquisition, and location estimation are written in C#, and are deployed in the Microsoft Azure cloud.

We choose to run our algorithms in the cloud because, first, signal processing is costly and especially our proposed robust acquisition algorithm has $10 - 100$ times more processing overhead (for its best result) which is not suitable for an embedded platform due to timing and energy constraints. Instead, it is done in the cloud to take advantage of its parallel processing capability which makes COIN-GPS both fast and energy efficient. Second, in an instant GPS technique we must use a web service to get ephemeris data anyway, so we believe having the signal processing tasks as part of a cloud-service is the right design choice.

8. EVALUATION

We describe a series of experiments which are categorized into four types: execution time, robustness of acquisition, location estimation, and five case studies.

8.1 Experimental Setup

We perform an in-depth evaluation of COIN-GPS by deploying the system in four single-storied stores (Starbucks, Home Depot, Fred Meyer, and Costco) and one multi-storied shopping mall (Bellevue Square Mall) which are located in the Bellevue, WA area. Inside each building, we capture and log GPS signals from $2 - 16$ spots, using COIN-GPS, and the same GPS logger with a Garmin 010-10702-00 omnidirectional external antenna. Our choice of spots is based on two things: first, since all the data were collected from public places, we could only take samples from those spots that are accessible by walking. An alternate and more exhaustive spot selection (e.g. a grid like arrangement of sample collection spots) was not possible in these places. Second, to obtain the ground truth of a spot, we had to take samples from spots which are later identifiable on maps (e.g., corners or junctions are easier to identify on a map).

At each location, COIN-GPS steers its antenna in nine different directions, and logs 100 ms of GPS signals from each direction. The baseline Garmin setup also logs 100 ms signals at each location. The main differences between our setup (Figure 10) and the baseline are: first, the baseline uses an omnidirectional antenna that is used in commercial Garmin GPS receivers. Second, the satellite acquisition algorithm in the baseline uses the technique as described in CO-GPS [22].

Since there is no GPS that works indoors, we had to rely upon Bing maps to obtain the ground truth of GPS coordinates. During our experiments, we note the distances (in meters) of a spot from at least two walls of the store with a high-sensitive laser-based distance measurement device having a range of 100 feet with 1/8 inch accuracy. These distances act as the relative coordinates of the spot with respect to the walls. By combining the absolute GPS coordinates of the walls of the stores on a Bing map with the relative displacements noted during the experiment, we compute the absolute GPS coordinates of a spot. To be able to exactly pin-point the location on the map, we often have chosen locations that are near a corner, or a junction, or in the middle of a section of the store that is identifiable on a map (e.g. frozen foods in Costco). Some of the stores (e.g. Home Depot and Bellevue Square Mall) provided us with their floor-plans which also helped us identify the spots.

8.2 Execution Time

We measure the execution times of different components in COIN-GPS and summarize them in Table 1. Each time the front-end antenna is steered to a particular direction, we give it about 100 ms to settle down. Collecting 100 ms signals and storing them takes an additional 200 ms. Considering nine directions, it takes about 3 seconds to complete one cycle of data logging. The back-end server that we have used is a Windows Server 2008 R2 PC having a Quad Core CPU @ 3.3 GHz and 16 GB RAM. The acquisition module takes 1.8 s per ms of signal; i.e., for the maximum 100 ms signals and assuming no parallel processing, the worst case acquisition time is as high as 3 minutes. The overhead is a one-time cost consisting of loading the C/A code tables, preparing caches, and ephemeris data, which require an update once a day. Compared to acquisition, location estimation is faster and takes 1.33 s on average. Overall, with parallelism, the end-to-end time is about 3.13 s. Without parallelism and a moderate $20 - 50$ ms of signals, the time is about $40 - 90$ s, which is on the same order of magnitude as GPS receivers in outdoor environments - 30 to 60 s for standalone GPS and 6+ s for AGPS.

Task	Module	Time (sec)
Front-End	Settling Time (per direction)	0.10
	Data Logger (per direction)	0.20
Acquisition	Acquire (per ms signal)	1.80
	Other Overhead (one time)	3.50
Localization	Estimate Location (per fix)	1.33

Table 1: Modules and Execution Times.

8.3 Robustness of Acquisition

8.3.1 Longer Signals and Acquired Satellites

In Section 5.2.1, we have described the benefit of integrating correlations from more than 1 ms of signals. In this experiment, we quantify this using our empirical data. Figure 13 shows the number of satellites acquired by both COIN-GPS and the Garmin setup, as we vary the amount of signals over which we integrate the correlation. We observe that the number of acquired satellites increases in both cases, however, COIN-GPS acquires 3 satellites (on average) when we integrate 50 or more correlation terms (shaded region in the figure). With the Garmin antenna, the average number hardly ever reaches 2, even when we integrate over 100 ms. The state-of-the-art CO-GPS (or any instant GPS), which uses $1 - 2$ ms signals, does not acquire even a single satellite. Thus, this result justifies the use of our high-gain directional antenna as well as our robust acquisition technique, which lets COIN-GPS acquire enough satellites to obtain a location fix in an indoor environment. Using only the robust acquisition algorithm alone would increase the number of acquired satellites from zero to two, but that wouldn't be sufficient. Using only the high-gain antenna alone would increase the number of acquired satellites from zero to one, which would also not be sufficient to estimate the location.

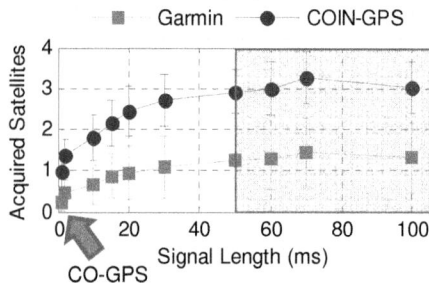

Figure 13: Signal length and acquired satellites.

The underlying reason that using a longer signal length helps is understood when we plot the peak ratios of a correlation plot for different amount of signals. Figure 14(a) shows that as we increase the amount of signals over which we integrate the correlation, the ratio between the highest two peaks (peak ratio) increases. However, after 50 ms, the increase is not significant and settles at around 7. Therefore, this number is used as a threshold in determining whether or not a satellite is acquired.

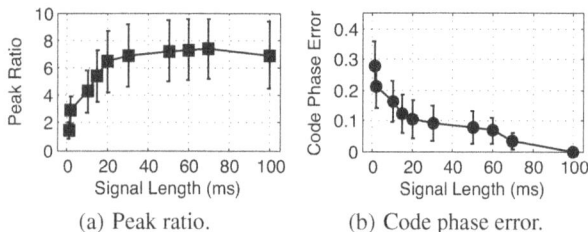

(a) Peak ratio. (b) Code phase error.

Figure 14: Peak ratio and code phase error.

Another important thing to notice is the errors in estimated code phases as we consider longer signals. This is because, ultimately, it is the code phase estimation error that determines the location estimation error in an instant GPS receiver by and large. Figure 14(b) shows that the relative code phase error diminishes as more and more correlation terms are integrated and becomes less than 5% when 70 or more correlation terms are integrated. Hence, this plot provides a guide in selecting a value of signal length to minimize the expected location estimation error. In COIN-GPS, we use 50 ms as our default integration length.

8.3.2 Indoor Satellite Distribution

COIN-GPS requires acquisition of at least 3 satellites to obtain a location fix. In this experiment, we empirically determine the distribution of the number of acquired satellites (from a single direction in COIN-GPS) for both COIN-GPS and CO-GPS (using a Garmin front-end). Figure 15 shows that CO-GPS acquires 2 or more satellites with only 10% probability, and never acquires 3 or more satellites and never obtains a location fix. On the other hand, COIN-GPS acquires at least 3 satellites 60% of the time, which means COIN-GPS is capable of obtaining a location fix in these cases. Compared to the state-of-the-art CO-GPS's 0% success rate, this is a significant improvement.

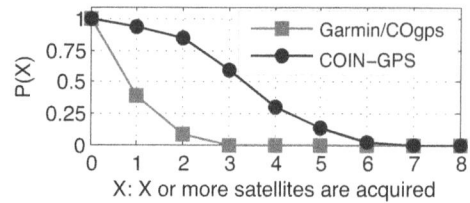

Figure 15: Distribution of acquired satellites.

8.4 Location Estimation Algorithm Evaluation

8.4.1 Combining Directional Acquisitions

COIN-GPS combines acquired satellites from up to nine directions to address the inadequate satellite problem. We empirically determine the number of directional acquisitions that are combined in COIN-GPS whenever there has been a successful location fix. Figure 16 shows the CDF of the number of directions combined. We see that, amongst all successful fixes, 63% use only one direction, 28% use 2, and 3 directions are required for the rest.

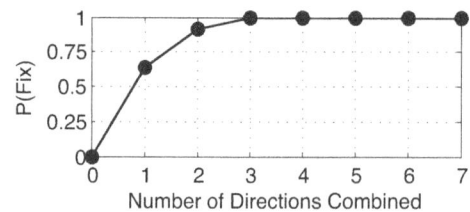

Figure 16: Distribution of location fixes.

8.4.2 Bias and Coarse Time Error Terms

In COIN-GPS, for M independent directional acquisitions, we assume there are M unknown bias terms and M unknown coarse time error terms. In this experiment, our goal is to see how different the biases and the coarse time offsets are and thus justify the assumption.

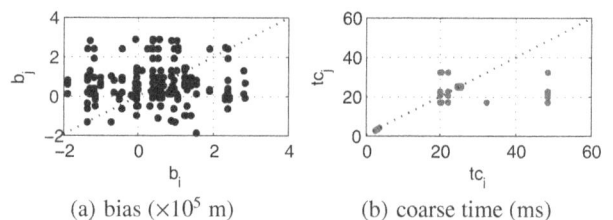

(a) bias ($\times 10^5$ m) (b) coarse time (ms)

Figure 17: Bias and Coarse Time.

Figure 17 shows all-pair biases and coarse time offsets obtained after solving the navigational equations. Each point (b_i, b_j) in Figure 17(a) represents two bias terms b_i and b_j from the same set of equations. Similarly, Figure 17(b) shows the coarse time offsets in pairs. If all M biases (or all M coarse time errors) were the same, the plot would be a straight line with a slope of 1. However, we see that the biases are highly scattered and most of the coarse time offsets are off the diagonal line. Making all M biases and all M coarse term offsets the same would result in estimated pseudo-range errors of 410 m and 25 m, respectively. Hence, by considering them as $2M$ independent unknown variables, COIN-GPS has eliminated such large errors.

8.5 Location Estimation Case Studies

We deploy COIN-GPS in five real-world indoor environments and summarize the results in Figures 18–21. In each figure, a pair of downward arrows on the map show the true (green) and estimated (red) locations, and the dotted line shows the displacement. The table on the right compares COIN-GPS with the baseline, and the plot shows the localization errors.

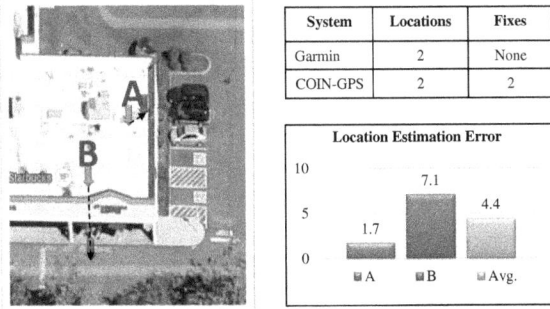

Figure 18: Starbucks.

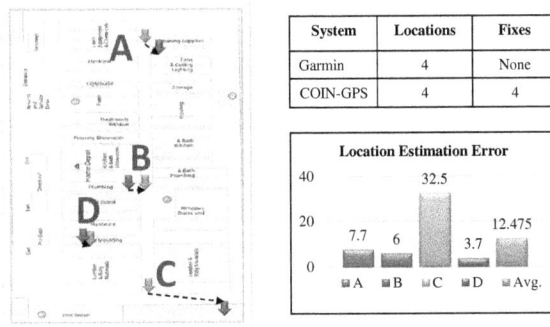

Figure 19: Home Depot.

COIN-GPS performs its best at Starbucks (Figure 18) and Home Depot (Figure 19), showing a 100% success rate in obtaining a location fix. These places are suitable for COIN-GPS as there is a large window at the front of Starbucks, and there are several skylights in Home Depot which are made of glass and framed with steel. In these locations, even some of the directional acquisitions (acquired satellites from a single direction with our antenna) had enough satellites to get a location fix. On average, COIN-GPS acquires 3.5 satellites per direction in both locations, and obtains location fixes with 4.4 – 12.5 m errors. With such errors, we can distinguish between a customer at Starbucks waiting in the line versus a customer sitting in the deep back of the store. We can also identify the section a customer is in Home Depot (e.g. cleaning, plumbing, moulding, or lumber). The baseline Garmin setup, on the other hand, sees < 1 satellite on average, and never gets a location fix.

The Bellevue Square Mall (Figure 20) is a large, multi-storied shopping mall. We conduct our experiment on its first and the second floors where a large walking area on the first floor shares the same roof with the top floor. Starting from A on the second floor, we take measurements from 8 spots on the second floor, 8 on the first floor, and stop at I. We get 6 successful fixes (A − F) on the second floor, and 3 on the first (G − I) with average errors of 21 m and 7.17 m, respectively. We get higher errors on the second floor

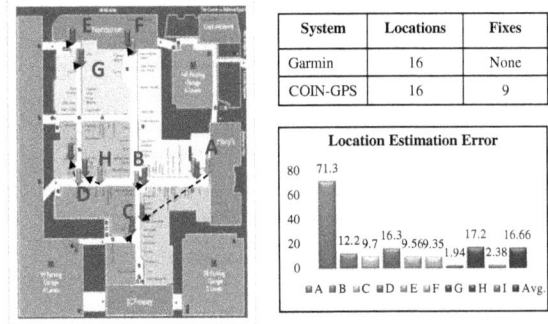

Figure 20: Bellevue Square Mall (two storied).

(e.g. A) than the first (e.g. I) as sometimes the signals are reflected by the lower floor before they reach the top floor. The Garmin receiver, on the other hand, hardly acquires a satellite at any spot and hence does not get any location fix.

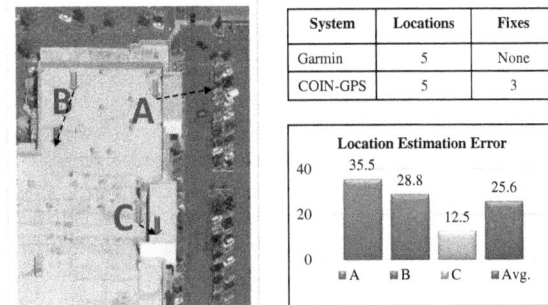

Figure 21: Fred Meyer.

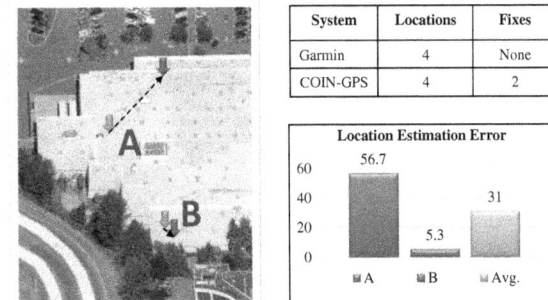

Figure 22: Costco.

The two most difficult cases for COIN-GPS have been the Fred Meyer (Figure 21) and the Costco (Figure 22). These buildings are somewhat sealed, having a ceiling made of concrete and a thick layer of steel framework, and they have no skylights. In these locations, we always had to combine multiple directions to obtain the required number of satellites. As this combination of directional acquisitions depends on the correct estimation of bias and coarse time errors, in general, their accuracy is lower. Out of a total of 9 spots inside these two buildings, COIN-GPS obtains 5 successful location fixes with an aggregate average error of 27.6 m. The received signals inside these buildings are so weak that COIN-GPS acquires 3 or more satellites in only about 30% of the directional acquisitions. The Garmin device acquires absolutely no satellite at all in these locations. Although COIN-GPS has its largest error in these scenarios, still the result is remarkable as it is capable of getting a location fix when the state-of-the-art does not even see a satellite.

Min	Median	Mean	P90	Max
1.70	9.63	17.37	46.10	71.30

Table 2: Summary of Localization Errors.

Table 2 shows the overall min, median, mean, 90th percentile, and max errors in our study. While a mean location estimation error of 17.3 m is comparable to the errors of an outdoor GPS, such an error is not suitable for most indoor location sensing applications in general. COIN-GPS with such an error may not be suitable to provide e.g. 'aisle-level' accuracy within a supermarket, but can provide a 'zone-level' accuracy. But this error is not a fundamental limit, rather a limitation of our implementation. There are scopes to improve the current solution, and the right way to proceed towards that is to understand the sources of errors.

One source of such errors is multipaths. We notice that most large errors occur when there are more than one received directions. It is possible that reflected signals from the same satellites caused pseudo-range errors. This can be eliminated to some extent by steering the directional antenna towards the predicted location of the satellites instead of steering the antenna towards a fixed set of directions as done in this paper. As each satellite orbits around the Earth in a somewhat regular pattern, it is possible to predict the direction of a satellite at a given time of the day. We did not apply this technique in COIN-GPS in order to keep our solution simple. This requires further investigation and we keep this as our future work.

Location	Spot	Satellites count	Directions count	Peak Ratio mean	Peak Ratio max	Error meters
Starbucks	A	5	1	5.27	18.64	1.7
	B	17	5	4.83	10.94	7.1
Home Depot	D	6	1	8.57	34.10	3.7
	B	5	1	3.88	4.81	6
	A	5	1	5.69	15.30	7.7
	C	10	2	5.71	16.30	32.5
Square Mall	G	5	1	6.72	18.74	1.94
	I	5	1	4.12	7.85	2.38
	F	5	1	12.37	21.72	9.35
	E	8	2	11.56	41.06	9.56
	C	7	2	4.57	9.94	9.7
	B	5	1	4.08	7.20	12.2
	D	7	1	12.31	55.95	16.3
	H	7	2	8.74	15.35	17.2
	A	9	3	3.87	12.00	71.3
Fred Meyer	C	5	1	9.66	22.88	12.5
	B	6	1	4.73	9.98	28.8
	A	7	2	3.10	5.42	35.5
Costco	B	5	1	11.49	38.55	5.3
	A	7	2	9.28	40.9	56.7

Table 3: Number of acquired satellites, number of directions combined to estimate the location, mean and max peak-ratios, and the location estimation error for each location are shown. For each location, spots are sorted by the location estimation errors.

Besides multipaths, the other possible causes of location estimation errors are the indoor SNR and the errors during combining the directional acquisitions. Due to the lack of proper instrumenta-

tion, we could not capture the actual SNR of the GPS signals during our field study. However, the peak-ratios of the correlation plots can be used as an alternative to the SNR. The larger the ratio, the better is SNR. Table 3 shows the number of acquired satellites, the number of directions combined to get a location fix, the mean peak-ratios in the correlation plots, and the location estimation errors for each of the 20 spots. For each location, we order the spots by the location estimation errors. We observe that the largest of the errors in each location happens whenever there is a need to combine two or more directional acquisitions and the total number of satellites is large. This can be somewhat compensated for if we consider the quality of acquired satellites when combining the directional acquisitions. The mean peak-ratio of a single directional acquisition can be used as an indication of the quality of the acquired satellites.

9. DISCUSSION

Steering the Antenna Electronically: Instead of using a programmable robot to steer the antenna physically, a more convenient alternative is to steer the beam electronically. We have implemented a prototype of such an electronically steerable antenna and tested its capability at a limited scale. As it was not used in our deployment experiments, we do not include this design while describing our implementation. Instead, we discuss it here for interested readers.

Figure 23: Electronically controllable antenna.

In Figure 23, the corporate feeding network is designed to provide excitation 'in-phase' to all 16 patches. When this 'in-phase' excitation occurs, the radiation pattern is broadside with maximal gain at around 0°. To enhance the reception of signals at different angles away from broadside without physically maneuvering the antenna, 16 voltage-controlled phase shifters (one for each antenna) are integrated to the network. The phase shifters offer 360° of phase delay controlled by a voltage that ranges from $0 - 13$ V. By changing these control voltages, the phases of the individual patches are shifted, and, in turn, the main beam of the radiation pattern is tilted. The voltage-controlled phase shifters are controlled by an externally-connected PCB that has a programmable SoC, and is powered through a USB cable connected to a laptop. By changing the duty cycle of a pulse-width modulated (PWM) voltage signal, different voltages between $0 - 13$ V are used to control the phase shifter. The PSoC allows 256-bit addressing; therefore, the control voltage increment for the phase shifter is ≈ 0.05 V.

Size of the Antenna: Compared to today's GPS receivers, which comfortably fit inside handheld devices, COIN-GPS along with its antenna are several orders of magnitude larger. This is a price that we are paying to compensate for the signal attenuation and multipath effects that we incur indoors. However, since we have chosen a 10×10 inches board having a thickness < 1 cm, the board with the electronically steerable antenna, at its current scale, can be fit nicely on the back cover of a laptop.

Usage in Indoor Mapping: COIN-GPS, in its current form, is not really suitable to be commercialized and sold as a consumer product. However, the system has other applications, such as providing the ground-truth for other indoor profiling techniques, or mapping indoor environments similar to Google's street-view car or Nokia's NAVTEQ system that are used outdoors. A limitation of COIN-GPS is that, in general, it does not work in multi-storied buildings. However, in a country like the USA, many commercial buildings are single-floored, such as stores, marts, warehouses, malls, schools, stations, and airports where COIN-GPS is usable.

Complementing COIN-GPS: COIN-GPS does not provide a guaranteed location fix at all times. Rather, it is highly likely that there will be several zones in a building where COIN-GPS may not acquire the required number of satellites. To handle such cases, relative location estimation techniques such as dead-reckoning [8, 40, 41] can be used to estimate locations between two consecutive fixes.

10. RELATED WORK

The GPS has been an active area of research ever since it was invented during the Cold War era. Our work in this paper is based on a rich body of work in GPS [24], A-GPS [37], and CO-GPS [22]. In particular, we adopt the concept of cloud-offloading from CO-GPS to save energy; however, our proposed front-end hardware, robust acquisition, and location estimation techniques are completely new and tailored to indoor environments. While we are the first to demonstrate an indoor GPS receiver that works in practical situations, there are some works that discuss indoor GPS challenges and opportunities [36, 35, 13, 4], signal characteristics [19], and achieving high sensitivity [5, 42].

Several indoor positioning systems have been proposed in the past. There are surveys [16, 21] that summarize, compare and contrast some early efforts on indoor localization. Techniques used in state-of-the-art indoor positioning systems include fingerprinting WiFi RSS (Radar [7], Horus [43], Large scale 802.11 [17], EZ [11], WiGEM [15], and ZEE [29]), ultrasonic beacons (Cricket [28]), acoustics and ambience fingerprinting (BatPhone [33] and Surround-Sense [6]), RFID (LandMarc [26]), and computer vision (SLAM [25], depth camera [9, 32]). All these systems have limitations, such as requiring an infrastructure setup and/or a characterization phase, and none of them provide a direct mapping to the real-world coordinates.

COIN-GPS, compared to the techniques mentioned above, does not require any extra infrastructure other than the existing GPS satellites, does not require any learning or characterization phase, and provides globally recognized GPS coordinates. Although the accuracy of COIN-GPS is not as good as most of the state-of-the-art techniques that we have mentioned above, the results in our work are remarkable as there have been no other GPS receivers that have achieved this much success. Some complementary techniques can further improve the accuracy of COIN-GPS. For example, pedestrian dead-reckoning techniques [8, 40, 41] or hybrid approaches like UnLoc [39] and GAC [44] can be used along with COIN-GPS to handle the corner cases where COIN-GPS does not get a location fix.

11. CONCLUSION

In this paper, we challenge the common belief that GPS receivers cannot work indoors due to weak signals and multipath effects. By incorporating a steerable directional antenna, leveraging the computing power of the cloud for robust acquisitions over long signals, and combining acquisition results from different directions over time, we devise a novel way of performing direct GPS-based localization in indoor environments. The COIN-GPS system has been shown to achieve acceptable location accuracy without any additional infrastructure in several real-world single-storied public spaces. While the current implementation is limited by its size and accuracy, the results are remarkable as there have been no other GPS receivers that have achieved this much success. We believe this work will be the basis for future portable, consumer grade indoor GPS receivers.

12. REFERENCES

[1] CST Microwave Studio. www.cts.com.
[2] SiGe GN3S Sampler. sparkfun.com/products/10981.
[3] WidowX Robot Turret. www.trossenrobotics.com.
[4] N. Agarwal, J. Basch, P. Beckmann, P. Bharti, S. Bloebaum, S. Casadei, A. Chou, P. Enge, W. Fong, N. Hathi, et al. Algorithms for gps operation indoors and downtown. *GPS solutions*, 6(3):149–160, 2002.
[5] D. Akopian. Fast fft based gps satellite acquisition methods. *IEE Proceedings-Radar, Sonar and Navigation*, 152(4):277–286, 2005.
[6] M. Azizyan, I. Constandache, and R. Roy Choudhury. SurroundSense: mobile phone localization via ambience fingerprinting. In *MobiCom '09*, Beijing, China.
[7] P. Bahl and V. N. Padmanabhan. Radar: An in-building rf-based user location and tracking system. In *INFOCOM 2000. Nineteenth Annual Joint Conference of the IEEE Computer and Communications Societies. Proceedings. IEEE*, volume 2, pages 775–784. Ieee, 2000.
[8] S. Beauregard and H. Haas. Pedestrian dead reckoning: A basis for personal positioning. In *Proceedings of the 3rd Workshop on Positioning, Navigation and Communication (WPNCŠ06)*, pages 27–35, 2006.
[9] J. Biswas and M. Veloso. Depth camera based indoor mobile robot localization and navigation. In *Robotics and Automation (ICRA), 2012 IEEE International Conference on*, pages 1697–1702. IEEE, 2012.
[10] Y. Chen, D. Lymberopoulos, J. Liu, and B. Priyantha. Fm-based indoor localization. In *Proceedings of the 10th International Conference on Mobile Systems, Applications, and Services*, MobiSys '12, pages 169–182, New York, NY, USA, 2012. ACM.
[11] K. Chintalapudi, A. Padmanabha Iyer, and V. N. Padmanabhan. Indoor localization without the pain. In *Proceedings of the sixteenth annual international conference on Mobile computing and networking*, pages 173–184. ACM, 2010.
[12] J. Chung, M. Donahoe, C. Schmandt, I.-J. Kim, P. Razavai, and M. Wiseman. Indoor location sensing using geo-magnetism. In *Proceedings of the 9th International Conference on Mobile Systems, Applications, and Services*, pages 141–154, 2011.
[13] G. Dedes and A. G. Dempster. Indoor gps positioning. In *Proceedings of the IEEE Semiannual Vehicular Technology Conference*, 2005.
[14] T. Denidni and Q. Rao. Design of single layer broadband slot antennas. *Electronics Letters*, 40(8):461–463, 2004.
[15] A. Goswami, L. E. Ortiz, and S. R. Das. WiGEM: a learning-based approach for indoor localization. In *Proceedings of the Seventh Conference on emerging Networking Experiments and Technologies*, 2011.
[16] Y. Gu, A. Lo, and I. Niemegeers. A survey of indoor positioning systems for wireless personal networks. *Communications Surveys & Tutorials, IEEE*, 11(1):13–32, 2009.

[17] A. Haeberlen, E. Flannery, A. M. Ladd, A. Rudys, D. S. Wallach, and L. E. Kavraki. Practical robust localization over large-scale 802.11 wireless networks. In *Proceedings of the 10th annual international conference on Mobile computing and networking*, pages 70–84. ACM, 2004.

[18] X. Jiang, C.-J. M. Liang, K. Chen, B. Zhang, J. Hsu, J. Liu, B. Cao, and F. Zhao. Design and evaluation of a wireless magnetic-based proximity detection platform for indoor applications. In *Proceedings of the 11th International Conference on Information Processing in Sensor Networks*, IPSN '12, pages 221–232, New York, NY, USA, 2012. ACM.

[19] M. B. Kjærgaard, H. Blunck, T. Godsk, T. Toftkjær, D. L. Christensen, and K. Grønbæk. Indoor positioning using gps revisited. In *Pervasive Computing*, pages 38–56. 2010.

[20] R. Li, G. DeJean, M. M. Tentzeris, and J. Laskar. Development and analysis of a folded shorted-patch antenna with reduced size. *Antennas and Propagation, IEEE Transactions on*, 52(2):555–562, 2004.

[21] H. Liu, H. Darabi, P. Banerjee, and J. Liu. Survey of wireless indoor positioning techniques and systems. *Systems, Man, and Cybernetics, Part C: Applications and Reviews, IEEE Transactions on*, 37(6):1067–1080, 2007.

[22] J. Liu, B. Priyantha, T. Hart, H. S. Ramos, A. A. Loureiro, and Q. Wang. Energy efficient gps sensing with cloud offloading. In *SenSys*, pages 85–98, 2012.

[23] D. López de Ipiña, P. R. S. Mendonça, and A. Hopper. Trip: A low-cost vision-based location system for ubiquitous computing. *Personal Ubiquitous Comput.*, 6(3):206–219, Jan. 2002.

[24] P. Misra and P. Enge. Global positioning system: Signals, measurements and. 2011.

[25] M. Montemerlo, S. Thrun, D. Koller, and B. Wegbreit. FastSLAM: A factored solution to the simultaneous localization and mapping problem. In *AAAI/IAAI*, pages 593–598, 2002.

[26] L. M. Ni, Y. Liu, Y. C. Lau, and A. P. Patil. Landmarc: indoor location sensing using active rfid. *Wireless networks*, 10(6):701–710, 2004.

[27] D. M. Pozar. Microstrip antennas. *Proceedings of the IEEE*, 80(1):79–91, 1992.

[28] N. B. Priyantha, A. Chakraborty, and H. Balakrishnan. The cricket location-support system. In *Proceedings of the 6th annual international conference on Mobile computing and networking*, pages 32–43. ACM, 2000.

[29] A. Rai, K. K. Chintalapudi, V. N. Padmanabhan, and R. Sen. Zee: Zero-effort crowdsourcing for indoor localization. In *Proceedings of the 18th annual international conference on Mobile computing and networking*, pages 293–304, 2012.

[30] S. K. Rao. Parametric design and analysis of multiple-beam reflector antennas for satellite communications. *Antennas and Propagation Magazine, IEEE*, 45(4):26–34, 2003.

[31] M. Redzic, C. Brennan, and N. E. O'Connor. Dual-sensor fusion for indoor user localisation. In *Proceedings of the 19th ACM International Conference on Multimedia*, MM '11, pages 1101–1104, New York, NY, USA, 2011. ACM.

[32] J. Shotton, T. Sharp, A. Kipman, A. Fitzgibbon, M. Finocchio, A. Blake, M. Cook, and R. Moore. Real-time human pose recognition in parts from single depth images. *Communications of the ACM*, 56(1):116–124, 2013.

[33] S. P. Tarzia, P. A. Dinda, R. P. Dick, and G. Memik. Indoor localization without infrastructure using the acoustic background spectrum. In *Proceedings of the 9th international conference on Mobile systems, applications, and services*, pages 155–168. ACM, 2011.

[34] G. Thiele. Analysis of yagi-uda-type antennas. *Antennas and Propagation, IEEE Transactions on*, 17(1):24–31, 1969.

[35] F. van Diggelen. Indoor gps theory & implementation. In *Position Location and Navigation Symposium, 2002 IEEE*, pages 240–247. IEEE, 2002.

[36] F. van Diggelen and C. Abraham. Indoor gps technology. *CTIA Wireless-Agenda, Dallas*, 2001.

[37] F. S. T. Van Diggelen. *A-gps: Assisted GPS, GNSS, and SBAS*. Artech House, 2009.

[38] D. Van Nee and A. Coenen. New fast gps code-acquisition technique using fft. *Electronics Letters*, 27(2):158–160, 1991.

[39] H. Wang, S. Sen, A. Elgohary, M. Farid, M. Youssef, and R. R. Choudhury. No need to war-drive: Unsupervised indoor localization. In *Proceedings of the 10th international conference on Mobile systems, applications, and services*, pages 197–210. ACM, 2012.

[40] O. Woodman and R. Harle. Pedestrian localisation for indoor environments. In *Proceedings of the 10th international conference on Ubiquitous computing*, pages 114–123. ACM, 2008.

[41] O. Woodman and R. Harle. Rf-based initialisation for inertial pedestrian tracking. In *Pervasive Computing*, pages 238–255. Springer, 2009.

[42] C. Yang, T. Nguyen, E. Blasch, and M. Miller. Post-correlation semi-coherent integration for high-dynamic and weak gps signal acquisition. In *Position, Location and Navigation Symposium, 2008 IEEE/ION*, pages 1341–1349. IEEE, 2008.

[43] M. Youssef and A. Agrawala. The horus wlan location determination system. In *Proceedings of the 3rd international conference on Mobile systems, applications, and services*, pages 205–218. ACM, 2005.

[44] M. Youssef, M. A. Yosef, and M. El-Derini. Gac: Energy-efficient hybrid gps-accelerometer-compass gsm localization. In *Global Telecommunications Conference (GLOBECOM 2010), 2010 IEEE*, pages 1–5. IEEE, 2010.

SAIL: Single Access Point-Based Indoor Localization

Alex Mariakakis
University of Washington

Souvik Sen
HP Labs

Jeongkeun Lee
HP Labs

Kyu-Han Kim
HP Labs

ABSTRACT

This paper presents *SAIL*, a Single Access Point Based Indoor Localization system. Although there have been advances in WiFi-based positioning techniques, we find that existing solutions either require a dense deployment of access points (APs), manual fingerprinting, energy hungry WiFi scanning, or sophisticated AP hardware. We design SAIL using a single commodity WiFi AP to avoid these restrictions. SAIL computes the distance between the client and an AP using the propagation delay of the signal traversing between the two, combines the distance with smartphone dead-reckoning techniques, and employs geometric methods to ultimately yield the client's location using a single AP. SAIL combines physical layer (PHY) information and human motion to compute the propagation delay of the direct path by itself, eliminating the adverse effect of multipath and yielding sub-meter distance estimation accuracy. Furthermore, SAIL systematically addresses some of the common challenges towards dead-reckoning using smartphone sensors and achieves $2 - 5$x accuracy improvements over existing techniques. We have implemented SAIL on commodity wireless APs and smartphones. Evaluation in a large-scale enterprise environment with 10 mobile users demonstrates that SAIL can capture the user's location with a mean error of 2.3m using just a single AP.

Categories and Subject Descriptors

H.3.4 [**Information Systems and Retrieval**]: Systems and Software; C.2.4 [**Computer-Communication Networks**]: Distributed Systems

Keywords

Indoor location; Smartphones; Dead-Reckoning; Time-of-Flight; Sensing

MobiSys'14, June 16–19, 2014, Bretton Woods, New Hampshire, USA.
Copyright 2014 ACM 978-1-4503-2793-0/14/06 ...$15.00.
http://dx.doi.org/10.1145/2594368.2594393.

1. INTRODUCTION

Precise indoor localization has received extensive interest due to the demand in location-based services. Innovative approaches [1] are constantly raising the bar; however, while trying to choose a positioning technique for real-world deployment that is both low cost and accurate, we find that the choices are quite limited. Accurate indoor positioning can be achieved using manual fingerprinting [2–6] or additional infrastructure [7–10], both of which are known to be costly propositions. Crowdsourcing solutions reduce the cost of fingerprinting [11, 12], but are slow to adapt to changes in the environment and depend on the willingness of the users to share sensitive sensor and location information.

Recently WiFi-based indoor localization has been revived by innovative triangulation and multilateration-based schemes [9, 13–15]. These approaches do not require any manual fingerprinting, but assume a high density of APs. For instance, EZ [14] leverages more than 100 APs and Arraytrack [9] requires several sophisticated WiFi APs with $7 - 8$ antennas. Given the pervasiveness of WiFi, the density requirement would seem to be an acceptable restriction. However, while trying to deploy our recent WiFi-based approach CUPID [15], we uncovered several practical limitations. First, multilateration requires distance estimation from at least $4 - 5$ reasonably strong WiFi APs with known locations, which are often unavailable at the edge of the enterprise network, in the developing world, and in small business locations. Second, even within the core of the enterprise network, it is difficult to find $4 - 5$ strong APs on the same channel. This is because nearby APs reside on different channels after the advent of the 802.11ac standard, which allows 21 channels in the 5GHz frequency band, and advancement in distributed channel assignment algorithms. This imposes a requirement on client devices to frequently scan across different channels to find a reliable set of APs. WiFi scanning is an energy hungry operation and can reduce the battery life of mobile devices by more than $2 - 3$ times [16], even if the scanning operation is invoked once every 10 seconds for continuous location tracking. Third, regular data communication cannot happen during the scanning operation, impacting the user experience, particularly for real-time traffic such as VoIP. To address these limitations, we need a positioning system that does not rely on multiple APs, thereby avoiding channel switching and network disruptions at the client. To achieve this, we design an *accurate single-AP localization system that works with commodity APs and avoids fingerprinting or crowdsourcing.*

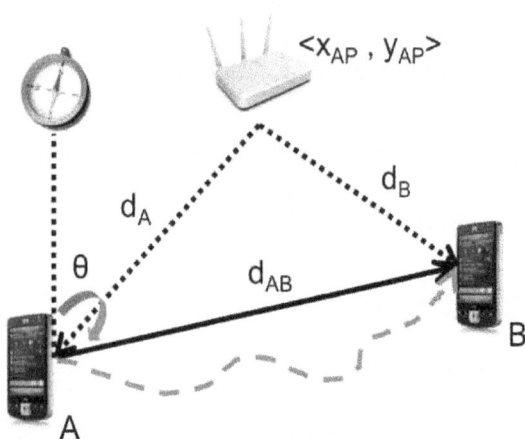

Figure 1: The triangle formed between an AP and a user walking from location A to location B.

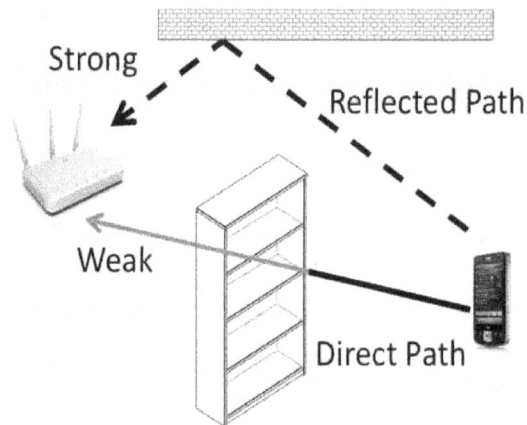

Figure 2: Wireless signal traverses through multiple paths, one direct, and a few reflected paths.

In search of a single-AP localization solution, we studied the possibility of combining the distance and the angle of the client from the AP to determine her location. However, we found that the angle estimation granularity with recent 3-antenna commodity APs is only 60 degrees [15], resulting in large location estimation errors of more than 7m on average. Instead of relying on coarse-grained angular information, we make a unique geometric observation that enables single AP-based positioning by leveraging user mobility.

We propose a scheme based on the triangle depicted in figure 1. Let us assume that the user has a smartphone connected to an AP, with a known location, and walks from location A to location B, both of which are unknown. It may be possible to estimate the distance of the user from the AP at these locations (d_A, d_B in figure 1) using WiFi. It may also be possible to compute the user's displacement between location A and B (d_{AB}), by using her phone's motion sensors – a method called *dead-reckoning*. Accurate estimation of d_A, d_B and d_{AB} will yield a unique triangle; however, this is not enough to find the location of the user. The triangle can be rotated around the AP in any direction and will still satisfy the side length constraints. However, if we can measure the overall compass heading of the user during the path AB (θ in figure 1), it is possible to determine the orientation of the triangle in the 2-D plane, ultimately yielding the location of the user.

To realize the above scheme, it is important to accurately estimate the distance of the client based on WiFi. It may be possible to estimate the distance using signal strength (RSSI), but RSSI is known to perform poorly indoors. CUPID [15] reduces the effect of multipath on signal strength, but is fundamentally susceptible to indoor shadowing. For example, whenever the AP and the client are in two separate rooms, most of the wireless paths are absorbed, causing a large distance estimation error of more than 10m. Rather than using signal strength, we find that the signal propagation time between the AP and the client is far less susceptible to shadowing. We use the Time-of-Flight (ToF) information from commodity WiFi APs that capture the round trip signal propagation time between the AP and the client. ToF is susceptible to multipath because it captures the propagation time of the

signal traversing through the strongest path and not necessarily the direct path [1](figure 2). Whenever the direct path is relatively weak due to a blockage, ToF is biased by stronger reflected components that traverse longer distances than the direct path. We exploit PHY layer information called *Channel Impulse Response (CIR)* to detect the presence of a stronger reflected path and appropriately correct the ToF value to obtain the arrival time of only the direct path. We further improve ToF-based ranging accuracy by carefully considering human mobility, ultimately reducing the median distance estimation error to 0.8m from 7m while using RSSI.

Our scheme requires precise dead-reckoning using smartphone motion sensors to determine the displacement of the user between two locations (e.g. A and B in figure 1). Although dead-reckoning techniques are quite mature [17], we find that existing techniques either impose restrictions on the user (e.g., holding the phone in a specific position), or employ map matching techniques to deal with the errors. Our new techniques are not without restrictions, but we believe that they are a step in the right direction. We design an accelerometer-based walking distance estimation algorithm that does not require user input for calibration. We detect random phone orientation changes using the smartphone's accelerometer and harness the gyroscope to identify physical turns. Our design also requires the compass heading of the user as she walks between two different locations. The compass on commodity smartphones is known to work poorly indoors due to ferromagnetic and electrical interference [12,18]. We show that by accounting for abnormalities in the magnetometer, it is possible to determine when the compass reading is most reliable. The compass reading alone is not enough because the phone may be held in such a way that the heading of the user does not correspond to heading of the phone. We employ the accelerometer to measure this offset and thereafter obtain the correct heading.

We combine the client's distance, dead-reckoning, and heading estimates geometrically (figure 1), yielding her location using a single WiFi AP. We prototype and deploy our system

---

[1]Direct path signal is the signal component that traverses along the straight line joining the client to the AP

called *SAIL* (Single AP-based Indoor Localization), using an HP enterprise AP and commodity smartphones. Testbed results from a 30,000ft² floor demonstrate that SAIL can achieve a median localization error of 2.3m using only a single AP. In addition to high accuracy and our deployment in multiple enterprises, we find that relying on only a single AP enables indoor location-based services in the developing world, small and medium business, etc.

Our main contributions are summarized as follows:

- **We utilize channel impulse responses and human mobility to eliminate the effect of multipath in ToF-based distance estimation:** By accounting for multipath, SAIL reduces the average error of ToF-based ranging from 5m to 0.8m.

- **We demonstrate how WiFi-based distance estimation can be improved by exploiting human mobility:** Our solution uses Kalman filtering to reduce the distance estimation error and adjusts its predictions after detecting physical turns using the smartphone's gyroscope.

- **We identify the opportunity to improve inertial dead-reckoning techniques using accelerometer hints:** SAIL distinguishes between most random orientation changes and physical turns. Furthermore, SAIL estimates the user's walking distance without any explicit inputs. In our experiments, these improvements reduced the mean dead-reckoning error of existing schemes from 7m to 4m.

- **We use the compass only when it is reliable to determine the user's heading:** SAIL reduces the heading estimation error to $5.9°$ from $27.4°$ when using raw compass values. It also identifies and nullifies the offset between the user's heading and the smartphone's heading.

- **We implement and demonstrate our solution using commodity WiFi APs and smartphones:** Our system exploits the PHY layer information obtained from Atheros wireless chipsets and is currently deployed at multiple enterprise locations.

In the following sections, we elaborate on our key intuitions and develop insights to design the SAIL system, followed by performance evaluation.

2. DISTANCE ESTIMATION USING WIRELESS TIME-OF-FLIGHT

This section elaborates on the key issues with Time-of-Flight-based distance estimation. We perform measurements in a busy office environment using HP MSM 460 APs using Atheros 9590 chipset and use these measurements to develop our key algorithms.

2.1 Wireless Signal Propagation

A wireless signal traverses in all radial directions and reflects off walls, furnitures, and other objects. Due to reflections, multiple copies of the same signal arrive at the receiver, each undergoing different delay and attenuation – a phenomena which is commonly called multipath. We define the *direct*

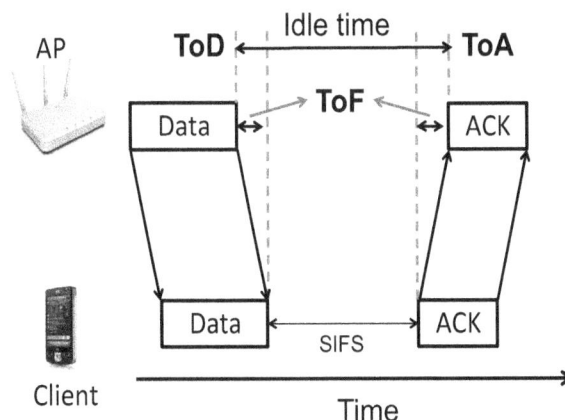

Figure 3: Computation of ToD and ToA in the PHY layer using data-ACK exchange.

path as the straight line joining the transmitter and the receiver. A wireless signal is composed of a direct path and other reflected components, each of which suffers its own delay as it propagates between the transmitter and the receiver.

Time-of-Flight (ToF) is defined as the round trip propagation time of a signal transmitted between the AP and the mobile device. WLAN ToF measurements are usually based on echo techniques [19]. These techniques employ a data-ACK exchange between the AP and the mobile device, relying on the extraction of timestamps from the main WLAN clock. The Atheros chipset can precisely compute the *Time-of-Departure (ToD)* of a data packet when it is sent out in the air at the PHY layer (figure 3). On correct reception of the packet, the client waits for an SIFS duration (a fixed value according to 802.11 standard) and starts responding with an ACK packet. The chipset also reports an estimated *Time-of-Arrival (ToA)* of the ACK packet at the AP as shown in figure 3. Both the ToD and ToA values are reported in terms of clock cycles using the 88MHz WLAN clock. Observe that the ToD and ToA values are recorded entirely at the AP and do not require any explicit synchronization between the mobile client and the AP. Moreover, since ToD and ToA are computed locally in the PHY layer of the AP, it is affected by neither clock drift between the AP and the mobile device nor the load on the main network processor.

The difference between ToA and ToD captures the channel idle time (t_{idle}) between the data and the ACK packets (figure 3). It is possible to estimate the ToF between the AP and a client based on t_{idle} because it only captures the ToF and the SIFS duration. Of course, the estimated ToF is susceptible to errors due to preamble synchronization and multipath. However, once the ToF is correctly determined, the distance between the AP and the client can be easily calculated as:

$$distance = c * ToF/2 \qquad (1)$$

where c is the speed of light and the ToF is expressed in seconds. Since the Atheros chipset employs a 88MHz WLAN clock, the resolution of distance estimation using ToF can be less than 1.7m.

2.2 Effect of Preamble Detection on ToF

It is important to precisely determine the ToA of the ACK packet; otherwise, even a small discrepancy can lead to large distance estimation errors. The ToA is determined based on preamble detection in the PHY layer; however, it is difficult to precisely detect the arrival of the preamble with nanosecond precision because of the limited bandwidth of the WLAN chipset. Figure 4(a) shows that ToA values can be quite random due to uncertainties in preamble detection.

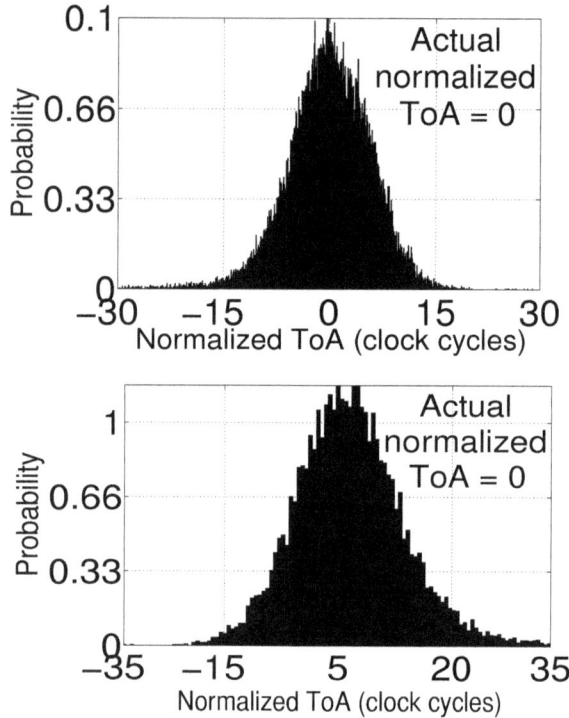

Figure 4: Distribution of normalized ToA values at the AP (a) for a static client, (b) for the same client when the LoS is blocked by a human standing in between (NLoS).

To address the randomness in preamble detection, we observe from figure 4(a) that the resultant error follows a Gaussian distribution whose mean is close to zero. This is because ToA estimates collected at different instances are subjected to independent sources of noise due to preamble detection. Thus, we use a Kalman filter [20] to minimize the effect of noise. The Kalman filter can optimally minimize the mean square error of the estimated distance based on ToF. Since the client can be mobile, we use a two-state Kalman filter that tracks both the estimated distance of the client as well as her relative speed w.r.t. the AP. In principle, the Kalman filter uses its relative speed estimate to predict the distance of the client. It then uses the current ToF-based distance value to update its distance and relative speed estimate. We will discuss in Section 5 how the Kalman filter is further optimized by correcting the relative speed estimate using dead-reckoning hints. Figure 5 shows that by addressing the errors due to preamble detection, it is possible to reduce the ToF-based distance estimation error. However, we find that the distance estimation error is still high in case of NLoS (non-LoS) environment because of the adverse effect of multipath. SAIL applies multipath correction to reduce the error due to multipath as described next.

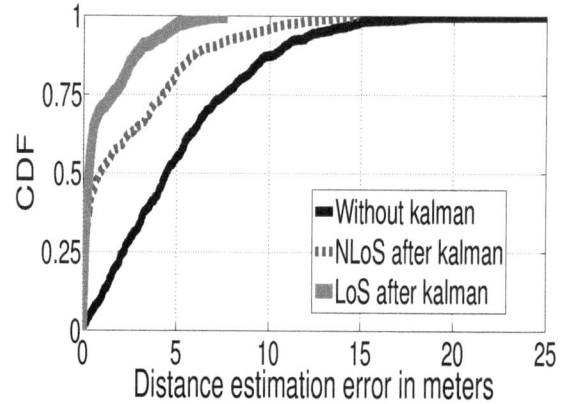

Figure 5: CDF of distance estimation error before and after applying Kalman filtering techniques for LoS and NLoS scenarios.

2.3 Effect of Multipath on ToF

Because of indoor multipath, multiple copies of the same signal arrive at the AP. The PHY layer reports the ToA value corresponding to the strongest arriving signal path, not necessarily the direct path, which has an effect on ToA estimation. ToA values can have lower error in Line-of-Sight (LoS) environments where the direct path signal is also the strongest arriving signal (figure 4(a)). However, in NLoS (non-LoS) environments where the direct path is blocked by a wall or the human carrying the mobile device, the estimated ToA may correspond to a later arriving stronger reflected path, causing a positive bias in the ToA readings (figure 4(b)). If it is possible to somehow determine the arrival time of only the direct path, distance estimation based on ToF can be significantly improved.

The direct path signal can be identified by using a PHY layer information called *Channel Impulse Response (CIR)* [15, 21]. The CIR captures the energy of the different wireless propagation paths, both direct and reflected, incident at increasing delays. Since the direct path traverses the minimum distance amongst all the received paths, it will likely appear in the earliest component of the CIR. Figure 6 shows the CIR at two different clients which are equidistant from the AP. For the first client (figure 6(a)), the direct path does not pass through obstructions, and thus yields the strongest component. However, for the second client (figure 6(b)), the direct path's trajectory is blocked by a human and hence is weaker than a later arriving reflected component. In this case, the PHY layer may report the arrival time of the reflected path as the ToA, resulting in a positive bias.

Our previous work, CUPID [15], exploited the energy of the direct path (EDP), extracted from the earliest component of the CIR to compute the distance between the AP and a client; however, its accuracy was limited because signal strength is inherently susceptible to indoor shadowing. Rather than depending on signal strength, we study the possibility of improving ToF-based ranging using CIR information. We find that by using the CIR, it is possible to estimate the positive bias in the ToA that is caused by a stronger reflected path. The difference in delay between the strongest and first component of the CIR captures the positive bias in the ToA (if any). In the

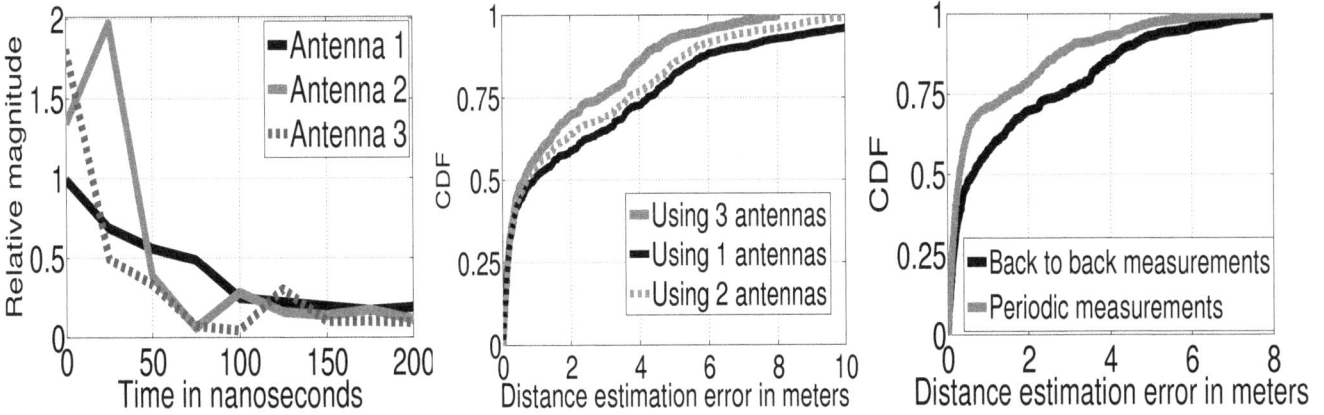

Figure 7: (a) Extracted CIR from 3 antennas. (b) Distance estimation performance improves due to multipath correction using multiple antennas. (c) Performance with distributing 10 ToF measurements over 1s.

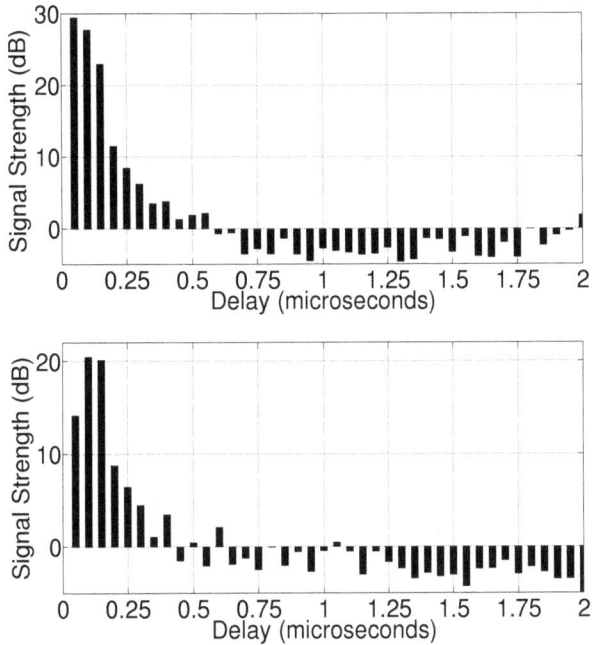

Figure 6: Estimating direct path using CIR: (a) Client is visible to the AP (LoS). (b) Client's direct signal path is blocked (NLoS).

NLoS scenario of figure 6(b), the stronger reflected path arrived 50ns later than the first (direct) path. Thus, the ToA can be reduced by 50ns to capture the arrival of the direct path in this example. However, the CIR-based correction depends on the resolution of the CIR itself. The resolution of the CIR is inversely proportional to the communication bandwidth. For example, the resolution of the CIR is only 25ns for an ACK packet received over a 40MHz bandwidth, causing distance estimation errors of up to 7.5m. As a consequence, we find that the above CIR-based correction only reduces the average distance estimation error marginally. We overcome the limitation of coarse CIR resolution by exploiting multiple antennas and human mobility as described next.

Exploiting multiple antennas: A mobile device typically transmits an ACK packet by using a single antenna, but most APs are MIMO capable and hence receive the ACK over multiple antennas. Since MIMO antennas are typically spaced apart by at least half a wavelength (6cm at 5.2GHz frequency band), the CIR varies across antennas (figure 7(a)). Nevertheless, the PHY layer reports a single ToA value of the ACK packet, even when multiple antennas are present. This is because the PHY layer synchronizes with the strongest arriving signal across all the antennas and reports the corresponding ToA. To reduce the multipath error by exploiting multiple antennas, we determine the relative arrival time (t_s) of the strongest component across all the CIRs (e.g., 2nd component of the 2nd antenna in figure 7(a)), and thereafter reduce the reported ToA by t_s. In figure 7(b) we apply the above technique to reduce the distance estimation error in NLoS scenarios where the direct path is blocked by a wall or a human being. Since increasing the number of antennas at the AP effectively increases the multipath detection resolution, we find that ToF-based distance estimation error decreases with increasing number of antennas. By correcting the error due to multipath using 3 antennas, we were able to reduce the mean distance estimation error from 2.8m to 1.6m.

Exploiting human mobility: We leverage natural human mobility to further reduce the effect of multipath. We observe that whenever the mobile device moves, the direct-path signal is usually stable, whereas reflected paths are quite random [9]. Therefore, if we compute multiple ToF snapshots over a short period, it may be possible to further reduce the error due to multipath. The multipath coherence time under mobility is typically more than 10ms [22]. Thus, it is difficult to exploit the effect of mobility on multipath by scheduling a few back-to-back measurements. Instead, we space the same measurements equally within a short time interval (1s in our implementation) to capture the arrival of the stable direct path. Figure 7(c) shows that by distributing the ToF measurements, SAIL is able to better deal with multipath reflections and hence improves the distance estimation accuracy. The performance can improve by increasing the number of ToF measurements per second; however, even with only 10 packets per second, the mean distance estimation error becomes less than 1m using an AP with 3 antennas.

319

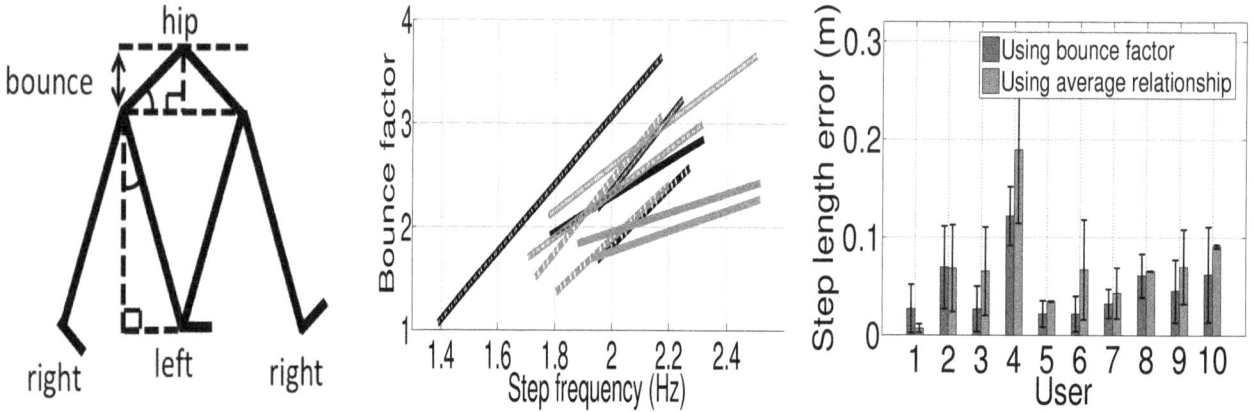

Figure 8: (a) Similar triangles are formed between the user's legs and hips while walking. (b) Step frequency vs. bounce factor relationship for ten users. (c) Step length determination accuracy across ten users.

3. SMARTPHONE DEAD-RECKONING

To enable indoor positioning using a single AP, SAIL needs to compute the displacement of the user as she walks between two locations. We use the smartphone's accelerometer to compute the walking distance and utilize the gyroscope to determine orientation changes, as described next.

3.1 Walking Distance Estimation using Accelerometer

To understand the issues with accelerometer-based walking distance estimation, we performed experiments in a 200ft corridor with 10 users for more than 4 hours. We find that when a person is walking, their body exhibits a natural periodic bounce that can be detected by the accelerometer. Counting the number of valleys in the acceleration magnitude signal allows us to track the number of steps taken by the user [12, 23]. The distance traveled by the user can be computed by multiplying the number of steps with the user's step length. We find that the step length of a user is directly proportional to her step frequency [23], which can be determined by counting the number of steps taken over a time interval. However, the step frequency vs. step length relationship varies across users (figure 9). This happens because step length depends on the physical build of the user (e.g., taller users typically take longer steps), which is difficult to ascertain without explicit user inputs [18] or personalization [23].

Rather than establishing the step length vs. step frequency relationship on a per user basis [23], we observe that users with similar physical builds are likely to exhibit similar walking behaviors. In other words, two users with similar physical build should exhibit similar lines in figure 9. We look to the vertical bounce of the user's hips as a quantifiable measurent of the user's build. Figure 8(a) illustrates how the bounce is directly proportional to step length through the geometry of similar triangles. The magnitude of the bounce manifests itself through the accelerometer. The accelerometer reports the total acceleration $\langle a_x, a_y, a_z \rangle$ experienced by the phone, which is the sum of the acceleration due to gravity $\langle g_x, g_y, g_z \rangle$ and the acceleration due to the force exerted by the user. The bounce is proportional to the variation of the acceleration component that is parallel to the gravity vector. Thus we

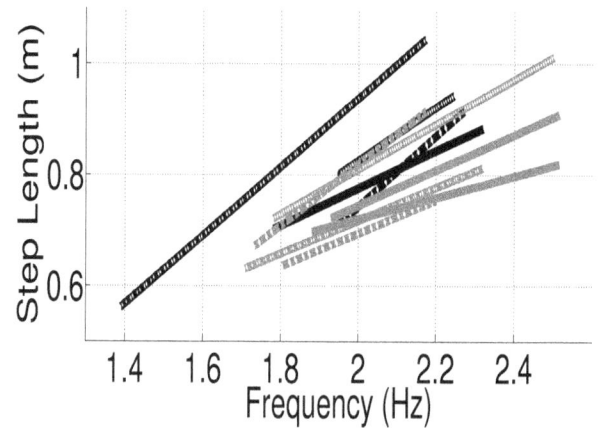

Figure 9: Step length vs. step frequency relationship for ten users.

define the standard deviation of the projections of the total acceleration onto the gravity vector as the *bounce factor*, BF:

$$BF = \text{std}\left(\frac{\langle a_x, a_y, a_z \rangle \cdot \langle g_x, g_y, g_z \rangle}{\langle g_x, g_y, g_z \rangle} \right) \quad (2)$$

Of course, the bounce factor is linearly related to step frequency (figure 8(b)) – the faster a person walks, the more their hips bounce. The position of the phone on the body also has an effect on the phone's acceleration. For instance, a phone in the user's pocket experiences more acceleration than a phone in the user's hand. SAIL's step length detection models only consider acceleration data when the phone is in the user's pocket because of the tight coupling between the phone and the user's leg motion. When a new user is tracked for the first time by SAIL, a constant step length is assumed. Once she places her phone in her pocket, it computes her step frequency and bounce factor. Thereafter, it identifies previous users who demonstrated the same bounce factor at the new user's step frequency. These users presumably share a similar build as the new user; hence, we assume that they share similar step length vs. step frequency lines, so we use an average of the ones in our model for the new user. The newly created step length vs. step frequency line can then be used to determine her step length independent of where she keeps the phone since step frequency is not affected by various poses.

Figure 8(c) displays the results of our step length estimation algorithm through cross-validation analysis across ten users. Our algorithm generally performs better than using an average step length vs. step frequency fit, which is agnostic of the physical build of the user.

3.2 Phone's Orientation Tracking using Gyroscope

Walking distance is not enough to find the displacement of the user between her past and current location. Since the user may take turns between those locations, orientation information is also necessary. Orientation changes can be detected using the smartphone compass, but it is known to be vulnerable to indoor magnetic interference [12]. Orientation changes can be determined from the gyroscope, which reports the relative angular velocity of the phone. When integrated over time, the gyroscope yields the relative angular displacement, which can·be used to detect the turns made by the user. This integration is affected by noise, causing the gyroscope to drift. The gyro drift can be addressed by performing the integration only when the gyroscope is changing substantially due to a turn [24]. However, not all the turns observed by the gyroscope correspond to physical turns made by the user. For instance, whenever the user raises her phone to take a phone call, the gyroscope may report a turn, although the user may have been walking straight during that time. Unless such events are detected, SAIL may report a turn whenever the user is toying with their phone.

We define a *pose change* as an event during which the user changes her phone's orientation without taking a physical turn (figure 10). We observe that during a pose change, the direction of the gravity vector with respect to the phone changes appreciably. For example, when the raises the phone to her ear to answer a phone call after texting with her friend, the direction of the gravity vector changes from the -z-axis to somewhere on the xy-plane. We use this observation to detect pose changes. If the direction of the gravity vector changes abruptly, we attribute any changes in the gyroscope reading during the same interval as a pose change and reset the integration of gyroscope values. Because gyroscope readings during that interval are ignored, any turns made by the user during a pose change are missed by the system. While these assumptions are less than ideal, reliable compass measurements can be used to correct the user's heading later on. Table 1 presents the results for pose change detection for 300 pose changes between five common poses. In a separate experiment, we also found that the false positive rate of the pose change detection scheme is close to zero. We conclude that regular walking seldom leads to any pose changes because the latter require a drastic change in the direction of the gravity vector.

3.3 User's Heading Estimation using Compass

Apart from the displacement of the user between her past and current location, SAIL also requires her overall compass head-

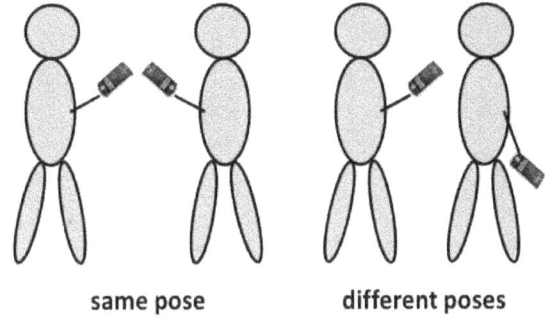

same pose   **different poses**

Figure 10: Pose changes occur during specific user initiated changes in phone orientation.

	Different poses				
	Head	Ear	Swinging	Purse	Pocket
Hand	X	100%	100%	100%	100%
Ear	100%	X	100%	100%	100%
Swinging	100%	100%	X	95%	100%
Purse	100%	100%	95%	X	100%
Pocket	100%	100%	85%	90%	X%

Table 1: Accuracy results for transitions between five different poses.

ing to determine the orientation of the triangle in figure 1 in the two-dimensional plane. The compass reading is based on the phone's magnetometer, which is seldom reliable indoors due to close proximity to ferromagnetic materials and electrical devices (figure 11(a)). Nevertheless, there are moments when the compass is accurate. If we can somehow detect these instances, we may be able to use the compass, along with the gyroscope, to determine the user's absolute heading.

In the absence of magnetic interference, the magnetometer should report the ideal geomagnetic field at a particular location. The World Magnetic Model [25] maintains an updated survey of this information every five years. If the user's magnetometer does not agree with the ideal geomagnetic conditions at her rough GPS location according to the survey, we may infer that there is some sort of electrical or ferromagnetic interference affecting the compass readings. Figure 11(b) shows the component of the magnetometer reading towards the earth from two different experiments. We observe that whenever the declination of the magnetic field was weak (i.e., magnitude towards earth was close to 0T), the compass was unreliable.

Not only are the magnitude and direction of the magnetometer readings important, but so too are the stability of those measurements. If the user is walking straight and the magnetometer is rapidly fluctuating between values, something is disturbing the nearby magnetic field and rendering any measurements useless. We gather the two above observations to design a *compass confidence metric* that ranges from 0 to 1, with higher values indicating more reliable readings. If m_{exp} represents the ideal magnitude of the geomagnetic field according to the World Magnetic Model and m_{meas} represents the magnitude reported by the magnetometer and projected in the direction of the ideal geomagnetic field vector, the compass confidence metric (M) is defined as:

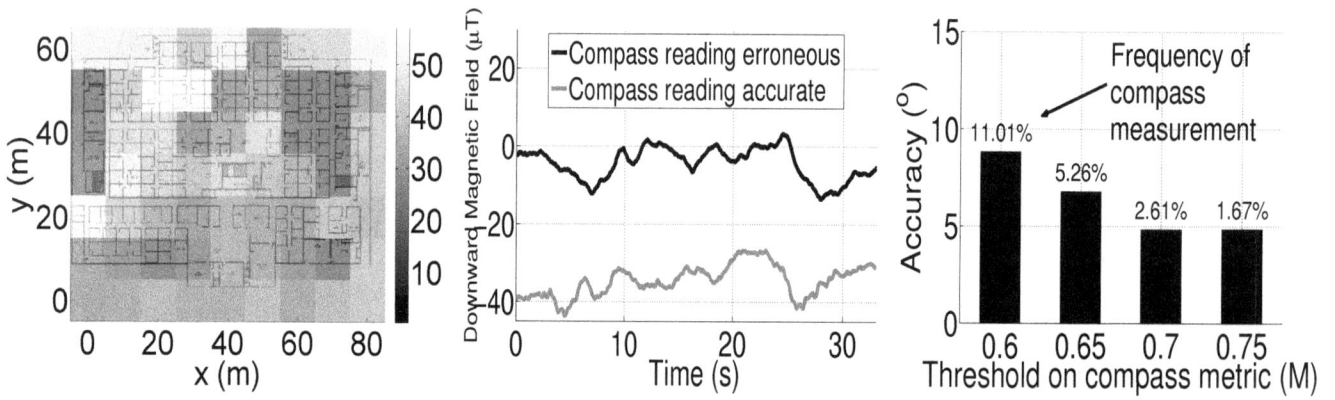

Figure 11: (a) Variation in compass error for different parts of a floor. (b) Magnetometer readings from two different locations with different compass accuracy. (c) Compass error as a function of confidence threshold.

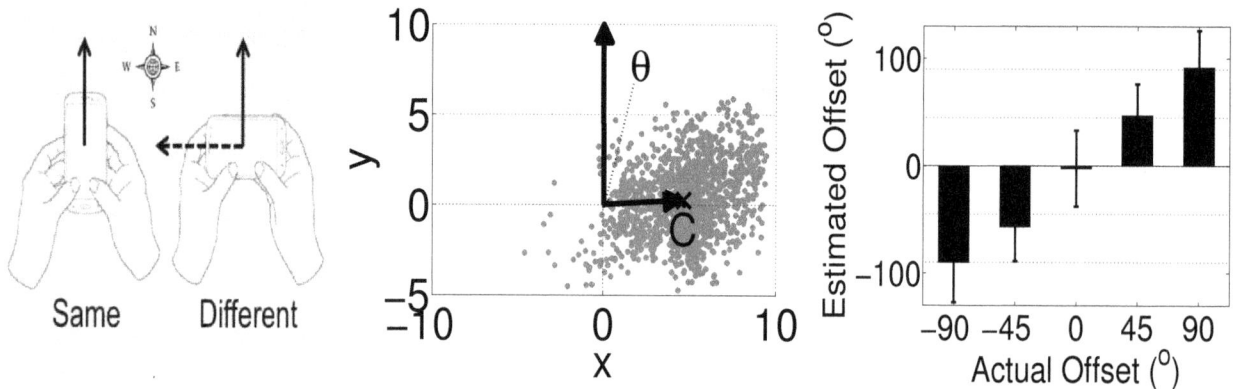

Figure 12: (a) The phone's heading is not always the same as the user's heading. (b) Force distribution while the phone is held in landscape mode. (c) Compass offset estimation accuracy.

$$M = \frac{1}{2}\left(\mu_1^{\frac{dm_{meas}}{dt}} + \mu_2^{|m_{meas}-m_{exp}|}\right) \quad (3)$$

where μ_1 and μ_2 are empirically determined constants. Intuitively, a higher threshold on the compass confidence metric will yield a more reliable compass (figure 11(c)). When the threshold is increased to 0.75, the median error for compass readings becomes 5°. However, higher compass reliability comes at the cost of reliable reading frequency (figure 11(c)). While more frequent compass readings would be desirable, SAIL requires an accurate compass reading early in the user's path at the very least. After a reliable compass reading, the gyroscope can be used to track the user's turns, and in turn, absolute heading direction. Of course, reliable compass readings later on can be used to update the user's heading. In fact, more periodic compass readings are required if the user changes the phone's pose while turning since SAIL ignores gyroscope readings during pose changes.

Compass Offset Correction

The compass value indicates the phone's heading and not necessarily the user's heading, causing an offset in the compass reading. For example, if the user holds her phone in landscape mode (figure 12(a)), any accurate compass reading would be 90° off of the user's heading. When the phone is in a more arbitrary orientation (e.g., pocket, purse, ear), finding the off-

set between the phone's and the user's heading, called the *compass offset*, is not trivial. Previous research has mostly assumed that the compass offset is zero, or address this problem indirectly by assuming that a map of the floorplan is available. SAIL does not make any such assumptions and addresses this issue by exploiting the smartphone's accelerometer.

We observe that as the user walks forward, she exerts a force that manifests itself on the accelerometer. The heading of the user with respect to the phone may be found by determining the component of that force that is parallel to the ground. Figure 12(b) shows the distribution of these force vectors for an experiment where the user held the phone in landscape mode. Observe that the distribution of the force lies primarily along the +x-axis of the phone, indicating that the user's walking force was being exerted to the longer side of the phone. The angle of the vector, formed by joining the origin and the centroid of the force distribution (θ in figure 12(b)), is the heading of the user relative to the phone. Since the +y-axis is representative of the phone's heading, the compass value can be compensated by using the angular difference between the vector C and the +y-axis. The same process applies for more random phone orientations. Figure 12(c) shows the accuracy of the offset detection for five different angles. Between the five cases, the average error was 4°, with the worst error of 12° appearing when the phone was held 45° counter-clockwise with respect to the user.

4. LOCATION ESTIMATION USING TRIANGLES

SAIL finds the user's location by forming a triangle between the user's past and current unknown location coordinates, and the known location of the AP to which her smartphone is connected (figure 1). It uses ToF to compute the distances, d_A and d_B, of the user from the AP at two unknown locations A and B respectively. It uses dead-reckoning to calculate the distance between locations A and B, called d_{AB} in figure 1. The length constraints (d_A, d_B, and d_{AB}) can determine a unique triangle, but are not enough to find the exact coordinates of the locations A and B. The triangle can be rotated at any angle around the AP, creating a large number of possibilities for locations A and B. However, the absolute heading of the line AB, as suggested by the user's compass, can determine the orientation of the triangle in the 2-D plane, ultimately yielding the user's location.

Even with the constraints discussed above, there can be ambiguity in location determination. Given a triangle that satisfies the above conditions, a second possibility can be made by reflecting that triangle across a line that is parallel to the side AB and passes through the AP coordinate (figure 13). If the user is walking straight, these triangles are identical and it is not possible to break the ambiguity. However, once the user turns, observe that the user is moving closer to the AP in one of the possibilities and further away in the other. This indicates that the distance of an intermediate point D from the AP will be different for the two candidate triangles (d_1 and d_2 in figure 13). Thus, the ambiguity can be broken by inspecting the WiFi distance at the intermediate point D and picking the triangle that satisfies this distance. In the case of figure 13, the top triangle will be selected if the distance estimate at the intermediate point of the trace is small. To avoid selecting the wrong triangle, we consider the intermediate instance when the WiFi distance measurement has the highest confidence.

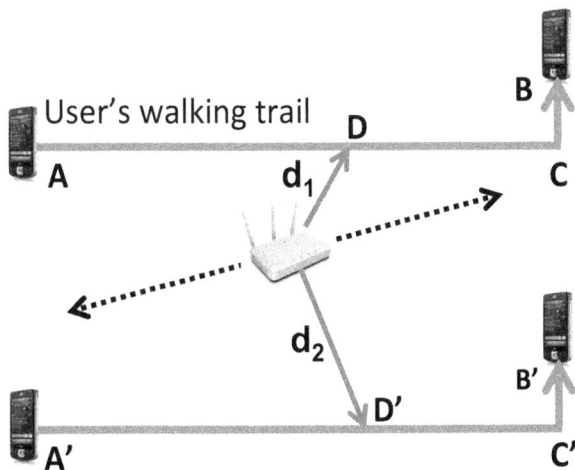

Figure 13: Two possible rotations of the triangle can still satisfy the side length and heading constraints.

5. IMPLEMENTATION AND EVALUATION

This section presents the implementation details of SAIL. We discuss SAIL's system details and end the section by evaluating SAIL's positioning performance.

5.1 CIR and ToF Processing

We obtain the CIR from the *Channel State Information* (CSI), available in the PHY layer. The Atheros 9590 chipset can export the CSI of any received packet. The reported CSI is a matrix containing one complex number per subcarrier and per receive antenna at the AP. Since the CSI captures the wireless channel in the frequency domain, an Inverse Fast Fourier Transform (IFFT) provides the CIR which captures the multipath components in the time domain. The chipset also reports the Time-of-Departure (ToD) value, in terms of clock cycles, in the transmit-complete descriptor of any data packet. Similarly, it exports the Time-of-Arrival (ToA) value of the ACK packet in its receive descriptor. For each data-ACK exchange, we estimate the ToF by using the ToA and ToD, as well as the chipset's clock frequency. We estimate the distance between the AP and a client based on ToF and further correct it using the computed CIR.

5.2 Configuring Kalman Filter States

The Kalman filter uses the past distance and relative speed estimates to correct the errors in current estimates. We initialize the filter's distance estimate using the first distance value available from the AP and the relative speed estimate as zero. Kalman filtering generally performs well, except in cases when the user is close to the AP and takes a turn. This is because the relative speed of the user w.r.t. the AP changes abruptly when she turns, confusing the Kalman filter and in turn injecting large errors in distance estimation. To solve this problem, we note that at any turn, it is possible to estimate the new relative speed by considering the user's relative speed right before the turn and the orientation change of the user from her gyroscope. Thus, whenever the user takes a physical turn, we correct the Kalman filter's relative speed estimate to account for the abrupt change. In section 5.4, we will show how this optimization can further reduce SAIL's distance estimation error.

5.3 SAIL System Details

Figure 14 plots the overall architecture of SAIL. As the user walks, the phone collects accelerometer, gyroscope, and magnetometer measurements. The phone performs calculations in real-time at every step to determine the user's step length and heading. A userspace process at the AP receives this step and heading information from the phone. It implements SAIL's distance estimation as well as triangle-based location determination. The AP schedules 10 probe packets per second to obtain the ToF estimates for the client. We use standard NULL data packets as probes because of their short length (60 bytes). Of course, if there is existing data traffic for the client, probe packets are not required. The AP receives the ToF, CSI, RSSI values from the driver and corrects the ToF using CSI to obtain the client's distance. SAIL is primarily targeted to track the location of a user as she walks. Initially, SAIL can only track the *change* in the user's location. Once she turns, however, the AP can decide between the two possible triangles and return a location estimate to the phone. From then on, the AP computes triangles only when it is confident about the WiFi-based distance estimation. Otherwise, it only uses dead-reckoning from the past estimated location and updates the user's location accordingly.

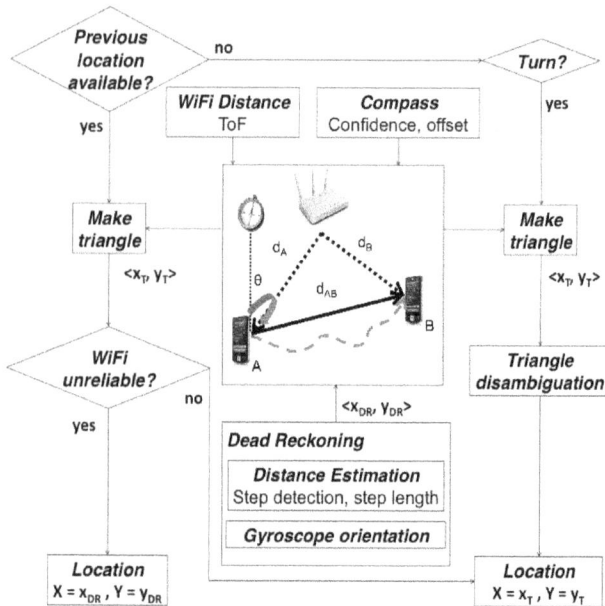

Figure 14: The architecture of SAIL.

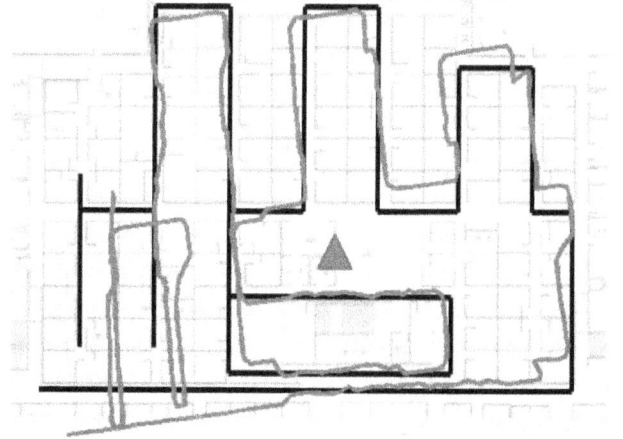

Figure 15: Evaluation floor plan with ground truth (black line), estimated walking path (blue line), and AP location (red triangle). The estimated path is slightly tilted due to compass error.

5.4 Evaluation Results

We evaluate SAIL using HP MSM 460 APs, with Atheros 9590 chipset tuned at 5.805GHz frequency using a 40MHz bandwidth. We recruited 10 users to evaluate SAIL and used 20 different types of mobile devices. Our evaluation includes Android-based mobile devices such as the Samsung Galaxy S3, Samsung Galaxy S4, Nexus 4, Sony Xperia Z, HTC One and iOS-based mobile devices such as the iPhone 5 and iPhone 5s.

Methodology

We design real-life experiments in an office environment with a single AP installed at a known location (figure 15). Users walked around arbitrarily in the building for an hour during normal office hours, with the smartphone in their pants pocket, covering approximately $30,000 \text{ft}^2$. As each user walks, the AP estimates and stores her location coordinates, which we use for our evaluation. We made separate arrangements to collect ground truth since GPS is not available indoors. Briefly, we pasted numbered markers at known locations. Whenever the user walked through a marker, she recorded its number and the current time. Since the locations of the markers are known, we did interpolation between the markers using step-count as the ground truth. The distance between the ground truth and the estimated location is SAIL's instantaneous localization error.

WiFi-based Distance Estimation

SAIL computes the distance of the client based on the propagation delay of only her direct path, called time-of-flight (ToF). Figure 16(a) shows the performance of SAIL's distance estimation error by using 10 packets per second and correcting the multipath infused error by using CIRs from 3 antennas at the AP. Further, by correcting the relative speed according to the Kalman filter whenever the user takes a phys-

ical turn, SAIL reduces the average distance estimation error to 0.8m. This is a step forward from current wireless ToF-based distance estimation schemes that suffer large errors (figure 16(a)) from being multipath and mobility agnostic [19]. Figure 16(a) also studies if signal strength can be used to determine the client's distance. We found that RSSI performs poorly because it is highly susceptible to indoor multipath and shadowing [15,21]. Recently, CUPID [15] reduced the effect of multipath on signal strength-based distance estimation by using the energy of the direct path (EDP). However, EDP is susceptible to shadowing caused by blockage of the signal paths between the AP and the client. EDP also suffers from large errors when the direct path is weak, and thus performs worse than ToF with an average distance estimation error of 5.4m. SAIL's ToF-based approach can precisely find the distance of the client, even when her direct path signal is weak. If the direct path does not exist due to complete blockage, ToF will indeed overestimate the client's distance. It is difficult to evaluate whether the direct path signal exists in our measurements. However, we find that the distance estimation accuracy falls sharply when the signal strength of a client at the AP is below 10dB (figure 16(b)), indicating the likely absence of a direct path.

Effect of Device Heterogeneity on Distance Estimation

The idle time between data frames and ACKs must be correctly accounted for in ToF calculations. Our measurements showed that some chipsets add an offset to the SIFS time. We found that this offset is not random, but is actually a manufacturer dependent *constant* value [19]. The first bits of the ACK MAC address identify the chipset manufacturer and thus can be used to look up and correct the predetermined offset. All mobile devices carrying the same chipset have the same offset. Because the offset is a chipset-specific parameter and is not affected by antenna configuration or phone orientation, we found that mobile devices of the same type have very similar distance estimation error (table 2). Even for mobile devices using different chipsets, once the predetermined offset

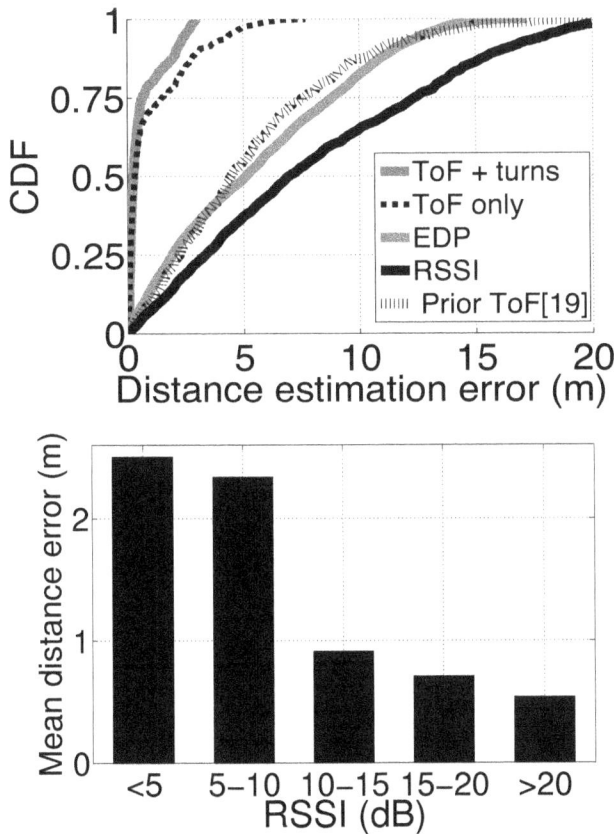

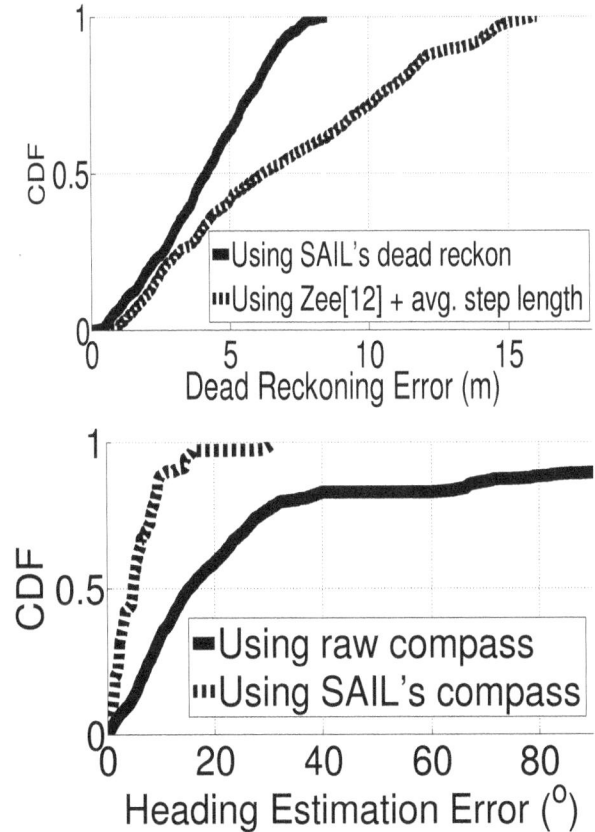

Figure 16: (a) Distance estimation error using ToF, RSSI, and EDP [15]. (b) Distance estimation improves with signal strength.

is corrected, the average distance estimation error is less than a meter (table 3).

	Distance estimation error (meters)			
Samsung Galaxy S4	0.71	0.68	0.75	0.63
iPhone 5	0.9	0.81	0.83	0.94

Table 2: Performance using 4 iPhone and 4 Samsung phones of the same type.

Galaxy S3	Xperia Z	iPhone 5S	HTC One	Nexus 4
0.93m	0.64m	0.82m	0.7m	0.9m

Table 3: Distance estimation error using different types of mobile devices.

Dead-Reckoning Performance

We use dead-reckoning techniques to determine the displacement of the user between two locations (e.g. A and B in figure 13). To evaluate the performance of dead-reckoning, we consider the distance between two random locations of the user spaced more than 20m apart. We find that existing dead-reckoning techniques are affected primarily by poor step length estimation (figure 17(a)). While most existing approaches using map matching techniques to deal with the er-

Figure 17: (a) CDF of dead-reckoning error between locations spaced more than 20m apart. (b) Heading estimation error can be large unless correct compass readings are carefully selected.

rors in step length estimation, SAIL does not impose any such restriction. By determining the user's physical build from her accelerometer readings, SAIL estimates her step length more accurately, resulting into significantly less estimation error.

SAIL also computes the user's absolute heading to determine the orientation of the triangle in figure 1. Smartphone compass-based heading estimation can be quite erroneous due to presence of electromagnetic materials indoors (figure 17(b)). SAIL improves heading estimation by harnessing the compass only when it is reliable. On average, SAIL reduces the heading estimation error to $5.9°$ from $27.4°$ while using the raw compass values.

Location Estimation

By combining WiFi distance and dead-reckoning, SAIL can successfully determine a client's location using a single AP. We evaluate the localization performance of the system by varying specific parameters and replacing our techniques with existing methods. Figure 15 and 18 shows SAIL's instantaneous location estimation error over a duration of 10 minutes. SAIL starts computing the user's location as soon as she makes the first turn. After the user's location has been determined for the first time, SAIL computes the triangle only when the WiFi distance is deemed reliable (RSSI > 10dB). Otherwise, it continues to dead-reckon from the past estimated location. We

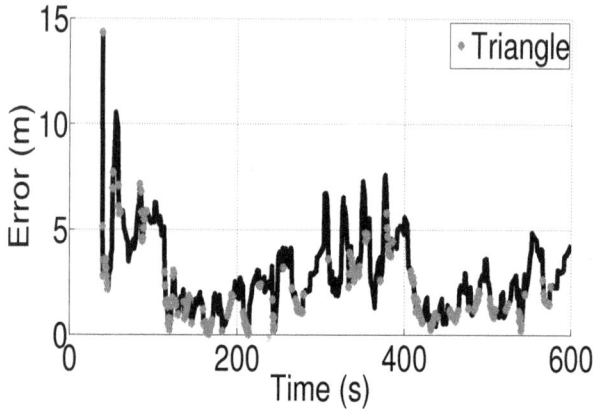

Figure 18: SAIL's location estimation error over time.

find that the errors are typically less than 5m except for a few locations where the client is far away from the AP. This is because SAIL's distance estimation is less accurate when the signal strength is weak, perhaps due to a less prominent presence of the direct path.

Impact of periodic WiFi probing: In general, SAIL probes the client every second and gathers the ToF and CIR values to compute her distance from the AP. Each such probe consists of 10 measurement packets resulting into a background traffic overhead of approximately 0.2% per client. It is important to address this overhead since it can grow quickly with the number of clients. To reduce the overhead, we study the possibility of reducing the frequency of probing in figure 19(a). We find that computing the client's distance at a reduced frequency affects our localization performance. However, with only 10 probe packets every 3.5 seconds, SAIL's average location estimation error is still less than 4m. Of course, SAIL can leverage any existing traffic between the AP and the client to further reduce the location estimation error.

Comparison with existing schemes: Location estimation based on SAIL's triangle can be performed by using existing dead-reckoning and WiFi-based distance estimation techniques at the cost of accuracy. Figure 19(b) shows how the performance is affected by using EDP-based [15] WiFi distance estimation, but maintaining SAIL's dead-reckoning techniques. EDP does not capture the client's distance as accurately as ToF does, increasing the median location estimation error to 7m. Figure 19(b) also evaluates if existing dead-reckoning schemes [18] can perform as well when augmented with SAIL's ToF-based distance estimation. We found that, unlike SAIL, existing schemes often get confused by erroneous compass measurements, resulting into large errors in location estimation.

It is also possible to find the location of the user by computing her angle-of-arrival (AoA [9,15]) at the AP and combining that information with the ToF-based distance estimate. AoA-based techniques suffer from multipath and their accuracy is fundamentally limited by the number of antennas (e.g., $60°$ granularity with recent 3-antenna APs). Thus, even after combining accurate distance estimation using ToF, AoA-based schemes such as CUPID [15] do not perform as well as SAIL.

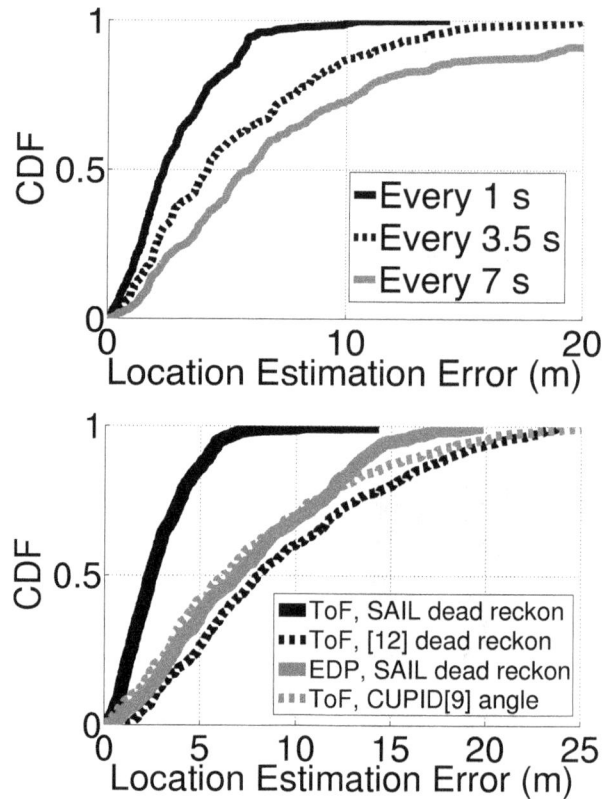

Figure 19: (a) CDF of location estimation error for different frequency of WiFi distance probing. (b) Comparison of SAIL's location estimation performance.

6. RELATED WORK

The indoor localization literature is vast [1,26,27], including techniques using fingerprinting [2,5,6,28,29], crowdsourcing [11,12,18,23,30], triangulation and trilateration [8,9,14,15,31,32]. In the interest of space, we heavily subsample this literature, focusing on systems related to SAIL.

RF signal strength-based: RSSI is a poor estimator of distance because it is susceptible to indoor multipath reflections and shadowing [15,21]. It may be possible to combine measurements from a large number of APs [14] to address the issues with RSSI, but comes at the cost of frequent scanning at the client or channel hopping at the APs. Fingerprinting techniques [2–5,33] also rely on the availability of several APs, but provide better accuracy. However, they need periodic wardriving because of environmental and automatic WLAN configuration changes, making them an expensive proposition. FILA [21] and CUPID [15] attempt to improve WiFi-based distance estimation using PHY layer information, but do so with limited success.

Time-based: Apart from signal strength, there have been attempts to harness the time-of-flight of wireless signal propagation. Most techniques either require expensive clock synchronization between the AP and the client or additional hardware modules [10,34,35]. Echo techniques based on packet exchanges were first proposed in [36] and refined in [37] and [19]. However, unlike SAIL, none of the previous approaches address the effect of multipath in WiFi ToF-based distance estimation. Centaur [13] supplements RSSI with acoustic ranging. Cricket [38] and AHLoS [39] mark the difference in propagation delays between RF signals and ultrasound to determine location. Whether using signal strength or time-of-flight to compute location, all of the above solutions require measurements from multiple access points. This either comes at the cost of battery life for the user's smartphone due to excessive scanning or increased overhead at the APs due to frequent channel hopping and coordination packets. SAIL avoids these costs by leveraging only a single AP, yet still providing high accuracy.

Angle-of-arrival-based techniques use multiple antennas to estimate the angle at which the signal is received, and then triangulate the location of the signal source [9, 15, 40–43]. However, acquiring accurate angle estimation requires large antenna arrays, known antenna spacings, and synchronized CSI reports across antennas [15]. Even with access to raw signal information and using 8 antennas [9, 41], AoA techniques can be derailed in multipath rich indoor environments. SAIL's localization performance will certainly improve when accurate angle estimation is available alongside distance estimation. However, the angle estimation granularity with recent 3-antenna 11n APs is only 60 degrees [15], adding little benefit to SAIL. Moreover, while SAIL may be able to operate strictly at the ToF-capable mobile device (section 7) without requiring any explicit user turns [44], angle estimation requires multiple antennas – unforeseeable for mobile devices in recent future.

Smartphone dead-reckoning: Dead-reckoning has often been used to improve the performance of WiFi-based localization [17]. Evennou et al. [45] combine WiFi fingerprinting and dead-reckoning to refine a map-based particle filter, but do so at the cost of expensive wardriving with knowledge of the building floorplan. UnLoc [18] uses WiFi as a dimension for generating landmarks that can correct dead-reckoning traces over time; however, UnLoc restricts the position of the phone since it relies on gyroscope readings for dead-reckoning and landmark matching. Dead-reckoning has been addressed on its own as well. Existing literature has attempted to eliminate the fixed step-length constraint by either requiring user personalization or leveraging periodic GPS reading to calibrate the correlation function [46]. Park et al. [47] apply machine learning to both estimate the user's walking speed and classify between four different pose classes. While their approach is robust for the trained poses, we suspect that previously unseen poses would lead to misclassification. Instead of looking for changes in pose classification, SAIL looks for large changes in the direction of the gravity vector. Heading estimation is another important aspect of dead-reckoning. Since the compass is unreliable for accurate estimation [12], existing techniques [12, 23, 30, 45, 48] correct the compass heading using map-based particle filtering. These systems rely on indoor walking paths like long hallways for corrections to be made, rendering them ineffective in open spaces.

7. DISCUSSION AND LIMITATIONS

Acquiring CSI/ToF: SAIL leverages CSI and ToF information, already calculated in the WiFi chipset hardware for channel estimation, calibration, etc. Recent 802.11n/ac systems report CSI estimation to drivers for advanced beamforming and MIMO [22, 49, 50]. ToF has also been available in various opensource WiFi platforms and used for distance estimation [19, 37].

Step length training: SAIL's automated step length estimation relies on the training data gathered from users with various physical builds. We performed this training through our own experiments, but we could have also gathered the data by observing GPS readings as the users walks outdoors [46]. SAIL does not require extensive training data collection since step lengths tend to have correlations between users with similar physical builds [51].

Dead-reckoning during pose changes: Pose changes indicate moments when the system is unsure about the dead-reckoning, so physical turns may be missed during these times. The compass may be able to correct the user's heading intermittently, but the orientation estimation algorithm needs to be extended for continuous dead-reckoning.

Diversity in human mobility: We recognize every user interaction with the phone is yet to be tested. Examples include when the user is walking backwards and when the phone is free to move in a user's backpack. Even so, SAIL applies fewer constraints upon the user mobility than its predecessors.

Interaction between AP and mobile device: For our implementation, we combined the dead-reckoning on the phone and WiFi distance estimation at the AP. However, if the right set of APIs are exposed, ToF-based distance computation can also be performed at the mobile device, allowing location estimation strictly at the client.

8. CONCLUSION

In this paper, we have presented SAIL, a system that methodically addresses many of the challenges towards practical WiFi-based positioning using only a single AP. While there have been numerous attempts to use pervasive WiFi for localization, most proposals impose limitations – extensive bootstrapping or dense AP deployments – that hinder their widespread adoption. To overcome the limitations, SAIL employs a single AP and still yields a decent positioning accuracy by improving WiFi ToF-based ranging and smartphone dead-reckoning. SAIL exploits PHY layer information to eliminate the effect of multipath in ToF-based ranging. SAIL advances smartphone dead-reckoning by designing robust techniques for step length, heading estimation, and pose change detection. To our best knowledge, SAIL is the first attempt to meet the single AP design goal using commodity APs and smartphones. The techniques proposed in SAIL are now operational in an enterprise network and achieve a median error of 2.3m.

9. ACKNOWLEDGMENT

We sincerely thank Prof. Rajesh Balan for shepherding our paper, as well as the anonymous reviewers for their valuable comments and feedback. We would also like to thank our colleagues at HP Labs who enthusiastically participated in our experimental evaluation.

10. REFERENCES

[1] Y. Gu et al. A survey of indoor positioning systems. *IEEE Communications Surveys & Tutorials*, 2009.
[2] V. Bahl et al. RADAR: An in-building rf-based user location and tracking system. In *INFOCOM*, 2000.

[3] S. Sen et al. Spot localization using phy layer information. In *MobiSys*, 2012.

[4] Yu-Chung et al. Accuracy characterization for metropolitan-scale wi-fi localization. In *MobiSys*, 2005.

[5] M. Youssef and A. Agrawala. The horus WLAN location determination system. In *MobiSys*, 2005.

[6] Y. Chen et al. Fm-based indoor localization. In *MobiSys*, 2012.

[7] G. Borriello et al. Walrus: wireless acoustic location with room-level resolution using ultrasound. In *MobiSys 2005*.

[8] P. Hu et al. Pharos: Enable physical analytics through visible light based indoor localization. 2013.

[9] J. Xiong and K. Jamieson. Arraytrack: A fine-grained indoor location system. In *USENIX NSDI*, 2013.

[10] M. Youssef et al. Pinpoint: An asynchronous time-based location determination system. In *ACM Mobisys 2006*.

[11] Z. Yang et al. Locating in fingerprint space: wireless indoor localization with little human intervention. In *MobiCom*, 2012.

[12] A. Rai et al. Zee: Zero-effort crowdsourcing for indoor localization. In *MobiCom*, 2012.

[13] R. Nandakumar et al. Centaur: locating devices in an office environment. In *MobiCom*, 2012.

[14] K. Chintalapudi, A. Iyer, and V. Padmanabhan. Indoor localization without the pain. In *MOBICOM*, 2010.

[15] S. Sen et al. Avoiding multipath to revive inbuilding wifi localization. In *MobiSys*, 2013.

[16] A. Anand et al. A quantitative analysis of power consumption for location-aware applications on smart phones. In *ISIE 2007*. IEEE.

[17] Robert Harle. A survey of indoor inertial positioning systems for pedestrians. 2013.

[18] H. Wang et al. Unsupervised indoor localization. MobiSys, 2012.

[19] D. Giustiniano et al. Caesar: carrier sense-based ranging in off-the-shelf 802.11 wireless lan. In *ACM CoNEXT 2011*.

[20] Greg Welch and Gary Bishop. An introduction to the kalman filter, 1995.

[21] K. Wu et al. Fila: Fine-grained indoor localization. In *INFOCOM*, 2012.

[22] D. Halperin. *Simplifying the Configuration of 802.11 Wireless Networks with Effective SNR*. PhD thesis, University of Washington, 2012.

[23] F. Li et al. A reliable and accurate indoor localization method using phone inertial sensors. 2012.

[24] Johann Borenstein et al. Heuristic reduction of gyro drift for personnel tracking systems. *Journal of Navigation*, 62(1):41, 2009.

[25] Stefan Maus, Susan Macmillan, Susan McLean, Brian Hamilton, A Thomson, M Nair, and C Rollins. *The US/UK world magnetic model for 2010-2015*. NOAA National Geophysical Data Center, 2010.

[26] J. Hightower and G. Borriello. Location systems for ubiquitous computing. *Computer*, 2001.

[27] G. Borriello et al. Delivering real-world ubiquitous location systems. *Communications of the ACM*, 48(3):36–41, 2005.

[28] J. Hightower et al. Learning and recognizing the places we go. In *UbiComp 2005*.

[29] Y. Gao et al. Zifind: Exploiting cross-technology interference signatures for energy-efficient indoor localization. *Scanning*, 120:140, 2013.

[30] J. Hightower et al. Particle filters for location estimation in ubiquitous computing: A case study. *UbiComp 2004*.

[31] N. Banerjee et al. Virtual compass: relative positioning to sense mobile social interactions. *Pervasive Computing*, 2010.

[32] K.K. Chintalapudi et al. Ad-hoc localization using ranging and sectoring. In *INFOCOM 2004*.

[33] Yi-Chao Chen et al. Sensor-assisted wi-fi indoor location system for adapting to environmental dynamics. In *MSWIM 2005*.

[34] M. Ciurana, F. Barcelo, and F. Izquierdo. A ranging system with ieee 802.11 data frames. In *RWS*, 2007.

[35] Golden S.A. et al. Sensor measurements for wi-fi location with emphasis on time-of-arrival ranging. *IEEE TMC*, 2007.

[36] D. McCrady et al. Mobile ranging using low-accuracy clocks. *IEEE Transactions on Microwave Theory and Techniques*, 38(6), 2000.

[37] C. Hoene et al. Four-way toa and software-based trilateration of ieee 802.11 devices. In *PIMRC 2008*.

[38] N. Priyantha, A. Chakraborty, and H. Balakrishnan. The cricket location-support system. In *MOBICOM*, 2000.

[39] A. Savvides et al. Dynamic fine-grained localization in ad-hoc networks of sensors. In *ACM MobiCom*, 2001.

[40] D. Niculescu and B. Nath. Ad hoc positioning system (APS) using AoA. In *IEEE Infocom*, 2003.

[41] J. Xiong and K. Jamieson. Towards fine-grained radio-based indoor location. In *HotMobile*. ACM, 2012.

[42] L. Cong et al. Hybrid tdoa/aoa mobile user location for wideband cdma cellular systems. *IEEE Transactions on Wireless Communications*, 1(3):439–447, 2002.

[43] A. Tarighat et al. Improved wireless location accuracy using antenna arrays and interference cancellation. In *ICASSP*, 2003.

[44] Z. Zhang et al. I am the antenna: accurate outdoor ap location using smartphones. In *ACM Mobicom*, 2011.

[45] Frédéric Evennou et al. Advanced integration of wifi and inertial navigation systems for indoor mobile positioning. *Eurasip journal on applied signal processing*, pages 164–164, 2006.

[46] D.K. Cho et al. Autogait: A mobile platform that accurately estimates the distance walked. In *PerCom*, 2010.

[47] J.G. Park et al. Online pose classification and walking speed estimation using handheld devices. In *UbiComp*, 2012.

[48] V Fox et al. Bayesian filtering for location estimation. *Pervasive Computing, IEEE*, 2(3):24–33, 2003.

[49] E.H. Ong et al. Ieee 802.11 ac: Enhancements for very high throughput wlans. In *IEEE PIMRC 2011*.

[50] Y. Xiao. Ieee 802.11 n: enhancements for higher throughput in wireless lans. *Wireless Communications, IEEE*, 2005.

[51] J. Ahn et al. Long-range correlations in stride intervals may emerge from non-chaotic walking dynamics. *PloS one*, 8(9), 2013.

I am a Smartphone and I can Tell my User's Walking Direction

Nirupam Roy
University of Illinois (UIUC)
nroy8@illinois.edu

He Wang
University of Illinois (UIUC)
hewang5@illinois.edu

Romit Roy Choudhury
University of Illinois (UIUC)
croy@illinois.edu

ABSTRACT

This paper describes *WalkCompass*, a system that exploits smartphone sensors to estimate the direction in which a user is walking. We find that several smartphone localization systems in the recent past, including our own, make a simplifying assumption that the user's walking direction is known. In trying to relax this assumption, we were not able to find a generic solution from past work. While intuition suggests that the walking direction should be detectable through the accelerometer, in reality this direction gets blended into various other motion patterns during the act of walking, including up and down bounce, side-to-side sway, swing of arms or legs, etc. Moreover, the walking direction is in the phone's local coordinate system (e.g., along Y axis), and translation to global directions, such as 45° North, can be challenging when the compass is itself erroneous. WalkCompass copes with these challenges and develops a stable technique to estimate the user's walking direction within a few steps. Results drawn from 15 different environments demonstrate median error of less than 8 degrees, across 6 different users, 3 surfaces, and 3 holding positions. While there is room for improvement, we believe our current system can be immediately useful to various applications centered around localization and human activity recognition.

Categories and Subject Descriptors

C.4 [**Performance of Systems**]: Measurement techniques; C.5.3 [**Computer System Implementation**]: Portable devices

General Terms

Design, Experimentation, Performance

Keywords

Heading direction; Force analysis; Mobile phones; Sensing; Compass correction; Localization; Activity recognition; Orientation; Magnetic field

MobiSys'14, June 16–19, 2014, Bretton Woods, New Hampshire, USA.
Copyright 2014 ACM 978-1-4503-2793-0/14/06 ...$15.00.
http://dx.doi.org/10.1145/2594368.2594392 .

1. INTRODUCTION

Despite tremendous amount of academic research, indoor localization is still struggling to come to mainstream. Based on numerous discussions with industries and start-ups, we are beginning to realize that much of the academic research has optimized for "location accuracy", while making simplifying assumptions about other aspects of the end-to-end system. Example assumptions include the availability of indoor maps, availability of dense WiFi infrastructure, orientation of the phone, known walking directions, etc. The consistent feedback we have received is that relaxing these assumptions is crucial at this point, perhaps even more than pushing the boundaries of location accuracy. Driven by this feedback, this paper concentrates on automatically sensing a user's global walking direction regardless of the orientation of the phone.

If solved well, a user's walking direction can offer benefits beyond inertial localization. Stitching crowd-sourced sensor data to infer detailed indoor maps is of increasing interest – the user's walking direction is a critical component in this. Elevator companies are envisioning that future elevators will be proactively fetched when the resident of a building begins to walk towards the elevator [2] – the walking direction is valuable here. Walking directions may also translate to the user's facing direction, enabling additional applications in augmented reality, social activities, and context-awareness. Of course, these benefits would be available only if walking direction is estimated through a generic stand-alone module, without relying on external information (such as maps, locations, WiFi access points). Moreover, to be able to tell the global walking direction (e.g., 45° North), the compass errors need to be mitigated. *WalkCompass* is focused on addressing these challenges.

It is natural to question the difficulty of solving this problem – one may ask *why not estimate the walking direction by projecting accelerometer signals to the horizontal plane?* While this is true in abstraction, the real situation is far more complicated when the phone is held in different orientations at various body positions. In pant pockets, for example, the phone swings along with the leg, continuously altering the phone's local coordinate system; free-flowing hands are similar. Users sway sideways in varying degrees while taking each step, which becomes pronounced when the phone is in the palm (e.g., when the user is checking emails). Inherent sensor noise further pollutes the signal. The precise walking direction is actually a micro-motion that needs to be carefully identified, weighted, and averaged over at least two steps.

Even if the user's walking direction is successfully extracted in the phone's local coordinate system, translating it to global directions, say $45°$ North East, is an additional challenge. This is because the global (magnetic) coordinate system relies on the compass, which itself is susceptible to ferromagnetic interference in many indoor environments. All in all, the accelerometer signal that corresponds to the direction of walking gets blended into various other motion patterns that vary across users, environments, and phone models. Solving it generically, we believe, is non-trivial.

The core intuitions in WalkCompass are simple and can be explained in two parts. First, when a user walks, her heel strikes the ground creating a distinct vibration that resonates through the entire body. This vibration reflects on the accelerometer data across all holding positions, even when the user is holding the phone against her ears. WalkCompass uses this vibration as a reference, scans the signal backwards, and extract specific samples from a time window when the body's movement is dominantly in the heading direction. The signal is then processed with the gyroscope data to compensate for instability of the phone's coordinate system, such as when the entire phone is swinging in the pant pocket. This motion vector is then projected to the plane orthogonal to gravity, and averaged over few steps to converge upon the *local* walking direction.

The second problem pertains to translating the walking direction to the global magnetic coordinate system, but for this, the compass needs to be improved. WalkCompass's intuition is to treat the compass measurements as a signal, shaped by the earth's magnetic field, and by (the resultant of) other interferers in the ambiance. While separating this resultant interference is a difficult problem, the opportunity arises from walking. Since the phone moves in small steps, it observes staggered snapshots of the same interference – as if watching an object from different viewing angles – thereby enabling the possibility of triangulation. Of course, triangulation is possible only when the signal exhibits certain properties. WalkCompass exploits these properties to correct the compass direction in certain locations, and uses gyroscope based dead reckoning to track the walking direction between these locations.

Of course, the above is an over-simplification of our designed algorithm – several constraints need to be accounted for that are detailed in the paper. WalkCompass incorporates these algorithms into a functional system, with certain optimization for human variations and holding positions. Experiment results from 15 different settings show that the main limitation of WalkCompass is in its time to convergence. While an ideal system should be able to offer the direction in 2 walking steps, WalkCompass sometimes requires up to 5 steps. However, the direction accuracy is promising, with the 75th percentile error being less than 12 degrees, in comparison to the compass which can be $26°$ even when held in the direction of walking. The accuracies scale across users, varying placements on the body, and while walking over different surfaces such as concrete, carpets, etc. Micro-benchmarks on magnetic interference

calculation also exhibit promising results, demonstrating that the native compass errors can be appreciably reduced (when the user is walking). While there is still room for improvement, we believe WalkCompass can already be useful to other applications. We have demonstrated the system to a few companies – an YouTube video of the demonstration is posted here [3].

The main contributions of WalkCompass may be briefly summarized as follows:

1. *Analyzing the anatomy of walking patterns from the perspective of smartphone sensors.* This is performed through a synchronized analysis of a walking video and sensor readings, revealing meanings of each short segment of accelerometer readings. We believe our analysis tool could benefit other smartphone-based activity recognition systems.

2. *Coping with magnetic interference in indoor environments.* Designing various techniques to localize, quantify, and isolate the interference, with certain inspirations borrowed from noise cancellation techniques in wireless communication.

3. *Implementation of a functional prototype on multiple models of Android phones.* Experiment results from 15 different buildings indicating median error of $8°$ with around 5 steps to achieve convergence.

2. FEW NATURAL QUESTIONS

(1) **Despite substantial research on activity recognition and phone orientations, why is walking direction still an unsolved problem?**
While we have been somewhat surprised as well, our literature survey revealed some insights into this question. Most papers that have attempted this problem have done so in the context of a broader application, and have leveraged application-specific opportunities to resolve the challenges. For instance, [9] analyzes human motion in indoor settings and inherently requires a map of the place; authors leverage the same map to estimate the user's walking direction. Authors in [30] perform localization using information about the WiFi AP's location, and use the same AP locations to infer crude walking direction. [22, 19] assumes that the phone's initial orientation is known, and tracks the user's heading direction for a short time window after that. Zee [28] is one of the localization papers that addresses the problem without other assumptions, but admit that the solution is not stable and offers ambiguity – they mention that using maps can solve the problem at the expense of some latency.

A recent paper [5] attempts to solve the problem as a stand-alone module but uses highly controlled conditions for testing, namely, phone held in hand. MATLAB results are presented for two path traces from outdoor environments. Moreover, the solution is only in the local coordinate frame. Finally, several papers estimate the orientation of a smartphone on the human body. Phone orientation, while necessary, is insufficient for translating a user's walking direction to a global coordinate system; moreover, detecting the (local) walking direction is a separate problem. Knowing the orientation does not make this problem any easier.

(2) Why not use the sequence of user's location to compute walking direction?

In outdoor environments, this is true and trivial (assuming GPS energy consumption is not an issue). For indoors, however, walking direction is needed to compute location in the first place. This reliance is growing stronger due to two reasons. First, with more systems moving away from manual war-driving to crowd-sourced approaches, it is important to understand the motion patterns of the crowd, so that sensed data can be appropriately oriented. Second, pedestrian dead reckoning is becoming increasingly popular for localization due to its ability to track fine scale human movements (otherwise difficult with say WiFi or cell tower signals). As a result, WalkCompass cannot assume the availability of the user's location – the estimated walking direction will be needed to facilitate localization.

3. SYSTEM OVERVIEW

Figure 1 shows the key building blocks underlying Walk-Compass, and their connections. We describe the flow of operation here, and expand on the technical details in the next sections.

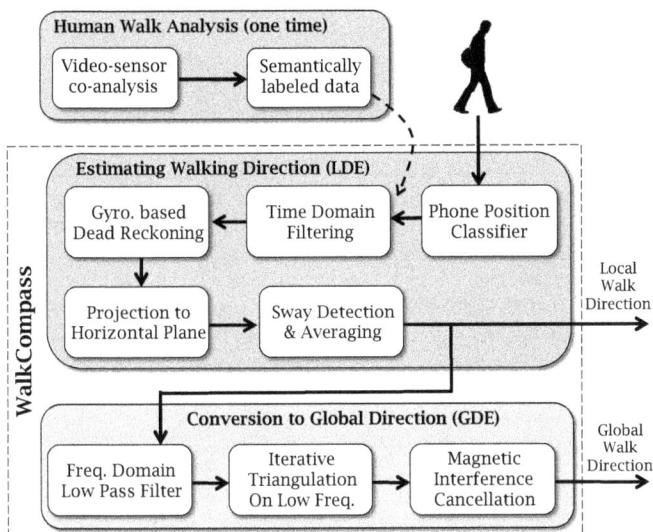

Figure 1: Flow of operations in WalkCompass. The input is the phone's sensor signals and the output is the local and global walking directions.

The overall WalkCompass system has 3 main modules, namely: (1) Human Walk Analysis (HWA), (2) Local Walk Direction Estimator (LDE), and (3) Global Walk Direction Estimator (GDE). HWA is a one-time analysis of human walking patterns that helps us understand how different forces act in different directions to keep the human body stable during a walk. We observe how these forces are manifested on the smartphone's accelerometer in different positions on the body, and use the insights to make key design decisions in LDE. Specifically, we identify the exact time-segment of the accelerometer signal that contains the forward motion of the body-part (e.g., leg, hand, chest) near which the phone is located.

The Local Walk Direction Estimator (LDE) receives the raw accelerometer reading from the smartphone, and first classifies the data to infer the phone's location on the body. The (time domain) accelerometer signal is then analyzed and the appropriate segment extracted based on HWA's recommendations. This segment contains the forces in the direction of the walk, but they are in 3D; moreover it is polluted by a constantly-rotating coordinate system (say when the upper leg swings while pivoted to the hips). The gyroscope is engaged to compensate for this rotation, and after some processing, the motion vector is projected to the horizontal plane, orthogonal to gravity.

Now, this vector is only for one step of one leg, and not necessarily the direction of the walk – humans extend their feet in side-ward directions, called sway, and the walking direction is an average of sway. The output from this averaging operation yields the walking direction in the phone's local coordinate system. Observe that this implies that with respect to the human's walking direction, the phone's orientation is now known.

The local walking direction may suffice for some applications; others need the global direction. In a perfect world, the global walking direction would be the angle subtended by the walking vector and the compass direction (i.e., North). For instance, if the walking vector points in the opposite direction of the phone's compass, then the global walking direction would be "South". However, the compass can be erroneous indoors due to ambient ferromagnetic interferences – the GDE module is tasked to compute the global walking direction despite these errors. To this end, the GDE module operates on the frequency domain, treating the sequence of compass readings as a digital signal.

As a person walks through indoor spaces, WalkCompass hypothesizes that the effect of nearby interferers would change quicker over time, and would be captured by the high frequency components in the compass signal. Filtering out the high frequency components, the low frequency components are expected to be from further away sources of interference, adding an offset to the compass reading. GDE employs an iterative algorithm that essentially attempts to localize this far-away interferer. The key intuition is to decompose the measured magnetic vector into the earth's magnetic vector (G) and the interference vector (I), and adjust the direction of G until all the I vectors intersect at the same point[1]. This value of G is inferred to be the actual earth's magnetic field. Of course, this triangulation may not be feasible in all locations (e.g., where many strong and opposing interfering sources are located far away). However, if some locations offer feasible results, the global walking direction can be computed there, and gyroscope-based tracking can be used at other (in-between) locations. The subsequent sections expand on each of the techniques, followed by micro-benchmark and full-scale system evaluation.

4. SYSTEM DESIGN

We describe the three modules, HWA, LDE, and GDE, for the case where the phone is carried in the pant pocket. This is actually the harder case, compared to the palm or in the

---

[1]Note that the magnitude of the earth's magnetic vector at a given location can be looked up in a database, so knowing the user's crude location, say the zip code, is adequate.

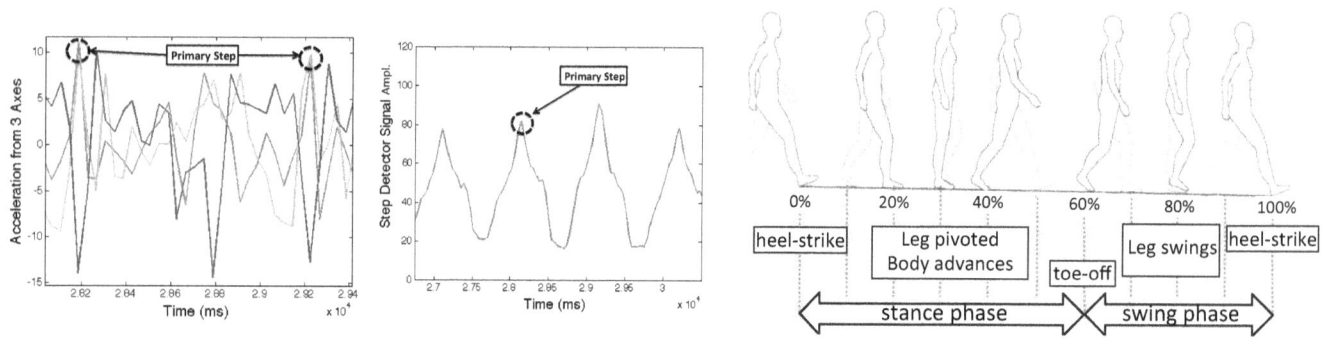

Figure 3: Accelerometer data from human walking patterns with the smartphone placed in the pocket: (a) Correlated jerks on all 3 axes on the accelerometer indicating a heel-strike on the ground. (b) The peak detection algorithm detects the timing of the heel-strikes. (c) The gait cycle of human walk composed of 2 phases: the first 60% between two heel strikes is called the *stance*, and the next 40% is called the *swing*.

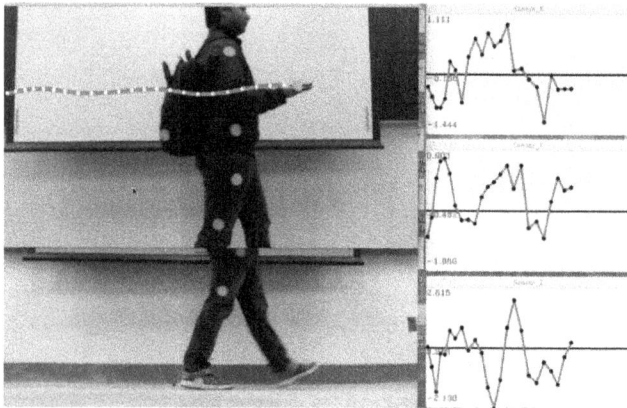

Figure 2: Matching video and accelerometer for labeling measured readings – the green circles are tracked across video frames to compute their respective motion vectors, and later matched against the vectors derived from the accelerometer.

swinging hand. At the end of this section, we will discuss how the techniques can be generalized to other placements with small modifications.

4.1 Human Walk Analysis (HWA)

Our goal in HWA is to be able to label the different parts of an accelerometer reading with the corresponding micro-actions that the user is performing at each time point. The hope is that this analysis would reveal at least one segment of the signal that is precisely along the walking direction, and more importantly, is least polluted by other micro-actions of the limbs. Of course, numerous studies, especially in the domains of physical therapy and computer animation, have analyzed the acceleration of various body parts during the walk cycle [13, 14, 12]. Our study, however, is from the view of the smartphone sensor, placed at different parts of the body, inside different outfits.

We set up a system in which 2 video cameras were placed focusing various body parts of a walking person, say John. John carried phones at multiple positions in the body – at each of these locations, we attached a green marker to help track the motion of the phone through the video frames. All

phones and the video cameras were time synchronized (to sub-milliseconds) by shining a bright light on all their cameras simultaneously. From the gathered videos, we tracked each green marker over time and translated them into motion in the X, Y, and Z axes of the phone. We matched the visually-computed motion with the accelerometer signal to synchronize them as well as possible. This process helps in matching the different ranges of motion (one in pixel space and the other in sensor signal space), as well as for synchronizing timing shifts due to fluctuations in accelerometer sampling (details omitted in the interest of space). Figure 2 shows the outcome – we are now able to click on any time window on the accelerometer signal and observe the corresponding video clip.

We distill 2 useful findings from this experiment that we use later to design the system. Here the limb that carries the phone is referred to as the *primary* limb, and the other is called *secondary*.

(1) Heel Strike is an Anchor Point

The maximum amplitude and fluctuation in the acceleration, along all the 3 axes, occurs when the heel of the human strikes the ground. This holds true across all positions on the body, including hand, backpack, pant pocket, shirt pocket, etc. – only the magnitude of the jerk is different in each of them. This general property serves as a valuable signal marker – an anchor point – from which other stages of the walk can be analyzed. To isolate this heel-strike with high reliability, we add all the 3 dimensions of the accelerometer signal, and take the signal envelope of this summation, and pass through a simple peak detection algorithm (Figure 3a and 3b). The outputs of the algorithm are the precise timings of the peaks.

(2) Swing Before Heel Strike

Between consecutive heel strikes, the legs go through two main phases – a "stance" and a "swing" as shown in Figure 3(c). Stance is the phase when the upper body and leg move forward while pivoted to the feet on the ground; swing is the phase when the leg swings forward, pivoted to the hip, to overtake the upper body. During the swing, the acceleration is positive in the first half of the swing, and negative in the second half (to bring the leg to a stop for a heel-strike).

Further, say the swing lasts from time t_1 to t_9 (Figure 4) – the acceleration is maximum at time t_3, then its zero at time t_5, and then the deceleration is maximum at time t_7.

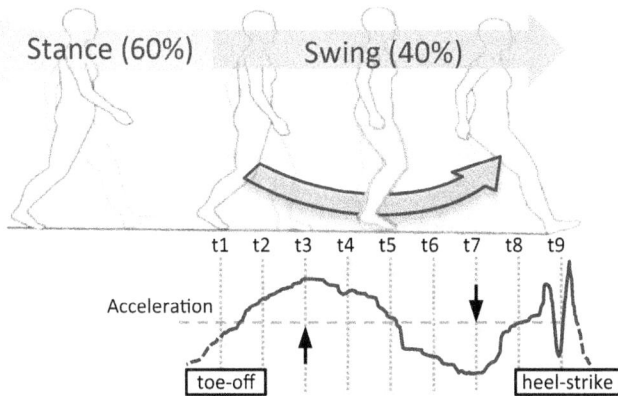

Figure 4: The acceleration at various points of the swing phase during the human walk cycle.

Our first approach was to extract the accelerometer data around t_3 and t_7, reverse the sign for the data at t_7, and average them to derive the user's walking direction. This should cope well with accelerometer noise since hardware noise is Gaussian with zero mean, hence should cancel well upon averaging. However, we observed that the data around t_3 is polluted by the motions of the secondary leg and the upper body. On the other hand, these secondary and upper body motions are much less prevalent around time t_7 – perhaps because the body is trying to stabilize – making the signal pristine. Hence, the Human Walk Analysis (HWA) module prescribes the region around this t_7 time point as the signal containing the walking direction. Of course, this is an approximation, since the above analysis assumes that the swing is occurring uniformly in time. To be accurate, we cannot assume that the mid point of the swing is at t_5, and the deceleration is maximum mid-way between t_5 and t_9. The subsequent discussions in LDE will account for these factors.

4.2 Local Walking Direction Estimator (LDE)

The LDE module receives a user's accelerometer readings as an input and runs the raw data through a position classifier to detect where the phone is located on the body. Past work has reliably solved this problem [29, 27] – we have borrowed these solutions, and depending on the placement, apply minor variants of LDE. For ease of explanation, we describe LDE entirely for the case of pant pockets, and discuss the variants at the end of the section.

Filtering: Assuming that the phone is in the pocket, the data is then received by the Time Domain Filtering module. This module computes the heal-strike peaks in the signal, looks back from the peak to extract the segment with maximum deceleration in the second half of the swing (as described earlier in HWA). More precisely, the start of the second half needs to be estimated first, for which Walk-Compass looks for the change in the sign of acceleration from positive to negative. Denote this time t_i and the time of next peak, t_j. WalkCompass extracts the time point of maximum deceleration within $[t_i, t_j]$ – denote this as time

t_x. To cope with accelerometer noise, typically Gaussian with zero mean, WalkCompass extracts a short segment around t_x[2]. WalkCompass passes this segment through a low pass filter to remove high frequency noise and potentially other signal pollutants, and forwards the samples to the gyroscope based dead reckoning module.

Dead Reckoning: The dead reckoning module fetches the gyroscope readings at these exact time points (corresponding to these signal samples) and observes the angular rotation of the phone. By rotating back the phone's coordinate system to a reference time point (i.e., rotating the phone in the reverse direction of the gyroscope readings), the samples are now brought to a stable coordinate system. The samples are now averaged, and the sign reversed. This is the walking vector in 3D space.

Projection to Horizontal: The walking direction in 3D space is then projected to the plane orthogonal to gravity, also called the *walk plane*. The gravity vector is of course not obvious from the raw accelerometer reading – we estimate the gravity vector by fusing the accelerometer and gyroscope data, and applying the complementary filter [1]. WalkCompass projects the 3D walking direction into the plane perpendicular to this computed gravity vector.

Sway Detection: In bipedal movement, each leg moves the body in a slightly lateral direction – the walking direction is actually a resultant of these two lateral motions. Thus, the walking direction computed so far is slightly offset from the actual walking direction. Further, the body also sways during the walk, introducing additional forces unaligned to the walking direction. Fortunately, all these movements are reasonably symmetric with respect to the heading direction in the horizontal plane. Therefore, the resultant of the primary and secondary movements mitigates these lateral movements and sway-induced errors. WalkCompass estimates the walking direction on the secondary leg using the same technique as the primary, except that it uses a second smaller peak in the accelerometer signal. These smaller peaks are indicative of when the secondary heel strikes the ground. The final resultant vector is passed through a median filter to remove random jerks on the phone during the walk. The output of the median filter is forwarded as the final output of LDE – this is WalkCompass's estimate of the walking direction in the phone's local coordinate system.

4.2.1 Coping with Phone Placement

Past work has developed classifiers that reliably discriminate the phone's location on the body (palm, pant pocket, swinging hands, etc.). The key technique is to observe the energy density from acceleration, as well as the magnitude of peaks during the walk. WalkCompass borrows this classifier with a few minor adjustments – this is not our contribution.

Once the phone's location is known, we apply a few minor modifications for the case when the phone is held in the hand (both palm and swing). Specifically, instead of summing the (x, y, z) accelerometer signals, we first compute the variation along the gravity dimension (which is

---

[2]Taking a sample only at t_x is susceptible to noise, instead averaging over a few samples is expected to dampen the noise.

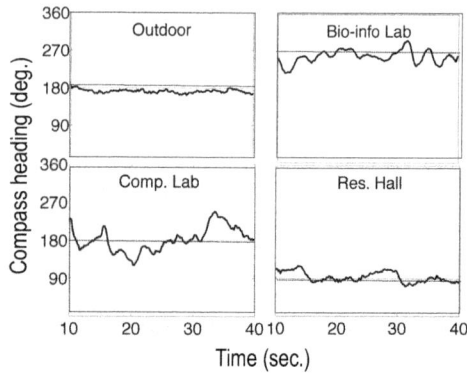

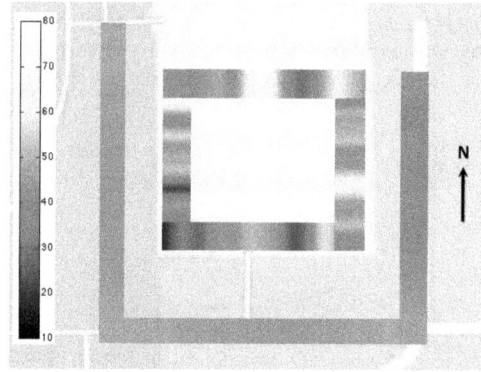

Figure 5: (a) Magnetic fluctuations in 3 indoor environments far higher than outdoors. (b) Heat map of magnetic intensity across the entire corridor of a science laboratory. WalkCompass performs evaluation in these settings.

not necessarily the z axis). The intuition is that the phone bounces maximally along the gravity, and the HWA module shows that the bounce-peaks are well correlated to the heel strikes. Thus, once we anchor the accelerometer signal to these bounces (which are symmetric for both legs), we apply the same segment extraction scheme. Fortunately, the time point when the leg's deceleration is maximum, is also the time when the upper body is getting stabilized from full-fledged forward motion. Selecting this time window is effective for hand-held phones. The case for shirt pockets is slightly more difficult, since the bounce is softer. Nonetheless, the bounce is still visible among the experiments we performed (but may be less reliable for a soft walker, or a child). We leave jacket pockets and bags to future work.

4.3 Global Direction Estimator (GDE)

Translating LDE's output to the global coordinate system entails 2 steps: (1) finding the true magnetic north in the phone's coordinate system, and (2) measuring the angle between the true magnetic north and LDE's output. Step 2 is trivial, and in an ideal world, even step 1 is simply the direction given by the smartphone's compass reading. In reality, however, the smartphone compass is heavily influenced by magnetic interferers in the surroundings, especially in indoor environments. Figure 5(a) shows the compass readings from Android and iPhones in 4 different environments – an outdoor sidewalk, a bio-engineering building, a computer science building and a residential hall. In 3 of these 4 cases, the compass deviates heavily from the actual walking direction. Figure 5(b) shows a more detailed view – a heat map of the magnetic intensity when the user walks with the phone in a rectangular corridor. The intensity varies frequently and ranges from 10 to 80 micro-tesla, indicating high magnetic interference. As a result more than 95% of the corridor incurs errors greater than 23 degree offset. However, on the outdoor path around the building, the magnetic intensity remains close to its expected value, around 53 micro-tesla at that location. In light of this, GDE concentrates on improving the compass, which is likely to benefit other applications that utilize the native compass app.

Background on the Magnetic Compass

The Earth behaves like a giant magnet surrounded by lines of magnetic flux [24]. A freely suspended magnetic needle aligns itself with these lines and directs itself towards the

magnetic North of the Earth. Although these magnetic flux lines converge at magnetic poles, they appear parallel in a given (small) region, due to Earth's large diameter. Thus, when we walk with a smartphone in outdoor settings with zero magnetic influence, we observe that the compass readings – a 3D vector – are parallel to each other. However, as we introduced an artificial interference near the phone[3], we observed that the measured compass vectors were distorted. The distortions were in the direction of the resultant of the Earth's magnetic field (G) and the field caused by the interferer (I) – shown in Figure 6(a). Now, with multiple interferers close to the phone, the measured compass readings changed quickly since small displacements brought the phone relatively closer to some interferers and further from others. When the interferers were moved far away, the magnitude of the interference reduced, and the fluctuations in the readings naturally subsided. The measured compass vector exhibited an offset from the actual magnetic north, and this offset changed slowly over time (Figure 6(b)).

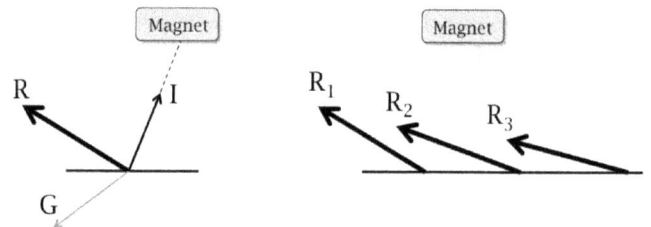

Figure 6: (a) Measured compass vector (R) is the resultant of earth's magnetic field (G) and the interference vector (I). (b) Compass vector R changing slowly as user moves.

Intuition for Compass Correction

The above observations, although unsurprising, offered us an intuition. We recognized that when the compass is moving, the data it records is essentially multiple snapshots of the magnetic interference from slightly changing angles. Assuming the interferer is far away and stationary, the consecutive compass vectors should make small angles between each other. Now, if the earth's magnetic north vector was

---

[3]Interferers can be permanent magnets, called *Hard Iron* interference, or any ferromagnetic material, called *Soft Iron* interference.

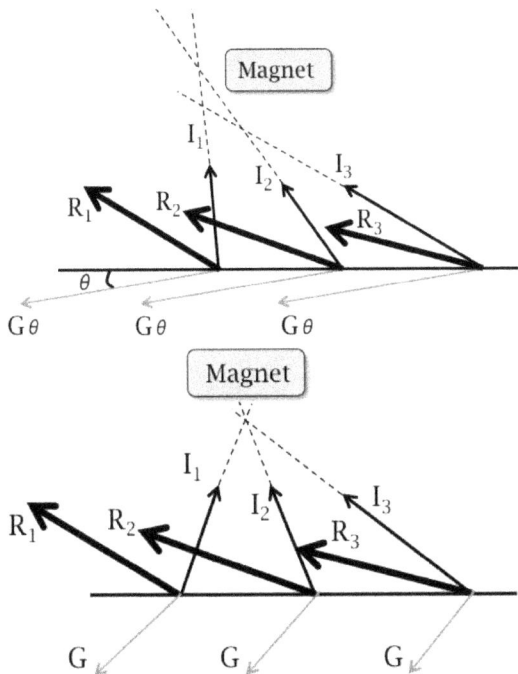

Figure 7: (a) With incorrect G vectors, the I vectors do not coincide. (b) Upon iterating over θ, for some value of G_θ, the vectors coincide.

indeed known, then subtracting this vector from the compass vectors, should have offered the interference vectors, and more importantly, these interference vectors should have intersected at the location of the interferer. In reality, since the earth's magnetic north is not known, we asked: *what if we iterate over all possible vectors of magnetic north until we find the interference vectors intersecting at one location.*

Figure 7 illustrates the idea graphically. Compass readings $[R_1, R_2, R_3...]$ correspond to a moving user recording the readings at times $[t_1, t_2, t_3...]$. Now, since the direction of G is not know, it is possible to assume an arbitrary direction, say G_θ, and subtract from the R vectors, resulting in interference vectors, I_1, I_2, and I_3. If G_θ is incorrect, the interference vectors are not expected to intersect at a common point. However, when iterated for all values of θ, the correct value of G may be expected to offer a common point of intersection, shown in Figure 7(b). If this intersection indeed occurs, then we can select the corresponding G_θ, and use that as an estimate of the true magnetic north.

A natural question is: *does the IMT algorithm assume only one interferer in the ambiance?* While it may appear to be so, observe that the interference vector we estimate could actually be the (vectorial) sum of all interferences in the ambiance. This is modeled under the principle that different force vectors can be linearly added and represented by a single resultant vector. Of course, there is no reason to believe that these resultant vectors would originate or culminate at a single source (the point of intersection). However, given that the spatial gaps between R_1, R_2, R_3 is small (say, three consecutive samples at 25 Hz), the resultant vectors are likely to be offset by small amounts, and hence, could be expected to meet at nearby points (a heuristic). The rest

of this section details this algorithm, called *Iterative Magnetic Triangulation* (IMT). Several pre-processing steps and fine-tuning are necessary to make the algorithm generic and robust to widely varying real-world conditions.

Iterative Magnetic Triangulation (IMT)

We describe 5 steps of the IMT algorithm next.

• Step 1: Vector Selection

The compass continuously provides a series of R_i vectors, however, not all these vectors are suitable for the IMT algorithm. For example, when the user is not moving, the compass reports unchanging magnetic vectors that are parallel to each other. The interference vectors for those samples will also be parallel, rendering triangulation infeasible. On the other hand, if the phone sways significantly (on the axis perpendicular to the of walking direction), then it breaks IMT's model that the phone is dominantly moving along the walking direction. Finally, the triangulation heuristic requires the interferers to be sufficiently far, so that within a small time window, the magnitudes of the interference vectors are almost equal. Recall that with nearby interferers, the magnitudes change much quicker.

In view of these constraints, IMT treats the compass data as a signal and first passes it through a low pass filter. This eliminates the high frequency components corresponding to nearby interferers, and leaves the influences of far away and strong interferers. On this residue signal, IMT opportunistically selects 3 consecutive vectors that are not parallel, and whose projections on the sway-axis have negligible variation. We find reasonable number of vector triplets $< R_i, R_{i+1}, R_{i+2} >$ that satisfy this criteria. Recall that even if WalkCompass obtains the global walking direction in a few spots, it can use the gyroscope to track the user in between those spots (since the gyroscope is not affected by magnetic interference).

• Step 2: Iteration and Triangulation

IMT has a reasonable (though not precise) estimate of the magnitude of G, based on the phone's crude location (at the granularity of, say, zip codes). This can be found from the International Geomagnetic Reference Field database [6]. However, the direction of G is unknown and IMT iterates over all possible values of θ. Thus, for a given θ, IMT subtracts G_θ from each of $< R_i, R_{i+1}, R_{i+2} >$ to compute $< I_i, I_{i+1}, I_{i+2} >$, and then observes how the interference vectors intersect. When the intersection points are tightly clustered (defined in more detail later), the corresponding G_θ is selected as the earth's magnetic field. If multiple values of θ present tight clusters, IMT chooses the values of θ that is closest to the compass reading. Finally, if no tight clusters are found, IMT attempts the same operation on the next valid vector triplet, or waits a few seconds to get fresh data from the walking user.

• Step 3: Refining Magnitude of G

Unfortunately, we observed that in some cases, the rough magnitude of G (looked up from the Reference Field database) provides unreliable results. This is due to inaccurate locations as well as unknown heights (i.e., a smartphone on the 5th floor of a building may observe different geomagnetic forces compared to sea level values from the

335

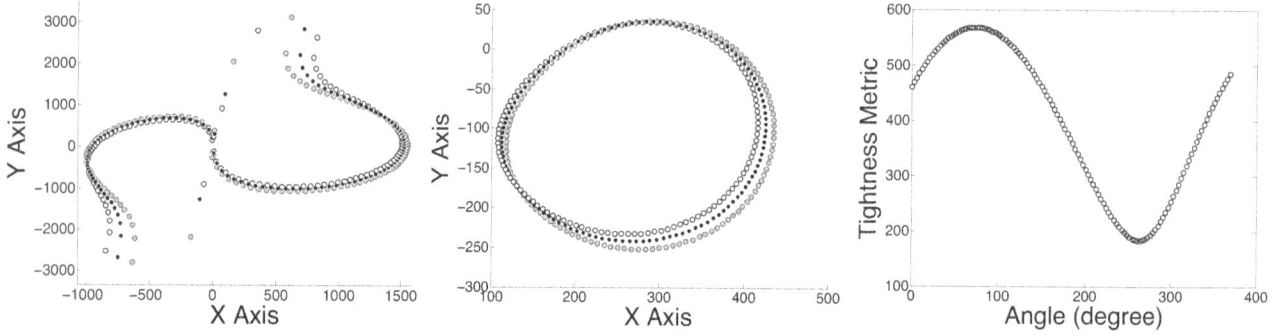

Figure 8: The locus of two interference vectors when iterating over geomagnetic vectors. If the magnitude of the geomagnetic vector is incorrect then the loci creates (a) an irregular shape, otherwise, (b) the loci creates a regular ellipse/circle shape. (c) Varying values of tightness with increasing θ – IMT picks G_θ corresponding to minimum tightness at around 260.

database). Importantly, we find that when the magnitude of G is erroneous, the locus of the intersection points of $< I_i, I_{i+1}, I_{i+2} >$, computed from all values of θ, follow erratic shapes (Figure 8(a)). On the other hand, when the magnitude of G is close to the correct value, this locus forms a reasonably closed-formed shape, resembling a circle or an ellipse (Figure 8(b)). In view of this, IMT checks the shape of the locus and iteratively reduces the magnitude of G until the locus forms the expected shape.

- **Step 4: Picking Tight Intersection Clusters**
Ideally, each pair in the inference vector triplet should intersect at the same point. In practice, however, the points of intersection form a cluster. IMT picks the value of θ for which it finds the tightest cluster of intersections. We define the "tightness" of a cluster as the sum of all pairs of points in that cluster.

- **Step 5: Final Global Walking Direction**
Figure 8(c) shows the variation of *tightness* values for a full iteration of G_θ for a given vector triplet. IMT finds the lowest point of this graph (i.e., the minimum value of tightness), and the corresponding G_θ (263° in this example) is announced as the estimated geomagnetic north. Note that this can also be used as the new compass output, improving the inherent quality of the compass. Finally, WalkCompass compares the local walking direction against this estimated north, and outputs the global walking direction of the user. Algorithm 1 presents the pseudo code for the IMT algorithm.

5. EVALUATION

5.1 Implementation and Methodology

WalkCompass has been implemented on Android, using the Jellybeans version, and tested using a variety of Samsung phones. The codebase has also been replicated on MATLAB to test optimization modules offline – the appropriate optimization have are ported back into the phone. Figure 9 shows a screenshot with the gray cone(thicker) showing the compass direction; the green cone(thinner) denotes the user's walking direction. The width of the cone is proportional to the variance of walking direction – a useful visualization for debugging in real conditions.

Algorithm 1: Pseudocode for the IMT algorithm

Data: continuous magnetometer data
Result: θ_{est}
$< R_i, R_{i+1}, R_{i+2} > =$ Vector Selection(filtered input);
$r_G =$ geomagnetic intensity;
while $r_G > threshold$ **do**
   for $\theta_G \leftarrow 0\circ$ **to** $360\circ$ **do**
      $G_\theta =$ vector with magnitude r_G and angle θ_G ;
      $I_i = R_i - G_\theta$;
      $I_{i+1} = R_{i+1} - G_\theta$;
      $I_{i+2} = R_{i+2} - G_\theta$;
      $< P_i, P_{i+1}, P_{i+2} > =$ pairwise intersections of $< I_i, I_{i+1}, I_{i+2} >$;
      $t_\theta =$ sum of all pairwise distances between P_i, P_{i+1} and P_{i+2}. ;
      Store $< (t_\theta, \theta_G) >$ in T ;
      if *Locus of* $< P_i, P_{i+1}, P_{i+2} >$ *goes irregular* **then**
         reduce r_G exponentially ;
         break ;
      end
   end
   $\theta_{est} = \theta_G$ for which t_θ is minimum in T ;
   return θ_{est} ;
end

WalkCompass experiments were performed with 6 users who volunteered to walk with the phone in different environments, using varying holding positions. The environments were mostly UIUC's science and engineering buildings with heavy magnetic influence – this subject's WalkCompass to a stronger test. For each test, we asked the users to walk along established corridors – this is because we used the Google satellite view to compute the global truth in walking directions. Some experiments were also performed in Wal-mart, houses, and apartments, and the global truths were computed similarly. We also walked along with the users noting down when they changed the orientation of the phone, or how they placed the phones in the pocket. We report results against the baseline of the phone's compass.

5.2 Performance Results

We intend to concentrate on the following questions:

336

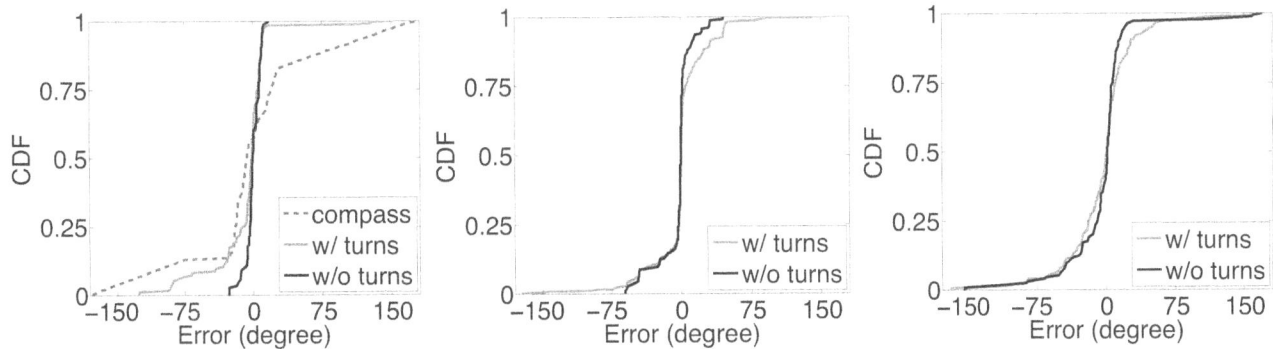

Figure 10: CDF of WalkCompass's LDE error with and without turns. (a) Phone held in the palm. (b) Phone carried in the pant pocket. (c) Phone held in swinging arms.

Figure 9: (a) WalkCompass screenshot. (b) QR code for WalkCompass demo.

- The accuracy of recognizing the walking direction in the phone's local coordinate system (i.e., results from outdoors and some interference-free indoor environments) – Figures 10, and 11. Speed of change detection, especially after sharp turns (Figure 12).

- Coping with different holding positions (Figure 13), and different orientations such as portraits to landscapes (Figure 14). Robustness when user is bear foot or wearing shoes, and walking on various surfaces, such as carpet, concrete, etc. (Figure 15).

- Accuracy of compass error correction with IMT – Figures 17, and 18. Its performance under various regimes of magnetic interference (in labs,office,house, and outdoor settings) – Figures 19, and 20.

Accuracy of Local Walk Direction (LDE)

Figure 10 plots the CDF of local walking direction error, estimated from all traces, across all users, and across all environments. Figure 10(a) plots the case when the phone is held in the palm (in the browsing position) – some are in portrait, some landscape, and some users held the phone at an angle to the walking direction. Figure 10(b) and (c) plot the case of pant pocket and swinging hands, respectively. WalkCompass's error is computed as the difference with the true walking direction (computed manually for every trace from Google's satellite view). Since we are unsure about the global truth near the turning positions (recall that users may be making soft turns), we show the error distributions including and excluding the turns. While excluding turns, we have removed 6 steps at the each turn.

We could not develop a meaningful baseline scheme for comparison, hence, we use the following. For the palm position in Figure 10(a), we record the orientation of the phone only when it is pointed in the direction of walking. We smoothen this data through a low pass filter (as a way of canceling out periodic perturbations) and plot its error CDF – denoted "compass". Evidently, even when the phone is pointing in the forward direction, and the data smoothened, the fluctuation is appreciable. Since we could not learn the phone's orientation in Figure 10(b) and (c), we do not plot the compass data in these two graphs.

Evident from the graph, WalkCompass exhibits low median error for a sizable fraction of the scenarios, and the errors are well distributed on both sides of the walking direction. This suggests that the heel-strike jerk manifests itself prominently across all these phone postures. The performance degrades when the hand swings – in fact, performance for one of the 5 users is poor, significantly skewing the distribution from the center. On close observation, we noticed that this user's hand-swings are embedded with several rotational motions of the wrist, and even though they are repetitive, WalkCompass is unable to cancel them out. For all other cases, the performance is reasonably consistent. For the palm, the median error is at $\pm 5°$, compared to $\pm 23°$ for the phone's native compass app (with low pass filtering). For the pant pocket, the median is at $\pm 3°$, and for the swinging-hand, $\pm 8°$.

Figure 11 breaks down the results for each individual user, demonstrating that the LDE module is fairly robust to different walking patterns. In all these traces, the user walked for around 20 steps on average before taking a turn, and has taken around 25 turns in total. We show both the median and the 75th percentile to reflect the robustness of the system. When carried in the palm or pant pocket, the errors are around $6°$, except for one user who experiences around $20°$ error. While this is not ideal, and leaves room for improvement, we believe it is still useful for various applications. An elevator company keen on automatically dispatching elevators based on approaching users finds such error margins tolerable.

Direction Change Detection

Figure 12 zooms into the turning behavior of users – this is a representative graph that plots the error when a user makes

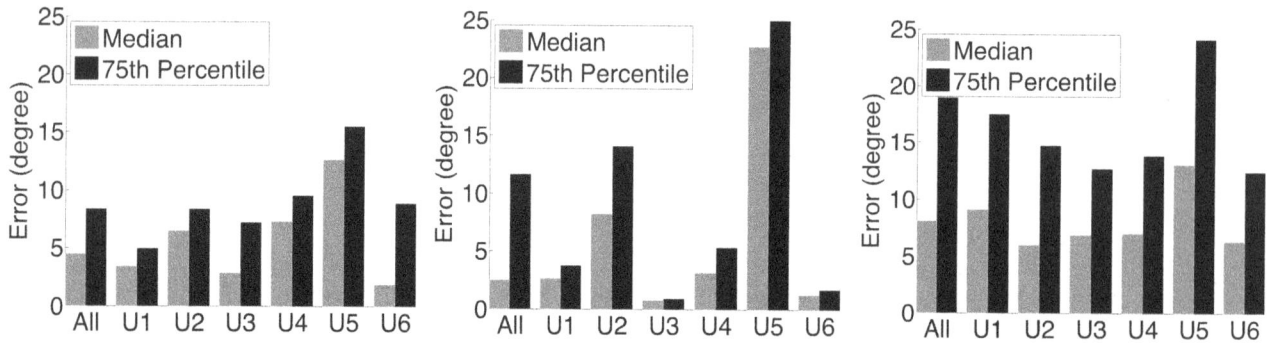

Figure 11: The median and 75th percentile of error per user without turns. Phone carried in (a) palm, (b) pocket, (c) swinging-hand.

a $180°$ turn. This is the worst case behavior, and the graph shows the time it takes to converge to the actual walking direction. Evidently, the error decreases at a steady pace with more number of steps after the turn, and converges at around 5 or 6 steps. We believe these results are slightly conservative since the ground truth is assumed to be the intended direction in which the user is walking, and does not account for how the user actually walked. WalkCompass measures each of the micro-deviations the user makes at each step, and is hence slightly penalized here.

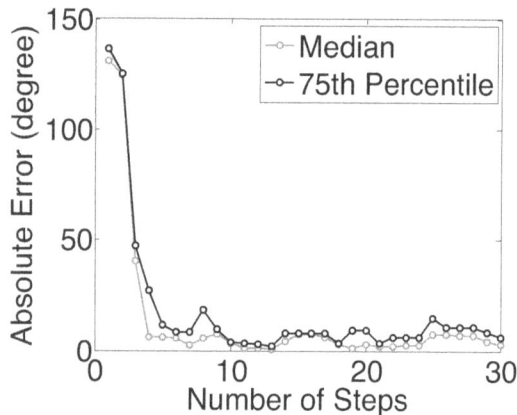

Figure 12: Error convergence after sharp turns. Both median and 75th percentile error converge after around 4 or 5 steps.

Toying with the Phone

Users orient their phones in various ways, perhaps changing from a portrait to landscape for a video, raising the phone for a phone call, or just tilting to check an email. Figure 13(a) shows the changes in the phone's compass directions, while WalkCompass's estimated direction continues to point in the user's heading direction. Since LDE computes the force in 3D, and takes the projection on to the horizontal plane, the walking direction is estimated for all orientations (even when the user is holding the phone against the ears for a call). Figure 13(b) plots the distribution of errors across all users and traces.

Figure 14(a) zooms in to the same results and shows a scatter plot from many users toying with the phone. For easier visualization, all the traces have been offset to a common walking direction of $250°$. Evidently, LDE copes consistently

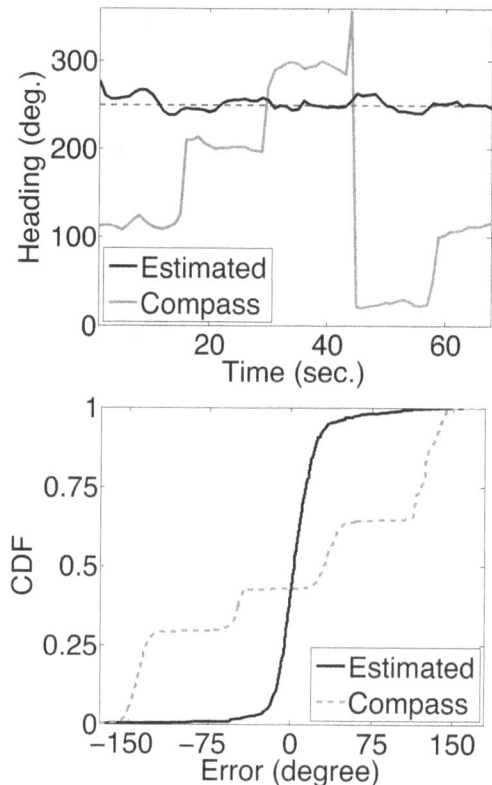

Figure 13: (a) Examples of traces in which users frequently changes the orientation of the phone. (b) CDF of error across all traces.

well with toying of phones and tracks the walking direction correctly. Some points fall far from the $250°$ line, however, observe that not too many points are consecutive, indicating that the large errors do not persist for long. To provide a sense of how much the phone was toyed with, Figure 14(b) shows the angles to which the phone was pointing across all the experiments.

Impact of Walking on Different Surfaces

Given that the success of LDE relies on correctly detecting the accelerometer signatures during a walk, we evaluate walking on various surfaces, with and without shoes. Users in our experiments walked barefoot and with shoes, on different surfaces, namely, carpet, and tiled floors. Figure 15

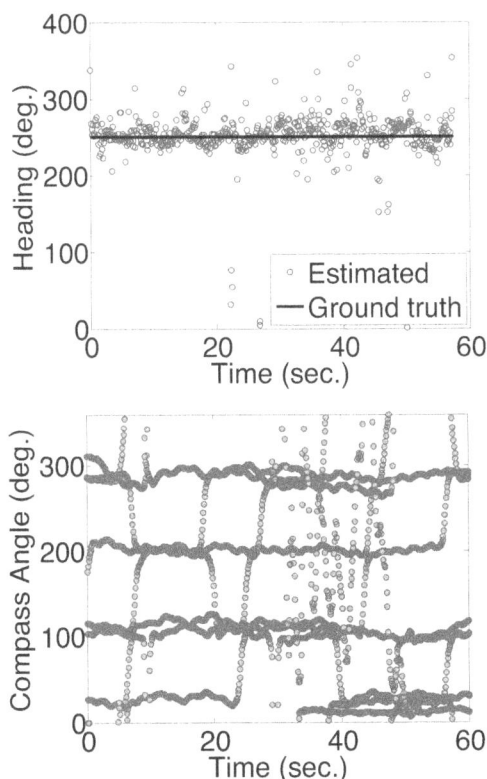

Figure 14: (a) Estimated heading for multiple users when they randomly change the phone's orientation. (b) Tracking the angle in which the phone is pointing to understand the extent of toying.

shows the median and 75th percentile errors for each of these [footwear, surface] tuples. Observe that the errors are not affected by any specific surface – the heel strike is reasonably robust and lends itself across all these scenarios.

Staircase and Backward Walk

We evaluate different modalities of walking, such as walking up and down staircases, and walking backwards. Figure 16(a) plots the CDF for staircases while Figure 16(b) shows the performance when the user walks backwards. For both scenarios, the phone was carried in different orientations and positions in the body. As with regular walking, the performance of a specific individual was relatively worst than others, especially for the hand-swing. Otherwise, the performance was stable. Finally, we note that in all cases, the error of walking did not accumulate over time; even when users walked for long duration and experienced some error due to some jerks on the phones or other actions, a new heel-strike would reset the errors. We believe this is a desirable resilience property in any sensing system, and WalkCompass possesses it. We have omitted these results in the interest of space.

Global Walking Direction Estimation (GDE)

This section focuses on evaluating the accuracy of the global walking direction estimator (GDE) module, and specifically the *Iterative Magnetic Triangulation* (IMT) algorithm. To test this algorithm in diverse conditions, we select 15 different locations from various regimes, including science and

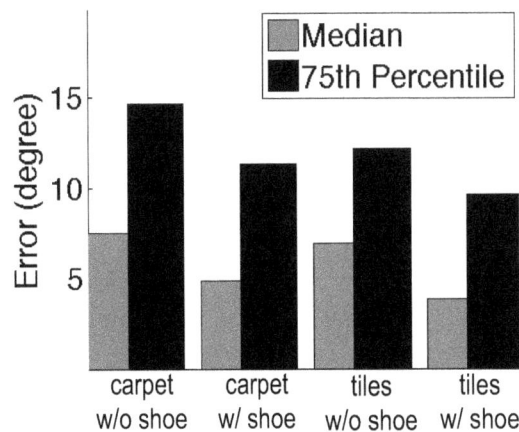

Figure 15: Walking on different surfaces (carpet and tiled floors) with and without shoes.

engineering laboratories, social places, houses, libraries, and outdoors. We apply the IMT algorithm on the magnetometer data and compare the results with the smartphone's native compass app. Since IMT's task is to only mitigate the magnetic interference (and not estimate walking directions), we hold the phone in the palm with the front of the phone facing the walking direction. We carefully record the ground truth from Google Satellite view.

5.2.1 Error distribution

Figure 17 plots the angle histogram across all traces, comparing IMT and the phone's compass against ground truth. Ideally this plot should have a spike only at $0°$, which is the ground truth. Evidently, the compass measurements scatters around $60°$ on both sides of $0°$, occasionally reaching up to $90°$. The long histogram bar around $25°$ suggest that that's the common case error. IMT, in contrast, produces errors of $10°$ from the ground truth. Figure 18 shows the cumulative distribution of absolute error for both IMT and compass. The curve rises steeply for IMT and its value remains less than $15°$ for 75% of the traces, whereas the raw compass is at $37°$ for the same 75th percentile. The median error of IMT is around $7°$, less than a third of compass error. However, for very high magnetic interference, where the compass error is more than $50°$, the performance of IMT degrades, although still remaining better than the compass. Figure 19 compares the median error of IMT and native compass for each of the 15 places. IMT is consistently half or one-third of the compass. This is encouraging since even outside WalkCompass, the techniques from this paper can be useful in improving the compass app in phones, especially in magnetic rich places where they are needed most.

5.2.2 Distribution of interval between effective triplets

Recall that IMT estimates the true compass direction on a set of three magnetic vectors, called a *triplet*. Ideally, many triplets should be available, so that WalkCompass can frequently estimate the true North. It is also advantageous to have the triplets evenly spread over the path of a walk – this allows better interpolation (using the gyroscope) between these correct points. Figure 20(a) shows the distribution of the intervals, in seconds, between two consecutive triplets found during the experiments. Although triplets tend to be collocated, we have found triplets separated by around 7 sec-

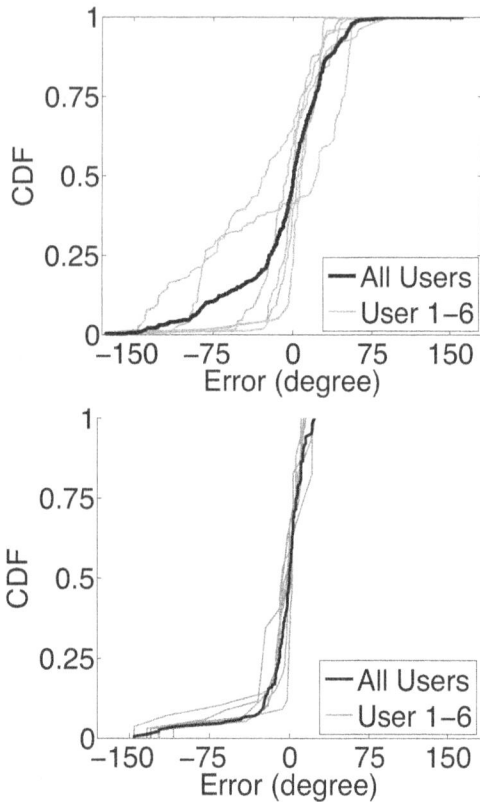

Figure 16: (a) The cumulative error distribution for walking up and down staircases. (b) CDF of error for walking backwards.

onds (i.e. every 7 steps) even at the 90th percentile. Figure 20(b) shows the number of triplets found in each individual experiment. The density is sufficient to continuously and reliably track the true geomagnetic North during the walk.

6. LIMITATIONS AND DISCUSSION

We discuss a few limitations and opportunities.

• **Tail of Error Distribution:** While median and 75th percentile of accuracy is quite reliable with WalkCompass, in certain settings the performance drops sharply. This is particularly evident in areas where the compass error is extremely high – greater than 45° – and in other cases where certain users vary the phone's orientation while swinging their arms. We do not have a strong handle on why these

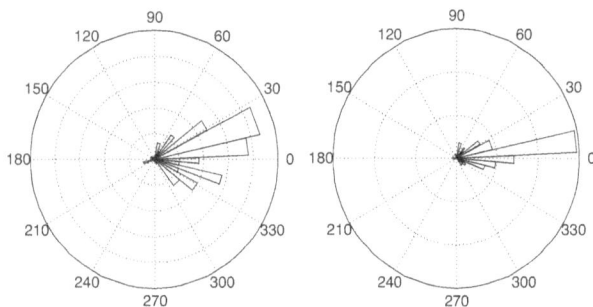

Figure 17: The angle histogram of (a) phone's native compass app, (b) IMT's estimates.

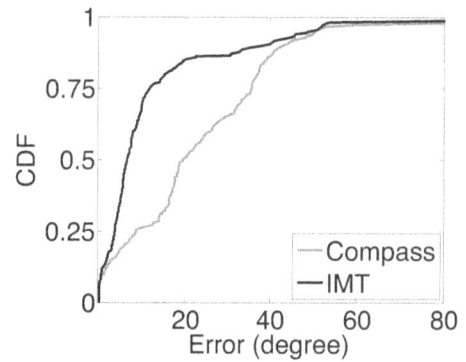

Figure 18: Comparing CDF of absolute error between the compass and IMT.

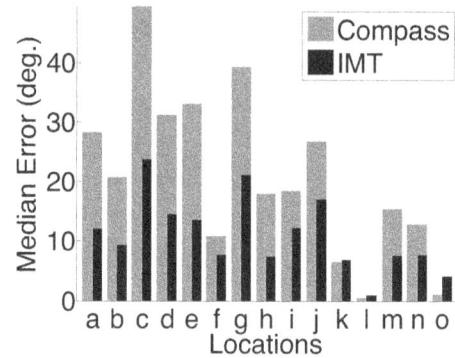

Figure 19: The median error comparison between IMT and compass across all 15 places.

cases occur – deeper engineering and fine tuning is necessary to cut-back on the tail of the error distribution.

• **Need to Walk a Few Steps:** The proposed IMT algorithm cannot use any magnetometer data to infer the magnetic north – only certain magnetometer snippets produce the correct answer. This indicates that the user would have to walk a distance before WalkCompass can estimate the magnetic North. While this may be tolerable for human walking applications, additional research is needed if the phone's native compass has to be improved. Our ongoing work is investigating methods to infer the true North from any snippet of magnetometer data.

• **Beyond Walking:** While WalkCompass has not been tested for other forms of human locomotion, such as wheel chairs, skate-boards, biking, etc., we believe the core techniques may still apply so long as there is a repetitive force in the heading direction. Pushing the wheel for wheel chairs, swinging the leg for skateboards, and rotation of the legs during cycling, all seem to offer this opportunity. We plan to test this in future.

• **3D WalkCompass:** This paper investigates human walking direction on 2D, but we believe that the core techniques can be scaled to 3D, albeit some additional complexity in the IMT algorithm. We leave this to future work.

7. RELATED WORK

We discuss past work on detecting walking directions.

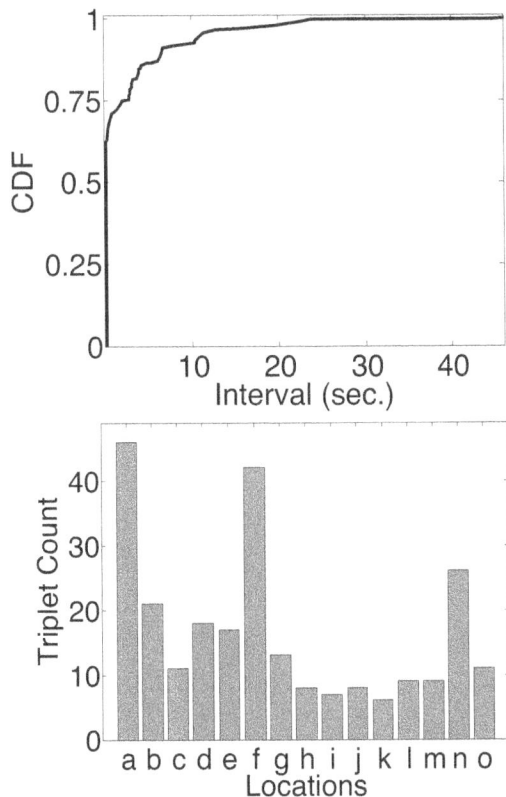

Figure 20: The distribution of the gap between two consecutive triplets(a) and number of triplets found per location(b).

Finding Heading Direction

Body-pasted sensors: Early work from anatomy analysis, skeletal parsing, and computer animation have studied the problem of walking direction using body-pasted sensors [16, 32, 17]. Smartphone sensors are characterized with far more degrees of freedom, given that it can be carried in different clothing, different parts of the body, or handled in unknown ways by the user. The challenges in coping with the variations are fundamentally different.

Sensor dead reckoning: Attempts have been made to solve the problem with smartphones, however, solutions make certain assumptions. Specifically, [22, 19] assume that the initial orientation of the phone is known, and the phone is held stable in the hands. Authors in [20] infer orientation by identifying specific gestures like texting, at which point the phone is assumed to be in a known stable orientation. In the outdoor setting, GPS can offer heading direction, although with limited responsiveness; GPS may also falter in Manhattan-like settings. WalkCompass relies only on the direction of the forces on the smartphone, thereby eliminating reliance on other technologies.

Map based: The application of particle filters on floorplans is a popular technique [7, 25, 28, 18, 11]. However, the approach fails in open spaces such as halls, airports, libraries, atriums of hotels, etc. Moreover, the reliance of floorplans restrict the applicability of these solutions. Zee [28] proposes an interesting stand-alone approach to infer the heading direction, essentially deriving hints from the

frequency response of the accelerometer. However, the technique alone is insufficient and leaves an ambiguity between two opposite directions. It relies on the map for disambiguation.

Vehicle dynamics: In essence, the analysis of vehicle dynamics using inertial sensors is also related to WalkCompass, despite differences in approach and methodology. Some recent papers in this domain have leveraged sensor data from smartphones to track the movement of vehicles for applications like driver detection [8], driving behavior analysis [15, 31, 10], and estimation of road conditions [23].

Correcting Compass Error

Geomagnetic fields and compass errors are well investigated areas of study – many surveying organizations [6, 26] precisely record and tracks the behavior of global magnetic fields and anomalies. For local magnetic distortions, some mathematical models are available [4] to quantify the error and apply corrective algorithms like *Ellipsoid Fitting* [21]. However, these approaches rely on calibrating the magnetic field at various locations using specific devices and methodology. These techniques are therefore suited for one-time applications, say robotic motion planning or war-driving, but does not scale to anywhere, anytime computing. WalkCompass attempts to correct the compass in a calibration-free, stand-alone manner.

8. CONCLUSION

This paper shows that the human's walking direction can be estimated from the smartphone's inertial sensors, regardless of the orientation of the phone on the body. The core techniques are rooted in analyzing the relationship between human walking and its effect on the phone, as well as methods to estimate and cancel magnetic interference from the compass data. We believe that WalkCompass can immediately help a variety of apps that make assumptions on the user's walking direction. More importantly, we believe that with some more effort, the phone's native compass can be dramatically improved, ultimately helping all applications that rely on the compass.

9. ACKNOWLEDGMENT

We sincerely thank our shepherd, Dr. Xiaofan Jiang as well as the anonymous reviewers for their invaluable feedback. We are also grateful to Intel and NSF for partially funding this research through the following grants: NSF 0910846 and NSF 1040043.

10. REFERENCES

[1] Complementary filter. http://web.mit.edu/scolton/www/filter.pdf.

[2] Unibros. http://hfid.olin.edu/sa2013/s_engr3220-unibros/inspirational.php.

[3] Walkcompass demo. http://synrg.csl.illinois.edu/projects/localization/walkcompass.

[4] AFZAL, M. H., RENAUDIN, V., AND LACHAPELLE, G. Assessment of indoor magnetic field anomalies using multiple magnetometers. *Proceedings of ION GNSS10* (2010), 1–9.

[5] AYUB, S., HERAVI, B. M., BAHRAMINASAB, A., AND HONARY, B. Pedestrian direction of movement

determination using smartphone. In *Next Generation Mobile Applications, Services and Technologies (NGMAST), 2012 6th International Conference on* (2012), IEEE, pp. 64–69.

[6] BARTON, C. International geomagnetic reference field: the seventh generation. *Journal of Geomagnetism and Geoelectricity 49* (1997), 123–148.

[7] CHINTALAPUDI, K., PADMANABHA IYER, A., AND PADMANABHAN, V. N. Indoor localization without the pain. In *Proceedings of the sixteenth annual international conference on Mobile computing and networking* (2010), ACM, pp. 173–184.

[8] CHU, H., RAMAN, V., SHEN, J., KANSAL, A., BAHL, V., AND CHOUDHURY, R. R. I am a smartphone and i know my user is driving.

[9] CONSTANDACHE, I., CHOUDHURY, R. R., AND RHEE, I. Towards mobile phone localization without war-driving. In *INFOCOM, 2010 Proceedings IEEE* (2010), IEEE, pp. 1–9.

[10] DAI, J., TENG, J., BAI, X., SHEN, Z., AND XUAN, D. Mobile phone based drunk driving detection. In *Pervasive Computing Technologies for Healthcare (PervasiveHealth), 2010 4th International Conference on-NO PERMISSIONS* (2010), IEEE, pp. 1–8.

[11] EVENNOU, F., MARX, F., AND NOVAKOV, E. Map-aided indoor mobile positioning system using particle filter. In *Wireless Communications and Networking Conference, 2005 IEEE* (2005), vol. 4, IEEE, pp. 2490–2494.

[12] FAURE, F., DEBUNNE, G., CANI-GASCUEL, M.-P., AND MULTON, F. Dynamic analysis of human walking. In *Computer Animation and SimulationâĂŹ97*. Springer, 1997, pp. 53–65.

[13] GAFUROV, D., HELKALA, K., AND SØNDROL, T. Gait recognition using acceleration from mems. In *Availability, Reliability and Security, 2006. ARES 2006. The First International Conference on* (2006), IEEE, pp. 6–pp.

[14] INMAN, V. T. Human locomotion. *Canadian Medical Association Journal 94*, 20 (1966), 1047.

[15] JOHNSON, D. A., AND TRIVEDI, M. M. Driving style recognition using a smartphone as a sensor platform. In *Intelligent Transportation Systems (ITSC), 2011 14th International IEEE Conference on* (2011), IEEE, pp. 1609–1615.

[16] KIM, J. W., JANG, H. J., HWANG, D.-H., AND PARK, C. A step, stride and heading determination for the pedestrian navigation system. *Journal of Global Positioning Systems 3*, 1-2 (2004), 273–279.

[17] KRACH, B., AND ROBERTSON, P. Integration of foot-mounted inertial sensors into a bayesian location estimation framework. In *Positioning, Navigation and Communication, 2008. WPNC 2008. 5th Workshop on* (2008), IEEE, pp. 55–61.

[18] KWON, W., ROH, K.-S., AND SUNG, H.-K. Particle filter-based heading estimation using magnetic compasses for mobile robot navigation. In *Robotics and Automation, 2006. ICRA 2006. Proceedings 2006 IEEE International Conference on* (2006), IEEE, pp. 2705–2712.

[19] LEE, S.-W., JUNG, P., AND SONG, S.-H. Hybrid indoor location tracking for pedestrian using a

smartphone. In *Robot Intelligence Technology and Applications 2012*. Springer, 2013, pp. 431–440.

[20] LI, F., ZHAO, C., DING, G., GONG, J., LIU, C., AND ZHAO, F. A reliable and accurate indoor localization method using phone inertial sensors. In *Proceedings of the 2012 ACM Conference on Ubiquitous Computing* (2012), ACM, pp. 421–430.

[21] LI, Q., AND GRIFFITHS, J. G. Least squares ellipsoid specific fitting. In *Geometric Modeling and Processing, 2004. Proceedings* (2004), IEEE, pp. 335–340.

[22] LINK, J. A. B., SMITH, P., VIOL, N., AND WEHRLE, K. Footpath: Accurate map-based indoor navigation using smartphones. In *Indoor Positioning and Indoor Navigation (IPIN), 2011 International Conference on* (2011), IEEE, pp. 1–8.

[23] MEDNIS, A., STRAZDINS, G., ZVIEDRIS, R., KANONIRS, G., AND SELAVO, L. Real time pothole detection using android smartphones with accelerometers. In *Distributed Computing in Sensor Systems and Workshops (DCOSS), 2011 International Conference on* (2011), IEEE, pp. 1–6.

[24] MERRILL, R. T., MCELHINNY, M. W., AND MCFADDEN, P. L. *Magnetic Field of the Earth*, vol. 63. Academic Press, 1996.

[25] NANDAKUMAR, R., CHINTALAPUDI, K. K., AND PADMANABHAN, V. N. Centaur: locating devices in an office environment. In *Proceedings of the 18th annual international conference on Mobile computing and networking* (2012), ACM, pp. 281–292.

[26] OLSEN, L., MAJOR, G., SHEIN, K., SCIALDONE, J., VOGEL, R., LEICESTER, S., WEIR, H., RITZ, S., STEVENS, T., MEAUX, M., ET AL. Nasa/global change master directory (gcmd) earth science keywords. *Version 6*, 0.0 (2007), 0.

[27] PEI, L., LIU, J., GUINNESS, R., CHEN, Y., KUUSNIEMI, H., AND CHEN, R. Using ls-svm based motion recognition for smartphone indoor wireless positioning. *Sensors 12*, 5 (2012), 6155–6175.

[28] RAI, A., CHINTALAPUDI, K. K., PADMANABHAN, V. N., AND SEN, R. Zee: Zero-effort crowdsourcing for indoor localization. In *Proceedings of the 18th annual international conference on Mobile computing and networking* (2012), ACM, pp. 293–304.

[29] SUSI, M., RENAUDIN, V., AND LACHAPELLE, G. Motion mode recognition and step detection algorithms for mobile phone users. *Sensors 13*, 2 (2013), 1539–1562.

[30] WANG, Y., JIA, X., LEE, H., AND LI, G. An indoors wireless positioning system based on wireless local area network infrastructure. In *6th Int. Symp. on Satellite Navigation Technology Including Mobile Positioning & Location Services* (2003), no. 54.

[31] WANG, Y., YANG, J., LIU, H., CHEN, Y., GRUTESER, M., AND MARTIN, R. P. Sensing vehicle dynamics for determining driver phone use. In *Proceeding of the 11th annual international conference on Mobile systems, applications, and services* (2013), ACM, pp. 41–54.

[32] WOODMAN, O., AND HARLE, R. Pedestrian localisation for indoor environments. In *Proceedings of the 10th international conference on Ubiquitous computing* (2008), ACM, pp. 114–123.

Demo: Rio: A System Solution for Sharing I/O between Mobile Systems

Ardalan Amiri Sani, Kevin Boos, Min Hong Yun, and Lin Zhong

Rice University, Houston, TX

Extended Abstract [1]

A user nowadays owns a variety of mobile systems, including smartphones, tablets, smart glasses, and smart watches, each equipped with a plethora of I/O devices, such as cameras, speakers, microphones, sensors, and cellular modems. There are many interesting use cases in which an application running on one mobile system accesses I/O on another system, for three fundamental reasons. (*i*) Mobile systems can be in different physical locations or orientations. For example, one can control a smartphone's high-resolution camera from a tablet camera application to more easily capture a self-portrait. (*ii*) Mobile systems can serve different users. For example, one can a play music for another user if one's smartphone can access the other device's speaker. (*iii*) Certain mobile systems have unique I/O devices due to their distinct form factor and targeted use cases. For example, a user can make a phone call from her tablet using the modem and SIM card in her smartphone.

Solutions exist for sharing I/O devices, e.g., for camera [1], speaker [2], and modem (for messaging) [3]. However, these solutions have three limitations. (*i*) They do not support unmodified applications. (*ii*) They do not expose all the functionality of an I/O device for sharing. (*iii*) They are I/O class-specific, requiring significant engineering effort to support new I/O devices.

We demonstrate Rio (*Remote I/O*), an I/O sharing solution for mobile systems that overcomes all three aforementioned limitations. Rio adopts a split-stack I/O sharing model, in which the I/O stack is split between the two mobile systems at a certain boundary. All communications that cross this boundary are intercepted on the mobile system hosting the application and forwarded to the mobile system with the I/O device, where they are served by the rest of the I/O stack. Rio uses *device files* as its boundary of choice. Device files are used in Unix-like OSes, such as Android and iOS, to abstract many classes of I/O devices, providing an I/O class-agnostic boundary. The device file boundary supports I/O sharing for unmodified applications, as it is transparent to the application layer. It also exposes the full functionality of each I/O device to other mobile systems by allowing processes in one system to directly communicate with the device drivers in another. Rio is not the first system to exploit the device file boundary; our previous work, Paradice [5], uses device files as the boundary for I/O virtualization inside a single system. However, Rio faces a different set of challenges regarding how to properly exploit this boundary, as explained in the full paper [6].

In this demo, we use a prototype implementation of Rio for Android systems. Our implementation supports four important I/O classes: camera, audio devices such as speaker and microphone, sensors such as accelerometer, and cellular modem (for phone calls and SMS). It consists of about 7100 lines of code, of which less than 500 are specific to I/O classes. Rio also supports I/O sharing between heterogeneous mobile systems, including tablets and smartphones. See [4] for a video of the demo.

Categories and Subject Descriptors

B.4.2 [**Input/Output and Data Communications**]: Input/Output Devices; C.0 [**Computer Systems Organization**]: General—System architectures; C.2.4 [**Computer-Communication Networks**]: Distributed Systems— Client/Server; K.8.0 [**Personal Computing**]: General

Keywords

I/O; Remote I/O; I/O Sharing; Mobile; Rio

---

[1] Full paper: [6]

MobiSys'14, June 16–19, 2014, Bretton Woods, New Hampshire, USA.
ACM 978-1-4503-2793-0/14/06.
http://dx.doi.org/10.1145/2594368.2601471.

1. REFERENCES

[1] Android IP Webcam application. https://play.google.com/store/apps/details?id=com.pas.webcam&hl=en.
[2] Android Wi-Fi Speaker application. https://play.google.com/store/apps/details?id=pixelface.android.audio&hl=en.
[3] MightyText application. http://mightytext.net.
[4] Rio Project Homepage (including a video demo). http://www.ruf.rice.edu/~mobile/rio.html.
[5] A. Amiri Sani, K. Boos, S. Qin, and L. Zhong. I/O Paravirtualization at the Device File Boundary. *Proc. ACM ASPLOS,* 2014.
[6] A. Amiri Sani, K. Boos, M. Yun, and L. Zhong. Rio: A System Solution for Sharing I/O between Mobile Systems. *Proc. ACM MobiSys,* 2014.

Demo: Open Data Kit 2.0 Tool Suite

Waylon Brunette, Samuel Sudar, Gaetano Borriello
University of Washington
Box 352350
Seattle, WA 98195
{wrb, sudars, gaetano}@cse.uw.edu

ABSTRACT

Open Data Kit (ODK) is an open-source, modular toolkit that enables organizations to build application-specific mobile information services in resource-constrained environments. Feedback from users and developers about limitations experienced with the ODK 1.x set of tools led to a redesign of the system architecture and the creation of new tools. This demonstration presents a revised tool suite called ODK 2.0. This expanded ODK toolkit aims to increase an organization's data collection and management capabilities by supporting data synchronization, adaptable workflows, more configurable presentation screens, and increasing the diversity of input types by enabling new data input methods on mobile devices.

1. DESCRIPTION

Building information systems in resource-constrained environments can be challenging because of the limited and diverse infrastructure available in different deployment contexts. Open Data Kit (ODK) [2] is designed to assist organizations in these challenged settings by enabling domain experts (e.g., doctors, foresters) to deploy mobile information systems with minimal assistance from IT professionals. ODK is an open-source toolkit that enables organizations to build application-specific (e.g., public health, environmental monitoring) information services for use in resource-constrained environments. ODK has been used by a wide variety of organizations, from small NGOs to large government ministries, with thousands of users in dozens of countries. While ODK lacks self-tracking usage statistics, other metrics such as the ODK's website receiving 180,000+ unique visitors from 217 different countries/territories (current average 15,000+ hits a month) help to show ODKs global usage. Additionally, over 40 companies offer ODK based products or consulting services located in a variety of countries.

While many organizations successfully leveraged ODK 1.x to build mobile information systems, other organizations struggled to adapt the tools to an increasingly diverse set of use cases. Feedback from users about their struggles adapting their use case to the JavaRosa's XForm standard demonstrated that ODK 1.x was not malleable enough for certain classes of applications. This revelation led to a redesign of the ODK system architecture to create new more customizable tools. This demonstration features the redesigned ODK tool suite, which is being released as "ODK 2.0". This demonstration showcases working implementations of the revised toolkit proposed in ODK's HotMobile 2013 paper [1]

that outlined the redesign rationale and highlighted new design principles. The expanded ODK toolkit aims to increase an organization's data collection and management capabilities by supporting: data synchronization, adaptable workflows, and increasing the diversity of input types by enabling new data input methods on mobile devices. Additionally, ODK 2.0's user interface widgets are implemented using JavaScript/HTML; thereby, enabling organizations to have a malleable system to make runtime customizable navigation, widgets, and question data types. These new capabilities increase the diversity of deployments that ODK supports and improves an organization's ability to build customized domain specific applications by: providing interactive, non-linear navigation capabilities; enabling users to curate data on the mobile device; and simplifying the process of collecting information from sensors.

This demonstration highlights the revised ODK 2.0 tools including: 1) *Tables* –customizable data viewer that includes synchronization and viewing and manipulating data in a simple row format. 2) *Survey* - flexible questionnaire-rendering with a customizable presentation layer that expands user-directed navigation and allows form designers to express non-linear workflow logic. 3) *Sensors* – simplifies the process of connecting sensors over both wired and wireless communication channels, thereby reducing the amount of manual data transcription from sensors into survey forms, and 4) *Scan* - facilitates the automatic conversion of information recorded on paper forms to a digital format using the camera of a mobile device.

While ODK's architecture was redesigned, the goals of ODK remain focused on the concept that for computing tools to address information gaps in developing regions, information services must be composable by non-programmers and be deployable by resource-constrained organizations (limited by either financial and/or technical resources) using commodity devices and cloud services. This demonstration showcases various ODK tools allowing conference attendees to experience and inquire about an academic open-source project that has successfully made it easier for organizations to utilize mobile devices to collect and aggregate data in resource-constrained environments.

2. ACKNOWLEDGMENTS

We gratefully acknowledge the support of Google Research, NSF Grant No. IIS-1111433, and an NSF Graduate Research Fellowship under Grant No. DGE-0718124.

3. REFERENCES

[1] W. Brunette, et al. "Open Data Kit 2.0: expanding and refining information services for developing regions." Proc. of the 14th Workshop on Mobile Computing Systems and Applications, 2013.

[2] C. Hartung, et al. "Open Data Kit: tools to build information services for developing regions," Proc. 4th ACM/IEEE Intl. Conf. on Information and Communication Technologies and Development (ICTD), 2010.

Demo: Kahawai: High-Quality Mobile Gaming Using GPU Offload

Eduardo Cuervo
Microsoft Research
cuervo@microsoft.com

Alec Wolman
Microsoft Research
alecw@microsoft.com

Landon Cox
Duke University
lpcox@cs.duke.edu

Stefan Saroiu
Microsoft Research
ssaroiu@microsoft.com

Madanlal Musuvathi
Microsoft Research
madanm@microsoft.com

Ali Razeen
Duke University
alrazeen@cs.duke.edu

1. INTRODUCTION

With the advent of consumer mobile devices equipped with high resolution touchscreens and powerful CPUs and GPUs, gaming has become one of the most popular activities on smartphones and tablets. As device screens grow larger and screen resolutions increase, finer graphical detail and advanced graphical effects are becoming more important for mobile applications, especially games.

To provide richer visual experiences, mobile devices have seen rapid improvements in their GPU processing capabilities, but today's devices cannot duplicate the sophisticated graphical detail provided by gaming consoles and high-end desktop GPUs. The primary reason for this performance gap is power consumption. A high-end desktop GPU may consume 500 Watts of power, whereas a high-end mobile GPU will consume less than 10 Watts. Furthermore, mobile GPUs will likely always lag behind their desktop contemporaries. The battery capacity of mobile devices is limited and growing slowly, and high power consumption requires sophisticated and bulky thermal dissipation mechanisms that are incompatible with mobile form factors.

In this demo, we present *Kahawai* a GPU offload system that overcomes the drawbacks of thin-client gaming. The main technique used by Kahawai is *collaborative rendering*. Collaborative rendering relies on a mobile GPU to generate low-fidelity output, which when combined with server-side GPU output allows a mobile device to display a high-fidelity result.

The key insight behind collaborative rendering is that while fine-grained details are prohibitively expensive for mobile GPUs to render at an acceptable frame rate, these details represent a small portion of the total information encoded within a stream. Thus, collaborative rendering relies on the mobile GPU to render low-fidelity output containing most of a stream's content, and relies on the server infrastructure to fill in the details.

Collaborative rendering in Kahawai addresses thin-client gaming's main shortcomings. First, when the mobile device is connected to a server, Kahawai provides high-quality gaming at significant network bandwidth savings relative to a thin-client. Second, disconnected Kahawai clients can play games offline using their own GPU, albeit with reduced visual quality. To enable collaborative rendering, Kahawai requires tight synchronization between an instance of the game executing on the mobile device and another instance of the same game executing on the server. To support this, we integrated partial deterministic replay into a popular open-source game engine, the idTech 4 game engine used by many commercial games.

We develop two separate collaborative rendering techniques as part of Kahawai, with each targeting a different aspect of the game stream's fidelity (i.e., per-frame detail and frame rate). In our first technique, *delta encoding*, the mobile device produces reduced-fidelity output by generating every frame at a lower level of detail. The server-side GPU concurrently renders two versions of the game output: a high-fidelity, finely detailed version, and a low-fidelity version that matches the mobile device's output. The server uses these two outputs to calculate delta frames representing the visual differences between the high-fidelity and low-fidelity frames. The server then sends a compressed video stream of delta frames to the client, and the mobile device decompresses the stream and applies the deltas to the frames that it rendered locally.

In our second technique, *client-side I-frame rendering*, the mobile device produces reduced-fidelity output by rendering highly detailed frames at a lower rate. The server renders the missing frames at a higher rate, and sends the missing frames as compressed video. The mobile device decodes the video, combines the frames in the correct order, and displays the results. Both of our techniques are compatible with the hardware-accelerated H.264 video decoders built in to many of today's mobile devices.

In the Kahawai prototype we will present. We will run a modified and playable version of a commercial game, Doom 3 [1] demonstrating the benefits of collaborative rendering using both of our techniques. We will use a powerful server using an Nvidia GTX 780 GPU and a Microsoft Surface Pro tablet as our client device. These devices will be connected directly through an ethernet cable and network latency will be emulated through software.

Categories and Subject Descriptors

C.2.4 [**Distributed Systems**]: Client/Server

Keywords

distributed systems; code offload; collaborative rendering; videogame streaming; video compression

2. REFERENCES

[1] IDSoftware. Doom 3, 2004.
    http://www.idsoftware.com/games/doom.

MobiSys'14, June 16–19, 2014, Bretton Woods, New Hampshire, USA.
ACM 978-1-4503-2793-0/14/06.
http://dx.doi.org/10.1145/2594368.2601482 .

Demo: Real-time Object Tagging and Retrieval

Puneet Jain
Duke University

Romit Roy Choudhury
University of Illinois, Urbana-Champaign

ABSTRACT

We propose an augmented reality system on off-the-shelves smartphones which allows random physical object tagging. At later times, such tags could be retrieved from different locations and orientations. Our approach does not require any additional infrastructure support, localization scheme, specialized camera, or modification to smartphone's operating system. Designed and developed for current generation smartphones, our application shows promising initial results with retrieval accuracy of 82% in indoor environment without noticeable impact on the user experience.

If made commercially available, such system could be used in city tourism, infrastructure maintenance, and enabling new kind of social interactions.

Demonstration Setup

We expect to demonstrate our system on Android smartphones in MobiSys 2014 main conference. The users shall be provided with smartphones and would be asked to tag any random object at the conference venue. We shall simultaneously allow other users to retrieve same objects from different location, orientation, and phones. The demonstration does not require any additional setup help except stable WiFi connectivity from the conference committee.

We have prototyped our system on Android 4.3 and tested it with Samsung Galaxy S4 phones. We have used Amazon EC2 for the data storage and offloading of computationally intensive tasks.

Challenges and Related Work

Object tagging and retrieval in real-time is a challenging problem for several reasons:

1. GPS-Compass-Accelerometers are too noisy – it is hard to infer precise pose of the tagger, triangulation based techniques on short distances do not work.
2. Smartphones still have limited processing power – image processing and computer vision algorithms are computation hungry.
3. Application layer end-to-end network latency is too high – per frame cloud offloading is not feasible.
4. The retriever continuously scans the environment for tags using viewfinder – no two video frames may be similar, selective frame processing may not work.

Our approach to solving this problem is hybrid: leverage smartphone sensors such as Accelerometer, Compass, GPS,

and Gyroscope to estimate quick and rough location-orientation of the phone and incrementally applying heavy-weight computer vision algorithms to reduce the search space of the matching tags. The former is used to build a rough and continuously changing in-device cache of tags in the vicinity, while the later is used to affirm the object matching using low to high fidelity algorithms.

Our system leverages a rich body of work in both the Mobile Computing and Computer Vision. Specifically, we use various sensor stabilization, filtering, triangulation, pose-estimation, and dead-reckoning techniques to continuously infer the rough pose using noisy inertial sensors. Ultimately to increase our object retrieval confidence, we have modified and customized several state-of-the-art image and scene analysis algorithms to run on Android operating system with minimal processing latency.

Real-time in-phone augmented reality is coming into realization with the projects like Google Tango [1] and Kinect-fusion [2]. While promising, these projects are in still in prototype stages, require specialized hardward and sensors such as depth camera and GPUs. Our approach to solving this problem is inexpensive, practical, and compatible to wide range of phones.

Evaluation

We have evaluated our system by tagging random 20 objects in the Coordinated Science Lab, UIUC. The objects are later retrieved 5 times each, from different locations and orientations. Each trial retrieves three best matched tags from the repository. Among 100 retrieval trials, 54 trials resulted best matched tag as the desired tag, while in 16 and 5 trials, same appeared on the second and third positions. The object confusion matrix is shown in Figure 1.

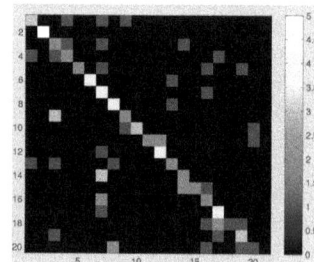

Figure 1: Tag retrieval accuracy in the form of confusion matrix – Tag X is confused with Y proportionate to intensity value

1. REFERENCES

[1] Project tango.
    https://www.google.com/atap/projecttango/, 2014.
[2] S. Izadi et al. Kinectfusion: real-time 3d reconstruction and interaction using a moving depth camera. In *UIST*. ACM, 2011.

MobiSys'14, June 16–19, 2014, Bretton Woods, New Hampshire, USA.
ACM 978-1-4503-2793-0/14/06.
http://dx.doi.org/10.1145/2594368.2601472 .

Demo: DeLorean: Using Speculation to Enable Low-Latency Continuous Interaction for Mobile Cloud Gaming

Kyungmin Lee*   David Chu†   Eduardo Cuervo†   Alec Wolman†   Jason Flinn*

*Univeristy of Michigan   †Microsoft Research

Playing games on mobile devices is very popular. Recently, cloud gaming – where datacenter servers execute the games on behalf of thin clients that merely transmit UI input events and display output rendered by the servers – has emerged as an interesting alternative to traditional client-side game execution. Cloud Gaming-as-a-Service (GaaS) offers several advantages salient to mobile clients. First, users with low end devices can get the same high quality experience as users with high end devices. Second, mobile game developers avoid two challenges that arise with the huge diversity of mobile devices: platform compatibility headaches and per-platform performance tuning. Third, upgrading servers (e.g., for bug fixes, game updates, etc.) becomes far easier than redeploying new software to clients. Finally, players can select from a vast library of games and instantly play any of them.

However, GaaS on mobile devices faces a key technical dilemma: how can players attain *real-time interactivity* in the face of wide-area latency? Real-time interactivity means client input events should be quickly reflected on the client display. User studies have shown that players are sensitive to as little as 60 ms latency, and are aggravated at latencies in excess of 100 ms [1]. A further delay degradation from 150 ms to 250 ms lowers user engagement by 75% [2].

Instead, we propose to mitigate wide-area latency via speculative execution. We present *DeLorean* a system that delivers real-time gaming interactivity as fast as traditional local client-side execution, despite with network latencies.

DeLorean's basic approach combines input prediction with speculative execution to render mulitple possible frame outputs which could occur RTT milliseconds in the future. DeLorean employs the following techniques to accomplish this.

Future Input Prediction: Given the user's historical tendencies and recent behavior, we show that some categories of user actions are highly predictable. We develop a Markov-based prediction model that examines recent user input to forecast expected future input. We use two techniques to improve prediction quality: supersampling of input events,

and constructing a Kalman filter to improve users' perception of smoothness.

State Space Subsampling and Time Shifting: Certain user inputs (e.g., firing a gun) cannot be easily predicted. For these, we use parallel speculative executions to explore multiple outcomes. However, the set of all possible frames over long RTTs can be very large due to state space explosion. To address this, we use two techniques: state space subsampling, and event stream time shifting. These greatly reduce possible outcomes with minimal impact on the quality of interaction, thereby permitting speculation within a reasonable budget.

Misprediction Compensation: When mispredictions occur, DeLorean enables the client to execute *error compensation* on the (mis)predicted frame. The resulting frame is very close to what the client ought to see. Our misprediction compensation uses *view interpolation*, a vision technique that transforms pre-rendered images from one viewpoint to a different viewpoint using only a small amount of additional 3D metadata.

To punctuate our emphasis on fast interaction, we evaluate DeLorean's prediction techniques using two *fast action games* where even small latencies are disadvantageous. Doom 3 is a twitch-based first person shooter where responsiveness is paramount. Fable 3 is a role playing game with frequent fast action combat. Both are high-quality, commercially-released games, and are very similar to mobile games in the first person shooter and role playing genres, respectively.

Through interactive gamer testing, we found that players perceived only minor differences in responsiveness on DeLorean even with some network latnecy when compared head-to-head to a system with no latency. Overall, player surveys indicated positive reception of gameplay on DeLorean.

Categories and Subject Descriptors

D.2.2 [**Software Engineering**]: Design Tools and Techniques

Keywords

Cloud gaming; Speculation

MobiSys'14, June 16–19, 2014, Bretton Woods, New Hampshire, USA.
ACM 978-1-4503-2793-0/14/06.
http://dx.doi.org/10.1145/2594368.2601474.

1. REFERENCES

[1] BEIGBEDER, T., COUGHLAN, R., LUSHER, C., PLUNKETT, J., AGU, E., AND CLAYPOOL, M. The effects of loss and latency on user performance in unreal tournament 2003. In *NetGames'04* (New York, NY, USA, 2004), ACM, pp. 144–151.

[2] CHEN, K.-T., HUANG, P., AND LEI, C.-L. How sensitive are online gamers to network quality? *Commun. ACM 49*, 11 (Nov. 2006), 34–38.

Demo: AuthPaper – Protecting Paper-based Documents/ Credentials Using Authenticated 2D Barcodes

Chak Man Li, Pili Hu and Wing Cheong Lau
Department of Information Engineering, The Chinese University of Hong Kong
Hong Kong
{cmli,hupili,wclau}@ie.cuhk.edu.hk

ABSTRACT

All printed documents and credentials are potentially subject to counterfeiting and forgery. Conventional counterfeiting solutions such as watermarking or printing with special-quality paper are not cost-effective. Certification via authorized chops/ stamps is low-cost but only provides a false sense of security/ authenticity. While embedding a serial number in the document for online verification is low-cost and secure, it is not applicable without Internet connection. We demonstrate AuthPaper (Authenticated Paper) to solve these problems by: 1) Digitally sign on the document to be protected; 2) Put the original content, digital signature and optionally the signer's certificate in a self-describing encapsulation; 3) Generate a 2D barcode (e.g. QR code) to carry the encapsulation and embed it as an integral part of the paper document. Note that the information carried in Authenticated QR Code is 40 to 50 times more than a typical one ($\approx$ 50 Bytes). The biggest technical challenge is to scan and decode such densely packed codes in a robust manner. We have developed an Android application to address the challenge. In short, AuthPaper provides a secure, low-cost and offline method for document authentication.

1. CHALLENGES, DESIGN AND IMPLEMENTATION OF AUTHPAPER

To realize AuthPaper, the biggest and foremost challenge is to scan and decode densely packed QR codes. Current off-the-shelf QR code decoding libraries, e.g. ZXing[1] cannot handle high-capacity QR codes very well, because they are designed for codes containing small amount of user data (e.g. less than 100 bytes). When the code is densely packed, the performance becomes very sensitive to the environment and scanning operation like uneven lighting, distortion and shaking. We implemented the prototype App by improv-

This research was supported in part by a grant from the Innovation and Technology Fund (ITF) of the Hong Kong SAR Government, (Project no. ITS/300/13).

[1] https://github.com/zxing

MobiSys'14, June 16–19, 2014, Bretton Woods, New Hampshire, USA.
ACM 978-1-4503-2793-0/14/06.
http://dx.doi.org/10.1145/2594368.2601468.

Table 1: Effect of Print-out Size and Content Size (bytes) on User Operation Time (seconds)

Input Size (bytes)	Physical Print-out Sizes					
	Large Op. Time (secs)			Small Op. Time (secs)		
	median	mean	stdev	median	mean	stdev
676	4.2	5.0	4.1	4.2	5.8	6.3
751	4.2	7.8	10.2	4.4	9.2	21.0
1606	4.7	8.8	16.9	4.8	8.6	16.5
1881	10.9	21.7	30.1	13.7	16.7	12.6
2100	8.0	14.4	21.6	11.7	19.4	20.5
2320	8.5	17.1	19.3	8.0	21.1	24.3

ing ZXing library: 1) We improved the binarizing stage by considering the illuminance from neighboring blocks and global average; 2) We improved the accuracy of finder pattern detection by a set of heuristics including color, thickness, and relative positions; 3) We improved the bit-matrix transformation by better dimension estimation from timing patterns. The improved algorithm can decode dense codes that original ZXing library fails to.

Other challenges include designing a proper encapsulation format and figure out the minimum print-out size. We enumerated the design space and obtained operational parameters for AuthPaper. More technical details and introduction video can be found at http://authpaper.net/.

We generated codes with different data size/ print-out size and conducted a usability test with our prototype scanner. The end-to-end user operation time is summarized in Table 1. We found that untrained users can quickly learn to verify AuthPaper documents and the median end-to-end operation time is less than 5 seconds for an Authenticated code carrying more than 1606 bytes of user data.

2. DEMO SETUP

In this demo, we will prepare many sample AuthPaper documents including real ones and forged ones. Conference attendees will try to verify those documents using our prototype. The prototype Android application will be available on Google Play and we will also prepare APK packages for offline distribution. To demonstrate the range of data capacity and printout size of the corresponding 2D barcodes and the robustness of our current implementation under real-world operating conditions, hardcopies of Authenticated 2D barcodes carrying different mixes of heterogeneous types of data will be provided. We will also invite the attendees to try scanning/ decoding the sample codes using their own application of choice under different lighting conditions and compare with our application. This gives the attendees a better idea how our optimized scanner can better handle hostile environments for high-capacity, densely packed QR codes.

DEMO: A Remote Sensor Placement Device for Scalable and Precise Deployment of Sensor Networks

[1]David Mascareñas
dmascarenas@lanl.gov

[1]Logan Ott
logan@lanl.gov

[2]Aaron Curtis
aarongc@nmt.edu

[1]Sara Brambilla
sbrambilla@lanl.gov

[1]Amy Larson
amylarson@lanl.gov

[1]Steve Brumby
brumby@lanl.gov

[1]Charles Farrar
farrar@lanl.gov

[1]Los Alamos National Laboratory, PO Box 1663, Los Alamos, NM, USA 87544
[2]New Mexico Tech, 801 Leroy Pl, Socorro, NM, USA, 87801

ABSTRACT

The goal of this work is to develop a new autonomous capability for remotely deploying precisely located sensor nodes without damaging the sensor nodes in the process. Over the course of the last decade there has been significant interest in research to deploy sensor networks. This research is driven by the fact that the costs associated with installing sensor networks can be very high. In order to rapidly deploy sensor networks consisting of large numbers of sensor nodes, alternative techniques must be developed to place the sensor nodes in the field.

Figure 1 Prototype intelligent gas gun with magazine to hold 3 sensor packages

To date much of the research on sensor network deployment has focused on strategies that involve the random dispersion of sensor nodes [1]. In addition other researchers have investigated deployment strategies utilizing small unmanned aerial helicopters for dropping sensor networks from the air. [2]. The problem with these strategies is that often sensor nodes need to be very precisely located for their measurements to be of any use. The reason for this could be that the sensor being used only have limited range, or need to be properly coupled to the environment which they are sensing. The problem with simply dropping sensor nodes is that for many applications it is necessary to deploy sensor nodes horizontally. In addition, to properly install many types of sensors, the sensor must assume a specific pose relative to the object being measured.

Figure 2. Remote sensor placement package embedded in a piece of fiber board using the remote sensor placement device

In order to address these challenges we are currently developing a technology to remotely and rapidly deploy precisely located sensor nodes. The remote sensor placement device being developed can be described as an intelligent gas gun (Figure 1). A laser rangefinder is used to measure the distance to a specified target sensor location. This distance is then used to estimate the amount of energy required to propel the sensor node to the target location with just enough additional energy left over to ensure the sensor node is able to attach itself to the target of interest. We are currently in the process of developing attachment mechanisms for steel, wood, fiberglass (Figure 2).

In this demonstration we will perform a contained, live demo of our prototype pneumatic remote sensor placement device along with some prototype sensor attachment mechanisms we are developing.

1. REFERENCES

[1] Wan, P.J., Yi, C.W., 2006. *Coverage by Randomly Deployed Wireless Sensor Networks.* IEEE Transactions on Information Theory, Vol 52, No 6.

[2] Corke, P., Hrabar, S., Peterson, R., Rus, D., Siripalli, S., Sukhatme, G., 2004. *The Autonomous Deployment and Repair of a Sensor Network Using an Unmanned Aerial Vehicle.* Robotics and Automation, Proceedings of ICRA 2004, IEEE International Conference on, Vol 4, (New Orleans, LA, USA, April 26-May 1, 2004).

MobiSys'14, Jun 16-19 2014, Bretton Woods, NH, USA
ACM 978-1-4503-2793-0/14/06.
http://dx.doi.org/10.1145/2594368.2601481.

Demo: Hand-to-Hand Communication Using Smartphones

Keisuke Murase, Ryo Kanaoka
Aoyama Gakuin University
5-10-1 Fuchinobe, Chuo-ku
Sagamihara, 252-5258, Japan
+81-42-759-6318
{mkei,ryoryo}@rcl-aoyama.jp

Niwat Thepvilojanapong
Mie University
1577 Kurimamachiya-cho
Tsu, Mie 514-8507
+81-59-231-9463
wat@net.info.mie-u.ac.jp

Tsubasa Ito
Aoyama Gakuin University
5-10-1 Fuchinobe, Chuo-ku
Sagamihara, 252-5258, Japan
+81-42-759-6318
tubasa@rcl-aoyama.jp

Teemu Leppänen
University of Oulu
P.O. BOX 4500
FI- 90014 University of Oulu, Finland
+358 294 482543
teemu.leppanen@ee.oulu.fi

Hiroki Saito
Meiji University
4-21-1 Nakano, Nakano-ku
Tokyo, 164-8525, Japan
+81-3-3296-4369
hrksaito@meiji.ac.jp

Yoshito Tobe
Aoyama Gakuin University
5-10-1 Fuchinobe, Chuo-ku
Sagamihara, 252-5258, Japan
+81-42-759-6318
ytobe88@gmail.com

ABSTRACT

We study an instant messaging system between two smartphones, without the need of visually following the screen of the smartphones. In the sending side, a Morse-code-type touchscreen input is used to encode the message and a vibration in the receiver side to perceive the message.

Categories and Subject Descriptors

H.4 [**Information Systems Application**]: Miscellaneous

General Terms

Design, Experimentation

Keywords

hand-to-hand communication; messaging with vibration; Bluetooth

1. INTRODUCTION

We propose an instant messaging system for smartphones called Hand-to-Hand-on-Bluetooth Communication (H2BCom), which relies on haptic interface as a tool for exchanging information. Among many issues in the design, the largest decision we have made is encoding of messages. Since we aim at sending any kind of message, we have chosen to use the Morse code, created by the touching behavior of a finger on a smartphone touchscreen and perceived by vibration at the receiver.

The related work includes ComTouch, trying to to enrich the inter-personal communication by complementing voice with a tactile channel [1]. The remote voice communication is

augmented by converting touching hand pressure into vibrational intensity between users in real-time. Pressages [2] is a mobile haptic communication system that aims to augment phone calls in which a user squeezes the side of the device and the pressure level is mapped to vibrations on the recipient's device.Vinteraction [3] leverages a combination of vibrator and accelerometer to send information from a smart device to another. Our work differs from the above in that any kind of message can be transferred.

2. Design of H2BCom

The messages are encoded into Morse-type codes. The symbols of 'dot' and 'dash' are decided corresponding on the length of touching the screen, as a 'short' on 'long'. Unlike normal Morse code, the boundaries between words are separated by the action of fling. Both smartphones can take turns as a sender by using abbreviation "AR" as indication of willingness to stop messaging, thus a half-duplex bidirectional communication is achieved. The receiver recognizes the message by the vibration of the above gestures. As the receiver may not keep up with the vibration rate, the user can either store the message into the phone memory to be played out later, or it can be played out immediately with his personal preferred vibration rate.

3. Demonstrations and Video Clip

In our demonstration, the participants can use the provided Android smartphones to send and receive messages by this method. Additionally, a video of application use can be found from http://rcl-aoyama.jp/mobisys14-demo.mp4.

4. REFERENCES

[1] Chang, A., O'Modhrain, S., Jacob, R., Gunther, E., and Ishii, H. *Comtouch: Design of a vibrotactile communication device.* In Proc. of DIS2002 (2002), 312-320.

[2] Hoggan, E., Stewart, C., Haverinen, L., Jacucci, G., and Lantz, V. *Pressages: Augmenting phone calls with non-verbal messages.* In Proc. of UIST2012 (2012), 555-562.

[3] Yonezawa, T., Ito, T., and Tokuda, H. *Transferring information from mobile devices to personal computers by using vibration and accelerometer.* In Proc. of the 13th Int. Conf. on Ubiquitous Computing (UbiComp 2011) (2011), 487-488

Demo: Zero Interaction Private Messaging with ZIPR

Ali Razeen
Duke University
alrazeen@cs.duke.edu

Landon Cox
Duke University
lpcox@cs.duke.edu

ABSTRACT

Messaging app developers are beginning to take the security and privacy of their users' communication more seriously [3]. Unfortunately, a recent study has shown that the developers of many popular apps incorrectly use cryptography [2]. As a result, they make mistakes that may result in trivially broken encryption schemes. For example, the developers of Snapchat use a constant symmetric encryption key hard-coded into the app and it only takes 12 lines of Ruby to crack the encryption [1].

In this work, we propose ZIPR (Zero-Interaction PRivacy), a system that relieves developers from the task of using cryptography correctly. Designed for text-messaging apps, ZIPR automatically negotiates shared secret keys, and encrypts and decrypts messages as users of these apps chat with each other. No manual intervention is required by users for them to enjoy secure messaging.

There are two key ideas behind ZIPR. First, most text-messaging apps follow a basic UI scheme that contains (i) a text box for users to compose their message, (ii) a "send" button which they click on to send the message, and (iii) a list view to display sent and received messages. By intercepting events on these UI elements, ZIPR can manipulate the composed message before it is sent and before it is displayed. This allows the system to transparently encrypt and decrypt message data.

The second key idea is that ZIPR can reuse the communication channel defined by an app to negotiate a shared secret key between two users. This is done by piggy-backing negotiation data on the messages users send to each other. A major advantage of this approach is that ZIPR can avoid the difficult task of establishing user identities. After all, a user of a text-messaging app is likely to carry out a conversation only with someone she knows, and both of them would have signed up for the chat service using some personal data such as their email addresses or phone numbers.

Developers use ZIPR by tagging UI elements; no changes to their source code are required. This is similar to HTTPS

MobiSys '14, Jun 16-19 2014, Bretton Woods, NH, USA
ACM 978-1-4503-2793-0/14/06
http://dx.doi.org/10.1145/2594368.2601470.

where web developers only need to configure their servers with SSL certificates to encrypt data transmission with their users. However, unlike HTTPS, the end-to-end encryption in ZIPR takes place between the two users carrying out a conversation and not between a server and a user. This ensures that even if the app servers are compromised, users' messages would remain secure.

ZIPR is implemented in Android 4.3 and works with existing apps with very few modifications. In this demo, we show that our current prototype works with several apps including Whatsapp, Facebook Messenger, and Skype. These apps required only four, five, and three lines of modification to their UI XML definition files, respectively.

Figure 1: **Whatsapp running under ZIPR.**

In Figure 1, we show a screenshot of Whatsapp running under ZIPR. In the first two messages exchanged between the users, a new shared secret key is negotiated. Subsequently, all following messages are securely transmitted, and these encrypted messages are prefixed with a "*" by ZIPR.

We are currently extending our prototype to use the Android Keystore API and the TrustZone hardware to allow users to identify MitM attacks, and to store the secret keys securely. We are also porting other messaging apps, such as Viber, to ZIPR.

1. REFERENCES

[1] Dmitri DB.
    https://security.stackexchange.com/q/52584/.

[2] M. Egele, D. Brumley, Y. Fratantonio, and C. Kruegel.
    An Empirical Study of Cryptographic Misuse in
    Android Applications. In *Proceedings of CCS '13*,
    November 2013.

[3] The New York Times - Molly Wood. Can You Trust
    'Secure' Messaging Apps? http://nyti.ms/1pbofVI.

Demo: Mapping Global Mobile Performance Trends with Mobilyzer and MobiPerf

Sanae Rosen*, Hongyi Yao*, Ashkan Nikravesh*, Yunhan Jia*, David Choffnes†,
Z. Morley Mao*
*University of Michigan, †Northeastern University
sanae,hyyao,ashnik,jackjia@umich.edu, choffnes@ccs.neu.edu, zmao@umich.edu

ABSTRACT

Mobilyzer is an open-source network measurement library that coordinates network measurement tasks among different applications, facilitates measurement task design, and allows for more effective measurement task management than in existing standalone approaches. Unifying various network tasks into one framework greatly simplifies the problem of developing, deploying and managing measurement tasks which may otherwise interfere with one another. An intelligent scheduler, coordinated by a central server, dynamically schedules tasks to run in the background, preserving the user's battery life and respecting limits set by the user on task frequency and data consumption. We will demo MobiPerf, an open-source mobile network measurement tool built using the Mobilyzer library. MobiPerf collects a wide range of network performance data, ranging from the latency and throughput measurements common in existing client-based measurement frameworks, to HTTP loading times for specific URLs, to inferring RRC state configuration parameters and their impact on performance. We will also demo an interface for viewing a large, open dataset of performance data from around the world collected by MobiPerf.

Categories and Subject Descriptors

C.2.1 [**Network Architecture and Design**]: Wireless communication; C.4 [**Performance of systems**]: Measurement techniques

Keywords

Network performance measurements; Cellular networks; LTE; 4G; network measurement libraries

1. DEMONSTRATION

We will demonstrate the Mobilyzer library [1] using MobiPerf [2], on several phones and three different carriers. Audience members will be able to schedule measurements from both the app and the web interface, and view results in real time. This demo shows how Mobilyzer enables on-demand measurements after the app release, and how it manages multiple simultaneous measurement requests. An example screenshot from a device running MobiPerf, as well

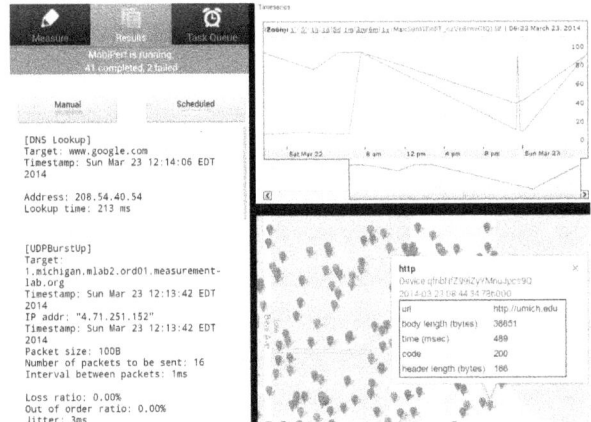

Figure 1: Screenshot of the MobiPerf application, and a map and timeline of data from one device in the web interface.

as data shown in the web interface, are shown in Figure 1. A wide range of measurements are suppported, including latency, the time to complete DNS lookups, and packet loss rates. Most recently, to demonstrate Mobilyzer's ability to support more complex measurements, we have introduced a task for inferring RRC state timers and their performance impact, which accounts for interfering traffic from all applications on the device.

We have collected data on network performance around the world, demonstrating the effectiveness of a global mobile network measurement platform for monitoring performance trends. We make anonymized data from MobiPerf publicly available, and will also demo an interactive visualization of the data collected to date (available on the MobiPerf website), adapted from work by Zarifis et al. [3].

2. REFERENCES

[1] Mobilyzer. http://mobilyzer-project.mobi/.
[2] MobiPerf. http://mobiperf.com.
[3] K. Zarifis, T. Flach, S. Nori, D. Choffnes, R. Govindan, E. Katz-Besset, Z. M. Mao, and M. Welsh. Diagnosing Path Inflation of Mobile Client Traffic. In *Passive and Active Measurement*, 2014.

MobiSys'14, June 16–19, 2014, Bretton Woods, NH, USA
ACM 978-1-4503-2793-0/14/06.
http://dx.doi.org/10.1145/2594368.2601469.

Demo: I am a Smartphone and I can Tell my User's Walking Direction

Nirupam Roy
University of Illinois at
Urbana-Champaign (UIUC)

He Wang
University of Illinois at
Urbana-Champaign (UIUC)

Romit Roy Choudhury
University of Illinois at
Urbana-Champaign (UIUC)

1. ABSTRACT

We present a demonstration of WalkCompass, a system to appear in the MobiSys 2014 main conference. WalkCompass exploits smartphone sensors to estimate the direction in which a user is walking. We find that several smartphone localization systems in the recent past, including our own, make a simplifying assumption that the user's walking direction is known. In trying to relax this assumption, we were not able to find a generic solution from past work. While intuition suggests that the walking direction should be detectable through the accelerometer, in reality this direction gets blended into various other motion patterns during the act of walking, including up and down bounce, side-to-side sway, swing of arms or legs, etc. WalkCompass analyzes the human walking dynamics to estimate the dominating forces and uses this knowledge to find the heading direction of the pedestrian. In the demonstration we will show the performance of this system when the user holds the smartphone on the palm. A collection of YouTube videos of the demo is posted at http://synrg.csl.illinois.edu/projects/localization/walkcompass.

2. SYSTEM OVERVIEW

The core intuitions in WalkCompass [1] are based on simple analysis of walking dynamics and can be explained with the following key points. First, we performed an analysis of human walking patterns that helps us understand how different forces act in different directions to keep the human body stable during a walk. We found that, when a user walks, her heel strikes the ground creating a distinct vibration that resonates through the entire body. This vibration reflects on the accelerometer data across all holding positions, even when the user is holding the phone against her ears. WalkCompass uses this vibration as a reference, scans the signal backwards, and extracts specific samples from a time window when the body's movement is dominantly in the heading direction. These samples represent the user's motion vector. The signal is then processed with the gy-roscope data to compensate for instability of the phone's coordinate system. This motion vector is projected to the plane orthogonal to gravity, and averaged over few steps to converge upon the *local* walking direction.

3. DEMONSTRATION

WalkCompass has been implemented on Android, using the Jellybeans version, and tested using a variety of Samsung phones. Figure 1(a) shows a screenshot of the tentative application with the (thicker) gray cone showing the compass direction; the (thinner) green cone denotes the user's walking direction. The width of the cone is proportional to the variance of error in the walking direction – a useful visualization for debugging in real conditions. In the demonstration we will have the WalkCompass application running on smartphones. The users can walk with a smartphone in hand and can observe the application indicating the correct walking direction on the screen, despite changes in orientation of the smartphone. We have observed that WalkCompass can estimate the walking direction even when the user is walking backward. Figure 1(b) shows a QR code for the WalkCompass webpage [2].

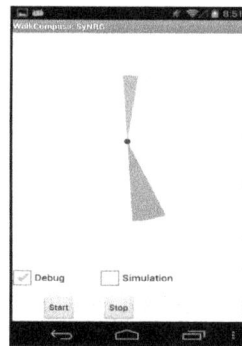

Figure 1: (a) WalkCompass screenshot. (b) QR code for WalkCompass demo.

MobiSys'14, June 16–19, 2014, Bretton Woods, New Hampshire, USA.
ACM 978-1-4503-2793-0/14/06.
http://dx.doi.org/10.1145/2594368.2601478 .

4. REFERENCES

[1] N. Roy, H. Wang, and R. Roy Choudhury, "I am a smartphone and i can tell my user's walking direction," in *Proceedings of the 12th international conference on Mobile systems, applications, and services*, ACM, 2014.

[2] "Walkcompass demo." http://synrg.csl.illinois.edu/projects/localization/walkcompass.

Demo: Ubiquitous Interaction with Smart Objects

Jan Rüth, Hanno Wirtz, Klaus Wehrle
Chair of Communication and Distributed Systems (COMSYS)
RWTH Aachen University
{rueth, wirtz, wehrle}@comsys.rwth-aachen.de

Categories and Subject Descriptors

C.2.1 [**Computer Communication Networks**]: Network Architecture and Design—*Wireless communication*

Keywords

ubiquitous computing; mobile communication

1. INTRODUCTION

Increasingly, everyday physical objects become "smart" by making their functionality accessible, controllable, and extensible for Internet-based users and services via a connection to the digital world. Deployed in scenarios that range from private households over offices to public spaces, smart objects enable ubiquitous "smart spaces" that build on interaction with mobile users. However, ubiquitous interaction with smart objects is currently complicated by three factors. 1) Communication with objects requires Internet or local network access, a requirement that is not met under ground, abroad, or when lacking access credentials to 802.11 networks. 2) Identifying a specific object from the envisioned billions of objects requires a suitable discovery mechanism, introducing delays and mandating object owners to disclose object semantics. 3) Interacting with object functionalities mandates an a-priori installation of a specific app, that provides a human-usable interface, per object and use case, resulting in an abundance of (redundant) apps. We argue that smart object interaction is thereby restricted to pre-defined scenarios and objects, e.g., at home or in offices.

In this demonstration, we strive to make smart object interaction ubiquitous. Current approaches abstract from user locations and contexts via the Internet but lack support for spontaneous discovery and interaction with possibly unknown objects in the immediate vicinity of the user. In order to enable such interaction, we address the aforementioned factors by 1) enabling *direct* communication and interaction with objects over Bluetooth 4.0 Low Energy (BLE), removing the need for network access and reducing the discovery scope to the intuitive local interaction scope of the user and 2) enable

MobiSys'14, June 16–19, 2014, Bretton Woods, New Hampshire, USA.
ACM 978-1-4503-2793-0/14/06
http://dx.doi.org/10.1145/2594368.2601477.

Figure 1: Discovery of nearby smart objects and their abilities. Objects can be recognized using a visual "Marker" or via computer vision ("Image").

smart objects to *unmediatedly* specify their functionality and interaction possibilities as well as their interface and its representation to users in a lightweight, generic, and extensible way, allowing for unrestricted, spontaneous interaction.

2. SYSTEM OVERVIEW

Recent approaches [1] show the benefit of smart object interaction via a tactile virtual GUI that provides an intuitive interface to the object functionality. Specifically, the visually recognized object in the camera view is virtually augmented with the GUI. Especially in unknown scenarios, virtual interfaces greatly assist in understanding object functionalities and interfaces. Moreover, a virtually augmented GUI allows for more complex and versatile interaction mechanisms than a static, non-modifiable hardware interface. We thus enable smart objects to provide their GUI and underlying commands directly to mobile users, mitigating the requirement of pre-distributed GUI descriptions and network access as in [1]. Objects thus store and transmit a visual fingerprint of themselves as well as a generic definition of the GUI elements and their position relative to the object's visual appearance in the camera view.

We build on BLE as the communication channel for its energy efficiency, lightweight protocol stack, low cost factor, and proliferation in current smartphones. We offer two mech-

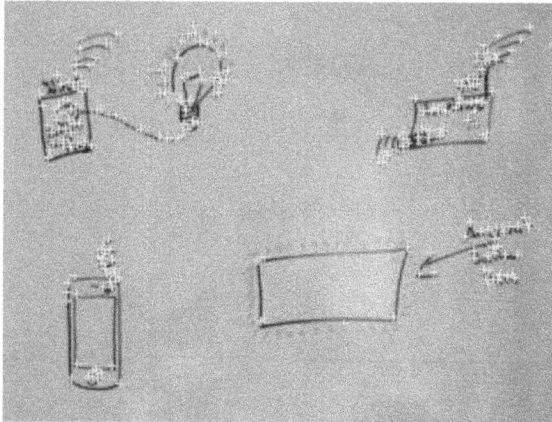

Figure 2: Artificial example of feature points (yellow plus signs) that the object transmits to the mobile device and that identify an object in computer vision recognition and subsequent GUI augmentation.

Figure 3: Visual marker attached to a computer screen. Augmented GUI elements relative to the marker provide an touch-based interface to interact with the underlying music player.

anisms for object discovery, cf. Figure 1, by mobile devices that present a tradeoff between obtrusiveness and communication overhead. First, objects can be visually recognized using a physically attached marker which is indicated to mobile devices using an marker ID and its dimensions. Alternatively, objects provide computer vision (CV) material, c.f. Figure 2, to enable CV-based recognition. CV recognition is physically less obtrusive at higher communication costs.

We utilize the Qualcomm Vuforia framework [2] to augment the camera view with 3D GUI elements as visible in Figure 3. The mobile user is able to interact with the GUI elements through the smartphone's touch screen. We then translate GUI actions into interaction commands transmitted to the object via BLE. Upon reception the smart object can trigger the requested functionality. Thereby the smartphone itself must not know the specific underlying technology of the smart objects thus enabling a generic and ubiquitous use.

3. DESCRIPTION OF DEMONSTRATION

We demonstrate our approach with iOS smartphones and a number of everyday objects to illustrate the design space of smart object interaction. The demonstration will allow discovery and selection of nearby objects and subsequent visual recognition and GUI interaction. We strive for a smart object setup that comprises "naturally" smart objects, such as a laptop, and objects whose physical functionality is extended using our approach. Conference participants will be able to interact with objects and change the interaction GUI of objects to show the flexibility and spontaneity of ubiquitous smart object interaction.

Acknowledgements

This work was funded by the DFG Cluster of Excellence on Ultra High-Speed Mobile Information and Communication (UMIC).

4. REFERENCES

[1] V. Heun, S. Kasahara, and P. Maes. Smarter Objects: Using AR Technology to Program Physical Objects and Their Interactions. In *CHI*. ACM, 2013.

[2] Qualcomm. Vuforia. https://www.vuforia.com/.

Demo: Protecting Visual Secrets with PrivateEye

Animesh Srivastava
Duke University
animeshs@cs.duke.edu

Landon Cox
Duke University
lpcox@cs.duke.edu

ABSTRACT

Consider the following scenario from the not-too-distant future: the CEO of a company is presenting his vision for the next quarter to a small group of co-workers. The CEO trusts everyone in the room, but many in attendance have smartphones and camera-equipped wearable computing devices running third-party apps. The CEO is worried that this third-party software could leak the highly confidential information in his slides and on the whiteboard. This raises the question: how can the CEO prevent apps with camera access from leaking company secrets?

First, the CEO must have a way of identifying or *marking* visual secrets. Markings should be: (1) easy to create by hand and with digital tools, and (2) easy and efficient to recognize by software. Marking visual secrets by placing QR-codes or badges near them makes real-time recognition difficult due to scaling problems (particularly at far distances). Moreover, precisely encoding a two-dimensional region surrounding a visual secret in a QR-code or badge would be too awkward and slow for users. Finally, general-purpose object recognition is too slow and consumes too much energy.

In this demo, we present PrivateEye, a system that prevents visual secrets from inadvertently leaking. PrivateEye consists of two pieces: (1) a specification for marking a two-dimensional space as secret, and (2) software on a recording device for recognizing markings and obscuring visual secrets in real-time. Figure 1(a) and 2(a) show examples of how PrivateEye users can define a region containing visual secrets by combining solid and dotted lines. Depending on the medium, users can define secret regions by hand (e.g., on a whiteboard) or use digital tools (e.g., within a presentation).

PrivateEye is based on the principle that preventing leaks requires visual information to be withheld from third-party apps until the system can be confident that it is safe to reveal. As a result, PrivateEye works in three phases. **Phase 1** requires the camera view to stabilize. During this phase,

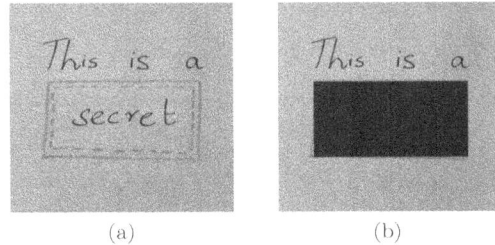

Figure 1: (a) A region on a whiteboard marked as secret by drawing the special marking around it. (b) The whiteboard scene captured by PrivateEye.

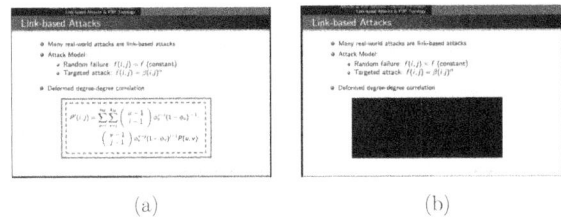

Figure 2: (a) A region on a presentation slide marked as secret by drawing the special marking around it. (b) The presentation scene captured by PrivateEye.

PrivateEye completely blurs the camera view so that apps cannot infer secret information from an image capture. Once the camera view stabilizes, PrivateEye enters **Phase 2**, in which the system detects all the rectangles in the camera view. At this point, all the detected rectangles appear blocked to the user (Figure 1(b) and 2(b)). PrivateEye then moves on to **Phase 3**. In this phase, the system searches each blocked rectangle for secret markings (i.e., dotted rectangles). PrivateEye can safely reveal the content of rectangles without secret markings to an app; however, the system must continue to block any rectangles containing secret markings. If PrivateEye detects that the camera view has changed, then it must return to **Phase 1**.

During the demo, PrivateEye will be running on Google Nexus 4 and Google Glass. We plan to invite the audience to use one of these devices and view some of the objects already marked secret. We will also let them draw the markers around some text on a whiteboard. This will help the audience to understand the usability and effectiveness of PrivateEye.

MobiSys'14, June 16–19, 2014, Bretton Woods, New Hampshire, USA.
ACM 978-1-4503-2793-0/14/06.
http://dx.doi.org/10.1145/2594368.2601467.

Demo: Crowd-Cache – Popular Content for Free

Kanchana Thilakarathna
UNSW & NICTA, Australia
kanchana.thilakarathna
@nicta.com.au

Fangzhou Jiang
USYD & NICTA, Australia
fangzhou.jiang
@nicta.com.au

Sirine Mrabet
NICTA Australia
sirine.mrabet
@nicta.com.au

Mohamed Ali Kaafar
INRIA France, NICTA Australia
dali.kaafar
@nicta.com.au

Aruna Seneviratne
UNSW & NICTA, Australia
aruna.seneviratne
@nicta.com.au

Prasant Mohapatra
UC Davis, USA
pmohapatra
@ucdavis.edu

ABSTRACT

Crowd-Cache is a novel crowd-sourced content caching system which provides cheap and convenient content access for mobile users. Our system exploits both transient colocation of devices and the spatial temporal correlation of content popularity, where users in a particular location and at specific times would be likely interested in similar content. We demonstrate the feasibility of Crowd-Cache system through a prototype implementation on Android smartphones.

Categories and Subject Descriptors

C.2.1 [**Computer-Communication Networks**]: Network Architecture and Design—*Network Communications*

Keywords

Distributed Caching; Crowd Sourcing; Mobile Content Distribution

1. INTRODUCTION

The emergence of smart mobile devices have led to an explosion in mobile data traffic [2]. This traffic is being generated by the user consuming rich media, especially video via the over the top services such as catch-up TV and YouTube. It has been reported that the current cellular network operators are struggling to cope with the increasing demand [1] and as a result, today a majority of cellular operators only provide capped data plans.

Content caching and peer-to-peer dissemination are two of the common approaches to address the needs of growing mobile data traffic. Traditional in-network caching exploits the locality of interest by storing the content as close to the location of the interest. However in mobile networks, as the delay and cost are incurred on the last hop wireless link, the traditional in-network caching helps in reducing the latency and bandwidth only in the backhaul links.

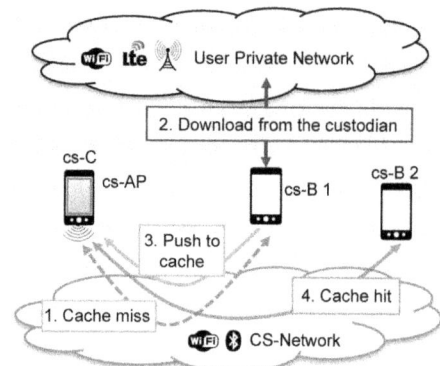

Figure 1: Operations of the Crowd-Cache System

We propose and demonstrate a novel content caching scheme which combines the concepts of traditional in-network caching, crowd-sourcing and peer-to-peer data delivery and harness the advanced capabilities of mobile devices rather than thin clients as traditional systems.

2. CROWD-CACHE: AN OVERVIEW

Our system exploits both transient colocation of devices and the epidemic nature of content popularity, where users in a particular location and at specific times would be likely interested in the same set of content. The key idea of the Crowd-Cache system is to leverage on the possibility to gather such content of interest into a localised cache so that further requests would not require any expensive bandwidth cost.

The architecture of the proposed system is illustrated in Figure 1. We consider two modes of operation: a browser-only mode, referred as *cc-B*, and a cache-mode, referred as *cc-C* for crowd-source caching. *cc-C* users will act as Crowd-Cache network access-points, denoted *(cc-APs)*. In practice, we envision several reward-based schemes to gratify *cc-C* users, which provides sufficient incentives for becoming a *cc-C*. The *cc-C* devices advertise their availability via specific SSIDs broadcast (e.g. cc-SSID), which is operated by simply activating the WiFi Hotspot mode. All mobile devices running a *cc-B* can then associate with the *cc-AP*. Associations to the *cc-APs* are handled by the *cc-B* app and is secured using e.g. existing standard WLAN security mechanisms such as WPA authentication mechanisms.

When a user requests a content via cc-B, the device associates with available cc-AP and then the corresponding cc-C app checks the cache for the requested content. In case of a cache hit, the content is delivered from the cc-C to the cc-B locally. In case of a miss, cc-B is informed which triggers a switch of the network connection from cc-AP to the user *private network* (e.g. LTE, 3G network). Then the cc-B downloads the content from the external content custodian as shown in step 2 in Figure 1.

Contribution to the crowd cache happens whenever a user downloads content via his *private network connection* due to a cache miss. When first connecting to a cc-AP, cc-B pushes the content that lies in the device local cache to cc-C of the cc-AP (step 3 in Figure 1). The cc-C makes a local decision as to whether it is useful or not to update its cache with the new content depending on the content replacement strategy adopted by the cc-C. Then, whenever another cc-B user requests the same content, a cache hit happens as illustrated in step 4 in Figure 1.

We model the crowd-cache system based on real-world video access patterns of mobile users. The preliminary results of real data-driven simulations show that it is possible to achieve up to approximately 90% cache hit rate, while more than 80% of users saving approximately 80% of cellular bandwidth without significant impact on the device energy consumption.

2.1 Application Scenario

We envisage several deployment scenarios of the Crowd-Cache system. In the following, we describe a real-life deployment which considers a public transport scenario (e.g. Bus), where users commute to work. Let's assume for simplicity, that the bus driver is a registered cc-C. Thus, the bus driver's mobile device will act as a cc-AP within the bus. Initially, the cache of the bus driver's cc-C only contains data that has been downloaded via the driver's own (private) network connection (for example for his/her own use). When a passenger who has subscribed to the Crowd-Cache service gets on the bus, the cc-B discovers the availability of a cc-AP (via the active discovery mode searching for specific AP beacons).

First, cc-B pushes locally cached content (e.g. videos downloaded whilst at home or at the bus stop via user own network connections) to the bus driver's cc-C. When a newcomer (a passenger in our scenario), sends a requests via the Crowd-Cache system to access some internet content (e.g. YouTube videoclips, hot trending news, etc.), cc-B first checks the bus driver's cc-C to verify whether the content is available. In case of a cache hit, the content is obtained through the bus driver's cc-C. Otherwise, the user request is served through his own network connection if available (the user is notified that the connection is redirected to outside the local cc-AP). More generally, each passenger who gets on the bus and has subscribed to the Crowd-Cache system, transfers its own cached data to the bus driver's cc-C cache. In such a semi transient environment, after a while the cache of the cc-C will most likely contain the popular videos, thus increasing the cache hit rates.

2.2 Incentives for users

The main incentive to use the cc-B is mainly driven by free access to popular content, while contributing from time to time to the cache. When users encounter a crowd cache miss,

there is no additional cost, except from contributing via a cheap connection (e.g. WiFi) to the crowd cache so that potential further requests for the same content from other users can be served from the cache. In fact, the crowd cache here is constituted by a collaborative effort from multiple users gathered in the same area for a particular lapse of time. In return, users could benefit from each others effort to save on downloads costs exploiting existing content in the "crowd-sourced" cache.

From the cc-C's perspective, the incentives for participating in the system are twofold. First, cc-C inherits all incentives from cc-B's as they still benefit from the content downloaded to the cc-AP. Second, we envision several ads-based reward schemes to gratify cc-Cs who contribute to the system. Whenever a cc-C serves for a cache hit, it also displays an advertisement. Since these ads are locally served from a cc-C, such data will not be accounted on the users private network quotas. The cc-Cs and cc-Bs will upload their impression counts whenever they have access to an Internet connection via a *private network connection*, e.g when they have access to a low cost network at home. cc-Cs with a high number of ads impressions get a monetary reward, as a portion of the ads monetary revenue generated by the ads clicks and/or impressions and affiliate ad campaigns. In the above model, the more a cc-C supplies content, the more likely it will get rewarded. This represents a clear incentives for cc-Cs to participate and operate as a cache contributor whenever they can.

Another important aspect to consider is the potential drain of battery from the content pushing process to the cc-C. However, the extra energy consumption of uploading will be offset by the reduction in energy consumption when cc-B downloads large volumes of data from the cc-C[1]. In the case of cc-C, we consider the device is connected to a power source during the hosting of cc-AP, e.g. bus driver's cc-C device needs to be connected to a power source.

3. DEMONSTRATION

We demonstrate the feasibility of Crowd-Cache system using a prototype Android app. Several Android smartphones are used to demonstrate the two operation scenarios of cache hit and cache miss, while another Android device is used as cc-C. We will ask interested conference participants to query and watch their preferred video clips on YouTube using Crowd-Cache app. Then, we revel among other metrics the actual cache hit rate achieved during the demonstration period based on the participants' transient co-location of content preference.

4. REFERENCES

[1] ByteMobile. Mobile analytics report. In *http://www.bytemobile.com*, oct 2011.
[2] Cisco. Cisco visual networking index: Global mobile data traffic forecast update, 2011–2016. In *http://www.cisco.com*.
[3] H. Petander. Energy-aware network selection using traffic estimation. In *Proc. of the 1st ACM workshop MICNET '09*, pages 55–60, Beijing, China, 2009.

---

[1]It has been shown that the energy consumed by WiFi is significantly lower than those of cellular networks mainly due to the heavy traffic load in cellular networks leading to lower speeds and thus taking longer time to complete data transfers [3].

Demo: Yalut – User-Centric Social Networking Overlay

Kanchana Thilakarathna, Xinlong Guan and Aruna Seneviratne
School of EE&T, UNSW and National ICT Australia (NICTA), Australia
first name.lastname@nicta.com.au

ABSTRACT

Yalut is a novel user-centric hybrid content sharing overlay for social networking. Yalut enables the users to retain control over their own data and preserve their privacy, whilst still using the popular centralized services. In this demonstration, we show the feasibility of Yalut by integrating the service with the popular social networking apps on Android devices, Mac and Windows desktop platforms. We show that it is possible to provide the benefits of distributed content sharing on top of the existing centralized services with minimal changes to the content sharing process.

Categories and Subject Descriptors

C.2.1 [**Computer-Communication Networks**]: Network Architecture and Design—*Store and forward networks*

Keywords

User Generated Content Sharing; Cellular Data Traffic Offloading; Mobile Social Networking

1. INTRODUCTION

Majority of user generated content, e.g. photos and videos, is being shared by uploading them to centralized online social networking (C-OSN) services such as Facebook and YouTube. Even though the cost of storage and distribution is high when using centralized architectures, the C-OSN providers prefer to host the service centrally as it allows the mining of user data and generating revenue from other sources, e.g. advertisements. Advantages for the user are; being able to access the content from any device, and not having to worry about maintenance. However, these advantages come at the cost of reduced privacy and losing the control of their data.

Decentralized social networking (D-OSN) have been proposed as the means to improve user privacy and the user losing control of their data [2, 1, 3]. However, none of these services have seen widespread use for a number of reasons. Firstly, because of most users have already subscribed to the C-OSNs. Secondly, because D-OSN services are too complicated and expensive for a typical user. Thirdly, because users are not being able to migrate from their current services, due to personal data being locked in with subscribed C-OSNs.

MobiSys'14, June 16–19, 2014, Bretton Woods, New Hampshire, USA.
ACM 978-1-4503-2793-0/14/06.
http://dx.doi.org/10.1145/2594368.2601465.

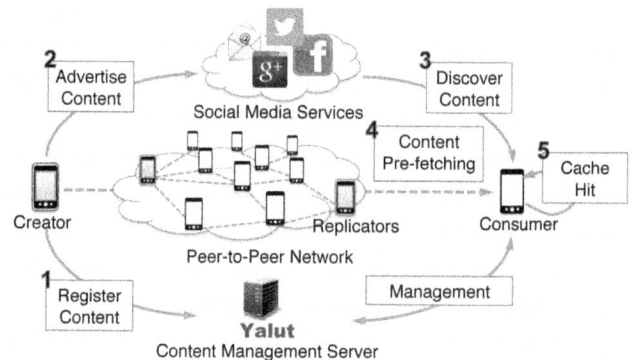

Figure 1: Yalut content sharing processes

Yalut[1] overcomes the above shortcomings by acting as an overly on top of the widely used C-OSNs and provides highly efficient content sharing and storage methods, ensures the same level of content availability as C-OSNs, reduces the cost of communication and battery usage [4].

2. YALUT: AN OVERVIEW

Yalut achieves the above whilst protecting user privacy by keeping user data away from third party service providers, using distributed content delivery and storage, delaying uploads, and predictive downloading of content. Although these concepts alone are not new, the novelty in Yalut stems from the integration of the availability of content is advertised, the content is stored and distributed.

Yalut relies on a centralized entity (Content Management Server - CMS) to manage the peer-to-peer content distribution. Consider a content creator who wants to share a content with his social networking friends on a given popular C-OSNs (Facebook, Twitter etc.). First, Yalut mobile app registers the content to be shared with the CMS as shown in step 1 in Figure 1. The registration is done through any available network connection at the time of sharing. Then, a link to the CMS is shared with friends on the C-OSN of their choice using the C-OSNs methods of advertising the content, e.g. posting on the wall in the case of Facebook. Yalut app provides the ability to select among number of popular services such as Facebook, Twitter, Google+, Email and Messages.

Other Yalut users discover the shared content through the notification appearing on as they normally do when using the C-OSN (step 3 in Figure 1). In addition, the Yalut mobile app monitors notification feeds in the background and pre-fetches the content and locally cache content when pre-fetching is enabled. When a user clicks on the shared notification, Yalut displays the content either by fetching it from the local cache (step 5) or initiating the content downloading process using a peer-to-peer protocol such as BitTorrent as shown in step 4 in Figure 1. The content

---

[1]http://www.yalut.com

creator and other friends who already have full or pieces of the content take part in the content uploading.

In addition, Yalut introduces the notion of ephemeral content, where the user can control the period of time the content is to be shared. This can be easily implemented as the user has full control of the content. After the specified expiry time, the content and the shared notifications will be deleted from all friends devices and other respective services. One of the main challenges is to ensure the same level of content availability without having a centralized store. This is achieved in Yalut by replicating content on a group devices selected among the intended consumers, i.e. on the social networking friends of the creator which is referred to as mTribe [4].

3. REPLICATING OF CONTENT

A mobile device may not be able to provide access to the content continuously due to three primary reasons, namely the communications costs, battery usage, and not being "on" all the time. This is overcome by replicating content on devices that have complementary connectivity, sufficient battery power and being "on". Moreover, through this process, if the traffic is routed through a low-cost and/or less congested network, it will result in significant benefits to both the mobile network service providers and the users.

Device grouping for content replication is performed by the CMS, as it has a global view of the system state in terms of both mobile devices and networking infrastructure. The CMS carries out the grouping periodically or in response to a significant degradation of the availability of a tribe's content. Each device periodically (daily) updates the CMS with its binary *Device Availability* pattern, i.e. its ability to host others' content based on the available network connection, spare storage and battery status[2].

Let the availability of a device i be A_i^t, where $A_i^t = 1$, if the device is capable of hosting others' content during the time slot t and $A_i^t = 0$ otherwise. Then, the probability of low-cost network availability of a tribe of devices (G) can be defined as follows, where $|T|$ represents the number of time slots considered to infer future availability, the "Training Period".

$$P_a(G) = \frac{\sum_{t \in T} \bigcup_{i \in G} A_i^t}{|T|}, \quad A_i^t = \begin{cases} 1 & \text{Available} \\ 0 & \text{Not available} \end{cases}$$

If users have regular behavioral patterns, it is possible to use $P_a(G)$ as a metric to predict future availability as discussed in [5]. If $P_a(G)$ is higher than a threshold, the *"Threshold of Pairing"* (P_{th}), we consider that tribe G satisfies the availability constraint and can be used to host others' content in the future. However, we cannot implicitly select tribes based on threshold of pairing due to the overheads associated with replication. Therefore, we consider two additional constraints in device grouping.

1) Minimum Replication: A high level of replication will disrupt the system performance by creating additional traffic flows and overheads, wasting battery life and storage of mobile devices. Hence, the device grouping trades-off replication to availability. The minimum replication is ensured by defining a *Limit of Replication*, i.e. the maximum allowed

size of a tribe. *2) Fairness:* If a device is selected by many users to host data, it would drain energy and storage of that device. The fairness of the system is ensured by defining the *Limit of Hosting*, i.e. the maximum number of tribes that a single device can belong to.

When these three constraints are satisfied, a device included in the mTribe is said to be *covered*. Thus, the content replication problem becomes *"how to find a maximum cover while satisfying minimum replication and fairness constraints"*. We showed that the problem of content replication to achieve maximum availability while satisfying minimum replication and fairness among users is NP-Hard [4]. Then we proposed and evaluated an approximation algorithm based on a combination of a bipartite b-matching and a greedy heuristic. Using real data traces, we showed the viability of the proposed algorithm, in fact it is possible to achieve persistent low-cost network availability with only two replicas per content. For the particular traces, we evaluated the cellular bandwidth and energy consumption of devices using realistic content creation and access modelling. In this demonstration, we show feasibility of the practical implementation of our system on Android smartphones, Mac and Windows desktop platforms.

4. DEMONSTRATION

The demonstration consists of several Android smartphones and a desktop computer, whose users are assumed to be online friends. One device is then used to take a photo, and availability of the photo for a period of time is advertised by posting it on the users' Facebook wall or through a Tweet using the Yalut mobile app. Using this, we first show how Yalut feeds appear through the chosen social network feeds in real-time. We also have one device pre-configured to pre-fetch the content, and highlight the benefits of pre-fetching. Finally, the ephemeral nature of the shared content is also demonstrated. This demo requires that all the devices have WLAN Internet access. Attendees will be able to actively participate in the demonstration either by downloading the app from Google Play store to their personal devices or using one of the demo devices.

5. REFERENCES

[1] L. Cutillo, R. Molva, and T. Strufe. Safebook: A privacy-preserving online social network leveraging on real-life trust. *Communications Magazine, IEEE*, 47(12):94–101, 2009.

[2] http://joindiaspora.org.

[3] A. Mahdian, J. Black, R. Han, and S. Mishra. Myzone: A next-generation online social network. In *Tech Report: Department of Computer Science, University of Colorado at Boulder*, 2011.

[4] K. Thilakarathna, H. Petander, J. Mestre, and A. Seneviratne. MobiTribe: Cost Efficient Distributed User Generated Content Sharing on Smartphones. *Mobile Computing, IEEE Transactions on*, jul 2013.

[5] K. Thilakarathna, H. Petander, and A. Seneviratne. Performance of Content Replication in MobiTribe: a Distributed Architecture for Mobile UGC Sharing. In *Proc. of IEEE LCN*, pages 558–566, oct 2011.

---

[2]We showed in [5], that the history of device availability patterns can be effectively used to infer future availability patterns of a device and groups of devices.

Demo: SaveAlert: Design for a Sensor-driven CrowdWatch Danger Detection System

Güliz Seray Tuncay
University of Illinois, at
Urbana-Champaign
tuncay2@illinois.edu

Kirill Varshavskiy
University of Illinois, at
Urbana-Champaign
varshav2@illinois.edu

Robin Kravets
University of Illinois, at
Urbana-Champaign
rhk@illinois.edu

ABSTRACT

SaveAlert is an adaptive framework for danger-detection using existing devices such as off-the-shelf smartphones and smartwatches. The framework can be extended to different sensors that could trigger distress signals to notify nearby users of potentially dangerous situations.

Categories and Subject Descriptors

C.2.4 [**Distribtued Systems**]: Distributed Applications; C.3 [**Special-Purpose and Application-Based Systems**]: Signal processing systems

Keywords

Safety; Danger detection; Crowd Monitoring; Crowd Sensing, Crowd Dynamics

1. INTRODUCTION

SaveAlert is a rugged system for identifying dangerous situations and informing users of hazardous occurrences in their vicinity. This system is very similar to the Amber Alert infrastructure [1] already implemented on many operating systems; however, SaveAlert is a completely autonomous system which relies on sensor information from its users to notify of impending danger. This is a framework that goes outside of the scope of relaying notifications to provide a systematic way to integrate various sensors and cautionary thresholds that can aid in quickened awareness of crisis. The frameworks interoperability yields a seamless integration into existing software with more room to grow as system adoption increases. This architecture is inspired by the crowd-dynamics research of the CrowdWatch team at the University of Illinois, and can be easily integrated into the current CrowdWatch [2] hierarchy.

2. ARCHITECTURE

The system has three entities: the sensor, the client, and the server. The sensors can be tied directly to the server or

MobiSys'14, June 16–19, 2014, Bretton Woods, New Hampshire, USA.
ACM 978-1-4503-2793-0/14/06.
http://dx.doi.org/10.1145/2594368.2601475.

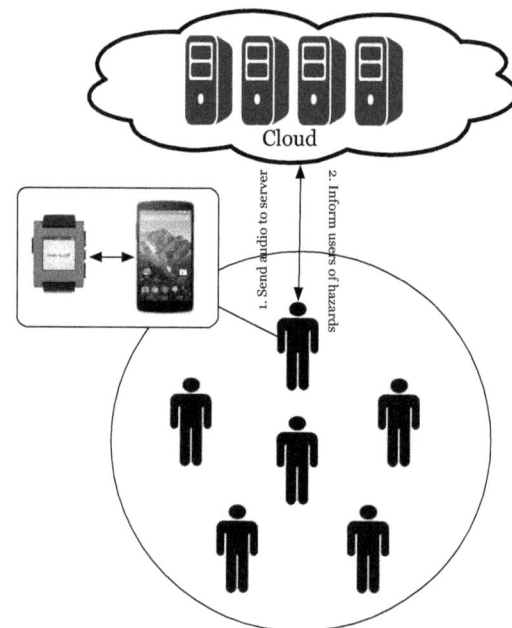

Figure 1: SaveAlert architecture.

to any of the clients, which will consequently pass on sensor information to the server. Once a sensor is deployed, it will consistently push updates to the server. A hierarchical structure as in CrowdWatch can be deployed within the crowd to ensure efficient data collection. The server will be in charge of analyzing all incoming data and making decisions based on any flags that are triggered during the analysis. The flags are pre-configured to be activated once data analysis show various parameters exceeding the threshold. This structure provides advanced customization and flexibility in danger-triggers. Once danger is detected, the server will send out a distress signal to clients within a certain geographical radius specified by the danger threshold. This will trigger a notification on the client and all its peripherals, which in the case of the demonstration, is a Pebble smartwatch. Fig. 1 shows the components of this architecture.

3. DEMONSTRATION

This demonstration approximates the full capabilities of this framework; however, we are still able to show that

SaveAlert is a powerful framework for potentially saving lives. In the demo, there are several Android smartphones running the SaveAlert service in the background. The phones' users are wearing a Pebble smartwatch [3] that can receive notifications from the phones and they are using their phones to collect audio data that will be analyzed by the server to detect any extraordinary situations (i.e., screaming). If such events are detected, the server will notify the users in the vicinity via their smartphones and then through the Pebble watches.

We will demonstrate sensor-triggered events in two ways, a simulated software sensor and a physical audio trigger. The software sensor will be a simulated sensor set up for possible real-life danger detection, i.e. a fire sensor. This simulated sensor will be implemented in code and act just like a normal sensing device by sending out updates and having a set location. It will send out scheduled distress calls and show how our framework reacts to the broadcast. Additionally, we will have one of the phones serving as an audio sensor, which will allow us to trigger its danger signal according to its pre-configured threshold. This could be accomplished with unprecedented screaming from the phone's user.

4. CONCLUSIONS

As peripherals get more adopted as an expansion to current device capabilities, their functionality could be utilized to provide a safer and danger-aware environment. SaveAlert is more than sending out notifications, it is about a rugged framework that provides an increased awareness of your surroundings. Additionally, it is highly customizable and can be used to create an interwoven system of sensor driven notifications. This opens up the framework to be capable of informing users and potentially organizations (i.e. firefighters, police) of danger even if the user involved is not capable of doing so him or herself. The demonstration is set up to show the ease of use and customizability of this system.

5. ACKNOWLEDGEMENTS

The authors would like to thank Klara Nahrstedt for supporting this project and being an integral part of the Crowd-Watch team, and also Cinda Heeren for providing Pebble smartwatches, which make this demonstration a reality.

6. REFERENCES

[1] http://www.amberalert.gov/.
[2] Robin Kravets, Hilfi Alkaff, Andrew Campbell, Karrie Karahalios, and Klara Nahrstedt. Crowdwatch: Enabling in-network crowd-sourcing. In *Proceedings of the Second ACM SIGCOMM Workshop on Mobile Cloud Computing*, MCC '13, pages 57–62, New York, NY, USA, 2013. ACM.
[3] http://www.getpebble.com/.

Demo: Recognizing Humans without Face Recognition

He Wang
University of Illinois at
Urbana-Champaign

Xuan Bao
Samsung Research, USA

Romit Roy Choudhury
University of Illinois at
Urbana-Champaign

Srihari Nelakuditi
University of South Carolina

1. INTRODUCTION

We envision augmented-reality applications in which an individual looks at other people through her camera-enabled glass (e.g., Google Glass) and obtains information about them. While face recognition would be one approach to this problem, we believe that it may not be always possible to see a person's face. Our technique is complementary to face recognition, and exploits the intuition that human motion patterns and clothing colors can together encode several bits of information. Treating this information as a "temporary fingerprint", it may be feasible to recognize an individual with reasonable consistency, while allowing her to *turn off* the fingerprint when privacy is of concern. We develop *InSight*, a system implemented using Android Galaxy smartphones and videos taken from Google Glasses. Results from real world experiments involving up to 21 people show that 8 seconds of their motion patterns together with their clothing colors can discriminate them. These results suggest that face recognition may not be the only option for recognizing humans; human diversity lends itself to sensing and could also serve as an effective identifier.

Imagine a near future where humans are carrying smartphones and wearing camera-embedded glasses, such as the Google Glass. This work intends to recognize a human by looking at him from any angle, even when his face is not visible. For instance, Alice may look at people around her in a social gathering and see the names of each individual – like a virtual badge – suitably overlaid on her Google Glass display. Where revealing names is undesirable, only a tweet message could be shared [1]. People at the airport could tweet "looking to share a cab ", recruiters in a job-fair could tweet "seeking app developers", and Alice could view each individual's tweet above their heads (Figure 1). In general, we intend to extend augmented reality [2] [3] to humans and the key challenge pertains to differentiating individuals. We explore options outside face recognition [4] [5].

Evaluations from real world experiments involving up to 21 people show that, 5 to 8 seconds of their motion patterns along with

Figure 1: An example scenario with InSight. Alice views the tweets of other people displayed on her Google Glass. The whole operation is orchestrated by the *InSight* server running in the cloud.

their clothing colors are sufficient for *InSight* to correctly recognize them in more than 80% of the cases.

On the day of the demonstration, we will invite participants to keep Android phones installed with our system in their pockets or hands to gather sensor readings. One user will take a short video of the participants with Google Glass or Android phone. Our system will process the video and sensor data to deliver the recognition results.

2. REFERENCES

[1] H. Wang, X. Bao, R. Roy Choudhury, and S. Nelakuditi, "Recognizing humans without face recognition," in *ACM HotMobile*, 2013.
[2] P. Mistry and P. Maes, "SixthSense: A wearable gestural interface," in *ACM SIGGRAPH ASIA 2009 Sketches*, 2009.
[3] D. Wagner, G. Reitmayr, A. Mulloni, T. Drummond, and D. Schmalstieg, "Real-time detection and tracking for augmented reality on mobile phones," in *Visualization and Computer Graphics, IEEE Transactions on*, 2010.
[4] M.A. Turk and A.P. Pentland, "Face recognition using eigenfaces," in *CVPR*, 1991.
[5] W. Zhao, R. Chellappa, P.J. Phillips, and A. Rosenfeld, "Face recognition: A literature survey," *ACM Computing Surveys (CSUR)*, 2003.

Demo: A Paper Keyboard for Mobile Devices

Junjue Wang, Kaichen Zhao and Xinyu Zhang
University of Wisconsin-Madison
{jwang283, kzhao25}@wisc.edu, xyzhang@ece.wisc.edu

Chunyi Peng
The Ohio State University
chunyi@cse.ohio-state.edu

ABSTRACT

A well-known bottleneck of contemporary mobile devices is the inefficient and error-prone touchscreen keyboard. We have developed UbiK, an alternative portable text-entry method that allows user to type on a piece of paper, placed on solid surfaces like wood desktop. UbiK leverages the microphones on a mobile device to accurately localize the keystrokes through fine-grained acoustic fingerprinting. We have implemented UbiK as an Android application. Our experiments demonstrate that UbiK is able to achieve above 95% of localization accuracy. In this demonstration, we will show how Ubik works with an external paper keyboard (Figure 1) for a smartphone and a 7-inch tablet. User participation will be welcome in this live demo.

Categories and Subject Descriptors

H.5.2 [**Information Interfaces and Presentation**]: User Interfaces—*Input devices and strategies*

Keywords

UbiK; mobile text-entry; paper keyboard; acoustic localization

1. INTRODUCTION

Modern digital hardware technologies keep pushing mobile devices to smaller form factors. As a result, on-screen keyboard, a daily part of life for many people, remains as an obstacle that prevents the anticipated role switching for mobile devices from information consumers to providers.

To circumvent this challenge, we have developed UbiK [1], a new approach to mobile text input that recognizes keystrokes through fine-grained localization. UbiK enables PC-like text-entry experience, by allowing users to click on solid surfaces, and then localizing the keystroke through its acoustic patterns. A keyboard outline can be drawn on the surface, or printed on a piece of paper atop. The keystrokes can be sensed using microphones that are readily available on today's mobile devices. With such simple setup, UbiK can serve as a spontaneous and efficient keyboard in a wide range of scenarios, *e.g.*, on an office desk, conference room table, or an airplane tray table.

We build UbiK as a prototype application for Android devices. Our implementation achieves real-time keystroke detection and localization without noticeable latency. UbiK is robust against minor

MobiSys'14, June 16–19, 2014, Bretton Woods, New Hampshire, USA.
ACM 978-1-4503-2793-0/14/06
http://dx.doi.org/10.1145/2594368.2601476.

Figure 1: A typical use case of UbiK.

displacement of the keyboard or mobile devices, and can rapidly converge to high accuracy after significant disturbance. Typing is not as rapid as on a mechanical keyboard but easily outperforms thumb-operated keyboards, especially for experienced users.

2. SYSTEM DEMONSTRATION

Figure 1 illustrates a typical use case of UbiK. The mobile device is placed near the printed keyboard, so as to capture the keystroke sound using its microphones. Before running UbiK, an initial setup is needed, whereby the user types all the printed keys at least once and generates "training sounds". UbiK runs a set of novel keystroke detection/localization mechanisms in the mobile device, which learn highly distinguishable acoustic features from the keystrokes, and then use such features to detect subsequent key-press events and localize the corresponding keys.

UbiK's fine-grained keystroke localization mechanism is based on the following experimental observations. First, finger clicks on the same spot exhibit highly consistent multi-path fading patterns, due to soundwave reflections cancelling or strengthening each other. Second, the frequency-domain profiles of different keystrokes reveal highly distinguishable features and can be conveniently used as location signatures. Such features exist even for keystrokes on a flat, homogeneous surface. Third, dual-microphone interface on typical mobile devices can be leveraged to improve the audio signal diversity and hence signature diversity.

In this demo, we will show the rationale and operations of UbiK from two perspectives. First, we present a real-time graphical illustration of the above three phenomenons, in consistent with [1]. Second, we will allow users to experience UbiK by running the corresponding Android application on a smartphone/tablet. A video exhibition will accompany our demo to showcase UbiK's working mechanisms and how an experienced user uses UbiK as a PC-like keyboard.

3. REFERENCES

[1] J. Wang, K. Zhao, X. Zhang, and C. Peng, "Ubiquitous Keyboard for Small Mobile Devices: Harnessing Multipath Fading for Fine-Grained Keystroke Localization," in *Proc. of ACM MobiSys*, 2014.

Demo: FaceBlock: Privacy-Aware Pictures for Google Glass

Roberto Yus[1], Primal Pappachan[2], Prajit Kumar Das[2],
Eduardo Mena[1], Anupam Joshi[2], Tim Finin[2]

University of Zaragoza, Spain[1], {ryus,emena}@unizar.es
University of Maryland, Baltimore County, USA[2], {primal1,prajit1,joshi,finin}@umbc.edu

Categories and Subject Descriptors

K.4.1 [**Public Policy Issues**]: Privacy

Keywords

Google Glass, privacy-aware pictures, policy sharing

1. INTRODUCTION

Wearable technology is changing the human-computer interaction paradigm by improving the user experience. For example, *eyewear* technology, such as Google Glass, is opening a new world of possibilities. One of the best capabilities of such devices is that they allow spontaneous and effortless photo taking. Instead of pulling out your camera, turning it on, aiming, taking a picture and putting it away, Google Glass makes it as easy as saying "Okay Glass, take a picture".

However, their strength has also become controversial: people worry that their pictures could be taken without their knowledge or consent, violating their privacy. These privacy concerns are not new and have existed since camera technology became accessible to everyone. But, Google Glass makes it difficult to know when someone is taking a picture of you. Resorting to drastic measures, like banning their use in public places, is not a good solution. We demonstrate FaceBlock[1], which protects the privacy rights of individuals by allowing them to choose whether or not to be included in pictures taken with Glass (see [1] for more information).

Our approach allows a user's mobile device to share privacy policies with nearby Glass devices using a P2P communication channel (our prototype uses Bluetooth). Along with the policy, users share information that helps identify them in a picture. When the Google Glass takes a picture the system recognizes faces on it, checks policies it has received, and obscures faces as necessary. In our prototype, users share their *eigenface* [2] as a way to identify them on the pictures. An eigenface is an "encoded" picture of a face

[1]Work supported by CICYT TIN2010-21387-C02-02, DGA-FSE, NSF 0910838 and MURI FA9550-08-1-0265.

MobiSys '14 Bretton Woods, NH, USA
ACM 978-1-4503-2793-0/14/06.
http://dx.doi.org/10.1145/2594368.2601473.

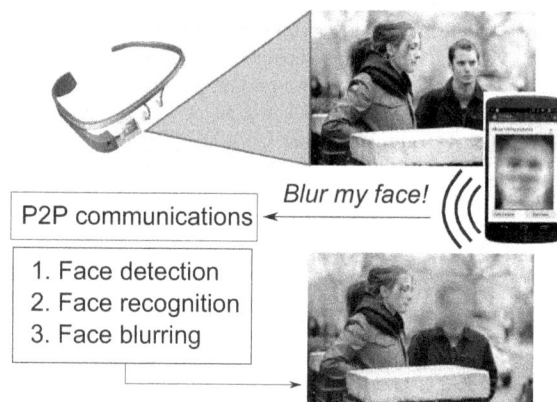

Figure 1: **High-level architecture of our system**

that showing its deviations with respect to a "mean face", which is composed of hundred of faces (Figure 1 shows an example). Other ways of recognizing people can also be used in such a system system, like unique clothes [3]. The use of a policy language grounded in semantic descriptions will enable context-aware constraints (e.g., "blur my picture except when I am at the office").

2. DEMO SETUP

The demo setup includes our prototype, a Google Glass, and two smart-phones. We will invite people to take privacy-aware pictures with FaceBlock. Figure 1 shows a possible scenario. Joel is using his Google Glass to take pictures of his girlfriend Clementine. Patrick is walking by and may be captured in Joel's picture. Patrick has FaceBlock on his smartphone and whenever it detects a Google Glass device, it will create a Bluetooth connection and shares Patrick's policy ("blur my face in pictures from strangers") and his face identifier (eigenface). Joel, who is also using FaceBlock, receives this information from Patrick and every time that Joel takes a picture, FaceBlock analyzes it and obscures Patrick's face if detected.

3. REFERENCES

[1] http://face-block.me.
[2] M. Turk and A. Pentland. Eigenfaces for recognition. *Journal of cognitive neuroscience*, 3(1):71–86, 1991.
[3] H. Wang, X. Bao, R. R. Choudhury, and S. Nelakuditi. Insight: Recognizing humans without face recognition. HotMobile'13.

Poster: A Robust Vehicular Accident Detection System using Inexpensive Portable Devices

Nicholas Capurso, Eric Elsken, Donnell Payne, Liran Ma
Computer Science Department
Texas Christian University
Fort Worth, TX 76129, USA
{Nick.Capurso, Eric.Elsken, D.Payne, L.Ma}@tcu.edu

In the event of a vehicular accident, there are many scenarios in which the occupants become incapacitated and unable to call for assistance. Currently, there exist systems such as OnStar [1] that provides accident detection and roadside assistance services. However, the cost of these proprietary systems and their availability for all vehicular models limit their use.

We propose an inexpensive and robust system that provides accurate accident detection and emergency responder notification as our senior capstone project at Texas Christian University. The proposed system contains three primary components: a smartphone, a single-on-board computer (the Raspberry Pi [2]), and Texas Instruments SensorTags [3] as shown in Figure 1.

Figure 1: System components.

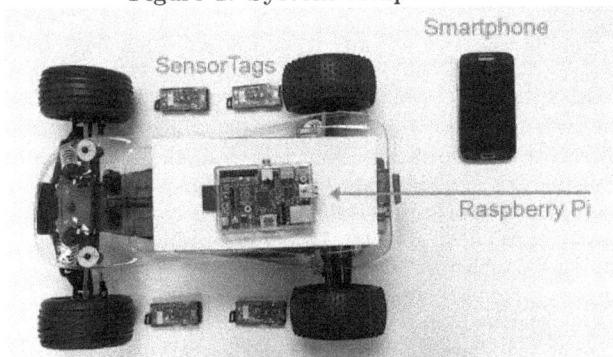

The smartphone provides a means for accident detection utilizing its own sensors and emergency notification. To be specific, we develop a smartphone application that continuously monitors the smartphone's gyroscope and linear accelerometer sensors. The gyroscope measures a change in the device's orientation and is used to detect accidents where a vehicle has a rapid and significant change in orientation, such as in a rollover. The linear accelerometer is a software-based sensor that functions as a standard accelerometer that excludes gravity and is used to detect forceful accidents, such as head-on collisions. Our prototype smartphone, the Samsung Galaxy S4 [4], runs Android 4.3 Jelly Bean (API 18).

The Raspberry Pi is also responsible for determining accidents based on multiple SensorTags' sensor readings so as to provide redundancy. The introduction of the Raspberry Pi and SensorTags is due to the following two reasons: i) Sensor readings on the smartphone alone may cause an unacceptable number of high false alarms; ii) The addition of readings from SensorTags can improve the accuracy. Yet, direct wireless communication between the SensorTags and the smartphone would quickly drain the smartphone's battery. Hence, the Raspberry Pi is employed as an on-board agent that communicates with the SensorTags. The Raspberry Pi runs the same accident detection algorithm as on the smartphone.

The detection algorithm compares accelerometer and gyroscope vector magnitudes as well as the individual vector components against multiple predetermined thresholds. These threshold values are obtained as a result of testing our prototype system in different driving situations. When an accident is detected by either party, it attempts to confirm the accident has occurred from the other party via a Bluetooth connection. If an accident is confirmed, the smartphone has the ability to contact emergency responders. Both the smartphone and the Raspberry Pi keep recent sensor readings in memory and will output them to a file in the event of an accident so they may be analyzed at a later time.

Currently, we have implemented our accident detection algorithm on the smartphone and are working on optimizing our threshold values and improving the detection algorithm to take other factors into consideration, such as noise. Once this is completed, we will begin extensive testing of the combined system.

MobiSys'14, June 16–19, 2014, Bretton Woods, New Hampshire, USA.
ACM 978-1-4503-2793-0/14/06.
http://dx.doi.org/10.1145/2594368.2601456 .

1. REFERENCES

[1] O. Corporation. OnStar Official Website. http://www.onstar.com.

[2] R. P. Foundation. Raspberry Pi Official Website. http://www.raspberrypi.org/.

[3] T. Instruments. Texas Instruments SensorTag CC2541 Product Information. http://www.ti.com/tool/cc2541dk-sensor.

[4] Samsung. The Galaxy S4 Smartphone Specifications. http://www.samsung.com/global/microsite/galaxys4/index.html.

Poster: SoftOffload: A Programmable Approach Toward Collaborative Mobile Traffic Offloading

Aaron Yi Ding§, Jon Crowcroft†, Sasu Tarkoma§

§University of Helsinki, Helsinki, Finland　　　　　†University of Cambridge, Cambridge, UK

{aaron.ding , sasu.tarkoma}@cs.helsinki.fi; jon.crowcroft@cl.cam.ac.uk

Categories and Subject Descriptors

C.2.1 [**Network Architecture and Design**]: Network communications

Keywords

Software Defined Networking; Mobile Data Offloading

ABSTRACT

The fast increase of mobile traffic from smartphone-like devices has created a huge pressure for the cellular operators to manage the network infrastructure and resources. Offloading the mobile traffic to alternative networks such as WiFi is sought as a promising direction to solve this problem cost-effectively. According to our study and experimental findings [1], existing research proposals are lack of concern for the complexity of network deployment and device limitations, which impedes the solution deployment. To overcome such challenge, we propose SoftOffload, a programmable framework for collaborative mobile traffic offloading. SoftOffload takes the advantage of software defined networking (SDN) paradigm in terms of openness and extensibility. We have implemented the first prototype utilising the open source Floodlight platform [2].

1. DESIGN AND IMPLEMENTATION

The design principle of SoftOffload is to improve the openness and deployability by adopting the open standard software defined solutions. As illustrated in Figure 1, the key elements include the SDN-based SoftOffload controller and the SoftOffload local agents. The central SoftOffload controller is built on top of the open source Floodlight platform on which we integrate our offloading algorithm and controlling logic [1] as an extension module to guide the mobile traffic offloading. The SoftOffload local agents utilise the modular Click router [3] where we implement a set of monitoring and sampling elements to assist the offloading procedure.

MobiSys '14, Bretton Woods, NH, USA
ACM 978-1-4503-2793-0/14/06.
http://dx.doi.org/10.1145/2594368.2601462.

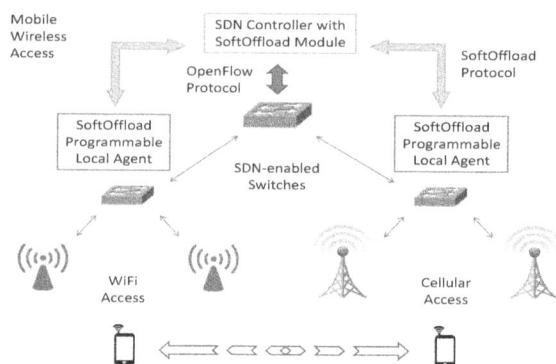

Figure 1: SoftOffload Architecture

SoftOffload aims at improving the offloading efficiency and the system responsiveness to the dynamic changes in a wireless mobile environment. The hierarchical design makes the system scalable by distributing the offloading functionality between the central controller and the local agents. This function splitting reduces the redundant signalling and the processing overhead comparing to the centralised approach. SoftOffload uses the OpenFlow protocol to manage the SDN-enabled switches and adopts our customised protocol to communicate with the local agents. In our testing environment, we utilise commodity hardware with Open vSwitch installation to enable OpenFlow support.

The beauty of SoftOffload comes from its open and programmable design which improves the extensibility and deployability. SoftOffload facilitates the adding of new extensions such as traffic inspecting and rate shaping for various access environment with different requirements. Our open source oriented approach combined with standardised SDN solutions can bring community contributions to drive the SoftOffload development further. We are planning to release the project package after thorough testing and evaluation.

2. REFERENCES

[1] A. Y. Ding, B. Han, Y. Xiao, P. Hui, A. Srinivasan, M. Kojo, and S. Tarkoma. Enabling Energy-Aware Collaborative Mobile Data Offloading for Smartphones. In *Proceedings of IEEE SECON 2013*.

[2] Floodlight OpenFlow Controller: http://www.projectfloodlight.org/

[3] Project Click: http://read.cs.ucla.edu/click/

Poster: Semi-automatic Monitoring Vital Parameters of Mobile Users

Zhanwei Du, Yongjian Yang, Wu Liao, Linlu Liu, Lipeng Liu
College of Computer Science and Technology
Jilin University, Changhun 130012
zwdu@acm.org, yyj@jlu.edu.cn, {lwliaowu, liulinlu91, peng_2516}@163.com

Categories and Subject Descriptors

H.3.4 [Systems and Software]: Distrbuted Systems

Keywords

Body area network, Ontology model, Mobile

1. INTRODUCTION

Body area network(BAN) technology, as an emerging technology, has a very short history. Initial applications of BANs are expected to appear primarily in the healthcare domain, especially for continuous monitoring and logging vital parameters of patients suffering from chronic diseases such as diabetes, asthma and heart attacks. However, many hospitals acquire electronic patient records systems in these years, with Electronic health record (EHR), which is a systematic collection of electronic health information about an individual patient.

While the BAN technology is still in its primitive stage it is being widely researched and once adopted. Considering the incomplete utilization of electronic health record lost in most BAN systems, we propose a technique to Semi-automatic monitor human body using wearable biosensors, with the help of ontology model for EHR knowledge. The system MobiEHR has some distinctive features different from the existing systems [1, 2]: The continuously information will be transmitted wirelessly to users' mobile phone first. Then this phone will instantly transmit all information in real or delayed time to the backend system. In the backend system, every user's health status is monitored and computed by EHR ontology model. If an emergency is detected, the system will immediately inform the patients' family and paramedic through the computer system by sending appropriate messages or alarms.

2. APPROACH

The design of the system, called MobiEHR, aims at introducing new mobile value-added services in the area of mobile

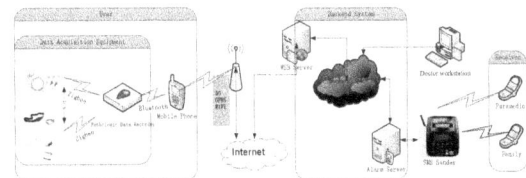

Figure 1: The architecture of MobiEHR.

healthcare, based on users' electronic health record. This is achieved by the integration of wearable biosensors and EHR ontology model. The architecture is described in Figure 1.

The EHR ontology model is so-called "semi-automatic", established and used to track users' health status, through different kinds of vital signs. Besides, the frequency of monitoring is adjustable. Once some emergencies are detected, the system will speed up the frequency and send the alarm messages to the doctors in first-aid center. Finally the doctors decided whether this alarm is true.

The system also contains smartphones with Android operating system. These biosensors form a self-organization network and continuously measure and transmit vital constants to backend system through mobile phone. These data allows on the other side the introduction of new value-added services in the areas of diagnostic, remote assistance, and so on. Furthermore, the MobiEHR system tries sparse coding to reduce the data size and support the fast and reliable application of remote assistance in case of accidents by "One-button Call" function to send reliable position data to the first-aid center.

3. ACKNOWLEDGMENTS

This work was supported by National Natural Science Foundation of China 61272412, Ph.D. Programs Foundation of Ministry of Education of China 20120061110044, Jilin province science and technology development plan item 20120303.

4. REFERENCES

[1] C. Wang, Q. Wang, and S. Shi. A distributed wireless body area network for medical supervision. In *Instrumentation and Measurement Technology Conference (I2MTC), 2012 IEEE International*, pages 2612–2616. IEEE, 2012.

[2] M. R. Yuce. Implementation of wireless body area networks for healthcare systems. *Sensors and Actuators A: Physical*, 162(1):116–129, 2010.

Poster: Motivating an Inter-networking Architecture for WSN/IoT

Laura Marie Feeney
Swedish Institute of Computer Science
http://www.sics.se/~lmfeeney

1. INTER-NETWORK INTERFERENCE

Growing commercial development of WSN/WBAN/IoT solutions will eventually lead to their ubiquitous deployment. Inevitably, there will be environments that contain many *independent, co-located networks* with overlapping areas of wireless coverage. Examples of high density scenarios include transit stations and urban housing.

Because these various networks and applications will be owned by different people and because they mostly operate in ISM bands, there is no trusted authority that can coordinate their activity. Cross-technology interference has been widely studied, e.g. between IEEE 802.11 and IEEE 802.15.4, but very little work has addressed inter-network interference between co-located WSNs using the same communication technology. However, the potentially large number of co-located networks and fairly small number of channels suggests that this will not be an unusual situation.

The risk of external frames being received and misinterpreted as local frames is studied in [2], which emphasized the need for authentication on all frames. Interference between co-located IEEE 802.15.4 PANs is demonstrated in [3]. This work reflects a similar interest in timing and interference interactions between networks that can receive and identify, but not decrypt, each other's frames.

The diversity of IEEE 802.15.4-based WSN protocols is the motivating use case. These protocols use the same PHY/MAC in very different ways, from pure unslotted CSMA to the scheduled mesh in WirelessHART. Such significant differences in channel access mechanisms can lead to adverse interactions between independent networks, which will not be able to explicitly negotiate (or even infer) how to share the channel efficiently.

Thus the long-term goal of this work-in-progress is to motivate the development of architecture and design principles that can mitigate problems of inter-network interference.

As a specific example, consider two kinds of asynchronous MAC layers. Figure 1 shows interactions between networks using an X-MAC [1] type protocol (i.e. sender strobes, receivers periodically listen) and an RI-MAC [4] type protocol

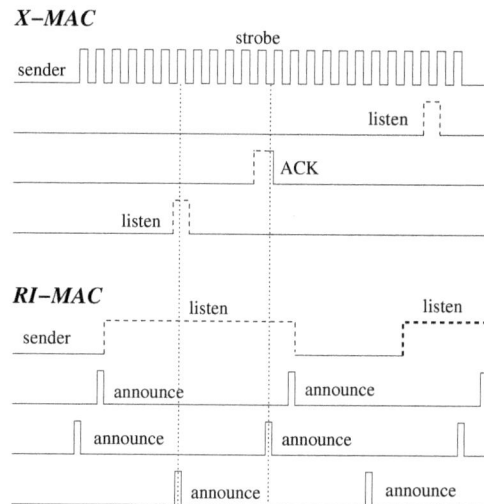

Figure 1: Interaction between X-MAC and RI-MAC (there are many variations of both protocols, the basic structure is shown). Dotted lines show conflicts.

(i.e. sender listens, receivers periodically strobe). The figure shows two specific collision scenarios in this case. If the networks have the same period, the listen intervals of X-MAC nodes and the RI-MAC node announcements should be de-synchronized, as should correlated data transmissions. Mechanisms providing this functionality would increase resilience in the presence of co-located networks.

2. REFERENCES

[1] M. Buettner, G. V. Yee, E. Anderson, and R. Han. X-MAC: a short preamble mac protocol for duty-cycled wireless sensor networks. In *4th ACM Conf on Embedded Networked Sensor Systems (SenSys)*, 2006.

[2] L. M. Feeney. Exploring semantic interference in heterogenous sensor networks. In *1st ACM Workshop on Heterogeneous Sensor and Actor Networks*, 2008.

[3] N. Nordin and F. Dressler. Effects and implications of beacon collisions in co-located IEEE 802.15. 4 networks. In *IEEE Vehicular Technology Conf (VTC Fall)*, 2012.

[4] Y. Sun, O. Gurewitz, and D. B. Johnson. RI-MAC: A receiver-initiated asynchronous duty cycle MAC protocol for dynamic traffic loads in wireless sensor networks. In *6th ACM Conf on Embedded Network Sensor Systems (SenSys)*, 2008.

MobiSys'14, June 16–19, 2014, Bretton Woods, New Hampshire, USA.
ACM 978-1-4503-2793-0/14/06.
http://dx.doi.org/10.1145/2594368.2601449.

Poster: A Virtual Sensing Framework for Mobile Phones

Jon C. Hammer, Tingxin Yan

Dept. of Computer Science and Engineering, University of Arkansas

{jhammer, tingxiny}@uark.edu

Categories and Subject Descriptors

C.5.3 [**Computer System Implementation**]: Microcomputers—*Portable devices*

Keywords

Mobile devices; Virtual Sensor; Sensing Framework; Behavior Inference

1. VIRTUAL SENSING FOR MOBILE PHONES

Much research has been done regarding the use of hardware sensors in smartphones, leading to the emergence of mobile sensing systems such as activity recognition, localization, and proximity sensing [2]. Although hardware sensors provide informative contextual information, continuous sensing and inference could incur prohibitive energy costs.

We argue that besides hardware sensors, there exist many *virtual* sensors on mobile phones that are continuously available and inexpensive to query from the operating system and services. Examples include screen status, mobile app usage, app notifications, and responses to notifications. Our core observation is that events triggered by the operating system or services provide continuous data streams that indicate user contexts. For example, the frequency and duration of screen sessions indicates how busy a mobile user is, and the frequency of application notification arrivals and departures indicates how mobile users communicate with others.

This work presents a virtual sensing framework by exploiting operating system events for energy efficient context inference. Specifically, we investigate features that can be extracted from virtual sensors and used to infer the *logical status* of mobile users, such as isWorking, isSocial, and isStressful. The preliminary results indicate promising performance and suggest several potential applications.

2. DESIGN AND IMPLEMENTATION

Our framework acts as a middleware between the OS and applications, as shown in Figure 1. The framework provides three core functionalities with negligible energy cost: (1) It continuously logs operating system events and abstracts them as *data probes*, and provides APIs to serve applications. (2) It extracts descriptive features from data probes to enable context inference. (3) It enables various applications by using the context inference results.

MobiSys'14, June 16–19, 2014, Bretton Woods, New Hampshire, USA.
ACM 978-1-4503-2793-0/14/06.
http://dx.doi.org/10.1145/2594368.2601457.

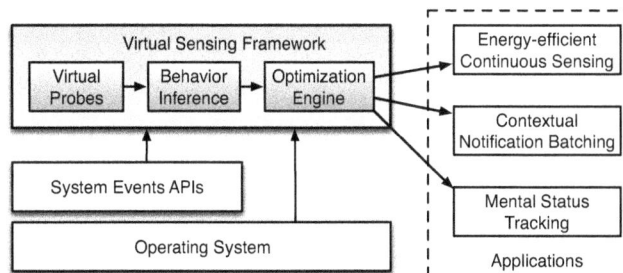

Figure 1: The system architecture of the proposed virtual sensing framework.

As a preliminary work, we present four virtual probes (summarized in Figure 2) for logical status inference. Our observations indicate strong correlation between many OS events and the logical status of mobile users, such as screen status and isWorking. Inspired by such observations, we designed a set of descriptive features for logical status inference. For example, queueing parameters, such as inter-arrival time and service rate, are often good features to classify isWorking and isSocial. Furthermore, connected network information, such as BSSID, would be useful for augmenting the isWorking prediction, as location is likely to be an important factor in such a classification.

Virtual Probes	Features	Logical Status
App Notification	Arrival/Departure Rate, # Responses, App Owners	IsWorking, IsSocial, IsStressful
Screen State	Duration, Frequency, App Sequence	IsWorking, IsStressful
Foreground Activity	App category, App Sequence, Trigger App, Trigger Method.	IsWorking, IsSocial, IsHappy
Network Connection	Connection ID, Session Duration	Logical Location

Figure 2: Virtual probes and their features in the proposed virtual sensing framework.

We implemented our virtual sensing framework for unmodified Android devices, inspired by the Funf Open Sensing Framework [1]. Our measurement results indicate that the continuous usage of our framework consumes 0.5% of total battery, an imperceptible amount for mobile users. Several applications can be enabled using our framework, including controlling hardware sensors for energy-efficient continuous sensing, mobile system performance optimization such as notification batching, and efficient logical status tracking such as isWorking, isSocial, and isStressful.

3. REFERENCES

[1] N. Aharony, W. Pan, C. Ip, I. Khayal, and A. Pentland. The social fMRI: measuring, understanding, and designing social mechanisms in the real world. In *Ubicomp*, 2011.
[2] N. D. Lane, E. Miluzzo, H. Lu, D. Peebles, T. Choudhury, and A. T. Campbell. A survey of mobile phone sensing. *IEEE Communications Magazine*, 2010.

Poster: M-SEven: Monitoring Smoking Event by Considering Time Sequence Information via iPhone M7 API

Bo-Jhang Ho and Mani B. Srivastava
Networked and Embedded System Lab
University of California, Los Angeles
{bojhang, mbs}@ucla.edu

1. INTRODUCTION

Smartphones are equipped with various sensors that provide rich context information. By leveraging these sensors, several interesting and practical applications have emerged. Accelerometer data has been used, for example, to detect transportation [3], exercise activities [2], etc. A typical approach is to classify activity directly based on features extracted from raw sensing data. Cheng *et. al.* implemented a different approach by using two-stage classification: the system first detects several sub-behaviors, and uses the combination of attributes to infer higher-level behaviors. Built upon this approach, we foucus on exploring the *time sequence* of activities, which is an underexplored, yet natural and information-rich indicator. In this work, we explore this time sequence concept through detection of smoking events.

In the public area, smoking is usually prohibited. Thus, smokers normally go to outdoor areas with fewer passerbys to smoke. Instead of detecting bio-signals through wearable sensors [1], we leverage movement patterns as indicators; smokers normally start from a stationary state (either the phone is on the desk or in their pocket), walk to the smoking spot which is usually outdoors, stand there for several minutes, then go back to their working area and resume stationary state. Although there are various activities with similar patterns that might cause false positives, e.g., buying lunch from an outdoor food truck, we believe there are subtleties in the sensor data to distinguish them apart, e.g. differences between standing casually (smoking), versus moving periodically when waiting in line (food truck). In this work we demonstrate the detection of the smoking movement pattern through data collected from the primary phone of one smoker for two days.

2. METHODOLOGY AND RESULT

We use iPhone 5S to collect the data from people's daily activities. The system collects 1) location information and 2) activities by M7 API. We use coordination accuracy to distinguish indoor from outdoor. An error larger than 20

MobiSys'14, June 16–19, 2014, Bretton Woods, New Hampshire, USA.
ACM 978-1-4503-2793-0/14/06.
http://dx.doi.org/10.1145/2594368.2601451.

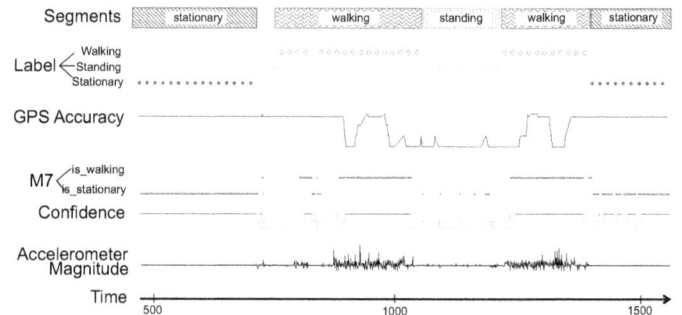

Figure 1: One example of how our system detects the smoking event. We put accelerometer data for your reference only.

meters is considered an indoor activity in our experiment. By querying M7 API we can get a list of records as activity history. Each activity record has attributes in a combination of the four states: *is_stationary*, *is_walking*, *is_running* and *is_driving*, along with start/end time and three-level confidence. The system overview is presented in Fig. 1. Building on top of these 4 low-level states, we segment into 3 different labels: *stationary*, *standing* and *walking*. We use a rule-based approach to get labels, that is to set thresholds to separate them. In our approach we consider high-confidence records before lower ones. Since there might be outliers, a sliding window filter based on majority voting is applied. Then we combine the same labels into one segment. If the system detects 5 continuous segments as follows: stationary => walking => 2-to-7-minute-outdoor standing => walking => stationary, such a pattern indicates a smoking behavior. Our system successfully detects 10 out of 12 events with no false alarms throughout working hours (8am-6pm).

3. REFERENCES

[1] A. A. Ali, S. M. Hossain, K. Hovsepian, M. M. Rahman, K. Plarre, and S. Kumar. mpuff: Automated detection of cigarette smoking puffs from respiration measurements. IPSN '12. ACM, 2012.

[2] H.-T. Cheng, F.-T. Sun, M. Griss, P. Davis, J. Li, and D. You. Nuactiv: Recognizing unseen new activities using semantic attribute-based learning. MobiSys '13. ACM, 2013.

[3] S. Hemminki, P. Nurmi, and S. Tarkoma. Accelerometer-based transportation mode detection on smartphones. SenSys '13. ACM, 2013.

Poster: Retro: An Automated, Application-Layer Record and Replay for Android

Taeyeon Ki, Satyaditya Munipalle, Karthik Dantu, Steven Y. Ko, Lukasz Ziarek
Department of Computer Science and Engineering
University at Buffalo, The State University of New York
{tki, satyadit, kdantu, stevko, lziarek}@buffalo.edu

Extended Abstract

Today's mobile applications operate in a diverse set of environments, where it is difficult for a developer to know beforehand what conditions his or her application will be put under. For example, once deployed on an online application store, an application can be downloaded on different types of hardware, ranging from budget smartphones to high-end tablets. In addition, network conditions can vary widely from Wi-Fi to 3G to 4G. Mobile applications also need to co-exist with other applications that compete for resources at different times.

Due to this diverse set of operating conditions, it is difficult to understand what problems are occurring in the wild for mobile applications. Moreover, it is even more difficult to reproduce problems in a lab environment where developers can debug the problems. Some platforms support bug reports and stack traces, but they are inadequate in scenarios when operating conditions and inputs are not consistent.

To address these issues, we propose Retro, an automated, application-layer record and replay system for Android. Unlike previous record and replay systems, Retro aims to support mobile Android applications with three features.

First, Retro provides an automated instrumentation framework that transforms a regular Android application into a traceable application. This means that Retro does not require any change in the Android platform; thus, it enables developers to distribute instrumented applications via online application stores. Through the instrumentation, Retro records application-layer events such as click events, sensor readings, method calls, and return values. In order to reduce the overhead of logging, Retro also uses a selective logging mechanism that decides which event types to log at runtime.

Second, Retro provides a replayer that a developer can use in a lab environment to faithfully replay a recorded run. To maximize the ease of use, Retro seamlessly integrates this replay functionality into Android's existing development workflow by adding the replayer into the Android platform. This means that a developer can replay using a regular phone as

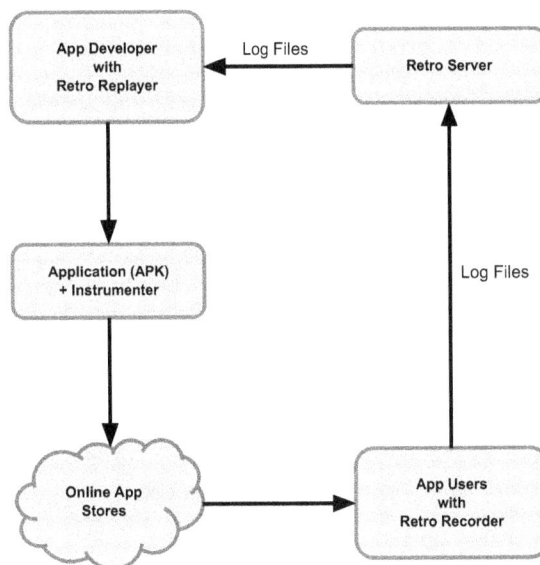

Figure 1: Overview of Retro

well as an emulator. Also, Retro provides a VCR-like interface for replaying that is capable of forwarding and rewinding executions.

Third, Retro examines Android-specific issues in enabling record and replay and incorporates design choices that are tailored towards Android. The goal for doing this is efficiency and faithfulness; by examining Android-specific issues, Retro can provide efficient recording and replaying functionalities as well as faithfulness in replaying.

Categories and Subject Descriptors

D.2.5 [**Software Engineering**]: Testing and Debugging—*Tracing*

Keywords

Record&Replay; Debugging; Android apps

Acknowledgments

We thank Aveek Karmakar for discussions and supports during Retro development. This work was supported in part by funding from National Science Foundation Awards, CNS-1350883 (CAREER) and CNS-1205656.

MobiSys'14, June 16–19, 2014, Bretton Woods, New Hampshire, USA.
ACM 978-1-4503-2793-0/14/06.
http://dx.doi.org/10.1145/2594368.2601453.

Poster: Enabling Computational Jewelry for mHealth Applications

Andres Molina-Markham
Dartmouth College

Ronald A. Peterson
Dartmouth College

Joseph Skinner
Dartmouth College

Ryan J. Halter
Dartmouth College

Jacob Sorber
Clemson University

David Kotz
Dartmouth College

Many of the most compelling mHealth applications are designed to enable long-term health monitoring for outpatients with chronic medical conditions, for individuals seeking to change behavior, for physicians seeking to quantify and detect behavioral aberrations for early diagnosis, for home-care providers needing to track movements of elders under their care in order to respond quickly to emergencies, or for athletes monitoring their physiology to improve performance. Developing BAHN applications that require consistent presence and strong security, without depending on a smartphone or without building lots of computation/communication resources into every BAHN device presents a critical challenge for the wide-spread adoption of mHealth technologies. The smartphone is not always with its user [1]: many people set aside their phone while at home or while driving, exercising, or bathing. According to a Pew study, a third of smartphones have been lost or stolen [2]! When the smartphone is not present, the BAHN could lose its foundation; valuable data could be lost, critical events may go unrecognized. Second, smartphones have limited means to authenticate or identify the person holding them; if the phone has been lost or stolen, an app could inappropriately disclose personal health information about the phone's owner. Third, smartphones are general-purpose devices, not dedicated to health-related applications; it is thus more difficult to evaluate the safety and security of a system when it is sharing resources with other applications.

For these reasons, we are developing wearable devices as the foundation for a consistently present and highly available body-area mHealth network. Our vision is that a small device, such as a bracelet or pendant, will provide the availability and reliability properties essential for successful body-area mHealth networks. We call this class of device *computational jewelry*, and expect it will be the next frontier of mobile systems.

MobiSys'14, June 16–19, 2014, Bretton Woods, New Hampshire, USA.
ACM 978-1-4503-2793-0/14/06.
http://dx.doi.org/10.1145/2594368.2601454.

We prototyped our first piece of computational jewelry, which we call *amulet*, to enable our previously proposed vision [3]. It runs applications that may collect sensor data from built-in sensors or from other devices, analyze and log the data, queue information for later upload, and interact with the wearer. Independent developers can develop applications that can be vetted and installed on an amulet.

We achieve our goal of allowing applications to run on a small ultra-low-power device by means of (1) a multiprocessor hardware architecture and (2) an event-driven software architecture that allows applications to survive routine processor shutdowns. (1) We use a two-processor architecture: an application processor capable of performing computationally intensive tasks and a coprocessor that manages radio communications and internal sensors (in our prototype: accelerometer, gyroscope, magnetometer, temperature sensor, light sensor, and microphone). To save power the application processor is powered off most of the time, while the coprocessor handles all real-time device interactions. Minutes or hours of sensor data and other messages from the coprocessor are staged in queues, stored in shared Ferroelectric RAM, until it is necessary to boot the application processor. (2) Most mHealth applications are reactive, running only when an event of interest occurs. Our architecture provides a state-machine event-driven programming model. Programmers define an application as a finite-state machine and a set of functions to handle events of interest. Our architecture allows applications to identify computational state that should be retained between events. Explicitly managing program state (rather than implicitly managing state in a thread's run-time stack) allows our run-time system to efficiently save application state to persistent memory and power down the main processor, with no harm to applications. This approach dramatically extends battery life, increasing overall application availability.

Prototype Implementation

Key goals of our previously proposed vision [3] were to create a system that is consistently present and highly available, while providing a flexible application programming model. To achieve consistent presence, an amulet must be able to be implemented in a small package so it will have a wearable form factor. Therefore, the battery must be small: e.g., a typical 150 mAh battery requires only 1.71 cm^3. To achieve high availability, despite a tiny battery, an amulet must be extremely power efficient so it can function for several days. To achieve independence from the smartphone, for interesting applications, an amulet must be capable of performing digital signal processing, cryptographic operations, and, sensor-data classification. Thus, our approach involves a dual-processor design: an ultra-low-power processor tends to communications and sensing (I/O coprocessor), and a more-capable application processor runs applications. Although this approach is not uncommon, our hardware-software architecture is specifically designed to shut down the application processor – not just put it to sleep – most of the time. This approach drives another requirement: the application processor (and its OS) must transition quickly from off mode to active mode. Our approach drives two requirements: first, applications must be able to survive routine system reboots; second, the application processor must be able to return from off state to active state, load its operating system, and reload an application extremely fast.[1] Our architecture achieves these requirements by providing an event-driven programming model. This approach works well for mHealth applications, many of which are idle most of the time, waiting for something to happen.

Amulet applications are defined as finite-state machines (FSMs) with memory. Thus, each application is defined as a set of *states*, a small set of *variables*, and a set of *event handlers* by which the application responds to events of interest. When an event is delivered to the application, the system calls the appropriate handler function and transitions the application to the designated next state. The non-blocking handler is a function that may consume data arriving with the event, update application variable(s), or send events to system services (or to itself), in any combination. The application subscribes to certain events when it is initialized, and can add or adjust subscriptions as part of the action in an event handler. This approach makes application state explicit; because handlers run to completion,[2] there are no threads with stack-based state information to preserve between events, let alone across processor reboots. Application code and variables are kept in persistent storage, as is a record of the current state of each application; thus, when the event queue becomes empty, the application processor simply shuts off.

The application processor remains off until the I/O coprocessor wakes it up. On request, the I/O coprocessor produces messages to carry the output from internal sensors (e.g., temperature, accelerometer), an input from the wearer (e.g., a button press), or the reception of a network message from an external mHealth device. The coprocessor inserts each new message into the interprocessor message queue; the memory controller uses a set of queue-management policies to determine when to wake the application processor (examples include the insertion of a high-priority message or the queue being near full). While the application processor is awake, it draws messages from the interprocessor queue and copies it into a new event message inserted into its internal event queue.

We implemented the following OS services and managers in C: Sensor Manager, Actuator Manager, Storage Manager, Network Manager, Interprocessor Communication Manager and Authorization Manager. Each consist of two parts, an event-driven application – which we implemented in a similar way to applications – and a set of routines that have access to lower level drivers. The event-driven part allows these managers to receive and process event messages. The set of routines with low level access are not available to applications. We implemented the I/O coprocessor as a single finite state machine with timers and hardware interrupts. We also implemented three devices to simulate a heart-rate monitor, a galvanic skin response sensor, and a nicotine sensor that communicate via ANT with our prototype. The three devices are development boards that use the same ANT SoC as in our prototype (Nordic Semi nRF51422). We implemented the message queue using an ultra-low-power MCU with FRAM (MSP430). FRAM offers persistent storage without power, and it is one hundred times faster than flash. On writes FRAM uses 250 times less power than flash ($\approx \mu A$ at 12kB/s). The FRAM MCU buffers data until one of two conditions are met: (i) the FRAM is full, or (ii) the I/O coprocessor observes an event that must wake up the application processor. This may happen when an application subscribes to a particular data value from a sensor.

Our first wearable prototype is 3.7×3.5 cm. We optimized it for development and not yet for size. Our programming model allows multiple independently-developed applications to run simultaneously and efficiently. Our current prototype provides 14 to 26 hours of battery life with a 150mAh battery when running two mHealth applications (for stress management and smoking cessation) with realistic workloads. For news about the Amulet project, visit amulet-project.org and 'follow' our blog.

Acknowledgements

We thank Kevin Freeman, Bhargav Golla, Emily Greene, Hilary Johnson, Adam Labrie, Tim Pierson, and Tianlong Yun for their participation in this project. This research results from a research program at the Institute for Security, Technology, and Society, supported by the National Science Foundation under award numbers CNS-1314281, CNS-1314342, and TC-0910842, and by the Department of Health and Human Services (SHARP program) under award number 90TR0003-01. The views and conclusions contained in this document are those of the authors and should not be interpreted as necessarily representing the official policies, either expressed or implied, of the sponsors.

1. REFERENCES

[1] A. K. Dey, K. Wac, D. Ferreira, K. Tassini, J. H. Hong, and J. Ramos. Getting closer: an empirical investigation of the proximity of user to their smart phones. In *Proceedings of the International Conference on Ubiquitous Computing (UbiComp)*, pages 163–172, Sept. 2011. DOI 10.1145/2030112.2030135.

[2] K. Hill. Sorry, smartphone owners, but you're more likely to have your privacy invaded. Forbes, Sept. 2012. Online at http://tinyurl.com/hill-smartphone.

[3] J. Sorber, M. Shin, R. Peterson, C. Cornelius, S. Mare, A. Prasad, Z. Marois, E. Smithayer, and D. Kotz. An Amulet for trustworthy wearable mHealth. In *Proceedings of the Workshop on Mobile Computing Systems and Applications (HotMobile)*, Feb. 2012. DOI 10.1145/2162081.2162092.

---

[1]In the applications we consider, an application may execute a task every few seconds and the task may only require a few milliseconds to complete.

[2]A supervisor enforces a timeout to prevent handlers from blocking or running too long.

Poster: Scalable Evaluations for Wireless Mobile Systems

Soumendra Nanda   Brian DeCleene   Victor Firoiu   May Leung

Yingbo Song   Charles Tao

BAE Systems
6 New England Executive Park
Burlington, MA, 01821, USA
(781) 273-3388
soumendra.nanda@baesystems.com

ABSTRACT

Wireless researchers face the practical challenge of evaluating the performance of new routing protocols for very large-scale heterogeneous mobile systems. While simulation platforms, tools and techniques have matured, doubts remain about the broad validity of simulated results when applied to real world situations. Wireless network emulation provides a middle ground between simulations and real-world testing. However, emulation environments are complex to run and cost-prohibitive for larger-scale tests. In order to maximize fidelity while managing complexity and costs, we developed a common framework that unifies simulation-based analysis and emulation experiment tools, in order to produce calibrated and scalable performance evaluations.

Categories and Subject Descriptors

C.2 [Computer-Communication Networks]: Wireless communications. C.4 [Performance of Systems]: Modeling techniques

General Terms

Algorithms, Management, Measurement, Performance, Design, Experimentation, Verification.

Keywords

Simulation, Emulation, Wireless, MANET, Scalability, EMANE

1. BACKGROUND

NRL's Extendable Mobile Ad-hoc Network Emulator (EMANE) is a modular framework that supports real-time modeling of link and physical layer connectivity [1]. EMANE executes networking and application software in-situ on allocated computer resources while exposing those resources to the same conditions that occur in real-world mobile and wireless communications. For example, BAE SYSTEMS collected position data along with network measurements from a series of outdoor field trials [2]. After each field test, position information (from GPS) and collected channel pathloss data were replayed within a customized version of EMANE. By comparing results from emulation and field experiments, we iteratively refined the configuration parameters of our emulation framework such that the deviation between real-

MobiSys'14, June 16–19, 2014, Bretton Woods, NH, USA.
ACM978-1-4503-2793-0/14/06.
http://dx.doi.org/10.1145/2594368.2601450

world results and mid-size emulation experiments (on the order of 40 nodes) was small.

2. EMULATION CHALLENGES

While field-based calibration was effective in mid-size emulation environments, new evaluation strategies are required to evaluate the performance of new protocols in large scale networks (between 100 to as many as 5000 mobile nodes). Beyond cost and coordination challenges with collecting field measurements at these scales, emulator performance suffered scalability issues as a result of increased $O(N^2)$ complexity necessary to model channel contention/access. Each emulation experiment runs in real time. Also, larger experiments require complex initial configuration and generate large volumes of data and logs upon completion. In fact, for short experiments, setup and post-processing time often equals or exceeds the experiment runtime. Logs for each node can take several GB (even for 10-minute experiments) – requiring additional download time as well as data storage. Collectively, these impediments limited our ability to rapidly research and test new ideas and algorithms.

3. SCALING AND CALIBRATION

To address the emulation scalability challenges, we developed a virtualized 500-node MANET system on EMANE with multiple radios by running multiple lightweight virtual machines (as many as 25 Linux containers) on each multicore emulation hosts and via additional optimizations [3].

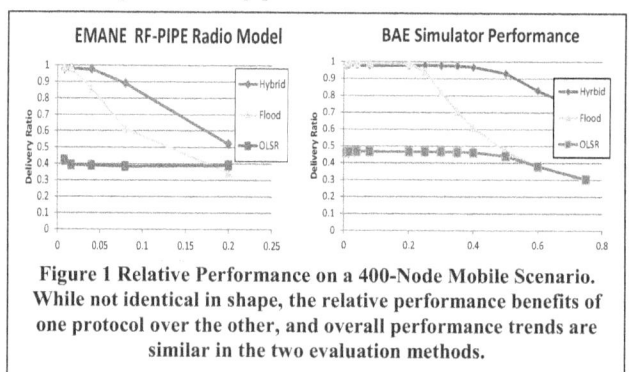

Figure 1 Relative Performance on a 400-Node Mobile Scenario. While not identical in shape, the relative performance benefits of one protocol over the other, and overall performance trends are similar in the two evaluation methods.

For larger networks on the order of 1000 nodes, our solution was to use the emulation-field trial calibration process as a methodology for calibrating larger environments, while replacing expensive field trials with low-cost simulation. Building upon on an in-house developed network simulator, we first calibrated the simulator's performance profile, to match that of our previously calibrated emulation-based system. This process required development of common tools to ensure comparative execution and the ability to compare/contrast collected results.

This process enabled us to execute simulation experiments that previously required about 30 minutes in emulation, to now less than 4 minutes, while showing comparable and similar results on both systems. This speedup allowed us to explore multiple new ideas and protocols for new MANET research efficiently, by first examining them in the simulator, and then more fully within the emulator. Figure 1 illustrates the results of this process and showcases how the results generated by the two approaches compare. While calibration and performance tuning challenges remain, our initial results suggest that our overall approach is viable for the performance evaluation of large scale mobile systems.

4. ACKNOWLEDGEMENTS

This work was supported by DARPA under contract FA8750-12-C-0229. This document does not necessarily constitute or imply its endorsement, recommendation, or favoring by the United States government.

5. REFERENCES

[1] Naval Research Laboratory, "EMANE," Available: http://cs.itd.nrl.navy.mil/work/emane/.

[2] Victor Firoiu, Greg Lauer, Brian DeCleene, and Soumendra Nanda. "Experiences with network coding within MANET field experiments." In In Military Communications Conference, MILCOM 2010, pp. 1363-1368.

[3] Victor Firoiu, Brian DeCleene, May Leung, Soumendra Nanda, and Charles Tao. "Scaling MANETs Using Long-Range Radios and Protocol Adaptation." In MILCOM 2013.

Poster: Towards Reducing Smartphone Application Delay through Read/Write Isolation

David T. Nguyen*, Gang Zhou*, Guoliang Xing†
*College of William and Mary, USA †Michigan State University, USA
{dnguyen, gzhou}@cs.wm.edu, glxing@cse.msu.edu

Categories and Subject Descriptors

C.4 [**Performance of Systems**]: Design studies

Keywords

Smartphone App Delay; I/O Optimizations; App Launch

1. INTRODUCTION AND APPROACH

A recent analysis[3] indicates that most user interactions with smartphones are short. Specifically, 80% of the apps are used for less than two minutes. With such brief interactions, apps should be rapid and responsive. However, the same study reports that many apps incur significant delays during launch and run-time. This work addresses two key research questions towards achieving rapid app response. (1) *How does disk I/O performance affect smartphone app response time?* (2) *How can we improve app performance with I/O optimization techniques?*

We address the questions via following contributions. First, through a large-scale measurement study based on the data collected within 130 days from 1009 Android devices using an app[2] we developed, we find that Android devices spend a significant portion of their CPU active time (up to 58%) waiting for storage I/Os to complete, also known as *iowait* (Figure 1). This negatively affects the smartphone's overall app performance, and results in slow response time. Further investigation reveals that a read experiences up to 626% slowdown when blocked by a concurrent write. Additionally, the results indicate significant asymmetry in the slowdown of one I/O type due to another. Finally, we study the speedup of concurrent I/Os, and the results suggest that reads benefit more from concurrency.

Second, we implement a system called SmartIO that shortens app delays by prioritizing reads over writes. SmartIO allows reads to be completed before writes, and delays writes as long as there are reads, while avoiding write starvation. To achieve this, a third level of I/O priority is added into the current block layer[1], assigning higher priority to reads and lower to writes. This third priority level has a lower priority than the original block layer's priorities.

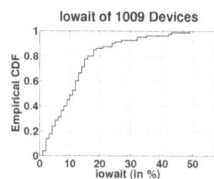

Figure 1: Iowait.

MobiSys'14, June 16–19, 2014, Bretton Woods, New Hampshire, USA.
ACM 978-1-4503-2793-0/14/06.
http://dx.doi.org/10.1145/2594368.2601458.

Write starvation is avoided by applying a maximal period of time assigned to a process (100ms). Additionally, SmartIO issues I/Os with optimized concurrency parameters that are obtained during installation. The parameters include the optimal number of sequential or random reads (writes) that benefit most from concurrency.

2. PERFORMANCE EVALUATION

We evaluate our system using 20 popular apps and show that SmartIO reduces launch delays by up to 37.8%, and run-time delays by up to 29.6% (Figure 2). SmartIO's performance gain during launch is due to its read-intensive nature. Specifically, the average number of reads observed during launch on the 20 apps is five times higher than writes. The smaller performance gain during the run-time is caused by its modest I/O activity. The average number of I/Os observed during launch is 2 times higher than during run-time. SmartIO's read performance improvement comes with little cost due to the read/write discrepancy nature of the flash storage (reads take much faster to complete). Although, writes may encounter slight slowdowns. In another experiment, we install the 20 apps researched, and the writes are on average 7.6% slower with SmartIO. However, at the same time, many other processes in the background may benefit from SmartIO. Based on our large-scale study, there are on average 255 processes running on each device at any point of time, from which 98 have some I/O activity and generate a workload. These processes are expected to have faster response time with SmartIO.

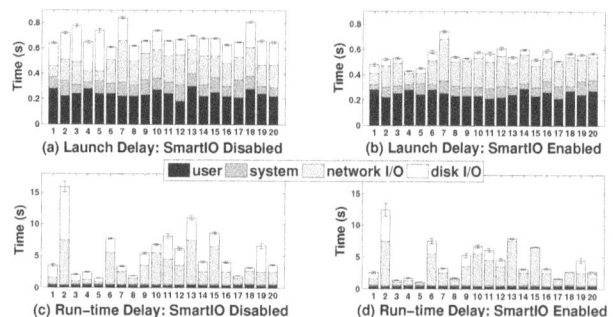

Figure 2: Launch and Run-time Delay. 1: Angry Birds; **2:**GTA; **3:**Need for Speed; **4:**Temple Run; **5:**The Simpsons; **6:**CNN; **7:**Nightly News; **8:**ABC News; **9:**YouTube; **10:**Pandora; **11:**Facebook; **12:**Twitter; **13:**Gmail; **14:**Google Maps; **15:**AccuWeather; **16:**Accelerometer M.; **17:**Gyroscope Log; **18:**Proximity Sensor; **19:**Compass; **20:**Barometer.

3. REFERENCES

[1] Block layer. http://goo.gl/SwdLZ5, 2014.
[2] Storebench download. http://goo.gl/ava9eV, 2014.
[3] T. Yan, D. Chu, D. Ganesan, A. Kansal, and J. Liu. Fast app launching for mobile devices. In *Proc. of ACM MobiSys, 2012.*

Poster: Ontology-Based Heartbeat Classification for Mobile Electrocardiogram Monitoring

Juyoung Park, Kuyeon Lee, Kyungtae Kang
Department of Computer Science & Engineering
Hanyang University, Republic of Korea
{parkjy, leekuyeon, ktkang}@hanyang.ac.kr

Categories and Subject Descriptors

H.4.0 [**Information Systems Applications**]: General; J.3 [**Life and Medical Sciences**]: Health

Keywords

Heartbeat classification, ontology, ECG, mobile device

1. INTRODUCTION

Recently, it has become possible to integrate a Holter monitor with mobile devices to supply the requirements of the monitoring function precisely to allow a person to continue with her/his normal routines. A person can lead a normal life while a sensor acquires electrocardiogram (ECG) data continuously and sends them to his/her mobile device using Bluetooth. Consequently, the individual's long-term ECG signal can be observed seamlessly.

We propose an ontology-based heartbeat classification method based on long-term observation of an individual's heart activity, which includes automatic ontology learning. Inspired by the fact that experts diagnose illness via their clinical experiences, as well as distinct individual characteristics, our classification system detects arrhythmia using *Arrhythmia/Profile Ontology* for distinct individual characteristics and *Universal Ontology* for clinical experience. Using these ontologies enables us to achieve analysis and systematic management for mobile ECG Holter monitoring.

2. ONTOLOGY-BASED CLASSIFIER

Decision trees constitute a non-parametric supervised learning method used for classification and can be converted to rules easily for inference. Learning a decision tree involves calculating the uncertainties of features and selecting the most general one. The uncertainty calculation is based on the concept of entropy, and the learning method selects the most general node of all the features. In our system, these steps are iterated until all heartbeats have been classified. Decision trees have three main components: a root node, leaf nodes, and branches. The root node is the starting point of the tree, and the leaf nodes represent the final result of a combination of branches. Thus, the root node is the most general feature, a branch is a condition, and a leaf node is a combination

This work was supported by Basic Science Research Program through the National Research Foundation of Korea funded by the Ministry of Science, ICT & Future Planning (NRF-2013R1A1A1059188).

of feature values as an annotation (the result of classification). In the first stage of our system, the *Arrhythmia Ontology* has only an annotation set. After learning the decision tree, combinations of the values from a root node to the leaf nodes are converted into inference rules. If similar leaf nodes exist in the decision tree, combinations of these nodes are joined by the OR operator as a rule.

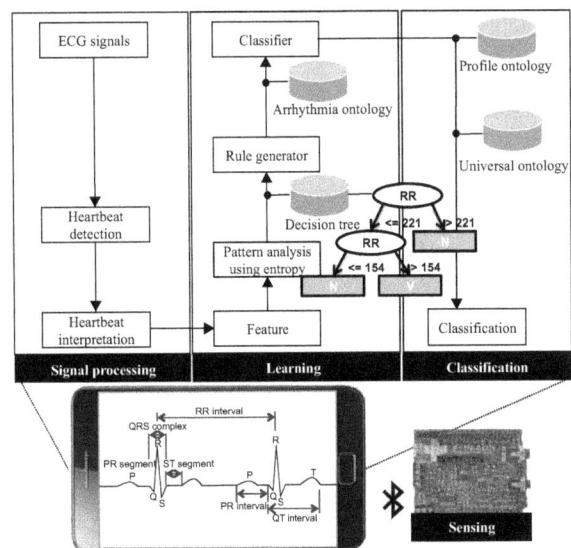

Figure 1. Functional architecture & example of a decision tree

3. CASE STUDY

As a case study, we applied a decision tree classifier to record ID 106 in the MIT-BIH Arrhythmia Database [1]. In our example of a decision tree (see Fig. 1), there are two branches that depend on the value of the RR interval I_{RR}, and there are three leaf nodes: two are for the normal heartbeat (N) class, and one is for the premature ventricular contraction (V) class. Thus, the decision tree is converted into two rules, one for each class:

$$\exists_x \{ N(x) \equiv (I_{RR}(x) \leq 154) \sqcup (I_{RR}(x) > 221) \},$$

$$\exists_x \{ V(x) \equiv (I_{RR}(x) \leq 221) \sqcap (I_{RR}(x) > 154) \}.$$

These rules are integrated into the *Arrhythmia/Profile Ontology* as individual characteristics. The *Universal Ontology* is used to verify the classification results using the *Arrhythmia Ontology* as reference and to classify a heartbeat in the absence of a rule in the *Arrhythmia Ontology* as clinical experiences.

4. REFERENCES

[1] G. B. Moody and R. G. Mark, "The impact of the MIT-BIH arrhythmia database," *IEEE Engineering in Medicine and Biology Magazine*, vol. 20, no. 3, pp. 45-50, May/Jun. 2001.

Poster: Balancing Disclosure and Utility of Personal Information

Aarathi Prasad
Institute for Security,
Technology and Society
Dartmouth College

Xiaohui Liang
Institute for Security,
Technology and Society
Dartmouth College

David Kotz
Institute for Security,
Technology and Society
Dartmouth College

ABSTRACT

The ubiquity of smartphones and mobile and wearable devices allow people to collect information about their health, wellness and lifestyle and share with others. If it is not clear what they need to share to receive benefits, *subjects* (people whose information is collected) might share too much, thus disclosing unnecessary private information. On the other hand, concerned about disclosing personal information, subjects might share less than what the recipient needs and lose the opportunity to enjoy the benefits. This balance of disclosure and utility is important when the subject wants to receive some benefits, but is concerned about disclosing private information.

We address this problem of balancing disclosure and utility of personal information collected by mobile technologies. We believe subjects can decide how best to share their information if they are aware of the benefits and risks of sharing. We developed ShareBuddy, a privacy-aware architecture that allows recipients to request information and specify the benefits the subjects will receive for sharing each piece of requested information; the architecture displays these benefits and warns subjects about the risks of sharing. We describe the ShareBuddy architecture in this poster.

Categories and Subject Descriptors

K.4 [**COMPUTERS AND SOCIETY**]: Privacy

Keywords

sharing controls, mobile devices, personal information

1. INTRODUCTION

Mobile technologies allow people to collect their personal information at any time to achieve some personal goals. Currently the most popular mobile technologies are health and wellness devices and applications which *subjects*, i.e., people whose information is collected, use to monitor their health information and improve their lifestyle. Some share their health and wellness information with family, friends and peers for emotional support, clinical advisors for diagnosis and health advice, employers and insurance companies for monetary benefits and researchers for contributing to the greater good. The people and groups that subjects share information with are collectively referred to as *recipients* and the benefits the subject wants to receive by sharing her information with the recipients, i.e., the value perceived by the subject in sharing is referred to as *utility*. Typically in such scenarios, the subject uses a sensor (e.g., a medical device or an activity tracker) to collect her information. The sensor forwards the subject's data to a networked device (her smartphone or laptop) which then uploads the data to her personal account on the cloud and shared with the recipients.

For the subject to receive the benefits they desire, i.e., to maximize the utility, the information disclosed must be useful to the recipients so they can help the subject achieve her goal. Unfortunately many subjects limit the information they share out of privacy concerns that stem from the fact that they are not aware of how their information will be used by the recipients; this leads to under-sharing of their information, i.e., limiting disclosure and utility of the information. On the other hand, most subjects are incapable of deducing what sensitive inferences could be made from their data. Also, to receive benefits, subjects might share more than necessary because it is unclear to them what information the recipients really need. The latter two cases might lead to over-sharing, i.e., increased disclosure of information but with almost no increase in utility. If the sharing does not reflect their privacy preferences, subjects might become frustrated and ultimately limit or stop using the device. Mobile technologies should strive for a balance, allowing subjects to limit disclosure of information but obtain meaningful utility, so that subjects can enjoy the benefits provided by the technologies without worrying about the disclosure of their sensitive information.

In this poster, we present ShareBuddy, a privacy-aware architecture that helps subjects achieve this balance; the architecture is shown in Figure 1. ShareBuddy allows subjects to review requests from recipients on their mobile phone; these requests describe what information they need to share and why. ShareBuddy also provides flexible sharing controls that warn subjects about sharing information that could be used to make sensitive inferences about them. We conducted a lab study with 21 participants using a prototype of ShareBuddy to explore the effect of displaying benefits and risks of requested information on subjects' sharing behavior.

MobiSys'14, June 16–19, 2014, Bretton Woods, New Hampshire, USA.
ACM 978-1-4503-2793-0/14/06.
http://dx.doi.org/10.1145/2594368.2601448.

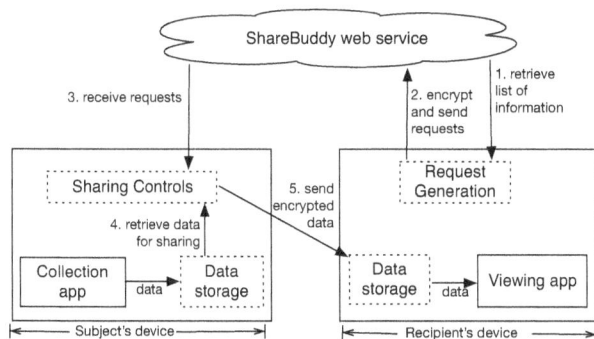

Figure 1: **Shapes in dotted lines are part of the ShareBuddy architecture. This diagram shows the workflow for recipients to request and view data and for subjects to share data.**

2. SHAREBUDDY

ShareBuddy is a privacy-aware architecture that helps subjects balance disclosure and utility of their information. ShareBuddy has three components:

ShareBuddy on the subject's phone stores data collected by the applications on the subject's phone (referred to as *collection* apps) and helps subjects decide what data to share and with whom,

ShareBuddy web service allows developers to register collection apps, recipients to request for data collected by these applications, requests and data to be sent between recipients and subjects, and

ShareBuddy on the recipient's device receives the data sent by the subject and allows the recipient to view the data on their mobile and/or web application (referred to as *viewing* app).

Before registering collection apps with ShareBuddy, the developers must add hooks to their collection app so that the ShareBuddy component on the subject's phone can access the information collected by it.

Both subjects and recipients need to register with Share-Buddy before using the service. ShareBuddy allows recipients to choose from the list of information collected by all registered collection apps. For every type of information they request, recipients must clearly state why they need it and what benefits the subject will receive for sharing the information. The recipient must also specify their level of need for the information, i.e., is the information *necessary*, *nice-to-have* or *unnecessary*. Once they create the request, the recipients enter the phone number of the subject whose information they are requesting for. Subjects who are not registered with ShareBuddy receive a request to install the component on their phone and to register with the Share-Buddy service. If the subject is already registered, the request generator on the recipient's device encrypts the request with the subject's public key (her phone number) and forwards the message to the subject's phone, along with a session key that the subject can use to send the data later.

The subject views the request on her device and decides how to share the information requested by the recipient. ShareBuddy provides an opt-out approach; the information

deemed as necessary by the recipient will be selected for sharing by default. These sharing defaults allow subjects to receive benefits without changing any settings, while also limiting their information disclosure. If subjects are not willing to share *necessary* information, they can opt out of sharing completely because they know that they will not receive any benefits. The request will also help subjects realize that they will not receive any benefits by sharing just the *nice-to-have* information without certain *necessary* information or by sharing any *unnecessary* information. *Nice-to-have* information is usually context associated with the *necessary* information that might be useful to recipients to better understand the *necessary* information; context could be used to make sensitive inferences about the subject when combined with associated target information. ShareBuddy uses visual clues to warn subjects about the risks of sharing if they choose any combination of information types that could be used to make sensitive inferences about them. The information sharing starts as soon as the subjects submit their sharing choices. Subjects can review and change the sharing settings at any time on their device.

The ShareBuddy component on the subject's device encrypts the information with the key provided by the recipient and forwards the message to the ShareBuddy component on the recipient's device. When the recipient wants to view the information, the viewing app retrieves the information from the data storage on the recipient's device; the viewing app developer can write their own visualization functions or use the visualization APIs that are submitted to the Share-Buddy server by the collection app developers.

The goal of ShareBuddy is to help subjects understand the benefits and risks of sharing, so that they can limit disclosure of their information but obtain meaningful utility. By design, it also guarantees confidentiality (only intended subjects can view the requests and intended recipients can view the data).

3. USER STUDY

We developed a prototype of the ShareBuddy architecture for wellness applications. We conducted a lab study with 21 participants to explore the effect of displaying benefits and risks of requested information on the subjects' sharing behavior. The study methods were approved by the Dartmouth Institutional Review Board. The study helped us confirm our hypothesis that knowing about benefits and risks of sharing helps subjects better balance the disclosure and utility of their information. We expect ShareBuddy to be useful to subjects in making sharing decisions that match their privacy preferences and so we plan to deploy the ShareBuddy system in real-world wellness and addiction programs.

4. ACKNOWLEDGMENTS

We wish to thank Denise Anthony, Celeste Campos-Castillo, Shrirang Mare and Andres Molina-Markham for their guidance and the anonymous reviewers for their comments. This research results from a research program at the Institute for Security, Technology and Society at Dartmouth College, supported by the National Science Foundation under award numbers CNS-1143548 and CNS-1329686.

Poster: *DriveBlue:* Can Bluetooth Enhance your Driving Experience?

Ahmed Salem, Tamer Nadeem
Department of Computer Science
Old Dominion University, VA, USA
{asalem, nadeem}@cs.odu.edu.com

Mecit Cetin
Civil & Environmental Engineering Department
Old Dominion University, VA, USA
mcetin@odu.edu

Categories and Subject Descriptors

I.5.4 [**Pattern Recognition**]: Applications
; C.2.3 [**Network Operations**]: Network Monitoring

Keywords

Bluetooth, Neighbour Discovery, Crowd-Sensing, Machine Learning, Android

1. INTRODUCTION

Bluetooth wide availability in vehicles either through passengers' smartphones or vehicles hardware have been poorly exploited by researchers[2]. Neighbor Discovery is an exclusive Bluetooth [3] feature can be utilized to enhance transportation services while maintaining vehicle's privacy. In this project, we advocate for using Bluetooth in developing intelligent transportation services. We name our project *DriveBlue*.

Traffic incidents (e.g. congestion, accidents) are likely to affect drivers daily commute. So far solutions to such problems are based on statistical analysis. Bluetooth was used to estimate the travel time by extrapolating the period used to travel between two points [1].

In this project, we exploit Bluetooth neighbor discovery to detect traffic conditions (e.g. average road speed, differentiate between vehicles on regular lanes versus HOV) with receivers placed in a single site as in Fig. 1a. Features are extracted, and classified revealing some of the current traffic conditions.

2. DATA COLLECTION

We have conducted two experiments to validate the feasibility of detecting vehicles' motion patterns. Four Android devices (Bluetooth ON) were loaded in a vehicle to emulate having multiple vehicles on the road. The vehicle then spanned the Bluetooth coverage area[1].

The first experiment, a controlled one performed inside Old Dominion University campus. The vehicle used two motion patterns: slow (<25mph), and fast (>30mph). We ran this experiment 12 times per motion pattern under the same traffic conditions. The collected data contains the following infor-

[1] For space limitations details can be found in [4]

MobiSys'14, June 16–19, 2014, Bretton Woods, New Hampshire, USA.
ACM 978-1-4503-2793-0/14/06.
http://dx.doi.org/10.1145/2594368.2601452 .

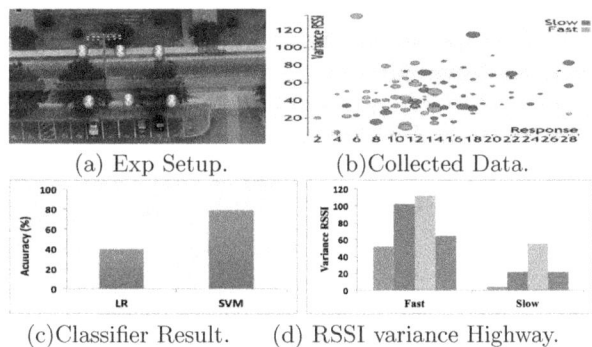

(a) Exp Setup.   (b)Collected Data.

(c)Classifier Result.   (d) RSSI variance Highway.

Figure 1: Experiment Results.

mation for every phone per run:number of collected responses, average appearance time (sec.), and RSSI variance.

Fig 1b plots the data with average number of responses on x-axis, RSSI variance on y-axis, and the size of the bubble represents the appearance time in seconds. Fig.1b depicts the feasibility of classifying the data into two classes.

The second experiment was conducted on the Interstate-64 to collect real traffic data. We performed two runs (for logistic and regulation constraints) at different times representing normal traffic condition (fast) and heavy traffic (slow).

3. PRELIMINARY RESULTS

Machine Learning classifiers with k-cross fold validation were applied on the extracted features from the controlled experiment. Logistic Regression (LR) was able to differentiate between the two motion patterns with an accuracy of 40%, while Support Vector Machine (SVM) achieved 79% accuracy Fig. 1c. SVM results proofs the possibility of using Bluetooth signals from a single site of reading for traffic applications.

Fig.1d shows data collected from the highway experiment, each column represent readings from a different Android device. The figure depicts the feasibility of applying Machine learning classification on the highway data [1].

4. REFERENCES

[1] B. Araghi. Improving accuracy of bluetooth-based travel time estimation using low-level sensor data. In *TRB 92nd Annual Meeting*, number 13-1922, 2013.

[2] C. Hughes. Automotive communications market forecast tables 2012, http://www.strategyanalytics.com.

[3] M. Rónai. A simple neighbour discovery procedure for bluetooth ad hoc networks. In *GLOBECOM'03. IEEE*, volume 2. IEEE, 2003.

[4] A. Salem, T. Nadeem, and M. Cetin. Technical report, http://swimsys.cs.odu.edu/driveBlue.php.

Poster: A Power-Aware Mobile App for Field Scientists

Bo Wang
Washington State University
bo.wang@wsu.edu

Xinghui Zhao
Washington State University
x.zhao@wsu.edu

David Chiu
Washington State University
david.chiu@wsu.edu

ABSTRACT

In this poster, we design and implement a mobile application and back-end management system to help field scientists manage data collection, improve real-time communication, and optimize power consumption during a scientific field study.

Categories and Subject Descriptors

H.4.0 [**Information Systems Applications**]: General

General Terms

Design, Measurement, Experimentation

Keywords

Mobile, Power

1. INTRODUCTION

Field research refers to the collection of data outside of a workplace setting. Managing such field studies in real-time is challenging. We have designed a power-aware mobile application that can simplify the management, data collection, and communication among team members during field studies. A key challenge of the application is to ensure that the devices would have enough power to carry out the study. To this end, we profile the energy consumption of our application on real mobile devices and propose a model that estimates the power usage of the application according to user actions. Based on this model, we develop a power controller module, which dynamically adjusts power usage of the application. It maximizes the user experience but saves enough battery life to meet the desired duration of the field study.

2. SYSTEM DESIGN

The design of our scientific field study application is shown in Figure 1. The power controller embedded in the application is used for monitoring current battery life, current running components, and current power usage. It uses these inputs to optimizes the power usage by dynamically adjusts the screen brightness to ensure that

MobiSys'14, June 16–19, 2014, Bretton Woods, New Hampshire, USA.
ACM 978-1-4503-2793-0/14/06.
http://dx.doi.org/10.1145/2594368.2601463.

the field experiment can last the desired duration. We plan to adjust other features in the near future, including the GPS update rate, and server communicate rates.

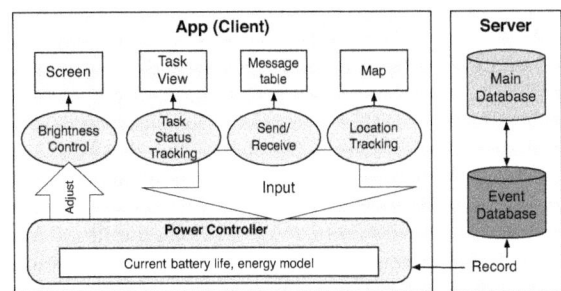

Figure 1: System Design

3. PRELIMINARY RESULTS

In our experiment, we set the desired field study duration to be 1 hour (= 3,600 secs). Then we optimize using different time-window sizes. For a window size τ, we use our power model to estimate the energy taken over the next $\tau + 1$ seconds. A smaller window may cause our algorithm to be to eager to keep brightness levels high, while a large window may be too conservative.

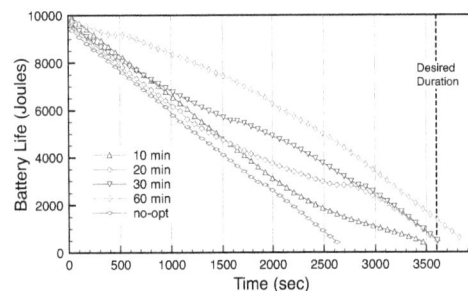

Figure 2: Power Optimization Results

4. RELATED EFFORTS

Our work was inspired by Rahul, *et al.* propose a general methodology for measuring power usage on smart phones [1]. The idea of their system is to account for the power usage of all of the primary hardware subsystems on the phone.

5. REFERENCES

[1] R. Murmuria, J. Medsger, A. Stavrou, and J. M. Voas, "Mobile application and device power usage measurements," in *SERE '12*, pp. 147–156, 2012.

Poster: Crowdsourcing for Video Traffic Surveillance

Hui Wen[1], Qiang Li[1], Qi Han[2], Shiming Ge[1],Limin Sun[1]*
[1]Beijing Key Laboratory of IOT Information Security Technology, Institute of Information Engineering, CAS, China
[2]Department of EECS, Colorado School of Mines, Golden, CO USA 80401
E-mails:{wenhui,liqiang43,geshiming,sunlimin}@iie.ac.cn, qhan@mines.edu

Categories and Subject Descriptors

H.4.m [Information Systems Applications]: Miscellaneous

Keywords

Crowdsourcing, Video traffic surveillance, Event detection

1. INTRODUCTION

Video traffic surveillance monitors traffic situations such as traffic jams, traffic accidents, or running a red light. Although automatic traffic event detection has been studied for years, current systems often fail to handle various situations and do not fully take advantage of existing video traffic surveillance data. Hence, there is a need for an approach that integrates labor resources with intelligent video analysis to enhance the robustness of video analysis models and fulfill the demands of traffic surveillance.

Motivated by the intuition that a driver or pedestrian often needs to know the exact traffic conditions before selecting a particular route, we propose a crowdsourcing [2] surveillance framework to assist existing traffic surveillance systems. In particular, people can use their smartphones to check the detected traffic situation and the corresponding video clips received from the video surveillance system, and make quick judgements about the received results. This fine-grained information provided by traffic surveillance system not only shows the detected traffic results but also presents live video clips. Furthermore, smartphone users can provide their feedback to the system for improving the intelligent video surveillance model or correcting errors that may be present in the current traffic event detection.

2. FRAMEWORK

Figure 1 shows our proposed framework. Basically, the system informs smartphone users of abnormal traffic situations and gets the feedback from users to improve the traffic event detection model. This crowdsourcing allows the surveillance tasks to be distributed among a large number of smartphone users who provide ground truth of the traffic conditions.

There are several key components in the framework. (1) *Traffic event detection.* Traffic video analysis is used to train

MobiSys'14, June 16–19, 2014, Bretton Woods, New Hampshire, USA.
ACM 978-1-4503-2793-0/14/06.
http://dx.doi.org/10.1145/2594368.2601460 .

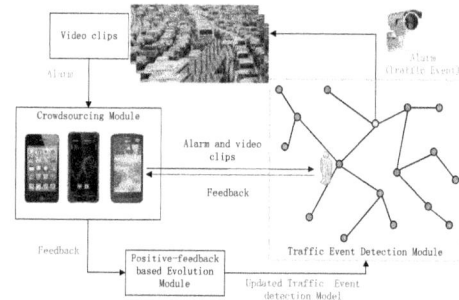

Figure 1. Overview of Proposed Framework

a model for detecting various traffic events. Our current work focuses on traffic accidents detection to validate the framework. This module applies subspace clustering or dictionary learning [1] techniques to first identify normal patterns and then detect traffic accidents based on deviation from these normal patterns. (2) *Crowdsourcing.* Different from a traditional video surveillance system, our framework allows smartphone users to get the video clips from the system via a push or pull based method. Smartphone users then become "traffic surveillance supervisors." Once they view live surveillance videos, they can provide feedback to the system to improve the robustness of the video analysis. (3) *Positive-feedback based evolution.* Simple yet valuable feedback is provided by smartphones users to indicate whether the traffic alert is right or wrong. The feedback module then updates the abnormal traffic event detection model online by positive judgment obtained from smartphone users. Specifically, the PN-learning method[3] is used for model self-learning. The method evaluates the crowdsourcing feedback with the features extracted from the video clips, identifies the motion feature that have been classified as being contradictory to structural constraints, and augments the sample set with the representative samples.

There are several key issues in implementing this framework. They include designing proper feedback strategies, developing an online abnormal traffic event detection model, solving the optimization problem of the subspace clustering or dictionary learning, considering the structure constraints of the positive and negative samples in PN-learning, and synchronization of feedback from a large number of users.

3. REFERENCES

[1] Y. Cong, J. Yuan, and J. Liu. Abnormal event detection in crowded scenes using sparse representation. *Pattern Recognition*, 46:1851–1864, 2013.

[2] J. Deng, J. Krause, and L. Fei-Fei. Fine-grained crowdsourcing for fine-grained recognition. In *CVPR*, pages 580–587, 2013.

[3] Z. Kalal, J. Matas, and K. Mikolajczyk. Pn learning: Bootstrapping binary classifiers by structural constraints. In *CVPR*, pages 49–56, 2010.

Poster: Improving Efficiency of Metropolitan-Scale Transit Systems with Multi-Mode Data Feeds

Desheng Zhang
zhang@cs.umn.edu
University of Minnesota

Tian He
tianhe@cs.umn.edu
University of Minnesota

Urban transit systems play a significant role in preventing daily commutes from becoming more congested than they are now, e.g., transit systems reduced 865 million hours of travel delay and 450 million gallons of gas during U.S. commutes in 2013. However, the previous theory and practice on urban transit research have typically focused on individual transit modes in isolation, and thus there is a lack of research on how to integrate real-time data feeds about different transit modes (e.g., taxicab, bus and subway) and other urban infrastructures (e.g., cellular networks) to improve transit efficiency. To address this issue, we propose and implement a novel architecture for multi-mode transit services based on the urban infrastructures in a Chinese city Shenzhen. The key contributions of this poster are as follows.

- We propose a novel three-layer architecture based on multi-mode real-time data feeds to tackle the unbalanced demand and supply in urban transit systems. It aims to provide unseen urban dynamics in fine-grained spatio-temporal resolutions to support real-world services, which cannot be achieved by monolithic urban transit systems in isolation.

- We design a demand/supply abstraction mechanism as an architectural bridge between the domain-independent urban transit infrastructures and the application-specific knowledge output, which is tailored by end users for various real-world application designs.

In particular, the proposed architecture is given in Figure 1.

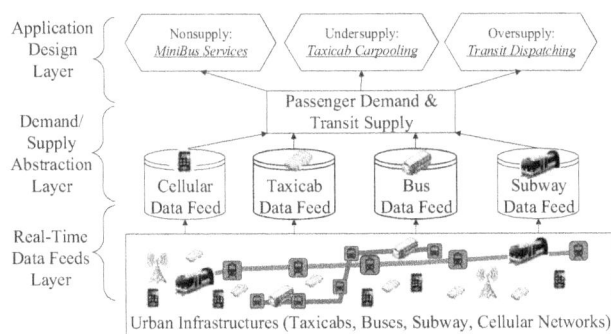

Figure 1: System Architecture

MobiSys'14, June 16–19, 2014, Bretton Woods, New Hampshire, USA.
ACM 978-1-4503-2793-0/14/06.
http://dx.doi.org/10.1145/2594368.2601459.

(i) **The Real-Time Data Feed Layer** ensures reliable collection of online data feeds from urban transit infrastructures. We establish a secure and reliable transmission mechanism, which feeds our server the above four kinds of data collected by service providers with a wired connection.

(ii) **The Demand/Supply Abstraction Layer** unifies heterogeneous online feeds from different modes to produce abstracted passenger demand and transit supply. Figure 2 gives region-level travel demand mined from our data.

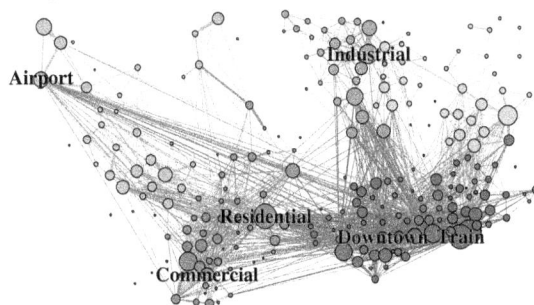

Figure 2: Passenger Travel Demand in Shenzhen

(iii) **The Application Design Layer** utilizes service interfaces provided by the demand/supply abstraction layer to enhance the passenger experience by real-world applications. In particular, the proposed services will cover a complete set of the demand-and-supply relationship (i.e., non-supply, undersupply and oversupply) as in Figure 1. For example, Figure 3 gives the relocated taxicab supply based on the passenger demand in region levels in order to balance the passenger demand and taxicab supply. The warmer the color of the regions, the higher the taxicab transit supply.

Figure 3: Relocated Taxicab Supply in Shenzhen

In short, the three-level architecture in Figure 1 suggests a horizontal view of building high-performance applications. Traditional stand-alone closed transit systems, e.g., taxicab or bus networks, do not have such capacities. As a narrow-waist, the demand/supply abstraction layer allows fellow researchers to add more transit modes (e.g., personal vehicles) or applications without redesigning the whole architecture.

Video: Rio: A System Solution for Sharing I/O between Mobile Systems

Ardalan Amiri Sani, Kevin Boos, Min Hong Yun, and Lin Zhong

Rice University, Houston, TX

Abstract [1]

Modern mobile systems are equipped with a diverse collection of I/O devices, including cameras, microphones, various sensors, and cellular modem. There exist many novel use cases for allowing an application on one mobile system to utilize I/O devices from another. This video demonstrates Rio, an I/O sharing solution that supports unmodified applications and realizes many of these novel use cases. Rio's design is common to many classes of I/O devices, significantly reducing the engineering effort to support new I/O devices. Moreover, it supports all the functionalities of an I/O device for sharing. Rio also supports I/O sharing between mobile systems of different form factors, including smartphones and tablets.

Categories and Subject Descriptors

B.4.2 [**Input/Output and Data Communications**]: Input/Output Devices; C.0 [**Computer Systems Organization**]: General—System architectures; C.2.4 [**Computer-Communication Networks**]: Distributed Systems—Client/Server; K.8.0 [**Personal Computing**]: General

Keywords

I/O; Remote I/O; I/O Sharing; Mobile; Rio

1. REFERENCES

[1] A. Amiri Sani, K. Boos, M. Yun, and L. Zhong. Rio: A System Solution for Sharing I/O between Mobile Systems. *Proc. ACM MobiSys*, 2014.

---

[1]Full paper: [1]

MobiSys'14, June 16–19, 2014, Bretton Woods, New Hampshire, USA.
ACM 978-1-4503-2793-0/14/06.
http://dx.doi.org/10.1145/2594368.2602434.

Video: WiFi-Honk – Smartphone-based Beacon Stuffed WiFi Car2X-Communication System for Vulnerable Road User Safety

Kaustubh Dhondge
University of Missouri - Kansas City
546 Flarsheim Hall
5110 Rockhill Road
Kansas City, MO, 64110, USA
kaustubh.dhondge@umkc.edu

Sejun Song
University of Missouri - Kansas City
546 Flarsheim Hall
5110 Rockhill Road
Kansas City, MO, 64110, USA
sjsong@umkc.edu

Younghwan Jang
University of Missouri - Kansas City
546 Flarsheim Hall
5110 Rockhill Road
Kansas City, MO, 64110, USA
yjvxf@mail.umkc.edu

Hyungbae Park
University of Missouri - Kansas City
546 Flarsheim Hall
5110 Rockhill Road
Kansas City, MO, 64110, USA
hpark@umkc.edu

Sunae Shin
University of Missouri - Kansas City
546 Flarsheim Hall
5110 Rockhill Road
Kansas City, MO, 64110, USA
sshin@umkc.edu

Baek-Young Choi
University of Missouri - Kansas City
546 Flarsheim Hall
5110 Rockhill Road
Kansas City, MO, 64110, USA
choiby@umkc.edu

ABSTRACT

As smartphones gain their popularity, vulnerable road users (VRUs) are increasingly distracted by activities with their devices such as listening to music, watching videos, texting or making calls while walking or bicycling on the road. In spite of the development of various high-tech Car-to-Car (C2C) and Car-to-Infrastructure (C2I) communications for enhancing the traffic safety, protecting such VRUs from vehicles still relies heavily on traditional sound warning methods. Furthermore, as smartphones continue to become highly ubiquitous, VRUs are increasingly oblivious to safety related warning sounds. A traffic accident study shows the number of headphone-wearing VRUs involved in roadside accidents has increased by 300% in the last 10 years. Although recently a few Car2Pedestrian-communication methods have been proposed by various car manufacturers, their practical usage is limited, as they mostly require special communication devices to cope with the wide range of mobility, and also assume VRUs' active attention to the communication while walking. We propose a smartphone-based Car2X-communication system, named WiFi-Honk, which can alert the potential collisions to both VRUs and vehicles in order to especially protect the distracted VRUs. WiFi-Honk provides a practical safety means for the distracted VRUs without requiring any special device using WiFi of smartphone. WiFi-Honk removes the WiFi association overhead using the beacon stuffed WiFi communication with the geographic location, speed, and direction information of the smartphone replacing its SSID while operating in WiFi Direct/Hotspot mode, and also provides an efficient collision estimation algorithm to issue appropriate warnings. Our experimental and simulation studies validate that WiFi-Honk can successfully alert VRUs within a sufficient reaction time frame, even in high mobility environments.

Categories and Subject Descriptors

H.4.0 [**Information Systems Applications**]: General

Keywords

Smartphone; WiFi; Car2X-Communication

REFERENCES

[1] "Honda Demonstrates Advanced Vehicle-to-Pedestrian and Vehicle-to-Motorcycle Safety Technologies," *http://www. honda.com/newsandviews/article.aspx?id=7352-en*, 2013.

[2] R. Chandra, J. Padhye, L. Ravindranath, and A. Wolman, "Beacon-Stuffing: Wi-Fi without Associations," *in Eighth IEEE Workshop on Mobile Computing Systems and Applications, HotMobile*, 2007, pp. 53–57.

[3] Kaustubh Dhondge, Sejun Song, Baek-Young Choi, Hyungbae Park, "WiFiHonk: Smartphone based Beacon Stuffed WiFi Car2X-Communication System for Vulnerable Road User Safety," *IEEE 79th Vehicular Technology Conference (VTC)*, Spring 2014.

[4] S. Engel, C. Kratzsch, and K. David, "Car2Pedestrian-Communication: Protection of Vulnerable Road Users Using Smartphones," *in Advanced Microsystems for Automotive Applications, Springer International Publishing*, 2013

MobiSys'14, Jun 16-19 2014, Bretton Woods, NH, USA
ACM 978-1-4503-2793-0/14/06.
http://dx.doi.org/10.1145/2594368.2602430

VIDEO: Remote Sensor Placement

[1]David Mascareñas   [1]Sara Brambilla   [1]Logan Ott   [1]Amy Larson
{dmascarenas, sbrambilla, logan, amylarson}@lanl.gov

[1]Charles Farrar   [2]Aaron Curtis   [1]Steve Brumby
farrar@lanl.gov, aarongc@nmt.edu, brumby@lanl.gov

[1]Los Alamos National Laboratory, PO Box 1663, Los Alamos, NM, USA 87544
[2]New Mexico Tech, 801 Leroy Pl, Socorro, NM, USA, 87801

ABSTRACT

The goal of this work is to develop a new autonomous capability for remotely deploying precisely located sensor nodes without damaging the sensor nodes in the process. Over the course of the last decade there has been significant interest in research to deploy sensor networks. This research is driven by the fact that the costs associated with installing sensor networks can be very high. In order to rapidly deploy sensor networks consisting of large numbers of sensor nodes, alternative techniques must be developed to place the sensor nodes in the field.

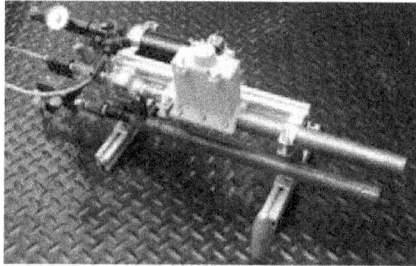

Figure 1 Prototype intelligent gas gun with magazine to hold 3 sensor packages.

To date much of the research on sensor network deployment has focused on strategies that involve the random dispersion of sensor nodes [1]. In addition other researchers have investigated deployment strategies utilizing small unmanned aerial helicopters for dropping sensor networks from the air. [2]. The problem with these strategies is that often sensor nodes need to be very precisely located for their measurements to be of any use. The reason for this could be that the sensor being used only have limited range, or need to be properly coupled to the environment which they are sensing. The problem with simply dropping sensor nodes is that for many applications it is necessary to deploy sensor nodes horizontally. In addition, to properly install many types of sensors, the sensor must assume a specific pose relative to the object being measured.

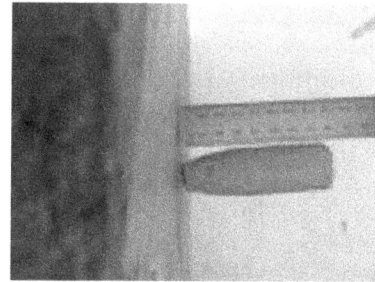

Figure 2. Remote sensor placement package embedded in a piece of fiber board using the remote sensor placement device.

In order to address these challenges we are currently developing a technology to remotely and rapidly deploy precisely located sensor nodes. The remote sensor placement device being developed can be described as an intelligent gas gun (Figure 1). A laser rangefinder is used to measure the distance to a specified target sensor location. This distance is then used to estimate the amount of energy required to propel the sensor node to the target location with just enough additional energy left over to ensure the sensor node is able to attach itself to the target of interest. We are currently in the process of developing attachment mechanisms for steel, wood, fiberglass (Figure 2).

In this demonstration we will perform a contained, live demo of our prototype pneumatic remote sensor placement device along with some prototype sensor attachment mechanisms we are developing.

1. REFERENCES

[1] Wan, P.J., Yi, C.W., 2006. *Coverage by Randomly Deployed Wireless Sensor Networks.* IEEE Transactions on Information Theory, Vol 52, No 6.

[2] Corke, P., Hrabar, S., Peterson, R., Rus, D., Siripalli, S., Sukhatme, G., 2004. *The Autonomous Deployment and Repair of a Sensor Network Using an Unmanned Aerial Vehicle.* Robotics and Automation, Proceedings of ICRA 2004, IEEE International Conference on, Vol 4, (New Orleans, LA, USA, April 26-May 1, 2004).

MobiSys'14, June 16-19, 2014, Bretton Woods, NH, USA.
ACM 978-1-4503-2793-0/14/06.
http://dx.doi.org/10.1145/2594368.2602433

Video: Study of Storage Impact on Smartphone Application Delay

David T. Nguyen
College of William and Mary
McGlothlin-Street Hall 126
Williamsburg
VA 23185, USA
dnguyen@cs.wm.edu

Gang Zhou
College of William and Mary
McGlothlin-Street Hall 126
Williamsburg
VA 23185, USA
gzhou@cs.wm.edu

Guoliang Xing
Michigan State University
3115 Engineering Building
East Lansing
MI 48824-1226, USA
glxing@cse.msu.edu

ABSTRACT

The smartphone has become an important part of our daily lives. However, the user experience is still far from being optimal. In particular, despite the rapid hardware upgrades, current smartphones often suffer various unpredictable delays during operation, e.g., when launching an application, leading to poor user experience. This video features our study of storage impact on smartphone application delay. We conduct the first large-scale measurement study on the I/O delay of Android using the data collected from our application running on 1009 devices within 130 days. We observe that Android devices spend up to 58% of their CPU active time waiting for storage I/Os to complete. This negatively affects the smartphone's overall application performance, and results in slow response time. Further investigation, among others, reveals that reads experience up to a 626% slowdown in the presence of concurrent writes. The obtained knowledge is used to design and implement a system called SmartIO that reduces the application delay by prioritizing reads over writes, and grouping them based on assigned priorities. SmartIO is implemented on the Android platform and evaluated extensively on several groups of popular applications. The results from the 20 researched applications demonstrate that SmartIO reduces launch delays by up to 37.8%, and run-time delays by up to 29.6%.

Categories and Subject Descriptors

C.4 [**Performance of Systems**]: Design studies; C.5.3 [**Computer System Implementation**]: Microcomputers-Portable devices.

General Terms

Experimentation, Design, Measurement

Keywords

Smartphone Application Delay; I/O Optimizations; Flash Storage; Application Launch

1. RESOURCES

The video is available on the homepage of the first author [4], and the project overview is presented in [5, 6]. Interested readers may download our StoreBench storage benchmark application used in the large-scale study from Google Play [2]. StoreBench requires a rooted device with Android 3.0 or higher, and installed BusyBox [1] on the device. The dataset of the large-scale storage performance study will be made available at [3].

2. ACKNOWLEDGEMENTS

The authors would like to thank Mai Anh Do from Christopher Newport University for her able assistance in creating this video. We also thank William & Mary LENS research lab members and anonymous reviewers for their valuable comments.

3. REFERENCES

[1] Busybox. http://goo.gl/CF6vJ, 2014.
[2] Storebench download. http://goo.gl/ava9eV, 2014.
[3] Storebench web. http://StoreBench.com, 2014.
[4] D. T. Nguyen. Homepage. http://www.cs.wm.edu/~dnguyen.
[5] D. T. Nguyen. Smartphone application delay optimizations. In *Proceedings of the 12th International Conference on Mobile Systems, Applications, and Services*, MobiSys '14, New York, NY, USA, 2014. ACM.
[6] D. T. Nguyen, G. Zhou, and G. Xing. Poster: Towards reducing smartphone application delay through read/write isolation. In *Proceedings of the 12th International Conference on Mobile Systems, Applications, and Services*, MobiSys '14, New York, NY, USA, 2014. ACM.

MobiSys'14, June 16–19, 2014, Bretton Woods, New Hampshire, USA.
ACM 978-1-4503-2793-0/14/06.
http://dx.doi.org/10.1145/2594368.2602431.

Video: Procrastinator: Pacing Mobile Apps' Usage of the Network

Lenin Ravindranath
lenin@csail.mit.edu
M.I.T.
Cambridge, MA, USA

Sharad Agarwal
sagarwal@microsoft.com
Microsoft Research
Redmond, WA, USA

Jitendra Padhye
padhye@microsoft.com
Microsoft Research
Redmond, WA, USA

Chris Riederer
cjr2149@columbia.edu
Columbia University
New York, NY, USA

"This app is too slow" is a phrase that app developers dread when reading user reviews for their apps. Over the last 5 years, smartphone users have forced app developers to optimize their apps for performance. App developers now rely heavily on threading and asynchronous programming patterns to keep their app's UI responsive. They rely on prefetching network content at the launch of an app to hide the network latency of cellular communication.

Apps that prefetch network content are downloading content before the user needs it - for example to populate images that are off screen. Those users that scroll or click through an app to visit that off-screen content will experience a more responsive app. However, for those users that do not visit that off-screen content, the penalty is wasted network consumption. This waste can harm three sets of users – (1) users that are always conscious about data consumption because they are on a pay-per-byte plan; (2) users that start their monthly cellular billing cycle with a large number of bytes (e.g. 2GB), but eventually run low and want the remaining bytes to last them through the end of their cycle; (3) users that have large data plans at home but are temporarily roaming internationally and are paying additional per-byte charges.

This problem cannot be solved by producing two versions of an app – data-light and data-heavy versions – for two different sets of users. A data-rich user can sometimes become data-poor, or vice-versa temporarily when the user connects to Wi-Fi (we assume that Wi-Fi connectivity is free or significantly cheaper) or starts running out of her monthly cellular allotment or is roaming. Alternatively, producing a single adaptive app is difficult for the app developer who has to manage multiple network transfers that affect different parts of the user interface. Worse, the user can be scrolling around in the app while some network transfers are ongoing and connectivity changes between cellular and Wi-Fi.

Our goal is to *automatically* delay prefetching of network content *when appropriate*, to reduce data usage. Our system is called *Procrastinator*. "Delaying" or "procrastination" of network content is done based on current network connectivity (cellular or Wi-Fi), the status of the user's cellular data plan, where in the app the user is (which parts of the UI are visible), and potential for impact on the functionality of the app beyond the UI (such as playing music or vibrating the phone).

MobiSys'14, June 16–19, 2014, Bretton Woods, New Hampshire, USA.
ACM 978-1-4503-2793-0/14/06.
http://dx.doi.org/10.1145/2594368.2602432.

In designing Procrastinator, we strive for *"immediate deployability"* – we do not require changes to the mobile OS, nor runtime. We also attempt to achieve *"zero effort"* for the app developer – we do not want her to write additional code, nor add code annotations. She may need to simply run our system, and can optionally choose to test her app under Procrastinator. We also strive for *"zero functionality impact"* – beyond appearing as though the network is occasionally slower, the user should not experience any other change in the functionality of the app.

We have implemented Procrastinator for the Windows Phone 8 platform. Our system automatically rewrites app binaries without requiring app source code. There are two key challenges in building Procrastinator. First, Procrastinator must automatically identify asynchronous network calls that are candidates for procrastination. This involves careful static analysis of the app code. Next, Procrastinator must rewrite the app code, so that at run time, it can decide (a) whether to procrastinate each candidate call, and (b) when to execute a previously procrastinated call, if at all.

Our system automatically identifies for each network transfer which part of the app UI it affects. For those parts of the UI that are not visible, it delays network transfers until they become visible. Our system works on arbitrary third party apps without source code nor app developer effort. At run time, it uses dynamic information about network connectivity and data plan information to automatically switch from prefetching behavior to procrastination. Our lab experiments identify the potential network usage savings in 6 popular, professionally-written Windows Phone apps, as well as additional savings that are untapped because of our conservative approach in avoiding any change to the functionality of the app. Our small study of 9 users with those 6 apps demonstrates savings in total network usage by each app ranging from none to 4X. A larger scale evaluation of 140 apps using automated UI behavior demonstrates 2.5X and higher savings in 20-40 apps, or 20% and higher savings in 60-75 apps. These savings for the data-poor user come with a 300ms median latency penalty on LTE if the user goes to a part of the app where Procrastinator did not allow data to be prefetched.

This video demonstrates Procrastinator running on typical, popular apps. It shows the normal behavior of the app when the user has a lot of cellular bytes left on her data plan. It later shows behavior when the user is running low on cellular bytes. In that case, the video shows how main content on the primary page of apps is unaffected, and the delay that the user will typically experience if she goes to secondary pages.

Video: User-Generated Free-Form Gestures for Authentication: Security and Memorability

Michael Sherman[†], Gradeigh Clark[†], Yulong Yang[†], Shridatt Sugrim[†], Arttu Modig[*],
Janne Lindqvist[†], Antti Oulasvirta[‡*], Teemu Roos[*]
[†]Rutgers University, [‡]Max Planck Institute for Informatics
[*]Saarland University, [*]University of Helsinki

ABSTRACT

This is a video demonstration for a full paper available in Mo-biSys'14 proceedings http://dx.doi.org/10.1145/2594368.2594375 [1]. The video demonstrates several forms of authentication on a common tablet, and compares them to our method for gesture-based authentication. Our method measures the security and memorability of user generated free-form gestures by estimating the mutual information of repeated gestures. We show examples of such gestures with high and low mutual information content. We also show what information from each is visible to a shoulder surfing attacker, and describe how our system is resistant to such an attack.

Categories and Subject Descriptors

H.5.m. [**Information Interfaces and Presentation (e.g. HCI)**]: Miscellaneous

Keywords

gestures; security; mutual information; memorability

Acknowledgments

This material is based upon work supported by the National Science Foundation under Grant Number 1228777. Any opinions, findings, and conclusions or recommendations expressed in this material are those of the author(s) and do not necessarily reflect the views of the National Science Foundation.

1. REFERENCES

[1] M. Sherman, G. Clark, Y. Yang, S. Sugrim, A. Modig, J. Lindqvist, A. Oulasvirta, and T. Roos. User-Generated Free-Form Gestures for Authentication: Security and Memorability. In *Proc. of Mobisys'14*. http://dx.doi.org/10.1145/2594368.2594375.

Video: Open Data Kit Tables

Samuel Sudar, Waylon Brunette, Gaetano Borriello
University of Washington
Box 352350
Seattle, WA 98195
{sudars, wrb, gaetano}@cs.washington.edu

ABSTRACT

Mobile devices are integral to the workflows of many organizations working in rural or disconnected contexts. Data is often collected on mobile phones and tablets using tools like Open Data Kit (ODK). However, some of the applications require users to revisit and update previously collected data, necessitating easy viewing of stored data. To make it easier for organizations to create flexible information services, we present ODK Tables, an Android tool that allows users to enter and curate data on mobile devices. Tables leverages web tools to make mobile app creation simple. It provides abstractions to make the process straightforward and allows app designers to access data through a JavaScript API. App designers can create a custom app using only a small number of HTML and JavaScript files. This facilitates the creation of a custom user interface but leaves storage, data management, and synchronization to the framework. The result is a fully featured Android app based on established web-based tools with full support for disconnected operation.

Categories and Subject Descriptors

K.6.3 [**Software Management**]: Software Development

General Terms

Management, Design, Human Factors.

Keywords

ICTD, mobile app, database viewing, synchronization, disconnected operation, Open Data Kit, ODK.

1. DESCRIPTION

Mobile computing devices have emerged as an increasingly indispensable tool for many organizations working in emerging regions. The devices serve as a mode of data collection, as well as the main data-browsing platform in the field. Tools like Open Data Kit (ODK) seek to make this process easier by providing a suite of tools designed to facilitate mobile data collection and management [1]. As mobile devices become more prevalent, organizations desire customizing these tools to create entire information management systems where they can control user interactions with data. The ODK 2.0 suite of tools has been designed with this goal in mind, allowing users to create highly configurable and customizable workflows and systems on mobile devices [2]. ODK Tables is a tool in the ODK 2.0 tool suite that focuses on make mobile app creation simple [3].

Tables is motivated by the insight that many mobile apps are essentially database viewers. Users interact with this database while and viewing and editing its contents. From the perspective of an app designer, even simple apps thus require the same boilerplate from a persistence and synchronization layer. Tables takes care of data management and synchronization with an ODK Aggregate server, allowing the app designer to focus on the flow of information and the user experience.

A Tables app comprises a number of HTML and JavaScript files that are rendered by the framework. JavaScript APIs are exposed as two variables on the global window object that give designers the ability to access their data and launch additional pages. In this sense a Tables app is a collection of webpages that is displayed and navigated like a website. Writing an app thus does not require knowledge of Android or a complex development environment and is more capable in disconnected environments than pure HTML5. All necessary development and debugging can be performed directly in a browser, provided that the browser supports developer tools and JavaScript debugging.

In this video we present the abstractions provided by ODK Tables that allow designers to treat mobile apps as websites. We also present Hope Study, a Tables app that serves as the main entry point to data collection and curation in a longitudinal HIV study in Kenya. It has been in successful daily use for over six months. The study protocol is complex, with different data required at different time points and for patients in different arms of the study. The workflow has been written into the app, allowing healthcare workers to follow the paradigm without requiring extensive training.

2. ACKNOWLEDGMENTS

We gratefully acknowledge the support of Google Research, NSF Grant No. IIS-1111433, and an NSF Graduate Research Fellowship under Grant No. DGE-0718124.

3. REFERENCES

[1] W. Brunette, M. Sundt, N. Dell, R. Chaudhri, N. Breit, and G. Borriello. "Open Data Kit 2.0: expanding and refining information services for developing regions." Proc. of the 14th Workshop on Mobile Computing Systems and Applications, 2013.

[2] C. Hartung, A. Lerer, Y. Anokwa, C. Tseng, W. Brunette, and G. Borriello. "Open Data Kit: tools to build information services for developing regions," Proc. 4th ACM/IEEE Intl. Conf. on Information and Communication Technologies and Development (ICTD), 2010.

[3] W. Brunette, S. Sudar, N. Worden, D. Price, R. Anderson, and G. Borriello. "ODK Tables: Building Easily Customizable Information Applications on Android Devices," in Proceedings of the 3rd ACM Symposium on Computing for Development (ACM DEV '13).

Video: Unsupervised Indoor Localization (UnLoc): Beyond the Prototype

He Wang
University of Illinois at
Urbana-Champaign

Souvik Sen
HP Labs

Alex Mariakakis
University of Washington

Ahmed Elgohary
University of Waterloo

Moustafa Farid
EJUST

Moustafa Youssef
EJUST

Romit Roy Choudhury
University of Illinois at
Urbana-Champaign

ABSTRACT

This video presents a demo of indoor localization in multiple settings. In the demo, a user walks with a smartphone and the user's location is shown on the phone's screen in real time. Our system, called Unsupervised Indoor Localization (UnLoc) [1] utilizes the sensor data from smartphones to learn "invisible landmarks" in the environment. Example landmarks could be a unique magnetic fluctuation experienced when the phone is near a watercooler, or a distinct gyroscope rotation when the user turns a corner. We use these indoor "landmarks" to periodically reset the user's location. To track the user between these landmarks, we use an optimized variant of dead reckoning, ultimately leading to a robust location tracking system. We call our system UnLoc, since the landmarks are generated in an unsupervised manner, requiring no manual effort or floorplan of the building. The demo describes the high level intuitions, shows UnLoc in operation, and shares experiences from running UnLoc in various real-world environments.

1. REFERENCES

[1] H. Wang, S. Sen, A. Elgohary, M. Farid, M. Youssef, and R. Roy Choudhury, "No need to war-drive: Unsupervised indoor localization," in *MobiSys*, 2012.

Author Index

395

www.ingramcontent.com/pod-product-compliance
Lightning Source LLC
Chambersburg PA
CBHW080657220326
41598CB00033B/5233